NOTE TO STUDENTS

This text was written with the objective of preparing you for your future professional career. Accounting is a stimulating, rewarding field of study. To be effective, professionals in all areas of business, such as finance, production, marketing, personnel, and general management, must have a good understanding of accounting. In addition, men and women whose careers are in nonbusiness areas can use a knowledge of accounting to perform more effectively in society.

As you begin your study of accounting, you may find the following suggestions helpful:

- Read each chapter objective before you begin studying a chapter.
- Take a few minutes and scan the chapter to get a flavor of the material before you begin a detailed reading of the chapter.
- As you read each chapter, you may wish to underline points that you feel are especially important. Also, you should give special attention to key terms which are identified in color when they first appear in the chapter.
- After reading the text of the chapter, carefully study the Chapter Review, giving special attention to the following items:

Key Points. You should thoroughly understand each of the key points presented in the chapter. If you have difficulty understanding any of the key points, review the section of the chapter where the key point is discussed and illustrated. The key points are organized according to the chapter objectives.

Key Terms. You should be able to define each key term. If you cannot, refer to the page of the chapter where the key term is first presented and discussed. You may also refer to the Glossary at the end of the text, where all of the key terms are listed in alphabetical order and defined.

Self-Examination Questions. Answer each of the self-examination questions and check your answers by referring to the explanation of the correct response, which is presented at the end of the chapter.

Illustrative Problem. Study the illustrative problem and its suggested solution. Each illustrative problem applies the concepts and principles discussed in the chapter to a problem situation. If you have difficulty understanding the illustrative problem, refer to the section of the chapter where the applicable concepts and principles are discussed and illustrated.

- Work all assigned homework. In many cases, the homework is related to specific chapter illustrations, and you may find it helpful to review the relevant chapter sections before you begin a homework assignment.
- Take notes during class lectures and discussions and give attention to the topics covered by your instructor.
- In reviewing for examinations, keep in mind those topics that your instructor has emphasized, and review your class notes and the text.
- If you feel you need additional aid, you may find the Study Guides that accompany this textbook helpful. The Study Guides can be ordered from South-Western Publishing Co. by your college or university bookstore.

ACCOUNTING
PRINCIPLES

16th EDITION

PHILIP E. FESS, Ph.D., C.P.A.
Professor Emeritus of Accountancy
University of Illinois, Champaign-Urbana

CARL S. WARREN, Ph.D., C.P.A., C.M.A., C.I.A.
Professor of Accounting
University of Georgia, Athens

AB70QA
PUBLISHED BY
SOUTH-WESTERN PUBLISHING CO.
CINCINNATI, OH   WEST CHICAGO, IL   DALLAS, TX   LIVERMORE, CA

Copyright © 1990
by South-Western Publishing Co.
Cincinnati, Ohio

ISBN: 0-538-80600-1

Library of Congress Catalog Card Number: 88-63689

1 2 3 4 5 6 7 8 9 KI 3 2 1 0 9

Printed in the United States of America

Library of Congress Cataloging-in-Publication Data

Fess, Philip E.
   Accounting principles / Philip E. Fess, Carl S. Warren. — 16th
ed.
      p.   cm.
   Includes bibliographical references and index.
   ISBN 0-538-80600-1
   1. Accounting.   I. Warren, C. S.   II. Title.
HF5635.F386   1990
657 — dc20   88-63689
                                                           CIP

PREFACE

The sixteenth edition of ACCOUNTING PRINCIPLES is a student-oriented text. It presents the fundamental accounting concepts and principles in a logical, concise, and clear manner. ACCOUNTING PRINCIPLES provides a solid educational foundation that allows instructors to focus on clarifying issues and increasing the student's understanding of accounting and its uses. This student orientation is one of the principal reasons why this text has been used by more students than any other for more than 50 years and why it is still the leader in teaching principles of accounting.

Fundamental accounting concepts and principles are presented in the text in a business setting that allows students to understand accounting as it is applied in serving not only the business world but all of society. Such an approach meets the needs of students planning careers in accounting as well as in business administration, in liberal arts areas, in law, or in other disciplines.

IMPORTANT FEATURES OF THE SIXTEENTH EDITION

The basic foundation of ACCOUNTING PRINCIPLES, which has served instructors and students so well over the years, has been retained in the sixteenth edition. However, new features have been added, based on extensive feedback from current users and on independent reviews by numerous scholars and educators. The most significant new features and the features retained from previous editions are:

Chapter Objectives

The chapter objectives have been integrated with the text presentation and the instructor's materials as follows:

- Each chapter begins with a listing of the chapter objectives. This listing provides a framework for the presentation of the chapter material.
- Each chapter objective is repeated in the margin next to the discussion to which the objective relates.
- The key points in each chapter review are organized by chapter objective.
- All end-of-chapter exercises and problems are identified by chapter objective.
- The teaching outlines provided in the *Instructor's Manual* are organized by chapter objective.
- All questions and problems in the test bank are identified by chapter objective.

Illustrations

Charts, graphs, and diagrams throughout the text enable students to visualize important concepts and principles. These charts, graphs, and diagrams are highlighted with color to enhance the learning process.

Real-World Examples

Additional real-world business examples have been integrated throughout the text to provide students with a flavor of the real-world impact of accounting. These examples add concrete meaning to concepts and principles which might otherwise appear abstract. Many of these examples were taken directly from the latest annual reports of companies such as Pepsico and General Motors. In addition, the American Institute of Certified Public Accountants' publication, *Accounting Trends & Techniques*, is cited where appropriate to indicate the frequency with which alternative accounting presentations and methods are used in the real world.

Enrichment Material

New excerpts from well-known business periodicals, such as the *Journal of Accountancy, The Wall Street Journal,* and *Forbes,* have been included in the text. Each excerpt is designed to stir the students' interest and enrich their learning experience by providing real-world information relevant to the topics that are discussed in the chapter.

Ethics Discussion Cases

An ethics discussion case has been added to each chapter of the sixteenth edition, in response to the business world's increasing emphasis on ethical conduct. As a basis for discussion, the American Institute of Certified Public Accountants' *Code of Professional Conduct* and the National Association of Accountants' *Standards of Ethical Conduct for Management Accountants* have been included in Appendix B. These codes of professional conduct supplement the presentation of professional ethics in Chapter 1.

Chapter Reviews

The chapter review at the end of each chapter is designed to increase and enhance student retention of important chapter concepts and principles. Each review includes key points, key terms, self-examination questions, and an illustrative problem and solution.

- The **key points,** organized by chapter objective, summarize the major concepts presented in a chapter. By studying the key points, students can quickly review the major concepts and principles of each chapter.
- Each **key term** listed in the chapter review is followed by the page number indicating where the term was first discussed in the chapter. Students may also refer to the Glossary at the end of the text, where all the key terms, with page references, are listed alphabetically and defined.
- Five **self-examination questions** are provided for each chapter. After studying the chapter, students can answer these questions and compare their answers with the correct ones. Explanations of both the correct and incorrect answers for each question, provided at the end of the chapter, increase students' understanding and enhance the learning process.
- The **illustrative problem** with suggested solution focuses on the concepts and principles discussed in the chapter. Students can use these problems as a means of building confidence in their ability to apply a chapter's concepts and principles to a problem situation. Each illustrative problem is similar to one or more end-of-chapter problems.

Real-World Focus Questions

At least one discussion question that requires students to interpret and respond to a real-world business situation is contained in each chapter. In some chapters, a real-world exercise or problem is also included. These questions, exercises, and problems, which are labeled "Real World Focus," are based on actual business data.

Comprehensive Problems

Five comprehensive problems are included—at the end of Chapters 3, 5, 6, 11, and 16. These problems integrate and summarize the concepts and principles of several chapters. They may be assigned as mini practice sets to be worked manually, or the first four problems can be worked with the Solutions software that may be purchased with the text.

Series B Problems

The alternate Series B problems appear at the end of each chapter in order to facilitate student and instructor usage.

Statement of Cash Flows

The sixteenth edition introduces the statement of cash flows in Chapter 1 as one of the four basic financial statements. Using the direct method, a simple statement of cash flows for a service enterprise is described and illustrated. Several exercises and problems at the end of Chapter 1 require students to prepare simple statements of cash flows.

An in-depth discussion of the statement of cash flows is presented in Chapter 18. Early in Chapter 18 an illustration of the statement of cash flows, using both the direct method and the indirect method, is presented as a basis for discussion.

Two appendixes are included at the end of Chapter 18. The first appendix further describes and illustrates the direct method of preparing the statement of cash flows. The second appendix describes and illustrates a work sheet approach to preparing the statement of cash flows. The work sheet approach presented in the sixteenth edition is completely revised.

Accounting for Merchandise Inventory

An alternate method of handling merchandise inventory at the end of an accounting period is included in Appendix C. This method, sometimes referred to as the closing method, can be used instead of the method presented in the merchandising chapters. The Solutions Manual includes solutions for both approaches.

Deferrals and Accruals

The deferrals and accruals material which appeared as a separate chapter in previous editions has been carefully integrated into several chapters of the sixteenth edition. An expanded discussion of adjustments for deferrals and accruals has been added to Chapter 4. The alternative methods of initially recording deferrals are presented in Chapter 6 in the context of the design of accounting systems. An appendix to Chapter 6 provides additional discussion and illustrations of the recording of deferrals. The appendix can be used in place of the discussion at the end of Chapter 6 or to supplement that discussion. Exercises and problems covering the appendix materials are included.

Internal Control Structure

The discussion of internal controls has been revised to incorporate *Statements on Auditing Standards, No. 55.* Accordingly, the discussion of internal controls describes the importance of the control environment, the control procedures, and the accounting system.

Future Value and Bond Sinking Funds

The discussion of sinking funds in Chapter 16 has been revised to include the consideration of future value concepts in determining sinking fund deposits. Future value tables and present value tables are included in Appendix A.

Accounting for International Operations

The special problems in accounting for transactions with foreign companies and in preparing consolidated statements for domestic and foreign corporations are presented in Chapter 17.

Managerial Accounting

The coverage of managerial accounting has been expanded and reorganized.

- Chapter 20, "Managerial Accounting Concepts and Principles," has been developed to facilitate the transition from financial accounting to managerial accounting. The chapter begins by distinguishing financial and managerial accounting. In addition, by describing and illustrating common managerial accounting terms, concepts, and principles, the chapter provides an overview of managerial accounting as a basis for the remaining managerial accounting chapters.
- Chapter 22, "Process Cost Systems," has been expanded to include a discussion of both the first-in, first-out (fifo) and average cost methods.

■ A discussion of cost behavior has been added to the beginning of Chapter 23, "Cost Behavior Concepts and Cost-Volume-Profit Analysis." This discussion includes a description of the variable, fixed, and mixed cost concepts. Cost estimation using the high-low method has also been added.

■ Chapter 24, "Profit Planning for Management Analysis," has been revised to reflect the current practice of utilizing contribution margin analysis rather than gross profit analysis. This discussion appears at the end of the chapter as an illustration of the use of variable costing.

■ Chapter 26, "Responsibility Accounting," now follows the budgeting and standard costs chapter.

■ Chapter 27, "Differential Analysis and Product Pricing," has been revised to include a discussion of the setting of normal product prices.

■ Chapter 28, "Capital Investment Analysis," is devoted to a single topic because of the importance of capital investment analysis. The chapter describes and illustrates the average rate of return, cash payback, discounted cash flow, and discounted internal rate of return methods of evaluating capital investments. Factors complicating capital investment analysis and capital rationing are also discussed.

■ In response to the increasing importance of service enterprises, examples of the application of traditional managerial concepts and principles to service enterprises have been added.

Codes of Ethics for Accountants

The American Institute of Certified Public Accountants' *Code of Professional Conduct* and the National Association of Accountants' *Standards of Ethical Conduct for Management Accountants* have been included in Appendix B. These codes of professional conduct supplement the presentation of professional ethics in Chapter 1 and provide a framework for students to answer the ethics discussion cases in each chapter.

Accounting for Individuals and Nonprofit Organizations

The discussions of accounting for individuals and accounting for nonprofit organizations have been moved to Appendix D and Appendix F, respectively. These appendixes include relevant discussion questions and exercises.

Income Taxes

The effect of income taxes on accounting has been incorporated throughout the text. The coverage of income taxes is presented in greater depth in Appendix E. This appendix, which incorporates the 1988 changes in the tax law, provides students with an understanding of the basic nature of the federal income tax system and its effects on personal and business income. The appendix includes discussion questions and exercises.

Major Trends in Manufacturing

Appendix G, which has been added to the sixteenth edition, describes and illustrates major trends in manufacturing in the United States. Some of the trends described and illustrated include just-in-time manufacturing, automation, total product quality control systems, materials planning requirement systems, and information technology. A selected bibliography is included in the *Instructor's Manual* for instructors who wish to assign additional reading in these areas. The appendix includes discussion questions.

Specimen Financial Statements

Appendix I includes a variety of examples of real world financial statements of large, publicly held corporations. These financial statements provide insight into the financial reporting of real companies.

End-of-Chapter Materials

The end-of-chapter exercises and problems have been carefully written and revised to be both practical and comprehensive. The variety and volume of the assignment materials presented at the end of each chapter provide a wide choice of subject matter and range of difficulty. In addition, selected problems may be solved using general ledger and spreadsheet software that is available from South-Western Publishing Co. As in previous editions, each chapter contains a mini-case for stimulating student interest. Each case, which presents situations with which students can easily identify, emphasizes important chapter concepts and principles. An ethics discussion case at the end of each chapter emphasizes an ethical issue related to the chapter.

SUPPLEMENTARY MATERIALS

ACCOUNTING PRINCIPLES is part of a well-integrated educational package that includes materials designed for the instructor's use and for the students' use. These materials are carefully prepared and reviewed to maintain consistency and high quality throughout.

Available to Instructors

Solutions Manuals. These manuals contain solutions to all end-of-chapter materials, including the discussion questions, exercises, problems, mini-cases, ethics cases, and comprehensive problems.

Instructor's Manual. This manual contains a summary of the chapter objectives, terminology, and concepts. In a section organized according to chapter objectives, a basis for developing class lectures and assigning homework is provided. In addition, exercise and problem descriptions, estimated time requirements for the problems, and suggestions for use of the appendixes and other supplementary items are included. The Instructor's Manual is also available on diskettes (**Electronic Instructor's Manual**), so that it can be tailored to individual class syllabi and objectives.

Spreadsheet Applications. These template diskettes are used with Lotus® 1-2-3®[1] for solving selected end-of-chapter exercises and problems that are identified with the symbol at the right. These diskettes, which also provide a Lotus 1-2-3 tutorial and "what if" analysis, may be ordered free of charge from South-Western Publishing Co.

Solutions Transparencies and Teaching Transparencies. Transparencies of solutions to all exercises and problems, including the comprehensive problems, are available. The teaching transparencies are designed to aid the instructor's focus on key concepts and principles discussed in the text. The transparencies are packaged in two boxes, one for Chapters 1–14 and one for Chapters 15–28 and Appendixes D, E, F, and H.

HyperGraphics.®[2] This instructional delivery system uses a microcomputer, a liquid crystal device (LCD), an overhead projector, and a hand-held remote control device to add graphics, color, and animation to class lectures. An Instructor's Manual explains how to install and use the program. A *ClassNotes and Study Guide* for students complements the classroom presentation. The addition of response pads adds interactivity to the class.

Videos. A set of instructional videos, prepared by Walter DeAguero of Saddleback College, are available. These videos may be used for student review of material or to enhance class lectures.

Test Bank. A collection of more than 2,500 examination problems, multiple-choice questions, and true or false questions, accompanied by solutions, is available in both printed and microcomputer (**MicroSWAT III**) versions. These items are identified by chapter objective and by level of difficulty. The Test Bank is designed to save

---

[1]Lotus 1-2-3 are registered trademarks of the Lotus Development Corporation. Any reference to Lotus or 1-2-3 refers to this footnote.

[2]HyperGraphics is a registered trademark of HyperGraphics Corporation.

time in preparing and grading periodic and final examinations. Individual items may also be selected for use as short quizzes. The number of questions and problems is sufficient to provide variety from year to year and from class section to class section. The printed version of the Test Bank also contains the solutions for the Achievement Tests.

Achievement Tests, prepared by Charles Rohr of Mt. San Jacinto College, Philip E. Fess, and Carl S. Warren. Three sets of preprinted objective tests are available. Each test in sets A and B covers a single chapter. Each test in set C contains 50 multiple-choice questions covering a group of chapters. Set C, which may be machine graded, also includes a comprehensive test covering each half of the text.

Keys for Practice Sets. Each key is a complete solution for its corresponding practice set.

Manual for Demonstration Problems and Notes. Solutions for problems contained in the student's *Demonstration Problems and Notes,* along with a set of correlating transparencies, are available. As the instructor works through each problem on the transparencies, students can follow the solution as they complete each problem in their workbook.

Available to Students

Solutions: Applications Software, prepared by Warren W. Allen and Dale H. Klooster of Educational Technical Systems. This software, which may be ordered with the textbook, is a general ledger program tailored specifically to ACCOUNTING PRINCIPLES. It may be used with the IBM® PC, IBM PS/2,[3] and the Tandy® 1000[4] microcomputers to solve selected end-of-chapter problems and four comprehensive problems, which are identified with the symbol at the right. It may also be used to solve most problems that require journal entries and a general ledger, as well as three manual practice sets, so that they in effect become computerized practice sets.

Working Papers. Appropriate forms on which to work end-of-chapter problems and mini-cases are available in bound volumes. The first volume for use with Chapters 1–14 and the second volume for use with Chapters 13–28 are preprinted for working specific problems. The third volume for use with Chapters 1–28 is a set of blank forms that may be used to work exercises and problems.

Study Guides, prepared by James A. Heintz of Indiana University and Carl S. Warren. The Study Guides are designed to assist in comprehending the concepts and principles presented in the text. These publications, which are printed in two volumes (one for Chapters 1–14 and one for Chapters 15–28), include an outline and a glossary for each chapter as well as brief objective questions and problems. Solutions to these questions and problems are presented at the back of the Study Guides.

Microcomputer Study Guides. These microcomputer versions of the manual Study Guides may be used with the IBM PC, IBM PS/2, and the Tandy 1000.

Financial Accounting Tutor and **Managerial Accounting Tutor, prepared by Thomas P. Lawler of Marist College.** These interactive computerized tutorials provide step-by-step explanations and examples for students' review of accounting principles.

Student Reference Card. This 3-hole-punched card provides students with a quick reference for basic accounting facts, such as the rules of debit and credit.

ClassNotes and Study Guide. This learning resource for use with HyperGraphics presents a structured outline for every lesson and includes questions and exercises for study and review.

Practice Sets. *Varsity Sporting Goods Co.,* prepared by Herman R. Andress of Santa Fe Community College, is a merchandising sole propietorship that uses special journals. ***Centurion Computer Systems,*** prepared by Edward E. Stumpf of Fullerton College, is a merchandising sole proprietorship that uses a voucher register and a payroll register. ***Treasure Chest Coins*** and ***Park Avenue Jewelers,*** prepared by Dale H. Klooster and Warren W. Allen, are automated sets for merchandising sole proprietorships. ***SEMO Sporting Goods Co.,*** prepared by Deborah F. Beard, Stephen C. DelVecchio, and John A. Elfrink of Southeast Missouri State University, requires the

---

[3]IBM is a registered trademark of International Business Machines Corporation. Any reference to the IBM Personal Computer or the IBM Personal System/2 refers to this footnote.
[4]Tandy® 1000 is a registered trademark of the Radio Shack Division of Tandy Corporation. Any reference to the Tandy 1000 microcomputer refers to this footnote.

preparation of correcting entries and financial statements for a wholesaling corpora-tion. ***Classic Designs Inc.,*** prepared by Herman R. Andress, is a departmentalized merchandising corporation that uses a voucher system. ***WeMake Toys Inc.,*** prepared by Stephen S. Hamilton of Lane Community College, is a manufacturing corporation that uses a job order cost system.

Demonstration Problems and Notes, prepared by L. Paden Neeley of The University of North Texas. A workbook of problems that emphasize important ac-counting concepts and principles of the textbook is available.

Integrated Accounting on Microcomputers, prepared by Dale H. Klooster and Warren W. Allen. This text-workbook with diskette is a stand-alone, automated ac-counting package that is intended for a first course in microcomputer accounting. Completion time is approximately 45–55 hours.

Electronic Spreadsheet Applications for Accounting Principles, Financial Accounting, and Managerial Accounting, prepared by Gaylord N. Smith of Albion College. These supplemental text-workbooks with template diskettes in-clude accounting applications and a Lotus 1-2-3 tutorial. Each text-workbook requires approximately 20–25 hours for completion.

ORGANIZATION OF THE SIXTEENTH EDITION

ACCOUNTING PRINCIPLES has been organized to facilitate the learning of accounting and the overall educational process. Concepts and principles are intro-duced in a logical, step-by-step way and are reinforced by applications from the busi-ness world.

Each chapter builds on the terminology, concepts, and principles introduced in previous chapters. The chapter objectives provide students with a basis for beginning their study of each chapter. In turn, each chapter is organized around the chapter ob-jectives in an educationally sound approach. The chapter reviews provide students with a means for review and a basis for assessing their knowledge of each chapter. The end-of-chapter discussion questions, exercises, problems, mini-cases, and ethics cases provide a vehicle for the instructor to discuss each chapter's concepts and prin-ciples and to assess the students' understanding of them. Periodic assigning of com-prehensive problems and the giving of examinations provide instructors with a means of assessing students' cumulative knowledge.

The organization of the sixteenth edition of ACCOUNTING PRINCIPLES is briefly summarized in the following paragraphs.

Introduction: Evolution of Accounting

The introduction presents a summary of the beginnings of accounting in 1494 and its development to the present. This overview provides students of all backgrounds an excellent perspective on the importance and influence of accounting on all phases of society.

Part 1 — Basic Structure of Accounting

Chapters 1–5 focus on the basic concepts and principles of accounting, includ-ing accounting for both service enterprises and merchandise enterprises. These chapters are presented without the complexities of special journals and subsidiary ledgers. The emphasis on different forms of organization is minimized by presenting simple owner equity structures and deferring complex owner equity structures to later chapters. The adjusting and closing process for a service enterprise is intentionally kept simple in Chapters 1–3 to facilitate student understanding. Chapters 4–5 build on the basic framework of Chapters 1–3 by describing and illustrating accounting for merchandise enterprises and deferrals and accruals.

Part 2 — Accounting Systems

Chapter 6 emphasizes the qualities of a properly designed accounting system, in-cluding the principles of internal control and the use of special journals and subsidiary ledgers. Chapters 7–11 build on this systems foundation, beginning with cash in Chapter 7 and, in balance sheet order, proceeding with receivables and temporary in-vestments (Chapter 8), inventories (Chapter 9), plant assets and intangible assets (Chapter 10), and current liabilities and payroll (Chapter 11).

Part 3 — Accounting Principles

Chapter 12, "Concepts and Principles," ties together the generally accepted accounting concepts and principles presented in the first 11 chapters, and expands the discussion to include additional accounting principles. Chapter 12 also includes a discussion of reporting changes in price levels.

Part 4 — Partnerships and Corporations

Chapter 13 discusses the characteristics of partnerships and the unique accounting concepts and principles related to partnerships. Chapter 14 discusses the characteristics of corporations and introduces basic accounting concepts and principles related to corporations.

Part 5 — Financial Reporting for Corporations

Chapters 15–19 focus on additional financial reporting issues for corporations. Chapters 15–17 describe and illustrate the reporting of paid-in capital and stockholders' equity, unusual items, income taxes, bonds, long-term investments in bonds and stocks, consolidated financial statements, and international accounting. Chapters 18 and 19 describe and illustrate the use of the statement of cash flows, financial statement analysis, and annual reports.

Part 6 — Managerial Accounting Principles and Systems

Chapters 20–22 open the discussion of managerial accounting concepts and principles. Chapter 20 provides an introduction to managerial accounting by distinguishing financial and managerial accounting and describing and illustrating common managerial accounting terms, concepts, and principles. Chapters 21 and 22 present the application of managerial accounting concepts to job order and process cost accounting systems.

Part 7 — Planning and Control

Chapters 23–26 present managerial accounting concepts and principles that are especially useful for planning and control. Chapter 23 focuses on cost behavior and cost-volume-profit analysis. Chapter 24 presents profit reporting for management analysis, including absorption costing, variable costing, and contribution margin analysis. Chapter 25 presents the concepts of budgeting and standard costs. Chapter 25 also includes an appendix on quantitative techniques useful for planning and control. Chapter 26 describes and illustrates responsibility accounting for cost, profit, and investment centers.

Part 8 — Decision Making

Chapters 27–28 present managerial accounting concepts and principles that are especially useful for decision making. Chapter 27 describes and illustrates differential analysis, including the analysis of acceptance of business at a special price. Chapter 27 concludes with a discussion of product pricing, including the setting of normal product prices. Chapter 28 describes and illustrates capital investment analysis.

Appendixes

- Appendix A contains interest tables for both present value and future value.
- Appendix B contains the professional codes of ethics for the American Institute of Certified Public Accountants and the National Association of Accountants.
- Appendix C presents an alternative method of recording merchandise inventory at the end of an accounting period. This method is sometimes referred to as the closing method. Solutions to problems using this method are presented in the Solutions Manual.
- Appendix D describes and illustrates accounting for individuals. Questions and exercises are included in the appendix.
- Appendix E discusses income taxes for individuals and business enterprises. Questions and exercises are included in the appendix.

- Appendix F describes and illustrates accounting for nonprofit organizations. Questions and exercises are included in the appendix.
- Appendix G discusses major trends in manufacturing and their impact on managerial accounting. Some of the trends described and illustrated include just-in-time manufacturing, automation, total product quality control systems, materials planning requirement systems, and the impact of information technology. The appendix includes discussion questions.
- Appendix H presents a work sheet approach to the preparation of financial statements for manufacturing enterprises using the periodic inventory method. Problem materials are included in the appendix.
- Appendix I contains selected financial statements for real companies.

ACKNOWLEDGEMENTS

Throughout the textbook, relevant professional statements of the Financial Accounting Standards Board and other authoritative publications are discussed, quoted, paraphrased, or footnoted. We are indebted to the American Accounting Association, the American Institute of Certified Public Accountants, the Financial Accounting Standards Board, and the National Association of Accountants for material from their publications.

We thank the following faculty who reviewed the previous edition or manuscript for this edition and provided helpful suggestions:

Diana Anderson
Baker College

Leonard J. Podsiadlik
Oakland Community College

John R. Blahnik
Lorain County Community College

La Donna Rhodes
Fullerton College

Ellen D. Cook
University of Southwestern Louisiana

Lawrence A. Roman
Cuyahoga Community College

Walter G. DeAguero
Saddleback College

William E. Smith
Xavier University

Larry F. Lofton
Hinds Community College

James Schnell
Monroe Community College

Paul Morgan
Gulf Coast Community College

Richard J. Sporleder
Moberly Area Junior College

Lyle R. Niemeyer
Marshalltown Community College

We also thank the following faculty who provided suggestions that have been incorporated in this edition: Anne R. Calo, Mattatuck Community College; Shelby W. Davis, Jr., University of Southwestern Louisiana; Mansir J. Edwards, Adirondack Community College; Stephen J. Greene, Mira Mar College; F. Clayton Hallett, Jackson Community College; Jack Klett, Indian River Community College; Albert T. Pasek, Delta College; and Jean Redfern, Golden West College.

We continue to welcome your comments and suggestions.

Philip E. Fess
Carl S. Warren

ABOUT THE AUTHORS

Professor Philip E. Fess is the Arthur Andersen & Co. Alumni Professor of Accountancy Emeritus at the University of Illinois, Champaign-Urbana. Professor Fess received his PhD from the University of Illinois and has been involved in textbook writing for over twenty-five years. In addition to having more than 30 years of teaching experience, he has won numerous teaching awards, including the University of Illinois, College of Commerce Alumni Association Excellence in Teaching Award and the Illinois CPA Society Educator of the Year Award.

Professor Fess is a CPA and a member of the American Institute of CPAs, the Illinois Society of CPAs, and the American Accounting Association. He has served many professional associations in a variety of ways, including a term as a member of the Auditing Standards Board, editorial advisor to the *Journal of Accountancy,* and chairperson of the American Accounting Association Committee on CPA Examinations. Professor Fess has written more than 100 books and articles, which have appeared in such journals as the *Journal of Accountancy*, the *Accounting Review*, the *CPA Journal*, and *Management Accounting*. He has also served as an expert witness before the U.S. Tax Court and as a member of the Cost Advisory Panel for the Secretary of the Air Force.

Professor Fess and his wife, Suzanne, have three daughters: Linda, who is an Assistant Professor of Accountancy at Temple University; Ginny, who is a CPA and is employed by Solar Turbine Co.; and Martha, who is also a CPA and is employed by Steres, Alpert, and Carne, CPAs. Professor Fess' hobby is tennis, and he has represented the United States in international tennis competition.

Professor Carl S. Warren is the Arthur Andersen & Co. Alumni Professor of Accounting at the J.M. Tull School of Accounting at the University of Georgia, Athens. Professor Warren received his PhD from Michigan State University in 1973 and has taught accounting at the University of Iowa, Michigan State University, the University of Chicago, and the University of Georgia. He has received teaching awards from three different student organizations at the University of Georgia.

Professor Warren is a CMA and a CPA. He was awarded a Certificate of Distinguished Performance for his scores on the CMA examination and a Certificate of Honorable Mention for his scores on the CPA examination. He is a member of the National Association of Accountants, the American Institute of CPAs, the Georgia Society of CPAs, the American Accounting Association, the Georgia Association of Accounting Educators, and the Financial Executives Institute. Professor Warren has served on numerous professional committees and editorial boards, including a term as editor of the American Accounting Association publication *Auditing: A Journal of Practice and Theory.* He has written nine textbooks and numerous articles in such journals as the *Journal of Accountancy,* the *Accounting Review,* the *Journal of Accounting Research,* the *CPA Journal, Corporate Accounting, Cost and Management,* and *Managerial Planning.* Professor Warren is also the Consulting Editor for South-Western Publishing Co.'s accounting series.

Professor Warren resides in Athens, Georgia, with his wife, Sharon, and two children, Stephanie (age 16) and Jeffrey (age 14). Professor Warren's hobbies include coaching Little League Baseball, golf, tennis, and fishing.

CONTENTS IN BRIEF

INTRODUCTION: EVOLUTION OF ACCOUNTING   1

1 BASIC STRUCTURE OF ACCOUNTING   6
   1 Accounting Principles and Practices   7
   2 The Accounting Cycle   48
   3 Completion of the Accounting Cycle   94
   4 Accounting for a Merchandising Enterprise   138
   5 Periodic Reporting for a Merchandising Enterprise   178

2 ACCOUNTING SYSTEMS   223
   6 Accounting Systems Design   224
   7 Cash   280
   8 Receivables and Temporary Investments   316
   9 Inventories   349
   10 Plant Assets and Intangible Assets   386
   11 Payroll, Notes Payable, and Other Current Liabilities   426

3 ACCOUNTING PRINCIPLES   465
   12 Concepts and Principles   466

4 PARTNERSHIPS AND CORPORATIONS   504
   13 Partnership Formation, Income Division, and Liquidation   505
   14 Corporations: Organization and Operations   536

5 FINANCIAL REPORTING FOR CORPORATIONS   567
   15 Stockholders' Equity, Earnings, and Dividends   568
   16 Long-Term Liabilities and Investments in Bonds   608
   17 Investments in Stocks; Consolidated Statements;
      International Operations   646
   18 Statement of Cash Flows   691
   19 Financial Statement Analysis and Annual Reports   745

6 MANAGERIAL ACCOUNTING PRINCIPLES
AND SYSTEMS   792
   20 Managerial Accounting Concepts and Principles   793
   21 Job Order Cost Systems   831
   22 Process Cost Systems   869

7 PLANNING AND CONTROL   905
   23 Cost Behavior Concepts and Cost-Volume-Profit Analysis   906
   24 Profit Planning for Management Analysis   943
   25 Budgeting and Standard Cost Systems   976
   26 Responsibility Accounting   1027

8 DECISION MAKING   1066
   27 Differential Analysis and Product Pricing   1067
   28 Capital Investment Analysis   1100

CONTENTS

INTRODUCTION: EVOLUTION OF ACCOUNTING   1

Primitive Accounting   1
Double-Entry System   1
Industrial Revolution   2
Corporate Organization   3
Public Accounting   3
Income Tax   4
Government Influence   4
Accounting's Future   5
     Computerized Accounting Systems   5
     International Accounting   5
     Socioeconomic Accounting   5

1 BASIC STRUCTURE OF ACCOUNTING   6

1 ACCOUNTING PRINCIPLES AND PRACTICES   7
Accounting as an Information System   7
     Users of Accounting Information   8
     Relationship of Accounting to Other Disciplines   9
Profession of Accountancy   10
     Private Accounting   10
     Public Accounting   11
     Specialized Accounting Fields   12
Principles and Practices   14
     Business Entity Concept   15
     The Cost Principle   15
Business Transactions   16
Assets, Liabilities, and Owner's Equity   17
Transactions and the Accounting Equation   17
Financial Statements for Sole Proprietorships   22
     Income Statement   22
     Statement of Owner's Equity   24
     Balance Sheet   24
     Statement of Cash Flows   25
Financial Statements for Corporations   26
     Retained Earnings Statement   26
     Balance Sheet   27
     Statement of Cash Flows   28

2 THE ACCOUNTING CYCLE   48
Classification of Accounts   49
     Assets   49
     Liabilities   49
     Owner's Equity   50
     Revenues   50
     Expenses   50
Chart of Accounts   50
Nature of an Account   51
     Balance Sheet Accounts   52
     Income Statement Accounts   55
     Normal Balances of Accounts   56
Journals and Accounts   57
     Two-Column Journal   57
     Two-Column Accounts and Four-Column Accounts   58
     Posting   60
     Illustration of Journalizing and Posting   60
Trial Balance   66
     Proof Provided by the Trial Balance   66
     Discovery of Errors   67

3 COMPLETION OF THE ACCOUNTING CYCLE   94
Matching Principle   94
Nature of the Adjusting Process   95
Illustrations of Adjusting Entries   96
     Prepaid Expenses   96
     Plant Assets   97
     Accrued Expenses (Liabilities)   99
Work Sheet for Financial Statements   100
     Trial Balance Columns   101
     Adjustments Columns   102
     Adjusted Trial Balance Columns   104
     Income Statement and Balance Sheet Columns   105
Financial Statements   108
     Income Statement   108
     Statement of Owner's Equity   108
     Balance Sheet   110
     Retained Earnings Statement   110
Journalizing and Posting Adjusting Entries   110
Nature of the Closing Process   111
     Journalizing and Posting Closing Entries   111
     Post-Closing Trial Balance   116
Fiscal Year   117
Accounting Cycle   118

**4 ACCOUNTING FOR A
    MERCHANDISING
    ENTERPRISE   138**
Accounting for Purchases   138
    Purchases Discounts   *139*
    *Purchases Returns and
    Allowances*   *141*
Accounting for Sales   142
    Sales Discounts   *144*
    Sales Returns and Allowances   *144*
Transportation Costs   145
Sales Taxes   147
    Sales Tax for Seller   *147*
    Sales Tax for Buyer   *147*
Periodic Reporting for
Merchandising Enterprises   148
Merchandise Inventory Systems   148
Cost of Merchandise Sold   149
Merchandise Inventory
Adjustments   150
Adjustments for Deferrals and
Accruals   151
    *Deferrals and Accruals on the
    Financial Statements*   *151*
    *Adjusting Entries for Prepaid
    Expenses (Deferrals)*   *151*
    *Adjusting Entries for Unearned
    Revenues (Deferrals)*   *152*
    *Adjusting Entries for Accrued
    Liabilities (Accrued Expenses)*   *153*
    *Adjusting Entries for Accrued
    Assets (Accrued Revenues)*   *154*
Work Sheet for Merchandising
Enterprises   154
    *Adjustments on the Work
    Sheet*   *154*
    Completing the Work Sheet   *155*
    *Completion of Year-End
    Procedures*   *156*

**5 PERIODIC REPORTING
    FOR A MERCHANDISING
    ENTERPRISE   178**
Financial Statements for
Merchandising Enterprises   179
    Income Statement   *179*
    Retained Earnings Statement   *184*
    Balance Sheet   *185*
Adjusting Entries   186
Closing Entries   186
Reversing Entries   188
    *Reversing Entries for Accrued
    Liabilities*   *188*
    *Reversing Entries for Accrued
    Assets*   *190*
    *Reversing Entries for a
    Merchandising Enterprise*   *191*
Interim Statements   192
Correction of Errors   193

2 ACCOUNTING SYSTEMS   223

**6 ACCOUNTING SYSTEMS
    DESIGN   224**
Principles of Accounting Systems   224
    Cost-Effectiveness Balance   *224*
    Flexibility to Meet Future Needs *224*
    Adequate Internal Controls   *225*
    Effective Reporting   *225*
    *Adaptation to Organizational
    Structure*   *225*
Accounting System Installation
and Revision   225
    Systems Analysis   *226*
    Systems Design   *226*
    Systems Implementation   *226*
Internal Control Structure   227
    The Control Environment   *227*
    The Control Procedures   *228*
    The Accounting System   *229*
Data Processing Methods   229
Subsidiary Ledgers and Special
Journals   230
    Subsidiary Ledgers   *230*
    Special Journals   *230*
    Purchases Journal   *232*
    Cash Payments Journal   *236*
    *Accounts Payable Control and
    Subsidiary Ledger*   *237*
    Sales Journal   *239*
    Cash Receipts Journal   *241*
    *Accounts Receivable Control
    and Subsidiary Ledger*   *242*
Other Accounting System
Modifications   243
    Accounting for Deferrals   *243*
    *Computerized Accounting
    Systems*   *246*
APPENDIX: Alternative Methods of
Recording Deferrals   246

PRACTICE SET: VARSITY SPORTING GOODS CO.
*This set is available with transactions in narrative
form or with business documents. The set provides
practice in accounting for a sole proprietorship that
uses five journals, a general ledger, and two subsidiary ledgers.*

7 CASH   280
Control over Cash   280
    *The Bank Account as a Tool
    for Controlling Cash*   *280*
    Bank Statement   *282*
    Bank Reconciliation   *283*
Internal Control of Cash Receipts   286
    Cash Short and Over   *287*
    Cash Change Funds   *287*

CONTENTS

Internal Control of Cash Payments 287
  Basic Features of the Voucher
  System 288
  Purchases Discounts 292
  Petty Cash 293
  Other Cash Funds 294
Cash Transactions and Electronic
Funds Transfer 294

8 RECEIVABLES AND TEMPORARY INVESTMENTS 316
Classification of Receivables 316
Control over Receivables 317
Characteristics of Notes
Receivable 318
  Due Date 318
  Interest-Bearing Notes and
  Non-Interest-Bearing Notes 319
  Interest 319
  Maturity Value 320
Accounting for Notes Receivable 320
  Discounting Notes Receivable 322
  Dishonored Notes Receivable 324
Uncollectible Receivables 324
Allowance Method of Accounting
for Uncollectibles 325
  Write-Offs to the Allowance
  Account 327
  Estimating Uncollectibles 328
Direct Write-Off Method of
Accounting for Uncollectibles 330
Temporary Investments 331
Temporary Investments and
Receivables in the Balance Sheet 332

9 INVENTORIES 349
Importance of Inventories 349
  The Effect of Inventory on the
  Current Period's Statements 350
  The Effect of Inventory on the
  Following Period's Statements 351
Inventory Systems 352
Determining Actual Quantities in
the Inventory 353
Determining the Cost of Inventory 354
Inventory Costing Methods Under
a Periodic System 354
  First-In, First-Out Method 356
  Last-In, First-Out Method 357
  Average Cost Method 357
  Comparison of Inventory
  Costing Methods 358
Accounting for and Reporting
Inventory Under a Perpetual
System 361
  Inventory Costing Methods
  Under a Perpetual System 362

  Internal Control and Perpetual
  Inventory Systems 364
  Automated Perpetual Inventory
  Systems 365
Valuation of Inventory at Other
Than Cost 366
  Valuation at Lower of Cost or
  Market 366
  Valuation at Net Realizable
  Value 367
Presentation of Merchandise
Inventory on the Balance Sheet 367
Estimating Inventory Cost 368
  Retail Method of Inventory
  Costing 368
  Gross Profit Method of
  Estimating Inventories 369

10 PLANT ASSETS AND INTANGIBLE ASSETS 386
Acquisition of Plant Assets 387
Nature of Depreciation 388
Accounting for Depreciation 388
  Straight-Line Method 390
  Units-of-Production Method 390
  Declining-Balance Method 391
  Sum-of-the-Years-Digits
  Method 392
  Comparison of Depreciation
  Methods 392
  Depreciation for Federal Income
  Tax 393
  Revision of Periodic
  Depreciation 394
  Recording Depreciation 395
  Subsidiary Ledgers for Plant
  Assets 396
  Depreciation of Plant Assets of
  Low Unit Cost 397
Composite-Rate Depreciation
Method 397
Capital and Revenue
Expenditures 398
  Capital Expenditures 398
  Revenue Expenditures 399
  Summary of Capital and
  Revenue Expenditures 399
Disposal of Plant Assets 400
  Discarding Plant Assets 400
  Sale of Plant Assets 401
  Exchange of Plant Assets 402
Acquisition of Plant Assets
Through Leasing 404
Depletion 404
Intangible Assets 405
  Patents 405
  Copyrights 406
  Goodwill 406
Reporting Depreciation Expense,
Plant Assets, and Intangible
Assets in the Financial Statements 407

11 PAYROLL, NOTES
PAYABLE, AND OTHER
CURRENT LIABILITIES   426
Payroll and Payroll Taxes   426
    Liability for Employee Earnings   426
    Deductions from Employee
    Earnings   429
    Computation of Employee Net
    Pay   430
    Liability for Employer's Payroll
    Taxes   432
Accounting Systems for Payroll
and Payroll Taxes   433
    Payroll Register   433
    Employee's Earnings Record   436
    Payroll Checks   437
    Payroll System Diagram   439
    Internal Controls for Payroll
    Systems   441
Liability for Employee's Fringe
Benefits   441
    Liability for Vacation Pay   441
    Liability for Pensions   442
Short-Term Notes Payable   443
Product Warranty Liability   445

PRACTICE SET: CENTURION
COMPUTER SYSTEMS

This set is available with transactions in narrative
form or with business documents. The set provides
practice in accounting for a sole proprietorship that
uses the voucher system.

3   ACCOUNTING PRINCIPLES   465

12 CONCEPTS AND PRINCIPLES   466
Development of Concepts and
Principles   466
    Financial Accounting
    Standards Board   467
    Governmental Accounting
    Standards Board   468
    Accounting Organizations   469
    Government Organizations   469
    Other Influential Organizations   469
Business Entity   470
Going Concern   470
Objective Evidence   471
Unit of Measurement   472
    Scope of Accounting Reports   472
    Changes in Price Levels   472
Accounting Period   474
Matching Revenue and Expired
Costs   474
    Recognition of Revenue   475
    Allocation of Costs   477
Adequate Disclosure   478
    Accounting Methods
    Employed   478
    Changes in Accounting
    Estimates   479
    Contingent Liabilities   479
    Segment of a Business   481
    Events Subsequent to Date of
    Statements   481
Consistency   482
Materiality   483
Conservatism   485

4   PARTNERSHIPS AND
CORPORATIONS   504

13 PARTNERSHIP
FORMATION, INCOME
DIVISION, AND
LIQUIDATION   505
Characteristics of Partnerships   505
Advantages and Disadvantages
of Partnerships   506
Accounting for Partnerships   507
Recording Investments   507
Division of Net Income or Net
Loss   508
    Income Division Recognizing
    Services of Partners   509
    Income Division Recognizing
    Services of Partners and
    Investments   510
    Income Division — Allowances
    Exceed Net Income   510
Statements for Partnerships   511
Partnership Dissolution   511
    Admission of a Partner   512
    Withdrawal of a Partner   515
    Death of a Partner   515
Liquidation of Partnerships   516
    Gain on Realization   516
    Loss on Realization; No Capital
    Deficiencies   517
    Loss on Realization; Capital
    Deficiencies   518

14 CORPORATIONS:
ORGANIZATION AND
OPERATIONS   536
Characteristics of a Corporation   537
Stockholders' Equity   538
Characteristics of Capital Stock   538
    Classes of Stock   539
    Participating and
    Nonparticipating Preferred
    Stock   540
    Cumulative and Noncumulative
    Preferred Stock   540
    Other Preferential Rights   541

Issuing Capital Stock   542
  *Premium and Discount on
  Stock*   *542*
  *Premium on Capital Stock on
  the Balance Sheet*   *543*
  *Issuing Stock for Assets Other
  Than Cash*   *544*
  No-Par Stock   *544*
  *Subscriptions and Stock
  Issuance*   *545*
Treasury Stock   547
Equity per Share   549
Organization Costs   550

5 FINANCIAL REPORTING FOR CORPORATIONS   567

15 STOCKHOLDERS' EQUITY, EARNINGS, AND DIVIDENDS   568
Paid-In Capital   568
Corporate Earnings and Income
Taxes   570
Allocation of Income Tax Between
Periods   571
Reporting Unusual Items in the
Financial Statements   574
  *Unusual Items that Affect the
  Income Statement*   *574*
  *Unusual Items that Affect the
  Retained Earnings Statement*   *576*
Earnings per Common Share   579
Appropriation of Retained
Earnings   581
Nature of Dividends   583
  Cash Dividends   *583*
  Stock Dividends   *585*
  Liquidating Dividends   *586*
Stock Splits   587
Dividends and Stock Splits for
Treasury Stock   587

PRACTICE SET: CLASSIC DESIGNS INC.
This set is available with transactions in narrative form. The set provides practice in accounting for a corporation that operates a departmentalized business.

16 LONG-TERM LIABILITIES AND INVESTMENTS IN BONDS   608
Financing Corporations   608
Characteristics of Bonds   610
Present Value Concepts   611
Present Value Concepts for
Bonds Payable   612
  Present Value of $1   *612*
  Present Value of Annuity of $1   *613*
Accounting for Bonds Payable   613
  Bonds Issued at Face Amount   *614*
  Bonds Issued at a Discount   *615*
  Bonds Issued at a Premium   *617*
  Zero-Coupon Bonds   *619*
Bond Sinking Fund   619
  Future Value Concepts   *619*
  *Accounting for Bond Sinking
  Fund*   *621*
Appropriation for Bonded
Indebtedness   623
Bond Redemption   623
Balance Sheet Presentation of
Bonds Payable   624
Investments in Bonds   624
  *Accounting for Bond
  Investments — Purchase,
  Interest, and Amortization*   *625*
  *Accounting for Bond
  Investments — Sale*   *626*

PRACTICE SET: SEMO SPORTING GOODS SUPPLY INC.
This set requires the preparation of correcting entries and financial statements for a corporation.

17 INVESTMENTS IN STOCKS; CONSOLIDATED STATEMENTS; INTERNATIONAL OPERATIONS   646
Investments in Stocks   646
Accounting for Long-Term
Investments in Stocks   647
  Cost Method   *647*
  Equity Method   *649*
  *Sale of Long-Term Investments
  in Stock*   *649*
Business Combinations   650
  Mergers and Consolidations   *651*
  *Parent and Subsidiary
  Corporations*   *651*
Accounting for Parent-Subsidiary
Affiliations   652
Basic Principles of Consolidation
of Financial Statements   652
  Purchase Method   *653*
  Pooling of Interests Method   *660*
  *Consolidated Income
  Statement and Other
  Statements*   *663*
Corporation Financial Statements   664
Accounting for International
Operations   665
  *Accounting for Transactions
  with Foreign Companies*   *666*
  *Consolidated Financial
  Statements with Foreign
  Subsidiaries*   *668*

18 STATEMENT OF CASH FLOWS 691

Nature of the Statement of Cash Flows 691
Reporting Cash Flows 693
  Cash Flows from Operating Activities 693
  Cash Flows from Investing Activities 694
  Cash Flows from Financing Activities 694
  Illustrations of the Statement of Cash Flows 694
  Noncash Investing and Financing Activities 696
  Cash Flow per Share 696
Assembling Data and Preparing the Statement of Cash Flows 696
  Retained Earnings 697
  Common Stock 703
  Preferred Stock 703
  Bonds Payable 703
  Equipment 704
  Building 705
  Land 705
  Investments 705
  Preparing the Statement of Cash Flows 706
APPENDIX: The Direct Method of Reporting Cash Flows from Operating Activities 707
APPENDIX: Work Sheet for Statement of Cash Flows 711

19 FINANCIAL STATEMENT ANALYSIS AND ANNUAL REPORTS 745

Basic Analytical Procedures 745
  Horizontal Analysis 746
  Vertical Analysis 749
  Common-Size Statements 751
  Other Analytical Measures 752
Focus of Financial Statement Analyses 752
Solvency Analysis 753
  Current Position Analysis 753
  Accounts Receivable Analysis 755
  Inventory Analysis 756
  Ratio of Plant Assets to Long-Term Liabilities 757
  Ratio of Stockholders' Equity to Liabilities 757
  Number of Times Interest Charges Earned 758
Profitability Analysis 758
  Ratio of Net Sales to Assets 758
  Rate Earned on Total Assets 759
  Rate Earned on Stockholders' Equity 760

  Rate Earned on Common Stockholders' Equity 761
  Earnings per Share on Common Stock 761
  Price-Earnings Ratio 762
  Dividend Yield 763
Summary of Analytical Measures 763
Corporate Annual Reports 765
  Financial Highlights 765
  President's Letter 766
  Independent Auditors' Report 766
  Management Report 769
  Historical Summary 770
  Other Information 770

6 MANAGERIAL ACCOUNTING PRINCIPLES AND SYSTEMS 792

20 MANAGERIAL ACCOUNTING CONCEPTS AND PRINCIPLES 793

Financial Accounting and Managerial Accounting 794
The Management Process 795
Characteristics of Managerial Accounting Reports 796
  Relevance 796
  Timeliness 796
  Accuracy 797
  Clarity 797
  Conciseness 797
  Costs vs. Benefits of Managerial Accounting Reports 798
Organization of the Managerial Accounting Function 798
Cost Concepts 801
Manufacturing Costs 802
  Direct Materials Cost 802
  Direct Labor Cost 803
  Factory Overhead Cost 803
  Prime Costs and Conversion Costs 803
Nonmanufacturing Costs 804
Product Costs and Period Costs 805
Financial Statements for Manufacturing Enterprises 805
  Balance Sheet for a Manufacturing Enterprise 806
  Income Statement for a Manufacturing Enterprise 807
Additional Cost Concepts for Managerial Planning 809
  Variable Costs and Fixed Costs 809
  Direct and Indirect Costs 810
  Controllable Costs and Noncontrollable Costs 810
  Differential Costs 811

Discretionary Costs   811
Sunk Costs   811
Opportunity Costs   812
Summary of Cost Concepts   812

21 JOB ORDER COST SYSTEMS   831
Usefulness of Product Costs   831
Types of Accounting Systems   832
  General Accounting Systems 832
  Cost Accounting Systems   834
  Perpetual Inventory Procedures 834
Job Order Cost Systems for Manufacturing Enterprises 835
  Materials   835
  Factory Labor   837
  Factory Overhead   838
  Work in Process   841
  Finished Goods and Cost of Goods Sold 844
  Sales   844
Illustration of Job Order Cost Accounting 845
Job Order Cost Systems for Service Enterprises 851

PRACTICE SET: WEMAKE TOYS INC.
The narrative accompanies the set, which is available without business papers. This set provides practice in accounting for a manufacturing business that uses a job order cost system.

22 PROCESS COST SYSTEMS   869
Flow of Costs in a Process Cost System 869
Inventories of Partially Processed Materials 871
  Flow of Materials   871
  Equivalent Units of Production 872
Cost of Production Report   873
Service Departments and Process Costs 875
Joint Products and By-Products   876
  Accounting for Joint Products 876
  Accounting for By-Products 877
Illustration of Process Cost Accounting 877
  Cost of Production Reports 882
  Financial Statements   883
Inventory Costing Methods   885
  First-In, First-Out (Fifo) Cost Method 885
  Average Cost Method   885

7 PLANNING AND CONTROL   905

23 COST BEHAVIOR CONCEPTS AND COST-VOLUME-PROFIT   906
Cost Behavior   907
  Fixed Costs   907
  Variable Costs   908
  Mixed Costs   909
  Summary of Cost Behavior Concepts 911
Cost-Volume-Profit Relationships   912
Mathematical Approach to Cost-Volume-Profit Analysis 912
  Break-Even Point   912
  Desired Profit   915
Graphic Approach to Cost-Volume-Profit Analysis 915
  Cost-Volume-Profit (Break-Even) Chart 915
  Profit-Volume Chart   917
Use of Computers in Cost-Volume-Profit Analysis 920
Sales Mix Considerations   921
Special Cost-Volume-Profit Relationships 922
  Margin of Safety   922
  Contribution Margin Ratio 923
Limitations of Cost-Volume-Profit Analysis 923

24 PROFIT PLANNING FOR MANAGEMENT ANALYSIS   943
Absorption Costing and Variable Costing 943
The Income Statement Under Variable Costing and Absorption Costing 944
  Income Reported When Units Manufactured Equal Units Sold 946
  Income Reported When Units Manufactured Exceed Units Sold 946
  Income Reported When Units Manufactured Are Less Than Units Sold 947
  Comparison of Income Reported Under the Two Concepts 948
Income Analysis Under Variable Costing and Absorption Costing 948
Management's Use of Variable Costing and Absorption Costing 951
  Cost Control   951
  Product Pricing   952
  Production Planning   953
  Sales Analysis   954
  Contribution Margin Analysis 956

**25 BUDGETING AND
STANDARD COST
SYSTEMS**   **976**
Nature and Objectives of
Budgeting   976
Budgeting Systems   977
    Sales Budget   979
    Production Budget   979
    Direct Materials Purchases
    Budget   980
    Direct Labor Cost Budget   981
    Factory Overhead Cost Budget   981
    Cost of Goods Sold Budget   982
    Operating Expenses Budget   982
    Budgeted Income Statement   983
    Capital Expenditures Budget   984
    Cash Budget   984
    Budgeted Balance Sheet   986
Budget Performance Reports   987
Flexible Budgets   987
Computerized Budgeting Systems   989
Budgeting and Human Behavior   989
Standard Costs   989
Variances from Standards   990
    Direct Materials Cost Variance   991
    Direct Labor Cost Variance   992
    Factory Overhead Cost
    Variance   993
Standards in the Accounts   997
Revision of Standards   998
**APPENDIX: Quantitative
Techniques for Inventory Control**   **998**

**26 RESPONSIBILITY
ACCOUNTING**   **1027**
Centralized and Decentralized
Operations   1027
    Advantages of Decentralization   1028
    Disadvantages of
    Decentralization   1029
Types of Decentralized
Operations   1029
    Cost Centers   1030
    Profit Centers   1030
    Investment Centers   1031
Responsibility Accounting for
Cost Centers   1032
Responsibility Accounting for
Profit Centers   1034
    Gross Profit by Departments   1035
    Operating Income by
    Departments   1035
    Departmental Margin   1039
Responsibility Accounting for
Investment Centers   1043
    Operating Income   1043
    Rate of Return on Investment   1043
    Residual Income   1046

8 DECISION MAKING   **1066**

**27 DIFFERENTIAL ANALYSIS
AND PRODUCT PRICING**   **1067**
Differential Analysis   1067
    Lease or Sell   1068
    Discontinuance of an
    Unprofitable Segment   1069
    Make or Buy   1071
    Equipment Replacement   1072
    Process or Sell   1073
    Acceptance of Business at a
    Special Price   1074
Setting Normal Product Prices   1075
    Total Cost Concept   1075
    Product Cost Concept   1077
    Variable Cost Concept   1078
    Choosing a Cost-Plus
    Approach Cost Concept   1079
Economic Theory of Product
Pricing   1080
    Maximization of Profits   1080
    Revenues   1080
    Costs   1080
    Product Price Determination   1081
    Pricing Strategies   1083

**28 CAPITAL INVESTMENT
ANALYSIS**   **1100**
Nature of Capital Investment
Analysis   1100
Methods of Evaluating Capital
Investment Proposals   1101
    Methods That Ignore Present
    Value   1101
    Present Value Methods   1104
Factors That Complicate Capital
Investment Analysis   1110
    Income Tax   1110
    Unequal Proposal Lives   1111
    Lease Versus Capital
    Investment   1112
    Uncertainty   1113
    Changes in Price Levels   1113
Capital Rationing   1113
Planning and Controlling Capital
Investment Expenditures   1115

APPENDIXES

A   **INTEREST TABLES**   **A-1**
B   **CODES OF ETHICS
   FOR ACCOUNTANTS**   **B-1**
C   **ALTERNATIVE METHOD
   OF RECORDING
   MERCHANDISE
   INVENTORIES**   **C-1**

D ACCOUNTING FOR
  INDIVIDUALS   D-1
E INCOME TAXES   E-1
F ACCOUNTING FOR
  NONPROFIT
  ORGANIZATIONS   F-1

G MAJOR TRENDS IN
  MANUFACTURING   G-1
H MANUFACTURING
  WORK SHEET   H-1
I SPECIMEN FINANCIAL
  STATEMENTS   I-1

TEXT OBJECTIVES

1 Describe the evolution of accounting.

2 Describe the basic structure of the accounting profession.

3 Describe and illustrate the basic financial accounting concepts and principles.

4 Describe and illustrate accounting systems for service and merchandising enterprises.

5 Describe and illustrate accounting concepts and principles for sole proprietorships, partnerships, and corporations.

6 Describe and illustrate financial accounting concepts and principles for analyzing business operations.

7 Describe the basic nature and structure of managerial accounting.

8 Describe and illustrate accounting systems for manufacturing enterprises.

9 Describe and illustrate managerial accounting concepts and principles for planning, control, and decision making.

INTRODUCTION
EVOLUTION OF ACCOUNTING

Accounting has evolved, as have medicine, law, and most other fields of human activity, in response to the social and economic needs of society. As business and society have become more complex over the years, accounting has developed new concepts and techniques to meet the ever increasing needs for financial information. Without such information, many complex economic developments and social programs might never have been undertaken. This introduction briefly describes the evolution of accounting.

PRIMITIVE ACCOUNTING

People in all civilizations have maintained various types of records of business activities. The oldest known are clay tablet records of the payment of wages in Babylonia around 3600 B.C. There are numerous evidences of record keeping and systems of accounting control in ancient Egypt and in the Greek city-states. The earliest known English records were compiled at the direction of William the Conqueror in the eleventh century to ascertain the financial resources of the kingdom.

For the most part, early accounting dealt only with limited aspects of the financial operations of private or governmental enterprises. There was no systematic accounting for all transactions of a particular unit, only for specific types or portions of transactions. Complete accounting for an enterprise developed somewhat later in response to the needs of the commercial republics of Italy.

DOUBLE-ENTRY SYSTEM

The evolution of the system of record keeping which came to be called "double entry" was strongly influenced by Venetian merchants. The first known description of the system was published in Italy in 1494. The author, a Franciscan monk by the name of Luca Pacioli, was a mathematician who taught in various universities in Perugia, Naples, Pisa, and Florence. Evidence of the position that Pacioli occupied among the intellectuals of his day was his close friendship with Leonardo da Vinci, with whom he collaborated on a mathematics book. Pacioli did the text and da Vinci the illustrations.

Goethe, the German poet, novelist, scientist, and universal genius, wrote about double entry as follows: "It is one of the most beautiful inventions of the human spirit, and every good businessman should use it in his economic undertakings."[1] Double entry provides for recording both aspects of a transaction in such a manner as to establish an equilibrium. For example, if an individual borrows $1,000 from a bank, the amount of the loan is recorded both as cash of $1,000 and as an obligation to repay $1,000. Either of the $1,000 amounts is balanced by the other $1,000 amount. As the basic principles are developed further in the early chapters of this book, it will become evident that "double entry" provides for the recording of all business transactions in a systematic manner. It also provides for a set of integrated financial statements reporting in monetary terms the amount of (1) the profit (net income) for a single venture or for a specified period, (2) the properties (assets) owned by the enterprise and the ownership rights (equities) to the properties, and (3) the flow of cash into and out of the enterprise.

When the resources of a number of people were pooled to finance a single venture, such as a voyage of a merchant ship, the double-entry system provided records and reports of the income of the venture and the equity of the various participants. As single ventures were replaced by more permanent business organizations, the double-entry system was easily adapted to meet their needs. In spite of the tremendous development of business operations since 1494, and the ever increasing complexities of business and governmental organizations, the basic elements of the double-entry system have continued virtually unchanged.

INDUSTRIAL REVOLUTION

The Industrial Revolution, which occurred in England from the mid-eighteenth to the mid-nineteenth century, brought many social and economic changes, notably a change from the handicraft method of producing marketable goods to the factory system. The use of machinery in turning out many identical products gave rise to the need to determine the cost of a large volume of machine-made products instead of the cost of a relatively small number of individually handcrafted products. The specialized field of cost accounting emerged to meet this need for the analysis of various costs and for recording techniques.

In the early days of manufacturing operations, when business enterprises were relatively small and often isolated geographically, competition was frequently not very keen. Cost accounting was primitive and focused primarily on providing management with records and reports on past operations. Most business decisions were made on the basis of this historical financial information combined with intuition or hunches about the potential success of proposed courses of action.

As manufacturing enterprises became larger and more complex and as competition among manufacturers increased, the "scientific management concept" evolved. This concept emphasized a systematic approach to the solution of management problems. Paralleling this trend was the development of more sophisticated cost accounting concepts to supply management with analytical techniques for measuring the efficiency of current operations and in planning for future operations. This trend was accelerated in the twentieth century by the advent of the electronic computer with its capacity for manipulating large masses of data and its ability to determine the potential effect of alternative courses of action.

[1]Goethe, Johann Wolfgang von, *Samtliche Werke*, edited by Edward von der Hellen (Stuttgart and Berlin: J. G. Cotta, 1902–07), Vol. XVII, p. 37.

CORPORATE ORGANIZATION

The expanded business operations initiated by the Industrial Revolution required increasingly large amounts of money to build factories and purchase machinery. This need for large amounts of capital resulted in the development of the corporate form of organization, which was first legally established in England in 1845. The Industrial Revolution spread rapidly to the United States, which became one of the world's leading industrial nations shortly after the Civil War. The accumulation of large amounts of capital was essential for establishment of new businesses in industries such as manufacturing, transportation, mining, electric power, and communications. In the United States, as in England, the corporation was the form of organization that facilitated the accumulation of the substantial amounts of capital needed.

Almost all large American business enterprises, and many small ones, are organized as corporations largely because ownership is evidenced by readily transferable shares of stock. The shareholders of a corporation control the management of corporate affairs only indirectly. They elect a board of directors, which establishes general policies and selects officers who actively manage the corporation. The development of a class of owners far removed from active participation in the management of the business created an additional dimension for accounting. Accounting information was needed not only by management in directing the affairs of the corporation but also by the shareholders, who required periodic financial statements in order to appraise management's performance.

As corporations became larger, an increasing number of individuals and institutions looked to accountants to provide economic information about these enterprises. Prospective shareholders and creditors sought information about a corporation's financial status and its prospects for the future. Government agencies required financial information for purposes of taxation and regulation. Employees, union representatives, and customers demanded information upon which to judge the stability and profitability of corporate enterprises. Thus accounting began to expand its function of meeting the needs of a relatively few owners to a public role of meeting the needs of a variety of interested parties.

PUBLIC ACCOUNTING

The development of the corporation also created a new social need—the need for an independent audit to provide some assurance that management's financial representations were reliable. This audit function, often referred to as the "attest function," was chiefly responsible for the creation and growth of the public accounting profession. Unlike private accountants, public accountants are independent of the enterprises for which they perform services.

Recognizing the need for accounting services of professional caliber, all of the states provide for the licensing of certified public accountants (*CPAs*). In 1944, fifty years after the enactment of the first CPA law, there were approximately 25,000 CPAs in the United States. During the next four decades the number increased tenfold, and currently the number exceeds 300,000.

Auditing is still a major service offered by CPAs, but presently they also devote much of their time to assisting their clients with problems related to planning, controlling, and decision making. Such consulting services, commonly known as management advisory services, have increased in volume over the years until today they comprise a significant part of the practice of most public accounting firms.

INCOME TAX

Enactment of the federal income tax law in 1913 resulted in a tremendous stimulus to accounting activity. All business enterprises organized as corporations or partnerships, as well as many individuals, were required to maintain sufficient records to enable them to file accurate tax returns. Since that time the income tax laws and regulations have become increasingly complex. As a consequence businesses have depended upon both private and public accountants for advice on legal methods of tax minimization, for preparing tax returns, and for representing them in tax disputes with governmental agencies.

It should also be noted that accounting has influenced the development of income tax law to a great degree. Had not accounting progressed to a point where periodic net income could be determined, the enactment and enforcement of any tax law undoubtedly would have been extremely difficult, if not impossible.

GOVERNMENT INFLUENCE

Over the years government at various levels has intervened to an increasing extent in economic and social matters affecting ever greater numbers of people. Accounting has played an important role by providing the financial information needed to achieve the desired goals.

As the number and size of corporate enterprises grew and an ever increasing number of shares of stock were traded in the market place, laws regulating the activities of stock exchanges, stockbrokers, and investment companies were enacted for the protection of investors. These regulations involve accounting requirements. To protect the public from excessive charges by railroads and other monopolies, commissions were established to limit their rates to levels yielding net income considered to be a "fair return" on invested capital. This rate-making process required extensive accounting information. Regulated banks and savings and loan associations also had to meet record-keeping and reporting requirements and permit periodic examination of their records by governmental agencies. As labor unions became larger and more powerful, regulatory laws were enacted requiring them to submit periodic financial reports. With the enactment of social security and medicare legislation came record-keeping and reporting requirements for almost all businesses and many individuals.

As the federal government exercised increasing control over economic activities, accounting information became more essential as a basis for formulating legislation. One of the areas in which the government has influenced economic and social behavior has been through the income tax. For example, contributions to charitable organizations have been encouraged by permitting their deduction in determining taxable income. Controls over wages and prices have also been enacted at various times in attempts to control the economy by reducing the rate of inflation. An enormous volume of accounting data must be reported, summarized, and studied before proceeding with the evaluation of various governmental proposals such as the foregoing.

ACCOUNTING'S FUTURE

Accounting is capable of supplying financial information that is essential for the efficient operation and for the evaluation of performance of any economic unit in society. Changes in the environment in which such organizations operate will inevitably be accompanied by alterations in accounting concepts and techniques. Although long-range predictions as to environmental changes are risky and of doubtful value, there are three areas that promise to receive increased attention in the immediate future — computerized accounting systems, international accounting, and socioeconomic accounting.

Computerized Accounting Systems

Since the electronic computer was first used to process business data in the middle of the twentieth century, it has played an ever increasing role in the design of accounting systems and the processing of economic data. It has generally enabled interested users of accounting information to receive relevant economic data on a more timely basis at a lower cost.

The integration of the electronic computer into accounting systems has created both opportunities and challenges for accountants. The computer provides opportunities for accountants to analyze efficiently a greater quantity of economic data for reporting to users. As the use of computers in business continues to accelerate, there will be an increasing demand for accountants to aid in the analysis, design, and implementation of these systems. This responsibility, in turn, will create ever greater challenges for accountants to obtain a complete understanding of business operations and the principles of designing systems that will gather all accurate, relevant data on a timely basis.

International Accounting

The rapid growth of multinational firms in recent years has had a significant impact on accounting because of the different environments existing in the various countries in which such firms operate. Currently, a major problem is the need to develop more uniform accounting standards among countries. Working toward this end are such international organizations as the International Accounting Standards Committee and the International Federation of Accountants.

Socioeconomic Accounting

The term socioeconomic accounting refers to the measurement and communication of information about the impact of various organizations on society. Three major areas of social measurement can be identified. First, at the societal level the interest is on the total impact of all institutions on matters that affect the quality of life. The second area is concerned with the programs undertaken by the government and socially oriented not-for-profit organizations to accomplish specific social objectives. The third area, sometimes referred to as corporate social responsibility, focuses on the public interest in corporate social performance in such areas as reduction of water and air pollution, conservation of natural resources, improvement in quality of product and customer service, and employment practices regarding minority groups and females. The concept of social measurement is relatively simple as a theory, but much additional study and research will be needed before measurement can be expressed in terms of monetary costs and benefits.

Basic
Structure of
Accounting

PART ONE

1

CHAPTER ONE
ACCOUNTING PRINCIPLES AND PRACTICES

CHAPTER OBJECTIVES

1 Describe accounting as an information system.

2 Describe the profession of accounting and its specialized fields.

3 Describe the development of accounting principles and their relation to practice.

4 Describe a business transaction.

5 Identify the accounting equation and its basic elements.

6 Describe and illustrate how all business transactions can be stated in terms of the resulting changes in the three basic elements of the accounting equation.

7 Identify and describe the financial statements of a sole proprietorship:
Income statement
Statement of owner's equity
Balance sheet
Statement of cash flows

8 Identify and describe the financial statements of a corporation.

Accounting plays an important role in our economic and social system. Sound decisions made by individuals, businesses, governments, and other entities are essential for the efficient distribution and use of the nation's scarce resources. To make such decisions, these groups must have reliable information provided by the accounting system. The objective of accounting, therefore, is to record, summarize, report, and interpret economic data for use by many groups within our economic and social system.

ACCOUNTING AS AN INFORMATION SYSTEM

OBJECTIVE 1
Describe accounting as an information system.

Accounting[1] is often called the "language of business." This language can be viewed as an information system that provides essential information about the financial activities of an entity to various individuals or groups for their use in making informed judgments and decisions. As such, accounting information is composed principally of financial data about business transactions, expressed in terms of money. The recording of transaction data may take various forms, such as pen or pencil markings made by hand, printing by mechanical and electronic devices, or magnetic impressions on tape or disks.

---

[1]A glossary of terms appears at the end of the text. The terms included in the glossary are printed in color the first time they appear in the text.

The mere records of transactions are of little use in making informed judgments and decisions. The recorded data must be sorted and summarized and then presented in significant reports. The usefulness of reports is often improved by various kinds of percentage and trend analyses.

Users of Accounting Information

Accounting provides the techniques for gathering economic data and the language for communicating these data to different individuals and institutions. Investors in a business enterprise need information about its financial status and its future prospects. Bankers and suppliers appraise the financial soundness of a business organization and assess the risks involved before making loans or granting credit. Government agencies are concerned with the financial activities of business organizations for purposes of taxation and regulation. Employees and their union representatives are also vitally interested in the stability and the profitability of the organization that hires them.

The individuals who depend upon and make the most use of accounting are those charged with the responsibility for directing the operations of enterprises. They are often referred to collectively as "management." Many types of data may be needed by management. For example, in the conduct of day-to-day operations, management relies upon accounting to provide the amount owed to each creditor and by each customer and the date each payment is due. Managers also rely upon accounting information to assist them in evaluating current operations and in planning future operations. For example, comparisons of past performance with planned objectives may reveal the means of accelerating favorable trends and reducing those that are unfavorable.

The process of using accounting to provide information to users is illustrated in the following diagram. First, user groups are identified and their

Accounting as a Provider of Information to Users

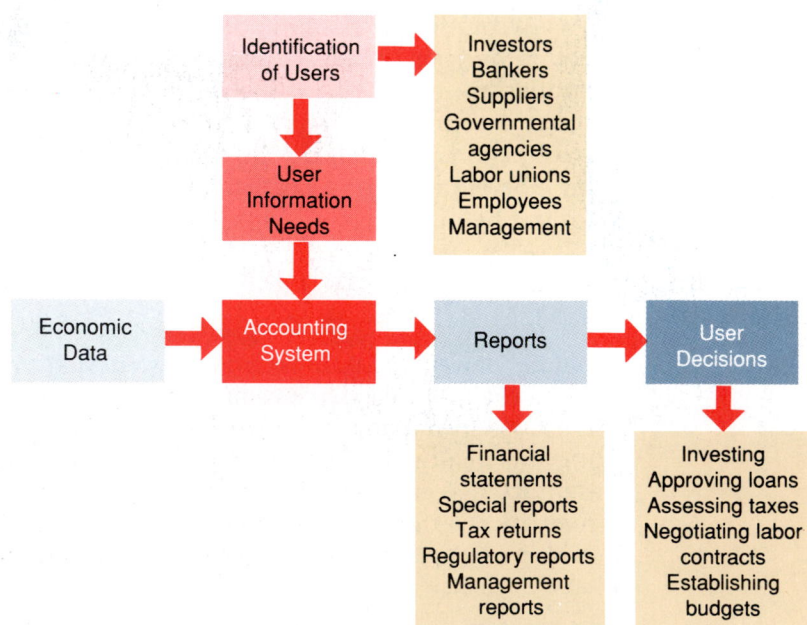

information needs determined. These needs determine which economic data are gathered and processed by the accounting system. Finally, the accounting system generates reports that communicate essential information to users. For example, investors need information on the financial condition and results of operations of an enterprise to assess the profitability and riskiness of their investments in the enterprise. The accounting system satisfies these needs by recording essential information and periodically summarizing this information in financial reports. Although the information for one category of users may differ markedly from that needed by other users, accounting can provide each user group with economic information to assist them in making decisions regarding future actions.

Relationship of Accounting to Other Disciplines

Individuals engaged in such areas of business as finance, production, marketing, personnel, and general management need not be expert accountants, but they are more effective if they have a good understanding of accounting principles. Everyone engaged in business activity, from the youngest employee to the manager and owner, comes into contact with accounting. The higher the level of authority and responsibility, the greater is the need for an understanding of accounting concepts and terminology.

A study of U.S. corporations revealed that finance and accounting were the most common backgrounds of chief executive officers. Interviews with corporate executives produced the following comments:[2]

> "... it's vital that the chief executive officer know the corporation and ... have an understanding of accounting."

> "... my training in accounting and auditing practice has been extremely valuable to me throughout."

> "A knowledge of accounting carries with it an understanding of the establishment and the maintenance of sound financial controls — an area which is absolutely essential to a chief executive officer."

> "I try to have my entire staff understand the financial function and how to use financial data."

The importance of understanding accounting is not limited to the business world. Many employees with specialized training in nonbusiness areas also make use of accounting data and need to understand accounting principles and terminology. For example, an engineer responsible for selecting the most desirable solution to a technical manufacturing problem may consider cost accounting data to be the deciding factor. Lawyers use accounting data in tax cases and in lawsuits involving property ownership and damages from breach of contract. Governmental agencies rely on accounting data in evaluating the efficiency of government operations and for appraising the feasibility of proposed taxation and spending programs. Finally, every adult engages in business transactions and must necessarily be concerned with the financial aspects of life. Accounting plays an important role in modern society and, broadly speaking, all citizens are affected by accounting in some way.

---

[2]John R. Linden, "Rising Corporate Stars: The Accountant as Chief Executive Officer," *The Journal of Accountancy* (September, 1978), pp. 64–71.

PROFESSION OF ACCOUNTANCY

OBJECTIVE 2
Describe the
profession of
accounting and its
specialized fields.

Accounting can be characterized as a profession that has experienced rapid development during the current century. This has been accompanied by an expansion of the career opportunities in accounting and an increasing number of professionally trained accountants. During the period 1960–1988, the profession of accountancy more than doubled in size. Among the factors contributing to this growth have been the increase in number, size, and complexity of business corporations; the frequent changes in the tax laws; and other governmental restrictions on business operations.

As the complexity of the business and social environment continues to increase, employment and advancement opportunities in the profession of accountancy are expected to continue to grow and expand. The following table indicates the projected growth of the profession of accountancy relative to the projected growth of the legal and medical professions:

Profession	Projected Rate of Increase 1986–2000
Accountancy	39.8%
Medical	38.2
Legal	35.4

Source: U.S. Department of Labor, Bureau of Labor Statistics, *Occupational Projections and Training Data: 1988 Edition* (Washington: U.S. Government Printing Office, April, 1988).

As professionals, accountants are typically engaged in either (1) private accounting or (2) public accounting. Accountants employed by a particular business firm or not-for-profit organization, perhaps as chief accountant, controller, or financial vice-president, are said to be engaged in **private accounting**. Accountants who render accounting services on a fee basis, and staff accountants employed by them, are said to be engaged in **public accounting**.

Both private and public accounting have long been recognized as excellent training for top managerial responsibilities. Many executive positions in government and in industry are held by men and women with education and experience in accounting.

Private Accounting

The scope of activities and responsibilities of private accountants varies widely. They are frequently referred to as managerial accountants, or, if they are employed by a manufacturing concern, as industrial or cost accountants. Various governmental units and other not-for-profit organizations also employ accountants.

The Institute of Certified Management Accountants, which is an affiliate of the National Association of Accountants, grants the Certified Management Accountant (CMA) designation as evidence of professional competence in that field. Requirements for the CMA designation include the baccalaureate degree or equivalent, two years of experience in management accounting, and successful completion of examinations occupying two and one-half days. Participation in a program of continuing professional education is also required for renewal of the certificate. The Institute of Internal Auditors administers a similar program for internal auditors—accountants who review the accounting and operating procedures prescribed by their firms. Accountants qualifying under this program are entitled to use the designation Certified Internal Auditor (CIA).

Public Accounting

In public accounting, an accountant may practice as an individual or as a member of a public accounting firm. Public accountants who have met a state's education, experience, and examination requirements may become **certified public accountants**, commonly called **CPAs**.

Qualifications of CPAs. The qualifications required for the CPA certificate differ among the various states. A specified level of education is required, often the completion of a collegiate course of study in accounting. All states require that a candidate pass an examination prepared by the **American Institute of Certified Public Accountants (AICPA)**. The examination is administered twice a year, in May and November. Many states permit candidates to take the examination upon graduation from college or during the term in which they will complete the educational requirements. The examination, which occupies one afternoon and two all-day sessions, is divided into four parts: Accounting Theory, Accounting Practice, Auditing, and Business Law. Some states also require an examination in an additional subject, such as Rules of Professional Conduct. Most states do not permit successful candidates to practice as independent CPAs until they have had from one to three years' experience in public accounting or in employment considered equivalent. Details regarding the requirements in any particular state can be obtained from the respective State Board of Accountancy.

In recent years a majority of the states have enacted laws requiring public practitioners to participate in a program of continuing professional education or forfeit their right to continue in public practice. According to the statutes of one of the states, the continuing education must be a "formal program of learning which contributes directly to the professional competence of an individual after he or she has been licensed to practice public accounting." The states differ as to some of the details of the requirement, such as the number of hours of formal education required for renewal of the permit to practice. The rules adopted by a number of State Boards of Accountancy require forty hours per year (a fifty-minute class period counts as one hour).

Professional Ethics for CPAs. CPAs have a duty not only to their clients but to their colleagues and the public to perform services competently and with integrity. However, many clients and much of the public do not have the capability of evaluating a CPA's performance. Therefore, standards of conduct have been established to guide CPAs in the conduct of their practices. These standards, called **codes of professional conduct** or **codes of professional ethics**, have been established by professional organizations of CPAs, such as the AICPA and state societies of CPAs, and by regulatory agencies, such as State Boards of Accountancy and the Securities and Exchange Commission.

The purpose of codes of professional conduct is to instill confidence in the quality of services rendered by public accountants by requiring them to commit to honorable behavior, even at the sacrifice of personal advantage. For example, under the current AICPA code of professional conduct, CPAs must act in a way that will serve the public interest, honor the public trust, and demonstrate commitment to professionalism.[3]

A CPA who violates the code of professional conduct is subject to disciplinary proceedings. The AICPA and state societies of CPAs have authority to revoke a CPA's membership in their organizations. If the violation also involves a regulatory agency, such as a State Board of Accountancy or the Securities and Exchange Commission, the CPA's ability to practice within the agency's jurisdiction may be revoked or otherwise limited. The combination of professional organization and regulatory agency sanctions guards against unethical behavior by the public accounting profession.

To meet the public's expectations of the role and responsibilities of the CPA, codes of professional conduct change as society changes. However, ethical conduct is more than simply conforming to written standards of professional behavior. In a true sense, ethical conduct requires a personal commitment to honorable behavior. This thought was best expressed by Marcus Aurelius, who said, "A man should *be* upright; not be *kept* upright."

ETHICS IN AMERICAN BUSINESS

In October, 1987, Touche Ross conducted a survey of 1,107 directors and top executives of corporations with $500 million or more in annual sales, deans of business schools, and members of Congress, seeking their opinions on ethics in American business. The survey's many interesting findings included the following:

—The United States has higher standards of business ethics than any other country in the world. Ethical standards are also considered high in the United Kingdom, Canada, Switzerland, and Germany, which respondents ranked in that order, followed by Japan.

—An enterprise actually strengthens its competitive position by maintaining high ethical standards.

—The four professions with the highest standards are clergy, accountants, teachers, and engineers, in that order. The ethical standards of business people as a professional group are well regarded, particularly by bankers and accountants.

—A vast majority of the respondents believe that American business is ethical.

—Though respondents believe almost unanimously that the business community is troubled by ethical problems, they are very far from seeing a wholesale breakdown in American business ethics. Indeed, compared to 100 years ago during the age of the robber barons, business ethics are definitely better today.

—Legislation is the least effective way of encouraging ethical business behavior. Rather, the adoption of business codes of ethics is the most effective way. Indeed, the main reason for high ethical standards in a profession is that profession's own standards and accreditation.

Source: *Ethics in American Business*, Touche Ross, January, 1988.

Specialized Accounting Fields

As in many other areas of human activity during the twentieth century, a number of specialized fields in accounting have evolved as a result of rapid

---

[3]*The Code of Professional Conduct*, American Institute of Certified Public Accountants (New York, 1988). The text of this code as well as the code of ethics for the National Association of Accountants are reproduced in Appendix B.

technological advances and accelerated economic growth. The most important accounting fields are described briefly in the following paragraphs.

Financial accounting is concerned with the recording of transactions for a business enterprise or other economic unit and the periodic preparation of various reports from such records. The reports, which may be for general purposes or for a special purpose, provide useful information for managers, owners, creditors, governmental agencies, and the general public. Of particular importance to financial accountants are the rules of accounting, termed **generally accepted accounting principles (GAAP)**. Corporate enterprises must employ such principles in preparing their annual reports on profitability and financial status for their stockholders and the investing public. Comparability of financial reports is essential if the nation's resources are to be divided among business organizations in a socially desirable manner.

Auditing is a field of activity involving an independent review of the accounting records. In conducting an audit, public accountants examine the records supporting the financial reports of an enterprise and give an opinion regarding their fairness and reliability. An important element of "fairness and reliability" is adherence to generally accepted accounting principles. In addition to retaining public accountants for a periodic audit, many corporations have their own permanent staff of internal auditors. Their principal responsibility is to determine if the various operating divisions are following management's policies and procedures.

Cost accounting emphasizes the determination and the control of costs. It is concerned primarily with the costs of manufacturing processes and of manufactured products. In addition, one of the most important duties of the cost accountant is to gather and explain cost data, both actual and prospective. Management uses these data in controlling current operations and in planning for the future.

Managerial accounting uses both historical and estimated data in assisting management in daily operations and in planning future operations. It deals with specific problems that confront enterprise managers at various organizational levels. The managerial accountant is frequently concerned with identifying alternative courses of action and then helping to select the best one. For example, the accountant may assist the company treasurer in preparing plans for future financing, or may develop data for use by management in determining the selling price to be placed on a new product. In recent years, public accountants have realized that their training and experience uniquely qualify them to advise management personnel on policies and administration. This rapidly growing field of specialization by CPAs is frequently called *management advisory services* or *administrative services*.

Tax accounting encompasses the preparation of tax returns and the consideration of the tax consequences of proposed business transactions or alternative courses of action. Accountants specializing in this field, particularly in the area of tax planning, must be familiar with the tax statutes affecting their employer or clients and must also keep up to date on administrative regulations and court decisions on tax cases.

Accounting systems is the special field concerned with the design and implementation of procedures for the accumulation and reporting of financial data. The systems accountant must devise appropriate "checks and balances" to safeguard business properties and provide for information flow that will be efficient and helpful to management. Familiarity with the uses and relative merits of various data processing methods, including computer hardware and software, is also essential.

Budgetary accounting presents the plan of financial operations for a period and, through records and summaries, provides comparisons of actual operations with the predetermined plan. A combination of planning and controlling future operations, it is sometimes considered to be a part of managerial accounting.

International accounting is concerned with the special problems associated with the international trade of multinational business organizations. Because of the increasing number of businesses and the volume of business activity in international trade, this field of accounting has rapidly increased in importance. Accountants specializing in this area must be familiar with the influences that custom, law, and taxation of various countries bring to bear on international operations and accounting principles.

Not-for-profit accounting specializes in recording, reporting, and planning the operations of various governmental units and other not-for-profit organizations such as churches, charities, and educational institutions. An essential element is an accounting system that will insure strict adherence on the part of management to restrictions and other requirements imposed by law, by other institutions, or by individual donors.

Social accounting is a relatively new field of accounting and is the most difficult to describe in a few words. There have been increasing demands on the profession for measurement of social costs and benefits which have previously been considered to be unmeasurable. One of the engagements in this field involved the measurement of traffic patterns in a densely populated section of the nation. This effort was part of a government study to determine the best use of transportation funds, not only in terms of facilitating trade but also of assuring a good environment for the area's residents. Other innovative engagements have dealt with the best use of welfare funds in a large city, with the public use of state parks, with wildlife in state game preserves, and with statewide water and air pollution.

Accounting instruction, as a field of specialization, requires no explanation. However, in addition to teaching, accounting professors often engage in research, auditing, tax accounting, or other areas of accounting on a part-time or consulting basis.

There is some overlapping among the various fields, and leaders in any particular field are likely to be well versed in related areas. There is also a considerable degree of specialization within a particular field. For example, in auditing one may become an expert in a single type of business enterprise such as department stores or public utilities. In tax accounting one may become a specialist in oil and gas producing companies. In systems one may become an expert in electronic data processing equipment.

PRINCIPLES AND PRACTICE

OBJECTIVE 3
Describe the development of accounting principles and their relation to practice.

In accounting, as in the physical and biological sciences, experimentation and change are never-ending. Capable scholars devote their lives and their intellectual energies to the development of accounting principles. Experienced professional accountants contribute their best thinking to the solution of problems continually confronting their clients or employers. Professional accounting associations periodically issue pronouncements on accounting principles. Authoritative accounting pronouncements are issued by such bodies as the **Financial Accounting Standards Board (FASB)**. It is from research, accepted accounting practices, and pronouncements of professional and authoritative bodies that generally accepted accounting principles evolve to form the underlying basis for accounting practice.

In the following paragraphs and throughout the text, accounting principles are discussed and illustrated. It is only through this emphasis on the "why" of accounting as well as on the "how" that the full significance of accounting can be learned.

Business Entity Concept

The **business entity concept** is based on the applicability of accounting to individual economic units in society. These individual economic units include all business enterprises organized for profit; numerous governmental units, such as states, cities, and school districts; other not-for-profit units, such as charities, churches, hospitals, and social clubs; and individual persons and family units.[4] The basic economic data for a unit must first be recorded, followed by analysis and summarization, and finally by periodic reporting. Thus, accounting applies to each separate economic unit.

It is possible, of course, to combine the data for similar economic units to obtain an overall view. For example, accounting data accumulated by each of the airline companies may be assembled and summarized to provide financial information about the entire industry. Similarly, reports on gross national product (GNP) are developed from the accounting records or reports of many separate economic units.

This textbook is concerned primarily with the accounting principles and techniques applicable to profit-making businesses. Such businesses are customarily organized as sole proprietorships, partnerships, or corporations. A **sole proprietorship** is owned by one individual. A **partnership** is owned by two or more individuals in accordance with a contractual arrangement. A **corporation**, organized in accordance with state or federal statutes, is a separate legal entity in which ownership is divided into shares of stock. Although the sole proprietorship is the most common business form, the corporation is the dominant form in terms of dollars of business activity, as indicated in the charts on the following page.

The Cost Principle

The records of properties and services purchased by a business are maintained in accordance with the **cost principle**, which requires that the monetary record be in terms of *cost*. For example, if a building is purchased at a cost of $150,000, that is the amount used in the buyer's accounting record. The seller may have been asking $170,000 for the building up to the time of the sale; the buyer may have initially offered $130,000 for it; the building may have been assessed at $125,000 for property tax purposes and insured for $135,000; and the buyer may have received an offer of $175,000 for the building the day after it was acquired. These latter amounts have no effect on the accounting records because they do not originate from an exchange. The exchange price, or cost, of $150,000 determines the monetary amount used in the records for the building.

---

[4]Accounting for individuals and accounting for not-for-profit units are described and illustrated in Appendixes D and F, respectively.

*Profit-Making
Businesses*

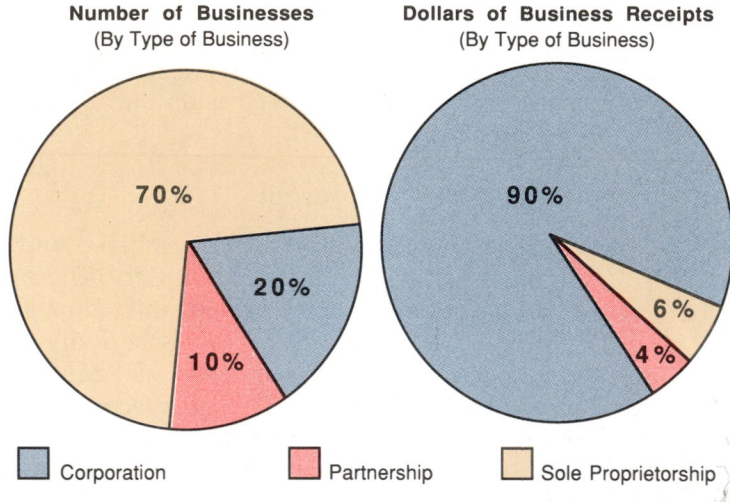

Number of Businesses
(By Type of Business)

Dollars of Business Receipts
(By Type of Business)

70%

20%

10%

90%

6%

4%

■ Corporation   ■ Partnership   ■ Sole Proprietorship

Source: U.S. Bureau of the Census, *Statistical Abstract of the United States: 1988* (108th edition; Washington: U.S. Government Printing Office, 1987).

Continuing the illustration, the $175,000 offer received by the buyer is an indication that the building was a bargain purchase at $150,000. To use $175,000 in the accounting records, however, would give recognition to an illusory or unrealized profit. If, after purchasing the building, the buyer should accept the offer and sell the building for $175,000, a profit of $25,000 would be realized, and the new owner would use $175,000 as the cost of the building.

The determination of costs incurred and revenues earned is fundamental to accounting. In exchanges between buyer and seller, both attempt to get the best price. Only the amount agreed upon is objective enough for accounting purposes. If the monetary amounts at which the accounting records for properties are maintained were constantly revised upward and downward on the basis of mere offers, appraisals, and opinions, accounting reports would soon become unstable and unreliable.

BUSINESS TRANSACTIONS

OBJECTIVE 4
Describe a business
transaction.

A **business transaction** is the occurrence of an event or of a condition that must be recorded. For example, the payment of a monthly telephone bill of $68, the purchase of $1,750 of merchandise on credit, and the acquisition of land and a building for $210,000 are illustrative of the variety of business transactions.

The first two transactions are relatively simple: a payment of money in exchange for a service, and a promise to pay within a short time in exchange for goods. The purchase of a building and the land on which it is situated is usually a more complex transaction. The total price agreed upon must be allocated between the land and the building, and the agreement usually provides for spreading the payment of a large part of the price over a period of years and for the payment of interest on the unpaid balance.

A particular business transaction may lead to an event or a condition that results in another transaction. For example, the purchase of merchandise on credit will be followed by payment to the creditor, which is another transaction. Each time a portion of the merchandise is sold, another transaction occurs. Similarly, partial payments for the land and the building are additional transactions, as are periodic payments of interest on the debt. Each of these events must be recorded.

The fact that the life of the building is limited must also be shown in the records. The wearing-out of the building is not an exchange of goods or services between the business and an outsider, but it is nevertheless a significant condition that must be recorded. Transactions of this type, as well as others that are not directly related to outsiders, are sometimes referred to as **internal transactions**.

ASSETS, LIABILITIES, AND OWNER'S EQUITY

OBJECTIVE 5
Identify the accounting equation and its basic elements.

The properties owned by a business enterprise are referred to as **assets** and the rights or claims to the properties are referred to as **equities**. If the assets owned by a business amount to $100,000, the equities in the assets must also amount to $100,000. The relationship between the two may be stated in the form of an equation, as follows:

Assets = Equities

Equities may be subdivided into two principal types: the rights of creditors and the rights of owners. The rights of creditors represent *debts* of the business and are called **liabilities**. The rights of the owner or owners are called **owner's equity**. Expansion of the equation to give recognition to the two basic types of equities yields the following, which is known as the **accounting equation**:

Assets = Liabilities + Owner's Equity

It is customary to place "Liabilities" before "Owner's Equity" in the accounting equation because creditors have preferential rights to the assets. The residual claim of the owner or owners is sometimes given greater emphasis by transposing liabilities to the other side of the equation, yielding:

Assets − Liabilities = Owner's Equity

TRANSACTIONS AND THE ACCOUNTING EQUATION

OBJECTIVE 6
Describe and illustrate how all business transactions can be stated in terms of the resulting changes in the three basic elements of the accounting equation.

All business transactions, from the simplest to the most complex, can be stated in terms of the resulting change in the three basic elements of the accounting equation. The effect of these changes on the accounting equation can be demonstrated by studying some typical transactions. As the basis of the illustration, assume that John Long establishes a sole proprietorship to be known as Long Taxi. Each transaction or group of similar transactions during the first month of operations is described, followed by an illustration of its effect on the accounting equation.

Transaction (a)

Long's first transaction is to deposit $10,000 in a bank account in the name of Long Taxi. The effect of this transaction is to increase the asset (cash), on the left side of the equation, by $10,000 and to increase the owner's equity, on the other side of the equation, by the same amount. As shown in the following illustration of this transaction's effect on Long Taxi's accounting equation, the equity of the owner is often referred to by using the owner's name and "Capital," such as "John Long, Capital."

Assets		Owner's Equity
Cash	=	John Long, Capital
(a) 10,000		10,000 Investment

It should be noted that the equation relates only to the business enterprise. Long's personal assets, such as his home and his personal bank account, and his personal liabilities are excluded from consideration. The business is treated as a separate entity, with cash of $10,000 and owner's equity of $10,000.

Transaction (b)

Long's next transaction is to purchase land as a future building site, for which $7,500 in cash is paid. This transaction changes the composition of the assets but does not change the total amount. The items in the equation prior to this transaction, the effects of the transaction, and the new balances after the transaction are as follows:

	Assets			Owner's Equity
	Cash	+	Land	John Long, Capital
Bal.	10,000			10,000
(b)	−7,500		+7,500	
Bal.	2,500		7,500	10,000

Long's current plans are to lease automobiles and other equipment and storage facilities from Ross Bus Company for several months until he can arrange financing for the purchase of automobiles and other equipment and for the construction of storage facilities.

Transaction (c)

During the month, Long purchases $850 of gasoline, oil, and other supplies from various suppliers, agreeing to pay in the near future. This type of transaction is called a purchase *on account* and the liability created is termed an **account payable**. Consumable goods purchased, such as supplies, are considered to be **prepaid expenses**, or assets.

In actual practice, each purchase would be treated as a separate transaction. In this illustration, however, the purchases are treated as a group. The effect is to increase assets and liabilities by $850, as follows:

	Assets						Liabilities	+	Owner's Equity
	Cash	+	Supplies	+	Land		Accounts Payable	+	John Long, Capital
Bal.	2,500				7,500	=			10,000
(c)			+850				+850		
Bal.	2,500		+850		7,500		+850		10,000

Transaction (d)

During the month, $400 is paid to creditors on account, thereby reducing both assets and liabilities. The effect on the equation is as follows:

	Assets				Liabilities	+	Owner's Equity
	Cash	+ Supplies	+ Land		Accounts Payable	+	John Long, Capital
Bal.	2,500	850	7,500	=	850		10,000
(d)	−400				−400		
Bal.	2,100	850	7,500		450		10,000

Transaction (e)

In general, the amount charged to customers for goods or services sold to them is called **revenue**. Other terms may be used for certain kinds of revenue, such as *sales* for the sale of merchandise or business services, *fees earned* for charges by a physician to patients, *rent earned* for the use of real estate or other property, and *fares earned* for Long Taxi.

During the first month of operations, Long Taxi earned fares of $4,500, receiving the amount in cash. The total effect of these transactions is to increase cash by $4,500 and to increase owner's equity by the same amount. In terms of the accounting equation, the effect of the receipt of cash for services performed is as follows:

	Assets				Liabilities +	Owner's Equity
	Cash	+ Supplies	+ Land		Accounts Payable +	John Long, Capital
Bal.	2,100	850	7,500	=	450	10,000
(e)	+4,500					+4,500 Fares earned
Bal.	6,600	850	7,500		450	14,500

Instead of requiring the payment of cash at the time goods or services are sold, a business may make sales *on account*, allowing the customer to pay later. In such cases the firm acquires an **account receivable**, which is a claim against the customer. An account receivable is as much an asset as cash, and the revenue is realized in exactly the same manner as if cash had been immediately received. At a later date, when the money is collected, there is only an exchange of one asset for another, with cash increasing and accounts receivable decreasing.

Transaction (f)

In a broad sense, the amount of assets consumed or services used in the process of earning revenue is called **expense**. Expenses would include supplies used, wages of employees, and other assets and services used in operating the business. For Long Taxi, various business expenses incurred and paid during the month were as follows: wages, $1,125; rent, $850; utilities, $150; miscellaneous, $75. The effect of this group of transactions is to reduce cash and to reduce owner's equity, as follows:

	Assets			Liabilities +	Owner's Equity
	Cash +	Supplies +	Land	Accounts Payable +	John Long, Capital
Bal.	6,600	850	7,500	450	14,500
(f)	−2,200				−1,125 Wages exp.
					−850 Rent expense
					−150 Utilities exp.
					−75 Misc. expense
Bal.	4,400	850	7,500	450	12,300

Transaction (g)

At the end of the month it is determined that the cost of the supplies on hand is $250, the remainder ($850 − $250) having been used in the operations of the business. This reduction of $600 in supplies and owner's equity may be shown as follows:

	Assets			Liabilities +	Owner's Equity
	Cash +	Supplies +	Land	Accounts Payable +	John Long, Capital
Bal.	4,400	850	7,500	450	12,300
(g)		−600			−600 Supplies exp.
Bal.	4,400	250	7,500	450	11,700

Transaction (h)

At the end of the month, Long withdraws from the business $1,000 in cash for his personal use. This transaction, which reduces cash and reduces owner's equity, is the exact opposite of an investment in the business by the owner. It is not a business expense, but a withdrawal of a portion of the owner's equity. The effect of the $1,000 withdrawal is as follows:

	Assets			Liabilities +	Owner's Equity
	Cash +	Supplies +	Land	Accounts Payable +	John Long, Capital
Bal.	4,400	250	7,500	450	11,700
(h)	−1,000				−1,000 Withdrawal
Bal.	3,400	250	7,500	450	10,700

Summary

The business transactions of Long Taxi are summarized in tabular form, as follows. The transactions are identified by letter, and the balance of each item is shown after each transaction.

	Assets			= Liabilities +	Owner's Equity
	Cash	+ Supplies +	Land =	Accounts Payable +	John Long, Capital
(a)	+10,000				+10,000 Investment
(b)	− 7,500		+7,500		
	2,500		7,500		10,000
(c)		+850		+850	
	2,500	850	7,500	850	10,000
(d)	− 400			−400	
	2,100	850	7,500	450	10,000
(e)	+ 4,500				+ 4,500 Fares earned
	6,600	850	7,500	450	14,500
(f)	− 2,200				− 1,125 Wages exp.
					− 850 Rent expense
					− 150 Utilities exp.
					− 75 Misc. expense
	4,400	850	7,500	450	12,300
(g)		−600			− 600 Supplies exp.
	4,400	250	7,500	450	11,700
(h)	− 1,000				− 1,000 Withdrawal
	3,400	250	7,500	450	10,700

The following observations, which apply to all types of businesses, should be noted:

1. The effect of every transaction can be stated in terms of increases and/or decreases in one or more of the accounting equation elements.
2. The equality of the two sides of the accounting equation is always maintained.
3. The owner's equity is increased by amounts invested by the owner and is decreased by withdrawals by the owner. In addition, owner's equity is increased by revenues and is decreased by expenses. The effect of these four types of transactions on owner's equity is illustrated as follows:

Effect of Transactions on Owner's Equity

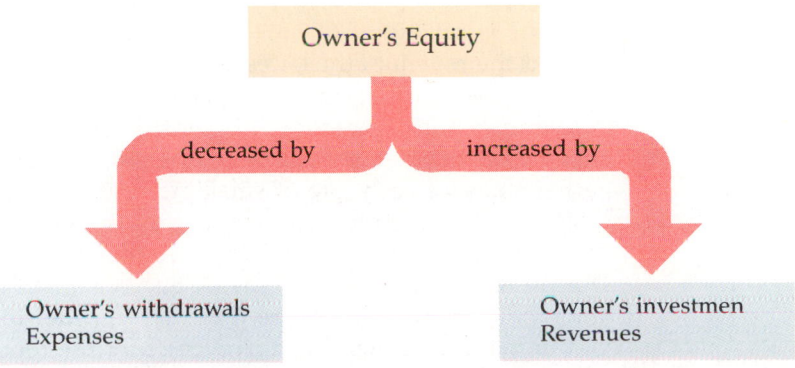

FINANCIAL STATEMENTS FOR SOLE PROPRIETORSHIPS

After the effect of the individual transactions has been determined, the essential information is communicated to users. The accounting statements that communicate this information are called **financial statements**. The principal financial statements are the income statement, the statement of owner's equity, the balance sheet, and the statement of cash flows. The nature of the data presented in each statement, in general terms, is as follows:

Income statement

A summary of the revenue and the expenses of a business entity for a specific period of time, such as a month or a year.

Statement of owner's equity

A summary of the changes in the owner's equity of a business entity that have occurred during a specific period of time, such as a month or a year.

Balance sheet

A list of the assets, liabilities, and owner's equity of a business entity as of a specific date, usually at the close of the last day of a month or a year.

Statement of cash flows

A summary of the cash receipts and cash payments of a business entity for a specific period of time, such as a month or a year.

The basic features of the four statements and their interrelationships are illustrated on the following page. The data for the statements were taken from the summary of transactions of Long Taxi previously presented.

All financial statements should be identified by the name of the business, the title of the statement, and the date or period of time. The data presented in the income statement, the statement of owner's equity, and the statement of cash flows are for a period of time. The data presented in the balance sheet are for a specific date.

The use of indentions, captions, dollar signs, and rulings in the financial statements should be noted. They aid the reader by emphasizing the various distinct sections of the statements.

Income Statement

The excess of the revenue over the expenses incurred in earning the revenue is called **net income** or **net profit**. If the expenses of the enterprise exceed the revenue, the excess is a **net loss**. It is ordinarily impossible to determine the exact amount of expense incurred in connection with each revenue transaction. Therefore, it is considered satisfactory to determine the net income or the net loss for a stated period of time, such as a month or a year, rather than for each sale or small group of sales.

As indicated, the determination of the periodic net income (or net loss) is a **matching** process involving two steps. First, revenues are recognized during the period. Second, the assets consumed in generating the revenues must be **matched** against the revenues in order to determine the net income or the net loss. Generally, the revenue for the rendering of a service is recognized after the service has been rendered to the customer. The assets con-

Income Statement

Long Taxi Income Statement For Month Ended August 31, 1990		
Fares earned		$4 5 0 0 00
Operating expenses:		
Wages expense	$1 1 2 5 00	
Rent expense	8 5 0 00	
Supplies expense	6 0 0 00	
Utilities expense	1 5 0 00	
Miscellaneous expense	7 5 00	
Total operating expenses		2 8 0 0 00
Net income		$1 7 0 0 00

Statement of Owner's Equity— Sole Proprietorship

Long Taxi Statement of Owner's Equity For Month Ended August 31, 1990		
Investment during the month		$10 0 0 0 00
Net income for the month	$1 7 0 0 00	
Less withdrawals	1 0 0 0 00	
Increase in owner's equity		7 0 0 00
John Long, capital, August 31, 1990		$10 7 0 0 00

Balance Sheet— Sole Proprietorship

Long Taxi Balance Sheet August 31, 1990		
Assets		
Cash		$ 3 4 0 0 00
Supplies		2 5 0 00
Land		7 5 0 0 00
Total assets		$11 1 5 0 00
Liabilities		
Accounts payable		$ 4 5 0 00
Owner's Equity		
John Long, capital		10 7 0 0 00
Total liabilities and owner's equity		$11 1 5 0 00

Statement of Cash Flows— Sole Proprietorship

Long Taxi Statement of Cash Flows For Month Ended August 31, 1990		
Cash flows from operating activities:		
Cash received from customers	$4 5 0 0 00	
Deduct cash payments for expenses and		
payments to creditors	2 6 0 0 00	
Net cash flow from operating activities		$1 9 0 0 00
Cash flows from investing activities:		
Cash payments for acquisition of land		(7 5 0 0 00)
Cash flows from financing activities:		
Cash received as owner's investment	$10 0 0 0 00	
Deduct cash withdrawal by owner	1 0 0 0 00	
Net cash flow from financing activities		9 0 0 0 00
Net cash flow and August 31, 1990 cash balance		$3 4 0 0 00

sumed in generating revenue during a period must be recognized as expenses. In this way, the expenses are properly **matched** against the revenues generated.

The effects of revenue earned and expenses incurred during the month for Long Taxi were shown in the equation as increases and decreases, respectively, in owner's equity. The details, together with net income in the amount of $1,700, are reported in the income statement on page 23.

The order in which the operating expenses are presented in the income statement varies among businesses. One of the arrangements commonly followed is to list them in the order of size, beginning with the larger items. Miscellaneous expense is usually shown as the last item, regardless of the amount.

Statement of Owner's Equity

Three types of transactions affected owner's equity for Long Taxi during the month: (1) the original investment of $10,000, (2) the revenues and expenses which resulted in net income of $1,700 for the month, and (3) a withdrawal of $1,000 by the owner. This information is presented in the statement of owner's equity on page 23, which serves as a connecting link between the balance sheet and the income statement.

Since Long Taxi had been in operation for only one month, it had no owner's equity at the beginning of August. For September and most subsequent periods, however, there would be a beginning balance that would be reported on the statement of owner's equity. To illustrate, assume that Long Taxi reported net income of $2,400, and the owner withdrew $2,000 during September. The statement of owner's equity for Long Taxi for September would appear as follows:

Long Taxi Statement of Owner's Equity For Month Ended September 30, 1990		
John Long, capital, September 1, 1990		$10 7 0 0 00
Net income for the month	$2 4 0 0 00	
Less withdrawals	2 0 0 0 00	
Increase in owner's equity		4 0 0 00
John Long, capital, September 30, 1990		$11 1 0 0 00

Balance Sheet

The amounts of Long Taxi's assets, liabilities, and owner's equity at the end of August, the first month of operations, appear on the last line of the summary on page 21. Minor rearrangements of these data and the addition of a heading yield the balance sheet illustrated on page 23. This form of balance sheet, with the liability and owner's equity sections presented below the asset section, is called the **report form**. Another arrangement in common use lists the assets on the left and the liabilities and owner's equity on the right. Because of its similarity to the account, a basic accounting device described in the next chapter, it is referred to as the **account form of balance sheet**.

It is customary to begin the asset section with cash. This item is followed by receivables, supplies, prepaid insurance, and other assets that will be converted into cash or used up in the near future. The assets of a relatively permanent nature, such as land, buildings, and equipment, follow in that order.

In the liabilities and owner's equity section of the balance sheet, it is customary to present the liabilities first, followed by owner's equity. In the illustration on page 23, liabilities are composed entirely of accounts payable. When there are two or more categories of liabilities, each should be listed and the total amount of liabilities presented in the following manner:

Liabilities

Accounts payable.............................	$1,100	
Salaries payable	300	
Total liabilities.................................		$1,400

Statement of Cash Flows

It is customary to report cash flows (cash receipts and cash payments) in three sections: (1) operating activities, (2) investing activities, and (3) financing activities. Data for the preparation of these three sections of the statement of cash flows for Long Taxi appear in the cash column of the summary on page 21.[5]

The cash flows from operating activities section includes cash transactions that enter into the determination of net income. For Long Taxi, the cash received from customers was $4,500 for fares earned. The cash payments totaled $2,600, which consisted of $400 paid to creditors for supplies purchased and $2,200 paid for wages, rent, utilities, and miscellaneous expense. The net cash flow from operating activities is $1,900 ($4,500 − $2,600).

The net cash flow from operating activities will normally differ from the amount of net income for the period. For Long Taxi, the net cash flow from operating activities ($1,900) differs from the net income ($1,700) by $200. This difference arises because $600 of supplies were used during August, but only $400 was paid to creditors on account. Thus, while the income statement reports supplies expense of $600, the statement of cash flows includes only $400 as cash payments for supplies.

The cash flows from investing activities section reports the cash transactions for the acquisition and sale of relatively long-term or permanent-type assets. Long Taxi's only cash flow related to investing activities was the acquisition of land for $10,000.

The cash flows from financing activities section reports the cash transactions related to cash investments by the owner, and borrowings and cash withdrawals of the owner. For Long Taxi, the cash flows from financing activities were $10,000 from the investment by the owner, less $1,000 of cash withdrawals by the owner. The net cash flow from financing activities, $9,000, is determined by subtracting the cash withdrawals of $1,000 from the $10,000 cash received from the owner as an investment.

---

[5]In practice, an alternative means may be used to accumulate the data needed to prepare the statement of cash flows. The discussion of this method and additional complexities are reserved until Chapter 18, after various necessary concepts and principles have been explained and illustrated.

Since August was Long Taxi's first month of operations, the increase in cash flows for August is the August 31, 1990 cash balance. In future statements, the cash balance at the beginning of the period is added to the increase (or decrease) in cash for the period to indicate the cash balance at the end of the period. To illustrate, assume that Long Taxi's net cash flows for September increased by $250. The increase resulted from the following cash transactions:

Cash received from customers	$6,000
Cash payments for expenses and	
payments to creditors...................................	3,750
Cash withdrawal by owner	2,000

The statement of cash flows for Long Taxi for September would be as follows:

Long Taxi		
Statement of Cash Flows		
For Month Ended September 30, 1990		
Cash flows from operating activities:		
Cash received from customers	$6 0 0 0 00	
Deduct cash payments for expenses and		
payments to creditors	3 7 5 0 00	
Net cash flow from operating activities		$2 2 5 0 00
Cash flows from financing activities:		
Cash withdrawal by owner		(2 0 0 0 00)
Increase in cash		$ 2 5 0 00
Cash balance, September 1, 1990		3 4 0 0 00
Cash balance, September 30, 1990		$3 6 5 0 00

FINANCIAL STATEMENTS FOR CORPORATIONS

OBJECTIVE 8
Identify and describe the financial statements of a corporation.

Business enterprises with large amounts of assets are usually organized as corporations and have many owners, called **stockholders**. The corporate form is also used by many small enterprises with a limited number of stockholders.

If Long Taxi had been organized as a corporation, with ownership represented by shares of stock, its income statement would be similar to the one shown on page 23. The other financial statements would be different in some respects from the corresponding statements for a sole proprietorship.

Retained Earnings Statement

In corporate enterprises, the emphasis in reporting changes in **stockholders' (owner's) equity** is on the changes in **retained earnings**, or net income retained in the business. The changes in retained earnings that have occurred during a period are reported in a **retained earnings statement**.[6]

If Long Taxi had been organized as a corporation, changes in the amount of earnings retained in the business would have resulted from (1) net income and (2) distributions of earnings, called **dividends**, to owners. The retained earnings statement for Long Taxi Corporation for August would appear as follows:

[6]If there have been significant changes related to shares of stock during a period, such data should be reported in a separate additional statement. The details of minor changes need not be reported.

Retained Earnings Statement — Corporation

Long Taxi Corporation Retained Earnings Statement For Month Ended August 31, 1990	
Net income for the month	$1,700
Less dividends..	1,000
Retained earnings, August 31, 1990	$ 700

Having been in existence only one month, Long Taxi Corporation had no retained earnings at the beginning of August. For September and most subsequent periods, however, there would be a beginning balance of retained earnings that would be reported on the retained earnings statement. To illustrate, assume that Long Taxi Corporation reported net income of $2,400 and paid dividends of $2,000 during September. The retained earnings statement for Long Taxi Corporation for September would appear as follows:

Long Taxi Corporation Retained Earnings Statement For Month Ended September 30, 1990		
Retained earnings, September 1, 1990		$ 700
Net income for the month	$2,400	
Less dividends...	2,000	
Increase in retained earnings		400
Retained earnings, September 30, 1990..................		$1,100

Balance Sheet

If Long Taxi had been organized as a corporation, its balance sheet at the end of August, the first month of operations, would appear as follows:

Balance Sheet — Corporation

Long Taxi Corporation Balance Sheet August 31, 1990		
Assets		
Cash...		$ 3,400
Supplies		250
Land...		7,500
Total assets		$11,150
Liabilities		
Accounts payable...		$ 450
Stockholders' Equity		
Capital stock	$10,000	
Retained earnings...	700	
Total stockholders' equity......................................		10,700
Total liabilities and stockholders' equity		$11,150

The only differences between the balance sheet shown above and the one illustrated on page 23 occur in the owner's equity section. In the corporation balance sheet, this section is referred to as the stockholders' equity section. In this section, the investment of the stockholders ($10,000 capital stock) and the net income retained in the business ($700 retained earnings) are reported separately, and the names of the stockholders (owners) are not shown.

Statement of Cash Flows

If Long Taxi had been organized as a corporation, its statement of cash flows for the month ended August 31, 1990, would appear as follows:

Statement of Cash Flows— Corporation

Long Taxi Corporation
Statement of Cash Flows
For Month Ended August 31, 1990

Cash flows from operating activities:		
Cash received from customers	$ 4,500	
Deduct cash payments for expenses and		
payments to creditors...................................	2,600	
Net cash flow from operating activities		$1,900
Cash flows from investing activities:		
Cash payments for acquisition of land................		(7,500)
Cash flows from financing activities:		
Cash received from sale of capital stock.............	$10,000	
Deduct cash payments for dividends..................	1,000	
Net cash flow from financing activities...............		9,000
Net cash flows and August 31, 1990 cash balance..		$3,400

The only differences between the statement of cash flows above and the one illustrated on page 23 occur in the cash flows from financing activities section. In the corporation statement of cash flows, the cash received as investments of stockholders (owners) arises from the sale of capital stock and the cash payments to stockholders (owners) are in the form of dividends.

CHAPTER REVIEW

KEY POINTS

OBJECTIVE 1   Accounting as an Information System

The objective of accounting is to record, summarize, report, and interpret economic data for use by many groups within our economic and social system. In this sense, accounting is often called the "language of business." This language can be viewed as an information system that provides essential information about the financial activities of an entity to various individuals or groups for their use in making informed judgments and decisions.

Accounting provides for the gathering of economic data and the communication of these data to different individuals and institutions. Examples of users of accounting information include investors, bankers, suppliers, government agencies, employees, and managers of the entity.

To be effective, individuals engaged in such areas of business as finance, production, marketing, personnel, and general management must have a good understanding of accounting concepts, principles, and terminology. In addition, the importance of understanding accounting is not limited to the business world, and many employees with specialized training in nonbusiness areas also make use of accounting data.

OBJECTIVE 2

Profession of Accountancy

Accountancy is a rapidly expanding profession whose members may be viewed as engaged in either (1) private accounting or (2) public accounting. Accountants employed by a particular business firm or not-for-profit organization, perhaps as a chief accountant, comptroller, or financial vice-president, are said to be engaged in private accounting. Accountants who render accounting services on a fee basis, and staff accountants employed by them, are said to be engaged in public accounting. Public accountants who meet a state's education, experience, and examination requirements may practice as certified public accountants (CPAs).

Specialized fields in accounting have evolved as a result of rapid technological advances and accelerated economic growth. The more important accounting fields are financial accounting, auditing, cost accounting, managerial accounting, tax accounting, accounting systems, budgetary accounting, international accounting, not-for-profit accounting, social accounting, and accounting instruction.

OBJECTIVE 3

Principles and Practice

Generally accepted accounting principles have evolved to form an underlying basis for accounting practice. Several professional accounting associations, with the dominant one being the Financial Accounting Standards Board, issue pronouncements on accounting principles.

The business entity concept is based upon the applicability of accounting to individual economic units in society. Profit-making businesses are customarily organized as sole proprietorships, partnerships, or corporations.

The cost principle requires that properties and services purchased by a business be recorded in terms of cost.

OBJECTIVE 4

Business Transactions

A business transaction is the occurrence of an event or a condition that must be recorded. Business transactions may be either simple or complex and may lead to an event or a condition that results in yet another transaction.

OBJECTIVE 5

Assets, Liabilities, and Owner's Equity

The properties owned by a business and the rights or claims to properties may be stated in the form of an equation as follows: Assets = Equities. The expansion of the equation to give recognition to two basic types of equities yields the following, which is known as the accounting equation: Assets = Liabilities + Owner's Equity.

OBJECTIVE 6

Transactions and the Accounting Equation

All transactions, from the simplest to the most complex, can be stated in terms of the resulting change in the three basic elements of the accounting equation. That is, the effect of every transaction can be stated in terms of increases and/or decreases in one or more of the accounting equation elements such that the equality of the two sides of the accounting equation is always maintained.

OBJECTIVE 7, 8   Accounting Statements

After the effect of individual transactions has been determined and recorded, accounting reports (financial statements) summarizing the effects of transactions are prepared and communicated to users. The principal financial statements of a sole proprietorship are the income statement, the statement of owner's equity, the balance sheet, and the statement of cash flows. The financial statements for a corporation are similar to those of a sole proprietorship, except that a retained earnings statement is prepared instead of a statement of owner's equity. The owner's equity section of the balance sheet is referred to as stockholders' equity rather than owner's equity. In addition, the cash flows from financing activities for a corporation arise from the sale of capital stock and the payment of dividends, rather than from owner's investment and drawings.

KEY TERMS

accounting 7
private accounting 10
public accounting 10
certified public accountants (CPAs) 11
codes of professional conduct 11
generally accepted accounting
    principles (GAAP) 13
Financial Accounting Standards Board
    (FASB) 15
business entity concept 15
sole proprietorship 15
partnership 15
corporation 15
cost principle 15
business transaction 16
assets 17
equities 17
liabilities 17
owner's equity 17

accounting equation 17
account payable 18
prepaid expenses 18
revenue 19
account receivable 19
expense 19
income statement 22
statement of owner's equity 22
balance sheet 22
statement of cash flows 22
net income 22
net loss 22
matching 22
report form of balance sheet 24
account form of balance sheet 24
stockholders' equity 26
retained earnings 26
retained earnings statement 26
dividends 26

SELF-EXAMINATION QUESTIONS

Answers at end of chapter.

1. A profit-making business that is a separate legal entity and in which ownership is divided into shares of stock is known as a:
    A. sole proprietorship
    B. single proprietorship
    C. partnership
    D. corporation

2. The properties owned by a business enterprise are called:
    A. assets
    B. liabilities
    C. stockholders' equity
    D. owner's equity

3. A list of assets, liabilities, and owner's equity of a business entity as of a specific date is:
    A. a balance sheet
    B. an income statement
    C. a statement of owner's equity
    D. a retained earnings statement

4. If total assets increased $20,000 during a period of time and total liabilities increased by $12,000 during the same period, the amount and direction (increase or decrease) of the period's change in owner's equity is:
    A. $32,000 increase   C. $8,000 increase
    B. $32,000 decrease   D. $8,000 decrease

5. If revenue was $45,000, expenses were $37,500, and the owner's withdrawals were $10,000, the amount of net income or net loss was:
    A. $45,000 net income   C. $37,500 net loss
    B. $7,500 net income   D. $2,500 net loss

ILLUSTRATIVE PROBLEM

The assets and liabilities of Morgan Dry Cleaners on October 1 of the current year are as follows: Cash, $1,000; Accounts Receivable, $2,200; Supplies, $850; Land, $11,450; Accounts Payable, $2,030. Morgan Dry Cleaners is a sole proprietorship owned and operated by M. A. Morgan. Currently, a building, delivery truck, and equipment are being rented, pending expansion to new facilities. The actual work of dry cleaning is done by another company at wholesale rates. Business transactions during October are summarized as follows:

(a) Received cash from cash customers for dry cleaning sales, $4,928.
(b) Paid creditors on account, $1,755.
(c) Received cash from M. A. Morgan as an additional investment, $3,700.
(d) Paid rent for the month, $1,200.
(e) Charged customers for dry cleaning sales on account, $1,025.
(f) Purchased supplies on account, $245.
(g) Received cash from customers on account, $2,000.
(h) Received monthly invoice for dry cleaning expense for October (to be paid on November 10), $1,635.
(i) Paid the following: wages expense, $850; truck expense, $250; utilities expense, $325; miscellaneous expense, $75.
(j) Determined, by taking an inventory, the cost of supplies used during the month, $115.

Instructions:
1. Determine the amount of owner's equity (M. A. Morgan's capital) as of October 1 of the current year.
2. State the assets, liabilities, and owner's equity as of October 1 in equation form similar to that shown in this chapter. In tabular form below the equation, indicate the increases and decreases resulting from each transaction and the new balances after each transaction. Explain the nature of each increase and decrease in owner's equity by an appropriate notation at the right of the amount.
3. Prepare (a) an income statement for October, (b) a statement of owner's equity for October, (c) a balance sheet as of October 31, and (d) a statement of cash flows for October.

SOLUTION

(1) Assets − Liabilities = Owner's Equity (M.A. Morgan, capital)
    $15,500 − $2,030 = Owner's Equity (M.A. Morgan, capital)
             $13,470 = Owner's Equity (M.A. Morgan, capital)

(2)

	Assets			=	Liabilities	+	Owner's Equity	
	Cash +	Accounts Receivable +	Supplies +	Land =		Accounts Payable +	M.A. Morgan, Capital	
Bal.	1,000	2,200	850	11,450		2,030	13,470	
(a)	+ 4,928						+ 4,928	Dry cleaning sales
Bal.	5,928	2,200	850	11,450		2,030	18,398	
(b)	− 1,755					−1,755		
Bal.	4,173	2,200	850	11,450		275	18,398	
(c)	+ 3,700						+ 3,700	Add. investment
Bal.	7,873	2,200	850	11,450		275	22,098	
(d)	− 1,200						− 1,200	Rent expense
Bal.	6,673	2,200	850	11,450		275	20,898	
(e)		+ 1,025					+ 1,025	Dry cleaning sales
Bal.	6,673	3,225	850	11,450		275	21,923	
(f)			+ 245			+ 245		
Bal.	6,673	3,225	1,095	11,450		520	21,923	
(g)	+ 2,000	−2,000						
Bal.	8,673	1,225	1,095	11,450		520	21,923	
(h)						+1,635	− 1,635	Dry cleaning exp.
Bal.	8,673	1,225	1,095	11,450		2,155	20,288	
(i)	− 1,500						− 850	Wages expense
							− 250	Truck expense
							− 325	Utilities expense
							− 75	Miscellaneous exp.
Bal.	7,173	1,225	1,095	11,450		2,155	18,788	
(j)			− 115				− 115	Supplies expense
Bal.	7,173	1,225	980	11,450		2,155	18,673	

(3)

Morgan Dry Cleaners
Income Statement
For Month Ended October 31, 19--

Dry cleaning sales		$5 9 5 3 00
Operating expenses:		
Dry cleaning expense	$1 6 3 5 00	
Rent expense	1 2 0 0 00	
Wages expense	8 5 0 00	
Utilities expense	3 2 5 00	
Truck expense	2 5 0 00	
Supplies expense	1 1 5 00	
Miscellaneous expense	7 5 00	
Total operating expenses		4 4 5 0 00
Net income		$1 5 0 3 00

Morgan Dry Cleaners
Statement of Owner's Equity
For Month Ended October 31, 19--

M.A. Morgan, capital, October 1, 19--		$13 4 7 0 00
Additional investment by owner	$3 7 0 0 00	
Net income for the month	1 5 0 3 00	
Increase in owner's equity		5 2 0 3 00
M.A. Morgan, capital, October 31, 19--		$18 6 7 3 00

Morgan Dry Cleaners
Balance Sheet
October 31, 19--

Assets			
Cash			$ 7 1 7 3 00
Accounts receivable			1 2 2 5 00
Supplies			9 8 0 00
Land			11 4 5 0 00
Total assets			$20 8 2 8 00
Liabilities			
Accounts payable			$ 2 1 5 5 00
Owner's Equity			
M. A. Morgan, capital			18 6 7 3 00
Total liabilities and owner's equity			$20 8 2 8 00

Morgan Dry Cleaners
Statement of Cash Flows
For Month Ended October 31, 19--

Cash flows from operating activities:		
Cash received from customers	$6 9 2 8 00*	
Deduct cash payments for expenses and		
to creditors	4 4 5 5 00**	
Net cash flow from operating activities		$2 4 7 3 00
Cash flows from financing activities:		
Cash received from owner's investment		3 7 0 0 00
Increase in cash		$6 1 7 3 00
Cash balance, October 1, 19--		1 0 0 0 00
Cash balance, October 31, 19--		$7 1 7 3 00

*$4,928 (transaction a) + $2,000 (transaction g) = $6,928
**$1,755 (transaction b) + $1,200 (transaction d) + $1,500 (transaction i) = $4,455

DISCUSSION QUESTIONS

1. What is the objective of accounting?

2. Name some of the categories of individuals and institutions who use accounting information.

3. Why is a knowledge of accounting concepts and terminology useful to all individuals engaged in business activities?

4. Distinguish between private accounting and public accounting.

5. Describe in general terms the requirements that an individual must meet (a) for the CMA designation and (b) for the CPA certificate.

6. Name some of the specialized fields of accounting activity.

7. (a) Name the three principal forms of profit-making business organizations. (b) Which of these forms is identified with the greatest number of businesses?

8. What is meant by the cost principle?

9. (a) Land with an assessed value of $100,000 for property tax purposes is acquired by a business enterprise for $175,000. At what amount should the land be recorded by the purchaser?
   (b) Five years later the plot of land in (a) has an assessed value of $140,000 and the business enterprise receives an offer of $250,000 for it. Should the monetary amount assigned to the land in the business records now be increased and, if so, by what amount?
   (c) Assuming that the land acquired in (a) was sold for $275,000, (1) how much would the owner's equity increase, and (2) at what amount would the purchaser record the land?

10. (a) If the assets owned by a business enterprise total $450,000, what is the amount of the equities of the enterprise? (b) What are the two principal types of equities?

11. Name the three elements of the accounting equation.

12. (a) An enterprise has assets of $250,000 and liabilities of $175,000. What is the amount of its owner's equity?
    (b) An enterprise has assets of $480,000 and owner's equity of $200,000. What is the total amount of its liabilities?
    (c) A corporation has assets of $995,000, liabilities of $590,000, and capital stock of $250,000. What is the amount of its retained earnings?
    (d) An enterprise has liabilities of $500,000 and owner's equity of $300,000. What is the total amount of its assets?

13. Describe how the following business transactions affect the three elements of the accounting equation.
    (a) Invested cash in the business.
    (b) Purchased supplies for cash.
    (c) Purchased supplies on account.
    (d) Received cash for services performed.
    (e) Paid for utilities used in the business.

14. (a) A vacant lot acquired for $75,000, on which there is a balance owed of $45,000, is sold for $90,000 in cash. What is the effect of the sale on the total amount of the seller's (1) assets, (2) liabilities, and (3) owner's equity?
    (b) After receiving the $90,000 cash in (a), the seller pays the $45,000 owed. What is the effect of the payment on the total amount of the seller's (1) assets, (2) liabilities, and (3) owner's equity?

15. Operations of a service enterprise for a particular month are summarized as follows:
    Service sales: on account, $24,000; for cash, $70,000
    Expenses incurred: on account, $36,000; for cash, $45,000
    What was the amount of the enterprise's (a) revenue, (b) expenses, and (c) net income?

16. A business enterprise had revenues of $85,000 and operating expenses of $92,750. Did the enterprise (a) incur a net loss or (b) realize a net income?

17. A business enterprise had revenues of $92,500 and operating expenses of $85,000. Did the enterprise (a) incur a net loss or (b) realize a net income?

18. Indicate whether each of the following types of transactions will (a) increase owner's equity or (b) decrease owner's equity:
    (1) owner's investments
    (2) owner's withdrawals
    (3) expenses
    (4) revenues

19. Give the title of a sole proprietorship's four major financial statements illustrated in this chapter, and briefly describe the nature of the information provided by each.

20. Indicate whether the data in each of the following financial statements (a) covers a period of time or (b) is for a specific date:
    (1) income statement
    (2) balance sheet
    (3) statement of owner's equity
    (4) statement of cash flows

21. Name the three types of activities reported in the statement of cash flows.

22. What particular item of financial or operating data for a service enterprise, organized as a corporation, appears on (a) both the income statement and the retained earnings statement, and (b) both the balance sheet and the retained earnings statement?

23. The income statement of a sole proprietorship for the month of October indicates a net income of $35,000. During the same period the owner withdrew $40,000 in cash from the business for personal use. Would it be correct to say that the owner incurred a *net loss* of $5,000 during the month? Discuss.

24. House of High Fidelity had an owner's equity balance of $180,000 at the beginning of the period. At the end of the period, the company had total assets of $245,000 and total liabilities of $75,000. (a) What was the net income or net loss for the period, assuming no additional investments or withdrawals? (b) What was the net income or net loss for the period, assuming a withdrawal of $25,000 had occurred during the period?

25. Indicate whether each of the following activities would be reported on the statement of cash flows as (a) operating activity, (b) investing activity, or (c) financing activity:
    (1) cash received as owner's investment
    (2) cash paid for land
    (3) cash received from fees earned
    (4) cash paid for expenses

Real World Focus
26. Based upon the annual report of Coca-Cola Enterprises Inc. presented in Appendix I, what are (a) the total assets at December 30, 1988, (b) the total liabilities and shareholders' equity at December 30, 1988, (c) the net operating revenues for the year ended December 30, 1988, (d) the net income for the year ended December 30, 1988, and (e) the ratio of the net income to the net operating revenues for the year ended December 30, 1988?

EXERCISES

Exercise 1–1
Transactions of sole proprietorship.
OBJ. 6

The following selected transactions were completed by Lopez Delivery Service during June:

(1) Received cash from owner as additional investment, $10,000.
(2) Purchased supplies of gas and oil for cash, $850.
(3) Billed customers for delivery services on account, $900.
(4) Received cash from cash customers, $1,750.
(5) Paid advertising expense, $750.
(6) Paid rent for June, $1,500.

(7) Paid creditors on account, $350.
(8) Received cash from customers on account, $700.
(9) Paid cash to owner for personal use, $1,000.
(10) Determined by taking an inventory that $575 of supplies of gas and oil had been used during the month.

Indicate the effect of each transaction on the accounting equation by listing the numbers identifying the transactions, (1) through (10), in a vertical column, and inserting at the right of each number the appropriate letter from the following list:

(a) Increase in one asset, decrease in another asset.
(b) Increase in an asset, increase in a liability.
(c) Increase in an asset, increase in owner's equity.
(d) Decrease in an asset, decrease in a liability.
(e) Decrease in an asset, decrease in owner's equity.

Exercise 1–2
Nature of transactions.
OBJ. 6

Ruth Tavel is engaged in a service business. Summary financial data for January are presented in equation form as follows. Each line designated by a number indicates the effect of a transaction on the equation. Each increase and decrease in owner's equity, except transaction (5), affects net income.

	Cash	+	Supplies	+	Land	=	Liabilities	+	Owner's Equity
Bal.	7,500		750		10,000		3,750		14,500
(1)	+9,000								+ 9,000
(2)	−2,750						−2,750		
(3)	−3,300								− 3,300
(4)			+900				+ 900		
(5)	− 950								− 950
(6)	−5,000				+ 5,000				
(7)			−980						− 980
Bal.	4,500		670		15,000		1,900		18,270

(a) Describe each transaction.
(b) What is the amount of net decrease in cash during the month?
(c) What is the amount of net increase in owner's equity during the month?
(d) What is the amount of the net income for the month?
(e) How much of the net income of the month was retained in the business?

Exercise 1–3
Net income for four sole proprietorships.
OBJ. 7

Four different sole proprietorships, A, B, C, and D, show the same balance sheet data at the beginning and end of a year. These data, exclusive of the amount of owner's equity, are summarized as follows:

	Total Assets	Total Liabilities
Beginning of the year	$410,000	$180,000
End of the year...	505,000	250,000

On the basis of the above data and the following additional information for the year, determine the net income (or loss) of each company for the year. (*Suggestion:* First determine the amount of increase or decrease in owner's equity during the year.)

Company A: The owner had made no additional investments in the business and had made no withdrawals from the business.
Company B: The owner had made no additional investments in the business but had withdrawn $30,000.
Company C: The owner had made an additional investment of $35,000 but had made no withdrawals.
Company D: The owner had made an additional investment of $35,000 and had withdrawn $30,000.

Exercise 1–4
Balance sheet items for sole proprietorship.
OBJ. 7

From the following list of selected items taken from the records of A-1 Appliance Service as of a specific date, identify those that would appear on the balance sheet:

(1) Jane Davis, Capital
(2) Fees Earned
(3) Land
(4) Wages Expense
(5) Accounts Payable
(6) Cash
(7) Utilities Expense
(8) Supplies Expense
(9) Wages Payable
(10) Supplies

Exercise 1–5
Missing amounts from balance sheet and income statement data.
OBJ. 7

One item is omitted in each of the following summaries of balance sheet and income statement data for four different sole proprietorships, A, B, C, and D.

	A	B	C	D
Beginning of the year:				
Assets	$250,000	$70,000	$99,000	(d)
Liabilities	140,000	30,000	76,000	$27,100
End of the year:				
Assets	290,000	95,000	96,000	73,000
Liabilities	160,000	20,000	77,000	42,000
During the year:				
Additional investment in the business	(a)	9,000	10,000	25,000
Withdrawals from the business	20,000	12,000	(c)	21,000
Revenue	95,000	(b)	88,100	99,000
Expenses	80,000	35,000	89,600	78,000

Determine the amounts of the missing items, identifying them by letter. (*Suggestion:* First determine the amount of increase or decrease in owner's equity during the year.)

Exercise 1–6
Balance sheets; net income for sole proprietorship.
OBJ. 7

Financial information related to the sole proprietorship of George Belmont Interiors for June and July of the current year is as follows:

	June 30, 19--	July 31, 19--
Accounts Payable	$ 6,520	$ 8,100
Accounts Receivable	9,900	13,400
George Belmont, Capital	?	?
Cash	9,500	11,400
Supplies	975	750

(a) Prepare balance sheets for George Belmont Interiors as of June 30 and as of July 31 of the current year.
(b) Determine the amount of net income for July, assuming that the owner had made no additional investments or withdrawals during the month.
(c) Determine the amount of net income for July, assuming that the owner had made no additional investments and had withdrawn $2,500 during the month.

Exercise 1–7
Income statement and statement of cash flows.
OBJ. 7

Barr Services was organized on June 1 with a cash investment of $2,000 by Robert Barr. A summary of the transactions for the remainder of June are as follows:

Fees earned	$4,900
Cash received from customers	4,900
Wages expense	1,200
Rent expense	900
Supplies expense	250
Miscellaneous expense	50
Cash payments for expenses and payments to creditors	2,300
Cash withdrawal by owner	1,750

(a) Prepare an income statement for the month ended June 30.
(b) Prepare a statement of cash flows for the month ended June 30.
(c) What is the reason that the net income for June was less than the net cash flow from operating activities for June?

Exercise 1–8
Transactions of corporation.
OBJ. 6, 8

Matlock Corporation, engaged in a service business, completed the following selected transactions during the period:

(1) Issued additional capital stock, receiving cash.
(2) Purchased supplies on account.
(3) Charged customers for services sold on account.
(4) Returned defective supplies purchased on account for which payment has not yet been made.
(5) Paid a creditor on account.
(6) Received cash from customers on account.
(7) Paid utilities expense.
(8) Received cash as a refund from the erroneous overpayment of an expense.
(9) Determined the amount of supplies used during the month.
(10) Paid cash dividends to stockholders.

Using a tabular form with four column headings entitled Transaction, Assets, Liabilities, and Owner's Equity, respectively, indicate the effect of each transaction. Use + for increase and − for decrease.

Exercise 1–9
Balance sheet items for corporation.
OBJ. 8

From the following list of selected items taken from the records of J. A. Buck Corporation as of a specific date, identify those that would appear on the balance sheet:

(1) Retained Earnings
(2) Cash
(3) Salaries Expense
(4) Land
(5) Accounts Payable
(6) Capital Stock
(7) Fees Earned
(8) Salaries Payable
(9) Supplies
(10) Utilities Expense

PROBLEMS

Series A

Problem 1–1A
Transactions for sole proprietorship.
OBJ. 6

SPREADSHEET PROBLEM

John Allen established a sole proprietorship on October 1 of the current year and completed the following transactions during October:

(a) Opened a business bank account with a deposit of $5,000.
(b) Paid rent on office and equipment for the month, $3,000.
(c) Purchased supplies on account, $925.
(d) Paid creditors on account, $625.
(e) Received cash from fees earned, $3,750.
(f) Paid automobile expenses for month, $780, and miscellaneous expenses, $250.
(g) Paid office salaries, $1,500.
(h) Determined that the cost of supplies on hand was $275; therefore, the cost of supplies used was $650.
(i) Billed customers for fees earned, $2,350.
(j) Withdrew cash for personal use, $1,000.

Instructions:

Indicate the effect of each transaction and the balances after each transaction, using the following tabular headings:

	Assets		Liabilities		Owner's Equity
Cash + Accounts Receivable + Supplies		=	Accounts Payable	+	John Allen, Capital

By appropriate notations at the right of each change, indicate the nature of each increase and decrease in owner's equity.

Problem 1–2A
Financial statements for sole proprietorship.
OBJ. 7

Joan Bowan established Joan Bowan Services on July 1 of the current year. The effect of each transaction and the balances after each transaction for July are as follows:

| | | Assets | | | = | Liabilities + | Owner's Equity |
| | | | Accounts | | | Accounts | Joan Bowan, |
	Cash	+ Receivable	+ Supplies =		Payable +	Capital
(a)	+3,000					+3,000 Investment
(b)	−2,000					−2,000 Rent expense
Bal.	1,000					1,000
(c)			+550		+550	
Bal.	1,000		550		550	1,000
(d)	+4,500					+4,500 Fees earned
Bal.	5,500		550		550	5,500
(e)	− 250				−250	
Bal.	5,250		550		300	5,500
(f)		+1,250				+1,250 Fees earned
Bal.	5,250	1,250	550		300	6,750
(g)	− 655					− 380 Auto expense
						− 275 Misc. expense
Bal.	4,595	1,250	550		300	6,095
(h)	−1,000					−1,000 Salaries expense
Bal.	3,595	1,250	550		300	5,095
(i)			−125			− 125 Supplies expense
Bal.	3,595	1,250	425		300	4,970
(j)	−1,200					−1,200 Withdrawal
Bal.	2,395	1,250	425		300	3,770

Instructions:

(1) Prepare an income statement for the month ended July 31.
(2) Prepare a statement of owner's equity for the month ended July 31.
(3) Prepare a balance sheet as of July 31.
(4) Prepare a statement of cash flows for the month ended July 31.

Problem 1–3A
Transactions for sole proprietorship; financial statements.
OBJ. 6, 7

On July 1 of the current year, Jill Hill established a sole proprietorship under the name Hill Realty. Hill completed the following transactions during the month of July:

(a) Opened a business bank account with a deposit of $5,000.
(b) Paid rent on office and equipment for the month, $3,600.
(c) Purchased supplies (stationery, stamps, pencils, etc.) on account, $750.
(d) Paid creditor on account, $500.
(e) Earned sales commissions, receiving cash, $11,100.
(f) Withdrew cash for personal use, $2,000.
(g) Paid automobile expenses (including rental charge) for month, $900, and miscellaneous expenses, $550.
(h) Paid office salaries, $3,150.
(i) Determined that the cost of supplies used was $425.

Instructions:

(1) Indicate the effect of each transaction and the balances after each transaction, using the following tabular headings:

Assets		Liabilities		Owner's Equity
Cash + Supplies	=	Accounts Payable	+	Jill Hill, Capital

By appropriate notations at the right of each change, indicate the nature of each increase and decrease in owner's equity.

(2) Prepare an income statement for July, a statement of owner's equity for July, a balance sheet as of July 31, and a statement of cash flows for July.

Problem 1–4A

Transactions for sole proprietorship; financial statements.

OBJ. 6, 7

Moore Dry Cleaners is a sole proprietorship owned and operated by Betty Moore. Currently, a building and equipment are being rented, pending expansion to new facilities. The actual work of dry cleaning is done by another company at wholesale rates. The assets and the liabilities of the business on June 1 of the current year are as follows: Cash, $9,400; Accounts Receivable, $4,750; Supplies, $560; Land, $15,000; Accounts Payable, $3,880. Business transactions during June are summarized as follows:

(a) Paid rent for the month, $1,250.
(b) Charged customers for dry cleaning sales on account, $6,450.
(c) Paid creditors on account, $1,680.
(d) Purchased supplies on account, $310.
(e) Received cash from cash customers for dry cleaning sales, $3,600.
(f) Received cash from customers on account, $3,750.
(g) Received monthly invoice for dry cleaning expense for June (to be paid on July 10), $3,400.
(h) Paid the following: wages expense, $1,300; truck expense, $725; utilities expense, $510; miscellaneous expense, $190.
(i) Determined the cost of supplies used during the month, $570.

Instructions:

(1) Determine the amount of Betty Moore's capital as of June 1 of the current year.
(2) State the assets, liabilities, and owner's equity as of June 1 in equation form similar to that shown in this chapter. In tabular form below the equation, indicate the increases and decreases resulting from each transaction and the new balances after each transaction. Explain the nature of each increase and decrease in owner's equity by an appropriate notation at the right of the amount.
(3) Prepare (a) an income statement for June, (b) a statement of owner's equity for June, (c) a balance sheet as of June 30, and (d) a statement of cash flows for June.

Problem 1–5A

Financial statements for sole proprietorship.

OBJ. 7

Following are the amounts of the assets and liabilities of Cole Personnel Service, a sole proprietorship, at June 30, the *end* of the current year, and its revenue and expenses for the year ended on that date. The capital of A. C. Cole, owner, was $13,350 at July 1, the *beginning* of the current year, and the owner withdrew $14,000 during the current year. Cash received from customers was $74,500 and cash paid for expenses and to creditors was $56,900.

Cash	$ 6,125
Accounts receivable	7,600
Supplies	675
Prepaid insurance	650
Accounts payable	1,100
Salaries payable	300
Fees earned	68,775
Salary expense	28,900
Rent expense	9,000

Advertising expense	$ 5,950
Utilities expense	4,500
Supplies expense	2,600
Taxes expense	1,800
Insurance expense	900
Miscellaneous expense	825

Instructions:

(1) Prepare an income statement for the current year ended June 30.
(2) Prepare a statement of owner's equity for the current year ended June 30.
(3) Prepare a balance sheet as of June 30 of the current year.
(4) Prepare a statement of cash flows for the current year ended June 30. The cash balance on July 1, beginning of the current year, was $2,525.

Problem 1–6A

Financial statements for corporation.

OBJ. 8

Following are the amounts of ACJ Corporation's assets and liabilities at October 31, the end of the current year, and its revenue and expenses for the year ended on that date, listed in alphabetical order. ACJ Corporation had capital stock of $50,000 and retained earnings of $16,765 on November 1, the beginning of the current year. During the current year, the corporation paid cash dividends of $15,000 and received cash from the sale of capital stock of $20,000. Cash received from customers was $189,500 and cash paid for expenses and to creditors was $185,500.

Accounts payable	$ 12,100
Accounts receivable	21,250
Advertising expense	5,500
Cash	16,500
Insurance expense	1,900
Land	80,000
Miscellaneous expense	1,750
Prepaid insurance	950
Rent expense	42,000
Salaries payable	2,250
Salary expense	85,500
Fees earned	206,500
Supplies	865
Supplies expense	6,125
Taxes expense	5,775
Utilities expense	24,500

Instructions:

(1) Prepare an income statement for the current year ended October 31.
(2) Prepare a retained earnings statement for the current year ended October 31.
(3) Prepare a balance sheet as of October 31 of the current year.
(4) Prepare a statement of cash flows for the current year ended October 31. The cash balance on November 1, the beginning of the current year, was $7,500.

Problem 1–7A

Transactions for corporation; financial statements.

OBJ. 6, 8

On July 1 of the current year, Shriver Delivery Inc. was organized as a corporation. The summarized transactions of the business for its first two months of operations, ending on August 31, are as follows:

(a) Received cash from stockholders for capital stock $75,000

(b) Purchased a portion of a delivery service that had been operating as a sole proprietorship in accordance with the following details:

Assets acquired by the corporation:

Accounts receivable	$15,600	
Truck supplies	7,500	
Office supplies	900	$24,000

Liabilities assumed by the corporation:

Accounts payable	9,000

Payment to be made as follows:

Cash	$7,500	
Three notes payable of $2,500 each, due at two-month intervals	7,500	$15,000

(c) Purchased truck supplies on account	$ 1,750
(d) Purchased office supplies for cash	250
(e) Paid creditors on account	5,000
(f) Received cash from customers on account	12,000
(g) Paid insurance premiums in advance	2,400
(h) Paid advertising expense	1,100
(i) Charged delivery service sales to customers on account	40,500
(j) Paid rent expense on office and trucks	4,100
(k) Paid utilities expense	925
(l) Paid first of the three notes payable	2,500
(m) Paid miscellaneous expenses	1,475
(n) Paid taxes expense	275
(o) Paid wages expense	19,200
(p) Truck supplies used	2,800
(q) Office supplies used	325
(r) Insurance premiums that expired and became an expense	500
(s) Purchased land as future building site, paying $25,000 cash and giving a note payable due in 5 years for the balance of $25,000	50,000
(t) Paid cash dividends to stockholders	2,000

Instructions:

(1) List the following captions in a single line at the top of a sheet turned sideways.

$$\underline{\text{Cash}} + \underline{\text{Accounts Receivable}} + \underline{\text{Truck Supplies}} + \underline{\text{Office Supplies}} + \underline{\text{Prepaid Insurance}} + \underline{\text{Land}} =$$

$$\underline{\text{Notes Payable}} + \underline{\text{Accounts Payable}} + \underline{\text{Capital Stock}} + \underline{\text{Retained Earnings}} \quad \underline{\text{Retained Earnings Notations}}$$

(2) In the appropriate columns, indicate the effect of the original investment and the remaining transactions, identifying each by letter. Indicate increases by + and decreases by −. *Do not determine the new balances of the items after each transaction.* In the space for retained earnings notations, identify each revenue and expense item and dividends paid to stockholders.

(3) Insert the final balances in each column and determine that the equation is in balance at August 31, the end of the period.

(4) Prepare the following: (a) income statement for the two months, (b) retained earnings statement for the two months, and (c) balance sheet as of August 31.

Series B

Problem 1–1B
Financial statements for sole proprietorship.

OBJ. 6

John Herr established a sole proprietorship on July 1 of the current year and completed the following transactions during July:

(a) Opened a business bank account with a deposit of $5,000.
(b) Paid rent on office and equipment for the month, $3,000.
(c) Purchased supplies (stationery, stamps, pencils, etc.) on account, $950.
(d) Received cash from fees earned, $2,500.
(e) Paid creditors on account, $650.
(f) Billed customers for fees earned, $1,250.
(g) Paid automobile expenses (including rental charges) for month, $480, and miscellaneous expenses, $275.
(h) Paid office salaries, $1,500.
(i) Determined that the cost of supplies on hand was $425; therefore, the cost of supplies used was $525.
(j) Withdrew cash for personal use, $1,200.

Instructions:

Indicate the effect of each transaction and the balances after each transaction, using the following tabular headings:

Assets	Liabilities	Owner's Equity
Cash + Accounts Receivable + Supplies =	Accounts Payable +	John Herr, Capital

By appropriate notations at the right of each change, indicate the nature of each increase and decrease in owner's equity.

Problem 1–2B
Financial statements for sole proprietorship.

OBJ. 7

Robert May established Robert May Services on May 1 of the current year. The effect of each transaction and the balances after each transaction for May are as follows:

		Assets			=	Liabilities	+	Owner's Equity	
		Cash	+ Accounts Receivable	+ Supplies	=	Accounts Payable	+	Robert May, Capital	
(a)		+4,000						+4,000	Investment
(b)		−1,800						−1,800	Rent expense
Bal.		2,200						2,200	
(c)				+425		+425			
Bal.		2,200		425		425		2,200	
(d)		− 225				−225			
Bal.		1,975		425		200		2,200	
(e)		+3,750						+3,750	Fees earned
Bal.		5,725		425		200		5,950	
(f)		− 600						− 350	Auto expense
								− 250	Misc. expense
Bal.		5,125		425		200		5,350	
(g)		− 900						− 900	Salaries expense
Bal.		4,225		425		200		4,450	
(h)				−250				− 250	Supplies expense
Bal.		4,225		175		200		4,200	
(i)			+1,350					+1,350	Fees earned
Bal.		4,225	1,350	175		200		5,550	
(j)		−1,500						−1,500	Withdrawal
Bal.		2,725	1,350	175		200		4,050	

Instructions:

(1) Prepare an income statement for the month ended May 31.
(2) Prepare a statement of owner's equity for the month ended May 31.
(3) Prepare a balance sheet as of May 31.
(4) Prepare a statement of cash flows for the month ended May 31.

Problem 1–4B
Transactions for sole proprietorship; financial statements.
OBJ. 6, 7

Moore Dry Cleaners is a sole proprietorship owned and operated by Betty Moore. Currently, a building and equipment are being rented, pending expansion to new facilities. The actual work of dry cleaning is done by another company at wholesale rates. The assets and the liabilities of the business on May 1 of the current year are as follows: Cash, $9,250; Accounts Receivable, $14,100; Supplies, $900; Land, $25,000; Accounts Payable, $9,800. Business transactions during May are summarized as follows:

(a) Received cash from cash customers for dry cleaning sales, $7,650.
(b) Paid rent for the month, $1,200.
(c) Purchased supplies on account, $320.
(d) Paid creditors on account, $7,700.
(e) Charged customers for dry cleaning sales on account, $5,020.
(f) Received monthly invoice for dry cleaning expense for May (to be paid on June 8), $6,500.
(g) Paid the following: wages expense, $1,400; truck expense, $580; utilities expense, $460; miscellaneous expense, $130.
(h) Received cash from customers on account, $8,100.
(i) Determined the cost of supplies used during the month, $470.

Instructions:

(1) Determine the amount of Betty Moore's capital as of May 1 of the current year.
(2) State the assets, liabilities, and owner's equity as of May 1 in equation form similar to that shown in this chapter. In tabular form below the equation, indicate increases and decreases resulting from each transaction and the new balances after each transaction. Explain the nature of each increase and decrease in owner's equity by an appropriate notation at the right of the amount.
(3) Prepare (a) an income statement for May, (b) a statement of owner's equity for May, (c) a balance sheet as of May 31, and (d) a statement of cash flows for May.

Problem 1–5B
Financial statements for sole proprietorship.
OBJ. 7

Following are the amounts of the assets and liabilities of Conrad Services, a sole proprietorship, at December 31, the *end* of the current year, and its revenue and expenses for the year ended on that date. The capital of Tom Conrad, owner, was $21,500 at January 1, the *beginning* of the current year, and the owner withdrew $24,000 during the current year. Cash received from customers was $97,000 and cash paid for expenses and to creditors was $72,100.

Cash...	$ 5,750
Accounts receivable..	21,000
Supplies..	4,950
Prepaid insurance..	1,500
Accounts payable...	2,750
Salaries payable..	1,500
Fees earned..	99,250
Salary expense...	28,600
Rent expense...	12,000
Utilities expense	7,000
Supplies expense	5,800
Taxes expense	5,500
Insurance expense...	3,750
Advertising expense..	3,000
Miscellaneous expense...	2,150

Instructions:

(1) Prepare an income statement for the current year ended December 31.
(2) Prepare a statement of owner's equity for the current year ended December 31.
(3) Prepare a balance sheet as of December 31 of the current year.
(4) Prepare a statement of cash flows for the current year ended December 31. The cash balance on January 1, beginning of the current year, was $4,850.

Problem 1–6B

Financial statements for corporation.

OBJ. 8

Following are the amounts of Borg Corporation's assets and liabilities at July 31, the end of the current year, and its revenue and expenses for the year ended on that date, listed in alphabetical order. Borg Corporation had capital stock of $50,000 and retained earnings of $97,890 on August 1, the beginning of the current year. During the current year, the corporation paid cash dividends of $40,000 and received cash from sale of capital stock of $50,000. Cash received from customers was $840,000 and cash paid for expenses and to creditors was $815,000.

Accounts payable	$ 84,000
Accounts receivable	69,750
Advertising expense	30,000
Cash	64,515
Insurance expense	22,500
Land	200,000
Miscellaneous expense	8,125
Prepaid insurance	6,000
Rent expense	165,000
Salaries payable	11,250
Salary expense	412,000
Fees earned	850,000
Supplies	6,250
Supplies expense	19,750
Taxes expense	33,500
Utilities expense	65,750

Instructions:

(1) Prepare an income statement for the current year ended July 31.
(2) Prepare a retained earnings statement for the current year ended July 31.
(3) Prepare a balance sheet as of July 31 of the current year.
(4) Prepare a statement of cash flows for the current year ended July 31. The cash balance on August 1, the beginning of the current year, was $29,515.

MINI-CASE 1

Chris Dunn, a junior in college, has been seeking ways to earn extra spending money. As an active sports enthusiast, Chris plays tennis regularly at the Vineyards Golf and Tennis Club, where her family has a membership. The president of the club recently approached Chris with the proposal that she manage the club's tennis courts on weekends. Chris's primary duty would be to supervise the operation of the club's two indoor and six outdoor courts, including court reservations. In return for her services, the club would pay Chris $50 per weekend, plus Chris could keep whatever she earned from lessons and the fees from the use of the ball machine. The club and Chris agreed to a one-month trial, after which both would consider an arrangement for the remaining two years of Chris's college career. On this basis, Chris organized Tennis Services Unlimited. During September, Chris managed the tennis courts and entered into the following transactions:

(a) Opened a business account by depositing $450.
(b) Paid $200 for tennis supplies (practice tennis balls, etc.).
(c) Paid $150 for the rental of video tape equipment to be used in offering lessons during September.
(d) Arranged for the rental of two ball machines during September for $100. Paid $50 in advance, with the remaining $50 due October 1.
(e) Received $950 for lessons given during September.
(f) Received $140 in fees from the use of the ball machines during September.
(g) Paid $250 for salaries of part-time employees who answered the telephone and took reservations while Chris was giving lessons.
(h) Paid $75 for miscellaneous expenses.
(i) Received $200 from the club for managing the tennis courts during September.
(j) Supplies on hand at the end of the month totaled $75.
(k) Chris withdrew $500 for personal use on September 30.

As a friend and accounting student, Chris has asked you to aid her in assessing the venture.

Instructions:

(1) Indicate the effect of each transaction and the balances after each transaction, using the following tabular headings:

Assets	Liabilities	Owner's Equity

Cash + Supplies = Accounts Payable + C. Dunn, Capital

(2) Prepare an income statement for September.
(3) Prepare a statement of owner's equity for September.
(4) Prepare a balance sheet as of September 30.
(5) (a) Assume that Chris Dunn could earn $6 per hour working 20 hours per weekend as a waitress. Evaluate which of the two alternatives, working as a waitress or operating Tennis Services Unlimited, would provide Chris with the most income per month.
     (b) Discuss any other factors that you believe Chris should consider before discussing a long-term arrangement with Vineyards Golf and Tennis Club.

ETHICS DISCUSSION CASE

John Eskew, the president of Eskew Enterprises, applied for a $100,000 loan from First National Bank. The bank requested financial statements from Eskew Enterprises as a basis for granting the loan. John Eskew has told his accountant to provide the bank with a balance sheet, an income statement, and a statement of owner's equity. John Eskew has decided to omit the statement of cash flows, since there was a net decrease in cash during the past year.

Discuss whether John Eskew is behaving in an ethical manner by omitting the statement of cash flows.

ANSWERS TO SELF-EXAMINATION QUESTIONS

1. D A corporation, organized in accordance with state or federal statutes, is a separate legal entity in which ownership is divided into shares of stock (answer D). A sole proprietorship, sometimes referred to as a single proprietorship (answers A and B), is an unincorporated business enterprise owned by one individual. A partnership (answer C) is an unincorporated business enterprise owned by two or more individuals.

2. A The properties owned by a business enterprise are referred to as assets (answer A). The debts of the business are called liabilities (answer B), and the equity of the owners is called stockholders' equity or owner's equity (answers C and D).

3. A The balance sheet is a listing of the assets, liabilities, and owner's equity of a business entity at a specific date (answer A). The income statement (answer B) is a summary of the revenue and expenses of a business entity for a specific period of time. The statement of owner's equity (answer C) summarizes the changes in owner's equity for a sole proprietorship or partnership during a specific period of time. The retained earnings statement (answer D) summarizes the changes in retained earnings for a corporation during a specific period of time.

4. C The accounting equation is:

$$\text{Assets} = \text{Liabilities} + \text{Owner's Equity}$$

Therefore, if assets increased by $20,000 and liabilities increased by $12,000, owner's equity must have increased by $8,000 (answer C) as indicated in the following computation:

$$\text{Assets} = \text{Liabilities} + \text{Owner's Equity}$$
$$\$20,000 = \$12,000 + \text{Owner's Equity}$$
$$\$20,000 - \$12,000 = \text{Owner's Equity}$$
$$\$\ 8,000 = \text{Owner's Equity}$$

5. B Net income is the excess of revenue over expenses, or $7,500 (answer B). If expenses exceed revenue, the difference is a net loss. Withdrawals by the owner are the opposite of the owner's investing in the business and do not affect the amount of net income or net loss.

CHAPTER TWO

THE ACCOUNTING CYCLE

CHAPTER OBJECTIVES

1 Describe the common classification of accounts for a small service enterprise.

2 Describe the nature of a chart of accounts and illustrate a chart of accounts for a small service enterprise.

3 Describe the nature of an account and the general rules of debit and credit and normal balances of accounts.

4 Describe and illustrate the use of a two-column journal, a two-column account and a four-column account, and the posting of transactions to the ledger.

5 Describe and illustrate the preparation of a trial balance and its use in the discovery of errors.

The transactions completed by an enterprise during a specific period may cause increases and decreases in many different asset, liability, and owner's equity items. To have the details of these transactions readily available and to prepare periodic financial statements, the effects of the transactions must be recorded in a systematic manner.

The nature of transactions and their effect on business enterprises were described and recorded in Chapter 1 by the use of the accounting equation, Assets = Liabilities + Owner's Equity. Although transactions can be analyzed and recorded in terms of their effect on the equation, such a format is not practical as a design for actual accounting systems.

Accountants must provide information on business transactions for use in directing operations and for the preparation of timely periodic financial statements. These goals are met by keeping a separate record for each item that appears on the financial statements. The individual records are then summarized at periodic intervals and the data thus obtained are presented in the financial statements or other reports. For example, a record would be used only for recording increases and decreases in cash, another record would be used only for recording increases and decreases in supplies, another for land, etc. Likewise, a separate record would be kept for sales, another record would be kept for salary expense, another for rent expense, etc. The type of record traditionally used for the purpose of recording individual transactions is called an **account**. A group of related accounts that comprise a complete unit, such as all of the accounts of a specific business enterprise, is called a **ledger**.

CLASSIFICATION OF ACCOUNTS

OBJECTIVE 1
Describe the common classification of accounts for a small service enterprise.

Accounts in the ledger are customarily listed in the order in which they appear in the financial statements and are classified according to common characteristics. Balance sheet accounts are classified as assets, liabilities, or owner's equity. Income statement accounts are classified as revenues or expenses. In addition, there may be subgroupings within the major categories. The classifications and accounts characteristically used by a small service enterprise are described in the paragraphs that follow. Additional classes and accounts are introduced in later chapters.

Assets

Any physical thing (tangible) or right (intangible) that has a monetary value is an asset. Assets are customarily divided into groups for presentation on the balance sheet. The two groups used most often are (1) current assets and (2) plant assets.

Current Assets. Cash and other assets that may reasonably be expected to be realized in cash or sold or used up usually within one year or less, through the normal operations of the business, are called **current assets**. In addition to cash, the current assets usually owned by a service business are notes receivable and accounts receivable, and supplies and other prepaid expenses.

Cash is any medium of exchange that a bank will accept at face value. It includes bank deposits, currency, checks, bank drafts, and money orders. **Notes receivable** are claims against debtors evidenced by a written promise to pay a sum of money at a definite time to the order of a specified person or to bearer. **Accounts receivable** are also claims against debtors, but are less formal than notes. They arise from sales of services or merchandise on account. **Prepaid expenses** include supplies on hand and advance payments of expenses such as insurance and property taxes.

Plant Assets. Tangible assets used in the business that are of a permanent or relatively fixed nature are called **plant assets** or **fixed assets**. Plant assets include equipment, machinery, buildings, and land. With the exception of land, such assets gradually wear out or otherwise lose their usefulness with the passage of time. They are said to *depreciate*. The concept of depreciation is discussed in more detail in Chapter 3.

Liabilities

Liabilities are debts owed to outsiders (creditors) and are frequently described on the balance sheet by titles that include the word "payable." The two categories occurring most frequently are (1) current liabilities and (2) long-term liabilities.

Current Liabilities. Liabilities that will be due within a short time (usually one year or less) and that are to be paid out of current assets are called **current liabilities**. The most common liabilities in this group are **notes payable** and **accounts payable**, which are exactly like their receivable counterparts except that the debtor-creditor relationship is reversed. Other current liability accounts commonly found in the ledger are Salaries Payable, Interest Payable, and Taxes Payable.

Long-Term Liabilities. Liabilities that will not be due for a comparatively long time (usually more than one year) are called **long-term liabilities** or **fixed liabilities**. As they come within the one-year range and are to be paid, such liabilities become current. If the obligation is to be renewed rather than paid at maturity, however, it would continue to be classed as long-term. When payment of a long-term debt is to be spread over a number of years, the installments due within one year from a balance sheet date are classed as a current liability. When a note is accompanied by security in the form of a mortgage, the obligation may be referred to as *mortgage note payable* or *mortgage payable*.

Owner's Equity

Owner's equity is the residual claim against the assets of the business after the total liabilities are deducted. For a corporation, owner's equity is frequently called **stockholders' equity**, *shareholders' equity,* or *stockholders' investment*.

Capital, Capital Stock, and Retained Earnings. Capital is the owner's equity in a sole proprietorship (and partnership). The owner's equity may also be described as **net worth**. For a corporation, **capital stock** represents the investment of the stockholders, and **retained earnings** represents the net income retained in the business.

Drawings and Dividends. Drawings represent the amount of withdrawals made by the owner of a sole proprietorship (and partnership). For a corporation, **dividends** represent the distribution of earnings to stockholders.

Revenues

Revenues are the gross increases in owner's equity as a result of the sale of merchandise, the performance of services for a customer or a client, the rental of property, the lending of money, and other business and professional activities entered into for the purpose of earning income. Revenue from sales of merchandise or sales of services is often identified merely as *sales*. Other terms employed to identify sources of revenue include *professional fees, commissions revenue, fares earned,* and *interest income.* If an enterprise has various types of revenue, a separate account should be maintained for each.

Expenses

Costs that have been consumed in the process of producing revenue are **expired costs** or **expenses.** The number of expense categories and individual expense accounts maintained in the ledger varies with the nature and the size of an enterprise. A large business with authority and responsibility spread among many employees may use an elaborate classification and hundreds of accounts as an aid in controlling expenses. For a small service business, a modest number of expense accounts is satisfactory.

CHART OF ACCOUNTS

OBJECTIVE 2
Describe the nature of a chart of accounts and illustrate a chart of accounts for a small service enterprise.

The number of accounts maintained by a specific enterprise is affected by the nature of its operations, its volume of business, and the extent to which details are needed for taxing authorities, managerial decisions, credit purposes, etc. For example, one enterprise may have separate accounts for executive salaries, office salaries, and sales salaries, while another may find it satisfactory to record all types of salaries in a single salary expense account.

A listing of the accounts in a ledger is called a **chart of accounts**. Insofar as possible, the order of the accounts in the chart of accounts should agree with the order of the items in the balance sheet and the income statement. The accounts are numbered to permit indexing and also for use as references.

Although accounts in the ledger may t numbered consecutively as in the pages of a book, a flexible system of indexing is preferable. In the following chart of accounts for a small service business, Hill Photographic Studio, each account number has two digits. The first digit indicates the major division of the ledger in which the account is placed. Accounts beginning with 1 represent assets; 2, liabilities; 3, owner's equity (owner's capital and drawing); 4, revenue; and 5, expenses. The second digit indicates the position of the account within its division. A numbering system of this type has the advantage of permitting the later insertion of new accounts in their proper sequence without disturbing the other account numbers. For a large enterprise with a number of departments or branches, it is not unusual for each account number to have four or more digits.

Chart of Accounts for Hill Photographic Studio

Balance Sheet Accounts	Income Statement Accounts
1. Assets	4. Revenue
11 Cash	41 Sales
12 Accounts Receivable	5. Expenses
14 Supplies	51 Supplies Expense
15 Prepaid Rent	52 Salary Expense
18 Photographic Equipment	53 Rent Expense
19 Accumulated Depreciation[1]	54 Depreciation Expense[1]
2. Liabilities	59 Miscellaneous Expense
21 Accounts Payable	
22 Salaries Payable	
3. Owner's Equity	
31 Ann Hill, Capital	
32 Ann Hill, Drawing	
33 Income Summary[1]	

The initial preparation of the ledger based on the chart of accounts is often referred to as *opening the ledger.*

NATURE OF AN ACCOUNT

OBJECTIVE 3
Describe the nature of an account and the general rules of debit and credit and normal balances of accounts.

The simplest form of an account has three parts: (1) a title, which is the name of the item recorded in the account; (2) a space for recording increases in the amount of the item, in terms of money; and (3) a space for recording decreases in the amount of the item, also in monetary terms. This form of an account, illustrated below, is known as a **T account** because of its similarity to the letter T.

T Account

Title	
Left side	Right side
debit	*credit*

[1]The accumulated depreciation, depreciation expense, and income summary accounts are discussed in Chapter 3, when the process of preparing financial statements for Hill Photographic Studio is discussed.

The left side of the account is called the **debit** side and the right side is called the **credit** side.[2] The word **charge** is sometimes used as a synonym for debit. Amounts entered on the left side of an account, regardless of the account title, are called **debits** or **charges** to the account, and the account is said to be **debited** or **charged**. Amounts entered on the right side of an account are called **credits**, and the account is said to be **credited**.

In the following illustration, receipts of cash during a period of time have been listed vertically on the debit side of the cash account. The cash payments for the same period have been listed in similar fashion on the credit side of the account. A memorandum total of the cash receipts for the period to date, $10,950 in the illustration, may be inserted below the last debit at any time the information is desired. The figures should be small and written in pencil in order to avoid mistaking the amount for an additional debit. (The procedure is sometimes referred to as **pencil footing**.) The total of the cash payments, $6,850 in the illustration, may be inserted on the credit side in a similar manner. Subtraction of the smaller sum from the larger, $10,950 − $6,850, yields the amount of cash on hand, which is called the **balance of the account**. The cash account in the illustration has a balance of $4,100. This amount may be inserted in pencil figures next to the larger pencil footing, which identifies it as a **debit balance**. If a balance sheet were to be prepared at this time, the amount of cash reported thereon would be $4,100.

Cash

	3,750		850
	4,300		1,400
	2,900		700
4,100	10,950		2,900
			1,000
			6,850

Balance Sheet Accounts

The manner of recording data in the accounts and the relationship of accounts to the balance sheet are presented in the two illustrations that follow. For the first illustration, assume that Carl Davis establishes a business venture, to be known as Davis Appliance Repair, by initially depositing $3,500 cash in a bank account for the use of the enterprise. Immediately after the deposit, the balance sheet for the business, in account form, would contain the following information:

Assets		Owner's Equity	
Cash..........................	$3,500	Carl Davis, capital..........	$3,500

Every business transaction affects a minimum of two accounts. The effect of the above transaction on accounts in the ledger can be described as a

---

[2]Often abbreviated as *Dr.* for "debit" and *Cr.* for "credit," derived from the Latin *debere* and *credere*.

$3,500 debit to Cash and a $3,500 credit to Carl Davis, Capital. This information is initially entered in a record called a **journal**. In the journal, the information is stated in a formalized manner by listing the title of the account and the amount to be debited, followed by a similar listing, below and to the right of the debit, of the title of the account and the amount to be credited. The process of recording a transaction in the journal is called **journalizing**. The form of presentation is called a **journal entry**, and is illustrated as follows:

Cash..	3,500
Carl Davis, Capital	3,500

The data in the journal entry are transferred to the appropriate accounts by a process known as **posting**. The accounts after posting the above journal entry appear as follows:

Cash		Carl Davis, Capital	
3,500			3,500

Note that the amount of the asset, which is reported on the left side of the account form of balance sheet, is posted to the left (debit) side of Cash. The owner's equity in the business, which is reported on the right side of the balance sheet, is posted to the right (credit) side of Carl Davis, Capital. When other assets are acquired, the increases will be recorded as debits to the appropriate accounts. As owner's equity is increased or liabilities are incurred, the increases will be recorded as credits.

For the second illustration, assume that after opening the checking account, Davis purchased equipment and tools at a cost of $2,800. Davis paid $1,800 in cash by writing a check on the bank account, and agreed to pay the remaining $1,000 within thirty days. After this transaction, the data reported in the balance sheet would be as follows:

Assets		Liabilities	
Cash...........................	$1,700	Accounts payable..........	$1,000
Equipment....................	2,800	Owner's Equity	
		Carl Davis, capital.........	3,500
		Total liabilities and	
Total assets...................	$4,500	owner's equity...........	$4,500

The effect of the transaction can be described as a $2,800 debit (increase) to Equipment, an $1,800 credit (decrease) to Cash, and a $1,000 credit (increase) to Accounts Payable. The same information can be presented in the form of the following journal entry. (An entry composed of two or more debits or of two or more credits is called a **compound journal entry**.)

Equipment..	2,800
Cash...	1,800
Accounts Payable	1,000

After the journal entry for the second transaction has been posted, the accounts of Davis Appliance Repair appear as follows:

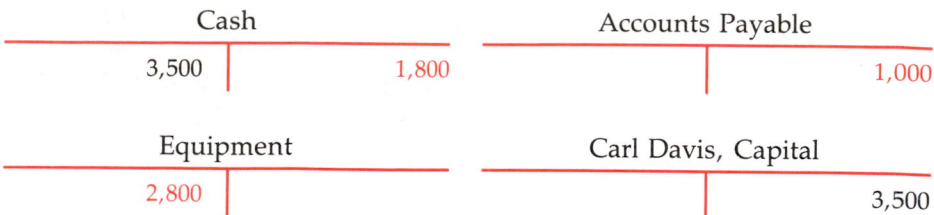

Cash		Accounts Payable	
3,500	1,800		1,000

Equipment		Carl Davis, Capital	
2,800			3,500

Note that the effect of the transaction was to increase one asset account, decrease another asset account, and increase a liability account. Note also that although the amounts, $2,800, $1,800, and $1,000, are different, the equality of debits and credits was maintained. Regardless of the complexity of a transaction or the number of accounts affected, the sum of the debits is always equal to the sum of the credits. This equality of debit and credit for each transaction is inherent in the equation A = L + OE. It is also because of this duality that the system is known as **double-entry accounting**.

TAKING THE HUMAN SPIRIT INTO ACCOUNT

Double-entry bookkeeping is one of the most beautiful discoveries of the human spirit. . . . It came from the same spirit which produced the systems of Galileo and Newton and the subject matter of modern physics and chemistry. By the same means, it organizes perceptions into a system, and one can characterize it as the first Cosmos constructed purely on the basis of mechanistic thought. . . . Without too much difficulty, we can recognize in double-entry bookkeeping the ideas of gravitation, of the circulation of the blood and of the conservation of matter.

Source: From the novel, *Wilhelm Meister's Lehrjahre* (Apprenticeship), written in 1795–6 by the German poet Johann Wolfgang von Goethe, translated by the German political economist Werner Sombart (1863–1941).

In the preceding paragraphs, it was observed that the left side of asset accounts is used for recording increases and the right side is used for recording decreases. It was also observed that the right side of liability and owner's equity accounts is used to record increases. It naturally follows that the left side of such accounts is used to record decreases. The left side of all accounts, whether asset, liability, or owner's equity, is the debit side and the right side is the credit side. Consequently, a debit may be either an increase or a decrease, depending on the nature of the account affected. A credit may likewise be either an increase or a decrease, depending on the nature of the account. The rules of debit and credit may therefore be stated as follows:

General Rules of Debit and Credit

Debit may signify:	*Credit* may signify:
Increase in asset accounts	Decrease in asset accounts
Decrease in liability accounts	Increase in liability accounts
Decrease in owner's equity accounts	Increase in owner's equity accounts

The rules of debit and credit may also be stated in relationship to the accounting equation and the account form of balance sheet, as in the following diagram:

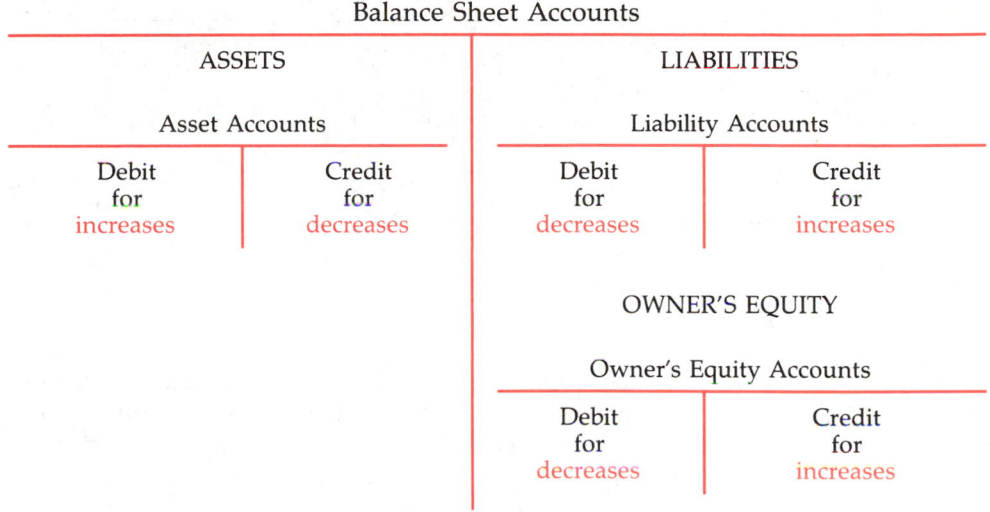

The owner of a sole proprietorship may from time to time withdraw cash from the business for personal use. This practice is common if the owner devotes full time to the business or if the business is the owner's principal source of income. Such withdrawals have the effect of decreasing owner's equity, and just as decreases in owner's equity are recorded as debits, withdrawals are recorded as debits. Withdrawals are debited to an account bearing the owner's name followed by Drawing or Personal. The balance in this account is periodically transferred to the owner's capital account. Thus, debits to the drawing account may be thought of as either decreasing owner's equity (negative sense) or increasing drawings (positive sense).

The dividends account of a corporation is comparable to the drawing account of a sole proprietorship. Distributions of earnings to the stockholders are debited to Dividends, which is periodically transferred to the retained earnings account. Debits to the dividends account have the effect of decreasing owner's equity (negative sense) or increasing dividends (positive sense).

Income Statement Accounts

The theory of debit and credit in its application to revenue and expense accounts is based on the relationship of these accounts to owner's equity. The net income or the net loss for a period, as reported on the income statement, is the net increase or the net decrease in owner's equity as a result of operations.

Revenue increases owner's equity. Just as increases in owner's equity are recorded as credits, increases in revenues during an accounting period are recorded as credits.

Expenses have the effect of decreasing owner's equity, and just as decreases in owner's equity are recorded as debits, increases in expense accounts are recorded as debits. Debits to expense accounts are usually referred to in the positive sense (as increases in expense) rather than in the negative sense (as decreases in owner's equity). The rules of debit and credit as applied to revenue and expense accounts are shown in the following diagram:

Income Statement Accounts	
Debit for *decreases in owner's equity*	*Credit for* *increases in owner's equity*

Expense Accounts		Revenue Accounts	
Debit for increases	Credit for decreases	Debit for decreases	Credit for increases

At the end of an accounting period, the revenue and expense account balances are reported in the income statement. Periodically, usually at the end of the accounting year, all revenue and expense account balances are transferred to a summarizing account and the accounts are then said to be *closed*. The balance in the summarizing account, which is the net income or net loss for the period, is then transferred to the owner's capital account (to the retained earnings account for a corporation) and the summarizing account is also closed. Because revenue and expense accounts are periodically closed, they are sometimes called **temporary accounts** or **nominal accounts**. The balances of the accounts reported in the balance sheet are carried forward from year to year and because of their permanence are sometimes referred to as **real accounts**.

Normal Balances of Accounts

The sum of the increases recorded in an account is usually equal to or greater than the sum of the decreases recorded in the account. For this reason, the normal balances of all accounts are positive rather than negative. For example, the total debits (increases) in an asset account will ordinarily be greater than the total credits (decreases). Thus, asset accounts normally have debit balances.

The rules of debit and credit and the normal balances of the various types of accounts are summarized as follows. Note that the drawing, dividends, and expense accounts are considered in the positive sense. Increases in these accounts, which represent decreases in owner's equity, are recorded as debits.

		Increase	Decrease	Normal Balance
Balance sheet accounts:				
Asset		Debit	Credit	Debit
Liability		Credit	Debit	Credit
Owner's Equity *or* Stockholders' Equity				
Capital	Capital Stock	Credit	Debit	Credit
	Retained Earnings	Credit	Debit	Credit
Drawing	Dividends	Debit	Credit	Debit
Income statement accounts:				
Revenue		Credit	Debit	Credit
Expense		Debit	Credit	Debit

When an account that normally has a debit balance actually has a credit balance, or vice versa, it is an indication of an accounting error or of an unusual situation. For example, a credit balance in the office equipment account could result only from an accounting error. On the other hand, a debit balance in an account payable account could result from an overpayment.

JOURNALS AND ACCOUNTS

OBJECTIVE 4
Describe and illustrate the use of a two-column journal, a two-column account and a four-column account, and the posting of transactions to the ledger.

The flow of accounting data from the time a transaction occurs to its recording in the ledger may be diagrammed as follows:

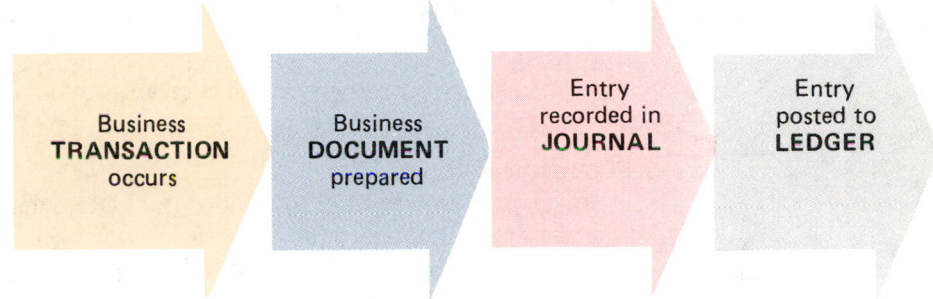

The initial record of each transaction, or of a group of similar transactions, is evidenced by a business document, such as a sales ticket, a bill, or a cash register tape. On the basis of the evidence provided by the business documents, the transactions are entered in chronological order in a journal. The amounts of the debits and the credits in the journal are then transferred or posted to the accounts in the ledger. The use of a two-column journal, two-column or four-column accounts, and posting from the journal to the ledger are discussed and illustrated in the following paragraphs.

Two-Column Journal

The basic features of a journal entry were illustrated earlier when the use of debit and credit was introduced. There is great variety in both the design of journals and the number of different journals that can be employed by an enterprise. A business may use a single all-purpose two-column journal, or it may use a number of multicolumn journals, restricting each to a single type of transaction. Examples of more sophisticated journal systems are discussed and illustrated in later chapters. Means by which business documents or various types of processing methods may entirely replace journals are also discussed.

Before a transaction is entered in the two-column journal, it should be analyzed according to the following sequence of steps:

1. Determine whether an asset, a liability, owner's equity, revenue, or expense is affected.
2. Determine whether the affected asset, liability, owner's equity, revenue, or expense increases or decreases.
3. Determine whether the effect of the transaction should be recorded as a debit or as a credit in an asset, liability, owner's equity, revenue, or expense account.

To illustrate the results of such analyses, assume that $1,822.25 is received from cash sales for May 1. The asset Cash increases and therefore should be debited for $1,822.25. The revenue account Sales also increases and therefore should be credited for $1,822.25. The two-column journal in which the transaction has been recorded would appear as follows:

	DATE		DESCRIPTION	POST. REF.	DEBIT	CREDIT	
1	1990 May	1	Cash		1 822 25		1
2			Sales			1 822 25	2
3			Cash sales for the day.				3
4							4

JOURNAL   PAGE 17

The process of recording a transaction in a two-column journal is summarized as follows:

1. Record the date:
   a. Insert the year at the top only of the Date column of each page, except when the year date changes.
   b. Insert the month on the first line only of the Date column of each page, except when the month date changes.
   c. Insert the day in the Date column on the first line used for each transaction, regardless of the number of transactions during the day.
2. Record the debit:
   Insert the title of the account to be debited at the extreme left of the Description column and enter the amount in the Debit column.
3. Record the credit:
   Insert the title of the account to be credited below the account debited, moderately indented, and enter the amount in the Credit column.
4. Write an explanation:
   Brief explanations may be written below each entry, moderately indented. Some accountants prefer that the explanation be omitted if the nature of the transaction is obvious. It is also permissible to omit a lengthy explanation of a complex transaction if a reference to the related business document can be substituted.

It should be noted that all transactions are recorded only in terms of debits and credits to specific accounts. The titles used in the entries should be the same as the titles of the accounts in the ledger. For example, supplies purchased should be entered as a debit to Supplies, not to "supplies purchased," and cash received should be entered as a debit to Cash, not to "cash received."

The line following an entry is left blank in order to clearly separate each entry. The column headed Post. Ref. (posting reference) is not used until the debits and credits are posted to the appropriate accounts in the ledger.

Two-Column Accounts and Four-Column Accounts

Accounts in the simple T form are used primarily for illustrative purposes. The addition of special rulings to the T form yields the standard two-column form illustrated as follows:

Standard Form of the
Two-Column Account

ACCOUNT Cash								ACCOUNT NO. 11				
DATE	ITEM	POST. REF.	DEBIT					DATE	ITEM	POST. REF.	CREDIT	
1990 May 1	Balance	✔	5	2 4 5	00			1990 May 1		17	3 5 0	00
1		17	1	8 2 2	25			1		17	9 9 5	50
3		17		9 6 0	40			3		17	1 9 2	00
								3		17	1 8 8 2	25
	4,607.90		8	0 2 7	65						3 4 1 9	75

The standard two-column account form distinguishes to the greatest possible extent between debit entries and credit entries. It is primarily because of this feature that the T form is used at the beginning of introductory accounting courses. In actual practice, there has been a tendency for account forms with balance columns to replace the simpler T form, though the latter is still used. A four-column form is shown as follows:

Standard Form of the
Four-Column Account

ACCOUNT Cash						BALANCE		ACCOUNT NO. 11
DATE	ITEM	POST. REF.	DEBIT	CREDIT	DEBIT		CREDIT	
1990 May 1	Balance	✔			5 2 4 5 00		
1		17	1 8 2 2 25		7 0 6 7 25		
1		17		3 5 0 00	6 7 1 7 25		
1		17		9 9 5 50	5 7 2 1 75		
3		17	9 6 0 40		6 6 8 2 15		
3		17		1 9 2 00	6 4 9 0 15		
3		17		1 8 8 2 25	4 6 0 7 90		

Among the significant advantages of the four-column account form are the following:

1. Only a single date column is required, with each debit and credit appearing in its chronological order.
2. The debit or credit nature of an account balance is more easily determined and more prominently displayed in the account.
3. Having immediately adjacent debit and credit columns makes it easier to examine the data in an account.

When posting is computerized and the four-column format is used, the new balance of an account is automatically computed in the proper column after each posting. The account balance is thus always readily available. The same procedure may be followed when the posting is done manually. An alternative is to postpone the computation of the balance until all postings for the month have been completed. When this is done, only the final month-end balance is inserted in the appropriate balance column. The exact procedure adopted in a particular situation will depend upon such factors as the availability of computers and the desirability of having current account balances visible at all times.

Posting

When posting is done manually, the debits and credits in the journal may be posted in the order that they occur or, if many items are to be posted at one time, all the debits may be posted first, followed by the credits. The posting of a debit journal entry or a credit journal entry to an account in the ledger is performed in the following manner:

1. Record the date and the amount of the entry in the account.
2. Insert the number of the journal page in the Posting Reference column of the account.
3. Insert the ledger account number in the Posting Reference column of the journal.

These procedures are illustrated as follows by the posting of a debit to the cash account. The posting of a credit uses the same sequence of procedures.

Diagram of the Posting of a Debit

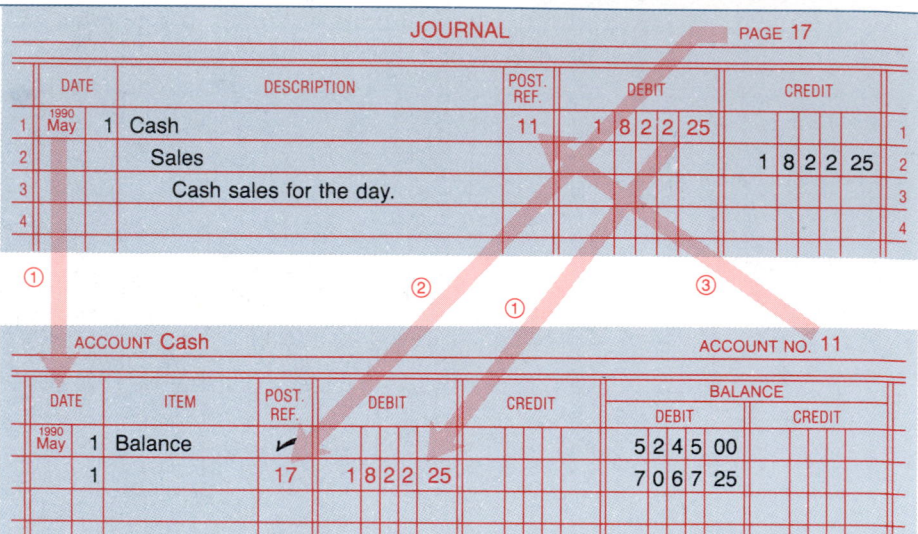

Illustration of Journalizing and Posting

To illustrate the journalizing and posting process, a month's transactions for Hill Photographic Studio are used. Hill Photographic Studio is the small service business whose chart of accounts was presented on page 51.

To reduce repetition, some of the following transactions are stated as a summary. For example, sales of services for cash are ordinarily recorded on a daily basis, but in the illustration, summary totals are given only at the middle and end of the month. Similarly, all sales of services on account during the month are summarized as a single transaction. In practice, each sale would be recorded separately.

Mar. 1. Ann Hill operated a photographic business in her home on a part-time basis. She decided to move to rented quarters as of March 1 and to devote full time to the business, which was to be known as Hill Photographic Studio. The following assets were invested in the enterprise: cash, $3,500; accounts receivable, $950; supplies, $1,200; and photographic equipment, $15,000. There were no liabilities transferred to the business.

Analysis: The four asset accounts, Cash, Accounts Receivable, Supplies, and Photographic Equipment, increase and are debited for $3,500, $950, $1,200, and $15,000, respectively. The owner's equity in these assets is equal to the sum of the assets, or $20,650; hence, Ann Hill, Capital is credited for that amount. (The use of individual accounts receivable from customers is described in a later chapter.)

	DATE		DESCRIPTION	POST. REF.	DEBIT	CREDIT	
	JOURNAL					PAGE 1	
1	1990 Mar.	1	Cash	11	3 5 0 0 00		1
2			Accounts Receivable	12	9 5 0 00		2
3			Supplies	14	1 2 0 0 00		3
4			Photographic Equipment	18	15 0 0 0 00		4
5			Ann Hill, Capital	31		20 6 5 0 00	5

(The ledger to which the illustrative entries are posted is presented on pages 64–66.)

Mar. 1. Paid $2,400 on a lease rental contract, the payment representing three months' rent of quarters for the studio.

Analysis: The asset acquired in exchange for the cash payment is the use of the property for three months. The asset Prepaid Rent increases and is debited for $2,400; the asset Cash decreases and is credited for $2,400. (When rent for a single month is prepaid at the beginning of a month, it is customarily debited to the rent expense account at the time of payment, thus avoiding the necessity of transferring the amount from Prepaid Rent to Rent Expense at the end of the month.)

6							6
7		1	Prepaid Rent	15	2 4 0 0 00		7
8			Cash	11		2 4 0 0 00	8

Mar. 4. Purchased additional photographic equipment on account from Palmer Photographic Equipment Inc. for $2,500.

Analysis: The asset Photographic Equipment increases and is therefore debited for $2,500. The liability Accounts Payable increases and is credited for $2,500. (The use of individual accounts payable to creditors is described in a later chapter.)

9							9
10		4	Photographic Equipment	18	2 5 0 0 00		10
11			Accounts Payable	21		2 5 0 0 00	11

Mar. 5. Received $850 from customers in payment of their accounts.

Analysis: The asset Cash increases and is debited for $850; the asset Accounts Receivable decreases and is credited for $850.

12							12
13		5	Cash	11	8 5 0 00		13
14			Accounts Receivable	12		8 5 0 00	14

Mar. 6. Paid $125 for a newspaper advertisement.

Analysis: Expense accounts are subdivisions of owner's equity. Increases in expense are decreases in owner's equity; hence, an expense account is debited for $125. The asset Cash was decreased by the transaction; therefore that account is credited for $125. (Miscellaneous Expense is debited because total expenditures for advertising during an accounting period are expected to be relatively minor.)

15					15
16	6	Miscellaneous Expense	59	1 2 5 00	16
17		Cash	11		1 2 5 00	17

Mar. 10. Paid $500 to Palmer Photographic Equipment Inc. to apply on the $2,500 debt owed them.

Analysis: This payment decreases the liability Accounts Payable, so that account is debited for $500. It also decreases the asset Cash, which is credited for $500.

18					18
19	10	Accounts Payable	21	5 0 0 00	19
20		Cash	11		5 0 0 00	20

Mar. 13. Paid receptionist $575 for two weeks' salary.

Analysis: Similar to transaction of March 6.

21					21
22	13	Salary Expense	52	5 7 5 00	22
23		Cash	11		5 7 5 00	23

Mar. 16. Received $1,980 from sales for the first half of March.

Analysis: Cash increases and is debited for $1,980. The revenue account Sales, which is a subdivision of owner's equity, increases and is credited for $1,980.

24					24
25	16	Cash	11	1 9 8 0 00	25
26		Sales	41		1 9 8 0 00	26

Mar. 20. Paid $650 for supplies.

Analysis: The asset Supplies increases and is debited for $650; the asset Cash decreases and is credited for $650.

27					27
28	20	Supplies	14	6 5 0 00	28
29		Cash	11		6 5 0 00	29

Mar. 27. Paid receptionist $575 for two weeks' salary.

Analysis: Similar to transaction of March 6.

30						30
31	27	Salary Expense	52	5 7 5 00		31
32		Cash	11		5 7 5 00	32

Mar. 31. Paid $69 for telephone bill for the month.

Analysis: Similar to transaction of March 6.

33						33
34	31	Miscellaneous Expense	59	6 9 00		34
35		Cash	11		6 9 00	35

Mar. 31. Paid $175 for electric bill for the month.

Analysis: Similar to transaction of March 6.

36						36
37	31	Miscellaneous Expense	59	1 7 5 00		37
38		Cash	11		1 7 5 00	38

Mar. 31. Received $1,870 from sales for the second half of March.

Analysis: Similar to transaction of March 16.

	DATE	DESCRIPTION	POST. REF.	DEBIT	CREDIT	
			JOURNAL		PAGE 2	
1	1990 Mar. 31	Cash	11	1 8 7 0 00		1
2		Sales	41		1 8 7 0 00	2

Mar. 31. Sales on account totaled $1,675 for the month.

Analysis: The asset Accounts Receivable increases and is debited for $1,675. The revenue account Sales increases and is credited for $1,675. (Note that the revenue is earned even though no cash is received; the claim against the customers is as much an asset as cash. As customers pay their accounts later, Cash will be debited and Accounts Receivable will be credited.)

3						3
4	31	Accounts Receivable	12	1 6 7 5 00		4
5		Sales	41		1 6 7 5 00	5

Mar. 31. Hill withdrew $1,500 for her personal use.

Analysis: The transaction resulted in a decrease in the amount of owner's equity invested in the business and is recorded by a $1,500 debit to Ann Hill, Drawing; the decrease in business cash is recorded by a $1,500 credit to Cash.

6						6
7	31	Ann Hill, Drawing	32	1 5 0 0 00		7
8		Cash	11		1 5 0 0 00	8

After all the entries for the month have been posted, the ledger will appear as shown below and on pages 65–66. In practice, each account would appear on a separate page in the ledger. Tracing each entry from the journal to the accounts in the ledger will give a clear understanding of the posting process.

The accounts are numbered in accordance with the chart shown on page 51. However, some of the accounts listed in the chart are not shown in the illustrative ledger. The additional accounts will be used later when the illustration for Hill Photographic Studio is completed in Chapter 3.

Ledger — Hill
Photographic Studio

ACCOUNT **Cash**   ACCOUNT NO. 11

DATE	ITEM	POST. REF.	DEBIT	CREDIT	BALANCE DEBIT	BALANCE CREDIT
1990 Mar. 1		1	3 5 0 0 00		3 5 0 0 00	
1		1		2 4 0 0 00	1 1 0 0 00	
5		1	8 5 0 00		1 9 5 0 00	
6		1		1 2 5 00	1 8 2 5 00	
10		1		5 0 0 00	1 3 2 5 00	
13		1		5 7 5 00	7 5 0 00	
16		1	1 9 8 0 00		2 7 3 0 00	
20		1		6 5 0 00	2 0 8 0 00	
27		1		5 7 5 00	1 5 0 5 00	
31		1		6 9 00	1 4 3 6 00	
31		1		1 7 5 00	1 2 6 1 00	
31		2	1 8 7 0 00		3 1 3 1 00	
31		2		1 5 0 0 00	1 6 3 1 00	

ACCOUNT **Accounts Receivable**   ACCOUNT NO. 12

DATE	ITEM	POST. REF.	DEBIT	CREDIT	BALANCE DEBIT	BALANCE CREDIT
1990 Mar. 1		1	9 5 0 00		9 5 0 00	
5		1		8 5 0 00	1 0 0 00	
31		2	1 6 7 5 00		1 7 7 5 00	

ACCOUNT **Supplies**   ACCOUNT NO. 14

DATE	ITEM	POST. REF.	DEBIT	CREDIT	BALANCE DEBIT	BALANCE CREDIT
1990 Mar. 1		1	1 2 0 0 00		1 2 0 0 00	
20		1	6 5 0 00		1 8 5 0 00	

Ledger—Hill Photographic Studio (continued)

ACCOUNT Prepaid Rent — ACCOUNT NO. 15

DATE	ITEM	POST. REF.	DEBIT	CREDIT	BALANCE DEBIT	BALANCE CREDIT
1990 Mar. 1		1	2 400 00		2 400 00	

ACCOUNT Photographic Equipment — ACCOUNT NO. 18

DATE	ITEM	POST. REF.	DEBIT	CREDIT	BALANCE DEBIT	BALANCE CREDIT
1990 Mar. 1		1	15 000 00		15 000 00	
4		1	2 500 00		17 500 00	

ACCOUNT Accounts Payable — ACCOUNT NO. 21

DATE	ITEM	POST. REF.	DEBIT	CREDIT	BALANCE DEBIT	BALANCE CREDIT
1990 Mar. 4		1		2 500 00		2 500 00
10		1	500 00			2 000 00

ACCOUNT Ann Hill, Capital — ACCOUNT NO. 31

DATE	ITEM	POST. REF.	DEBIT	CREDIT	BALANCE DEBIT	BALANCE CREDIT
1990 Mar. 1		1		20 650 00		20 650 00

ACCOUNT Ann Hill, Drawing — ACCOUNT NO. 32

DATE	ITEM	POST. REF.	DEBIT	CREDIT	BALANCE DEBIT	BALANCE CREDIT
1990 Mar. 31		2	1 500 00		1 500 00	

ACCOUNT Sales — ACCOUNT NO. 41

DATE	ITEM	POST. REF.	DEBIT	CREDIT	BALANCE DEBIT	BALANCE CREDIT
1990 Mar. 16		1		1 980 00		1 980 00
31		2		1 870 00		3 850 00
31		2		1 675 00		5 525 00

ACCOUNT Salary Expense — ACCOUNT NO. 52

DATE	ITEM	POST. REF.	DEBIT	CREDIT	BALANCE DEBIT	BALANCE CREDIT
1990 Mar. 13		1	575 00		575 00	
27		1	575 00		1 150 00	

Ledger—Hill Photographic Studio (concluded)

| ACCOUNT Miscellaneous Expense | | | | | | ACCOUNT NO. 59 | |

DATE	ITEM	POST. REF.	DEBIT	CREDIT	BALANCE DEBIT	BALANCE CREDIT
1990 Mar. 6		1	1 2 5 00		1 2 5 00	
31		1	6 9 00		1 9 4 00	
31		1	1 7 5 00		3 6 9 00	

TRIAL BALANCE

OBJECTIVE 5
Describe and illustrate the preparation of a trial balance and its use in the discovery of errors.

The equality of debits and credits in the ledger should be verified at the end of each accounting period, if not more often. Such a verification, which is called a **trial balance,** may be in the form of a calculator tape or in the form illustrated as follows. The summary listing of both the balances and the titles of the accounts is also useful in preparing the financial statements.

Hill Photographic Studio Trial Balance March 31, 1990		
Cash	1 6 3 1 00	
Accounts Receivable	1 7 7 5 00	
Supplies	1 8 5 0 00	
Prepaid Rent	2 4 0 0 00	
Photographic Equipment	17 5 0 0 00	
Accounts Payable		2 0 0 0 00
Ann Hill, Capital		20 6 5 0 00
Ann Hill, Drawing	1 5 0 0 00	
Sales		5 5 2 5 00
Salary Expense	1 1 5 0 00	
Miscellaneous Expense	3 6 9 00	
	28 1 7 5 00	28 1 7 5 00

As the first step in preparing the trial balance, the balance of each account in the ledger should be determined. If two-column accounts are used, memorandum pencil footings and balances are inserted in accordance with the procedure illustrated on page 52. If the four-column account form is employed, the balance of each account must be indicated in the appropriate balance column on the same line as the last posting to the account. (In the illustrative ledger, the balances were extended after each posting.)

Proof Provided by the Trial Balance

The trial balance does not provide complete proof of the accuracy of the ledger. It indicates only that the *debits* and the *credits* are *equal*. This proof is of value, however, because errors frequently affect the equality of debits and credits. If the two totals of a trial balance are not equal, it is probably due to one or more of the following types of errors:

1. Error in preparing the trial balance, such as:
   a. One of the columns of the trial balance was incorrectly added.
   b. The amount of an account balance was incorrectly recorded on the trial balance.
   c. A debit balance was recorded on the trial balance as a credit, or vice versa, or a balance was omitted entirely.

2. Error in determining the account balances, such as:
    a. A balance was incorrectly computed.
    b. A balance was entered in the wrong balance column.
3. Error in recording a transaction in the ledger, such as:
    a. An erroneous amount was posted to the account.
    b. A debit entry was posted as a credit, or vice versa.
    c. A debit or a credit posting was omitted.

Among the types of errors that will not cause an inequality in the trial balance totals are the following:

1. Failure to record a transaction or to post a transaction.
2. Recording the same erroneous amount for both the debit and the credit parts of a transaction.
3. Recording the same transaction more than once.
4. Posting a part of a transaction correctly as a debit or credit but to the wrong account.

It is readily apparent that care should be exercised both in recording transactions in the journal and in posting to the accounts. The desirability of accuracy in determining account balances and reporting them on the trial balance is equally obvious.

Discovery of Errors

The existence of errors in the accounts may be determined in various ways: (1) by audit procedures, (2) by chance discovery, or (3) through the medium of the trial balance. If the debit and the credit totals of the trial balance are not in agreement, the exact amount of the difference between the totals should be determined before proceeding to search for the error.

The amount of the difference between the two totals of a trial balance sometimes gives a clue as to the nature of the error or where it occurred. For example, a difference of 10, 100, or 1,000 between two totals is frequently the result of an error in addition. A difference between totals can also be due to the omission of a debit or a credit posting or, if it is divisible evenly by 2, to the posting of a debit as a credit, or vice versa. For example, if the debit and the credit totals of a trial balance are $20,640 and $20,236 respectively, the difference of $404 may indicate that a credit posting of that amount was omitted or that a credit of $202 was erroneously posted as a debit.

Two other common types of errors are known as **transpositions** and **slides**. A transposition is the erroneous rearrangement of digits, such as writing $542 as $452 or $524. In a slide, the entire number is erroneously moved one or more spaces to the right or the left, such as writing $542.00 as $54.20 or $5,420.00. If an error of either type has occurred and there are no other errors, the discrepancy between the two trial balance totals will be evenly divisible by 9.

A preliminary examination along the lines suggested by the preceding paragraphs will frequently disclose the error. If it does not, the general procedure is to retrace the various steps in the accounting process, beginning with the last step and working back to the original entries in the journal. Ordinarily, errors that have caused the trial balance totals to be unequal will be discovered before all of the steps are retraced. While there are no rigid rules governing the procedures, the following plan is suggested:

1. Verify the accuracy of the trial balance totals by re-adding the columns.
2. Compare the listings in the trial balance with the balances shown in the ledger, making certain that no accounts have been omitted.
3. Recompute the balance of each account in the ledger.
4. Trace the postings in the ledger back to the journal, placing a small check mark by the item in the ledger and also in the journal. If the error is not found, examine each account to see if there is an entry without a check mark. Do the same with the entries in the journal.
5. Verify the equality of the debits and the credits in the journal.

ERRORS!

Chasing errors in a trial balance is not a fascinating sport like chasing a golf ball. It is tedious and uninteresting. The only way for an accountant to avoid it is to make no mistakes — and that standard is too high for most of us to maintain continuously. The penalty for one little slip may be a night or two at the office, checking an interminable mass of postings. For this reason, any hint that may aid in tracking an error to its diabolically well concealed lair, any straw that may be floated out for a submerged accountant to grasp, is a kindness and a charity.

Some day, perhaps, the mechanical accountant will entirely supplant the human article, but for a long time yet many a set of accounts will be posted by hand, and many a balance will be taken off without the aid of even an adding machine. Moreover, when the mechanical millennium — or whatever it is — arrives, there will still be balances to chase, for the machine will chew and digest only what is fed to it, and if its diet be not perfectly balanced, neither will be the result, and still will be heard the old familiar question, "How much are you out?"

This quarry is, of course, the mistake that threw out the balance, and it is the difference between what was written and what should have been written. For the sake of brevity, I shall call this the "error", which strictly speaking it is not, for the error is really the mistake itself and not its result.

Now, when a balance doesn't balance, there are several obvious things to be done. The footings all have to be checked; one must be certain that each ledger account is correctly computed and the right amount carried into the trial-balance book in the proper column; one must be assured that the totals have been carried forward correctly from one page to another; that the journal is in balance; that no posting checks are missing. Then all the items that are the same as the error must be looked up for a skipped posting, and, if it happens to be an even number, all items that are one-half the error, in case something has been posted on the wrong side. These things are simple routine, and before the list is complete the cause of the trouble has probably been found, and the happy discoverer has gone contentedly home to help Willie with his arithmetic.

If not, if the two columns simply will not add up the same, things begin to look serious. The accountant phones his wife that he will not be home to dinner. Then he begins to analyze his error and see if there are any sign-posts sticking up out of it. If none is found, he may as well begin to check postings. The sooner he starts, the sooner he gets through, and he has my sympathy, especially if he has to do it by himself.

Source: Adapted from F. Howard Seely, "The Transposition of Figures," *The Journal of Accountancy* (June, 1932).

CHAPTER REVIEW

KEY POINTS

OBJECTIVE 1

Classification of Accounts

The record traditionally kept for each item that appears on the financial statements is the account. A group of related accounts that comprise a complete unit, such as all the accounts of a specific business enterprise, is called the ledger.

Accounts in the ledger are customarily listed in the order in which they appear in the financial statements and are classified according to common characteristics. Balance sheet accounts are classified as asset, liability, or owner's equity accounts. Income statement accounts are classified as revenues or expenses. There may also be subgroupings within the major categories.

OBJECTIVE 2

Chart of Accounts

Accounts in the ledger are numbered consecutively so as to permit easy indexing and for use in posting. A listing of the accounts used by a specific enterprise in its ledger is referred to as a chart of accounts.

OBJECTIVE 3

Nature of an Account

The simplest form of an account is the T account. Increases and decreases in an account are recorded as debits (entries on the left side of the account) and credits (entries on the right side of the account). Periodically, the debits and the credits in an account are summed and the difference between the two sums is determined. This difference is called the balance of the account. General rules of debit and credit have been established for recording increases or decreases to asset, liability, owner's equity, revenue, expense, drawing, and dividend accounts. Regardless of the complexity of a transaction or the number of accounts affected, each transaction is recorded in a manner so that the sum of the debits is always equal to the sum of the credits.

The effects of transactions are initially entered in a record called a journal. Periodically, transactions that have been journalized are transferred to the accounts by a process known as posting.

The sum of the increases recorded in an account is usually equal to or greater than the sum of the decreases recorded in the account. For this reason, the normal balance of an account is indicated by the side of the account (debit or credit) that receives the increases.

The rules of debit and credit and normal account balances are summarized in the following table:

		Increase	Decrease	Normal Balance
Balance sheet accounts:				
Asset		Debit	Credit	Debit
Liability		Credit	Debit	Credit
Owner's Equity *or* Stockholders' Equity				
Capital	Capital Stock	Credit	Debit	Credit
	Retained Earnings	Credit	Debit	Credit
Drawing	Dividends	Debit	Credit	Debit
Income statement accounts:				
Revenue		Credit	Debit	Credit
Expense		Debit	Credit	Debit

OBJECTIVE 4

Journals and Accounts

The flow of accounting data from the time a transaction occurs to its recording in the ledger is diagrammed as follows:

Business *TRANSACTION* occurs $\longrightarrow$ Business *DOCUMENT* prepared $\longrightarrow$ Entry recorded in *JOURNAL* $\longrightarrow$ Entry posted to *LEDGER*

A two-column journal with a debit column and a credit column may be used for recording initial transactions in an accounting system. Before a transaction is entered in a journal, it should be analyzed according to the following sequence of steps:

1. Determine whether an asset, a liability, owner's equity, revenue, or expense is affected.
2. Determine whether the affected asset, liability, owner's equity, revenue, or expense increases or decreases.
3. Determine whether the effect of the transaction should be recorded as a debit or as a credit in an asset, liability, owner's equity, revenue, or expense account.

T accounts are used primarily for illustrative purposes, but are seldom used in practice. Special rulings may be added to the basic T account form to yield a two-column account. A four-column account that provides debit balance and credit balance columns is used widely in practice.

OBJECTIVE 5

Trial Balance

The equality of the debits and credits in a ledger are verified periodically by the preparation of a trial balance. The trial balance does not provide complete proof of accuracy of the ledger, but only indicates that the debits and credits are equal.

KEY TERMS

account 48
ledger 48
current assets 49
cash 49
notes receivable 49
accounts receivable 49
prepaid expenses 49
plant assets 49
current liabilities 49
notes payable 49
accounts payable 49
long-term liabilities 49
owner's equity 50
stockholders' equity 50
capital 50
net worth 50
capital stock 50
retained earnings 50
drawings 50

dividends 50
revenues 50
expenses 50
chart of accounts 51
T account 51
debit 52
credit 52
balance of the account 52
journal 53
journalizing 53
posting 53
double-entry accounting 54
temporary accounts 56
nominal accounts 56
real accounts 56
trial balance 66
transpositions 67
slides 67

SELF-EXAMINATION QUESTIONS

Answers at end of chapter.

1. A debit may signify:
   A. an increase in an asset account
   B. a decrease in an asset account
   C. an increase in a liability account
   D. an increase in the owner's capital account

2. The type of account with a normal credit balance is:
   A. an asset   C. a revenue
   B. a drawing   D. an expense

3. The current asset category would include:
   A. cash   C. supplies on hand
   B. accounts receivable   D. all of the above

4. The receipt of cash from customers in payment of their accounts would be recorded by a:
   A. debit to Cash; credit to Accounts Receivable
   B. debit to Accounts Receivable; credit to Cash
   C. debit to Cash; credit to Accounts Payable
   D. debit to Accounts Payable; credit to Cash

5. The form listing the balances and the titles of the accounts in the ledger on a given date is the:
   A. income statement   C. retained earnings statement
   B. balance sheet   D. trial balance

ILLUSTRATIVE PROBLEM

Judy K. Schmidt, M.D., has been practicing as a pediatrician for three years. During June, she completed the following transactions in her practice of pediatrics:

June 1. Paid office rent for June, $600.
      2. Purchased equipment on account, $2,100.
      5. Received cash on account from patients, $4,150.
      8. Purchased X-ray film and other supplies on account, $145.
      9. One of the items of equipment purchased on June 2 was defective. It was returned with the permission of the supplier, who agreed to reduce the account for the amount charged for the item, $125.
     12. Paid cash to creditors on account, $1,250.
     16. Sold X-ray film to another doctor at cost, as an accommodation, receiving cash, $63.
     17. Paid cash for renewal of a 2-year property insurance policy, $370.
     20. Discovered that the balance of the cash account and of the accounts payable account as of June 1 were overstated by $50. A payment of that amount to a creditor in May had not been recorded. Journalize the $50 payment as of June 20.
     23. Paid cash for laboratory analyses, $245.
     27. Paid cash from business bank account for personal and family expenses, $1,250.
     30. Recorded the cash received in payment of services (on a cash basis) to patients during June, $1,720.
     30. Paid salaries of receptionist and nurses, $1,725.
     30. Paid gas and electricity expense, $157.
     30. Paid water expense, $29.
     30. Recorded fees charged to patients on account for services performed in June, $4,145.

30. Paid telephone expense, $74.

30. Paid miscellaneous expenses, $132.

Schmidt's account titles, numbers, and balances as of June 1 (all normal balances) are listed as follows: Cash, 11, $3,123; Accounts Receivable, 12, $6,725; Supplies, 13, $290; Prepaid Insurance, 14, $365; Equipment, 18, $19,745; Accounts Payable, 22, $765; Judy K. Schmidt, Capital, 31, $29,483; Judy K. Schmidt, Drawing, 32; Professional Fees, 41; Salary Expense, 51; Rent Expense, 53; Laboratory Expense, 55; Utilities Expense, 56; Miscellaneous Expense, 59.

Instructions:

1. Open a ledger of four-column accounts for Dr. Schmidt as of June 1 of the current year. Enter the balances in the appropriate balance columns and place a check mark (√) in the posting reference column. (It is advisable to verify the equality of the debit and credit balances in the ledger before proceeding with the next instruction.)
2. Record each transaction in a two-column journal.
3. Post the journal to the ledger, extending the month-end balances to the appropriate balance columns after all posting is completed.
4. Prepare a trial balance as of June 30.

SOLUTION

(2) and (3)

JOURNAL   PAGE 27

	DATE		DESCRIPTION	POST. REF.	DEBIT	CREDIT	
1	19-- June	1	Rent Expense	53	6 0 0 00		1
2			Cash	11		6 0 0 00	2
3							3
4		2	Equipment	18	2 1 0 0 00		4
5			Accounts Payable	22		2 1 0 0 00	5
6							6
7		5	Cash	11	4 1 5 0 00		7
8			Accounts Receivable	12		4 1 5 0 00	8
9							9
10		8	Supplies	13	1 4 5 00		10
11			Accounts Payable	22		1 4 5 00	11
12							12
13		9	Accounts Payable	22	1 2 5 00		13
14			Equipment	18		1 2 5 00	14
15							15
16		12	Accounts Payable	22	1 2 5 0 00		16
17			Cash	11		1 2 5 0 00	17
18							18
19		16	Cash	11	6 3 00		19
20			Supplies	13		6 3 00	20
21							21
22		17	Prepaid Insurance	14	3 7 0 00		22
23			Cash	11		3 7 0 00	23
24							24
25		20	Accounts Payable	22	5 0 00		25
26			Cash	11		5 0 00	26

			POST. REF.	DEBIT					CREDIT					
27														27
28	23	Laboratory Expense	55		2	4	5	00						28
29		Cash	11							2	4	5	00	29
30														30
31	27	Judy K. Schmidt, Drawing	32	1	2	5	0	00						31
32		Cash	11						1	2	5	0	00	32
33														33
34	30	Cash	11	1	7	2	0	00						34
35		Professional Fees	41						1	7	2	0	00	35
36														36

JOURNAL   PAGE 28

	DATE	DESCRIPTION	POST. REF.	DEBIT					CREDIT					
1	30	Salary Expense	51	1	7	2	5	00						1
2		Cash	11						1	7	2	5	00	2
3														3
4	30	Utilities Expense	56		1	5	7	00						4
5		Cash	11							1	5	7	00	5
6														6
7	30	Utilities Expense	56			2	9	00						7
8		Cash	11								2	9	00	8
9														9
10	30	Accounts Receivable	12	4	1	4	5	00						10
11		Professional Fees	41						4	1	4	5	00	11
12														12
13	30	Utilities Expense	56			7	4	00						13
14		Cash	11								7	4	00	14
15														15
16	30	Miscellaneous Expense	59		1	3	2	00						16
17		Cash	11							1	3	2	00	17

(1) and (3)

ACCOUNT Cash   ACCOUNT NO. 11

DATE		ITEM	POST. REF.	DEBIT					CREDIT					BALANCE DEBIT					BALANCE CREDIT				
19-- June	1	Balance	✓											3	1	2	3	00					
	1		27							6	0	0	00										
	5		27	4	1	5	0	00															
	12		27						1	2	5	0	00										
	16		27			6	3	00															
	17		27							3	7	0	00										
	20		27								5	0	00										
	23		27							2	4	5	00										
	27		27						1	2	5	0	00										
	30		27	1	7	2	0	00															
	30		28						1	7	2	5	00										
	30		28							1	5	7	00										
	30		28								2	9	00										
	30		28								7	4	00										
	30		28							1	3	2	00	3	1	7	4	00					

ACCOUNT **Accounts Receivable**   ACCOUNT NO. **12**

DATE		ITEM	POST. REF.	DEBIT	CREDIT	BALANCE	
						DEBIT	CREDIT
19-- June	1	Balance	✔			6 7 2 5 00	
	5		27		4 1 5 0 00		
	30		28	4 1 4 5 00		6 7 2 0 00	

ACCOUNT **Supplies**   ACCOUNT NO. **13**

DATE		ITEM	POST. REF.	DEBIT	CREDIT	BALANCE	
						DEBIT	CREDIT
19-- June	1	Balance	✔			2 9 0 00	
	8		27	1 4 5 00			
	16		27		6 3 00	3 7 2 00	

ACCOUNT **Prepaid Insurance**   ACCOUNT NO. **14**

DATE		ITEM	POST. REF.	DEBIT	CREDIT	BALANCE	
						DEBIT	CREDIT
19-- June	1	Balance	✔			3 6 5 00	
	17		27	3 7 0 00		7 3 5 00	

ACCOUNT **Equipment**   ACCOUNT NO. **18**

DATE		ITEM	POST. REF.	DEBIT	CREDIT	BALANCE	
						DEBIT	CREDIT
19-- June	1	Balance	✔			19 7 4 5 00	
	2		27	2 1 0 0 00			
	9		27		1 2 5 00	21 7 2 0 00	

ACCOUNT **Accounts Payable**   ACCOUNT NO. **22**

DATE		ITEM	POST. REF.	DEBIT	CREDIT	BALANCE	
						DEBIT	CREDIT
19-- June	1	Balance	✔				7 6 5 00
	2		27		2 1 0 0 00		
	8		27		1 4 5 00		
	9		27	1 2 5 00			
	12		27	1 2 5 0 00			
	20		27	5 0 00			1 5 8 5 00

ACCOUNT **Judy K. Schmidt, Capital**   ACCOUNT NO. **31**

DATE		ITEM	POST. REF.	DEBIT	CREDIT	BALANCE	
						DEBIT	CREDIT
19-- June	1	Balance	✔				29 4 8 3 00

ACCOUNT Judy K. Schmidt, Drawing   ACCOUNT NO. 32

DATE	ITEM	POST. REF.	DEBIT	CREDIT	BALANCE DEBIT	BALANCE CREDIT
19-- June 27		27	1 2 5 0 00		1 2 5 0 00	

ACCOUNT Professional Fees   ACCOUNT NO. 41

DATE	ITEM	POST. REF.	DEBIT	CREDIT	BALANCE DEBIT	BALANCE CREDIT
19-- June 30		27		1 7 2 0 00		
30		28		4 1 4 5 00		5 8 6 5 00

ACCOUNT Salary Expense   ACCOUNT NO. 51

DATE	ITEM	POST. REF.	DEBIT	CREDIT	BALANCE DEBIT	BALANCE CREDIT
19-- June 30		28	1 7 2 5 00		1 7 2 5 00	

ACCOUNT Rent Expense   ACCOUNT NO. 53

DATE	ITEM	POST. REF.	DEBIT	CREDIT	BALANCE DEBIT	BALANCE CREDIT
19-- June 1		27	6 0 0 00		6 0 0 00	

ACCOUNT Laboratory Expense   ACCOUNT NO. 55

DATE	ITEM	POST. REF.	DEBIT	CREDIT	BALANCE DEBIT	BALANCE CREDIT
19-- June 23		27	2 4 5 00		2 4 5 00	

ACCOUNT Utilities Expense   ACCOUNT NO. 56

DATE	ITEM	POST. REF.	DEBIT	CREDIT	BALANCE DEBIT	BALANCE CREDIT
19-- June 30		28	1 5 7 00			
30		28	2 9 00			
30		28	7 4 00		2 6 0 00	

ACCOUNT Miscellaneous Expense   ACCOUNT NO. 59

DATE	ITEM	POST. REF.	DEBIT	CREDIT	BALANCE DEBIT	BALANCE CREDIT
19-- June 30		28	1 3 2 00		1 3 2 00	

(4)

Judy K. Schmidt, M.D.															
Trial Balance															
June 30, 19--															
Cash	3	1	7	4	00										
Accounts Receivable	6	7	2	0	00										
Supplies		3	7	2	00										
Prepaid Insurance		7	3	5	00										
Equipment	21	7	2	0	00										
Accounts Payable							1	5	8	5	00				
Judy K. Schmidt, Capital							29	4	8	3	00				
Judy K. Schmidt, Drawing	1	2	5	0	00										
Professional Fees							5	8	6	5	00				
Salary Expense	1	7	2	5	00										
Rent Expense		6	0	0	00										
Laboratory Expense		2	4	5	00										
Utilities Expense		2	6	0	00										
Miscellaneous Expense		1	3	2	00										
	36	9	3	3	00		36	9	3	3	00				

DISCUSSION QUESTIONS

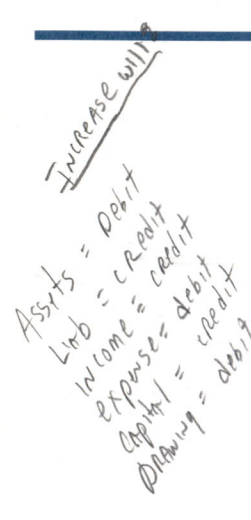

1. What is an account?

2. Differentiate between an account and a ledger.

3. Identify each of the following accounts as asset, liability, owner's equity, revenue, or expense, and state in each case whether the normal balance is a debit or a credit. If the account is an owner's equity account, also state whether it is capital or drawing. (a) Accounts Payable, (b) Supplies, (c) Rent Expense, (d) Ann Mann, Drawing, (e) Cash, (f) Accounts Receivable, (g) Sales, (h) Ann Mann, Capital, (i) Equipment, (j) Salary Expense.

4. Describe the nature of the assets that compose the following categories: (a) current assets, (b) plant assets.

5. Identify each of the following as (a) a current asset or (b) a plant asset: (1) equipment, (2) cash, (3) building, (4) accounts receivable, (5) supplies, (6) land.

6. As of the time a balance sheet is being prepared, a business enterprise owes a mortgage note payable of $200,000, the terms of which provide for monthly payments of $5,000. How should the liability be classified on the balance sheet?

7. Describe in general terms the sequence of accounts in the ledger.

8. What is the name of the record in which a transaction is initially recorded?

9. Do the terms *debit* and *credit* signify increase or decrease, or may they signify either? Explain.

10. Define posting.

11. Indicate whether each of the following is recorded by a debit or by a credit: (a) increase in an asset account, (b) decrease in a liability account, (c) increase in a revenue account.

12. What is the effect (increase or decrease) of debits to expense accounts (a) in terms of owner's equity and (b) in terms of expense?

13. What is the effect (increase or decrease) of credits to revenue accounts (a) in terms of owner's equity and (b) in terms of revenue?

14. John Collins Company adheres to a policy of depositing all cash receipts in a bank account and making all payments by check. The cash account as of March 31 has a credit balance of $925 and there is no undeposited cash on hand. (a) Assuming that there were no errors in journalizing or posting, what is the explanation of this unusual balance? (b) Is the $925 credit balance in the cash account an asset, a liability, owner's equity, a revenue, or an expense?

15. During the month, a business enterprise has a substantial number of transactions affecting each of the following accounts. State for each account whether it is likely to have (a) debit entries only, (b) credit entries only, or (c) both debit and credit entries.
    (1) Rent Expense   (5) Betty Moxley, Drawing
    (2) Sales   (6) Accounts Receivable
    (3) Miscellaneous Expense   (7) Notes Payable
    (4) Accounts Payable   (8) Cash

16. Rearrange the following in proper sequence: (a) entry posted to ledger, (b) business transaction occurs, (c) entry recorded in journal, (d) business document prepared.

17. Describe the three procedures required to post the credit portion of the following journal entry (Sales is account no. 41):

JOURNAL   PAGE 29

19--					
May	30	Accounts Receivable..........	12	1,200	
		Sales			1,200

18. Boswell Company performed services in May for a specific customer and the fee was $12,500. Payment was received in the following June. (a) Was the revenue earned in May or June? (b) What accounts should be debited and credited in (1) May and (2) June?

19. As of April 1, Jane Thomas, Capital had a credit balance of $15,000. During the year, the owner's withdrawals totaled $12,000 and the business incurred a net loss of $6,000. There were no additional investments in the business. Assuming that there have been no recording errors, will the balance sheet prepared at March 31 balance? Explain.

20. During the month, a business corporation received $925,000 in cash and paid out $790,000 in cash. Do the data indicate that the corporation earned $135,000 during the month? Explain.

21. (a) Describe the form known as a trial balance. (b) What proof is provided by a trial balance?

22. When a trial balance is prepared, an account balance of $36,750 is listed as $63,750, and an account balance of $54,000 is listed as $5,400. Identify the transposition and the slide.

23. When a purchase of supplies of $950 for cash was recorded, both the debit and the credit were journalized and posted as $590. (a) Would this error cause the trial balance to be out of balance? (b) Would the answer be the same if the $950 entry had been journalized correctly, but the credit to Cash had been posted as $590?

24. Indicate which of the following errors, each considered individually, would cause the trial balance totals to be unequal:

(a) A payment of $25,000 for equipment purchased was posted as a debit of $25,000 to Equipment and a credit of $52,000 to Cash.

(b) A withdrawal of $1,000 by the owner was journalized and posted as a debit of $100 to Salary Expense and a credit of $100 to Cash.

(c) A payment of $750 to a creditor was posted as a credit of $750 to Accounts Payable and a credit of $750 to Cash.

(d) A receipt of $950 from an account receivable was journalized and posted as a debit of $950 to Cash and a credit of $950 to Sales.

(e) A fee of $7,500 earned and due from a client was not debited to Accounts Receivable or credited to a revenue account, because the cash had not been received.

Real World Focus

25. The current asset and current liability data adapted from The Pillsbury Company balance sheet as of May 31, 1988, are as follows:

Current assets (in millions):

Cash and equivalents	$ 102.1
Receivables	575.3
Inventories	551.7
Prepaid expenses and other assets	83.5
	$1,312.6

Current liabilities (in millions):

Notes payable	$ 41.9
Long-term debt, current portion	40.1
Accounts and drafts payable	572.6
Advances on sales	145.0
Employee compensation	122.4
Other liabilities	383.1
	$1,305.1

(a) Based upon the preceding data, determine (1) the difference between the total current assets and the total current liabilities as of May 31, 1988, and (2) the ratio of the total current assets to the total current liabilities as of May 31, 1988.

(b) Based upon the solution in (a), is it likely that The Pillsbury Company will be able to pay its current liabilities as they become due?

EXERCISES

Exercise 2–1
Identify transactions for sole proprietorship.
OBJ. 1, 3

Eight transactions are recorded in the following T accounts:

Cash				Accounts Receivable			Supplies		
(1) 25,000	(2)	2,500		(5) 17,500	(7) 12,500		(3)	905	
(7) 12,500	(3)	950							
	(4)	1,225							
	(6)	5,000							
	(8)	2,500							

Equipment	John Adams, Capital	Service Revenue
(2) 10,000	(1) 25,000	(5) 17,500

Accounts Payable		John Adams, Drawing	Operating Expenses
(6) 5,000	(2) 7,500	(8) 2,500	(4) 1,225

Indicate for each debit and each credit: (a) whether an asset, liability, capital, drawing, revenue, or expense account was affected and (b) whether the account was increased (+) or decreased (−). Answers should be presented in the following form (transaction (1) is given as an example):

	Account Debited		Account Credited	
Transaction	Type	Effect	Type	Effect
(1)	asset	+	capital	+

Exercise 2–2
Chart of accounts for sole proprietorship.
OBJ. 2

Wilson Co. is a newly organized enterprise. The list of accounts to be opened in the general ledger is as follows:

Accounts Payable	Miscellaneous Expense
Accounts Receivable	Prepaid Rent
Accumulated Depreciation	Rent Expense
Ann Wilson, Capital	Salaries Payable
Ann Wilson, Drawing	Salary Expense
Cash	Sales
Depreciation Expense	Supplies
Equipment	Supplies Expense

List the accounts in the order in which they should appear in the ledger of Wilson Co. and assign account numbers. Each account number is to have two digits: the first digit is to indicate the major classification ("1" for assets, etc.), and the second digit is to identify the specific account within each major classification ("11" for Cash, etc.).

Exercise 2–3
Chart of accounts for sole proprietorship.
OBJ. 2

JR Co. is a newly organized enterprise with the following list of asset, liability, and owner's equity accounts, arranged in alphabetical order:

Accounts Payable	Notes Payable (long-term)
Accounts Receivable	Notes Receivable (short-term)
Accumulated Depreciation — Building	Office Equipment
Accumulated Depreciation — Office Equipment	Office Supplies
Accumulated Depreciation — Store Equipment	Prepaid Insurance
Building	Salaries Payable
Cash	Sales Commissions Payable
Interest Receivable	Store Equipment
J. R. Gorgio, Capital	Store Supplies
J. R. Gorgio, Drawing	Taxes Payable
Land	

Construct a chart of accounts, assigning account numbers and arranging the accounts in balance sheet order, as illustrated on page 51. Each account number is to be composed of three digits: the first digit is to indicate the major classification ("1" for assets, etc.), the second digit is to indicate the subclassification ("11" for current assets, etc.), and the third digit is to identify the specific account ("111" for Cash, etc.).

Exercise 2–4
Chart of accounts
for corporation.
OBJ. 2

C. D. Highland Co. is a newly organized enterprise. The list of accounts to be opened in the general ledger is as follows:

Retained Earnings	Accounts Receivable
Miscellaneous Expense	Equipment
Sales	Salary Expense
Accumulated Depreciation	Cash
Capital Stock	Accounts Payable
Supplies	Supplies Expense
Prepaid Rent	Salaries Payable
Rent Expense	Depreciation Expense

List the accounts in the order in which they should appear in the ledger of C. D. Highland Co. and assign account numbers. Each account number is to have two digits: the first digit is to indicate the major classification ("1" for assets, etc.), and the second digit is to identify the specific account within each major classification ("11" for Cash, etc.).

Exercise 2–5
Transactions for sole
proprietorship.
OBJ. 4

Dunston Company has the following accounts in its ledger: Cash; Accounts Receivable; Supplies; Office Equipment; Accounts Payable; Jane Dunston, Capital; Jane Dunston, Drawing; Fees Earned; Rent Expense; Advertising Expense; Utilities Expense; Miscellaneous Expense.

Record the following selected transactions, completed during July of the current year, in a two-column journal:

July　1. Paid rent for the month, $1,000.
　　　2. Paid advertising expense, $350.
　　　5. Paid cash for supplies, $125.
　　　7. Purchased office equipment on account, $3,750.
　　10. Received cash from customers on account, $5,600.
　　12. Paid creditor on account, $2,150.
　　14. Withdrew cash for personal use, $1,200.
　　15. Paid cash for repairs to office equipment, $75.
　　27. Paid telephone bill for the month, $195.
　　29. Fees earned and billed to customers for the month, $9,150.
　　31. Paid electricity bill for the month, $430.

Exercise 2–6
Transactions for
corporation.
OBJ. 4

Snyder Inc. has the following accounts in its ledger: Cash; Accounts Receivable; Supplies; Office Equipment; Accounts Payable; Capital Stock; Retained Earnings; Dividends; Fees Earned; Salary Expense; Rent Expense; Advertising Expense; Utilities Expense; Miscellaneous Expense.

Record the following selected transactions, completed during February of the current year, in a two-column journal:

Feb.　1. Paid advertising expense, $1,500.
　　　2. Paid rent for the month, $2,750.
　　　5. Paid cash for supplies, $275.
　　　7. Purchased office equipment on account, $10,500.
　　10. Received cash from customers on account, $9,700.
　　11. Paid cash for repairs to office equipment, $175.
　　12. Paid creditor on account, $7,150.
　　14. Paid cash dividend, $2,000.
　　24. Paid telephone bill for the month, $475.
　　27. Fees billed to customers for the month, $17,200.
　　28. Paid electricity bill for the month, $950.
　　28. Paid salaries, $4,900.

Exercise 2–7
Trial balance for
sole proprietorship.

OBJ. 5

The accounts in the ledger of Dobbs Realty as of June 30 of the current year are listed in alphabetical order as follows. All accounts have normal balances. The balance of the cash account has been intentionally omitted.

Accounts Payable	$ 21,910
Accounts Receivable	28,500
Cash	?
H. Dobbs, Capital	150,000
H. Dobbs, Drawing	28,000
Fees Earned	350,000
Insurance Expense	5,000
Land	125,000
Miscellaneous Expense	9,900
Notes Payable	25,000
Prepaid Insurance	3,150
Rent Expense	48,000
Salary Expense	215,000
Supplies	3,900
Supplies Expense	6,100
Utilities Expense	41,500

Prepare a trial balance, listing the accounts in their proper order and inserting the missing figure for cash.

Exercise 2–8
Errors in trial
balance.

OBJ. 5

The following preliminary trial balance of King Carpet Services does not balance:

King Carpet Services
Trial Balance
December 31, 19--

Cash	67,500	
Accounts Receivable	17,000	
Prepaid Insurance		3,300
Equipment	4,500	
Accounts Payable		9,850
Salaries Payable		590
Jane Dillow, Capital	61,250	
Jane Dillow, Drawing		24,000
Service Revenue		64,940
Salary Expense		33,400
Advertising Expense	5,200	
Miscellaneous Expense		1,490
	155,450	137,570

When the ledger and other records are reviewed, you discover the following: (1) the debits and credits in the cash account total $67,500 and $62,300, respectively; (2) a sale of $500 to a customer on account was not posted to the accounts receivable account; (3) a payment of $1,900 made to a creditor on account was not posted to the accounts payable account; (4) the balance of the salaries payable account is $950; (5) the correct balance of the equipment account is $45,000; and (6) each account has a normal balance. Prepare a corrected trial balance.

Exercise 2–9
Effect of errors on
trial balance.

OBJ. 5

The following errors occurred in posting from a two-column journal:

(1) A debit of $7,500 to Equipment was posted twice.
(2) A credit of $200 to Cash was posted as $2,000.
(3) A debit of $1,000 to Cash was posted to Salary Expense.
(4) A credit of $400 to Accounts Payable was posted as a debit.
(5) An entry debiting Cash and crediting Fees Earned for $2,250 was not posted.

(6) A debit of $810 to Supplies was posted as $180.

(7) A credit of $725 to Accounts Receivable was not posted.

Considering each case individually (i.e., assuming that no other errors had occurred), indicate: (a) by "yes" or "no" whether the trial balance would be out of balance; (b) if answer to (a) is "yes", the amount by which the trial balance totals would differ; and (c) the column of the trial balance that would have the larger total. Answers should be presented in the following form (error (1) is given as an example):

Error	(a) Out of Balance	(b) Difference	(c) Larger Total
(1)	yes	$7,500	debit

PROBLEMS

Problem 2–1A

Entries into T accounts for sole proprietorship.

OBJ. 3, 5

Frank Moyer, architect, opened an office on May 1 of the current year. During the month he completed the following transactions connected with his professional practice:

(a) Transferred cash from a personal bank account to an account to be used for his business, $7,500.

(b) Purchased used automobile for $6,800, paying $1,400 cash and giving a non-interest-bearing note for the remainder.

(c) Paid May rent for office and workroom, $800.

(d) Paid cash for supplies, $225.

(e) Purchased office and drafting room equipment on account, $4,200.

(f) Paid cash for insurance policies on automobile and equipment, $392.

(g) Received cash from a client for plans delivered, $1,725.

(h) Paid cash to creditors on account, $2,100.

(i) Paid cash for miscellaneous expenses, $40.

(j) Received invoice for blueprint service, due in following month, $75.

(k) Recorded fee earned on plans delivered, payment to be made in following month, $2,500.

(l) Paid salary of assistant, $1,000.

(m) Paid cash for miscellaneous expenses, $68.

(n) Paid installment due on note payable, $150.

(o) Paid gas, oil, and repairs on automobile for May, $70.

Instructions:

(1) Record the foregoing transactions in the following T accounts: Cash; Accounts Receivable; Supplies; Prepaid Insurance; Automobiles; Equipment; Notes Payable; Accounts Payable; Frank Moyer, Capital; Professional Fees; Salary Expense; Rent Expense; Automobile Expense; Blueprint Expense; Miscellaneous Expense. To the left of each amount entered in the accounts, place the appropriate letter to identify the transactions.

(2) Determine the balances of the accounts in the ledger, pencil footing all accounts having two or more debits or credits. A memorandum balance should also be inserted in accounts having both debits and credits, in the manner illustrated on

page 52. For accounts with entries on one side only (such as Professional Fees), there is no need to insert the memorandum balance in the item column. Accounts containing only a single debit and a single credit (such as Notes Payable) need no pencil footings; the memorandum balance should be inserted in the appropriate item column. Accounts containing a single entry only (such as Prepaid Insurance) need neither a pencil footing nor a memorandum balance.

(3) Prepare a trial balance for Frank Moyer, Architect, as of May 31 of the current year.

Problem 2–2A

Journal entries and trial balance for sole proprietorship.

OBJ. 3, 4, 5

Pam Conrad established a sole proprietorship, to be known as Conrad Decorators, on March 10 of the current year. During the remainder of the month, Conrad completed the following business transactions:

Mar. 10. Conrad transferred cash from a personal bank account to an account to be used for the business, $10,000.
- 10. Paid rent for period of March 10 to end of month, $800.
- 11. Purchased a truck for $10,000, paying $2,000 cash and giving a note payable for the remainder.
- 12. Purchased equipment on account, $1,700.
- 14. Paid premiums on property and casualty insurance, $510.
- 14. Purchased supplies for cash, $925.
- 15. Received cash for job completed, $850.
- 16. Purchased supplies on account, $240.
- 17. Paid wages of employees, $650.
- 21. Paid creditor for equipment purchased on March 12, $1,700.
- 24. Recorded sales on account and sent invoices to customers, $1,900.
- 26. Received an invoice for truck expenses, to be paid in April, $225.
- 28. Received cash for job completed, $1,050. This sale had not been recorded previously.
- 29. Paid utilities expense, $205.
- 29. Paid miscellaneous expenses, $80.
- 29. Received cash from customers on account, $1,420.
- 31. Paid wages of employees, $1,350.
- 31. Withdrew cash for personal use, $1,500.

Instructions:

(1) Open a ledger of two-column accounts for Conrad Decorators, using the following titles and account numbers: Cash, 11; Accounts Receivable, 12; Supplies, 13; Prepaid Insurance, 14; Equipment, 16; Truck, 18; Notes Payable, 21; Accounts Payable, 22; Pam Conrad, Capital, 31; Pam Conrad, Drawing, 32; Sales, 41; Wages Expense, 51; Rent Expense, 53; Utilities Expense, 54; Truck Expense, 55; Miscellaneous Expense, 59.

(2) Record each transaction in a two-column journal, referring to the above list of accounts or to the ledger in selecting appropriate account titles to be debited and credited. (Do not insert the account numbers in the journal at this time.)

(3) Post the journal to the ledger, inserting appropriate posting references as each item is posted.

(4) Determine the balances of the accounts in the ledger, pencil footing all accounts having two or more debits or credits. A memorandum balance should also be inserted in accounts having both debits and credits, in the manner illustrated on page 52. For accounts with entries on one side only (such as Sales), there is no need to insert the memorandum balance in the item column. Accounts containing only a single debit and a single credit (such as Accounts Receivable) need no pencil footings; the memorandum balance should be inserted in the appropriate item column. Accounts containing a single entry only (such as Prepaid Insurance) need neither a pencil footing nor a memorandum balance.

(5) Prepare a trial balance for Conrad Decorators as of March 31.

Problem 2–3A
Journal entries and
trial balance for
sole proprietorship.

OBJ. 3, 4, 5

SOLUTIONS
SOFTWARE

Ann Kane, M.D., completed the following transactions in the practice of her profession during May of the current year:

May   1. Paid office rent for May, $1,900.
        2. Purchased equipment on account, $9,000.
        5. Purchased X-ray film and other supplies on account, $850.
        6. Received cash on account from patients, $9,125.
        7. Paid cash to creditors on account, $6,120.
     10. Sold X-ray film to another doctor at cost as an accommodation, receiving cash, $75.
     10. Paid cash for renewal of property insurance policy, $545.
     15. Paid cash for laboratory analyses, $345.
     20. Discovered that the balance of the cash account was understated and the accounts receivable account was overstated as of May 1 by $100. A cash receipt of that amount on account from a patient in April had not been recorded. Journalized the $100 receipt as of May 20.
     24. One of the items of equipment purchased on May 2 was defective. It was returned with the permission of the supplier, who agreed to reduce the account for the amount charged for the item, $250.
     26. Paid cash from business bank account for personal and family expenses, $2,200.
     28. Paid miscellaneous expenses, $420.
     30. Paid gas and electricity expense, $510.
     30. Paid water expense, $130.
     30. Paid telephone expense, $225.
     31. Recorded fees charged to patients on account for services performed in May, $8,200.
     31. Recorded the cash received in payment of services (on a cash basis) to patients during May, $9,910.
     31. Paid salaries of receptionist and nurses, $4,750.

Kane's account titles, numbers, and balances as of May 1 (all normal balances) are listed as follows: Cash, 11, $6,125; Accounts Receivable, 12, $14,960; Supplies, 13, $1,240; Prepaid Insurance, 14, $3,500; Equipment, 18, $55,600; Accounts Payable, 22, $9,850; Ann Kane, Capital, 31, $71,575; Ann Kane, Drawing, 32; Professional Fees, 41; Salary Expense, 51; Rent Expense, 53; Utilities Expense, 55; Laboratory Expense, 56; Miscellaneous Expense, 59.

Instructions:

(1) Open a ledger of four-column accounts for Dr. Kane as of May 1 of the current year. Enter the balances in the appropriate balance columns and place a check mark (√) in the posting reference column. (It is advisable to verify the equality of the debit and credit balances in the ledger before proceeding with the next instruction.)
(2) Record each transaction in a two-column journal.
(3) Post the journal to the ledger, extending the month-end balances to the appropriate balance columns after all posting is completed.
(4) Prepare a trial balance as of May 31.
(5) Assuming that the expenses which have not been recorded (such as supplies expense and insurance expense) amount to a total of $1,950 for the month, determine the following amounts:
   (a) Net income for the month of May.
   (b) Increase or decrease in owner's equity during May.
   (c) Owner's equity as of May 31.

Problem 2–4A

Journal entries and trial balance for corporation.

OBJ. 3, 4, 5

The following business transactions were completed by Kim Theatre Corporation during May of the current year:

May 1. Received and deposited in a bank account $50,000 cash for capital stock.
2. Purchased the Coastland Drive-In Theatre for $150,000, divided as follows: land, $60,000; buildings, $60,000; equipment, $30,000. Paid $45,000 in cash and gave a note payable for the remainder.
4. Entered into a contract for the operation of the refreshment stand concession at a rental of 20% of the concessionaire's sales, with a guaranteed minimum of $750 a month, payable in advance. Received cash of $750 as the advance payment for the month of May.
6. Purchased supplies, $450, and equipment, $4,800, on account.
7. Paid premiums for property and casualty insurance policies, $2,250.
8. Paid for May billboard and newspaper advertising, $750.
10. Cash received from admissions for the week, $3,100.
12. Paid miscellaneous expense, $265.
17. Paid semimonthly wages, $1,450.
17. Cash received from admissions for the week, $2,980.
19. Paid miscellaneous expenses, $310.
20. Returned a portion of the supplies purchased on May 6 to the supplier, receiving full credit for the cost, $75.
23. Paid cash to creditors on account, $2,250.
24. Cash received from admissions for the week, $3,420.
26. Purchased supplies for cash, $210.
26. Paid for advertising leaflets for special promotion during last week in May, $375.
28. Recorded invoice of $5,400 for rental of film for May. Payment is due on June 7.
29. Paid electricity and water bills, $890.
31. Paid semimonthly wages, $1,610.
31. Cash received from admissions for remainder of the month, $3,600.
31. Recorded additional amount owed by the concessionaire for the month of May; sales for the month totaled $4,500. Rental charges in excess of the advance payment of $750 are not due and payable until June 10.

Instructions:

(1) Open a ledger of four-column accounts for Kim Theatre Corporation, using the following account titles and numbers: Cash, 11; Accounts Receivable, 12; Prepaid Insurance, 13; Supplies, 14; Land, 17; Buildings, 18; Equipment, 19; Accounts Payable, 21; Note Payable, 24; Capital Stock, 31; Admissions Income, 41; Concession Income, 42; Wages Expense, 51; Film Rental Expense, 52; Advertising Expense, 53; Electricity and Water Expense, 54; Miscellaneous Expense, 59.
(2) Record the transactions in a two-column journal.
(3) Post the journal to the ledger, extending the month-end balances to the appropriate balance columns after all posting is completed.
(4) Prepare a trial balance as of May 31.
(5) Determine the following:
  (a) Amount of total revenue recorded in the ledger.
  (b) Amount of total expenses recorded in the ledger.
  (c) Amount of net income for May, assuming that additional unrecorded expenses (including supplies used, insurance expired, etc.) totaled $950.
  (d) The understatement or overstatement of net income for May that would have resulted from failure to record the invoice for film rental until it was paid in June. (See transaction of May 28.)
  (e) The understatement or overstatement of liabilities as of May 31 that would have resulted from failure to record the invoice for film rental in May. (See transaction of May 28.)

Problem 2–5A
Journal entries and trial balance for corporation.

OBJ. 3, 4, 5

Park Realty Inc. acts as an agent in buying, selling, renting, and managing real estate. The account balances at the end of April of the current year are as follows:

11 Cash	44,500	
12 Accounts Receivable	31,600	
13 Prepaid Insurance	750	
14 Office Supplies	625	
16 Land	—0—	
21 Accounts Payable		5,250
22 Notes Payable		—0—
31 Capital Stock		50,000
32 Retained Earnings		22,025
33 Dividends	20,000	
41 Fees Earned		157,750
51 Salary and Commission Expense	122,100	
52 Rent Expense	6,000	
53 Advertising Expense	4,900	
54 Automobile Expense	3,950	
59 Miscellaneous Expense	600	
	235,025	235,025

The following business transactions were completed by Park Realty Inc. during May of the current year:

May 1. Paid rent on office for month, $1,500.
2. Purchased office supplies on account, $425.
3. Paid insurance premiums, $1,925.
9. Received cash from clients on account, $21,000.
15. Paid salaries and commissions, $19,650.
15. Purchased land for a future building site for $50,000, paying $10,000 in cash and giving a note payable for the remainder.
15. Recorded revenue earned and billed to clients during first half of month, $20,900.
18. Paid creditors on account, $4,150.
20. Returned a portion of the office supplies purchased on May 2, receiving full credit for their cost, $50.
29. Received cash from clients on account, $16,700.
29. Paid advertising expense, $2,150.
29. Discovered an error in computing a commission; received cash from the salesperson for the overpayment, $500.
30. Paid automobile expense (including rental charges for an automobile), $850.
30. Paid miscellaneous expenses, $215.
31. Recorded revenue earned and billed to clients during second half of month, $19,300.
31. Paid salaries and commissions, $19,850.
31. Paid dividends, $10,000.

Instructions:

(1) Open a ledger of four-column accounts for the accounts listed. Record the balances in the appropriate balance columns as of May 1, write "Balance" in the item section, and place a check mark (√) in the posting reference column.
(2) Record the transactions for May in a two-column journal.
(3) Post to the ledger, extending the month-end balances to the appropriate balance columns after all posting is completed.
(4) Prepare a trial balance of the ledger as of May 31.

If the working papers correlating with the textbook are not used, omit Problem 2–6A.

Problem 2–6A

Errors in trial balance for sole proprietorship.

OBJ. 5

The following records of Evans TV Repair are presented in the working papers:
    Journal containing entries for the period July 1–31.
    Ledger to which the July entries have been posted.
    Preliminary trial balance as of July 31, which does not balance.

    Locate the errors, supply the information requested, and prepare a corrected trial balance, proceeding in accordance with the following detailed instructions. The balances recorded in the accounts as of July 1 and the entries in the journal are correctly stated. If it is necessary to correct any posted amounts in the ledger, a line should be drawn through the erroneous figure and the correct amount inserted above. Corrections or notations may be inserted on the preliminary trial balance in any manner desired. It is not necessary to complete all of the instructions if equal trial balance totals can be obtained earlier. However, the requirements of instructions (6) and (7) should be completed in any event.

Instructions:

(1) Verify the totals of the preliminary trial balance, inserting the correct amounts in the schedule provided in the working papers.
(2) Compute the difference between the trial balance totals.
(3) Compare the listings in the trial balance with the balances appearing in the ledger and list the errors found in the space provided in the working papers.
(4) Verify the accuracy of the balance of each account in the ledger and list the errors found in the space provided in the working papers.
(5) Trace the postings in the ledger back to the journal, using small check marks to identify items traced. Correct any amounts in the ledger that may be necessitated by errors in posting and list the errors in the space provided in the working papers.
(6) Journalize as of July 31 the payment of $210 for advertising expense. The bill had been paid on July 31 but was inadvertently omitted from the journal. Post to the ledger. (Revise any amounts necessitated by posting this entry.)
(7) Prepare a new trial balance.

Problem 2–7A

Corrected trial balance for sole proprietorship.

OBJ. 5

Lakeview Carpet Installation, a sole proprietorship, has the following trial balance as of September 30 of the current year:

Cash	8,820	
Accounts Receivable	17,825	
Supplies	1,800	
Prepaid Insurance	400	
Equipment	22,500	
Notes Payable		25,000
Accounts Payable		5,000
Joan Key, Capital		36,720
Joan Key, Drawing	8,000	
Sales		59,750
Wages Expense	31,500	
Rent Expense	1,800	
Advertising Expense	5,700	
Gas, Electricity, and Water Expense	5,650	
	103,995	126,470

The debit and credit totals are not equal as a result of the following errors:
(a) The balance of cash was understated by $700.
(b) A cash receipt of $470 was posted as a debit to Cash of $740.
(c) A credit of $325 to Accounts Receivable was not posted.
(d) A return of $245 of defective supplies was erroneously posted as a $425 credit to Supplies.

(e) An insurance policy acquired at a cost of $400 was posted as a credit to Pre-paid Insurance.
(f) The balance of Notes Payable was overstated by $5,000.
(g) A credit of $910 in Accounts Payable was overlooked when determining the balance of the account.
(h) A debit of $1,000 for a withdrawal by the owner was posted as a debit to Wages Expense.
(i) The balance of $18,000 in Rent Expense was entered as $1,800 in the trial balance.
(j) Miscellaneous Expense, with a balance of $1,100, was omitted from the trial balance.

Instructions:

Prepare a corrected trial balance as of September 30 of the current year.

Series B

Problem 2–1B
Entries into T accounts for sole proprietorship.
OBJ. 3, 5

Fran Adams, architect, opened an office on July 1 of the current year. During the month she completed the following transactions connected with her professional practice:

(a) Transferred cash from personal bank account to an account to be used for the business, $10,000.
(b) Paid July rent for office and workroom, $1,250.
(c) Purchased used automobile for $7,500, paying $2,250 cash and giving a non-interest-bearing note for the remainder.
(d) Purchased office and drafting room equipment on account, $6,000.
(e) Paid cash for supplies, $900.
(f) Paid cash for insurance policies, $850.
(g) Received cash from client for plans delivered, $1,600.
(h) Paid cash for miscellaneous services, $75.
(i) Paid cash to creditors on account, $3,000.
(j) Paid installment due on note payable, $500.
(k) Received invoice for blueprint service, due in August, $110.
(l) Recorded fee earned on plans delivered, payment to be made in August, $3,750.
(m) Paid salary of assistant, $1,250.
(n) Paid gas, oil, and repairs on automobile for July, $95.

Instructions:

(1) Record the foregoing transactions in the following T accounts: Cash; Accounts Receivable; Supplies; Prepaid Insurance; Automobiles; Equipment; Notes Payable; Accounts Payable; Fran Adams, Capital; Professional Fees; Salary Expense; Rent Expense; Automobile Expense; Blueprint Expense; Miscellaneous Expense. To the left of the amount entered in the accounts, place the appropriate letter to identify the transaction.
(2) Determine the balances of the accounts in the ledger, pencil footing all accounts having two or more debits or credits. A memorandum balance should also be inserted in accounts having both debits and credits, in the manner illustrated on

page 52. For accounts with entries on one side only (such as Professional Fees), there is no need to insert the memorandum balance in the item column. Accounts containing only a single debit and a single credit (such as Notes Payable) need no pencil footings; the memorandum balance should be inserted in the appropriate item column. Accounts containing a single entry only (such as Prepaid Insurance) need neither a pencil footing nor a memorandum balance.

(3) Prepare a trial balance for Fran Adams, Architect, as of July 31 of the current year.

Problem 2–2B
Journal entries and trial balance for sole proprietorship.

OBJ. 3, 4, 5

SOLUTIONS SOFTWARE

Laura Mead established a sole proprietorship, to be known as Mead Decorators, on June 10 of the current year. During the remainder of the month, Mead completed the following business transactions:

June 10. Mead transferred cash from a personal bank account to an account to be used for the business, $15,000.
10. Paid rent for period of June 10 to end of month, $800.
12. Purchased office equipment on account, $5,500.
14. Purchased a used truck for $15,000, paying $7,500 cash and giving a note payable for the remainder.
15. Purchased supplies for cash, $525.
16. Received cash for job completed, $500.
16. Paid wages of employees, $600.
20. Paid premiums on property and casualty insurance, $725.
22. Recorded sales on account and sent invoices to customers, $1,950.
24. Received an invoice for truck expenses, to be paid in July, $310.
26. Received cash for job completed, $650. This sale had not been recorded previously.
28. Purchased supplies on account, $190.
29. Paid utilities expense, $390.
29. Paid miscellaneous expenses, $95.
30. Received cash from customers on account, $1,300.
30. Paid wages of employees, $1,250.
30. Paid creditor a portion of the amount owed for equipment purchased on June 12, $2,500.
30. Withdrew cash for personal use, $2,000.

Instructions:

(1) Open a ledger of two-column accounts for Mead Decorators, using the following titles and account numbers: Cash, 11; Accounts Receivable, 12; Supplies, 13; Prepaid Insurance, 14; Equipment, 16; Truck, 18; Notes Payable, 21; Accounts Payable, 22; Laura Mead, Capital, 31; Laura Mead, Drawing, 32; Sales, 41; Wages Expense, 51; Rent Expense, 53; Utilities Expense, 54; Truck Expense, 55; Miscellaneous Expense, 59.

(2) Record each transaction in a two-column journal, referring to the above list of accounts or to the ledger in selecting appropriate account titles to be debited and credited. (Do not insert the account numbers in the journal at this time.)

(3) Post the journal to the ledger, inserting appropriate posting references as each item is posted.

(4) Determine the balances of the accounts in the ledger, pencil footing all accounts having two or more debits or credits. A memorandum balance should also be inserted in accounts having both debits and credits, in the manner illustrated on page 52. For accounts with entries on one side only (such as Sales), there is no need to insert the memorandum balance in the item column. Accounts containing only a single debit and a single credit (such as Accounts Receivable) need no pencil footings; the memorandum balance should be inserted in the appropriate item column. Accounts containing a single entry only (such as Prepaid Insurance) need neither a pencil footing nor a memorandum balance.

(5) Prepare a trial balance for Mead Decorators as of June 30.

Problem 2–4B
Journal entries and
trial balance for
corporation.

OBJ. 3, 4, 5

The following business transactions were completed by Midway Theatre Corporation during June of the current year:

June 1. Deposited in a bank account $75,000 cash received for capital stock.
     3. Purchased the Lakeview Drive-In Theatre for $250,000, divided as follows: land, $125,000; buildings, $75,000; equipment, $50,000. Paid $60,000 in cash and gave a note payable for the remainder.
     4. Entered into a contract for the operation of the refreshment stand concession at a rental of 25% of the concessionaire's sales, with a guaranteed minimum of $1,000 a month, payable in advance. Received cash of $1,000 as the advance payment for the month of June.
     5. Paid for advertising leaflets for June, $250.
     6. Paid premiums for property and casualty insurance policies, $3,500.
     8. Purchased supplies, $750, and equipment, $4,150, on account.
     8. Paid for June billboard and newspaper advertising, $1,500.
    10. Paid miscellaneous expense, $250.
    12. Cash received from admissions for the week, $5,600.
    15. Paid semimonthly wages, $2,950.
    19. Cash received from admissions for the week, $5,900.
    19. Paid miscellaneous expenses, $210.
    19. Returned a portion of the supplies purchased on June 8 to the supplier, receiving full credit for the cost, $90.
    21. Paid cash to creditors on account, $2,950.
    26. Cash received from admissions for the week, $4,910.
    26. Purchased supplies for cash, $300.
    29. Recorded invoice of $5,800 for rental of film for June. Payment is due on July 9.
    30. Paid electricity and water bills, $625.
    30. Paid semimonthly wages, $3,450.
    30. Cash received from admissions for remainder of the month, $3,100.
    30. Recorded additional amount owed by the concessionaire for the month of June; sales for the month totaled $6,000. Rental charges in excess of the advance payment of $1,000 are not due and payable until July 10.

Instructions:

(1) Open a ledger of four-column accounts for Midway Theatre Corporation, using the following account titles and numbers: Cash, 11; Accounts Receivable, 12; Prepaid Insurance, 13; Supplies, 14; Land, 17; Buildings, 18; Equipment, 19; Accounts Payable, 21; Note Payable, 24; Capital Stock, 31; Admissions Income, 41; Concession Income, 42; Wages Expense, 51; Film Rental Expense, 52; Advertising Expense, 53; Electricity and Water Expense, 54; Miscellaneous Expense, 59.
(2) Record the transactions in a two-column journal.
(3) Post the journal to the ledger, extending the month-end balances to the appropriate balance columns after all posting is completed.
(4) Prepare a trial balance as of June 30.
(5) Determine the following:
   (a) Amount of total revenue recorded in the ledger.
   (b) Amount of total expenses recorded in the ledger.
   (c) Amount of net income for June, assuming that additional unrecorded expenses (including supplies used, insurance expired, etc.) totaled $2,750.
   (d) The understatement or overstatement of net income for June that would have resulted from failure to record the additional amount owed by the concessionaire for the month of June until it was paid in July. (See transaction of June 30.)
   (e) The understatement or overstatement of assets as of June 30 that would have resulted from failure to record the additional amount owed by the concessionaire in June. (See transaction of June 30.)

If the working papers correlating with the textbook are not used, omit Problem 2–6B.

Problem 2–6B

Errors in trial balance for sole proprietorship.

OBJ. 5

The following records of Evans TV Repair are presented in the working papers:

Journal containing entries for the period July 1–31.

Ledger to which the July entries have been posted.

Preliminary trial balance as of July 31, which does not balance.

Locate the errors, supply the information requested, and prepare a corrected trial balance, proceeding in accordance with the following detailed instructions. The balances recorded in the accounts as of July 1 and the entries in the journal are correctly stated. If it is necessary to correct any posted amounts in the ledger, a line should be drawn through the erroneous figure and the correct amount inserted above. Corrections or notations may be inserted on the preliminary trial balance in any manner desired. It is not necessary to complete all of the instructions if equal trial balance totals can be obtained earlier. However, the requirements of instructions (6) and (7) should be completed in any event.

Instructions:

(1) Verify the totals of the preliminary trial balance, inserting the correct amounts in the schedule provided in the working papers.
(2) Compute the difference between the trial balance totals.
(3) Compare the listings in the trial balance with the balances appearing in the ledger and list the errors found in the space provided in the working papers.
(4) Verify the accuracy of the balance of each account in the ledger and list the errors found in the space provided in the working papers.
(5) Trace the postings in the ledger back to the journal, using small check marks to identify items traced. Correct any amounts in the ledger that may be necessitated by errors in posting, and list the errors in the space provided in the working papers.
(6) Journalize as of July 31 the payment of $250 for gas and electricity. The bill had been paid on July 31 but was inadvertently omitted from the journal. Post to the ledger. (Revise any amounts necessitated by posting this entry.)
(7) Prepare a new trial balance.

Problem 2–7B

Corrected trial balance for sole proprietorship.

OBJ. 5

Gursoy Photography, a sole proprietorship, prepared the following trial balance as of July 31 of the current year:

Cash	5,935	
Accounts Receivable	9,800	
Supplies	1,450	
Prepaid Insurance	220	
Equipment	11,750	
Notes Payable		10,000
Accounts Payable		4,750
Alice Gursoy, Capital		12,390
Alice Gursoy, Drawing	9,000	
Sales		86,950
Wages Expense	52,400	
Rent Expense	750	
Advertising Expense	5,250	
Gas, Electricity, and Water Expense	4,950	
	101,505	114,090

The debit and credit totals are not equal as a result of the following errors:

(a) The balance of cash was overstated by $1,000.
(b) A cash payment of $750 was posted as a credit to Cash of $570.
(c) A debit of $175 to Accounts Receivable was not posted.
(d) A return of $725 of defective supplies was erroneously posted as a $275 credit to Supplies.

(e) An insurance policy acquired at a cost of $400 was posted as a credit to Prepaid Insurance.

(f) The balance of Notes Payable was overstated by $2,500.

(g) A debit of $150 in Accounts Payable was overlooked when the balance of the account was determined.

(h) A debit of $1,500 for a withdrawal by the owner was posted as a <u>credit</u> to Alice Gursoy, Capital.

(i) The balance of $7,500 in Rent Expense was entered as $750 in the trial balance.

(j) Miscellaneous Expense, with a balance of $840, was omitted from the trial balance.

Instructions:

Prepare a corrected trial balance as of July 31 of the current year.

MINI-CASE 2

During June through August, Ron Wood is planning to manage and operate Wood Caddy Services at the Vineyards Country Club. Ron will rent a small maintenance building from the country club for $100 per month and will offer caddy services, including cart rentals, to golfers. Ron has had no formal training in record keeping. During June, he kept notes of all receipts and expenses in a shoe box.

An examination of Ron's shoe box records for June revealed the following:

June 1. Withdrew $1,000 from personal bank account to be used to operate the caddy service.
1. Paid rent to Vineyards Country Club, $100.
1. Paid for golf supplies (practice balls, etc.), $300.
1. Paid miscellaneous expenses, $50.
1. Arranged for the rental of forty regular (pulling) golf carts and ten gasoline-driven carts for $1,000 per month. Paid $500 in advance, with the remaining $500 due June 30.
2. Purchased supplies, including gasoline, for the golf carts on account, $375. Vineyards Country Club has agreed to allow Ron to store the gasoline in one of their fuel tanks at no cost.
15. Cash receipts for June 1–15, $1,110.
15. For June 1–15, accepted IOUs from customers on account, $250.
15. Paid salary of part-time employees, $190.
17. Paid cash to creditors on account, $175.
22. Purchased supplies, including gasoline, on account, $250.
25. Received cash in payment of IOUs on account, $150.
28. Paid miscellaneous expenses, $60.
30. Cash receipts for June 16–30, $1,650.
30. For June 16–30, accepted IOUs from customers on account, $150.
30. Paid electricity (utilities) expense, $75.
30. Paid telephone (utilities) expense, $30.
30. Paid salary of part-time employees, $210.
30. Supplies on hand at the end of June, $350.
30. Paid remaining rental on golf carts, $500.

Ron has asked you several questions concerning his financial affairs to date, and he has asked you to assist him with his record keeping and reporting of financial data.

Instructions:

(1) To assist Ron with his record keeping, prepare a chart of accounts that would be appropriate for Wood Caddy Services.
(2) Prepare an income statement for June to help Ron assess the profitability of Wood Caddy Services. For this purpose, the use of T accounts may be useful in analyzing the effects of each of the June transactions.
(3) At various times throughout June, Ron took cash from the cash receipts of the caddy service for personal use. If $750 of cash were on hand on June 30, how much did Ron withdraw from the enterprise for personal use?

ETHICS DISCUSSION CASE

At the end of the current month, Fran Briscoe prepared a trial balance for Witt Services. The debit side of the trial balance exceeds the credit side by a significant amount. Fran has decided to subtract the difference from the balance of the miscellaneous expense account in order to complete the preparation of the current month's financial statements by a 5 o'clock deadline. Fran will look for the difference next week when there is more time.

Discuss whether Fran Briscoe is behaving in an ethical manner.

ANSWERS TO SELF-EXAMINATION QUESTIONS

1. A A debit may signify an increase in asset accounts (answer A) or a decrease in liability and owner's capital accounts. A credit may signify a decrease in asset accounts (answer B) or an increase in liability and owner's capital accounts (answers C and D).
2. C Liability, capital, capital stock, retained earnings, and revenue (answer C) accounts have normal credit balances. Asset (answer A), drawing (answer B), dividend, and expense (answer D) accounts have normal debit balances.
3. D The current asset category includes cash and other assets that may reasonably be expected to be realized in cash or sold or consumed usually within a year or less, and therefore would include cash (answer A), accounts receivable (answer B), and supplies on hand (answer C).
4. A The receipt of cash from customers on account increases the asset Cash and decreases the asset Accounts Receivable as indicated by answer A. Answer B has the debit and credit reversed, and answers C and D involve transactions with creditors (accounts payable) and not customers (accounts receivable).
5. D The trial balance (answer D) is a listing of the balances and the titles of the accounts in the ledger on a given date, so that the equality of the debits and credits in the ledger can be verified. The income statement (answer A) is a summary of revenue and expenses for a period of time, the balance sheet (answer B) is a presentation of the assets, liabilities, and owner's equity on a given date, and the retained earnings statement (answer C) is a summary of the changes in retained earnings for a corporation over a period of time.

CHAPTER THREE

COMPLETION OF THE ACCOUNTING CYCLE

CHAPTER OBJECTIVES

1 Discuss the matching principle as it relates to the cash basis and the accrual basis of accounting.

2 Describe the nature of the adjusting process.

3 Describe and illustrate basic procedures for adjusting the accounting records prior to the preparation of the financial statements.

4 Describe and illustrate the work sheet for summarizing the accounting data for use in preparing financial statements.

5 Describe and illustrate the preparation of financial statements.

6 Describe and illustrate journalizing and posting adjusting entries.

7 Describe and illustrate the basic procedures for preparing the accounting records for use in accumulating data for the following accounting period.

8 Describe what is meant by a fiscal year and a natural business year.

9 Describe and diagram the basic phases of the accounting cycle.

During an accounting period, transactions are recorded as they occur, as was demonstrated in the preceding chapter. At the end of the period, the ledger accounts must be brought up to date, so that revenues and expenses are properly matched and the financial statements fairly present the results of operations for a period and the financial condition at the end of that period.

MATCHING PRINCIPLE

OBJECTIVE 1
Discuss the matching principle as it relates to the cash basis and the accrual basis of accounting.

Revenues and expenses may be reported on the income statement by (1) the **cash basis** or (2) the **accrual basis** of accounting. When the cash basis is used, revenues are reported in the period in which cash is received, and expenses are reported in the period in which cash is paid. For example, sales would be recorded only when cash is received from customers, and salaries expense would be recorded only when cash is paid to employees. Net income (or net loss) would be the difference between the cash receipts (revenues) and the cash disbursements (expenses). Small service enterprises which have few receivables and payables, as well as practicing professionals (such as accountants, physicians, and attorneys), may use the cash basis. For most businesses, however, the cash basis is not considered an acceptable method. For this reason, the cash basis will not be discussed in the remainder of the text.

Most enterprises use the accrual basis of accounting. Under the accrual method, revenues are reported in the period in which they are earned, and expenses are reported in the period in which they are incurred in an attempt to produce revenues. For example, revenue would be recognized as services are provided to customers and not when the cash is received from customers. Likewise, supplies expense would be recognized when the supplies are used and not when the cash is paid for supplies purchased. Generally accepted accounting principles require the use of the accrual basis, so that revenues recognized are **matched** with the related expenses incurred in producing the revenues.

The accrual basis of accounting requires the use of an adjusting process at the end of the accounting period to match revenues and expenses for the period properly. The common characteristics of the adjusting process are discussed in the following paragraphs.

NATURE OF THE ADJUSTING PROCESS

OBJECTIVE 2
Describe the nature of the adjusting process.

At the end of the accounting period, many of the amounts listed on the trial balance can be transferred, without change, to the financial statements. For example, the balance of the cash account is normally the amount of that asset owned by the enterprise on the last day of the accounting period. Similarly, the balance in Notes Payable is likely to be the total amount of that type of liability owed by the enterprise on the last day of the accounting period.

All trial balance amounts are not necessarily correct. The amounts listed for prepaid expenses are normally overstated. The reason for the overstatement is that the day-to-day consumption or expiration of these assets has not been recorded. For example, the balance in the supplies account represents the cost of the inventory of supplies at the beginning of the period plus the cost of those acquired during the period. Some of the supplies would have been used during the period; hence, the balance listed on the trial balance is overstated. In the same manner, the balance in Prepaid Insurance represents the beginning balance plus the cost of insurance policies acquired during the period, and no entries were made for the premiums as they expired. To make entries on a day-to-day basis would be costly and unnecessary. There are two effects on the ledger when the daily reduction in prepaid expenses is not recorded: (1) asset accounts are overstated and (2) expense accounts are understated.

Other data needed for the financial statements may be entirely omitted from the trial balance because revenue or expense related to the period has not been recorded. For example, salary expense incurred between the last payday and the end of the accounting period would not ordinarily be recorded in the accounts because salaries are customarily recorded only when they are paid. However, such accrued salaries are an expense of the period because the services were rendered during the period. They also represent a liability as of the last day of the period because they are owed to the employees. The entries required at the end of an accounting period to bring the accounts up to date and to assure the proper matching of revenues and expenses are called adjusting entries. In a broad sense, they may be called corrections to the ledger. But bringing the ledger up to date at the end of a period is part of the accounting procedure; it is not caused by errors. The term "adjusting entries" is therefore more appropriate than the term "correcting entries."

ILLUSTRATIONS OF ADJUSTING ENTRIES

OBJECTIVE 3
Describe and illustrate basic procedures for adjusting the accounting records prior to the preparation of the financial statements.

The illustrations of adjusting entries that follow are based on the ledger of Hill Photographic Studio, as reported in the March 31 trial balance presented below. T accounts are used for illustrative purposes and the adjusting entries, which are shown in the accounts, appear in color to separate them from items that were posted during the month.

Hill Photographic Studio Trial Balance March 31, 1990		
Cash	1 6 3 1 00	
Accounts Receivable	1 7 7 5 00	
Supplies	1 8 5 0 00	
Prepaid Rent	2 4 0 0 00	
Photographic Equipment	17 5 0 0 00	
Accounts Payable		2 0 0 0 00
Ann Hill, Capital		20 6 5 0 00
Ann Hill, Drawing	1 5 0 0 00	
Sales		5 5 2 5 00
Salary Expense	1 1 5 0 00	
Miscellaneous Expense	3 6 9 00	
	28 1 7 5 00	28 1 7 5 00

Prepaid Expenses

According to Hill's trial balance, the balance in the supplies account on March 31 is $1,850. Some of these supplies (film, developing agents, etc.) have been used during the past month and some are still in stock. If the amount of either is known, the other can be readily determined. It is more practical to determine the cost of the supplies on hand at the end of the month than it is to keep a record of those used from day to day. Assuming that the inventory of supplies on March 31 is determined to be $890, the amount to be moved from the asset account to the expense account is computed as follows:

Supplies available (balance of account)............	$1,850
Supplies on hand (inventory)..........................	890
Supplies used (amount of adjustment)	$ 960

Increases in expense accounts are recorded as debits and decreases in asset accounts are recorded as credits. Hence at the end of March, the supplies expense account should be debited for $960 and the supplies account should be credited for $960 to recognize the supplies used during March. The adjusting entry is illustrated in the following T accounts:

Adjustment of Prepaid Expense — Supplies

Supplies					Supplies Expense	
Mar. 1	1,200	**Mar. 31**	**960**	➡	**Mar. 31**	**960**
20	650					
890	*1,850*					

After the adjustment, the asset account has a debit balance of $890 and the expense account has a debit balance of $960.

The debit balance of $2,400 in Hill's prepaid rent account represents a prepayment on March 1 of rent for three months: March, April, and May. At the end of March, the rent expense account should be increased (debited) and the prepaid rent account should be decreased (credited) by $800, the rental for one month. The adjusting entry is illustrated in the following T accounts:

Adjustment of Prepaid Expense — Rent

Prepaid Rent		Rent Expense	
Mar. 1 2,400	**Mar. 31** 800 ⟶	**Mar. 31** 800	
1,600			

The prepaid rent account now has a debit balance of $1,600, which is an asset. The rent expense account has a debit balance of $800, which is an expense.

If the preceding adjustments for supplies ($960) and rent ($800) are not recorded, the financial statements prepared as of March 31 will be incorrect to the extent indicated as follows:

Income statement
Expenses will be understated	$1,760
Net income will be overstated	1,760

Statement of owner's equity
Net income will be overstated	$1,760
Ending owner's equity will be overstated	1,760

Balance sheet
Assets will be overstated	$1,760
Owner's equity will be overstated	1,760

The cost of supplies, prepaid rent, and other prepayments of expenses of future periods may be recorded as expenses at the time of payment, rather than as assets. This alternative treatment will be considered in a later chapter. Meanwhile, all such expenditures will be assumed to be recorded first as assets, as in the preceding illustration.

Prepayments of expenses of one accounting period are sometimes made at the beginning of the period to which they apply. When this is the case, the expenditure is ordinarily recorded as an expense rather than as an asset. During the accounting period, the expense account debited will include an amount that represents an asset, but it will be wholly expense at the end of the period. For example, if rent for March is paid on March 1, it is an asset at the time of payment. The asset expires gradually from day to day, and at the end of the month the entire amount has become an expense. Therefore, if the expenditure is initially recorded as a debit to Rent Expense, no additional entries are needed at the end of the period.

Plant Assets

Like supplies, the photographic equipment was used in the operations of Hill Photographic Studio. Unlike supplies, there is no visible reduction in the quantity of the equipment. As time passes, however, equipment does lose its capacity to provide useful services. This decrease in usefulness is a business expense, which is called depreciation. The factors involved in computing depreciation are discussed in a later chapter.

The adjusting entry to record depreciation is similar to the entry illustrated in the preceding section, in which an expense account is debited and an asset account is credited. The account debited is a depreciation expense account, which is reported on the income statement. However, because it is common practice to report on the balance sheet both the original cost of a plant asset and the amount of depreciation recorded since its acquisition, the account credited is an **accumulated depreciation** account. An accumulated depreciation account is a **contra account** because it is "offset against" another account. Accumulated depreciation accounts may be referred to as **contra asset accounts** because they are offset against asset accounts.

Typical titles for plant asset accounts and their related contra asset accounts are as follows:

Plant Asset	*Contra Asset*
Land	———
Buildings	Accumulated Depreciation—Buildings
Equipment	Accumulated Depreciation—Equipment

The ledger could show more detail by having a separate account for each of a number of buildings. Equipment may also be subdivided according to function, such as Delivery Equipment, Store Equipment, and Office Equipment, with a related accumulated depreciation account for each plant asset account.

The adjusting entry to record depreciation for March for Hill Photographic Studio is illustrated in the following T accounts. The estimated amount of depreciation for the month is assumed to be $175.

Adjustment for Depreciation

Photographic Equipment		Accumulated Depreciation	
Mar. 1 15,000			Mar. 31 175
4 2,500			
17,500			

Depreciation Expense	
Mar. 31 175	

The $175 increase in the accumulated depreciation account represents a subtraction from the $17,500 cost recorded in the related plant asset account. The difference between the two balances is the unexpired or undepreciated cost and is called the **book value of the asset**. The book value may be presented on the balance sheet in the following manner:

Plant assets:		
Photographic equipment...................................	$17,500	
Less accumulated depreciation......................	175	$17,325

If the previous adjustment for depreciation ($175) is not recorded, the financial statements as of March 31 will be incorrect to the extent indicated as follows:

Income statement	
Expenses will be understated...	$175
Net income will be overstated	175

Statement of owner's equity

Net income will be overstated $175
Ending owner's equity will be overstated............................. 175

Balance Sheet

Assets will be overstated... $175
Owner's equity will be overstated....................................... 175

Accrued Expenses (Liabilities)

It is customary to pay for some types of services, such as insurance and rent, before they are used. Other types of services are paid for after the service has been performed. Services performed by employees is an example of this type of situation. The wage or salary expense accumulates or accrues as a legal claim hour by hour and day by day, but payment is made only weekly, biweekly, or in accordance with some other period of time. Such an accumulated expense that is unpaid and unrecorded is referred to as an **accrued expense.** In the case of the wage or salary expense, if the last day of a pay period is not the last day of the accounting period, the accrued expense and the related liability must be recorded in the accounts by an adjusting entry.

The data in the following T accounts were taken from the ledger of Hill Photographic Studio. The debits of $575 on March 13 and 27 in the salary expense account were biweekly payments on alternate Fridays for the payroll periods ended on those days. The salaries earned on Monday and Tuesday, March 30 and 31, total $115. This amount is an additional expense of March and is debited to the salary expense account. It is also a liability as of March 31 and is therefore credited to Salaries Payable.

Adjustment for Accrued Expense

Salaries Payable		Salary Expense	
	Mar. 31 **115**	Mar. 13 575	
		27 575	
		1,150	
		31 **115**	
		1,265	

After the adjustment, the debit balance of the salary expense account is $1,265, which is the actual expense for the month. The credit balance of $115 in Salaries Payable is the amount of the liability for salaries owed as of March 31. If the previous adjustment for salaries ($115) is not recorded, the financial statements as of March 31 will be incorrect to the extent indicated as follows:

Income statement

Expenses will be understated... $115
Net income will be overstated 115

Statement of owner's equity

Net income will be overstated $115
Ending owner's equity will be overstated....................................... 115

Balance sheet

Liabilities will be understated $115
Owner's equity will be overstated.. 115

WORK SHEET FOR FINANCIAL STATEMENTS

OBJECTIVE 4
Describe and
illustrate the
work sheet for
summarizing the
accounting data for
use in preparing
financial statements.

Before journalizing and posting adjustments similar to those just described, it is necessary to determine and assemble the relevant data. For example, it is necessary to determine the cost of supplies on hand and the salaries accrued at the end of the period. Such collections of data, preliminary drafts of financial statements, and other useful analyses prepared by accountants are generally called **working papers**.

A type of working paper frequently used by accountants prior to the preparation of financial statements is called a **work sheet** Its use reduces the possibility of overlooking the need for an adjustment, provides a convenient means of verifying arithmetical accuracy, provides for the arrangement of data in a logical form, and provides the source data for the financial statements.

The work sheet is identified by (1) the name of the enterprise, (2) the nature of the form (work sheet), and (3) the period of time involved. A form commonly used has an account title column and ten money columns arranged in five pairs of debit and credit columns. The main headings of the five sets of money columns are as follows:

Work Sheet with Trial Balance Recorded

Hill Photographic
Work
For Month Ended

	ACCOUNT TITLE	TRIAL BALANCE		ADJUSTMENTS	
		DEBIT	CREDIT	DEBIT	CREDIT
1	Cash	1 6 3 1 00			
2	Accounts Receivable	1 7 7 5 00			
3	Supplies	1 8 5 0 00			
4	Prepaid Rent	2 4 0 0 00			
5	Photographic Equipment	1 7 5 0 0 00			
6	Accounts Payable		2 0 0 0 00		
7	Ann Hill, Capital		2 0 6 5 0 00		
8	Ann Hill, Drawing	1 5 0 0 00			
9	Sales		5 5 2 5 00		
10	Salary Expense	1 1 5 0 00			
11	Miscellaneous Expense	3 6 9 00			
12		2 8 1 7 5 00	2 8 1 7 5 00		
13					
14					
15					
16					
17					
18					
19					
20					
21					
22					
23					

1. Trial Balance
2. Adjustments
3. Adjusted Trial Balance
4. Income Statement
5. Balance Sheet

The preparation of work sheets is facilitated by the use of a computer software program, especially a spreadsheet program. Using computers, the procedures described and illustrated in the following paragraphs are programmed into the software, so that the completion of work sheets requires only the entry of data.

Trial Balance Columns

The trial balance data may be assembled directly on the work sheet form or they may be prepared on another sheet first and then copied onto the work sheet form. The work sheet for Hill Photographic Studio, with the trial balance data recorded, is presented below and on page 100.

Studio

Sheet

March 31, 1990

ADJUSTED TRIAL BALANCE		INCOME STATEMENT		BALANCE SHEET		
DEBIT	CREDIT	DEBIT	CREDIT	DEBIT	CREDIT	
						1
						2
						3
						4
						5
						6
						7
						8
						9
						10
						11
						12
						13
						14
						15
						16
						17
						18
						19
						20
						21
						22
						23

Adjustments Columns

Both the debit and the credit parts of an adjustment should be inserted on the appropriate lines before going on to another adjustment, as indicated on the work sheet for Hill Photographic Studio appearing below. Cross-referencing the related debit and credit of each adjustment by letters is useful to anyone who may have occasion to review the work sheet. It is also helpful later when the adjusting entries are recorded in the journal. The sequence of adjustments is not important, except that there is a time and accuracy advantage in following the order in which the adjustment data are assembled. If the titles of some of the accounts to be adjusted do not appear in the trial balance because they had no balance prior to adjustment, they should be inserted in the Account Title column, below the trial balance totals, as they are needed.

The adjusting entries for Hill Photographic Studio were explained and illustrated by T accounts earlier in the chapter. In practice, the adjustments are inserted directly on the work sheet on the basis of the data assembled by the accounting department.

Explanatory notes for the entries in the Adjustments columns of the work sheet follow:

Work Sheet with Trial Balance and Adjustments Recorded

Hill Photographic
Work
For Month Ended

	ACCOUNT TITLE	TRIAL BALANCE DEBIT	TRIAL BALANCE CREDIT	ADJUSTMENTS DEBIT	ADJUSTMENTS CREDIT
1	Cash	1 6 3 1 00			
2	Accounts Receivable	1 7 7 5 00			
3	Supplies	1 8 5 0 00			(a) 9 6 0 00
4	Prepaid Rent	2 4 0 0 00			(b) 8 0 0 00
5	Photographic Equipment	1 7 5 0 0 00			
6	Accounts Payable		2 0 0 0 00		
7	Ann Hill, Capital		2 0 6 5 0 00		
8	Ann Hill, Drawing	1 5 0 0 00			
9	Sales		5 5 2 5 00		
10	Salary Expense	1 1 5 0 00		(d) 1 1 5 00	
11	Miscellaneous Expense	3 6 9 00			
12		2 8 1 7 5 00	2 8 1 7 5 00		
13	Supplies Expense			(a) 9 6 0 00	
14	Rent Expense			(b) 8 0 0 00	
15	Depreciation Expense			(c) 1 7 5 00	
16	Accumulated Depreciation				(c) 1 7 5 00
17	Salaries Payable				(d) 1 1 5 00
18				2 0 5 0 00	2 0 5 0 00
19					
20					
21					
22					
23					

(a) Supplies. The supplies account has a debit balance of $1,850; the cost of the supplies on hand at the end of the period is $890; therefore, the supplies expense for March is the difference between the two amounts, or $960. The adjustment is entered by writing (1) *Supplies Expense* in the Account Title column, (2) *$960* in the Adjustments Debit column on the same line, and (3) *$960* in the Adjustments Credit column on the line with Supplies.

(b) Rent. The prepaid rent account has a debit balance of $2,400, which represents a payment for three months beginning with March; therefore, the rent expense for March is $800. The adjustment is entered by writing (1) *Rent Expense* in the Account Title column, (2) *$800* in the Adjustments Debit column on the same line, and (3) *$800* in the Adjustments Credit column on the line with Prepaid Rent.

(c) Depreciation. Depreciation of the photographic equipment is estimated at $175 for the month. This expired portion of the cost of the equipment is both an expense and a reduction in the asset. The adjustment is entered by writing (1) *Depreciation Expense* in the Account Title column, (2) *$175* in the Adjustments Debit column on the same line, (3) *Accumulated Depreciation* in the Account Title column, and (4) *$175* in the Adjustments Credit column on the same line.

Studio

Sheet

March 31, 1990

ADJUSTED TRIAL BALANCE		INCOME STATEMENT		BALANCE SHEET		
DEBIT	CREDIT	DEBIT	CREDIT	DEBIT	CREDIT	
						1
						2
						3
						4
						5
						6
						7
						8
						9
						10
						11
						12
						13
						14
						15
						16
						17
						18
						19
						20
						21
						22
						23

(d) Salaries. Salaries accrued but not paid at the end of March amount to $115. This is an increase in expense and an increase in liabilities. The adjustment is entered by writing (1) *$115* in the Adjustments Debit column on the same line with Salary Expense, (2) *Salaries Payable* in the Account Title column, and (3) *$115* in the Adjustments Credit column on the same line.

The final step in completing the Adjustments columns is to prove the equality of debits and credits by totaling and ruling the two columns.

Adjusted Trial Balance Columns

The data in the Trial Balance columns are combined with the adjustments data and extended to the Adjusted Trial Balance columns as indicated on the work sheet for Hill Photographic Studio below. For example, the cash and accounts receivable accounts are extended at their original amounts of $1,631 and $1,775, since no adjustments affected either account. Supplies has an initial balance of $1,850 and a credit adjustment (decrease) of $960. The amount to be extended is the debit balance of $890. The same procedure is continued until all account balances have been extended to the Adjusted Trial Balance columns. The Debit and Credit columns are then totaled to prove that no arithmetical errors have been made up to this point.

Work Sheet with Trial Balance, Adjustments, and Adjusted Trial Balance Recorded

Hill Photographic
Work
For Month Ended

	ACCOUNT TITLE	TRIAL BALANCE DEBIT	TRIAL BALANCE CREDIT	ADJUSTMENTS DEBIT	ADJUSTMENTS CREDIT
1	Cash	1 631 00			
2	Accounts Receivable	1 775 00			
3	Supplies	1 850 00			(a) 960 00
4	Prepaid Rent	2 400 00			(b) 800 00
5	Photographic Equipment	17 500 00			
6	Accounts Payable		2 000 00		
7	Ann Hill, Capital		20 650 00		
8	Ann Hill, Drawing	1 500 00			
9	Sales		5 525 00		
10	Salary Expense	1 150 00		(d) 115 00	
11	Miscellaneous Expense	369 00			
12		28 175 00	28 175 00		
13	Supplies Expense			(a) 960 00	
14	Rent Expense			(b) 800 00	
15	Depreciation Expense			(c) 175 00	
16	Accumulated Depreciation				(c) 175 00
17	Salaries Payable				(d) 115 00
18				2 050 00	2 050 00
19	Net Income				
20					
21					
22					
23					

Income Statement and Balance Sheet Columns

The data in the Adjusted Trial Balance columns are extended to one of the remaining four columns as indicated on the work sheet for Hill Photographic Studio appearing on pages 106 and 107. The amounts of assets, liabilities, owner's equity, and drawing (or dividends) are extended to the Balance Sheet columns, and the revenues and expenses are extended to the Income Statement columns. An advantage in time and accuracy can be achieved by beginning at the top and proceeding down the page in sequential order.

In the illustrative work sheet, the first account listed is Cash and the balance appearing in the Adjusted Trial Balance Debit column is $1,631. This amount should be extended to the appropriate column. Cash is an asset, it is listed on the balance sheet, and it has a debit balance. Accordingly, the $1,631 amount is extended to the Debit column of the balance sheet section. The balance of Accounts Receivable is extended in similar fashion. The $890 adjusted balance of Supplies is extended to the Balance Sheet Debit column. The same procedure is continued until all account balances have been extended to the appropriate columns. The balances of the capital and drawing accounts are extended to the Balance Sheet columns, because this work sheet does not provide for separate Statement of Owner's Equity columns.

Studio

Sheet

March 31, 1990

ADJUSTED TRIAL BALANCE		INCOME STATEMENT		BALANCE SHEET		
DEBIT	CREDIT	DEBIT	CREDIT	DEBIT	CREDIT	
1 631 00						1
1 775 00						2
890 00						3
1 600 00						4
17 500 00						5
	2 000 00					6
	20 650 00					7
1 500 00						8
	5 525 00					9
1 265 00						10
369 00						11
						12
960 00						13
800 00						14
175 00						15
	175 00					16
	115 00					17
28 465 00	28 465 00					18
						19
						20
						21
						22
						23

After all of the balances have been extended, each of the four columns is
totaled. The net income or the net loss for the period is the amount of the difference between the totals of the two Income Statement columns. If the
Credit column total is greater than the Debit column total, the excess is the net
income. For the work sheet presented below, the computation of net income
is as follows:

Total of Credit column (revenue)	$5,525
Total of Debit column (expenses)	3,569
Net income (excess of revenue over expenses)	$1,956

Revenue and expense accounts, which are subdivisions of owner's
equity, are temporary in nature. They are used during the accounting period
to aid in the accumulation of detailed operating data. After they have served
their purpose, the net balance will be transferred to the capital account (or

Work Sheet Completed For Hill Photographic Studio

Hill Photographic
Work
For Month Ended

	ACCOUNT TITLE	TRIAL BALANCE DEBIT	TRIAL BALANCE CREDIT	ADJUSTMENTS DEBIT	ADJUSTMENTS CREDIT
1	Cash	1631 00			
2	Accounts Receivable	1775 00			
3	Supplies	1850 00			(a) 960 00
4	Prepaid Rent	2400 00			(b) 800 00
5	Photographic Equipment	17500 00			
6	Accounts Payable		2000 00		
7	Ann Hill, Capital		20650 00		
8	Ann Hill, Drawing	1500 00			
9	Sales		5525 00		
10	Salary Expense	1150 00		(d) 1150 00	
11	Miscellaneous Expense	369 00			
12		28175 00	28175 00		
13	Supplies Expense			(a) 960 00	
14	Rent Expense			(b) 800 00	
15	Depreciation Expense			(c) 175 00	
16	Accumulated Depreciation				(c) 175 00
17	Salaries Payable				(d) 1150 00
18				2050 00	2050 00
19					
20					
21					
22					
23					

the retained earnings account) in the ledger. This transfer is accomplished on the work sheet by entries in the Income Statement Debit column and the Balance Sheet Credit column, with the description of the amount, "Net Income," inserted in the Account Title column, as illustrated below. If there had been a net loss instead of a net income, the amount would have been entered in the Income Statement Credit column and the Balance Sheet Debit column, and described as "Net Loss" in the Account Title column.

After the final entry is made on the work sheet, each of the four statement columns is totaled to verify the arithmetic accuracy of the amount of net income or net loss transferred from the income statement to the balance sheet. The totals of the two Income Statement columns must be equal, as must the totals of the two Balance Sheet columns. The work sheet may be expanded by the addition of a pair of columns solely for the statement of owner's equity (or retained earnings statement) data. However, because of the very few items involved, this variation is not illustrated.

Studio
Sheet
March 31, 1990

	ADJUSTED TRIAL BALANCE		INCOME STATEMENT		BALANCE SHEET		
	DEBIT	CREDIT	DEBIT	CREDIT	DEBIT	CREDIT	
	1 631 00				1 631 00		1
	1 775 00				1 775 00		2
	890 00				890 00		3
	1 600 00				1 600 00		4
	17 500 00				17 500 00		5
		2 000 00				2 000 00	6
		20 650 00				20 650 00	7
	1 500 00				1 500 00		8
		5 525 00		5 525 00			9
	1 265 00		1 265 00				10
	369 00		369 00				11
							12
	960 00		960 00				13
	800 00		800 00				14
	175 00		175 00				15
		175 00				175 00	16
		115 00				115 00	17
	28 465 00	28 465 00	3 569 00	5 525 00	24 896 00	22 940 00	18
			1 956 00			1 956 00	19
			5 525 00	5 525 00	24 896 00	24 896 00	20
							21
							22
							23

FINANCIAL STATEMENTS ━━━━━━━━━━━━━━━━━━━━━━

The work sheet is an aid in preparing the financial statements. The income statement, statement of owner's equity, and balance sheet prepared from the work sheet of Hill Photographic Studio appear on page 109.[1] Their basic forms correspond to the statements presented in Chapter 1. Some minor variations are illustrated; others will be introduced in later chapters. The remaining portions of this section are devoted to the sources of the data and the manner in which they are reported on the statements.

Income Statement

The work sheet is the source of all of the data reported on the income statement. The sequence of expenses as listed on the work sheet may be changed in order to present them on the income statement in the order of size.

Statement of Owner's Equity

The amount listed on the work sheet as the capital of a sole proprietor does not always represent the account balance at the beginning of the accounting period. The proprietor may have invested additional assets in the business during the period. Hence, it is necessary to refer to the account in the ledger to determine the beginning balance and any additional investments. The amount of net income (or net loss) and the amount of the drawings appearing in the Balance Sheet columns of the work sheet are then used to determine the ending capital account balance.

The form of the statement of owner's equity can be changed to meet the circumstances of any particular case. In the illustration on page 109, the amount withdrawn by the owner was less than the net income. If the withdrawals had exceeded the net income, the order of the two items could have been reversed. The difference between the two would then be deducted from the beginning capital account balance.

Other factors, such as additional investments or a net loss, also require changes in form, as in the following example:

Allan Johnson, capital, January 1, 19--..................	$45,000.00	
Additional investment during the year...................	6,000.00	
Total...		$51,000.00
Net loss for the year..	$ 7,500.00	
Withdrawals	8,600.00	
Decrease in owner's equity		16,100.00
Allan Johnson, capital, December 31, 19--		$34,900.00

In an incorporated business, it is necessary to show the difference between changes in capital stock and changes in retained earnings. If the change in the amount of capital stock issued during the period is significant, a capital stock statement should be prepared. Otherwise, such a statement is unnecessary.

---

[1] The basic nature of the statement of cash flows was also discussed in Chapter 1. An in-depth discussion of the preparation and use of the statement of cash flows is presented in Chapter 18 after various necessary concepts and principles have been explained and illustrated.

Income Statement

Hill Photographic Studio
Income Statement
For Month Ended March 31, 1990

Sales		$ 5,525.00
Operating expenses:		
Salary expense..................................	$ 1,265.00	
Supplies expense.............................	960.00	
Rent expense....................................	800.00	
Depreciation expense	175.00	
Miscellaneous expense	369.00	
Total operating expenses.................		3,569.00
Net income		$ 1,956.00

*Statement of
Owner's Equity*

Hill Photographic Studio
Statement of Owner's Equity
For Month Ended March 31, 1990

Ann Hill, capital, March 1, 1990		$20,650.00
Net income for the month......................	$ 1,956.00	
Less withdrawals..................................	1,500.00	
Increase in owner's equity......................		456.00
Ann Hill, capital, March 31, 1990..............		$21,106.00

Balance Sheet

Hill Photographic Studio
Balance Sheet
March 31, 1990

Assets

Current assets:		
Cash...	$ 1,631.00	
Accounts receivable...........................	1,775.00	
Supplies	890.00	
Prepaid rent	1,600.00	
Total current assets		$ 5,896.00
Plant assets:		
Photographic equipment.....................	$17,500.00	
Less accumulated depreciation..........	175.00	17,325.00
Total assets		$23,221.00

Liabilities

Current liabilities:		
Accounts payable..............................	$ 2,000.00	
Salaries payable	115.00	
Total liabilities.....................................		$ 2,115.00

Owner's Equity

Ann Hill, capital....................................		21,106.00
Total liabilities and owner's equity.............		$23,221.00

Balance Sheet

The balance sheet illustrated on page 109 was expanded by the addition of subcaptions for current assets, plant assets, and current liabilities. If there were any liabilities that were not due until more than a year from the balance sheet date, they would be listed under the caption "Long-term liabilities." An example of a balance sheet illustrating a long-term liabilities section appears on page 185.

In the illustration on page 109, the plant assets are made up entirely of photographic equipment. When there are two or more categories of plant assets, the cost, accumulated depreciation, and book value of each category should be listed, and the total amount of plant assets should be shown. This presentation is illustrated as follows:

Plant assets:		
Equipment	$40,600	
Less accumulated depreciation	12,100	$28,500
Automobiles	$22,500	
Less accumulated depreciation	9,600	12,900
Total plant assets		$41,400

The work sheet is the source of all the data reported on the balance sheet, with the exception of the amount of the sole proprietor's capital, which can be obtained from the statement of owner's equity. The stockholders' equity section of the balance sheet of a corporation is subdivided into capital stock and retained earnings. The amount to be reported for the latter is obtained from the retained earnings statement.

Retained Earnings Statement

The basic form of a retained earnings statement for a corporation was illustrated on page 27. If dividend payments are debited to Dividends, the amount will appear on the work sheet. However, some accountants prefer to debit dividends directly to Retained Earnings. When this is the case, it is necessary to refer to the ledger to determine the beginning balance of Retained Earnings and the amount of the dividends debited during the period.

JOURNALIZING AND POSTING ADJUSTING ENTRIES

OBJECTIVE 6
Describe and illustrate journalizing and posting adjusting entries.

At the end of the accounting period, the adjusting entries appearing in the work sheet are recorded in the journal and posted to the ledger. This procedure brings the ledger into agreement with the data reported on the financial statements. The adjusting entries are dated as of the last day of the period, even though they are usually recorded at a later date. Each entry may be supported by an explanation, but a suitable caption above the first adjusting entry is sufficient.

The adjusting entries in the journal of Hill Photographic Studio are presented as follows. The accounts to which they have been posted appear in the ledger beginning on page 113.

Adjusting Entries

				JOURNAL	POST. REF.		DEBIT					CREDIT				PAGE 2
		DATE	DESCRIPTION													
11			Adjusting Entries													11
12	Mar.	31	Supplies Expense	51		9	6	0	00							12
13			Supplies	14							9	6	0	00		13
14																14
15		31	Rent Expense	53		8	0	0	00							15
16			Prepaid Rent	15							8	0	0	00		16
17																17
18		31	Depreciation Expense	54		1	7	5	00							18
19			Accumulated Depreciation	19							1	7	5	00		19
20																20
21		31	Salary Expense	52		1	1	5	00							21
22			Salaries Payable	22							1	1	5	00		22
23																23

NATURE OF THE CLOSING PROCESS

OBJECTIVE 7
Describe and
illustrate the basic
procedures for
preparing the
accounting records
for use in
accumulating data
for the following
accounting period.

The revenue, expense, and drawing (or dividends) accounts are temporary accounts used in classifying and summarizing changes in the owner's equity during the accounting period. At the end of the period, the net effect of the balances in these accounts must be recorded in the permanent capital (or retained earnings) account. The balances must also be removed from the temporary accounts, so that they will be ready for use in accumulating data for the following accounting period. Both of these goals are accomplished by a series of entries called **closing entries**.

Journalizing and Posting Closing Entries

An account titled **Income Summary** is used for summarizing the data in the revenue and expense accounts. It is used only at the end of the accounting period and is both opened and closed during the closing process. Other account titles used for the summarizing account are Expense and Revenue Summary, Profit and Loss Summary, and Income and Expense Summary.

Four entries are required in order to close the temporary accounts of a sole proprietorship at the end of the period. They are as follows:

1. Each revenue account is debited for the amount of its balance, and Income Summary is credited for the total revenue.
2. Each expense account is credited for the amount of its balance, and Income Summary is debited for the total expense.
3. Income Summary is debited for the amount of its balance (net income), and the capital account is credited for the same amount. (Debit and credit are reversed if there is a net loss.)
4. The drawing account is credited for the amount of its balance, and the capital account is debited for the same amount.

The procedure for closing the temporary accounts of a corporation differs only slightly from the outline described above. Income Summary is closed (entry 3) to Retained Earnings, and Dividends is closed (entry 4) to Retained Earnings.

The account titles and amounts needed in journalizing the closing entries may be obtained from any one of three sources: (1) work sheet, (2) income statement and statement of owner's equity, and (3) ledger. When the work sheet is used, the data for the first two entries are taken from the Income Statement columns. The amount for the third entry is the net income or net loss appearing at the bottom of the work sheet. Reference to the drawing account balance appearing in the Balance Sheet Debit column of the work sheet supplies the information for the fourth, and final, entry.

The process of closing the temporary accounts of Hill Photographic Studio is illustrated by the following flowchart:

Flowchart of Closing Process

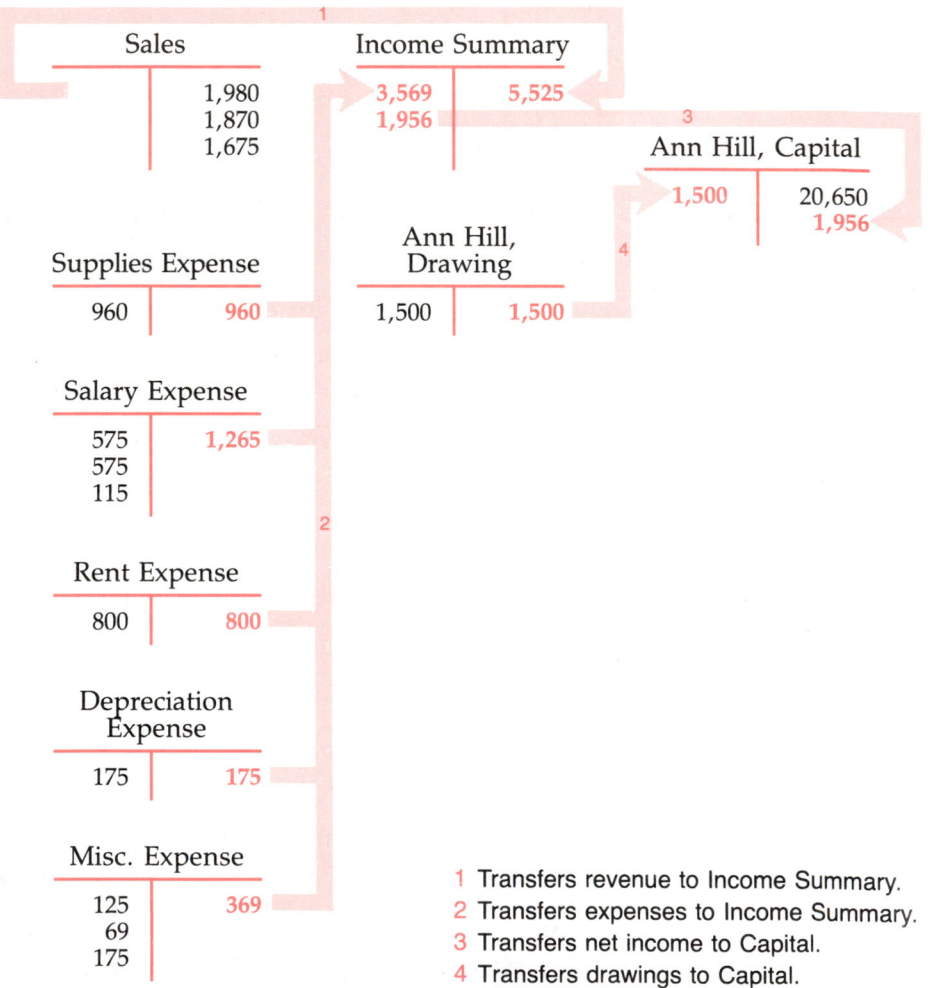

1 Transfers revenue to Income Summary.
2 Transfers expenses to Income Summary.
3 Transfers net income to Capital.
4 Transfers drawings to Capital.

After the closing entries have been journalized, illustrated as follows, and posted to the ledger, the balance in the capital account will correspond to the amounts reported on the statement of owner's equity and balance sheet. In addition, the revenue, expense, and drawing accounts will have zero balances.

Closing Entries

	JOURNAL				PAGE 2	
	DATE	DESCRIPTION	POST. REF.	DEBIT	CREDIT	
24		Closing Entries				24
25	Mar. 31	Sales	41	5 5 2 5 00		25
26		Income Summary	33		5 5 2 5 00	26
27						27
28	31	Income Summary	33	3 5 6 9 00		28
29		Salary Expense	52		1 2 6 5 00	29
30		Miscellaneous Expense	59		3 6 9 00	30
31		Supplies Expense	51		9 6 0 00	31
32		Rent Expense	53		8 0 0 00	32
33		Depreciation Expense	54		1 7 5 00	33
34						34
35	31	Income Summary	33	1 9 5 6 00		35
36		Ann Hill, Capital	31		1 9 5 6 00	26
37						37
38	31	Ann Hill, Capital	31	1 5 0 0 00		38
39		Ann Hill, Drawing	32		1 5 0 0 00	39
40						40
41						41

The ledger of Hill Photographic Studio after the adjusting and closing entries have been posted begins below and continues on pages 114–116. Each posting of an adjusting entry and a closing entry is identified in the item section of the account as an aid to the student. It is not necessary that this be done in actual practice.

Ledger after the Accounts Have Been Adjusted and Closed

ACCOUNT Cash						ACCOUNT NO. 11	
DATE	ITEM	POST. REF.	DEBIT	CREDIT	BALANCE		
					DEBIT	CREDIT	
1990 Mar. 1		1	3 5 0 0 00		3 5 0 0 00		
1		1		2 4 0 0 00	1 1 0 0 00		
5		1	8 5 0 00		1 9 5 0 00		
6		1		1 2 5 00	1 8 2 5 00		
10		1		5 0 0 00	1 3 2 5 00		
13		1		5 7 5 00	7 5 0 00		
16		1	1 9 8 0 00		2 7 3 0 00		
20		1		6 5 0 00	2 0 8 0 00		
27		1		5 7 5 00	1 5 0 5 00		
31		1		6 9 00	1 4 3 6 00		
31		1		1 7 5 00	1 2 6 1 00		
31		2	1 8 7 0 00		3 1 3 1 00		
31		2		1 5 0 0 00	1 6 3 1 00		

Ledger after the Accounts Have Been Adjusted and Closed (Continued)

ACCOUNT **Accounts Receivable** ACCOUNT NO. **12**

DATE	ITEM	POST. REF.	DEBIT	CREDIT	BALANCE DEBIT	BALANCE CREDIT
1990 Mar. 1		1	9 50 00		9 50 00	
5		1		8 50 00	1 00 00	
31		2	1 6 75 00		1 7 75 00	

ACCOUNT **Supplies** ACCOUNT NO. **14**

DATE	ITEM	POST. REF.	DEBIT	CREDIT	BALANCE DEBIT	BALANCE CREDIT
1990 Mar. 1		1	1 2 00 00		1 2 00 00	
20		1	6 50 00		1 8 50 00	
31	Adjusting	2		9 60 00	8 90 00	

ACCOUNT **Prepaid Rent** ACCOUNT NO. **15**

DATE	ITEM	POST. REF.	DEBIT	CREDIT	BALANCE DEBIT	BALANCE CREDIT
1990 Mar. 1		1	2 4 00 00		2 4 00 00	
31	Adjusting	2		8 00 00	1 6 00 00	

ACCOUNT **Photographic Equipment** ACCOUNT NO. **18**

DATE	ITEM	POST. REF.	DEBIT	CREDIT	BALANCE DEBIT	BALANCE CREDIT
1990 Mar. 1		1	15 0 00 00		15 0 00 00	
4		1	2 5 00 00		17 5 00 00	

ACCOUNT **Accumulated Depreciation** ACCOUNT NO. **19**

DATE	ITEM	POST. REF.	DEBIT	CREDIT	BALANCE DEBIT	BALANCE CREDIT
1990 Mar. 31	Adjusting	2		1 75 00		1 75 00

ACCOUNT **Accounts Payable** ACCOUNT NO. **21**

DATE	ITEM	POST. REF.	DEBIT	CREDIT	BALANCE DEBIT	BALANCE CREDIT
1990 Mar. 4		1		2 5 00 00		2 5 00 00
10		1	5 00 00			2 0 00 00

ACCOUNT **Salaries Payable** ACCOUNT NO. **22**

DATE	ITEM	POST. REF.	DEBIT	CREDIT	BALANCE DEBIT	BALANCE CREDIT
1990 Mar. 31	Adjusting	2		1 1 5 00		1 1 5 00

Ledger after the Accounts Have Been Adjusted and Closed (Continued)

ACCOUNT Ann Hill, Capital — ACCOUNT NO. 31

DATE		ITEM	POST. REF.	DEBIT	CREDIT	BALANCE DEBIT	BALANCE CREDIT
1990 Mar.	1		1		20 650 00		20 650 00
	31	Closing	2		1 956 00		22 606 00
	31	Closing	2	1 500 00			21 106 00

ACCOUNT Ann Hill, Drawing — ACCOUNT NO. 32

DATE		ITEM	POST. REF.	DEBIT	CREDIT	BALANCE DEBIT	BALANCE CREDIT
1990 Mar.	31		2	1 500 00		1 500 00	
	31	Closing	2		1 500 00	—	—

ACCOUNT Income Summary — ACCOUNT NO. 33

DATE		ITEM	POST. REF.	DEBIT	CREDIT	BALANCE DEBIT	BALANCE CREDIT
1990 Mar.	31	Closing	2		5 525 00		5 525 00
	31	Closing	2	3 569 00			1 956 00
	31	Closing	2	1 956 00		—	—

ACCOUNT Sales — ACCOUNT NO. 41

DATE		ITEM	POST. REF.	DEBIT	CREDIT	BALANCE DEBIT	BALANCE CREDIT
1990 Mar.	16		1		1 980 00		1 980 00
	31		2		1 870 00		3 850 00
	31		2		1 675 00		5 525 00
	31	Closing	2	5 525 00		—	—

ACCOUNT Supplies Expense — ACCOUNT NO. 51

DATE		ITEM	POST. REF.	DEBIT	CREDIT	BALANCE DEBIT	BALANCE CREDIT
1990 Mar.	31	Adjusting	2	960 00		960 00	
	31	Closing	2		960 00	—	—

ACCOUNT Salary Expense — ACCOUNT NO. 52

DATE		ITEM	POST. REF.	DEBIT	CREDIT	BALANCE DEBIT	BALANCE CREDIT
1990 Mar.	13		1	575 00		575 00	
	27		1	575 00		1 150 00	
	31	Adjusting	2	115 00		1 265 00	
	31	Closing	2		1 265 00	—	—

ACCOUNT Rent Expense — ACCOUNT NO. 53

DATE		ITEM	POST. REF.	DEBIT	CREDIT	BALANCE DEBIT	BALANCE CREDIT
1990 Mar.	31	Adjusting	2	800 00		800 00	
	31	Closing	2		800 00	—	—

Ledger after the Accounts Have Been Adjusted and Closed (Concluded)

ACCOUNT Depreciation Expense							ACCOUNT NO. 54	
DATE	ITEM	POST. REF.	DEBIT	CREDIT	BALANCE			
					DEBIT		CREDIT	
1990 Mar. 31	Adjusting	2	1 75 00		1 75 00			
31	Closing	2		1 75 00	—		—	

ACCOUNT Miscellaneous Expense							ACCOUNT NO. 59	
DATE	ITEM	POST. REF.	DEBIT	CREDIT	BALANCE			
					DEBIT		CREDIT	
1990 Mar. 6		1	1 25 00		1 25 00			
31		1	69 00		1 94 00			
31		1	1 75 00		3 69 00			
31	Closing	2		3 69 00	—		—	

As the entry to close an account is posted, a line should be inserted in both Balance columns opposite the final entry, as illustrated by Ann Hill, Drawing and the remaining temporary accounts. Transactions affecting the accounts in the following period will be posted in the spaces immediately below the closing entry.

Post-Closing Trial Balance

The last procedure of the accounting cycle is the preparation of a trial balance after all of the temporary accounts have been closed. The purpose of the **post-closing** (after closing) **trial balance**, which is illustrated as follows, is to make sure that the ledger is in balance at the beginning of the new accounting period. The accounts and amounts should agree exactly with the accounts and amounts listed on the balance sheet at the end of the period.

Post-Closing Trial Balance

Hill Photographic Studio		
Post-Closing Trial Balance		
March 31, 1990		
Cash	1 6 3 1 00	
Accounts Receivable	1 7 7 5 00	
Supplies	8 9 0 00	
Prepaid Rent	1 6 0 0 00	
Photographic Equipment	17 5 0 0 00	
Accumulated Depreciation		1 7 5 00
Accounts Payable		2 0 0 0 00
Salaries Payable		1 1 5 00
Ann Hill, Capital		21 1 0 6 00
	23 3 9 6 00	23 3 9 6 00

Instead of preparing a formalized post-closing trial balance, it is possible to proceed directly from the ledger to a calculator to determine the equality of debit and credit balances in the ledger. A calculator providing a tape record of the amounts should be used—the tape becoming, in effect, the post-closing trial balance. Without such a tape, there are no efficient means of determining whether the cause of an inequality of trial balance totals is due to errors in manipulating the keys or to errors in the ledger.

FISCAL YEAR

OBJECTIVE 8
Describe what is
meant by a fiscal
year and a natural
business year.

The maximum length of an accounting period is usually one year, which includes a complete cycle of the seasons and of business activities. Income and property taxes are also based on yearly periods and thus require that annual determinations be made.

The annual accounting period adopted by an enterprise is known as its **fiscal year**. Fiscal years ordinarily begin with the first day of the particular month selected and end on the last day of the twelfth month hence. The period most commonly adopted is the calendar year, although other periods are not unusual, particularly for incorporated businesses. For example, an enterprise may adopt a fiscal year that ends when business activities have reached the lowest point in the enterprise's annual operating cycle. Such a fiscal year is termed the **natural business year**.

The 1988 edition of *Accounting Trends & Techniques*, published by the American Institute of Certified Public Accountants, reported the following results of a survey of 600 industrial and merchandising companies concerning the month of their fiscal year end:

Percentage of companies with fiscal years ending in the month of:

January...	4%
February......................................	2
March	2
April...	1
May..	2
June...	7
July	2
August	3
September....................................	6
October.......................................	4
November.....................................	3
December.....................................	64

CLOSING THE BOOKS

Habit is a wonderful saver of mental effort. But too close adherence to habit in business limits efficiency by shutting off initiative.

This is particularly true in the adherence of general business to the habit of following a fixed date for closing the so-called "fiscal" year.

The best date for closing the books and preparing financial statements for the "fiscal" year is when business is in its most liquid condition — when bank loans and other liabilities are lowest, accounts receivable reduced, and, especially, when the inventory is at a minimum.

Source: Management and Administration (May, 1924), p. 503.

The most logical date for closing *your* "fiscal" year is that time when *your* business is logically over for the twelve months — when stocks are lowest — when prices are normal — when selling is not being forced — when you are not buying heavily — when profits can be most accurately determined — when your accounting department is not working nights, or your bank is not burdened with December 31st reports. In other words, close *your* books when *your* business is most naturally through with the rush of *your* year, when proper time and attention can be given, and your public accountants can serve you best.

The long-term financial history of a business enterprise may be shown by a succession of balance sheets, prepared every year. The history of operations for the intervening periods is presented in a series of income statements. If the life of a business enterprise is represented by a line moving from left to right, a series of balance sheets and income statements may be diagrammed as follows:

THE LIFE OF A BUSINESS

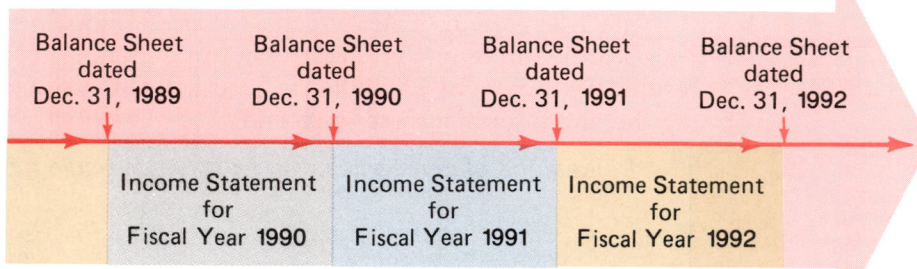

| Balance Sheet dated Dec. 31, 1989 | Balance Sheet dated Dec. 31, 1990 | Balance Sheet dated Dec. 31, 1991 | Balance Sheet dated Dec. 31, 1992 |

| Income Statement for Fiscal Year 1990 | Income Statement for Fiscal Year 1991 | Income Statement for Fiscal Year 1992 |

ACCOUNTING CYCLE

OBJECTIVE 9
Describe and diagram the basic phases of the accounting cycle.

The principal accounting procedures of a fiscal period have been presented in this and the preceding chapter. The sequence of procedures is frequently called the **accounting cycle.** It begins with the analysis and the journalizing of transactions and ends with the post-closing trial balance. The most significant output of the accounting cycle is, of course, the financial statements.

An understanding of all phases of the accounting cycle is essential as a foundation for further study of accounting principles and the uses of accounting data by management. The following basic phases of the cycle are shown, by number, in the flowchart on page 119:

1. Transactions are analyzed and recorded in a journal.
2. Transactions are posted to the ledger.
3. Trial balance is prepared, data needed to adjust the accounts are assembled, and the work sheet is completed.
4. Financial statements are prepared.
5. Adjusting and closing entries are journalized.
6. Adjusting and closing entries are posted to the ledger.
7. Post-closing trial balance is prepared.

Accounting Cycle

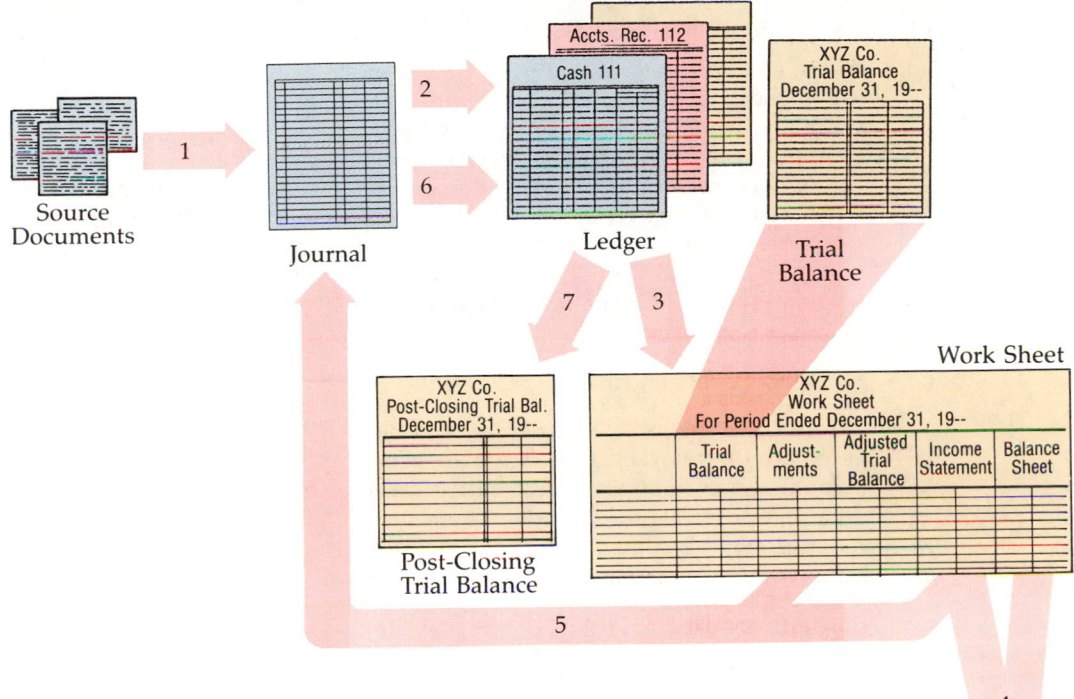

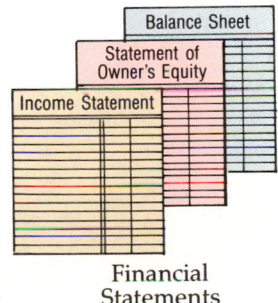

Financial
Statements

1. Transactions analyzed and recorded in journal.
2. Transactions posted to ledger.
3. Trial balance prepared, adjustment data assembled, and work sheet completed.
4. Financial statements prepared.
5. Adjusting and closing entries journalized.
6. Adjusting and closing entries posted to ledger.
7. Post-closing trial balance prepared.

CHAPTER REVIEW

KEY POINTS

Matching Principle

Revenues and expenses may be reported on the income statement by (1) the cash basis or (2) the accrual basis of accounting. When the cash basis is used, revenues are reported in the period in which cash is received, and expenses are reported in the period in which cash is paid. Most enterprises, however, use the accrual basis of accounting. Under the accrual method, revenues are reported in the period in which they are earned, and expenses are reported in the period in which they are incurred in an attempt to produce revenues. The accrual basis of accounting requires the use of an adjusting process at the end of the accounting period to match revenues and expenses within the period properly.

OBJECTIVE 2, 3

Nature of the Adjusting Process

At the end of the accounting period, some of the amounts listed on the trial balance are not necessarily correct. For example, amounts listed for prepaid expenses are normally overstated because the day-to-day consumption or expiration of these assets has not been recorded. Likewise, some revenue or expense items related to the period may not be recorded, since these items are customarily recorded only when cash has been received or paid. The entries required at the end of the accounting period to bring the accounts up to date and to insure the proper matching of revenues and expenses under the accrual method are called adjusting entries. The posting of the adjusting entries will bring the ledger up to date as a planned part of the accounting cycle.

OBJECTIVE 4, 5

Work Sheet and Financial Statements

Before adjustments are journalized and posted, it is necessary to determine and assemble the relevant data. A type of working paper that is used frequently by accountants to summarize these data is called a work sheet. The work sheet is also an aid in preparing the financial statements, including the income statement, statement of owner's equity, and balance sheet. For a corporation, a retained earnings statement can be prepared from the work sheet.

OBJECTIVE 6

Journalizing and Posting Adjusting Entries

At the end of the accounting period, the adjusting entries are recorded in the journal and posted to the ledger. This procedure brings the ledger into agreement with the data reported on the financial statements.

OBJECTIVE 7

Nature of the Closing Process

The revenue, expense, and drawing (dividends) accounts are temporary accounts used in classifying and summarizing changes in owner's equity during an accounting period. At the end of the period, the net effect of the balances in these accounts must be recorded in a permanent capital (or retained earnings) account. The balances must also be removed from the temporary accounts so that they will be ready for use to accumulate data for the following accounting period. Both of these goals are accomplished by the journalizing and posting of closing entries.

In preparing the closing entries, an account titled Income Summary is used for summarizing the data in the revenue and expense accounts. The balance of this account is then closed to the owner's capital account (or retained earnings account for a corporation). Finally, the drawing (dividends) account is closed to the capital account (retained earnings account for a corporation). After the closing entries have been journalized and posted to the ledger, the balance in the owner's capital account (or retained earnings account for a corporation) will correspond to the amounts reported on the statement of owner's equity (retained earnings statement for a corporation) and balance sheet.

The last procedure of the accounting cycle is the preparation of a trial balance after all of the temporary accounts have been closed. The purpose of the post-closing trial balance is to make sure the ledger is in balance at the beginning of the new accounting period. The accounts and amounts should agree exactly with the accounts and amounts listed on the balance sheet at the end of the period.

OBJECTIVE 8

Fiscal Year

The annual accounting period adopted by an enterprise is known as the fiscal year. The period most commonly adopted is the calendar year, although other periods corresponding to the enterprise's natural business year may be used, particularly for incorporated enterprises.

OBJECTIVE 9

Accounting Cycle

The sequence of accounting procedures during a fiscal period is called the accounting cycle. It begins with the analysis of transactions and ends with the post-closing trial balance. The most significant outputs of the accounting cycle are the financial statements.

KEY TERMS

matching principle 94
cash basis 94
accrual basis 94
adjusting entries 95
depreciation 97
accumulated depreciation 98
contra account 98
accrued expense 99

work sheet 100
closing entries 111
Income Summary 111
post-closing trial balance 116
fiscal year 117
natural business year 117
accounting cycle 118

SELF-EXAMINATION QUESTIONS

Answers at end of chapter.

1. If the supplies account, before adjustment on May 31, indicated a balance of $2,250, and an inventory of supplies on hand at May 31 totaled $950, the adjusting entry would be:
    A. debit Supplies, $950; credit Supplies Expense, $950
    B. debit Supplies, $1,300; credit Supplies Expense, $1,300
    C. debit Supplies Expense, $950; credit Supplies, $950
    D. debit Supplies Expense, $1,300; credit Supplies, $1,300

2. If the estimated amount of depreciation on equipment for a period is $2,000, the adjusting entry to record depreciation would be:
    A. debit Depreciation Expense, $2,000; credit Equipment, $2,000
    B. debit Equipment, $2,000; credit Depreciation Expense, $2,000
    C. debit Depreciation Expense, $2,000; credit Accumulated Depreciation, $2,000
    D. debit Accumulated Depreciation, $2,000; credit Depreciation Expense, $2,000

3. If the equipment account has a balance of $22,500 and its accumulated depreciation account has a balance of $14,000, the book value of the equipment is:
    A. $36,500   C. $14,000
    B. $22,500   D. $8,500

4. Which of the following accounts would be closed to the income summary account at the end of a period?
    A. Sales   C. Both Sales and Salary Expense
    B. Salary Expense   D. Neither Sales nor Salary Expense

5. The post-closing trial balance would include which of the following accounts?
    A. Cash   C. Salary Expense
    B. Sales   D. All of the above

ILLUSTRATIVE PROBLEM

Two years ago, K. L. Waters organized Star Laundromat as a sole proprietorship. At March 31, 1991, the end of the current fiscal year, the trial balance of Star Laundromat is as follows:

Star Laundromat
Trial Balance
March 31, 1991

	Debit	Credit
Cash	2 4 2 5 00	
Laundry Supplies	1 8 7 0 00	
Prepaid Insurance	6 2 0 00	
Laundry Equipment	37 6 5 0 00	
Accumulated Depreciation		9 7 0 0 00
Accounts Payable		9 2 5 00
K. L. Waters, Capital		22 1 8 0 00
K. L. Waters, Drawing	10 2 0 0 00	
Laundry Revenue		39 1 2 5 00
Wages Expense	12 4 1 5 00	
Rent Expense	3 6 0 0 00	
Utilities Expense	2 7 1 5 00	
Miscellaneous Expense	4 3 5 00	
	71 9 3 0 00	71 9 3 0 00

(Continued at top of next page)

SOLUTION

(1)

Star
Work
For Year Ended

	ACCOUNT TITLE	TRIAL BALANCE		ADJUSTMENTS	
		DEBIT	CREDIT	DEBIT	CREDIT
1	Cash	2 4 2 5 00			
2	Laundry Supplies	1 8 7 0 00			(a) 1 3 9 0 00
3	Prepaid Insurance	6 2 0 00			(b) 3 1 5 00
4	Laundry Equipment	37 6 5 0 00			
5	Accumulated Depreciation		9 7 0 0 00		(c) 1 9 5 0 00
6	Accounts Payable		9 2 5 00		
7	K. L. Waters, Capital		22 1 8 0 00		
8	K. L. Waters, Drawing	10 2 0 0 00			
9	Laundry Revenue		39 1 2 5 00		
10	Wages Expense	12 4 1 5 00		(d) 1 4 0 00	
11	Rent Expense	3 6 0 0 00			
12	Utilities Expense	2 7 1 5 00			
13	Miscellaneous Expense	4 3 5 00			
14		71 9 3 0 00	71 9 3 0 00		
15	Laundry Supplies Expense			(a) 1 3 9 0 00	
16	Insurance Expense			(b) 3 1 5 00	
17	Depreciation Expense			(c) 1 9 5 0 00	
18	Wages Payable				(d) 1 4 0 00
19				3 7 9 5 00	3 7 9 5 00
20	Net Income				
21					
22					
23					

The data needed to determine year-end adjustments are as follows:

(a)	Inventory of laundry supplies at March 31, 1991	$ 480
(b)	Insurance premiums expired during the year............................	315
(c)	Depreciation on equipment during the year.............................	1,950
(d)	Wages accrued but not paid at March 31, 1991........................	140

Instructions:

1. Record the trial balance on a ten-column work sheet and complete the work sheet.
2. Prepare an income statement, a statement of owner's equity (no additional investments were made during the year), and a balance sheet.
3. On the basis of the adjustments data in the work sheet, journalize the adjusting entries.
4. On the basis of the data in the work sheet, journalize the closing entries.

Laundromat

Sheet

March 31, 1991

ADJUSTED TRIAL BALANCE		INCOME STATEMENT		BALANCE SHEET		
DEBIT	CREDIT	DEBIT	CREDIT	DEBIT	CREDIT	
2425 00				2425 00		1
480 00				480 00		2
305 00				305 00		3
3765 00				3765 00		4
	11650 00				11650 00	5
	925 00				925 00	6
	22180 00				22180 00	7
10200 00				10200 00		8
	39125 00		39125 00			9
12555 00		12555 00				10
3600 00		3600 00				11
2715 00		2715 00				12
435 00		435 00				13
						14
1390 00		1390 00				15
315 00		315 00				16
1950 00		1950 00				17
	140 00				140 00	18
74020 00	74020 00	22960 00	39125 00	51060 00	34895 00	19
		16165 00			16165 00	20
		39125 00	39125 00	51060 00	51060 00	21
						22
						23

(2)

Star Laundromat
Income Statement
For Year Ended March 31, 1991

Laundry revenue						$39	1	2 5	00
Operating expenses:									
Wages expense	$12	5	5 5	00					
Rent expense	3	6	0 0	00					
Utilities expense	2	7	1 5	00					
Depreciation expense	1	9	5 0	00					
Laundry supplies expense	1	3	9 0	00					
Insurance expense		3	1 5	00					
Miscellaneous expense		4	3 5	00					
Total operating expenses						22	9	6 0	00
Net income						$16	1	6 5	00

Star Laundromat
Statement of Owner's Equity
For Year Ended March 31, 1991

K. L. Waters, capital, April 1, 1990						$22	1	8 0	00
Net income for the year	$16	1	6 5	00					
Less withdrawals	10	2	0 0	00					
Increase in owner's equity						5	9	6 5	00
K. L. Waters, capital, March 31, 1991						$28	1	4 5	00

Star Laundromat
Balance Sheet
March 31, 1991

Assets									
Current assets:									
Cash	$ 2	4	2 5	00					
Laundry supplies		4	8 0	00					
Prepaid insurance		3	0 5	00					
Total current assets						$ 3	2	1 0	00
Plant assets:									
Laundry equipment	$37	6	5 0	00					
Less accumulated depreciation	11	6	5 0	00		26	0	0 0	00
Total assets						$29	2	1 0	00
Liabilities									
Current liabilities:									
Accounts payable	$	9	2 5	00					
Wages payable		1	4 0	00					
Total liabilities						$ 1	0	6 5	00
Owner's Equity									
K. L. Waters, capital						28	1	4 5	00
Total liabilities and owner's equity						$29	2	1 0	00

(3)

	DATE		DESCRIPTION	POST. REF.	DEBIT					CREDIT					
			JOURNAL										PAGE		
1			Adjusting Entries												1
2	1991 Mar.	31	Laundry Supplies Expense		1	3	9	0	00						2
3			Laundry Supplies							1	3	9	0	00	3
4															4
5		31	Insurance Expense			3	1	5	00						5
6			Prepaid Insurance								3	1	5	00	6
7															7
8		31	Depreciation Expense		1	9	5	0	00						8
9			Accumulated Depreciation							1	9	5	0	00	9
10															10
11		31	Wages Expense			1	4	0	00						11
12			Wages Payable								1	4	0	00	12

(4)

	DATE		DESCRIPTION	POST. REF.	DEBIT					CREDIT					
14			Closing Entries												14
15	1991 Mar.	31	Laundry Revenue		39	1	2	5	00						15
16			Income Summary							39	1	2	5	00	16
17															17
18		31	Income Summary		22	9	6	0	00						18
19			Wages Expense							12	5	5	5	00	19
20			Rent Expense							3	6	0	0	00	20
21			Utilities Expense							2	7	1	5	00	21
22			Miscellaneous Expense								4	3	5	00	22
23			Laundry Supplies Expense							1	3	9	0	00	23
24			Insurance Expense								3	1	5	00	24
25			Depreciation Expense							1	9	5	0	00	25
26															26
27		31	Income Summary		16	1	6	5	00						27
28			K. L. Waters, Capital							16	1	6	5	00	28
29															29
30		31	K. L. Waters, Capital		10	2	0	0	00						30
31			K. L. Waters, Drawing							10	2	0	0	00	31

DISCUSSION QUESTIONS

1. How are revenues and expenses reported on the income statement under (a) cash basis accounting and (b) accrual basis accounting?

2. Is the balance listed on the trial balance for supplies, before the accounts have been adjusted, normally the amount that should be reported on the balance sheet? Explain.

3. Why are adjusting entries needed at the end of an accounting period?

4. What is the nature of the balance in the prepaid insurance account at the end of the accounting period (a) before adjustment? (b) after adjustment?

5. If the effect of the credit portion of an adjusting entry is to increase the balance of a liability account, which of the following statements describes the effect of the debit portion of the entry?
(a) Increases the balance of a revenue account.
(b) Increases the balance of an expense account.
(c) Increases the balance of an asset account.

6. Does every adjusting entry have an effect on the determination of the amount of net income for a period? Explain.

7. On July 1 of the current year, an enterprise paid the July rent on the building that it occupies. (a) Do the rights acquired at July 1 represent an asset or an expense? (b) What is the justification for debiting Rent Expense at the time of payment?

8. At the end of January, the first month of the fiscal year, the usual adjusting entry transferring supplies used to an expense account is inadvertently omitted. Which items will be incorrectly stated, because of the error, on (a) the income statement for January and (b) the balance sheet as of January 31? Also indicate whether the items in error will be overstated or understated.

9. In accounting for depreciation on equipment, what is the name of the account that would be referred to as a contra asset account?

10. (a) Explain the purpose of the two accounts: Depreciation Expense and Accumulated Depreciation. (b) What is the normal balance of each account? (c) Is it customary for the balances of the two accounts to be equal in amount? (d) In what financial statements, if any, will each account appear?

11. What term is applied to the difference between the balance in a plant asset account and its related accumulated depreciation account?

12. If the balance in the equipment account is $25,000 and the balance in the accumulated depreciation — equipment account is $10,000, what is the book value of the equipment?

13. Accrued salaries of $7,500 owed to employees for December 29, 30, and 31 are not taken into consideration in preparing the financial statements for the fiscal year ended December 31. Which items will be erroneously stated, because of the error, on (a) the income statement for the year and (b) the balance sheet as of December 31? Also indicate whether the items in error will be overstated or understated.

14. Assume that the error in Question 13 was not corrected and that the $7,500 of accrued salaries was included in the first salary payment in January. Which items will be erroneously stated, because of failure to correct the initial error, on (a) the income statement for the month of January and (b) the balance sheet as of January 31?

15. Is the work sheet a substitute for the financial statements? Discuss.

16. In the Balance Sheet columns of the work sheet for C. D. Parker Company for the current year, the Debit column total is $29,750 greater than the Credit column total. Would the income statement report a net income or a net loss? Explain.

17. Why are closing entries required at the end of an accounting period?

18. What type of accounts are closed by transferring their balances to Income Summary (a) as a debit, (b) as a credit?

19. To what account is the income summary account closed for (a) a sole proprietorship? (b) a corporation?

20. To what account in the ledger of a corporation is the account Dividends periodically closed?

21. From the following list, identify the accounts that should be closed to Income Summary at the end of the fiscal year: (a) Accounts Payable, (b) Salaries Payable, (c) Capital Stock, (d) Salaries Expense, (e) Depreciation Expense—Buildings, (f) Supplies, (g) Equipment, (h) Supplies Expense, (i) Retained Earnings, (j) Sales, (k) Land, (l) Accumulated Depreciation—Buildings.

22. Are adjusting and closing entries in the journal dated as of the last day of the fiscal period or as of the day the entries are actually made? Explain.

23. Which of the following accounts in the ledger of a corporation will ordinarily appear in the post-closing trial balance? (a) Accounts Receivable, (b) Accumulated Depreciation, (c) Cash, (d) Supplies, (e) Depreciation Expense, (f) Wages Payable, (g) Equipment, (h) Retained Earnings, (i) Dividends, (j) Capital Stock, (k) Wages Expense, (l) Sales.

24. What term is applied to the annual accounting period adopted by a business enterprise?

Real World Focus

25. The fiscal years for several well-known companies were as follows:

Company	Fiscal Year Ending
K Mart	January 30
J. C. Penney	January 26
Zayre Corp.	January 26
Toys "R" Us, Inc.	February 3
Federated Department Stores	February 2
The Limited, Inc.	February 2

What general characteristic of these companies explains why they do not have fiscal years ending December 31?

EXERCISES

Exercise 3–1

Adjusting entries for prepaid insurance.

OBJ. 3

The balance in the prepaid insurance account, before adjustment at the end of the year, is $7,225. Journalize the adjusting entry required under each of the following alternatives for determining the amount of the adjustment: (a) the amount of insurance expired during the year is $4,900; (b) the amount of unexpired insurance applicable to future periods is $2,325.

Exercise 3–2

Adjusting entries for accrued salaries.

OBJ. 3

A business enterprise pays weekly salaries of $12,000 on Friday for a five-day week ending on that day. Journalize the necessary adjusting entry at the end of the fiscal period, assuming that the fiscal period ends (a) on Monday, (b) on Wednesday.

Exercise 3–3

Adjusting entries for prepaid and accrued taxes.

OBJ. 3

A business enterprise was organized on April 1 of the current year. On April 2, the enterprise paid $9,600 to the city for taxes (license fees) for the next 12 months, and debited the prepaid taxes account. The same enterprise is also required to pay in January an annual tax (on property) for the previous calendar year. The estimated amount of the property tax for the current year is $9,950. (a) Journalize the two adjusting entries required to bring the accounts affected by the two taxes up to date as of December 31, the end of the current year. (b) What is the amount of tax expense for the current year?

Exercise 3–4
Adjusting entries for supplies and depreciation.
OBJ. 3

The balance in the supplies account, before adjustment at the end of the year, is $2,750. The inventory of supplies at the end of the year was determined to be $600. The estimated depreciation on equipment used during the year is $1,600. Journalize the adjusting entries required at the end of the year to recognize (a) supplies used during the year and (b) depreciation expense for the year.

Exercise 3–5
Adjusting entries for depreciation; effect of error.
OBJ. 3

On December 31, a business enterprise estimates depreciation on equipment used during the first year of operations to be $3,200. (a) Journalize the adjusting entry required as of December 31. (b) If the adjusting entry in (a) were omitted, which items would be erroneously stated on (1) the income statement for the year and (2) the balance sheet as of December 31?

Exercise 3–6
Statement of owner's equity.
OBJ. 5

Selected accounts from the ledger of L. E. Pruitt Company, for the current fiscal year ended December 31, are as follows:

Lisa E. Pruitt, Capital				Lisa E. Pruitt, Drawing		
Dec. 31	48,000	Jan. 1	87,750	Mar. 31	12,000	Dec. 31 48,000
		Dec. 31	43,250	June 30	12,000	
				Sept. 30	12,000	
				Dec. 31	12,000	

Income Summary			
Dec. 31	569,650	Dec. 31	612,900
31	43,250		

Prepare a statement of owner's equity for the year.

Exercise 3–7
Balance sheet for sole proprietorship.
OBJ. 5

After all of the accounts have been closed on June 30, the end of the current fiscal year, the balances of selected accounts from the ledger of Bards Company are as follows:

Accounts Payable	$ 9,250
Accounts Receivable	9,920
Accumulated Depreciation — Equipment	21,100
Cash	6,150
Equipment	57,600
Prepaid Insurance	3,100
Prepaid Rent	2,400
Salaries Payable	2,750
Supplies	4,750
Robert Bards, Capital	50,820

Prepare a balance sheet in report form.

Exercise 3–8
Retained earnings statement.
OBJ. 5

Selected accounts from the ledger of Bennett-Hill Inc., for the current fiscal year ended June 30, 1991, are as follows:

Capital Stock				Dividends		
		July 1	200,000	Aug. 1	8,000	June 30 36,000
				Nov. 1	8,000	
				Feb. 1	10,000	
				May 1	10,000	

Retained Earnings				Income Summary		
June 30	36,000	July 1	94,500	June 30	808,300	June 30 851,150
		June 30	42,850	30	42,850	

Prepare a retained earnings statement for the year.

Exercise 3–9
Closing entries for
sole proprietorship.
OBJ. 7

After all revenue and expense accounts have been closed at the end of the fiscal year, Income Summary has a debit of $845,500 and a credit of $917,500. As of the same date, Betty Moxley, Capital has a credit balance of $182,200, and Betty Moxley, Drawing has a balance of $48,000. (a) Journalize the entries required to complete the closing of the accounts. (b) State the amount of Moxley's capital at the end of the period.

Exercise 3–10
Closing entries for
corporation.
OBJ. 7

After all revenue and expense accounts have been closed at the end of the fiscal year, Income Summary has a debit of $992,150 and a credit of $980,000. As of the same date, Retained Earnings has a credit balance of $245,750, and Dividends has a balance of $25,000. (a) Journalize the entries required to complete the closing of the accounts. (b) State the amount of Retained Earnings at the end of the period.

PROBLEMS

Series A

Problem 3–1A
Work sheet and
related items for
sole proprietorship.
OBJ. 3, 4, 5, 6, 7

SPREADSHEET
PROBLEM

The trial balance of Westside Laundromat at July 31, 1991, the end of the current fiscal year, and the data needed to determine year-end adjustments are as follows:

Westside Laundromat
Trial Balance
July 31, 1991

Cash..	7,790	
Laundry Supplies..	4,750	
Prepaid Insurance...	2,825	
Laundry Equipment...	85,600	
Accumulated Depreciation.......................................		55,700
Accounts Payable...		4,950
Ana Perez, Capital..		30,900
Ana Perez, Drawing...	18,000	
Laundry Revenue..		76,900
Wages Expense..	24,500	
Rent Expense...	15,575	
Utilities Expense...	8,500	
Miscellaneous Expense...	910	
	168,450	168,450

Adjustment data:

(a) Inventory of laundry supplies at July 31	$1,840
(b) Insurance premiums expired during the year................................	1,500
(c) Depreciation on equipment during the year.................................	5,720
(d) Wages accrued but not paid at July 31	850

Instructions:

(1) Record the trial balance on a ten-column work sheet and complete the work sheet.
(2) Prepare an income statement, a statement of owner's equity (no additional investments were made during the year), and a balance sheet.
(3) On the basis of the adjustment data in the work sheet, journalize the adjusting entries.
(4) On the basis of the data in the work sheet, journalize the closing entries.

Problem 3–2A
Adjusting and
closing entries;
statement of
owner's equity.

OBJ. 3, 5, 6, 7

SPREADSHEET
PROBLEM

As of December 31, the end of the current fiscal year, the accountant for Buchanan Company prepared a trial balance, journalized and posted the adjusting entries, prepared an adjusted trial balance, prepared the statements, and completed the other procedures required at the end of the accounting cycle. The two trial balances as of December 31, one before adjustments and the other after adjustments, are as follows:

Buchanan Company
Trial Balance
December 31, 19--

	Unadjusted		Adjusted	
Cash	19,750		19,750	
Supplies	9,880		3,460	
Prepaid Rent	10,400		800	
Prepaid Insurance	2,700		700	
Land	47,500		47,500	
Buildings	118,000		118,000	
Accumulated Depreciation — Buildings		79,600		84,400
Trucks	72,000		72,000	
Accumulated Depreciation — Trucks		32,800		50,900
Accounts Payable		8,920		9,520
Salaries Payable		—		1,450
Taxes Payable		—		920
John Buchanan, Capital		101,390		101,390
John Buchanan, Drawing	24,000		24,000	
Service Fees Earned		170,680		170,680
Salary Expense	81,200		82,650	
Depreciation Expense — Trucks	—		18,100	
Rent Expense	—		9,600	
Supplies Expense	—		6,420	
Utilities Expense	6,200		6,800	
Depreciation Expense — Buildings	—		4,800	
Taxes Expense	800		1,720	
Insurance Expense	—		2,000	
Miscellaneous Expense	960		960	
	393,390	393,390	419,260	419,260

Instructions:

(1) Present the eight journal entries that were required to adjust the accounts at December 31. None of the accounts was affected by more than one adjusting entry.
(2) Present the journal entries that were required to close the accounts at December 31.
(3) Prepare a statement of owner's equity for the fiscal year ended December 31. There were no additional investments during the year.

If the working papers correlating with this textbook are not used, omit Problem 3–3A.

Problem 3–3A
Ledger accounts,
work sheet, and
related items for
sole proprietorship.

OBJ. 3, 4, 5, 6, 7

The ledger and trial balance of Eastland Household Services as of July 31, 1991, the end of the first month of its current fiscal year, are presented in the working papers.

Instructions:

(1) Complete the ten-column work sheet. Data needed to determine the necessary adjusting entries are as follows:

Inventory of supplies at July 31	$590.00
Insurance premiums expired during July.........................	95.00
Depreciation on the building during July	125.00
Depreciation on equipment during July............................	140.00
Wages accrued but not paid at July 31............................	975.00

(2) Prepare an income statement, a statement of owner's equity, and a balance sheet. (Note: The owner made an additional investment during the period.)

(3) Journalize and post the adjusting entries, inserting balances in the accounts affected.

(4) Journalize and post the closing entries. Indicate closed accounts by inserting a line in both Balance columns opposite the closing entry. Insert the new balance of the capital account.

(5) Prepare a post-closing trial balance.

Problem 3–4A

Ledger accounts, work sheet, and related items for sole proprietorship.

OBJ. 3, 4, 5, 6, 7

SOLUTIONS SOFTWARE

The trial balance of Lopez Machine Repairs at December 31, 1991, the end of the current year, and the data needed to determine year-end adjustments are as follows:

Lopez Machine Repairs
Trial Balance
December 31, 1991

Cash..	7,525	
Supplies..	4,870	
Prepaid Insurance...	1,950	
Equipment...	31,500	
Accumulated Depreciation — Equipment..............................		9,750
Trucks..	42,000	
Accumulated Depreciation — Trucks...................................		26,400
Accounts Payable...		4,015
Al Lopez, Capital		25,800
Al Lopez, Drawing...	18,000	
Service Revenue...		99,950
Wages Expense..	37,925	
Rent Expense..	9,600	
Truck Expense...	9,350	
Miscellaneous Expense..	3,195	
	165,915	165,915

Adjustment data:

(a) Inventory of supplies at December 31	$ 910
(b) Insurance premiums expired during year.......................	1,050
(c) Depreciation on equipment during year.........................	5,380
(d) Depreciation on truck during year...............................	6,200
(e) Wages accrued but not paid at December 31.................	700

Instructions:

(1) Open a ledger of four-column accounts, using the following account titles and numbers: Cash, 11; Supplies, 13; Prepaid Insurance, 14; Equipment, 16; Accumulated Depreciation — Equipment, 17; Trucks, 18; Accumulated Depreciation — Trucks, 19; Accounts Payable, 21; Wages Payable, 22; Al Lopez, Capital, 31; Al Lopez, Drawing, 32; Income Summary, 33; Service Revenue, 41; Wages Expense, 51; Supplies Expense, 52; Rent Expense, 53; Depreciation Expense — Equipment, 54; Truck Expense, 55; Depreciation Expense — Trucks, 56; Insurance Expense, 57; Miscellaneous Expense, 59.

(2) For the accounts listed in the trial balance, enter the balances in the appropriate balance columns and place a check mark (√) in the posting reference column.
(3) Record the trial balance on a ten-column work sheet and complete the work sheet.
(4) Prepare an income statement, statement of changes in owner's equity (no additional investments were made during the year), and a balance sheet.
(5) Journalize and post the adjusting entries, inserting balances in the accounts affected.
(6) Journalize and post the closing entries. Indicate closed accounts by inserting a line in both Balance columns opposite the closing entry. Insert the new balance of the capital account.
(7) Prepare a post-closing trial balance.

Problem 3–5A
Work sheet and statements for corporation.
OBJ. 4, 5

Berkshire Bowl Inc. prepared the following trial balance at June 30, 1991, the end of the current fiscal year:

Berkshire Bowl Inc.
Trial Balance
June 30, 1991

Cash	13,700	
Prepaid Insurance	3,400	
Supplies	1,950	
Land	50,000	
Building	137,500	
Accumulated Depreciation — Building		51,700
Equipment	90,100	
Accumulated Depreciation — Equipment		35,300
Accounts Payable		7,500
Capital Stock		100,000
Retained Earnings		66,700
Dividends	20,000	
Bowling Revenue		198,400
Salaries and Wages Expense	80,200	
Utilities Expense	28,200	
Advertising Expense	19,000	
Repairs Expense	11,500	
Miscellaneous Expense	4,050	
	459,600	459,600

The data needed to determine year-end adjustments are as follows:

(a) Insurance expired during the year $2,700
(b) Inventory of supplies at June 30 450
(c) Depreciation of building for the year 1,620
(d) Depreciation of equipment for the year 5,500
(e) Accrued salaries and wages at June 30 2,000

Instructions:

(1) Record the trial balance on a ten-column work sheet and complete the work sheet.
(2) Prepare an income statement for the year ended June 30.
(3) Prepare a retained earnings statement for the year ended June 30.
(4) Prepare a balance sheet as of June 30.
(5) Compute the percent of net income to revenue for the year.
(6) Compute the percent of net income for the year ended June 30 to total stockholders' equity as of the beginning of the fiscal year. The capital stock account remained unchanged during the year.

Series B

Problem 3–1B
Work sheet and
related items for
sole proprietorship.

OBJ. 3, 4, 5, 6, 7

The trial balance of Parkview Coin Laundry at October 31, 1991, the end of the current fiscal year, and the data needed to determine year-end adjustments are as follows:

Parkview Coin Laundry
Trial Balance
October 31, 1991

Cash..	9,950	
Laundry Supplies...	7,200	
Prepaid Insurance..	2,750	
Laundry Equipment..	72,500	
Accumulated Depreciation..		37,100
Accounts Payable..		6,100
Jane Powers, Capital...		26,500
Jane Powers, Drawing...	18,000	
Laundry Revenue...		151,800
Wages Expense..	50,150	
Rent Expense..	36,000	
Utilities Expense..	22,250	
Miscellaneous Expense..	2,700	
	221,500	221,500

Adjustment data:

(a)	Inventory of laundry supplies at October 31	$1,600
(b)	Insurance premiums expired during the year.................	1,800
(c)	Depreciation on equipment during the year...................	7,700
(d)	Wages accrued but not paid at October 31...................	1,750

Instructions:

(1) Record the trial balance on a ten-column work sheet and complete the work sheet.
(2) Prepare an income statement, a statement of owner's equity (no additional invest- ments were made during the year), and a balance sheet.
(3) On the basis of the adjustment data in the work sheet, journalize the adjusting entries.
(4) On the basis of the data in the work sheet, journalize the closing entries.

Problem 3–2B
Adjusting and
closing entries;
statement of
owner's equity.

OBJ. 3, 5, 6, 7

As of June 30, 1991, the end of the current fiscal year, the accountant for Fidelity Com- pany prepared a trial balance, journalized and posted the adjusting entries, pre- pared an adjusted trial balance, prepared the statements, and completed the other procedures required at the end of the accounting cycle. The two trial balances as of June 30, one before adjustments and the other after adjustments, are shown on page 134.

Instructions:

(1) Present the eight journal entries that were required to adjust the accounts at June 30. None of the accounts was affected by more than one adjusting entry.
(2) Present the journal entries that were required to close the accounts at June 30.
(3) Prepare a statement of owner's equity for the fiscal year ended June 30, 1991. There were no additional investments during the year.

Fidelity Company
Trial Balance
June 30, 1991

	Unadjusted		Adjusted	
Cash..................................	12,825		12,825	
Supplies.............................	8,950		3,635	
Prepaid Rent.......................	19,500		1,500	
Prepaid Insurance................	3,750		1,250	
Equipment..........................	92,150		92,150	
Accumulated Depreciation — Equipment...		53,480		66,270
Automobiles........................	56,500		56,500	
Accumulated Depreciation — Automobiles		28,250		36,900
Accounts Payable.................		8,310		8,730
Salaries Payable..................		—		3,400
Taxes Payable.....................		—		1,225
Mary Hoover, Capital.............		41,245		41,245
Mary Hoover, Drawing...........	18,600		18,600	
Service Fees Earned.............		261,200		261,200
Salary Expense....................	172,300		175,700	
Rent Expense......................	—		18,000	
Supplies Expense.................	—		5,315	
Depreciation Expense — Equipment.......	—		12,790	
Depreciation Expense — Automobiles.....	—		8,650	
Utilities Expense..................	4,700		5,120	
Taxes Expense....................	1,500		2,725	
Insurance Expense...............	—		2,500	
Miscellaneous Expense.........	1,710		1,710	
	392,485	392,485	418,970	418,970

If the working papers correlating with this textbook are not used, omit Problem 3–3B.

Problem 3–3B

Ledger accounts, work sheet, and related items for sole proprietorship.

OBJ. 3, 4, 5, 6, 7

SOLUTIONS SOFTWARE

The ledger and trial balance of Eastland Household Services as of July 31, 1991, the end of the first month of its current fiscal year, are presented in the working papers.

Instructions:

(1) Complete the ten-column work sheet. Data needed to determine the necessary adjusting entries are as follows:

Inventory of supplies at July 31	$900.00
Insurance premiums expired during July....................................	80.10
Depreciation on the building during July....................................	125.00
Depreciation on equipment during July......................................	95.00
Wages accrued but not paid at July 31	250.00

(2) Prepare an income statement, a statement of owner's equity, and a balance sheet. (Note: The owner made an additional investment during the period.)

(3) Journalize and post the adjusting entries, inserting balances in the accounts affected.

(4) Journalize and post the closing entries. Indicate closed accounts by inserting a line in both Balance columns opposite the closing entry. Insert the new balance of the capital account.

(5) Prepare a post-closing trial balance.

MINI-CASE 3

Assume that you recently accepted a position with the American National Bank as an assistant loan officer. As one of your first duties, you have been assigned the responsibility of evaluating a loan request for $100,000 from Antipest, a small sole proprietorship. In support of the loan application, Don Shuman, owner, submitted the following "Statement of Accounts" (trial balance) for the first year of operations ended December 31, 1990:

Antipest
Statement of Accounts
December 31, 1990

Cash	5,765	
Billings Due from Others	10,835	
Supplies (chemicals, etc.)	20,930	
Trucks	45,850	
Equipment	22,610	
Amounts Owed to Others		6,580
Investment in Business		66,500
Service Revenue		136,710
Wages Expense	84,140	
Utilities Expense	9,660	
Rent Expense	6,720	
Insurance Expense	1,960	
Other Expenses	1,320	
	209,790	209,790

Instructions:

(1) Explain to Don Shuman why a set of financial statements (income statement, statement of owner's equity, and a balance sheet) would be useful to you in evaluating the loan request.

(2) In discussing the "Statement of Accounts" with Don Shuman, you discovered that the accounts had not been adjusted at December 31. Through analysis of the "Statement of Accounts," indicate possible adjusting entries that might be necessary before an accurate set of financial statements could be prepared.

(3) Assuming that an accurate set of financial statements will be submitted by Don Shuman in a few days, what other considerations or information would you require before making a decision on the loan request?

ETHICS DISCUSSION CASE

McRee Company's fiscal year ends October 31. During the first week of November, McRee Company's accountant prepared the work sheet for the year ended October 31, 1990. After the financial statements were prepared, the accountant journalized and posted the adjusting and closing entries. The accountant dated the adjusting and closing entries October 31, 1990, even though the entries were actually prepared and entered on November 6, 1990.

Evaluate whether the accountant behaved in an ethical manner by dating the adjusting and closing entries October 31, 1990.

COMPREHENSIVE PROBLEM 1

For the past several years, John Abrams has operated a television repair service in his home on a part-time basis. As of September 1, Abrams decided to move to rented quarters and to devote full time to the business, which was to be known as A-1 TV. A-1 TV entered into the following transactions during September:

Sept. 1. The following assets were received from John Abrams: cash, $7,500; accounts receivable, $900; supplies, $1,250; and service equipment, $11,000. There were no liabilities received.
   1. Paid three months' rent on a lease rental contract, $2,250.
   2. Paid the premiums on property and casualty insurance policies, $1,740.
   4. Purchased additional service equipment on account from Halsted Company, $2,500.
   6. Received cash from customers on account, $500.
   9. Paid cash for a newspaper advertisement, $110.
   11. Paid Halsted Company for part of the debt incurred on September 4, $1,250.
   12. Recorded sales on account for the period September 1–12, $1,000.
   13. Paid receptionist for two weeks' salary, $500.
   17. Recorded cash from cash customers for service revenue earned during the first half of September, $1,100.
   17. Paid cash for supplies, $950.
   20. Recorded sales on account for the period September 13–20, $700.
   24. Recorded cash from cash customers for service revenue earned for the period September 17–24, $1,850.
   27. Received cash from customers on account, $1,200.
   27. Paid receptionist for two weeks' salary, $500.
   30. Paid telephone bill for September, $75.
   30. Paid electricity bill for September, $140.
   30. Recorded cash from cash customers for service revenue earned for the period September 25–30, $950.
   30. Recorded sales on account for the remainder of September, $800.
   30. Abrams withdrew $1,500 for personal use.

Instructions:

(1) Open a ledger of four-column accounts for A-1 TV, using the following titles and account numbers: Cash, 11; Accounts Receivable, 12; Supplies, 14; Prepaid Rent, 15; Prepaid Insurance, 16; Service Equipment, 18; Accumulated Depreciation, 19; Accounts Payable, 21; Salaries Payable, 22; John Abrams, Capital, 31; John Abrams, Drawing, 32; Income Summary, 33; Service Revenue, 41; Salary Expense, 51; Rent Expense, 52; Supplies Expense, 53; Depreciation Expense, 54; Insurance Expense, 55; Miscellaneous Expense, 59.
(2) Record the transactions in a two-column journal.
(3) Post the journal to the ledger, extending the month-end balances to the appropriate balance columns after all posting is completed.
(4) Prepare a trial balance as of September 30, on a ten-column work sheet, listing all the accounts in the order given in the ledger. Complete the work sheet, using the following adjustment data:

(a) Insurance expired during September	$ 145
(b) Inventory of supplies on September 30	1,520
(c) Depreciation of store equipment for September	200
(d) Accrued receptionist salary on September 30	100
(e) Rent expired during September	750

(Continued)

(5) Prepare an income statement, a statement of owner's equity, and a balance sheet.
(6) Journalize and post the adjusting entries.
(7) Journalize and post the closing entries. Indicate closed accounts by inserting a line in both Balance columns opposite the closing entry. Insert the new balance in the capital account.
(8) Prepare a post-closing trial balance.

ANSWERS TO SELF-EXAMINATION QUESTIONS

1. D The balance in the supplies account, before adjustment, represents the amount of supplies available. From this amount ($2,250) is subtracted the amount of supplies on hand ($950) to determine the supplies used ($1,300). Since increases in expense accounts are recorded by debits and decreases in asset accounts are recorded by credits, answer D is the correct entry.

2. C Since increases in expense accounts (such as depreciation expense) are recorded by debits and it is customary to record the decreases in usefulness of plant assets as credits to accumulated depreciation accounts, answer C is the correct entry.

3. D The book value of a plant asset is the difference between the balance in the asset account and the balance in the related accumulated depreciation account, or $22,500 − $14,000, as indicated by answer D ($8,500).

4. C Since all revenue and expense accounts are closed at the end of the period, both Sales (revenue) and Salary Expense (expense) would be closed to Income Summary (answer C).

5. A Since the post-closing trial balance includes only balance sheet accounts (all of the revenue, expense, and drawing accounts have been previously closed), Cash (answer A) would appear on the trial balance. Both Sales (answer B) and Salary Expense (answer C) are temporary accounts that are closed prior to the preparation of the post-closing trial balance.

CHAPTER FOUR

ACCOUNTING FOR A MERCHANDISING ENTERPRISE

CHAPTER OBJECTIVES

1 Describe and illustrate the accounting for merchandising transactions, including:
  a Purchases of merchandise
  b Sales of merchandise
  c Transportation costs
  d Sales taxes

2 Describe the sequence of year-end procedures for a merchandising enterprise.

3 Describe two merchandise inventory systems.

4 Describe and illustrate the cost of merchandise sold section of an income statement.

5 Describe and illustrate the journal entries for merchandise inventory adjustments at year end.

6 Describe and illustrate the adjustments for deferrals and accruals at year end.

7 Describe and illustrate the preparation and completion of a work sheet for a merchandising enterprise.

Merchandising enterprises acquire merchandise for resale to customers. It is the selling of merchandise, instead of a service, that makes the activities of merchandising enterprises differ from the activities of service enterprises. This chapter focuses on the accounting principles and concepts that are unique to merchandising enterprises—accounting for transactions between the buyers and sellers of merchandise. In addition, the necessary year-end adjustments and the work sheet for a merchandising enterprise are presented.

Although the procedures described are commonly used by merchandising enterprises, these procedures may vary from business to business. For example, purchases and sales may be made for cash or on credit (on account), and many different arrangements may be made for making payments on account. In addition, policies for the return of merchandise and for the payment of transportation costs may be different.

ACCOUNTING FOR PURCHASES

OBJECTIVE 1a
Describe and illustrate the accounting for purchases of merchandise.

Purchases of merchandise are usually identified in the ledger as *Purchases*. A more exact account title, such as "Purchases of Merchandise," could be used, but the briefer title is customarily used. Thus a merchandising enterprise can accumulate in the purchases account the cost of all merchandise purchased for resale during the accounting period.

When purchases are made for cash, the transaction could be recorded as follows:

Beg9g *Inventory-supplies*

Jan. 3	Purchases..	510	
	Cash...		510
	Purchases from supplier, Bowen Co.		

Most purchases of merchandise are made on account and could be recorded as follows:

Jan. 4	Purchases..	925	
	Accounts Payable		925
	Purchases from supplier,		
	Thomas Corporation.		

Purchases Discounts

The arrangements agreed upon by the buyer and the seller as to when payments for merchandise are to be made are called the **credit terms**. If payment is required immediately upon delivery, the terms are said to be "cash" or "net cash." Otherwise, the buyer is allowed a certain amount of time, known as the **credit period**, in which to pay.

It is usual for the credit period to begin with the date of the sale as shown by the date of the **invoice** or **bill**. If payment is due within a stated number of days after the date of the invoice, for example 30 days, the terms are said to be "net 30 days," which may be written as "n/30."[1] If payment is due by the end of the month in which the sale was made, it may be expressed as "n/eom."

As a means of encouraging payment before the end of the credit period, the seller may offer a discount for the early payment of cash. Thus the expression "2/10, n/30" means that, although the credit period is 30 days, the buyer may deduct 2% of the amount of the invoice if payment is made within 10 days of the invoice date. This deduction is known as a **cash discount**. The essentials of credit terms of 2/10, n/30 are summarized in the following diagram:

Credit Terms

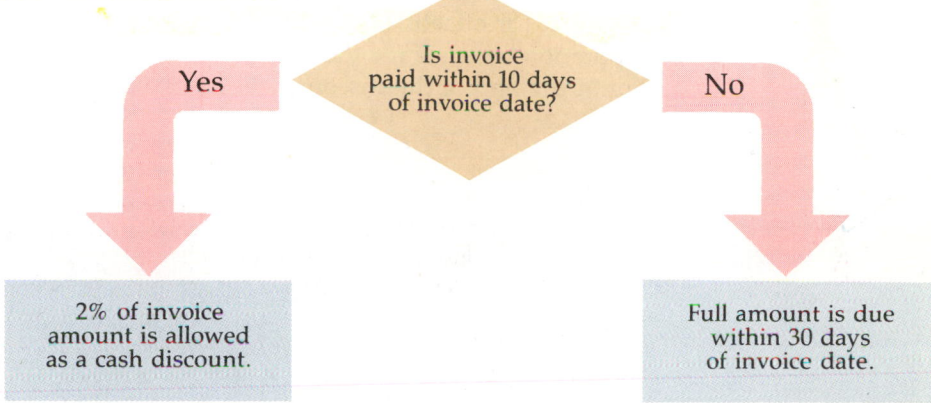

---

[1] The word "net" in this context does not have the usual meaning of a remainder after all relevant deductions have been subtracted, as in "net income," for example.

From the buyer's standpoint, it is important to take advantage of all available discounts, even though it may be necessary to borrow the money to make the payment. To illustrate, assume that the following invoice for $1,500 is received by Valley Electric Corporation:

Invoice

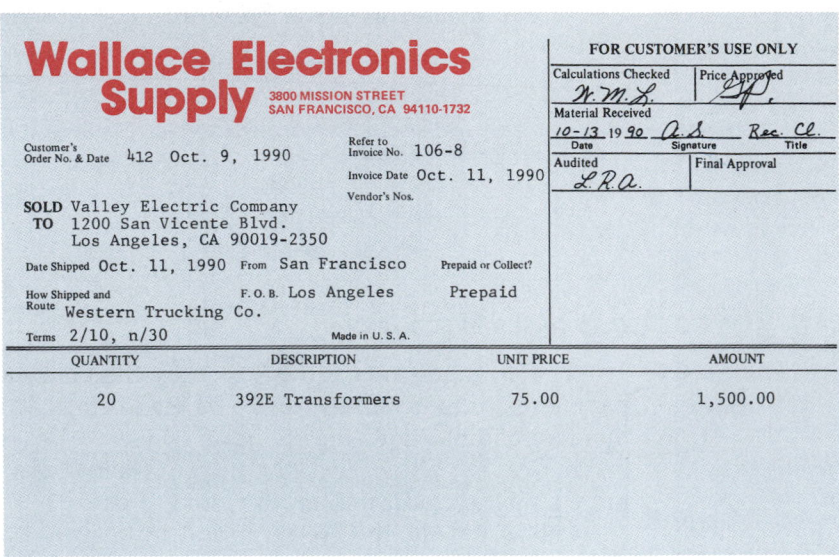

The invoice, with terms of 2/10, n/30, is to be paid within the discount period with money borrowed for the remaining 20 days of the credit period. If an annual interest rate of 12% is assumed, the net savings to the buyer is $20.20, determined as follows:

Discount of 2% on $1,500	$30.00
Interest for 20 days at rate of 12% on $1,470 ($1,500 − $30)	9.80
Savings effected by borrowing	$20.20

Discounts taken by the buyer for early payment of an invoice are called **purchases discounts**. They are recorded by crediting the purchases discounts account and are usually viewed as a deduction from the amount initially recorded in Purchases. In this sense, the purchases discounts account is a contra (or offsetting) account to Purchases. To illustrate, Valley Electric Corporation's entries for the purchase invoice presented above and its payment at the end of the discount period could be recorded as follows:

Oct. 11	Purchases...	1,500	
	Accounts Payable..............................		1,500
	Invoice 106-8 from Wallace Electronics Supply.		
Oct. 21	Accounts Payable.................................	1,500	
	Cash...		1,470
	Purchases Discounts............................		30
	Invoice 106-8 from Wallace Electronics Supply.		

Purchases Returns and Allowances

When merchandise is returned (purchases return) or a price adjustment (purchases allowance) is requested, the buyer usually communicates with the seller in writing. The details may be stated in a letter, or the buyer (debtor) may use a debit memorandum form. This form, illustrated as follows, is a convenient medium for informing the seller (creditor) of the amount the buyer proposes to debit to the accounts payable account. It also states the reasons for the return or request for a price reduction.

Debit Memorandum

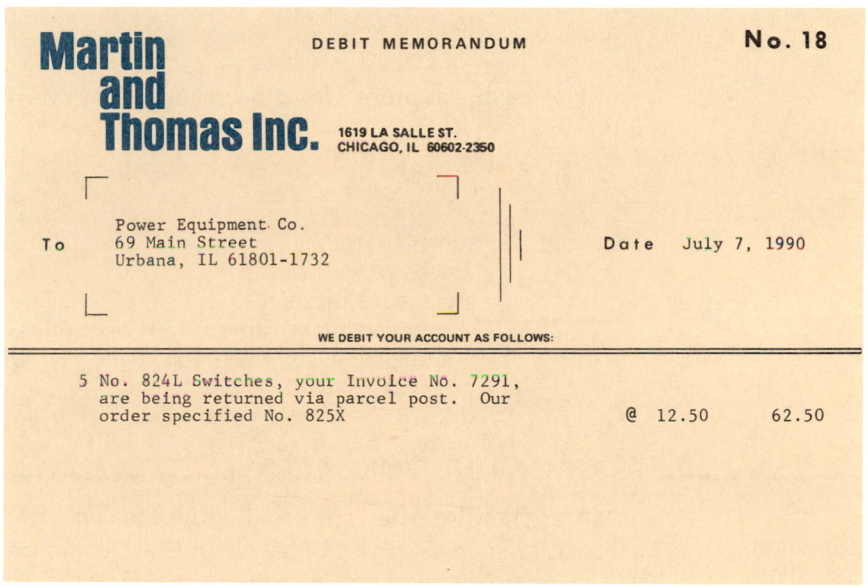

credit memo –
Debit Accts. Payable
credit Purchases Return & Allowances

The debtor may use a copy of the debit memorandum as the basis for an entry or may wait for confirmation from the creditor, which is usually in the form of a credit memorandum. In either event, Accounts Payable must be debited and Purchases Returns and Allowances must be credited.[2] The purchases returns and allowances account can be viewed as a deduction from the amount initially recorded in Purchases. In this sense, like Purchases Discounts, the purchases returns and allowances account is a contra (or offsetting) account to Purchases. To illustrate, the entry by Martin and Thomas Inc. to record the return of the merchandise identified in the debit memo above would be as follows:

July 7	Accounts Payable.................................	62.50	
	Purchases Returns and Allowances........		62.50
	Debit Memo No. 18.		

[2]Many businesses credit the purchases returns and allowances account for merchandise returned and allowances granted. However, some businesses prefer to credit the purchases account. If this alternative is used, the balance of the purchases account will be a net amount—the total purchases less the total returns and allowances for the period.

When a buyer returns merchandise or has been granted an allowance prior to the payment of the invoice, the amount of the debit memorandum is deducted from the invoice amount before the purchases discount is computed. For example, assume that the details related to the amount payable to Power Equipment Co., for which the debit memo illustrated above was issued, are as follows:

Invoice No. 7291 dated July 1 (terms 2/10, n/30)......................	$2,045.00
Debit Memo No. 18 dated July 7	62.50
Balance of account	$1,982.50
Discount (2% of $1,982.50)...	39.65
Cash payment, July 11..	$1,942.85

The cash payment could be recorded by Martin and Thomas Inc. as follows:

July 11	Accounts Payable.................................	1,982.50	
	Cash...		1,942.85
	Purchases Discounts............................		39.65
	Payment of Invoice No. 7291 from Power Equipment Co., less Debit Memo No. 18.		

ACCOUNTING FOR SALES

OBJECTIVE 1b
Describe and illustrate the accounting for sales of merchandise.

Merchandise sales are usually identified in the ledger as *Sales*. A more exact title, such as "Sales of Merchandise," could be used.

A business may sell merchandise for cash. These sales are generally "rung up" on a cash register and totaled at the end of the day. Such sales could be recorded as follows:

Jan. 7	Cash..	1,872.50	
	Sales..		1,872.50
	Cash sales for the day.		

Sales to customers who use bank credit cards (such as MasterCard and VISA) are generally treated as cash sales. The credit card invoices representing these sales are deposited by the seller directly into the bank, along with the currency and checks received from customers. Periodically, the bank charges a service fee for handling these credit card sales. The service fee should be debited to an expense account.

A business may also sell merchandise on account. Such sales result in a debit to Accounts Receivable and a credit to Sales, as illustrated in the following entry:

Jan. 12	Accounts Receivable	510	
	Sales..		510
	Invoice No. 7172 to Sims Co.		

Sales made by the use of nonbank credit cards (such as American Express) generally must be reported periodically to the card company before cash is received. Therefore, such sales create a receivable with the card company. Before the card company remits cash, it normally deducts a service fee. To illustrate, assume that nonbank credit card sales of $1,000 are made and reported to the card company on January 20. On January 27, the company deducts a service fee of $50 and remits $950. The transactions could be recorded as follows:

Jan. 20	Accounts Receivable	1,000	
	Sales...		1,000
	American Express credit sales.		
Jan. 27	Cash...	950	
	Credit Card Collection Expense	50	
	Accounts Receivable		1,000
	Receipt of cash from American Express for sales reported on January 20.		

CREDIT CARDS AND CASH DISCOUNTS

The extensive use of credit cards by the American consumer has led some analysts to predict that the "cashless society" is on the horizon. In an effort to reduce operating costs, however, many businesses have encouraged consumers to use cash rather than credit cards. For example, some oil companies are now offering incentives for their customers to use cash, described as follows in an article that appeared in the *Harvard Business Review*:

...Exxon, Amoco, Sohio, and Mobil have been trying out various ways of offering discounts for cash in lieu of credit card sales. Mobil has lowered its wholesale price while adding a 3% processing fee for credit card sales to induce station managers to favor cash sales. As a result,... Mobil stations [are] offering consumers gasoline at 4 cents a gallon less if they pay cash....

The idea received a boost in the summer of 1981 when Congress passed the Cash Discount Act, permitting businesses to give discounts exceeding 5% to consumers paying cash. Previously, a rebate of more than 5% was considered a finance charge levied against credit card users and was therefore illegal.

The retailer incurs two costs in each credit card transaction: the [collection] fee to convert the charge to cash and the interest expense arising from the time lag between the sale and collection of funds. If, for example, [the retailer's] cost of [funds] is 20%, if an average six days elapse between the sale and the collection of the proceeds, and if the [collector's] fee is 5%, then $10,000 in credit sales are equivalent to $9,472 in cash sales. The retailer could offer a cash discount of 5.3% and still be as well off as with a credit card sale.

Although many retailers might like to reject credit cards altogether because of their expense, up to now they have been ill-advised to take this step unless most of their competitors followed suit. Otherwise, they could suffer a...disadvantage.

The retailer should consider four elements before adopting a discount-for-cash policy:

The reasons why...customers use credit cards. If it's just because they like the convenience of not carrying cash or consider it an advantage to buy now and pay later, they are candidates for a cash discount strategy. If, however, customers need the credit in order to make a purchase, a small cash reduction for cash payment probably would not deter their use of credit cards.

The proportion of [the retailer's] volume made up by cash sales. If the proportion is high, a dis-

count-for-cash policy would give many customers who would have paid cash anyway a "free" deduction. Obviously, the effect on the retailer's earnings would not be healthy.

The cost of implementing the new policy. Computerized cash registers permit programming of a discount. Without electronic cash-handling technology, calculating the rebates could result in

slower checkouts and clerical errors.

...Customers' attitudes toward such an incentive—if [they] can [be ascertained.] If ...competitors have a cash discount policy, the retailer could match this and wait for customer reaction. This "competitive parity" assumes, however, that rivals have determined an optimal discount policy that is applicable to others..."

Source: Michael Levy and Charles A. Ingene, "Retailers: Head off Credit Cards with Cash Discounts?" *Harvard Business Review* (May–June, 1983), pp. 18–22.

Sales Discounts

Sales discounts — debit "sales dis." Acct to offset "Sales" Acct

The seller refers to the discounts taken by the buyer for early payment of an invoice as **sales discounts.** They are recorded by debiting the sales discounts account and are considered to be a reduction in the amount initially recorded in Sales. In this sense, the balance of the sales discounts account is viewed as a contra (or offsetting) account to Sales. To illustrate, if cash is received within the discount period from a previously recorded credit sale of $500, 2/10, n/30, the transaction could be recorded as follows:

June 10	Cash......................................	490	
	Sales Discounts	10	
	Accounts Receivable		500
	Collection on Invoice No. 8722 to		
	Carver Co., less discount.		

Sales Returns and Allowances

debit — Sales Account

Merchandise sold may be returned by the buyer **(sales return)** or, because of defects or for other reasons, the buyer may be allowed a reduction from the original price at which the goods were sold **(sales allowance)**. If the return or allowance is for a sale on account, the seller usually gives the buyer a **credit memorandum**. This memorandum shows the amount for which the buyer is to be credited and the reason therefor. A typical credit memorandum is illustrated at the top of page 145.

The effect of a sales return or allowance is a reduction in sales revenue and a reduction in cash or accounts receivable. If the sales account is debited, however, the balance of the account at the end of the period will represent net sales, and the volume of returns and allowances will not be disclosed. Because of the loss in revenue resulting from allowances, and the various expenses (transportation, unpacking, repairing, reselling, etc.) related to returns, it is advisable that management know the amount of such transactions. Such a policy will allow management to determine the causes of returns and allowances, should they become excessive, and to take corrective action. It is therefore preferable to debit an account entitled Sales Returns and Allowances. If the original sale is on account, the remainder of the transaction is recorded as a credit to Accounts Receivable. Because sales returns and allowances are viewed as reductions of the amount initially recorded in Sales, the sales returns and allowances account is a contra (or

Credit Memorandum

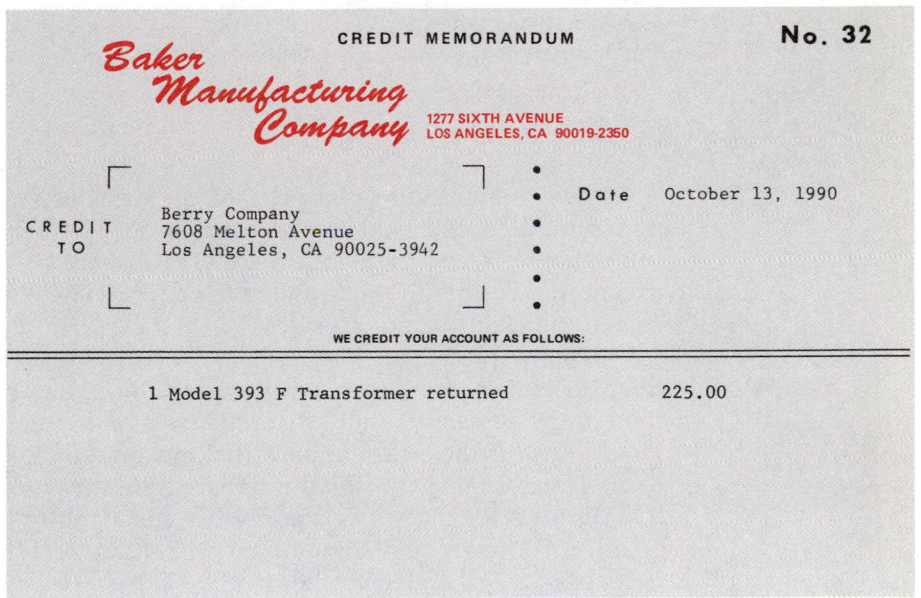

offsetting) account to Sales. To illustrate, the entry made by Baker Manufacturing Company for the credit memo presented above could be recorded as follows:

Oct. 13	Sales Returns and Allowances...................	225	
	Accounts Receivable		225
	Credit Memo No. 32.		

Cash Refund
Debit – "Sales Return & Allowances"
Credit – "Cash"

If a cash refund is made because of merchandise returned or for an allowance, Sales Returns and Allowances is debited and Cash is credited.

TRANSPORTATION COSTS

OBJECTIVE 1c
Describe and illustrate the accounting for transportation costs for merchandise purchases and sales.

The terms of the agreement between buyer and seller include provisions concerning (1) when the ownership (title) of the merchandise passes to the buyer and (2) which party is to bear the cost of delivering the merchandise to the buyer. If the ownership passes to the buyer when the seller delivers the merchandise to the shipper, the buyer is to absorb the transportation costs and the terms are said to be **FOB shipping point**. FOB shipping point means that the seller places the merchandise "free on board" at the shipping point and the buyer is responsible for the transportation costs beyond that point. If ownership passes to the buyer when the merchandise is received by the buyer, the seller is to assume the costs of transportation and the terms are said to be **FOB destination**. FOB destination means that the seller places the merchandise "free on board" to its destination by paying the delivery costs. The relationship of the shipping terms to the passage of ownership and who is to bear the costs of transportation is summarized in the following table:

Shipping Terms	FOB Shipping Point	FOB Destination
Ownership (title) passes to buyer when merchandise is	delivered to shipper	delivered to buyer
Transportation costs are borne by	buyer	seller

When merchandise is purchased on terms of FOB shipping point, the transportation costs paid by the buyer should be debited to Transportation In or Freight In and credited to Cash. The balance of the transportation in or freight in account should be added to net purchases in determining the total cost of merchandise purchased.[3]

In some cases, the seller may prepay the transportation costs and add them to the invoice, as an accommodation or courtesy to the buyer, even though the agreement states that the buyer bear such costs (terms FOB shipping point). If the seller prepays the transportation charges, the buyer will debit Transportation In for the transportation costs. To illustrate, assume that on June 10, Durban Co. purchases merchandise from Bell Corp. on account, $900, terms FOB shipping point, 2/10, n/30, with prepaid transportation costs of $50 added to the invoice. The entry by Durban Co. could be recorded as follows:

June 10	Purchases...	900	
	Transportation In	50	
	Accounts Payable................................		950

When the terms provide for a discount for early payment, the discount is based on the amount of the sale rather than on the invoice total. To illustrate, if Durban Co. pays the amount due on the purchase of June 10 within 10 days, the amount of the discount and the amount of the payment could be determined as follows:

Invoice from Bell Corp., including prepaid transportation of $50		$950
Amount subject to discount	$900	
Rate of discount	2%	
Amount of purchases discount		18
Amount of payment		$932

Durban Co. could record the payment as follows:

June 20	Accounts Payable.................................	950	
	Cash...		932
	Purchases Discounts..........................		18
	Invoice 73B from Bell Corp.		

[3]Some businesses prefer to debit the purchases account for transportation charges paid on merchandise purchased FOB shipping point. If this alternative is used, the balance of the purchases account will include the transportation costs borne by the buyer. The total cost of merchandise purchased will be the same as when a separate transportation in or freight in account is used.

When the seller prepays the transportation costs and the terms are FOB shipping point, as in the illustration above, the seller adds these costs to the invoice that is sent to the buyer. Therefore, the seller records the payment of the transportation costs by debiting Accounts Receivable. In the illustration above, for example, Bell Corp. records the following entry on June 10, in addition to the entry to record the sale to Durban Co.:

| June 10 | Accounts Receivable .... | 50 | |
| | Cash .... | | 50 |

When the agreement states that the seller is to bear the delivery costs (FOB destination), the amounts paid by the seller for delivery are debited to Transportation Out, Delivery Expense, or a similarly titled account. The total of such costs incurred during a period is reported on the seller's income statement as a selling expense.

SALES TAXES

OBJECTIVE 1d Describe and illustrate the accounting for sales taxes on merchandise purchases and sales.

Almost all states and many other taxing units levy a tax on sales of merchandise. The liability for the sales tax is ordinarily incurred at the time the sale is made, regardless of the terms of the sale.

Sales Tax for Seller

At the time of a cash sale, the seller collects the sales tax. When a sale is made on account, the buyer is charged for the tax. The seller credits the sales account for only the amount of the sale, and credits the tax to Sales Tax Payable. For example, a sale of $100 on account, subject to a tax of 4%, could be recorded by the following entry:

Aug. 12	Accounts Receivable	104	
	Sales		100
	Sales Tax Payable		4
	Invoice No. 339.		

Periodically, the appropriate amount of the sales tax is paid to the taxing unit, and Sales Tax Payable is debited.

Sales Tax for Buyer

The buyer debits the purchases account for the full amount of the merchandise acquired, including the sales tax. For example, a purchase of $100 on account, subject to a tax of 4%, could be recorded by the following entry:

Aug. 12	Purchases	104	
	Accounts Payable		104
	Invoice No. 339.		

PERIODIC REPORTING FOR MERCHANDISING ENTERPRISES

At yearly intervals throughout the life of a business enterprise, the operating data for the fiscal year must be summarized and reported for the use of managers, owners, creditors, various governmental agencies, and other interested persons. Summaries of the various assets of the enterprise on the last day of the fiscal year, together with the status of the equities of creditors and owners, must also be reported. The ledger, which contains the basic data for the reports, must then be brought up to date through proper adjusting entries. Finally, the accounts must be prepared to receive entries for transactions that will occur in the following year. The sequence of year-end procedures may be changed slightly, but in general the following outline is typical:

1. Prepare a trial balance of the ledger on a work sheet form.
2. Review the accounts and gather the data required for the adjustments.
3. Insert the adjustments and complete the work sheet.
4. Prepare financial statements from the data in the work sheet.
5. Journalize the adjusting entries and post to the ledger.
6. Journalize the closing entries and post to the ledger.
7. Prepare a post-closing trial balance of the ledger.

Although the summarizing and reporting procedures described and illustrated in the remainder of this chapter and in Chapter 5 are similar to those discussed in the preceding chapter, a number of differences should be noted. For the most part these differences relate to the type of business enterprise being discussed. In Chapter 3, the importance of properly matching revenues and expenses for a service enterprise was discussed. In Chapters 4 and 5, the discussion relates to a merchandising enterprise.

In a merchandising business, merchandise purchased during the period has been recorded in the purchases account. Some of this merchandise may have been sold during the period, and some may be unsold at the end of the period (ending inventory). This ending inventory becomes the beginning inventory for the next period. The accounting for this inventory in order to match revenues and expenses properly is discussed in the remainder of the chapter. In addition, an in-depth discussion of the adjustments for prepaid and accrued items and the use of the work sheet in the year-end procedures for a merchandising enterprise are presented.

MERCHANDISE INVENTORY SYSTEMS

There are two main systems for accounting for merchandise held for sale: **periodic** and **perpetual**. Many merchandising enterprises use the periodic system. In this system, the revenues from sales are recorded when sales are made, but no attempt is made on the sales date to record the cost of the merchandise sold. It is only by a detailed listing of the merchandise on hand (called a **physical inventory**) at the end of the accounting period that a determination is made of (1) the cost of the merchandise sold during the period and (2) the cost of the inventory on hand at the end of the period. The periodic system is used in illustrations in this chapter.

Under the perpetual system, both the sales amount and the cost of merchandise sold amount are recorded when each item of merchandise is sold. In this manner, the accounting records continuously (perpetually) disclose the inventory on hand. The perpetual system is discussed in later chapters.

COST OF MERCHANDISE SOLD

OBJECTIVE 4
Describe and illustrate the cost of merchandise sold section of an income statement.

For merchandising enterprises that use the periodic system, the cost of merchandise sold during a period is reported in a separate section in the income statement. To illustrate, assume that Cox Co. began its business operations on January 3, 1989, and purchased $340,000 of merchandise during the year. If the inventory at December 31, 1989, the end of the year, is **$59,700**, the cost of merchandise sold during 1989 would be reported as follows:

Cost of Merchandise Sold—Ending Inventory but No Beginning Inventory

Cost of merchandise sold:	
Purchases	$340,000
Less merchandise inventory, December 31, 1989	59,700
Cost of merchandise sold	$280,300

To continue the illustration, assume that during 1990 Cox Co. purchases additional merchandise of $521,980, receives credit for purchases returns and allowances of $9,100, takes purchases discounts of $2,525, and pays transportation costs of $17,400. The purchases returns and allowances and the purchases discounts are deducted from the total purchases to yield the **net purchases**, and the transportation costs are added to the net purchases to yield the **cost of merchandise purchased**. These amounts would be reported in the cost of merchandise sold section of Cox Co.'s income statement for 1990 as follows:

Purchases		$521,980
Less: Purchases returns and allowances	$9,100	
Purchases discounts	2,525	11,625
Net purchases		$510,355
Add transportation in		17,400
Cost of merchandise purchased		$527,755

The ending inventory of Cox Co. on December 31, 1989, **$59,700**, becomes the beginning inventory for 1990. In the cost of merchandise sold section of the income statement for 1990, this beginning inventory is added to the cost of merchandise purchased to yield the **merchandise available for sale**. The ending inventory, which is assumed to be **$62,150**, is then subtracted from the merchandise available for sale to yield the cost of merchandise sold. The cost of merchandise sold during 1990 would be reported as follows:

Cost of Merchandise Sold—Beginning and Ending Inventories

Cost of merchandise sold:			
Merchandise inventory, January 1, 1990			$ 59,700
Purchases		$521,980	
Less: Purchases returns and allowances	$9,100		
Purchases discounts	2,525	11,625	
Net purchases		$510,355	
Add transportation in		17,400	
Cost of merchandise purchased			527,755
Merchandise available for sale			$587,455
Less merchandise inventory, December 31, 1990			62,150
Cost of merchandise sold			$525,305

MERCHANDISE INVENTORY ADJUSTMENTS

OBJECTIVE 5
Describe and
illustrate the
journal entries
for merchandise
inventory
adjustments
at year end.

The best method of making the data readily available for reporting the cost of merchandise sold is to maintain a separate account entitled Merchandise Inventory. Throughout an accounting period, this account shows the inventory at the beginning of the period. Purchases of merchandise during the period are then debited to the account entitled Purchases. As explained previously, returns and allowances are recorded in the purchases returns and allowances account. Cash discounts are recorded in a purchases discounts account, and transportation costs are recorded in the transportation in account.

At the end of the period it is necessary to remove from Merchandise Inventory the amount representing the inventory at the beginning of the period and to replace it with the amount representing the inventory at the end of the period. This is accomplished by two adjusting entries.[4] The first entry transfers the beginning inventory to Income Summary. Since this beginning inventory is part of the cost of merchandise sold, it is debited to Income Summary. It is also a subtraction from the asset account, Merchandise Inventory, and hence is credited to that account. Continuing with the illustration for Cox Co. from the preceding section, the first adjusting entry for the beginning inventory of $59,700 at January 1, 1990, would be as follows:

| Dec. 31 | Income Summary .... | 59,700 | |
| | Merchandise Inventory .... | | 59,700 |

The second adjusting entry debits the cost of the merchandise inventory at the end of the period to the asset account, Merchandise Inventory. The credit portion of the entry effects a deduction of the unsold merchandise from the total cost of the merchandise available for sale during the period. In terms of the illustration of the partial income statement above for Cox Co., the credit portion of the second entry accomplishes the subtraction of $62,150 from $587,455 to yield the $525,305 cost of merchandise sold. The second adjusting entry is as follows:

| Dec. 31 | Merchandise Inventory .... | 62,150 | |
| | Income Summary .... | | 62,150 |

The effect of the two inventory adjustments is indicated by the following T accounts for Merchandise Inventory and Income Summary:

Merchandise Inventory

| Dec. 31 Preceding year | 59,700 | Dec. 31 Current year | 59,700 |
| Dec. 31 Current year | 62,150 | | |

Income Summary

| Dec. 31 Current year | 59,700 | Dec. 31 Current year | 62,150 |

---

[4]An alternative method of recording merchandise inventory is presented in Appendix C. This alternative method is sometimes referred to as the closing method.

In the accounts, the inventory of $59,700 at the end of the preceding year (beginning of current year) has been transferred to Income Summary as a part of the cost of merchandise available for sale. It is replaced by a debit of $62,150, the merchandise inventory at the end of the current year. The credit of the same amount to Income Summary is a deduction from the cost of merchandise available for sale.

ADJUSTMENTS FOR DEFERRALS AND ACCRUALS

The use of adjusting entries at the end of the accounting period to match properly the revenues and expenses for the period was first discussed in Chapter 3. Prepaid expenses (deferrals), such as supplies and rent, and accruals of expenses, such as wages, were described and illustrated. A **deferral** is a delay of the recognition of an expense already paid or of a revenue already received. An **accrual** is an expense that has not been paid or a revenue that has not been received. This section further discusses deferrals and accruals of expenses, as well as revenues.

Deferrals and Accruals on the Financial Statements

Deferred expenses expected to benefit a short period of time are listed on the balance sheet among the current assets, where they are called **prepaid expenses**. Long-term prepayments that can be charged to the operations of several years are presented on the balance sheet in a section called **deferred charges**.

Deferred revenues may be listed on the balance sheet as a current liability, where they are called **unearned revenues** or **revenues received in advance**. If a long period of time is involved, they are presented on the balance sheet in a section called **deferred credits**.

Any unrecorded accruals must be recorded before financial statements are prepared. Accrued expenses may be described on the balance sheet as **accrued liabilities**, or reference to the accrual may be omitted from the title, as in "Wages payable." The liabilities for accrued expenses are ordinarily due within a year and are listed as current liabilities.

Accrued revenues may be described on the balance sheet as **accrued assets**, or reference to the accrual may be omitted from the title, as in "Interest receivable" and "Fees receivable." The amounts receivable for accrued revenues are usually due within a short time and are classified as current assets.

Adjusting Entries for Prepaid Expenses (Deferrals)

Prepaid expenses are the costs of goods and services that have been purchased but not used at the end of the accounting period. The portion of the asset that has been used during the period has become an expense; the remainder will not become an expense until some time in the future. Prepaid expenses include such items as prepaid insurance, prepaid rent, prepaid advertising, prepaid interest, and various kinds of supplies.

Insurance premiums or other services or supplies that are used may be debited to asset accounts when purchased, even though all or a part of them are expected to be consumed during the accounting period.[5] The amount actually used is then determined at the end of the period and the accounts ad-

---

[5] The concepts and procedures for recording prepaid expenses initially as expenses are presented in Chapter 6.

justed accordingly. To illustrate, assume that the office supplies account of Cox Co. has a balance of $1,090 at December 31, 1990, the end of the year. This amount represents the cost of office supplies on hand at the beginning of the year and the cost of supplies purchased during the year. If the physical inventory at the end of the year indicated office supplies on hand totaling $480, the cost of the office supplies used during the year is $610 ($1,090 − $480). The adjusting entry to record the $610 decrease of the asset and the corresponding increase in expense is as follows:

	Adjusting Entry		
Dec. 31	Office Supplies Expense..........................	610	
	Office Supplies		610

After the entry has been posted, the office supplies expense account will have a balance of $610 and that amount will be reported as an expense on the income statement. The office supplies account will have a balance of $480 and that amount will be reported as an asset on Cox Co.'s balance sheet.

To illustrate further, assume that the prepaid insurance account for Cox Co. has a balance of $4,560 at December 31, 1990. This amount represents the unexpired insurance at the beginning of the year plus the total of premiums on policies purchased during the year. Assume further that $1,910 of insurance premiums have expired during the year, leaving $2,650 of unexpired premiums ($4,560 − $1,910). The adjusting entry to record the $1,910 decrease of the asset and the corresponding increase in expense is as follows:

	Adjusting Entry		
Dec. 31	Insurance Expense................................	1,910	
	Prepaid Insurance		1,910

After this entry has been posted, the insurance expense account will have a balance of $1,910 and that amount will be reported as an expense on the income statement. The prepaid insurance account balance will be $2,650 and that amount will be reported as an asset on Cox Co.'s balance sheet.

Adjusting Entries for Unearned Revenues (Deferrals)

Revenue received during a particular period may be only partly earned by the end of the period. Items of revenue that are received in advance represent a liability that may be termed **unearned revenue**. The portion of the liability that is discharged during the period through delivery of goods or services has been earned; the remainder will be earned in the future. For example, magazine publishers usually receive advance payment for subscriptions covering periods ranging from a few months to a number of years. At the end of an accounting period, that portion of the receipts which is related to future periods has not been earned and should, therefore, appear in the balance sheet as a liability.

Other examples of unearned revenue are rent received in advance on property rented, premiums received in advance by an insurance company, tuition received in advance by a school, an annual retainer fee received in advance by an attorney, and amounts received in advance by an advertising firm for advertising services to be rendered in the future.

By accepting advance payment of a good or service, a business commits itself to furnish the good or the service at some future time. At the end of the accounting period, if some portion of the good or the service has been furnished, part of the revenue has been earned. The earned portion appears in the income statement. The unearned portion represents a liability of the business to furnish the good or the service in a future period and is reported in the balance sheet as a liability.

When revenue is received in advance, it may be credited to a liability account.[6] To illustrate, assume that on October 1, 1990, Cox Co. rents a portion of a building that it has been leasing for a period of one year, receiving $2,400 in payment for the entire year's rental. Assume also that the transaction was originally recorded by a debit to Cash and a credit to the liability account Unearned Rent. On December 31, 1990, the end of the fiscal year, one fourth of the amount has been earned and three fourths of the amount remains a liability. The entry to record the revenue and reduce the liability appears as follows:

	Adjusting Entry		
Dec. 31	Unearned Rent........................	600	
	Rent Income.........................		600

After this entry has been posted, the unearned rent account will have a balance of $1,800 ($2,400 − $600), which will be reported as a liability on Cox Co.'s balance sheet. The rent income account will have a balance of $600 and that amount will be reported on the income statement.

Adjusting Entries for Accrued Liabilities (Accrued Expenses)

Some expenses accrue from day to day but are usually recorded only when they are paid. Examples are salaries paid to employees and interest paid on notes payable. The amounts of such accrued but unpaid items at the end of the fiscal period are both an expense and a liability. It is for this reason that such accruals are called **accrued liabilities** or **accrued expenses**.

To illustrate the adjusting entry for an accrued liability, assume that on December 31, 1990, the end of the fiscal year, the sales salaries expense account for Cox Co. has a debit balance of $59,250, and the office salaries expense account has a balance of $20,660. During the year, salaries have been paid every two weeks. For this particular fiscal year, the records of the business show that the accruals for sales salaries and office salaries are $780 and $360, respectively, at the end of the year. The entry to record the additional expense and liability is as follows:

	Adjusting Entry		
Dec. 31	Sales Salaries........................	780	
	Office Salaries.......................	360	
	Salaries Payable..................		1,140

[6]The concepts and procedures for recording unearned revenues initially as revenues are discussed in Chapter 6.

After the adjusting entry has been posted to the accounts, the sales salaries expense totals $60,000 ($59,220 + $780), and the office salaries expense totals $21,020 ($20,660 + $360). These amounts will appear as expenses on the income statement. The balance in Salaries Payable will be $1,140 and that amount will be reported as a liability on Cox Co.'s balance sheet.

Adjusting Entries for Accrued Assets (Accrued Revenues)

All assets belonging to the business at the end of an accounting period and all revenues earned during the period should be recorded in the ledger. But during a fiscal period it is common to record some types of revenue only as the cash is received; consequently, at the end of the period there may be items of revenue that have not been recorded. In such cases, the amount of the accrued revenue must be recorded by debiting an asset account and crediting a revenue account. Because of the dual nature of such accruals, they are called **accrued assets** or **accrued revenues**.

To illustrate the adjusting entry for an accrued asset, assume that on December 31, 1990, the end of the fiscal year, Cox Co. has an interest-bearing note receivable. All interest income will be collected in 1991, when payment is due on the note. Assume further that the interest earned but not collected as of December 31, 1990, is $200. The entry to record this increase in the amount of interest due (receivable) on the note and the revenue earned is as follows:

	Adjusting Entry		
Dec. 31	Interest Receivable	200	
	Interest Income		200

After the entry has been posted, the interest receivable account will have a balance of $200, which would be reported as an asset in the balance sheet for Cox Co. The interest income would be reported on the income statement.

WORK SHEET FOR MERCHANDISING ENTERPRISES

OBJECTIVE 7
Describe and illustrate the preparation and completion of a work sheet for a merchandising enterprise.

After year-end posting of the journal is completed, a work sheet is used to assist in preparing the adjusting entries, closing entries, and financial statements.[7] In the work sheet presented on pages 156 and 157, the trial balance for Cox Co. as of December 31, 1990, differs slightly from trial balances illustrated earlier. All of the accounts in the ledger are listed in sequential order, including titles of accounts that have no balances. This variation in format has the advantage of listing accounts in the order in which they will be used when the statements are prepared.

Adjustments on the Work Sheet

The data needed for adjusting the accounts of Cox Co. are summarized as follows:

---

[7]As discussed in Chapter 3, computer software packages may be used to facilitate the preparation of the work sheet.

Interest accrued on notes receivable on		
December 31, 1990..		$ 200
Merchandise inventory as of December 31, 1990		62,150
Office supplies as of December 31, 1990.........................		480
Insurance expired during 1990......................................		1,910
Depreciation during 1990 on:		
Store equipment		3,100
Office equipment		2,490
Salaries accrued on December 31, 1990:		
Sales salaries...	$780	
Office salaries	360	1,140
Rent income earned during 1990....................................		600

Although there is no specific order in which the accounts need to be analyzed, the adjustment data assembled, and the adjusting entries made, time can be saved and greater accuracy achieved by selecting the accounts in the order in which they appear on the trial balance. The nature of and the amounts for the adjusting entries are presented below the work sheet as an aid to understanding.

Completing the Work Sheet

After all of the necessary adjustments are entered on the work sheet, the two adjustments columns are totaled to prove the equality of debits and credits. As illustrated in the preceding chapter, the balances of the accounts in the Trial Balance columns and the amount of any adjustments are added or deducted as appropriate. The adjusted balances are then extended into the Adjusted Trial Balance columns, which are totaled to prove the equality of debits and credits. Both the debit and credit amounts for Income Summary are extended.

Some accountants prefer to eliminate the Adjusted Trial Balance columns and to extend the adjusted account balances directly to the appropriate statement column. Such an alternative form of work sheet is especially popular if there are only a few items involved.

The process of extending the balances, as adjusted, to the statement columns is accomplished best by beginning with Cash at the top and moving down the work sheet, item by item, in sequential order. An exception to the usual practice of extending only the account balances should be noted. Both the debit and credit amounts for Income Summary are extended to the Income Statement columns. Since both the amount of the debit adjustment (beginning inventory of $59,700) and the amount of the credit adjustment (ending inventory of $62,150) may be reported on the income statement, there is no need to determine the difference between the two amounts.

After all of the items have been extended into the statement sections of the work sheet, the four columns are totaled and the net income or net loss is determined. In the illustration, the difference between the credit and the debit columns of the Income Statement section is $75,400, the amount of the net income. The difference between the debit and the credit columns of the Balance Sheet section is also $75,400, which is the increase in owner's equity as a result of the net income. Agreement between the two balancing amounts is evidence of debit-credit equality and arithmetical accuracy.

Work Sheet

Cox
Work
For Year Ended

	ACCOUNT TITLE	TRIAL BALANCE		ADJUSTMENTS		
		DEBIT	CREDIT	DEBIT		CREDIT
1	Cash	62,950				
2	Notes Receivable	40,000				
3	Accounts Receivable	60,880				
4	Interest Receivable			(a) 200		
5	Merchandise Inventory	59,700		(c) 62,150	(b)	59,700
6	Office Supplies	1,090			(d)	610
7	Prepaid Insurance	4,560			(e)	1,910
8	Store Equipment	27,100				
9	Accumulated Depreciation—Store Equipment		2,600		(f)	3,100
10	Office Equipment	15,570				
11	Accumulated Depreciation—Office Equipment		2,230		(g)	2,490
12	Accounts Payable		22,420			
13	Salaries Payable				(h)	1,140
14	Unearned Rent		2,400	(i) 600		
15	Note Payable (final payment, 1994)		25,000			
16	Capital Stock		100,000			
17	Retained Earnings		53,800			
18	Dividends	18,000				
19	Income Summary			(b) 59,700	(c)	62,150
20	Sales		720,185			
21	Sales Returns and Allowances	6,140				
22	Sales Discounts	5,790				
23	Purchases	521,980				
24	Purchases Returns and Allowances		9,100			
25	Purchases Discounts		2,525			
26	Transportation In	17,400				
27	Sales Salaries Expense	59,250		(h) 780		
28	Advertising Expense	10,860				
29	Depreciation Expense—Store Equipment			(f) 3,100		
30	Miscellaneous Selling Expense	630				
31	Office Salaries Expense	20,660		(h) 360		
32	Rent Expense	8,100				
33	Depreciation Expense—Office Equipment			(g) 2,490		
34	Insurance Expense			(e) 1,910		
35	Office Supplies Expense			(d) 610		
36	Miscellaneous Administrative Expense	760				
37	Rent Income				(i)	600
38	Interest Income		3,600		(a)	200
39	Interest Expense	2,440				
40		943,860	943,860	131,900		131,900
41						
42	Net Income					

(a) Interest earned but not received on notes receivable, $200.
(b) Beginning merchandise inventory, $59,700.
(c) Ending merchandise inventory, $62,150.
(d) Office supplies used, $610 ($1,090 − $480).
(e) Insurance expired, $1,910.

(f) Depreciation of store equipment, $3,100.
(g) Depreciation of office equipment, $2,490.
(h) Salaries accrued but not paid (sales salaries, $780; office salaries, $360), $1,140.
(i) Rent earned from amount received in advance, $600.

Completion of Year-End Procedures

The year-end accounting procedures that are necessary for a merchandising enterprise include the preparation of financial statements, adjusting entries, and closing entries. These items, which are discussed and illustrated in Chapter 5, are prepared from the data in the statement sections of the work sheet.

Co.
Sheet
December 31, 1990

#	ADJUSTED TRIAL BALANCE DEBIT	CREDIT	INCOME STATEMENT DEBIT	CREDIT	BALANCE SHEET DEBIT	CREDIT	#
1	62,950				62,950		1
2	40,000				40,000		2
3	60,880				60,880		3
4	200				200		4
5	62,150				62,150		5
6	480				480		6
7	2,650				2,650		7
8	27,100				27,100		8
9		5,700				5,700	9
10	15,570				15,570		10
11		4,720				4,720	11
12		22,420				22,420	12
13		1,140				1,140	13
14		1,800				1,800	14
15		25,000				25,000	15
16		100,000				100,000	16
17		53,800				53,800	17
18	18,000				18,000		18
19	59,700	62,150	59,700	62,150			19
20		720,185		720,185			20
21	6,140		6,140				21
22	5,790		5,790				22
23	521,980		521,980				23
24		9,100		9,100			24
25		2,525		2,525			25
26	17,400		17,400				26
27	60,030		60,030				27
28	10,860		10,860				28
29	3,100		3,100				29
30	630		630				30
31	21,020		21,020				31
32	8,100		8,100				32
33	2,490		2,490				33
34	1,910		1,910				34
35	610		610				35
36	760		760				36
37		600		600			37
38		3,800		3,800			38
39	2,440		2,440				39
40	1,012,940	1,012,940	722,960	798,360	289,980	214,580	40
41			75,400			75,400	41
42			798,360	798,360	289,980	289,980	42

CHAPTER REVIEW

KEY POINTS

Merchandising enterprises acquire merchandise for resale to customers. It is the selling of merchandise, instead of a service, that makes the activities of merchandising enterprises differ from the activities of service enterprises. The accounting system for a merchandising enterprise must accommodate the recording of transactions between buyers and sellers of merchandise.

OBJECTIVE 1a

Accounting for Purchases

Purchases of merchandise, which may be made for cash or on account, are usually identified in the ledger as Purchases. For purchases of merchandise on account, the credit terms may allow cash discounts for early payment. Such discounts are recorded by the buyer as purchases discounts and are usually viewed as a deduction from the amount initially recorded in Purchases. Likewise, when merchandise is returned or a price adjustment is granted, the buyer records the adjustment as a purchases return and allowance.

OBJECTIVE 1b

Accounting for Sales

Merchandise sales, which may be for cash or on account, are usually identified in the ledger as Sales. The seller refers to the discounts taken by the buyer for early payment as sales discounts, which are viewed as a reduction in the amount initially recorded in Sales. Merchandise returned or an allowance for reduction in the original price at which the goods were sold is treated as a sales return or allowance. Like sales discounts, sales returns and allowances are treated as a reduction in the initial amount recorded in Sales.

OBJECTIVE 1c

Transportation Costs

The terms of a sale between a buyer and seller will include provisions concerning when ownership of the merchandise passes to the buyer and which party is to bear the cost of delivering merchandise to the buyer. If the ownership passes to the buyer when the seller delivers the merchandise to the shipper, the buyer is to absorb the transportation costs and the terms are said to be FOB shipping point. If the ownership passes to the buyer when the merchandise is received by the buyer, the seller is to assume the cost of transportation and the terms are said to be FOB destination.

OBJECTIVE 1d

Sales Taxes

The liability for the sales tax is ordinarily incurred at the time the sale is made and is recorded by the seller as a credit to the sales tax payable account. The offsetting debit will be to Accounts Receivable if the merchandise is purchased on account, or to Cash if the cash is collected at the time of the sale. From the buyer's perspective, the cost of the purchases will include the original list price of the merchandise plus the sales tax.

OBJECTIVE 2

Periodic Reporting for Merchandising Enterprises

The summarization and reporting procedures for a merchandising enterprise are similar to those of a service enterprise. In a merchandising enterprise, however, merchandise purchased during the period will be recorded in a purchases account. Because some of this merchandise may be unsold at the end of the period, an adjustment to the merchandise inventory account is necessary.

OBJECTIVE 3

Merchandise Inventory Systems

Under the periodic system of accounting for merchandise, no attempt is made to record the cost of merchandise sold until the end of the period. It is only by a detailed listing of merchandise on hand (called a physical inventory) at the end of the accounting period that a determination is made of (1) the cost of merchandise sold during the period and (2) the cost of inventory on hand at the end of the period. Under the perpetual system of accounting for merchandise inventory, both the sales amount and the cost of merchandise sold amount are recorded when each item of merchandise is sold.

OBJECTIVE 4, 5

Cost of Merchandise Sold and Inventory Adjustments

For merchandising enterprises using the periodic system, the cost of merchandise sold and the beginning and ending inventories are reported in the income statement.

Two adjusting entries are required to adjust the merchandise inventory to its proper balance as of the end of the accounting period. These adjusting entries are recorded through the use of the income summary account.

OBJECTIVE 6

Adjustments for Deferrals and Accruals

A deferral is a delay of the recognition of an expense already paid or a revenue already received. Deferred expenses expected to benefit a short period of time are called prepaid expenses, while long-term prepayments are called deferred charges. Deferred revenues are called unearned revenues. Unearned revenues to be earned over a short period of time are current liabilities, while long-term deferred revenues are classified as deferred credits.

An accrual is an expense that has not been paid or a revenue that has not been received. Accrued expenses may be referred to as accrued liabilities, and accrued revenues may be called accrued assets.

Prepaid expenses are the costs of goods and services that have been purchased but not used. An adjustment is necessary at the end of the period so that the portion of the asset that has been used during the period becomes an expense; the remainder is an asset.

Items of revenue that are received in advance represent a liability that may be termed unearned revenue. An adjustment is necessary at the end of the period so that the portion of the liability that is discharged during the period, through the delivery of goods or services, is reported as earned; the remainder is reported as a liability.

Some expenses accrue from day to day but are usually recorded only when paid. The amounts of such accrued but unpaid items at the end of the fiscal period must be recorded by an adjusting entry that debits an expense account and credits a liability account.

Some revenues accrue from day to day, but are recorded only when cash is received. Consequently, at the end of the period the amount of the accrued revenue must be recorded by an adjusting entry which debits an asset account and credits a revenue account.

OBJECTIVE 7

Work Sheet

The work sheet for a merchandising enterprise is completed in a similar fashion to that of a service enterprise. The primary difference is that the beginning and ending merchandise inventories, which are shown in the income summary account, appear in both the debit and credit income statement columns of the work sheet.

KEY TERMS

invoice 139	perpetual inventory system 148
cash discount 139	physical inventory 148
purchases discounts 140	deferral 151
purchases returns and allowances 141	accrual 151
debit memorandum 141	prepaid expenses 151
credit memorandum 141	unearned revenues 152
sales discounts 144	accrued liabilities 153
sales returns and allowances 144	accrued expenses 153
FOB shipping point 145	accrued assets 154
FOB destination 145	accrued revenue 154
periodic inventory system 148	

SELF-EXAMINATION QUESTIONS

Answers at end of chapter.

1. If merchandise purchased on account is returned, the buyer may inform the seller of the details by issuing:
   A. a debit memorandum   C. an invoice
   B. a credit memorandum   D. a bill

2. If merchandise is sold on account to a customer for $1,000, terms FOB shipping point, 1/10, n/30, and the seller prepays $50 in transportation costs, the amount of the discount for early payment would be:
   A. $0   C. $10.00
   B. $5.00   D. $10.50

3. Merchandise is sold on account to a customer for $1,000, terms FOB destination, 1/10, n/30. If the seller pays $50 in transportation costs and the customer returns $100 of the merchandise prior to payment, what is the amount of the discount for early payment?
   A. $0   C. $10.00
   B. $9.00   D. $10.50

4. For an enterprise using the periodic inventory system, which of the following is added to merchandise inventory at the beginning of the period in computing the cost of merchandise sold?
   A. Purchases discounts
   B. Purchases returns and allowances
   C. Merchandise inventory at the end of the period
   D. None of the above

5. The balance in Unearned Rent at the end of a period represents:
   A. an asset   C. a revenue
   B. a liability   D. an expense

ILLUSTRATIVE PROBLEM

MacBride Discount Stores Inc. entered into the following selected transactions during August of the current year:

Aug. 1. Purchased merchandise on account, terms 2/10, n/30, FOB shipping point, $28,500.
     1. Paid rent for August, $4,500.
     2. Paid transportation charges on purchase of August 1, $1,180.
     5. Purchased office supplies for cash, $600.
     7. Sold merchandise on account, terms 1/10, n/30, FOB destination, $12,400.
     8. Paid transportation charges on sale of August 7, $550.
    11. Paid for merchandise purchased on August 1, less discount.
    12. Received merchandise returned from sale of August 7, $3,200.
    14. Purchased merchandise on account, terms 4/15, n/30, FOB shipping point, $18,300 with prepaid transportation costs of $750 added to the invoice.
    16. Returned merchandise purchased on August 14, $5,200.
    17. Received cash on account from sale of August 7, less return and discount.
    18. Sold merchandise on account, terms 1/10, n/30, FOB shipping point, $8,800. Prepaid transportation costs as an accommodation to the customer, $250.
    26. Sold merchandise on bank credit cards, $3,700.
    29. Paid for merchandise purchased on August 14, less return and discount.
    31. Received cash on account from sale of August 18, $9,050.

Instructions:

1. Record the August transactions in a two-column journal.
2. The merchandise inventory on hand at September 1, 1990, the beginning of the current fiscal year, was $250,000. A physical inventory taken on August 31, 1991, determined that merchandise on hand was $274,600. Prepare the adjusting entries for merchandise inventory for the current fiscal year ended August 31, 1991.

SOLUTION

(1)

Aug.	1	Purchases	28,500	
		Accounts Payable		28,500
	1	Rent Expense	4,500	
		Cash		4,500
	2	Transportation In	1,180	
		Cash		1,180
	5	Office Supplies	600	
		Cash		600
	7	Accounts Receivable	12,400	
		Sales		12,400
	8	Transportation Out	550	
		Cash		550
	11	Accounts Payable	28,500	
		Purchases Discounts		570
		Cash		27,930
	12	Sales Returns and Allowances	3,200	
		Accounts Receivable		3,200
	14	Purchases	18,300	
		Transportation In	750	
		Accounts Payable		19,050
	16	Accounts Payable	5,200	
		Purchases Returns and Allowances		5,200
	17	Cash	9,108	
		Sales Discounts	92	
		Accounts Receivable		9,200
	18	Accounts Receivable	8,800	
		Sales		8,800
	18	Accounts Receivable	250	
		Cash		250
	26	Cash	3,700	
		Sales		3,700
	29	Accounts Payable	13,850	
		Purchases Discounts*		524
		Cash		13,326
	31	Cash	9,050	
		Accounts Receivable		9,050

* ($18,300 − $5,200) × 4% = $524

(2)

Aug. 31	Income Summary...	250,000	
	Merchandise Inventory		250,000
31	Merchandise Inventory	274,600	
	Income Summary.....................................		274,600

DISCUSSION QUESTIONS

1. What distinguishes a merchandising enterprise from a service enterprise?

2. What is the name of the account in which purchases of merchandise are recorded?

3. The credit period during which the purchaser of merchandise is allowed to pay usually begins with what date?

4. Pruitt Inc. ordered $5,000 of merchandise on account on May 12, terms 2/10, n/30. Although the supplier shipped the merchandise on May 13, the merchandise was not received by Pruitt Inc. until May 16. The invoice received with the merchandise by Pruitt Inc. was dated May 13. What is the last date Pruitt Inc. could pay the invoice and still receive the discount?

5. What is the meaning of (a) 2/10, n/60; (b) n/30; (c) n/eom?

6. What is the term applied to discounts for early payment by (a) the buyer; (b) the seller?

7. Carter Company purchased merchandise on account from a supplier for $5,000, terms 1/10, n/30. Carter Company returned $500 of the merchandise and received full credit. (a) If Carter Company pays the invoice within the discount period, what is the amount of cash required for the payment? (b) What accounts are credited by Carter Company to record the return and the cash discount?

8. The debits and credits from four related transactions are presented in the following T accounts. (a) Describe each transaction. (b) What is the rate of the discount and on what amount was it computed?

Cash				Accounts Payable			
		(2)	175	(3)	500	(1)	7,500
		(4)	6,860	(4)	7,000		

Purchases				Purchases Discounts			
(1)	7,500					(4)	140

Transportation In				Purchases Returns and Allowances			
(2)	175					(3)	500

9. How does the accounting for sales to customers using bank credit cards, such as MasterCard and VISA, differ from accounting for sales to customers using nonbank credit cards, such as American Express?

10. After the amount due on a sale of $2,000, terms 2/10, n/eom, is received from a customer within the discount period, the seller consents to the return of the entire shipment. (a) What is the amount of the refund owed to the customer? (b) What accounts should be debited and credited by the seller to record the return and the refund?

11. Who bears the transportation costs when the terms of sale are (a) FOB shipping point, (b) FOB destination?

12. Merchandise is sold on account to a customer for $10,000, terms FOB shipping point, 2/10, n/30, the seller paying the transportation costs of $400. Determine the following: (a) amount of the sale, (b) amount debited to Accounts Receivable, (c) amount of the discount for early payment, (d) amount of the remittance due within the discount period.

13. A retailer is considering the purchase of 20 units of a specific commodity from either of two suppliers. Their offers are as follows:
A: $100 a unit, total of $2,000, 2/10, n/30, plus transportation costs of $250.
B: $110 a unit, total of $2,200, 1/10, n/30, no charge for transportation.
Which of the two offers, A or B, yields the lower price?

14. A sale of merchandise on account for $500 is subject to a 6% sales tax. (a) Should the sales tax be recorded at the time of sale or when payment is received? (b) What is the amount of the sale? (c) What is the amount debited to Accounts Receivable? (d) What is the title of the account to which the $30 is credited?

15. What is the name of the account in which unsold merchandise at the end of a period is recorded?

16. In which type of system for accounting for merchandise held for sale is there no attempt to record the cost of merchandise sold until the end of the period, when a physical inventory is taken?

17. In the following questions, identify the items designated by "X":
(a) Purchases − (X + X) = Net purchases
(b) Net purchases + X = Cost of merchandise purchased
(c) X + Cost of merchandise purchased = Merchandise available for sale
(d) Merchandise available for sale − X = Cost of merchandise sold

18. What account is used in a periodic inventory system to remove from the merchandise inventory account the inventory at the beginning of the period and replace it with the amount representing the inventory at the end of the period?

19. What term is used to describe a delay of the recognition of an expense already paid or of a revenue already received?

20. What term is used to describe an expense that has not been paid or a revenue that has not been received?

21. Where would (a) accrued expenses and (b) accrued revenues, both due within a year, appear on the balance sheet?

22. On June 30, the end of its fiscal year, an enterprise owed salaries of $12,500 for an incomplete payroll period. On the first payday in July, salaries of $20,900 are paid. (a) Is the $12,500 a deferral or an accrual as of June 30? (b) Which of the following types of accounts will be affected by the related adjusting entry: (1) asset, (2) liability, (3) revenue, (4) expense?

23. On January 2, an enterprise receives $24,000 from a tenant as rent for the current calendar year. The fiscal year of the enterprise is from April 1 to March 31. (a) Will the enterprise's adjusting entry for the rent as of March 31 of the current year be a deferral or an accrual? (b) Which of the following types of accounts will be affected

by the adjusting entry as of March 31: (1) asset, (2) liability, (3) revenue, (4) expense? (c) How much of the $24,000 rent should be allocated to the current fiscal year ending March 31?

24. From time to time during the fiscal year, an enterprise makes an advance payment of premiums on three-year and one-year property insurance policies. (a) At the end of such fiscal year, will there be a deferral or an accrual for the enterprise? (b) Which of the following types of accounts will be affected by the related adjusting entry at the end of the fiscal year: (1) asset, (2) liability, (3) revenue, (4) expense?

25. Classify the following items as (a) prepaid expense, (b) unearned revenue, (c) accrued expense, or (d) accrued revenue.
    (1) Utilities owed but not yet paid.
    (2) Fees received but not yet earned.
    (3) Salary owed but not yet due.
    (4) Storage fees earned but not yet received.
    (5) Fees earned but not yet received.
    (6) Taxes owed but payable in the following period.
    (7) Receipts from sales of meal tickets by a restaurant.
    (8) Supplies on hand.
    (9) Property taxes paid in advance.
    (10) Life insurance premiums received by an insurance company.
    (11) A two-year premium paid on a fire insurance policy.
    (12) Tuition collected in advance by a university.

26. There are balances in each of the following accounts after adjustments have been made at the end of the fiscal year. Identify each as (a) asset, (b) liability, (c) revenue, or (d) expense.
    (1) Prepaid Insurance   (7) Unearned Subscriptions
    (2) Supplies   (8) Rent Receivable
    (3) Salary Expense   (9) Fees Receivable
    (4) Rent Income   (10) Supplies Expense
    (5) Prepaid Advertising   (11) Taxes Payable
    (6) Insurance Expense   (12) Fees Earned

27. The account Merchandise Inventory is listed at $225,000 on the trial balance (before adjustments) as of July 31, the end of the first month in the fiscal year. Which one of the following phrases describes the item correctly?
    (a) Inventory of merchandise at July 1, beginning of the month.
    (b) Purchases of merchandise during July.
    (c) Merchandise available for sale during July.
    (d) Inventory of merchandise at July 31, end of the month.
    (e) Cost of merchandise sold during July.

28. The following data appear in a work sheet as of December 31, the end of the fiscal year:

	Adjustments		Income Statement	
	Dr.	Cr.	Dr.	Cr.

| Income Summary | (a) 180,000 | (b) 195,000 | 180,000 | 195,000 |

(a) To what account was the $180,000 credited in adjustment (a)?
(b) To what account was the $195,000 debited in adjustment (b)?

(c) What was the amount of the merchandise inventory at January 1, the beginning of the fiscal year?

(d) What amount will be listed for merchandise inventory on the balance sheet at December 31, the end of the fiscal year?

(e) If the totals of the Income Statement columns of the work sheet are $1,375,000 debit and $1,500,000 credit, what is the amount of the net income for the year?

(f) Would the amount determined to be net income be affected by extending only the net amount of $15,000 ($195,000 − $180,000) into the Income Statement column?

Real World Focus

29. It is not unusual for a customer to drive into a Texaco, Mobil, or Gulf gasoline station and discover that the cash price per gallon is 3 or 4 cents lower than the credit price per gallon. As a result, many customers pay cash rather than use their credit cards. Why would a gasoline station owner establish such a policy?

Real World Focus

30. The balance sheet for Tandy Corporation as of June 30, 1988, includes the following accrued expenses as current liabilities:

Accrued payroll and bonuses	$75,500,000
Accrued sales and payroll taxes...	20,176,000
Accrued insurance...	22,115,000
Accrued interest	13,256,000

The net income for Tandy Corporation for the year ended June 30, 1988, was $316,354,000. (a) If the accrued expenses had *not* been recorded at June 30, 1988, how much would net income have been misstated for the fiscal year ended June 30, 1988? (b) What is the percentage of the misstatement in (a) to the reported net income of $316,354,000?

EXERCISES

Exercise 4–1

Purchase-related transactions.

OBJ. 1

Kramer Co. purchases $5,000 of merchandise from a supplier on account, terms FOB shipping point, 1/10, n/30. The supplier adds transportation charges of $180 to the invoice. Kramer Co. returns some of the merchandise, receiving a credit memorandum for $500, and then pays the amount due within the discount period. Present Kramer Co.'s entries to record (a) the purchase, (b) the merchandise return, and (c) the payment.

Exercise 4–2

Determination of amounts to be paid on invoices.

OBJ. 1

Determine the amount to be paid in full settlement of each of the following invoices, assuming that credit for returns and allowances was received prior to payment and that all invoices were paid within the discount period.

	Purchase Invoice Merchandise	Transportation	Terms	Returns and Allowances
(a)	$8,000	—	FOB destination, n/30	$ 500
(b)	5,000	—	FOB destination, 1/10, n/30	—
(c)	7,500	—	FOB shipping point, 2/10, n/30	1,000
(d)	4,000	$50	FOB shipping point, 1/10, n/30	.50
(e)	4,750	90	FOB shipping point, 2/10, n/30	750

Exercise 4–3
Sales-related transactions, including the use of credit cards.
OBJ. 1

Present entries for the following transactions of C. D. McDonald Inc.:

(a) Sold merchandise for cash, $7,500.
(b) Sold merchandise on account, $16,000.
(c) Sold merchandise to customers who used MasterCard and VISA, $4,250.
(d) Sold merchandise to customers who used American Express, $2,750.
(e) Paid an invoice from First National Bank for $250, representing a service fee for processing of MasterCard and VISA sales.
(f) Received $2,590 from American Express Company after a $160 collection fee had been deducted.

Exercise 4–4
Sales-related transactions.
OBJ. 1

Present entries for the following related transactions:

Oct.   2. Sold merchandise to a customer for $10,000, terms FOB shipping point, 1/10, n/30.
       2. Paid the transportation charges of $195, debiting the amount to Accounts Receivable.
       6. Issued a credit memorandum for $1,000 to the customer for merchandise returned.
      12. Received a check for the amount due from the sale.

Exercise 4–5
Sales-related transactions.
OBJ. 1

Tavel Corp. sells merchandise to Graf Co. on account, $8,500, FOB shipping point, 1/10, n/30. Tavel Corp. pays the transportation charges of $250 as an accommodation and adds it to the invoice. Tavel Corp. issues a credit memorandum for $500 for merchandise returned and subsequently receives the amount due within the discount period. Present Tavel Corp.'s entries to record (a) the sale and the transportation costs, (b) the credit memorandum, and (c) the receipt of the check for the amount due.

Exercise 4–6
Purchase-related transactions.
OBJ. 1

Based upon the data presented in Exercise 4–5, present Graf Co.'s entries to record (a) the purchase, including the transportation charges, (b) the return of the merchandise for credit, and (c) the payment of the invoice within the discount period.

Exercise 4–7
Purchase-related transactions.
OBJ. 1

Present entries for the following related transactions of R & R Inc.:

(a) Purchased $9,000 of merchandise from Baxter Co. on account, terms 2/10, n/30.
(b) Paid the amount owed on the invoice within the discount period.
(c) Discovered that some of the merchandise was defective and returned items with an invoice price of $1,000, receiving credit.
(d) Purchased an additional $750 of merchandise from Baxter Co. on account, terms 2/10, n/30.
(e) Received a check for the balance owed from the return in (c), after deducting for the purchase in (d).

Exercise 4–8
Sales tax-related transactions.
OBJ. 1

Present entries to record the following related transactions of Collier Electric Co.:

(a) Purchased merchandise on account, $15,000, terms 2/10, n/30.
(b) Sold $3,000 of merchandise on account, subject to a sales tax of 6%.
(c) Paid the amount owed in (a) within the discount period.
(d) Paid $1,650 to the state revenue department for sales taxes collected.

Exercise 4–9

Cost of merchandise
sold section of
income statement.

OBJ. 4

On the basis of the following data, prepare the cost of merchandise sold section of the income statement for the fiscal year ended July 31, 1991, for Coldwell Inc.

Merchandise Inventory, July 31, 1991	$125,000
Merchandise Inventory, August 1, 1990	115,000
Purchases	550,000
Purchases Returns and Allowances	4,250
Purchases Discounts	3,200
Transportation In	3,950

Exercise 4–10

Merchandising
adjusting entries.

OBJ. 5

Data needed for adjusting the periodic merchandise inventory for Lights of Naples for the fiscal year ended December 31, 1990, are as follows:

Merchandise inventory as of January 1, 1990	$115,000
Merchandise inventory as of December 31, 1990	130,000

Journalize the necessary adjusting entries for merchandise inventory.

Exercise 4–11

Adjusting entries
for deferrals.

OBJ. 6

The prepaid insurance account had a balance of $4,750 at the beginning of the year. The account was debited for $5,150 for premiums on policies purchased during the year. Prepare the adjusting entry required at the end of the year under each of the following alternatives: (a) the amount of unexpired insurance applicable to future periods is $4,300, (b) the amount of insurance expired during the year is $5,550.

Exercise 4–12

Adjusting entries
for deferrals.

OBJ. 6

In their first year of operations, the Buckley Gazette received $172,500 from magazine subscriptions, crediting the amount to Unearned Subscriptions. At the end of the year, $47,500 was unearned. Prepare the adjusting entry that should be made at the end of the year.

Exercise 4–13

Adjusting entries
for accruals.

OBJ. 6

A business enterprise owes accrued salaries of $1,450 for the last two days of the current year. It also has interest of $425 earned but not collected at the end of the current year. Prepare the adjusting entries to record (a) the salaries owed at the end of the year, (b) the interest income accrued at the end of the year.

Exercise 4–14

Adjusting entries
for deferrals
and accruals.

OBJ. 6

At the end of the current fiscal year, the unearned rent account has a balance of $18,000 and the unbilled fees for services performed for clients totaled $11,250. Assuming that $6,000 of the amount in the unearned rent account has been earned, prepare the adjusting entries necessary at the end of the year to record (a) the earned rent income, (b) unbilled fees.

PROBLEMS

Series A

Problem 4–1A

Purchase-related
and sales-related
transactions.

OBJ. 1

The following selected transactions were completed during July between Norman Company and Ruiz Inc.:

July 2. Norman Company sold merchandise on account to Ruiz Inc., $15,000, terms FOB shipping point, 1/10, n/30. Norman Company prepaid transportation costs of $500 which were added to the invoice.

8. Norman Company sold merchandise on account to Ruiz Inc., $10,000, terms FOB destination, 1/15, n/eom.

8. Norman Company paid transportation costs of $300 for delivery of merchandise sold to Ruiz Inc. on July 8.

11. Ruiz Inc. returned merchandise purchased on account on July 8 from Norman Company, $4,000.

12. Ruiz Inc. paid Norman Company for purchases of July 2, less discount.

July 23. Ruiz Inc. paid Norman Company for purchases of July 8, less discount and less return of July 11.

23. Norman Company sold merchandise on account to Ruiz Inc., $8,000, terms FOB shipping point, n/eom.

24. Ruiz Inc. paid transportation charges of $300 on July 23 purchase from Norman Company.

31. Ruiz Inc. paid Norman Company on account for purchases of July 23.

Instructions:

Journalize the July transactions in a two-column journal for (1) Norman Company and (2) Ruiz Inc.

Problem 4–2A
Purchase-related and sales-related transactions.
OBJ. 1

The following were selected from among the transactions completed by Varro Company during May of the current year:

May 1. Purchased merchandise on account from Green Inc., $5,000, terms FOB shipping point, 2/10, n/30, with prepaid transportation costs of $225 added to the invoice.

5. Purchased merchandise on account from Faulk Co., $7,500, terms FOB destination, 1/10, n/30.

6. Sold merchandise on account to R & R Inc., $4,100, terms 2/10, n/30.

8. Purchased office supplies for cash, $475.

10. Returned merchandise purchased on May 5 from Faulk Co., $1,500.

11. Paid Green Inc. on account for purchases of May 1, less discount.

14. Purchased merchandise for cash, $14,000.

15. Paid Faulk Co. on account for purchases of May 5, less return of May 10 and discount.

16. Received cash on account from sale of May 6 to R & R Inc., less discount.

21. Sold merchandise on nonbank credit cards and reported accounts to the card company, $3,750.

22. Sold merchandise on account to Comer Co., $3,480, terms 2/10, n/30.

26. Sold merchandise for cash, $6,125.

26. Received merchandise returned by Comer Co. from sale of May 22, $1,480.

30. Received cash from card company for nonbank credit card sales of May 21, less $215 service fee.

Instructions:

Journalize the transactions for Varro Company in a two-column journal.

Problem 4–3A
Purchase-related and sales-related transactions for a sole proprietorship.
OBJ. 1
SOLUTIONS SOFTWARE

The account balances at June 1 of the current year of Allen Company are as follows:

11 Cash	$ 17,990
12 Accounts Receivable	32,350
13 Merchandise Inventory	81,100
14 Prepaid Insurance	3,000
15 Store Supplies	2,200
21 Accounts Payable	28,300
31 W. A. Allen, Capital	108,340
32 W. A. Allen, Drawing	—
33 Income Summary	—
41 Sales	—
42 Sales Returns and Allowances	—
43 Sales Discounts	—
51 Purchases	—
52 Purchases Returns and Allowances	—
53 Purchases Discounts	—
54 Transportation In	—
55 Sales Salaries Expense	—
56 Advertising Expense	—

57 Store Supplies Expense .... —
58 Miscellaneous Selling Expense.. —
59 Office Salaries Expense .... —
60 Rent Expense.. —
61 Insurance Expense.. —
62 Miscellaneous Administrative Expense............................... —

The following transactions were completed during June of the current year:

June 1. Paid rent for month, $3,000.
2. Purchased merchandise on account, $12,500.
4. Purchased merchandise on account, FOB shipping point, $20,100.
7. Sold merchandise on account, $16,000.
9. Paid transportation charges on the purchase of June 4, $525.
10. Received $12,250 cash from customers on account, after discounts of $250 were deducted.
11. Paid creditors $16,700 on account, after discounts of $280 had been deducted.
14. Sold merchandise for cash, $9,500.
15. Received merchandise returned on account, $800.
16. Paid sales salaries of $3,950 and office salaries of $1,280.
17. Paid creditors $12,750 on account, after discounts of $200 had been deducted.
18. Received $9,800 cash from customers on account, after discounts of $200 had been deducted.
21. Purchased merchandise on account, $15,200.
22. Paid advertising expense, $4,250.
23. Sold merchandise for cash, $11,600.
24. Returned merchandise purchased on account, $2,200.
25. Sold merchandise on account, $30,200.
28. Sold merchandise for cash, $8,200.
28. Refunded $350 cash on sales made for cash.
29. Paid sales salaries of $3,800 and office salaries of $1,280.
30. Paid creditors $10,900 on account, no discount.
30. Received $12,500 cash from customers on account, no discount.

Instructions:

(1) Open a ledger of four-column accounts for the accounts listed. Record the balances in the appropriate balance column as of June 1, write "Balance" in the item section, and place a check mark (√) in the posting reference column.
(2) Record the transactions for June in a two-column journal.
(3) Post to the ledger, extending the month-end balances to the appropriate balance columns after all posting is completed.
(4) Prepare a trial balance of the ledger as of June 30.

Problem 4–4A
Adjusting entries.
OBJ. 6

The following information was obtained from a review of the ledger (before adjustments) and other records of Deland Company at December 31, the end of the current fiscal year:

(a) As advance premiums have been paid on insurance policies during the year, they have been debited to Prepaid Insurance, which has a balance of $3,258 at December 31. Details of premium expirations are as follows:

Policy No.	Premium Cost per Month	Period in Effect During Year
SB106	$50	Jan. 1–June 30
C84DE	45	Jan. 1–Oct. 31
01CF2	55	July 1–Dec. 31
Z149C	40	Nov. 1–Dec. 31

(b) The unbilled management fees at December 31 total $9,500.
(c) As office supplies have been purchased during the year, they have been debited to Office Supplies, which has a balance of $1,280 at December 31. The inventory of supplies at that date totals $390.
(d) Sales commissions are uniformly 2% of net sales and are paid on the tenth of the month following the sales. Net sales for the month ended December 31 were $120,500. Only commissions paid have been recorded during the year.
(e) Prepaid Advertising has a debit balance of $13,000 at December 31, which represents the advance payment on April 1 of a yearly contract for a uniform amount of space in 52 consecutive issues of a weekly publication. As of December 31, advertisements had appeared in 39 issues.
(f) Unearned Rent has a credit balance of $18,900, composed of the following: (1) January 1 balance of $4,500, representing rent that the tenant prepaid for four months, January through April, and (2) a credit of $14,400, representing the tenant's advance payment of rent for twelve months at $1,200 a month, beginning with May.

Instructions:

(1) Determine the amount of each adjustment, identifying all principal figures used in the computations.
(2) Journalize the adjusting entries as of December 31 of the current fiscal year, identifying each entry by letter.

Problem 4–5A
Adjusting entries from ledger account balances.
OBJ. 6

Selected accounts from the ledger of Keiko Asano Inc. at the end of the fiscal year are as follows. The account balances are shown before and after adjustment.

	Unadjusted Balance	Adjusted Balance
Fees Receivable	—	$ 4,200
Supplies	$ 3,250	810
Prepaid Insurance	7,620	4,645
Wages Payable	—	3,560
Utilities Payable	—	570
Unearned Rent	9,360	720
Fees Earned	109,500	113,700
Wages Expense	69,100	72,660
Utilities Expense	5,940	6,510
Insurance Expense	—	2,975
Supplies Expense	—	2,440
Rent Income	—	8,640

Instructions:

Journalize the adjusting entries that were posted to the ledger at the end of the fiscal year.

Problem 4–6A
Work sheet for merchandising sole proprietorship.
OBJ. 4, 7

The accounts and their balances in the ledger of Miller Company on December 31 of the current year are as follows:

Cash	$ 38,500
Accounts Receivable	88,300
Merchandise Inventory	113,800
Prepaid Insurance	9,500
Store Supplies	2,300
Office Supplies	1,500
Store Equipment	86,600
Accumulated Depreciation—Store Equipment	28,000
Office Equipment	29,300
Accumulated Depreciation—Office Equipment	12,000
Accounts Payable	89,500
Salaries Payable	—

Unearned Rent	$ 2,400
Note Payable (due 1999)	100,000
W. A. Miller, Capital	79,800
W. A. Miller, Drawing	48,000
Income Summary	—
Sales	760,000
Sales Returns and Allowances	12,000
Sales Discounts	7,500
Purchases	500,000
Purchases Returns and Allowances	12,500
Purchases Discounts	6,500
Transportation In	2,400
Sales Salaries Expense	64,000
Advertising Expense	18,000
Depreciation Expense—Store Equipment	—
Store Supplies Expense	—
Miscellaneous Selling Expense	1,400
Office Salaries Expense	31,000
Rent Expense	24,000
Depreciation Expense—Office Equipment	—
Insurance Expense	—
Office Supplies Expense	—
Miscellaneous Administrative Expense	1,100
Rent Income	—
Interest Expense	11,500

The data for year-end adjustments on December 31 are as follows:

Merchandise inventory on December 31		$107,500
Insurance expired during the year		6,900
Inventory of supplies on December 31:		
Store supplies		900
Office supplies		500
Depreciation for the year:		
Store equipment		8,100
Office equipment		3,000
Salaries payable on December 31:		
Sales salaries	$2,500	
Office salaries	1,200	3,700
Rent income earned for the year		600

Instructions:

(1) Prepare a work sheet for the fiscal year ended December 31. List all accounts in the order given.

(2) Prepare the cost of merchandise sold section of the income statement from the data presented in the income statement columns of the work sheet.

Problem 4–7A
Work sheet for merchandising corporation.

OBJ. 7

The accounts in the ledger of Dugan Company, with the unadjusted balances on August 31, the end of the current fiscal year, are as follows:

Cash	$ 19,960
Notes Receivable	50,000
Accounts Receivable	53,340
Interest Receivable	—
Merchandise Inventory	120,200
Prepaid Insurance	2,980
Store Supplies	2,620
Store Equipment	164,200
Accumulated Depreciation—Store Equipment	84,600
Accounts Payable	32,000
Salaries Payable	—

Unearned Rent	$ 3,600
Capital Stock	150,000
Retained Earnings	95,950
Dividends	16,000
Income Summary	—
Sales	790,500
Purchases	513,700
Sales Salaries Expense	79,800
Advertising Expense	24,800
Depreciation Expense — Store Equipment	—
Store Supplies Expense	—
Miscellaneous Selling Expense	1,600
Office Salaries Expense	53,700
Rent Expense	25,000
Heating and Lighting Expense	17,400
Taxes Expense	7,850
Insurance Expense	—
Miscellaneous Administrative Expense	3,500
Rent Income	—
Interest Income	—

The data needed for year-end adjustments on August 31 are as follows:

Interest earned on notes receivable as of August 31		$ 2,500
Merchandise inventory on August 31		100,000
Insurance expired during the year		2,060
Store supplies inventory on August 31		1,020
Depreciation for the current year		9,300
Accrued salaries on August 31:		
Sales salaries	$1,500	
Office salaries	1,200	2,700
Rent income earned during the year		2,800

Instructions:

Prepare a work sheet for the fiscal year ended August 31. List all accounts in the order given.

Series B

Problem 4–1B
Purchase-related and sales-related transactions.

The following selected transactions were completed during February between Cary Company and Lynn Inc.:

Feb. 3. Cary Company sold merchandise on account to Lynn Inc., $15,000, terms FOB destination, 2/15, n/eom.

3. Cary Company paid transportation costs of $300 for delivery of merchandise sold to Lynn Inc. on February 3.

10. Cary Company sold merchandise on account to Lynn Inc., $10,000, terms FOB shipping point, n/eom.

12. Lynn Inc. returned merchandise purchased on account on February 10 from Cary Company, $2,000.

12. Lynn Inc. paid transportation charges of $700 on February 10 purchase from Cary Company.

18. Cary Company sold merchandise on account to Lynn Inc., $18,000, terms FOB shipping point, 2/10, n/30. Cary Company prepaid transportation costs of $1,500 which were added to the invoice.

18. Lynn Inc. paid Cary Company on account for purchases of February 3, less discount.

Feb. 24. Lynn Inc. paid Cary Company on account for purchases of February 18, less discount.

28. Lynn Inc. paid Cary Company on account for purchases of February 10, less return of February 12.

Instructions:

Journalize the February transactions in a two-column journal for (1) Cary Company and (2) Lynn Inc.

Problem 4–2B

Purchase-related and sales-related transactions.

OBJ. 1

SOLUTIONS SOFTWARE

The following were selected from among the transactions completed by Langerman Co. during November of the current year:

Nov. 1. Purchased office supplies for cash, $850.

2. Purchased merchandise on account from Gant Co., $10,500, terms FOB destination, 1/10, n/30.

6. Sold merchandise for cash, $4,450.

7. Purchased merchandise on account from Liebman Co., $6,900, terms FOB shipping point, 2/10, n/30, with prepaid transportation costs of $190 added to the invoice.

7. Returned merchandise purchased on November 2 from Gant Co., $500.

11. Sold merchandise on account to Bowles Co., $1,800, terms 1/10, n/30.

12. Paid Gant Co. on account for purchases of November 2, less return of November 7 and discount.

16. Sold merchandise on nonbank credit cards and reported accounts to the card company, $3,850.

17. Paid Liebman Co. on account for purchases of November 7, less discount.

19. Purchased merchandise for cash, $3,500.

21. Received cash on account from sale of November 11 to Bowles Co., less discount.

24. Sold merchandise on account to Hall Inc., $4,800, terms 1/10, n/30.

28. Received cash from card company for nonbank credit card sales of November 16, less $220 service fee.

30. Received merchandise returned by Hall Inc. from sale of November 24, $1,750.

Instructions:

Journalize the transactions for Langerman Co. in a two-column journal.

Problem 4–5B

Adjusting entries from ledger account balances.

OBJ. 6

Selected accounts from the ledger of Anderson Company at the end of the fiscal year are as follows. The account balances are shown before and after adjustment.

	Unadjusted Balance	Adjusted Balance
Fees Receivable	—	$ 9,000
Supplies	$ 2,980	900
Prepaid Insurance	4,720	2,120
Wages Payable	—	2,425
Advertising Payable	—	3,300
Unearned Rent	5,200	400
Fees Earned	129,600	138,600
Wages Expense	63,280	65,705
Insurance Expense	—	2,600
Advertising Expense	16,200	19,500
Supplies Expense	—	2,080
Rent Income	—	4,800

Instructions:

Journalize the adjusting entries that were posted to the ledger at the end of the fiscal year.

Problem 4–6B
Work sheet for merchandising sole proprietorship.
OBJ. 4, 7

The accounts and their balances in the ledger of Orion Company on December 31 of the current year are as follows:

Cash	$ 34,400
Accounts Receivable	86,300
Merchandise Inventory	111,300
Prepaid Insurance	10,500
Store Supplies	2,800
Office Supplies	1,200
Store Equipment	79,600
Accumulated Depreciation — Store Equipment	23,000
Office Equipment	27,300
Accumulated Depreciation — Office Equipment	12,000
Accounts Payable	50,500
Salaries Payable	—
Unearned Rent	2,400
Note Payable (due 1999)	100,000
F. L. Farr, Capital	89,400
F. L. Farr, Drawing	48,000
Income Summary	—
Sales	760,000
Sales Returns and Allowances	7,000
Sales Discounts	8,500
Purchases	500,000
Purchases Returns and Allowances	12,500
Purchases Discounts	6,500
Transportation In	2,400
Sales Salaries Expense	70,000
Advertising Expense	18,000
Depreciation Expense — Store Equipment	—
Store Supplies Expense	—
Miscellaneous Selling Expense	1,400
Office Salaries Expense	25,000
Rent Expense	10,000
Depreciation Expense — Office Equipment	—
Insurance Expense	—
Office Supplies Expense	—
Miscellaneous Administrative Expense	1,100
Rent Income	—
Interest Expense	11,500

The data for year-end adjustments on December 31 are as follows:

Merchandise inventory on December 31		$115,200
Insurance expired during the year		6,500
Inventory of supplies on December 31:		
Store supplies		1,600
Office supplies		450
Depreciation for the year:		
Store equipment		7,500
Office equipment		2,800
Salaries payable on December 31:		
Sales salaries	$3,200	
Office salaries	900	4,100
Rent income earned for the year		600

Instructions:

(1) Prepare a work sheet for the fiscal year ended December 31. List all accounts in the order given.
(2) Prepare the cost of merchandise sold section of the income statement from the data presented in the income statement columns of the work sheet.

Problem 4–7B
Work sheet for merchandising corporation.

OBJ. 7

The accounts in the ledger of Terrel Company, with the unadjusted balances on April 30, the end of the current fiscal year, are as follows:

Cash...	$ 25,100
Notes Receivable..	50,000
Accounts Receivable...	57,600
Interest Receivable...	—
Merchandise Inventory..	87,150
Prepaid Insurance..	5,800
Store Supplies..	4,950
Store Equipment...	50,500
Accumulated Depreciation—Store Equipment.........................	30,130
Accounts Payable...	26,800
Salaries Payable...	—
Unearned Rent...	3,600
Capital Stock..	100,000
Retained Earnings...	69,020
Dividends...	15,000
Income Summary..	—
Sales...	587,500
Purchases..	375,000
Sales Salaries Expense..	51,500
Advertising Expense..	15,800
Depreciation Expense—Store Equipment...............................	—
Store Supplies Expense...	—
Miscellaneous Selling Expense..	2,750
Office Salaries Expense..	35,000
Rent Expense...	24,000
Heating and Lighting Expense...	9,660
Taxes Expense..	5,100
Insurance Expense..	—
Miscellaneous Administrative Expense..................................	2,140
Rent Income..	—
Interest Income..	—

The data needed for year-end adjustments on April 30 are as follows:

Interest earned on notes receivable as of April 30............		$ 2,500
Merchandise inventory on April 30.................................		90,000
Insurance expired during the year		3,800
Store supplies inventory on April 30		1,250
Depreciation for the current year		11,500
Accrued salaries on April 30:		
Sales salaries..	$1,600	
Office salaries	750	2,350
Rent income earned during the year		2,800

Instructions:

Prepare a work sheet for the fiscal year ended April 30, listing all of the accounts in the order given.

MINI-CASE 4

DISCOUNT   INC.

For the past twenty years, your father has managed and operated Giant Discount Inc., a regional chain of retail stores. You have recently accepted a position with Giant Discount Inc. as a special assistant to the president. As a first assignment, you are to review the purchasing and disbursing policies of the enterprise.

For your analysis, the controller has gathered the following data covering the past three years:

	19X3	19X2	19X1
Purchases	$22,500,000	$20,200,000	$17,900,000
Purchases returns and allowances	300,000	250,000	100,000
Transportation in	562,200	534,200	489,000

After reviewing these data, you ask the controller why no purchases discounts are shown for the three-year period. The controller responded as follows:

Your father won't let us take purchases discounts. It doesn't make sense to me. The industry standard is 2/10, n/30. Your father always has believed in paying the bills on the final due date and not a day before. I've tried to convince him that we should take the discounts, but he won't budge.

The controller also indicated that the company has recently entered into a store expansion program that will likely create a cash shortage. Because of this situation, the company has negotiated a $1,250,000 line of credit with its bank at an interest rate of 12%.

Instructions:

(1) Prepare an analysis indicating the net savings that the company could have earned from taking all discounts for the past three years. Assume that discounts are available on all purchases. In addition, assume that the company had sufficient cash to pay all invoices without borrowing and that the average rates at which the excess cash could have been invested in each of the past three years were as follows:

19X3...	10%
19X2...	12%
19X1...	13%

(Hint: You should take into consideration the interest income the company would have forgone by paying the invoices within the discount period.)

(2) Assume that you are able to convince your father to use the new line of credit to pay all invoices within the discount period during 19X4. The net purchases for 19X4 are projected to increase 10% over the net purchases for 19X3. Compute the expected net savings for 19X4 by taking all the available purchases discounts.

(3) Based upon the purchase data for 19X3, 19X2, and 19X1, what other questions might you raise concerning the company's purchasing and disbursing policies?

ETHICS DISCUSSION CASE	On March 1, 1990, Henning Inc. purchased $10,000 of merchandise, terms 2/10, n/30, from Dodson Company. Even though the discount period had expired on March 15, 1990, Kay Williams subtracted the discount of $200 when she processed the documents for payment by the treasurer.
	Discuss whether Kay Williams behaved in an ethical manner by subtracting the discount, even though the discount period had expired.

ANSWERS TO SELF-EXAMINATION QUESTIONS

1. **A** A debit memorandum (answer A), issued by the buyer, indicates the amount the buyer proposes to debit to the accounts payable account. A credit memorandum (answer B), issued by the seller, indicates the amount the seller proposes to credit to the accounts receivable account. An invoice (answer C) or a bill (answer D), issued by the seller, indicates the amount and terms of the sale.

2. **C** The amount of discount for early payment is $10 (answer C), or 1% of $1,000. Although the $50 of transportation costs paid by the seller are debited to the customer's account, the customer is not entitled to a discount on that amount.

3. **B** The customer is entitled to a discount of $9 (answer B) for early payment. This amount is 1% of $900, which is the sales price of $1,000 less the return of $100. The $50 of transportation costs is an expense of the seller.

4. **D** Purchases discounts (answer A), purchases returns and allowances (answer B), and merchandise inventory at the end of the period (answer C) are all subtracted from the sum of merchandise inventory at the beginning of the period and purchases in determining the cost of merchandise sold.

5. **B** Unearned revenues are revenues received in advance that will be earned in the future. They represent a liability (answer B) of the business to furnish goods or services in a future period.

CHAPTER FIVE

PERIODIC REPORTING FOR A MERCHANDISING ENTERPRISE

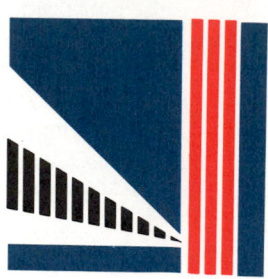

CHAPTER OBJECTIVES

1 Describe and illustrate alternative formats and terminology for the income statement, retained earnings statement, and balance sheet of a merchandising enterprise.

2 Describe and illustrate the preparation of adjusting entries for a merchandising enterprise.

3 Describe and illustrate the preparation of closing entries for a merchandising enterprise.

4 Describe and illustrate the preparation of reversing entries.

5 Describe the preparation of interim financial statements.

6 Describe and illustrate the procedures for correcting errors in accounting records.

Accounting for merchandising enterprises, including the year-end adjustment procedures and the preparation of the work sheet, was discussed in Chapter 4. The discussion is continued in this chapter by describing and illustrating the preparation of financial statements, adjusting entries, closing entries, and a post-closing trial balance for a merchandising enterprise. Alternative formats and terminology which can be used in preparing financial statements are also described and illustrated.

In connection with the discussion of adjusting entries, the purpose and use of reversing entries is presented and illustrated. A discussion of interim financial statements and their preparation is also presented. Finally, recognition is given to the fact that occasional errors in journalizing and posting transactions will occur. Procedures necessary to correct such errors are discussed and illustrated.

FINANCIAL STATEMENTS FOR MERCHANDISING ENTERPRISES

OBJECTIVE 1
Describe and illustrate alternative formats and terminology for the income statement, retained earnings statement, and balance sheet of a merchandising enterprise.

The basic financial statements for a merchandising enterprise, including the income statement, statement of owner's equity, and balance sheet, are similar to those of a service enterprise. For a corporate enterprise, the financial statements would include the retained earnings statement rather than the statement of owner's equity. The basic differences between the financial statements of a merchandising enterprise and a service enterprise include the cost of merchandise sold section of the income statement, which was illustrated in Chapter 4, and the inclusion of merchandise inventory on the balance sheet as a current asset.

To simplify the presentation, the work sheet of Cox Co., presented in Chapter 4 and reproduced on pages 180 and 181, is used as a basis for illustration and discussion. From this work sheet, alternative formats and terminology for the financial statements of Cox Co. are illustrated.[1]

Income Statement

There are two widely used forms for the income statement: multiple-step and single-step. The 1988 edition of *Accounting Trends & Techniques* reported that 57% of the 600 industrial and merchandising companies surveyed use the multiple-step form, while 43% use the single-step form.

Multiple-Step Form. The **multiple-step income statement** is so called because of its many sections, subsections, and intermediate balances. In practice, there is considerable variation in the amount of detail presented in these sections. For example, instead of reporting separately the gross sales and the related returns, allowances, and discounts, the statement may begin with net sales. Similarly, the supporting data for the determination of the cost of merchandise sold may be omitted from the statement. The various sections of a multiple-step income statement for Cox Co., presented on page 182, are discussed briefly in the paragraphs that follow.

Revenue From Sales. The total of all charges to customers for merchandise sold, both for cash and on account, is reported in this section. Sales returns and allowances and sales discounts are deducted from the gross amount to yield net sales.

Cost of Merchandise Sold. The determination of this important figure was explained and illustrated in Chapter 4. Other descriptive terms frequently employed are **cost of goods sold** and **cost of sales**.

Gross Profit. The excess of the net revenue from sales over the cost of merchandise sold is called **gross profit,** **gross profit on sales**, or **gross margin**. It is called *gross* because operating expenses must be deducted from it.

Operating Expenses. The operating expenses of a business may be grouped under any desired number of headings and subheadings. In a retail

---

[1]Examples of alternative forms are also presented in Appendix I, Specimen Financial Statements.

business of the kind that has been used for illustrative purposes, it is usually satisfactory to subdivide operating expenses into two categories: selling and administrative.

Expenses that are incurred directly and entirely in connection with the sale of merchandise are classified as **selling expenses**. They include such expenses as salaries of the sales force, store supplies used, depreciation of store equipment, and advertising.

Expenses incurred in the administration or general operations of the business are classified as **administrative expenses** or **general expenses**. Examples of these expenses are office salaries, depreciation of office equipment, and office supplies used. Expenses that are partly connected with

Work Sheet

Cox
Work
For Year Ended

	ACCOUNT TITLE	TRIAL BALANCE DEBIT	TRIAL BALANCE CREDIT	ADJUSTMENTS DEBIT	ADJUSTMENTS CREDIT	
1	Cash	62,950				1
2	Notes Receivable	40,000				2
3	Accounts Receivable	60,880				3
4	Interest Receivable			(a) 200		4
5	Merchandise Inventory	59,700		(c) 62,150	(b) 59,700	5
6	Office Supplies	1,090			(d) 610	6
7	Prepaid Insurance	4,560			(e) 1,910	7
8	Store Equipment	27,100				8
9	Accumulated Depreciation—Store Equipment		2,600		(f) 3,100	9
10	Office Equipment	15,570				10
11	Accumulated Depreciation—Office Equipment		2,230		(g) 2,490	11
12	Accounts Payable		22,420			12
13	Salaries Payable				(h) 1,140	13
14	Unearned Rent		2,400	(i) 600		14
15	Note Payable (final payment, 1994)		25,000			15
16	Capital Stock		100,000			16
17	Retained Earnings		53,800			17
18	Dividends	18,000				18
19	Income Summary			(b) 59,700	(c) 62,150	19
20	Sales		720,185			20
21	Sales Returns and Allowances	6,140				21
22	Sales Discounts	5,790				22
23	Purchases	521,980				23
24	Purchases Returns and Allowances		9,100			24
25	Purchases Discounts		2,525			25
26	Transportation In	17,400				26
27	Sales Salaries Expense	59,250		(h) 780		27
28	Advertising Expense	10,860				28
29	Depreciation Expense—Store Equipment			(f) 3,100		29
30	Miscellaneous Selling Expense	630				30
31	Office Salaries Expense	20,660		(h) 360		31
32	Rent Expense	8,100				32
33	Depreciation Expense—Office Equipment			(g) 2,490		33
34	Insurance Expense			(e) 1,910		34
35	Office Supplies Expense			(d) 610		35
36	Miscellaneous Administrative Expense	760				36
37	Rent Income				(i) 600	37
38	Interest Income		3,600		(a) 200	38
39	Interest Expense	2,440				39
40		943,860	943,860	131,900	131,900	40
41						41
42	Net Income					42

selling and partly connected with the administrative operations of the business may be divided between the two categories. In a small business, however, such expenses as rent, insurance, and taxes are commonly reported as administrative expenses.

Expenses of relatively small amounts that cannot be identified with the principal accounts are usually accumulated in accounts entitled Miscellaneous Selling Expense and Miscellaneous Administrative Expense.

Income from Operations. The excess of gross profit over total operating expenses is called **income from operations,** or **operating income**. The amount of the income from operations and its relationship to capital investment and

Co.
Sheet
December 31, 1990

	ADJUSTED TRIAL BALANCE		INCOME STATEMENT		BALANCE SHEET		
	DEBIT	CREDIT	DEBIT	CREDIT	DEBIT	CREDIT	
1	62,950				62,950		1
2	40,000				40,000		2
3	60,880				60,880		3
4	200				200		4
5	62,150				62,150		5
6	480				480		6
7	2,650				2,650		7
8	27,100				27,100		8
9		5,700				5,700	9
10	15,570				15,570		10
11		4,720				4,720	11
12		22,420				22,420	12
13		1,140				1,140	13
14		1,800				1,800	14
15		25,000				25,000	15
16		100,000				100,000	16
17		53,800				53,800	17
18	18,000				18,000		18
19	59,700	62,150	59,700	62,150			19
20		720,185		720,185			20
21	6,140		6,140				21
22	5,790		5,790				22
23	521,980		521,980				23
24		9,100		9,100			24
25		2,525		2,525			25
26	17,400		17,400				26
27	60,030		60,030				27
28	10,860		10,860				28
29	3,100		3,100				29
30	630		630				30
31	21,020		21,020				31
32	8,100		8,100				32
33	2,490		2,490				33
34	1,910		1,910				34
35	610		610				35
36	760		760				36
37		600		600			37
38		3,800		3,800			38
39	2,440		2,440				39
40	1,012,940	1,012,940	722,960	798,360	289,980	214,580	40
41			75,400			75,400	41
42			798,360	798,360	289,980	289,980	42

Multiple-Step Form of Income Statement

Cox Co.
Income Statement
For Year Ended December 31, 1990

Revenue from sales:			
Sales...		$720,185	
Less: Sales returns and allowances ..	$ 6,140		
Sales discounts....................	5,790	11,930	
Net sales			$708,255
Cost of merchandise sold:			
Merchandise inventory, January 1, 1990		$ 59,700	
Purchases..................................	$521,980		
Less: Purchases returns and allowances.................	$9,100		
Purchases discounts..............	2,525	11,625	
Net purchases.............................		$510,355	
Add transportation in		17,400	
Cost of merchandise purchased......		527,755	
Merchandise available for sale		$587,455	
Less merchandise inventory, December 31, 1990		62,150	
Cost of merchandise sold.............			525,305
Gross profit			$182,950
Operating expenses:			
Selling expenses:			
Sales salaries expense...............	$ 60,030		
Advertising expense....................	10,860		
Depreciation expense— store equipment	3,100		
Miscellaneous selling expense	630		
Total selling expenses		$ 74,620	
Administrative expenses:			
Office salaries expense...............	$ 21,020		
Rent expense	8,100		
Depreciation expense— office equipment.....................	2,490		
Insurance expense......................	1,910		
Office supplies expense..............	610		
Miscellaneous administrative expense................................	760		
Total administrative expenses		34,890	
Total operating expenses			109,510
Income from operations			$ 73,440
Other income:			
Interest income	$ 3,800		
Rent income	600		
Total other income......................		$ 4,400	
Other expense:			
Interest expense...........................		2,440	1,960
Net income[2]...................................			$ 75,400

[2]This amount is further reduced by corporation income tax. The discussion of income taxes levied on corporate entities is reserved for later chapters.

to net sales are important factors in judging the efficiency of management and the degree of profitability of an enterprise. If operating expenses are greater than the gross profit, the excess is called **loss from operations**.

Other Income. Revenue from sources other than the principal activity of a business is classified as other income, or **nonoperating income**. In a merchandising business, this category often includes income from interest, rent, dividends, and gains resulting from the sale of plant assets.

Other Expense. Expenses that cannot be associated definitely with operations are identified as other expense, or **nonoperating expense**. Interest expense that results from financing activities and losses incurred in the disposal of plant assets are examples of items that are reported in this section.

The two categories of nonoperating items are offset against each other on the income statement. If the total of other income exceeds the total of other expense, the difference is added to income from operations. If the reverse is true, the difference is subtracted from income from operations.

Net Income. The final figure on the income statement is labeled **net income** (or **net loss**). It is the net increase (or net decrease) in owner's equity as a result of profit-making activities. (As noted on the preceding page, the reporting of corporation income tax is discussed later.)

Single-Step Form. The **single-step form of income statement** derives its name from the fact that the total of all expenses is deducted from the total of all revenues. Such a statement is illustrated as follows for Cox Co. The illustration has been condensed to focus attention on its principal features. Such condensation is not an essential characteristic of the single-step form.

Single-Step Form of Income Statement

Cox Co. Income Statement For Year Ended December 31, 1990		
Revenues:		
Net sales...		$708,255
Interest income..		3,800
Rent income...		600
Total revenues...		$712,655
Expenses:		
Cost of merchandise sold	$525,305	
Selling expenses..	74,620	
Administrative expenses..	34,890	
Interest expense	2,440	
Total expenses		637,255
Net income		$ 75,400

The single-step form has the advantage of being simple and it emphasizes total revenues and total expenses as the factors that determine net income. An objection to the single-step form is that such relationships as gross profit to sales and income from operations to sales are not as readily determinable as they are when the multiple-step form is used.

Retained Earnings Statement

The **retained earnings statement** summarizes the changes which have occurred in the retained earnings account during the fiscal period. It serves as a connecting link between the income statement and the balance sheet. The retained earnings statement for Cox Co. is illustrated as follows:

Retained Earnings Statement

Cox Co.
Retained Earnings Statement
For Year Ended December 31, 1990

Retained earnings, January 1, 1990...............................		$ 53,800
Net income for the year...	$75,400	
Less dividends...	18,000	
Increase in retained earnings		57,400
Retained earnings, December 31, 1990.........................		$111,200

The analysis of retained earnings may be added at the bottom of the income statement to form a **combined income and retained earnings statement**. This combined form was used by 8% of the 600 industrial and merchandising companies surveyed in the 1988 edition of *Accounting Trends & Techniques*. The income statement portion of the combined statement may be shown either in multiple-step form or in a single-step form, as in the following illustration:

Combined Income and Retained Earnings Statement

Cox Co.
Income and Retained Earnings Statement
For Year Ended December 31, 1990

Revenues:		
Net sales...		$708,255
Interest income...		3,800
Rent income...		600
Total revenues...		$712,655
Expenses:		
Cost of merchandise sold	$525,305	
Selling expenses..	74,620	
Administrative expenses.......................................	34,890	
Interest expense	2,440	
Total expenses		637,255
Net income		$ 75,400
Retained earnings, January 1, 1990...........................		53,800
		$129,200
Less dividends...		18,000
Retained earnings, December 31, 1990.......................		$111,200

The combined statement form emphasizes net income as the connecting link between the income statement and the retained earnings portion of owner's equity and thus helps the reader's understanding. A criticism of the combined statement is that the net income figure is buried in the body of the statement.

Balance Sheet

The traditional arrangement of assets on the left-hand side of the balance sheet, with the liabilities and owner's equity on the right-hand side, is referred to as the **account form**.[3] If the entire statement is presented on a single page, it is customary to present the three sections in a downward sequence, with the total of the assets section equaling the combined totals of the other two sections. The latter form, called the **report form**, is illustrated in the following balance sheet for Cox Co.:

Report Form of Balance Sheet

Cox Co.
Balance Sheet
December 31, 1990

Assets

Current assets:			
Cash		$ 62,950	
Notes receivable		40,000	
Accounts receivable		60,880	
Interest receivable		200	
Merchandise inventory		62,150	
Office supplies		480	
Prepaid insurance		2,650	
Total current assets			$229,310
Plant assets:			
Store equipment	$27,100		
Less accumulated depreciation	5,700	$ 21,400	
Office equipment	$15,570		
Less accumulated depreciation	4,720	10,850	
Total plant assets			32,250
Total assets			$261,560

Liabilities

Current liabilities:			
Accounts payable		$ 22,420	
Note payable (current portion)		5,000	
Salaries payable		1,140	
Unearned rent		1,800	
Total current liabilities			$ 30,360
Long-term liabilities:			
Note payable (final payment, 1994)			20,000
Total liabilities			$ 50,360

Stockholders' Equity

Capital stock		$100,000	
Retained earnings		111,200	
Total stockholders' equity			211,200
Total liabilities and stockholders' equity			$261,560

[3]An account form of balance sheet is illustrated on pages 664 and 665.

ADJUSTING ENTRIES

The analyses required to make the adjustments were completed during the process of preparing the work sheet. It is therefore unnecessary to refer again to the basic data when recording the adjusting entries in the journal. After the entries are posted, the balances of all asset, liability, revenue, and expense accounts correspond exactly to the amounts reported in the financial statements. The adjusting entries for Cox Co. are as follows:[4]

Adjusting Entries

	DATE	DESCRIPTION	POST. REF.	DEBIT	CREDIT
1		Adjusting Entries			
2	1990 Dec. 31	Interest Receivable	114	2 0 0 00	
3		Interest Income	811		2 0 0 00
5	31	Income Summary	313	59 7 0 0 00	
6		Merchandise Inventory	114		59 7 0 0 00
8	31	Merchandise Inventory	114	62 1 5 0 00	
9		Income Summary	313		62 1 5 0 00
11	31	Office Supplies Expense	717	6 1 0 00	
12		Office Supplies	116		6 1 0 00
14	31	Insurance Expense	716	1 9 1 0 00	
15		Prepaid Insurance	117		1 9 1 0 00
17	31	Depreciation Expense—Store Equip.	613	3 1 0 0 00	
18		Accumulated Depr.—Store Equip.	122		3 1 0 0 00
20	31	Depreciation Expense—Office Equip.	715	2 4 9 0 00	
21		Accumulated Depr.—Office Equip.	124		2 4 9 0 00
23	31	Sales Salaries Expense	611	7 8 0 00	
24		Office Salaries Expense	711	3 6 0 00	
25		Salaries Payable	213		1 1 4 0 00
27	31	Unearned Rent	214	6 0 0 00	
28		Rent Income	812		6 0 0 00

JOURNAL   PAGE 28

CLOSING ENTRIES

The closing entries are recorded in the journal immediately following the adjusting entries. All of the temporary owner's equity accounts are cleared of their balances, reducing them to zero. The final effect of closing out such balances is a net increase or a net decrease in the retained earnings account. The closing entries for Cox Co. are as follows:

[4]An alternative method of recording merchandise inventory is presented in Appendix C. This alternative method is sometimes referred to as the closing method. Under this method, the entries for beginning and ending merchandise inventory are classified as closing entries rather than adjusting entries.

Closing Entries

JOURNAL

PAGE 29

	DATE	DESCRIPTION	POST. REF.	DEBIT	CREDIT	
1		Closing Entries				1
2	1990 Dec. 31	Sales	411	720 1 8 5 00		2
3		Purchases Returns and Allowances	512	9 1 0 0 00		3
4		Purchases Discounts	518	2 5 2 5 00		4
5		Interest Income	811	3 8 0 0 00		5
6		Rent Income	812	6 0 0 00		6
7		Income Summary	313		736 2 1 0 00	7
8						8
9	31	Income Summary	313	663 2 6 0 00		9
10		Sales Returns and Allowances	412		6 1 4 0 00	10
11		Sales Discounts	413		5 7 9 0 00	11
12		Purchases	511		521 9 8 0 00	12
13		Transportation In	514		17 4 0 0 00	13
14		Sales Salaries Expense	611		60 0 3 0 00	14
15		Advertising Expense	612		10 8 6 0 00	15
16		Depreciation Exp. — Store Equip.	613		3 1 0 0 00	16
17		Miscellaneous Selling Expense	619		6 3 0 00	17
18		Office Salaries Expense	711		21 0 2 0 00	18
19		Rent Expense	712		8 1 0 0 00	19
20		Depreciation Exp. — Office Equip.	715		2 4 9 0 00	20
21		Insurance Expense	716		1 9 1 0 00	21
22		Office Supplies Expense	717		6 1 0 00	22
23		Miscellaneous Administrative				23
24		Expense	719		7 6 0 00	24
25		Interest Expense	911		2 4 4 0 00	25
26						26
27	31	Income Summary	313	75 4 0 0 00		27
28		Retained Earnings	311		75 4 0 0 00	28
29						29
30	31	Retained Earnings	311	18 0 0 0 00		30
31		Dividends	312		18 0 0 0 00	31
32						32

The effect of each of these four entries may be described as follows:

1. The first entry closes all income statement accounts with *credit* balances by transferring the total to the *credit* side of Income Summary.
2. The second entry closes all income statement accounts with *debit* balances by transferring the total to the *debit* side of Income Summary.
3. The third entry closes Income Summary by transferring its balance, the net income for the year, to Retained Earnings.
4. The fourth entry closes Dividends by transferring its balance to Retained Earnings.

The income summary account, as it will appear after the merchandise inventory adjustments and the closing entries have been posted, is as follows. Each item in the account is identified as an aid to understanding. Such notations are not an essential part of the posting procedure.

Income Summary Account

ACCOUNT Income Summary								**ACCOUNT NO.** 313	

DATE		ITEM	POST. REF.	DEBIT	CREDIT	BALANCE	
						DEBIT	CREDIT
1990 Dec.	31	Mer. inv.,					
		Jan. 1	28	59 700 00		59 700 00	
	31	Mer. inv.,					
		Dec. 31	28		62 150 00		2 450 00
	31	Revenue, etc.	29		736 210 00		738 660 00
	31	Expense, etc.	29	663 260 00			75 400 00
	31	Net income	29	75 400 00			

After all temporary owner's equity accounts have been closed, the only accounts with balances are the asset, contra asset, liability, capital stock, and retained earnings accounts. It is advisable to take a post-closing trial balance to verify the debit-credit equality of the balances of these accounts, which should correspond exactly with the amounts appearing on the balance sheet on page 185.

REVERSING ENTRIES

OBJECTIVE 4
Describe and illustrate the preparation of reversing entries.

Some of the adjusting entries recorded at the end of a fiscal year have an important effect on otherwise routine transactions that occur in the following year. Typical examples are the adjusting entries for accrued salaries owed to employees at the end of the year and for accrued interest earned but not collected at the end of the year. To simplify the analysis and recording of subsequent transactions related to such adjusting entries, an optional procedure—the use of **reversing entries**—may be used. As the term implies, a reversing entry is the exact reverse of the adjusting entry to which it relates. The amounts and the accounts are the same as the adjusting entry; the debits and credits are merely reversed, as discussed in the following paragraphs.

Reversing Entries for Accrued Liabilities

Some expenses accrue from day to day but are recorded only when they are paid. For example, the wage or salary expense of an enterprise and the accompanying liability to employees actually accumulates or accrues day by day, or even hour by hour, during any part of the fiscal year. Nevertheless, the practice of recording the expense only at the time of payment is more efficient. When salaries are paid weekly, an entry debiting Salary Expense and crediting Cash will be recorded 52 or 53 times during the year. If there has been an adjusting entry for accrued salaries at the end of the year, however, the first payment of salaries in the following year will include such year-end accrual. In the absence of some special provision, it will be necessary to debit Salaries Payable for the amount owed for the earlier year and Salary Expense for the portion of the payroll that represents expense for the later year.

To illustrate, assume the following facts for an enterprise that pays salaries weekly and ends its fiscal year on December 31:

1. Salaries are paid on Friday for the five-day week ending on Friday.
2. The balance in Salary Expense as of Friday, December 27, is $62,500.
3. Salaries accrued for Monday and Tuesday, December 30 and 31, total $500.
4. Salaries paid on Friday, January 3, of the following year total $1,250.

The foregoing data may be diagrammed as follows:

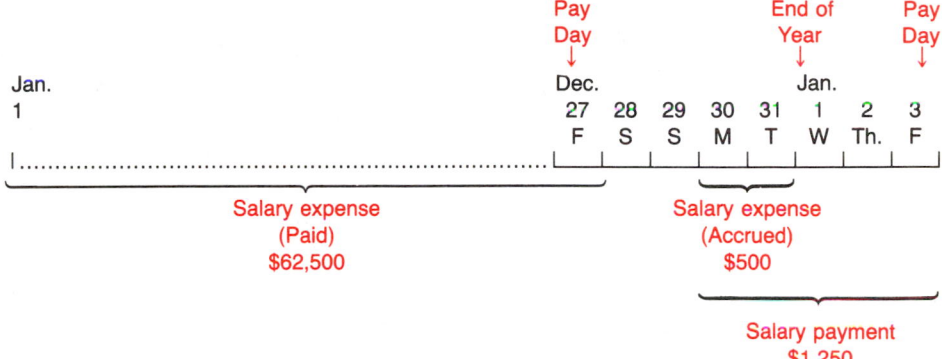

The adjusting entry to record the accrued salary expense and salaries payable for Monday and Tuesday, December 30 and 31, is as follows:

Dec. 31	Salary Expense	611	500	
	Salaries Payable	213		500

After the adjusting entry has been posted, Salary Expense will have a debit balance of $63,000 ($62,500 + $500) and Salaries Payable will have a credit balance of $500. After the closing process is completed, Salary Expense is in balance and ready for entries of the following year, but Salaries Payable continues to have a credit balance of $500. As matters now stand, it would be necessary to record the $1,250 payroll on January 3 as a debit of $500 to Salaries Payable and a debit of $750 to Salary Expense. This means that the employee who records payroll entries must not only record this particular payroll in a different manner from all other weekly payrolls for the year, but must also refer to the adjusting entries in the journal or the ledger to determine the amount of the $1,250 payment to be debited to each of the two accounts.

The need to refer to earlier entries and to divide the debit between two accounts can be avoided by recording a reversing entry as of the first day of the following fiscal period. Continuing with the illustration, the reversing entry for the accrued salaries is as follows:

Jan. 1	Salaries Payable	213	500	
	Salary Expense	611		500

The effect of the reversing entry is to transfer the $500 liability from Salaries Payable to the credit side of Salary Expense. The real nature of the $500 balance is unchanged; it remains a liability. When the payroll is paid on January 3, Salary Expense will be debited and Cash will be credited for

$1,250, the entire amount of the weekly salaries. After the entry is posted, Salary Expense will have a debit balance of $750, which is the amount of expense incurred for January 1–3. The sequence of entries, including adjusting, closing, and reversing entries, may be traced in the following accounts:

Adjustment and Reversal for Accrued Salaries

ACCOUNT **SALARY EXPENSE**   ACCOUNT NO. 611

Date		Item	Post. Ref.	Debit	Credit	Balance Debit	Balance Credit
1990 Jan.	5		1	1,240		1,240	
Dec.	6		25	1,300		58,440	
	13		26	1,450		59,890	
	20		27	1,260		61,150	
	27		28	1,350		62,500	
	31	Adjusting	28	500		63,000	
	31	Closing	29		63,000	—	—
1991 Jan.	1	Reversing	29		500		500
	3		29	1,250		750	

ACCOUNT **SALARIES PAYABLE**   ACCOUNT NO. 213

Date		Item	Post. Ref.	Debit	Credit	Balance Debit	Balance Credit
1990 Dec.	31	Adjusting	28		500		500
1991 Jan.	1	Reversing	29	500		—	—

Reversing Entries for Accrued Assets

For efficiency's sake, it is common to record some types of revenues only as the cash is received. For example, the interest income earned on an interest-bearing note receivable actually accumulates or accrues from day to day, or even moment by moment. Nevertheless, the practice of recording the interest income only at the time of the cash receipt of the interest is more efficient. However, when this procedure is used, an adjusting entry is needed at the end of the year to recognize any interest that is accrued and unpaid. In the adjusting entry, Interest Receivable is debited and Interest Income is credited for the amount accrued. In this case, the first cash receipt in the following year will include the year-end accrual. In the absence of some special provision, it would be necessary to credit Interest Receivable for the amount received for the earlier year and Interest Income for the portion of the cash receipt that represents income for the later year.

To illustrate, assume that an enterprise has a note receivable on which $6,000 of interest is due every six months. If $4,000 of interest income has been earned (accrued) on December 31, the end of the year, the adjusting entry would be as follows:

Dec. 31	Interest Receivable............................	114	4,000	
	Interest Income............................	811		4,000

When the next $6,000 of interest income is received, it would be necessary to credit $4,000 to Interest Receivable and $2,000 to Interest Income. This means that the employee who records the interest entries must record this receipt in a different manner from all other receipts of interest income. It also means that for this particular receipt, the employee must refer to the adjusting entries to determine the proper amount to be credited to each of the two accounts — Interest Receivable and Interest Income. The need to refer to earlier entries and to divide the credit between two accounts can be avoided by the use of reversing entries, as previously discussed. Continuing with the illustration, the reversing entry for the accrued interest income is as follows:

| Jan. 1 | Interest Income................................ | 811 | 4,000 | |
| | Interest Receivable....................... | 114 | | 4,000 |

The effect of the reversing entry is to transfer the $4,000 asset from Interest Receivable to the debit side of Interest Income. The real nature of the $4,000 balance is unchanged; it remains an asset. When the $6,000 of interest is received on March 1 of the following year, Interest Income will be credited for the entire amount. After the entry is posted, Interest Income will have a balance of $2,000, which is the amount of income realized for the period January 1–March 1. The sequence of entries may be traced in the following accounts:

ACCOUNT **INTEREST INCOME** ACCOUNT NO. 811

Date		Item	Post. Ref.	Debit	Credit	Balance Debit	Balance Credit
1990 Dec.	31	Adjusting	28		4,000		4,000
	31	Closing	29	4,000		—	—
1991 Jan.	1	Reversing	29	4,000		4,000	
Mar.	1		31		6,000		2,000

ACCOUNT **INTEREST RECEIVABLE** ACCOUNT NO. 114

Date		Item	Post. Ref.	Debit	Credit	Balance Debit	Balance Credit
1990 Dec.	31	Adjusting	28	4,000		4,000	
1991 Jan.	1	Reversing	29		4,000	—	—

Reversing Entries for a Merchandising Enterprise

The year-end procedures for Cox Co. are completed by journalizing and posting the reversing entries for accrued salaries and accrued interest income. The entries are as follows:

Reversing Entries

	DATE		DESCRIPTION	POST. REF.	DEBIT	CREDIT	
30			Reversing Entries				30
31	1991 Jan.	1	Salaries Payable	213	1 1 4 0 00		31
32			Sales Salaries Expense	611		7 8 0 00	32
33			Office Salaries Expense	711		3 6 0 00	33
34							34
35							35
36		1	Interest Income	811	2 0 0 00		36
37			Interest Receivable	114		2 0 0 00	37

JOURNAL   PAGE 29

After the reversing entry for accrued salaries is posted, Salaries Payable is in balance and the liabilities for sales and office salaries appear as credits in the respective expense accounts. The entire amount of the first payroll in January will be debited to the salary expense accounts, and the balances of the accounts will then automatically represent the expense of the new period. After the reversing entry for accrued interest income is posted, Interest Receivable is in balance and the asset for interest earned appears as a debit in Interest Income. The entire amount of the first receipt of interest in 1991 will be credited to the interest income account and its balance will then automatically represent the interest income for 1991 to that date.

REVERSING ENTRIES: ONCE OR TWICE?

The use of reversing entries is an optional procedure designed to simplify the recording of transactions that follow, reduce the time required to record such transactions, avoid errors, and promote efficiency in general. In one case, however, a reversing entry created rather than prevented an error from occurring.

The error occurred when two companies merged and combined their accounting systems. The accounting systems for the two companies were incompatible—and so, unfortunately, were the chief accounting personnel of the two companies, who were jockeying for position and scarcely speaking to each other. Competent enough to perform routine functions for the separate companies, they were unable to cope with the change brought about by the merger. Furthermore, the basic data which the accounting systems provided were suspect; one company's computerized accounting system was badly programmed and almost nightmarishly erratic.

Amid the confusion of closing and opening the books while the two accounting departments were being combined, an accrued liability was reversed twice instead of once. The net effect was that earnings were overstated by $790,000 and accounts payable were understated by the same amount.

Source: Richard J. Whalen, "The Big Skid at Yale Express," *Fortune* (November, 1965).

INTERIM STATEMENTS

Service and merchandising enterprises frequently prepare financial statements at intervals within the fiscal year, such as monthly, quarterly, or semiannually. Statements issued for periods covering less than a fiscal year are called **interim statements**.

The analysis and recording of transactions is performed on a continuous basis throughout the fiscal year, regardless of when financial statements are to be prepared. When interim financial statements are to be prepared, the adjustment data are assembled and a work sheet is completed as of the end of the interim period. The work sheet then serves as a basis for preparing the interim statements. However, adjusting and closing entries are not recorded in the accounts. These entries are recorded only at the end of the fiscal year.

The amounts of the asset and liability accounts appearing in the balance sheet section of the work sheet for an interim period are the balances as of the last day of that period. The amounts of the revenue and expenses appearing in the income statement section, however, are the total amounts accumulated since the beginning of the fiscal year. To illustrate, assume that the fiscal year of an enterprise is the calendar year. The work sheet prepared at the end of February provides data for an income statement for the two-month period, January–February, and data for a balance sheet as of February 28(29). The work sheet at the end of March provides data for an income statement for the three-month period, January–March, and data for a balance sheet as of March 31. Data for the income statement for a single month only are obtained by subtracting from the amount of each revenue and expense of the current cumulative income statement the corresponding amount from the preceding cumulative income statement. Continuing the illustration, if sales are reported at $190,000 on the cumulative January–March income statement and at $120,000 on the cumulative January–February income statement, the sales reported on the March income statement will be $70,000 ($190,000 − $120,000). The amount of each expense incurred in March and the net income for March is determined in the same manner.

CORRECTION OF ERRORS

OBJECTIVE 6
Describe and illustrate the procedures for correcting errors in accounting records.

Occasional errors in journalizing and posting transactions are unavoidable. Procedures used to correct errors in the journal and ledger vary according to the nature of the error and the phase of the accounting cycle in which it is discovered.

When an error in an account title or amount in the journal is discovered before the entry is posted, the correction may be made by drawing a line through the error and inserting the correct title or amount immediately above. If there is any likelihood of questions arising later, the person responsible may initial the correction. To illustrate, assume that a purchase of office equipment for cash was erroneously journalized as a $500 debit to Office Supplies but correctly journalized as a $500 credit to Cash. If the journal entry has not been posted to the ledger, then the correction may be made as follows:

Journal with Corrected Entry

	DATE		DESCRIPTION	POST. REF.	DEBIT	CREDIT	
1	1990 Oct.	5	Office Equipment ~~Office Supplies~~	DC	5 0 0 00		1
2			Cash			5 0 0 00	2
3							3

When an entry in the journal is prepared correctly, but the debit portion is incorrectly posted to the account as a credit (or vice versa), the incorrect posting may be corrected by drawing a line through the error and posting the item correctly. If the amount of a single debit or credit posting is in error, such as posting a journal debit of $500 as $50, the correction may be made in a similar manner. As indicated in the preceding paragraph, if there is any likelihood of questions arising later, the person responsible may initial the correction, as in the following illustration in which a debit of $500 for office equipment was erroneously posted as a $50 debit.

Account with Corrected Posting

ACCOUNT	Office Equipment						ACCOUNT NO.	18	
DATE	ITEM	POST. REF.	DEBIT	CREDIT	BALANCE				
					DEBIT		CREDIT		
1990 Oct. 5	DC	1	5̶0̶ 00 500 00		5̶0̶ 00 500 00				

When an erroneous account title appears in a journal entry and the error is not discovered until after posting is completed, the preferable procedure is to journalize and post a correcting entry. To illustrate, assume that a purchase of office equipment, which was paid in cash, was erroneously journalized and posted as a $500 debit to Office Supplies but correctly journalized and posted as a $500 credit to Cash. Before a correcting entry is made, it is advisable to establish clearly both (1) the debit(s) and credit(s) of the entry in which the error occurred and (2) the debit(s) and credit(s) that should have been recorded. T accounts may be helpful in making this analysis, as in the following example:

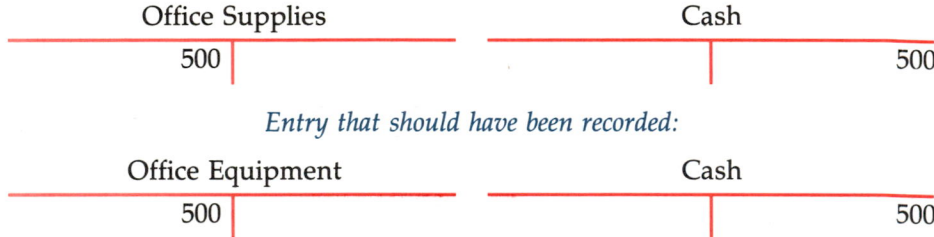

Entry in which error occurred:

Office Supplies		Cash	
500			500

Entry that should have been recorded:

Office Equipment		Cash	
500			500

Comparison of the two sets of T accounts shows that the erroneous debit of $500 to Office Supplies may be corrected by a $500 credit to that account and that Office Equipment should be debited for $500. The following correcting entry is then journalized and posted:

Correcting Entry

	JOURNAL				PAGE 22	
	DATE	DESCRIPTION	POST. REF.	DEBIT	CREDIT	
1	1990 Oct. 31	Office Equipment	18	5 0 0 00		1
2		Office Supplies	15		5 0 0 00	2
3		To correct erroneous debit to				3
4		Office Supplies on Oct. 5.				4
5		See invoice from Allen				5
6		Supply Company. CRN				6
7						7

The preceding procedures for correction of errors are summarized in the following table:

Procedures for Correcting Errors	Error	Correction Procedure
	Journal entry incorrect, but not posted.	Draw line through the error and insert correct title or amount.
	Journal entry correct, but posted incorrectly.	Draw line through the error and post correctly.
	Journal entry incorrect and posted.	Journalize and post a correcting entry.

CHAPTER REVIEW

KEY POINTS

OBJECTIVE 1

Financial Statements for Merchandising Enterprises

The basic financial statements for a merchandising enterprise are the income statement, statement of owner's equity or retained earnings statement, and balance sheet.

There are two widely used forms for the income statement: multiple-step and single-step. The multiple-step income statement is so called because of its many sections, subsections, and intermediate balances. The single-step income statement derives its name from the fact that the total of all expenses is deducted from the total of all revenues.

The retained earnings statement summarizes the changes that have occurred in the retained earnings account during a fiscal period. It is not unusual to add the analysis of retained earnings at the bottom of the income statement to form a combined income and retained earnings statement.

The balance sheet may be prepared using the account form or the report form. The account form lists assets on the left-hand side of the statement, with liabilities and owner's equity on the right-hand side. The report form lists assets, liabilities, and owner's equity in a downward sequence.

OBJECTIVE 2

Adjusting Entries

The adjusting entries are prepared for a merchandising enterprise from the work sheet adjustments columns. After the adjusting entries have been posted, the balances of all asset, liability, revenue, and expense accounts correspond exactly to the amounts reported in the financial statements.

OBJECTIVE 3

Closing Entries

The closing entries are recorded in the journal immediately following the adjusting entries. All the temporary owner's equity accounts are cleared of their balances, reducing them to zero. The final effect of closing out such balances is a net increase or decrease in the retained earnings (owner's capital) account. The final closing entry reduces the dividends (drawing) account to a zero balance by transferring it to retained earnings (owner's capital).

After the adjusting and closing entries have been recorded, it is advisable to take another trial balance to verify the debit-credit equality of the ledger as of the beginning of the following year.

OBJECTIVE 4

Reversing Entries

Some of the adjusting entries recorded at the end of the fiscal year have an important effect on otherwise routine transactions that occur in the following year. To simplify the recording of transactions in the following year, to reduce the time required to record such transactions, to avoid errors, and to promote efficiency, reversing entries may be prepared. As the term implies, a reversing entry is the exact reverse of the adjusting entry to which it relates. The amounts are the same; the debits and credits are merely reversed.

OBJECTIVE 5   Interim Statements

Financial statements issued for periods covering less than a fiscal year are called interim statements. When interim financial statements are to be prepared, the adjustment data are assembled and a work sheet is completed as of the end of the interim period. Interim adjusting and closing entries are not recorded in the accounts.

OBJECTIVE 6   Correction of Errors

Occasional errors in journalizing and posting transactions are unavoidable. The procedures for correction of errors are summarized in the table on page 195.

KEY TERMS

multiple-step income statement 179   net income 183
cost of merchandise sold 179   net loss 183
gross profit 179   single-step income statement 183
selling expenses 180   retained earnings statement 184
administrative expenses 180   account form of balance sheet 185
income from operations 181   report form of balance sheet 185
other income 183   reversing entry 188
other expense 183   interim statements 192

SELF-EXAMINATION QUESTIONS

Answers at end of chapter.

1. The income statement in which the total of all expenses is deducted from the total of all revenues is termed:
   A. multiple-step form   C. account form
   B. single-step form   D. report form

2. On a multiple-step income statement, the excess of net sales over the cost of merchandise sold is called:
   A. operating income   C. gross profit
   B. income from operations   D. net income

3. Which of the following expenses would normally be classified as "other expense" on a multiple-step income statement?
   A. Depreciation expense—   C. Insurance expense
      office equipment   D. Interest expense
   B. Sales salaries expense

4. On July 1, the first day of the fiscal year, Salary Expense has a credit balance of $5,500. On July 3, the first payday in the year, salaries of $21,700 are paid. What is the salary expense for July 1–3?
   A. $5,500   C. $21,700
   B. $16,200   D. $27,200

5. At the end of the fiscal year, the adjusting entry for accrued salaries was inadvertently omitted. The effect of the error (assuming that it is not corrected) would be to:
   A. understate expenses for the year
   B. overstate net income for the year
   C. understate liabilities at the end of the year
   D. all of the above

ILLUSTRATIVE PROBLEM

A partially completed work sheet for Hadley Inc., including all adjustments, is presented below.

Hadley Inc.
Work Sheet
For Year Ended October 31, 1991

	ACCOUNT TITLE	TRIAL BALANCE DEBIT	TRIAL BALANCE CREDIT	ADJUSTMENTS DEBIT	ADJUSTMENTS CREDIT
1	Cash	26400 00			
2	Accounts Receivable	62200 00			
3	Merchandise Inventory	141300 00		(b) 156000 00	(a) 141300 00
4	Prepaid Insurance	6800 00			(c) 4300 00
5	Store Supplies	1250 00			(d) 660 00
6	Office Supplies	800 00			(e) 480 00
7	Store Equipment	65000 00			
8	Accumulated Depreciation—Store Equipment		20100 00		(f) 5850 00
9	Office Equipment	19600 00			
10	Accumulated Depreciation—Office Equipment		8100 00		(g) 2160 00
11	Accounts Payable		36400 00		
12	Salaries Payable				(h) 2700 00
13	Unearned Rent		1000 00	(i) 500 00	
14	Note Payable (final payment, 2001)		75000 00		
15	Capital Stock		50000 00		
16	Retained Earnings		62420 00		
17	Dividends	8000 00			
18	Income Summary			(a) 141300 00	(b) 156000 00
19	Sales		540000 00		
20	Sales Returns and Allowances	4300 00			
21	Sales Discounts	2500 00			
22	Purchases	360000 00			
23	Purchases Returns and Allowances		9000 00		
24	Purchases Discounts		4680 00		
25	Transportation In	1800 00			
26	Sales Salaries Expense	43200 00		(h) 1800 00	
27	Advertising Expense	15000 00			
28	Depreciation Expense—Store Equipment			(f) 5850 00	
29	Store Supplies Expense			(d) 660 00	
30	Miscellaneous Selling Expense	970 00			
31	Office Salaries Expense	30000 00		(h) 900 00	
32	Rent Expense	8500 00			
33	Insurance Expense			(c) 4300 00	
34	Depreciation Expense—Office Equipment			(g) 2160 00	
35	Office Supplies Expense			(e) 480 00	
36	Miscellaneous Administrative Expense	830 00			
37	Rent Income				(i) 500 00
38	Interest Expense	8250 00			
39		806700 00	806700 00	313950 00	313950 00
40	Net Income				

Instructions:

1. Complete the work sheet for Hadley Inc.
2. Prepare a multiple-step income statement.
3. Prepare a retained earnings statement.

(Continued at top of next page)

SOLUTION

(1)

Hadley

Work

For Year Ended

	ACCOUNT TITLE	TRIAL BALANCE		ADJUSTMENTS	
		DEBIT	CREDIT	DEBIT	CREDIT
1	Cash	2 6 4 0 0 00			
2	Accounts Receivable	6 2 2 0 0 00			
3	Merchandise Inventory	14 1 3 0 0 00		(b) 15 6 0 0 00	(a) 14 1 3 0 0 00
4	Prepaid Insurance	6 8 0 0 00			(c) 4 3 0 0 00
5	Store Supplies	1 2 5 0 00			(d) 6 6 0 00
6	Office Supplies	8 0 0 00			(e) 4 8 0 00
7	Store Equipment	6 5 0 0 0 00			
8	Accumulated Depreciation—Store Equipment		2 0 1 0 0 00		(f) 5 8 5 0 00
9	Office Equipment	1 9 6 0 0 00			
10	Accumulated Depreciation—Office Equipment		8 1 0 0 00		(g) 2 1 6 0 00
11	Accounts Payable		3 6 4 0 0 00		
12	Salaries Payable				(h) 2 7 0 0 00
13	Unearned Rent		1 0 0 0 00	(i) 5 0 0 00	
14	Note Payable (final payment, 2001)		7 5 0 0 0 00		
15	Capital Stock		5 0 0 0 0 00		
16	Retained Earnings		6 2 4 2 0 00		
17	Dividends	8 0 0 0 00			
18	Income Summary			(a) 14 1 3 0 0 00	(b) 15 6 0 0 00
19	Sales		54 0 0 0 0 00		
20	Sales Returns and Allowances	4 3 0 0 00			
21	Sales Discounts	2 5 0 0 00			
22	Purchases	36 0 0 0 0 00			
23	Purchases Returns and Allowances		9 0 0 0 00		
24	Purchases Discounts		4 6 8 0 00		
25	Transportation In	1 8 0 0 00			
26	Sales Salaries Expense	4 3 2 0 0 00		(h) 1 8 0 0 00	
27	Advertising Expense	1 5 0 0 0 00			
28	Depreciation Expense—Store Equipment			(f) 5 8 5 0 00	
29	Store Supplies Expense			(d) 6 6 0 00	
30	Miscellaneous Selling Expense	9 7 0 00			
31	Office Salaries Expense	3 0 0 0 0 00		(h) 9 0 0 00	
32	Rent Expense	8 5 0 0 00			
33	Insurance Expense			(c) 4 3 0 0 00	
34	Depreciation Expense—Office Equipment			(g) 2 1 6 0 00	
35	Office Supplies Expense			(e) 4 8 0 00	
36	Miscellaneous Administrative Expense	8 3 0 00			
37	Rent Income				(i) 5 0 0 00
38	Interest Expense	8 2 5 0 00			
39		80 6 7 0 0 00	80 6 7 0 0 00	31 3 9 5 0 00	31 3 9 5 0 00
40	Net Income				
41					

4. Prepare a report form of balance sheet, assuming that the current portion of the note payable is $7,500.
5. Journalize the adjusting entries.
6. Journalize the closing entries.
7. Journalize any reversing entries as of November 1, 1991.

Inc.

Sheet

October 31, 1991

	ADJUSTED TRIAL BALANCE		INCOME STATEMENT		BALANCE SHEET		
	DEBIT	CREDIT	DEBIT	CREDIT	DEBIT	CREDIT	
	2 6 4 0 0 00				2 6 4 0 0 00		1
	6 2 2 0 0 00				6 2 2 0 0 00		2
	15 6 0 0 0 00				15 6 0 0 0 00		3
	2 5 0 0 00				2 5 0 0 00		4
	5 9 0 00				5 9 0 00		5
	3 2 0 00				3 2 0 00		6
	6 5 0 0 0 00				6 5 0 0 0 00		7
		2 5 9 5 0 00				2 5 9 5 0 00	8
	1 9 6 0 0 00				1 9 6 0 0 00		9
		1 0 2 6 0 00				1 0 2 6 0 00	10
		3 6 4 0 0 00				3 6 4 0 0 00	11
		2 7 0 0 00				2 7 0 0 00	12
		5 0 0 00				5 0 0 00	13
		7 5 0 0 0 00				7 5 0 0 0 00	14
		5 0 0 0 0 00				5 0 0 0 0 00	15
		6 2 4 2 0 00				6 2 4 2 0 00	16
	8 0 0 0 00				8 0 0 0 00		17
	14 1 3 0 0 00	15 6 0 0 0 00	14 1 3 0 0 00	15 6 0 0 0 00			18
		54 0 0 0 0 00		54 0 0 0 0 00			19
	4 3 0 0 00		4 3 0 0 00				20
	2 5 0 0 00		2 5 0 0 00				21
	36 0 0 0 0 00		36 0 0 0 0 00				22
		9 0 0 0 00		9 0 0 0 00			23
		4 6 8 0 00		4 6 8 0 00			24
	1 8 0 0 00		1 8 0 0 00				25
	4 5 0 0 0 00		4 5 0 0 0 00				26
	1 5 0 0 0 00		1 5 0 0 0 00				27
	5 8 5 0 00		5 8 5 0 00				28
	6 6 0 00		6 6 0 00				29
	9 7 0 00		9 7 0 00				30
	3 0 9 0 0 00		3 0 9 0 0 00				31
	8 5 0 0 00		8 5 0 0 00				32
	4 3 0 0 00		4 3 0 0 00				33
	2 1 6 0 00		2 1 6 0 00				34
	4 8 0 00		4 8 0 00				35
	8 3 0 00		8 3 0 00				36
		5 0 0 00		5 0 0 00			37
	8 2 5 0 00		8 2 5 0 00				38
	97 3 4 1 0 00	97 3 4 1 0 00	63 2 8 0 0 00	71 0 1 8 0 00	34 0 6 1 0 00	26 3 2 3 0 00	39
			7 7 3 8 0 00			7 7 3 8 0 00	40
			71 0 1 8 0 00	71 0 1 8 0 00	34 0 6 1 0 00	34 0 6 1 0 00	41

(2)

Hadley Inc.
Income Statement
For Year Ended October 31, 1991

Revenue from sales:			
Sales		$540,000	
Less: Sales returns and allowances	$ 4,300		
Sales discounts	2,500	6,800	
Net sales			$533,200
Cost of merchandise sold:			
Merchandise inventory, November 1, 1990		$141,300	
Purchases		$360,000	
Less: Purchases returns and allowances	$9,000		
Purchases discounts	4,680	13,680	
Net purchases		$346,320	
Add transportation in		1,800	
Cost of merchandise purchased		348,120	
Merchandise available for sale		$489,420	
Less merchandise inventory, October 31, 1991		156,000	
Cost of merchandise sold			333,420
Gross profit			$199,780
Operating expenses:			
Selling expenses:			
Sales salaries expense	$ 45,000		
Advertising expense	15,000		
Depreciation expense—store equipment	5,850		
Store supplies expense	660		
Miscellaneous selling expense	970		
Total selling expenses		$ 67,480	
Administrative expenses:			
Office salaries expense	$ 30,900		
Rent expense	8,500		
Insurance expense	4,300		
Depreciation expense—office equipment	2,160		
Office supplies expense	480		
Miscellaneous administrative expense	830		
Total administrative expenses		47,170	
Total operating expenses			114,650
Income from operations			$ 85,130
Other income:			
Rent income		$ 500	
Other expense:			
Interest expense		8,250	7,750
Net income			$ 77,380

(3)

Hadley Inc.
Retained Earnings Statement
For Year Ended October 31, 1991

Retained earnings, November 1, 1990		$ 62,420
Net income for the year	$77,380	
Less dividends	8,000	
Increase in retained earnings		69,380
Retained earnings, October 31, 1991		$131,800

(4)
Hadley Inc.
Balance Sheet
October 31, 1991

Assets

Current assets:

Cash..........		$ 26,400
Accounts receivable..........		62,200
Merchandise inventory..........		156,000
Prepaid insurance..........		2,500
Store supplies..........		590
Office supplies..........		320
Total current assets..........		$248,010

Plant assets:

Store equipment..........	$65,000	
Less accumulated depreciation..........	25,950	$ 39,050
Office equipment..........	$19,600	
Less accumulated depreciation..........	10,260	9,340
Total plant assets..........		48,390
Total assets..........		$296,400

Liabilities

Current liabilities:

Accounts payable..........		$ 36,400
Note payable (current portion)..........		7,500
Salaries payable..........		2,700
Unearned rent..........		500
Total current liabilities..........		$ 47,100

Long-term liabilities:

Note payable (final payment, 2001)..........		67,500
Total liabilities..........		$114,600

Stockholders' Equity

Capital stock..........		$ 50,000
Retained earnings..........		131,800
Total stockholders' equity..........		181,800
Total liabilities and stockholders' equity..........		$296,400

(5)

JOURNAL   PAGE 27

	DATE		DESCRIPTION	POST. REF.	DEBIT						CREDIT						
1			Adjusting Entries														1
2	1991 Oct.	31	Income Summary		141	3	0	0	00								2
3			Merchandise Inventory								141	3	0	0	00		3
4																	4
5		31	Merchandise Inventory		156	0	0	0	00								5
6			Income Summary								156	0	0	0	00		6
7																	7
8		31	Insurance Expense			4	3	0	0	00							8
9			Prepaid Insurance									4	3	0	0	00	9
10																	10
11		31	Store Supplies Expense				6	6	0	00							11
12			Store Supplies										6	6	0	00	12
13																	13
14		31	Office Supplies Expense				4	8	0	00							14
15			Office Supplies										4	8	0	00	15

16										16
17	31	Depr. Expense — Store Equipment	5 8 5 0	00						17
18		Accumulated Depr. — Store Equip.				5 8 5 0	00			18
19										19
20	31	Depr. Expense — Office Equipment	2 1 6 0	00						20
21		Accumulated Depr. — Office Equip.				2 1 6 0	00			21
22										22
23	31	Sales Salaries Expense	1 8 0 0	00						23
24		Office Salaries Expense	9 0 0	00						24
25		Salaries Payable				2 7 0 0	00			25
26										26
27	31	Unearned Rent	5 0 0	00						27
28		Rent Income				5 0 0	00			28

(6)

29		Closing Entries								29
30	31	Sales	540 0 0 0	00						30
31		Purchases Returns and Allowances	9 0 0 0	00						31
32		Purchases Discounts	4 6 8 0	00						32
33		Rent Income	5 0 0	00						33
34		Income Summary				554 1 8 0	00			34
35										35
36	31	Income Summary	491 5 0 0	00						36
37		Sales Returns and Allowances				4 3 0 0	00			37
38		Sales Discounts				2 5 0 0	00			38
39		Purchases				360 0 0 0	00			39
40		Transportation In				1 8 0 0	00			40
41		Sales Salaries Expense				45 0 0 0	00			41
42		Advertising Expense				15 0 0 0	00			42
43		Depr. Expense — Store Equipment				5 8 5 0	00			43
44		Store Supplies Expense				6 6 0	00			44
45		Miscellaneous Selling Expense				9 7 0	00			45
46		Office Salaries Expense				30 9 0 0	00			46
47		Rent Expense				8 5 0 0	00			47
48		Insurance Expense				4 3 0 0	00			48
49		Depr. Expense — Office Equipment				2 1 6 0	00			49
50		Office Supplies Expense				4 8 0	00			50
51		Miscellaneous Administrative								51
52		Expense				8 3 0	00			52
53		Interest Expense				8 2 5 0	00			53
54										54
55	31	Income Summary	77 3 8 0	00						55
56		Retained Earnings				77 3 8 0	00			56
57										57
58	31	Retained Earnings	8 0 0 0	00						58
59		Dividends				8 0 0 0	00			59

(7)

	DATE		DESCRIPTION	POST. REF.	DEBIT	CREDIT	
1			Reversing Entry				1
2	1991 Nov.	1	Salaries Payable		2 7 0 0 00		2
3			Sales Salaries Expense			1 8 0 0 00	3
4			Office Salaries Expense			9 0 0 00	4

JOURNAL   PAGE 28

DISCUSSION QUESTIONS

1. What is the primary characteristic of the multiple-step income statement?

2. Is there uniformity in the amount of detail presented in a multiple-step income statement? Explain.

3. For the fiscal year, net sales were $895,000 and the cost of merchandise purchased was $625,000. Merchandise inventory at the beginning of the year was $80,000, and at the end of the year it was $70,000. Determine the following amounts:
   (a) Merchandise available for sale. *705,000*
   (b) Cost of merchandise sold. *635*
   (c) Gross profit. *260*
   (d) Merchandise inventory listed on the balance sheet as of the end of the year. *70,000*

4. Into what two categories are operating expenses of a merchandising enterprise usually separated?

5. The following expenses were incurred by a merchandising enterprise during the year. In which expense section of the income statement should each be reported: (a) selling, (b) administrative, or (c) other?
   (1) Interest income on notes receivable. *C*
   (2) Salaries of office personnel. *B*
   (3) Insurance expense on store equipment. *A*
   (4) Advertising expense. *A*
   (5) Office supplies used. *B*
   (6) Depreciation expense on office equipment. *B*
   (7) Rent expense on office building. *B*
   (8) Salary of sales manager. *A*

6. Differentiate between the multiple-step and the single-step forms of the income statement.

7. What major advantages and disadvantages does the single-step form of income statement have in comparison to the multiple-step statement?

8. (a) What two financial statements are frequently combined and presented as a single statement? (b) What is the major criticism directed at the combined statement?

9. Differentiate between the account form and the report form of balance sheet.

10. Describe the four entries to close the accounts of a corporation.
   Income statement accts
   Credit balances & debit of income summary
   Retained earnings of income summary
   Close Dividends

A. Net Income or loss
   of Retained Earnings
B. Bal. sheet accts

11. (a) What is the effect of closing the revenue, expense, and dividends accounts of a corporation at the end of a fiscal year? (b) After the closing entries have been posted, what type of accounts remain with balances?

12. Why is it advisable, after closing the accounts at the end of a year, to reverse the adjusting entries that had been made for accrued salaries, accrued interest income, and other accrued expenses and revenues?

13. Before adjustment at June 30, the end of the fiscal year, the salary expense account has a debit balance of $462,500. The amount of salary accrued (owed but not paid) on the same date is $8,150. Indicate the necessary (a) adjusting entry, (b) closing entry, and (c) reversing entry.

14. Before adjustment at December 31, the end of the fiscal year, the interest income account has a credit balance of $18,000. The amount of the interest accrued (earned but not received) on the same date is $4,000. Indicate the necessary (a) adjusting entry, (b) closing entry, and (c) reversing entry.

Liability

15. Immediately after the reversing entries have been recorded, Salary Expense has a credit balance of $8,750. Assuming that there have been no errors, does the balance represent an asset, expense, revenue, liability, contra asset, or contra expense?

16. As of July 1, the first day of the fiscal year, Salary Expense has a credit balance of $7,800. On July 3, the first payday of the year, salaries of $13,100 are paid. (a) What is the salary expense for July 1–3? (b) What entry should be made to record the payment on July 3?

Intermi
     Statements

17. What are financial statements issued for periods covering less than a fiscal year called?

18. How is a correction made when an error in an account title or amount in the journal is discovered before the entry is posted?

19. In preparing and posting the journal entry to record the purchase of land by issuing a note payable, the capital stock account was erroneously credited. What is the preferred procedure to correct the error?

Real World Focus

20. A recent trend in retailing is the establishment of warehouse clubs. These clubs offer name-brand merchandise at prices ranging from 20 to 40 percent below discount store prices to their members who pay a nominal yearly fee. The Price Club, with projected annual sales of over $1 billion, is one of the leaders in this growing area of retailing. The following graph compares the gross profit as a percent of sales of The Price Club with that of K Mart Corp.:

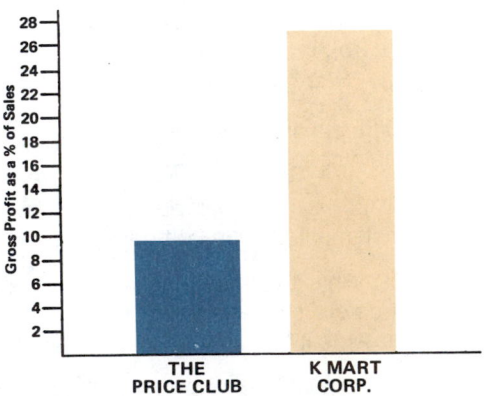

How can the Price Club remain profitable with a gross profit percentage less than one half that of K Mart Corp.?

EXERCISES

Exercise 5–1

Identification of items missing from income statement.

OBJ. 1

For (a) through (i), identify the items designated by "X".

(a) Sales − (X + X) = Net sales
(b) Purchases − (X + X) = Net purchases
(c) Net purchases + X = Cost of merchandise purchased
(d) Merchandise inventory (beginning) + cost of merchandise purchased = X
(e) Merchandise available for sale − X = Cost of merchandise sold
(f) Net sales − cost of merchandise sold = X
(g) X + X = Operating expenses
(h) Gross profit − operating expenses = X
(i) Income from operations + X − X = Net income

Exercise 5–2

Determination of amounts for items omitted from income statement.

OBJ. 1

Three items are omitted in each of the following tabulations of income statement data. Determine the amounts of the missing items, identifying them by letter.

Sales	$ (a)	$575,000	$985,000	$755,000
Sales returns and allowances..	12,000	17,000	(g)	28,000
Sales discounts	2,000	8,000	5,000	(j)
Net sales...........................	110,000	(d)	965,000	(k)
Beginning inventory..............	(b)	125,000	215,000	(l)
Cost of merchandise purchased	70,000	(e)	600,000	580,000
Ending inventory...................	30,000	105,000	(h)	120,000
Cost of merchandise sold.......	65,000	340,000	(i)	540,000
Gross profit........................	(c)	(f)	390,000	180,000

Exercise 5–3

Multiple-step income statement, merchandise inventory adjustments, and closing entries.

OBJ. 1, 2, 3

Selected account titles and related amounts appearing in the income statement and balance sheet columns of the work sheet of Shuman Company for the year ended December 31 are listed in alphabetical order as follows:

Administrative Expenses	$ 87,200
Building..	295,000
Capital Stock...	300,000
Cash..	60,600
Dividends	55,000
Interest Expense...	2,500
Merchandise Inventory (1/1)......................................	225,000
Merchandise Inventory (12/31)	230,000
Notes Payable..	25,000
Office Supplies...	8,500
Purchases	850,000
Purchases Discounts	8,000
Purchases Returns and Allowances.............................	12,000
Retained Earnings...	148,080
Salaries Payable...	3,720
Sales	1,275,000
Sales Discounts..	9,500
Sales Returns and Allowances	35,000
Selling Expenses	125,000
Store Supplies..	7,200
Transportation In...	11,300

All selling expenses have been recorded in the account entitled "Selling Expenses," and all administrative expenses have been recorded in the account entitled "Administrative Expenses."

(a) Prepare a multiple-step income statement for the year.
(b) Determine the amount of retained earnings to be reported in the balance sheet at the end of the year.
(c) Journalize the entries to adjust the merchandise inventory.
(d) Journalize the closing entries.

Exercise 5–4
Single-step income statement.
OBJ. 1

Summary operating data for X-L Inc. during the current year ended September 30, 1991, are as follows: cost of merchandise sold, $895,000; administrative expenses, $150,000; interest expense, $27,500; rent income, $30,000; net sales, $1,470,000; and selling expenses, $205,000. Prepare a single-step income statement.

Exercise 5–5
Combined income and retained earnings statement.
OBJ. 1

From the data presented in Exercise 5–4 and assuming that the balance of Retained Earnings was $425,000 on October 1, 1990, and that $80,000 of dividends were paid during the year, prepare a combined income and retained earnings statement for X-L Inc. (Use the single-step form for the income statement portion.)

Exercise 5–6
Adjusting and reversing entries.
OBJ. 2, 4

On the basis of the following data, journalize (a) the adjusting entries at June 30, 1991, the end of the current fiscal year, and (b) the reversing entry on July 1, 1991, the first day of the following year.

(1) Sales salaries are uniformly $10,000 for a five-day workweek, ending on Friday. The last payday of the year was Friday, June 27.
(2) Merchandise inventory: July 1, 1990 (beginning), $79,900; June 30, 1991 (ending), $85,400.
(3) Store supplies account balance before adjusting, $4,250; store supplies physical inventory, June 30, $870.
(4) The prepaid insurance account before adjustment on June 30 has a balance of $11,325. An analysis of the policies indicates that $7,825 of premiums has expired during the year.
(5) Unearned rent account balance before adjustment, $4,800; unearned rent income, June 30, $1,200.

Exercise 5–7
Entries posted to the salary expense account.
OBJ. 2, 3, 4

Portions of the salary expense account of an enterprise are as follows:

ACCOUNT Salary Expense   ACCOUNT NO. 54

Date		Item	Post. Ref.	Dr.	Cr.	Balance Dr.	Balance Cr.
19--							
Jan.	1		24		1,375		1,375
	5		24	6,500		5,125	
Dec.	27	(1)	51	7,500		245,500	
	31	(2)	51	2,500		248,000	
	31	(3)	52		248,000	—	—
19--							
Jan.	1	(4)	52		2,500		2,500
	4	(5)	53	7,500		5,000	

(a) Indicate the nature of the entry (payment, adjusting, closing, reversing) from which each numbered posting was made. (b) Present the complete journal entry from which each numbered posting was made.

Exercise 5–8
Entries to correct errors.
OBJ. 6

A number of errors in journalizing and posting transactions are described as follows:

(a) A $500 purchase of supplies on account was recorded as a debit to Cash and a credit to Accounts Payable.

(b) A payment of $1,500 to a supplier on account, terms 1/10, n/30, within the discount period was recorded as a debit to Accounts Receivable, $1,500, a credit to Cash, $1,485, and a credit to Purchases Discounts, $15.

(c) Payment of $2,500 cash dividend was recorded as a debit to Miscellaneous Expense and a credit to Cash.

(d) Rent of $800 paid for the current month was recorded as a debit to Supplies Expense and a credit to Cash.

(e) Land of $50,000 purchased through the issuance of a note payable was recorded as a debit to Buildings and a credit to Accounts Payable.

Present the journal entries to correct the errors.

PROBLEMS

Series A

Problem 5–1A
Preparation of multiple-step income statement and report form of balance sheet for corporation.
OBJ. 1

The following selected accounts and their normal balances appear in the income statement and balance sheet columns of the work sheet of Wilcox Inc. for the fiscal year ended December 31, 1991:

Cash	$ 87,750
Notes Receivable	50,000
Accounts Receivable	97,000
Merchandise Inventory, Jan. 1, 1991	75,000
Merchandise Inventory, Dec. 31, 1991	85,000
Office Supplies	2,600
Prepaid Insurance	9,800
Office Equipment	27,750
Accumulated Depreciation — Office Equipment	10,800
Store Equipment	50,000
Accumulated Depreciation — Store Equipment	18,900
Accounts Payable	35,000
Salaries Payable	2,500
Note Payable (final payment, 2001)	25,000
Capital Stock	150,000
Retained Earnings	140,210
Dividends	25,000
Sales	975,000
Sales Returns and Allowances	9,000
Sales Discounts	8,500
Purchases	775,000
Purchases Returns and Allowances	16,200
Purchases Discounts	3,800
Transportation In	10,300
Sales Salaries Expense	83,000
Advertising Expense	16,300
Depreciation Expense — Store Equipment	4,800
Miscellaneous Selling Expense	1,000
Office Salaries Expense	25,900
Rent Expense	12,150
Depreciation Expense — Office Equipment	3,500
Insurance Expense	2,750
Office Supplies Expense	900
Miscellaneous Administrative Expense	1,150
Interest Income	5,000
Interest Expense	3,260

Instructions:

(1) Prepare a multiple-step income statement.
(2) Prepare a retained earnings statement.
(3) Prepare a report form of balance sheet, assuming that the current portion of the note payable is $2,500.

Problem 5–2A

Preparation of single-step income statement and combined income and retained earnings statement.

OBJ. 1

Selected accounts and related amounts for Wilcox Inc. for the fiscal year ended December 31, 1991, are presented in Problem 5–1A.

Instructions:

(1) Prepare a single-step income statement.
(2) Prepare a combined income and retained earnings statement, using the single-step form for the income statement portion.

Problem 5–3A

Combined income and retained earnings statement; balance sheet.

OBJ. 1

The following data for Marr Co. were selected from the ledger after adjustment at December 31, the end of the current fiscal year:

Accounts payable	$ 70,900
Accounts receivable	161,100
Accumulated depreciation — office equipment	40,800
Accumulated depreciation — store equipment	75,200
Administrative expenses	247,250
Capital stock	200,000
Cash	105,600
Cost of merchandise sold	825,500
Dividends	75,000
Dividends payable	15,000
Interest expense	18,000
Merchandise inventory	200,000
Note payable (due in 2003)	150,000
Office equipment	72,200
Prepaid insurance	10,700
Rent income	15,500
Retained earnings	156,100
Salaries payable	9,750
Sales	1,470,000
Selling expenses	283,250
Store equipment	204,650

Instructions:

(1) Prepare a combined income and retained earnings statement, using the single-step form for the income statement portion.
(2) Prepare a balance sheet in report form.

If the working papers correlating with this textbook are not used, omit Problem 5–4A.

Problem 5–4A

Completion of work sheet and preparation of financial statements for corporation.

OBJ. 1

A partially completed work sheet for Magan Inc. is presented in the working papers. All adjustments have been entered on the work sheet.

Instructions:

(1) Complete the work sheet.
(2) Prepare a multiple-step income statement.
(3) Prepare a retained earnings statement.
(4) Prepare a report form of balance sheet, assuming that the current portion of the note payable is $10,000.

Problem 5–5A
Adjusting entries from work sheet for sole proprietorship.
OBJ. 2

A portion of the work sheet of Keaton Co. for the current year ended March 31 is as follows:

Account Title	Income Statement Debit	Income Statement Credit	Balance Sheet Debit	Balance Sheet Credit
Cash			46,150	
Notes Receivable			25,000	
Accounts Receivable			103,250	
Interest Receivable			500	
Merchandise Inventory			295,000	
Prepaid Rent			4,000	
Prepaid Insurance			3,560	
Supplies			1,380	
Store Equipment			112,300	
Accumulated Depr.—Store Equipment				71,000
Office Equipment			44,520	
Accumulated Depr.—Office Equipment				35,000
Accounts Payable				95,100
Sales Salaries Payable				3,750
Note Payable				250,000
B.C. Keaton, Capital				150,620
B.C. Keaton, Drawing			40,000	
Income Summary	315,000	295,000		
Sales		995,000		
Sales Returns and Allowances	17,000			
Sales Discounts	10,500			
Purchases	590,720			
Purchases Returns and Allowances		15,950		
Purchases Discounts		8,840		
Transportation In	5,730			
Sales Salaries Expense	114,000			
Depreciation Expense—Store Equipment	15,960			
Supplies Expense	960			
Miscellaneous Selling Expense	3,800			
Office Salaries Expense	61,000			
Rent Expense	48,000			
Heating and Lighting Expense	21,750			
Insurance Expense	4,100			
Depreciation Expense—Office Equipment	5,180			
Miscellaneous Administrative Expense	2,900			
Interest Income		2,000		
Interest Expense	30,000			
	1,246,600	1,316,790	675,660	605,470

Instructions:

(1) From the partial work sheet, determine the nine entries that appeared in the adjustments columns and present them in journal form. The only accounts affected by more than one adjusting entry were Merchandise Inventory and Income Summary. The balance in Prepaid Rent before adjustment was $52,000, representing 13 months' rent at $4,000 per month.

(2) Determine the following:
   (a) Amount of net income for the year.
   (b) Balance of the owner's capital account at the end of the year.

Problem 5–6A
Closing entries
from work sheet
for corporation.
OBJ. 3

The account balances taken from the Income Statement columns of the work sheet for Wagner Corporation at the end of the current fiscal year are as follows:

	Debit	Credit
Income Summary	260,500	241,650
Sales		1,240,700
Sales Returns and Allowances	31,400	
Sales Discounts	12,900	
Purchases	770,650	
Purchases Returns and Allowances		18,050
Purchases Discounts		8,600
Transportation In	12,100	
Sales Salaries Expense	120,750	
Depreciation Expense—Store Equipment	11,800	
Supplies Expense	2,040	
Miscellaneous Selling Expense	1,600	
Office Salaries Expense	50,300	
Rent Expense	33,600	
Heating and Lighting Expense	13,420	
Insurance Expense	11,500	
Depreciation Expense—Office Equipment	5,180	
Miscellaneous Administrative Expense	1,900	
Interest Expense	21,600	
	1,361,240	1,509,000

Instructions:

Journalize the closing entries, assuming that the balance in the dividends account at the end of the current fiscal year was $60,000.

Problem 5–7A
Preparation of work
sheet, financial
statements, and
adjusting, closing,
and reversing
entries for sole
proprietorship.
OBJ. 1, 2, 3, 4

SOLUTIONS
SOFTWARE

The accounts and their balances in the ledger of Carter Company on December 31 of the current year are as follows:

Cash	$ 68,175
Accounts Receivable	112,500
Merchandise Inventory	180,000
Prepaid Insurance	10,600
Store Supplies	3,750
Office Supplies	1,700
Store Equipment	112,000
Accumulated Depreciation—Store Equipment	40,300
Office Equipment	50,000
Accumulated Depreciation—Office Equipment	17,200
Accounts Payable	66,700
Salaries Payable	—
Unearned Rent	1,200
Note Payable (final payment, 1997)	105,000
C. C. Carter, Capital	220,510
C. C. Carter, Drawing	40,000
Income Summary	—
Sales	995,000
Sales Returns and Allowances	12,500
Sales Discounts	6,500
Purchases	635,000
Purchases Returns and Allowances	9,500
Purchases Discounts	5,500
Transportation In	6,200
Sales Salaries Expense	86,400

Advertising Expense	$ 30,000
Depreciation Expense—Store Equipment	—
Store Supplies Expense	—
Miscellaneous Selling Expense	1,335
Office Salaries Expense	60,000
Rent Expense	30,000
Insurance Expense	—
Depreciation Expense—Office Equipment	—
Office Supplies Expense	—
Miscellaneous Administrative Expense	1,650
Rent Income	—
Interest Expense	12,600

The data for year-end adjustments on December 31 are as follows:

Merchandise inventory on December 31		$220,000
Insurance expired during the year		7,260
Inventory of supplies on December 31:		
Store supplies		1,700
Office supplies		400
Depreciation for the year:		
Store equipment		9,500
Office equipment		4,800
Salaries payable on December 31:		
Sales salaries	$2,750	
Office salaries	1,150	3,900
Unearned rent on December 31		400

Instructions:

(1) Prepare a work sheet for the fiscal year ended December 31, listing all accounts in the order given.
(2) Prepare a multiple-step income statement.
(3) Prepare a statement of owner's equity.
(4) Prepare a report form of balance sheet, assuming that the current portion of the note payable is $15,000.
(5) Journalize the adjusting entries.
(6) Journalize the closing entries.
(7) Journalize the reversing entries as of January 1.

Problem 5–8A
Preparation of work sheet, financial statements, and adjusting, closing, and reversing entries for corporation.

The accounts and their balances in the ledger of Gove Company on December 31 of the current year are as follows:

Cash	$ 61,075
Accounts Receivable	114,600
Merchandise Inventory	180,000
Prepaid Insurance	10,600
Store Supplies	3,750
Office Supplies	1,700
Store Equipment	115,000
Accumulated Depreciation—Store Equipment	40,300
Office Equipment	52,000
Accumulated Depreciation—Office Equipment	17,200
Accounts Payable	66,700
Salaries Payable	—
Unearned Rent	1,200
Note Payable (final payment, 1997)	105,000
Capital Stock	150,000
Retained Earnings	70,510
Dividends	40,000
Income Summary	—

Sales	$997,500
Sales Returns and Allowances	15,000
Sales Discounts	6,500
Purchases	637,500
Purchases Returns and Allowances	9,500
Purchases Discounts	8,000
Transportation In	6,200
Sales Salaries Expense	86,400
Advertising Expense	29,450
Depreciation Expense—Store Equipment	—
Store Supplies Expense	—
Miscellaneous Selling Expense	1,885
Office Salaries Expense	60,000
Rent Expense	30,000
Insurance Expense	—
Depreciation Expense—Office Equipment	—
Office Supplies Expense	—
Miscellaneous Administrative Expense	1,650
Rent Income	—
Interest Expense	12,600

The data for year-end adjustments on December 31 are as follows:

Merchandise inventory on December 31		$220,000
Insurance expired during the year		7,260
Inventory of supplies on December 31:		
Store supplies		1,700
Office supplies		400
Depreciation for the year:		
Store equipment		9,500
Office equipment		4,800
Salaries payable on December 31:		
Sales salaries	$2,750	
Office salaries	1,150	3,900
Unearned rent on December 31		400

Instructions:

(1) Prepare a work sheet for the fiscal year ended December 31, listing all accounts in the order given.
(2) Prepare a multiple-step income statement.
(3) Prepare a retained earnings statement.
(4) Prepare a report form of balance sheet, assuming that the current portion of the note payable is $15,000.
(5) Journalize the adjusting entries.
(6) Journalize the closing entries.
(7) Journalize the reversing entries as of January 1.

Problem 5-9A
Work sheet and interim financial statements for sole proprietorship.
OBJ. 5

R. D. Myers Co. prepares interim statements at the end of each month and closes its accounts annually as of December 31. The trial balance at September 30 of the current year, the adjustment data needed at September 30, and the interim income statement for the eight months ended August 31 of the current year are as follows:

R. D. Myers Co.
Trial Balance
September 30, 19--

Cash	10,490	
Prepaid Insurance	1,250	
Supplies	1,070	
Land	25,000	
Building	74,500	
Accumulated Depreciation—Building		21,725
Equipment	61,250	
Accumulated Depreciation—Equipment		35,200
Accounts Payable		3,170
R. D. Myers, Capital		86,255
R. D. Myers, Drawing	16,000	
Service Revenue		85,600
Salaries and Wages Expense	30,650	
Advertising Expense	5,000	
Utilities Expense	4,380	
Repairs Expense	1,320	
Miscellaneous Expense	1,040	
	231,950	231,950

Adjustment data at September 30:

(a) Insurance expired for the period January 1–September 30 .... $ 950
(b) Inventory of supplies on September 30 220
(c) Depreciation of building for the period January 1–September 30 .. 1,620
(d) Depreciation of equipment for the period
      January 1–September 30 5,150
(e) Accrued salaries and wages on September 30 1,820

R. D. Myers Co.
Income Statement
For Eight Months Ended August 31, 19--

Service revenue		$73,000
Operating expenses:		
Salaries and wages expense	$28,250	
Depreciation expense—equipment	4,400	
Advertising expense	3,955	
Utilities expense	3,702	
Depreciation expense—building	1,440	
Repairs expense	1,148	
Insurance expense	825	
Supplies expense	700	
Miscellaneous expense	827	
Total operating expenses		45,247
Net income		$27,753

Instructions:

(1) Record the trial balance on a ten-column work sheet and complete the work sheet.
(2) Prepare an interim income statement for the nine months ended September 30. (For this problem, it is not necessary to distinguish between selling and administrative expenses.)
(3) Prepare an interim statement of owner's equity for the nine months ended September 30. *(Continued)*

214   PART ONE Basic Structure of Accounting

(4) Prepare an interim balance sheet as of September 30.
(5) On the basis of the income statement for the nine-month period and the income statement for the eight-month period, prepare an interim income statement for the month of September.

Problem 5–10A
Entries for transactions and corrections.
OBJ. 6

The following selected transactions and errors relate to the accounts of Lupo Co. during the current fiscal year:

March 12. Marcia Lupo established the business with an investment of $50,000 in cash and $15,000 in store equipment, on which there was a balance owed of $7,150. The account payable is to be recorded in the ledger of the enterprise.

April 3. Acquired land to be used as a future building site at a contract price of $65,000. The property was encumbered by a note for $50,000. Paid the seller $15,000 in cash and agreed to assume the responsibility for paying the note.

May 22. Discovered that a cash payment of $2,150 in partial payment of the account payable incurred with the equipment acquired on March 12 had been journalized and posted as a debit to Accounts Payable of $2,150 and a credit to Equipment of $2,150.

June 15. Discovered that a payment of a $5,000 invoice, terms 1/10, n/30, within the discount period had been recorded as a debit to Accounts Payable of $4,950 and a credit to Cash of $4,950.

July 18. Discovered that a withdrawal of $2,000 by the owner had been debited to Salary Expense.

Oct. 3. Discovered that cash of $2,000, received from a customer on account, had been journalized and posted as a debit to Cash and a credit to Sales.

Nov. 30. Sold to an employee for cash $200 of store supplies at cost for the employee's personal use.

Dec. 5. Discovered that a purchase of merchandise of $1,200 returned to the supplier for credit had been journalized and posted as a debit to Cash and a credit to Miscellaneous Expense.

31. Discovered that depreciation of $1,750 on the equipment acquired on March 12 had been journalized and posted as a debit to Miscellaneous Expense of $1,570 and a credit to Equipment of $1,570.

Instructions:

Journalize the transactions and the corrections. When there are more than two items in an entry, present the entry in compound form.

Series B

Problem 5–1B
Preparation of multiple-step income statement and report form of balance sheet for corporation.
OBJ. 1

SOLUTIONS SOFTWARE

The following selected accounts and their normal balances appear in the income statement and balance sheet columns of the work sheet of Maddox Inc. for the fiscal year ended March 31, 1991:

Cash	$ 43,750
Notes Receivable	100,000
Accounts Receivable	225,000
Merchandise Inventory, April 1, 1990	125,000
Merchandise Inventory, March 31, 1991	120,000
Office Supplies	7,900
Prepaid Insurance	4,500
Office Equipment	35,000
Accumulated Depreciation — Office Equipment	12,800

Store Equipment	$ 77,500
Accumulated Depreciation—Store Equipment	29,700
Accounts Payable	50,000
Salaries Payable	3,900
Note Payable (final payment, 1999)	80,000
Capital Stock	250,000
Retained Earnings	147,250
Dividends	40,000
Sales	1,450,000
Sales Returns and Allowances	12,100
Sales Discounts	11,900
Purchases	1,125,000
Purchases Returns and Allowances	24,600
Purchases Discounts	15,400
Transportation In	10,000
Sales Salaries Expense	133,200
Advertising Expense	22,800
Depreciation Expense—Store Equipment	6,400
Miscellaneous Selling Expense	1,600
Office Salaries Expense	40,150
Rent Expense	26,350
Depreciation Expense—Office Equipment	12,700
Insurance Expense	3,900
Office Supplies Expense	1,300
Miscellaneous Administrative Expense	1,600
Interest Income	12,000
Interest Expense	8,000

Instructions:

(1) Prepare a multiple-step income statement.
(2) Prepare a retained earnings statement.
(3) Prepare a report form balance sheet, assuming that the current portion of the note payable is $10,000.

Problem 5–2B
Preparation of single-step income statement and combined income and retained earnings statement.

OBJ. 1

Selected accounts and related amounts for Maddox Inc. for the fiscal year ended March 31, 1991, are presented in Problem 5–1B.

Instructions:

(1) Prepare a single-step income statement.
(2) Prepare a combined income and retained earnings statement, using the single-step form for the income statement portion.

Problem 5–3B
Combined income and retained earnings statement; balance sheet.

OBJ. 1

SPREADSHEET PROBLEM

The following data for Lusk Co. were selected from the ledger after adjustment at April 30, 1991, the end of the current fiscal year:

Accounts payable	$ 83,700
Accounts receivable	122,100
Accumulated depreciation—office equipment	30,750
Accumulated depreciation—store equipment	91,050
Administrative expenses	113,220
Capital stock	100,000
Cash	40,100
Cost of merchandise sold	990,890
Dividends	60,000
Dividends payable	15,000
Interest expense	18,000
Merchandise inventory	280,200
Note payable (due in 2001)	150,000
Office equipment	111,000
Prepaid insurance	5,250

Rent income	$	8,700
Retained earnings		281,500
Salaries payable		4,640
Sales		1,390,750
Selling expenses		175,080
Store equipment		240,250

Instructions:

(1) Prepare a combined income and retained earnings statement, using the single-step form for the income statement portion.
(2) Prepare a balance sheet in report form.

Problem 5–5B
Adjusting entries from work sheet for corporation.
OBJ. 2

A portion of the work sheet of C. C. Schultz Inc. for the current year ended June 30 is as follows:

Account Title	Income Statement		Balance Sheet	
	Debit	Credit	Debit	Credit
Cash			61,050	
Notes Receivable			50,000	
Accounts Receivable			125,000	
Interest Receivable			1,000	
Merchandise Inventory			241,650	
Prepaid Rent			9,000	
Prepaid Insurance			8,000	
Supplies			3,360	
Store Equipment			99,750	
Accumulated Depr. — Store Equipment				33,490
Office Equipment			63,600	
Accumulated Depr. — Office Equipment				15,750
Accounts Payable				84,550
Sales Salaries Payable				4,100
Note Payable				200,000
Capital Stock				150,000
Retained Earnings				107,760
Dividends			30,000	
Income Summary	250,000	241,650		
Sales		1,234,700		
Sales Returns and Allowances	40,900			
Sales Discounts	12,900			
Purchases	818,250			
Purchases Returns and Allowances		18,050		
Purchases Discounts		8,400		
Transportation In	12,900			
Sales Salaries Expense	120,750			
Depreciation Expense — Store Equipment	12,000			
Supplies Expense	2,040			
Miscellaneous Selling Expense	1,600			
Office Salaries Expense	50,300			
Rent Expense	36,000			
Heating and Lighting Expense	13,420			
Insurance Expense	11,500			
Depreciation Expense — Office Equipment	5,980			
Miscellaneous Administrative Expense	1,900			
Interest Income		6,000		
Interest Expense	21,600			
	1,412,040	1,508,800	692,410	595,650

Instructions:

(1) From the partial work sheet, determine the nine entries that appeared in the adjustments columns and present them in journal form. The only accounts affected by more than one adjusting entry were Merchandise Inventory and Income Summary. The balance in Prepaid Rent before adjustment was $45,000, representing 15 months' rent at $3,000 per month.
(2) Determine the following:
   (a) Amount of net income for the year.
   (b) Balance of the retained earnings account at the end of the year.

Problem 5–6B

Closing entries from work sheet for corporation.

OBJ. 3

The account balances taken from the Income Statement columns of the work sheet for Woodward Corporation at the end of the current fiscal year are as follows:

	Debit	Credit
Income Summary	354,000	335,000
Sales		1,020,000
Sales Returns and Allowances	12,000	
Sales Discounts	8,500	
Purchases	617,720	
Purchases Returns and Allowances		14,650
Purchases Discounts		10,140
Transportation In	7,230	
Sales Salaries Expense	124,000	
Depreciation Expense—Store Equipment	16,460	
Supplies Expense	960	
Miscellaneous Selling Expense	3,800	
Office Salaries Expense	70,000	
Rent Expense	36,000	
Heating and Lighting Expense	21,750	
Insurance Expense	4,100	
Depreciation Expense—Office Equipment	5,180	
Miscellaneous Administrative Expense	2,900	
Interest Expense	30,000	
	1,314,600	1,379,790

Instructions:

Journalize the closing entries, assuming that the balance in the dividends account at the end of the current fiscal year was $40,000.

MINI-CASE 5

HARMON VIDEO INC.

Your sister operates Harmon Video Inc., a video tape distributorship that is in its third year of operation. Recently, Jack Davis, the firm's accountant, resigned. Before leaving, he completed the work sheet for the year ended April 30, 1991, and recorded the necessary adjusting entries. From this work sheet, your sister prepared the following financial statements:

Harmon Video Inc.
Income Statement
For Year Ended April 30, 1991

Sales		$340,000
Less cost of merchandise sold:		
Purchases	$261,600	
Net increase in merchandise inventory	17,500	244,100
Gross profit		$ 95,900
Operating expenses:		
Salaries expense	$ 30,050	
Heat and lighting expense	7,750	
Insurance expense	4,500	
Depreciation expense—building	3,100	
Depreciation expense—office equipment	1,260	
Depreciation expense—store equipment	3,060	
Supplies expense	2,440	
Miscellaneous expense	1,620	
Transportation in	4,100	57,880
		$ 38,020
Selling expenses:		
Advertising expense	$ 11,940	
Transportation out	14,160	26,100
Income from operations		$ 11,920
Other income:		
Purchases discounts	$ 2,480	
Purchases returns and allowances	8,770	
Interest income	500	11,750
		$ 23,670
Other expenses:		
Sales returns	$ 1,500	
Dividends	15,000	
Interest expense	6,000	22,500
Net income		$ 1,170

Harmon Video Inc.
Retained Earnings Statement
For Year Ended April 30, 1991

Retained earnings, May 1, 1990	$29,750
Net income for the year	1,170
Retained earnings, April 30, 1991	$30,920

Harmon Video Inc.
Balance Sheet
April 30, 1991

Assets

Cash	$ 14,520
Merchandise inventory	58,300
Supplies	1,820
Prepaid insurance	1,680
Accounts receivable	20,600
Store equipment	12,800
Office equipment	6,300
Building	57,900
Land	30,000
Notes receivable	5,000
Total assets	$208,920

Liabilities and Stockholders' Equity	
Accumulated depreciation—store equipment	$ 4,320
Accumulated depreciation—office equipment	2,520
Accumulated depreciation—building	5,760
Accounts payable	13,800
Salaries payable	1,600
Note payable—	
First National Bank (due in 1999)	50,000
Capital stock	100,000
Retained earnings	30,920
Total liabilities and stockholders' equity	$208,920

As part of the existing loan agreement with First National Bank, Harmon Video Inc. must submit financial statements annually to the bank. In reviewing your sister's statements and supporting records before she submits the statements to the bank, you discover the following information:

Merchandise inventory:	
May 1, 1990	$40,800
April 30, 1991	58,300
Salaries expense:	
Sales salaries	$25,050
Office salaries	5,000
Supplies expense:	
Store supplies	$ 1,600
Office supplies	840
Miscellaneous expense:	
Selling	$ 1,020
Administrative	600

Instructions:

(1) Revise your sister's statements as necessary to conform to proper form for a multiple-step income statement, a retained earnings statement, and a report form of balance sheet.

(2) Prepare a projected single-step income statement based upon the following data: Your sister is considering a proposal to increase net income by offering sales discounts of 2/10, n/30, and by shipping all merchandise FOB shipping point. Currently, no sales discounts are allowed and merchandise is shipped FOB destination. It is estimated that these credit terms will increase net sales by 10%. The ratio of cost of merchandise sold to net sales is 70% and is not expected to change under the proposed plan. All selling and administrative expenses are expected to remain unchanged, except for store supplies, miscellaneous selling, office supplies, and miscellaneous administrative expenses, which are expected to increase proportionately with increased net sales. The other income and other expense items will remain unchanged. The shipment of all merchandise FOB shipping point will eliminate all transportation out expenses.

(3) (a) Based upon the projected income statement in (2), would you recommend the implementation of the proposed changes?
   (b) Describe any possible concerns you may have related to the proposed changes described in (2).

ETHICS DISCUSSION CASE	Ruth Baird, president of Kirby Inc., has decided to use the single-step format rather than the multiple-step format for Kirby Inc.'s income statement for the year ended December 31, 1990. Evaluate whether Ruth Baird has behaved in an ethical manner by using the single-step income statement format rather than the multiple-step format.

COMPREHENSIVE PROBLEM 2

The account balances for Dyson Inc. are as follows. All balances are stated as of May 1, 1991, unless otherwise indicated.

11	Cash	34,060
12	Notes Receivable	10,000
13	Accounts Receivable	45,320
14	Interest Receivable	—
15	Merchandise Inventory, June 1, 1990	123,900
16	Prepaid Insurance	4,250
17	Store Supplies	2,550
18	Store Equipment	43,800
19	Accumulated Depreciation	12,600
21	Accounts Payable	38,500
22	Salaries Payable	—
31	Capital Stock	100,000
32	Retained Earnings, June 1, 1990	59,420
33	Dividends	6,000
34	Income Summary	—
41	Sales	792,000
42	Sales Returns and Allowances	13,600
43	Sales Discounts	5,200
51	Purchases	570,000
52	Purchases Returns and Allowances	15,600
53	Purchases Discounts	5,760
54	Transportation In	5,800
55	Sales Salaries Expense	74,400
56	Advertising Expense	18,000
57	Depreciation Expense	—
58	Store Supplies Expense	—
59	Miscellaneous Selling Expense	2,800
60	Office Salaries Expense	29,400
61	Rent Expense	33,000
62	Insurance Expense	—
63	Miscellaneous Administrative Expense	1,800
70	Interest Income	—

During May, the last month of Dyson Inc.'s fiscal year, the following transactions were completed:

May 1. Paid rent for May, $3,000.

       1. Received a $10,000 note receivable from a customer on account.

       2. Purchased merchandise on account, terms 1/10, n/30, FOB shipping point, $25,000.

May 3. Paid transportation charges on purchase of May 2, $710.
     4. Purchased merchandise on account, terms 2/10, n/30, FOB destination, $17,500.
     5. Sold merchandise on account, terms 2/10, n/30, FOB shipping point, $8,000.
     8. Received $14,750 cash from customers on account, no discount.
    10. Sold merchandise for cash, $19,500.
    11. Paid $12,800 to creditors on account, after discounts of $200 had been deducted.
    12. Paid for merchandise purchased on May 2, less discount.
    13. Received merchandise returned on sale of May 5, $500.
    14. Paid advertising expense for last half of May, $1,500.
    15. Received cash from sale of May 5, less return and discount.
    15. Paid sales salaries of $3,500 and office salaries of $900.
    18. Received $28,500 cash from customers on account, after discounts of $400 had been deducted.
    19. Purchased merchandise for cash, $6,400.
    19. Paid $13,150 to creditors on account, after discounts of $250 had been deducted.
    20. Sold merchandise on account, terms 1/10, n/30, FOB shipping point, $16,000.
    21. Purchased merchandise on account, terms 1/10, n/30, FOB destination, $15,000.
    22. Paid for merchandise purchased on May 4.
    24. Returned damaged merchandise purchased on May 21, receiving credit from the seller, $3,000.
    25. Refunded cash on sales made for cash, $400.
    29. Paid sales salaries of $3,500 and office salaries of $900.
    29. Sold merchandise on account, terms 2/10, n/30, FOB shipping point, $24,700.
    29. Purchased store supplies for cash, $350.
    30. Received cash from sale of May 20, less discount.
    31. Paid for purchase of May 21, less return and discount.
    31. Sold merchandise on account, terms 2/10, n/30, FOB shipping point, $19,250.
    31. Purchased merchandise on account, terms 1/10, n/30, FOB destination, $18,150.

Instructions:

(1) Record the balances of each of the accounts as of May 1 in the appropriate balance column of a four-column account. Write "Balance" in the item section, and place a check mark (√) in the posting reference column.
(2) Record the transactions for May in a two-column journal.
(3) Post to the ledger, extending the month-end balances to the appropriate balance columns after all posting is completed.
(4) Prepare a trial balance as of May 31 on a ten-column work sheet, listing all the accounts in the order given in the ledger. Complete the work sheet for the fiscal year ended May 31, using the following adjustment data:

(a) Interest accrued on notes receivable on May 31	$	100
(b) Merchandise inventory on May 31		134,150
(c) Insurance expired during the year		2,750
(d) Store supplies inventory on May 31		750
(e) Depreciation for the current year		5,360
(f) Accrued salaries on May 31:		
Sales salaries...	$700	
Office salaries...	175	875

(Continued)

(5) Prepare a multiple-step income statement, a retained earnings statement, and a report form of balance sheet.

(6) Journalize and post the adjusting entries.

(7) Journalize and post the closing entries. Indicate closed accounts by inserting a line in both balance columns opposite the closing entry. Insert the new balance in the retained earnings account.

(8) Prepare a post-closing trial balance.

(9) Journalize and post any reversing entries as of June 1, 1991.

ANSWERS TO SELF-EXAMINATION QUESTIONS

1. **B** The single-step form of income statement (answer B) is so named because the total of all expenses is deducted from the total of all revenues. The multiple-step form (answer A) includes numerous sections and subsections with several intermediate balances before arriving at net income. The account form (answer C) and the report form (answer D) are two common forms of the balance sheet.

2. **C** Gross profit (answer C) is the excess of net sales over the cost of merchandise sold. Operating income (answer A) or income from operations (answer B) is the excess of gross profit over operating expenses. Net income (answer D) is the final figure on the income statement after all revenues and expenses have been reported.

3. **D** Expenses such as interest expense (answer D) that cannot be associated definitely with operations are identified as other expense or nonoperating expense. Depreciation expense—office equipment (answer A) is an administrative expense. Sales salaries expense (answer B) is a selling expense. Insurance expense (answer C) is a mixed expense with elements of both selling expense and administrative expense. For small businesses, however, insurance expense is usually reported as an administrative expense.

4. **B** The salaries paid on July 3, $21,700 (answer C), include salary expense incurred prior to July 1, $5,500 (answer A). Therefore, the salary expense for July 1–3 is the difference between the amount paid and the credit balance in Salary Expense on July 1, or $16,200 (answer B).

5. **D** The omission of the adjustment for accrued salaries at the end of the year understates expenses (answer A) and consequently overstates net income (answer B) for the year. The liability for salaries payable is also omitted and results in understating liabilities at the end of the year (answer C).

Accounting Systems

PART TWO

2

CHAPTER SIX

ACCOUNTING SYSTEMS DESIGN

CHAPTER OBJECTIVES

1 Describe the principles of properly designed accounting systems.

2 Describe the three phases of accounting system installation and revision.

3 Describe and illustrate the principles of internal control.

4 Describe data processing methods that may be used in accounting systems.

5 Describe and illustrate the use of subsidiary ledgers and the following special journals to process accounting data:
Purchases journal
Cash payments journal
Sales journal
Cash receipts journal

6 Describe and illustrate the modification of accounting systems for accounting for deferrals and for using computers.

The way in which management is given the information for use in conducting the affairs of the business and in reporting to owners, creditors, and other interested parties is called the **accounting system**. In a general sense, an accounting system includes the entire network of communications used by a business organization to provide needed information.

PRINCIPLES OF ACCOUNTING SYSTEMS

OBJECTIVE 1
Describe the principles of properly designed accounting systems.

Because of differences in businesses, in the number of transactions to be processed, and in the uses made of accounting data, accounting systems will vary from business to business. However, there are a number of broad principles discussed in the paragraphs that follow that apply to all systems.

Cost-Effectiveness Balance

An accounting system must be tailored to meet the specific needs of each business. Since costs must be incurred in meeting these needs, one of the major considerations in developing an accounting system is cost effectiveness. For example, although the reports produced by an accounting system are a valuable end product of the system, the value of the reports produced should be at least equal to the cost of producing them. No matter how detailed or informational a report may be, it should not be produced if it costs more than the benefits received by those who use it.

Flexibility to Meet Future Needs

A characteristic of the modern business environment is change. Each business must adapt to the constantly changing environment in which it operates. Whether the changes are the result of new government regulations, changes in accounting principles, organizational changes necessary to meet practices of competing businesses, changes in data processing technology, or other factors, the accounting system must be flexible enough to meet the changing demands made of it. For example, regulatory agencies, such as the Securities and Exchange Commission, often require a continually changing variety of reports that require changes in the accounting system.

Adequate Internal Controls

An accounting system must provide the information needed by management in reporting to owners, creditors, and other interested parties. In addition, the system should aid management in directing operations. The detailed policies and procedures used to direct operations and provide reasonable assurance that the entity's objectives are achieved are called **internal controls**. The broad principles for an internal control structure are discussed later in the chapter.

Effective Reporting

Users of the information provided by the accounting system rely on various reports for relevant information presented in an understandable manner. When these reports are prepared, the requirements and knowledge of the user should be recognized. For example, management may need detailed reports for directing operations on a weekly or even daily basis, and regulatory agencies often require uniform data and establish certain deadlines for the submission of certain reports.

Adaptation to Organizational Structure

Only by effectively using and adapting to the human resources of a business can the accounting system meet information needs at the lowest cost. Since no two businesses are structured alike, the accounting system must be tailored to the organizational structure of each business. The lines of authority and responsibility will affect the information requirements of each business. In addition, an effective system needs the approval and support of all levels of management.

ACCOUNTING SYSTEM INSTALLATION AND REVISION

OBJECTIVE 2
Describe the three phases of accounting system installation and revision.

Before designing and installing an accounting system for an enterprise, the designer must have a complete knowledge of the business' operations. However, the designer should recognize that some areas of the system, such as the types and design of the forms needed and the number and titles of the accounts required, may be affected by factors that are not known when a business is first organized. As new information about a business is obtained and as a business "outgrows" its accounting system when it expands to new operational areas, the system will need to be revised.

Many large businesses continually review their accounting system and may constantly be involved in changing some part of it. The job of installing or changing an accounting system, either in its entirety or only in part, is made up of three phases: (1) analysis, (2) design, and (3) implementation.

Systems Analysis

The goal of **systems analysis** is to determine information needs, the sources of such information, and the deficiencies in procedures and data processing methods presently used. The analysis usually begins with a review of the organizational structure and the job descriptions of the personnel affected. This review is followed by a study of the forms, records, procedures, processing methods, and reports used by the enterprise. The source of such information is usually the firm's *Systems Manual.*

In addition to looking at the shortcomings of the present system, the analyst should determine management's plans for changes in operations (volume, products, territories, etc.).

Systems Design

Accounting systems are changed as a result of the kind of analysis previously described. The design of the new system may involve only minor changes from the existing system, such as revision of a particular form and the related procedures and processing methods, or it may be a complete revision of the entire system. Systems designers must have a general knowledge of the qualities of different kinds of data processing equipment, and the ability to evaluate alternatives. Although successful systems design depends to a large extent upon the creativity, imagination, and general capabilities of the designer, observance of the broad principles previously discussed is necessary.

Systems Implementation

The final phase of the creation or revision of an accounting system is to carry out, or implement, the proposals. New or revised forms, records, procedures, and equipment must be installed, and any that are no longer useful must be withdrawn. All personnel responsible for operating the system must be carefully trained and closely supervised until satisfactory efficiency is achieved.

For a large organization, a major revision such as a change from an obsolete to a modern computer processing system is usually done gradually over an extended period rather than all at once. With such a procedure, there is less likelihood that the flow of useful data will be seriously slowed down during the critical phase of implementation. Weaknesses and conflicting or unnecessary elements in the design may also become apparent during the implementation phase. They are more easily seen and corrected when changes in a system are adopted gradually, and possible chaos is thereby avoided.

ACCOUNTING SYSTEMS, PROFIT MEASUREMENT, AND MANAGEMENT

A Greek restaurant owner in Canada had his own system of accounting. He kept his accounts payable in a cigar box on the left-hand side of his cash register, his daily cash returns in the cash register, and his receipts for paid bills in another cigar box on the right.

When his youngest son graduated as an accountant, he was appalled by his father's primitive methods. "I don't know how you can run a business that way," he said. "How do you know what your profits are?"

"Well, son," the father replied, "when I

got off the boat from Greece, I had nothing but the pants I was wearing. Today, your brother is a doctor. You are an accountant. Your sister is a speech therapist. Your mother and I have a nice car, and city house, a coun-

try home. We have a good business, and everything is paid for..."

"So, you add all that together, subtract the pants, and there's your profit!"

Source: Anonymous.

INTERNAL CONTROL STRUCTURE

OBJECTIVE 3
Describe and illustrate the principles of internal control.

An enterprise's internal control structure consists of the policies and procedures established to provide reasonable assurance that the enterprise's goals and objectives will be achieved. This internal control structure can be divided into three elements: (1) the control environment, (2) the control procedures, and (3) the accounting system.[1] The basic principles underlying an effective internal control structure are briefly discussed in the following paragraphs. It should be noted that the policies and procedures of an internal control structure will vary according to the size and type of business enterprise. In a small business where it is possible for the owner-manager to supervise the employees personally and direct the affairs of the business, few control policies and procedures are necessary. As the number of employees and the complexities of an enterprise increase, it becomes more difficult for management to maintain control over all phases of operations. As a firm grows, management needs to delegate authority and to place more reliance on the control structure in order to achieve adherence to enterprise goals and objectives.

The Control Environment

The control environment of an enterprise represents an overall attitude toward and awareness of the importance of controls by both management and other employees. Factors influencing the control environment of an enterprise include management's philosophy and operating style, the organizational structure of the enterprise, and personnel policies and practices.

Management's philosophy and operating style includes management's attitude concerning controls. For example, if top management routinely violates established control policies and procedures, the control environment could be adversely affected because lower management and employees may view controls as unimportant. On the other hand, a top management that emphasizes the importance of controls in dealing with operating personnel and encourages adherence to control policies and procedures will create a favorable control environment.

The organizational structure of an enterprise establishes the framework for planning and controlling operations. For example, a merchandising enterprise might organize each of its stores as relatively separate business units, with each store manager given full authority over pricing and other operating activities. Included with this authority is the responsibility for establishing a control environment for achieving the enterprise's goals and objectives.

---

[1] *Statements on Auditing Standards, No. 55,* "Consideration of the Internal Control Structure in a Financial Statement Audit" (New York: American Institute of Certified Public Accountants, 1988).

Personnel policies and procedures includes the hiring, training, evaluation, promotion, and compensation of employees to accomplish an enterprise's goals and objectives. Common personnel policies that impact on the control environment include the establishment of codes of ethics for employee conduct and conflict of interest policies.

The Control Procedures

Control procedures are those policies and procedures that management has established within the control environment in order to provide reasonable assurance that enterprise goals will be achieved. General control procedures which can be integrated throughout the accounting system and which apply to all enterprises are briefly discussed in the following sections.

Competent Personnel and Rotation of Duties. The successful operation of an accounting system requires procedures to ensure that people are able to perform the duties to which they are assigned. Hence, it is necessary that all accounting employees be adequately trained and supervised to perform their jobs. It is also advisable to rotate clerical personnel periodically from job to job. In addition to broadening their understanding of the system, the knowledge that others may in the future perform their jobs tends to discourage deviations from prescribed procedures. Rotation of duties is also very helpful in disclosing any irregularities that may have occurred.

Assignment of Responsibility. If employees are to work efficiently, their responsibilities must be clearly defined. Control procedures should exist to guarantee that no overlapping or undefined areas of responsibility exist. For example, if a certain cash register is to be used by two or more salesclerks, each one should be assigned a separate cash drawer and register key. Thus, a daily proof of cash can be obtained for each clerk.

Separation of Responsibility for Related Operations. To decrease the possibility of inefficiency, errors, and fraud, control procedures should exist to guarantee that responsibility for a sequence of related operations is divided among two or more persons. For example, no one individual should be authorized to order merchandise, verify the receipt of the merchandise, and pay the supplier. To do so would invite abuses such as the following:

1. Placing orders with a supplier on the basis of friendship rather than on price, quality, and other objective factors.
2. Indifferent and routine verification of the quantity and the quality of goods received.
3. Conversion of goods to the personal use of the employee.
4. Carelessness in verifying the validity and the accuracy of invoices.
5. Payment of false invoices.

When the responsibility for purchasing, receiving, and paying are divided among three persons or departments, the possibilities of such abuses are minimized.

The "checks and balances" provided by distributing responsibility among various departments requires no duplication of effort. The business documents prepared as a result of the work of each department must "fit" with those prepared by the other departments.

Separation of Operations and Accounting. Control procedures should exist to ensure that responsibility for maintaining the accounting records are separated from the responsibility for engaging in business transactions and for the custody of the firm's assets. By such separation, the accounting records serve as an independent check on the business operations. For example, the employees entrusted with handling cash receipts from credit customers should not have access to the journal or ledger. Separation of the two functions reduces the possibilities of errors and embezzlement.

Proofs and Security Measures. Proofs and security measures should be used to safeguard business assets and assure reliable accounting data. This control procedure applies to many different techniques, such as the use of a bank account and other safekeeping measures for cash and other valuable documents. Cash registers are widely used in making the initial record of cash sales. The conditioning of the public to observe the amount recorded as the sale or to accept a printed receipt from the salesclerk increases the machine's effectiveness as a part of the internal control structure.

The use of fidelity insurance is also an aid to developing an effective internal control structure. It insures against losses caused by fraud on the part of employees who are entrusted with company assets.

Independent Review. To determine whether internal control procedures are being effectively applied, the control structure should be periodically reviewed and evaluated by internal auditors. These auditors must be independent of the employees responsible for operations. An example of the use of internal auditors for review of internal control procedures is described in the annual report of Rose's Stores Inc., as follows:

> To meet its responsibilities with respect to financial information, management maintains and enforces internal accounting policies, procedures, and controls which are designed to provide reasonable assurance that assets are safeguarded and that transactions are properly recorded and executed in accordance with management's authorization. The concept of reasonable assurance is based on the recognition that the cost of controls should not exceed the expected benefits. Management maintains an internal audit function and an internal control function which are responsible for evaluating the adequacy and application of financial and operating controls and for testing compliance with Company policies and procedures.

Internal auditors should report any weaknesses and recommend changes to correct them. For example, a review of cash disbursements may disclose that invoices were not paid within the discount period, even though enough cash was available.

The Accounting System

The accounting system is an integral part of the internal control structure of an enterprise. Without the information generated by the accounting system, management would lack the ability to plan and direct operations in achieving enterprise goals. The principles of an effective accounting system were discussed earlier in this chapter.

DATA PROCESSING METHODS

OBJECTIVE 4
Describe data processing methods that may be used in accounting systems.

The entire amount of data needed by an enterprise is called its **data base**. Depending upon the variety and the amount of data included in the data base, various processing methods—manual and computerized—may be used. Whether the accounting system for a particular enterprise uses one or a combination of these methods, the basic principles of accounting systems as discussed are applicable.

In preceding chapters, manual accounting systems were used to process accounting data because they are the easiest systems to understand. If the data base is relatively small, manually kept records may serve a business reasonably well. However, as the data base increases, manual processing becomes too costly and takes too much time. In such a case, the manual system can be changed, or it may be replaced or supplemented by a computerized system in order to reduce costs and process accounting data more efficiently. In the following paragraphs, changes that can make an accounting system more efficient will be described and illustrated.

SUBSIDIARY LEDGERS AND SPECIAL JOURNALS

OBJECTIVE 5
Describe and illustrate the use of subsidiary ledgers and the following special journals to process accounting data:
Purchases journal
Cash payments journal
Sales journal
Cash receipts journal

In preceding chapters, all transactions were initially recorded in a two-column journal, then posted individually to the appropriate accounts in the ledger. Applying such detailed procedures to a large number of transactions that are often repeated is impractical. For example, if many credit sales are made, each of these transactions would require an entry debiting Accounts Receivable and crediting Sales. In addition, the accounts receivable account in the ledger would include receivables from a large number of customers. In such cases, subsidiary ledgers and special journals may be useful.

Subsidiary Ledgers

As the number of purchases and sales on account increase, the need for maintaining a separate account for each creditor and debtor is clear. If such accounts are numerous, their inclusion in the same ledger with all other accounts would cause the ledger to become unmanageable. The chance of posting errors would also be increased and the preparation of the trial balance and the financial statements would be delayed.

When there are a large number of individual accounts with a common characteristic, it is common to place them in a separate ledger called a **subsidiary ledger**. The principal ledger, which contains all of the balance sheet and income statement accounts, is then called the **general ledger**. Each subsidiary ledger is represented in the general ledger by a summarizing account, called a **controlling account**. The sum of the balances of the accounts in a subsidiary ledger must agree with the balance of the related controlling account. Thus, a subsidiary ledger may be said to be *controlled* by its controlling account.

The individual accounts with creditors are arranged in alphabetical order in a subsidiary ledger called the **accounts payable ledger** or **creditors ledger**. The related controlling account in the general ledger is Accounts Payable. The subsidiary ledger containing the individual accounts for credit customers is called the **accounts receivable ledger** or **customers ledger**. The controlling account in the general ledger that summarizes the debits and credits to the individual customers accounts is Accounts Receivable. The accounts payable ledger is illustrated and further discussed on pages 237–239, and the accounts receivable ledger is further discussed on page 243.

Special Journals

One of the simplest methods of processing data more efficiently in a manual accounting system is to expand the two-column journal to a **multicolumn** journal. Each amount column included in a multicolumn journal is restricted to the recording of transactions affecting a certain account. For example, a special column could be used only for recording debits to the cash account and another special column could be used only for recording credits to the cash account. The addition of the two special columns would eliminate the writing of "Cash" in the journal for every receipt and payment of cash. Furthermore, there would be no need to post each individual debit and credit to the cash account. Instead, the "Cash Dr." and "Cash Cr." columns could be totaled periodically and only the totals posted, yielding additional economies. In a similar manner, special columns could be added for recording credits to Sales, debits and credits to Accounts Receivable and Accounts Payable, and for other entries that are repeated. Although there is no exact number of columns that may be effectively used in a multicolumn journal, there is a maximum number beyond which the journal would become unmanageable. Also, the possibilities of errors in recording become greater as the number of columns and the width of the page increase.

An all-purpose multicolumn journal is usually satisfactory for a small business enterprise that needs the services of only one accountant. If the number of transactions is enough to require two or more accountants, the use of a single journal is usually not efficient. The next logical development in expanding the system is to replace an all-purpose journal with a number of **special journals**, each designed to record a single kind of transaction. Special journals would be needed only for the kinds of transactions that occur frequently. Since most enterprises have many transactions in which cash is received and many in which cash is paid out, it is common practice to use a special journal for recording cash receipts and another special journal for recording cash payments. An enterprise that sells services or merchandise to customers on account might use a special journal designed for recording only such transactions. On the other hand, a business that does not give credit would have no need for such a journal.

The transactions that occur most often in a medium-size merchandising firm and the special journals in which they are recorded are as follows:

Purchase of merchandise or other items *on account*	recorded in	Purchases journal
Payments of cash for *any* purpose	recorded in	Cash payments journal
Sale of merchandise *on account*	recorded in	Sales journal
Receipt of cash from *any* source	recorded in	Cash receipts journal

Sometimes the business documents evidencing purchases and sales transactions are used as special journals. When there are a large number of such transactions on a credit basis, the use of this procedure may result in a substantial savings in record keeping expenses and a reduction of record keeping errors.

The two-column form illustrated in earlier chapters can be used for miscellaneous entries, such as adjusting and closing entries, that do not "fit" in any of the special journals. The two-column form is commonly called the **general journal** or simply the **journal**.

Purchases Journal

Property most frequently purchased on account by a merchandising concern is of the following types: (1) merchandise for resale to customers, (2) supplies for use in conducting the business, and (3) equipment and other plant assets. Because of the variety of items acquired on credit terms, the purchases journal should be designed to allow for the recording of everything purchased on account. The form of purchases journal used by Kannon Corporation is illustrated below.

For each transaction recorded in the purchases journal, the credit is entered in the Accounts Payable Cr. column. The next three amount columns are used for accumulating debits to the particular accounts most frequently affected. Invoice amounts for merchandise purchased for sale to customers are recorded in the Purchases Dr. column. The purpose of the Store Supplies Dr. and Office Supplies Dr. columns is readily apparent. If supplies of these two categories were purchased only once in a while, the two columns could be omitted from the journal.

The final set of columns, under the main heading Sundry Accounts Dr., is used to record acquisitions, on account, of items not provided for in the special debit columns. The title of the account to be debited is entered in the Account column and the amount is entered in the Amount column. A separate posting reference column is provided for this section of the purchases journal.

Posting the Purchases Journal. The special journals used in recording most of the transactions affecting creditors accounts are designed to allow the posting of individual transactions to the accounts payable ledger and a single monthly total to Accounts Payable. The basic techniques of posting credits from a purchases journal to an accounts payable ledger and the controlling account are shown in the flowchart at the top of page 233.

Purchases Journal

PAGE 19   PURCHASES

	DATE		ACCOUNT CREDITED	POST. REF.	ACCOUNTS PAYABLE CR.
1	1990 Oct.	2	Video Co.	✓	5 7 2 4 00
2		3	Marsh Inc.	✓	7 4 0 6 00
3		9	Parker Supply Co.	✓	2 5 7 00
4		11	Marsh Inc.	✓	3 2 0 8 00
5		16	Dunlap Corporation	✓	3 5 9 3 00
6		17	Robinson Supply	✓	1 5 0 0 00
7		20	Walton Co.	✓	15 1 2 5 00
8		23	Parker Supply Co.	✓	1 3 2 00
9		27	Dunlap Corporation	✓	6 3 7 5 00
10		31			43 3 2 0 00
11					(2 1 1)

Flow of Credits from Purchases Journal to Ledgers

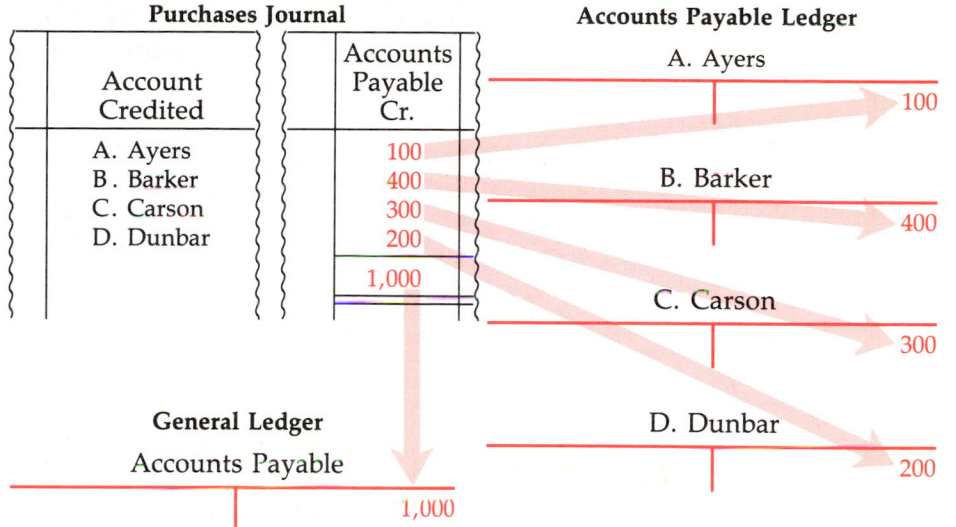

The individual credits of $100, $400, $300, and $200 to Ayers, Barker, Carson, and Dunbar respectively are posted to their accounts in the accounts payable ledger. The sum of the credits to the four individual accounts in the subsidiary ledger is posted as a single $1,000 credit to Accounts Payable, the controlling account in the general ledger.

Since the balances in the creditors accounts are usually credit balances, a three-column account form is used instead of the four-column account form illustrated earlier. When a creditor's account is overpaid and a debit balance occurs, that fact should be indicated by an asterisk or parentheses in the Balance column. When an account's balance is zero, a line may be drawn in the Balance column.

JOURNAL   PAGE 19

PURCHASES DR.	STORE SUPPLIES DR.	OFFICE SUPPLIES DR.	SUNDRY ACCOUNTS DR. ACCOUNT	POST. REF.	AMOUNT	
5 7 24 00						1
7 4 06 00						2
	1 31 00	1 26 00				3
3 2 08 00						4
3 5 93 00						5
1 5 00 00						6
			Store Equipment	121	15 1 25 00	7
	75 00	57 00				8
6 3 75 00						9
27 8 06 00	2 06 00	1 83 00			15 1 25 00	10
(5 1 1)	(1 1 5)	(1 1 6)			(✓)	11

The source of the entries posted to the subsidiary and general ledgers is indicated in the posting reference column of each account by inserting the letter "P" and the page number of the purchases journal. An account in the accounts payable ledger of Kannon Corporation is presented as an example.

An Account in the Accounts Payable Ledger

NAME Robinson Supply
ADDRESS 3800 Mission Street, San Francisco, CA 94110-1732

DATE	ITEM	POST. REF.	DEBIT	CREDIT	BALANCE
1990 Oct. 17		P19		1 5 0 0 00	1 5 0 0 00

The creditors accounts in the subsidiary ledger are not numbered, because the order changes each time a new account is inserted alphabetically or an old account is removed. Thus, instead of a number, a check mark (✔) is inserted in the posting reference column of the purchases journal after a credit is posted.

The amounts in the Sundry Accounts Dr. column of the purchases journal are posted to the appropriate accounts in the general ledger and the posting reference ("P" and page number) is inserted in the accounts. As each amount is posted, the related general ledger account number is inserted in the posting reference column of the Sundry Accounts section.

At the end of each month, the purchases journal is totaled and ruled in the manner illustrated on pages 232 and 233. Before posting the totals to the general ledger, the sum of the totals of the four debit columns should be compared with the total of the credit column to prove their equality.

The totals of the four special columns are posted to the appropriate general ledger accounts in the usual manner, with the related account numbers inserted below the columnar totals. Because each amount in the Sundry Accounts Dr. column was posted individually, a check mark is placed below the $15,125 total to show that no further action is needed.

Two of the general ledger accounts to which postings were made are presented as examples. The debit posting to Store Equipment was from the Sundry Accounts Dr. column; the credit posting to Accounts Payable was from the total of the Accounts Payable Cr. column.

General Ledger Accounts after Posting from Purchases Journal

ACCOUNT Store Equipment   ACCOUNT NO. 121

DATE	ITEM	POST. REF.	DEBIT	CREDIT	BALANCE DEBIT	BALANCE CREDIT
1990 Oct. 1	Balance	✔			11 9 7 5 00	
20		P19	15 1 2 5 00		27 1 0 0 00	

ACCOUNT Accounts Payable   ACCOUNT NO. 211

DATE	ITEM	POST. REF.	DEBIT	CREDIT	BALANCE DEBIT	BALANCE CREDIT
1990 Oct. 1	Balance	✔				21 9 7 5 00
31		P19		43 3 2 0 00		65 2 9 5 00

The flow of data from the purchases journal of Kannon Corporation to its two related ledgers is presented graphically in the diagram on page 235. Two procedures revealed by the flow diagram should be given special attention:

1. Postings are made from the purchases journal to both (a) accounts in the subsidiary ledger and (b) accounts in the general ledger.
2. The sum of the postings to individual accounts payable in the subsidiary ledger equals the columnar total posted to Accounts Payable (controlling account) in the general ledger.

Flow of Data from Purchases Journal to Ledgers

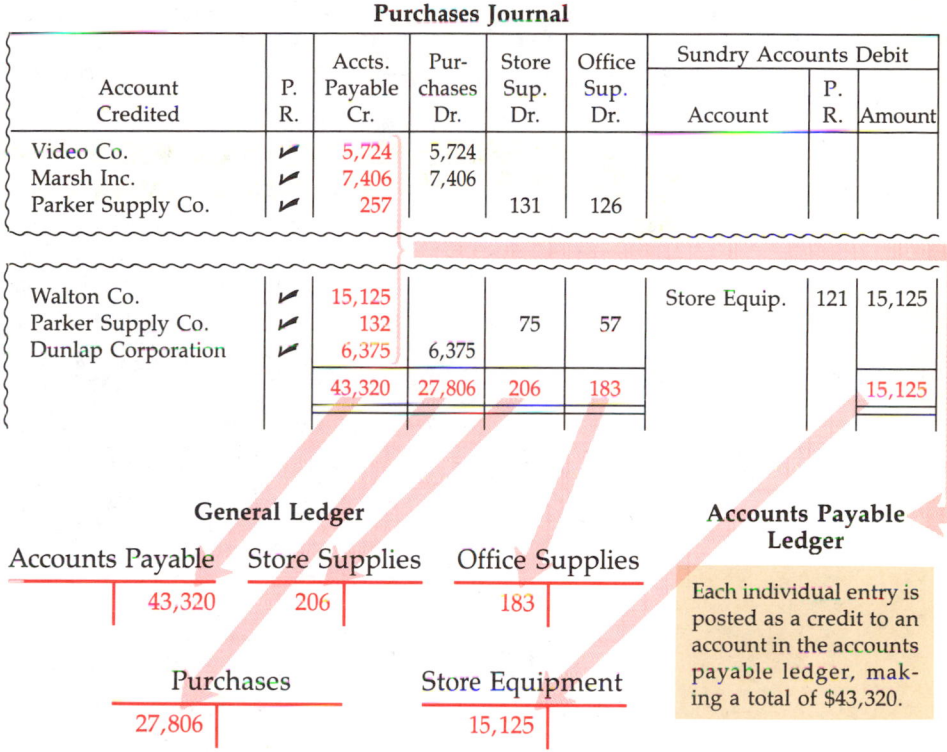

Purchases Returns and Allowances. When merchandise purchased is returned or a price adjustment is granted, an entry is made in the general journal according to the principles described in Chapter 4. To illustrate, assume that during October, Kannon Corporation issued a debit memorandum for a return of merchandise. The entry may be recorded in a two-column general journal, as follows:

General Journal Entry for Purchases Returns and Allowances

	DATE		DESCRIPTION	POST. REF.	DEBIT	CREDIT	
17	Oct.	20	Accounts Payable — Dunlap Corp.	211	9 7 50		17
18			Purchases Returns and Allowances	512		9 7 50	18
19			Debit Memo No. 20.				19

JOURNAL   PAGE 18

The debit portion of the entry is posted to the accounts payable account in the general ledger (No. 211) and also to the creditor's account in the subsidiary ledger (✔). The need for posting the debits to two different accounts is indicated, at the time these entries are journalized, by drawing a *diagonal line* in the posting reference column. The account number and check mark are inserted, in the usual manner, at the time the entry is posted.

After the entry has been recorded, the memorandum is attached to the related unpaid invoice. If the invoice had been paid before the return or allowance was granted, the settlement might be a cash refund.

If goods other than merchandise are returned or a price adjustment is granted, the account to which the goods were first debited should be credited. For example, if a purchase of office equipment is returned, the credit would be to Office Equipment rather than Purchases Returns and Allowances.

Cash Payments Journal

The standards for determining the special columns to be provided in the **cash payments journal** are the same as for the purchases journal, namely, the kind of transactions to be recorded and the frequency of their occurrence. It is necessary to have a Cash Cr. column. Payments to creditors on account happen often enough to require columns for Accounts Payable Dr. and Purchases Discounts Cr. The cash payments journal illustrated below has these three columns and an additional column for Sundry Accounts Dr.

Cash Payments Journal after Posting

CASH PAYMENTS JOURNAL   PAGE 16

	DATE	CK. NO.	ACCOUNT DEBITED	POST. REF.	SUNDRY ACCOUNTS DR.	ACCOUNTS PAYABLE DR.	PURCHASES DISCOUNTS CR.	CASH CR.	
1	1990 Oct. 2	312	Purchases	511	1 2 7 5 00			1 2 7 5 00	1
2	4	313	Store Equipment	121	3 5 0 00			3 5 0 00	2
3	12	314	Marsh Inc.	✔		7 4 0 6 00	7 4 06	7 3 3 1 94	3
4	12	315	Sales Salaries Exp.	611	2 5 6 0 00			2 5 6 0 00	4
5	12	316	Office Salaries Exp.	711	8 8 0 00			8 8 0 00	5
6	14	317	Misc. Admin. Exp.	719	5 6 40			5 6 40	6
7	16	318	Prepaid Insurance	117	9 8 4 00			9 8 4 00	7
8	20	319	Marsh Inc.	✔		3 2 0 8 00	3 2 08	3 1 7 5 92	8
9	20	320	Heath Co.	✔		4 8 5 0 00		4 8 5 0 00	9
10	21	321	Sales Ret. & Allow.	412	4 6 2 00			4 6 2 00	10
11	23	322	Robinson Supply	✔		1 5 0 0 00	3 0 00	1 4 7 0 00	11
12	23	323	Video Co.	✔		7 6 0 0 00		7 6 0 0 00	12
13	23	324	Rent Expense	712	7 8 9 20			7 8 9 20	13
14	24	325	Walton Co.	✔		9 5 2 5 00		9 5 2 5 00	14
15	26	326	Sales Salaries Exp.	611	2 5 6 0 00			2 5 6 0 00	15
16	26	327	Office Salaries Exp.	711	8 8 0 00			8 8 0 00	16
17	26	328	Advertising Expense	612	7 8 6 00			7 8 6 00	17
18	27	329	Misc. Selling Exp.	619	4 1 50			4 1 50	18
19	28	330	Office Equipment	123	9 0 0 00			9 0 0 00	19
20	31				12 5 2 4 10	34 0 8 9 00	1 3 6 14	46 4 7 6 96	20
21					(✔)	(2 1 1)	(5 1 3)	(1 1 1)	21

All payments by Kannon Corporation are made by check. As each transaction is recorded in the cash payments journal, the related check number is entered in the column at the right of the Date column. The check numbers provide a convenient cross-reference, and their use also is helpful in controlling cash payments.

The Sundry Accounts Dr. column is used to record debits to any account for which there is no special column. On October 2, for example, Kannon Corporation paid $1,275 for a cash purchase of merchandise. The transaction was recorded by writing "Purchases" in the space provided and $1,275 in the Sundry Accounts Dr. and the Cash Cr. columns. The posting reference (511) was inserted later, at the time the debit was posted.

Debits to creditors accounts for invoices paid are recorded in the Accounts Payable Dr. column and credits for the amounts paid are recorded in the Cash Cr. column. If a discount is taken, the debit to the account payable will, of course, differ from the amount of the payment. Cash discounts taken on merchandise purchased for resale are recorded in the Purchases Discounts Cr. column.

At frequent intervals during the month, the amounts entered in the Accounts Payable Dr. column are posted to the creditors accounts in the accounts payable ledger. After each posting, "CP" and the page number of the journal are inserted in the posting reference column of the account. Check marks are placed in the posting reference column of the cash payments journal to indicate that the amounts have been posted. The items in the Sundry Accounts Dr. column are also posted to the appropriate accounts in the general ledger at frequent intervals. The posting is indicated by writing the account numbers in the posting reference column of the cash payments journal. At the end of the month, each of the amount columns in the cash payments journal is totaled, the sum of the two debit totals is compared with the sum of the two credit totals to determine their equality, and the journal is ruled.

A check mark is placed below the total of the Sundry Accounts Dr. column to indicate that it is not posted. As each of the totals of the other three columns is posted to a general ledger account, the proper account numbers are inserted below the column totals.

Accounts Payable Control and Subsidiary Ledger

During October, the following postings were made to Accounts Payable in the general ledger of Kannon Corporation:

Credits to Accounts Payable

Oct. 31 Total purchases on account (purchases journal) $43,320.00

Debits to Accounts Payable

Oct. 20 A return of merchandise (general journal) 97.50
     31 Total cash payments on account
          (cash payments journal) 34,089.00

The accounts payable controlling account and the subsidiary accounts payable ledger of Kannon Corporation as of October 31 are presented below and on pages 238 and 239.

GENERAL LEDGER

Accounts Payable Account in the General Ledger at the End of the Month

ACCOUNT Accounts Payable   ACCOUNT NO. 211

DATE	ITEM	POST. REF.	DEBIT	CREDIT	BALANCE DEBIT	BALANCE CREDIT
1990 Oct. 1	Balance	✔				21 975 00
20		J18	97 50			21 877 50
31		P19		43 320 00		65 197 50
31		CP16	34 089 00			31 108 50

ACCOUNTS PAYABLE LEDGER

Accounts Payable Ledger at the End of the Month

NAME Dunlap Corporation
ADDRESS 521 Scottsdale Blvd., Phoenix, AZ 85004-1100

DATE	ITEM	POST. REF.	DEBIT	CREDIT	BALANCE
1990 Oct. 16		P19		3 5 9 3 00	3 5 9 3 00
20		J18	9 7 50		3 4 9 5 50
27		P19		6 3 7 5 00	9 8 7 0 50

NAME Heath Co.
ADDRESS 9950 Ridge Ave., Los Angeles, CA 90048-3694

DATE	ITEM	POST. REF.	DEBIT	CREDIT	BALANCE
1990 Sept. 21		P18		4 8 5 0 00	4 8 5 0 00
Oct. 20		CP16	4 8 5 0 00		———

NAME Marsh Inc.
ADDRESS 650 Wilson, Portland, OR 97209-1406

DATE	ITEM	POST. REF.	DEBIT	CREDIT	BALANCE
1990 Oct. 3		P19		7 4 0 6 00	7 4 0 6 00
11		P19		3 2 0 8 00	10 6 1 4 00
12		CP16	7 4 0 6 00		3 2 0 8 00
20		CP16	3 2 0 8 00		———

NAME Parker Supply Co.
ADDRESS 142 West 8th, Los Angeles, CA 90014-1225

DATE	ITEM	POST. REF.	DEBIT	CREDIT	BALANCE
1990 Oct. 9		P19		2 5 7 00	2 5 7 00
23		P19		1 3 2 00	3 8 9 00

NAME Robinson Supply
ADDRESS 3800 Mission Street, San Francisco, CA 94110-1732

DATE	ITEM	POST. REF.	DEBIT	CREDIT	BALANCE
1990 Oct. 17		P19		1 5 0 0 00	1 5 0 0 00
23		CP16	1 5 0 0 00		———

Accounts Payable Ledger at the End of the Month — Concluded

NAME Video Co.
ADDRESS 1200 Capital Ave., Sacramento, CA 95814-1048

DATE		ITEM	POST. REF.	DEBIT	CREDIT	BALANCE
1990 Sept.	25		P18		7 6 0 0 00	7 6 0 0 00
Oct.	2		P19		5 7 2 4 00	13 3 2 4 00
	23		CP16	7 6 0 0 00		5 7 2 4 00

NAME Walton Co.
ADDRESS 9554 W. Colorado Blvd., Pasadena, CA 91107-1318

DATE		ITEM	POST. REF.	DEBIT	CREDIT	BALANCE
1990 Sept.	28		P18		9 5 2 5 00	9 5 2 5 00
Oct.	20		P19		15 1 2 5 00	24 6 5 0 00
	24		CP16	9 5 2 5 00		15 1 2 5 00

After all posting has been completed for the month, the sum of the balances in the accounts payable ledger should be compared with the balance of the accounts payable account in the general ledger. If the controlling account and the subsidiary ledger do not agree, the error or errors must be located and corrected. The balances of the individual creditors accounts may be summarized on a calculator tape, or a schedule such as the following may be prepared. The total of the schedule, $31,108.50, agrees with the balance of the accounts payable account shown on page 237.

Schedule of Accounts Payable

Kannon Corporation
Schedule of Accounts Payable
October 31, 1990

Dunlap Corporation	$ 9,870.50
Parker Supply Co.	389.00
Video Co.	5,724.00
Walton Co.	15,125.00
Total accounts payable	$31,108.50

Sales Journal

The sales journal is used only for recording *sales of merchandise on account*; sales of merchandise for cash are recorded in the cash receipts journal. Sales of nonmerchandise assets are recorded in the cash receipts journal or the general journal, depending upon whether the sale was made for cash or on account. The sales journal of Kannon Corporation for October is shown at the top of page 240.

Details of the first sale recorded by Kannon Corporation in October are taken from Invoice No. 615. The customer is Barnes Inc. and the invoice total is $9,350. Since the amount of the debit to Accounts Receivable is the

Sales Journal after Posting

	DATE		INVOICE NO.	ACCOUNT DEBITED	POST. REF.	ACCTS. REC. DR. SALES CR.	
1	1990 Oct.	2	615	Barnes Inc.	✔	9 3 5 0 00	1
2		3	616	Standard Supply Co.	✔	1 6 0 4 00	2
3		5	617	David T. Mattox	✔	15 3 0 5 00	3
4		9	618	Barnes Inc.	✔	1 3 9 6 00	4
5		10	619	Adler Company	✔	6 7 5 0 00	5
6		17	620	Hamilton Inc.	✔	7 8 6 5 00	6
7		23	621	Cooper & Co.	✔	1 5 0 2 00	7
8		26	622	Tracy & Lee Inc.	✔	3 2 6 0 00	8
9		27	623	Standard Supply Co.	✔	1 9 0 8 00	9
10		31				48 9 4 0 00	10
11						(113)　　(411)	11

SALES JOURNAL　　　　PAGE 35

same as the credit to Sales, a single amount column in the sales journal is sufficient. However, if sales are subject to a sales tax, a special column may be added to the sales journal for recording the credit to Sales Tax Payable.

Posting the Sales Journal. The principles used in posting the sales journal compare to those used in posting the purchases journal. The source of the entry being posted is shown in the posting reference column of an account by the letter "S" and the proper page number. A customer's account with a posting from the sales journal is as follows:

An Account in the Accounts Receivable Ledger

NAME Adler Company

ADDRESS 7608 Melton Ave., Los Angeles, CA 90025-3942

DATE		ITEM	POST. REF.	DEBIT	CREDIT	BALANCE
1990 Oct.	10		S35	6 7 5 0 00		6 7 5 0 00

As each debit to a customer's account is posted, a check mark (✔) is inserted in the posting reference column of the sales journal. At the end of each month, the amount column of the sales journal is added, the journal is ruled, and the total is posted as a debit to Accounts Receivable and a credit to Sales. The respective account numbers are then inserted below the total to indicate that the posting is completed.

Sales Returns and Allowances. When merchandise sold is returned or a price adjustment is granted, an entry is made in the general journal according to the principles described in Chapter 4. During October, Kannon Corporation issued a credit memorandum and prepared the following entry in a two-column general journal:

General Journal Entry for Sales Returns and Allowances

JOURNAL　　　　PAGE 18

	DATE		DESCRIPTION	POST. REF.	DEBIT	CREDIT	
1	1990 Oct.	13	Sales Returns and Allowances	412	2 2 5 00		1
2			Accounts Receivable—				2
3			Adler Company	113 ✔		2 2 5 00	3
4			Credit Memo No. 32				4

Note the *diagonal line* and *double posting* in the entry to record the credit memorandum. The diagonal line is placed in the posting reference column *at the time the entry is recorded in the general journal.*

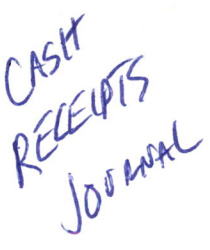

If a cash refund is made because of merchandise returned or for an allowance, Sales Returns and Allowances is debited and Cash is credited. The entry would be recorded in the cash payments journal.

Cash Receipts Journal

All transactions that increase the amount of cash are recorded in a **cash receipts journal.** In a typical merchandising business, the most frequent sources of cash receipts are likely to be cash sales and collections from customers on account.

The cash receipts journal has a special column entitled Cash Dr. The frequency of the various kinds of transactions in which cash is received determines the titles of the other columns. The cash receipts journal of Kannon Corporation for October is as follows:

Cash Receipts Journal after Posting

CASH RECEIPTS JOURNAL   PAGE 14

	DATE	ACCOUNT CREDITED	POST. REF.	SUNDRY ACCOUNTS CR.	SALES CR.	ACCOUNTS REC. CR.	SALES DISCOUNTS DR.	CASH DR.	
1	1990 Oct. 2	Notes Receivable	112	2 400 00				2 544 00	1
2		Interest Income	812	1 44 00					2
3	5	Barnes Inc.	✔			5 800 00	1 16 00	5 684 00	3
4	6	Fogarty & Jacobs	✔			2 625 00	52 50	2 572 50	4
5	7	Sales	✔		3 700 00			3 700 00	5
6	10	David T. Mattox	✔			6 00 00	12 00	5 88 00	6
7	13	Standard Supply Co.	✔			1 604 00	32 08	1 571 92	7
8	14	Sales	✔		1 632 00			1 632 00	8
9	17	Adler Company	✔			6 525 00	1 30 50	6 394 50	9
10	19	Hamilton Inc.	✔			4 850 00		4 850 00	10
11	21	Sales	✔		1 920 30			1 920 30	11
12	23	Purchases Returns							12
13		and Allowances	512	8 6 20				8 6 20	13
14	24	Wallace Corporation	✔			2 200 00		2 200 00	14
15	27	Hamilton Inc.	✔			7 865 00	1 57 30	7 707 70	15
16	28	Sales	✔		2 086 00			2 086 00	16
17	31	Sales	✔		2 423 40			2 423 40	17
18	31			2 630 20	11 761 70	32 069 00	5 00 38	45 960 52	18
19				(✔)	(411)	(113)	(413)	(111)	19

The Sundry Accounts Cr. column is used for recording credits to any account for which there is no special column. For example, as of October 2, in the illustration, the receipt of $2,544 in payment of an interest-bearing note was recorded by a credit to Notes Receivable of $2,400 and a credit to Interest Income of $144. Both amounts were entered in the Sundry Accounts Cr. column. The posting references for the credits were inserted at the time the amounts were posted.

The Sales Cr. column is used for recording sales of merchandise for cash. Each individual sale is recorded on a cash register, and the totals thus accumulated are recorded in the cash receipts journal daily, weekly, or at other regular intervals. This is illustrated by the entry of October 7 recording weekly sales and cash receipts of $3,700. Since the total of the Sales Cr. column will be posted at the end of the month, a check mark is inserted in the posting reference column to show that the $3,700 item needs no further attention.

Credits to customers accounts for payments of invoices are recorded in the Accounts Receivable Cr. column. The amount of the cash discount granted, if any, is recorded in the Sales Discounts Dr. column, and the amount of cash actually received is recorded in the Cash Dr. column. The entry on October 5 illustrates the use of these columns. Cash in the amount of $5,684 was received from Barnes Inc. in payment of its account of $5,800, the cash discount being 2% of $5,800 or $116.

Each amount in the Sundry Accounts Cr. column of the cash receipts journal is posted to the proper account in the general ledger at frequent intervals during the month. The posting is indicated by inserting the account number in the posting reference column. At regular intervals the amounts in the Accounts Receivable Cr. column are posted to the customers accounts in the subsidiary ledger, and "CR" and the proper page number are inserted in the posting reference columns of the accounts. Check marks are placed in the posting reference column of the journal to show that the amounts have been posted. None of the individual amounts in the remaining three columns of the cash receipts journal are posted.

At the end of the month, all of the amount columns are totaled, the equality of the debits and credits is proved, and the journal is ruled. Because each amount in the Sundry Accounts Cr. column has been posted individually to a general ledger account, a check mark is inserted below the column total to indicate that no further action is needed. The totals of the other four columns are posted to the proper accounts in the general ledger and their account numbers are inserted below the totals to show that the posting has been completed.

The flow of data from the cash receipts journal to the ledgers of Kannon Corporation is illustrated in the following diagram:

Flow of Data from Cash Receipts Journal to Ledgers

Cash Receipts Journal

Account Credited	P. R.	Sundry Accounts Cr.	Sales Cr.	Accounts Receivable Cr.	Sales Discounts Dr.	Cash Dr.
Notes Receivable	112	2,400.00				2,544.00
Interest Income	811	144.00				
Barnes Inc.	✔			5,800.00	116.00	5,684.00
Fogarty & Jacobs	✔			2,625.00	52.50	2,572.50
Sales	✔		3,700.00			3,700.00
David T. Mattox	✔			600.00	12.00	588.00
Sales	✔		2,423.40			2,423.40
		2,630.20	11,761.70	32,069.00	500.38	45,960.52

General Ledger

Notes Receivable
2,400.00

Sales
11,761.70

Sales Discounts
500.38

Interest Income
144.00

Accounts Receivable
32,069.00

Cash
45,960.52

Accounts Receivable Ledger

Each individual entry is posted as a credit to an account in the accounts receivable ledger, making a total of $32,069.

Accounts Receivable Control and Subsidiary Ledger

During October, the following postings were made to Accounts Receivable in the general ledger of Kannon Corporation:

Debits

Oct. 31 Total sales on account (sales journal)............................ $48,940.00

Credits

Oct. 13 A sales return (general journal) 225.00

Oct. 31 Total cash received on account (cash receipts journal) 32,069.00

The accounts receivable controlling account of Kannon Corporation as of October 31 is as follows:

Accounts Receivable Account in the General Ledger at the End of the Month

GENERAL LEDGER

ACCOUNT Accounts Receivable   ACCOUNT NO. 113

DATE		ITEM	POST. REF.	DEBIT	CREDIT	BALANCE DEBIT	BALANCE CREDIT
1990 Oct.	1	Balance	✔			17 2 6 0 00	
	13		J18		2 2 5 00	17 0 3 5 00	
	31		S35	48 9 4 0 00		65 9 7 5 00	
	31		CR14		32 0 6 9 00	33 9 0 6 00	

The posting procedures and determination of the balances of the accounts in the accounts receivable ledger and the preparation of the schedule of accounts receivable are comparable to those for accounts payable and are therefore not illustrated.

OTHER ACCOUNTING SYSTEM MODIFICATIONS

The preceding paragraphs have described and illustrated the use of subsidiary ledgers and special journals to make an accounting system more efficient in the processing of financial information. Depending on the type of business and the needs of management, other modifications of the accounting system can be made in order to increase the efficiency of the accounting system. These modifications might include procedures for recording deferrals and the use of computers to automate the recording process.

Accounting for Deferrals

A deferral was defined in Chapter 4 as an expense that has already been paid or a revenue that has already been received for services to be rendered or merchandise to be shipped. At the time an expense is prepaid, it can be recorded as either an asset (as described in Chapter 4) or an expense. At the time a prepaid revenue is received, it can be recorded as either a liability (as described in Chapter 4) or a revenue. The only difference between the alternative methods of recording these deferrals is the entries used. Their effect on the financial statements will be the same. The choice of method will, however, affect the design of the accounting system.[2]

---

[2] The alternative procedures for recording deferrals are described and illustrated in more detail in the appendix at the end of the chapter.

To illustrate the alternative methods of recording prepaid expenses and their implications for the design of the accounting system, assume that premiums on insurance policies acquired during the first year of operation were $2,034. Also, assume that $906 of the premiums had expired during the year, leaving $1,128 as unexpired premiums, computed as follows:

Premiums on insurance policies acquired during the year..................	$2,034
Premiums expired during the year..	906
Unexpired premiums at the end of year..	$1,128

Prepaid Expenses Recorded Initially as Assets. Insurance premiums may be debited to an asset account when the insurance is acquired, even though all or part of the insurance coverage is expected to expire during the accounting period. If the prepaid insurance account had been debited for premiums of $2,034 on insurance policies acquired during the year, the following adjusting entry to record the insurance expense of $906, representing the expired insurance and the corresponding decrease of the asset, would be made:

	Adjusting Entry		
Dec. 31	Insurance Expense.................................	906	
	Prepaid Insurance		906

After the expired insurance of $906 is transferred to the expense account, the balance of $1,128 in Prepaid Insurance ($2,034 − $906) represents the cost of premiums on various policies that apply to future periods. The expense of $906 appears on the income statement for the period and the asset of $1,128 appears on the balance sheet as of the end of the period.

Prepaid Expenses Recorded Initially as Expenses. Instead of being debited to an asset account, the $2,034 for policies acquired during the year may be debited to an expense account at the time of the expenditure, even though all or part of the prepayment is expected to be unused at the end of the accounting period. In this illustration, the following adjusting entry is necessary at the end of the year to recognize the unexpired insurance of $1,128 and the corresponding decrease of $1,128 in the expense account:

	Adjusting Entry		
Dec. 31	Prepaid Insurance	1,128	
	Insurance Expense..............................		1,128

After the unexpired insurance of $1,128 is transferred to the asset account, the balance of $906 in Insurance Expense ($2,034 − $1,128) represents the cost of premiums that has expired during the year on various policies. The asset of $1,128 appears on the balance sheet at the end of the period and the expense of $906 appears on the income statement for the period.

In future periods, the unexpired insurance becomes insurance expense. Therefore, some provision must be made in future periods to transfer the expiration of the insurance from the asset account to the expense account. Although it would be possible to transfer daily the cost of the expiration, a more efficient way of assuring proper allocations in future periods is to add

reversing entries to the summarizing procedures. Although reversing entries are optional, their use eliminates the need to refer to earlier adjustment data to record the expiration of insurance. It also lessens the possibilities of error. The effect of the reversing entry is to transfer the entire balance of the asset account to the expense account immediately after the temporary accounts have been closed for the period. Continuing with the illustration, the reversing entry is as follows:

	Reversing Entry		
Jan. 1	Insurance Expense	1,128	
	Prepaid Insurance		1,128

The reversing entry does not change the basic nature of the $1,128, only its location in the ledger. It is unexpired insurance on January 1, just as it was unexpired insurance on December 31.

After the reversing entry has been posted, the unexpired insurance at January 1 is in the expense account. Furthermore, since past expenditures were debited to the expense account, all expenditures for insurance policies in force during the following year may also be recorded in the expense account. At the end of the following year, the adjusting and reversing procedures would be repeated in the manner illustrated.

The Choice of Method and the Accounting System. The choice between the two methods of recording prepaid expenses depends upon which method would normally result in fewer entries and would be least likely to create errors in the recording process. Prepaid expenses such as rent expense, which will be consumed during the accounting period, are usually recorded initially as expenses. In this way, only one entry will be required and no adjusting entry is necessary. Because only one entry is required, there is less likelihood of overlooking an adjusting entry. On the other hand, prepaid expenses such as insurance premiums, which will only be partially used or consumed during the accounting period, are usually recorded initially as assets and an adjustment is made at the end of the period for the amount consumed. As illustrated above, the recording of insurance premiums initially as assets requires only an adjusting entry. In contrast, a company that records insurance premiums initially as expenses would normally make both an adjusting entry and a reversing entry.

The method selected for recording the various types of transactions should be documented in the systems manual. In many accounting systems, both methods of recording prepaid expenses will be used for different types of prepaid expenses. For example, insurance premiums and office supplies could be recorded initially as assets, while advertising and rent could be recorded initially as expenses.

Unearned Revenues. The considerations for choosing among the methods illustrated for recording prepaid expenses also apply to the recording of unearned revenues. For this reason, the recording of unearned revenues is not illustrated. The major difference is that unearned revenue may be recorded initially as revenue or as a liability. For example, rent received in advance could be recorded either as rent income or as unearned rent.[3]

---

[3]Alternative procedures for recording unearned revenues are described and illustrated in the appendix at the end of the chapter.

Computerized Accounting Systems

Most business enterprises use computers to process accounting data. These computers may be large computers or small microcomputers. Regardless of the size of the system, however, the concepts, methods, and procedures described throughout this chapter for a manual system also apply to computerized systems. Even in the most advanced computer system, special journals, subsidiary ledgers, and control accounts may be maintained and periodically printed for use by management.

To illustrate, when an advanced computer system is used to process data related to sales made on account, a clerk enters the customer's account number, merchandise quantities, sales prices, discount terms, and shipping directions directly into the computer through a terminal. The computer then updates the customer's account in the subsidiary ledger and the inventory records. Periodically, perhaps at the end of each day, the computer summarizes the transactions, posts to the general ledger accounts, verifies the equality of debits and credits, and prints a summary of the day's transactions, including a printout of sales activity in a format similar to that of a sales journal.

The speed and accuracy of computerized accounting systems allows greater flexibility in the generation of reports for management's use. For example, the computerized system described above allows for up-to-date reporting of inventory quantities, thus enabling management to reorder merchandise on a timely basis and keep the inventory level at a minimum.

Although the availability of inexpensive micro- and minicomputers has made computerized processing of accounting data affordable to small and medium-size businesses, a thorough understanding of the flow of data through a manual accounting system is essential. Such an understanding allows management to design sound accounting systems that provide accurate data upon which to base decisions. In addition, since all computerized accounting systems include the concepts and principles inherent in a manual system, an understanding of a manual system allows managers to recognize more clearly the interrelationships which exist within accounting data and reports. This understanding enables managers to anticipate how decisions may affect operations and the financial statements of an enterprise.

APPENDIX

ALTERNATIVE METHODS OF RECORDING DEFERRALS

In Chapters 4 and 6 it was noted that a prepaid expense may be debited to either an asset account or an expense account at the time of payment, and unearned revenue may be credited to either a liability account or a revenue account at the time of receipt. This appendix describes and illustrates these alternatives in greater detail.

PREPAID EXPENSES

On page 244, insurance premiums paid in advance were used as the basis for illustrating the alternative methods of recording prepaid expenses.

In this illustration the amount of insurance premiums paid during the year, expired during the year, and unexpired at the end of the year were as follows:

Premiums on insurance policies acquired during the year..................	$2,034
Premiums expired during the year...	906
Unexpired premiums at the end of the year......................................	$1,128

Based on these amounts, the entries to record the prepaid insurance initially as an asset and initially as an expense can be summarized as follows:

Systems of Recording Prepaid Expenses

Prepaid Expense **Recorded Initially as Asset**	Prepaid Expense **Recorded Initially as Expense**

Initial entries (to record initial expenditures):
  Prepaid Insurance 225
    Cash............................ 225
	Initial entries (to record initial expenditures):
	  Insurance Expense............. 225
	    Cash............................ 225

Prepaid Insurance 180
    Cash............................ 180
	Insurance Expense............. 180
	    Cash............................ 180

Adjusting entry (to transfer amount **used** to appropriate **expense** account):
  Insurance Expense............. 906
    Prepaid Insurance 906
	Adjusting entry (to transfer amount **unused** to the appropriate **asset** account):
	  Prepaid Insurance 1,128
	    Insurance Expense.......... 1,128

Closing entry (to close income statement accounts with debit balances):
  Income Summary XXXXXX
    Purchases...................... XXXXXX
 	
  Insurance Expense 906
	Closing entry (to close income statement accounts with debit balances):
	  Income Summary XXXXXX
	    Purchases...................... XXXXXX
	
	  Insurance Expense 906

Reversing entry (**not required** because amount prepaid at beginning of new period is in the asset account):
None.
	Reversing entry (to transfer amount **unused** back to **expense** account for the beginning of the new period):
	
	  Insurance Expense............. 1,128
	    Prepaid Insurance 1,128

The posting of the entries to record the prepaid insurance initially as an asset affects the prepaid insurance and insurance expense accounts as shown below and on the following page:

Prepaid Expense Recorded as Asset

ACCOUNT PREPAID INSURANCE   ACCOUNT NO. 118

Date		Item	Post. Ref.	Debit	Credit	Balance Debit	Balance Credit
1990							
Jan.	1		CP1	1,250		1,250	
Mar.	18		CP6	225		1,475	
Aug.	26		CP16	379		1,854	
Nov.	11		CP20	180		2,034	
Dec.	31	Adjusting	J25		906	1,128	

Prepaid Expense Recorded as Asset— Continued

ACCOUNT INSURANCE EXPENSE   ACCOUNT NO. 716

Date		Item	Post. Ref.	Debit	Credit	Balance Debit	Balance Credit
1990 Dec.	31	Adjusting	J25	906		906	
	31	Closing	J26		906	—	

The posting of the entries to record the prepaid insurance initially as an expense is shown in the following insurance expense and prepaid insurance accounts:

Prepaid Expense Recorded as Expense

ACCOUNT INSURANCE EXPENSE   ACCOUNT NO. 716

Date		Item	Post. Ref.	Debit	Credit	Balance Debit	Balance Credit
1990 Jan.	1		CP1	1,250		1,250	
Mar.	18		CP6	225		1,475	
Aug.	26		CP16	379		1,854	
Nov.	11		CP20	180		2,034	
Dec.	31	Adjusting	J25		1,128	906	
	31	Closing	J25		906	—	
1991 Jan.	1	Reversing	J26	1,128		1,128	

ACCOUNT PREPAID INSURANCE   ACCOUNT NO. 118

Date		Item	Post. Ref.	Debit	Credit	Balance Debit	Balance Credit
1990							
Dec.	31	Adjusting	J25	1,128		1,128	
1991 Jan.	1	Reversing	J26		1,128	—	—

Either of the two systems illustrated above may be used for all of the prepaid expenses of an enterprise, or one system may be used for prepayment of some kinds of expenses and the other system for other kinds. Initial debits to the asset account seem to be logical for prepayments of insurance, which are usually for periods of from one to three years. On the other hand, interest charges on notes payable are usually for short periods. Some charges may be recorded when a note is issued; other charges may be recorded when a note is paid; and few, if any, of the debits for interest may require adjustment at the end of the period. It therefore seems logical to record all interest charges initially by debiting the expense account rather than the asset account.

As indicated in the illustration, both methods will result in the same account balances after the adjusting entries are recorded. Therefore, the amounts reported as expenses in the income statement and as assets on the balance sheet will not be affected by the system used. To avoid confusion, the system adopted by an enterprise for each kind of prepaid expense should be followed consistently from year to year.

UNEARNED REVENUES

As a basis for illustrating the two systems for recording revenues received in advance, assume that on October 1 a business rents a portion of its building for a period of one year, receiving $7,200 in payment for the entire term of the lease. On December 31, the end of the fiscal year, $1,800 (1/4 of $7,200) has been earned and $5,400 (3/4 of $7,200) has not yet been earned. The entry to record the receipt of the rent and the related adjusting entry under each of the two systems are described and illustrated in the following paragraphs.

Unearned Revenues Recorded Initially as Liabilities

If the business in this illustration records the receipt of the rent as a liability, it will debit Cash and credit Unearned Rent for $7,200 on October 1. On December 31, the following adjusting entry will record the revenue and reduce the liability:

	Adjusting Entry			
Dec. 31	Unearned Rent..................................	218	1,800	
	Rent Income..................................	812		1,800

After this entry has been posted, the unearned rent account and the rent income account appear as follows:

Adjustment for Unearned Revenue Recorded as Liability

ACCOUNT UNEARNED RENT   ACCOUNT NO. 218

Date		Item	Post. Ref.	Debit	Credit	Balance Debit	Balance Credit
1990 Oct.	1		CR18		7,200		7,200
Dec.	31	Adjusting	J25	1,800			5,400

ACCOUNT RENT INCOME   ACCOUNT NO. 812

Date		Item	Post. Ref.	Debit	Credit	Balance Debit	Balance Credit
1990 Dec.	31	Adjusting	J25		1,800		1,800

After the amount earned, $1,800, is transferred to Rent Income, the balance of $5,400 remaining in Unearned Rent is a liability to render a service in the future. It appears as a current liability in the balance sheet because the service is to be rendered within the next accounting period. Rent Income is reported in the Other Income section of the income statement.

Unearned Revenues Recorded Initially as Revenues

To illustrate the alternative of recording the receipt of the rent as revenue, assume that Cash was debited and Rent Income was credited for $7,200 on October 1. On December 31, the end of the fiscal year, three fourths of the balance in Rent Income is still unearned and the remaining one fourth has been earned. The entry to record the transfer to the liability account appears as follows:

		Adjusting Entry			
Dec. 31	Rent Income..	812	5,400	
	Unearned Rent.............................	218		5,400

After this entry has been posted, the rent income account and the unearned rent account appear as follows:

Adjustment for Unearned Revenue Recorded as Revenue

ACCOUNT RENT INCOME   ACCOUNT NO. 812

Date		Item	Post. Ref.	Debit	Credit	Balance	
						Debit	Credit
1990							
Oct.	1		CR18		7,200		7,200
Dec.	31	Adjusting	J25	5,400			1,800

ACCOUNT UNEARNED RENT   ACCOUNT NO. 218

Date		Item	Post. Ref.	Debit	Credit	Balance	
						Debit	Credit
1990							
Dec.	31	Adjusting	J25		5,400		5,400

The unearned rent of $5,400 is listed in the current liability section of the balance sheet, and the rent income of $1,800 is reported in the income statement. The $5,400 of unearned rent at the end of the year will be earned during the following year. If it is transferred to the income account by a reversing entry immediately after the accounts are closed, no further action will be needed either month by month or at the end of the nine-month period. Furthermore, since the $7,200 rent was credited initially to the income account, all such payments received in the following year may also be treated the same way. If a reversing entry is not made, there may be balances in both the liability account and the income account at the end of the following year. This would require analysis of both accounts and possibly cause confusion. The reversing entry for the unearned rent, which is the exact reverse of the adjusting entry, is as follows:

		Reversing Entry			
Jan. 1	Unearned Rent...................................	218	5,400	
	Rent Income....................................	812		5,400

After the foregoing entry is posted to the two accounts, they will appear as shown below and on the following page:

Adjustment and Reversal for Unearned Revenue Recorded as Revenue

ACCOUNT RENT INCOME   ACCOUNT NO. 812

Date		Item	Post. Ref.	Debit	Credit	Balance	
						Debit	Credit
1990							
Oct.	1		CR18		7,200		7,200
Dec.	31	Adjusting	J25	5,400			1,800
	31	Closing	J25	1,800		—	—
1991							
Jan.	1	Reversing	J26		5,400		5,400

ACCOUNT UNEARNED RENT   ACCOUNT NO. 218

Date		Item	Post. Ref.	Debit	Credit	Balance	
						Debit	Credit
1990 Dec.	31	Adjusting	J25		5,400		5,400
1991 Jan.	1	Reversing	J26	5,400		—	—

At the beginning of the new fiscal year, there is a credit balance of $5,400 in Rent Income. Although the balance is in reality a liability at this time, it will become revenue before the end of the year. Whenever a revenue account needs adjustment for an unearned amount at the end of a period, the adjusting entry should be reversed after the accounts have been closed.

Comparison of the Two Systems

The basic features of the two systems of recording unearned revenue, including the related entries at the end of the accounting period, can be summarized as follows, using the data in the preceding illustration:

Systems of Recording Unearned Revenue

Unearned Revenue **Recorded Initially as Liability**	Unearned Revenue **Recorded Initially as Revenue**

Initial entries (to record initial receipt):
Cash................................ 7,200
    Unearned Rent   7,200
	Initial entries (to record initial receipt):
	Cash............................... 7,200
	    Rent Income................... 7,200

Adjusting entry (to transfer amount **earned** to appropriate **revenue** account):
Unearned Rent 1,800
    Rent Income...................   1,800
	Adjusting entry (to transfer amount **unearned** to appropriate **liability** account):
	Rent Income...................... 5,400
	    Unearned Rent 5,400

Closing entry (to close income statement accounts with credit balances):
Sales XXXXX
〰〰〰〰〰〰
〰〰〰〰〰〰
Rent Income 1,800
    Income Summary   XXXXXX
	Closing entry (to close income statement accounts with credit balances):
	Sales XXXXX
	〰〰〰〰〰〰
	〰〰〰〰〰〰
	Rent Income..................... 1,800
	    Income Summary XXXXXX

Reversing entry (**not required** because amount unearned at beginning of new period is in the liability account): None.	Reversing entry (to transfer amount **unearned** back to **revenue** account for the beginning of the new period): Unearned Rent .... 5,400 Rent Income.................. 5,400

Either of the systems may be used for all revenues received in advance, or the first system may be used for advance receipts of some kinds of revenue and the second system for other kinds. The results obtained are the same under both systems, but to avoid confusion the system used should be followed consistently from year to year.

USE OF REVERSING ENTRIES

As discussed in this chapter, the use of reversing entries is optional. However, the use of reversing entries generally simplifies the analysis of transactions and reduces the likelihood of errors in the subsequent recording of transactions. The following table summarizes those situations in which reversing entries of adjustments for deferrals will be prepared:

Reversing entries should be prepared:

■ when a prepaid expense has been initially recorded as an expense
■ when an unearned revenue has been initially recorded as a revenue

CHAPTER REVIEW

KEY POINTS

OBJECTIVE 1　　　### Principles of Accounting Systems

Although accounting systems will vary from business to business, the following broad principles will apply to all systems: cost-effectiveness balance, flexibility to meet future needs, adequate internal controls, effective reporting, and adaptation to organizational structure.

OBJECTIVE 2　　　### Accounting System Installation and Revision

Accounting system installation and revision involves three phases: (1) analysis of information needs, (2) design of the new system, and (3) implementation of proposals.

OBJECTIVE 3　　　### Internal Control Structure

The internal control structure of an enterprise consists of the detailed policies and procedures which provide reasonable assurance that an entity's objectives will be achieved. The internal control structure consists of three elements: (1) the control environment, (2) the control procedures, and (3) the accounting system.

The control environment refers to the overall attitude toward and awareness of the importance of controls by both management and other employees. Control procedures are those policies and procedures that management has established within the control environment in order to provide reasonable assurance that enterprise goals will be achieved. General control procedures which can be integrated throughout the accounting system include the following: competent personnel and rotation of duties, assignment of responsibility, separation of responsibility for related operations, separation of operations and accounting, proofs and security measures, and independent review. The accounting system is an integral part of the control structure because it provides the information needed by management to plan and direct operations in achieving enterprise goals.

OBJECTIVE 4　　　### Data Processing Methods

The entire amount of data needed by an enterprise is called its data base. Depending upon the variety and the amount of data included in the data base, various processing methods—manual and computerized—may be used.

OBJECTIVE 5　　　### Subsidiary Ledgers and Special Journals

Subsidiary ledgers may be used to maintain separate records for each creditor and debtor. When subsidiary ledgers are used, each subsidiary ledger is represented in the general ledger by a summarizing account, called a controlling account. The sum of the balances of the accounts in a subsidiary ledger must agree with the balance of the related controlling account.

One of the simplest methods of reducing the processing time and expense of recording a large number of transactions in a manual system is to use special journals. Special journals commonly used in medium-size merchandising firms include the following: purchases journal, cash payments journal, sales journal, and cash receipts journal.

The purchases journal is used to record purchases of merchandise or other items on account. The cash payments journal is used to record the payment of cash for any purpose. The sales journal is used to record the sale of merchandise on account. The cash receipts journal is used to record the receipt of cash from any source. The two-column general journal is used for recording transactions that do not "fit" in any of the four special journals.

OBJECTIVE 6

Accounting System Modifications

An accounting system can be modified in many ways to increase the efficiency of the system in processing financial information. One such modification is the use of computers to automate the recording process. Alternative procedures can also be used to record deferrals of expenses and revenues. For example, at the time a prepaid expense is incurred it can be recorded as an expense or as an asset. The only difference between these alternatives is the entries used; their effect on the financial statements is the same. The choice made by an enterprise in designing the accounting system depends upon which alternative will make that enterprise's system the most efficient.

KEY TERMS

accounting system 224
internal controls 225
subsidiary ledger 230
general ledger 230
controlling account 230
accounts payable ledger 230
accounts receivable ledger 230

special journals 231
general journal 231
purchases journal 232
cash payments journal 236
sales journal 239
cash receipts journal 241

SELF-EXAMINATION QUESTIONS
Answers at end of chapter.

1. The final phase of the revision of an accounting system that involves carrying out the proposals for changes in the system is termed:
   A. systems analysis
   B. systems design
   C. systems implementation
   D. none of the above

2. The detailed procedures used by management to direct operations so that enterprise goals can be achieved are termed:
   A. internal controls
   B. systems analysis
   C. systems design
   D. systems implementation

3. A payment of cash for the purchase of merchandise would be recorded in the:
   A. purchases journal
   B. cash payments journal
   C. sales journal
   D. cash receipts journal

4. When there are a large number of individual accounts with a common characteristic, it is common to place them in a separate ledger called a:
   A. subsidiary ledger
   B. creditors ledger
   C. accounts payable ledger
   D. accounts receivable ledger

5. The controlling account in the general ledger that summarizes the debits and credits to the individual customers accounts in the subsidiary ledger is entitled:
   A. Accounts Payable
   B. Accounts Receivable
   C. Sales
   D. Purchases

ILLUSTRATIVE PROBLEM

Selected transactions of O'Malley Inc. for the month of May are as follows:

(a) May 1 Issued Check No. 1001 in payment of rent for May, $1,200.
(b)   2 Purchased merchandise on account from McMillan Co., terms 2/10, n/30, FOB shipping point, $3,600.
(c)   4 Issued Check No. 1003 in payment of transportation charges on the merchandise purchased on May 2, $320.
(d)   8 Sold merchandise on account to Waller Inc., Invoice No. 51, terms 1/10, n/eom, FOB shipping point, $4,500.
(e)   9 Issued Check No. 1005 for office supplies purchased, $450.
(f)   10 Received cash for office supplies sold to employees at cost, $120.
(g)   11 Purchased office equipment on account from Fender Office Products, $15,000.
(h)   12 Issued Credit Memorandum No. 801 for $400 to Waller Inc. for merchandise returned.
(i)   12 Issued Check No. 1010 in payment of the merchandise purchased from McMillan Co. on May 2, less discount, $3,528.
(j)   16 Sold merchandise on account to Riepe Co., Invoice No. 58, terms 1/10, n/30, FOB shipping point, $8,000.
(k)   18 Received $4,059 from Waller Inc. in payment of May 8 invoice, less return of May 12 and discount.
(l)   20 Issued additional capital stock for cash, $100,000.
(m)   23 Issued Credit Memorandum No. 802 for $220 to Riepe Co. for a price adjustment on damaged merchandise sold on May 16.
(n)   24 Sold merchandise on nonbank credit cards, $16,700.
(o)   25 Sold merchandise for cash, $15,900.
(p)   30 Issued Check No. 1040 in payment of dividends to stockholders, $10,000.
(q)   30 Issued Check No. 1041 in payment of electricity and water bills, $690.
(r)   30 Issued Check No. 1042 in payment of office and sales salaries for May, $15,800.
(s)   31 Recorded adjusting entries from the work sheet prepared for the fiscal year ended May 31.

O'Malley Inc. maintains a purchases journal, a cash payments journal, a sales journal, a cash receipts journal, and a general journal. In addition, accounts receivable and accounts payable subsidiary ledgers are used.

Instructions:

1. Indicate the journal in which each of the preceding transactions [(a) through (s)] would be recorded.
2. Indicate whether an account in the accounts receivable or accounts payable subsidiary ledger would be affected for each of the preceding transactions.
3. Record transactions (b), (c), (d), (h), (i), and (k) in the appropriate journals.

SOLUTION

	(1)	(2)
(a)	Cash payments journal	
(b)	Purchases journal	Accounts payable ledger
(c)	Cash payments journal	
(d)	Sales journal	Accounts receivable ledger
(e)	Cash payments journal	
(f)	Cash receipts journal	
(g)	Purchases journal	Accounts payable ledger
(h)	General journal	Accounts receivable ledger
(i)	Cash payments journal	Accounts payable ledger

	(1)	(2)
(j)	Sales journal	Accounts receivable ledger
(k)	Cash receipts journal	Accounts receivable ledger
(l)	Cash receipts journal	
(m)	General journal	Accounts receivable ledger
(n)	Sales journal	Accounts receivable ledger
(o)	Cash receipts journal	
(p)	Cash payments journal	
(q)	Cash payments journal	
(r)	Cash payments journal	
(s)	General journal	

(3)

Transaction (b):

PURCHASES JOURNAL

DATE	ACCOUNT CREDITED	POST. REF.	ACCOUNTS PAYABLE CR.	PURCHASES DR.	STORE SUPPLIES DR.
May 2	McMillan Co.		3 6 0 0 00	3 6 0 0 00	

Transactions (c) and (i):

CASH PAYMENTS JOURNAL

DATE	CK. NO.	ACCOUNT DEBITED	POST. REF.	SUNDRY ACCOUNTS DR.	ACCOUNTS PAYABLE DR.	PURCHASES DISCOUNTS CR.	CASH CR.
May 4	1003	Transportation In		3 2 0 00			3 2 0 00
12	1010	McMillan Co.			3 6 0 0 00	7 2 00	3 5 2 8 00

Transaction (d):

SALES JOURNAL

DATE	INVOICE NO.	ACCOUNT DEBITED	POST. REF.	ACCTS. REC. DR. SALES CR.
May 8	51	Waller Inc.		4 5 0 0 00

Transaction (h):

JOURNAL

DATE	DESCRIPTION	POST. REF.	DEBIT	CREDIT
May 12	Sales Returns and Allowances		4 0 0 00	
	Accounts Receivable — Waller Inc.			4 0 0 00
	Credit Memo No. 801.			

Transaction (k):

CASH RECEIPTS JOURNAL

DATE	ACCOUNT CREDITED	POST. REF.	SUNDRY ACCOUNTS CR.	SALES CR.	ACCOUNTS REC. CR.	SALES DISCOUNTS DR.	CASH DR.
May 18	Waller Inc.				4 1 0 0 00	4 1 00	4 0 5 9 00

DISCUSSION QUESTIONS

1. Why is the accounting system of an enterprise an information system?

2. What are internal controls?

3. What is the objective of systems analysis?

4. What is included in an enterprise's *Systems Manual*?

5. Name and describe the three elements of the internal control structure.

6. How does a policy of rotating clerical employees from job to job aid in strengthening the control procedures within the control environment?

7. Why should the responsibility for a sequence of related operations be divided among different persons?

8. The ticket seller at a movie theater doubles as ticket taker for a few minutes each day while the ticket taker is on a break. Which control procedure of an enterprise's system of internal control is violated in this situation?

9. Why should the responsibility for maintaining the accounting records be separated from the responsibility for operations?

10. How can the use of fidelity insurance aid internal control?

11. How does a periodic review by internal auditors strengthen the internal control structure?

12. What is the term applied (a) to the ledger containing the individual customers accounts and (b) to the single account summarizing accounts receivable?

13. The following items were purchased on account by a retail hardware store. Indicate the account to which each purchase should be debited.
    (a) Ten stepladders
    (b) Two dozen electric drills
    (c) Three cash registers
    (d) One gross of pads of sales tickets
    (e) Forty cans of cement block sealer
    (f) Two kegs of nails
    (g) Two-year fire insurance policy on building
    (h) One electronic calculator for office use
    (i) Two display cases

14. During the current month, the following errors occurred in recording transactions in the purchases journal or in posting therefrom:
    (a) An invoice for $650 of merchandise from Johnson Co. was recorded as having been received from Jones Inc., another supplier.

(b) A credit of $640 to Nash Co. was posted as $460 in the subsidiary ledger.

(c) An invoice for merchandise of $6,500 was recorded as $5,600.

(d) The accounts payable column of the purchases journal was overadded by $1,000.

How will each error come to the bookkeeper's attention, other than by chance discovery?

15. The accounts payable and cash columns in the cash payments journal were unknowingly overadded by $100 at the end of the month. (a) Assuming no other errors in recording or posting, will the error cause the trial balance totals to be unequal? (b) Will the creditors ledger agree with the accounts payable controlling account?

16. In recording a cash payment, the bookkeeper enters the correct amount of $500 in the Accounts Payable Dr. column and the correct amount of $490 in the Cash Cr. column, but omits the entry for Purchases Discounts. How will the error be found, other than by chance discovery?

17. Assuming the use of a two-column general journal and a purchases journal and a cash payments journal as illustrated in this chapter, indicate the journal in which each of the following transactions should be recorded:
(a) Payment of cash on account to creditor.
(b) Purchase of office supplies on account.
(c) Purchase of merchandise for cash.
(d) Return of portion of merchandise purchased in (c).
(e) Purchase of store equipment on account.
(f) Withdrawal of cash by owner.

18. In recording 200 sales of merchandise on account during a single month, how many times will it be necessary to write "Sales" (a) if each transaction, including sales, is recorded individually in a two-column general journal; (b) if each sale is recorded in a sales journal?

19. How many individual postings to Sales for the month would be needed in Question 18 if the procedure described in (a) had been used; if the procedure described in (b) had been used?

20. In posting the following general journal entry, the bookkeeper posted correctly to Dailey's account but failed to post to the controlling account.

Feb. 15 Sales Returns and Allowances..................... 402   625
                Accounts Receivable—T. N. Dailey............   ✔   625

(a) How will the error be discovered? (b) Describe the procedure that is designed to prevent oversights of this type.

21. What does a check mark (✔) in the posting reference column of the cash receipts journal, which is illustrated in this chapter, signify (a) when the account being credited is an account receivable, (b) when the account credited is Sales?

22. Assuming the use of a two-column general journal and a sales journal and a cash receipts journal as illustrated in this chapter, indicate the journal in which each of the following transactions should be recorded:
(a) Investment of additional cash in the business by the owner.
(b) Sale of merchandise for cash.
(c) Receipt of cash refund for an overcharge on a purchase of merchandise.
(d) Sale of office supplies on account, at cost, to a neighboring business.
(e) Receipt of cash from sale of office equipment.
(f) Receipt of cash on account from customer.
(g) Sale of merchandise on account.   *(Continued)*

(h) Closing of the owner's drawing account at the end of the year.

(i) Adjustment to record accrued salaries at the end of the year.

(j) Issuance of credit memorandum to customer.

23. A purchase of office supplies can be debited to one of two types of accounts. Name the two types of accounts that can be debited.

24. (a) Will a business enterprise almost always have prepaid property and casualty insurance at the end of each fiscal year? Explain.

(b) Will a business enterprise that occasionally places advertisements in the local newspaper, for which it makes advance payments, always have prepaid advertising at the end of each fiscal year? Explain.

(c) Would it be logical to record prepayments of the type referred to in (a) as assets and prepayments of the type referred to in (b) as expenses? Discuss.

25. The accountant uses the following uniform procedures in recording certain transactions:

(1) Premiums on fire insurance are debited to Prepaid Insurance.

(2) Advertising, which is paid in advance, is debited to Advertising Expense.

Assuming that an adjusting entry is required at the end of the fiscal year as a result of each of the foregoing recording procedures, (a) give the accounts to be debited and credited for each adjustment and (b) state whether or not each of the adjusting entries should be reversed as of the beginning of the following year.

Real World Focus

26. One of the largest single company frauds in history was perpetrated against Equity Funding Corporation of America. Approximately $2 billion of insurance policies that were claimed to have been sold by the company were bogus. The bogus policies, which were supported by falsified policy applications, were listed along with real policies on Equity Funding's computer tapes (records). These computer tapes were kept in a separate room where they were easily accessible by Equity Funding personnel, including the computer programmers. In addition, computer programmers and other company personnel had access to the computer. What general weaknesses in Equity Funding's internal controls contributed to the occurrence and the size of the fraud?

EXERCISES

Exercise 6–1
Identification of postings from purchases journal.
OBJ. 5

Using the following purchases journal, identify each of the posting references, indicated by a letter, as representing (1) a posting to a general ledger account, (2) a posting to a subsidiary ledger account, or (3) that no posting is required.

(Left Page) 49   PURCHASES JOURNAL

Date	Account Credited	Post. Ref.	Accounts Payable Cr.
19--			
Nov. 1	Greenburg Co.	(a)	4,925
3	C. T. Davis Co.	(b)	4,600
10	Palmer Products	(d)	2,450
14	Young and Young	(e)	7,300
19	Greenburg Co.	(f)	3,775
25	C. T. Davis Co.	(g)	9,100
30			32,150
			(i)

(Continued on page 259)

Purchases Dr.	Store Supplies Dr.	Office Supplies Dr.	Sundry Accounts Dr.		
			Account	Post. Ref.	Amount
4,925	....	....	....	......	....
....	....	....	Office Equipment......	(c)	4,600
....	2,000	450	....	......	....
7,300	....	....	....	......	....
3,775	....	....	....	......	....
....	....	....	Store Equipment.......	(h)	9,100
16,000	2,000	450			13,700
(j)	(k)	(l)			(m)

Exercise 6–2

Identification of postings from cash payments journal.

OBJ. 5

Using the following cash payments journal, identify each of the posting references, indicated by a letter, as representing (1) a posting to a general ledger account, (2) a posting to a subsidiary ledger account, or (3) that no posting is required.

CASH PAYMENTS JOURNAL

Page 51

Date	Ck. No.	Account Debited	Post. Ref.	Sundry Accounts Dr.	Accounts Payable Dr.	Purchases Discounts Cr.	Cash Cr.
19--							
Jan. 4	712	P. C. Rose Co..........	(a)	....	5,000	50	4,950
5	713	Sales Returns and Allowances..........	(b)	400	....	....	400
10	714	Purchases.............	(c)	9,000	....	....	9,000
15	715	Kinard Co..............	(d)	....	2,500	50	2,450
20	716	Office Equipment.....	(e)	5,500	....	....	5,500
24	717	Advertising Expense	(f)	750	....	....	750
25	718	Office Supplies	(g)	250	....	....	250
27	719	R & D Inc.	(h)	....	5,500	55	5,445
31	720	Salaries Expense.....	(i)	2,050	....	....	2,050
31				17,950	13,000	155	30,795
				(j)	(k)	(l)	(m)

Exercise 6–3

Identification of transactions in accounts payable ledger account.

OBJ. 5

The debits and credits from three related transactions are presented in the following account taken from the accounts payable ledger:

NAME Cramptron Co.

ADDRESS 1402 Fifth Avenue

Date	Item	Post. Ref.	Debit	Credit	Balance
19--					
June 4		P42		15,750.00	15,750.00
15		J14	750.00		15,000.00
29		CP48	15,000.00		—

Describe each transaction.

Exercise 6–4

Error in accounts payable ledger and schedule of accounts payable.

OBJ. 5

After Swanson Company had completed all posting for the month of November in the current year, the sum of the balances in the following accounts payable ledger did not agree with the balance of the appropriate controlling account in the general ledger.

NAME Baker Products Co.

ADDRESS 919 Prospect Ave.

Date	Item	Post. Ref.	Debit	Credit	Balance
19--					
Nov. 1	Balance	✔			5,250
10		CP29	5,250		—
20		P32		1,750	1,750
29		J9	250		2,000

NAME David Caldwell Inc.

ADDRESS 1942 Elm Street

Date	Item	Post. Ref.	Debit	Credit	Balance
Nov. 1	Balance	✔			7,250
18		CP30	7,250		—
29		P32		9,500	9,500

NAME Karen Golden and Daughter

ADDRESS 313 Sixth Avenue

Date	Item	Post. Ref.	Debit	Credit	Balance
Nov. 8		P31		3,750	3,750
27		P32		7,000	10,750

NAME P. C. Palmisino Supply

ADDRESS 1410 Kirby Street

Date	Item	Post. Ref.	Debit	Credit	Balance
Nov. 1	Balance	✔			7,900
7		P31		4,900	12,700
12		J9	250		12,450
20		CP29	7,700		4,750

NAME Grant Yost Co.

ADDRESS 616 E. Mattis Ave.

Date	Item	Post. Ref.	Debit	Credit	Balance
Nov. 2		P31		5,000	5,000

Assuming that the controlling account balance of $31,600 has been verified as correct, (a) determine the error(s) in the preceding accounts and (b) prepare a schedule of accounts payable.

Exercise 6–5

Identification of transactions in accounts receivable ledger.

OBJ. 5

The debits and credits from three related transactions are presented in the following account taken from the accounts receivable ledger:

NAME Dystra and Diaz

ADDRESS 1340 Bald Eagle Drive

Date	Item	Post. Ref.	Debit	Credit	Balance
19--					
Feb. 5		S69	9,000.00		9,000.00
7		J19		800.00	8,200.00
14		CR60		8,200.00	—

Describe each transaction.

Exercise 6–6

Entries to record memorandums and correction of errors.

OBJ. 5

Present general journal entries to record the following transactions:

May 2. Issued credit memorandum for return of merchandise sold on account to D. C. Leonard Co. on May 1, $1,250.
  6. Received credit memorandum for return of equipment purchased on account from Harris Equipment Co. on April 27, $4,750.
 12. Issued debit memorandum for return of merchandise purchased on account from C. Kiner Inc. on May 9, $900.
 20. Issued credit memorandum for allowance made to Alice Gates for defective merchandise sold on account on May 13, $400.
 30. Corrected error of April 30 when a note received from L. L. Bacon Co. for $10,000 on account was not recorded.

Exercise 6–7

Entries to correct errors.

OBJ. 5

Present the general journal entries to correct the following errors, assuming that the incorrect entries had been posted and that the corrections are recorded in the same period in which the errors occurred.

(a) A cash sale of $620 to S. D. Strawberry was recorded as a sale on account.
(b) A cash receipt of $980 ($1,000 less 2% discount) from John Sabo was recorded as a $980 debit to Cash and a $980 credit to the subsidiary account John Sabo (and to Accounts Receivable).
(c) A cash remittance of $675 received from Vega Co. as payment on account was recorded as a cash sale.
(d) Transportation costs of $90 incurred on purchases of merchandise had been debited to Office Supplies.
(e) A $720 cash purchase of merchandise from Paul O'Neil Co. had been recorded as a purchase on account.

Exercise 6–8

Two methods of recording store supplies.

OBJ. 6

The store supplies inventory at the beginning of the fiscal year is $1,540, purchases of store supplies during the year total $3,970, and the inventory at the end of the year is $1,685.

(a) Set up T accounts for Store Supplies and Store Supplies Expense and record the following directly in the accounts, employing the system of initially recording store supplies as an expense (identify each entry by number): (1) beginning balance; (2) purchases for the period; (3) adjusting entry at end of the period; (4) closing entry.
(b) Set up T accounts for Store Supplies and Store Supplies Expense and record the following directly in the accounts, employing the system of initially recording store supplies as an asset (identify each entry by number): (1) beginning balance; (2) purchases for the period; (3) adjusting entry at the end of the period; (4) closing entry.

Exercise 6–9

Two methods of recording store supplies.

OBJ. 6

For the first year of operations, purchases of store supplies on account total $3,670, and the inventory at the end of the year is $1,485.

(a) Employing the system of initially recording store supplies as an expense, prepare entries (identify each entry by number) to record (1) purchases for the period; (2) adjusting entry at the end of the period; (3) closing entry; and (4) reversing entry, if appropriate.
(b) Employing the system of initially recording store supplies as an asset, prepare entries (identify each entry by number) to record (1) purchases for the period; (2) adjusting entry at the end of the period; (3) closing entry; and (4) reversing entry, if appropriate.

Exercise 6–10

Two methods of recording insurance expense.

OBJ. 6

Because of a lack of consistency in recording the payment of premiums on property and casualty insurance, there are balances in both the asset and expense accounts at the end of the year, before adjustments. Prepaid Insurance has a debit balance of $2,225, and Insurance Expense has a debit balance of $4,200. You determine that the total amount of insurance premiums allocable to future periods is $2,950.

(a) Assuming that all future insurance premiums will be recorded as an asset, present journal entries (1) to adjust the accounts and (2) to close the appropriate account.
(b) Assuming that all future insurance premiums will be recorded as an expense, present journal entries (1) to adjust the accounts, (2) to close the appropriate account, and (3) to transfer the balance in Prepaid Insurance to Insurance Expense.
(c) (1) What is the amount of insurance expense for the year?
(2) What is the amount of prepaid insurance at the end of the year?

Exercise 6–11

Identification of entries in Rent Expense.

OBJ. 6

The entries identified by numbers in the following account are related to the summarizing process at the end of the year. (a) Identify each entry as adjusting, closing, or reversing, and (b) present for each entry the title of the account to which the related debit or credit was posted.

RENT EXPENSE

Date		Item	Debit	Credit	Balance Debit	Balance Credit
Jan.	1	(1)	2,000		2,000	
Jan. to Dec.	1 ... 31	Transactions during the year	26,200		28,200	
	31	(2)		2,200	26,000	
	31	(3)		26,000	—	—
Jan.	1	(4)	2,200		2,200	

Appendix Exercise 6–12

Year-end entries for deferred revenues.

In their first year of operations, Easterly Publishing Co. received $600,000 from advertising contracts and $975,000 from magazine subscriptions, crediting the two amounts to Advertising Revenue and Circulation Revenue respectively. At the end of the year, the deferral of advertising revenue amounts to $125,000, and the deferral of circulation revenue amounts to $250,000. (a) If no adjustments are made at the end of the year, will revenue for the year be overstated or understated, and by what amount? (b) Present the adjusting entries that should be made at the end of the year. (c) Present the entries to close the two revenue accounts. (d) Present the reversing entries if appropriate.

Appendix Exercise 6–13

Two methods of recording advertising revenue.

The unearned advertising revenue of Hill Advertising Agency at the beginning of the fiscal year is $45,500, revenues received during the year total $414,500, and the unearned advertising revenue at the end of the year is $53,120.

(a) Set up T accounts for Unearned Advertising Revenue and Advertising Revenue and record the following directly in the accounts, employing the system of initially recording advertising fees as a revenue (identify each entry by number): (1) beginning balance; (2) revenues received during the period; (3) adjusting entry at the end of the period; (4) closing entry.

(b) Set up T accounts for Unearned Advertising Revenue and Advertising Revenue and record the following directly in the accounts, employing the system of initially recording advertising fees as a liability (identify each entry by number): (1) beginning balance; (2) revenues received during the period; (3) adjusting entry at the end of the period; (4) closing entry.

Appendix Exercise 6–14
Adjusting and reversing entries.

From a review of the ledger (before adjustment) and other records of Long Company, the following data were obtained for the current fiscal year ending May 31:

(1) As insurance premiums are paid, they have been debited to Prepaid Insurance, which has a balance of $4,120 at May 31. An analysis of the insurance policies and premiums indicates that $2,940 of the insurance has expired during the year.

(2) Rent Income has a balance at May 31 of $20,320, composed of the following:
(a) the beginning balance at June 1 of $7,420, representing rent prepaid for six months;
(b) a credit of $12,900, representing advance payment of rent for twelve months beginning December 1.

(3) Sales salaries are uniformly $16,800 for a six-day workweek ending on Saturday. The last payday of the year was Saturday, May 27.

(4) Unbilled service fees total $13,600 at May 31.

Journalize (a) the adjusting entries as of May 31 of the current fiscal year, identifying each entry by number, and (b) the reversing entries that should be made on June 1 of the succeeding fiscal year, identifying each entry by the corresponding number used in (a).

PROBLEMS

Series A

Problem 6–1A
Purchases and purchases returns, accounts payable account, and accounts payable ledger.

OBJ. 5

Purchases on account and related returns and allowances completed by Gladen Co. during May of the current year are as follows:

May 1. Purchased merchandise on account from Vero Co., $5,775.20.
  3. Purchased merchandise on account from Lane Corp., $11,552.50.
  4. Received a credit memorandum from Vero Co. for merchandise returned, $200.
  8. Purchased office supplies on account from Tyler Supply, $175.30.
  12. Purchased merchandise on account from Vero Co., $4,370.50.
  13. Purchased office equipment on account from Foster Equipment Co., $11,900.
  15. Purchased merchandise on account from James Co., $3,100.
  18. Received a credit memorandum from Tyler Supply for office supplies returned, $22.50.
  19. Purchased merchandise on account from Ames Co., $2,500.
  23. Purchased store supplies on account from Tyler Supply, $325.
  26. Received a credit memorandum from Lane Corp. as an allowance for damaged merchandise, $500.
  26. Purchased merchandise on account from James Co., $475.15.
  30. Purchased office supplies on account from Tyler Supply, $375.10.

Instructions:

(1) Open the following accounts in the general ledger and enter the balances as of May 1:

114	Store Supplies...	$ 572.50
115	Office Supplies...	319.50
122	Office Equipment..	33,500.00
211	Accounts Payable...	11,855.10
511	Purchases...	107,313.30
512	Purchases Returns and Allowances	3,050.25

(2) Open the following accounts in the accounts payable ledger and enter the balances in the balance columns as of May 1: Ames Co., $3,150; Foster Equipment Co.; James Co., $3,220.75; Lane Corp., $5,484.35; Tyler Supply; Vero Co.

(3) Record the transactions for May, posting to the creditors accounts in the accounts payable ledger immediately after each entry. Use a purchases journal, similar to the one illustrated on pages 232 and 233, and a two-column general journal.

(4) Post the general journal and the purchases journal to the accounts in the general ledger.

(5) (a) What is the sum of the balances in the subsidiary ledger at May 31?
    (b) What is the balance of the controlling account at May 31?

Problem 6–2A

Purchases and cash payments journals; accounts payable and general ledgers.

OBJ. 5

Ashe Co. was established on March 16 of the current year. Transactions related to purchases, returns and allowances, and cash payments during the remainder of March are as follows:

Mar. 16. Issued Check No. 1 in payment of rent for the remainder of March, $2,250.
   17. Purchased store equipment on account from Midtown Co., $7,750.
   18. Purchased merchandise on account from Carter Clothing, $3,250.
   19. Issued Check No. 2 in payment of store supplies, $210, and office supplies, $125.
   20. Purchased merchandise on account from Norris Clothing Co., $6,420.
   21. Purchased merchandise on account from Agassi Co., $4,900.
   22. Received a credit memorandum from Norris Clothing Co. for returned merchandise, $720.
       Post the journals to the accounts payable ledger.
   24. Issued Check No. 3 to Midtown Co. in payment of invoice of $7,750.
   25. Received a credit memorandum from Agassi Co. for defective merchandise, $600.
   26. Issued Check No. 4 to Carter Clothing in payment of invoice of $3,250, less 2% discount.
   28. Issued Check No. 5 to a cash customer for merchandise returned, $90.
   28. Issued Check No. 6 to Norris Clothing Co. in payment of the balance owed, less 2% discount.
   28. Purchased merchandise on account from Agassi Co., $7,100.
       Post the journals to the accounts payable ledger.
   30. Purchased the following from Midtown Co. on account: store supplies, $110; office supplies, $42; office equipment, $3,450.
   30. Issued Check No. 7 to Agassi Co. in payment of invoice of $4,900, less the credit of $600 and 1% discount.
   30. Purchased merchandise on account from Carter Clothing, $2,150.
   31. Issued Check No. 8 in payment of store supplies, $170.
   31. Issued Check No. 9 in payment of sales salaries, $2,200.
   31. Received a credit memorandum from Midtown Co. for defect in office equipment, $125.
       Post the journals to the accounts payable ledger.

Instructions:

(1) Open the following accounts in the general ledger, using the account numbers indicated:

111	Cash	412	Sales Returns and Allowances
116	Store Supplies	511	Purchases
117	Office Supplies	512	Purchases Returns and Allowances
121	Store Equipment	513	Purchases Discounts
122	Office Equipment	611	Sales Salaries Expense
211	Accounts Payable	712	Rent Expense

(2) Open the following accounts in the accounts payable ledger: Agassi Co.; Carter Clothing; Midtown Co.; Norris Clothing Co.

(3) Record the transactions for March, using a purchases journal similar to the one illustrated on pages 232 and 233, a cash payments journal similar to the one illustrated on page 236, and a two-column general journal. Post to the accounts payable ledger at the points indicated in the narrative of transactions.

(4) Post the appropriate individual entries to the general ledger (Sundry Accounts columns of the purchases journal and the cash payments journal; both columns of the general journal).

(5) Total each of the columns of the purchases journal and the cash payments journal and post the appropriate totals to the general ledger. (Because the problem does not include transactions related to cash receipts, the cash account in the ledger will have a credit balance.)

(6) Prepare a schedule of accounts payable.

Problem 6–3A

Sales journal; accounts receivable and general ledgers.

OBJ. 5

SKL Company was established on May 12 of the current year. Its sales of merchandise on account and related returns and allowances during the remainder of the month are as follows. Terms of all sales were 2/10, n/30, FOB destination.

May 15. Sold merchandise on account to Downs Co., Invoice No. 1, $2,000.
  20. Sold merchandise on account to Reese Inc., Invoice No. 2, $2,750.
  22. Sold merchandise on account to Innis Co., Invoice No. 3, $3,375.
  23. Issued Credit Memorandum No. 1 for $250 to Downs Co. for merchandise returned.
  27. Sold merchandise on account to D. L. Victor Co., Invoice No. 4, $3,000.
  28. Sold merchandise on account to Unisac Inc., Invoice No. 5, $500.
  28. Issued Credit Memorandum No. 2 for $150 to Reese Inc. for merchandise returned.
  30. Sold merchandise on account to Reese Inc., Invoice No. 6, $1,925.
  30. Issued Credit Memorandum No. 3 for $75 to D. L. Victor Co. for damages to merchandise caused by faulty packing.
  31. Sold merchandise on account to Innis Co., Invoice No. 7, $1,495.

Instructions:

(1) Open the following accounts in the general ledger, using the account numbers indicated: Accounts Receivable, 113; Sales, 411; Sales Returns and Allowances, 412.

(2) Open the following accounts in the accounts receivable ledger: Downs Co.; Innis Co.; Reese Inc.; Unisac Inc.; D. L. Victor Co.

(3) Record the transactions for May, posting to the customers accounts in the accounts receivable ledger and inserting the balance immediately after recording each entry. Use a sales journal, similar to the one illustrated on page 240, and a two-column general journal.

(4) Post the general journal and the sales journal to the three accounts opened in the general ledger, inserting the account balances only after the last postings.

(Continued)

(5) (a) What is the sum of the balances of the accounts in the subsidiary ledger at May 31?
      (b) What is the balance of the controlling account at May 31?

If the working papers correlating with the textbook are not used, omit Problem 6–4A.

Problem 6–4A

Sales and cash receipts journals; accounts receivable and general ledgers.

OBJ. 5

Three journals, the accounts receivable ledger, and portions of the general ledger of Larkin Company are presented in the working papers. Sales invoices and credit memorandums were entered in the journals by an assistant. Terms of sales on account are 1/10, n/30, FOB shipping point. Transactions in which cash and notes receivable were received during July are as follows:

July 3. Received $5,445 from G. L. Powell Co. in payment of June 23 invoice, less discount.
      6. Received $25,500 in payment of $25,000 note receivable and interest of $500.
         Post transactions of July 2, 3, and 6 to accounts receivable ledger.
      7. Received $6,930 from Marion Rau Co. in payment of June 29 invoice, less discount.
     10. Received $2,200 from W. A. Edwards Co. in payment of June 10 invoice, no discount.
     15. Cash sales for first half of July totaled $16,250.
         Post transactions of July 7, 10, 12, and 15 to accounts receivable ledger.
     19. Received $800 refund for return of defective equipment purchased for cash in June.
     20. Received $3,168 from G. L. Powell Co. in payment of balance due on July 10 invoice, less discount.
     22. Received $5,445 from W. A. Edwards Co. in payment of July 12 invoice, less discount.
         Post transactions of July 17, 20, 22, and 23 to accounts receivable ledger.
     28. Received $50 for sale of office supplies at cost.
     31. Received $1,250 cash and a $2,500 note receivable from Bob Harris and Son in settlement of the balance due on the invoice of July 2, no discount. (Record receipt of note in the general journal.)
     31. Cash sales for the second half of July totaled $16,100.
         Post transactions of July 27, 28, 30, and 31 to accounts receivable ledger.

Instructions:

(1) Record the cash receipts in the cash receipts journal and the note in the general journal. Before recording a receipt of cash on account, determine the balance of the customer's account. Post the entries from the three journals, in date sequence, to the accounts receivable ledger in accordance with the instructions in the narrative of transactions. Insert the new balance after each posting to an account.
(2) Post the appropriate individual entries from the cash receipts journal and the general journal to the general ledger.
(3) Total each of the columns of the sales journal and the cash receipts journal and post the appropriate totals to the general ledger. Insert the balance of each account after the last posting.
(4) Prepare a schedule of the accounts receivable as of July 31 and compare the total with the balance of the controlling account.

Problem 6–5A

Sales and cash receipts journals; accounts receivable and general ledgers.

OBJ. 5

SPREADSHEET PROBLEM

Transactions related to sales and cash receipts completed by Menter Company during the period June 16–30 of the current year are as follows. The terms of all sales on account are 1/10, n/30, FOB shipping point.

June 16. Issued Invoice No. 808 to Thomas Co., $7,250.
    16. Received cash from T. A. Davis Co. for the balance owed on its account, less discount.
    17. Issued Invoice No. 809 to Jackson Co., $3,500.
    18. Issued Invoice No. 810 to R. D. Reed Inc., $5,100.
        Post all journals to the accounts receivable ledger.
    21. Received cash from Jackson Co. for the balance owed on June 16, no discount.
    22. Issued Credit Memorandum No. 55 to Thomas Co., $250.
    24. Issued Invoice No. 811 to Jackson Co., $7,000.
    24. Received $1,050 in payment of a $1,000 note receivable and interest of $50.
        Post all journals to the accounts receivable ledger.
    25. Received cash from Thomas Co. for the balance due on invoice of June 16, less discount.
    27. Received cash from Jackson Co. for invoice of June 17, less discount.
    29. Issued Invoice No. 812 to T. A. Davis Co., $8,000.
    30. Recorded cash sales for the second half of the month, $11,750.
    30. Issued Credit Memorandum No. 56 to T. A. Davis Co., $150.
        Post all journals to the accounts receivable ledger.

Instructions:

(1) Open the following accounts in the general ledger, inserting the balances indicated, as of June 1:

111	Cash	$19,222
112	Notes Receivable	7,500
113	Accounts Receivable	14,650
411	Sales	—
412	Sales Returns and Allowances	—
413	Sales Discounts	—
811	Interest Income	—

(2) Open the following accounts in the accounts receivable ledger, inserting the balances indicated, as of June 16: T. A. Davis Co., $7,400; Jackson Co., $9,925; R. D. Reed Inc.; Thomas Co.

(3) In a sales journal similar to the one illustrated on page 240 and a cash receipts journal similar to the one illustrated on page 241, insert "June 16 Total(s) Forwarded" on the first line of the Account Debited or Account Credited column, "✔" in the Post. Ref. column, and the following dollar figures in the respective amount columns:

    Sales journal: 25,350
    Cash receipts journal: 3,442; 13,420; 22,675; 185; 39,352.

(4) Using the two special journals and a two-column general journal, record the transactions for the remainder of June. Post to the accounts receivable ledger and insert the balances at the points indicated in the narrative of transactions. *Determine the balance in the customer's account before recording a cash receipt.*

(5) Total each of the columns of the special journals and post the individual entries and totals to the general ledger. Insert account balances after the last posting.

(6) Determine that the subsidiary ledger agrees with the controlling account in the general ledger.

Problem 6–6A

All journals and general ledger for sole proprietorship; trial balance.

OBJ. 5

The transactions completed by F. C. Marr Co. during July, the first month of the current fiscal year, were as follows:

July   1. Issued Check No. 830 for July rent, $2,500.
    3. Purchased equipment on account from Olin Co., $5,800.
    3. Purchased merchandise on account from Polk Inc., $3,950.
    6. Issued Invoice No. 922 to Wallace Co., $2,125.
    7. Received check for $4,950 from Dunn Corp. in payment of $5,000 invoice, less discount.
    7. Issued Check No. 831 for miscellaneous selling expense, $225.
    8. Received credit memorandum from Polk Inc. for returned merchandise, $450.
    8. Issued Invoice No. 923 to Green Co., $6,000.
    9. Issued Check No. 832 to Engles Co. in payment of $7,500 invoice, less 2% discount.
    9. Received check for $9,405 from Baker Manufacturing Co. in payment of $9,500 invoice, less discount.
   10. Issued Check No. 833 to Davis Enterprises in payment of $4,250 invoice, no discount.
   12. Issued Invoice No. 924 to Dunn Corp., $3,500.
   12. Issued Check No. 834 for $930 to Ross Corp. in payment of account, no discount.
   12. Received check for $775 from Wallace Co. on account, no discount.
   14. Issued credit memorandum to Dunn Corp. for damaged merchandise, $500.
   15. Issued Check No. 835 for $3,465 to Polk Inc. in payment of $3,500 balance, less 1% discount.
   15. Issued Check No. 836 for $2,250 for cash purchase of merchandise.
   15. Cash sales for July 1–15, $19,650.
   18. Purchased merchandise on account from Davis Enterprises, $6,420.
   18. Received check for return of merchandise that had been purchased for cash, $110.
   19. Issued Check No. 837 for miscellaneous administrative expense, $175.
   21. Purchased the following on account from Cass Supply Inc.: store supplies, $225; office supplies, $195.
   23. Issued Check No. 838 in payment of advertising expense, $850.
   23. Issued Invoice No. 925 to Baker Manufacturing Co., $1,950.
   24. Purchased the following on account from Engles Co.: merchandise, $4,170; store supplies, $130.
   25. Issued Invoice No. 926 to Gnatt Corp., $4,600.
   25. Received check for $2,970 from Dunn Corp. in payment of $3,000 balance, less discount.
   29. Issued Check No. 839 for $5,800 to Olin Co. in payment of invoice of July 3, no discount.
   30. Issued Check No. 840 to F. C. Marr as a personal withdrawal, $3,000.
   31. Issued Check No. 841 for monthly salaries as follows: sales salaries, $11,100; office salaries, $4,500.
   31. Cash sales for July 16–31, $26,150.
   31. Issued Check No. 842 in payment of transportation charges for merchandise purchased during the month, $350.

Instructions:

(1) Open the following accounts in the general ledger, entering the balances indicated as of July 1:

111	Cash	$11,350
113	Accounts Receivable	15,275
114	Merchandise Inventory	31,450
115	Store Supplies	745
116	Office Supplies	410
117	Prepaid Insurance	2,100

121	Equipment	$47,250
122	Accumulated Depreciation	22,250
211	Accounts Payable	12,680
311	F. C. Marr, Capital	73,650
312	F. C. Marr, Drawing	—
411	Sales	—
412	Sales Returns and Allowances	—
413	Sales Discounts	—
511	Purchases	—
512	Purchases Returns and Allowances	—
513	Purchases Discounts	—
514	Transportation In	—
611	Sales Salaries Expense	—
612	Advertising Expense	—
619	Miscellaneous Selling Expense	—
711	Office Salaries Expense	—
712	Rent Expense	—
719	Miscellaneous Administrative Expense	—

(2) Record the transactions for July, using a purchases journal (as on pages 232 and 233), a sales journal (as on page 240), a cash payments journal (as on page 236), a cash receipts journal (as on page 241), and a two-column general journal. The terms of all sales on account are FOB shipping point, 1/10, n/30. Assume that an assistant makes daily postings to the individual accounts in the accounts payable ledger and the accounts receivable ledger.

(3) Post the appropriate individual entries to the general ledger.

(4) Total each of the columns of the special journals and post the appropriate totals to the general ledger; insert the account balances.

(5) Prepare a trial balance.

(6) Balances of the accounts in the subsidiary ledgers as of July 31 are as follows:

Accounts receivable: 1,950; 6,000; 4,600; 2,125.
Accounts payable: 420; 6,420; 4,300.

Verify the agreement of the subsidiary ledgers with their respective controlling accounts.

Appendix Problem 6–7A
Adjusting and reversing entries.

The following selected accounts appear in the ledger of Kandel Company at April 30, the end of the current fiscal year. None of the year-end adjustments have been recorded.

113	Fees Receivable	—
114	Supplies	$ 1,560
115	Prepaid Insurance	3,840
116	Prepaid Advertising	—
215	Unearned Rent	—
313	Income Summary	—
411	Fees Earned	152,000
513	Advertising Expense	20,400
514	Insurance Expense	—
515	Supplies Expense	—
611	Rent Income	15,600

The following information relating to adjustments at April 30 is obtained from physical inventories, supplementary records, and other sources:

(1) Unbilled fees at April 30, $6,800.
(2) Rent collected in advance that will not be earned until the following year, $1,200.
(3) The insurance record indicates that $1,300 of insurance relates to future years.

(4) Inventory of supplies at April 30, $540.

(5) Of a prepayment of $6,000 for advertising space on a billboard, 60% of the time has expired, and the remainder will expire in the following year. The payment of the $6,000 was recorded in Advertising Expense.

Instructions:

(1) Journalize the adjusting entries for April 30.
(2) Journalize the reversing entries for May 1.

Appendix
Problem 6–8A
Two methods of recording advertising expense and rent income; financial statement presentation.

The following transactions relate to advertising and rent. Accounts are adjusted and closed only at December 31, the end of the fiscal year.

Advertising

Jan.   1.   Debit balance of $2,750 (allocable to January–May).
June 1.   Payment of $7,200 (allocable at $600 a month for 12 months beginning June 1).

Rent

Jan.   1.   Credit balance of $12,800 ($2,400 allocable to January–February; $10,400 allocable to January–August).
Mar. 1.   Receipt of $14,400 (allocable at $1,200 a month for 12 months beginning March 1).
Sept. 1.   Receipt of $15,600 (allocable at $1,300 a month for 12 months beginning September 1).

Instructions:

(1) Open accounts for Prepaid Advertising, Advertising Expense, Unearned Rent, and Rent Income. Using the system of initially recording prepaid expense as an asset and unearned revenue as a liability, record the following directly in the accounts: (a) beginning balances as of January 1; (b) transactions of March 1, June 1, and September 1; (c) adjusting entries at December 31; (d) closing entries at December 31; and (e) reversing entries at January 1, if appropriate. Identify each entry in the item section of the accounts as balance, transaction, adjusting, closing, or reversing, and extend the balance after each entry.

(2) Open a duplicate set of accounts and follow the remaining instructions in Instruction (1), except to employ the system of initially recording prepaid expense as an expense and unearned revenue as revenue.

(3) Determine the amounts that would appear in the balance sheet at December 31 as asset and liability respectively, and in the income statement for the year as expense and revenue respectively, according to the system employed in Instruction (1) and the system employed in Instruction (2). Present your answers in the following form:

System	Asset	Expense	Liability	Revenue
Instruction (1)	$	$	$	$
Instruction (2)				

Series B

Problem 6–2B
Purchases and cash payments journals; accounts payable and general ledgers.

OBJ. 5

SPREADSHEET PROBLEM

Check Clothiers began operations on June 15 of the current year. Transactions related to purchases, returns and allowances, and cash payments during the remainder of June are as follows:

June 15.   Issued Check No. 1 in payment of rent for the remainder of June, $1,150.
      16.   Purchased office equipment on account from Drysdale Equipment Corp., $8,100.

June 17. Purchased merchandise on account from Reid Clothing Co., $14,800.
     17. Issued Check No. 2 in payment of store supplies, $410, and office supplies, $290.
     18. Purchased merchandise on account from Bryan Clothing, $9,720.
     19. Purchased merchandise on account from Abrams Co., $2,150.
     20. Received a credit memorandum from Bryan Clothing for returned merchandise, $720.
         Post the journals to the accounts payable ledger.
     23. Issued Check No. 3 to Drysdale Equipment Corp. in payment of invoice of $8,100.
     23. Received a credit memorandum from Abrams Co. for defective merchandise, $150.
     24. Issued Check No. 4 to Reid Clothing Co. in payment of invoice of $14,800, less 1% discount.
     25. Issued Check No. 5 to a cash customer for merchandise returned, $175.
     26. Issued Check No. 6 to Bryan Clothing in payment of the balance owed, less 2% discount.
     27. Purchased merchandise on account from Abrams Co., $1,950.
         Post the journals to the accounts payable ledger.
     30. Purchased the following from Drysdale Equipment Corp. on account: store supplies, $150; office supplies, $75; store equipment, $1,500.
     30. Issued Check No. 7 to Abrams Co. in payment of invoice of $2,150, less the June 23 credit of $150.
     30. Purchased merchandise on account from Reid Clothing Co., $6,200.
     30. Issued Check No. 8 in payment of sales salaries, $2,110.
     30. Received a credit memorandum from Drysdale Equipment Corp. for defect in office equipment, $150.
         Post the journals to the accounts payable ledger.

Instructions:

(1) Open the following accounts in the general ledger, using the account numbers indicated:

111	Cash	412	Sales Returns and Allowances
116	Store Supplies	511	Purchases
117	Office Supplies	512	Purchases Returns and Allowances
121	Store Equipment	513	Purchases Discounts
122	Office Equipment	611	Sales Salaries Expense
211	Accounts Payable	712	Rent Expense

(2) Open the following accounts in the accounts payable ledger: Abrams Co.; Bryan Clothing; Drysdale Equipment Corp.; and Reid Clothing Co.

(3) Record the transactions for June, using a purchases journal similar to the one illustrated on pages 232 and 233, a cash payments journal similar to the one illustrated on page 236, and a two-column general journal. Post to the accounts payable ledger at the points indicated in the narrative of transactions.

(4) Post the appropriate individual entries to the general ledger (Sundry Accounts columns of the purchases journal and the cash payments journal; both columns of the general journal).

(5) Total each of the columns of the purchases journal and the cash payments journal, and post the appropriate totals to the general ledger. (Because the problem does not include transactions related to cash receipts, the cash account in the ledger will have a credit balance.)

(6) Prepare a schedule of accounts payable.

If the working papers correlating with the textbook are not used, omit Problem 6–4B.

Problem 6–4B

Sales and cash receipts journals; accounts receivable and general ledgers.

OBJ. 5

Three journals, the accounts receivable ledger, and portions of the general ledger of Eagle Company are presented in the working papers. Sales invoices and credit memorandums were entered in the journals by an assistant. Terms of sales on account are 1/10, n/30, FOB shipping point. Transactions in which cash and notes receivable were received during July are as follows:

July 3. Received $5,445 from G. L. Powell Co. in payment of June 23 invoice, less discount.

     6. Received $10,100 in payment of $10,000 note receivable and interest of $100.
Post transactions of July 2, 3, and 6 to accounts receivable ledger.

     8. Received $6,930 from Marion Rau Co. in payment of June 29 invoice, less discount.

     9. Received $2,200 from W. A. Edwards Co. in payment of June 10 invoice, no discount.
Post transactions of July 8, 9, 10, 12, and 15 to accounts receivable ledger.

   16. Cash sales for first half of July totaled $4,610.

   19. Received $1,000 refund for return of defective equipment purchased for cash in June.

   20. Received $3,168 from G. L. Powell Co. in payment of balance due on July 10 invoice, less discount.

   22. Received $5,445 from W. A. Edwards Co. in payment of July 12 invoice, less discount.
Post transactions of July 17, 20, 22, and 23 to accounts receivable ledger.

   27. Received $40 for sale of office supplies at cost.

   31. Received $1,250 cash and a $2,500 note receivable from Bob Harris and Son in settlement of the balance due on the invoice of July 2, no discount. (Record receipt of note in the general journal.)

   31. Cash sales for second half of July totaled $4,150.
Post transactions of July 27, 28, 30, and 31 to accounts receivable ledger.

Instructions:

(1) Record the cash receipts in the cash receipts journal and the note in the general journal. Before recording a receipt of cash on account, determine the balance of the customer's account. Post the entries from the three journals, in date sequence, to the accounts receivable ledger in accordance with the instructions in the narrative of transactions. Insert the new balance after each posting to an account.

(2) Post the appropriate individual entries from the cash receipts journal and the general journal to the general ledger.

(3) Total each of the columns of the sales journal and the cash receipts journal and post the appropriate totals to the general ledger. Insert the balance of each account after the last posting.

(4) Prepare a schedule of the accounts receivable as of July 31 and compare the total with the balance of the controlling account.

Problem 6–5B

Sales and cash receipts journals; accounts receivable and general ledgers.

OBJ. 5

Transactions related to sales and cash receipts completed by Cross Company during the period June 16–30 of the current year are as follows. The terms of all sales on account are 2/10, n/30, FOB shipping point.

June 16. Issued Invoice No. 793 to Thomas Co., $5,575.

     16. Received cash from T. A. Davis Co. for the balance due on its account, less discount.

     19. Issued Invoice No. 794 to Jackson Co., $3,900.

June 20. Issued Invoice No. 795 to R. D. Reed Inc., $3,200.
Post all journals to the accounts receivable ledger.
  23. Received cash from Jackson Co. for the balance owed on June 16, no discount.
  24. Issued Credit Memorandum No. 35 to Thomas Co., $275.
  24. Issued Invoice No. 796 to Jackson Co., $6,500.
  24. Received $1,560 in payment of a $1,500 note receivable and interest of $60.
Post all journals to the accounts receivable ledger.
  25. Received cash from Thomas Co. for the balance due on invoice of June 16, less discount.
  28. Received cash from Jackson Co. for invoice of June 19, less discount.
  28. Issued Invoice No. 797 to T. A. Davis Co., $2,100.
  30. Issued Credit Memorandum No. 36 to T. A. Davis Co., $250.
  30. Recorded cash sales for the second half of the month, $8,155.
Post all journals to the accounts receivable ledger.

Instructions:

(1) Open the following accounts in the general ledger, inserting the balances indicated, as of June 1:

111	Cash	$19,222
112	Notes Receivable...	7,500
113	Accounts Receivable...	14,650
411	Sales...	—
412	Sales Returns and Allowances	—
413	Sales Discounts..	—
811	Interest Income	—

(2) Open the following accounts in the accounts receivable ledger, inserting the balances indicated, as of June 16: T. A. Davis Co. $7,400; Jackson Co., $9,925; R. D. Reed Inc.; Thomas Co.

(3) In a sales journal similar to the one illustrated on page 240 and a cash receipts journal similar to the one illustrated on page 241, insert "June 16 Total(s) Forwarded" on the first line of the Account Debited or Account Credited column, "✔" in the Post. Ref. column, and the following dollar figures in the respective amount columns:

Sales journal: 25,350
Cash receipts journal: 3,442; 13,420; 22,675; 185; 39,352.

(4) Using the two special journals and a two-column general journal, record the transactions for the remainder of June. Post to the accounts receivable ledger, and insert the balances at the points indicated in the narrative of transactions. *Determine the balance in the customer's account before recording a cash receipt.*

(5) Total each of the columns of the special journals and post the individual entries and totals to the general ledger. Insert account balances after the last posting.

(6) Determine that the subsidiary ledger agrees with the controlling account in the general ledger.

Problem 6–6B

All journals and general ledger for sole proprietorship; trial balance.

OBJ. 5

The transactions completed by F. C. Marr Co. during July, the first month of the current fiscal year, were as follows:

July 1. Issued Check No. 610 for July rent, $1,800.
  2. Purchased merchandise on account from Jacobs Co., $3,690.
  3. Purchased equipment on account from Ross Equipment Co., $9,750.
  5. Issued Invoice No. 940 to C. C. Martin Inc., $1,700.
  6. Received check for $5,940 from Towers Co. in payment of $6,000 invoice, less discount.

July 6. Issued Check No. 611 for miscellaneous selling expense, $310.
9. Received credit memorandum from Jacobs Co. for returned merchandise, $290.
9. Issued Invoice No. 941 to Franco Corp., $8,500.
10. Issued Check No. 612 for $4,606 to Bunn Co. in payment of $4,700 invoice, less 2% discount.
10. Received check for $6,275 from Cedeno Manufacturing Co. in payment of account, no discount.
10. Issued Check No. 613 to Haller Enterprises in payment of $6,100 invoice, no discount.
11. Issued Invoice No. 942 to Kline Corp., $3,120.
11. Issued Check No. 614 for $1,880 to Willis Co. in payment of account, no discount.
12. Received check for $1,683 from C. C. Martin Inc. in payment of $1,700 invoice, less discount.
13. Issued credit memorandum to Kline Corp. for damaged merchandise, $320.
13. Issued Check No. 615 for $3,332 to Jacobs Co. in payment of $3,400 balance, less 2% discount.
16. Issued Check No. 616 for $2,725 for cash purchase of merchandise.
16. Cash sales for July 1–16, $21,520.
17. Purchased merchandise on account from Haller Enterprises, $7,920.
18. Received check for return of merchandise that had been purchased for cash, $790.
18. Issued Check No. 617 for miscellaneous administrative expense, $238.
19. Purchased the following on account from Moore Supply Inc.: store supplies, $248; office supplies, $197.
20. Issued Check No. 618 in payment of advertising expense, $1,850.
23. Issued Invoice No. 943 to Cedeno Manufacturing Co., $8,172.
24. Purchased the following on account from Bunn Co.: merchandise, $5,127; store supplies, $292.
25. Issued Invoice No. 944 to Franco Corp., $4,650.
25. Received check from Franco Corp. in payment of $3,000 July 1 balance, no discount.
26. Issued Check No. 619 to Ross Equipment Co. in payment of $9,750 invoice of July 3, no discount.
27. Issued Check No. 620 to F. C. Marr as a personal withdrawal, $3,500.
30. Issued Check No. 621 for monthly salaries as follows: sales salaries, $9,100; office salaries, $3,800.
31. Cash sales for July 17–31, $18,150.
31. Issued Check No. 622 in payment of transportation charges for merchandise purchased during the month, $930.

Instructions:

(1) Open the following accounts in the general ledger, entering the balances indicated as of July 1:

111	Cash	$11,350
113	Accounts Receivable	15,275
114	Merchandise Inventory	31,450
115	Store Supplies	745
116	Office Supplies	410
117	Prepaid Insurance	2,100
121	Equipment	47,250
122	Accumulated Depreciation	22,250
211	Accounts Payable	12,680
311	F. C. Marr, Capital	73,650

312	F. C. Marr, Drawing	—
411	Sales	—
412	Sales Returns and Allowances	—
413	Sales Discounts	—
511	Purchases	—
512	Purchases Returns and Allowances	—
513	Purchases Discounts	—
514	Transportation In	—
611	Sales Salaries Expense	—
612	Advertising Expense	—
619	Miscellaneous Selling Expense	—
711	Office Salaries Expense	—
712	Rent Expense	—
719	Miscellaneous Administrative Expense	—

(2) Record the transactions for July, using a purchases journal (as on pages 232 and 233), a sales journal (as on page 240), a cash payments journal (as on page 236), a cash receipts journal (as on page 241), and a two-column general journal. The terms of all sales on account are FOB shipping point, 1/10, n/30. Assume that an assistant makes daily postings to the individual accounts in the accounts payable ledger and the accounts receivable ledger.

(3) Post the appropriate individual entries to the general ledger.

(4) Total each of the columns of the special journals and post the appropriate totals to the general ledger; insert the account balances.

(5) Prepare a trial balance.

(6) Balances of the accounts in the subsidiary ledgers as of July 31 are as follows:

Accounts receivable: 13,150; 8,172; 2,800.
Accounts payable: 5,419; 7,920; 445.

Verify the agreement of the subsidiary ledgers with their respective controlling accounts.

Appendix Problem 6–8B

Two methods of recording insurance expense and rent income; financial statement presentation.

The following transactions relate to insurance and rent. Accounts are adjusted and closed only at December 31, the end of the fiscal year.

Insurance

Jan. 1. Debit balance of $1,850 (allocable to January–May).
June 1. Payment of $6,600 (allocable at $550 a month for 12 months beginning June 1).

Rent

Jan. 1. Credit balance of $12,220 ($2,300 allocable to January–February; $9,920 allocable to January–August).
Mar. 1. Receipt of $14,400 (allocable at $1,200 a month for 12 months beginning March 1).
Sept. 1. Receipt of $15,300 (allocable at $1,275 a month for 12 months beginning September 1).

Instructions:

(1) Open accounts for Prepaid Insurance, Insurance Expense, Unearned Rent, and Rent Income. Using the system of initially recording prepaid expense as an asset and unearned revenue as a liability, record the following directly in the accounts: (a) beginning balances as of January 1; (b) transactions of March 1, June 1, and September 1; (c) adjusting entries at December 31; (d) closing entries at December 31; and (e) reversing entries at January 1, if appropriate. Identify each entry in the item section of the accounts as balance, transaction, adjusting, closing, or reversing, and extend the balance after each entry.

(Continued)

(2) Open a duplicate set of accounts and follow the remaining instructions in Instruction (1), except to employ the system of initially recording prepaid expense as an expense and unearned revenue as revenue.

(3) Determine the amounts that would appear in the balance sheet at December 31 as asset and liability respectively, and in the income statement for the year as expense and revenue respectively, according to the system employed in Instruction (1) and the system employed in Instruction (2). Present your answers in the following form:

System	Asset	Expense	Liability	Revenue
Instruction (1)	$	$	$	$
Instruction (2)				

MINI-CASE 6

REED JEWELERS

For the past few years, your aunt has operated a small jewelry store, Reed Jewelers. Its current annual revenues are approximately $525,000. Because the company's accountant has been taking more and more time each month to record all transactions in a two-column journal and to prepare the financial statements, your aunt is considering improving the company's accounting system by adding special journals and subsidiary ledgers. Your aunt has asked you to help her with this project. She has compiled the following information:

(1)

Type of Transaction	Estimated Frequency per Month
Purchases of merchandise on account	100
Sales on account	225
Cash receipts from customers on account	210
Daily cash register summaries of cash sales	25
Purchases of merchandise for cash	20
Purchases of office supplies on account	5
Purchases of store supplies on account	5
Cash payments for utilities expenses	4
Cash purchases of office supplies	4
Cash purchases of store supplies	4

(2) For merchandise purchases of high dollar-value items, Reed Jewelers issues notes payable at current interest rates to vendors. These notes are issued because many of the high-value items may not sell immediately and the issuance of the notes reduces the need to maintain large balances of cash or assets that can be readily converted to cash. Notes are issued for approximately 10% of the purchases on account.

(3) All purchases discounts are taken when available.
(4) A sales discount of 1/10, n/30 is offered to all credit customers.
(5) A local sales tax of 6% is collected on all intrastate sales of merchandise.
(6) Monthly financial statements are prepared.

Instructions:

(1) Based upon the preceding description of Reed Jewelers, indicate which special journals you would recommend as part of Reed Jewelers' accounting system.
(2) Assume that your aunt has decided to use a sales journal and a purchases journal. Design the format for each journal, giving special consideration to the needs of Reed Jewelers.
(3) Which subsidiary ledgers would you recommend for Reed Jewelers?

ETHICS DISCUSSION CASE

Ed Hoard, a systems analyst for Fortney Inc., is currently helping a neighbor set up an accounting system for a new business venture. Ed has agreed to set up the system for a fee of $800. In designing the new system, Ed has utilized several special journal and subsidiary ledger formats especially developed for Fortney Inc. by its public accountants.

Discuss whether Ed Hoard is behaving in an ethical manner.

COMPREHENSIVE PROBLEM 3

The transactions completed by Jefferson Enterprises during January, the first month of the current fiscal year, were as follows:

Jan. 2. Issued Check No. 810 for January rent, $2,000.
      2. Purchased merchandise on account from Dane Corp., $3,150.
      3. Purchased equipment on account from Lee Equipment Co., $5,000.
      4. Issued Invoice No. 990 to C. L. Frank Inc., $1,575.
      6. Received check for $2,744 from Nichols Corp. in payment of $2,800 invoice, less discount.
      7. Issued Check No. 811 for miscellaneous selling expense, $230.
      8. Received credit memorandum from Dane Corp. for merchandise returned to them, $150.
      8. Issued Invoice No. 991 to Jackson Co., $6,500.
      9. Issued Check No. 812 for $9,310 to Easterly Inc. in payment of $9,500 invoice, less 2% discount.
      9. Received check for $8,624 from Allen Co. in payment of $8,800 invoice, less discount.
     10. Issued Check No. 813 to Beaman Co. in payment of $3,620 invoice, no discount.
     10. Issued Invoice No. 992 to Nichols Corp., $3,225.
     11. Issued Check No. 814 to Peak Corp. in payment of account, $705, no discount.

Jan. 12. Received check for $3,275 from C. L. Frank Inc. on account, no discount.

14. Issued credit memorandum to Nichols Corp. for damaged merchandise, $225.

15. Issued Check No. 815 for $2,940 to Dane Corp. in payment of $3,000 balance, less 2% discount.

15. Issued Check No. 816 for $2,550 for cash purchase of merchandise.

15. Cash sales for January 2–15, $18,942.

17. Purchased merchandise on account from Beaman Co., $6,420.

18. Received check for return of merchandise that had been purchased for cash, $130.

18. Issued Check No. 817 for miscellaneous administrative expense, $130.

21. Purchased the following on account from Acme Supply Inc.: store supplies, $215; office supplies, $170.

22. Issued Check No. 818 in payment of advertising expense, $610.

23. Issued Invoice No. 993 to Allen Co., $1,950.

24. Purchased the following on account from Easterly Inc.: merchandise, $3,125; store supplies, $110.

25. Issued Invoice No. 994 to Jackson Co., $3,290.

25. Received check for $2,940 from Nichols Corp. in payment of $3,000 balance, less discount.

26. Issued Check No. 819 to Lee Equipment Co. in payment of $5,000 invoice of January 3, no discount.

29. Issued Check No. 820 to Joan Jefferson as a personal withdrawal, $2,500.

30. Issued Check No. 821 for monthly salaries as follows: sales salaries, $9,600; office salaries, $3,800.

31. Cash sales for January 16–31, $19,250.

31. Issued Check No. 822 for cash purchase of merchandise, $610.

Instructions:

(1) Open the following accounts in the general ledger, entering the balances indicated as of January 1:

111	Cash	$10,600
113	Accounts Receivable	17,700
114	Merchandise Inventory	30,000
115	Store Supplies	410
116	Office Supplies	225
117	Prepaid Insurance	2,100
121	Equipment	40,650
122	Accumulated Depreciation	11,250
211	Accounts Payable	13,825
311	Joan Jefferson, Capital	76,610
312	Joan Jefferson, Drawing	—
411	Sales	—
412	Sales Returns and Allowances	—
413	Sales Discounts	—
511	Purchases	—
512	Purchases Returns and Allowances	—
513	Purchases Discounts	—
611	Sales Salaries Expense	—
612	Advertising Expense	—
619	Miscellaneous Selling Expense	—
711	Office Salaries Expense	—
712	Rent Expense	—
719	Miscellaneous Administrative Expense	—

Open the following accounts in the accounts receivable ledger and enter the balances in the balance columns as of January 1: Allen Co., $8,800; C. L. Frank Inc., $3,275; Jackson Co.; Nichols Corp., $2,800; Wilson and Son, $2,825. Open the following accounts in the accounts payable ledger and enter the balances in the balance columns as of January 1: Acme Supply Inc.; Beaman Co., $3,620; Dane Corp.; Easterly Inc., $9,500; Lee Equipment Co.; Peak Corp., $705.

(2) Record the transactions for January, using a purchases journal (as on pages 232 and 233), a sales journal (as on page 240), a cash payments journal (as on page 236), a cash receipts journal (as on page 241), and a two-column general journal. The terms of all sales on account are 2/15, n/60, FOB shipping point. Post to the accounts receivable and accounts payable ledgers and insert the balances immediately after recording each entry.

(3) Post the appropriate individual entries to the general ledger.

(4) Add the columns of the special journals and post the appropriate totals to the general ledger; insert the account balances.

(5) Prepare a trial balance.

(6) Prepare schedules of accounts receivable and accounts payable as of January 31 and compare the total of each schedule with the balance of the appropriate controlling account.

ANSWERS TO SELF-EXAMINATION QUESTIONS

1. **C** The task of revising an accounting system is composed of three phases. Systems analysis (answer A) is the initial phase involving the determination of the informational needs, sources of such information, and deficiencies in the procedures and data processing methods currently employed. Systems design (answer B) is the phase in which proposals for changes are developed. Systems implementation (answer C) is the final phase involving carrying out or implementing the proposals for changes.

2. **A** The policies and procedures established by an enterprise to provide reasonable assurance that the enterprise's goals will be achieved are called internal controls (answer A). The three phases of installing or changing an accounting system are (1) analysis (answer B), (2) design (answer C), and (3) implementation (answer D). Systems analysis is the determination of the informational needs, sources of such information, and deficiencies in the procedures and data processing methods presently used. Systems design refers to the design of a new system or change in the present system based on the systems analysis. The carrying out of proposals for the design of a system is referred to as systems implementation.

3. **B** All payments of cash for any purpose are recorded in the cash payments journal (answer B). Only purchases of merchandise or other items *on account* are recorded in the purchases journal (answer A). All sales of merchandise on account are recorded in the sales journal (answer C), and all receipts of cash are recorded in the cash receipts journal (answer D).

4. **A** The general term used to describe the type of separate ledger that contains a substantial number of individual accounts with a common characteristic is subsidiary ledger (answer A). The creditors ledger (answer B), sometimes called the accounts payable ledger (answer C), is a specific subsidiary ledger containing only individual accounts with creditors. Likewise, the accounts receivable ledger (answer D), also referred to as the customers ledger, is a specific subsidiary ledger containing only individual accounts with customers.

5. **B** The controlling account for the customers ledger (the ledger that contains the individual accounts with customers) is Accounts Receivable (answer B). The accounts payable account (answer A) is the controlling account for the creditors ledger. There are no subsidiary ledgers for the sales (answer C) and purchases (answer D) accounts.

CHAPTER SEVEN
CASH

CHAPTER OBJECTIVES

1 Describe and illustrate the use of a bank account for controlling cash, including the preparation of a bank reconciliation.

2 Describe and illustrate internal controls for cash receipts, including:
Use of a cash short and over account
Use of cash change funds

3 Describe and illustrate internal controls for cash payments, including use of a:
Voucher system
Discounts lost account
Petty cash account

4 Describe recent trends in the use of electronic funds transfer to process cash transactions.

In Chapter 6, the qualities of a properly designed accounting system and the principles of internal control for directing operations were discussed. This chapter presents the application of these internal control principles to the design of an effective system for controlling cash and the accounting for cash transactions.

CONTROL OVER CASH

OBJECTIVE 1
Describe and illustrate the use of a bank account for controlling cash, including the preparation of a bank reconciliation.

Because of the ease with which money can be transferred, cash is the asset most likely to be diverted and used improperly by employees. In addition, many transactions either directly or indirectly affect the receipt or payment of cash. It is therefore necessary that cash be effectively safeguarded by special controls.

The Bank Account as a Tool for Controlling Cash

One of the major devices for maintaining control over cash is the bank account. To get the most benefit from a bank account, all cash received must be deposited in the bank and all payments must be made by checks drawn on the bank or from special cash funds. When such a system is strictly followed, there is a double record of cash, one maintained by the business and the other by the bank.

In some cases, a bank may require a business to maintain in a bank account a minimum cash balance, called a **compensating balance**. This requirement is generally imposed by the bank as a part of a loan agreement or line of credit (an amount the bank is willing to lend). Compensating balance requirements should be disclosed in notes to the financial statements, as indicated in the following note taken from the financial statements for K mart Corporation:

> *... In support of lines of credit, it is expected that compensating balances will be maintained on deposit with the banks, which will average 10% of the line to the extent that it is not in use and an additional 10% on the portion in use, whereas other lines require fees in lieu of compensating balances....*

The forms used by a business in connection with a bank account are a signature card, deposit ticket, check, and record of checks drawn. These forms are described in the following paragraphs.

Signature Card. At the time an account is opened, an identifying number is assigned to the account, and a **signature card** must be signed by each person authorized to sign checks drawn on the account. The card is used by the bank to determine the authenticity of the signature on checks presented to it for payment.

Deposit Ticket. The details of a deposit are listed by the depositor on a printed form supplied by the bank. **Deposit tickets** may be prepared in duplicate, in which case the copy is stamped or initialed by the bank's teller and given to the depositor as a receipt. The receipt of a deposit may be indicated by means other than a duplicate deposit ticket, but all methods give the depositor written proof of the date and the total amount of the deposit.

Check. A **check** is a written instrument signed by the depositor, ordering the bank to pay a certain sum of money to the order of a designated person. There are three parties to a check: the **drawer**, the one who signs the check; the **drawee**, the bank on which the check is drawn; and the **payee**, the one to whose order the check is drawn. When checks are issued to pay bills, they are recorded as credits to Cash on the day issued, even though they are not presented to the drawer's bank until some later time. When checks are received from customers, they are recorded as debits to Cash, on the assumption that the customer has enough money on deposit.

Check forms may be obtained in many styles. The name and the address of the depositor are often printed on each check, and the checks are usually numbered in sequence to facilitate the depositor's internal control. Most banks use automatic sorting and posting equipment and, therefore, provide check forms on which the bank's identification number and the depositor's account number are printed along the lower margin in machine-readable magnetic ink. When the check is presented for payment, the amount for which it is drawn is inserted next to the account number, also in magnetic ink.

Record of Checks Drawn. A memorandum record of the basic details of a check should be prepared at the time the check is written. The record may be a stub from which the check is detached or it may be a small booklet designed to be kept with the check forms. Each type of record also provides spaces for recording deposits and the current bank balance.

Business firms may prepare a copy of each check drawn and then use it as a basis for recording the transaction in the cash payments journal. Checks issued to a creditor on account are usually accompanied by a notification of the specific invoice that is being paid. The purpose of such notification, sometimes called a **remittance advice**, is to make sure that proper credit is recorded in the accounts of the creditor. Mistakes are less likely to happen and the possible need for exchanges of correspondence is reduced. The invoice number or other descriptive data may be inserted in spaces provided on the face or on the back of the check or on an attachment to the check, as in the following illustration:

Check and Remittance Advice

MONROE COMPANY			363
813 Greenwood Street	Detroit, MI 48206-4070 _____ April 12 _____ 19 90		9-42 / 720

Pay to the Order of ___ Hammond Office Products Inc. _____ $ 921.20 ___

Nine hundred twenty-one 20/100-- Dollars

ANB AMERICAN NATIONAL BANK OF DETROIT

DETROIT, MI 48201-2500   (313)933-8547   MEMBER FDIC

K. R. Simms ___ Treasurer
Earl M. Hartman ___ Vice President

⑆072000423⑆ ⑈627042 363

DETACH THIS PORTION BEFORE CASHING

DATE	DESCRIPTION	GROSS AMOUNT	DEDUCTIONS	NET AMOUNT
4/12/90	Invoice No. 529482	940.00	18.80	921.20

MONROE COMPANY

Before depositing the check at the bank, the payee removes the part of the check containing the remittance information. The removed part may then be used by the payee as written proof of the details of the cash receipt.

Bank Statement

Although there are some differences in procedure, banks usually maintain an original and a copy of all checking account transactions. When this is done, the original becomes the statement of account that is mailed to the depositor, usually once each month. Like any account with a customer or a creditor, the bank statement shows the beginning balance, checks and other debits (deductions by the bank), deposits and other credits (additions by the bank), and the balance at the end of the period. The depositor's checks received by the bank during the period may accompany the bank statement, arranged in the order of payment. The paid or canceled checks are perforated or stamped "Paid," together with the date of payment.

Debit or credit memorandums describing other entries in the depositor's account may also be enclosed with the statement. For example, the bank may have debited the depositor's account for service charges or for deposited checks returned because of insufficient funds. It may have credited the account for receipts from notes receivable left for collection, for loans to the depositor, or for interest.[1] A typical bank statement is illustrated as follows:

---

[1]Although interest-bearing checking accounts are common for individuals, Federal Reserve Regulation Q prohibits the paying of interest on corporate checking accounts.

Bank Statement

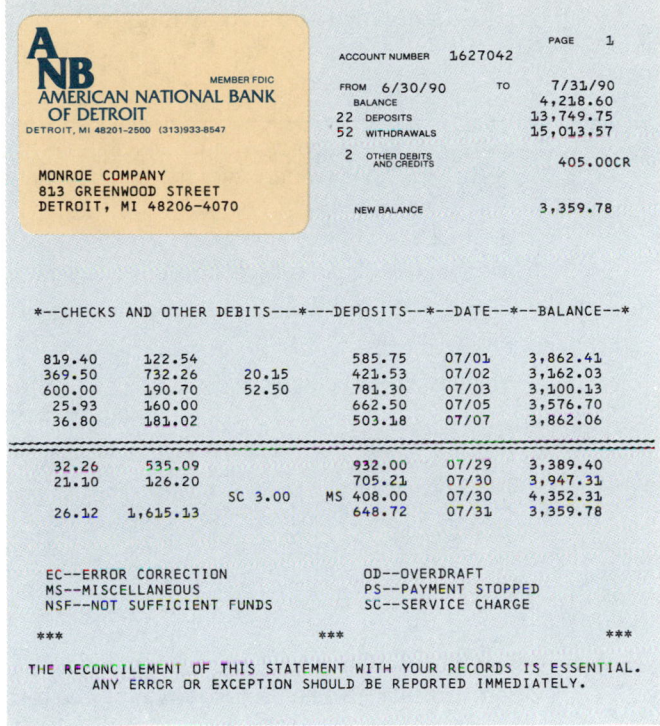

Bank Reconciliation

When all cash receipts are deposited in the bank and all payments are made by check, the cash account is often called Cash in Bank. This account in the depositor's ledger is the reciprocal of the account with the depositor in the bank's ledger. Cash in Bank in the depositor's ledger is an asset with a debit balance, and the account with the depositor in the bank's ledger is a liability with a credit balance.

It might seem that the two balances should be equal, but they are not likely to be equal on any specific date because of either or both of the following: (1) delay by either party in recording transactions and (2) errors by either party in recording transactions. Ordinarily, there is a time lag of one day or more between the date a check is written and the date that it is presented to the bank for payment. If the depositor mails deposits to the bank or uses the night depository, a time lag between the date of the deposit and the date that it is recorded by the bank is also probable. Conversely, the bank may debit or credit the depositor's account for transactions about which the depositor will not be informed until later. Examples are service or collection fees charged by the bank and the proceeds of notes receivable sent to the bank for collection.

To determine the reasons for any difference and to correct any errors that may have been made by the bank or the depositor, the depositor's own records should be reconciled with the bank statement. The **bank reconciliation** is divided into two major sections: one section begins with the balance according to the bank statement and ends with the adjusted balance; the other section begins with the balance according to the depositor's records and also ends with the adjusted balance. The two amounts designated as the adjusted balance must be equal. The form and the content of the bank reconciliation are outlined as follows:

Bank balance according to bank statement............................		$XXX
Add: Additions by depositor not on bank statement................	$XX	
Bank errors..	XX	XX
		$XXX
Deduct: Deductions by depositor not on bank statement..........	$XX	
Bank errors...	XX	XX
Adjusted balance..		$XXX
Bank balance according to depositor's records......................		$XXX
Add: Additions by bank not recorded by depositor	$XX	
Depositor errors...	XX	XX
		$XXX
Deduct: Deductions by bank not recorded by depositor...........	$XX	
Depositor errors...	XX	XX
Adjusted balance..		$XXX

The following procedures are used in finding the reconciling items and determining the adjusted balance of Cash in Bank:

1. Individual deposits listed on the bank statement are compared with unrecorded deposits appearing in the preceding reconciliation and with deposit receipts or other records of deposits. Deposits not recorded by the bank are added to the balance according to the bank statement.
2. Paid checks are compared with outstanding checks appearing on the preceding reconciliation and with checks listed in the cash payments journal. Checks issued that have not been paid by the bank are outstanding and are deducted from the balance according to the bank statement.
3. Bank credit memorandums are traced to the cash receipts journal. Credit memorandums not recorded in the cash receipts journal are added to the balance according to the depositor's records.
4. Bank debit memorandums are traced to the cash payments journal. Debit memorandums not recorded in the cash payments journal are deducted from the balance according to the depositor's records.
5. Errors discovered during the process of making the foregoing comparisons are listed separately on the reconciliation. For example, if the amount for which a check was written had been recorded erroneously by the depositor, the amount of the error should be added to or deducted from the balance according to the depositor's records. Similarly, errors by the bank should be added to or deducted from the balance according to the bank statement.

Illustration of Bank Reconciliation. The bank statement for Monroe Company, reproduced on page 283, indicates a balance of $3,359.78 as of July 31. The balance in Cash in Bank in Monroe Company's ledger as of the same date is $2,234.99. Use of the procedures outlined above reveals the following reconciling items:

Deposit of July 31 not recorded on bank statement		$ 816.20
Checks outstanding: No. 812, $1,061.00; No. 878, $435.39; No. 883, $48.60..		1,544.99
Note plus interest of $8 collected by bank (credit memorandum), not recorded in cash receipts journal		408.00
Bank service charges (debit memorandum) not recorded in cash payments journal		3.00
Check No. 879 for $732.26 to Taylor Co. on account, recorded in cash payments journal as $723.26......................................		9.00

The bank reconciliation based on the bank statement and the reconciling items is as follows:

Monroe Company
Bank Reconciliation
July 31, 1990

Balance per bank statement......................................		$3,359.78
Add deposit of July 31, not recorded by bank............		816.20
		$4,175.98
Deduct outstanding checks:		
No. 812	$1,061.00	
No. 878	435.39	
No. 883	48.60	1,544.99
Adjusted balance		$2,630.99
Balance per depositor's records.............................		$2,234.99
Add note and interest collected by bank...................		408.00
		$2,642.99
Deduct: Bank service charges	$ 3.00	
Error in recording Check No. 879.................	9.00	12.00
Adjusted balance		$2,630.99

Entries Based on Bank Reconciliation. Bank memorandums not recorded by the depositor and depositor's errors shown by the bank reconciliation require that entries be made in the accounts. The entries may be recorded in the appropriate special journals if they have not already been posted for the month, or they may be recorded in the general journal.

The entries for Monroe Company, based on the bank reconciliation above, are as follows:

July 31	Cash in Bank...	408	
	Notes Receivable		400
	Interest Income..................................		8
	Note collected by bank.		
31	Miscellaneous Administrative Expense	3	
	Accounts Payable—Taylor Co.................	9	
	Cash in Bank.....................................		12
	Bank service charges and error in recording Check No. 879.		

The data needed for these adjustments are provided by the section of the bank reconciliation that begins with the balance per depositor's records. No adjusting entries are necessary on the depositor's books as a result of the information included in the section that begins with the balance per bank statement.

After the foregoing entries are posted, the cash in bank account will have a debit balance of $2,630.99, which agrees with the adjusted balance shown on the bank reconciliation. This is the amount of cash available for use as of July 31 and the amount that would be reported on the balance sheet on that date.

Importance of Bank Reconciliation. The bank reconciliation is an important part of the system of internal control because it is a means of comparing recorded cash, as shown by the accounting records, with the amount of cash reported by the bank. It thus provides for finding and correcting errors and irregularities. Greater internal control is achieved when the bank reconciliation is prepared by an employee who does not take part in or record cash transactions with the bank. Without a proper separation of these duties, cash is more likely to be embezzled. For example, an employee who takes part in all of these duties could prepare an unauthorized check, omit it from the accounts, and cash it. Then to account for the canceled check when returned by the bank, the employee could understate the amount of the outstanding checks on future bank reconciliations by the amount of the embezzlement.

INTERNAL CONTROL OF CASH RECEIPTS

Department stores and other retail businesses ordinarily receive cash from two main sources: (1) over the counter from cash customers and (2) by mail from charge customers making payments on account. At the end of the business day, each salesclerk counts the cash in the assigned cash drawer and records the amount on a memorandum form. An employee from the cashier's department removes the cash register tapes on which total receipts were recorded for each cash drawer, counts the cash, and compares the total with the memorandum and the tape, noting any differences. The cash is then taken to the cashier's office and the tapes and memorandum forms are forwarded to the accounting department, where they become the basis for entries in the cash receipts journal.

The employees who open incoming mail compare the amount of cash received with the amount shown on the accompanying remittance advice (or remittance notice) to be certain that the two amounts agree. If there is no separate remittance advice, an employee prepares one on a form designed for such use. All cash received, usually in the form of checks and money orders, is sent to the cashier's department, where it is combined with the receipts from cash sales and a deposit ticket is prepared. The remittance advices are delivered to the accounting department, where they become the basis for entries in the cash receipts journal and for posting to the customers accounts in the subsidiary ledger.

The duplicate deposit tickets or other bank receipt forms obtained by the cashier are sent to the controller or other financial officer, who compares the total amount with that reported by the accounting department as the total debit to Cash in Bank for the period.

Cash Short and Over

The amount of cash actually received during a day often does not agree with the record of cash receipts. Whenever there is a difference between the record and the actual cash and no error can be found in the record, it must be assumed that the mistake occurred in making change. The cash shortage or overage is recorded in an account entitled Cash Short and Over. A common method for handling such mistakes is to include in the cash receipts journal a Cash Short and Over Debit column into which all cash shortages are entered, and a Cash Short and Over Credit column into which all cash overages are entered. For example, if the actual cash received from cash sales is less than the amount indicated by the cash register tally, the entry in the cash receipts journal would include a debit to Cash Short and Over. An example for one day's receipts, in general journal form, follows:

Cash in Bank	4,577.60	
Cash Short and Over	3.16	
Sales		4,580.76

If there is a debit balance in the cash short and over account at the end of the fiscal period, it is an expense and may be included in "Miscellaneous administrative expense" on the income statement. If there is a credit balance, it is revenue and may be listed in the "Other income" section. If the balance becomes larger than may be accounted for by minor errors in making change, management should take corrective measures.

Cash Change Funds

Retail stores and other businesses that receive cash directly from customers must maintain a fund of currency and coins in order to make change. The fund may be established by drawing a check for the required amount, debiting the account Cash on Hand and crediting Cash in Bank. No additional charges or credits to the cash on hand account are necessary unless the amount of the fund is to be increased or decreased. At the end of each business day, the total amount of cash received during the day is deposited and the original amount of the change fund is retained. The desired composition of the fund is maintained by exchanging bills or coins for those of other denominations at the bank.

INTERNAL CONTROL OF CASH PAYMENTS

OBJECTIVE 3
Describe and
illustrate internal
controls for cash
payments,
including use of a:
Voucher system
Discounts lost
   account
Petty cash account

It is common practice for business enterprises to require that every payment of cash be evidenced by a check signed by a designated official. As an additional control, some firms require two signatures on all checks or only on checks which are larger than a certain amount. It is also common to use a check protector, which produces amounts on the check that are not easily removed or changed.

When the owner of a business has personal knowledge of all goods and services purchased, the owner may sign checks, with the assurance that the creditors have followed the terms of their contracts and that the exact amount of the obligation is being paid. Disbursing officials are seldom able to have such a complete knowledge of affairs, however. In enterprises of even moderate size, the responsibility for issuing purchase orders, inspecting goods received, and verifying contractual and arithmetical details of invoices is divided among the employees of several departments. It is desirable, therefore, to coordinate these related activities and to link them with the final issuance of checks to creditors. One of the best systems used for this purpose is the voucher system.

Basic Features of the Voucher System

A **voucher system** is made up of records, methods, and procedures used in proving and recording liabilities and in making and recording cash payments. A voucher system uses (1) vouchers, (2) a voucher register, (3) a file for unpaid vouchers, (4) a check register, and (5) a file for paid vouchers. As in all areas of accounting systems and internal controls, many differences in detail are possible. The discussion that follows refers to a medium-size merchandising enterprise with separate departments for purchasing, receiving, accounting, and disbursing.

Vouchers. The term **voucher** is widely used in accounting. In a general sense, it means any document that serves as proof of authority to pay cash, such as an invoice approved for payment, or as evidence that cash has been paid, such as a canceled check. The term has a narrower meaning when applied to the voucher system: a voucher is a special form on which is recorded relevant data about a liability and the details of its payment.

An important characteristic of the voucher system is the requirement that a voucher be prepared for each expenditure. In fact, a check may not be issued except in payment of a properly authorized voucher. Vouchers may be paid immediately after they are prepared or at a later date, depending upon the circumstances and the credit terms.

A voucher form is illustrated below. The face of the voucher provides space for the name and address of the creditor, the date and number of the voucher, and basic details of the invoice or other supporting document, such as the vendor's invoice number and the amount and terms of the invoice. One half of the back of the voucher is devoted to the account distribution and the other half to summaries of the voucher and the details of payment. Spaces are also provided for the signature or initials of certain employees.

Voucher

JANSEN AUTO SUPPLY INC.

VOUCHER

Date July 1, 1990   Voucher No. 451

Payee   Allied Manufacturing Company
        683 Fairmont Road
        Chicago, IL 60630-3168

DATE	DETAILS	AMOUNT
June 28, 1990	Invoice No. 4693-C FOB Chicago, 2/10, n/30	450.00

Attach Supporting Documents

ACCOUNT DISTRIBUTION

DEBIT	AMOUNT
PURCHASES	450 00
SUPPLIES	
ADVERTISING EXPENSE	
DELIVERY EXPENSE	
MISC. SELLING EXPENSE	
MISC. GENERAL EXPENSE	
CREDIT ACCOUNTS PAYABLE	450 00

DISTRIBUTION APPROVED L. Donnelly

NO. 451
DATE 7/1/90   DUE 7/8/90

PAYEE
Allied Manufacturing Company
683 Fairmont Road
Chicago, IL 60630-3168

VOUCHER SUMMARY

AMOUNT	450 00
ADJUSTMENT	
DISCOUNT	9 00
NET	441 00
APPROVED M. C. Leshou	CONTROLLER
RECORDED WB	

PAYMENT SUMMARY

DATE	7/8/90
AMOUNT	441.00
CHECK NO.	863
APPROVED A. T. Wood	
RECORDED L. K. R.	a.s.

Vouchers are customarily prepared by the accounting department on the basis of an invoice or a memorandum that serves as proof of an expenditure. This is usually done only after the following comparisons and verifications have been completed and noted on the invoice:

1. Comparison of the invoice with a copy of the purchase order to verify quantities, prices, and terms.
2. Comparison of the invoice with the receiving report to verify receipt of the items billed.
3. Verification of the arithmetical accuracy of the invoice.

After all data except details of payment have been inserted, the invoice or other supporting evidence is attached to the voucher. The voucher is then given to the designated official or officials for final approval.

Voucher Register. After approval by the designated official, each voucher is recorded in a journal known as a *voucher register*. It is similar to and replaces the purchases journal described in Chapter 6.

A typical form of a voucher register is illustrated at the bottom of pages 290 and 291. The vouchers are entered in numerical order, each being recorded as a credit to Accounts Payable (sometimes entitled Vouchers Payable) and as a debit to the account or accounts to be charged for the expenditure.

When a voucher is paid, the date of payment and the number of the check are inserted in the proper columns in the voucher register. These notations provide a ready means of determining at any time the amount of an individual unpaid voucher or of the total amount of unpaid vouchers.

Unpaid Voucher File. After a voucher has been recorded in the voucher register, it is filed in an unpaid voucher file, where it remains until it is paid. The amount due on each voucher represents the credit balance of an account payable, and the voucher itself is like an individual account in a subsidiary accounts payable ledger. Accordingly, a separate subsidiary ledger is not needed.

All voucher systems include some way to assure payment within the discount period or on the last day of the credit period. A simple but effective method is to file each voucher in the unpaid voucher file according to the earliest date that consideration should be given to its payment. The file may be made up of a group of folders, numbered from 1 to 31, the numbers representing the days of a month. Such a system brings to the attention of the disbursing official the vouchers that are to be paid on each day. It also provides management with a convenient means of forecasting the amount of cash needed to meet maturing obligations.

When a voucher is to be paid, it is removed from the unpaid voucher file and a check is issued in payment. The date, the number, and the amount of the check are listed on the back of the voucher for use in recording the payment in the check register. Paid vouchers and the supporting documents are often run through a canceling machine to prevent accidental or intentional reuse.

An exception to the general rule that vouchers be prepared for all expenditures may be made for bank charges shown by debit memorandums or notations on the bank statement. For example, such items as bank service charges, safe-deposit box rentals, and returned NSF (Not Sufficient Funds) checks from customers may be charged to the depositor's account without either a formal voucher or a check. For large expenditures, such as the repayment of a bank loan, a supporting voucher may be prepared, if desired, even though a check is not written. The paid note may then be attached to the voucher as evidence of the obligation. All bank debit memorandums are the equivalent of checks as evidence of payment.

Check Register. The payment of a voucher is recorded in a check register, an example of which is illustrated below. The <mark>check register</mark> is a modi-

Check Register

	CK.		VOU.	ACCOUNTS PAYABLE	PURCHASES DISCOUNTS	CASH IN BANK	BANK	
DATE	NO.	PAYEE	NO.	DR.	CR.	CR.	DEPOSITS	BALANCE
19--								8,743.10
JULY 1	856	CHAVEZ REALTORS	452	600.00		600.00	1,240.30	9,383.40
2	857	FOSTER PUBLICATIONS	453	52.50		52.50		9,330.90
2	858	HILL AND DAVIS	436	1,420.00	14.20	1,405.80	865.70	8,790.80
3	859	BENSON EXPRESS CO.	454	36.80		36.80	942.20	9,696.20
30	879	VOIDED						
30	880	STONE & CO.	460	14.30		14.30		9,521.80
30	881	EVANS CORP.	448	1,015.00		1,015.00	765.50	9,272.30
31	882	GRAHAM & CO.	469	830.00	16.60	813.40		8,458.90
31	883	PETTY CASH	478	48.60		48.60	938.10	9,348.40
31				17,322.90	198.20	17,124.70		
				(212)	(513)	(111)		

CHECK REGISTER   PAGE 14

<mark>fied form of the cash payments journal and is so called because it is a complete record of all checks.</mark> It is common to record all checks in the check register in sequential order, including occasional checks that are voided because of an error in their preparation.

Voucher Register

PAGE 11   VOUCHER

DATE	VOU. NO.	PAYEE	DATE PAID	CK. NO.	ACCOUNTS PAYABLE CR.	PURCHASES DR.
19--						
JULY 1	451	ALLIED MFG. CO.	7-8	863	450.00	450.00
1	452	CHAVEZ REALTORS	7-1	856	600.00	
2	453	FOSTER PUBLICATIONS	7-2	857	52.50	
3	454	BENSON EXPRESS CO.	7-3	859	36.80	24.20
3	455	ROBERSON'S SUPPLY CO.			784.20	
3	456	MOORE & CO.	7-11	866	1,236.00	1,236.00
6	457	J. L. BROWN CO.	7-6	860	22.50	
6	458	TURNER CORP.			395.30	395.30
31	477	CENTRAL MOTORS			112.20	
31	478	PETTY CASH	7-31	883	48.60	
31					15,551.60	11,640.30
					(212)	(511)

Each check issued is in payment of a voucher that has previously been recorded as an account payable in the voucher register. The effect of each entry in the check register is a debit to Accounts Payable and a credit to Cash in Bank (and Purchases Discounts, when appropriate).

The memorandum columns for Bank Deposits and Bank Balance appearing in the illustration of the check register are optional. They provide a convenient means of determining the cash available at all times.

When check forms with a remittance advice are prepared in duplicate, the copies retained may make up the check register. At the end of each month, summary totals can be readily obtained for Accounts Payable debit, Purchases Discounts credit, and Cash credit, and the entry recorded in the general journal. If the volume of checks issued is large, a significant amount of clerical expenses may be saved by eliminating the copying of data in a columnar check register.

Paid Voucher File. After payment, vouchers are usually filed in numerical order in a paid voucher file. They are then readily available for examination by employees or independent auditors needing information about a certain expenditure. Eventually the paid vouchers are destroyed according to the firm's policies concerning the retention of records.

The Voucher System and Management. The voucher system not only provides effective accounting controls but also aids management in discharging other responsibilities. For example, the voucher system gives greater assurance that all payments are in liquidation of valid liabilities. In addition, current information is always available for use in determining future cash requirements. This in turn enables management to make the best use of cash resources. Invoices on which cash discounts are allowed can be paid within the discount period and other invoices can be paid on the final day of the credit period, thus reducing costs and maintaining a favorable credit standing. Seasonal borrowing can also be planned more accurately, with a consequent saving in interest costs.

REGISTER							PAGE 11
STORE SUPPLIES DR.	ADV. EXP. DR.	DEL. EXP. DR.	MISC. SELLING EXP. DR.	MISC. ADMIN. EXP. DR.	SUNDRY ACCOUNTS DR. ACCOUNT	POST. REF.	AMOUNT
					RENT EXPENSE	712	600.00
	52.50						
		12.60					
34.20					OFFICE EQUIPMENT	122	750.00
				22.50			
		112.20					
4.30		16.20	19.50	8.60			
59.80	176.40	286.10	48.30	64.90			3,275.80
(116)	(012)	(013)	(018)	(718)			(✔)

Purchases Discounts

In earlier chapters, purchases of merchandise were recorded at the invoice price, and cash discounts taken were credited to the purchases discounts account at the time of payment. There are two opposing views on how discounts taken should be reported in the income statement.

The most widely accepted view, which has been followed in this textbook, is that purchases discounts should be reported as a deduction from purchases. For example, the cost of merchandise with an invoice price of $1,000, subject to terms of 2/10, n/30, is recorded initially at $1,000. If payment is made within the discount period, the discount of $20 reduces the cost to $980. If the invoice is not paid within the discount period, the cost of the merchandise remains $1,000. This treatment of purchases discounts may be attacked on the grounds that the date of payment should not affect the cost of a commodity. The additional payment required beyond the discount period adds nothing to the value of the commodities purchased.

The second view reports discounts taken as "other income." In terms of the preceding example, the cost of the merchandise is considered to be $1,000, regardless of the time of payment. If payment is made within the discount period, revenue of $20 is considered to be realized. The objection to this procedure lies in the recognition of revenue from the act of purchasing and paying for a commodity. Theoretically, an enterprise might make no sales of merchandise during an accounting period and yet might report as revenue the amount of cash discounts taken.

A major disadvantage of recording purchases at the invoice price and recognizing purchases discounts at the time of payment is that this method does not measure the cost of failing to take discounts. Well-managed enterprises maintain enough cash to pay within the discount period all invoices subject to a discount, and view the failure to take a discount as an inefficiency. To measure the cost of this inefficiency, purchases invoices may be recorded at the net amount, assuming that all discounts will be taken. Any discounts *not* taken are then recorded in an expense account called Discounts Lost. This method measures the cost of failure to take cash discounts and gives management an opportunity to take remedial action. Again assuming the same data, the invoice for $1,000 would be recorded as a debit to Purchases of $980 and a credit to Accounts Payable for the same amount. If the invoice is not paid until after the discount period has passed, the entry in general journal form would be as follows:

Accounts Payable...	980	
Discounts Lost...	20	
Cash in Bank		1,000

When this method is used with the voucher system, all vouchers are prepared and recorded at the net amount. Any discount lost is noted on the related voucher and recorded in a special column in the check register when the voucher is paid.

Another advantage of this treatment of purchases discounts is that all merchandise purchased is recorded initially at the net price, and hence no later adjustments to cost are necessary. An objection, however, is that the amount reported as accounts payable in the balance sheet may be less than the amount needed to discharge the liability.

Petty Cash

In most businesses there is a frequent need for the payment of relatively small amounts, such as for postage due, for transportation charges, or for the purchase of urgently needed supplies at a nearby retail store. Payment by check in such cases would result in delay, annoyance, and excessive expense of maintaining the records. Yet because these small payments may occur frequently and therefore amount to a considerable total sum, it is desirable to retain close control over such payments. This may be done by maintaining a special cash fund called petty cash.

In establishing a petty cash fund, the first step is to estimate the amount of cash needed for disbursements of relatively small amounts during a certain period, such as a week or a month. If the voucher system is used, a voucher is then prepared for this amount and it is recorded in the voucher register as a debit to Petty Cash and a credit to Accounts Payable. The check drawn to pay the voucher is recorded in the check register as a debit to Accounts Payable and a credit to Cash in Bank.

The money obtained from cashing the check is placed in the custody of a specific employee who is authorized to disburse the fund according to restrictions as to maximum amount and purpose. Each time a disbursement is made from the fund, the employee records the essential details on a receipt form, obtains the signature of the payee as proof of the payment, and initials the completed form. A typical petty cash receipt is illustrated as follows:

Petty Cash Receipt

PETTY CASH RECEIPT

NO. 121 DATE August 1, 1990

PAID TO Metropolitan Times AMOUNT 3 | 70

FOR Daily newspaper

CHARGE TO Miscellaneous Administrative Expense

PAYMENT RECEIVED: S. O. Hall   APPROVED BY N.E.R.

When the amount of money in the petty cash fund is reduced to the predetermined minimum amount, the fund is replenished. If the voucher system is used, the accounts debited on the replenishing voucher are those indicated by a summary of expenditures. The voucher is then recorded in the voucher register as a debit to the various expense and asset accounts and a credit to Accounts Payable. The check in payment of the voucher is recorded in the check register in the usual manner.

To illustrate the entries that would be made in accounting for petty cash, assume that a voucher system is used and that a petty cash fund of $100 is established on August 1. At the end of August, the petty cash receipts indicate expenditures for the following items: office supplies, $28; postage (office supplies), $22; store supplies, $35; and daily newspaper (miscellaneous administrative expense), $3.70. To record the establishment and replenishment of the petty cash fund, the entries in general journal form would be as follows:

Aug.	1	Petty Cash 100.00	
		Accounts Payable	100.00
	1	Accounts Payable 100.00	
		Cash in Bank...	100.00
	31	Office Supplies 50.00	
		Store Supplies 35.00	
		Miscellaneous Administrative Expense........... 3.70	
		Accounts Payable	88.70
	31	Accounts Payable 88.70	
		Cash in Bank...	88.70

Replenishing the petty cash fund restores it to its original amount. It should be noted that the only entry in the petty cash account will be the initial debit, unless at some later time the standard amount of the fund is increased or decreased.

Because disbursements are not recorded in the accounts until the fund is replenished, petty cash funds and other special funds that operate in a like manner should always be replenished at the end of an accounting period. The amount of money actually in the fund will then agree with the balance in the related fund account, and the expenses and the assets for which payment has been made will be recorded in the proper period.

Other Cash Funds

Cash funds may also be established to meet other special needs of a business. For example, money may be advanced for travel expenses as needed. Then periodically, after expense reports have been received, the expenses are recorded and the fund is replenished. A similar procedure may be used to provide a working fund for a sales office located in another city. The amount of the fund may be deposited in a local bank and the sales representative may be authorized to draw checks for payment of rent, salaries, and other operating expenses. Each month, the representative sends the invoices, bank statement, paid checks, bank reconciliation, and other business documents to the home office. The data are audited, the expenditures are recorded, and a reimbursing check is returned for deposit in the local bank.

CASH TRANSACTIONS AND ELECTRONIC FUNDS TRANSFER

OBJECTIVE 4
Describe recent trends in the use of electronic funds transfer to process cash transactions.

Currently most cash transactions are in the form of currency or check. The broad principles discussed in earlier sections provide the basis for developing an effective system to control such cash transactions. However, the development of **electronic funds transfer (EFT)** may eventually change the form in which many cash transactions are executed and could affect the processing and controlling of cash transactions.

EFT can be defined as a payment system that uses computerized electronic impulses rather than paper (money, checks, etc.) to effect a cash transaction. For example, a business may pay its employees by means of EFT. Under such a system, employees who want their payroll checks deposited directly in a checking account sign an authorization form. For each pay period, the business' computer produces a payroll file with computer-sensitive notations for relevant payroll data. The file is transmitted over telephone lines to the banks designated by the employees. The banks then credit each employee's account. Similar cash payments might be made for other preauthorized payments. The federal government currently processes several million social security checks through EFT.

EFT is also beginning to play a role in retail sales. Through a point-of-sale (POS) system, a customer pays for goods at the time of purchase by presenting a plastic card. The card is used to activate a terminal in the store and thereby effect an immediate transfer from the customer's checking account to the retailer's account at the bank.

Some companies are using EFT systems to process both cash payments and cash receipts. For example, General Electric Co. estimates that 40–50% of its payments to creditors and its collections from customers are processed by EFT systems. Studies have indicated that EFT systems may reduce the cost of processing certain cash transactions and contribute to better control over cash receipts and cash payments. Offsetting these potential advantages are problems of protecting the privacy of information stored in computers, and difficulties in documenting purchase and sale transactions. In any event, developments with EFT systems are likely to be followed very closely by most businesses over the next few years.

CONTROLLING EFT SYSTEMS

Many companies use EFT to transfer cash among various corporate bank accounts, to make investments, and to pay vendors. Control weaknesses and some relatively simple steps to safeguard electronically transferred funds were described in a *Journal of Accountancy* article, as follows:

The key element in most EFT systems is the telephone. Once a corporate cash manager has established an EFT facility with a bank, he or she usually only needs to call the bank (or make contact through a computer hookup), identify himself and specify the dollar amount to be transferred from a particular account at the disbursing bank, as well as the account and bank to which funds are to be transferred.... As a result of these calls, hundreds of billions of dollars are transferred through the banking system every business day....

...When cash disbursements are made by written check, most companies' control procedures...[provide] reasonable assurance that cash disbursements...are being made [properly. When an EFT system is used]...several relatively inexpensive and easily implemented control procedures can be added to traditional controls to reduce the risk of losing funds during electronic transfers....

■ *Passwords. Companies should instruct banks not to accept transfer instructions from any caller who is unable to provide an established password....*

■ *Additional authorization. The vast majority of fund transfers by most companies are routine, such as transfers between their own bank accounts and transfers to investment accounts in the company's name. These reasonably could be considered relatively low risk, since funds never leave the company's accounts. Transfers to outside ac-*

counts, on the other hand, generally are much less frequent and obviously involve much higher risk.

To minimize the risk of lost funds . . . additional authorizations [should be required] before unusual transfers are completed. . . .

■ *After the transfer. The traditional bank account reconciliation process is an effective control except for the time lag involved. . . . To overcome this weakness, an ongoing reconciliation system can*

be used with EFTs. Banks should be instructed to provide the transaction advice for each fund transfer on a timely basis. . . .

Transaction advices should be sent directly to a person not involved in the EFT process. This person should be instructed to match the advices on the day they are received with the internal cash receipt or disbursement records, as well as with required internal documentation. . . .

Source: Michael J. Fischer, "Electronic Funds Transfers: Controlling the Risk," *The Journal of Accountancy* (June 1988), pp. 130–134.

CHAPTER REVIEW

KEY POINTS

OBJECTIVE 1

Control Over Cash

It is necessary to safeguard cash effectively because of the ease with which it can be transferred. One of the major devices for maintaining control over cash is the bank account. To obtain the most benefit from a bank account, all cash received must be deposited in the bank and all payments must be made by checks drawn on the bank or from special cash funds.

Periodically, the bank mails to the depositor a statement of account. This statement of account should be reconciled with the depositor's records by preparing a bank reconciliation. The bank reconciliation is divided into two major sections: one section begins with the balance according to the bank statement and ends with an adjusted balance; the other section begins with the balance according to the depositor's records and also ends with an adjusted balance. After all reconciling items have been considered, the two amounts designated as the adjusted balance must be equal.

After a bank reconciliation has been prepared, the items which appear in the section of the bank reconciliation beginning with the balance according to the depositor's records must be entered into the accounting records through the use of adjusting journal entries.

OBJECTIVE 2

Internal Control of Cash Receipts

The bank reconciliation is an important part of the system of internal control over cash. Other controls of cash receipts include the separation of responsibilities for recording cash transactions from the handling of cash, the use of a cash short and over account for differences between recorded receipts and actual receipts, and the use of cash change funds.

OBJECTIVE 3

Internal Control of Cash Payments

One of the best systems for establishing control of cash payments is the use of a voucher system. A voucher system is made up of records, methods, and procedures used in proving and recording liabilities and in making and recording cash payments. A voucher system uses (1) vouchers, (2) a voucher register, (3) a file for unpaid vouchers, (4) a check register, and (5) a file for paid vouchers.

Because of the importance of taking advantage of all purchases discounts, a business may use a separate account, called Discounts Lost, to account for any discounts not taken during the discount period. When this method is used with the voucher system, all vouchers are prepared and recorded at the net amount, assuming that the discount will be taken.

A special cash fund, called petty cash, may be used by a business to make small payments that occur frequently, for which payment by check would cause delay, annoyance, and excessive expense of maintaining records. The amount of money maintained in a petty cash fund is placed in the custody of a specific employee, who authorizes disbursement of the fund according to specific restrictions as to maximum amount and purpose. When the amount of money in the petty cash fund is reduced to a predetermined minimum amount, the fund is replenished. Other cash funds may be established by businesses for purposes such as travel expenses.

OBJECTIVE 4   Cash Transactions and Electronic Funds Transfer

Electronic funds transfer is a payment system that uses computerized electronic impulses rather than paper (money, checks, etc.) to effect cash transactions. EFT is beginning to play an important role in retail sales and in processing cash payments and cash receipts.

KEY TERMS

bank reconciliation 283
voucher system 288
voucher 288
voucher register 289

check register 290
petty cash 293
electronic funds transfer (EFT) 294

SELF-EXAMINATION QUESTIONS
Answers at end of chapter.

1. In preparing a bank reconciliation, the amount of checks outstanding would be:
   A. added to the bank balance according to the bank statement
   B. deducted from the bank balance according to the bank statement
   C. added to the bank balance according to the depositor's records
   D. deducted from the bank balance according to the depositor's records

2. Journal entries based on the bank reconciliation are required for:
   A. additions to the bank balance according to the depositor's records
   B. deductions from the bank balance according to the depositor's records
   C. both A and B
   D. neither A nor B

3. The journal used to record liabilities when a voucher system is used is called:
   A. a voucher   C. a check register
   B. an unpaid voucher file   D. a voucher register

4. A voucher system is used, all vouchers for purchases are recorded at the net amount, and a purchase is made for $500 under terms 1/10, n/30.
    A. Purchases would be debited for $495 to record the purchase.
    B. Discounts Lost would be debited for $5 if the voucher is not paid within the discount period.
    C. If the voucher is not paid until after the discount period has expired, the discount lost would be reported as an expense on the income statement.
    D. All of the above

5. A petty cash fund is:
    A. used to pay relatively small amounts
    B. established by estimating the amount of cash needed for disbursements of relatively small amounts during a specified period
    C. reimbursed when the amount of money in the fund is reduced to a predetermined minimum amount
    D. all of the above

ILLUSTRATIVE PROBLEM

The bank statement for Dunlap Company for April 30 indicates a balance of $10,443.11. The Dunlap Company employs the voucher system in controlling expenditures and disbursements. All cash receipts are deposited each evening in a night depository, after banking hours. The accounting records indicate the following summary data for cash receipts and disbursements for April:

CASH IN BANK ACCOUNT
    Balance as of April 1 .... $ 5,143.50

CASH RECEIPTS JOURNAL
    Total cash receipts for April $28,971.60

CHECK REGISTER
    Total amount of checks issued in April................. $26,060.85

Comparison of the bank statement and the accompanying canceled checks and memorandums with the records revealed the following reconciling items:

(a) The bank had collected for Dunlap Company $912 on a note left for collection. The face of the note was $900.
(b) A deposit of $1,852.21, representing receipts of April 30, had been made too late to appear on the bank statement.
(c) Checks outstanding totaled $3,265.27.
(d) A check drawn for $79 had been erroneously charged by the bank as $97.
(e) A check for $10 returned with the statement had been recorded in the check register as $100. The check was for the payment of an obligation to Davis Equipment Company for the purchase of office supplies on account.
(f) Bank service charges for April amounted to $8.20.

Instructions:
1. Prepare a bank reconciliation for April.
2. Journalize the entries that should be made by Dunlap Company.

SOLUTION

(1)

Dunlap Company
Bank Reconciliation
April 30, 19--

Balance per bank statement		$10,443.11
Add: Deposit of April 30 not recorded		
by bank..	$1,852.21	
Bank error in charging check for $97		
instead of $79..................................	18.00	1,870.21
		$12,313.32
Deduct: Outstanding checks..........................		3,265.27
Adjusted balance...		$ 9,048.05
Balance per depositor's records......................		$ 8,054.25*
Add: Proceeds of note collected by bank,		
including $12 interest	$ 912.00	
Error in recording check.........................	90.00	1,002.00
		$ 9,056.25
Deduct: Bank service charges.........................		8.20
Adjusted balance...		$ 9,048.05

*$5,143.50 + $28,971.60 − $26,060.85

(2)

Cash in Bank...	1,002.00	
Notes Receivable..		900.00
Interest Income..		12.00
Accounts Payable		90.00
Miscellaneous Administrative Expense	8.20	
Cash in Bank...		8.20

DISCUSSION QUESTIONS

1. Why is cash the asset that often warrants the most attention in the design of an effective internal control structure?

2. (a) What is meant by the term *compensating balance* as applied to the checking account of a firm? (b) How is the compensating balance reported in the financial statements?

3. Distinguish between the drawer and payee of a check.

4. What name is often given to the notification attached to a check that indicates the specific invoice that is being paid?

5. When checks are received, they are recorded as debits to Cash, the assumption being that the drawer has sufficient funds on deposit. What entry should be made if a check received from a customer and deposited is returned by the bank for lack of sufficient funds (NSF)?

6. Do items reported on the bank statement as debits represent (a) additions made by the bank to the depositor's balance, or (b) deductions made by the bank from the depositor's balance?

7. What is the purpose of preparing a bank reconciliation?

8. Identify each of the following reconciling items as: (a) an addition to the balance per bank statement, (b) a deduction from the balance per bank statement, (c) an addition to the balance per depositor's records, or (d) a deduction from the balance per depositor's records. (None of the transactions reported by bank debit and credit memorandums have been recorded by the depositor.)
   (1) Deposit in transit, $4,725.10.
   (2) Note collected by bank, $6,090.00.
   (3) Outstanding checks, $8,515.50.
   (4) Check for $100 charged by bank as $1,000.
   (5) Check drawn by depositor for $25 but recorded as $250.
   (6) Bank service charges, $30.15.
   (7) Check of a customer returned by bank to depositor because of insufficient funds, $83.20.

9. Which of the reconciling items listed in Question 8 necessitate an entry in the depositor's accounts?

10. The procedures employed for over-the-counter receipts are as follows: At the close of each day's business, the salesclerks count the cash in their respective cash drawers, after which they determine the amount recorded by the register and prepare the memorandum cash form, noting any discrepancies. An employee from the cashier's office counts the cash, compares the total with the memorandum, and takes the cash to the cashier's office. (a) Indicate the weak link in internal control. (b) How can the weakness be corrected?

11. The mailroom employees send all remittances and remittance advices to the cashier. The cashier deposits the cash in the bank and forwards the remittance advices and duplicate deposit slips to the accounting department. (a) Indicate the weak link in internal control in the handling of cash receipts. (b) How can the weakness be corrected?

12. The combined cash count of all cash registers at the close of business is $3.50 more than the cash sales indicated by the cash register tapes. (a) In what account is the cash overage recorded? (b) Are cash overages debited or credited to this account?

13. In which section of the income statement would a credit balance in Cash Short and Over be reported?

14. The accounting clerk pays all obligations by prenumbered checks. What are the strengths and weaknesses in the internal control over cash disbursements in this situation?

15. What is meant by the term *voucher* as applied to the voucher system?

16. Before a voucher for the purchase of merchandise is approved for payment, three documents should be compared to verify the accuracy of the liability. Name these three documents.

17. (a) When the voucher system is employed, is the accounts payable account in the general ledger a controlling account? (b) Is there a subsidiary creditors ledger?

18. The controller approves all vouchers before they are submitted to the treasurer for payment. What procedure can the controller add to the system to assure that the documents accompanying the vouchers and supporting the expenditures are not "reused" to support future vouchers improperly?

19. In what order are vouchers ordinarily filed (a) in the unpaid voucher file, and (b) in the paid voucher file? Give reasons for the answers.

20. What are the two possibilities for reporting purchases discounts on the income statement?

21. Merchandise with an invoice price of $2,000 is purchased subject to terms of 1/10, n/30. Determine the cost of the merchandise according to each of the following systems:

(a) Discounts taken are treated as deductions from the invoice price.
   (1) The invoice is paid within the discount period.
   (2) The invoice is paid after the discount period has expired.
(b) Discounts taken are treated as other income.
   (1) The invoice is paid within the discount period.
   (2) The invoice is paid after the discount period has expired.
(c) Discounts allowable are treated as deductions from the invoice price, regardless of when payment is made.
   (1) The invoice is paid within the discount period.
   (2) The invoice is paid after the discount period has expired.

22. What account or accounts are debited when recording the voucher (a) establishing a petty cash fund and (b) replenishing a petty cash fund?

23. The petty cash account has a debit balance of $500. At the end of the accounting period, there is $42 in the petty cash fund along with petty cash receipts totaling $458. Should the fund be replenished as of the last day of the period? Discuss.

24. What is meant by electronic funds transfer?

Real World Focus
25. Between September 3 and September 22, seventeen prenumbered checks totaling $1,129,232.39 were forged and cashed on the accounts of Perini Corporation, a construction company based in the Boston suburb of Framingham. Perini Corporation kept its supply of blank prenumbered checks in an unlocked storeroom with items such as styrofoam coffee cups. Every clerk and secretary had access to this storeroom. It was later discovered that someone had apparently stolen two boxes of prenumbered checks. The numbers of the missing checks matched the numbers of the out-of-sequence checks cashed by the banks. What fundamental principle of control over cash was violated in this case?

EXERCISES

Exercise 7–1
Bank reconciliation.
OBJ. 1

The following data are accumulated for use in reconciling the bank account of Meg Nance and Company for June:

(a) Balance per bank statement at June 30, $7,929.50.
(b) Balance per depositor's records at June 30, $6,017.05.
(c) Checks outstanding, $2,510.40.
(d) A check for $230 in payment of a voucher was erroneously recorded in the check register as $320.
(e) Deposit in transit, not recorded by bank, $671.25.
(f) Bank debit memorandum for service charges, $16.70.

Prepare a bank reconciliation.

Exercise 7–2
Entries for bank reconciliation.
OBJ. 1

Using the data presented in Exercise 7–1, prepare in general journal form the entry or entries that should be made by the depositor.

Exercise 7–3
Entries for note collected by bank.
OBJ. 1

Accompanying a bank statement for Conrad Company is a credit memorandum for $4,080, representing the principal ($4,000) and interest ($80) on a note that had been collected by the bank. The depositor had been notified by the bank at the time of the collection, but had made no entries. In general journal form, present the entry that should be made by the depositor.

Exercise 7–4
Entry for cash sales.
OBJ. 2

The actual cash received from cash sales for D. D. Clausen Company was $5,754.75, and the amount indicated by the cash register total was $5,750.25. Prepare the entry, in general journal form, to record the cash receipts and cash sales.

Exercise 7–5
Entries for vouchers and checks; purchases at gross amount.
OBJ. 3

Record in general journal form the following selected transactions, indicating above each entry the name of the register in which it should be recorded. Assume the use of a voucher register and a check register similar to those illustrated in this chapter. All invoices are recorded at invoice price.

June 1. Recorded Voucher No. 421 for $5,000, payable to Wilson Co., for merchandise purchased, terms 2/10, n/30.
 7. Recorded Voucher No. 430 for $1,500, payable to J. J. Franco Co., for merchandise purchased, terms 1/10, n/30.
16. Issued Check No. 419 in payment of Voucher No. 430.
17. Recorded Voucher No. 450 for $2,500, payable to Glos Inc., for merchandise purchased, terms 2/10, n/30.
26. Issued Check No. 441 in payment of Voucher No. 450.
30. Recorded Voucher No. 459 for $221.90 to replenish the petty cash fund for the following disbursements: store supplies, $77.50; office supplies, $51.25; miscellaneous administrative expense, $46.10; miscellaneous selling expense, $47.05.
30. Issued Check No. 448 in payment of Voucher No. 459.
30. Issued Check No. 449 in payment of Voucher No. 421.

Exercise 7–6
Entries for purchases at net amount.
OBJ. 3

Record in general journal form the following related transactions, assuming that invoices for commodities purchased are recorded at their net price after deducting the allowable discount:

May 5. Voucher No. 799 is prepared for merchandise purchased from Close Co., $6,000, terms 2/10, n/30.
15. Voucher No. 811 is prepared for merchandise purchased from Bridge's Co., $2,500, terms 1/10, n/30.
25. Check No. 798 is issued in payment of Voucher No. 811.
June 3. Check No. 808 is issued in payment of Voucher No. 799.

Exercise 7–7
Petty cash fund entries.
OBJ. 3

Prepare in general journal form the entries to record the following:

(a) Voucher No. 8 is prepared to establish a petty cash fund of $250.
(b) Check No. 6 is issued in payment of Voucher No. 8.
(c) The amount of cash in the petty cash fund is now $27.30. Voucher No. 62 is prepared to replenish the fund, based on the following summary of petty cash receipts: office supplies, $82.15; miscellaneous selling expense, $80.60; miscellaneous administrative expense, $58.70. (Since the amount of the check to replenish the fund plus the balance in the fund do not equal $250, record the discrepancy in the cash short and over account.)
(d) Check No. 57 is issued by the disbursing officer in payment of Voucher No. 62. The check is cashed and the money is placed in the fund.

Exercise 7–8
Cash change fund entries.
OBJ. 3

Record in general journal form the following transactions:

(a) Voucher No. 126 is prepared to establish a change fund of $500.
(b) Check No. 120 is issued in payment of Voucher No. 126.
(c) Cash sales for the day, according to the cash register tapes, were $4,655.30, and cash on hand is $5,153.50. A bank deposit ticket was prepared for $4,653.50.

PROBLEMS

Series A

Problem 7–1A

Bank reconciliation and entries.

OBJ. 1

SPREADSHEET PROBLEM

The cash in bank account for J. D. Casler Co. at May 31 of the current year indicated a balance of $13,215.80 after both the cash receipts journal and the check register for May had been posted. The bank statement indicated a balance of $19,513.90 on May 31. Comparison of the bank statement and the accompanying canceled checks and memorandums with the records revealed the following reconciling items:

(a) Checks outstanding totaled $7,070.10.
(b) A deposit of $3,915.20, representing receipts of May 31, had been made too late to appear on the bank statement.
(c) The bank had collected $3,120 on an interest-bearing note left for collection. The face of the note was $3,000.
(d) A check for $69 returned with the statement had been recorded erroneously in the check register as $96. The check was for the payment of an obligation to Lee & Co. for the purchase of office supplies on account.
(e) A check drawn for $42 had been erroneously charged by the bank as $24.
(f) Bank service charges for May amounted to $21.80.

Instructions:

(1) Prepare a bank reconciliation.
(2) Record the necessary entries in general journal form. The accounts have not been closed. The voucher system is used.

Problem 7–2A

Bank reconciliation determined from listings in check register and bank statement; related entries.

OBJ. 1

Pierce Company employs the voucher system in controlling expenditures and disbursements. All cash receipts are deposited each Wednesday and Friday in a night depository after banking hours. The data required to reconcile the bank statement as of July 31 have been abstracted from various documents and records and are reproduced as follows. The sources of the data are printed in capital letters.

CASH IN BANK ACCOUNT:
    Balance as of July 1 .... $10,705.50

CASH RECEIPTS JOURNAL:
    Total of Cash in Bank Debit column for month of July .... $ 6,105.10

DUPLICATE DEPOSIT TICKETS:
    Date and amount of each deposit in July:

Date	Amount	Date	Amount	Date	Amount
July 2	$725.40	July 12	$516.70	July 23	$731.45
5	634.90	16	697.60	26	601.50
9	819.24	19	701.26	30	677.05

CHECK REGISTER:
    Number and amount of each check issued in July:

Check No.	Amount	Check No.	Amount	Check No.	Amount
614	$132.50	621	$399.50	628	$737.70
615	700.10	622	VOID	629	329.90
616	279.90	623	VOID	630	882.80
617	395.50	624	818.01	631	981.56
618	535.40	625	658.63	632	62.40
619	220.10	626	550.03	633	310.08
620	238.87	627	318.73	634	103.30

Total amount of checks issued in July $8,655.01

JULY BANK STATEMENT:

Balance as of July 1	$10,550.30
Deposits and other credits	11,308.85
Checks and other debits	(8,623.61)
Balance as of July 31	$13,235.54

Date and amount of each deposit in July:

Date	Amount	Date	Amount	Date	Amount
July 1	$780.80	July 11	$819.24	July 21	$701.26
3	725.40	13	516.70	24	731.45
6	634.90	17	697.60	28	601.50

CHECKS ACCOMPANYING JULY BANK STATEMENT:
Number and amount of each check, rearranged in numerical sequence:

Check No.	Amount	Check No.	Amount	Check No.	Amount
580	$310.10	618	$535.40	626	$550.03
612	92.50	619	220.10	627	318.73
613	137.50	620	238.87	629	339.90
614	132.50	621	399.50	630	882.80
615	700.10	624	818.01	631	981.56
616	279.90	625	658.63	632	62.40
617	395.50			633	310.08

BANK MEMORANDUMS ACCOMPANYING JULY BANK STATEMENT:
Date, description, and amount of each memorandum:

Date	Description	Amount
July 9	Bank credit memo for note collected:	
	Principal	$5,000.00
	Interest	100.00
16	Bank debit memo for check returned because of insufficient funds	240.10
31	Bank debit memo for service charges	19.40

BANK RECONCILIATION FOR PRECEDING MONTH:

Pierce Company
Bank Reconciliation
June 30, 19--

Balance per bank statement		$10,550.30
Add deposit of June 30, not recorded by bank		780.80
		$11,331.10
Deduct outstanding checks:		
No. 580	$310.10	
602	85.50	
612	92.50	
613	137.50	625.60
Adjusted balance		$10,705.50
Balance per depositor's records		$10,723.20
Deduct service charges		17.70
Adjusted balance		$10,705.50

Instructions:

(1) Prepare a bank reconciliation as of July 31. If errors in recording deposits or checks are discovered, assume that the errors were made by the company. Assume that all deposits are from cash sales. All checks are in payment of vouchers.
(2) Record the necessary entries in general journal form. The accounts have not been closed.
(3) What is the amount of cash in bank that should appear on the balance sheet as of July 31?

If the working papers correlating with the textbook are not used, omit Problem 7–3A.

Problem 7–3A

Voucher and check registers; accounts payable account; bank reconciliation.

OBJ. 1, 3

Portions of the voucher register, check register, and accounts payable account of Roley Co. are presented in the working papers. Cash disbursements and other selected transactions completed during the period May 26–31 of the current year are described as follows:

May 26. Recorded Voucher No. 635, payable to Voris Co. for merchandise, $11,000, terms 1/10, n/30. (Purchases invoices are recorded at the invoice price.)
26. Issued Check No. 616 to Morris Co. in payment of Voucher No. 623 for $4,000, less cash discount of 2%.
27. Recorded Voucher No. 636, payable to Acme Automobile Insurance Co. for an insurance policy, $1,584.
27. Issued Check No. 617 in payment of Voucher No. 636.
27. Recorded Voucher No. 637, payable to Trier Co. for merchandise, $1,500, terms 2/10, n/30.
28. Recorded Voucher No. 638 for $5,250, payable to Queens National Bank for note payable, $5,000, and interest, $250.
28. Issued Check No. 618 in payment of Voucher No. 638.
28. Issued Check No. 619 to Henry Stevens Co. in payment of Voucher No. 631 for $1,550, less cash discount of 2%.
29. Recorded Voucher No. 639, payable to Sidney News for advertising for May, $500.
29. Issued Check No. 620 in payment of Voucher No. 639.
31. Recorded Voucher No. 640, payable to Petty Cash for $179.90, distributed as follows: office supplies, $42.50; advertising expense, $31.45; delivery expense, $22.50; miscellaneous selling expense, $47.22; miscellaneous administrative expense, $36.23.
31. Issued Check No. 621 in payment of Voucher No. 640.

After the journals are posted at the end of the month, the cash in bank account has a debit balance of $17,245.50.

The bank statement indicates a May 31 balance of $20,933.50. A comparison of paid checks with the check register reveals that Check Nos. 617, 619, and 620 are outstanding. Check No. 593 for $610, which appeared on the April reconciliation as outstanding, is still outstanding. A debit memorandum accompanying the bank statement indicates a charge of $525 for a check drawn by Bird Co., a customer, which was returned because of insufficient funds.

Instructions:

(1) Record the transactions for May 26–31 in the appropriate journals.
(2) Total and rule the voucher register and the check register, and post totals to the accounts payable account.
(3) Complete the schedule of unpaid vouchers. (Compare the total with the balance of the accounts payable account as of May 31.)
(4) Prepare a bank reconciliation and journalize any necessary entries.

Problem 7–4A
Transactions for petty cash, advances to salespersons fund; cash short and over.

OBJ. 2, 3

Martin Company has just adopted the policy of depositing all cash receipts in the bank and of making all payments by check in conjunction with the voucher system. The following transactions were selected from those completed in June of the current year:

June 1. Recorded Voucher No. 1 to establish a petty cash fund of $200 and a change fund of $500.
1. Issued Check No. 725 in payment of Voucher No. 1.
3. Recorded Voucher No. 4 to establish an advances to salespersons fund of $1,000.
4. Issued Check No. 728 in payment of Voucher No. 4.
15. The cash sales for the day, according to the cash register tapes, totaled $3,097.40. The combined count of all cash on hand (including the change fund) totaled $3,600.
27. Recorded Voucher No. 40 to reimburse the petty cash fund for the following disbursements, each evidenced by a petty cash receipt:
June 4. Store supplies, $16.50.
6. Express charges on merchandise purchased, $15.50.
8. Office supplies, $14.75.
9. Office supplies, $9.20.
12. Postage stamps, $25 (Office Supplies).
12. Repair to adding machine, $29.50 (Miscellaneous Administrative Expense).
16. Repair to typewriter, $21.50 (Miscellaneous Administrative Expense).
18. Postage due on special delivery letter, $1.05 (Miscellaneous Administrative Expense).
20. Express charges on merchandise purchased, $19.50.
26. Telegram charges, $7.75 (Miscellaneous Selling Expense).
27. Issued Check No. 759 in payment of Voucher No. 40.
28. The cash sales for the day, according to the cash register tapes, totaled $2,609.50. The count of all cash on hand (including the change fund) totaled $3,105.60.
30. Recorded Voucher No. 43 to replenish the advances to salespersons fund for the following expenditures for travel: Gloria Griffin, $202.50; Nick Lane, $297.40; Teresa Palmer, $311.15.
30. Issued Check No. 765 in payment of Voucher No. 43.

Instructions:

Record the transactions in general journal form.

Problem 7–5A
Voucher and check registers; accounts payable account; schedule of unpaid vouchers.

OBJ. 3

Lang Company began business on June 20 of the current year. The following selected transactions were completed during the remainder of June:

June 21. Recorded Voucher No. 1, payable to Glaze Co. for merchandise, $7,500, terms 2/10, n/30.
22. Recorded Voucher No. 2, payable to Dahl Supplies Co. for office supplies, $515.
23. Recorded Voucher No. 3, payable to Adams and Sims for merchandise, $3,550, terms n/30.
23. Issued Check No. 1 for $515 to Dahl Supplies Co. in payment of Voucher No. 2.
25. Recorded Voucher No. 4, payable to Bunker Co. for store supplies, $490, terms cash.
25. Issued Check No. 2 for $490 to Bunker Co. in payment of Voucher No. 4.
27. Recorded Voucher No. 5, payable to Ramos Co. for merchandise, $4,500, terms 1/10, n/30.

June 28. Recorded Voucher No. 6, payable to Hoffman Office Equipment Co. for office equipment, $6,500, terms n/30.

29. Recorded Voucher No. 7, payable to Ace Express for transportation on merchandise purchases, $65.

30. Issued Check No. 3 for $65 to Ace Express in payment of Voucher No. 7.

30. Issued Check No. 4 for $7,500 to Glaze Co. in payment of Voucher No. 1, less cash discount of 2%.

Instructions:

(1) Set up a four-column account for Accounts Payable, Account No. 211.

(2) Record the June vouchers in a voucher register similar to the one illustrated in this chapter, with the following amount columns: Accounts Payable Cr., Purchases Dr., Store Supplies Dr., Office Supplies Dr., and Sundry Accounts Dr. Purchases invoices are recorded at the gross amount.

(3) Record the June checks in a check register similar to the one illustrated in this chapter, but omit the Bank Deposits and Balance columns. As each check is recorded in the check register, the date and check number should be inserted in the appropriate columns of the voucher register.

(4) Total and rule the registers and post to Accounts Payable.

(5) Prepare a schedule of unpaid vouchers.

Problem 7–6A

Voucher and check registers; accounts payable account; schedule of unpaid vouchers.

OBJ. 3

Conley Clothiers had the following vouchers in its unpaid voucher file at May 31 of the current year:

Due Date	Voucher No.	Creditor	Date of Invoice	Amount	Terms
June 5	510	Tomas Fashions	May 26	$7,500	1/10, n/30
June 12	498	Ace Shoes	May 13	2,700	n/30
June 13	500	Cox Co.	May 14	4,750	n/30

The vouchers prepared and the checks issued during the month of June were as follows:

VOUCHERS

Date	Voucher No.	Payee	Amount	Terms	Account(s) Debited
June 1	518	Fuller Co.	$ 9,500	1/10, n/30	Purchases
4	519	R and M Supply	90	n/10	Store supplies
5	520	Barr Co.	1,250	2/10, n/30	Purchases
8	521	C. C. Glass Inc.	900	2/10, n/30	Purchases
13	522	First National Bank	10,500		Note payable, $10,000 Interest, $500
15	523	Evans Office Supply	4,100	n/30	Office equipment
20	524	Sax Printers	215	cash	Office supplies
22	525	Bach Sportswear	1,250	2/10, n/30	Purchases
25	526	The Blouse Shop	1,900	1/10, n/30	Purchases
28	527	Eastman Inc.	550	n/30	Purchases
30	528	Parkhill Motors	22,000	cash	Delivery equipment
30	529	Petty Cash	130		Office supplies, $40 Store supplies, $34 Miscellaneous selling expense, $29 Miscellaneous administrative expense, $27

CHECKS

Date	Check No.	Payee	Voucher Paid	Amount
June 1	390	Fuller Co.	518	$ 9,405
5	391	Tomas Fashions	510	7,425
12	392	Ace Shoes	498	2,700
13	393	Cox Co.	500	4,750
13	394	First National Bank	522	10,500
14	395	R and M Supply	519	90
15	396	Barr Co.	520	1,225
18	397	C. C. Glass Inc.	521	882
20	398	Sax Printers	524	215
30	399	Parkhill Motors	528	22,000
30	400	Petty Cash	529	130

Instructions:

(1) Set up a four-column account for Accounts Payable, Account No. 205, and record the balance of $14,950 as of June 1. Place a ✔ in the Post. Ref. column.
(2) Record the June vouchers in a voucher register similar to the one illustrated in this chapter, with the following amount columns: Accounts Payable Cr., Purchases Dr., Store Supplies Dr., Office Supplies Dr., and Sundry Accounts Dr. Purchases invoices are recorded at the gross amount.
(3) Record the June checks in a check register similar to the one illustrated in this chapter, but omit the Bank Deposits and Balance columns. As each check is recorded in the check register, the date and check number should be inserted in the appropriate columns of the voucher register. (Assume that notations for payment of the May vouchers are made in the voucher register for May.)
(4) Total and rule the registers and post to Accounts Payable.
(5) Prepare a schedule of unpaid vouchers.

Series B

Problem 7–1B
Bank reconciliation and entries.

OBJ. 1

The cash in bank account for C. M. Ennis Co. at June 30 of the current year indicated a balance of $19,650.30 after both the cash receipts journal and the check register for June had been posted. The bank statement indicated a balance of $30,606.30 on June 30. Comparison of the bank statement and the accompanying canceled checks and memorandums with the records revealed the following reconciling items:

(a) Checks outstanding totaled $14,941.50.
(b) A deposit of $6,467.75, representing receipts of June 30, had been made too late to appear on the bank statement.
(c) The bank had collected $3,090 on a note left for collection. The face of the note was $3,000.
(d) A check for $91 returned with the statement had been recorded erroneously in the check register as $19. The check was for the payment of an obligation to Allen Supply Company for the purchase of office equipment on account.
(e) A check drawn for $55 had been erroneously charged by the bank as $550.
(f) Bank service charges for June amounted to $40.75.

Instructions:

(1) Prepare a bank reconciliation.
(2) Record the necessary entries in general journal form. The accounts have not been closed. The voucher system is used.

Problem 7–2B

Bank reconciliation from listings in check register and bank statement; related entries.

OBJ. 1

Pinter Corporation employs the voucher system in controlling expenditures and disbursements. All cash receipts are deposited each Wednesday and Friday in a night depository after banking hours. The data required to reconcile the bank statement as of April 30 have been abstracted from various documents and records and are reproduced as follows. To facilitate identification, the sources of the data are printed in capital letters.

CASH IN BANK ACCOUNT:
    Balance as of April 1 .... $7,817.40

CASH RECEIPTS JOURNAL:
    Total of Cash in Bank Debit column for month of April................. 7,829.58

DUPLICATE DEPOSIT TICKETS:
    Date and amount of each deposit in April:

Date	Amount	Date	Amount	Date	Amount
April 1	$848.63	April 10	$971.71	April 22	$897.34
3	914.04	15	957.85	24	942.71
8	840.50	17	946.74	29	510.06

CHECK REGISTER:
    Number and amount of each check issued in April:

Check No.	Amount	Check No.	Amount	Check No.	Amount
740	$287.50	747	Void	754	$249.75
741	555.15	748	$490.90	755	172.75
742	501.90	749	640.13	756	113.95
743	671.30	750	376.77	757	907.95
744	506.88	751	299.37	758	359.60
745	117.25	752	537.01	759	601.50
746	298.66	753	380.95	760	486.39

Total amount of checks issued in April... $8,555.66

APRIL BANK STATEMENT:
Balance as of April 1 .... $ 7,947.20
Deposits and other credits... 10,652.77
Checks and other debits .... (8,232.21)
Balance as of April 30 .... $10,367.76

Date and amount of each deposit in April:

Date	Amount	Date	Amount	Date	Amount
April 1	$690.25	April 9	$840.50	April 18	$946.74
2	848.63	11	971.71	23	897.34
4	914.04	16	975.85	25	942.71

CHECKS ACCOMPANYING APRIL BANK STATEMENT:
    Number and amount of each check, rearranged in numerical sequence:

Check No.	Amount	Check No.	Amount	Check No.	Amount
731	$162.15	744	$506.88	751	$299.37
738	251.40	745	117.25	752	537.01
739	60.55	746	298.66	753	380.95
740	287.50	748	490.90	754	249.75
741	555.15	749	640.13	756	113.95
742	501.90	750	376.77	757	907.95
743	671.30			760	486.39

BANK MEMORANDUMS ACCOMPANYING APRIL BANK STATEMENT:
Date, description, and amount of each memorandum:

Date	Description	Amount
April 4	Bank credit memo for note collected:	
	Principal...	$2,500.00
	Interest..	125.00
24	Bank debit memo for check returned because of insufficient funds..	311.80
30	Bank debit memo for service charges	24.50

BANK RECONCILIATION FOR PRECEDING MONTH:

Pinter Corporation
Bank Reconciliation
March 31, 19--

Balance per bank statement		$7,947.20
Add deposit for March 31, not recorded by bank		690.25
		$8,637.45
Deduct outstanding checks:		
No. 731..	$162.15	
736..	345.95	
738..	251.40	
739..	60.55	820.05
Adjusted balance...		$7,817.40
Balance per depositor's records		$7,832.50
Deduct service charges		15.10
Adjusted balance...		$7,817.40

Instructions:

(1) Prepare a bank reconciliation as of April 30. If errors in recording deposits or checks are discovered, assume that the errors were made by the company. Assume that all deposits are from cash sales. All checks are in payment of vouchers.
(2) Record the necessary entries in general journal form. The accounts have not been closed.
(3) What is the amount of cash in bank that should appear on the balance sheet as of April 30?

If the working papers correlating with the textbook are not used, omit Problem 7–3B.

Problem 7–3B
Voucher and check registers; accounts payable account; bank reconciliation.
OBJ. 1, 3

Portions of the voucher register, check register, and accounts payable account of Roley Co. are presented in the working papers. Cash disbursements and other selected transactions completed during the period May 26–31 of the current year are described as follows:

May 26. Issued Check No. 754 to Hyde Co. in payment of Voucher No. 609 for $4,000, less cash discount of 2%.
26. Recorded Voucher No. 617, payable to Towne Co. for merchandise, $6,000, terms 1/10, n/30. (Purchases invoices are recorded at the invoice price.)
26. Recorded Voucher No. 618, payable to United Auto Insurance Co. for an insurance policy, $1,975.
26. Issued Check No. 755 in payment of Voucher No. 618.
27. Recorded Voucher No. 619, payable to Gleason Co. for merchandise, $2,250, terms 1/10, n/30.
27. Recorded Voucher No. 620 for $10,100, payable to Second National Bank for note payable, $10,000, and interest, $100.
27. Issued Check No. 756 in payment of Voucher No. 620.

May 28. Recorded Voucher No. 621, payable to Naples News for advertising for May, $510.
28. Issued Check No. 757 in payment of Voucher No. 621.
29. Recorded Voucher No. 622, payable to Petty Cash for $189.05, distributed as follows: office supplies, $57.40; advertising expense, $20.55; delivery expense, $40.10; miscellaneous selling expense, $31.95; miscellaneous administrative expense, $39.05.
29. Issued Check No. 758 in payment of Voucher No. 622.
31. Issued Check No. 759 to Marcus Co. in payment of Voucher No. 608 for $1,550, no discount.

After the journals are posted at the end of the month, the cash in bank account has a debit balance of $19,992.70.

The bank statement indicates a May 31 balance of $23,425.10. A comparison of paid checks with the check register reveals that Check Nos. 755 and 759 are outstanding. Check No. 723 for $150, which appeared on the April reconciliation as outstanding, is still outstanding. Debit memorandums accompanying the bank statement indicate a charge of $222.50 for a check drawn by Lou Palmer, a customer, which was returned because of insufficient funds, and $20.10 for service charges.

Instructions:

(1) Record the transactions for May 26–31 in the appropriate journals.
(2) Total and rule the voucher register and the check register, and post totals to the accounts payable account.
(3) Complete the schedule of unpaid vouchers. (Compare the total with the balance of the accounts payable account as of May 31.)
(4) Prepare a bank reconciliation and journalize any necessary entries.

Problem 7–4B
Transactions for petty cash, advances to salespersons fund; cash short and over.

OBJ. 2, 3

Perkins Company has just adopted the policy of depositing all cash receipts in the bank and of making all payments by check in conjunction with the voucher system. The following transactions were selected from those completed in June of the current year:

June 2. Recorded Voucher No. 1 to establish a petty cash fund of $250 and a change fund of $500.
2. Issued Check No. 350 in payment of Voucher No. 1.
7. Recorded Voucher No. 6 to establish an advances to salespersons fund of $1,000.
7. Issued Check No. 353 in payment of Voucher No. 6.
10. The cash sales for the day, according to the cash register tapes, totaled $4,707.90. The combined count of all cash on hand (including the change fund) totaled $5,210.50.
25. Recorded Voucher No. 35 to reimburse the petty cash fund for the following disbursements, each evidenced by a petty cash receipt:
June 3. Store supplies, $19.00.
7. Express charges on merchandise purchased, $16.00.
8. Office supplies, $12.75.
9. Office supplies, $9.20.
12. Postage stamps, $45 (Office Supplies).
15. Repair to adding machine, $37.50 (Miscellaneous Administrative Expense).
16. Repair to typewriter, $30.50 (Miscellaneous Administrative Expense).
18. Postage due on special delivery letter, $1.05 (Miscellaneous Administrative Expense).
20. Express charges on merchandise purchased, $19.50.
24. Telegram charges, $7.75 (Miscellaneous Selling Expense).
25. Issued Check No. 383 in payment of Voucher No. 35.

June 28. The cash sales for the day, according to the cash register tapes, totaled $4,205.50. The count of all cash on hand (including the change fund) totaled $4,701.60.

30. Recorded Voucher No. 40 to replenish the advances to salespersons fund for the following expenditures for travel: Liz Geraci, $207.50; Mark Felix, $287.40; Sara Duffin, $351.15.

30. Issued Check No. 390 in payment of Voucher No. 40.

Instructions:

Record the transactions in general journal form.

Problem 7–5B

Voucher and check registers; accounts payable account; schedule of unpaid vouchers.

OBJ. 3

McMann Company began business on June 20 of the current year. The following selected transactions were completed during the remainder of June:

June 21. Recorded Voucher No. 1, payable to Pine Co. for merchandise, $9,000, terms 1/10, n/30.

22. Recorded Voucher No. 2, payable to Flower Company for office supplies, $350.

23. Recorded Voucher No. 3, payable to Butt Co. for merchandise, $8,550, terms n/30.

23. Issued Check No. 1 for $350 to Flower Company in payment of Voucher No. 2.

25. Recorded Voucher No. 4, payable to Bunker Co. for store supplies, $490, terms cash.

25. Issued Check No. 2 for $490 to Bunker Co. in payment of Voucher No. 4.

27. Recorded Voucher No. 5, payable to Reese Co. for merchandise, $9,500, terms 1/10, n/30.

28. Recorded Voucher No. 6, payable to Hoffman Office Equipment Co. for office equipment, $6,500, terms n/30.

29. Recorded Voucher No. 7, payable to Flash Express for transportation on merchandise purchases, $85.

30. Issued Check No. 3 for $85 to Flash Express in payment of Voucher No. 7.

30. Issued Check No. 4 for $9,000 to Pine Co. in payment of Voucher No. 1, less cash discount of 1%.

Instructions:

(1) Set up a four-column account for Accounts Payable, Account No. 211.
(2) Record the June vouchers in a voucher register similar to the one illustrated in this chapter, with the following amount columns: Accounts Payable Cr., Purchases Dr., Store Supplies Dr., Office Supplies Dr., and Sundry Accounts Dr. Purchases invoices are recorded at the gross amount.
(3) Record the June checks in a check register similar to the one illustrated in this chapter, but omit the Bank Deposits and Balance columns. As each check is recorded in the check register, the date and check number should be inserted in the appropriate columns of the voucher register.
(4) Total and rule the registers and post to Accounts Payable.
(5) Prepare a schedule of unpaid vouchers.

Problem 7–6B

Voucher and check registers; accounts payable account; schedule of unpaid vouchers.

OBJ. 3

Baxter Co. had the following vouchers in its unpaid voucher file at May 31 of the current year:

Due Date	Voucher No.	Creditor	Date of Invoice	Amount	Terms
June 3	706	Garbo Co.	May 24	$1,700	1/10, n/30
June 12	690	Little Inc.	May 13	3,300	n/30
June 28	719	Action Co.	May 29	2,450	n/30

The vouchers prepared and the checks issued during the month of June were as follows:

VOUCHERS

Date	Voucher No.	Payee	Amount	Terms	Account(s) Debited
June 1	723	Haller Co.	$1,800	2/10, n/30	Purchases
2	724	Adams Bros.	110	cash	Office supplies
6	725	Walls Co.	750	2/10, n/30	Purchases
7	726	Mann Supply	105	cash	Store supplies
9	727	Ramos Co.	1,250	2/10, n/30	Purchases
12	728	Ace Express	52	cash	Delivery expense
15	729	American Savings	6,300		Note payable, $6,000 Interest, $300
18	730	Collins Office Co.	2,600	n/30	Office equipment
19	731	Ross & Co.	950	2/10, n/30	Purchases
23	732	L. M. Carr Co.	2,200	cash	Store equipment
25	733	Temple Co.	3,100	2/10, n/30	Purchases
30	734	Petty Cash	152		Store supplies, $45 Office supplies, $39 Miscellaneous selling expense, $38 Miscellaneous administrative expense, $30

CHECKS

Date	Check No.	Payee	Voucher Paid	Amount
June 2	690	Adams Bros.	724	$ 110
3	691	Garbo Co.	706	1,683
7	692	Mann Supply	726	105
11	693	Haller Co.	723	1,764
12	694	Ace Express	728	52
12	695	Little Inc.	690	3,300
15	696	American Savings	729	6,300
16	697	Walls Co.	725	735
19	698	Ramos Co.	727	1,225
23	699	L. M. Carr Co.	732	2,200
28	700	Action Co.	719	2,450
29	701	Ross & Co.	731	931
30	702	Petty Cash	734	152

Instructions:

(1) Set up a four-column account for Accounts Payable, Account No. 205, and record the balance of $7,450 as of June 1. Place a ✓ in the Post. Ref. column.
(2) Record the June vouchers in a voucher register similar to the one illustrated in this chapter, with the following amount columns: Accounts Payable Cr., Purchases Dr., Store Supplies Dr., Office Supplies Dr., and Sundry Accounts Dr. Purchases invoices are recorded at the gross amount.
(3) Record the June checks in a check register similar to the one illustrated in this chapter, but omit the Bank Deposits and Balance columns. As each check is recorded in the check register, the date and check number should be inserted in the appropriate columns of the voucher register. (Assume that notations for payment of the May vouchers are made in the voucher register for May.)
(4) Total and rule the registers and post to Accounts Payable.
(5) Prepare a schedule of unpaid vouchers.

MINI-CASE 7

ROSSITER COMPANY

The records of Rossiter Company indicate a May 31 cash in bank balance of $24,231.05, which includes undeposited receipts for May 30 and 31. The cash balance on the bank statement as of May 31 is $22,540. This balance includes a note of $3,000 plus $90 interest collected by the bank but not recorded in the cash receipts journal. Checks outstanding on May 31 were as follows: No. 421, $843.40; No. 488, $430; No. 522, $652.40; No. 992, $955.15; No. 995, $457.70; and No. 996, $596.10.

On May 12, the cashier resigned, effective at the end of the month. Before leaving on May 31, the cashier prepared the following bank reconciliation:

Balance per books, May 31......................................		$24,231.05
Add outstanding checks:		
992..	$955.15	
995..	457.70	
996..	596.10	1,808.95
		$26,040.00
Less undeposited receipts		3,500.00
Balance per bank, May 31		$22,540.00
Deduct unrecorded note with interest		3,090.00
True cash, May 31		$19,450.00

Calculator Tape of Outstanding Checks

```
            0.    *

          955.15  +

          457.70  +

          596.10  +

        1,808.95  *
```

Subsequently, the owner of Rossiter Company discovered that the cashier had stolen all undeposited receipts in excess of the $3,500 on hand on May 31. The owner, a close family friend, has asked your help in determining the amount that the former cashier has stolen.

Instructions:

(1) Determine the amount the cashier stole from Rossiter Company. Show your computations in good form.
(2) How did the cashier attempt to conceal the theft?
(3) (a) Identify two major weaknesses in Rossiter Company's internal controls which allowed the cashier to steal the undeposited cash receipts.
(b) Recommend improvements in Rossiter Company's internal controls, so that similar types of thefts of undeposited cash receipts could be prevented.

(AICPA adapted)

ETHICS DISCUSSION CASE	During the reconciliation of Hibbitt Co.'s bank statement, Mark Wetzstein, assistant to the controller, discovered that Jones County National Bank erroneously recorded a $1,500 check written by Hibbitt Co. as $1,000. Mark has decided not to notify the bank, but to wait for the bank to detect the error. Mark plans to record the $500 error as Other Income if the bank fails to detect the error within the next three months. Discuss whether Mark Wetzstein is behaving in an ethical manner.

ANSWERS TO SELF-EXAMINATION QUESTIONS

1. **B** On any specific date, the cash in bank account in a depositor's ledger may not agree with the reciprocal account in the bank's ledger because of delays and/or errors by either party in recording transactions. The purpose of a bank reconciliation, therefore, is to determine the reasons for any discrepancies between the two account balances. All errors should then be corrected by the depositor or the bank as appropriate. In arriving at the adjusted (correct) balance according to the bank statement, outstanding checks must be deducted (answer B) to adjust for checks that have been written by the depositor but that have not yet been presented to the bank for payment.

2. **C** All reconciling items that are added to and deducted from the "balance per depositor's records" on the bank reconciliation (answer C) require that journal entries be made by the depositor to correct errors made in recording transactions or to bring the cash account up to date for delays in recording transactions.

3. **D** A voucher (answer A) is the form on which is recorded pertinent data about a liability. After a voucher is approved by the designated official, it is recorded in the voucher register (answer D). The voucher is filed in an unpaid vouchers file (answer B) until it is due for payment. It is then removed from the file and a check is issued in payment and an entry is made in the check register (answer C).

4. **D** A major advantage of recording purchases at the net amount (answer A) is that the cost of failing to take discounts is recorded in the accounts (answer B) and then reported as an expense on the income statement (answer C).

5. **D** To avoid the delay, annoyance, and expense that is associated with paying all obligations by check, relatively small amounts (answer A) are paid from a petty cash fund. The fund is established by estimating the amount of cash needed to pay these small amounts during a specified period (answer B) and it is then reimbursed when the amount of money in the fund is reduced to a predetermined minimum amount (answer C).

CHAPTER EIGHT

RECEIVABLES AND TEMPORARY INVESTMENTS

CHAPTER OBJECTIVES

1 Describe the common classifications of receivables.

2 Describe the basic principles of internal control over receivables.

3 Describe the common characteristics of notes receivable.

4 Describe and illustrate the accounting for notes receivable, including the discounting of notes receivable and dishonored notes receivable.

5 Describe the basic concepts in accounting for uncollectible receivables.

6 Describe and illustrate the allowance method of accounting for uncollectible receivables, including the estimation of uncollectibles based on sales and on an analysis of receivables.

7 Describe and illustrate the direct write-off method of accounting for uncollectible receivables.

8 Describe and illustrate the accounting for temporary investments.

9 Describe and illustrate the presentation of temporary investments and receivables in the balance sheet.

For many businesses, the revenue from sales on a credit basis is the largest factor influencing the amount of net income. As credit is granted, businesses must account for the resulting receivables, which may represent a substantial portion of the total current assets. As the receivables are collected, the cash realized is accounted for in the manner discussed in Chapter 7. If the amount of cash on hand exceeds immediate cash requirements, the excess cash might be invested in securities until needed. These securities are accounted for as temporary investments.

CLASSIFICATION OF RECEIVABLES

OBJECTIVE 1
Describe the common classifications of receivables.

The term **receivables** includes all money claims against people, organizations, or other debtors. Receivables are acquired by a business enterprise in various kinds of transactions, the most common being the sale of merchandise or services on a credit basis.

Credit may be granted on open account or on the basis of a formal instrument of credit, such as a promissory note. A **promissory note**, frequently referred to as a **note**, is a written promise to pay a sum of money on demand or at a definite time. Notes are usually used for credit periods of more than sixty days, as in sales of equipment on the installment plan, and for transactions of relatively large dollar amounts. Notes may also be used in settlement of an open account and in borrowing or lending money.

From the point of view of the creditor, a claim evidenced by a note has some advantages over a claim in the form of an account receivable. By signing a note, the debtor acknowledges the debt and agrees to pay it according to the terms given. The note is therefore a stronger legal claim if there is court action. It is also more liquid than an open account because the holder can usually transfer it more readily to a bank or other financial agency in exchange for cash.

The enterprise owning a note refers to it as a **note receivable**. If notes and accounts receivable originate from sales transactions, they are sometimes called **trade receivables**. In the absence of other descriptive words or phrases, accounts and notes receivable may be assumed to have originated from sales in the usual course of the business.

Other receivables include interest receivable, loans to officers or employees, and loans to affiliated companies. To facilitate their classification and presentation on the balance sheet, a general ledger account should be maintained for each type of receivable, with proper subsidiary ledgers.

All receivables that are expected to be realized in cash within a year are presented in the current assets section of the balance sheet. Those that are not currently collectible, such as long-term loans, should be listed under the caption "Investments" below the current assets section.

CONTROL OVER RECEIVABLES

OBJECTIVE 2
Describe the basic principles of internal control over receivables.

As is the case for all assets, the broad principles of internal control discussed in Chapter 6 can be used to establish procedures to safeguard receivables. These controls would include the separation of the business operations and the accounting for receivables, so that the accounting records can serve as an independent check on operations. Thus the employee who handles the accounting for notes and accounts receivable should not be involved with credit approvals or collections of receivables. Separation of these functions reduces the possibility of errors and embezzlement. The controls would also include the separation of responsibility for related functions, so that the work of one employee can serve as a check on the work of another employee. For example, the handling of the accounts receivable ledger and the general ledger should be separated. In this way, the work of the accounts receivable clerk can be checked by comparing the total of the individual account balances in the accounts receivable subsidiary ledger with the balance of the accounts receivable controlling account that is maintained by the general ledger clerk.

For most businesses, the principal receivables are notes receivable and accounts receivable. Generally, notes receivable are recorded in a single general ledger account. If there are numerous notes, the general ledger account can be supported by a notes receivable register. The register would contain details of each note, such as the name of the maker, place of payment, amount, term, interest rate, and due date. Frequent reference to the due date section directs attention to those notes that are due for payment. In this way, the maker of the note can be notified when the note is due, and the risk that the maker will overlook the due date can be minimized.

Adequate control over accounts receivable begins with the approval of the sale by a responsible company official or the credit department, after the customer's credit rating has been reviewed. Likewise, adjustments of accounts receivable, such as for sales returns and allowances and sales discounts, should be authorized or reviewed by a responsible party. Effective collection procedures should also be established to ensure timely collection of accounts receivable and to minimize losses from uncollectible accounts. The proper use of the controlling account and the accounts receivable ledger, as discussed in Chapter 6, also increases the effectiveness of the control over accounts receivable.

CHARACTERISTICS OF NOTES RECEIVABLE

OBJECTIVE 3
Describe the common characteristics of notes receivable.

As indicated earlier in the chapter, a note is a written promise to pay a sum of money on demand or at a definite time. As in the case of a check, it must be payable to the order of a certain person or firm, or to bearer. It must also be signed by the person or firm that makes the promise. The one to whose order the note is payable is called the **payee**, and the one making the promise is called the **maker**. In the following illustration, Pearland Company is the payee and Selig Corporation is the maker.

Promissory Note

$ 2,500.00	Fresno, California___March 16___ 19 90
Ninety days _____ AFTER DATE ___We___ PROMISE TO PAY TO	
THE ORDER OF___Pearland Company	
Two thousand five hundred 00/100---------------------- DOLLARS	
PAYABLE AT ___First National Bank	
VALUE RECEIVED WITH INTEREST AT___10%___	SELIG CORPORATION
NO.__14__ DUE ___June 14, 1990	H.B. Lane TREASURER

Notes have several characteristics that have accounting implications. These characteristics are described in the following paragraphs.

Due Date

The date a note is to be paid is called the due date or maturity date. The period of time between the issuance date and the due date of a short-term note may be stated in either days or months. When the term of a note is stated in days, the due date is the specified number of days after its issuance. To illustrate, the due date of the 90-day note presented above may be determined as follows:

Determination of Due Date of Note

Term of the note		90
March (days).........................	31	
Date of note.........................	16	15
Number of days remaining........		75
April (days)		30
		45
May (days)............................		31
Due date, June......................		14

When the term of a note is stated as a certain number of months after the issuance date, the due date is determined by counting the number of months from the issuance date. Thus, a 3-month note dated June 5 would be due on September 5. In those cases in which there is no date in the month of maturity that corresponds to the issuance date, the due date becomes the last day of the month. For example, a 2-month note dated July 31 would be due on September 30.

Interest-Bearing Notes and Non-Interest-Bearing Notes

A note that provides for the payment of interest for the period between the issuance date and the due date is called an **interest-bearing note**. If a note makes no provision for interest, it is said to be **non-interest-bearing**. The note illustrated on page 318 is an interest-bearing note.

Interest

Interest rates for interest-bearing notes are usually stated in terms of a period of one year, regardless of the actual period of time involved. Thus the interest on $2,000 for one year at 12% would be $240 (12% of $2,000); the interest on $2,000 for one fourth of one year at 12% would be $60 (¼ of $240).

Notes covering a period of time longer than one year ordinarily provide that the interest be paid semiannually, quarterly, or at some other stated interval. The time involved in commercial credit transactions is usually less than one year, and the interest provided for by a note is payable at the time the note is paid. In computing interest for a period of less than one year, agencies of the federal government use the actual number of days in the year. For example, 90 days is considered to be 90/365 of one year. The usual commercial practice is to use 360 as the denominator of the fraction; thus 90 days is considered to be 90/360 of one year.

The basic formula for computing interest is as follows:

$$\text{Principal} \times \text{Rate} \times \text{Time} = \text{Interest}$$

To illustrate the use of the formula, the $62.50 interest for the $2,500, 90-day, 10% note presented on page 318 is computed as follows:

$$\$2,500 \times \frac{10}{100} \times \frac{90}{360} = \$62.50 \text{ interest}$$

One of the commonly used shortcut methods of computing interest is called the 60-day, 6% method. The 6% annual rate is converted to the effective rate of 1% for a 60-day period (60/360 of 6%). Accordingly, the interest on any amount for 60 days at 6% is determined by moving the decimal point in the principal two places to the left. For example, the interest on $1,500 at 6% for 60 days is $15. The amount obtained by moving the decimal point must be adjusted (1) for interest rates greater or less than 6% and (2) for periods of time greater or less than 60 days. For example, the interest on $1,500 at 6% for 90 days is $22.50 (90/60 of $15). The interest on $1,500 at 12% for 60 days is $30 (12/6 of $15).

Comprehensive interest tables are available and are commonly used by financial institutions and other enterprises that require frequent interest calculations. Nevertheless, students of business should know the mechanics of interest computations well enough to use them with complete accuracy and to recognize major errors in interest amounts that come to their attention.

When the term of a note is stated in months instead of in days, each month may be considered as being 1/12 of a year, or, alternatively, the actual number of days in the term may be counted. For example, the interest on a 3-month note dated June 1 could be computed on the basis of 3/12 of a year or on the basis of 92/360 of a year. It is the usual commercial practice to use the first method, while banks usually charge interest for the exact number of days. For the sake of simplicity, the usual commercial practice will be assumed in all cases.

THE BOBTAILED YEAR

The practice of using the 360-day year for determining interest has a surprisingly significant effect on the economy as a whole. Both the background of the practice and its effect are described in the following excerpts from an article in *The Wall Street Journal*:

In 46 B.C., Julius Caesar proclaimed that a year would be pegged at 365 days, with an extra day added every fourth year. What was good enough for Caesar has been good enough for the rest of us ever since except for the nation's bankers.

A lot of bankers are using a 360-day year to compute the interest they charge to borrowers on commercial and corporate loans. This means, in effect, that they are collecting a smidgin more interest on these loans than their stated "annual" interest rates would indicate. . . .

Though only small amounts of money are involved in the difference between 365- and 360-day charges on any one loan, the nickels and dimes add up to an impressive pile. . . . [In fact, the overcharges that result from the use of the bobtailed year have been estimated to be at least $145 million a year.]

According to the bankers, use of the bobtailed year began before the widespread use of adding machines; clerks who had to do the computations with pencil and paper found it a lot easier to multiply and divide by 360 rather than 365 or 366. Since nobody seemed to care much, the 360-day base continued in use through the age of calculators and now is imbedded in the banks' computer programs. "Converting our computers to a 365-day year would be a massive job," says one officer of a major bank.

Source: James F. Carberry, "365 Days May Have Been Good Enough For Caesar, But Lenders Find That 360 Provide More Profit," *The Wall Street Journal*, March 30, 1973.

Maturity Value

The amount that is due at the maturity or due date is called the **maturity value.** The maturity value of a non-interest-bearing note is the face amount. The maturity value of an interest-bearing note is the sum of the face amount and the interest. In the note presented on page 318, the maturity value is $2,562.50 ($2,500 face amount plus $62.50 interest).

ACCOUNTING FOR NOTES RECEIVABLE

OBJECTIVE 4
Describe and illustrate the accounting for notes receivable, including the discounting of notes receivable and dishonored notes receivable.

The typical retail enterprise makes most of its sales for cash or on account. If the account of a customer becomes delinquent, the creditor may insist that the account be converted into a note. In this way, the debtor is given more time, and if the creditor needs more funds, the note may be endorsed and transferred to a bank or other financial agency. Notes may also be received by retail firms that sell merchandise on long-term credit. For example, a dealer in household appliances may require a down payment at the time of sale and accept a note or a series of notes for the remainder. Such arrangements usually provide for monthly payments. Wholesale firms and manufacturers are likely to receive notes more often than retailers, although here, too, much depends upon the kind of product and the length of the credit period.

When a note is received from a customer to apply on account, the facts are recorded by debiting the notes receivable account and crediting the accounts receivable controlling account and the account of the customer from whom the note is received. To illustrate, assume that the account of Glenn Enterprises, which has a balance of $9,200, is past due. A 90-day non-interest-bearing note for that amount, dated May 16, 1990, is accepted in settlement of the account. The note receivable is recorded at its face value and the entry to record the transaction is as follows:

May 16	Notes Receivable	9,200	
	Accounts Receivable—		
	Glenn Enterprises............................		9,200
	Received 90-day, non-interest-bearing		
	note dated May 16, 1990.		

When the $9,200 due on the note is collected, the following entry would be recorded in the cash receipts journal:

| Aug. 14 | Cash... | 9,200 | |
| | Notes Receivable .... | | 9,200 |

Interest-Bearing Notes Receivable

If the note received from a customer on account is interest bearing, interest must be recorded as appropriate. To illustrate, assume that a 30-day, 12% note dated December 21, 1990, is accepted in settlement of the account of W. A. Bunn Co., which has a balance of $6,000. The entry to record the transaction is as follows:

Dec. 21	Notes Receivable	6,000	
	Accounts Receivable—W. A. Bunn Co. ...		6,000
	Received 30-day, 12% note dated		
	December 21, 1990.		

On December 31, 1990, the end of the fiscal year, an adjusting entry would be recorded for the accrual of the interest from December 21 to December 31. The entry to record the accrued revenue of $20 ($6,000 × 12/100 × 10/360) is as follows:

	Adjusting Entry		
Dec. 31	Interest Receivable...............................	20	
	Interest Income....................................		20

Interest receivable is reported on the balance sheet at December 31, 1990, as a current asset. The interest income account is closed at December 31 and the amount is reported in the Other Income section of the income statement for the year ended December 31, 1990.

When the amount due on the note is collected in 1991, part of the interest received will effect a reduction of the interest that was receivable at December 31, 1990, and the remainder will represent revenue for 1991. To avoid the possibility of failing to recognize this division and to avoid the inconvenience of analyzing the receipt of interest in 1991, a reversing entry is made after the accounts are closed. The effect of the entry, which is illustrated as follows, is to transfer the debit balance in the interest receivable account to the debit side of the interest income account.

	Reversing Entry		
Jan. 1	Interest Income......................................	20	
	Interest Receivable.............................		20

At the time the note matures and payment is received, the entire amount of the interest received is credited to Interest Income, as illustrated by the following entry that would be recorded in the cash receipts journal:

Jan. 20	Cash..	6,060	
	Notes Receivable		6,000
	Interest Income..................................		60

After the foregoing entries are posted, the interest income account will appear as follows:

ACCOUNT INTEREST INCOME   ACCOUNT NO. 811

Date		Item	Post. Ref.	Debit	Credit	Balance Debit	Balance Credit
1990							
Dec.	12		CR20		120		946
	31	Adjusting	J17		20		966
	31	Closing	J17	966		—	—
1991							
Jan.	1	Reversing	J18	20		20	
	20		CR21		60		40

The adjusting and reversing process divided the $60 of interest received on January 20, 1991, into two parts for accounting purposes: (1) **$20** representing the interest income for 1990 (recorded by the adjusting entry) and (2) **$40** representing the interest income for 1991 (the balance in the interest income account at January 20, 1991).

Discounting Notes Receivable

Although it is not a common transaction, a company in need of cash may transfer its notes receivable to a bank by endorsement. The **discount** (interest) charged by the bank is computed on the maturity value of the note for the period of time the bank must hold the note, namely the time that will pass between the date of the transfer and the due date of the note. The amount of the **proceeds** paid to the endorser is the excess of the maturity value over the discount.

To illustrate, assume that a 90-day, 12% note receivable for $1,800, dated November 8, is discounted at the payee's bank on December 3 at the rate of 14%. The data used in determining the effect of the transaction are as follows:

Face value of note dated Nov. 8	$1,800.00
Interest on note—90 days at 12%	54.00
Maturity value of note due Feb. 6	$1,854.00
Discount period—Dec. 3 to Feb. 6 ....65 days	
Discount on maturity value—65 days at 14%	46.87
Proceeds	$1,807.13

The same information is presented graphically in the following flow diagram. In reading the data, follow the direction of the arrows.

Diagram of Discounting a Note Receivable

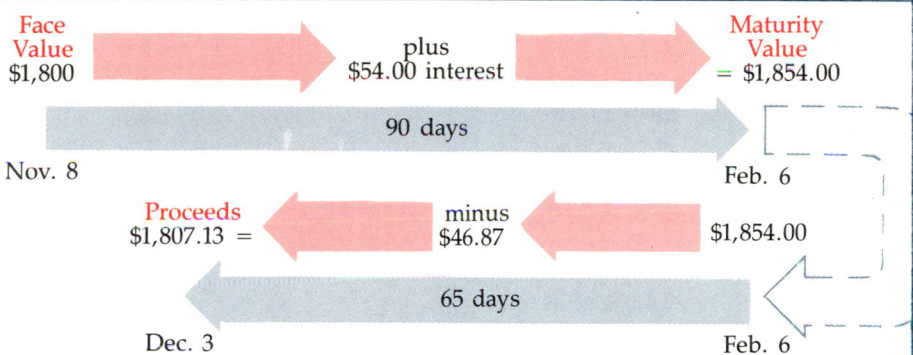

The excess of the proceeds from discounting the note, $1,807.13, over its face value, $1,800, is recorded as interest income. The entry for the transaction, in general journal form, is as follows:

Dec. 3	Cash	1,807.13	
	Notes Receivable		1,800.00
	Interest Income		7.13

It should be observed that the proceeds from discounting a note receivable may be less than the face value. When this situation occurs, the excess of the face value over the proceeds is recorded as interest expense. The amount and direction of the difference between the interest rate and the discount rate will affect the result, as will the relationship between the full term of the note and the length of the discount period.

Without a statement limiting responsibility, the endorser of a note is committed to paying the note if the maker should default. Such potential obligations that will become actual liabilities only if certain events occur in the future are called **contingent liabilities**. Thus, the endorser of a note that has been discounted has a contingent liability that is in effect until the due date. If the maker pays the promised amount at maturity, the contingent liability is removed without any action on the part of the endorser. If, on the other hand, the maker defaults and the endorser is notified according to legal requirements, the liability becomes an actual one.

Significant contingent liabilities should be disclosed on the balance sheet or in an accompanying note. Disclosure requirements for contingent liabilities are discussed and illustrated in Chapter 12.

Dishonored Notes Receivable

If the maker of a note fails to pay the debt on the due date, the note is said to be **dishonored**. A dishonored note receivable is no longer negotiable, and for that reason the holder usually transfers the claim, including any interest due, to the accounts receivable account. For example, if the $6,000, 30-day, 12% note received and recorded on December 21 (page 321) had been dishonored at maturity, the entry to charge the note, including the interest, back to the customer's account would have been as follows:

Jan. 20	Accounts Receivable—W. A. Bunn Co.	6,060	
	Notes Receivable		6,000
	Interest Income		60
	Dishonored note and interest.		

If there had been some assurance that the maker would pay the note within a relatively short time, action would have been delayed until the matter was resolved. However, for future guidance in extending credit, it may be desirable that the customer's account in the subsidiary ledger disclose the dishonor of the note.

When a discounted note receivable is dishonored, the holder usually notifies the endorser of such fact and asks for payment. If the request for payment and notification of dishonor are timely, the endorser is legally obligated to pay the amount due on the note. The entire amount paid to the holder by the endorser, including the interest, should be debited to the account receivable of the maker. To illustrate, assume that the $1,800, 90-day, 12% note discounted on December 3 (page 323) is dishonored at maturity by the maker, Pryor & Co. The entry to record the payment by the endorser, in general journal form, would be as follows:

Feb. 6	Accounts Receivable—Pryor & Co............	1,854	
	Cash		1,854

In some cases, the holder of a dishonored note gives the endorser a notarized statement of the facts of the dishonor. The fee for this statement, known as a **protest fee**, is charged to the endorser, who in turn charges it to the maker of the note. If there had been a protest fee of $12 in connection with the dishonor and the payment previously recorded, the debit to the maker's account and the credit to Cash would have been $1,866.

UNCOLLECTIBLE RECEIVABLES

OBJECTIVE 5
Describe the
basic concepts
in accounting
for uncollectible
receivables.

When merchandise or services are sold without the immediate receipt of cash, a part of the claims against customers usually proves to be uncollectible. This situation is common, regardless of the care used in granting credit and the effectiveness of the collection procedures used. The operating expense incurred because of the failure to collect receivables is called an expense or a loss from **uncollectible accounts**, **doubtful accounts**, or **bad debts**.[1]

---

[1]If both notes and accounts are involved, both may be included in the title, as in "uncollectible notes and accounts expense," or the general term "uncollectible receivables expense" may be substituted. Because of its wide usage and simplicity, "uncollectible accounts expense" will be used in this text.

There is no single general rule for determining when an account or a note becomes uncollectible. The fact that a debtor fails to pay an account according to a sales contract or dishonors a note on the due date does not necessarily mean that the account will be uncollectible. Bankruptcy of the debtor is one of the most significant indications of partial or complete worthlessness of a receivable. Other evidence includes closing of the debtor's business, disappearance of the debtor, failure of repeated attempts to collect, and the barring of collection by the statute of limitations.

There are two methods of accounting for receivables that are believed to be uncollectible. The **allowance method**, which is sometimes called the **reserve method**, provides in advance for uncollectible receivables.[2] The other procedure, called the **direct write-off method** or **direct charge-off method**, recognizes the expense only when certain accounts are judged to be worthless.

ALLOWANCE METHOD OF ACCOUNTING FOR UNCOLLECTIBLES

OBJECTIVE 6
Describe and illustrate the allowance method of accounting for uncollectible receivables, including the estimation of uncollectibles based on sales and on an analysis of receivables.

Most large business enterprises provide currently for the amount of their trade receivables estimated to become uncollectible in the future. The advance provision for future uncollectibility is made by an adjusting entry at the end of the fiscal period. As with all periodic adjustments, the entry serves two purposes. In this instance, it provides for (1) the reduction of the value of the receivables to the amount of cash expected to be realized from them in the future and (2) the allocation to the current period of the expected expense resulting from such reduction.

Assumed data for a new business firm, Richards Company, will be used to explain and illustrate the allowance method. The enterprise began business in August and chose to use the calendar year as its fiscal year. The accounts receivable account, illustrated as follows, has a balance of $105,000 at the end of the period.

ACCOUNT ACCOUNTS RECEIVABLE   ACCOUNT NO. 114

Date		Item	Post. Ref.	Debit	Credit	Balance Debit	Balance Credit
19--							
Aug.	31		S3	20,000		20,000	
Sept.	30		S6	25,000		45,000	
	30		CR4		15,000	30,000	
Oct.	31		S10	40,000		70,000	
	31		CR7		25,000	45,000	
Nov.	30		S13	38,000		83,000	
	30		CR10		23,000	60,000	
Dec.	31		S16	75,000		135,000	
	31		CR13		30,000	105,000	

Among the individual customers accounts making up the $105,000 balance in Accounts Receivable are a number of balances which are a varying

---

[2] The allowance (reserve) method is not acceptable for determining the federal income tax.

number of days past due. No specific accounts are believed to be wholly un-collectible at this time, but it seems likely that some will be collected only in part and that others are likely to become entirely worthless. Based on a care-ful study, it is estimated that a total of $3,000 will eventually prove to be un-collectible. The amount expected to be realized from the accounts receivable is, therefore, $102,000 ($105,000 − $3,000), and the $3,000 reduction in value is the uncollectible accounts expense for the period.

The $3,000 reduction in accounts receivable cannot yet be identified with specific customer accounts in the subsidiary ledger and should there-fore not be credited to the controlling account in the general ledger. The cus-tomary practice is to use a contra asset account entitled Allowance for Doubtful Accounts. The adjusting entry to record the expense and the re-duction in the asset is as follows:

	Adjusting Entry			
Dec. 31	Uncollectible Accounts Expense	717	3,000	
	Allowance for Doubtful Accounts..	115		3,000

The two accounts to which the entry is posted are illustrated as follows:

ACCOUNT UNCOLLECTIBLE ACCOUNTS EXPENSE   ACCOUNT NO. 717

Date		Item	Post. Ref.	Debit	Credit	Balance Debit	Balance Credit
19--							
Dec.	31	Adjusting	J4	3,000		3,000	

ACCOUNT ALLOWANCE FOR DOUBTFUL ACCOUNTS   ACCOUNT NO. 115

Date		Item	Post. Ref.	Debit	Credit	Balance Debit	Balance Credit
19--							
Dec.	31	Adjusting	J4		3,000		3,000

The debit balance of $105,000 in Accounts Receivable is the amount of the total claims against customers on open account, and the credit balance of $3,000 in Allowance for Doubtful Accounts is the amount to be deducted from Accounts Receivable to determine the **expected realizable value**, fre-quently called the **net realizable value**. The $3,000 reduction in the asset was transferred to Uncollectible Accounts Expense, which will in turn be closed to Income Summary.

Uncollectible accounts expense is generally reported on the income statement as an administrative expense, because the credit-granting and col-lection duties are the responsibilities of departments within the general ad-ministrative framework. The accounts receivable may be listed on the balance sheet at the net amount of $102,000, with a notation in parentheses showing the amount of the allowance, or the details may be presented as shown on the following partial balance sheet. When the allowance account includes provision for doubtful notes as well as accounts, it should be de-ducted from the total of Notes Receivable and Accounts Receivable.

*Accounts Receivable
on the Balance Sheet*

**Richards Company
Balance Sheet
December 31, 19--**

Assets

Current assets:		
Cash...		$ 21,600
Accounts receivable...	$105,000	
Less allowance for doubtful accounts.................	3,000	102,000

Write-Offs to the Allowance Account

When an account is believed to be uncollectible, it is written off against the allowance account as in the following entry:

Jan. 21	Allowance for Doubtful Accounts...............	110	
	Accounts Receivable — John Parker		110
	To write off the uncollectible account.		

During the year, as more accounts or portions of accounts are determined to be uncollectible, they are written off against Allowance for Doubtful Accounts in the same manner. Instructions for write-offs should originate with the credit manager or other designated official. The authorizations, which should always be written, serve as objective evidence in support of the accounting entry.

Naturally enough, the total amount written off against the allowance account during the period will rarely be equal to the amount in the account at the beginning of the period. The allowance account will have a credit balance at the end of the period if the write-offs during the period amount to less than the beginning balance. It will have a debit balance if the write-offs exceed the beginning balance. After the year-end adjusting entry is recorded, the allowance account will have a credit balance.

An account receivable that has been written off against the allowance account may later be collected. In such cases, the account should be reinstated by an entry that is the exact reverse of the write-off entry. For example, assume that the account of $110 written off in the preceding journal entry is later collected. The entry to reinstate the account would be as follows:

June 10	Accounts Receivable — John Parker	110	
	Allowance for Doubtful Accounts.............		110
	To reinstate account written off earlier in the year.		

The cash received in payment would be recorded as a receipt on account. Although it is possible to combine the reinstatement and the receipt of cash into a single debit and credit, the entries in the customer's account, with a proper notation, provide useful credit information.

Estimating Uncollectibles

The estimate of uncollectibles at the end of the fiscal period is based on past experience and forecasts of future business activity. When the trend of general sales volume is upward and there is relatively full employment, the amount of the expense should usually be less than when the trend is in the opposite direction. The estimate is customarily based on either (1) the amount of sales for the entire fiscal period or (2) the amount and the age of the receivable accounts at the end of the fiscal period.

Estimate Based on Sales. Accounts receivable are acquired as a result of sales on account. The amount of such sales during the year may therefore be used to determine the probable amount of the accounts that will be uncollectible. The amount of this estimate is added to whatever balance exists in Allowance for Doubtful Accounts. To illustrate, assume that the allowance account has a credit balance of $700 before adjustment. If it is known from past experience that about 1% of charge sales will be uncollectible and the charge sales for a certain year amount to $300,000, the adjusting entry for uncollectible accounts at the end of the year would be as follows:

	Adjusting Entry		
Dec. 31	Uncollectible Accounts Expense	3,000	
	Allowance for Doubtful Accounts............		3,000

After the adjusting entry is posted, the balance in the allowance account is $3,700. If there had been a debit balance of $200 in the allowance account before the year-end adjustment, the amount of the adjustment would still have been $3,000. The balance in the allowance account, after the adjusting entry is posted, would be $2,800 ($3,000 − $200).

Instead of charge sales, total sales (including those made for cash) may be used in developing the percentage. Total sales is obtainable from the ledger without the analysis that may be needed to determine charge sales. If the ratio of sales on account to cash sales does not change very much from year to year, the results obtained will be equally satisfactory. If in the above example the balance of the sales account at the end of the year is assumed to be $400,000, the application of 3/4 of 1% to that amount would also yield an estimate of $3,000.

If it becomes apparent over a period of time that the amount of write-offs is always greater or less than the amount provided by the adjusting entry, the percentage applied to sales data should be changed accordingly. A newly established business enterprise, having no record of credit experience, may obtain data on the probable amount of the expense from trade association journals and other publications containing information on credit and collections.

The estimate-based-on-sales method of determining the uncollectible accounts expense is widely used. It is simple and it provides the best basis for charging uncollectible accounts expense to the period in which the related sales were made.

Estimate Based on Analysis of Receivables. The process of analyzing the receivable accounts in terms of the length of time past due is sometimes called **aging the receivables**. The base point for determining age is the due date of the account. The number and breadth of the time intervals used will vary according to the credit terms granted to customers. A portion of a typical analysis is as follows:

Analysis of Accounts Receivable

CUSTOMER	BALANCE	NOT DUE	DAYS PAST DUE					
			1–30	31–60	61–90	91–180	181–365	over 365
Ashby & Co. ...	$ 150			$ 150				
B. T. Barr	610					$ 350	$260	
Brock Co........	470	$ 470						
J. Zimmer Co. ..	160							160
Total...........	$86,300	$75,000	$4,000	$3,100	$1,900	$1,200	$800	$300

The analysis is completed by adding the columns to determine the total amount of receivables in each age group. A sliding scale of percentages, based on experience, is next applied to obtain the estimated amount of uncollectibles in each group. The manner in which the data may be presented is illustrated as follows:

Estimate of Uncollectible Accounts

Age Interval	Balance	Estimated Uncollectible Accounts	
		Percent	*Amount*
Not due.........................	$75,000	2%	$1,500
1–30 days past due.........	4,000	5	200
31–60 days past due.......	3,100	10	310
61–90 days past due.......	1,900	20	380
91–180 days past due	1,200	30	360
181–365 days past due....	800	50	400
Over 365 days past due ...	300	80	240
Total.........................	$86,300		$3,390

The estimate of uncollectible accounts, $3,390 in the example above, is the amount to be deducted from accounts receivable to yield their expected realizable value. It is thus the amount of the desired balance of the allowance account after adjustment. The excess of this figure over the balance of the allowance account before adjustment is the amount of the current provision to be made for uncollectible accounts expense.

To continue the illustration, assume that the allowance account has a credit balance of $510 before adjustment. The amount to be added to this balance is therefore $2,880 ($3,390 − $510), and the adjusting entry is as follows:

	Adjusting Entry		
Dec. 31	Uncollectible Accounts Expense	2,880	
	Allowance for Doubtful Accounts............		2,880

After the adjusting entry is posted, the credit balance in the allowance account will be $3,390, which is the desired amount. If there had been a debit balance of $300 in the allowance account before the year-end adjustment, the amount of the adjustment would have been $3,690 ($3,390 desired balance + $300 negative balance).

Estimations of uncollectible accounts expense based on an analysis of receivables are less common than estimations based on sales volume. Estimations based on receivables analyses are sometimes preferred because they give more accurate estimates of the current realizable values of the receivables.

THE OLDER IT GETS

A properly designed accounting system should provide for the careful screening of credit, prompt reporting of delinquent accounts, and effective collection procedures for delinquent accounts. As illustrated in the following article from a public accounting firm's newsletter, collection success depends on quick collection efforts.

There is a direct relationship between the age of outstanding receivables and the chance of successfully collecting [them]. Recently the Commercial Law League of America published the fol-

lowing data showing the precise correlation between the age of the receivable and the chance of collection:

Period of Delinquency	Collection Likelihood
1 month	94%
2 months	85%
3 months	74%
6 months	48%
9 months	43%
1 year	27%
2 years	14%

Source: "The Older It Gets," *The Advisor* (Spring, 1988), p. 2.

DIRECT WRITE-OFF METHOD OF ACCOUNTING FOR UNCOLLECTIBLES

OBJECTIVE 7
Describe and illustrate the direct write-off method of accounting for uncollectible receivables.

The use of the allowance method, as previously illustrated, results in the uncollectible accounts expense being reported in the period in which the sales are made. This matching of expenses with related revenue is the preferred method of accounting for uncollectible receivables. However, there are situations in which it is impossible to estimate, with reasonable accuracy, the uncollectibles at the end of the period. Also, if an enterprise sells most of its goods or services on a cash basis, the amount of its expense from uncollectible accounts is usually small in relation to its revenue. The amount of its receivables at any time is also likely to represent a relatively small part of its total current assets. In such cases, it is satisfactory to delay recognition of uncollectibility until the period in which certain amounts are believed to be worthless and are actually written off as an expense. Accordingly, an allowance account or an adjusting entry is not needed at the end of the period. The entry to write off an account when it is believed to be uncollectible is as follows:

May 10	Uncollectible Accounts Expense	42	
	Accounts Receivable—D. L. Ross..........		42
	To write off uncollectible account.		

If an account that has been written off is collected later, the account should be reinstated. If the recovery is in the same fiscal year as the write-off, the earlier entry should be reversed to reinstate the account. To illustrate, assume that the account written off in the May 10 entry is collected in November of the same fiscal year. The entry to reinstate the account would be as follows:

Nov. 21	Accounts Receivable—D. L. Ross.............	42	
	Uncollectible Accounts Expense		42
	To reinstate account written off earlier in the year.		

The receipt of cash in payment of the reinstated amount would be recorded in the usual manner.

When an account that has been written off is collected in a later fiscal year, it may be reinstated by an entry like that just illustrated. An alternative is to credit some other appropriately titled account, such as Recovery of Uncollectible Accounts Written Off. The credit balance in such an account at the end of the year may then be reported on the income statement as a deduction from Uncollectible Accounts Expense, or the net expense only may be reported. Such amounts are likely to be small compared to net income.

TEMPORARY INVESTMENTS

OBJECTIVE 8
Describe and illustrate the accounting for temporary investments.

A business may have a large amount of cash on hand that is not needed immediately, but this cash may be needed later in operating the business, possibly within the coming year. Rather than allow this excess cash to lie idle until it is actually needed, the business may put all or a part of it into income-yielding investments, such as certificates of deposit and money market funds. In many cases, the idle cash is invested in securities that can be quickly sold when cash is needed. Such securities are known as **temporary investments** or **marketable securities**. Although they may be retained as an investment for a number of years, they continue to be classified as temporary, provided that (1) the securities are readily marketable and thus can be sold for cash at any time and (2) management intends to sell them at such time as the enterprise needs more cash for normal operations.

Temporary investments in securities include stocks and bonds. **Stocks** are equity securities issued by corporations, and **bonds** are debt securities issued by corporations and various government agencies. Stocks and bonds held as temporary investments are classified on the balance sheet as current assets. They may be listed after "Cash," or they may be combined with cash and described as "Cash and marketable securities."

A temporary investment in a portfolio of debt securities is usually carried at cost. However, the **carrying amount** (also called **basis**) of a temporary investment in a portfolio of equity securities is the lower of its total cost or market value, determined at the date of the balance sheet.[3] Note that in the following illustration, the carrying amount is based on the comparison between the *total* cost and the *total* market value of the portfolio, rather than the lower of cost or market price of *each item*.

Temporary Investment Portfolio	Cost	Market	Unrealized Gain (Loss)
Equity security A.............................	$150,000	$100,000	$(50,000)
Equity security B.............................	200,000	200,000	—
Equity security C.............................	180,000	210,000	30,000
Equity security D.............................	160,000	150,000	(10,000)
Total	$690,000	$660,000	$(30,000)

[3]*Statement of Financial Accounting Standards, No. 12*, "Accounting for Certain Marketable Securities" (Stamford: Financial Accounting Standards Board, 1975), par. 8.

The marketable equity securities would be reported in the current assets section of the balance sheet at a cost of $690,000, less an allowance for decline to market value of $30,000, to yield a carrying amount of $660,000. The unrealized loss of $30,000 is included in the determination of net income and reported as a separate item on the income statement. If the market value of the portfolio later rises, the unrealized loss is reversed and included in net income, but only to the extent that it does not exceed the original cost. In such cases, the increase is reported separately in the Other Income section of the income statement, and the amount reported on the balance sheet is likewise adjusted.[4]

TEMPORARY INVESTMENTS AND RECEIVABLES IN THE BALANCE SHEET

OBJECTIVE 9
Describe and illustrate the presentation of temporary investments and receivables in the balance sheet.

Temporary investments and all receivables that are expected to be realized in cash within a year are presented in the Current Assets section of the balance sheet. It is customary to list the assets in the order of their liquidity, that is, in the order in which they can be converted to cash in normal operations. An illustration of the presentation of receivables and temporary investments is shown in the following partial balance sheet for Pilar Enterprises Inc.:

Temporary Investments and Receivables in Balance Sheet

Pilar Enterprises Inc. Balance Sheet December 31, 19--		
Assets		
Current assets:		
Cash...		$119,500
Marketable equity securities.................................	$690,000	
Less allowance for decline to market..................	30,000	660,000
Notes receivable...		250,000
Accounts receivable...	$445,000	
Less allowance for doubtful accounts..................	15,000	430,000
Interest receivable...		14,500

CHAPTER REVIEW

KEY POINTS

OBJECTIVE 1

Classification of Receivables

The term receivables includes all money claims against people, organizations, or other debtors. A promissory note is a written promise to pay a sum of money on demand or at a definite time. Accounts and notes receivable originating from sales transactions are called trade receivables.

---

[4] The discussion of temporary investments in this chapter focuses on the concepts applicable to their presentations on the financial statements. Other aspects of accounting for investments, such as dividend income and interest income, are discussed in Chapter 17.

OBJECTIVE 2

Control Over Receivables

The internal controls that apply to receivables include the separation of responsibility for related functions, so that the work of one employee can serve as a check on the work of another employee. For most businesses, the principal receivables are notes receivable and accounts receivable. If there are numerous notes receivable, a general ledger account for notes receivable should be supported by a notes receivable register.

OBJECTIVE 3

Characteristics of Notes Receivable

The period of time between the issuance date and the maturity date of a short-term note may be stated in either days or months. When the term of a note is stated in days, the due date is the specified number of days after its issuance. When the term of a note is stated as a number of months after the issuance date, the due date is determined by counting the number of months from the issuance date.

Interest rates for interest-bearing notes are usually stated in terms of a period of one year, regardless of the actual period of time involved. Notes covering a period of time longer than one year ordinarily provide that the interest be paid semiannually, quarterly, or at some other stated interval. The basic formula for computing interest is as follows: Principal × Rate × Time = Interest.

The amount that is due at the maturity date of a note is the maturity value. The maturity value of an interest-bearing note is the sum of the face amount and the interest.

OBJECTIVE 4

Accounting for Notes Receivable

Notes may be received by retail firms that sell merchandise on long-term credit. Such notes usually provide for monthly payments. In addition, if an account receivable becomes delinquent, the account may be converted to a note. Instead of retaining the note receivable until maturity, a note receivable may be transferred to a bank by endorsement. This transfer to a bank is called discounting the note receivable. The discount (interest) charged by the bank is computed on the maturity value of the note for the period of time the bank must hold the note until the due date. The amount of the proceeds paid to the endorser is the excess of the maturity value over the discount. Without a statement limiting responsibility, the endorser of a note is committed to paying the note if the maker should default. Such potential obligations that will become actual liabilities only if certain events occur in the future are called contingent liabilities.

If the maker of a note fails to pay the debt on the due date, the note is said to be dishonored. A dishonored note receivable is no longer negotiable, and the amount of the claim against the maker is transferred to an accounts receivable account.

OBJECTIVE 5

Uncollectible Receivables

When merchandise or services are sold on credit, a part of the claims against customers may prove to be uncollectible. The operating expense incurred because of the failure to collect receivables is called uncollectible accounts expense. There are two methods of accounting for receivables that are believed to be uncollectible: the allowance method and the direct write-off method.

OBJECTIVE 6

Allowance Method of Accounting for Uncollectibles

Most large business enterprises provide currently for the amount of their trade receivables estimated to become uncollectible. The estimate of the amount of uncollectibles may be based on either (1) the amount of sales for the entire fiscal period or (2) the amount and the age of the receivable accounts at the end of the fiscal period. An adjusting entry made at the end of the fiscal period provides for (1) the reduction of the value of the receivables to the amount of cash expected to be realized from them in the future and (2) the allocation to the current period of the expected expense resulting from such reduction. The adjusting entry debits Uncollectible Accounts Expense and credits Allowance for Doubtful Accounts. When an account is believed to be uncollectible, it is written off against the allowance account.

The allowance account, which will normally have a credit balance after the adjusting entry has been posted, is a contra asset account. The uncollectible accounts expense is generally reported on the income statement as an administrative expense.

OBJECTIVE 7   Direct Write-Off Method of Accounting for Uncollectibles

If it is impossible to estimate uncollectibles with reasonable accuracy or if most sales are made on a cash basis, it is satisfactory to delay recognition of the uncollectibility of accounts receivable until the period in which certain accounts are believed to be worthless and are actually written off as an expense. Accordingly, under this method neither an allowance account nor an adjusting entry is needed at the end of the period. The entry in this case to write off an account debits Uncollectible Accounts Expense and credits Accounts Receivable.

OBJECTIVE 8   Temporary Investments

A business may put all or part of any excess cash on hand into income-yielding investments that are readily marketable and are known as temporary investments or marketable securities. These investments may include stocks and bonds. Stocks are equity securities and bonds are debt securities issued by corporations and various governmental agencies. A temporary investment of debt securities is usually carried in the records at cost. However, a temporary investment in equity securities must be carried at the lower of its total cost or market value at the balance sheet date.

OBJECTIVE 9   Temporary Investments and Receivables in the Balance Sheet

Temporary investments and all receivables that are expected to be realized in cash within a year are presented in the Current Assets section of the balance sheet. It is customary to list the assets in the order of their liquidity, that is, in the order in which they can be converted to cash in normal operations.

KEY TERMS

promissory note 316
note receivable 317
maturity value 320
discount 322
proceeds 322
contingent liabilities 323
dishonored 324

allowance method 325
direct write-off method 325
aging the receivables 328
temporary investments 331
marketable securities 331
carrying amount 331

SELF-EXAMINATION QUESTIONS
Answers at end of chapter.

1. What is the maturity value of a 90-day, 12% note for $10,000?
    A. $8,800
    B. $10,000
    C. $10,300
    D. $11,200

2. On June 16, an enterprise discounts a 60-day, 10% note receivable for $15,000, dated June 1, at the rate of 12%. The proceeds are:
    A. $15,000.00
    B. $15,021.25
    C. $15,250.00
    D. $15,478.75

3. At the end of the fiscal year, before the accounts are adjusted, Accounts Receivable has a balance of $200,000 and Allowance for Doubtful Accounts has a credit balance of $2,500. If the estimate of uncollectible accounts determined by aging the receivables is $8,500, the current provision to be made for uncollectible accounts expense would be:
    A. $2,500   C. $8,500
    B. $6,000   D. $200,000

4. At the end of the fiscal year, Accounts Receivable has a balance of $100,000 and Allowance for Doubtful Accounts has a balance of $7,000. The expected realizable value of the accounts receivable is:
    A. $7,000   C. $100,000
    B. $93,000   D. $107,000

5. Under what caption would a temporary investment in stock be reported in the balance sheet?
    A. Current assets   C. Investments
    B. Plant assets   D. None of the above

ILLUSTRATIVE PROBLEM

Selected transactions completed by Rodriguez Company are as follows. Rodriguez Company uses the allowance method of accounting for uncollectible accounts receivable.

Jan. 28. Sold merchandise on account to Lakeland Inc., $10,000.
Mar. 1. Accepted a 60-day, 12% note for $10,000 from Lakeland Inc. on account.
Apr. 11. Wrote off a $4,500 account from Exdel Inc. as uncollectible.
     16. Loaned $7,500 cash to Thomas Glazer, receiving a 90-day, 14% note.
     30. Received the interest due from Lakeland Inc. and a new 90-day, 14% note as a renewal of the loan. (Record both the debit and credit to the notes receivable account.)
May   1. Discounted the note from Thomas Glazer at the First National Bank at 10%.
June 13. Reinstated the account of Exdel Inc., written off on April 11, and received $4,500 in full payment.
July 15. Received notice from First National Bank that Thomas Glazer dishonored his note. Paid the bank the maturity value of the note plus a $20 protest fee.
     29. Received from Lakeland Inc. the amount due on its note of April 30.
Aug. 14. Received from Thomas Glazer the amount owed on the dishonored note, plus interest for 30 days at 15%, computed on the maturity value of the note and the protest fee.
Dec. 31. It is estimated that 2% of the credit sales of $958,600 for the year ended December 31 will be uncollectible.

Instructions:

Record the transactions in general journal form.

SOLUTION

Jan. 28	Accounts Receivable — Lakeland Inc.	10,000.00	
	Sales.......................................		10,000.00
Mar. 1	Notes Receivable — Lakeland Inc. ...	10,000.00	
	Accounts Receivable —		
	Lakeland Inc..........................		10,000.00
Apr. 11	Allowance for Doubtful Accounts ...	4,500.00	
	Accounts Receivable — Exdel Inc..		4,500.00

Apr. 16	Notes Receivable—Thomas Glazer .	7,500.00	
	Cash.........................		7,500.00
30	Notes Receivable—Lakeland Inc. ...	10,000.00	
	Cash.........................	200.00	
	Notes Receivable—Lakeland Inc.		10,000.00
	Interest Income		200.00
May 1	Cash.........................	7,600.78	
	Notes Receivable—Thomas Glazer		7,500.00
	Interest Income		100.78

Face value.....................	$7,500.00	
Interest on note (90 days		
at 14%)	262.50	
Maturity value	$7,762.50	
Discount on maturity value		
(75 days at 10%)..........	161.72	
Proceeds	$7,600.78	

June 13	Accounts Receivable—Exdel Inc.....	4,500.00	
	Allowance for Doubtful Accounts		4,500.00
13	Cash.........................	4,500.00	
	Accounts Receivable—Exdel Inc..		4,500.00
July 15	Accounts Receivable—Thomas Glazer	7,782.50	
	Cash.........................		7,782.50
29	Cash.........................	10,350.00	
	Notes Receivable—Lakeland Inc.		10,000.00
	Interest Income		350.00
Aug. 14	Cash.........................	7,879.78	
	Accounts Receivable—		
	Thomas Glazer......................		7,782.50
	Interest Income		
	($7,782.50 × 15% × 30/360)		97.28
Dec. 31	Uncollectible Accounts Expense	19,172.00	
	Allowance for Doubtful Accounts		19,172.00

DISCUSSION QUESTIONS

1. What are the advantages, to the creditor, of a note receivable in comparison to an account receivable?

2. What are trade receivables?

3. In what section of the balance sheet should a note receivable be listed if its term is (a) 60 days, (b) 3 years?

4. The accounts receivable clerk is also responsible for handling cash receipts. Which principle of internal control is violated in this situation?

5. Robinson Corporation issued a promissory note to Gantt Company. (a) Who is the payee? (b) What is the title of the account employed by Gantt Company in recording the note?

6. If a note provides for payment of principal of $5,000 and interest at the rate of 10%, will the interest amount to $500? Explain.

7. The following questions refer to a 60-day, 12% note for $10,000, dated July 1: (a) What is the face value of the note? (b) What is the amount of interest payable at maturity? (c) What is the maturity value of the note? (d) What is the due date of the note?

8. At the end of the fiscal year, an enterprise holds a 60-day note receivable accepted from a customer fifteen days earlier. (a) Which of the following types of accounts will be affected by the related adjusting entry at the end of the year: (1) asset, (2) liability, (3) revenue, (4) expense? (b) If the note is held until maturity, what fraction of the total interest should be allocated to the year in which the note is collected?

9. The payee of a 90-day, 10% note for $5,000, dated April 10, endorses it to a bank on May 10. The bank discounts the note at 12%, paying the endorser $5,022.50. Identify or determine the following as they relate to the note: (a) face value, (b) maturity value, (c) due date, (d) number of days in the discount period, (e) proceeds, (f) interest income or expense recorded by endorser, (g) amount payable to the bank if the maker should default.

10. During the year, notes receivable of $175,000 were discounted at a bank by an enterprise. By the end of the year, $150,000 of these notes have matured. What is the amount of the endorser's contingent liability for notes receivable discounted at the end of the year?

11. The maker of a $4,000, 12%, 60-day note receivable failed to pay the note on the due date. What entry should be made in the accounts of the payee to record the dishonored note receivable?

12. A discounted note receivable is dishonored by the maker and the endorser pays the bank the face of the note, $5,000, the interest, $300, and a protest fee of $15. What entry should be made in the accounts of the endorser to record the payment?

13. The series of six transactions recorded in the following T accounts were related to a sale to a customer on account and receipt of the amount owed. Briefly describe each transaction.

Cash				Notes Receivable				Accounts Receivable			
(4)	9,420	(5)	9,155	(3)	9,500	(4)	9,500	(1)	10,000	(2)	500
(6)	9,200							(5)	9,155	(3)	9,500
										(6)	9,155

Sales				Interest Income				Interest Expense			
(2)	500	(1)	10,000			(6)	45	(4)	80		

14. Which of the two methods of accounting for uncollectible accounts provides for the recognition of the expense at the earlier date?

15. What kind of an account (asset, liability, etc.) is Allowance for Doubtful Accounts, and is its normal balance a debit or a credit?

16. Give the adjusting entry to increase Allowance for Doubtful Accounts by $7,225.

17. After the accounts are adjusted and closed at the end of the fiscal year, Accounts Receivable has a balance of $197,500 and Allowance for Doubtful Accounts has a balance of $8,500.
    (a) What is the expected realizable value of the accounts receivable?
    (b) If an account receivable of $900 is written off against the allowance account, what will be the expected realizable value of the accounts receivable after the write-off, assuming that no other changes in either account have occurred in the meantime?

18. A firm has consistently adjusted its allowance account at the end of the fiscal year by adding a fixed percent of the period's net sales on account. After five years, the balance in Allowance for Doubtful Accounts has become disproportionately large in relationship to the balance in Accounts Receivable. Give two possible explanations.

19. The $400 balance of an account owed by a customer is considered to be uncollectible and is to be written off. Give the entry to record the write-off in the general ledger (a) assuming that the allowance method is used and (b) assuming that the direct write-off method is used.

20. Which of the two methods of estimating uncollectibles, when advance provision for uncollectible receivables is made, provides for the most accurate estimate of the current realizable value of the receivables?

21. Under what caption should securities held as a temporary investment be reported on the balance sheet?

22. A corporation has two equity securities which it holds as a temporary investment. If they have a total cost of $190,000 and a fair market value of $185,000, at what amount should these securities be reported in the Current Assets section of the corporation's balance sheet?

Real World Focus

23. Hilton Hotels Corporation owns and operates casinos at several of its hotels, located primarily in Nevada. For the year ended December 31, 1987, the following accounts and notes receivable were reported:

(In thousands)	1987	1986
Hotel accounts and notes receivable	$75,796	$75,946
Less allowance for doubtful accounts	3,256	1,915
	$72,540	$74,031
Casino accounts receivable	$26,334	$18,205
Less allowance for doubtful accounts	6,654	4,910
	$19,680	$13,295

(a) Compute the December 31, 1987 percentage of allowance for doubtful accounts to the gross hotel accounts and notes receivable. (b) Compute the December 31, 1987 percentage of the allowance for doubtful accounts to the gross casino accounts receivable. (c) Explain any difference in the two ratios computed in (a) and (b).

EXERCISES

Exercise 8–1
Determination of due date and interest on notes.
OBJ. 3

Determine the due date and the amount of interest due at maturity on the following notes:

Date of Note	Face Amount	Term of Note	Interest Rate
(a) April 5	$ 5,000	60 days	9%
(b) May 20	8,000	90 days	11%
(c) June 30	10,000	75 days	12%
(d) August 9	3,000	120 days	10%
(e) October 11	7,500	60 days	12%

Exercise 8–2
Entries for notes receivable.
OBJ. 3, 4

Winger Company issued a 60-day, 12% note for $10,000, dated May 10, to Loggia Corporation on account.

(a) Determine the due date of the note.
(b) Determine the maturity value of the note.
(c) Present entries, in general journal form, to record the following:
    (1) Receipt of the note by the payee.
    (2) Receipt by payee of payment of the note at maturity.

Exercise 8–3
Entries for note receivable and related year-end adjustments.
OBJ. 4

The following selected transactions were completed by Boothe Co. during the current year:

Dec. 1. Received from Adams Co., on account, a $5,000, 120-day, 12% note dated December 1.
    31. Recorded an adjusting entry for accrued interest on the note of December 1.
    31. Closed the interest income account. The only entry in this account originated from the December 31 adjustment.
Jan. 1. Recorded a reversing entry for accrued interest.
Mar. 31. Received $5,200 from Adams Co. for the note due today.

(a) Record the transactions in general journal form.
(b) What is the balance in interest income after the entry of March 31?
(c) How many days' interest on $5,000 at 12% does the amount reported in (b) represent?

Exercise 8–4
Discounting note receivable.
OBJ. 4

Bosley Co. holds a 90-day, 10% note for $20,000, dated April 20, that was received from a customer on account. On May 20, the note is discounted at the First National Bank at the rate of 12%.

(a) Determine the maturity value of the note.
(b) Determine the number of days in the discount period.
(c) Determine the amount of the discount.
(d) Determine the amount of the proceeds.
(e) Present the entry, in general journal form, to record the discounting of the note on May 20.

Exercise 8–5
Entries for receipt and discounting of note receivable and dishonored note.
OBJ. 4

Record the following transactions, in general journal form, in the accounts of L. Keaton and Daughter.

March 1. Received an $8,000, 60-day, 12% note dated March 1 from Hoskins Company on account.
    21. Discounted the note at Paxton National Bank at 13%.
April 30. The note is dishonored; paid the bank the amount due on the note plus a protest fee of $15.
May 20. Received the amount due on the dishonored note plus interest for 20 days at 12% on the total amount charged to Hoskins Company on April 30.

Exercise 8–6
Entries for receipt
and dishonor of
notes receivable.
OBJ. 4

Record the following transactions, in general journal form, in the accounts of Rein-hold Co.

May 1. Received a $25,000, 30-day, 12% note dated May 1 from Southwest Corp. on account.
10. Received a $12,000, 60-day, 14% note dated May 10 from Cara Young Co. on account.
31. The note dated May 1 from Southwest Corp. is dishonored and the customer's account is charged for the note, including interest.
July 9. The note dated May 10 from Cara Young Co. is dishonored and the customer's account is charged for the note, including interest.
Aug. 11. Cash is received for the amount due on the dishonored note dated May 1 plus interest for 72 days at 12% on the total amount debited to Southwest Corp. on May 31.
30. Wrote off against the allowance account the amount charged to Cara Young Co. on July 9 for the dishonored note dated May 10.

Exercise 8–7
Provision for
doubtful accounts.
OBJ. 6

At the end of the current year, the accounts receivable account has a debit balance of $112,500, and net sales for the year total $1,200,000. Determine the amount of the adjusting entry to record the provision for doubtful accounts under each of the following assumptions:
(a) The allowance account before adjustment has a credit balance of $750.
(1) Uncollectible accounts expense is estimated at 1% of net sales.
(2) Analysis of the accounts in the customers ledger indicates doubtful accounts of $12,450.
(b) The allowance account before adjustment has a debit balance of $500.
(1) Uncollectible accounts expense is estimated at 3/4 of 1% of net sales.
(2) Analysis of the accounts in the customers ledger indicates doubtful accounts of $8,850.

Exercise 8–8
Entries for
uncollectible
receivables using
allowance method.
OBJ. 6

In general journal form, record the following transactions in the accounts of Baker Corporation, which uses the allowance method of accounting for uncollectible receivables.

Jan. 30. Sold merchandise on account to C. F. Danson, $3,300.
July 11. Received $1,980 from C. F. Danson and wrote off the remainder owed on the sale of January 30 as uncollectible.
Dec. 15. Reinstated the account of C. F. Danson that had been written off on July 11 and received $1,320 cash in full payment.

Exercise 8–9
Entries for
uncollectible
accounts, using
direct write-off
method.
OBJ. 7

In general journal form, record the following transactions in the accounts of F. L. Winston and Co., which uses the direct write-off method of accounting for uncollectible receivables.

Feb. 20. Sold merchandise on account to J. P. Sands, $2,500.
July 1. Received $1,500 from J. P. Sands and wrote off the remainder owed on the sale of February 20 as uncollectible.
Dec. 10. Reinstated the account of J. P. Sands that had been written off on July 1 and received $1,000 cash in full payment.

Exercise 8–10
Temporary equity
securities in financial
statements.
OBJ. 8

As of December 31 of the first year of operations, Godell Corporation has the following portfolio of temporary equity securities:

	Cost	Market
Security M	$30,500	$28,750
Security N	19,200	22,100
Security O	21,600	23,900
Security P	70,300	65,250

Describe how the portfolio of temporary equity securities would affect the year-end balance sheet and income statement of Godell Corporation.

PROBLEMS

Series A

Problem 8–1A

Sales, notes receivable, discounting notes receivable transactions.

OBJ. 4

The following were selected from among the transactions completed by C. J. Yeager Co. during the current year:

Mar.	1.	Sold merchandise on account to Kerr Co., $15,000.
	30.	Accepted a 60-day, 12% note for $15,000 from Kerr Co. on account.
May	29.	Received from Kerr Co. the amount due on the note of March 30.
June	1.	Sold merchandise on account to Robeson's for $5,000.
	5.	Loaned $6,000 cash to Frank Nelson, receiving a 30-day, 14% note.
	11.	Received from Robeson's the amount due on the invoice of June 1, less 1% discount.
July	5.	Received the interest due from Frank Nelson and a new 60-day, 14% note as a renewal of the loan of June 5. (Record both the debit and the credit to the notes receivable account.)
Sept.	3.	Received from Frank Nelson the amount due on his note of July 5.
	16.	Sold merchandise on account to Alice Rijo, $4,000.
Oct.	16.	Accepted a 60-day, 12% note for $4,000 from Alice Rijo on account.
Nov.	15.	Discounted the note from Alice Rijo at the Second National Bank at 10%.
Dec.	15.	Received notice from Second National Bank that Alice Rijo had dishonored its note. Paid the bank the maturity value of the note.
	30.	Received from Alice Rijo the amount owed on the dishonored note, plus interest for 15 days at 10% computed on the maturity value of the note.

Instructions:

Record the transactions in general journal form.

Problem 8–2A

Details of notes receivable, including discounting.

OBJ. 4

During the last six months of the current fiscal year, Mitchell Co. received the following notes. Notes (1), (2), (3), and (4) were discounted on the dates and at the rates indicated.

Date	Face Amount	Term	Interest Rate	Date Discounted	Discount Rate
(1) April 10	$15,000	60 days	12%	April 30	10%
(2) May 30	8,000	60 days	12%	June 9	15%
(3) July 1	45,000	90 days	10%	July 31	12%
(4) Sept. 1	10,800	60 days	11%	Oct. 11	12%
(5) Dec. 11	18,000	30 days	14%	—	—
(6) Dec. 21	36,000	60 days	13%	—	—

Instructions:

(1) Determine for each note (a) the due date and (b) the amount of interest due at maturity, identifying each note by number.

(2) Determine for each of the first four notes (a) the maturity value, (b) the discount period, (c) the discount, (d) the proceeds, and (e) the interest income or interest expense, identifying each note by number.

(3) Present, in general journal form, the entries to record the discounting of notes (2) and (3) at a bank.

(4) Assuming that notes (5) and (6) are held until maturity, determine for each the amount of interest earned (a) in the current fiscal year and (b) in the following fiscal year.

Problem 8–3A
Notes receivable entries and year-end entries; general ledger accounts.
OBJ. 4

Moore Co. closes its accounts annually as of December 31, the end of the fiscal year. The following data relate to notes receivable and interest from November 1, 1990, through March 16, 1991. (All notes are dated as of the day they are received.)

Nov. 1. Received a $30,000, 12%, 60-day note on account.
    21. Received an $18,000, 14%, 90-day note on account.
Dec. 16. Received a $12,000, 15%, 90-day note on account.
    21. Received a $10,800, 13%, 30-day note on account.
    31. Received $30,600 on note of November 1.
    31. Recorded an adjusting entry for the interest accrued on the notes dated November 21, December 16, and December 21. There are no other notes receivable on this date.
    31. Closed the interest income account.
Jan. 1. Recorded a reversing entry for the accrued interest.
    20. Received $10,917 on note of December 21.
    21. Received a $7,000, 12%, 30-day note on account.
Feb. 19. Received $18,630 on note of November 21.
    20. Received $7,070 on note of January 21.
Mar. 16. Received $12,450 on note of December 16.

Instructions:

(1) Open accounts for Interest Receivable (Account No. 116) and Interest Income (Account No. 611), and record a credit balance of $3,750 in the latter account as of November 1 of the current year.
(2) Present entries in general journal form to record the transactions and other data, posting to the two accounts after each entry affecting them.
(3) If the reversing entry had not been recorded as of January 1, indicate how each interest receipt in January, February, and March should be allocated. Submit the data in the following form:

Note (Face Amount)	Total Interest Received	Cr. Interest Receivable	Cr. Interest Income
$18,000	$	$	$
12,000			
10,800			
7,000			
Total	$	$	$

(4) Do the March 16 balances of Interest Receivable and Interest Income obtained by the use of the reversing entry technique correspond to the balances that would have been obtained by analyzing each receipt?

Problem 8–4A
Entries related to uncollectible accounts.
OBJ. 6

The following transactions, adjusting entries, and closing entries were completed during the current fiscal year ended December 31:

Jan. 19. Reinstated the account of Andrew Bowen, which had been written off in the preceding year as uncollectible. Recorded the receipt of $565 cash in full payment of Bowen's account.
Feb. 28. Wrote off the $4,650 balance owed by Picci Co., which is bankrupt.
May 7. Received 40% of the $5,000 balance owed by C. D. Clark Corp., a bankrupt business, and wrote off the remainder as uncollectible.
Oct. 19. Reinstated the account of Bob Johnson, which had been written off two years earlier as uncollectible. Recorded the receipt of $750 cash in full payment.
Dec. 30. Wrote off the following accounts as uncollectible (compound entry): Adams Co., $910; Dawson Co., $1,900; Keck Furniture, $2,775; Briana Parker, $620.

Dec. 31. Based on an analysis of the $212,750 of accounts receivable, it was estimated that $12,500 will be uncollectible. Recorded the adjusting entry.

31. Recorded the entry to close the appropriate account to Income Summary.

Instructions:

(1) Open the following selected accounts, recording the credit balance indicated as of January 1 of the current fiscal year:

115	Allowance for Doubtful Accounts	$12,900
313	Income Summary	—
718	Uncollectible Accounts Expense	—

(2) Record in general journal form the transactions and the adjusting and closing entries described. After each entry, post to the three selected accounts affected and extend the new balances.

(3) Determine the expected realizable value of the accounts receivable as of December 31.

(4) Assuming that, instead of basing the provision for uncollectible accounts on an analysis of receivables, the adjusting entry on December 31 had been based on an estimated loss of 1/2 of 1% of the net sales of $2,500,000 for the year, determine the following:

(a) Uncollectible accounts expense for the year.

(b) Balance in the allowance account after the adjustment of December 31.

(c) Expected realizable value of the accounts receivable as of December 31.

Problem 8–5A

Comparison of two methods of accounting for uncollectible receivables.

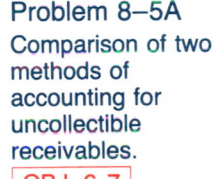

Reissen Corporation has just completed its fourth year of operations. The direct write-off method of recording uncollectible accounts expense has been employed during the entire period. Because of substantial increases in sales volume and amount of uncollectible accounts, the firm is considering the possibility of changing to the allowance method. Information is requested as to the effect that an annual provision of 1% of sales would have had on the amount of uncollectible accounts expense reported for each of the past four years. It is also considered desirable to know what the balance of Allowance for Doubtful Accounts would have been at the end of each year. The following data have been obtained from the accounts:

Year	Sales	Uncollectible Accounts Written Off	Year of Origin of Accounts Receivable Written off as Uncollectible			
			1st	2d	3d	4th
1st	$500,000	$2,250	$2,250			
2d	750,000	3,300	1,750	$1,550		
3d	850,000	5,600	1,200	2,900	$1,500	
4th	950,000	6,550		2,800	1,950	$1,800

Instructions:

(1) Assemble the desired data, using the following columnar captions:

	Uncollectible Accounts Expense			Balance of
Year	Expense Actually Reported	Expense Based on Estimate	Increase in Amount of Expense	Allowance Account, End of Year

(2) Experience during the first four years of operation indicated that the receivables were either collected within two years or had to be written off as uncollectible. Does the estimate of 1% of sales appear to be reasonably close to the actual experience with uncollectible accounts originating during the first two years?

Problem 8–6A
Financial statements for corporation.
OBJ. 9

The following data for B. N. Collins Company were selected from the ledger, after adjustment at December 31, the end of the current fiscal year:

Accounts payable	$ 24,250
Accounts receivable	48,000
Accumulated depreciation — building	162,500
Accumulated depreciation — office equipment	47,250
Administrative expenses	72,250
Allowance for decline to market of marketable securities	1,400
Allowance for doubtful accounts	2,400
Building	310,000
Capital stock	250,000
Cash	34,600
Cost of merchandise sold	514,000
Dividends	60,000
Interest and dividend income	6,100
Land	80,000
Marketable equity securities	55,000
Merchandise inventory	75,000
Notes receivable	40,000
Office equipment	79,750
Office supplies	5,500
Prepaid insurance	7,000
Retained earnings	203,400
Salaries payable	3,950
Sales	795,000
Sales discounts	6,500
Selling expenses	107,250
Unrealized loss from decline to market of marketable securities	1,400

Instructions:

(1) Prepare an income statement in multiple-step form.
(2) Prepare a retained earnings statement.
(3) Prepare a balance sheet in report form.

Series B

Problem 8–1B
Sales, notes receivable, discounting notes receivable transactions.
OBJ. 4

The following were selected from among the transactions completed by Drysdale Co. during the current year:

Jan. 10. Loaned $5,000 cash to Susan Butler, receiving a 90-day, 12% note.
Feb. 8. Sold merchandise on account to Warren Enterprises, $8,000.
20. Sold merchandise on account to C. D. Connors Co., $7,100.
Mar. 2. Received from C. D. Connors Co. the amount of the invoice of February 20, less 2% discount.
10. Accepted a 60-day, 15% note for $8,000 from Warren Enterprises on account.
Apr. 10. Received the interest due from Susan Butler and a new 90-day, 14% note as a renewal of the loan of January 10. (Record both the debit and the credit to the notes receivable account.)
May 9. Received from Warren Enterprises the amount due on the note of March 10.
July 2. Sold merchandise on account to Swartz and Sons, $20,000.
9. Received from Susan Butler the amount due on her note of April 10.

Aug. 1. Accepted a 60-day, 12% note for $20,000 from Swartz and Sons on account.
   31. Discounted the note from Swartz and Sons at the American National Bank at 14%.
Sept. 30. Received notice from the American National Bank that Swartz and Sons had dishonored its note. Paid the bank the maturity value of the note.
Oct. 30. Received from Swartz and Sons the amount owed on the dishonored note, plus interest for 30 days at 12% computed on the maturity value of the note.

Instructions:

Record the transactions in general journal form.

Problem 8–2B
Details of notes receivable, including discounting.
OBJ. 4

During the last three months of the current fiscal year, Donahoe Co. received the following notes. Notes (1), (2), (3), and (4) were discounted on the dates and at the rates indicated.

	Date	Face Amount	Term	Interest Rate	Date Discounted	Discount Rate
(1)	Oct. 10	$ 9,600	60 days	14%	Oct. 30	12%
(2)	Oct. 21	19,000	30 days	12%	Nov. 5	14%
(3)	Oct. 28	6,200	90 days	14%	Dec. 27	15%
(4)	Nov. 8	8,000	60 days	12%	Nov. 23	16%
(5)	Dec. 16	12,000	60 days	11%	—	—
(6)	Dec. 21	15,000	30 days	12%	—	—

Instructions:

(1) Determine for each note (a) the due date and (b) the amount of interest due at maturity, identifying each note by number.
(2) Determine for each of the first four notes (a) the maturity value, (b) the discount period, (c) the discount, (d) the proceeds, and (e) the interest income or interest expense, identifying each note by number.
(3) Present, in general journal form, the entries to record the discounting of notes (2) and (4) at a bank.
(4) Assuming that notes (5) and (6) are held until maturity, determine for each the amount of interest earned (a) in the current fiscal year and (b) in the following fiscal year.

Problem 8–3B
Notes receivable entries and year-end entries; general ledger accounts.
OBJ. 4

Southern Corporation closes its accounts annually as of December 31, the end of the fiscal year. The following data relate to notes receivable and interest from November 1, 1990, through March 11, 1991. (All notes are dated as of the day they are received.)

Nov. 1. Received a $7,500, 14%, 60-day note on account.
   11. Received a $30,000, 12%, 120-day note on account.
Dec. 16. Received a $24,000, 13%, 60-day note on account.
   21. Received a $12,000, 12%, 30-day note on account.
   31. Received $7,675 on note of November 1.
   31. Recorded an adjusting entry for the interest accrued on the notes dated November 11, December 16, and December 21. There are no other notes receivable on this date.
   31. Closed the interest income account.
Jan. 1. Recorded a reversing entry for the accrued interest.
   20. Received $12,120 on note of December 21.
   26. Received a $9,000, 12%, 30-day note on account.
Feb. 14. Received $24,520 on note of December 16.
   25. Received $9,090 on note of January 26.
Mar. 11. Received $31,200 on note of November 11.

Instructions:

(1) Open accounts for Interest Receivable (Account No. 116) and Interest Income (Account No. 611), and record a credit balance of $5,200 in the latter account as of November 1 of the current year.

(2) Present entries in general journal form to record the transactions and other data, posting to the two accounts after each entry affecting them.

(3) If the reversing entry had not been recorded as of January 1, indicate how each interest receipt in January, February, and March should be allocated. Submit the data in the following form:

Note (Face Amount)	Total Interest Received	Cr. Interest Receivable	Cr. Interest Income
$12,000	$	$	$
24,000			
9,000			
30,000			
Total	$	$	$

(4) Do the March 10 balances of Interest Receivable and Interest Income obtained by use of the reversing entry technique correspond to the balances that would have been obtained by analyzing each receipt?

Problem 8–4B
Entries related to uncollectible accounts.
OBJ. 6

The following transactions, adjusting entries, and closing entries were completed during the current fiscal year ended December 31:

Jan. 22. Received 70% of the $5,000 balance owed by White Co., a bankrupt business, and wrote off the remainder as uncollectible.

Mar. 5. Reinstated the account of Patrick Lynskey, which had been written off in the preceding year as uncollectible. Recorded the receipt of $725 cash in full payment of Lynskey's account.

July 27. Wrote off the $8,900 balance owed by Martin Corp., which has no assets.

Sept. 7. Reinstated the account of W. W. Bacon Inc., which had been written off in the preceding year as uncollectible. Recorded the receipt of $2,950 cash in full payment of the account.

Dec. 30. Wrote off the following accounts as uncollectible (compound entry): Davis Co., $3,950; Nance Inc., $4,600; Powell Distributors, $6,500; J. J. Stevens, $4,200.

31. Based on an analysis of the $580,000 of accounts receivable, it was estimated that $31,250 will be uncollectible. Recorded the adjusting entry.

31. Recorded the entry to close the appropriate account to Income Summary.

Instructions:

(1) Open the following selected accounts, recording the credit balance indicated as of January 1 of the current fiscal year:

115	Allowance for Doubtful Accounts	$28,250
313	Income Summary	—
718	Uncollectible Accounts Expense	—

(2) Record in general journal form the transactions and the adjusting and closing entries previously described. After each entry, post to the three selected accounts affected and extend the new balances.

(3) Determine the expected realizable value of the accounts receivable as of December 31.

(Continued)

(4) Assuming that, instead of basing the provision for uncollectible accounts on an analysis of receivables, the adjusting entry on December 31 had been based on an estimated loss of 1/2 of 1% of the net sales of $5,500,000 for the year, determine the following:

(a) Uncollectible accounts expense for the year.
(b) Balance in the allowance account after the adjustment of December 31.
(c) Expected realizable value of the accounts receivable as of December 31.

MINI-CASE 8

For several years, Myers' sales have been on a "cash only" basis. On January 1, 1987, however, Myers began offering credit on terms of n/30. The amount of the adjusting entry to record the estimated uncollectible receivables at the end of each year has been 1/2 of 1% of credit sales, which is the rate reported as the average for the industry. Credit sales and the year-end credit balances in Allowance for Doubtful Accounts for the past four years are as follows:

Year	Credit Sales	Allowance for Doubtful Accounts
1987	$5,000,000	$ 7,500
1988	4,700,000	10,000
1989	5,200,000	14,500
1990	4,500,000	18,000

Ethyl Myers, president of Myers, is concerned that the method used to account for and write off uncollectible receivables is unsatisfactory. She has asked for your advice in the analysis of past operations in this area and for recommendations for change.

Instructions:

(1) Determine the amount of (a) the addition to Allowance for Doubtful Accounts and (b) the accounts written off for each of the four years.
(2) Advise Ethyl Myers as to whether the estimate of 1/2 of 1% of credit sales appears reasonable.
(3) Assume that after discussing item (2) with Ethyl Myers, she asked you what action might be taken to determine what the balance of Allowance for Doubtful Accounts should be at December 31, 1990, and possible changes, if any, you might recommend in accounting for uncollectible receivables. How would you respond?

ETHICS DISCUSSION CASE

Cathy Stanfield, controller of Federal Savings Bank of Bogart, has instructed the bank's computer programmer to program the bank's computers to calculate interest on depository accounts (payables) using the 365-day year and to calculate interest on loans (receivables) using the 360-day year.

Discuss whether Cathy Stanfield is behaving in an ethical manner.

ANSWERS TO SELF-EXAMINATION QUESTIONS

1. C Maturity value is the amount that is due at the maturity or due date. The maturity value of $10,300 (answer C) is determined as follows:

Face amount of note	$10,000
Plus interest ($10,000 × 12/100 × 90/360)	300
Maturity value of note	$10,300

2. B The proceeds of $15,021.25 (answer B) are determined as follows:

Face value of note dated June 1	$15,000.00
Interest on note (60 days at 10%)	250.00
Maturity value of note due July 31	$15,250.00
Discount on maturity value (45 days, from June 16 to July 31 at 12%)	228.75
Proceeds	$15,021.25

3. B The estimate of uncollectible accounts, $8,500 (answer C), is the amount of the desired balance of Allowance for Doubtful Accounts *after adjustment*. The amount of the current provision to be made for uncollectible accounts expense is thus $6,000 (answer B), which is the amount that must be added to the Allowance for Doubtful Accounts credit balance of $2,500 (answer A), so that the account will have the desired balance of $8,500.

4. B The amount expected to be realized from accounts receivable is the balance of Accounts Receivable, $100,000, less the balance of Allowance for Doubtful Accounts, $7,000, or $93,000 (answer B).

5. A Securities held as temporary investments are classified on the balance sheet as current assets (answer A).

CHAPTER NINE
INVENTORIES

CHAPTER OBJECTIVES

1 Describe and illustrate the effect of inventory on the financial statements of the current period and the following period.

2 Identify and describe the two principal inventory systems.

3 Identify and illustrate the procedures for determining the actual quantities in inventory.

4 Describe and illustrate the determination of the cost of inventory.

5 Describe and illustrate the most common inventory costing methods under a periodic system, including the comparison

of the effect of the methods on operating results.

6 Describe and illustrate the accounting for inventory under the perpetual system.

7 Describe and illustrate the valuation of inventory at other than cost, including valuation at the lower of cost or market.

8 Identify and illustrate the proper presentation of inventory in the financial statements.

9 Describe and illustrate methods of estimating the cost of inventory.

The term **inventories** is used to designate (1) merchandise held for sale in the normal course of business, and (2) materials in the process of production or held for such use. This chapter discusses the determination of the inventory of merchandise purchased for resale, commonly called **merchandise inventory.** Inventories of raw materials and partially processed materials of a manufacturing enterprise will be considered in a later chapter.

IMPORTANCE OF INVENTORIES

OBJECTIVE 1
Describe and illustrate the effect of inventory on the financial statements of the current period and the following period.

Merchandise, being continually purchased and sold, is one of the most active elements in the operation of wholesale and retail businesses. The sale of merchandise provides the principal source of revenue for such enterprises. When the net income is determined, the cost of merchandise sold is normally the largest deduction from sales. In fact, it is usually larger than all other deductions combined. In addition, a substantial part of a merchandising firm's resources is invested in inventory. It is frequently the largest of the current assets of such a firm.

The Effect of Inventory on the Current Period's Statements

Inventory determination plays an important role in matching expired costs with revenues of the period. As was explained and illustrated in Chapter 4, the total cost of merchandise available for sale during a period of time must be divided into two parts at the end of the period. The cost of the merchandise determined to be in the inventory will appear on the balance sheet as a current asset. The other element, which is the cost of the merchandise sold, will be reported on the income statement as a deduction from net sales to yield gross profit. An error in the determination of the inventory amount at the end of the period will cause an equal misstatement of gross profit and net income, and the amount reported for both assets and owner's equity in the balance sheet will be incorrect by the same amount. The effects of understatements and overstatements of merchandise inventory at the end of the period are demonstrated in the following three sets of condensed income statements and balance sheets. The first set of statements is based on a correct ending inventory of $20,000; the second set, on an *incorrect ending inventory of $12,000;* and the third set, on an *incorrect ending inventory of $27,000.* In all three cases, net sales are $200,000, merchandise available for sale is $140,000, and expenses are $55,000.

Income Statement for the Year   Balance Sheet at End of Year

1. Inventory at end of period correctly stated at $20,000.

Net sales	$200,000	Merchandise inventory	$ 20,000
Cost of merchandise sold	120,000	Other assets	80,000
Gross profit	$ 80,000	Total	$100,000
Expenses	55,000		
		Liabilities	$ 30,000
Net income	$ 25,000	Owner's equity	70,000
		Total	$100,000

2. Inventory at end of period incorrectly stated at $12,000; (understated by $8,000).

Net sales	$200,000	Merchandise inventory	$ 12,000
Cost of merchandise sold	128,000	Other assets	80,000
Gross profit	$ 72,000	Total	$ 92,000
Expenses	55,000		
		Liabilities	$ 30,000
Net income	$ 17,000	Owner's equity	62,000
		Total	$ 92,000

3. Inventory at end of period incorrectly stated at $27,000; (overstated by $7,000).

Net sales	$200,000	Merchandise inventory	$ 27,000
Cost of merchandise sold	113,000	Other assets	80,000
Gross profit	$ 87,000	Total	$107,000
Expenses	55,000		
		Liabilities	$ 30,000
Net income	$ 32,000	Owner's equity	77,000
		Total	$107,000

Note that in the illustration the total cost of merchandise available for sale was constant at $140,000. It was the way in which the cost was allocated that varied. The variations in allocating the $140,000 of merchandise cost are summarized as follows:

	Merchandise Available		
	Total	*Inventory*	*Sold*
1. Inventory correctly stated............................	$140,000	$20,000	$120,000
2. Inventory understated by $8,000..................	140,000	12,000	128,000
3. Inventory overstated by $7,000....................	140,000	27,000	113,000

The effect of the errors on net income, assets, and owner's equity may also be summarized. Comparison of the financial statements in *2* and *3* with the financial statements in *1* yields the following:

	Net Income	Assets	Owner's Equity
2. Ending inventory understated $8,000	Understated $8,000	Understated $8,000	Understated $8,000
3. Ending inventory overstated $7,000	Overstated $7,000	Overstated $7,000	Overstated $7,000

The Effect of Inventory on the Following Period's Statements

The inventory at the end of one period becomes the inventory for the beginning of the following period. Thus, if the inventory is incorrectly stated at the end of the period, the net income of that period will be misstated and so will the net income for the following period. The amount of the two misstatements will be equal and in opposite directions. Therefore, the effect on net income of an incorrectly stated inventory, if not corrected, is limited to the period of the error and the following period. At the end of this following period, assuming no additional errors, both assets and owner's equity will be correctly stated. To illustrate, assume that the ending inventory for period *1* was understated by $10,000, and no other errors are made. The gross profit (and net income) would be understated for period *1* and overstated for period *2* by $10,000, indicated as follows:

	Period 1				Period 2			
	No Error		*Error*		*Error*		*No Error*	
Net sales		$90,000		$90,000		$85,000		$85,000
Cost of merchandise sold:								
Beginning inventory...............	$25,000				**$20,000**		$30,000	
Purchases.............................	70,000		70,000		65,000		65,000	
Merchandise available for sale .	$95,000		$95,000		$85,000		$95,000	
Less ending inventory.............	30,000		**20,000**		28,000		28,000	
Cost of merchandise sold.....		65,000		75,000		57,000		67,000
Gross profit		$25,000		$15,000		$28,000		$18,000

Understated $10,000   Overstated $10,000

In the illustration, the $10,000 understatement of inventory at the end of period *1* resulted in an overstatement of the cost of merchandise sold and thus an understatement of gross profit by $10,000. On the balance sheet, merchandise inventory and owner's equity would both be understated by $10,000. Because the ending inventory of period *1* becomes the beginning inventory for period *2*, the cost of merchandise sold was understated and gross profit was overstated by $10,000 for period *2*. Both merchandise inventory and owner's equity will be correct at the end of period *2*.

FALSIFIED INVENTORY AND INCOME INFLATE COMPANY'S VALUE

The importance of inventory to financial statements is recognized even by those who attempt to manipulate a company's statements in a fraudulent manner. One example of such inventory fraud is described in the following excerpt from an article in *The Wall Street Journal*:

Until last year, Crazy Eddie Inc. steadily recorded superb gains in sales and earnings, apparently because of rapid expansion of its electronics stores, adept sales-floor techniques and catchy commercials.

But the now-troubled company's latest court and regulatory filings suggest another element: a possible scheme by founder Eddie Antar and others to falsify inventory and profit reports....

...Crazy Eddie says its former management—led by Mr. Antar—created "phantom" inventory and profits, then destroyed records in a cover-up. The purpose, the company says...was to "artificially inflate the net worth of the company" and the value of stock owned by Mr. Antar and others.

For instance, Crazy Eddie says the former management inflated the March 1987 inventory count at one warehouse by $10 million, by drafting phony count sheets and, among other things, improperly including $4 million in merchandise that was [recorded as] being returned to suppliers. Stores were also packed with unrecorded [purchases] prior to physical [inventory] counts....

Source: Jeffrey A. Tannenbaum, "Filings by Crazy Eddie Suggest Founder Led Scheme to Inflate Company's Value," *The Wall Street Journal* (May 31, 1988), p. 28.

INVENTORY SYSTEMS

OBJECTIVE 2
Identify and describe the two principal inventory systems.

There are two principal systems of inventory accounting—periodic and perpetual. When the **periodic inventory system** is used, only the revenue from sales is recorded each time a sale is made. No entry is made at the time of the sale to record the cost of the merchandise that has been sold. Consequently, a **physical inventory** must be taken in order to determine the cost of the inventory at the end of an accounting period. Ordinarily, it is practical to take a complete physical inventory only at the end of the fiscal year. In the earlier chapters dealing with purchases and sales of merchandise, the use of the periodic system was assumed.

In contrast to the periodic system, the **perpetual inventory system** uses accounting records that continuously disclose the amount of the inventory. A separate account for each type of merchandise is maintained in a subsidiary ledger. Increases in inventory items are recorded as debits to the proper accounts, and decreases are recorded as credits. The balances of the accounts are called the **book inventories** of the items on hand. Regardless of the care with which the perpetual inventory records are maintained, their accuracy must be tested by taking a physical inventory of each type of commodity at least once a year. The records are then compared with the actual quantities on hand and any differences are corrected.

The periodic inventory system is often used by retail enterprises that sell many kinds of low unit cost merchandise, such as groceries, hardware, and drugs. The expense of maintaining perpetual inventory records may be prohibitive in such cases. In recent years, however, the use of computerized systems in such businesses has reduced this expense considerably. Firms selling a relatively small number of high unit cost items, such as office equipment, automobiles, or fur garments, are more likely to use the perpetual system.

Although much of the discussion that follows applies to both systems, the use of the periodic inventory system will be assumed. Later in the chapter, principles and procedures related only to the perpetual inventory system will be presented.

DETERMINING ACTUAL QUANTITIES IN THE INVENTORY

OBJECTIVE 3
Identify and illustrate the procedures for determining the actual quantities in inventory.

The first stage in the process of "taking" an inventory is to determine the quantity of each kind of merchandise owned by the enterprise. When the periodic system is used, the counting, weighing, and measuring should be done at the end of the accounting period. To accomplish this, the inventory crew may work during the night, or business operations may be stopped until the count is finished.

The details of the specific procedures for determining quantities and assembling the data differ among companies. A common practice is to use teams made up of two persons. One person counts, weighs, or otherwise determines quantity, and the other lists the description and the quantity on inventory sheets. The quantity indicated for high-cost items is verified by a third person at some time during the inventory-taking period. It is also advisable for the third person to verify other items selected at random from the inventory sheets.

All of the merchandise owned by the business on the inventory date, and only such merchandise, should be included in the inventory. It may be necessary to examine purchase and sales invoices of the last few days of the accounting period and the first few days of the following period to determine who has legal title to merchandise in transit on the inventory date. As discussed in Chapter 4, the shipping terms are an indication of when title passes. When goods are purchased or sold **FOB shipping point**, title usually passes to the buyer when the goods are shipped. When the terms are **FOB destination**, title usually does not pass to the buyer until the goods are delivered. To illustrate, assume that merchandise purchased FOB shipping point is shipped by the seller on the last day of the buyer's fiscal period. The merchandise does not arrive until the following period and hence is not available for "counting" by the inventory crew. However, such merchandise should be included in the buyer's inventory because title has passed. It is also evident that a debit to Purchases and a credit to Accounts Payable should be recorded by the buyer as of the end of the current period, rather than recording it as a transaction of the following period.

Another example, although less common, will further show the importance of closely examining transactions involving shipments of merchandise. Manufacturers sometimes ship merchandise on a consignment basis to retailers who act as the manufacturer's agent when selling the merchandise. The manufacturer retains title until the goods are sold. Obviously, such unsold merchandise is a part of the manufacturer's (consignor's) inventory, even though the manufacturer does not have physical possession. It is just as obvious that the consigned merchandise should not be included in the retailer's (consignee's) inventory.

DETERMINING THE COST OF INVENTORY

The cost of merchandise inventory is made up of the purchase price and all expenditures incurred in acquiring such merchandise, including transportation, customs duties, and insurance against losses in transit. The purchase price can be readily determined, as may some of the other costs. Those that are difficult to associate with specific inventory items may be prorated on some equitable basis. Minor costs that are difficult to allocate may be left out entirely from inventory cost and treated as operating expenses of the period.

If purchases discounts are treated as a deduction from purchases on the income statement, they should also be deducted from the purchase price of items in the inventory. If it is not possible to determine the exact amount of discount applicable to each inventory item, a pro rata amount of the total discount for the period may be deducted instead. For example, if net purchases and purchases discounts for the period amount to $200,000 and $3,000 respectively, the discounts represent 1½% of net purchases. If the inventory cost before considering the cash discounts is $30,000, the amount may be reduced by 1½%, or $450, to yield an inventory cost of $29,550.

INVENTORY COSTING METHODS UNDER A PERIODIC SYSTEM

One of the most significant problems in determining inventory cost comes about when identical units of a certain commodity have been acquired at different unit cost prices during the period. In such cases, it is necessary to determine the unit prices of the items still on hand. To illustrate this problem and its relationship to the determination of net income and inventory cost, assume that three identical units of Commodity X were available for sale to customers during the fiscal year. One of these units was in the inventory at the beginning of the year, and the other two were purchased on March 4 and May 9 respectively. The costs per unit are as follows:

Commodity X	Units	Cost
Jan. 1 Inventory..............................	1	$ 9
Mar. 4 Purchase	1	13
May 9 Purchase	1	14
Total...	3	$36
Average cost per unit.......................		$12

During the year, two units of Commodity X were sold, leaving one unit in the inventory at the end of the year. In the illustration, the units are easily identified with specific expenditures because both the variety of merchandise carried in stock and the volume of sales are relatively small. Since these conditions do not usually exist in actual practice, businesses are not likely to use **specific identification** procedures except with the aid of computerized accounting systems and equipment that can read inventory labels (bar codes). When specific identification procedures are too costly to justify their use, it is customary to use an arbitrary assumption as to the *flow of costs* of merchandise through the enterprise. The three most common assumptions of determining the cost of the merchandise sold are as follows:

1. Cost flow is in the order in which the expenditures were made — first-in, first-out.
2. Cost flow is in the reverse order in which the expenditures were made — last-in, first-out.
3. Cost flow is an average of the expenditures.

Details of the cost of the two units of Commodity X assumed to be sold and the cost of the one unit remaining, determined in accordance with each of these assumptions, are as follows:

	Commodity X Costs		
	Units Available	*Units Sold*	*Unit Remaining*
1. In order of expenditures (first-in, first-out)	$36 −	($ 9 + $13) =	$14
2. In reverse order of expenditures (last-in, first-out).	36 −	(14 + 13) =	9
3. In accordance with average expenditures	36 −	(12 + 12) =	12

The three most widely used inventory costing methods (which correspond to the three assumptions of cost flows illustrated) are:

1. **First-in, first-out (fifo)**
2. **Last-in, first-out (lifo)**
3. **Average**

The extent of the use of these three methods is indicated by the following chart:

Inventory Costing Methods

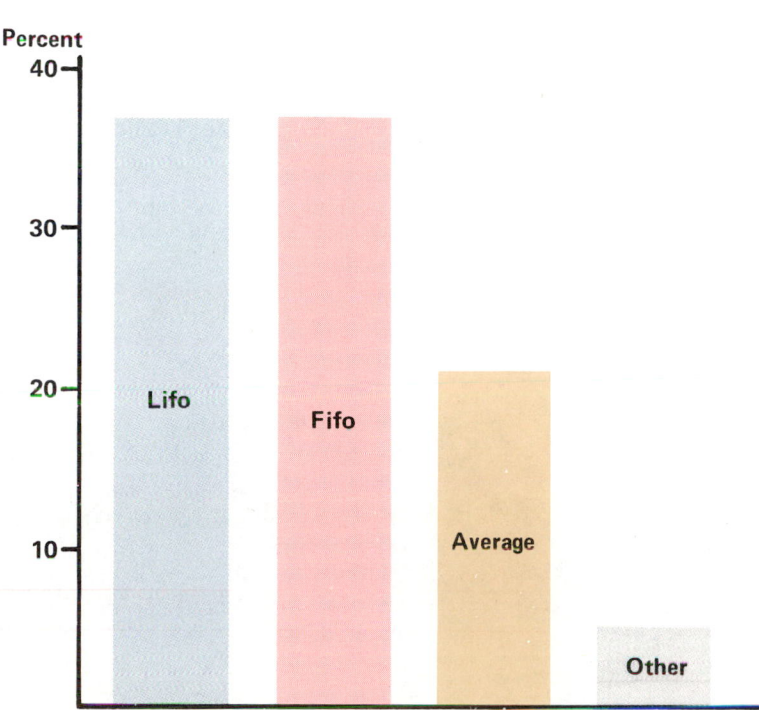

Source: *Accounting Trends & Techniques,* 42d ed. (New York: American Institute of Certified Public Accountants, 1988).

First-In, First-Out Method

The **first-in, first-out (fifo) method** of costing inventory is based on the assumption that costs should be charged against revenue in the order in which they were incurred. Hence the inventory remaining is assumed to be made up of the most recent costs. The illustration of the application of this method is based on the following data for a particular commodity:

Jan.	1	Inventory	200 units at $ 9	$ 1,800
Mar.	10	Purchase	300 units at 10	3,000
Sept.	21	Purchase	400 units at 11	4,400
Nov.	18	Purchase	100 units at 12	1,200
		Available for sale during year	1,000	$10,400

The physical count on December 31 shows that 300 units of the particular commodity are on hand. In accordance with the assumption that the inventory is composed of the most recent costs, the cost of the 300 units is determined as follows:

Most recent costs, Nov. 18	100 units at $12	$1,200
Next most recent costs, Sept. 21	200 units at 11	2,200
Inventory, Dec. 31	300	$3,400

Deduction of the inventory of **$3,400** from the **$10,400** of merchandise available for sale yields **$7,000** as the cost of merchandise sold, which represents the earliest costs incurred for this commodity. The relationship of the inventory at December 31 and the cost of merchandise sold during the year is illustrated in the following diagram:

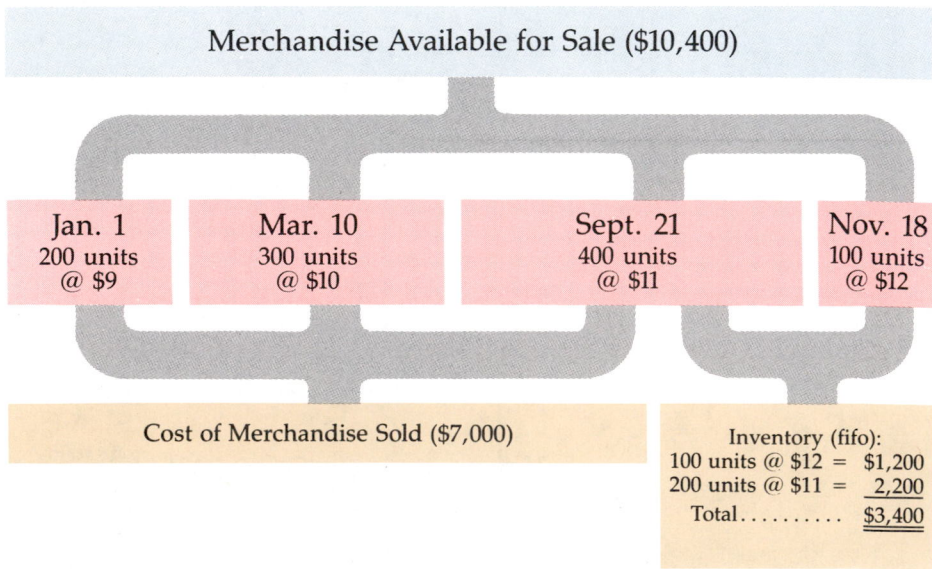

In most businesses, there is a tendency to dispose of goods in the order of their acquisition. This would be particularly true of perishable merchandise and goods in which style or model changes are frequent. Thus, the fifo method is generally in harmony with the physical movement of merchandise in an enterprise. To the extent that this is the case, the fifo method approximates the results that would be obtained by the specific identification of costs.

Last-In, First-Out Method

The **last-in, first-out (lifo) method** is based on the assumption that the most recent costs incurred should be charged against revenue. Hence the inventory remaining is assumed to be composed of the earliest costs. Based on the illustrative data presented in the preceding section, the cost of the 300 units of inventory is determined in the following manner:

Earliest costs, Jan. 1	200 units at $ 9................	$1,800
Next earliest costs, Mar. 10..............	100 units at 10................	1,000
Inventory, Dec. 31	300...............................	$2,800

Deduction of the inventory of **$2,800** from the **$10,400** of merchandise available for sale yields **$7,600** as the cost of merchandise sold, which represents the most recent costs incurred for this particular commodity. The relationship of the inventory at December 31 and the cost of merchandise sold during the year is illustrated in the following diagram:

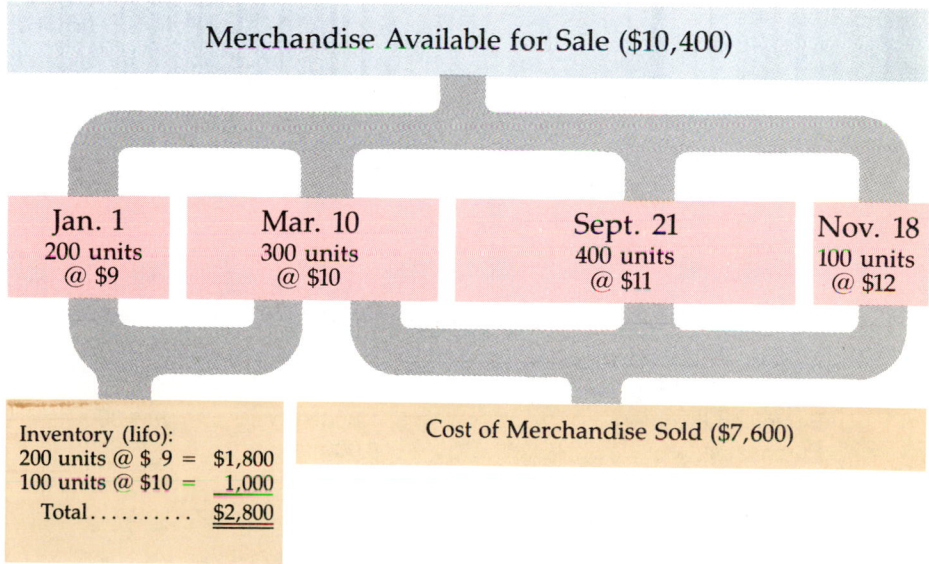

The use of the lifo method was originally confined to the relatively rare situations in which the units sold were taken from the most recently acquired stock. Because of tax considerations, its use has greatly increased during the past few decades, and it is now often used even when it does not represent the physical flow of goods.

Average Cost Method

The **average cost method,** sometimes called the **weighted average method,** is based on the assumption that costs should be charged against revenue according to the weighted average unit costs of the goods sold. The same weighted average unit costs are used in determining the cost of the merchandise remaining in the inventory. The weighted average unit cost is determined by dividing the total cost of the identical units of each commodity available for sale during the period by the related number of units of that commodity. Assuming the same cost data as in the preceding illustrations, the average cost of the 1,000 units and the cost of the 300 units in inventory are determined as follows:

Average unit cost.............. $10,400 ÷ 1,000 = $10.40
Inventory, Dec. 31 .... 300 units at $10.40 .... $3,120

Deduction of the inventory of $3,120 from the $10,400 of merchandise available for sale yields $7,280 as the cost of merchandise sold, which represents the average of the costs incurred for this commodity.

For businesses in which various purchases of identical units of a commodity are mingled, the average method has some relationship to the physical flow of goods.

Comparison of Inventory Costing Methods

Each of the three alternative methods of costing inventories under the periodic system is based on a different assumption as to the flow of costs. If the cost of units and prices at which they were sold had remained stable, all three methods would have yielded the same results. Prices do change, however, and as a consequence the three methods will usually yield different amounts for (1) the inventory reported on the balance sheet at the end of the period, (2) the cost of the merchandise sold for the period, and (3) the gross profit (and net income) reported for the period. Using the examples presented in the preceding sections and assuming that net sales were $15,000, the following partial income statements indicate the effects of each method when prices are rising:

	First-In, First-Out		Average Cost		Last-In, First-Out	
Net sales.......................................		$15,000		$15,000		$15,000
Cost of merchandise sold:						
Beginning inventory.....................	$ 1,800		$ 1,800		$ 1,800	
Purchases	8,600		8,600		8,600	
Merchandise available for sale......	$10,400		$10,400		$10,400	
Less ending inventory	3,400		3,120		2,800	
Cost of merchandise sold		7,000		7,280		7,600
Gross profit.............................		$ 8,000		$ 7,720		$ 7,400

As shown in the income statements, the fifo method yielded the lowest amount for the cost of merchandise sold and the highest amount for gross profit (and net income). It also yielded the highest amount for the ending inventory. On the other hand, the lifo method yielded the highest amount for the cost of merchandise sold, the lowest amount for gross profit (and net income), and the lowest amount for ending inventory. The average cost method yielded results that were between those of fifo and lifo.

Use of the First-In, First-Out Method. During a period of inflation or rising prices, the use of the fifo method will result in the effects shown in the illustration because the costs of the units sold are assumed to be in the order in which they were incurred, and the earlier unit costs were lower than the more recent unit costs. Much of the benefit of the larger amount of gross profit is lost, however, as the inventory is continually replenished at ever higher prices. During the 1970s, when the rate of inflation increased to double-digit percentages, the larger gross profits that resulted were frequently referred to as *inventory profits* or *illusory profits.*

In a period of deflation or declining prices, the effect described above is reversed, and the fifo method yields the lowest amount of gross profit. The major criticism of the fifo method is this tendency to maximize the effect of inflationary and deflationary trends on amounts reported as gross profit. However, the dollar amount reported as merchandise inventory on the balance sheet will usually be about the same as its current replacement cost.

Use of the Last-In, First-Out Method. During a period of rising prices, the use of the last-in, first-out method will result in a lower amount of inventory at the end of the period, a higher amount of cost of merchandise sold, and a lower amount of gross profit than the other two methods. The reason for these effects is that the cost of the most recently acquired units most nearly approximates the cost of their replacement, and the more recent unit costs were higher than the earlier unit costs. Thus, it can be argued that the use of the lifo method more nearly matches current costs with current revenues. This latter point was one reason that Chrysler Corporation changed from the fifo method to the lifo method in 1984, as stated in the following footnote that accompanied Chrysler's financial statements for 1984:

Effective January 1, 1984, Chrysler changed its method of accounting from first-in, first-out (fifo) to last-in, first-out (lifo) for substantially all of its domestic productive inventories. The change to lifo was made to more accurately match current costs with current revenues. Had the inventory, at December 31, 1984, been valued on the fifo basis, it would have been $29.7 million higher than reported.

During periods of rising prices, the use of lifo offers a savings in income taxes. The income tax savings results because lifo reports the lowest amount of net income of the three methods. During the accelerated inflationary trend of the 1970s, many business enterprises changed from fifo to lifo to take advantage of this tax savings.

In a period of deflation or falling price levels, the effect described above is reversed and the lifo method yields the highest amount of gross profit. The major justification for lifo is this tendency to minimize the effect of price trends on reported gross profit and, therefore, to exert a stabilizing influence on the economy. A criticism of the use of lifo is that the dollar amount reported for merchandise inventory on the balance sheet may be quite far removed from the current replacement cost. In such situations, however, it is customary to indicate in a note accompanying the published financial statements the approximate difference between the lifo inventory amount and the inventory amount if fifo had been used. The following note accompanying the 1988 statements of The Walgreen Co. is illustrative:

Inventories are valued on a last-in, first-out (LIFO) cost basis. At August 31, 1988 and 1987, inventories would have been greater by $208,894,000 and $179,282,000 respectively, if they had been valued on a lower of first-in, first-out (FIFO) cost or market basis.

INFLATION AND ADOPTION OF LIFO

The effects of using lifo and some of the reasons that the method is adopted (or not adopted) by businesses were discussed in an article in *Management Accounting*. Some excerpts from that article follow.

...The primary advantage of lifo is that in today's inflationary environment lifo defers (not avoids) income taxes by reducing income. The improved cash flow, then, can be profitably invested or used to reduce borrowings....

In addition to deferring income taxes, though, lifo has a great deal of theoretical justification. By matching current costs against current sales, lifo produces a truer picture of income; that is, the quality of income produced by the use of lifo is higher because it more nearly approximates disposable income....

Even though the primary advantage of lifo—reduced tax payments—is a function of lower income, the negative earnings impact ironically continues to cloud corporate managers' decisions about the adoption of lifo. Managers fear that lower reported earnings will [have unfavorable effects on the stock price, executive compensation contracts, and credit ratings. However,] there is little evidence to suggest that stock price is adversely affected by lifo adoption. Furthermore, [lifo should have no effect on executive compensation contracts or credit ratings.]

The Internal Revenue Code...and Treasury Regulations...[mandate] that taxpayers who avail themselves of the federal income tax benefits of the lifo method also must use lifo "...for credit purposes or for purposes of reports to shareholders, partners, or other proprietors, or to beneficiaries...." Thus, the lifo conformity requirement is the culprit behind the negative earnings impact issue. However, regulations adopted in January, 1981, although not going to the extent of allowing the use of lifo in tax returns and a non-lifo method elsewhere, did relax the conformity requirement significantly, such that it is now possible to present non-lifo information very favorably in lifo-based reports....

...[The] non-lifo data may be presented in the notes to the financial statements as in the...Merck & Co. Inc. Annual Report: "...Lifo had the effect of reducing...net income by $21,108,000 ($.28 per share)...with a positive increase to cash flow of $19,500,000...as a result of decreased U.S. taxes."

...Another concern about lifo commonly expressed by corporate managers is misstatement of the inventories on the lifo balance sheet. Particularly over a period of rapidly rising inventory quantities and prices, the use of lifo can lead to a valuation of inventories that is significantly less than current replacement cost. However, this misstatement can be mitigated by presenting inventories valued on a non-lifo basis and deducting the lifo valuation [allowance to reduce the balance sheet inventory to the lifo amount, as follows:]

Inventory	XXX
Less reduction to lifo cost	XXX
Total	XXX

Source: Clayton T. Rumble, "So You Still Have Not Adopted Lifo," *Management Accounting* (October, 1983), pp. 59–67.

Use of the Average Cost Method. The average cost method of inventory costing is, in a sense, a compromise between fifo and lifo. The effect of price trends is averaged, both in the determination of gross profit and in the determination of inventory cost. For any given series of acquisitions, the average cost will be the same, regardless of the direction of price trends. For example, a complete reversal of the sequence of unit costs presented in the illustration on page 356 would not affect the reported gross profit or the inventory cost. The time required to assemble the data is likely to be greater for the average cost method than for the other two methods. The additional expense incurred could be large if there are many purchases of a wide variety of merchandise items.

Selection of an Inventory Costing Method. The foregoing comparisons show the importance attached to the selection of the inventory costing method. It is not unusual for manufacturing enterprises to apply one method to a particular class of inventory, such as merchandise ready for sale, and a different method to another class, such as raw materials purchased. The method(s) used may be changed for a valid reason. The effect of any change in method and the reason for the change should be fully disclosed in the financial statements for the fiscal period in which the change occurred.

ACCOUNTING FOR AND REPORTING INVENTORY UNDER A PERPETUAL SYSTEM

OBJECTIVE 6
Describe and illustrate the accounting for inventory under the perpetual system.

Under the periodic inventory system, as described in earlier chapters, the merchandise inventory account at the beginning of an accounting period reflects the merchandise on hand on that date. Purchases of merchandise are recorded in the purchases account, and sales of merchandise are recorded in the sales account. The cost of the merchandise sold is not determined for each sale. Instead, at the end of an accounting period, when a physical inventory is taken, two adjusting entries are made.[1] With these entries, the beginning inventory is removed from the merchandise inventory account and is replaced by the ending inventory. This adjusted balance of merchandise inventory is reported on the balance sheet. The cost of merchandise sold is then determined, and this amount is reported on the income statement.

Under the perpetual inventory system, all merchandise increases and decreases are recorded in a manner somewhat similar to the recording of increases and decreases in cash. The merchandise inventory account at the beginning of an accounting period reflects the merchandise on hand on that date. Sales are recorded in the sales account and, on the date of each sale, the cost of the merchandise sold is recorded by debiting Cost of Merchandise Sold and crediting Merchandise Inventory. Thus, in the perpetual system, the merchandise inventory account continuously (perpetually) discloses the balance of merchandise on hand. At the end of the period, the balance in the merchandise inventory account is reported on the balance sheet, and the balance in the cost of merchandise sold account is reported on the income statement.

The accounting for and reporting of merchandise inventory transactions under the periodic and perpetual systems are compared and illustrated below and on page 362:

Comparison of Periodic and Perpetual Systems

Inventory, Purchases, and Sales Data

January 1	Merchandise inventory (beginning)	$52,500
1–31	Purchases (on account)	26,200
1–31	Sales (on account)—selling price	49,750
	Sales—cost price	28,000
31	Merchandise inventory (ending)	50,700

Periodic	Perpetual
January 1 Merchandise Inventory	
Merchandise inventory account reflects inventory on hand, $52,500.	Merchandise inventory account reflects inventory on hand, $52,500.

[1]An alternative method of recording merchandise inventory is presented in Appendix C.

*Comparison of
Periodic and Perpetual
Systems (Continued)*

| | Periodic | | Perpetual | |

Entries to Record Purchases, January 1–31

Periodic			Perpetual		
Purchases	26,200		Merchandise Inventory	26,200	
Accounts Payable		26,200	Accounts Payable......		26,200

Entries to Record Sales, January 1–31

Periodic			Perpetual		
Accounts Receivable	49,750		Accounts Receivable.....	49,750	
Sales......................		49,750	Sales......................		49,750
			Cost of Merchandise		
			Sold........................	28,000	
			Merchandise Inventory		28,000

Adjusting Entries for January 31 Merchandise Inventory

Periodic			Perpetual
Income Summary.........	52,500		No entries necessary
Merchandise Inventory		52,500	
Merchandise Inventory ..	50,700		
Income Summary......		50,700	

Reporting Cost of Merchandise Sold in January on Income Statement

Periodic			Perpetual	
Cost of merchandise sold:			Cost of merchandise sold............	$28,000
Jan. 1 inventory........	$52,500			
January purchases....	26,200			
Merchandise available				
for sale................	$78,700			
Less Jan. 31				
inventory	50,700			
Cost of merchandise				
sold....................		$28,000		

Reporting Merchandise Inventory, January 31, on Balance Sheet

Periodic		Perpetual	
Merchandise inventory	$50,700	Merchandise inventory................	$50,700

Inventory Costing Methods Under a Perpetual System

Unlike cash, merchandise is a mixed mass of goods. Details of the cost of each type of merchandise purchased and sold, together with such related transactions as returns and allowances, must be maintained in a subsidiary **inventory ledger**, with a separate account for each type. Whether this ledger is computerized or maintained manually, it is customary to use one of the three costing methods—first-in, first-out; last-in, first-out; or average.

In the following paragraphs, the fifo and lifo methods in a perpetual system are discussed and illustrated. The average cost method is briefly discussed also, but an illustration is reserved for advanced texts.

The basis for the fifo and lifo illustrations is the following data for merchandise identified as Commodity 127B:

			Units	Cost
Jan.	1	Inventory	10	$20
	4	Sale	7	
	10	Purchase	8	21
	22	Sale	4	
	28	Sale	2	
	30	Purchase	10	22

First-In, First-Out Method. To illustrate the first-in, first-out method of cost flow in a perpetual inventory system, the inventory ledger account for Commodity 127B is as follows. The number of units on hand after each transaction, together with total costs and unit costs, appear in the inventory section of the account.

Perpetual Inventory Account (FIFO)

Commodity 127B

Date	Purchases			Cost of Merchandise Sold			Inventory		
	Quantity	Unit Cost	Total Cost	Quantity	Unit Cost	Total Cost	Quantity	Unit Cost	Total Cost
Jan. 1							10	20	200
4				7	20	140	3	20	60
10	8	21	168				3 8	20 21	60 168
22				3 1	20 21	60 21	7	21	147
28				2	21	42	5	21	105
30	10	22	220				5 10	21 22	105 220

Note that after the 7 units of the commodity were sold on January 4, there was a remaining inventory of 3 units at $20 each. The 8 units purchased on January 10 were acquired at a unit cost of $21, instead of $20, and hence could not be combined with the 3 units. The inventory after the January 10 purchase is therefore reported on two lines, 3 units at $20 each and 8 units at $21 each. Next, it should be noted that the $81 cost of the 4 units sold on January 22 is composed of the remaining 3 units at $20 each and 1 unit at $21. At this point, 7 units remain in inventory at a cost of $21 per unit. The remainder of the illustration is explained in a similar manner.

Last-In, First-Out Method. When the last-in, first-out method is used in a perpetual inventory system, the cost of the units sold is the cost of the most recent purchases. To illustrate, the ledger account for Commodity 127B, prepared on a lifo basis, is as follows:

Perpetual Inventory Account (LIFO)

Commodity 127B

Date	Purchases			Cost of Merchandise Sold			Inventory		
	Quantity	Unit Cost	Total Cost	Quantity	Unit Cost	Total Cost	Quantity	Unit Cost	Total Cost
Jan. 1							10	20	200
4				7	20	140	3	20	60
10	8	21	168				3 8	20 21	60 168
22				4	21	84	3 4	20 21	60 84
28				2	21	42	3 2	20 21	60 42
30	10	22	220				3 2 10	20 21 22	60 42 220

A comparison of the ledger accounts for the fifo perpetual system and the lifo perpetual system indicates that the accounts are the same through the January 10 purchase. Using the lifo perpetual system, however, the cost of the 4 units sold on January 22 is the cost of the units from the January 10 purchase ($21 per unit). The cost of the 7 units in inventory after the sale on January 22 is the cost of the 3 units remaining from the beginning inventory and the cost of the 4 units remaining from the January 10 purchase. The remainder of the lifo illustration is explained in a similar manner.

Average Cost Method. When the average cost method is used in a perpetual inventory system, an average unit cost for each type of commodity is computed each time a purchase is made, rather than at the end of the period. This unit cost is then used to determine the cost of each sale, until another purchase is made and a new average is computed. This averaging technique is called a **moving average.**

Internal Control and Perpetual Inventory Systems

The use of a perpetual inventory system for merchandise provides the most effective means of control over this important asset. Although it is possible to maintain a perpetual inventory in memorandum records only or to limit the data to quantities, a complete set of records integrated with the general ledger is preferable. With the widespread use of computers, integrated perpetual inventory systems are being used by more and more companies.

The control feature is the most important advantage of the perpetual system. The inventory of each type of merchandise is always readily available in the subsidiary ledger. A physical count of any type of merchandise can be made at any time and compared with the balance of the subsidiary account to determine the existence and seriousness of any shortages. When a shortage is discovered, an entry is made debiting Inventory Shortages and crediting Merchandise Inventory for the cost. If the balance of the inventory shortages account at the end of a fiscal period is relatively small, it may be included in miscellaneous administrative expense on the income statement. Otherwise it may be separately reported in the administrative expense section.

In addition to the usefulness of the perpetual inventory system in the preparation of interim statements, the subsidiary ledger can be an aid in maintaining inventory quantities at an optimum level. Frequent comparisons of balances with predetermined maximum and minimum levels facilitate the timely reordering of merchandise to avoid both excess inventory and the loss of sales.

Automated Perpetual Inventory Systems

A perpetual inventory system may be maintained using manually kept records. However, such a system is often too costly and too time consuming for enterprises with a large number of inventory items and/or with many purchase and sales transactions. In such cases, because of the mass of data to be processed, the frequently recurring and routine nature of the processing, and the importance of speed and accuracy, the record keeping is often computerized. A computerized inventory system operates with little human intervention.

One use of computers in maintaining perpetual inventory records for retail stores is described in the following outline:

1. The quantity of inventory for each commodity, along with its color, unit size or other descriptive data, and any other information desired, is stored in the computer.
2. Each time a commodity is purchased or returned by a customer, the data are recorded and processed by the computer, so that the inventory records are updated.
3. Each time a commodity is sold, a salesclerk passes an electronic wand over the price tag attached to the merchandise. The electronic wand "reads" the magnetic code on the price tag. The information provided in the magnetic code is used by the computer to update the inventory records.
4. Data from a physical inventory count are periodically entered into the computer. These data are compared with the current balances and a listing of the overages and shortages is printed. The appropriate commodity balances are adjusted to the quantities determined by the physical count.

By entering additional data, the system described above can be extended to aid in maintaining inventory quantities at optimal levels. For example, data on the most economical quantity to be purchased in a single order and the minimum quantity to be maintained for each commodity can be entered into the computer. The computer is then programmed to compare these data with data on actual inventory and to start the purchasing activity by preparing purchase orders.

The system can also be extended to aid in processing the related accounting transactions. For example, as cash sales are entered on an electronic cash register, the sales data can be accumulated and used for the appropriate accounting entries. These entries would include a debit to Cash and a credit to Sales as well as a debit to Cost of Merchandise Sold and a credit to Merchandise Inventory.

VALUATION OF INVENTORY
AT OTHER THAN COST

OBJECTIVE 7
Describe and
illustrate the
valuation of
inventory at other
than cost, including
valuation at the
lower of cost or
market.

As discussed in the preceding sections, cost is the primary basis for the valuation of inventories. Under certain circumstances, however, inventory is valued at other than cost. Two such circumstances arise when (1) the cost of replacing items in inventory is below recorded cost, and (2) the inventory is not salable at normal sales prices because of imperfections, shop wear, style changes, or other causes.

Valuation at Lower of Cost or Market

If the market price of an item in inventory is lower than its cost, the **lower of cost or market** method is used to value inventory. It should be noted that regardless of the method used (cost, or lower of cost or market), it is first necessary to determine the cost of the inventory. "Market," as used in the phrase *lower of cost or market*, is interpreted to mean the cost to replace the merchandise on the inventory date, based on quantities typically purchased from the usual source of supply. In the discussion that follows, the salability of the merchandise at normal sales prices will be assumed. Articles that have to be sold at a price below their cost would be valued at their net realizable value, as described on page 367.

If the replacement price of an item in the inventory is lower than its cost, the use of the lower of cost or market method provides two advantages: (1) the gross profit (and net income) are reduced for the period in which the decline occurred and (2) an approximately normal gross profit is realized during the period in which the item is sold. To illustrate, assume that merchandise with a unit cost of $70 has sold at $100 during the period, yielding a gross profit of $30 a unit, or 30% of sales. Assume also that at the end of the year, there is a single unit of the commodity in the inventory and that its replacement price has declined to $63. Under such circumstances it would be reasonable to expect that the selling price would also decline, if indeed it had not already done so. Assuming a reduction in selling price to $90, the gross profit based on replacement cost of $63 would be $27, which is also 30% of the selling price. Accordingly, valuation of the unit in the inventory at $63 reduces gross profit of the past period by $7 and permits a normal gross profit of $27 to be realized on its sale in the following period. If the unit had been valued at its original cost of $70, the gross profit determined for the past year would have been $7 greater, and the gross profit attributable to the sale of the item in the following period would have been $7 less.

It would be possible to apply the lower of cost or market basis (1) to each item in the inventory, (2) to major classes or categories, or (3) to the inventory as a whole. The first procedure is the one usually followed in practice. To illustrate the application of the lower of cost or market to individual items, assume that there are 400 identical units of Commodity A in the inventory, each acquired at a unit cost of $10.25. If at the inventory date the commodity would cost $10.50 to replace, the cost price of $10.25 would be multiplied by 400 to determine the inventory value. On the other hand, if the commodity could be replaced at $9.50 a unit, the replacement price of $9.50 would be used for valuation purposes. The following tabulation illustrates one of the forms that may be followed in assembling inventory data:

Determination of Inventory at Lower of Cost or Market

Description	Quantity	Unit Cost Price	Unit Market Price	Total Cost	Total Lower of C or M
Commodity A	400	$10.25	$ 9.50	$ 4,100	$ 3,800
Commodity B	120	22.50	24.10	2,700	2,700
Commodity C	600	8.00	7.75	4,800	4,650
Commodity D	280	14.00	14.00	3,920	3,920
Total..				$15,520	$15,070

Although it is not essential to accumulate the data for total cost, as in the illustration, it permits the measurement of the reduction in inventory value as a result of a decline in market prices. When the amount of the market decline is known ($15,520 − $15,070, or $450), it may be reported as a separate item on the income statement. Otherwise, the market decline will be included in the amount reported as the cost of merchandise sold and will reduce gross profit by a corresponding amount. In any event, the amount reported as net income will not be affected. It will be the same, regardless of whether the amount of the market decline is determined and separately stated.

Valuation at Net Realizable Value

Obsolete, spoiled, or damaged merchandise and other merchandise that can be sold only at prices below cost should be valued at **net realizable value**. For this purpose, net realizable value is the estimated selling price less any direct cost of disposition, such as sales commissions. To illustrate, assume that damaged merchandise that had a cost of $1,000 can be sold for only $800, and direct selling expenses are estimated at $150. This inventory would be valued at $650 ($800 − $150), which is its net realizable value.

PRESENTATION OF MERCHANDISE INVENTORY ON THE BALANCE SHEET

OBJECTIVE 8
Identify and illustrate the proper presentation of inventory in the financial statements.

Merchandise inventory is usually presented on the balance sheet immediately following receivables. Both the method of determining the cost of the inventory (fifo, lifo, or average) and the method of valuing the inventory (cost, or lower of cost or market) should be shown. Both are important to the reader. The details may be disclosed by a parenthetical notation or a footnote. The use of a parenthetical notation is illustrated by the following partial balance sheet:

Merchandise Inventory on Balance Sheet

Afro-Arts Company
Balance Sheet
December 31, 1990

Assets

Current assets:

Cash...		$ 19,400
Accounts receivable...	$80,000	
Less allowance for doubtful accounts..................	3,000	77,000
Merchandise inventory—at lower of cost (first-in, first-out method) or market.....................................		216,300

It is not unusual for large enterprises with diversified activities to use different costing methods for different segments of their inventories. The following note taken from the financial statements of Chrysler Corp. is illustrative:

> Automotive inventories are valued at the lower of cost or market. The cost of substantially all domestic automotive inventories is recorded on a Last-In, First-Out (LIFO) basis.
>
> Aerospace inventories are stated at the lower of cost or market, with cost recognized on a First-In, First-Out (FIFO) basis.

ESTIMATING INVENTORY COST

OBJECTIVE 9
Describe and illustrate methods of estimating the cost of inventory.

In practice, an inventory amount may be needed in order to prepare an income statement when it is impractical or impossible to take a physical inventory or to maintain perpetual inventory records. For example, taking a physical inventory each month may be too costly, even though monthly income statements are desired. Taking a physical inventory may be impossible when a catastrophe, such as a fire, has destroyed the inventory. In such cases, the inventory cost might be estimated for use in preparing the income statement. Two commonly used methods of estimating inventory cost are (1) the retail method and (2) the gross profit method.

Retail Method of Inventory Costing

The **retail inventory method** of inventory costing is widely used by retail businesses, particularly department stores. It is based on the relationship of the cost of merchandise available for sale to the retail price of the same merchandise. The retail prices of all merchandise acquired are accumulated in supplementary records, and the inventory at retail is determined by deducting sales for the period from the retail price of the goods that were available for sale during the period. The inventory at retail is then converted to cost on the basis of the ratio of cost to selling (retail) price for the merchandise available for sale. Determination of inventory by the retail method is illustrated as follows:

Determination of Inventory by Retail Method

	Cost	Retail
Merchandise inventory, January 1	$19,400	$ 36,000
Purchases in January (net)	42,600	64,000
Merchandise available for sale	$62,000	$100,000
Ratio of cost to retail price: $\dfrac{\$62,000}{\$100,000} = 62\%$		
Sales for January (net)		70,000
Merchandise inventory, January 31, at retail		$ 30,000
Merchandise inventory, January 31, at estimated cost ($30,000 × 62%)		$ 18,600

There is an inherent assumption in the retail method of inventory costing that the composition or "mix" of the commodities in the ending inventory, in terms of percent of cost to selling price, is comparable to the entire stock of merchandise available for sale. In the illustration, for example, it is unlikely that the retail price of every item was composed of exactly 62% cost and 38% gross profit. It is assumed, however, that the weighted average of the cost percentages of the merchandise in the inventory ($30,000) is the same as in the merchandise available for sale ($100,000). When the inventory is made up of different classes of merchandise with very different gross profit rates, the cost percentages and the inventory should be developed separately for each class.

One of the major advantages of the retail method is that it provides inventory figures for use in preparing interim statements. Department stores and similar merchandisers usually determine gross profit and operating income each month but take a physical inventory only once a year. In addition to facilitating frequent income determinations, a comparison of the computed ending inventory with the physical ending inventory, both at retail prices, will help identify inventory shortages resulting from shoplifting and other causes. The appropriate corrective measures can then be taken.

The retail method can also be used in conjunction with the periodic system when a physical inventory is taken at the end of the year. In such a case, the items counted are recorded on the inventory sheets at their selling prices instead of their cost prices. The physical inventory at selling price is then converted to cost by applying the ratio of cost to selling (retail) price for the merchandise available for sale. To illustrate, assume that the data presented in the example above are for an entire fiscal year rather than for the first month of the year only. If the physical inventory taken on December 31 totaled $29,000, priced at retail, it would be this amount rather than the $30,000 that would be converted to cost. Accordingly, the inventory at cost would be $17,980 ($29,000 × 62%) instead of $18,600 ($30,000 × 62%). The $17,980 is generally accepted for use on the year-end financial statements and for income tax purposes.

Gross Profit Method of Estimating Inventories

The **gross profit method** uses an estimate of the gross profit realized during the period to estimate the inventory at the end of the period. By using the rate of gross profit, the dollar amount of sales for a period can be divided into its two components: (1) gross profit and (2) cost of merchandise sold. The latter may then be deducted from the cost of merchandise available for sale to yield the estimated inventory of merchandise on hand.

To illustrate this method, assume that the inventory on January 1 is $57,000, that net purchases during the month are $180,000, that net sales during the month are $250,000, and finally that gross profit is *estimated* to be 30% of net sales. The inventory on January 31 may be estimated as follows:

Estimate of Inventory by Gross Profit Method

Merchandise inventory, January 1		$ 57,000
Purchases in January (net)		180,000
Merchandise available for sale		$237,000
Sales in January (net)	$250,000	
Less estimated gross profit ($250,000 × 30%)	75,000	
Estimated cost of merchandise sold		175,000
Estimated merchandise inventory, January 31		$ 62,000

The estimate of the rate of gross profit is ordinarily based on the actual rate for the preceding year, adjusted for any changes made in the cost and sales prices during the current period. Inventories estimated in this manner are useful in preparing interim statements. The method may also be used in establishing an estimate of the cost of merchandise destroyed by fire or other disaster.

CHAPTER REVIEW

KEY POINTS

OBJECTIVE 1

Importance of Inventories

Inventory determination plays an important role in matching expired costs with revenues of the period. An error in the determination of the inventory amount at the end of the period will cause an equal misstatement of gross profit and net income. The amount reported for both assets and owner's equity in the balance sheet will also be incorrect by the same amount. In addition, because the inventory at the end of one period becomes the inventory for the beginning of the following period, an error in inventory at the end of the period will cause the net income of the following period to be misstated. The effect of the two misstatements in income will be equal and in opposite directions. Therefore, the effect on net income of an incorrectly stated inventory is limited to the period of the error and the following period. At the end of this following period, assuming no additional errors, both assets and owner's equity will be correctly stated.

OBJECTIVE 2

Inventory Systems

There are two principal systems of inventory accounting—periodic and perpetual. In the periodic system, only the revenue from sales is recorded at the time a sale is made. No entry is made until the end of the period to record the cost of merchandise sold. In the perpetual inventory system, sales and cost of merchandise sold are recorded at the time each sale is made. In this way, the accounting records continuously disclose the amount of inventory on hand. In a perpetual inventory system, a subsidiary ledger is maintained with a separate account for each type of merchandise.

OBJECTIVE 3

Determining Actual Quantities in the Inventory

All the merchandise owned by a business on the inventory date, and only such merchandise, should be included in the inventory. The first step in "taking" an inventory is to count the merchandise on hand. To this count is added merchandise in transit that is owned. Therefore, it is normally necessary to examine purchases and sales invoices of the last few days of the accounting period and the first few days of the following period to determine who has legal title to merchandise in transit on the inventory date.

OBJECTIVE 4

Determining the Cost of Inventory

The cost of merchandise inventory is made up of the purchase price and all expenditures incurred in acquiring such merchandise, including transportation, customs duties, and insurance against losses in transit.

OBJECTIVE 5

Inventory Costing Methods Under a Periodic System

In determining the cost of merchandise sold and the inventory cost at the end of the period, it is customary to use an assumption as to the flow of costs of merchandise through an enterprise. The three most common assumptions of determining the cost of merchandise sold are as follows: first-in, first-out (fifo); last-in, first-out (lifo); and average cost. The fifo method of costing inventory is based on the assumption that costs should be charged against revenue in the order in which they were incurred. The lifo method is based on the assumption that the most recent costs incurred should be charged against revenues. The average cost method, sometimes called the weighted average method, is based on the assumption that costs should be charged against revenue according to the weighted average unit costs of the goods sold.

If the cost of units and the prices at which they are sold remain stable, all three inventory costing methods will yield the same results. However, during a period of rising prices, the use of the fifo method will result in a higher amount of gross profit than the other two methods. In a period of declining prices, the use of the lifo method will result in a higher amount of gross profit than the other two methods. The average cost method of inventory costing is often viewed as a compromise between the fifo and lifo methods.

OBJECTIVE 6

Accounting for and Reporting Inventory Under a Perpetual System

Under a perpetual inventory system, sales are recorded in the sales account. On the date of each sale, the cost of the merchandise sold is also recorded by debiting Cost of Merchandise Sold and crediting Merchandise Inventory.

In a perpetual system, the details of merchandise increases and decreases are maintained in a subsidiary ledger, called an inventory ledger, with a separate account for each type of merchandise. As in a periodic system, it is customary to use one of the three costing methods—fifo, lifo, or average.

The use of a perpetual inventory system for merchandise provides the most effective means of control over this important asset. In a perpetual system, the existence of shortages can be determined by taking a physical count of the merchandise and comparing the count with the balance of the subsidiary ledger. The timely reordering of merchandise to avoid excess inventory and loss of sales can be accomplished by comparing the balance of the subsidiary ledger with predetermined maximum and minimum levels of inventory.

The basic inventory records in a perpetual inventory system may be maintained by using a computer. The system can be extended to aid in maintaining inventory quantities at optimal levels and in processing the inventory-related accounting transactions.

OBJECTIVE 7

Valuation of Inventory at Other than Cost

If the market price of an item of inventory is lower than its cost, the lower of cost or market method is used to value inventory. Market, as used in the phrase *lower of cost or market*, is interpreted to mean the cost to replace the merchandise on the inventory date. It is possible to apply the lower of cost or market basis to each item in the inventory, to major classes or categories, or to the inventory as a whole.

Merchandise that can be sold only at prices below cost should be valued at net realizable value, which is the estimated selling price less any direct cost of disposition.

OBJECTIVE 8

Presentation of Merchandise Inventory on the Balance Sheet

Merchandise inventory is usually presented in the Current Assets section of the balance sheet immediately following receivables. Both the method of determining the cost of the inventory (lifo, fifo, or average) and the method of valuing the inventory (cost, or lower of cost or market) should be shown.

OBJECTIVE 9

Estimating Inventory Cost

When it is impractical or impossible to take a physical inventory or to maintain perpetual inventory records, two commonly used methods of estimating inventory may be used: (1) the retail method and (2) the gross profit method. The retail method of inventory estimation is based on the relationship of the cost of merchandise available for sale to the retail price of the same merchandise. The inventory at retail is determined by deducting sales for the period from the retail price of the goods that were available for sale during the period. The inventory at retail is then converted to cost on the basis of the ratio of cost to selling (retail) price for the merchandise available for sale.

The gross profit method of estimating inventory is based upon the historical relationship of the gross profit to the dollar amount of sales. The rate of gross profit is multiplied by the current period sales in order to estimate the gross profit for the period. To determine the estimate of the cost of merchandise sold, the estimated gross profit is then subtracted from the sales of the period. The estimated cost of merchandise sold can then be subtracted from the merchandise available for sale for the period to determine an estimate of the ending inventory.

KEY TERMS

merchandise inventory 349
periodic inventory system 352
physical inventory 352
perpetual inventory system 352
first-in, first-out (fifo) method 356
last-in, first-out (lifo) method 357

average cost method 357
lower of cost or market 366
net realizable value 367
retail inventory method 368
gross profit method 369

SELF-EXAMINATION QUESTIONS

Answers at end of chapter.

1. If the merchandise inventory at the end of the year is overstated by $7,500, the error will cause an:
   A. overstatement of cost of merchandise sold for the year by $7,500
   B. understatement of gross profit for the year by $7,500
   C. overstatement of net income for the year by $7,500
   D. understatement of net income for the year by $7,500

2. The inventory system employing accounting records that continuously disclose the amount of inventory is called:
   A. periodic   C. physical
   B. perpetual   D. retail

3. The inventory costing method that is based on the assumption that costs should be charged against revenue in the order in which they were incurred is:
   A. fifo   C. average cost
   B. lifo   D. perpetual inventory

4. The following units of a particular commodity were available for sale during the period:

   Beginning inventory.. 40 units at $20
   First purchase .... 50 units at $21
   Second purchase .... 50 units at $22
   Third purchase.. 50 units at $23

What is the unit cost of the 35 units on hand at the end of the period as determined under the periodic system by the fifo costing method?

A. $20   C. $22
B. $21   D. $23

5. If merchandise inventory is being valued at cost and the price level is steadily rising, the method of costing that will yield the highest net income is:

A. lifo   C. average
B. fifo   D. periodic

ILLUSTRATIVE PROBLEM

Stewart Inc.'s beginning inventory and purchases during the fiscal year ended March 31, 1991, were as follows:

April 1, 1990	Inventory	1,000	$50.00	$ 50,000
April 10, 1990	Purchase	1,200	52.50	63,000
May 30, 1990	Purchase	800	55.00	44,000
August 26, 1990	Purchase	2,000	56.00	112,000
October 15, 1990	Purchase	1,500	57.00	85,500
December 31, 1990	Purchase	700	58.00	40,600
January 18, 1991	Purchase	1,350	60.00	81,000
March 21, 1991	Purchase	450	62.00	27,900
Total		9,000		$504,000

Stewart Inc. uses the periodic inventory system, and there are 3,200 units of inventory on hand on March 31, 1991.

Instructions:

1. Determine the cost of inventory on March 31, 1991, under each of the following inventory costing methods:
   a. First-in, first-out
   b. Last-in, first-out
   c. Average cost
2. Assume that during the fiscal year ended March 31, 1991, sales of $536,000 were made at an estimated gross profit rate of 40%. Estimate the ending inventory at March 31, 1991, using the gross profit method.

SOLUTION

(1)

(a) First-in, first-out method:

450 units @ $62	$ 27,900
1,350 units @ $60	81,000
700 units @ $58	40,600
700 units @ $57	39,900
3,200 units	$189,400

(b) Last-in, first-out method:

1,000 units @ $50.00	$ 50,000
1,200 units @ $52.50	63,000
800 units @ $55.00	44,000
200 units @ $56.00	11,200
3,200 units	$168,200

(c) Average cost method:

| Average cost per unit—$504,000 ÷ 9,000 units. | | $56 |
| Inventory, March 31, 1991—3,200 units at $56.. | | $179,200 |

(2) Merchandise inventory, April 1, 1990		$ 50,000
Purchases (net), April 1, 1990–March 31, 1991...		454,000
Merchandise available for sale........................		$504,000
Sales (net), April 1, 1990–March 31, 1991	$536,000	
Less estimated gross profit ($536,000 × 40%)....	214,400	
Estimated cost of merchandise sold.................		321,600
Estimated merchandise inventory, March 31, 1991		$182,400

DISCUSSION QUESTIONS

1. The merchandise inventory at the end of the year was inadvertently understated by $10,000. (a) Did the error cause an overstatement or an understatement of the gross profit for the year? (b) Which items on the balance sheet at the end of the year were overstated or understated as a result of the error?

2. The $10,000 inventory error in Question 1 was not discovered, and the inventory at the end of the following year was correctly stated. (a) Will the earlier error cause an overstatement or an understatement of the gross profit for the following year? (b) Which items on the balance sheet at the end of the following year will be overstated or understated as a result of the error in the earlier year?

3. Under which inventory accounting system—periodic or perpetual—must a physical inventory be taken to determine the cost of inventory at the end of an accounting period?

4. (a) Differentiate between the periodic system and the perpetual system of inventory determination. (b) Which system is more costly to maintain?

5. If the perpetual inventory system is used, is it desirable to take a physical inventory? Discuss.

6. What is the meaning of the following terms: (a) physical inventory; (b) book inventory?

7. In which of the following types of businesses would a perpetual inventory system ordinarily be used: (a) retail hardware store, (b) retail yacht dealer, (c) retail sports car dealer, (d) retail drugstore?

8. When does title to merchandise pass from the seller to the buyer if the terms of shipment are (a) FOB shipping point; (b) FOB destination?

9. A manufacturer ships merchandise to a retailer on a consignment basis. If the merchandise is unsold at the end of the period, in whose inventory should the merchandise be included?

10. Which of the three methods of inventory costing—fifo, lifo, or average cost—is based on the assumption that costs should be charged against revenue in the reverse order in which they were incurred?

11. Do the terms *fifo* and *lifo* refer to techniques employed in determining quantities of the various classes of merchandise on hand? Explain.

12. Does the term *last-in* in the lifo method mean that the items in the inventory are assumed to be the most recent (last) acquisitions? Explain.

13. Under which method of cost flow are (a) the earliest costs assigned to inventory; (b) the most recent costs assigned to inventory; (c) average costs assigned to inventory?

14. The following units of a particular commodity were available for sale during the year:

    Beginning inventory................................. 6 units at $111
    First purchase .... 10 units at $117
    Second purchase..................................... 5 units at $120

    The firm uses the periodic system, and there are 4 units of the commodity on hand at the end of the year. What is their unit cost according to (a) fifo, (b) lifo, (c) average cost?

15. If merchandise inventory is being valued at cost and the price level is steadily rising, which of the three methods of costing — fifo, lifo, or average cost — will yield (a) the highest inventory cost, (b) the lowest inventory cost, (c) the highest gross profit, (d) the lowest gross profit?

16. Which of the three methods of inventory costing — fifo, lifo, or average cost — will in general yield an inventory cost most nearly approximating current replacement cost?

17. An enterprise using a perpetual inventory system sells merchandise to a customer on account for $360; the cost of the merchandise was $270.
    (a) What entries would be made on the general ledger accounts as a result of the transaction?
    (b) What is the amount and direction of the net change in the amount of assets and owner's equity resulting from the transaction?

18. What are the three most important advantages of the perpetual inventory system over the periodic system?

19. In the phrase *lower of cost or market,* what is meant by "market"?

20. The cost of a particular inventory item is $275, the current replacement cost is $260, and the selling price is $350. At what amount should the item be included in the inventory according to the lower of cost or market basis?

21. Because of imperfections, an item of merchandise cannot be sold at its normal selling price. How should this item be valued for financial statement purposes?

22. An enterprise using the retail method of inventory costing determines that merchandise inventory at retail is $300,000. If the ratio of cost to retail price is 65%, what is the amount of inventory to be reported on the financial statements?

23. What uses can be made of the estimate of the cost of inventory determined by the gross profit method?

Real World Focus   24. The following footnote was taken from the 1988 financial statements of The Walgreen Co.:

    Inventories are valued on a last-in, first-out (LIFO) cost basis. At August 31, 1988 and 1987, inventories would have been greater by $208,894,000 and $179,282,000 respectively, if they had been valued on a lower of first-in, first-out (FIFO) cost or market basis.

Additional data are as follows:

Earnings before income taxes, 1988............ $208,970,000
Total lifo inventories, August 31, 1988......... 655,376,000

Based on the preceding data, determine (a) what the total inventories at August 31, 1988, would have been, using the fifo method, and (b) what the earnings before income taxes for the year ended August 31, 1988, would have been if fifo had been used instead of lifo.

EXERCISES

Exercise 9–1
Periodic inventory by three methods.
OBJ. 5

The beginning inventory and the purchases of an item during the year were as follows:

Jan.	1.	Inventory...	20 units at $78
Mar.	15.	Purchase..	15 units at $80
June	1.	Purchase..	20 units at $84
Sept.	30.	Purchase..	15 units at $82

There are 25 units of the commodity in the physical inventory at December 31. The periodic system is used. Determine the inventory cost and the cost of merchandise sold by three methods, presenting your answers in the following form:

	Cost	
Inventory Method	Merchandise Inventory	Merchandise Sold
(1) First-in, first-out	$	$
(2) Last-in, first-out		
(3) Average cost		

Exercise 9–2
Perpetual inventory using fifo.
OBJ. 6

Beginning inventory, purchases, and sales data for Commodity D45 are as follows:

Jan.	1.	Inventory	15 units at $40
	5.	Sold..	5 units
	10.	Purchased	10 units at $41
	17.	Sold..	12 units
	22.	Sold..	3 units
	30.	Purchased	10 units at $42

The enterprise maintains a perpetual inventory system, costing by the first-in, first-out method. Determine the cost of the merchandise sold in each sale and the inventory balance after each sale, presenting the data in the form illustrated on page 363.

Exercise 9–3
Perpetual inventory using lifo.
OBJ. 6

Beginning inventory, purchases, and sales data for Commodity R71 for July are as follows:

Inventory:		
July	1	25 units at $50
Sales:		
July	7	15 units
	18	10 units
	27	12 units
Purchases:		
July	3	20 units at $51
	20	15 units at $52

Assuming that the perpetual inventory system is used, costing by the lifo method, determine the cost of the inventory balance at July 31, presenting data in the form illustrated on page 364.

Exercise 9–4
Perpetual inventory entries.
OBJ. 6

The perpetual inventory system is used, and the merchandise inventory account (controlling) had a balance of $175,500 on January 1, the beginning of the current year. The account was debited for $659,500 for purchases made during the year.

(a) Journalize the entries required to record sales for the year (all sales are made on account): sales price, $995,000; cost, $676,600.

(b) If a physical count of inventory on December 31 revealed a cost of $157,150, prepare the entry to record the inventory shortage.

Exercise 9–5
Lower of cost or market inventory.
OBJ. 7

On the basis of the following data, determine the value of the inventory at the lower of cost or market. Assemble the data in the form illustrated on page 367.

Commodity	Inventory Quantity	Unit Cost	Unit Market Price
27C	12	$ 90	$ 92
42H	6	550	525
91K	25	110	115
11S	35	70	65
50V	20	250	260

Exercise 9–6
Retail inventory method.
OBJ. 9

On the basis of the following data, estimate the cost of the merchandise inventory at July 31 by the retail method:

		Cost	Retail
July 1	Merchandise inventory	$283,970	$417,500
July 1–31	Purchases (net)	215,150	316,500
July 1–31	Sales (net)		330,000

Exercise 9–7
Gross profit inventory method.
OBJ. 9

The merchandise inventory of Armstead Company was destroyed by fire on April 29. The following data were obtained from the accounting records:

Jan. 1	Merchandise inventory	$110,650
Jan. 1–April 29	Purchases (net)	175,150
	Sales (net)	300,000
	Estimated gross profit rate	35%

Estimate the cost of the merchandise destroyed.

PROBLEMS

Series A

Problem 9–1A
Corrections to inventory; revised income statement.
OBJ. 1, 3

The following preliminary income statement of Saxton Company was prepared before the accounts were adjusted or closed at the end of the fiscal year. The company uses the periodic inventory system.

Saxton Company
Income Statement
For Year Ended December 31, 19--

Sales (net)		$917,500
Cost of merchandise sold:		
Merchandise inventory, January 1, 19--	$195,000	
Purchases (net)	625,000	
Merchandise available for sale	$820,000	
Less merchandise inventory, December 31, 19--	187,500	
Cost of merchandise sold		632,500
Gross profit		$285,000
Operating expenses		202,500
Net income		$ 82,500

The following errors in the ledger and on the inventory sheets were discovered by the independent CPA retained to conduct the annual audit:

(a) A number of errors were discovered in pricing inventory items, in extending amounts, and in footing inventory sheets. The net effect of the errors, exclusive of those described below, was to understate by $7,500 the amount of ending inventory on the income statement.

(b) A purchases invoice for merchandise of $2,000, dated December 30, was not received until January 3 and had not been recorded by December 31. However, the merchandise, to which title had passed, had arrived and had been included in the December 31 inventory.

(c) A purchases invoice for merchandise of $2,500, dated December 31, had been received and correctly recorded, but the merchandise was not received until January 4 and had not been included in the December 31 inventory. Title had passed to Saxton Company on December 31.

(d) A sales invoice for $1,750, dated December 30, had not been recorded. The merchandise was shipped on December 30, FOB shipping point, and its cost, $1,150, was excluded from the December 31 inventory.

(e) A sales order for $7,500, dated December 31, had been recorded as a sale on that date, but title did not pass to the buyer until shipment was made on January 3. The merchandise, which had cost $5,000, was excluded from the December 31 inventory.

(f) An item of office equipment, received on December 27, was erroneously included in the December 31 merchandise inventory at its cost of $4,750. The invoice had been recorded correctly.

Instructions:

(1) Journalize the entries to correct the general ledger accounts as of December 31, inserting the identifying letters in the date column. All purchases and sales were made on account.

(2) Determine the correct inventory for December 31, beginning your analysis with the $187,500 inventory shown on the preliminary income statement. Assemble the corrections in two groupings, "Additions" and "Deductions," allowing six lines for each group. Identify each correction by the appropriate letter.

(3) Prepare a revised income statement.

Problem 9–2A
Periodic inventory by three methods.
OBJ. 5

Allen Stereo employs the periodic inventory system. Details regarding the inventory of television sets at January 1, purchases invoices during the year, and the inventory count at December 31 are summarized as follows:

Model	Inventory, January 1	Purchases Invoices 1st	2d	3d	Inventory Count, December 31
A24	6 at $240	6 at $241	8 at $245	7 at $245	5
C11	3 at 305	3 at 310	5 at 317	4 at 320	3
F35	2 at 520	2 at 530	2 at 530	2 at 536	3
H51	6 at 520	8 at 531	4 at 549	6 at 542	9
L60	9 at 213	7 at 215	6 at 222	6 at 225	8
R71	6 at 305	3 at 310	3 at 316	4 at 321	5
V82	—	4 at 570	4 at 600	—	2

Instructions:

(1) Determine the cost of the inventory on December 31 by the first-in, first-out method. Present data in columnar form, using the following headings:

Model	Quantity	Unit Cost	Total Cost

(Continued)

If the inventory of a particular model is composed of an entire lot plus a portion of another lot acquired at a different unit cost, use a separate line for each lot.

(2) Determine the cost of the inventory on December 31 by the last-in, first-out method, following the procedures indicated in (1).

(3) Determine the cost of the inventory on December 31 by the average cost method, using the columnar headings indicated in (1).

Problem 9–3A
Fifo and lifo
perpetual inventory.
OBJ. 6

The beginning inventory of Commodity CB9 and data on purchases and sales for a three-month period are as follows:

Date	Transaction	Number of Units	Per Unit	Total
April 1.	Inventory	12	$220	$2,640
8.	Purchase	20	225	4,500
12.	Sale	15	340	5,100
22.	Sale	5	340	1,700
May 4.	Purchase	10	230	2,300
11.	Sale	5	350	1,750
21.	Sale	4	350	1,400
28.	Purchase	15	235	3,525
June 5.	Sale	7	355	2,485
13.	Sale	10	355	3,550
19.	Purchase	10	240	2,400
26.	Sale	8	360	2,880

Instructions:

(1) Record the inventory, purchases, and cost of merchandise sold data in a perpetual inventory record similar to the one illustrated on page 363, using the first-in, first-out method.

(2) Determine the total sales and the total cost of Commodity CB9 sold for the period and indicate their effect on the general ledger by two entries in general journal form. Assume that all sales were on account.

(3) Determine the gross profit from sales of Commodity CB9 for the period.

(4) Record the inventory, purchases, and cost of merchandise sold data in a perpetual inventory record similar to the one illustrated on page 364, using the last-in, first-out method.

If the working papers correlating with the textbook are not used, omit Problem 9–4A.

Problem 9–4A
Lower of cost or
market inventory.
OBJ. 7

SPREADSHEET
PROBLEM

Data on the physical inventory of E. W. Mahan Co. as of December 31, the end of the current fiscal year, are presented in the working papers. The quantity of each commodity on hand has been determined and recorded on the inventory sheet. Unit market prices have also been determined as of December 31 and recorded on the sheet. The inventory is to be determined at cost and also at the lower of cost or market, using the first-in, first-out method. Quantity and cost data from the last purchases invoice of the year and the next-to-the-last purchases invoice are summarized at the top of page 380.

Instructions:

Record the appropriate unit costs on the inventory sheet and complete the pricing of the inventory. When there are two different unit costs applicable to a commodity, proceed as follows:

(1) Draw a line through the quantity and insert the quantity and unit cost of the last purchase.

(2) On the following line, insert the quantity and unit cost of the next-to-the-last purchase. The first item on the inventory sheet has been completed as an example.

	Last Purchases Invoice		Next-to-the-Last Purchases Invoice	
Description	Quantity Purchased	Unit Cost	Quantity Purchased	Unit Cost
A96	10	$ 40	15	$ 39
C11	15	290	15	290
E37	15	145	15	142
F52	100	30	75	31
H90	6	550	15	540
J19	150	12	100	13
K41	8	800	5	790
P21	500	7	500	8
P72	70	17	50	16
T15	5	250	4	260
V55	1,000	5	500	5
BC4	80	45	100	46
DD7	5	410	5	400
EA4	100	20	100	19
FB3	50	15	40	16
HH2	40	29	50	28
JB9	25	30	25	29
MN5	6	690	5	700

Problem 9–5A
Adjusting entries; statements for sole proprietorship.
OBJ. 7, 8

Little Imports is a distributor of imported motorcycles. Its unadjusted trial balance as of the end of the current fiscal year is as follows:

Cash	18,050	
Accounts Receivable	37,500	
Allowance for Doubtful Accounts		275
Merchandise Inventory	89,700	
Equipment	37,500	
Accumulated Depreciation—Equipment		20,000
Accounts Payable		24,500
Notes Payable		10,000
Jens Little, Capital		82,675
Jens Little, Drawing	36,000	
Sales		845,700
Purchases	705,800	
Operating Expenses (controlling account)	58,700	
Rent Income		1,200
Interest Expense	1,100	
	984,350	984,350

Data needed for adjustments at December 31:

(a) Merchandise inventory at December 31, at lower of cost (first-in, first-out method) or market, $94,100.
(b) Uncollectible accounts expense for current year, estimated at $2,500.
(c) Depreciation on equipment for current year, $6,200.

Instructions:

(1) Journalize the necessary adjusting entries. All selling and administrative expenses are included in the operating expenses controlling account.
(2) Prepare the following without the use of a conventional work sheet: (a) an income statement, (b) a statement of owner's equity, and (c) a balance sheet in report form.

Problem 9–6A
Retail method; gross profit method.
OBJ. 9

Selected data on merchandise inventory, purchases, and sales for Morheim Co. and Queens Supply Co. are as follows:

Morheim Co.

	Cost	Retail
Merchandise inventory, January 1	$292,520	$456,000
Transactions during January:		
Purchases	177,250 ⎤	274,500
Purchases discounts	2,250 ⎦	
Sales		267,500
Sales returns and allowances		5,000

Queens Supply Co.

Merchandise inventory, July 1	$425,200
Transactions during July and August:	
Purchases	310,500
Purchases discounts	5,500
Sales	476,900
Sales returns and allowances	3,900
Estimated gross profit rate	35%

Instructions:

(1) Determine the estimated cost of the merchandise inventory of Morheim Co. on January 31 by the retail method, presenting details of the computations.
(2) Estimate the cost of the merchandise inventory of Queens Supply Co. on August 31 by the gross profit method, presenting details of the computations.

Series B

Problem 9–2B
Periodic inventory by three methods.
OBJ. 5

A-1 Television employs the periodic inventory system. Details regarding the inventory of television sets at July 1, 1990, purchases invoices during the year, and the inventory count at June 30, 1991, are summarized as follows:

Model	Inventory, July 1	Purchases Invoices 1st	2d	3d	Inventory Count, June 30
B44	2 at $253	4 at $255	4 at $260	4 at $265	5
E17	8 at 80	10 at 84	8 at 90	8 at 99	10
G32	2 at 510	2 at 521	3 at 526	3 at 530	3
J60	8 at 120	4 at 105	3 at 105	6 at 99	8
M91	2 at 250	2 at 260	4 at 271	4 at 275	4
R55	5 at 160	4 at 170	4 at 175	7 at 180	8
T20	—	4 at 320	4 at 330	2 at 340	3

Instructions:

(1) Determine the cost of the inventory on June 30, 1991, by the first-in, first-out method. Present data in columnar form, using the following headings:

Model	Quantity	Unit Cost	Total Cost

If the inventory of a particular model is composed of an entire lot plus a portion of another lot acquired at a different unit cost, use a separate line for each lot.

(2) Determine the cost of the inventory on June 30, 1991, by the last-in, first-out method, following the procedures indicated in (1).
(3) Determine the cost of the inventory on June 30, 1991, by the average cost method, using the columnar headings indicated in (1).

Problem 9–3B
Fifo and lifo
perpetual inventory.
OBJ. 6

The beginning inventory of soybeans at the Savoy Co-Op and data on purchases and sales for a three-month period are as follows:

Date		Transaction	Number of Bushels	Per Unit	Total
July	1.	Inventory...	35,000	$7.50	$262,500
	6.	Purchase..	70,000	7.55	528,500
	16.	Sale..	40,000	8.50	340,000
	25.	Sale..	30,000	8.50	255,000
Aug.	8.	Sale..	10,000	8.60	86,000
	12.	Purchase..	50,000	7.60	380,000
	20.	Sale..	35,000	8.70	304,500
	28.	Sale..	25,000	8.65	216,250
Sept.	5.	Purchase..	60,000	7.55	453,000
	11.	Sale..	40,000	8.50	340,000
	20.	Purchase..	30,000	7.40	222,000
	30.	Sale..	45,000	8.50	382,500

Instructions:

(1) Record the inventory, purchases, and cost of merchandise sold data in a perpetual inventory record similar to the one illustrated on page 363, using the first-in, first-out method.
(2) Determine the total sales and the total cost of soybeans sold for the period and indicate their effect on the general ledger by two entries in general journal form. Assume that all sales were on account.
(3) Determine the gross profit from sales of soybeans for the period.
(4) Record the inventory, purchases, and cost of merchandise sold data in a perpetual inventory record similar to the one illustrated on page 364, using the last-in, first-out method.

If the working papers correlating with the textbook are not used, omit Problem 9–4B.

Problem 9–4B
Lower of cost or
market inventory.
OBJ. 7

Data on the physical inventory of Dent Corporation as of December 31, the end of the current fiscal year, are presented in the working papers. The quantity of each commodity on hand has been determined and recorded on the inventory sheet. Unit market prices have also been determined as of December 31 and recorded on the sheet. The inventory is to be determined at cost and also at the lower of cost or market, using the first-in, first-out method. Quantity and cost data from the last purchases invoice of the year and the next-to-the-last purchases invoice are summarized as follows:

	Last Purchases Invoice		Next-to-the-Last Purchases Invoice	
Description	Quantity Purchased	Unit Cost	Quantity Purchased	Unit Cost
A96	10	$ 40	15	$ 39
C11	5	315	5	325
E37	10	145	10	142
F52	100	30	100	29
H90	10	560	10	570
J19	150	15	100	13
K41	5	800	5	785
P21	500	6	500	6
R72	80	17	50	18

(Continued)

	Last Purchases Invoice		Next-to-the-Last Purchases Invoice	
Description	Quantity Purchased	Unit Cost	Quantity Purchased	Unit Cost
T15	5	$250	4	$260
V55	1,000	6	500	6
BC4	75	45	75	46
DD7	5	420	5	425
EA4	100	20	75	19
FB3	60	16	40	17
HH2	50	29	25	28
JB9	50	26	50	25
MN5	5	710	5	715

Instructions:

Record the appropriate unit costs on the inventory sheet and complete the pricing of the inventory. When there are two different unit costs applicable to a commodity, proceed as follows:

(1) Draw a line through the quantity and insert the quantity and unit cost of the last purchase.
(2) On the following line, insert the quantity and unit cost of the next-to-the-last purchase. The first item on the inventory sheet has been completed as an example.

Problem 9–6B
Retail method; gross profit method.
OBJ. 9

Selected data on merchandise inventory, purchases, and sales for Alton Co. and Zimmer Co. are as follows:

Alton Co.

	Cost	Retail
Merchandise inventory, July 1	$214,000	$307,500
Transactions during July:		
Purchases	175,500⎤	242,500
Purchases discounts	4,500⎦	
Sales		250,000
Sales returns and allowances		5,000

Zimmer Co.

Merchandise inventory, April 1	$602,500
Transactions during April and May:	
Purchases	399,750
Purchases discounts	2,750
Sales	625,000
Sales returns and allowances	5,000
Estimated gross profit rate	40%

Instructions:

(1) Determine the estimated cost of the merchandise inventory of Alton Co. on July 31 by the retail method, presenting details of the computations.
(2) Estimate the cost of the merchandise inventory of Zimmer Co. on May 31 by the gross profit method, presenting details of the computations.

MINI-CASE 9

DREW company

Drew Company began operations in 1990 by selling a single product. Data on purchases and sales for the year were as follows:

Purchases

Date	Units Purchased	Unit Cost	Total Cost
April 12	2,500	$26.40	$ 66,000
May 17	3,000	27.25	81,750
June 8	2,000	29.00	58,000
July 18	2,000	30.00	60,000
August 20	2,000	31.00	62,000
October 25	1,000	31.00	31,000
November 20	500	31.50	15,750
December 15	500	34.00	17,000
	13,500		$391,500

Sales

April.................................	1,000 units	September................	1,475 units
May...............................	1,000	October...................	1,400
June.............................	1,750	November................	1,125
July...............................	2,000	December................	500
August	1,750		

Total sales $501,000

On January 2, 1991, the president of the company, Becky Drew, asked for your advice on costing the 1,500-unit physical inventory that was taken on December 31, 1990. Also, since the firm plans to expand its product line, she asked for your advice on the use of a perpetual inventory system in the future.

Instructions:

(1) Determine the cost of the December 31, 1990 inventory under the periodic system, using the (a) first-in, first-out method, (b) last-in, first-out method, and (c) average cost method.
(2) Determine the gross profit for the year under each of the three methods in (1).
(3) (a) In your opinion, which of the three inventory costing methods best reflects the results of operations for 1990? Why?
   (b) In your opinion, which of the three inventory costing methods best reflects the replacement cost of the inventory on the balance sheet as of December 31, 1990? Why?
   (c) Which inventory costing method would you choose to use for income tax purposes? Why?
(4) Discuss the advantages and disadvantages of using a perpetual inventory system. From the data presented in this case, is there any indication of the adequacy of inventory levels during the year?

ETHICS DISCUSSION CASE	Webb Inc. is experiencing a decrease in sales and operating income for the fiscal year ending December 31, 1990. Shirley Gilreath, controller of Webb Inc., has suggested that all orders received before the end of the fiscal year be shipped by midnight, December 31, 1990, even if the shipping department must work overtime. Since Webb Inc. ships all merchandise FOB shipping point, Webb Inc. would record all such shipments as sales for the year ending December 31, 1990, thereby offsetting some of the decreases in sales and operating income. Discuss whether Shirley Gilreath is behaving in an ethical manner.

ANSWERS TO SELF-EXAMINATION QUESTIONS

1. **C** The overstatement of inventory by $7,500 at the end of a period will cause the cost of merchandise sold for the period to be understated by $7,500, the gross profit for the period to be overstated by $7,500, and the net income for the period to be overstated by $7,500 (answer C).

2. **B** The perpetual system (answer B) continuously discloses the amount of inventory. The periodic inventory system (answer A) relies upon a detailed listing of the merchandise on hand, called a physical inventory (answer C), to determine the cost of inventory at the end of a period. The retail inventory method (answer D) is employed in connection with the periodic system and is based on the relationship of the cost of merchandise available for sale to the retail price of the same merchandise.

3. **A** The fifo method (answer A) is based on the assumption that costs are charged against revenue in the order in which they were incurred. The lifo method (answer B) charges the most recent costs incurred against revenue, and the average cost method (answer C) charges a weighted average of unit costs of commodities sold against revenue. The perpetual inventory system (answer D) is a system that continuously discloses the amount of inventory.

4. **D** The fifo method of costing is based on the assumption that costs should be charged against revenue in the order in which they were incurred (first-in, first-out). Thus the most recent costs are assigned to inventory. The 35 units would be assigned a unit cost of $23 (answer D).

5. **B** When the price level is steadily rising, the earlier unit costs are lower than recent unit costs. Under the fifo method (answer B), these earlier costs are matched against revenue to yield the highest possible net income. The periodic inventory system (answer D) is a system and not a method of costing.

CHAPTER TEN

PLANT ASSETS AND INTANGIBLE ASSETS

CHAPTER OBJECTIVES

1 Describe and illustrate the accounting for the acquisition of plant assets.

2 Describe the nature of depreciation.

3 Describe and illustrate the accounting for depreciation.

4 Describe and illustrate the composite-rate depreciation method.

5 Describe and illustrate the accounting for capital and revenue expenditures.

6 Describe and illustrate the accounting for plant asset disposals.

7 Describe and illustrate the accounting for the leasing of plant assets.

8 Describe and illustrate the accounting for depletion.

9 Describe and illustrate the accounting for intangible assets.

10 Describe and illustrate the reporting of depreciation expense, plant assets, and intangible assets in the financial statements.

Long-lived is a general term that may be applied to assets of a permanent or relatively fixed nature owned by a business enterprise. As discussed in previous chapters, long-lived tangible assets that are of a permanent nature, used in the operations of the business, and not held for sale in the ordinary course of the business are classified on the balance sheet as **plant assets** or **fixed assets**. Other descriptive titles frequently used are **property, plant, and equipment**, used either alone or in various combinations. The properties most frequently included in plant assets may be described in more specific terms as equipment, furniture, tools, machinery, buildings, and land. Long-lived assets that are without physical characteristics, are not held for sale, but are useful in the operations of an enterprise are classified as **intangible assets**. Intangible assets often include patents, copyrights, and goodwill. This chapter focuses on the accounting principles and concepts for both tangible (plant) assets and intangible assets.

Although there is no standard criterion as to the minimum length of life necessary for classification as plant assets or intangible assets, such assets must be capable of repeated use or benefit and are ordinarily expected to last more than a year. However, the asset need not actually be used continuously or even often. For example, items of standby equipment held for use in the event of a breakdown of regular equipment or for use only during peak periods of activity are included in plant assets.

Assets acquired for resale in the normal course of business cannot be characterized as plant assets, regardless of their durability or the length of time they are held. For example, undeveloped land or other real estate acquired as a speculation should be listed on the balance sheet in the asset section entitled "Investments."

ACQUISITION OF PLANT ASSETS

OBJECTIVE 1
Describe and illustrate the accounting for the acquisition of plant assets.

The cost of acquiring a plant asset includes all expenditures *necessary* to get it in place and ready for use. Sales tax, transportation charges, insurance on the asset while in transit, special foundations, and installation costs should be added to the purchase price of the related plant asset. Similarly, when a secondhand asset is purchased, the initial costs of getting it ready for use, such as expenditures for new parts, repairs, and painting, are debited to the asset account. On the other hand, costs associated with the acquisition of a plant asset should be excluded from the asset account if they are not necessary for getting the asset ready for use and therefore do not increase the asset's usefulness. Expenditures resulting from carelessness or errors in installing the asset, from vandalism, or from other unusual occurrences do not increase the usefulness of the asset and should be treated as an expense.

The cost of constructing a building includes the fees paid to architects and engineers for plans and supervision, insurance incurred during construction, and all other needed expenditures related to the project. Generally, interest incurred during the construction period on money borrowed to finance construction should also be treated as part of the cost of the building.[1]

The cost of land includes not only the negotiated price but also broker's commissions, title fees, surveying fees, and other expenditures connected with securing title. If delinquent real estate taxes are assumed by the buyer, they also are chargeable to the land account. If unwanted buildings are located on land acquired for a plant site, the cost of their razing or removal, less any salvage recovered, is properly chargeable to the land account. The cost of leveling or otherwise permanently changing the contour is also an additional cost of the land.

Other expenditures related to the land may be charged to Land, Buildings, or Land Improvements, depending upon the circumstances. If the property owner bears the initial cost of paving the public street bordering the land, either by direct payment or by special tax assessment, the paving may be considered to be as permanent as the land. On the other hand, the cost of constructing walkways to and around the building may be added to the building account if the walkways are expected to last as long as the building. Expenditures for improvements that are neither as permanent as the land nor directly associated with the building may be set apart in a land improvements account and depreciated according to their different life spans. Some of the more usual items of this nature are trees and shrubs, fences, outdoor lighting systems, and paved parking areas.

---

[1]*Statement of Financial Accounting Standards*, No. 34, "Capitalization of Interest Cost" (Stamford: Financial Accounting Standards Board, 1979), par. 6.

NATURE OF DEPRECIATION

OBJECTIVE 2
Describe the nature of depreciation.

As time passes, all plant assets with the exception of land lose their capacity to yield services.[2] Accordingly, the cost of such assets should be transferred to the related expense accounts in an orderly manner during their expected useful life. This periodic cost expiration is called **depreciation**.

Factors contributing to a decline in usefulness may be divided into two categories: *physical* depreciation, which includes wear from use and deterioration from the action of the elements, and *functional* depreciation, which includes inadequacy and obsolescence. A plant asset becomes inadequate if its capacity is not sufficient to meet the demands of increased production. A plant asset is obsolete if the commodity that it produces is no longer in demand or if a newer machine can produce a commodity of better quality or at a great reduction in cost. The continued growth of technological progress during this century has made obsolescence an increasingly important part of depreciation. Although the several factors comprising depreciation can be defined, it is not feasible to identify them when recording depreciation expense.

The meaning of the term "depreciation" as used in accounting is often misunderstood because the same term is also commonly used in business to mean a decline in the market value of an asset. The amount of unexpired cost of plant assets reported in the balance sheet is not likely to agree with the amount that could be realized from their sale. Plant assets are held for use in the enterprise rather than for sale. It is assumed that the enterprise will continue forever as a **going concern**. Consequently, the decision to dispose of a plant asset is based mainly on its usefulness to the enterprise and not on its market value.

Another common misunderstanding is that depreciation accounting automatically provides the cash needed to replace plant assets as they wear out. The cash account is neither increased nor decreased by the periodic entries that transfer the cost of plant assets to depreciation expense accounts. The misconception probably occurs because depreciation expense, unlike most expenses, does not require an equivalent outlay of cash in the period in which the expense is recorded.

ACCOUNTING FOR DEPRECIATION

OBJECTIVE 3
Describe and illustrate the accounting for depreciation.

If a plant asset is expected to have no value at the time that it is retired from service, its entire initial cost should be spread over the expected useful life of the asset as depreciation expense. Also, if a plant asset's value at the time of retirement is expected to be very small in comparison with the cost of the asset, this value may be ignored and the entire cost spread over the asset's expected useful life. If a plant asset is expected to have a significant value at the time that it is retired from service, the difference between its initial cost and this value is the cost (depreciable cost) that should be spread over the useful life of the asset as depreciation expense. The plant asset's estimated value at the time that it is to be retired from service is called its **residual value**, **scrap value**, **salvage value**, or **trade-in value**.

---

[2]Land is here assumed to be used only as a site. Consideration will be given later in the chapter to land acquired for its mineral deposits or other natural resources.

In determining the amount of depreciable cost that is to be recognized as periodic depreciation expense, three factors need to be considered: the plant asset's (a) initial cost, (b) residual value, and (c) useful life. The relationship between these three factors and the periodic depreciation expense is presented in the following diagram:

Factors that Determine Depreciation Expense

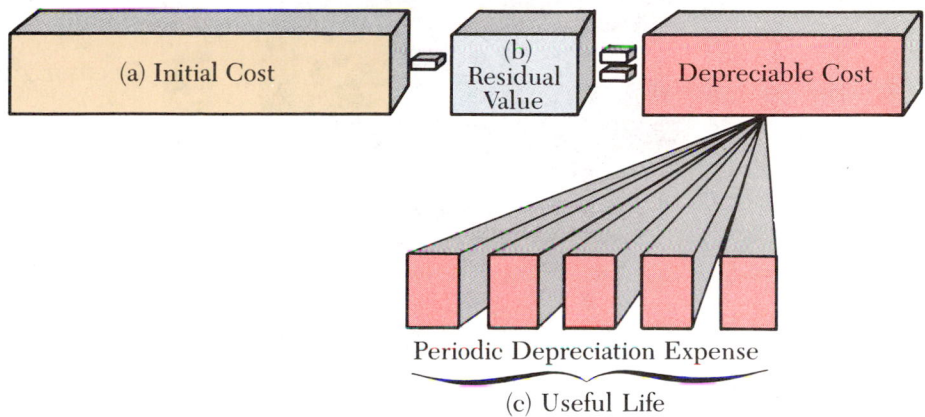

Neither the period of usefulness of a plant asset nor its residual value at the end of that period can be accurately determined until the asset is retired. However, in determining the amount of the periodic depreciation, these two related factors must be estimated at the time the asset is placed in service.

There are no hard-and-fast rules for estimating either factor, and both factors may be greatly affected by management policies. For example, the estimates of a company that provides its sales representatives with a new automobile every year will differ from those of a firm that keeps its cars for three years. Such variables as climate, frequency of use, maintenance, and minimum standards of efficiency will also affect the estimates.

Life estimates for depreciable assets are available in various trade association and other publications. For federal income tax purposes, the Internal Revenue Service has also established guidelines for life estimates. These guidelines may be useful in determining depreciation for financial reporting purposes.

In addition to the many factors that may influence the life estimate of an asset, there is a wide range in the degree of exactness used in the computation. A calendar month is ordinarily the smallest unit of time used. When this period of time is used, all assets placed in service or retired from service during the first half of a month are treated as if the event had occurred on the first day of that month. Similarly, all plant asset additions and reductions during the second half of a month are considered to have occurred on the first day of the next month. In the absence of any statement to the contrary, this practice will be assumed throughout this chapter.

It is not necessary that an enterprise use a single method of computing depreciation for all classes of its depreciable assets. The methods used in the accounts and financial statements may also differ from the methods used in determining income taxes and property taxes. The four methods used most often are straight-line, units-of-production, declining-balance, and sum-of-the-years-digits. The extent of the use of these methods in financial statements is presented in the following chart:

Use of Depreciation Methods

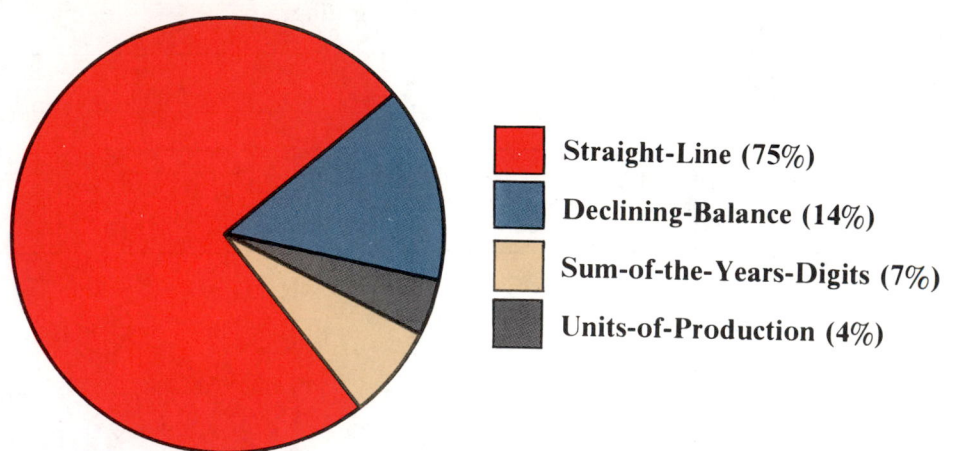

- ■ **Straight-Line (75%)**
- ■ **Declining-Balance (14%)**
- ■ **Sum-of-the-Years-Digits (7%)**
- ■ **Units-of-Production (4%)**

Source: Accounting Trends & Techniques, 42d ed. (New York: American Institute of Certified Public Accountants, 1988).

Straight-Line Method

The **straight-line method** of determining depreciation provides for equal periodic charges to expense over the estimated life of the asset. To illustrate this method, assume that the cost of a depreciable asset is $16,000, its estimated residual value is $1,000, and its estimated life is 5 years. The annual depreciation is computed as follows:

Straight-Line Method of Depreciation

$$\frac{\$16,000 \text{ cost} - \$1,000 \text{ estimated residual value}}{5 \text{ years estimated life}} = \$3,000 \text{ annual depreciation}$$

The annual depreciation of $3,000 would be prorated for the first and the last partial years of use. Assuming a fiscal year ending on December 31 and first use of the asset on October 15, the depreciation for that fiscal year would be $750 (3 months). If usage had begun on October 16, the depreciation for the year would be $500 (2 months).

The annual straight-line depreciation may be converted to a percentage rate, determined on the basis of cost and the estimated life of the asset without regard to residual value. The conversion to an annual percentage rate is accomplished by dividing 100 by the number of years of life. Thus a life of 50 years is equivalent to a 2% depreciation rate, 20 years is equivalent to a 5% rate, 8 years is equivalent to a 12½% rate, and so on.

The straight-line method is widely used because of its simplicity. In addition, it provides a reasonable allocation of costs to periodic revenue when usage is relatively the same from period to period.

Units-of-Production Method

The **units-of-production method** yields a depreciation charge that varies with the amount of asset usage. To apply this method, the length of life of the asset is expressed in terms of productive capacity, such as hours, miles, or number of units. Depreciation is first computed for the appropriate unit of production, and the depreciation for each accounting period is then determined by multiplying the unit depreciation by the number of units used during the period. To illustrate, assume that a machine with a cost of $16,000 and estimated residual value of $1,000 is expected to have an estimated life of 10,000 operating hours. The depreciation for a unit of one hour is computed as follows:

Units of Production Method of Depreciation

$$\frac{\$16,000 \text{ cost} - \$1,000 \text{ estimated residual value}}{10,000 \text{ estimated hours}} = \$1.50 \text{ hourly depreciation}$$

Assuming that the machine was in operation for 2,200 hours during a particular year, the depreciation for that year would be $3,300 ($1.50 × 2,200).

When the amount of usage of a plant asset changes from year to year, the units-of-production method is more logical than the straight-line method. It may yield fairer allocations of cost against periodic revenue.

Declining-Balance Method

The **declining-balance method** yields a declining periodic depreciation charge over the estimated life of the asset. The most common technique is to double the straight-line depreciation rate, computed as explained previously, and apply the resulting rate to the cost of the asset less its accumulated depreciation. For example, the declining-balance rate for an asset with an estimated life of 5 years would be double the straight-line rate of 20%, or 40%. This rate is then applied to the cost of the asset for the first year of its use and thereafter to the declining book value (cost minus accumulated depreciation). The method is illustrated in the following table:

Declining-Balance Method of Depreciation

Year	Cost	Accumulated Depreciation at Beginning of Year	Book Value at Beginning of Year	Rate	Depreciation for Year	Book Value at End of Year
1	$16,000	—	$16,000.00	40%	$6,400.00	$9,600.00
2	16,000	$ 6,400.00	9,600.00	40%	3,840.00	5,760.00
3	16,000	10,240.00	5,760.00	40%	2,304.00	3,456.00
4	16,000	12,544.00	3,456.00	40%	1,382.40	2,073.60
5	16,000	13,926.40	2,073.60	40%	829.44	1,244.16

Note that estimated residual value is not considered in determining the depreciation rate. It is also ignored in computing periodic depreciation, except that the asset should not be depreciated below the estimated residual value. In the above example, it was assumed that the estimated residual value at the end of the fifth year approximates the book value of $1,244.16. If the residual value had been estimated at $1,500, the depreciation for the fifth year would have been $573.60 ($2,073.60 − $1,500) instead of $829.44.

There was an implicit assumption in the above illustration that the first use of the asset coincided with the beginning of the fiscal year. This would usually not occur in actual practice, however, and would require a slight change in the computation for the first partial year of use. If the asset in the example had been placed in service at the end of the third month of the fiscal year, only the pro rata portion of the first full year's depreciation, $4,800 (9/12 × 40% × $16,000), would be allocated to the first fiscal year. The method of computing the depreciation for the following years would not be affected. Thus, the depreciation for the second fiscal year would be $4,480 [40% × ($16,000 − $4,800)].

Sum-of-the-Years-Digits Method

The **sum-of-the-years-digits method** yields results like those obtained by use of the declining-balance method. The periodic charge for depreciation declines steadily over the estimated life of the asset because a successively smaller fraction is applied each year to the original cost of the asset less the estimated residual value. The denominator of the fraction, which remains the same, is the sum of the digits representing the years of life. The numerator of the fraction, which changes each year, is the number of years of life remaining at the beginning of the year for which depreciation is being computed. For an asset with an estimated life of 5 years, the denominator is 5 + 4 + 3 + 2 + 1, or 15.[3] For the first year, the numerator is 5, for the second year 4, and so on. The method is illustrated by the following depreciation schedule for an asset with an assumed cost of $16,000, residual value of $1,000, and life of 5 years:

Sum-of-the-Years-Digits Method of Depreciation				Accumulated Depreciation at End of	Book Value at End of
Year	Cost Less Residual Value	Rate	Depreciation for Year	Year	Year
1	$15,000	5/15	$5,000	$ 5,000	$11,000
2	15,000	4/15	4,000	9,000	7,000
3	15,000	3/15	3,000	12,000	4,000
4	15,000	2/15	2,000	14,000	2,000
5	15,000	1/15	1,000	15,000	1,000

When the first use of the asset does not coincide with the beginning of a fiscal year, it is necessary to allocate each full year's depreciation between the two fiscal years benefited. Assuming that the asset in the example was placed in service after three months of the fiscal year had elapsed, the depreciation for that fiscal year would be $3,750 (9/12 × 5/15 × $15,000). The depreciation for the second year would be $4,250, computed as follows:

3/12 × 5/15 × $15,000	$1,250
9/12 × 4/15 × $15,000	3,000
Total, second fiscal year	$4,250

Comparison of Depreciation Methods

The straight-line method provides for uniform periodic charges to depreciation expense over the life of the asset. The units-of-production method provides for periodic charges to depreciation expense that may vary considerably, depending upon the amount of usage of the asset.

Both the declining-balance and the sum-of-the-years-digits methods provide for a higher depreciation charge in the first year of use of the asset and a gradually declining periodic charge thereafter. For this reason they are frequently referred to as **accelerated depreciation methods**. These methods are most appropriate for situations in which the decline in productivity or earning power of the asset is proportionately greater in the early years of its use than in later years. Further justification for their use is based on the ten-

---

[3]The denominator can also be determined from the following formula, where S = sum of the digits and N = number of years of estimated life: S = N[(N + 1) ÷ 2].

dency of repairs to increase with the age of an asset. The reduced amounts of depreciation in later years are therefore offset to some extent by increased maintenance expenses.

The periodic depreciation charges for the straight-line method and the accelerated methods are compared in the following chart. This chart is based on an asset cost of $16,000, an estimated life of 5 years, and an estimated residual value of $1,000.

Comparison of Depreciation Methods

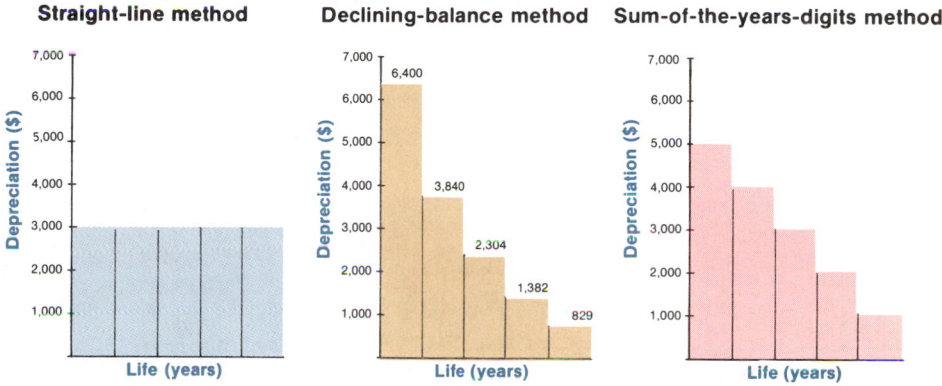

Depreciation for Federal Income Tax

Each of the four depreciation methods described in the preceding paragraphs can be used to determine the amount of depreciation for federal income tax purposes for plant assets acquired prior to 1981. The accelerated depreciation methods are widely used. Acceleration of the "write-off" of the asset reduces the income tax liability in the earlier years and thus increases the amount of cash available in those years to pay for the asset or for other purposes.

For plant assets acquired after 1980 and before 1987, either the straight-line method or the Accelerated Cost Recovery System (ACRS) could be used for federal income tax purposes. ACRS provided for depreciation deductions that approximated the depreciation calculated by the 150-percent declining-balance method. For most business property, ACRS also provided for three classes of useful life. Each class of useful life was often much shorter than the actual useful life of the asset in that class.

Under the Tax Reform Act of 1986, Modified ACRS (MACRS) provides for eight classes of useful life for plant assets acquired after 1986. The two most common classes, other than real estate, are the 5-year class and the 7-year class.[4] The 5-year class includes automobiles and light-duty trucks, and the 7-year class includes most machinery and equipment. The depreciation deduction for these two classes approximates the use of the 200-percent declining-balance method.

The Internal Revenue Service has prescribed methods that result in annual percentages to be used in determining depreciation for each class. In using these rates, residual value is ignored, and all plant assets are assumed to be placed in service in the middle of the year and taken out of service in

---

[4]Real estate is classified into 27 1/2-year classes and 31 1/2-year classes and is depreciated by the straight-line method.

the middle of the year. Thus, for the 5-year class assets, for example, depreciation is spread over six years, as shown in the following schedule of MACRS depreciation rates:

MACRS Depreciation Rate Schedule

Year	5-Year-Class Depreciation Rates
1	20.0%
2	32.0
3	19.2
4	11.5
5	11.5
6	5.8
	100.0%

TWO (LEGAL) SETS OF BOOKS

Many companies use one method of depreciation for financial reporting purposes (frequently the straight-line method) and a different method of depreciation for income tax purposes (often an accelerated method). The advantages of maintaining two sets of accounts is addressed in the following excerpts from an article in *The Wall Street Journal*:

... When you're dealing with the tax folks, quick depreciation... of equipment outlays makes a lot of sense. It cuts... profits and [therefore cuts] taxes.... [Such a policy also] leaves more cash for other uses. But good tax strategy can be bad business strategy.

David A. Tonneson, a Wakefield, Mass., accountant who specializes in advising small businesses, says the biggest mistake his clients make is to immediately deduct too much from profits [for depreciation on] equipment and installation costs. This results in undervalued [bases for] assets and makes borrowing more funds or selling the company more difficult. Small start-up companies would be wiser to [spread depreciation over future years more evenly]. Though this boosts reported income [in the early years], it boosts their asset base, permitting them to borrow more and sell their concern for more.

Mr. Tonneson says one of his clients lost a chance for a $1 million contract because it had used accelerated depreciation for its equipment. Using straight-line depreciation, the equipment would have been valued on the books at $525,000, or enough to collateralize a $420,000 loan from a bank. But after accelerated depreciation, the books only showed the equipment at $300,000, so the bank would supply only a $240,000 loan. The company needed $400,000 to gear up for the new order. It lost the sale.

Many new small-business owners aren't aware that they can use accelerated depreciation [MACRS] to report income to the tax authorities but can keep their asset [book] values up by using straight-line depreciation to report to shareholders.... While this does entail keeping two sets of books, "it's well worth it."

Source: Lee Berton, "Dos and Don'ts," *The Wall Street Journal* (June 10, 1988), p. 34R.

Revision of Periodic Depreciation

Earlier in this chapter, it was noted that two of the factors that must be considered in computing the periodic depreciation of a plant asset—its residual value at the time it is retired from service and its useful life—must be estimated at the time the asset is placed in service. Minor errors resulting from the use of these estimates are normal and tend to be recurring.[5] When

---

[5] The correction of material or large errors made in computing depreciation in prior periods is discussed in Chapter 15.

such errors occur, the revised estimates are used to determine the amount of the remaining undepreciated asset cost to be charged as an expense in future periods.

To illustrate, assume that a plant asset purchased for $130,000 and originally estimated to have a useful life of 30 years and a residual value of $10,000 has been depreciated for 10 years by the straight-line method. At the end of ten years, its book value (undepreciated cost) would be $90,000, determined as follows:

Asset cost...	$130,000
Less accumulated depreciation ($4,000 per year × 10 years)..	40,000
Book value (undepreciated cost), end of tenth year	$ 90,000

If during the eleventh year it is estimated that the remaining useful life is 25 years (instead of 20) and that the residual value is $5,000 (instead of $10,000), the depreciation expense for each of the remaining 25 years would be $3,400, determined as follows:

Book value (undepreciated cost), end of tenth year	$90,000
Less revised estimated residual value............................	5,000
Revised remaining depreciation	$85,000
Revised annual depreciation expense ($85,000 ÷ 25)	$ 3,400

Note that the correction of minor errors in the estimates used in the determination of depreciation does not affect the amounts of depreciation expense recorded in earlier years. The use of estimates, and the resulting likelihood of minor errors in such estimates, is inherent in the accounting process. Therefore when such errors do occur, the amounts recorded for depreciation expense in the past are not corrected; only future depreciation expense amounts are affected.

Recording Depreciation

Depreciation may be recorded by an entry at the end of each month, or the adjustment may be delayed until the end of the year. As illustrated on page 98, the part of the entry that records the decrease in the plant asset is credited to a contra asset account entitled Accumulated Depreciation or Allowance for Depreciation. The use of a contra asset account permits the original cost to remain unchanged in the plant asset account. This facilitates the computation of periodic depreciation, the listing of both cost and accumulated depreciation on the balance sheet, and the reporting required for property tax and income tax purposes.

An exception to the general procedure of recording depreciation monthly or annually is often made when a plant asset is sold, traded in, or scrapped. As discussed and illustrated later in the chapter, the disposal is recorded by removing from the accounts both the cost of the asset and its related accumulated depreciation as of the date of the disposal. Hence, it is advisable to record the additional depreciation on the item for the current period before recording the transaction disposing of the asset. A further advantage of recording the depreciation at the time of the disposal of the asset is that no additional attention need be given the transaction when the amount of the periodic depreciation adjustment for the other plant assets is later determined.

Subsidiary Ledgers for Plant Assets

When depreciation is to be computed individually on a large number of assets making up a functional group, it is advisable to maintain a subsidiary ledger. To illustrate, assume that an enterprise owns about 200 items of office equipment with a total cost of about $100,000. Unless the business is newly organized, the equipment would have been acquired over a number of years. The individual cost, estimated residual value, and estimated useful life would be different in each case, and the makeup of the group will continually change because of acquisitions and disposals.

There are many variations in the form of subsidiary records for depreciable assets. Multicolumn analysis sheets may be used, or a separate ledger account may be maintained for each asset. The form should be designed to provide spaces for recording the acquisition and the disposal of the asset, the depreciation charged each period, the accumulated depreciation to date, and any other pertinent data desired. Following is an example of a subsidiary ledger account for a plant asset:

An Account in the Office Equipment Ledger

Plant Asset Record

Account No.: 123-215   General Ledger Account: Office Equipment
Item: SF 490 COPIER
Serial No.: AT 47-3926
From Whom Purchased: Hamilton Office Machines Co. Inc.
Estimated Useful Life: 10 Years   Estimated Residual Value: $500   Depreciation per Year: $240

Date	Asset Debit	Asset Credit	Asset Balance	Accum. Depr. Debit	Accum. Depr. Credit	Accum. Depr. Balance	Book Value
04/08/90	2,900		2,900				2,900
12/31/90					180	180	2,720
12/31/91					240	420	2,480

The number assigned to the account illustrated is made up of the number of the office equipment account in the general ledger (123) followed by the number assigned to the specific item of office equipment purchased (215). An identification tag or plaque with the corresponding account number is attached to the asset. Depreciation for the year in which the asset was acquired, computed for nine months on a straight-line basis, is $180; for the following year it is $240. These amounts, together with the corresponding amounts from all other accounts in the subsidiary ledger, provide the figures for the respective year-end adjusting entries debiting the depreciation expense account and crediting the accumulated depreciation account.

The sum of the asset balances and the sum of the accumulated depreciation balances in all of the accounts should be compared periodically with the balances of their respective controlling accounts in the general ledger. When a certain asset is disposed of, the asset section of the subsidiary account is credited and the accumulated depreciation section is debited. This reduces the balances of both sections to zero. The account is then removed from the ledger and filed for possible future reference.

Subsidiary ledgers for plant assets are useful to the accounting department in (1) determining the periodic depreciation expense, (2) recording the disposal of individual items, (3) preparing tax returns, and (4) preparing insurance claims in the event of insured losses. The forms may also be expanded to provide spaces for accumulating data on the operating efficiency of the asset. Such information as number of breakdowns, length of time out of service, and cost of repairs is useful in comparing similar equipment produced by different manufacturers. When new equipment is to be purchased, the data are useful to management in deciding upon size, model, and other specifications and the best source of supply.

Regardless of whether subsidiary equipment ledgers are maintained, plant assets should be inspected periodically in order to determine their state of repair and whether or not they are still in use.

Depreciation of Plant Assets of Low Unit Cost

Subsidiary ledgers are not usually maintained for classes of plant assets that are made up of individual items of low unit cost, such as hand tools and other small portable equipment. Because of hard usage, breakage, and pilferage, such assets may be relatively short-lived and may require constant replacement. In such cases, the usual depreciation methods are not practical. One common method of determining cost expiration is to take a periodic inventory of the items on hand, estimate their fair value based on original cost, and transfer the remaining amount from the asset account to an appropriately titled account, such as Tools Expense. Other categories to which the same method is often applied are dies, molds, patterns, and spare parts.

COMPOSITE-RATE DEPRECIATION METHOD

OBJECTIVE 4
Describe and illustrate the composite-rate depreciation method.

In the preceding illustrations, depreciation has been computed on each individual plant asset and, unless otherwise stated, this procedure will be assumed in the problem materials at the end of the chapter. Another procedure, called the **composite-rate depreciation method**, is to determine depreciation for entire groups of assets by use of a single rate. The basis for grouping may be similarity in life estimates or other common traits, or it may be broadened to include all assets within a functional class, such as office equipment or factory equipment.

When depreciation is computed on the basis of a composite group of assets of differing life spans, a rate based on averages must be developed. This may be done by (1) computing the annual depreciation for each asset, (2) determining the total annual depreciation, and (3) dividing the sum thus determined by the total cost of the assets. The procedure is illustrated as follows:

Composite-Rate Method of Depreciation

Asset No.	Cost	Estimated Residual Value	Estimated Life	Annual Depreciation
101	$ 20,000	$4,000	10 years	$ 1,600
102	15,600	1,500	15 years	940
147	41,000	1,000	8 years	5,000
Total	$473,400			$49,707

$$\frac{\$49,707 \text{ annual depreciation}}{\$473,400 \text{ cost}} = 10.5\% \text{ composite rate}$$

Although new assets of differing life spans and residual values will be added to the group and old assets will be retired, the "mix" is assumed to remain relatively unchanged. Accordingly, a depreciation rate based on averages (10.5% in the illustration) also remains unchanged for an indefinite time in the future.

When a composite rate is used, it may be applied against total asset cost on a monthly basis, or some reasonable assumption may be made regarding the timing of increases and decreases in the group. A common practice is to assume that all additions and retirements have occurred uniformly throughout the year. The composite rate is then applied to the average of the beginning and the ending balances of the account. Another acceptable averaging technique is to assume that all additions and retirements during the first half of the year occurred as of the first day of the year, and that all additions and retirements during the second half of the year occurred on the first day of the following year.

When assets within the composite group are retired, no gain or loss should be recognized. Instead, the asset account is credited for the cost of the asset and the accumulated depreciation account is debited for the excess of cost over the amount realized from the disposal. Any deficiency in the amount of depreciation recorded on the shorter-lived assets is presumed to be balanced by excessive depreciation on the longer-lived assets.

Regardless of whether depreciation is computed for each individual unit or for composite groups, the periodic depreciation charge is based on estimates. The effect of obsolescence and inadequacy on the life of plant assets is particularly difficult to forecast. Any system that provides for the allocation of depreciation in a systematic and rational manner fulfills the requirements of good accounting.

CAPITAL AND REVENUE EXPENDITURES

OBJECTIVE 5
Describe and illustrate the accounting for capital and revenue expenditures.

Expenditures for acquiring plant assets or for additions to plant assets and expenditures that add to the utility of plant assets for more than one accounting period are called **capital expenditures**. Such expenditures are debited to the asset account or to a related accumulated depreciation account. Expenditures that benefit only the current period and that are made in order to maintain normal operating efficiency are called **revenue expenditures**. Such expenditures are debited to expense accounts. Although it may be difficult to distinguish between capital and revenue expenditures, care should be exercised so that revenues and expenses will be matched properly. Capital expenditures will affect the depreciation expense of more than one period, while revenue expenditures will affect the expenses of only the current period.

Capital Expenditures

The accounting for the initial costs of acquiring plant assets was discussed earlier in the chapter. The accounting for other common capital expenditures related to plant assets—(a) additions, (b) betterments, and (c) extraordinary repairs—are discussed in the following paragraphs.

Additions to Plant Assets. Expenditures for additions to existing plant assets would be debited to the plant asset accounts as discussed earlier in the chapter for the initial costs of acquiring plant assets. The costs of additions would be depreciated over the estimated useful life of the additions.

For example, the costs of adding an air conditioning system to a building or of adding a wing to a building would be treated as capital expenditures.

Betterments. Expenditures that increase operating efficiency or capacity for the remaining useful life of a plant asset are called **betterments**. Such expenditures would be added to the plant asset account. For example, if the power unit attached to a machine is replaced by one of greater capacity, the cost would be debited to the plant asset account. Also, the cost and the accumulated depreciation related to the old power unit would be removed from the accounts. The cost of the new power unit would be depreciated over its estimated useful life.

Extraordinary Repairs. Expenditures that increase the useful life of an asset beyond the original estimate are called **extraordinary repairs**. They should be debited to the appropriate accumulated depreciation account, however, rather than to the asset account. In such circumstances, the extraordinary repairs may be said to restore or "make good" a portion of the depreciation accumulated in prior years. In addition, the periodic depreciation for future periods would be redetermined on the basis of the revised book value of the asset and the revised estimate of the remaining useful life.

To illustrate, assume that a machine costing $50,000, with no residual value and a useful life of 10 years, has been depreciated for 6 years by the straight-line method ($5,000 annual depreciation). If at the beginning of the seventh year, an $11,500 extraordinary repair increases the remaining useful life of the machine to 7 years (instead of 4), the $11,500 would be debited to accumulated depreciation. The annual depreciation for the remaining 7 years of use would be $4,500, determined as follows:

Cost of machine...		$50,000
Less accumulated depreciation balance:		
Depreciation for first 6 years ($5,000 × 6)...........	$30,000	
Deduct debit for extraordinary repairs	11,500	
Balance of accumulated depreciation..................		18,500
Revised book value of machine after extraordinary repair		$31,500
Annual depreciation ($31,500 ÷ 7 years remaining useful life)..		$ 4,500

Revenue Expenditures

Expenditures for ordinary maintenance and repairs of a recurring nature should be classified as revenue expenditures and debited to expense accounts. For example, the cost of replacing spark plugs in an automobile or the cost of repainting a building should be debited to proper expense accounts.

Small expenditures are usually treated as repair expense, even though they may have the characteristics of capital expenditures. The saving in time and clerical expenses justifies the sacrifice of the small degree of accuracy. Some businesses establish a minimum dollar amount required to classify an item as a capital expenditure.

Summary of Capital and Revenue Expenditures

The initial cost of acquiring a plant asset is debited to a plant asset account. Subsequent to the initial expenditures, the accounting for expenditures related to the plant asset is summarized in the following diagram:

Capital and Revenue Expenditures

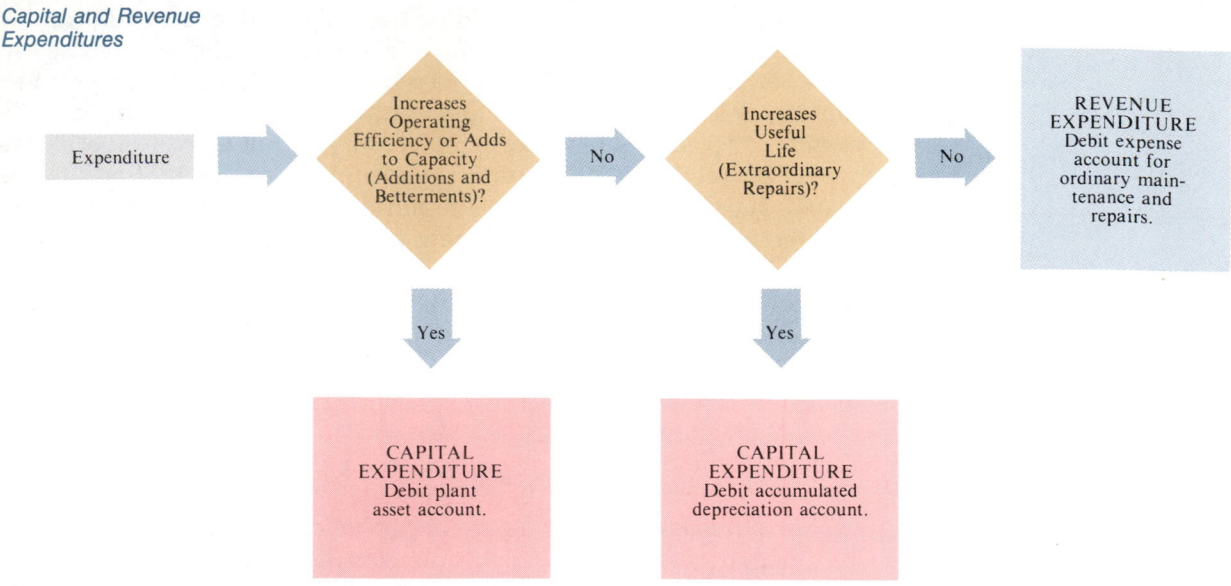

DISPOSAL OF PLANT ASSETS

OBJECTIVE 6
Describe and illustrate the accounting for plant asset disposals.

Plant assets that are no longer useful may be discarded, sold, or applied toward the purchase of other plant assets. The details of the entry to record a disposal will vary, but in all cases it is necessary to remove the book value of the asset from the accounts. This is done by debiting the proper accumulated depreciation account for the total depreciation to the date of disposal and crediting the asset account for the cost of the asset.

A plant asset should not be removed from the accounts only because it has been depreciated for the full period of its estimated life. If the asset is still useful to the enterprise, the cost and accumulated depreciation should remain in the ledger. Otherwise the accounts would contain no evidence of the continued existence of such plant assets and the control function of the ledger would be impaired. In addition, the cost and the accumulated depreciation data on such assets are often needed in reporting for property tax and income tax purposes.

Discarding Plant Assets

When plant assets are no longer useful to the business and have no market value, they are discarded. If the asset has been fully depreciated, no loss is realized. To illustrate, assume that an item of equipment acquired at a cost of $6,000 became fully depreciated at December 31, the end of the preceding fiscal year, and is now to be discarded as worthless. The entry to record the disposal is as follows:

Mar. 24	Accumulated Depreciation—Equipment.....	6,000	
	Equipment..		6,000
	To write off equipment discarded.		

If the accumulated depreciation applicable to the $6,000 of discarded equipment had been less than $6,000, there would have been a loss on its disposal. Furthermore, it would have been necessary to record depreciation for the three months of use in the current period before recording the disposal. To illustrate these differences, assume that annual depreciation on the equipment is computed at 10% of cost and that the accumulated depreciation balance is $4,750 after the annual adjusting entry at the end of the preceding year. The entry to record depreciation of $150 for the three months of the current period is as follows:

Mar. 24	Depreciation Expense—Equipment...........	150	
	Accumulated Depreciation—Equipment..		150
	To record current depreciation on		
	equipment discarded.		

The equipment is then removed from the accounts and the loss is recorded by the following entry:

Mar. 24	Accumulated Depreciation—Equipment.....	4,900	
	Loss on Disposal of Plant Assets..............	1,100	
	Equipment.......................................		6,000
	To write off equipment discarded.		

Ordinary losses and gains on the disposal of plant assets are nonoperating items and may be reported in the Other Expense and Other Income sections, respectively, of the income statement.

Sale of Plant Assets

The entry to record the sale of a plant asset is like the entries illustrated in the preceding section, except that the cash or other asset received must also be recorded. If the selling price is more than the book value of the asset, the transaction results in a gain; if the selling price is less than the book value, there is a loss. To illustrate some possibilities, assume that equipment acquired at a cost of $10,000 and depreciated at the annual rate of 10% of cost is sold for cash on October 12 of the eighth year of its use. The accumulated depreciation in the account as of the preceding December 31 is $7,000. The entry to record the depreciation for the nine months of the current year is as follows:

Oct. 12	Depreciation Expense—Equipment...........	750	
	Accumulated Depreciation—Equipment..		750
	To record current depreciation on		
	equipment sold.		

After the current depreciation is recorded, the book value of the asset is $2,250. In general journal form, entries to record the sale under three different assumptions as to selling price are as follows:

Sold at book value, for $2,250. No gain or loss.	Oct. 12	Cash...	2,250	
		Accumulated Depreciation—Equipment.....	7,750	
		Equipment...		10,000

Sold below book value, for $1,000. Loss of $1,250.	Oct. 12	Cash...	1,000	
		Accumulated Depreciation—Equipment.....	7,750	
		Loss on Disposal of Plant Assets..............	1,250	
		Equipment...		10,000

Sold above book value, for $3,000. Gain of $750.	Oct. 12	Cash...	3,000	
		Accumulated Depreciation—Equipment.....	7,750	
		Equipment...		10,000
		Gain on Disposal of Plant Assets............		750

Exchange of Plant Assets

Old equipment is often traded in for new equipment having a similar use. The trade-in allowance is deducted from the price of the new equipment, and the balance owed **(boot)** is paid according to the credit terms. The trade-in allowance given by the seller is often greater or less than the book value of the old equipment traded in. In the past, it was acceptable for financial reporting purposes to recognize the difference between the trade-in allowance and the book value as a gain or a loss. For example, a trade-in allowance of $1,500 on equipment with a book value of $1,000 would have yielded a recognized gain of $500. Such treatment is no longer acceptable for financial reporting purposes on the theory that revenue occurs from the production and sale of items produced by plant assets and not from the exchange of similar plant assets. However, if the trade-in allowance is less than the book value of the old equipment, the loss is recognized immediately.

Nonrecognition of Gain. The acceptable method of accounting for an exchange in which the trade-in allowance exceeds the book value of the old plant asset requires that the cost of the new asset be determined by adding the amount of boot given to the book value of the old asset. To illustrate, assume an exchange based on the following data:

Equipment traded in (old):

Cost of old equipment..	$4,000
Accumulated depreciation at date of exchange........................	3,200
Book value at June 19, date of exchange	$ 800

Similar equipment acquired (new):

Price of new equipment..	$5,000
Trade-in allowance on old equipment....................................	1,100
Boot given (cash)...	$3,900

The cost basis of the new equipment is $4,700, which is determined by adding the boot given ($3,900) to the book value of the old equipment ($800). The compound entry to record the exchange and the payment of cash, in general journal form, is as follows:

June 19	Accumulated Depreciation—Equipment.....	3,200	
	Equipment...	4,700	
	Equipment...		4,000
	Cash...		3,900

It should be noted that the nonrecognition of the $300 gain ($1,100 trade-in allowance minus $800 book value) at the time of the exchange is really a postponement. The periodic depreciation expense is based on a cost of $4,700 rather than on the quoted price of $5,000. The unrecognized gain of $300 at the time of the exchange will be matched by a reduction of $300 in the total amount of depreciation taken during the life of the equipment.

Recognition of Loss. To illustrate the accounting for a loss on the exchange of one plant asset for another which is similar in use, assume an exchange based on the following data:

Equipment traded in (old):

Cost of old equipment...	$ 7,000
Accumulated depreciation at date of exchange	4,600
Book value at September 7, date of exchange......................	$ 2,400

Similar equipment acquired (new):

Price of new equipment.......................................	$10,000
Trade-in allowance on old equipment.................................	2,000
Boot given (cash)...	$ 8,000

The amount of the loss to be recognized on the exchange is the excess of the book value of the equipment traded in ($2,400) over the trade-in allowance ($2,000), or $400. The entry to record the exchange, in general journal form, is as follows:

Sept. 7	Accumulated Depreciation—Equipment.....	4,600	
	Equipment...	10,000	
	Loss on Disposal of Plant Assets..............	400	
	Equipment...		7,000
	Cash...		8,000

Federal Income Tax Requirements. The Internal Revenue Code (IRC) requires that neither gains nor losses be recognized for income tax purposes if (1) the asset acquired by the taxpayer is similar in use to the asset given in exchange and (2) any boot involved is given (rather than received) by the taxpayer. Thus, the treatment of a nonrecognized gain corresponds to the acceptable method prescribed for financial reporting purposes, the boot given being added to the book value of the old equipment. In the first illustration, the cost basis for federal income tax purposes corresponds to the amount recorded as the cost of the new equipment, namely $4,700.

The cost basis of the new equipment in the second illustration, for federal income tax purposes, is determined in a like manner. The boot given ($8,000) is added to the book value of the old equipment ($2,400), yielding a cost basis of $10,400. The unrecognized loss of $400 at the time of the exchange will be matched by an increase of $400 in the total amount of depreciation allowed for income tax purposes during the life of the asset.

ACQUISITION OF PLANT ASSETS THROUGH LEASING

OBJECTIVE 7
Describe and illustrate the accounting for the leasing of plant assets.

Instead of owning a plant asset, a business may acquire the use of a plant asset through a lease. A **lease** is a contractual agreement that conveys the right to use an asset for a stated period of time. The two parties to a lease contract are the **lessor** and the **lessee**. The lessor is the party who legally owns the asset and who conveys the rights to use the asset to the lessee. Typical lease transactions include the leasing of automobiles, computers, airplanes, and communication satellites.

In agreeing to a lease, the lessee incurs an obligation to make periodic rent payments for the lease term. In accounting for lease obligations, all leases are classified by the lessee as either capital leases or operating leases. **Capital leases** are defined as leases which include one or more of the following provisions: (1) the lease transfers ownership of the leased asset to the lessee at the end of the lease term, (2) the lease contains an option for a bargain purchase of the leased asset by the lessee, (3) the lease term extends over most of the economic life of the leased asset, or (4) the lease requires rental payments which approximate the fair market value of the leased asset.[6] Leases which do not meet the preceding criteria for a capital lease are classified as **operating leases**.

A capital lease is accounted for as if the lessee has, in fact, purchased the asset. Accordingly, when a lease is executed, the lessee would debit an asset account for the fair market value of the leased asset and would credit a long-term lease liability account. The complex accounting procedures applicable to capital leases are discussed in detail in more advanced accounting texts.

In accounting for operating leases, rent expense is recognized as the leased asset is used. Neither future lease obligations nor the future rights to use the leased asset are recognized in the accounts. However, the lessee must disclose future lease commitments in footnotes to the financial statements.[7]

DEPLETION

OBJECTIVE 8
Describe and illustrate the accounting for depletion.

The periodic allocation of the cost of metal ores and other minerals removed from the earth is called **depletion**. The amount of the periodic cost allocation is based on the relationship of the cost to the estimated size of the mineral deposit and on the quantity extracted during the particular period. To illustrate, assume that the cost of certain mineral rights is $400,000 and that the deposit is estimated at 1,000,000 tons of ore of uniform grade. The

[6]*Statement of Financial Accounting Standards, No. 13,* "Accounting for Leases" (Stamford: Financial Accounting Standards Board, 1976), par. 7.

[7]*Ibid.*, par. 16.

depletion rate would be $400,000 ÷ 1,000,000, or $.40 a ton. If 90,000 tons are mined during the year, the depletion, amounting to $36,000, would be recorded by the following entry:

	Adjusting Entry			
Dec. 31	Depletion Expense.................................		36,000	
	Accumulated Depletion			36,000

The accumulated depletion account is a contra asset account. It is presented in the balance sheet as a deduction from the cost of the mineral deposit.

In determining income subject to the federal income tax, the IRC permits, with certain limitations, a depletion deduction equal to a specified percent of gross income from the extractive operations. Thus, for income tax purposes, it is possible for total depletion deductions to be more than the cost of the property. A detailed examination of the tax law and regulations regarding "percentage depletion" is beyond the scope of this discussion, however.

INTANGIBLE ASSETS

OBJECTIVE 9
Describe and illustrate the accounting for intangible assets.

The basic principles of accounting for intangible assets are like those described earlier for plant assets. The major concerns are the determination of the acquisition costs and the recognition of periodic cost expiration, called **amortization,** due to the passage of time or a decline in usefulness. These concerns as they affect patents, copyrights, and goodwill are discussed in the following paragraphs.

Patents

Manufacturers may acquire exclusive rights to produce and sell goods with one or more unique features. Such rights are evidenced by **patents,** which are issued to inventors by the federal government. They continue in effect for 17 years. An enterprise may purchase patent rights from others or it may obtain patents on new products developed in its own research laboratories.

The initial cost of a purchased patent should be debited to an asset account and then written off, or amortized, over the years of its expected usefulness. This period of time may be less than the remaining legal life of the patent, and the expectations are also subject to change in the future. The straight-line method of amortization should be used unless it can be shown that another method is more appropriate.[8]

A separate contra asset account is normally not credited for the write-off or amortization of patents. In most situations, the credit is recorded directly in the patents account. This practice is common for all intangible assets. To illustrate, assume that at the beginning of its fiscal year an enterprise acquires for $100,000 a patent granted six years earlier. Although the patent will not expire for another eleven years, it is expected to be of value for only five years. The entry to amortize the patent at the end of the fiscal year is as follows:

[8]*Opinions of the Accounting Principles Board, No. 17*, "Intangible Assets" (New York: American Institute of Certified Public Accountants, 1970), par. 30.

		Adjusting Entry		
Dec. 31	Amortization Expense — Patents................		20,000	
	Patents			20,000

Continuing the illustration, assume that after two years of use it appears that the patent will have no value at the end of an additional two years. The cost to be amortized in the third year would be the balance of the asset account, $60,000, divided by the remaining two years, or $30,000.

An enterprise that develops patentable products in its own research laboratories often incurs substantial costs for the experimental work involved. In theory, some accountants believe that such costs, normally referred to as **research and development costs**, should be treated as an asset in the same manner as patent rights purchased from others. However, business enterprises are generally required to treat expenditures for research and development as current operating expenses.[9] The reason for this requirement is that there is a high degree of uncertainty about their future benefits, and therefore expensing these costs as incurred seems most appropriate. In addition, from a practical standpoint, a reasonably fair cost figure for each patent is difficult to establish because a number of research projects may be in process at the same time or work on some projects may extend over a number of years. As a result, a specific relationship between research and development costs and future revenue seldom can be established.

Whether patent rights are purchased from others or result from the effort of its own research laboratories, an enterprise often incurs substantial legal fees related to the patents. For example, legal fees may be incurred in establishing the legal validity of the patents. Such fees should be debited to an asset account and then amortized over the years of the usefulness of the patents.

Copyrights

The exclusive right to publish and sell a literary, artistic, or musical composition is obtained by a **copyright**. Copyrights are issued by the federal government and extend for 50 years beyond the author's death. The costs assigned to a copyright include all costs of creating the work plus the cost of obtaining the copyright. A copyright that is purchased from another should be recorded at the price paid for it. Because of the uncertainty regarding the useful life of a copyright, it is usually amortized over a relatively short period of time.

Goodwill

In the sense that it is used in business, **goodwill** is an intangible asset that attaches to a business as a result of such favorable factors as location, product superiority, reputation, and managerial skill. Its existence is evidenced by the ability of the business to earn a rate of return on the investment that is in excess of the normal rate for other firms in the same line of business.

---

[9]*Statement of Financial Accounting Standards, No. 2,* "Accounting for Research and Development Costs" (Stamford: Financial Accounting Standards Board, 1974), par. 12.

Accountants are in general agreement that goodwill should be recognized in the accounts only if it can be objectively determined by an event or transaction, such as the purchase or sale of a business. Accountants also agree that the value of goodwill eventually disappears and that the recorded costs should be amortized over the years during which the goodwill is expected to be of value. This period should not, however, exceed 40 years.[10]

REPORTING DEPRECIATION EXPENSE, PLANT ASSETS, AND INTANGIBLE ASSETS IN THE FINANCIAL STATEMENTS

OBJECTIVE 10
Describe and illustrate the reporting of depreciation expense, plant assets, and intangible assets in the financial statements.

The amount of depreciation expense of a period should be set forth separately in the income statement or disclosed in some other manner. A general description of the method or methods used in computing depreciation should also accompany the financial statements.[11]

The balance of each major class of depreciable assets should be disclosed in the balance sheet or in notes thereto, together with the related accumulated depreciation, either by major class or in total.[12] When there are too many classes of plant assets to permit such a detailed listing in the balance sheet, a single figure may be presented, supported by a separate schedule.

Intangible assets are usually presented in the balance sheet in a separate section immediately following plant assets. The balance of each major class of intangible assets should be disclosed at an amount net of amortization taken to date.

An illustration of the presentation of plant assets and intangible assets is shown in the following partial balance sheet:

Plant Assets and Intangible Assets in the Balance Sheet

Clinton Door Inc.
Balance Sheet
December 31, 19--

Assets

	Cost	Accumulated Depreciation	Book Value	
Total current assets ...				$462,500
Plant assets:				
Land	$ 30,000	—	$ 30,000	
Buildings	110,000	$ 26,000	84,000	
Factory equipment........	650,000	192,000	458,000	
Office equipment..........	120,000	13,000	107,000	
Total plant assets	$910,000	$231,000		679,000
Intangible assets:				
Patents			$ 75,000	
Goodwill			50,000	
Total intangible assets.				125,000

---

[10]*Opinions of the Accounting Principles Board, No. 17,* "Intangible Assets," *op. cit.,* par. 29.

[11]*Opinions of the Accounting Principles Board, No. 22,* "Disclosure of Accounting Policies" (New York: American Institute of Certified Public Accountants, 1972), par. 13.

[12]*Opinions of the Accounting Principles Board, No. 12,* "Omnibus Opinion—1967" (New York: American Institute of Certified Public Accountants, 1967), par. 5.

CHAPTER REVIEW

KEY POINTS

Acquisition of Plant Assets

Long-lived assets that are tangible in nature, used in the operations of the business, and not held for sale in the ordinary course of the business are called plant assets or fixed assets. The initial cost of a plant asset includes all expenditures necessary to get it in place and ready for use. Such expenditures include sales taxes, transportation charges, insurance on the asset while in transit, special foundations, installation costs, broker's commissions, and title fees.

Nature of Depreciation

As time passes, all plant assets with the exception of land lose their capacity to yield services. This expiration of the cost of plant assets is called depreciation.

Accounting for Depreciation

In determining the amount of depreciation, three factors need to be considered: (1) the plant asset's initial cost, (2) the residual value of the asset, and (3) the useful life of the asset. The difference between a plant asset's initial cost and its residual value is the cost that is to be spread over the useful life of the asset.

The four methods of depreciation used most often are summarized as follows:

Straight-line...................... Provides for equal periodic charges to expense over the estimated useful life of the asset.

Units-of-production............. Yields a depreciation charge that varies with the amount of asset usage. Length of useful life of asset expressed in terms of productive capacity.

Declining-balance .... Yields a declining periodic depreciation charge over the estimated useful life of the asset. Rate of depreciation usually twice the straight-line rate computed without regard to residual value. Resulting rate applied to cost of asset less accumulated depreciation.

Sum-of-the-years-digits........ Yields a steadily declining periodic depreciation charge over the estimated useful life of the asset. Successively smaller fraction applied each year to the original cost of the asset less the estimated residual value.

All four depreciation methods will yield the same total depreciation over the life of the asset. However, each method will yield periodic charges which may vary significantly. Because the declining-balance and the sum-of-the-years-digits methods provide a higher depreciation charge in the early years of the life of the asset and a gradually declining charge thereafter, they are referred to as accelerated depreciation methods.

Each of the four depreciation methods can be used to determine the amount of depreciation for federal income tax purposes for plant assets acquired prior to 1981. For plant assets acquired after 1980 and before 1987, either the straight-line method or the Accelerated Cost Recovery System (ACRS) may be used. Under the Tax Reform Act of 1986, modified ACRS (MACRS) must be used for plant assets acquired after 1986.

Minor errors resulting from incorrect estimates of a plant asset's useful life and residual value are corrected by revising estimates used to determine the amount of remaining undepreciated asset cost to be charged to expense in future periods.

When depreciation is to be computed individually on a large number of assets making up a functional group, it is advisable to maintain a subsidiary ledger. Subsidiary ledgers for plant assets are useful in determining the periodic depreciation expense, recording the disposal of individual items, preparing tax returns, and preparing insurance claims in the event of insured losses.

Subsidiary ledgers are not usually maintained for classes of plant assets that are made up of individual items of low unit cost. For such items, depreciation is often determined by periodically taking an inventory of items on hand, estimating their fair value based on original cost, and transferring the remaining amount from the asset account to an expense account.

OBJECTIVE 4

Composite-Rate Depreciation Method

Depreciation determined for an entire group of assets by use of a single rate is referred to as composite-rate depreciation. When this method is used to compute depreciation on a group of assets of differing life spans, a rate based on averages must be developed.

OBJECTIVE 5

Capital and Revenue Expenditures

In addition to the initial cost of acquiring a plant asset, costs for additions made to the asset and other costs related to its efficiency or capacity are called capital expenditures. Costs for additions are debited to an asset account. Costs that add to the utility of the asset for more than one period (called betterments) are also debited to an asset account. Expenditures that increase the useful life of an asset beyond the original estimate are called extraordinary repairs and are debited to the appropriate accumulated depreciation account. Expenditures that benefit only the current period and that maintain normal operating efficiency are chargeable to expense accounts and are called revenue expenditures.

OBJECTIVE 6

Disposal of Plant Assets

Plant assets that are no longer useful may be discarded, sold, or traded in on other plant assets. When disposal of a plant asset occurs, the cost of the plant asset and the accumulated depreciation must be removed from the accounts and any related gain or loss recognized.

OBJECTIVE 7

Acquisition of Plant Assets Through Leasing

Instead of owning a plant asset, a business may acquire the use of a plant asset through a lease. A lease agreement conveys the right to use an asset for a stated period of time. A capital lease is accounted for as if the lessee has, in fact, purchased the asset. An operating lease recognizes lease payments as rent expense for the lessee and as rent income for the lessor.

OBJECTIVE 8

Depletion

The periodic allocation of the cost of metal ores and other minerals removed from the earth is called depletion. The amount of the periodic cost allocation is based on the relationship of the cost to the estimated size of the mineral deposit, and on the quantity extracted during the particular period. An accumulated depletion account is maintained as a contra account to the original cost of the mineral deposit.

OBJECTIVE 9

Intangible Assets

Long-lived assets that are useful in the operations of an enterprise, not held for sale, and without physical qualities are usually classified as intangible assets. The initial cost of an intangible asset is normally amortized over its useful life. Intangible assets include patents, copyrights, and goodwill.

OBJECTIVE 10   Reporting Depreciation Expense, Plant Assets, and Intangible Assets
                             in the Financial Statements.

The amount of depreciation expense and the method or methods used in computing depreciation should be disclosed in the financial statements. In addition, each major class of depreciable assets should be disclosed, along with the related accumulated depreciation. Intangible assets are usually presented in the balance sheet in a separate section immediately following plant assets. Each major class of intangible assets should be disclosed at an amount net of amortization taken to date.

KEY TERMS

plant assets 386
intangible assets 386
depreciation 388
residual value 388
straight-line method 390
units-of-production method 390
declining-balance method 391
sum-of-the-years-digits method 392
accelerated depreciation methods 392
composite-rate depreciation
    method 397

capital expenditures 398
revenue expenditures 398
betterments 399
extraordinary repairs 399
boot 402
capital leases 404
operating leases 404
depletion 404
amortization 405
goodwill 406

SELF-EXAMINATION QUESTIONS

Answers at end of chapter.

1. Which of the following expenditures incurred in connection with the acquisition of machinery is a proper charge to the asset account?
    A. Transportation charges
    B. Installation costs
    C. Both A and B
    D. Neither A nor B

2. What is the amount of depreciation, using the sum-of-the-years-digits method, for the first year of use for equipment costing $9,500, with an estimated residual value of $500 and an estimated life of 3 years?
    A. $4,500.00
    B. $3,166.67
    C. $3,000.00
    D. None of the above

3. An example of an accelerated depreciation method is:
    A. straight-line
    B. sum-of-the-years-digits
    C. units-of-production
    D. none of the above

4. A plant asset priced at $100,000 is acquired by trading in a similar asset that has a book value of $25,000. Assuming that the trade-in allowance is $30,000 and that $70,000 cash is paid for the new asset, what is the cost basis for the new asset for financial reporting purposes?
    A. $100,000
    B. $70,000
    C. $30,000
    D. None of the above

5. Which of the following is an example of an intangible asset?
    A. Patents
    B. Goodwill
    C. Copyrights
    D. All of the above

ILLUSTRATIVE PROBLEM

Florence Company acquired new equipment at a cost of $75,000 at the beginning of the fiscal year. The equipment has an estimated life of 5 years and an estimated residual value of $6,000. The president, Patrick Florence, has requested information regarding the alternative depreciation methods.

Instructions:

1. Determine the annual depreciation for each of the five years of estimated useful life of the equipment, the accumulated depreciation at the end of each year, and the book value of the equipment at the end of each year by (a) the straight-line method, (b) the declining-balance method (at twice the straight-line rate), and (c) the sum-of-the-years-digits method.

2. Assume that the equipment was depreciated under the declining-balance method. In the first week of the fifth year, the equipment was traded in for similar equipment priced at $90,000. The trade-in allowance on the old equipment was $8,000, and cash was paid for the balance.
    a. Prepare the journal entry to record the exchange.
    b. What is the cost basis of the new equipment for computing the amount of depreciation allowable for income tax purposes?

———————————— SOLUTION ————————————

(1)

	Year	Depreciation Expense	Accumulated Depreciation, End of Year	Book Value, End of Year
(a)	1	$13,800	$13,800	$61,200
	2	13,800	27,600	47,400
	3	13,800	41,400	33,600
	4	13,800	55,200	19,800
	5	13,800	69,000	6,000
(b)	1	$30,000	$30,000	$45,000
	2	18,000	48,000	27,000
	3	10,800	58,800	16,200
	4	6,480	65,280	9,720
	5	3,720*	69,000	6,000
(c)	1	$23,000	$23,000	$52,000
	2	18,400	41,400	33,600
	3	13,800	55,200	19,800
	4	9,200	64,400	10,600
	5	4,600	69,000	6,000

*The asset is not depreciated below the estimated residual value of $6,000.

(2)(a) Accumulated Depreciation—Equipment 65,280
        Equipment................................. 90,000
        Loss on Disposal of Plant Assets................... 1,720
            Equipment...   75,000
            Cash..   82,000

(b) Book value of old equipment...................................... $ 9,720
     Boot given (cash)...   82,000
     Cost basis of new equipment for income tax purposes..... $91,720

or

     Price of new equipment.. $90,000
     Plus unrecognized loss on old equipment....................   1,720
     Cost basis of new equipment for income tax purposes $91,720

DISCUSSION QUESTIONS

1. Which of the following qualities are characteristic of plant assets? (a) intangible, (b) tangible, (c) capable of repeated use in the operations of the business, (d) held for sale in the normal course of business, (e) used continuously in the operations of the business, (f) long-lived.

2. Walton Office Equipment Co. has a fleet of automobiles and trucks for use by salespersons and for delivery of office supplies and equipment. Sullivan Auto Sales Inc. has automobiles and trucks for sale. Under what caption would the automobiles and trucks be reported on the balance sheet of (a) Walton Office Equipment Co., (b) Sullivan Auto Sales Inc.?

3. Tomlin Company acquired an adjacent vacant lot as a speculation. The lot will hopefully be sold in the future at a gain. Where should such real estate be listed in the balance sheet?

4. Which of the following expenditures incurred in connection with the acquisition of a lathe should be charged to the asset account? (a) sales tax on purchase price, (b) freight charges, (c) cost of special foundation, (d) new parts to replace those damaged in unloading, (e) fee paid to factory representative for installation, (f) insurance while in transit.

5. Which of the following expenditures incurred in connection with the purchase of a secondhand printing press should be debited to the asset account? (a) freight charges, (b) repair of vandalism damages that occurred during installation, (c) replacement of worn-out parts, (d) installation costs.

6. To increase its parking area, Westex Shopping Center acquired adjoining land for $70,000 and a building located on the land for $35,000. The net cost of razing the building and leveling the land was $8,000, after amounts received from the sale of salvaged building materials were deducted. What accounts should be debited for (a) the cost of the land ($70,000), (b) the cost of the building ($35,000), (c) the net cost of preparing the land ($8,000)?

7. Are the amounts at which plant assets are reported in the balance sheet their approximate market values as of the balance sheet date? Discuss.

8. (a) Does the recognition of depreciation in the accounts provide a special cash fund for the replacement of plant assets? Explain. (b) Describe the nature of depreciation as the term is used in accounting.

9. Name the three factors that need to be considered in determining the amount of periodic depreciation.

10. Is it necessary for an enterprise to use the same method of computing depreciation (a) for all classes of its depreciable assets, (b) in the financial statements and in the determination of income taxes?

11. Of the four common depreciation methods, which is most widely used?

12. Convert each of the following estimates of useful life to a straight-line depreciation rate, stated as a percent, assuming that the residual value of the plant asset is to be ignored: (a) 4 years, (b) 5 years, (c) 10 years, (d) 20 years, (e) 25 years, (f) 40 years, (g) 50 years.

13. A plant asset with a cost of $95,000 has an estimated residual value of $5,000 and an estimated useful life of 6 years. What is the amount of the annual depreciation, computed by the straight-line method?

14. A plant asset with a cost of $65,000 has an estimated residual value of $5,000 and an estimated productive capacity of 600,000 units. What is the amount of annual depreciation, computed by the units-of-production method, for a year in which production is (a) 60,000 units, (b) 90,000 units?

15. The declining-balance method, at double the straight-line rate, is to be used for an asset with a cost of $100,000, estimated residual value of $10,000, and estimated useful life of 5 years. What is the depreciation for the first fiscal year, assuming that the asset was placed in service at the beginning of the year?

16. An asset with a cost of $22,000, an estimated residual value of $1,000, and an estimated useful life of 6 years is to be depreciated by the sum-of-the-years-digits method. (a) What is the denominator of the depreciation fraction? (b) What is the amount of depreciation for the first full year of use? (c) What is the amount of depreciation for the second full year of use?

17. (a) Name the two accelerated depreciation methods described in this chapter. (b) Why are the accelerated depreciation methods used frequently for income tax purposes? (c) What is the Modified Accelerated Cost Recovery System (MACRS), and under what conditions is it used?

18. A plant asset with a cost of $245,000 has an estimated residual value of $5,000, an estimated useful life of 40 years, and is depreciated by the straight-line method. (a) What is the amount of the annual depreciation? (b) What is the book value at the end of the twentieth year of use? (c) If at the start of the twenty-first year it is estimated that the remaining life is 25 years and that the residual value is $5,000, what is the depreciation expense for each of the remaining 25 years?

19. The cost of a composite group of equipment is $600,000 and the annual depreciation, computed on the individual items, totals $60,000. (a) What is the composite straight-line depreciation rate? (b) What would the rate be if the total depreciation amounted to $66,000 instead of $60,000?

20. (a) Differentiate between capital expenditures and revenue expenditures. (b) Why are some items that have the characteristics of capital expenditures treated as revenue expenditures?

21. Immediately after a used truck is acquired, a new motor is installed and the tires are replaced at a total cost of $4,150. Is this a capital expenditure or a revenue expenditure?

22. For a number of plant asset ledger accounts of an enterprise, the balance in accumulated depreciation is exactly equal to the cost of the asset. (a) Is it permissible to record additional depreciation on the assets if they are still useful to the enterprise? Explain. (b) When should an entry be made to remove the cost and accumulated depreciation from the accounts?

23. In what sections of the income statement are gains and losses from the disposal of plant assets presented?

24. A plant asset priced at $100,000 is acquired by trading in a similar asset and paying cash for the remainder. (a) Assuming that the trade-in allowance is $20,000, what is the amount of boot given? (b) Assuming that the book value of the asset traded in is $30,000, what is the cost basis of the new asset for financial reporting purposes? (c) What is the cost basis of the new asset for the computation of depreciation for federal income tax purposes?

25. Assume the same facts as in Question 24, except that the book value of the asset traded in is $10,000. (a) What is the cost basis of the new asset for financial reporting purposes? (b) What is the cost basis of the new asset for the computation of depreciation for federal income tax purposes?

26. Differentiate between a capital lease and an operating lease.

27. What is the term applied to the periodic charge for (a) ore removed from a mine, (b) the write-off of the cost of an intangible asset?

28. (a) Over what period of time should the cost of a patent acquired by purchase be amortized? (b) In general, what is the required treatment for research and development costs?

Real World Focus

29. A corporation purchased land and the building on the land with the intent of razing the building. Would the costs of demolition be reflected as part of the cost of the land? (Adapted from "Technical Issues Feature," *Journal of Accountancy* (December, 1987), p. 80.)

Real World Focus

30. A company has developed a tract of land into a skiing resort. The company has cut the trees, cleared and graded the land and hills, and constructed ski lifts. (a) Should the tree cutting, land clearing, and grading costs of constructing the ski slopes be debited to the land account? (b) If such costs are debited to Land, should they be depreciated? (Adapted from "Technical Issues Feature," *Journal of Accountancy* (December, 1987), p. 82.)

Real World Focus

31. The financial statements of La-Z-Boy Chair Company contain the following footnote:

> The Company has several long-term leases covering manufacturing facilities. The lease agreements require the Company to insure and maintain the facilities and provide for annual payments, which include interest. These leases give the Company the option to purchase the facilities for nominal amounts, or in some instances to renew the leases for extended periods at nominal annual rentals.

Would these leases be classified as operating or capital leases? Discuss.

EXERCISES

Exercise 10–1

Depreciation by three methods.

OBJ. 3

A plant asset acquired on January 2 at a cost of $275,000 has an estimated useful life of 10 years. Assuming that it will have no residual value, determine the depreciation for each of the first two years (a) by the straight-line method, (b) by the declining-balance method, using twice the straight-line rate, and (c) by the sum-of-the-years-digits method.

Exercise 10–2

Depreciation by units-of-production method.

OBJ. 3

A diesel-powered generator with a cost of $170,000 and estimated salvage value of $10,000 is expected to have a useful operating life of 40,000 hours. During May, the generator was operated 320 hours. Determine the depreciation for the month.

Exercise 10–3

Depreciation by units-of-production method.

OBJ. 3

Balances in Trucks and in Accumulated Depreciation—Trucks at the end of the year, prior to adjustment, are $159,500 and $49,600, respectively. Details of the subsidiary ledger are as follows:

Truck No.	Cost	Estimated Residual Value	Estimated Useful Life in Miles	Accumulated Depreciation at Beginning of Year	Miles Operated During Year
1	$67,500	$7,500	200,000	$18,600	30,000
2	45,000	5,000	200,000	7,700	20,000
3	28,000	4,000	150,000	23,300	4,500
4	19,000	1,000	150,000	—	17,500

(a) Determine the depreciation rates per mile and the amount to be credited to the accumulated depreciation section of each of the subsidiary accounts for the current year. (b) Present the journal entry to record depreciation for the year.

Exercise 10–4
Depreciation by three methods.
OBJ. 3

An item of equipment acquired at the beginning of the fiscal year at a cost of $52,400 has an estimated residual value of $2,000 and an estimated useful life of 8 years. Determine the following: (a) the amount of annual depreciation by the straight-line method, (b) the amount of depreciation for the second year computed by the declining-balance method (at twice the straight-line rate), (c) the amount of depreciation for the second year computed by the sum-of-the-years-digits method.

Exercise 10–5
Depreciation by accelerated depreciation methods.
OBJ. 3

A piece of machinery acquired at a cost of $40,000 has an estimated residual value of $4,000 and an estimated useful life of 5 years. It was placed in service on April 1 of the current fiscal year, which ends on December 31. Determine the depreciation for the current fiscal year and for the following fiscal year by (a) the declining-balance method, at twice the straight-line rate, and (b) the sum-of-the-years-digits method.

Exercise 10–6
Revision of depreciation.
OBJ. 3

An item of equipment acquired on January 4, 1987, at a cost of $35,000 has an estimated residual value of $5,000 and an estimated useful life of 10 years. Depreciation has been recorded for the first four years ended December 31, 1990, by the straight-line method. Determine the amount of depreciation for the current year ended December 31, 1991, if the revised estimated residual value is $3,800 and the revised estimated remaining useful life (including the current year) is 8 years.

Exercise 10–7
Composite depreciation rate.
OBJ. 4

A composite depreciation rate of 15% is applied annually to a plant asset account. Details of the account for the fiscal year ended December 31 are as follows:

Delivery Equipment

Jan.	1	Balance	297,750	Feb.	27		16,500
Feb.	19		19,650	Aug.	15		10,700
May	3		21,600	Dec.	20		16,550
July	30		17,000				
Dec.	1		21,000				

Determine the depreciation for the year according to each of the following assumptions: (a) that all additions and retirements have occurred uniformly throughout the year, (b) that additions and retirements during the first half of the year occurred on the first day of that year and those during the second half occurred on the first day of the succeeding year.

Exercise 10–8
Major repair to plant asset.
OBJ. 5

A number of major structural repairs completed at the beginning of the current fiscal year at a cost of $130,000 are expected to extend the life of a building 10 years beyond the original estimate. The original cost of the building was $1,000,000, and it has been depreciated by the straight-line method for 25 years. Residual value is expected to be negligible and has been ignored. The balance of the related accumulated depreciation account after the depreciation adjustment at the end of the preceding year is $500,000. (a) What has the amount of annual depreciation been in past years? (b) To what account should the cost of repairs ($130,000) be debited? (c) What is the book value of the building after the repairs have been recorded? (d) What is the amount of depreciation for the current year, using the straight-line method (assume that the repairs were completed at the very beginning of the year)?

Exercise 10–9
Entries for sale of plant asset.
OBJ. 6

A piece of equipment acquired on January 2, 1988, at a cost of $55,000 has an estimated useful life of 5 years, an estimated residual value of $5,000, and is depreciated by the straight-line method. (a) What was the book value of the equipment at December 31, 1991, the end of the fiscal year? (b) Assuming that the equipment was sold on July 1, 1992, for $7,500, prepare journal entries to record (1) depreciation for the six months of the current year ending December 31, 1992, and (2) the sale of the equipment.

Exercise 10–10
Disposal of plant asset.
OBJ. 6

A piece of equipment acquired on January 3, 1988, at a cost of $22,500 has an estimated useful life of 4 years and an estimated residual value of $2,500. (a) What was the annual amount of depreciation for the years 1988, 1989, and 1990, assuming the use of the straight-line method of depreciation? (b) What was the book value of the equipment on January 1, 1991? (c) Assuming that the equipment was sold on January 2, 1991, for $6,000, prepare the journal entry to record the sale. (d) Assuming that the equipment had been sold for $9,000 on January 2, 1991, instead of $6,000, prepare the journal entry to record the sale.

Exercise 10–11
Entries for loss on trade of plant asset.
OBJ. 6

On July 1, Farrell Co. acquired a new computer with a list price of $75,000. Farrell received a trade-in allowance of $15,000 on an old computer of a similar type, paid cash of $10,000, and gave a series of five notes payable for the remainder. The following information about the old computer is obtained from the account in the office equipment ledger: cost, $53,750; accumulated depreciation on December 31, the end of the preceding fiscal year, $32,500; annual depreciation, $10,000. Present entries to record: (a) the current depreciation on the old computer to the date of trade-in, (b) the transaction on July 1 for financial reporting purposes.

Exercise 10–12
Entries for gain on trade of plant asset.
OBJ. 6

On July 1, Ross Co. acquired a new computer with a list price of $125,000. Ross received a trade-in allowance of $15,000 on an old computer of a similar type, paid cash of $30,000, and gave a series of five notes payable for the remainder. The following information about the old computer is obtained from the account in the office equipment ledger: cost, $82,500; accumulated depreciation on December 31, the end of the preceding fiscal year, $62,500; annual depreciation, $15,000. Present entries to record: (a) the current depreciation on the old computer to the date of trade-in, (b) the transaction on July 1 for financial reporting purposes.

Exercise 10–13
Depreciation on asset acquired by exchange.
OBJ. 6

On the first day of the fiscal year, a delivery truck with a list price of $32,000 was acquired in an exchange for an old delivery truck and $27,500 cash. The old truck has a book value of $3,000 at the date of the exchange. The new truck is to be depreciated over 5 years by the straight-line method. The estimated residual value is $2,000. Determine the following: (a) annual depreciation for financial reporting purposes, (b) annual depreciation for income tax purposes, (c) annual depreciation for financial reporting purposes, assuming that the book value of the old delivery truck was $5,500, (d) annual depreciation for income tax purposes, assuming the same book value as indicated in (c).

Exercise 10–14
Amortization and depletion entries.
OBJ. 8, 9

On July 1 of the current fiscal year ended December 31, Stone Co. acquired a patent for $75,000 and mineral rights for $250,000. The patent, which expires in 7 years, is expected to have value for 5 years. The mineral deposit is estimated at 500,000 tons of ore of uniform grade. Present entries to record the following for the current year: (a) amortization of the patent, (b) depletion, assuming that 75,000 tons were mined during the year.

Exercise 10–15
Amortization and depletion entries.
OBJ. 8, 9

For each of the following unrelated transactions, (a) determine the amount of the amortization or depletion expense for the current year, and (b) present the adjusting entries required to record each expense.

(1) Timber rights on a tract of land were purchased for $90,000. The stand of timber is estimated at 300,000 board feet. During the current year, 50,000 board feet of timber were cut.

(2) Governmental and legal costs of $34,100 were incurred at midyear in obtaining a patent with an estimated economic life of 11 years. Amortization is to be for one-half year.

(3) Goodwill in the amount of $120,000 was purchased on January 5, the first month of the fiscal year. It is decided to amortize over the maximum period allowable.

PROBLEMS

Series A

Problem 10–1A
Allocation of expenditures and receipts to plant asset accounts.

OBJ. 1

The following expenditures and receipts are related to land, land improvements, and buildings acquired for use in a business enterprise. The receipts are identified by an asterisk.

(a)	Cost of real estate acquired as a plant site: Land........................	$ 210,000
	Building...................	60,000
(b)	Finder's fee paid to real estate agency	18,900
(c)	Fee paid to attorney for title search...	1,500
(d)	Delinquent real estate taxes on property, assumed by purchaser..	11,250
(e)	Cost of razing and removing the building..................................	8,500
(f)	Proceeds from sale of salvage materials from old building	1,500*
(g)	Cost of land fill and grading...	13,500
(h)	Architect's and engineer's fees for plans and supervision.............	95,000
(i)	Premium on 1-year insurance policy during construction..............	9,000
(j)	Cost of paving parking lot to be used by customers	17,500
(k)	Cost of trees and shrubbery planted	15,000
(l)	Special assessment paid to city for extension of water main to the property	7,500
(m)	Cost of repairing windstorm damage during construction.............	2,250
(n)	Cost of repairing vandalism damage during construction.............	500
(o)	Proceeds from insurance company for windstorm and vandalism damage	2,200*
(p)	Interest incurred on building loan during construction	85,000
(q)	Money borrowed to pay building contractor..............................	1,000,000*
(r)	Paid to building contractor for new building..............................	1,250,000
(s)	Refund of premium on insurance policy (i) canceled after 11 months..	600*

Instructions:

Assign each expenditure and receipt (indicate receipts by an asterisk) to Land (permanently capitalized), Land Improvements (limited life), Building, or Other Accounts. Identify each item by letter and list the amounts in columnar form, as follows:

Item	Land	Land Improvements	Building	Other Accounts
	$	$	$	$

Problem 10–2A
Depreciation by four methods.

OBJ. 3

Jacobsen Company purchased equipment on July 1, 1990, for $90,000. The equipment was expected to have a useful life of 3 years, or 7,000 operating hours, and a residual value of $6,000. The equipment was used for 700 hours during 1990 and for 2,800, 2,400 and 1,100 hours for 1991, 1992, and 1993 respectively.

Instructions:

Determine the amount of depreciation expense for the years ended December 31, 1990, 1991, 1992, and 1993 by (a) the straight-line method, (b) the declining-balance method, using twice the straight-line rate, (c) the sum-of-the-years-digits method, and (d) the units-of-production method.

Problem 10–3A
Determination of depreciation by three methods; trade of plant asset.

OBJ. 3, 6

SPREADSHEET PROBLEM

An item of new equipment, acquired at a cost of $160,000 at the beginning of a fiscal year, has an estimated useful life of 4 years and an estimated residual value of $10,000. The manager requested information regarding the effect of alternative methods on the amount of depreciation expense each year. Upon the basis of the data presented to the manager, the declining-balance method was selected.

In the first week of the fourth year, the equipment was traded in for similar equipment priced at $225,000. The trade-in allowance on the old equipment was $25,000, cash of $50,000 was paid, and a note payable was issued for the balance.

Instructions:

(1) Determine the annual depreciation expense for each of the estimated 4 years of use, the accumulated depreciation at the end of each year, and the book value of the equipment at the end of each year by (a) the straight-line method, (b) the declining-balance method (at twice the straight-line rate), and (c) the sum-of-the-years-digits method. The following columnar headings are suggested for each schedule:

Year	Depreciation Expense	Accumulated Depreciation, End of Year	Book Value, End of Year

(2) For financial reporting purposes, determine the cost basis of the new equipment acquired in the exchange.
(3) Present the entry to record the exchange.
(4) What is the cost basis of the new equipment for purposes of computing the amount of depreciation allowable for income tax purposes?
(5) Present the entry to record the exchange, assuming that the trade-in allowance was $15,000 instead of $25,000.
(6) What is the cost basis of the new equipment for purposes of computing the amount of depreciation allowable for income tax purposes, assuming the data presented in Instruction (5)?

Problem 10–4A
Correcting entries.

OBJ. 1, 5, 6

The following recording errors occurred and were discovered during the current year:

(a) The $1,100 cost of repairing factory equipment damaged in the process of installation was charged to Factory Equipment.
(b) Office equipment with a book value of $6,700 was traded in for similar equipment with a list price of $50,000. The trade-in allowance on the old equipment was $10,500, and a note payable was given for the balance. A gain on disposal of plant assets of $3,800 was recorded.
(c) Property taxes of $5,000 were paid on real estate acquired during the year and were debited to Property Tax Expense. Of this amount, $2,000 was for taxes that were delinquent at the time the property was acquired.
(d) The sale of a computer for $875 was recorded by an $875 credit to Office Equipment. The original cost of the computer was $3,900, and the related balance in Accumulated Depreciation at the beginning of the current year was $3,000. Depreciation of $400 accrued during the current year, prior to the sale, had not been recorded.
(e) The $1,900 cost of a major motor overhaul expected to prolong the life of a truck two years beyond the original estimate was debited to Delivery Expense. The truck was acquired new four years earlier.

(f) The $11,100 cost of repainting several interior rooms of a building was debited to Building. The building had been owned and occupied for 20 years.

(g) The cost of a razed building, $25,000, was debited to Loss on Disposal of Plant Assets and credited to Building. The building and the land on which it was located had been acquired at a total cost of $100,000 ($75,000 debited to Land, $25,000 debited to Building) as a parking area for the adjacent plant.

(h) The fee of $7,500 paid to the wrecking contractor to raze the building in (g) was debited to Miscellaneous Expense.

(i) A $350 charge for incoming transportation on an item of factory equipment was debited to Transportation In.

Instructions:

Journalize the entries to correct the errors during the current year. Identify each entry by letter.

Problem 10–5A
Transactions for plant assets, including trade.
OBJ. 1, 5, 6

The following transactions, adjusting entries, and closing entries were completed by Rhodes Furniture Co. during 3 fiscal years ending on June 30. All are related to the use of delivery equipment. The declining-balance method (twice the straight-line rate) of depreciation is used:

1990–1991 Fiscal Year

July   1. Purchased a used delivery truck for $18,500, paying cash.

3. Paid $1,500 to replace the automatic transmission and install new brakes on the truck. (Debit Delivery Equipment.)

Dec. 20. Paid garage $220 for changing the oil, replacing the oil filter, and tuning the engine on the delivery truck.

June 30. Recorded depreciation on the truck for the fiscal year. The estimated useful life of the truck is 8 years, with a residual value of $3,000.

30. Closed the appropriate accounts to the income summary account.

1991–1992 Fiscal Year

Sept. 2. Paid garage $235 to tune the engine and make other minor repairs on the truck.

Oct. 31. Traded in the used truck for a new truck priced at $30,250, receiving a trade-in allowance of $14,000 and paying the balance in cash. (Record depreciation to date in 1991.)

June 30. Recorded depreciation on the truck. It has an estimated trade-in value of $2,750 and an estimated life of 10 years.

30. Closed the appropriate accounts to the income summary account.

1992–1993 Fiscal Year

Apr.   1. Purchased a new truck for $36,000, paying cash.

2. Sold the truck purchased October 31, 1991, for $22,500. (Record depreciation for the year.)

June 30. Recorded depreciation on the remaining truck. It has an estimated residual value of $4,500 and an estimated useful life of 8 years.

30. Closed the appropriate accounts to the income summary account.

Instructions:

(1) Open the following accounts in the ledger:
    122 Delivery Equipment
    123 Accumulated Depreciation—Delivery Equipment
    616 Depreciation Expense—Delivery Equipment
    617 Truck Repair Expense
    812 Gain on Disposal of Plant assets

(2) Record the transactions and the adjusting and closing entries. Post to the accounts and extend the balances after each posting.

If the working papers correlating with the textbook are not used, omit Problem 10–6A.

Problem 10–6A
Plant asset
transactions and
subsidiary plant
ledger.

OBJ. 3, 6

Lasorta Press Co. maintains a subsidiary equipment ledger for the printing equipment and accumulated depreciation accounts in the general ledger. A small portion of the subsidiary ledger, the two controlling accounts, and a journal are presented in the working papers. The company computes depreciation on each individual item of equipment. Transactions and adjusting entries affecting the printing equipment are described as follows:

1990
July   2. Purchased a binder (Model G, Serial No. 19752) from Maas Manufacturing Co. on account for $102,000. The estimated useful life of the asset is 12 years, it is expected to have no residual value, and the straight-line method of depreciation is to be used. (This is the only transaction of the year that directly affected the printing equipment account.)

Dec. 31. Recorded depreciation for the year in subsidiary accounts 120-22 to 120-24, and inserted the new balances. (An assistant recorded the depreciation and the new balances in accounts 120-1 to 120-21.)

31. Journalized and posted the annual adjusting entry for depreciation on printing equipment. The depreciation for the year, recorded in subsidiary accounts 120-1 to 120-21, totaled $51,500 to which was added the depreciation entered in accounts 120-22 to 120-24.

1991
Sept. 30. Purchased a Model P rotary press from Birk Press Inc., priced at $60,000, giving the Model 11 Linotype (Account No. 120-23) in exchange, plus $15,000 cash and a series of ten $3,000 notes payable, maturing at 6-month intervals. The estimated useful life of the new press is 10 years, and it is expected to have a residual value of $6,250. (Recorded depreciation to date in 1991 on item traded in.)

Instructions:

(1) Journalize the transaction of July 2. Post to Printing Equipment in the general ledger and to Account No. 120-24 in the subsidiary ledger.

(2) Journalize the adjusting entry on December 31 and post to Accumulated Depreciation—Printing Equipment in the general ledger.

(3) Journalize the entries required by the purchase of printing equipment on September 30. Post to Printing Equipment and to Accumulated Depreciation—Printing Equipment in the general ledger and to Account Nos. 120-23 and 120-25 in the subsidiary ledger.

(4) If the rotary press purchased on September 30 had been depreciated by the declining-balance method at twice the straight-line rate, determine the depreciation on this press for the fiscal years ending (a) December 31, 1991, and (b) December 31, 1992.

Problem 10–7A
Income statement
and balance sheet
for corporation.

OBJ. 4, 9, 10

The trial balance of Staub Corporation at the end of the current calendar year, before adjustments, is as follows:

Cash	27,700	
Accounts Receivable	62,600	
Allowance for Doubtful Accounts		500
Merchandise Inventory	179,200	
Prepaid Expense	10,750	
Land	50,000	
Buildings	225,000	
Accumulated Depreciation—Buildings		90,000
Office Equipment	41,100	
Accumulated Depreciation—Office Equipment		17,600
Store Equipment	52,200	
Accumulated Depreciation—Store Equipment		22,100
Delivery Equipment	57,850	
Accumulated Depreciation—Delivery Equipment		21,750
Patents	18,000	
Accounts Payable		40,200
Notes Payable (short-term)		25,000
Capital Stock		250,000
Retained Earnings		180,250
Dividends	70,000	
Sales (net)		999,750
Purchases (net)	706,550	
Operating Expenses (controlling account)	144,600	
Interest Expense	1,600	
	1,647,150	1,647,150

Data needed for year-end adjustments:

(a) Estimated uncollectible accounts at December 31, $7,200.
(b) Merchandise inventory at December 31, $171,000.
(c) Insurance and other prepaid operating expenses expired during the year, $6,750.
(d) Depreciation is computed at composite rates on the average of the beginning and the ending balances of the plant asset accounts. The beginning balances and rates are as follows:

Office Equipment, $37,900; 10%   Delivery Equipment, $57,150; 20%
Store Equipment, $49,200; 8%   Buildings, $225,000; 2%

(e) Amortization of patents computed for the year, $3,000.
(f) Accrued liabilities at the end of the year, $2,000, of which $250 is for interest on the notes and $1,750 is for wages and other operating expenses.

Instructions:

(1) Prepare a multiple-step income statement for the current year.
(2) Prepare a balance sheet in report form, presenting the plant assets in the manner illustrated in this chapter.

Series B

Problem 10–1B
Allocation of expenditures and receipts to plant asset accounts.
OBJ. 1

The following expenditures and receipts are related to land, land improvements, and buildings acquired for use in a business enterprise. The receipts are identified by an asterisk.

(a)	Cost of real estate acquired as a plant site: Land	$140,000
	Building	65,000
(b)	Delinquent real estate taxes on property assumed by purchaser	11,250
(c)	Cost of razing and removing the building	6,400
(d)	Fee paid to attorney for title search	2,750

(e) Cost of land fill and grading...	$ 14,500
(f) Architect's and engineer's fees for plans and supervision	54,000
(g) Premium on 1-year insurance policy during construction...............	5,500
(h) Paid to building contractor for new building................................	600,000
(i) Cost of repairing windstorm damage during construction..............	1,250
(j) Cost of paving parking lot to be used by customers	20,000
(k) Cost of trees and shrubbery planted	32,500
(l) Special assessment paid to city for extension of water main to the property...	7,500
(m) Cost of repairing vandalism damage during construction..............	500
(n) Interest incurred on building loan during construction	40,000
(o) Cost of floodlights installed on parking lot	13,500
(p) Proceeds from sale of salvage materials from old building	1,100*
(q) Money borrowed to pay building contractor.................................	500,000*
(r) Proceeds from insurance company for windstorm damage...........	1,000*
(s) Refund of premium on insurance policy (g) canceled after 11 months..	350*

Instructions:

Assign each expenditure and receipt (indicate receipts by an asterisk) to Land (permanently capitalized), Land Improvements (limited life), Building, or Other Accounts. Identify each item by letter and list the amount in columnar form, as follows:

Item	Land	Land Improvements	Building	Other Accounts
	$	$	$	$

Problem 10–2B

Depreciation by four methods.

OBJ. 3

Thompson Company purchased equipment on January 2, 1991, for $80,000. The equipment was expected to have a useful life of 4 years, or 14,800 operating hours, and a residual value of $6,000. The equipment was used for 3,200 hours during 1991 and for 4,000, 3,800, and 3,800 hours for 1992, 1993, and 1994 respectively.

Instructions:

Determine the amount of depreciation expense for the fiscal years ending December 31, 1991, 1992, 1993, and 1994 by (a) the straight-line method, (b) the declining-balance method, using twice the straight-line rate, (c) the sum-of-the-years-digits method, and (d) the units-of-production method.

Problem 10–3B

Depreciation by three methods; trade of plant asset.

OBJ. 3, 6

An item of new equipment, acquired at a cost of $150,000 at the beginning of a fiscal year, has an estimated useful life of 5 years and an estimated residual value of $15,000. The manager requested information regarding the effect of alternative methods on the amount of depreciation expense each year. Upon the basis of the data presented to the manager, the declining-balance method was selected.

In the first week of the fifth year, the equipment was traded in for similar equipment priced at $170,000. The trade-in allowance on the old equipment was $20,000, cash of $25,000 was paid, and a note payable was issued for the balance.

Instructions:

(1) Determine the annual depreciation expense for each of the estimated 5 years of use, the accumulated depreciation at the end of each year, and the book value of the equipment at the end of each year by (a) the straight-line method, (b) the sum-of-the-years-digits method, and (c) the declining-balance method (at twice the straight-line rate). The following columnar headings are suggested for each schedule:

Year	Depreciation Expense	Accumulated Depreciation, End of Year	Book Value, End of Year

(2) For financial reporting purposes, determine the cost basis of the new equipment acquired in the exchange.
(3) Present the entry to record the exchange.
(4) What is the cost basis of the new equipment for purposes of computing the amount of depreciation allowable for income tax purposes?
(5) Present the entry to record the exchange, assuming that the trade-in allowance was $10,000 instead of $20,000.
(6) What is the cost basis of the new equipment for purposes of computing the amount of depreciation allowable for income tax purposes, assuming the data presented in Instruction (5)?

Problem 10–5B
Transactions for plant assets, including trade.
OBJ. 1, 5, 6

SOLUTIONS SOFTWARE

The following transactions, adjusting entries, and closing entries were completed by Robb Furniture Co. during a 3-year period. All are related to the use of delivery equipment. The declining-balance method (twice the straight-line rate) of depreciation is used.

1990
Jan.   4. Purchased a used delivery truck for $12,800, paying cash.
       7. Paid $1,600 for major repairs to the truck.
Aug. 11. Paid garage $195 for miscellaneous repairs to the truck.
Dec. 31. Recorded depreciation on the truck for the fiscal year. The estimated useful life of the truck is 4 years, with a residual value of $2,000.
      31. Closed the appropriate accounts to the income summary account.
1991
June 30. Traded in the used truck for a new truck priced at $26,000, receiving a trade-in allowance of $6,000 and paying the balance in cash. (Record depreciation to date in 1991.)
Nov.   4. Paid garage $195 for miscellaneous repairs to the truck.
Dec. 31. Recorded depreciation on the truck. It has an estimated residual value of $5,250 and an estimated useful life of 5 years.
      31. Closed the appropriate accounts to the income summary account.
1992
Oct.   1. Purchased a new truck for $24,400, paying cash.
       2. Sold the truck purchased in 1991 for $16,000. (Record depreciation to date in 1992.)
Dec. 31. Recorded depreciation on the remaining truck. It has an estimated residual value of $1,500 and an estimated useful life of 8 years.
      31. Closed the appropriate accounts to the income summary account.

Instructions:

(1) Open the following accounts in the ledger:

    122 Delivery Equipment
    123 Accumulated Depreciation—Delivery Equipment
    616 Depreciation Expense—Delivery Equipment
    617 Truck Repair Expense
    812 Gain on Disposal of Plant Assets

(2) Record the transactions and the adjusting and closing entries. Post to the accounts and extend the balances after each posting.

If the working papers correlating with the textbook are not used, omit Problem 10–6B.

Problem 10–6B
Plant asset transactions and subsidiary plant asset ledger.
OBJ. 3, 6

Cosby Press Inc. maintains a subsidiary equipment ledger for the printing equipment and accumulated depreciation accounts in the general ledger. A small portion of the subsidiary ledger, the two controlling accounts, and a journal are presented in the working papers. The company computes depreciation on each individual item of equipment. Transactions and adjusting entries affecting the printing equipment are described as follows:

1990

Sept. 1. Purchased a binder (Model C6, Serial No. 2795) from Weiss Manufacturing Co. on account for $90,000. The estimated useful life of the asset is 10 years, it is expected to have no residual value, and the straight-line method of depreciation is to be used. (This is the only transaction of the year that directly affected the printing equipment account.)

Dec. 31. Recorded depreciation for the year in subsidiary accounts 120-22 to 120-24, and inserted the balances. (An assistant recorded the depreciation and the new balances in accounts 120-1 to 120-21.)

      31. Journalized and posted the annual adjusting entry for depreciation on printing equipment. The depreciation for the year, recorded in subsidiary accounts 120-1 to 120-21, totaled $56,200, to which was added the depreciation entered in accounts 120-22 to 120-24.

1991

Mar. 31. Purchased a Model 17 rotary press from Clark Press Inc., priced at $50,000, giving the Model 11 Linotype (Account No. 120-23) in exchange plus $7,500 cash and a series of four $5,000 notes payable, maturing at 6-month intervals. The estimated useful life of the new press is 10 years, and it is expected to have a residual value of $1,750. (Recorded depreciation to date in 1991 on item traded in.)

Instructions:

(1) Journalize the transaction of September 1. Post to Printing Equipment in the general ledger and to Account No. 120-24 in the subsidiary ledger.

(2) Journalize the adjusting entry required on December 31 and post to Accumulated Depreciation — Printing Equipment in the general ledger.

(3) Journalize the entries required by the purchase of printing equipment on March 31. Post to Printing Equipment and to Accumulated Depreciation — Printing Equipment in the general ledger and to Account Nos. 120-23 and 120-25 in the subsidiary ledger.

(4) If the rotary press purchased on March 31 had been depreciated by the declining-balance method at twice the straight-line rate, determine the depreciation on this press for the fiscal years ending (a) December 31, 1991, and (b) December 31, 1992.

MINI-CASE 10

FRANK
CRAMER
& company

Frank Cramer, president of Frank Cramer and Company, is considering the purchase of twelve light-duty trucks on July 1, 1991, for $120,000. The trucks have a useful life of 5 years and no residual value. In the past, all plant assets have been leased. For tax purposes, Cramer was considering depreciating the trucks by the straight-line method. He discussed the matter with his CPA and learned that, although the straight-line method could be elected, it was to his advantage to use the modified accelerated cost recovery system (MACRS) for tax purposes. He has asked for your advice as to which method to use for tax purposes.

Instructions:

(1) Compute depreciation for each of the years (1991, 1992, 1993, 1994, 1995, and 1996) of useful life by (a) the straight-line method and (b) MACRS. In using the straight-line method, one-half year's depreciation should be computed for 1991 and 1996. The rates to be used for MACRS are presented on page 394.

(2) Assuming that income before depreciation and income tax is estimated to be $100,000 uniformly per year, and that the income tax rate is 30%, compute the net income for each of the years 1991, 1992, 1993, 1994, 1995, and 1996 if (a) the straight-line method is used and (b) MACRS is used.

(3) What factors would you present for Cramer's consideration in the selection of a depreciation method?

ETHICS DISCUSSION CASE

Ken Cantrell, CPA, is an assistant to the controller of Sinclair Inc. In his spare time, Ken also prepares tax returns and performs general accounting services for clients. Frequently, Ken performs these services after his normal working hours, using Sinclair Inc.'s microcomputers and laser printers. Occasionally, Ken's clients will call him at the office during regular working hours.

Discuss whether Ken Cantrell is performing in an ethical manner.

ANSWERS TO SELF-EXAMINATION QUESTIONS

1. **C** All expenditures necessary to get a plant asset (such as machinery) in place and ready for use are proper charges to the asset account. In the case of machinery acquired, the transportation costs (answer A) and the installation costs (answer B) are both (answer C) proper charges to the machinery accounts.

2. **A** The periodic charge for depreciation under the sum-of-the-years-digits method is determined by multiplying a fraction by the original cost of the asset after the estimated residual value has been subtracted. The denominator of the fraction, which remains constant, is the sum of the digits representing the years of life, or 6(3 + 2 + 1), in the question. The numerator of the fraction, which changes each year, is the number of years of life remaining at the beginning of the year for which depreciation is being computed, or 3 for the first year, 2 for the second year, and 1 for the third year in the question. The $4,500 (answer A) of depreciation for the first year is determined as follows:

$$\frac{\text{Years of Life Remaining at Beginning of Year}}{\text{Sum of Digits for Years of Life}} \times \left[\text{Cost} - \frac{\text{Estimated}}{\text{Residual Value}} \right]$$

$$\frac{3}{3 + 2 + 1} \times (\$9,500 - \$500)$$

$$= \frac{1}{2} \times \$9,000 = \$4,500$$

3. **B** Depreciation methods that provide for a higher depreciation charge in the first year of the use of an asset and a gradually declining periodic charge thereafter are referred to as accelerated depreciation methods. Examples of such methods are the sum-of-the-years-digits (answer B) and the declining-balance methods.

4. **D** The acceptable method of accounting for an exchange of similar assets in which the trade-in allowance ($30,000) exceeds the book value of the old asset ($25,000) requires that the cost of the new asset be determined by adding the amount of boot given ($70,000) to the book value of the old asset ($25,000), which totals $95,000.

5. **D** Long-lived assets that are useful in operations, not held for sale, and without physical qualities are referred to as intangible assets. Patents, goodwill, and copyrights are examples of intangible assets (answer D).

CHAPTER ELEVEN
PAYROLL, NOTES PAYABLE, AND OTHER CURRENT LIABILITIES

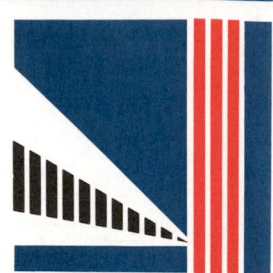

CHAPTER OBJECTIVES

1 Describe and illustrate the determination of payrolls, including liabilities arising from employee earnings and deductions from earnings.

2 Describe and illustrate accounting systems for payroll and payroll taxes.

3 Describe and illustrate accounting for employee fringe benefits, including vacation pay and pensions.

4 Describe and illustrate accounting for short-term notes payable.

5 Describe and illustrate accounting for product warranties.

Payables are the opposite of receivables. They are debts owed by an enterprise to its creditors. Money claims against a firm may originate in many ways, such as purchases of merchandise or services on account, loans from banks, and purchases of equipment and marketable securities on a credit basis. At any particular moment, a business may also owe its employees for wages or salaries accrued, banks or other creditors for interest accrued on notes, and governmental agencies for taxes.

Some types of current liabilities, such as accounts payable, have been discussed in earlier chapters. Additional types of current liabilities, including liabilities arising from payrolls, vacation pay, pensions, notes payable, and product warranties, are discussed in this chapter.

PAYROLL AND PAYROLL TAXES

OBJECTIVE 1
Describe and illustrate the determination of payrolls, including liabilities arising from employee earnings and deductions from earnings.

The term **payroll** is often used to refer to the total amount paid to employees for a certain period. Payroll expenditures are usually significant for several reasons. First, employees are sensitive to payroll errors or irregularities, and maintaining good employee morale requires that the payroll be paid on a timely, accurate basis. Second, payroll expenditures are subject to various federal and state regulations. Finally, the amount of these payroll expenditures and related payroll taxes has a significant effect on the net income of most business enterprises. Although the degree of importance of such expenses varies widely, it is not unusual for a business to expend nearly a third of its sales revenue for payroll and payroll-related expenses. These expenses and their related liabilities are discussed in the following sections.

Liability for Employee Earnings

The term **salary** is usually applied to payment for managerial, administrative, or similar services. The rate of salary is ordinarily expressed in terms of

426

a month or a year. Remuneration for manual labor, both skilled and unskilled, is commonly called **wages** and is stated on an hourly, weekly, or piecework basis. In practice, the terms salary and wages are often used interchangeably.

The basic salary or wage of an employee may be supplemented by commissions, bonuses, profit sharing, or cost-of-living adjustments. The form in which remuneration is paid generally has no effect on the manner in which it is treated by either the employer or the employee. Although payment is usually in terms of cash, it may take such forms as securities, notes, lodging, or other property or services.

Salary and wage rates are determined, in general, by agreement between the employer and the employees. Enterprises engaged in interstate commerce must also follow the requirements of the Fair Labor Standards Act. Employers covered by this legislation, which is commonly called the Federal Wage and Hour Law, are required to pay a minimum rate of $1\frac{1}{2}$ times the regular rate for all hours worked in excess of 40 hours per week. Exemptions from the requirements are provided for executive, administrative, and certain supervisory positions. Premium rates for overtime or for working at night or other less desirable times are fairly common, even when not required by law, and the premium rates may be as much as twice the base rate.

Determination of Employee Earnings. To illustrate the computation of the earnings of an employee, it is assumed that Thomas C. Johnson is employed at the rate of $20 per hour for the first 40 hours in the weekly pay period and at $30 ($20 + $10) per hour for any additional hours. His time card shows that he worked 46 hours during the week ended December 27. His earnings for that week are computed as follows:

Earnings at base rate (40 × $20).....................	$800.00
Earnings at overtime rate (6 × $30)	180.00
Total earnings..	$980.00

The foregoing computations can be stated in generalized arithmetic formulas or algorithms. If the hours worked during the week are less than or equal to ($\leq$) 40, the formula may be expressed by the following equation, where E represents total earnings, H represents hours worked, and R represents hourly rate:

$$E = H \times R$$

This equation cannot be used to determine the earnings of an employee who has worked more than (>) 40 hours during the week, because the overtime rate differs from the basic rate. The expansion of the equation to include the additional factor of overtime yields the following:

$$E = 40 R + 1.5 R(H - 40)$$

The two equations can be expressed as shown in the following algorithm:

If	Then
$H \leq 40$	$E = H \times R$
$H > 40$	$E = 40R + 1.5R(H - 40)$

After the value of H and R are known for each employee at the end of a payroll period, the earnings of each employee can be computed accurately and speedily. Application of the standardized procedure of the algorithm to computers makes it possible to process a payroll routinely, regardless of its size.

Determination of Profit-Sharing Bonuses. Many enterprises pay their employees an annual bonus in addition to their regular salary or wage. The amount of the bonus is often based on the productivity of the employees, as measured by the net income of the enterprise. Such profit-sharing bonuses are treated in the same manner as wages and salaries.

The method used in determining the amount of a profit-sharing bonus is usually stated in the agreement between the employer and the employees. When the amount of the bonus is measured by a certain percentage of income, there are four basic formulas for the computation. The percentage may be applied (1) to income before deducting the bonus and income taxes, (2) to income after deducting the bonus but before deducting income taxes, (3) to income before deducting the bonus but after deducting income taxes, or (4) to net income after deducting both the bonus and income taxes.

Determination of a 10% bonus according to each of the four methods is illustrated as follows, based on the assumption that the employer's income before deducting the bonus and income taxes amounts to $150,000, and that income taxes are levied at the rate of 40% of income. Bonus and income taxes are abbreviated as B and T respectively.

(1) Bonus based on income before deducting bonus and taxes.

$$B = .10 (\$150,000)$$
Bonus = $15,000

(2) Bonus based on income after deducting bonus but before deducting taxes.

$$B = .10 (\$150,000 - B)$$

Simplifying: $B = \$15,000 - .10B$
Transposing: $1.10B = \$15,000$
Bonus = $13,636.36

(3) Bonus based on income before deducting bonus but after deducting taxes.

B equation: $B = .10 (\$150,000 - T)$
T equation: $T = .40 (\$150,000 - B)$

Substituting for T in the B equation and solving for B:
$$B = .10 [\$150,000 - .40 (\$150,000 - B)]$$
Simplifying: $B = .10 (\$150,000 - \$60,000 + .40B)$
Simplifying: $B = \$15,000 - \$6,000 + .04B$
Transposing: $.96B = \$9,000$
Bonus = $9,375

(4) Bonus based on net income after deducting bonus and taxes.

B equation: $B = .10 (\$150,000 - B - T)$
T equation: $T = .40 (\$150,000 - B)$

Substituting for T in the B equation and solving for B:
$$B = .10 [\$150,000 - B - .40 (\$150,000 - B)]$$
Simplifying: $B = .10 (\$150,000 - B - \$60,000 + .40B)$
Simplifying: $B = \$15,000 - .10B - \$6,000 + .04B$
Transposing: $1.06B = \$9,000$
Bonus = $8,490.57

With the amount of the bonus possibilities ranging from the high of $15,000 to the low of $8,490.57, the importance of strictly following the bonus agreement is evident. If the bonus is to be shared by all of the employees, the agreement must also provide for the manner by which the bonus is divided among them. A common method is to express the bonus as a percentage of total earnings for the year. For example, if the bonus were computed to be $15,000 and employee earnings before the bonus had been $100,000, the bonus for each of the employees could be stated as 15% of their earnings.

MANAGER'S REWARDS FOR CORPORATE PERFORMANCE

The role of bonuses in compensation plans is becoming increasingly important in many companies. Examples of how and why companies are using bonuses, particularly for their executives, were given in articles in *The Wall Street Journal*, excerpts from which are as follows:

David Margolis works for a [very] generous company ... [In 1985,] Mr. Margolis, the president, chairman and chief executive officer of Colt Industries Inc., received a bonus of $555,000, more than double the average bonus for chief executives of similar-sized companies. And that bonus was $115,680 more than his base salary. Total compensation: close to $1 million.

... On top of his regular salary of $363,931, [Paul Fireman, Chairman of Reebok International Ltd.] received a bonus of $12.7 million ... [for 1986.]

That sum reflects an agreement under which Mr. Fireman is entitled to an annual bonus equal to 5% of the amount by which the company's annual pre-tax earnings exceeds $20 million. Pre-tax earnings for the maker of athletic shoes soared to $261.2 million in 1986 from $78.1 million in 1985 ...

... After years of regularly receiving hefty increases in salary and bonus — regardless of their company's success or failure — more top execu-

tives are now finding their compensation linked directly to corporate performance ...

"There's been so much scrutiny that boards have been taking a closer look" at compensation, says Pete Smith, national director of Wyatt Co.'s compensation consulting business. As a result, companies are relying less on salary and more on bonuses and other performance-linked compensation to reward executives. They are also tightening the criteria for earning those rewards .... [For example,] more compensation is being pegged to three-year or five-year gains in ... performance ....

Some companies also want to extend bonuses, which are usually limited to senior executives, to lower-level managers. Specialists believe that bonuses work successfully as incentives only if they amount to 15% or more of total compensation. But most lower-level managers are unwilling to risk that large a portion of their income ....

The solution — adding bonuses to existing salaries — means a big increase in costs. But some executives say those costs are worth it to retain first-class management. Says David Jones, chairman and chief executive of Humana Corp.: "You don't pay executives with cornflakes. There's always costs of employing executives. If the costs are reasonable, you pay them. You have to pay what the marketplace demands."

Source: Amanda Bennet, "More Managers Find Salary, Bonus Are Tied Directly to Performance," *The Wall Street Journal*, February 28, 1986 and Christopher J. Chipello, "Reebok's Chairman Got Bonuses Totaling $12.7 Million in '86, "*The Wall Street Journal*, April 14, 1987.

Deductions from Employee Earnings

The total earnings of an employee for a payroll period, including bonuses and overtime pay, are often called the **gross pay**. From this amount is subtracted one or more **deductions** to arrive at the **net pay**, which is the amount the employer must pay the employee. The deductions for federal taxes are of the widest applicability and usually the largest in amount. Deductions may also be needed for state or local income taxes and for contributions to state unemployment compensation programs. Other deductions may be made for contributions to pension plans and for items authorized by individual employees.

FICA Tax. Most employers are required by the Federal Insurance Contributions Act (FICA) to withhold a portion of the earnings of each of their employees. The amount of **FICA** tax withheld is the employees' contribution to the combined federal programs for old-age and disability benefits, insurance benefits to survivors, and health insurance for the aged (medicare). With very few exceptions, employers are required to withhold from each employee a tax at a specified rate on earnings up to a specified amount paid in the calendar year. Although both the schedule of future tax rates and the maximum amount subject to tax are revised often by Congress, such changes have no effect on the basic outline of the payroll system.[1] For purposes of illustration, a rate of 7.5% on maximum annual earnings of $50,000, or a maximum annual tax of $3,750, will be assumed.

Federal Income Tax. Except for certain types of employment, all employers must withhold a portion of the earnings of their employees for payment of the employees' liability for federal income tax. The amount that must be withheld from each employee differs according to the amount of gross pay, marital status, and the estimated deductions and exemptions claimed when filing the annual income tax return.

Other Deductions. Deductions from gross earnings for payment of taxes are compulsory. Neither the employer nor the employee has any choice in the matter. In addition, however, there may be other deductions authorized by individual employees or by the union representing them. For example, an employee may authorize deductions for the purchase of United States savings bonds, for contributions to a United Fund or other charitable organization, for payment of premiums on various types of employee insurance, or for the purchase of a retirement annuity. The union contract may also require the deduction of union dues or other deductions for group benefits.

Computation of Employee Net Pay

Gross earnings for a payroll period less the payroll deductions yields the amount to be paid to the employee, which is often called the **net pay** or **take-home pay**. The amount to be paid Thomas C. Johnson for the week ended December 27 is $730.80, based on the following summary:

Gross earnings for the week		$980.00
Deductions:		
FICA tax....................................	$ 37.50	
Federal income tax.....................	186.70	
U.S. savings bonds	20.00	
United Fund	5.00	
Total deductions......................		249.20
Net pay		$730.80

As has been indicated, there is a ceiling on the annual earnings subject to the FICA tax, and consequently the amount of the annual tax is also lim-

---

[1]Current tax rates and the amount of earnings subject to tax may be located in Internal Revenue Service publications and in standard tax reporting services.

ited. Therefore, when the amount of FICA tax to withhold from an employee is determined for a payroll period, it is necessary to refer to one of the following cumulative amounts:

1. Employee gross earnings for the year up to, but not including, the current payroll period, or
2. Employee tax withheld for the year up to, but not including, the current payroll period.

To continue with the illustration, reference to Johnson's earnings record shows cumulative earnings of $49,500 prior to the current week's earnings of $980. The amount of the current week's earnings subject to FICA tax is therefore the maximum of $500 ($50,000 − $49,500), and the FICA tax to be withheld is $37.50 (7.5% of $500). Alternatively, the determination could be based on the amount of FICA tax withheld from Johnson prior to the current payroll period. This amount, according to the employee record, is $3,712.50, and the amount to be withheld is the maximum of $37.50 ($3,750.00 − $3,712.50).

There is no ceiling on the amount of earnings subject to withholding for income taxes and hence no need to consider the cumulative earnings. The amount of federal income tax withheld would be determined by reference to official withholding tax tables issued by the Internal Revenue Service. For purposes of this illustration, the amount of federal income tax withheld was assumed to be $186.70. The deductions for the purchase of bonds and for the charitable contribution were in accordance with Johnson's authorizations.

As in the determination of gross earnings when overtime rates are a factor, the computation of some deductions can be generalized in the form of algorithms. The algorithm for the determination of the FICA tax deduction, based on the maximum deduction approach, is as follows, where E represents current period's earnings, F represents current period's FICA deduction, and f represents cumulative FICA deductions prior to the current period:

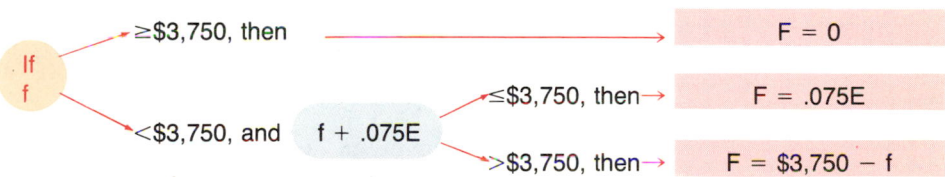

An alternative generalization of the method of determining FICA deductions, based on the maximum taxable earnings approach, is illustrated by the following decision diagram. The additional symbol "e" represents cumulative earnings prior to the current period.

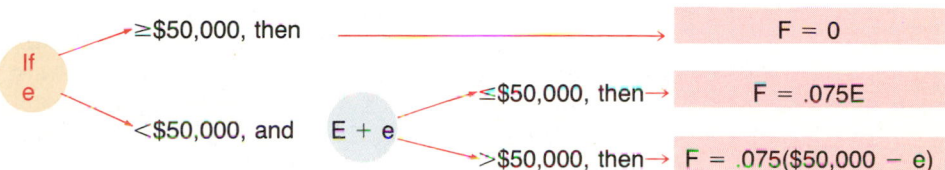

The elements of the decision diagram are examples of standardized instructions that can be applied to computations involving many variables. They are used in many situations as an aid to routine processing of repetitive data, regardless of whether the processing is performed manually or with a computer.

Liability for Employer's Payroll Taxes

Thus far the discussion of taxes has been limited to those levied against employees and withheld by employers. Most employers are subject to federal and state taxes based on the amount of remuneration earned by their employees. Such taxes are an operating expense of the business and may amount to a relatively large sum.

FICA Tax. Employers are required to contribute to the Federal Insurance Contributions Act program for each employee. The tax rate and the maximum amount of employee remuneration entering into an employer's tax base are the same as those applicable to employees, which for purposes of illustration are assumed to be 7.5% and $50,000 respectively.

YOUR SOCIAL SECURITY TAXES

In its 1936 publication, *Security in Your Old Age,* the Social Security Board set forth the following explanation of how the social security tax would affect a worker's paycheck:

The taxes called for in this law will be paid both by your employer and by you. For the next 3 years you will pay maybe 15 cents a week, maybe 25 cents a week, maybe 30 cents or more, according to what you earn. That is to say, during the next 3 years, beginning January 1, 1937, you will pay 1 cent for every dollar you earn, and at the same time your employer will pay 1 cent for every dollar you earn, up to $3,000 a year. Twenty-six million other workers and their employers will be paying at the same time.

After the first 3 years—that is to say, beginning in 1940—you will pay, and your employer will pay, 1½ cents for each dollar you earn, up to $3,000 a year. This will be the tax for 3 years, and then beginning in 1943, you will pay 2 cents, and so will your employer, for every dollar you earn for the next three years. After that, you and your employer will each pay half a cent more for 3 years, and finally, beginning in 1949, twelve years from now, you and your employer will each pay 3 cents on each dollar you earn, up to $3,000 a year. That is the most you will ever pay.

The rate on January 1, 1990, is estimated to be 7.65 cents per dollar earned (7.65%) up to the first $52,000 of earnings.

Source: Adapted from Arthur Lodge, "That Is the Most You Will Ever Pay," *Journal of Accountancy* (October, 1985), p. 44.

Federal Unemployment Compensation Tax. Unemployment insurance provides temporary relief to those who become unemployed as a result of economic forces beyond their control. Types of employment subject to the unemployment insurance program are similar to those covered by the FICA tax. The tax of .8% is levied on employers only, rather than on both employers and employees.[2] It is applicable only to the first $7,000 of the remuneration of each covered employee during a calendar year. As with the FICA tax, the rate and the maximum amount subject to federal unemployment compensation tax are revised often by Congress. The funds collected by the federal government are not paid out as benefits to the unemployed, but are allocated among the states for use in administering state programs.

State Unemployment Compensation Tax. The amounts paid as benefits to unemployed persons are obtained, for the most part, by taxes levied upon employers only. A very few states also require employee contributions. The rates of tax and the tax base vary, and in most states, employers who pro-

---

[2] The rate on January 1, 1990 was 6.2%, which may be reduced to .8% for credits for state unemployment compensation tax.

vide steady employment for their employees are awarded reduced rates. The employment experience and the status of each employer's tax account are reviewed annually, and the merit ratings and tax rates are revised accordingly.[3]

ACCOUNTING SYSTEMS FOR PAYROLL AND PAYROLL TAXES

OBJECTIVE 2
Describe and
illustrate accounting
systems for payroll
and payroll taxes.

Accounting systems for payroll and payroll taxes are concerned with the records and reports associated with the employer-employee relationship. It is important that the accounting system provide safeguards to insure that payments are in accord with management's general plans and its specific authorizations.

All employees of a firm expect and are entitled to receive their remuneration at regular intervals following the close of each payroll period. Regardless of the number of employees and the difficulties in computing the amounts to be paid, the payroll system must be designed to process the necessary data quickly and assure payment of the correct amount to each employee. The system must also provide adequate safeguards against payments to fictitious persons and other misappropriations of funds.

Various federal, state, and local laws require that employers accumulate certain specified data in their payroll records, not only for each payroll period but also for each employee. Periodic reports of such data must be submitted to the appropriate governmental agencies and remittances made for amounts withheld from employees and for taxes levied on the employer. The records must be retained for specified periods of time and be available for inspection by those responsible for enforcement of the laws. In addition, payroll data may be useful in negotiations with labor unions, in settling employee grievances, and in determining rights to vacations, sick leaves, and retirement pensions.

Although complex organizational structures may necessitate the use of detailed subsystems, the major parts common to most payroll systems are the payroll register, employee's earnings record, and payroll checks. Each of these major payroll components is illustrated and discussed in the following sections. Although the illustrations are relatively simple, many modifications might be introduced in actual practice.

Payroll Register

The multicolumn form used in assembling and summarizing the data needed at the end of each payroll period is called the **payroll register**. Its design varies according to the number and classes of employees and the extent to which computers are used. A form suitable for a small number of employees is illustrated on pages 434 and 435.

The nature of most of the data appearing in the illustrative payroll register is evident from the columnar headings. The number of hours worked and the earnings and deduction data are inserted in the appropriate columns. The sum of the deductions applicable to an employee is then deducted from the total earnings to yield the amount to be paid. Recording the check numbers in the payroll register as the checks are written eliminates the need to maintain other detailed records of the payments.

---

[3]As of January 1, 1990, the maximum state rate recognized by the federal unemployment system was 5.4% of the first $7,000 of each employee's earnings during a calendar year.

Payroll Register

PAYROLL FOR WEEK ENDING

| | TOTAL | EARNINGS | | | TAXABLE EARNINGS | |
NAME	HOURS	REGULAR	OVERTIME	TOTAL	UNEMPLOY-MENT COMP.	FICA
ARKIN, JOAN E.	40	500.00		500.00	500.00	500.00
DAWSON, LOREN A.	44	392.00	58.80	450.80		450.80
GREEN, MINDY M.		840.00		840.00		
JOHNSON, THOMAS C.	46	800.00	180.00	980.00		500.00
WYATT, WILLIAM R.	40	480.00		480.00		480.00
ZACHS, ANNA H.		600.00		600.00	150.00	600.00
TOTAL		13,328.70	574.00	13,902.70	2,710.00	11,354.70

The two columns under the general heading of Taxable Earnings are used in accumulating data needed to compute the employer's payroll taxes. The last two columns of the payroll register are used to accumulate the total wages or salaries to be charged to the expense accounts. This process is usually termed **payroll distribution**. If there is an extensive account classification of labor expense, the charges may be analyzed on a separate payroll distribution sheet.

The format of the illustrative payroll register aids the determination of arithmetic accuracy before checks are issued to employees and before the summary amounts are formally recorded. Specifically, all columnar totals except those in the Taxable Earnings columns should be cross-verified. The miscellaneous deductions must also be summarized by account classification. The following tabulation illustrates the method of cross-verification:

Earnings:		
Regular	$13,328.70	
Overtime	574.00	
Total		$13,902.70
Deductions:		
FICA tax	$ 851.60	
Federal income tax	3,332.18	
U.S. savings bonds	680.00	
United Fund	470.00	
Accounts receivable	50.00	
Total		5,383.78
Paid — net amount		$ 8,518.92
Accounts debited:		
Sales Salaries Expense		$11,122.16
Office Salaries Expense		2,780.54
Total (as above)		$13,902.70

DECEMBER 27, 19--

| | DEDUCTIONS | | | | | PAID | | ACCOUNTS DEBITED | |
FICA TAX	FEDERAL INCOME TAX	U.S. SAVINGS BONDS	MISCEL-LANEOUS	TOTAL	NET AMOUNT	CHECK NO.	SALES SALARIES EXPENSE	OFFICE SALARIES EXPENSE
37.50	74.10	20.00	UF 10.00	141.60	358.40	6857	500.00	
33.81	62.60		AR 50.00	146.41	304.39	6858		450.80
	186.30	25.00	UF 10.00	221.30	618.70	6859	840.00	
37.50	186.70	20.00	UF 5.00	249.20	730.80	6860	980.00	
36.00	69.20	10.00		115.20	364.80	6880	480.00	
45.00	71.36	5.00	UF 2.00	123.36	476.64	6881		600.00
851.60	3,332.18	680.00	UF 470.00	5,383.78	8,518.92		11,122.16	2,780.54
			AR 50.00					

MISCELLANEOUS DEDUCTIONS: AR—ACCOUNTS RECEIVABLE   UF—UNITED FUND

Recording Employees' Earnings. The payroll register may be used as a posting medium in a manner like that in which the voucher register and check register are used. Alternatively, it may be used as a supporting record for a compound journal entry that records the payroll data. The entry based on the payroll register illustrated is as follows:

Dec. 27	Sales Salaries Expense 950.0	11,122.16	
	Office Salaries Expense................ 450.00	2,780.54	
	FICA Tax Payable................................		851.60
	Employees Federal Income Tax Payable...		3,332.18
	Bond Deductions Payable......................		680.00
	United Fund Deductions Payable		470.00
	Accounts Receivable—Loren A. Dawson..		50.00
	Salaries Payable..................................		8,518.92
	Payroll for week ended December 27.		

The total expense incurred for the services of employees is recorded by the debits to the salary expense accounts. Amounts withheld from employees' earnings have no effect on the debits to these accounts. Five of the credits in the entry represent increases in specific liability accounts and one represents a decrease in the accounts receivable account.

Recording and Paying Payroll Taxes. Each time the payroll register is prepared, the amounts of all employees' current earnings entering the tax base are listed in the respective taxable earnings columns. As explained earlier, the cumulative amounts of each employee's earnings just prior to the current period are available in the employee's earnings record.

According to the payroll register illustrated for the week ended December 27, the amount of remuneration subject to FICA tax was $11,354.70, and the amount subject to state and federal unemployment compensation taxes was $2,710. Multiplication by the applicable tax rates yields the following amounts:

FICA tax..	$ 851.60
State unemployment compensation tax (5.4% × $2,710)......	146.34
Federal unemployment compensation tax (.8% × $2,710)	21.68
Total payroll taxes expense..	$1,019.62

The journal entry to record the payroll tax expense for the week and the liability for the taxes accrued is as follows:

Dec. 27	Payroll Taxes Expense.............................	1,019.62	
	FICA Tax Payable.................................		851.60
	State Unemployment Tax Payable		146.34
	Federal Unemployment Tax Payable		21.68
	Payroll taxes for week ended December 27.		

Payment of the liability for each of the taxes is recorded in the same manner as the payment of other liabilities. Employers are required to compute and report all payroll taxes on the calendar-year basis, regardless of the fiscal year they may use for financial reporting and income tax purposes. Details of the federal income tax and FICA tax withheld from employees are combined with the employer's FICA tax on a single return accompanied by the amount of tax due. Payments are required on a weekly, semimonthly, monthly, or quarterly basis, depending on the amount of the combined taxes. Unemployment compensation tax returns and payments are required by the federal government on an annual basis. Earlier payments are required when the tax exceeds a certain minimum. Unemployment compensation tax returns and payments are required by most states on a basis similar to that required by the federal government.

All payroll taxes levied against employers become liabilities at the time the related remuneration is *paid* to employees, rather than at the time the liability to the employees is incurred. Observance of this requirement may cause a problem of expense allocation between fiscal periods. To illustrate, assume that an enterprise using the calendar year as its fiscal year pays its employees on Friday for a weekly payroll period ending the preceding Wednesday, the two-day lag between Wednesday and Friday being needed to process the payroll. Regardless of the day of the week on which the year ends, there will be some accrued wages. If it ends on a Thursday, the accrual will cover a full week plus an extra day. Logically, the unpaid wages and the related payroll taxes should both be charged to the period that benefited from the services performed by the employees. On the other hand, there is legally no liability for the payroll taxes until the wages are paid in January, when a new cycle of earnings subject to tax is begun. The distortion of net income that would result from failure to accrue the payroll taxes might well be insignificant. The practice adopted should be followed consistently.

Employee's Earnings Record

The necessity of having the cumulative amount of each employee's earnings readily available at the end of each payroll period was discussed earlier. Without such information or the related data on the cumulative amount of FICA tax previously withheld, there would be no means of determining the appropriate amount to withhold from current earnings. It is essential, therefore, that detailed records be maintained for each employee.

A portion of the **employee's earnings record** is illustrated on pages 438 and 439. The relationship between this record and the payroll register can be seen by tracing the amounts entered on Johnson's earnings record for December 27 back to its source, which is the fourth line of the payroll register illustrated on pages 434 and 435.

In addition to spaces for recording data for each payroll period and the cumulative total of earnings, there are spaces for quarterly totals and the yearly total. These totals are used in various reports for tax, insurance, and other purposes. Copies of one such annual report, known as Form W-2 Wage and Tax Statement, must be given to each employee as well as to the Social Security Administration.

The source of the amounts inserted in the following statement was the employee's earnings record.

Wage and Tax Statement

1 Control number		OMB No. 1545-0008		
2 Employer's name, address, and ZIP code Langford Supply Co. 560 Hudson Avenue Cedar Rapids, IA 52731-6148		3 Employer's identification number 61-843652	4 Employer's state I.D. number	
		5 Statutory employee □ Deceased □ Pension plan □ Legal rep. □	942 emp. □ Subtotal □ Deferred compensation □ Void □	
		6 Allocated tips	7 Advance EIC payment	
8 Employee's social security number 381-48-9120	9 Federal income tax withheld $8,942.06	10 Wages, tips, other compensation $50,480.00	11 Social security tax withheld $3,750.00	
12 Employee's name, address, and ZIP code Thomas C. Johnson 4990 Columbus Avenue Statesville, IA 52732-6142		13 Social security wages $50,000.00	14 Social security tips	
		16	16a Fringe benefits incl. in Box 10	
		17 State income tax	18 State wages, tips, etc.	19 Name of state
		20 Local income tax	21 Local wages, tips, etc.	22 Name of locality

Form **W-2 Wage and Tax Statement 19--**
This information is being furnished to the Internal Revenue Service.
Copy B To be filed with employee's FEDERAL tax return   Dept. of the Treasury—IRS

Payroll Checks

One of the principal outputs of most payroll systems is a series of **payroll checks** at the end of each pay period. The data needed for this purpose are provided by the payroll register, each line of which applies to an individual employee. It is possible to prepare the checks solely by reference to the Net Amount column of the register. However, the customary practice is to provide each employee with a statement of the details of the computation. The statement may be entirely separate from the check or it may be in the form of a detachable stub attached to the check.

When employees are paid by checks drawn on the regular bank account and the voucher system is used, it is necessary to prepare a voucher for the net amount to be paid the employees. The voucher is then recorded in the voucher register as a debit to Salaries Payable and a credit to Accounts Payable, and payment is recorded in the check register in the usual manner. If the voucher system is not used, the payment would be recorded by a debit to Salaries Payable and a credit to Cash.

*Employee's Earnings
Record*

THOMAS C. JOHNSON
4990 COLUMBUS AVENUE   PHONE: 555-3148
STATESVILLE, IA 52732-6142

MARRIED	NUMBER OF WITHHOLDING ALLOWANCES: 4	PAY RATE: $800.00 PER WEEK
OCCUPATION: SALESPERSON		EQUIVALENT HOURLY RATE: $20

EARNINGS

LINE NO.	PERIOD ENDED	TOTAL HOURS	REGULAR EARNINGS	OVERTIME	TOTAL EARNINGS	CUMULATIVE TOTAL
39	SEPT. 27	51	800.00	330.00	1,130.00	38,250.00
THIRD QUARTER			10,400.00	1,770.00	12,170.00	
40	OCT. 4	40	800.00		800.00	39,050.00
46	NOV. 15	41	800.00	30.00	830.00	45,020.00
47	NOV. 22	40	800.00		800.00	45,820.00
48	NOV. 29	42	800.00	60.00	860.00	46,680.00
49	DEC. 6	50	800.00	300.00	1,100.00	47,780.00
50	DEC. 13	40	800.00		800.00	48,580.00
51	DEC. 20	44	800.00	120.00	920.00	49,500.00
52	DEC. 27	46	800.00	180.00	980.00	50,480.00
FOURTH QUARTER			10,400.00	1,830.00	12,230.00	
YEARLY TOTAL			41,600.00	8,880.00	50,480.00	

It should be understood that the journal entry derived from the payroll register, such as the compound entry illustrated on page 435, would precede the entries just described. It should also be noted that the entire amount paid may be recorded as a single item, regardless of the number of employees. There is no need to record each check separately because all of the details are available in the payroll register for future reference.

Most employers with a large number of employees use a special bank account and payroll checks designed specifically for the purpose. After the data for the payroll period have been recorded and summarized in the payroll register, a single check for the total amount to be paid is drawn on the firm's regular bank account and deposited in a special account. The individual payroll checks are then drawn against the special payroll account, and the numbers of the payroll checks are inserted in the payroll register.

The use of special payroll checks relieves the treasurer or other executives of the task of signing a large number of regular checks each payday. The responsibility for signing payroll checks may be given to the paymaster, or mechanical means of signing the checks may be used. Another advantage of this system is that reconciling the regular bank statement is simplified. The paid payroll checks are returned by the bank separately from regular checks and are accompanied by a statement of the special bank account. Any balance shown on the bank's statement will correspond to the sum of the pay-

SOC. SEC. NO.: 381-48-9120   EMPLOYEE NO.: 814

DATE OF BIRTH: OCTOBER 4, 1952

DATE EMPLOYMENT TERMINATED:

| | DEDUCTIONS | | | | PAID | | |
FICA TAX	FEDERAL INCOME TAX	U.S. BONDS	OTHER	TOTAL	NET AMOUNT	CHECK NO.	LINE NO.
84.75	213.60	20.00		318.35	811.65	6175	39
912.75	2,238.30	260.00	AR 40.00	3,451.05	8,718.95		
60.00	150.82	20.00	UF 5.00	235.82	564.18	6225	40
62.25	156.11	20.00		238.36	591.64	6530	46
60.00	150.82	20.00		230.82	569.18	6582	47
64.50	162.41	20.00		246.91	613.09	6640	48
82.50	210.00	20.00	UF 5.00	317.50	782.50	6688	49
60.00	150.82	20.00		230.82	569.18	6743	50
69.00	174.99	20.00		263.99	656.01	6801	51
37.50	186.70	20.00	UF 5.00	249.20	730.80	6860	52
881.25	2,244.60	260.00	UF 15.00	3,400.85	8,829.15		
3,750.00	8,942.06	1,040.00	AR 40.00	13,832.06	36,647.94		
			UF 60.00				

roll checks outstanding because the amount of each deposit is exactly the same as the total amount of checks drawn. The recording procedures are the same as when checks on the regular bank account are used.

Currency is sometimes used as the medium of payment when the payroll is paid each week or when the business location or the time of payment is such that banking or check-cashing facilities are not readily available to employees. In such cases, a single check, payable to Payroll, is drawn for the entire amount to be paid. The check is then cashed at the bank and the money is inserted in individual pay envelopes. Each employee should be required to sign a receipt which serves as evidence of payment. The procedures for recording the payment correspond to those outlined for payroll checks.

Payroll System Diagram

The flow of data within segments of an accounting system may be shown by diagrams such as the one illustrated on page 440. It depicts the interrelationships of the principal parts of the payroll system described in this chapter. The requirement of constant updating of the employee's earnings record is indicated by the dotted line.

Flow Diagram of a Payroll System

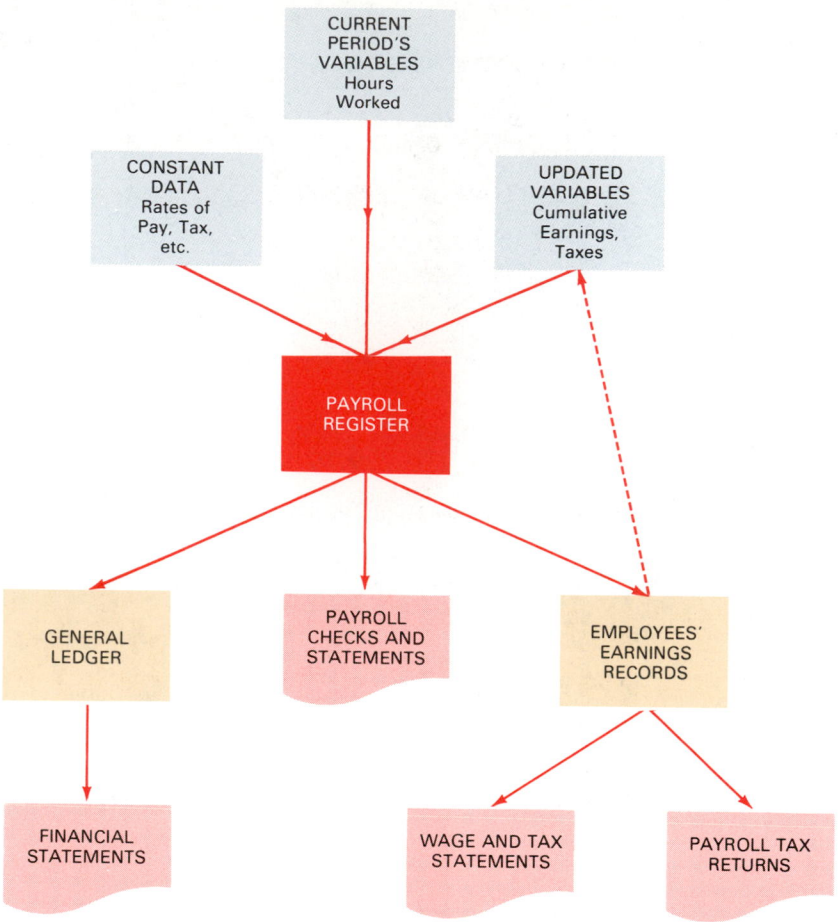

Attention thus far has been directed to the end product or *output* of a payroll system, namely the payroll register, the checks payable to individual employees, the earnings records for each employee, and reports for tax and other purposes. The basic data entering the payroll systems are sometimes called the *input* of the system. Input data that remain relatively unchanged and do not need to be reintroduced into the system for each payroll period are characterized as *constants*. Those data that differ from period to period are termed *variables*.

Constants include such data for each employee as name and social security number, marital status, number of income tax withholding allowances claimed, rate of pay, functional category (office, sales, etc.), and department where employed. The FICA tax rate, maximum earnings subject to tax, and various tax tables are also constants which apply to all employees. The variable data for each employee include the number of hours or days worked during each payroll period, days of sick leave with pay, vacation credits, and cumulative amounts of earnings and taxes withheld. If salespersons are employed on a commission basis, the amount of their sales would also vary from period to period. The forms used in initially recording both the constant and the variable data vary widely according to the complexities of the payroll system and the processing methods used.

Internal Controls for Payroll Systems

The large amount of data and the computations necessary to process the payroll are evident. As the number of employees and the mass of data increase, the number of individuals needed to manage and process payroll data likewise increases. Such characteristics, together with the relative magnitude of labor costs, indicate the need for controls that will assure the reliability of the data and minimize the opportunity for misuse of funds.

The cash disbursement controls discussed in Chapter 7 are applicable to payrolls. Thus, the use of the voucher system and the requirement that all payments be supported by vouchers are desirable. The addition or deletion of names on the payroll should be supported by written authorizations from the personnel department. It is also essential that employees' attendance records be controlled in such a manner as to prevent errors and abuses. Perhaps the most basic and widely used records are "In and Out" cards, whereby employees indicate, often by "punching" a time clock, their time of arrival and departure. Employee identification cards or badges may also be used in this connection to assure that all salaries and wages are paid to the proper individuals.

LIABILITY FOR EMPLOYEES' FRINGE BENEFITS

OBJECTIVE 3
Describe and illustrate accounting for employee fringe benefits, including vacation pay and pensions.

Many companies provide their employees a variety of benefits in addition to salary and wages earned. These benefits, often referred to as **fringe benefits**, may take many forms, such as vacations, employee pension plans, and health, life, and disability insurance. If the employer pays part or all of the cost of the fringe benefits and revenues and expenses are to be matched properly, the estimated cost of these benefits must be recognized as an expense of the period during which the employee earns the benefit. The application of accounting principles to fringe benefits is described in the following paragraphs, using vacation pay and pensions as examples.

Liability for Vacation Pay

Most employees are granted some vacation privileges. To match revenue and expense properly, the employer should accrue the vacation pay liability as the vacation privilege is earned, if the payment is probable and can be reasonably estimated.[4] To illustrate the accounting for vacation absences, frequently referred to as compensated absences, assume that all employees earn two weeks of vacation for each 50 weeks worked during the year, and the total vacation pay expense for the year is $100,000. Since this expense is actually incurred during the 50 weeks the employees work during the year, the expense and the liability could be recorded by an adjusting entry at the end of the accounting period, or recorded each pay period, illustrated as follows:

May 5	Vacation Pay Expense............................	2,000	
	Vacation Pay Payable...........................		2,000
	Vacation pay for week ended May 5		
	(1/50 of annual vacation pay of $100,000).		

[4]*Statement of Financial Accounting Standards*, No. 43, "Accounting for Compensated Absences" (Stamford: Financial Accounting Standards Board, 1980), par. 6.

Depending upon when it is to be paid, the vacation liability will be classified in the balance sheet as either a current liability or a long-term liability. When the payroll in which the employees are paid for their vacations is prepared, Vacation Pay Payable would be debited, and Salaries Payable and the appropriate accounts for recording taxes and withholdings would be credited.

Liability for Pensions

In recent years, retirement pension plans have increased rapidly in number, variety, and complexity. Although the details of the plans vary from employer to employer, pension benefits are usually based on factors such as employee age, years of service, and salary level. In 1974, Congress enacted the Employee Retirement Income Security Act (ERISA), which established guidelines for safeguarding employee benefits.

Pension plans may be classified as contributory or noncontributory, funded or unfunded, and qualified or unqualified. A **contributory plan** requires the employer to withhold a portion of each employee's earnings as a contribution to the plan. The employer then makes a contribution according to the provisions of the plan. A **noncontributory plan** requires the employer to bear the entire cost. A **funded plan** requires the employer to set aside funds to meet future pension benefits by making payments to an independent funding agency. The funding agency is responsible for managing the assets of the pension fund and for disbursing the pension benefits to employees. For many pension plans, insurance companies serve as the funding agency. An **unfunded plan** is managed entirely by the employer instead of by an independent agency. A **qualified plan** is designed to comply with federal income tax requirements which allow the employer to deduct pension contributions for tax purposes and which exempt pension fund income from tax. Most pension plans are qualified.

The accounting for pension plans can be complex due to the uncertainties of projecting future pension obligations. Future pension obligations depend upon such factors as employee life expectancies, expected employee compensation levels, and investment income on pension contributions. Pension funding requirements are estimated by individuals known as actuaries, who use sophisticated mathematical and statistical models.

The employer's cost of an employee's pension plan in a given year, referred to as the **net periodic pension cost**, is debited to an operating expense account, Pension Expense.[5] The credit is to Cash if the pension cost is fully funded. If the pension cost is partially funded, any unfunded amount is credited to Unfunded Accrued Pension Cost. To illustrate, assume that the pension plan of Flossmoor Industries requires an annual pension cost of $25,000, and Flossmoor Industries pays $15,000 to the fund trustee, Equity Insurance Company. The entry to record the transaction is as follows:

Pension Expense	25,000	
Cash		15,000
Unfunded Accrued Pension Cost		10,000

[5]*Statement of Financial Accounting Standards, No. 87,* "Employers' Accounting for Pensions" (Stamford: Financial Accounting Standards Board, 1985), par. 6.

Depending upon when the pension liability (unfunded accrued pension cost) is to be paid, the $10,000 will be classified on the balance sheet as either a long-term or a current liability.

An entity's financial statements should fully disclose the nature of its pension plans and pension obligations. The financial statement disclosures should include the net periodic pension cost for the year and a description of the pension plan, including such items as the employee groups covered, the entity's accounting and funding policies, and any pension changes affecting comparability among years.

When an employer first adopts or changes a pension plan, the employer must consider whether to grant employees credit for prior years service. If a company does grant credit to employees for prior service, a prior service cost obligation must be recognized. The funding of prior service cost is normally provided for over a number of years, thus creating a long-term prior service pension cost liability. The complex nature of accounting for prior service costs is left for more advanced accounting study.

SHORT-TERM NOTES PAYABLE

OBJECTIVE 4
Describe and illustrate accounting for short-term notes payable.

Notes may be issued to creditors in temporary satisfaction of an account payable created earlier, or they may be issued at the time merchandise or other assets are purchased. To illustrate the former, assume that an enterprise issues to Murray Co. a 90-day, 12% note for $1,000, dated December 1, 1990, in settlement of a $1,000 overdue account. The entry to record the transaction is as follows:

Dec. 1	Accounts Payable — Murray Co................	1,000	
	Notes Payable		1,000
	Issued a 90-day, 12% note on account.		

On December 31, 1990, the end of the fiscal year, an adjusting entry would be recorded for the accrual of the interest from December 1 to December 31. The entry to record the accrued expense of $10 ($1,000 × 12/100 × 30/360) is as follows:

	Adjusting Entry		
Dec. 31	Interest Expense	10	
	Interest Payable		10

Interest payable is reported on the balance sheet at December 31, 1990, as a current liability. The interest expense account is closed at December 31, and the amount is reported in the Other Expense section of the income statement for the year ended December 31, 1990.

When the amount due on the note is paid in 1991, part of the interest paid will effect a reduction of the interest that was payable at December 31, 1990, and the remainder will represent expense for 1991. To avoid the possibility of failing to recognize this division and to avoid the inconvenience of analyzing the payment of interest in 1991, a reversing entry is made after the accounts are closed. The effect of the entry, illustrated as follows, is to transfer the credit balance in the interest payable account to the credit side of the interest expense account.

Jan. 1	*Reversing Entry*		
	Interest Payable	10	
	Interest Expense		10

At the time the note matures and payment is made, the entire amount of the interest payment is debited to Interest Expense, as illustrated by the following entry:

Mar. 1	Notes Payable	1,000	
	Interest Expense	30	
	Cash..		1,030

After the foregoing entries are posted, the interest expense account will appear as follows:

ACCOUNT INTEREST EXPENSE   ACCOUNT NO. 911

Date		Item	Post. Ref.	Debit	Credit	Balance	
						Debit	Credit
1990							
Nov.	10		CP40	250		890	
Dec.	31	Adjusting	J17	10		900	
	31	Closing	J17		900	—	—
1991							
Jan.	1	Reversing	J18		10		10
Mar.	1		CP42	30		20	

The adjusting and reversing process divided the $30 of interest paid on March 1, 1991, into two parts for accounting purposes: (1) $10 representing the interest expense for 1990 (recorded by the adjusting entry) and (2) $20 representing the interest expense for 1991 (the balance in the interest expense account at March 1, 1991).

Notes may also be issued when money is borrowed from banks. Although there are many variations in interest and repayment terms, the most direct procedure is for the borrower to issue an interest-bearing note for the amount of the loan. For example, assume that on September 19 a firm borrows $4,000 from the First National Bank, with the loan evidenced by the firm's 90-day, 15% note. The effect of this transaction is as follows:

Sept. 19	Cash...	4,000	
	Notes Payable		4,000

On the due date of the note, ninety days later, the borrower owes $4,000, the face amount of the note, and interest of $150. The accounts are affected by the payment as follows:

Dec. 18	Notes Payable	4,000	
	Interest Expense	150	
	Cash...		4,150

A variant of the bank loan transaction just illustrated is to issue a non-interest-bearing note for the amount that is to be paid at maturity. Although the note issued is non-interest-bearing, interest is deducted from the maturity value of the note and the borrower receives the remainder. The deduction of interest from a future value is termed **discounting**. The rate used in computing the interest may be termed the **discount rate**, the deduction may be called the **discount**, and the net amount available to the borrower is called the **proceeds**.

To illustrate the discounting of a note payable, assume that on August 10 an enterprise issued to a bank a $4,000, 90-day, non-interest-bearing note and that the bank discount rate is 15%. The amount of the discount is $150, and the proceeds are $3,850. The entry to record the transaction is as follows:

Aug. 10	Cash...	3,850	
	Interest Expense	150	
	Notes Payable		4,000

The note payable is recorded at its face value, which is also its maturity value, and the interest expense is recorded at the time the note is issued. When the note is paid, the following entry is recorded:

| Nov. 8 | Notes Payable .... | 4,000 | |
| | Cash... | | 4,000 |

PRODUCT WARRANTY LIABILITY

At the time of sale, a company may grant a warranty on a product. If revenues and expenses are to be matched properly, a liability to cover the warranty must be recorded in the period of the sale.[6] Later, when the product is repaired or replaced, the liability will be reduced. To illustrate, assume that during June a company sells $60,000 of a product, on which there is a 36-month warranty for repairing defects in the product. If past experience indicates that the average cost to repair defects is 5% of the sales price, the entry to record the product warranty liability would be as follows:

June 30	Product Warranty Expense.......................	3,000	
	Product Warranty Payable.....................		3,000
	Product warranty for June,		
	5% × $60,000.		

When the defective product is repaired, the repair costs would be recorded by debiting Product Warranty Payable and crediting Cash, Supplies, or other appropriate account.

---

[6]*Statement of Financial Accounting Standards, No. 5,* "Accounting for Contingencies" (Stamford: Financial Accounting Standards Board, 1975), pars. 8, 24.

CHAPTER REVIEW

KEY POINTS

OBJECTIVE 1

Payroll and Payroll Taxes

The term payroll is used to refer to the total amount paid to employees for a certain period. Payroll includes amounts paid for salaries to managerial or administrative employees as well as wages paid for manual labor.

Many enterprises pay their employees an annual bonus in addition to their regular salary or wage. The amount of the bonus may be measured by a certain percentage of income, which may be computed in a variety of ways.

The total earnings of an employee for a payroll period, including bonuses and overtime pay, are often called the gross pay. From this amount is subtracted one or more deductions to arrive at the net pay. Deductions normally include FICA tax, federal income tax, and state and local income taxes, and may include union dues, charitable contributions, or employee insurance.

Most employers are subject to federal and state taxes based on the amount of remuneration earned by their employees. Such taxes include FICA tax, federal unemployment compensation tax, and state unemployment compensation tax.

OBJECTIVE 2

Accounting Systems for Payroll and Payroll Taxes

Although payroll systems will vary, the major parts common to most payroll systems include the payroll register, payroll checks, and employee's earnings record. Based upon the data in the payroll register, a compound journal entry is usually prepared to record the payroll for a period. This entry recognizes employer and employee payroll taxes as well as the liability for the net pay to the employees. The payment of the payroll liabilities is recorded in the usual manner. The payment of the payroll is usually accomplished through the use of payroll checks.

The employee's earnings record is updated after each payroll period and is used for preparing reports for tax, insurance, and other purposes.

Cash disbursement controls are applicable to payrolls. Thus, the use of the voucher system and the requirement that all payments be supported by vouchers is desirable. Additional controls, such as the maintenance of employees' attendance records, are also desirable.

OBJECTIVE 3

Liability for Employees' Fringe Benefits

Most companies provide their employees a variety of benefits in addition to salary and wages earned. These benefits are referred to as fringe benefits and may take the form of vacations, employee pension plans, health insurance, etc. The estimated cost of these benefits should be recognized as an expense of the period during which the employee earns the benefit.

OBJECTIVE 4

Short-Term Notes Payable

Notes may be issued to creditors in temporary satisfaction of an account payable created earlier, or they may be issued at the time merchandise or other assets are purchased. At the end of the fiscal period, an adjusting entry is normally prepared for the accrual of interest. The interest payable is reported on the balance sheet as a current liability. The adjusting entry for accrued interest at the end of the period is normally reversed to simplify the accounting process in the following period.

Notes may also be issued to borrow money from banks. The notes may be interest-bearing or non-interest-bearing. In the case of non-interest-bearing notes, the interest (discount) is deducted from the face of the note and the borrower receives the balance (proceeds).

OBJECTIVE 5   Product Warranty Liability

At the time of sale, a company may grant a warranty on a product. A liability to cover the warranty should be recorded during the period of the sale.

KEY TERMS

payroll 426
gross pay 429
net pay 429
FICA tax 430
payroll register 433

employee's earnings record 437
discount rate 445
discount 445
proceeds 445

SELF-EXAMINATION QUESTIONS
Answers at end of chapter.

1. An employee's rate of pay is $20 per hour, with time and a half for all hours worked in excess of 40 during a week. The following data are available:

Hours worked during current week................................... 45
Year's cumulative earnings prior to current week.................. $49,400
FICA rate, on maximum of $50,000 of annual earnings............ 7.5%
Federal income tax withheld... $ 212

Based on these data, the amount of the employee's net pay for the current week is:
A. $600   C. $800
B. $693   D. $950

2. Which of the following taxes are employers usually required to withhold from employees?
A. Federal income tax
B. Federal unemployment compensation tax
C. State unemployment compensation tax
D. All of the above

3. With limitations on the maximum earnings subject to the tax, employers incur operating costs for which of the following payroll taxes?
A. FICA tax
B. Federal unemployment compensation tax
C. State unemployment compensation tax
D. All of the above

4. An enterprise issued a $5,000, 60-day, 12% note to the bank. The amount due at maturity is:
A. $4,900   C. $5,100
B. $5,000   D. $5,600

5. An enterprise issued a $5,000, 60-day, non-interest-bearing note to the bank, and the bank discounts the note at 12%. The proceeds are:
A. $4,400   C. $5,000
B. $4,900   D. $5,100

ILLUSTRATIVE PROBLEM

Selected transactions of Grainger Company, completed during the fiscal year ended December 31, are as follows:
Mar. 1. Purchased merchandise on account from Perry Inc., $15,000.
Apr. 10. Issued a 60-day, 12% note for $15,000 to Perry Inc., on account.
June 9. Paid Perry Inc. the amount owed on the note of April 10.

Aug. 1. Issued a 90-day, non-interest-bearing note for $30,000 to Atlantic Coast National Bank. The bank discounted the note at 15%.

Oct. 30. Paid Atlantic Coast National Bank the amount due on the note of August 1.

Dec. 27. Prepared the journal entry to record the biweekly payroll. A summary of the payroll record follows:

Deductions:
FICA tax	$ 4,820
Federal income tax withheld	13,280
State income tax withheld	3,840
Savings bond deductions	630
Medical insurance deductions	960

Salary distribution:
Sales	$50,800
Officers	25,800
Office	6,400
Net amount	$59,470

30. Issued a check in payment of employees' federal income tax of $13,280 and FICA tax of $9,640 due.

31. Issued a check for $8,600 to the pension fund trustee to fully fund the pension cost for December.

31. Prepared a journal entry to record the employees' accrued vacation pay, $32,200.

31. Prepared a journal entry to record the estimated accrued product warranty liability, $41,360.

Instructions:

Record the preceding transactions, using a general journal.

SOLUTION

Mar. 1	Purchases	15,000	
	Accounts Payable — Perry Inc.		15,000
Apr. 10	Accounts Payable — Perry Inc.	15,000	
	Notes Payable		15,000
June 9	Notes Payable	15,000	
	Interest Expense	300	
	Cash		15,300
Aug. 1	Cash	28,875	
	Interest Expense	1,125	
	Notes Payable		30,000
Oct. 30	Notes Payable	30,000	
	Cash		30,000
Dec. 27	Sales Salaries Expense	50,800	
	Officers Salaries Expense	25,800	
	Office Salaries Expense	6,400	
	FICA Tax Payable		4,820
	Employees Federal Income Tax Payable		13,280
	Employees State Income Tax Payable		3,840
	Bond Deductions Payable		630
	Medical Insurance Payable		960
	Salaries Payable		59,470

Dec. 30	Employees Federal Income Tax Payable	13,280	
	FICA Tax Payable	9,640	
	Cash...		22,920
31	Pension Expense	8,600	
	Cash...		8,600
31	Vacation Pay Expense................................	32,200	
	Vacation Pay Payable		32,200
31	Product Warranty Expense..........................	41,360	
	Product Warranty Payable........................		41,360

DISCUSSION QUESTIONS

1. What term is frequently used to refer to the total amount paid to employees for a certain period?

2. If an employee is granted a profit-sharing bonus, is the amount of the bonus (a) part of the employee's earnings and (b) deductible as an expense of the enterprise in determining the federal income tax?

3. The general manager of a business enterprise is entitled to an annual profit-sharing bonus of 8%. For the current year, income before bonus and income taxes is $200,000, and income taxes are estimated at 35% of income before income taxes. Determine the amount of the bonus, assuming that the bonus is based on net income after deducting both bonus and income taxes.

4. What is (a) gross pay? (b) net or take-home pay?

5. (a) Identify the federal taxes that most employers are required to withhold from employees. (b) Give the titles of the accounts to which the amounts withheld are credited.

6. For each of the following payroll-related taxes, indicate whether there is a ceiling on the annual earnings subject to the tax: (a) FICA tax, (b) federal income tax, (c) federal unemployment compensation tax.

7. An employee earns $20 per hour with 1½ times the regular rate for all hours in excess of 40 per week. If the employee worked 50 hours during the current week, what was the gross pay for the week?

8. Based on the data presented in Question 7, determine the net pay for the current week, assuming that gross pay prior to the current week totaled $49,760, the FICA tax rate was 7.5% (with earnings up to $50,000 subject to the tax), and federal income tax to be withheld was $215.

9. Identify the payroll taxes levied against employers.

10. Do payroll taxes levied against employers become liabilities at the time the liabilities for wages are incurred or at the time the wages are paid?

11. Prior to the last weekly payroll period of the calendar year, the cumulative earnings of employees A and B are $50,800 and $49,500, respectively. Their earnings for the last completed payroll period of the year are $1,000 each, which will be paid in January. If the amount of earnings subject to FICA tax is $50,000 and the tax rate is 7.5%, (a) what will be the employer's FICA tax on the earnings of employees A and B in the last payroll period; (b) what is the employer's total FICA tax expense for employees A and B for the calendar year just ended?

12. Indicate the principal functions served by the employee's earnings record.

13. An employer pays the employees in currency and the pay envelopes are prepared by an employee rather than by the bank. (a) Why would it be advisable to obtain from the bank the exact amount of money needed for a payroll? (b) How could the exact number of each bill and coin denomination needed be determined efficiently in advance?

14. A company uses a weekly payroll period and a special bank account for payroll. (a) When should deposits be made in the account? (b) How is the amount of the deposit determined? (c) Is it necessary to have in the general ledger an account entitled "Cash—Special Payroll Account"? Explain. (d) The bank statement for the payroll bank account for the month ended July 31 indicates a bank balance of $9,972.50. Assuming that the bank has made no errors, what does this amount represent?

15. In a payroll system diagram, what type of input data are referred to as (a) constants, (b) variables?

16. To strengthen internal controls, what department should provide written authorizations for the addition of names to the payroll?

17. Explain how a payroll system that is properly designed and operated tends to give assurance (a) that wages paid are based upon hours actually worked, and (b) that payroll checks are not issued to fictitious employees.

18. To match revenues and expenses properly, should the expense for employee vacation pay be recorded in the period during which the vacation privilege is earned or during the period in which the vacation is taken? Discuss.

19. Differentiate between a contributory and a noncontributory pension plan.

20. Identify several factors which influence the future pension obligation of an enterprise.

21. How does prior service cost arise in a new or revised pension plan?

22. Where should the unfunded accrued pension cost be reported on the balance sheet?

23. A business enterprise issued a 60-day, 12% note for $15,000 to a creditor on account. Give the entries to record (a) the issuance of the note and (b) the payment of the note at maturity, including interest of $300.

24. In borrowing money from a bank, an enterprise issued a $75,000, 90-day, non-interest-bearing note, which the bank discounted at 13%. Are the proceeds $75,000? Explain.

25. When should the liability associated with a product warranty be recorded? Discuss.

Real World Focus

26. The 1988 annual report for Whirlpool Corporation reported in the liability section of the December 31, 1988 balance sheet the following data with respect to product warranties:

Current Liabilities:
  Product warranty... 24,100,000
Other Liabilities:
  Product warranty... 13,300,000

(a) What entry would have been made to record the accrued product warranty costs at December 31, 1988, assuming that no entry had been made in prior years? (b) How would costs of repairing a defective product be recorded?

Real World Focus

27. The "Questions and Answers Technical Hotline" in the June, 1988 *Journal of Accountancy* included the following question:

> Several years ago, Company B instituted legal action against Company A. Under a memorandum of settlement and agreement, Company A agreed to pay Company B a total of $17,500 in three installments—$5,000 on March 1, $7,500 on July 1 and the remaining $5,000 on December 31. Company A paid the first two installments during its fiscal year ended September 30. Should the unpaid amount of $5,000 be presented as a current liability at September 30?

> How would you answer this question?

EXERCISES

Exercise 11–1
Algorithm.
OBJ. 1

Develop an algorithm, in the form illustrated in this chapter, to compute the amount of each employee's weekly earnings subject to state unemployment compensation tax. Assume that the tax is 4.2% on the first $7,000 of each employee's earnings during the year and that the following symbols are to be used:

e — Cumulative earnings subject to state unemployment compensation tax prior to current week
E — Current week's earnings
S — Amount of current week's earnings subject to state unemployment compensation tax

Exercise 11–2
Profit-sharing bonus.
OBJ. 1

The general manager of a business enterprise is entitled to an annual profit-sharing bonus of 6%. For the current year, income before bonus and income taxes is $500,000, and income taxes are estimated at 35% of income before income taxes. Determine the amount of the bonus, assuming that (a) the bonus is based on income before deductions for bonus and income taxes and (b) the bonus is based on income after deduction for both bonus and income taxes.

Exercise 11–3
Summary payroll data.
OBJ. 1, 2

In the following summary of data for a payroll period, some amounts have been intentionally omitted:

Earnings:		Deductions:	
(1) At regular rate......	?	(4) FICA tax..............	$ 4,962.25
(2) At overtime rate....	$ 4,760.00	(5) Income tax withheld.	10,673.15
(3) Total earnings	?	(6) Medical insurance..	816.50
		(7) Union dues...........	?
		(8) Total deductions....	18,130.90
		(9) Net amount paid....	67,948.50

Accounts debited:	
(10) Factory Wages ...	$62,080.50
(11) Sales Salaries.....	?
(12) Office Salaries....	5,600.00

(a) Determine the amounts omitted in lines (1), (3), (7), and (11). (b) Present the journal entry to record the payroll. (c) Present, in general journal form, the entry to record the voucher for the payroll. (d) Present, in general journal form, the entry to record the payment of the voucher. (e) From the data given in this exercise and your answer to (a), would you conclude that this payroll was paid sometime during the first few weeks of the calendar year? Explain.

Exercise 11–4
Payroll tax entries.
OBJ. 2

According to a summary of the payroll of McFarlane Publishing Co., the amount of earnings for the four weekly payrolls paid in November of the current year was $540,000, of which $30,000 was not subject to FICA tax and $525,000 was not subject to state and federal unemployment taxes. (a) Determine the employer's payroll taxes expense for the month, using the following rates: FICA, 7.5%; state unemployment, 4.8%; federal unemployment, .8%. (b) Present the general journal entry to record the accrual of payroll taxes for the month of November.

Exercise 11–5
Accrued vacation pay and product warranty.
OBJ. 3, 5

A business enterprise provides its employees with varying amounts of vacation per year, depending on the length of employment. It also warrants its products for one year. The estimated total amount of the current year's vacation pay is $216,000, and the estimated product warranty is 2% of sales. If sales were $950,000 for January, prepare the adjusting entries required at January 31, the end of the first month of the current year, to record (a) the accrued vacation pay and (b) the accrued product warranty.

Exercise 11–6
Pension plan entries.
OBJ. 3

Bair Corporation maintains a funded pension plan for its employees. The plan requires quarterly installments to be paid to the funding agent, Powers Insurance Company, by the fifteenth of the month following the end of each quarter. If the pension cost is $60,000 for the quarter ended December 31, prepare entries to record (a) the accrued pension liability on December 31 and (b) the payment to the funding agent on January 15.

Exercise 11–7
Entries for discounting notes.
OBJ. 4

Gerhardt Co. issues a 90-day, non-interest-bearing note for $100,000 to Tyson Bank and Trust Co., and the bank discounts the note at 14%. (a) Present the maker's entries to record (1) the issuance of the note and (2) the payment of the note at maturity. (b) Present the payee's entries to record (1) the receipt of the note and (2) the receipt of payment of the note at maturity.

Exercise 11–8
Determination of interest on notes issued.
OBJ. 4

In negotiating a 90-day loan, an enterprise has the option of either (1) issuing a $250,000, non-interest-bearing note that will be discounted at the rate of 12%, or (2) issuing a $250,000 note that bears interest at the rate of 12% and that will be accepted at face value.

(a) Determine the amount of the interest expense for each option.
(b) Determine the amount of the proceeds for each option.
(c) Indicate the option that is more favorable to the borrower.

Exercise 11–9
Plant asset purchases with note.
OBJ. 4

On September 1, Jenkins Company purchased land for $120,000 and a building for $480,000, paying $150,000 cash and issuing a 12% note for the balance, secured by a mortgage on the property. The terms of the note provide for 18 semiannual payments of $25,000 on the principal plus the interest accrued from the date of the preceding payment. Present the entry to record (a) the transaction on September 1, (b) the adjustment for accrued interest on December 31, (c) the reversal of the adjustment on January 1, (d) the payment of the first installment on February 28, and (e) the payment of the second installment the following August 31.

PROBLEMS

Series A

Problem 11–1A
Profit-sharing bonuses.
OBJ. 1

The Chief Operating Officer (COO) of Shulman Company is entitled to an annual profit-sharing bonus of 4%. For the current year, income before bonus and income taxes is $750,000, and income taxes are estimated at 35% of income before income taxes.

Instructions:

(1) Determine the amount of the bonus, assuming that:
    (a) The bonus is based on income before deductions for bonus and income taxes.
    (b) The bonus is based on income after deduction for bonus but before deduction for income taxes.
    (c) The bonus is based on income after deduction for income taxes but before deduction for bonus.
    (d) The bonus is based on income after deduction for both bonus and income taxes.
(2) (a) Which bonus plan would the COO prefer? (b) Would this plan always be the COO's choice, regardless of Shulman Company's income level?

Problem 11–2A
Entries for payroll and payroll taxes.
OBJ. 1, 2

The following information relative to the payroll for the week ended December 30 was obtained from the records of Griffin Enterprises Inc.:

Salaries:		Deductions:	
Sales salaries................	$150,250	Income tax withheld	$34,200
Warehouse salaries	22,500	U.S. savings bonds........	4,500
Office salaries	15,250	Group insurance............	3,300
	$188,000	FICA tax withheld totals the same amount as the employer's tax.	

Tax rates assumed:
    FICA, 7.5%
    State unemployment (employer only), 3.8%
    Federal unemployment, .8%

Instructions:

(1) Assuming that the payroll for the last week of the year is to be paid on December 31, present the following entries:
    (a) December 30, to record the payroll. Of the total payroll for the last week of the year, $152,000 is subject to FICA tax and $15,000 is subject to unemployment compensation taxes.
    (b) December 30, to record the employer's payroll taxes on the payroll to be paid on December 31.
(2) Assuming that the payroll for the last week of the year is to be paid on January 6 of the following year, present the following entries:
    (a) December 30, to record the payroll.
    (b) January 6, to record the employer's payroll taxes on the payroll to be paid on January 6.

If the working papers correlating with the textbook are not used, omit Problem 11–3A.

Problem 11–3A
Payroll register.
OBJ. 1, 2

The payroll register for Ayres Company for the week ended December 21 of the current fiscal year is presented in the working papers.

Instructions:

(1) Journalize the entry to record the payroll for the week.
(2) Assuming the use of a voucher system and payment by regular check, present the entries, in general journal form, to record the payroll voucher and the issuance of the checks to employees.   *(Continued)*

(3) Journalize the entry to record the employer's payroll taxes for the week. Assume the following tax rates: FICA, 7.5%; state unemployment, 3.8%; federal unemployment, .8%.

(4) Present the entries, in general journal form, to record the following selected transactions:

Dec. 15. Prepared a voucher, payable to Arnaz National Bank, for employees income taxes, $1,275.40, and FICA taxes, $616.50.

15. Issued a check to Arnaz National Bank in payment of the voucher.

Problem 11–4A

Payroll accounts, entries with voucher and check registers, and year-end entries.

OBJ. 1, 2

The following accounts, with the balances indicated, appear in the ledger of Zeigler Company on December 1 of the current year:

212	Salaries Payable	—
213	FICA Tax Payable	$ 7,100
214	Employees Federal Income Tax Payable	8,520
215	Employees State Income Tax Payable	14,586
216	State Unemployment Tax Payable	1,881
217	Federal Unemployment Tax Payable	396
218	Bond Deductions Payable	750
219	Medical Insurance Payable	4,265
611	Sales Salaries Expense	694,430
711	Officers Salaries Expense	342,980
712	Office Salaries Expense	94,050
719	Payroll Taxes Expense	101,673

The following transactions relating to payroll, payroll deductions, and payroll taxes occurred during December:

Dec. 2. Prepared Voucher No. 749 for $750, payable to Monroe National Bank, to purchase United States savings bonds for employees.

2. Issued Check No. 732 in payment of Voucher No. 749.

3. Prepared Voucher No. 750 for $15,620, payable to Monroe National Bank for $8,520 of employees' federal income tax and $7,100 of FICA tax due.

3. Issued Check No. 733 in payment of Voucher No. 750.

14. Prepared a journal entry to record the biweekly payroll. A summary of the payroll record follows:

Deductions:	
FICA tax	$ 3,575
Federal income tax withheld	8,569
State income tax withheld	2,112
Savings bond deductions	375
Medical insurance deductions	528

Salary distributions:	
Sales	$33,660
Officers	16,720
Office	4,180

Net amount	$39,401

14. Prepared Voucher No. 757, payable to Payroll Bank Account, for the net amount of the biweekly payroll.

14. Issued Check No. 738 in payment of Voucher No. 757.

14. Prepared a journal entry to record employer's payroll taxes on earnings of December 14: FICA, $3,575; state unemployment tax, $162; federal unemployment tax, $35.

17. Prepared Voucher No. 758 for $15,719, payable to Monroe National Bank for $8,569 of employees' federal income tax and $7,150 of FICA tax due.

17. Issued Check No. 744 in payment of Voucher No. 758.

18. Prepared Voucher No. 760 for $4,265, payable to Wilson Insurance Company, for the semiannual premium on the group medical insurance policy.

19. Issued Check No. 750 in payment of Voucher No. 760.

28. Prepared a journal entry to record the biweekly payroll. A summary of the payroll record follows:

Deductions:	
FICA tax...	$ 3,311
Federal income tax withheld..................................	8,322
State income tax withheld	2,029
Savings bond deductions......................................	375
Salary distribution:	
Sales..	$31,350
Officers..	16,720
Office	4,180
Net amount...	$38,213

28. Prepared Voucher No. 795, payable to Payroll Bank Account, for the net amount of the biweekly payroll.

28. Issued check No. 782 in payment of Voucher No. 795.

28. Prepared a journal entry to record the employer's payroll taxes on earnings of December 28: FICA, $3,311; state unemployment tax, $161; federal unemployment tax, $33.

30. Prepared Voucher No. 801 for $750, payable to Monroe National Bank, to purchase United States savings bonds for employees.

30. Issued Check No. 791 in payment of Voucher No. 801.

30. Prepared Voucher No. 802 for $14,586, payable to Monroe National Bank, for employees' state income tax due on December 31.

30. Issued Check No. 792 in payment of Voucher No. 802.

Instructions:

(1) Open the accounts listed and enter the account balances as of December 1.

(2) Record the transactions, using a voucher register, a check register, and a general journal. The only amount columns needed in the voucher register are Accounts Payable Cr. and Sundry Accounts Dr. (subdivided into Account, Post. Ref., and Amount). The only amount columns needed in the check register are Accounts Payable Dr. and Cash in Bank Cr. Post to the accounts.

(3) Journalize the adjusting entry on December 31 to record salaries for the incomplete payroll period. Salaries accrued are as follows: sales salaries, $3,245; officers salaries, $1,800; office salaries, $450. The payroll taxes are immaterial and are not accrued. Post to the accounts.

(4) Journalize the entry to close the salary expense and payroll taxes expense accounts to Income Summary, and post to the accounts.

(5) Journalize the entry on January 1 to reverse the adjustment of December 31 and post to the accounts.

Problem 11–5A
Wage and Tax Statement data and employer FICA tax.

OBJ. 1, 2

Dilla Company began business on January 2 of last year. Salaries were paid to employees on the last day of each month, and both FICA tax and federal income tax were withheld in the required amounts. An employee who is hired in the middle of the month receives half the monthly salary for that month. All required payroll tax reports were filed and the correct amount of payroll taxes was remitted by the company for the calendar year. Before the Wage and Tax Statements (Form W-2) could be prepared for distributing to employees and filing with the Social Security Administration, the employees' earnings records were inadvertently destroyed.

None of the employees resigned or were discharged during the year, and there were no changes in salary rates. The FICA tax was withheld at the rate of 7.5% on the first $50,000 of salary. Data on dates of employment, salary rates, and employees' income taxes withheld, which are summarized as follows, were obtained from personnel records and payroll records.

Employee	Date First Employed	Monthly Salary	Monthly Income Tax Withheld
Brown	Jan. 2	$4,200	$ 854.50
Davis	June 2	2,500	417.50
Jung	Apr. 15	2,800	461.10
O'Leary	Jan. 2	4,000	810.10
Silhan	Dec. 1	3,600	652.30
Reese	Mar. 1	3,800	748.15
Silvas	Feb. 1	5,200	1,261.40

Instructions:

(1) Determine the amounts to be reported on each employee's Wage and Tax Statement (Form W-2) for the year, arranging the data in the following form:

Employee	Gross Earnings	Federal Income Tax Withheld	Earnings Subject to FICA Tax	FICA Tax Withheld

(2) Determine the following employer payroll taxes for the year: (a) FICA; (b) state unemployment compensation at 3.8% on the first $7,000 of each employee's earnings; (c) federal unemployment compensation at .8% of the first $7,000 of each employee's earnings; (d) total.

(3) In a manner similar to the illustrations in this chapter, develop four algorithms to describe the computations required to determine the four amounts in (1), using the following symbols:

n = Number of payroll periods
g = Monthly gross earnings
f = Monthly federal income tax withheld
G = Total gross earnings

F = Total federal income tax withheld
T = Total earnings subject to FICA tax
S = Total FICA tax withheld

Problem 11–6A

Notes payable, vacation pay, product warranty, and pension transactions.

OBJ. 3, 4, 5

The following items were selected from among the transactions completed by Brokow Co. during the current year:

Feb. 6. Purchased merchandise on account from Matlock Company, $7,500.
Mar. 18. Issued a 60-day, 12% note for $7,500 to Matlock Company, on account.
May 10. Issued a 120-day, non-interest-bearing note for $45,000 to Garden City Bank. The bank discounted the note at the rate of 14%.
       17. Paid Matlock Company the amount owed on the note of March 18.
Aug. 5. Borrowed $15,000 from First Federal Savings, issuing a 60-day, 14% note for that amount.
Sept. 7. Paid Garden City Bank the amount due on the note of May 10.
Oct. 4. Paid First Federal Savings the interest due on the note of August 5 and renewed the loan by issuing a new 30-day, 16% note for $15,000. (Record both the debit and the credit to the notes payable account.)
Nov. 3. Paid First Federal Savings the amount due on the note of October 4.
     15. Purchased store equipment from Ames Equipment Co. for $50,000, paying $15,000 and issuing a series of seven 12% notes for $5,000 each, coming due at 30-day intervals.

Dec. 15. Paid the amount due Ames Equipment Co. on the first note in the series issued on November 15.

31. Paid $27,500 of the annual pension cost of $40,000. (Record both the payment and the unfunded pension cost.)

Instructions:

(1) Record the transactions.
(2) Record the adjusting journal entries for each of the following accrued expenses for the current year:
   (a) Vacation pay... $15,000
   (b) Product warranty cost   12,750
(3) Record the adjusting journal entry for the accrued interest at December 31 on the six notes owed to Ames Equipment Co.
(4) Assume that a single note for $35,000 had been issued on November 15 instead of the series of seven notes, and that its terms required principal payments of $5,000 each 30 days, with interest at 12% on the principal balance before applying the $5,000 payment. Determine the amount that would have been due and payable on December 15.

Series B

Problem 11–1B
Profit-sharing bonuses.

OBJ. 1

The president of Beaver Products is entitled to an annual profit-sharing bonus of 5%. For the current year, income before bonus and income taxes is $500,000, and income taxes are estimated at 35% of income before income taxes.

Instructions:

(1) Determine the amount of the bonus, assuming that:
   (a) The bonus is based on income before deductions for bonus and income taxes.
   (b) The bonus is based on income after deduction for bonus but before deduction for income taxes.
   (c) The bonus is based on income after deduction for income taxes but before deduction for bonus.
   (d) The bonus is based on income after deduction for both bonus and income taxes.
(2) (a) Which bonus would the president prefer? (b) Would this plan always be the president's choice, regardless of Beaver Product's income level?

Problem 11–2B
Entries for payroll and payroll taxes.

OBJ. 1, 2

The following information relative to the payroll for the week ended December 30 was obtained from the records of T. T. Grasso Co.:

Salaries:		Deductions:	
Sales salaries...............	$ 90,000	Income tax withheld	$19,250
Warehouse salaries	18,980	Group insurance............	1,500
Office salaries	11,020	U.S. savings bonds........	1,200
	$120,000	FICA tax withheld totals the same amount as the employer's tax.	

Tax rates assumed:
   FICA, 7.5%
   State unemployment (employer only), 4.2%
   Federal unemployment, .8%

Instructions:

(1) Assuming that the payroll for the last week of the year is to be paid on December 31, present the following entries:

    (a) December 30, to record the payroll. Of the total payroll for the last week of the year, $109,000 is subject to FICA tax and $9,000 is subject to unemployment compensation taxes.

    (b) December 30, to record the employer's payroll taxes on the payroll to be paid on December 31.

(2) Assuming that the payroll for the last week of the year is to be paid on January 6 of the following fiscal year, present the following entries:

    (a) December 31, to record the payroll.

    (b) January 6, to record the employer's payroll taxes on the payroll to be paid on January 6.

If the working papers correlating with the textbook are not used, omit Problem 11–3B.

Problem 11–3B
Payroll register.
OBJ. 1, 2

The payroll register for Amy Garrow Co. for the week ending December 21 of the current fiscal year is presented in the working papers.

Instructions:

(1) Journalize the entry to record the payroll for the week.

(2) Assuming the use of a voucher system and payment by regular check, present the entries, in general journal form, to record the payroll voucher and the issuance of the checks to employees.

(3) Journalize the entry to record the employer's payroll taxes for the week. Assume the following tax rates: FICA, 7.5%; state unemployment, 3.1%; federal unemployment, .8%.

(4) Present the entries, in general journal form, to record the following selected transactions:

    Dec. 16. Prepared a voucher, payable to Weiss National Bank, for employees income taxes, $1,217.50, and FICA taxes, $301.50.

         16. Issued a check to Weiss National Bank in payment of the above voucher.

Problem 11–5B
Wage and Tax Statement data and employer FICA tax.
OBJ. 1, 2

Stoner Company began business on January 2 of last year. Salaries were paid to employees on the last day of each month, and both FICA tax and federal income tax were withheld in the required amounts. An employee who is hired in the middle of the month receives half the monthly salary for that month. All required payroll tax reports were filed and the correct amount of payroll taxes was remitted by the company for the calendar year. Before the Wage and Tax Statements (Form W-2) could be prepared for distributing to employees and filing with the Social Security Administration, the employees' earnings records were inadvertently destroyed.

None of the employees resigned or were discharged during the year, and there were no changes in salary rates. The FICA tax was withheld at the rate of 7.5% on the first $50,000 of salary. Data on dates of employment, salary rates, and employees' income taxes withheld, which are summarized as follows, were obtained from personnel records and payroll records.

Employee	Date First Employed	Monthly Salary	Monthly Income Tax Withheld
Allan	Mar. 1	$3,220	$ 541.88
Bork	Jan. 2	4,200	895.60
Faulk	Nov. 1	2,500	394.25
Helms	Aug. 1	3,740	700.15
Omar	Jan. 2	5,400	1,374.10
Ruiz	May 1	3,600	652.30
Yeager	Feb. 16	4,000	864.10

Instructions:

(1) Determine the amounts to be reported on each employee's Wage and Tax Statement (Form W-2) for the year, arranging the data in the following form:

Employee	Gross Earnings	Federal Income Tax Withheld	Earnings Subject to FICA Tax	FICA Tax Withheld

(2) Determine the following employer payroll taxes for the year: (a) FICA; (b) state unemployment compensation at 4.2% on the first $7,000 of each employee's earnings; (c) federal unemployment compensation at .8% of the first $7,000 of each employee's earnings; (d) total.

(3) In a manner similar to the illustrations in this chapter, develop four algorithms to describe the computations required to determine the four amounts in (1), using the following symbols:

n = Number of payroll periods   F = Total federal income tax withheld
g = Monthly gross earnings   T = Total earnings subject to FICA tax
f = Monthly federal income tax withheld   S = Total FICA tax withheld
G = Total gross earnings

Problem 11–6B
Notes payable, vacation pay, product warranty, and pension transactions.

OBJ. 3, 4, 5

SOLUTIONS SOFTWARE

The following items were selected from among the transactions completed by Douglas Co. during the current year:

Jan. 15. Purchased merchandise on account from Davis Co., $7,800.
Feb. 28. Issued a 60-day, 12% note for $7,800 to Davis Co., on account.
Apr. 29. Paid Davis Co. the amount owed on the note of February 28.
July 15. Borrowed $8,000 from Keyes National Bank, issuing a 90-day, 13% note for that amount.
      25. Issued a 120-day, non-interest-bearing note for $40,000 to Mid-State Bank. The bank discounted the note at the rate of 15%.
Oct. 13. Paid Keyes National Bank the interest due on the note of July 15 and renewed the loan by issuing a new 30-day, 15% note for $8,000. (Record both the debit and credit to the notes payable account.)
Nov. 12. Paid Keyes State Bank the amount due on the note of October 13.
      22. Paid Mid-State Bank the amount due on the note of July 25.
Dec. 1. Purchased office equipment from Bunn Equipment Co. for $60,000, paying $10,000 and issuing a series of ten 12% notes for $5,000 each, coming due at 30-day intervals.
      31. Paid the amount due Bunn Equipment Co. on the first note in the series issued on December 1.
      31. Paid $32,400 of the year's pension cost of $45,000. (Record both the payment and the unfunded pension cost.)

Instructions:

(1) Record the transactions.
(2) Record the adjusting journal entries for each of the following accrued expenses for the current year:
   (a) Vacation pay.. $17,900
   (b) Product warranty cost   15,000
(3) Record the adjusting entry for the accrued interest at December 31 on the nine notes owed to Bunn Equipment Co.
(4) Assume that a single note for $50,000 had been issued on December 1 instead of the series of ten notes, and that its terms required principal payments of $5,000 each 30 days, with interest at 12% on the principal balance before applying the $5,000 payment. Determine the amount that would have been due and payable on December 31.

MINI-CASE 11

In 1989, your father retired as president of the family-owned business, MG Inc., and a new president was recruited by an executive search firm. The new president's contract called for an annual base salary of $60,000 plus a bonus of 12% of income after deducting the bonus but before deducting income taxes.

In 1990, the first full year under the new president, MG Inc. reported income of $966,000 before deducting the bonus and income taxes. After being fired on January 2, 1991, the new president demanded immediate payment of a $115,920 bonus for 1990.

Your father was concerned about the accounting practices used during 1990, and he has asked you to help him in reviewing the accounting records before the bonus is paid. Upon investigation, you have discovered the following facts:

(a) The payroll for December 28–31, 1990, was not accrued at the end of the year. The salaries for the four-day period and the applicable payroll taxes are as follows:

Sales salaries	$7,000
Office salaries	3,000
FICA tax	7.5%
State unemployment tax (employer only)	3.2%
Federal unemployment tax	.8%

The payroll was paid on January 4, 1991, for the period December 28, 1990, through January 3, 1991.

(b) The semiannual pension cost of $25,000 was not accrued for the last half of 1990. The pension cost was paid to Equity Insurance Company on January 15, 1991, and was recorded by a debit to Pension Expense and a credit to Cash for $25,000.

(c) The estimated product warranty liability of $12,500 for products sold during the year ended December 31, 1990, was not recorded.

(d) On April 1, 1990, MG Inc. purchased a one-year insurance policy for $9,640, debiting the cost to Prepaid Insurance. No adjusting entry was made for insurance expired at December 31, 1990.

(e) The vacation pay liability of $10,120 for the year ended December, 1990, was not recorded.

Instructions:

(1) Based on reported 1990 income of $966,000 before deducting the bonus and income taxes, was the president's calculation of the $115,920 bonus correct? Explain.

(2) What accounting errors were made in 1990 which would affect the amount of the president's bonus?

(3) Based on the employment contract and your answer to (2), what is the correct amount of the president's bonus for 1990?

(4) How much did the president's demand for a $115,920 bonus exceed the correct amount of the bonus under the employment contract?

(5) Describe the major advantage and disadvantage of using profit-sharing bonuses in employment contracts.

ETHICS DISCUSSION CASE	Ed Kirkland, a CPA and staff assistant for a local CPA firm, noticed on his payroll stub covering the two-week period of March 2–March 16 that his overtime pay had been computed on the basis of 2 times his regular pay rate, rather than 1 1/2 times his regular rate. Ed has decided to cash the payroll check. If his employer later catches the error, Ed plans to deny having originally noticed the mistake. Discuss whether Ed Kirkland is behaving in an ethical manner.

COMPREHENSIVE PROBLEM 4

Selected transactions completed by Hogan Company during its first fiscal year ending December 31 were as follows:

(a) Prepared a voucher to establish a petty cash fund of $250 and issued a check in payment of the voucher. (Prepare two journal entries.)

(b) Prepared a voucher to replenish the petty cash fund, based on the following summary of petty cash receipts: office supplies, $55; miscellaneous selling expense, $97; miscellaneous administrative expense, $80.

(c) Prepared a voucher to record the purchase of $10,000 of merchandise, 2/10, n/30. Purchase invoices are recorded at the net amount.

(d) Paid the invoice in (c) after the discount period had passed.

(e) Received cash from daily cash sales for $8,750. The amount indicated by the cash register tally was $8,755.

(f) Received a 60-day, 10% note for $30,000 on account.

(g) Discounted note received in (f) at bank, 30 days prior to maturity, at 12%.

(h) Received notice from bank that note discounted in (g) had been dishonored. Paid the bank the maturity value of the note.

(i) Received amount owed on dishonored note in (h) plus interest for 36 days at 10% computed on the maturity value of the note.

(j) Received $1,200 on account and wrote off the remainder owed on a $2,000 accounts receivable balance. (The allowance method is used in accounting for uncollectible receivables.)

(k) Reinstated the account written off in (j) and received $800 cash in full payment.

(l) Traded office equipment on July 1 for new equipment with a list price of $125,000. A trade-in allowance of $80,000 was received on the old equipment that had cost $90,000 and had accumulated depreciation of $15,000 as of July 1. A voucher was prepared for the amount owed of $45,000.

(m) Recorded the monthly payroll for November, based on the following data:

Salaries:		Deductions:	
Sales salaries.................	$ 9,500	Income tax withheld	$2,950
Office salaries	4,500	FICA tax withheld totals	
	$14,000	the same amount as the	
		employer's tax.	

Tax rates assumed:
  FICA, 7.5%
  State unemployment, 3.8%
  Federal unemployment, .8%
  Amount subject to payroll taxes:

FICA.........................	$12,000
State unemployment....	2,000
Federal unemployment..	2,000

(n) Recorded the employer's payroll taxes on the payroll in (m).
(o) Issued a 90-day, non-interest-bearing note for $50,000 to the bank, which discounted it at 12%.
(p) Recorded voucher for payment of the note in (o) at maturity.
(q) The pension cost for the year was $12,000 and a voucher was prepared for $10,000, payable to the trustee for the funded portion.

Instructions:

(1) Record the selected transactions in general journal form.
(2) Based on the following data, prepare a bank reconciliation for November of the current year:
    (a) Balance per bank statement at November 30, $90,530.
    (b) Balance per ledger at November 30, $58,340.
    (c) Checks outstanding at November 30, $60,500.
    (d) Deposit in transit, not recorded by bank, $28,200.
    (e) Bank debit memorandum for service charges, $20.
    (f) A check for $100 in payment of a voucher was erroneously recorded in the accounts as $10.
(3) Based on the bank reconciliation prepared in (2), prepare in general journal form the entry or entries to be made by Hogan Company.
(4) Based on the following selected data, prepare the adjusting entries as of December 31 of the current year:
    (a) Estimated uncollectible accounts at December 31, $6,100. The balance of Allowance for Doubtful Accounts at December 31 was $1,500 (debit).
    (b) Merchandise inventory data are indicated in the following schedule:

Item	Purchases Invoices 1st	2d	3d	Inventory Count at December 31
C10	50 at $1,940	30 at $1,950	60 at $2,000	45
D35	25 at 1,100	20 at 1,185	25 at 1,200	30
L11	75 at 550	100 at 575	100 at 575	80
K72	10 at 2,600	10 at 2,600	10 at 2,675	15
V17	5 at 4,100	7 at 4,200	—	4

    The inventory is determined by the periodic method and is costed by the last-in, first-out method.
    (c) Prepaid insurance expired during the year, $17,250.
    (d) Office supplies used during the year, $4,500.
    (e) Depreciation is computed as follows:

Asset	Cost	Residual Value	Acquisition Date	Useful Life in Years	Depreciation Method Used
Buildings	$225,000	0	January 2	50	Straight-line
Office Equipment	120,000	$12,000	July 1	5	Sum-of-the-years-digits
Store Equipment	60,000	10,000	January 3	8	Declining-balance (at twice the straight-line rate)

    (f) A patent costing $18,000 when acquired on January 2 has a remaining legal life of 9 years, and was expected to have value for 6 years.
    (g) The cost of mineral rights was $50,000. Of the estimated deposit of 25,000 tons of ore, 6,000 tons were mined during the year.
    (h) Total vacation pay expense for the year, $7,000.
    (i) A product warranty was granted beginning December 1 and covering a one-year period. The estimated cost is 3% of sales, which totaled $150,000 in December.
(5) Based on the following post-closing trial balance and other data, prepare a balance sheet in report form at December 31 of the current year:

Hogan Company
Post-Closing Trial Balance
December 31, 19--

Petty Cash	250	
Cash	60,500	
Marketable Equity Securities	40,000	
Allowance for Decline to Market		4,360
Notes Receivable	50,000	
Accounts Receivable	151,100	
Allowance for Doubtful Accounts		6,100
Merchandise Inventory	220,250	
Prepaid Insurance	13,750	
Office Supplies	1,500	
Land	50,000	
Buildings	225,000	
Accumulated Depreciation — Buildings		4,500
Office Equipment	120,000	
Accumulated Depreciation — Office Equipment		18,000
Store Equipment	60,000	
Accumulated Depreciation — Store Equipment		15,000
Mineral Rights	50,000	
Accumulated Depletion		12,000
Patents	15,000	
FICA Tax Payable		2,100
Employees Federal Income Tax Payable		2,950
State Unemployment Tax Payable		1,520
Federal Unemployment Tax Payable		320
Salaries Payable		14,000
Accounts Payable		88,000
Product Warranty Payable		4,500
Vacation Pay Payable		7,000
Unfunded Accrued Pension Cost		2,000
Notes Payable		450,000
Capital Stock		320,000
Retained Earnings		105,000
	1,057,350	1,057,350

The following information relating to the balance sheet accounts at December 31 is obtained from supplementary records:

Notes receivable, current asset
Merchandise inventory, at cost by lifo method
Product warranty payable, current liability
Vacation pay payable:

Current liability	$ 5,000
Long-term liability	2,000

Unfunded accrued pension cost, long-term liability
Notes payable:

Current liability	50,000
Long-term liability	400,000

(6) Assuming that the general manager had been granted a 5% profit-sharing bonus (based on income after deduction for the bonus) and income before the bonus was $105,000, what would have been the amount of the bonus?   *(Continued)*

(7) On February 15 of the following year, the merchandise inventory was destroyed by fire. Based on the following data obtained from the accounting records, estimate the cost of the merchandise destroyed:

Jan. 1	Merchandise inventory	$220,250
Jan. 1–Feb. 15	Purchases (net)	192,250
	Sales (net)	380,000
	Estimated gross profit rate	40%

ANSWERS TO SELF-EXAMINATION QUESTIONS

1. **B** The amount of net pay of $693 (answer B) is determined as follows:

Gross pay:		
40 hours at $20	$800	
5 hours at $30	150	$950
Deductions:		
Federal income tax withheld	$212	
FICA ($600 × .075)	45	257
Net pay		$693

2. **A** Employers are usually required to withhold a portion of the earnings of their employees for payment of federal income taxes (answer A). Generally, federal (answer B) and state (answer C) unemployment compensation taxes are levied against the employer only and thus are not deducted from employee earnings.

3. **D** The employer incurs operating costs for FICA tax (answer A), federal unemployment compensation tax (answer B), and state unemployment compensation tax (answer C). These costs add significantly to the total labor costs for most businesses.

4. **C** The maturity value is $5,100, determined as follows:

Face amount of note	$5,000
Plus interest ($5,000 × 12/100 × 60/360)	100
Maturity value	$5,100

5. **B** The net amount available to a borrower from discounting a note payable is termed the proceeds. The proceeds of $4,900 (answer B) is determined as follows:

Face amount of note	$5,000
Less discount ($5,000 × 12/100 × 60/360)	100
Proceeds	$4,900

Accounting Principles

PART THREE

3

CHAPTER TWELVE
CONCEPTS AND PRINCIPLES

CHAPTER OBJECTIVES

1 Describe the development of accounting concepts and principles.

2 Identify and illustrate the application of ten basic accounting concepts and principles:
   a Business entity
   b Going concern

   c Objective evidence
   d Unit of measurement
   e Accounting period
   f Matching revenue and expired costs
   g Adequate disclosure
   h Consistency
   i Materiality
   j Conservatism

The historical development of accounting practice has been closely related to the economic development of the country. In the earlier stages of the American economy, a business enterprise was very often managed by its owner, and the accounting records and reports were used mainly by the owner-manager in conducting the business. Bankers and other lenders often relied on their personal relationship with the owner rather than on financial statements as the basis for making loans for business purposes. If a large amount was owed to a bank or supplier, the creditor often participated in management decisions.

As business organizations grew in size and complexity, "management" and "outsiders" became more clearly differentiated. From the latter group, which includes owners (stockholders), creditors, government, labor unions, customers, and the general public, came the demand for accurate financial information for use in judging the performance of management. In addition, as the size and complexity of the business unit increased, the accounting problems involved in the issuance of financial statements became more and more complex. With these developments came an awareness of the need for a framework of concepts and generally accepted accounting principles to serve as guidelines for the preparation of the basic financial statements.

DEVELOPMENT OF CONCEPTS AND PRINCIPLES

OBJECTIVE 1
Describe the development of accounting concepts and principles.

The word "principle" as used in the context of generally accepted accounting principles does not have the same authoritativeness as universal principles or natural laws relating to the study of astronomy, physics, or other physical sciences. Accounting principles have been developed by individuals to help make accounting data more useful in an ever-changing society. They represent the best possible guides, based on reason, observation, and experimentation, to the achievement of the desired results. The selection of the best method from among many alternatives has come about gradually, and in some subject matter areas a clear consensus is still lacking. These principles are continually reexamined and revised to keep pace with the increasing complexity of business operations. General acceptance among the members of the accounting profession is the criterion for determining an accounting principle.

Responsibility for the development of accounting principles has rested primarily on practicing accountants and accounting educators, working both independently and under the sponsorship of various accounting organizations. These principles are also influenced by business practices and customs, ideas and beliefs of the users of the financial statements, governmental agencies, stock exchanges, and other business groups.

Financial Accounting Standards Board

In 1973, the **Financial Accounting Standards Board (FASB)** was appointed by the Financial Accounting Foundation (FAF). The FAF is an independent, nonprofit organization that was created in 1972 to oversee the standard-setting process, to appoint members of standard-setting boards (the FASB and the Governmental Accounting Standards Board) and advisory councils, and to raise funds for the operation of the standard-setting process.

The FASB replaced the **Accounting Principles Board (APB)**, which provided much of the leadership in the development of generally accepted accounting principles from 1959 to 1973. The APB was composed of eighteen accountants who were members of the American Institute of Certified Public Accountants and who served without pay and continued their affiliations with their firms or institutions. The FASB, which is presently the dominant body in the development of generally accepted accounting principles, is composed of seven members, four of whom must be CPAs drawn from public practice. These seven members serve full time, receive a salary, and must resign from the firm or institution with which they have been affiliated. The FASB is assisted by an advisory council of approximately forty members, whose major responsibilities include the recommendation of priorities and agenda and the review of FASB plans, activities, and statements proposed for issuance. The FASB employs a full-time research staff and administrative staff as well as task forces to study specific matters from time to time.

As problems in financial reporting are identified, the FASB conducts extensive research to identify the principal issues involved and the possible solutions. Generally, after issuing discussion memoranda and preliminary proposals and evaluating comments from interested parties, the Board issues *Statements of Financial Accounting Standards,* which become part of generally accepted accounting principles. To explain, clarify, or elaborate on existing pronouncements, the Board also issues *Interpretations,* which have the same authority as the standards.

Presently, the Board is in the process of developing a broad conceptual framework for financial accounting. This project, which is expected to take many years to complete, is an attempt to develop a "constitution" that can be used to evaluate current standards and can serve as the basis for future standards. The results of the completed portion of this project have been published as six *Statements of Financial Accounting Concepts,* which are briefly described as follows:

■ **Objectives of Financial Reporting by Business Enterprises (No. 1)**
Sets forth three broad objectives of financial reporting:
1. To provide financial information that is useful in making rational investment, credit, and similar decisions;
2. To provide financial information to enable users to predict cash flows to the business and subsequently to themselves;
3. To provide financial information about business resources (assets), claims to these resources (liabilities and owner's equity), and changes in these resources and claims.

■ **Qualitative Characteristics of Accounting Information (No. 2)**
Identifies the essential qualities of the accounting information included in financial reports as follows: usefulness, understandability, relevance, reliability, verifiability, timeliness, neutrality, completeness, and comparability.

■ **Elements of Financial Statements of Business Enterprises (No. 3)**
Replaced by Statement No. 6.

■ **Objectives of Financial Reporting by Nonbusiness Organizations (No. 4)**
Sets forth the objectives that guide the preparation of the financial statements for nonbusiness organizations.

■ **Recognition and Measurement in Financial Statements of Business Enterprises (No. 5)**
Identifies the financial statements that should be prepared to meet the objectives of financial reporting for business enterprises.

■ **Elements of Financial Statements (No. 6)**
Replaces Statement No. 3 and defines the interrelated elements of financial statements that are directly related to measuring the performance and status of businesses and nonprofit organizations.

THE IMPORTANCE OF ACCOUNTING STANDARDS

No amount of policing by the public accounting profession or regulatory agencies to prevent abuses in financial reporting can satisfy the public need for comparable information from all companies. Only financial accounting and reporting standards can satisfy that need. The challenge to the FASB is to strike a reasonable balance between the prevention of abuses and the portrayal of economic reality. As standard setters, we must try to avoid the concern about potential abuses leading to standards that make significantly different situations look the same — in other words, forcing square pegs into round holes.

Source: Donald J. Kirk, FASB chairman (From a speech before the National Association of Accountants Second Annual International-European Conference, Paris, April 19, 1985).

Governmental Accounting Standards Board

The **Governmental Accounting Standards Board (GASB)** was formed in 1984 as an arm of the Financial Accounting Foundation. The GASB has a full-time chairperson and four part-time members who have responsibility for establishing the accounting standards to be followed by state and municipal governments. The GASB employs a full-time research staff and administrative staff. An advisory council of approximately 20 members assists the GASB and also has fund-raising responsibilities.

Accounting Organizations

Among the oldest and most influential organizations of accountants are the **American Institute of Certified Public Accountants (AICPA)** and the **American Accounting Association (AAA)**. Each organization publishes monthly or quarterly periodicals and, from time to time, issues other publications in the form of research studies, technical opinions, and monographs. There are also other national accounting organizations as well as many state societies and local chapters of the national and state organizations. These groups provide forums for the interchange of ideas and discussion of accounting principles.

Government Organizations

Of the various governmental agencies with an interest in the development of accounting principles, the **Securities and Exchange Commission (SEC)** has been the most influential. Established by an act of Congress in 1934, the SEC issues regulations that must be observed in the preparation of financial statements and other reports filed with the Commission.

The **Internal Revenue Service (IRS)** issues regulations that govern the determination of income for purposes of federal income taxation. Because these regulations sometimes conflict with financial accounting principles, many enterprises maintain two sets of accounts to satisfy both reporting requirements. To avoid this increased record keeping, there have been times when firms have adopted practices that are acceptable for tax purposes as generally accepted accounting principles.[1]

Other regulatory agencies exercise a dominant influence on the accounting principles of the industries under their jurisdiction. In rare situations, Congress may also enact legislation that dictates accounting principles. These situations usually involve controversial issues on which no clear consensus has been reached within the profession.

Other Influential Organizations

The **Financial Executives Institute (FEI)** has influenced the development of accounting principles by encouraging and sponsoring accounting research. The FEI also comments on proposed pronouncements of the FASB, the SEC, and other organizations.

The **National Association of Accountants (NAA)** is one of the largest organizations of accountants. It is primarily concerned with management's use of accounting information in directing business operations. Since management is responsible for the preparation of the basic financial statements, however, the NAA communicates its recommendations on generally accepted accounting principles to appropriate organizations.

Although the organizations mentioned above have traditionally had the most influence upon the establishment of accounting principles, other organizations representing users of accounting reports are increasingly making their views known. Prominent in this group are the **Financial Analysts**

---

[1] A discussion of the nature of the income tax is presented in more detail in Appendix E.

Federation (investors and investment advisors) and the **Securities Industry Associates** (investment bankers).

Many accounting principles have been introduced and integrated with discussions in earlier chapters. The remainder of this chapter is devoted to the underlying assumptions, concepts, and principles of the greatest importance and widest applicability. Attention will also be directed to applications of principles to specific situations in order to facilitate better understanding of accounting practices.

BUSINESS ENTITY

OBJECTIVE 2a
Describe and illustrate the application of the business entity concept.

The **business entity concept** assumes that a business enterprise is separate and distinct from the persons who supply its assets. This distinction exists regardless of the legal form of the business organization. The accounting equation, Assets = Equities, or Assets = Liabilities + Owner's Equity, is an expression of the entity concept; i.e., the business owns the assets and owes the various claimants. Thus, the accounting process is primarily concerned with the enterprise as a productive economic unit and only secondarily concerned with the investor as a claimant to the assets of the business.

The business entity concept used in accounting for a sole proprietorship is distinct from the legal concept of a sole proprietorship. The nonbusiness assets, liabilities, revenues, and expenses of a sole proprietor are excluded from the business accounts.[2] If a sole proprietor owns two or more dissimilar enterprises, each one is treated as a separate business entity for accounting purposes. Legally, however, a sole proprietor is personally liable for all business debts and may be required to use nonbusiness assets to satisfy the business creditors. Conversely, business assets are not immune from the claims of the sole proprietor's personal creditors.

Differences between the business entity concept and the legal nature of other forms of business organization will be considered in later chapters. For accounting purposes, however, revenues and expenses of any enterprise are viewed as affecting the business assets and liabilities, not the investors' assets and liabilities.

GOING CONCERN

OBJECTIVE 2b
Describe and illustrate the application of the going concern concept.

Only in rare cases is a business organized with the expectation of operating for only a certain period of time. In most cases, it is not possible to determine in advance the length of life of an enterprise, and so an assumption must be made. The nature of the assumption will affect the manner of recording some of the business transactions, which in turn will affect the data reported in the financial statements.

It is customary to assume that a business entity has a reasonable expectation of continuing in business at a profit for an indefinite period of time. This **going concern concept** provides much of the justification for recording plant assets at acquisition cost and depreciating them in an orderly manner without reference to their current realizable values. If there is no immediate expectation of selling them, plant assets should not be reported on the balance sheet at their estimated realizable values regardless of whether their current market value is less than their book value or greater than their book value. If the firm continues to use the assets, the change in market value

---

[2]Accounting for an individual's assets, liabilities, income, and expenditures is discussed in Appendix D.

causes no gain or loss, nor does it increase or decrease the usefulness of the assets. Thus, if the going concern assumption is a valid concept, the investment in plant assets will serve the purpose for which it was made — the investment in the assets will be recovered even though they may be individually marketable only at a loss.

The going concern assumption similarly supports the treatment of prepaid expenses as assets, even though they may not be salable. To illustrate, assume that on the last day of its fiscal year, a wholesale firm receives from a printer a $20,000 order of sales catalogs. If there were no assumption that the firm is to continue in business, the catalogs would be merely scrap paper and the value reported for them on the balance sheet would be small.

Doubt as to the continued existence of a firm may be disclosed in a note to the financial statements, as indicated in the following note from the 1987 statements of The Wurlitzer Company:

> The Company's . . . financial statements have been presented on the basis that it is a going concern, which contemplates the realization of assets and the satisfaction of liabilities in the normal course of business. . . .
>
> The Company's continued existence is dependent upon its ability to resolve its liquidity problems, principally by obtaining additional debt financing and equity capital. While pursuing additional debt and equity funding, the Company must continue to operate on limited cash flow generated internally. The Company has experienced a net loss from continuing operations for the quarter ended June 30, 1987 of $926,000 (unaudited) compared to a net loss from continuing operations for the quarter ended June 30, 1986 of $1,580,000 (unaudited).

When there is conclusive evidence that a business entity has a limited life, the accounting procedures should be appropriate to the expected terminal date of the entity. Changes in the application of normal accounting procedures may be needed for business organizations in receivership or bankruptcy, for example. In such cases, the financial statements should clearly disclose the limited life of the enterprise and should be prepared from the "quitting concern" or liquidation point of view, rather than from a "going concern" point of view.

OBJECTIVE EVIDENCE

OBJECTIVE 2c
Describe and illustrate the application of the objective evidence concept.

Entries in the accounting records and data reported on financial statements must be based on objectively determined evidence. If this principle is not followed, the confidence of the many users of the financial statements could not be maintained. For example, objective evidence such as invoices and vouchers for purchases, bank statements for the amount of cash in bank, and physical counts for merchandise on hand supports much of accounting. Such evidence is completely objective and can be verified.

Evidence is not always conclusively objective, for there are many cases in accounting in which judgments, estimates, and other subjective factors must be taken into account. In such situations, the most objective evidence available should be used. For example, the provision for doubtful accounts is an estimate of the losses expected from failure to collect sales made on account. The estimation of this amount should be based on such objective factors as past experience in collecting accounts receivable and reliable forecasts of future business activities. To provide accounting reports that can be accepted with confidence, evidence should be developed that will minimize the possibility of error, intentional bias, or fraud.

UNIT OF MEASUREMENT

All business transactions are recorded in terms of money. Other pertinent information of a nonfinancial nature may also be recorded, such as the description of assets acquired, the terms of purchase and sale contracts, and the purpose, amount, and term of insurance policies. But it is only through the record of dollar amounts that the diverse transactions and activities of a business may be measured, reported, and periodically compared. Money is both the common factor of all business transactions and the only feasible unit of measurement that can be used to achieve uniform financial oata.

The generally accepted use of the monetary unit for accounting for and reporting the activities of an enterprise has two major limitations: (1) it limits the scope of accounting reports and (2) it assumes a stability of the measurement unit.

Scope of Accounting Reports

Many factors affecting the activities and the future prospects of an enterprise cannot be expressed in monetary terms. In general, accounting does not attempt to report such factors. For example, information regarding the capabilities of the management, the state of repair of the plant assets, the effectiveness of the employee welfare program, the attitude of the labor union, the effectiveness of antipollution measures, and the relative strengths and weaknesses of the firm's competitors cannot be expressed in monetary terms. Although such matters are important to those concerned with enterprise operations, at the present time, accountancy does not assume responsibility for reporting information of this kind.

Changes in Price Levels

As a unit of measurement, the dollar differs from such quantitative standards as the kilogram, liter, or meter, which have not changed for centuries. The instability of the purchasing power of the dollar is well known, and the disruptive effect of the declining value of the dollar is acknowledged by accountants. In the past, however, this declining value generally has not been given recognition in the accounts or in conventional financial statements.

To indicate the nature of the problem, assume that the plant assets acquired by an enterprise for $100,000 twenty years ago are now to be replaced with similar assets which will cost $200,000 at present price levels. Assume further that during the twenty-year period the plant assets had been fully depreciated and the net income of the enterprise had amounted to $300,000. Although the initial outlay of $100,000 for the plant assets was recovered through depreciation charges, the amount represents only half of the cost of replacing the assets. Instead of considering the current value of the new assets to have increased to double the value of two decades earlier, the dollars recovered can be said to have declined to one half of their earlier value. From either point of view, the firm has suffered a loss in purchasing power, which is the same as a loss of capital. In addition, $100,000 of the net income reported during the period might be said to be illusory, since it must be used to replace the assets.

The use of a monetary unit that is assumed to be stable insures objectivity. In spite of the inflationary trend in the United States, historical-dollar financial statements are considered to be better than statements based on movements of the general price level. There are, however, two widely discussed recommendations for supplementing conventional statements and thus resolving financial reporting problems created by increasing price levels: (1) supplemental financial data based on current costs and (2) supplemental financial data based on constant dollars. The discussion in the following sections is confined to the basic concepts and problems of these recommendations.

Current Cost Data. Current cost is the amount of cash that would have to be paid currently to acquire assets of the same age and in the same condition as existing assets. When current costs are used as the basis for financial reporting, assets, liabilities, and owner's equity are stated at current values, and expenses are stated at the current cost of doing business. The use of current costs permits the identification of gains and losses that result from holding assets during periods of changes in price levels. To illustrate, assume that a firm acquired land at the beginning of the fiscal year for $50,000 and that at the end of the year its current cost (value) is $60,000. The land could be reported at its current cost of $60,000, and the $10,000 increase in value could be reported as an unrealized gain from holding the land.

The major disadvantage in the use of current costs is the absence of established standards and procedures for determining such costs. However, many accountants believe that adequate standards and procedures will evolve through experimentation with actual applications.

Constant Dollar Data. Constant dollar data, also known as general price-level data, are historical costs that have been converted to constant dollars through the use of a price-level index. In this manner, financial statement elements are reported in dollars, each of which has the same (that is, constant) general purchasing power.

A **price-level index** is the ratio of the total cost of a group of commodities prevailing at a particular time to the total cost of the same group of commodities at an earlier base time. The total cost of the commodities at the base time is assigned a value of 100 and the price-level indexes for all later times are expressed as a ratio to 100. For example, assume that the cost of a selected group of commodities amounted to $12,000 at a particular time and $13,200 today. The price index for the earlier, or base, time becomes 100 and the current price index is 110 [(13,200 ÷ 12,000) × 100].

A general price-level index may be used to determine the effect of changes in price levels on certain financial statement items. To illustrate, assume a price index of 120 at the time of purchase of a plot of land for $10,000 and a current price index of 150. The **constant dollar equivalent** of the original cost of $10,000 may be computed as follows:

$$\frac{\text{Current Price Index}}{\text{Price Index at Date of Purchase}} \times \text{Original Cost} = \text{Constant Dollar Equivalent}$$

$$\frac{150}{120} \times \$10,000 = \$12,500$$

Current Annual Reporting Requirements for Price-Level Changes. In 1979, the Financial Accounting Standards Board undertook an experimental program for reporting the effects of changing prices by requiring approximately 1,300 large, publicly held enterprises to disclose certain current cost information and constant dollar information annually as supplemental data. In 1984, after reviewing the experiences with these 1979 disclosure requirements, the FASB concluded that current cost information was more useful than constant dollar information as a supplement to the basic financial statements. In 1986, the FASB eliminated the requirement to disclose the effects of changing prices, but encouraged companies to disclose such information voluntarily.[3] The information that is now being disclosed includes elements of both current cost and constant dollar data, as shown in the following footnote from the 1986 annual report of The Pillsbury Company:

> Information on effects of changing prices and inflation
>
> Financial statements, prepared using historical costs as required by generally accepted accounting principles, may not reflect the full impact of current costs and general inflation.
>
> The following supplementary disclosures attempt to remeasure certain historical financial information to recognize the effects of changes in current costs using specific price indices. The current cost information is then expressed in average Fiscal 1986 dollars to reflect the effects of general inflation based on the U.S. Consumer Price Index. . . .

ACCOUNTING PERIOD

OBJECTIVE 2e
Describe and illustrate the application of the accounting period concept.

A complete and accurate picture of an enterprise's success or failure cannot be obtained until it discontinues operations, converts its assets into cash, and pays off its debts. Then, and only then, is it possible to determine its true net income. But many decisions regarding the business must be made by management and interested outsiders during its existence. It is therefore necessary to prepare periodic reports on operations, financial position, and cash flows.

Reports may be prepared when a certain job or project is completed, but more often they are prepared at specified time intervals. For a number of reasons, including custom and various legal requirements, the longest interval between reports is one year.

This element of periodicity creates many of the problems of accountancy. The basic problem is the determination of periodic net income. For example, the need for adjusting entries discussed in earlier chapters is directly attributable to the division of the life of an enterprise into arbitrary time periods. Problems of inventory costing, of recognizing the uncollectibility of receivables, and of selecting depreciation methods are also directly related to the periodic measurement process. Furthermore, the amounts of the assets and the equities reported on the balance sheet will also be affected by the methods used in determining net income. For example, the cost flow assumption used in determining the cost of merchandise sold during the accounting period will have a direct effect on the amount of cost assigned to the remaining inventory.

MATCHING REVENUE AND EXPIRED COSTS

OBJECTIVE 2f
Describe and illustrate the application of the principle of matching revenue and expired costs.

During the early stages of accounting development, accountants viewed the balance sheet as the principal financial statement. Over the years, the emphasis has shifted to the income statement as the users of financial statements have become more concerned with the results of business operations than with financial position.

The determination of periodic net income is a two-fold problem involving (1) the revenue recognized during the period and (2) the expired costs to be

[3]*Statement of Financial Accounting Standards, No. 89,* "Financial Reporting and Changing Prices" (Stamford: Financial Accounting Standards Board, 1986).

allocated to the period. It is thus a problem of **matching** revenue and expired costs, the residual amount being the net income or net loss for the period.

Recognition of Revenue

Revenue is measured by the amount charged to customers for merchandise delivered or services rendered to them. The problem created by periodicity is one of timing; that is, at what point is the revenue realized? For any particular accounting period, the question is whether revenue items should be recognized and reported as such in the current period or whether their recognition should be delayed to a future period.

Various criteria are acceptable for determining when revenue is realized. In any case, the criteria used should reasonably agree with the terms of the contractual arrangements with the customer and be based insofar as possible on objective evidence. The criteria most often used are described in the remaining paragraphs of this section.

Point of Sale. Revenue from the sale of merchandise is usually determined by the **point of sale method**, under which revenue is realized at the time title passes to the buyer. At point of sale, the sale price has been agreed upon, the buyer acquires the right of ownership in the merchandise, and the seller has a legal claim against the buyer. The realization of revenue from the sale of services may be determined in a like manner, although there is often a time lag between the time of the initial agreement and the completion of the service. For example, assume that a contract provides that certain repair services be performed, either for a specified price or on a time and materials basis. The price or terms agreed upon in the initial contract do not become revenue until the work has been performed.

Theoretically, revenue from the production and sale of merchandise and services emerges continuously as effort is expended. As a practical matter, however, it is usually not possible to make an objective determination until both (1) the contract price has been agreed upon and (2) the seller's portion of the contract has been completed.

Receipt of Payment. The recognition of revenue may be delayed until payment is received. When this criterion is used, revenue is considered to be realized at the time the cash is collected, regardless of when the sale was made. The cash basis is widely used by physicians, attorneys, and other enterprises in which professional services are the source of revenue. It has little theoretical justification but has the practical advantage of simplicity of operation and avoidance of the problem of estimating losses from uncollectible accounts. Its acceptability as a fair method of timing the recognition of revenue from personal services is influenced somewhat by the fact that it may be used in determining income subject to the federal income tax. It is not an appropriate method of measuring revenue from the sale of merchandise.

Installment Method. In some businesses, especially in the retail field, it is common to make sales on the installment plan. In the typical installment sale, the buyer makes a down payment and agrees to pay the remainder in specified amounts at stated intervals over a period of time. The seller may retain technical title to the goods or may take other means to make repossession easier in the event that the buyer defaults on the payments. Despite such provisions, installment sales should ordinarily be treated in the same manner as any other sale on account, in which case the revenue is considered to be realized at the point of sale.

In some exceptional cases, the circumstances are such that the collection of receivables is not reasonably assured. In these cases, the **installment method** of determining revenue may be used.[4] Under this method, each receipt of cash is considered to be revenue and to be composed of partial amounts of (1) the cost of merchandise sold and (2) gross profit on the sale.

As a basis for illustration, assume that in the first year of operations, a dealer in household appliances had total installment sales of $300,000, and the cost of the merchandise sold amounted to $180,000. Assume also that collections of the installment accounts receivable were spread over three years as follows: 1st year, $140,000; 2d year, $100,000; 3d year, $60,000. According to the point of sale method, all of the revenue would be recognized in the first year and the gross profit realized in that year would be determined as follows:

Point of Sale Method

Installment sales	$300,000
Cost of merchandise sold	180,000
Gross profit	$120,000

Under the installment method, gross profit is allocated according to the amount of receivables collected in each year, based on the percent of gross profit to sales. The rate of gross profit to sales is determined as follows:

$$\frac{\text{Gross Profit}}{\text{Installment Sales}} = \frac{\$120,000}{\$300,000} = 40\%$$

The amounts reported as gross profit for each of the three years in the illustration, based on collections of installment accounts receivable, are as follows:

Installment Method

1st year collections:	$140,000 × 40%	$ 56,000
2d year collections:	$100,000 × 40%	40,000
3d year collections:	$ 60,000 × 40%	24,000
Total	$300,000	$120,000

Percentage of Completion. Enterprises engaged in large construction projects may devote several years to the completion of a particular contract. To illustrate, assume that a contractor engages in a project that will require three years to complete, for a contract price of $50,000,000. Further assume that the total cost to be incurred, which will also be spread over the three-year period, is estimated at $44,000,000. According to the point of sale criterion, neither the revenue nor the related costs would be recognized until the project is completed. Therefore, using the **completed-contract method** of determining revenue, the entire net income from the contract would be reported in the third year.

Whenever the total cost of a long-term contract and the extent of the project's progress can be reasonably estimated, it is preferable to consider the revenue as being realized over the entire life of the contract.[5] The amount of revenue to be recognized in any particular period is then deter-

---

[4]*Opinions of the Accounting Principles Board, No. 10,* "Omnibus Opinion—1966" (New York: American Institute of Certified Public Accountants, 1966), par. 12.

[5]*Accounting Research and Terminology Bulletins—Final Edition,* "No. 45, Long-term Construction-type Contracts" (New York: American Institute of Certified Public Accountants, 1961), par. 15.

mined on the basis of the estimated percentage of the contract that has been completed during the period. The estimated percentage of completion can be developed by comparing the incurred costs with the most recent estimates of total costs or by estimates by engineers, architects, or other qualified personnel of the progress of the work performed. To continue with the illustration, assume that by the end of the first fiscal year the contract is estimated to be one-fourth completed and the costs incurred during the year were $11,200,000. According to the **percentage-of-completion method,** the revenue to be recognized and the income for the year would be determined as follows:

Revenue ($50,000,000 × 25%)	$12,500,000
Costs incurred	11,200,000
Income (Year 1)	$ 1,300,000

The costs actually incurred during the year (rather than one fourth of the original cost estimate of $44,000,000, or $11,000,000) are deducted from the revenue recognized.

The 1988 edition of *Accounting Trends & Techniques* indicated that 94% of the surveyed companies with long-term contracts used the percentage-of-completion method. Although the use of this method involves some subjectivity, and hence possible error, in the determination of the amount of reported revenue, the financial statements may be more informative and more useful than they would be if none of the revenue was recognized until completion of the contract.

The method used to recognize revenue on a long-term contract should be noted in the financial statements, as indicated in the following excerpt taken from a note to the financial statements of Martin Marietta Corporation:

> Revenue Recognition. Sales under long-term contracts generally are recognized under the percentage-of-completion method, and include a proportion of the earnings expected to be realized on the contract.... Other sales are recorded upon shipment of products or performance of services.

Allocation of Costs

Properties and services acquired by an enterprise are generally recorded at cost. "Cost" is the amount of cash or equivalent given to acquire the property or the service. If property other than cash is given to acquire properties or services, the cost is the cash equivalent of the property given. When the properties or the services acquired are sold or used, the costs are deducted from the related revenue to determine the amount of net income or net loss. The costs of properties or services acquired and on hand at any particular time represent assets. Such costs may also be called "unexpired costs." As the assets are sold or used, they become "expired costs" or "expenses."

The techniques of determining and recording cost expirations have been described and illustrated in earlier chapters. In general, there are two approaches to cost allocations: (1) compute the amount of the expired cost or (2) compute the amount of the unexpired cost. For example, it is customary to determine the portion of plant assets that have expired. After the depreciation for the period has been recorded, the balances of the plant asset accounts minus the balances of the related accumulated depreciation accounts represent the unexpired cost of the assets. The alternative approach must be used for merchandise and supplies, unless perpetual inventory records are maintained. If the cost of the merchandise or supplies on hand at the end of the period is determined by taking a physical inventory, the remaining costs in the related accounts are assumed to have expired. It might appear that the first approach emphasizes expired costs and the second emphasizes unexpired costs. This is not the case, however, since the selection of the method is based merely on convenience or practicality.

Many of the costs allocable to a period are treated as an expense at the time of incurrence because they will be wholly expired at the end of the period. For example, when a monthly rent is paid at the beginning of a month, the cost incurred is unexpired and hence it is an asset; but, since the cost incurred will be wholly expired at the end of the month, the rental is usually charged directly to the appropriate expense account. This process makes a subsequent adjusting entry unnecessary. The proper allocation of costs among periods is the most important consideration. Any one of many accounting techniques may be used in achieving this objective.

ADEQUATE DISCLOSURE

OBJECTIVE 2g
Describe and illustrate the application of the adequate disclosure concept.

Financial statements and their accompanying footnotes or other explanatory materials should contain all of the pertinent data believed essential to the reader's understanding of the enterprise's financial status. Criteria for **adequate disclosure,** or **full disclosure**, often must be based on value judgments rather than on objective facts.

Financial statements are made more useful by the use of headings and subheadings, and by merging items in significant categories. Although all essential data should be disclosed within these categories, judgment must be exercised by excluding nonessential information to avoid clutter. For example, detailed information as to the amount of cash in various special and general funds, the amount on deposit in each of several banks, and the amount invested in various marketable government securities is not needed by the reader of financial statements. Such information displayed on the balance sheet would hinder rather than aid understanding.

In most cases, all of the pertinent data needed by the reader cannot be presented in the financial statements themselves. The statements therefore normally include essential or explanatory information in accompanying notes. For example, on page 474 a note was used to present supplemental information related to the effects of inflation on the financial statements of The Pillsbury Company. Additional matters that accountants agree should be adequately disclosed in the accompanying notes are briefly described and illustrated in the following paragraphs. The illustrations quoted were taken from corporations' annual reports to stockholders, where they appeared in a section often titled "Notes to Financial Statements."

Accounting Methods Employed

When there are several acceptable alternative methods that could have a significant effect on amounts reported on the statements, the particular method used should be disclosed. Examples include inventory cost flow and pricing methods, depreciation methods, and various criteria of revenue recognition. There is considerable variation in the format used to disclose accounting methods employed. One form of disclosure is to present "Significant Accounting Policies" as the initial note. Some of the variations are illustrated by the following examples extracted from selected financial statements:

Digital Equipment Corporation

Note A—Significant Accounting Policies

Inventories—Inventories are stated at the lower of cost (first-in, first-out) or market.

Property, Plant and Equipment—Depreciation expense is computed principally on the following basis:

Classification	Depreciation Lives and Methods
Buildings	33 years (straight-line)
Machinery and equipment..................	8 and 10 years (sum-of-years), 4 and 5 years (double declining-balance)

Atico Financial Corporation

Sales of homesites are recorded under the installment method of accounting.

All depreciable assets are recorded at cost; depreciation is calculated using the straight-line method.

Changes in Accounting Estimates

There are many cases in accounting in which the use of estimates is necessary. These estimates should be revised when additional information or subsequent developments permit better insight or improved judgment upon which to base the estimates. If the effect of such a change on net income is material, it should be disclosed in the financial statements for the year in which the change is adopted.[6] An example of such a disclosure appeared in the 1987 financial statements of Time Incorporated:

Change in Estimate

In the first quarter of 1986 the Company changed the rate of amortization of its pay-TV programming costs to more closely reflect audience viewing patterns. The effect of this change was to reduce programming costs by $58 million and $57 million, resulting in increased net income of $35 million and $31 million, or $.58 per share and $.49 per share, during 1987 and 1986, respectively.

Contingent Liabilities

As discussed previously, contingent liabilities are potential obligations that will materialize only if certain events occur in the future. If the liability is probable and the amount of the liability can be reasonably estimated, it should be recorded in the accounts. Such liabilities discussed in preceding chapters include vacation pay payable and product warranty payable. Although the vacation pay liability is dependent on employees taking vacations, the

[6]*Opinions of the Accounting Principles Board, No. 20,* "Accounting Changes" (New York: American Institute of Certified Public Accountants, 1971), pars. 31–33.

liability is probable and is reasonably estimated. Likewise, although the product warranty liability is dependent upon customers presenting products for repair, the product warranty liability is probable and is reasonably estimated.

If the amount of the potential obligation cannot be reasonably estimated, the details of the contingency should be disclosed.[7] The most common contingent liabilities disclosed in notes to the financial statements — from litigation, guarantees, and discounting receivables — are discussed in the following paragraphs. The 1988 edition of *Accounting Trends & Techniques* indicated that 67% of the surveyed companies disclosed contingencies for litigations, 33% for guarantees, and 15% for discounting receivables.

Litigation. Lawsuits are being filed against companies with increasing frequency. In many cases, litigation takes many months or years to complete. Although it is often difficult to estimate the amount of the liability, the details should be disclosed. Following is an example of a note in the 1987 financial statements of Apple Computer Inc., disclosing a contingent liability arising from litigation:

Litigation (in part)

In May 1987, an action was commenced against Apple and certain of its current and former directors and officers, alleging that in 1985 Apple entered into and breached an alleged oral and written agreement to acquire the business of Woodside Design Associates, Inc. The complaint seeks up to $25 million in compensatory damages and up to $1 billion in punitive damages from Apple. Although discovery has only recently commenced in this action, Apple believes that the suit is without merit, and Apple intends to litigate vigorously the asserted claims, and, in the opinion of management, this litigation will not have a material effect on results of operations or financial condition.

Guarantees. Companies sometimes guarantee a loan for another company, often a supplier or favored customer. In such cases, the company is obligated to pay the loan if the borrower fails to make payment. Such a contingency can be disclosed as illustrated in the following note from the 1987 financial statements of Bethlehem Steel Corporation:

G (in part): Commitments and Contingent Liabilities:

We have guaranteed debt of various businesses, including that of certain associated enterprises, totaling $55.9 million at December 31, 1987. One of these businesses is currently experiencing financial difficulty and we may be required to fund up to $38.8 million under certain of these guarantees. We cannot currently estimate the losses, if any, that might result from these guarantees.

Discounted Receivables. In Chapter 8, the contingent liability arising from discounting a note receivable was discussed. A similar potential obligation may also arise from the sale of receivables. The contingent liability that exists until the due date for discounted receivables can be disclosed as illustrated by the following note from the 1987 financial statements of The Wurlitzer Company:

---

[7]*Statement of Financial Accounting Standards, No. 5,* "Accounting for Contingencies" (Stamford: Financial Accounting Standards Board, 1975), pars. 8, 10, 12.

7 (in part): Commitments and Contingent Liabilities

During the year ended March 31, 1987, the Company negotiated an agreement to sell at face value approximately $6,100,000 of accounts receivable to an outside finance company. Cash proceeds of the sale were approximately $6,000,000: the remaining $100,000 is held by the outside finance company as security for the uncollected recourse receivables. At March 31, 1987, the Company remained contingently liable on approximately $1,900,000 of the sold receivables; however, management believes that the allowance for doubtful accounts will be adequate for any such uncollectible receivables.

Segment of a Business

Many companies diversify their operations; that is, they are involved in more than one type of business activity. These companies may also operate in foreign markets. The individual segments of such diversified companies ordinarily experience differing rates of profitability, degrees of risk, and opportunities for growth. To help financial statement users in assessing past performance and future potential of diversified companies, financial statements should disclose such information as the enterprise's operations in different industries, its foreign markets, and its major customers. The required information for each significant reporting segment includes the following: revenue, income from operations, and identifiable assets associated with the segment.[8] An example of financial reporting for segments of a business is illustrated by the note adapted from the 1988 financial statements of The Walt Disney Company shown at the top of page 482.

Events Subsequent to Date of Statements

Events occuring or becoming known after the close of the period may have a significant effect on the financial statements and should be disclosed.[9] For example, if an enterprise should suffer a crippling loss from a fire or other catastrophe between the end of the year and the issuance of the statements, the facts should be disclosed. Similarly, such occurrences as the issuance of long-term debt or capital stock, or the purchase of another business enterprise after the close of the period should be made known. The Washington Post Company reported a subsequent event in a note to its 1987 financial statements as follows:

M. Subsequent Events

On January 4, 1988, the company sold its 100 percent interest in the Miami-Ft. Lauderdale cellular telephone system and its minority interest in the Palm Beach cellular system at an after-tax gain of approximately $115,500,000, or $9.00 per share. This gain will be recorded in the company's earnings for the first quarter of 1988.

---

[8]*Statement of Financial Accounting Standards, No. 14*, "Financial Reporting for Segments of a Business Enterprise" (Stamford: Financial Accounting Standards Board, 1976). Nonpublic corporations are exempted from this requirement by *Statement of Financial Accounting Standards, No. 21*, "Suspension of the Reporting of Earnings per Share and Segment Information by Nonpublic Enterprises" (Stamford: Financial Accounting Standards Board, 1978).

[9]*Statement on Auditing Standards, No. 1*, "Codification of Auditing Standards and Procedures" (New York: American Institute of Certified Public Accountants, 1988), section 560.

10. Business Segments

(In millions)	1988	1987	1986
Capital Expenditures			
Theme parks and resorts	$ 559.0	$ 249.1	$ 160.0
Filmed entertainment	16.9	15.7	4.5
Consumer products	6.6	1.0	.3
Corporate	13.2	14.3	9.3
	$ 595.7	$ 280.1	$ 174.1
Depreciation Expense			
Theme parks and resorts	$ 137.2	$ 134.0	$ 113.4
Filmed entertainment	6.8	5.5	5.0
Consumer products	.6	.2	.2
Corporate	4.0	3.4	2.0
	$ 148.6	$ 143.1	$ 120.6
Identifiable Assets			
Theme parks and resorts	$3,074.0	$2,291.3	$2,158.0
Filmed entertainment	609.5	483.0	413.3
Consumer products	127.0	30.6	25.0
Corporate	1,298.4	549.2	121.2
	5,108.9	3,354.1	2,717.5
Discontinued operations		452.2	403.5
	$5,108.9	$3,806.3	$3,121.0
Supplemental Revenue Data			
Theme Parks and Resorts			
Admissions and rides	$ 816.3	$ 757.4	$ 607.1
Merchandise	449.6	428.4	353.2
Food	379.5	336.0	288.7
Other	396.6	312.4	274.9
	$2,042.0	$1,834.2	$1,523.9
Filmed Entertainment			
Theatrical	$ 456.1	$ 284.6	$ 151.7
Other	693.1	591.0	360.0
	$1,149.2	$ 875.6	$ 511.7

CONSISTENCY

OBJECTIVE 2h
Describe and illustrate the application of the consistency concept.

A number of accepted alternative principles affecting the determination of income statement and balance sheet amounts have been presented in earlier sections of the text. Recognizing that different methods may be used under varying circumstances and that the comparison of an enterprise's current financial statements with those of the preceding year is common practice, some guide or standard is needed to assure that the enterprise's periodic financial statements can be compared.

The amount and the direction of change in net income and financial position from period to period is very important to readers and may greatly influence their decisions. Therefore, interested persons should be able to assume that successive financial statements of an enterprise are based consistently on the same generally accepted accounting principles. If the principles are not applied consistently, the trends indicated could be the result of changes in the principles used rather than the result of changes in business conditions or managerial effectiveness.

The concept of **consistency** does not completely prohibit changes in the accounting principles used. Changes are permissible when it is believed that the use of a different principle will more fairly state net income and financial position. Examples of changes in accounting principles include a change in the method of inventory pricing, a change in depreciation method for previously recorded assets, and a change in the method of accounting for long-term construction contracts. Consideration of changes in accounting principles must be accompanied by consideration of the general rule for disclosure of such changes, which is as follows:

> *The nature of and justification for a change in accounting principle and its effect on income should be disclosed in the financial statements of the period in which the change is made. The justification for the change should explain clearly why the newly adopted accounting principle is preferable.* [10]

There are various methods of reporting the effect of a change in accounting principle on net income. The cumulative effect of the change on net income may be reported on the income statement of the period in which the change is adopted. In some cases, the effect of the change could be applied retroactively to past periods by presenting revised income statements for the earlier years affected. The methods of disclosure are discussed in more detail in Chapter 15.

The application of the consistency concept does not require that a specific accounting method be used uniformly throughout an enterprise. For example, it is not unusual for large enterprises to use different costing and pricing methods for different segments of their inventories, as illustrated by the following note that appeared in the 1987 financial statements of Tribune Company:

> *Inventories*
>
> Inventories are stated at the lower of cost or market. Cost is determined on the first-in, first-out ("FIFO") or average basis for pulpwood, supplies, materials and Canadian newsprint and on the last-in, first-out ("LIFO") basis for U.S. newsprint.

MATERIALITY

OBJECTIVE 2i
Describe and illustrate the application of the materiality concept.

In following generally accepted accounting principles, the accountant must consider the relative importance of any event, accounting procedure, or change in procedure that affects items on the financial statements. Absolute accuracy in accounting and full disclosure in reporting are not ends in themselves, and there is no need to exceed the limits of practicality. The determination of what is significant and what is not requires the exercise of judgment. Precise criteria cannot be formulated.

To determine **materiality,** the size of an item and its nature must be considered in relationship to the size and the nature of other items. The erroneous classification of a $10,000 asset on a balance sheet exhibiting total assets of $10,000,000 would probably be immaterial. If the assets totaled only $100,000, however, it would certainly be material. If the $10,000 represented a note receivable from an officer of the enterprise, it might well be material even in the first assumption. If the loan was increased to $100,000 between

---

[10]*Opinions of the Accounting Principles Board,* No. 20, "Accounting Changes" (New York: American Institute of Certified Public Accountants, 1971), par. 17.

the close of the period and the issuance of the statements, both the nature of the item at the balance sheet date and the subsequent increase in amount would require disclosure.

The concept of materiality may be applied to procedures used in recording transactions. As was stated in an earlier chapter, small expenditures for plant assets may be treated as an expense of the period rather than as an asset. The saving in clerical costs is justified if the practice does not materially affect the financial statements. In establishing a dollar amount as the dividing line between a revenue expenditure and a capital expenditure, consideration would need to be given to such factors as (1) amount of total plant assets, (2) amount of plant assets in relationship to other assets, (3) frequency of occurrence of expenditures for plant assets, (4) nature and expected life of plant assets, and (5) probable effect on the amount of periodic net income reported.

Custom and practicality also influence criteria of materiality. Corporate financial statements seldom report the cents amounts or even the hundreds of dollars. A common practice is to round to the nearest thousand. For large corporations, there is an increasing tendency to report the financial data in terms of millions, carrying figures to one decimal. For example, the 1988 edition of *Accounting Trends & Techniques* indicated that 55 of 600 companies reported amounts to the nearest dollar, 412 to the nearest thousand dollars, and 133 to the nearest million dollars.

A technique known as "whole-dollar" accounting, which is used by some businesses, eliminates the cents amounts from accounting entries at the earliest possible point in the accounting sequence. There are some accounts, such as those with customers and creditors, in which it is not feasible to round to the nearest dollar. Nevertheless, the technique yields savings in office costs and improved productivity. The errors introduced into other accounts by rounding the amounts of individual entries at the time of recording tend to be compensating in nature, and the amount of the final error is not material.

It should not be inferred from the foregoing that whole-dollar accounting encourages or condones errors. The unrecorded cents are not lost; they are merely reported in a manner that reduces recording costs without materially affecting the accuracy of accounting data.

CONCERNING THE GNAT AND THE CAMEL

This is the story as it comes to us: An accountant . . . was [asked] to check the cash of a concern, which may be called the XYZ Corporation. This concern among its activities included a selling department where goods of small value were sold in fairly large quantities. When the cash of the selling department was counted it was found that the amount on hand was, let us say, $2.04—a fictitious amount greater than the actual sum—more than it should have been. Now this incident happened in the city of New York where, as all citizens know to their sorrow, there is a two percent tax on sales. Evidently, therefore, this excessive sum of $2.04 represented the sale of some article for $2, plus a tax of four cents. . . . Apparently a careless member of the staff had sold such an article, placed the proceeds in the till and forgotten to make the proper record of the whole stupendous transaction. The carelessness was unpardonable, of course. No member of any staff *anywhere should forget anything. However, the error occurred and the perspicacious young [accountant] discovered it, as he could not very well avoid doing. He found the unaccountable excess and, like a well-trained man, conscious of his complete efficiency, he set to work to trace the mistake and to expose the guilty person. Here was a chance for him to demonstrate his incalculable value to his firm.... Such wrongdoing must not escape unchallenged. Relying upon his supposed authority he began a search, a veritable inquisition, and after two or three days of earnest effort, during which he had interrupted the work of the entire...office and had...considerable...time expended, he was compelled to admit that he could not find a shortage in the inventory to account for the surplus cash, nor could he rightfully determine who had committed the crime. At last he regretfully reported the matter to his superior and confessed himself defeated. What the superior had to say about the matter is not recorded; but one can imagine the attitude of the [superior] and can*

form a reasonably accurate notion of the comments which were made....

This little story bears a moral which every accountant may well take to heart. It might be unwise to say that errors should be overlooked or that carelessness should be condoned. But surely there is no sense whatever in a ridiculous adherence to meticulous detail when the sole purpose is to trace something which is not worth tracing.... What the [accountant] should have done in the present case is clear. He should have made a note of the excess, and, after spending a few minutes in trying to trace it to its source, he should have gone on to weightier things. It is a great pity that this sort of incident ever occurs; but we are told that the case before us is not unique. There are many little fellows who revel in the most microscopic minutiae. They can't help it. They probably were born that way, but they should never, never, be employed in the work of accountancy, which, after all, is a matter of principles, not of pin points.

Source: A. P. Richardson, *The Journal of Accountancy* (October, 1936), pp. 233–235.

CONSERVATISM

OBJECTIVE 2j
Describe and illustrate the application of the conservatism concept.

Periodic statements are affected to a great degree by the selection of accounting procedures and other value judgments. Historically, accountants have tended to be conservative, and in selecting among alternatives they have often favored the method or the procedure that yielded the lesser amount of net income or of asset value. This attitude of **conservatism** was often expressed in the statement to "anticipate no profits and provide for all losses." For example, it is acceptable to price merchandise inventory at lower of cost or market. If market price is higher than cost, the higher amount is ignored in the accounts and, if presented in the financial statements, is presented parenthetically. Such an attitude of pessimism has been due in part to the need for an offset to the optimism of business management. It could also be argued that potential future losses to an enterprise from poor management decisions would be lessened if net income and assets were understated.

Current accounting thought has shifted somewhat from this philosophy of conservatism. Conservatism is no longer considered to be a dominant factor in selecting among alternatives. Revenue should be recognized when realized, and expired costs should be matched against revenue according to the principles based on reason and logic. The element of conservatism may be considered only when other factors affecting a choice of alternatives are neutral. The concepts of objectivity, consistency, disclosure, and materiality are more important than conservatism, and the latter should be a factor only when the others do not play a significant role.

CHAPTER REVIEW

KEY POINTS

Development of Concepts and Principles

As the American economy developed and as business organizations grew in size and complexity, there came an awareness of the need for a framework of concepts and generally accepted accounting principles to serve as guidelines for the preparation of the basic financial statements. These principles represent the best possible guides, based on reason, observation, and experimentation, to help make accounting data more useful in an ever-changing society.

Currently, the Financial Accounting Standards Board establishes accounting standards for business enterprises. The Governmental Accounting Standards Board has responsibility for establishing accounting standards to be followed by state and municipal governments.

Among the other organizations which have had an effect on the development of accounting principles are the American Institute of Certified Public Accountants, the American Accounting Association, the Securities and Exchange Commission, the Internal Revenue Service, the Financial Executives Institute, and the National Association of Accountants.

a   Business Entity

The business entity concept assumes that a business enterprise is separate and distinct from the persons who supply its assets. This distinction exists regardless of the legal form of the organization.

b   Going Concern

In most cases, it is not possible to determine in advance the length of life of an enterprise, and so an assumption must be made. It is customary to assume that a business entity has a reasonable expectation of continuing in business at a profit for an indefinite period of time.

c   Objective Evidence

Entries in the accounting records and data reported on financial statements must be based on objectively determined evidence. If this principle is not followed, the confidence of the many users of the financial statements could not be maintained.

d   Unit of Measurement

All business transactions are recorded in terms of money. The use of the monetary unit in accounting for and reporting the activities of an enterprise has two major limitations: (1) it limits the scope of accounting reports and (2) it assumes stability of the measurement unit. Factors affecting the activities and the future prospects of an enterprise that cannot be expressed in monetary terms may be disclosed in descriptions in notes to the financial statements. There are two widely discussed recommendations for supplementing conventional financial statements and thus resolving financial reporting problems created by the instability of the monetary unit: (1) supplemental financial data based on current costs and (2) supplemental financial data based on constant dollars.

e   Accounting Period

A complete and accurate picture of an enterprise's success or failure cannot be obtained until it discontinues operations, converts its assets into cash, and pays off its debts. However, many decisions regarding the business must be made by management and interested outsiders during its existence. It is therefore necessary to prepare periodic reports on operations, financial position, and cash flows.

f   Matching Revenue and Expired Costs

The determination of periodic net income is a two-fold problem involving (1) the revenue recognized during the period and (2) the expired costs to be allocated to the period. Thus, revenue and expired costs must be matched to determine net income or net loss for the period.

Revenue may be recognized at the point of sale, upon receipt of payment, or under the installment method. In addition, for enterprises engaged in large construction projects, revenue may be recognized under the percentage-of-completion method.

Properties and services acquired by an enterprise are generally recorded at cost. As the cost expires, it must be recognized as an expense of the period. Many costs are treated as an expense at the time of occurrence because they will be wholly expired at the end of the period.

g   Adequate Disclosure

Financial statements and their accompanying footnotes or other explanatory materials should contain all of the pertinent data believed essential to the reader's understanding of the enterprise's financial status. When there are several acceptable alternative accounting methods that could have a significant effect on amounts reported on the statements, the particular method used should be disclosed. When accounting estimates are revised because of additional information or subsequent developments, their effect on net income should be disclosed in the financial statements for the period in which the change is adopted. Any contingent liabilities that exist and are significant in nature should also be disclosed in financial statements. Companies with diversified segments should disclose their operations in different industries, their foreign markets, and their major customers. Events occurring or becoming known after the close of the period that have a significant effect on the financial statements should be disclosed.

h   Consistency

A number of acceptable alternative principles affecting the determination of income statement and balance sheet amounts exist. The concept of consistency implies that the financial statements should be prepared by applying the same principles year after year. If changes in principles do occur, their effect on the financial statements should be disclosed.

i   Materiality

In following generally accepted accounting principles, the accountant must consider the relative importance of any event, accounting procedure, or change in procedure that affects items on the financial statements. The concept of materiality implies that accountants need not strictly adhere to generally accepted accounting principles if the amounts involved are not significant.

j　Conservatism

The concept of conservatism implies that, in selecting among alternative accounting principles, the principle that yields the lesser amount of net income or asset value should be chosen. Current accounting thought has shifted somewhat from this philosophy of conservatism, and it is no longer considered to be a dominant factor in selecting among alternatives.

KEY TERMS

Financial Accounting Standards Board (FASB)　467
Governmental Accounting Standards Board　468
American Institute of Certified Public Accountants (AICPA)　469
Securities and Exchange Commission (SEC)　469
Internal Revenue Service (IRS)　469
business entity concept　470
going concern concept　470
current cost　473

constant dollar　473
price-level index　473
matching　475
point of sale method　475
installment method　476
completed-contract method　476
percentage-of-completion method　477
adequate disclosure　478
consistency　483
materiality　483
conservatism　485

SELF-EXAMINATION QUESTIONS

Answers at end of chapter.

1. Equipment that was acquired for $250,000 has a current book value of $100,000 and an estimated market value of $120,000. If the replacement cost of the equipment is $350,000, at what amount should the equipment be reported in the balance sheet?
   A. $120,000
   B. $150,000
   C. $350,000
   D. None of the above

2. Merchandise costing $140,000 was sold on the installment plan for $200,000 during the current year. Down payments of $40,000 and installment payments of $35,000 were received during the current year. If the installment method of accounting is employed, what is the amount of gross profit to be realized in the current year?
   A. $22,500
   B. $60,000
   C. $75,000
   D. None of the above

3. The total contract price for the construction of an ocean liner was $20,000,000, and the estimated construction costs were $17,000,000. During the current year, the project was estimated to be 40% completed and the costs incurred totaled $7,050,000. Under the percentage-of-completion method of accounting, what amount of income would be recognized for the current year?
   A. $950,000
   B. $1,200,000
   C. $3,000,000
   D. None of the above

4. The concept of consistency requires that the nature of and justification for a change in accounting principle and its effect on income be disclosed in the financial statements of the period in which a change is made. An example of a change in accounting principle is a:
   A. change in method of inventory pricing
   B. change in depreciation method for previously recorded plant assets
   C. change in method of accounting for installment sales
   D. all of the above

5. A corporation's financial statements do not report cents amounts. This is an example of the application of which of the following concepts?
    A. Business entity
    B. Going concern
    C. Consistency
    D. Materiality

ILLUSTRATIVE PROBLEM

Town and Country Furniture Company makes all sales on the installment basis and recognizes revenue at the point of sale. Condensed income statements and the amounts collected from customers for each of the first three years of operations are as follows:

	1990	1991	1992
Sales	$190,000	$240,000	$170,000
Cost of merchandise sold	133,000	163,200	122,400
Gross profit	$ 57,000	$ 76,800	$ 47,600
Operating expenses	33,900	41,500	30,000
Net income	$ 23,100	$ 35,300	$ 17,600
Collected from sales of first year	$ 50,000	$110,000	$ 30,000
Collected from sales of second year		80,000	120,000
Collected from sales of third year			60,000

Instructions:

Determine the amount of net income that would have been reported in each year if the installment method of recognizing revenue had been used. Ignore the possible effects of uncollectible accounts on the computations.

SOLUTION

		1990	1991	1992
Gross profit realized on collections from sales of:				
First year:	30%[1] × $ 50,000	$ 15,000		
	30% × $110,000		$33,000	
	30% × $ 30,000			$ 9,000
Second year:	32%[2] × $ 80,000		25,600	
	32% × $120,000			38,400
Third year:	28%[3] × $ 60,000			16,800
Total gross profit realized		$ 15,000	$58,600	$64,200
Operating expenses		33,900	41,500	30,000
Income (loss) from operations		$(18,900)	$17,100	$34,200

[1]$57,000 ÷ $190,000 = 30% gross profit
[2]$76,800 ÷ $240,000 = 32% gross profit
[3]$47,600 ÷ $170,000 = 28% gross profit

DISCUSSION QUESTIONS

1. Accounting principles are broad guides to accounting practice. (a) How do these principles differ from the principles relating to the physical sciences? (b) Of what significance is acceptability in the development of accounting principles? (c) Why must accounting principles be continually reexamined and revised?

2. What role does the Financial Accounting Foundation play in the development of accounting principles?

3. What body is currently dominant in the development of (a) generally accepted accounting principles for business enterprises and (b) principles for state and municipal governments?

4. Briefly discuss the process by which the Financial Accounting Standards Board (FASB) develops *Statements of Financial Accounting Standards*.

5. For accounting purposes, what is the nature of the assumption as to the length of life of an enterprise?

6. Why should the most objective evidence available be used as the basis for data reported on financial statements?

7. Plant assets are reported on the balance sheet at a total cost of $750,000, less accumulated depreciation of $300,000. (a) Is it possible that the assets might realize considerably more or considerably less than $450,000 if the business were discontinued and the assets were sold separately? (b) Why aren't plant assets reported on the balance sheet at their estimated market values?

8. During the current year, a mortgage note payable for $750,000, issued by Mills Company 10 years ago, became due and was paid. Assuming that the general price level had increased by 50% during the 10-year period, did the loan result in an increase or a decrease in Mills Company's purchasing power? Explain.

9. A machine with a cost of $70,000 and accumulated depreciation of $60,000 will soon need to be replaced by a similar machine that will cost $100,000. (a) At what amount should the machine presently owned be reported on the balance sheet? (b) What amount should management use in planning for the cash required to replace the machine?

10. During July, merchandise costing $100,000 was sold for $175,000 in cash. Because the purchasing power of the dollar has declined, it will cost $110,000 to replace the merchandise. (a)What is the amount of gross profit in July? (b) Assuming that all operating expenses for the month are paid in cash and that the owner withdraws cash in the amount of the net income, would there be enough cash remaining from the $175,000 of sales to replace the merchandise sold? Discuss.

11. Conventional financial statements do not give recognition to the instability of the purchasing power of the dollar. How can the effect of the fluctuating dollar on business operations be presented to the users of the financial statements?

12. What is the current cost of an asset?

13. If land was purchased for $50,000 when the general price-level index was 150, and the general price-level index has risen to 225, what is the constant dollar equivalent of the original cost of the land?

14. If a complete and accurate picture of an enterprise's success or failure is desired, what accounting period must be used to report on operations?

15. Is revenue from sales of merchandise on account more commonly recognized at the time of sale or at the time of cash receipt?

16. During the current year, merchandise costing $450,000 was sold on the installment plan for $750,000. The down payments and the installment payments received during the current year totaled $375,000. What is the amount of gross profit considered to be realized in the current year, applying (a) the point of sale method and (b) the installment method of revenue recognition?

17. During the current year, Mueller Construction Company obtained a contract to build an apartment building. The total contract price was $8,000,000, and the estimated construction costs were $6,950,000. During the current year, the project was estimated to be 40% completed, and the costs incurred totaled $2,910,000. Under the percentage-of-completion method of revenue recognition, what amount of (a) revenue, (b) cost, and (c) income should be recognized from the contract for the current year?

18. On January 4 of the current year, Hobbs Realty Company acquired a 5-acre tract of land for $100,000. Before the end of the year, $60,000 was spent in subdividing the tract and in paving streets. The market value of the land at the end of the year was estimated at $200,000. Although no lots were sold during the year, the income statement for the year reported revenue of $100,000, expenses of $60,000, and net income of $40,000 from the project. Were generally accepted accounting principles followed? Discuss.

19. Mini-Storage Company constructed a warehouse at a cost of $150,000, after a local contractor had submitted a bid of $170,000. The building was recorded at $170,000, and income of $20,000 was recognized. Were generally accepted accounting principles followed? Discuss.

20. Oslow Company purchased equipment for $150,000 at the beginning of a fiscal year. The equipment could be sold for $160,000 at the end of the fiscal year. It was proposed that since the equipment was worth more at the end of the year than at the beginning of the year, (a) no depreciation should be recorded for the current year, and (b) the gain of $10,000 should be recorded. Discuss the propriety of the proposals.

21. When there are several acceptable alternative accounting methods that could be used, the method used by an enterprise should be disclosed in the financial statements. Give examples of accounting methods that fall in this category.

22. If significant changes are made in the accounting principles applied from one period to the next, why should the effect of these changes be disclosed in the financial statements?

23. You have just been employed by a relatively small merchandising business that records its revenues only when cash is received and its expenses only when cash is paid. You are aware of the fact that the enterprise should record its revenues and expenses on the accrual basis. Would changing to the accrual basis violate the principle of consistency? Discuss.

24. For many years, Root Company has used the sum-of-the-years-digits method of computing depreciation. For the current year, the straight-line method was used, depreciation expense amounted to $65,000, and net income amounted to $75,000. Depreciation computed by the sum-of-the-years-digits method would have been $90,000. (a) What is the quantitative effect of the change in method on the net income for the current year? (b) Is the effect of the change material? (c) Should the effect of the change in method be disclosed in the financial statements?

25. The accountant for a large department store charged the acquisition of a pencil sharpener to an expense account, even though the asset had an estimated useful life of 10 years. Which accounting concept supports this treatment of the expenditure?

26. In 1960, Falk Corporation acquired a building, with a useful life of 50 years, and depreciated it by the declining-balance method. Is this practice conservative (a) for the year 1960 and (b) for the year 2009? Explain.

Real World Focus

27. The following footnote was taken from the 1988 annual report of Fay's Drug Company Inc.:

   Inventories—Inventory is stated at the lower of cost or market. The cost of substantially all the inventory is determined on a last-in, first-out (LIFO) basis. If these inventories had been valued at current replacement costs, total inventory values would have been approximately $21,290,000, $19,029,000 and $17,321,000 higher at January 31, 1988, 1987, and 1986, respectively.

   Fay's Drug Company Inc. reported "earnings before taxes on income" of $10,251,016 and $6,835,034 for years ending January 31, 1988 and 1987, respectively. Based upon the preceding data, determine the "earnings before taxes on income" that would have been reported in 1988 and 1987 if inventories had been valued using current (replacement) costs.

EXERCISES

Exercise 12–1
Effect of price-level change on investment in land.
OBJ. 2d

Several years ago, Peterson Company purchased land as a future building site for $50,000. The price-level index at that time was 120. On October 11 of the current year, when the price-level index was 192, the land was sold for $90,000.

   (a) Determine the amount of the gain that would be realized according to conventional accounting.
   (b) Indicate the amount of the gain that may be (1) attributed to the change in purchasing power and (2) considered a true gain in terms of current dollars.

Exercise 12–2
Recognition of revenue.
OBJ. 2f

Indicate for each of the following items the amount of revenue that should be reported for the current year and the amount of revenue that should be postponed to a future period. Give a reason for your answer.

   (a) Merchandise on hand at the end of the current fiscal year, costing $212,250, is expected to be sold in the following year for $340,500.
   (b) Thirty days before the end of the current fiscal year, $100,000 was loaned at 12% for 90 days.
   (c) Sales of merchandise made on terms 2/10, n/60 and delivered during the current year totaled $955,000. Cash received on credit sales totaled $910,000 during the current year.
   (d) Season tickets for a series of five concerts were sold for $90,000. Three concerts were played during the current year.
   (e) The contract price for building a bridge is $11,000,000. During the current year, the first year of construction, the bridge is estimated to be 25% completed and the costs incurred totaled $2,450,000. Revenue is to be recognized by the percentage-of-completion method.
   (f) A tract of land was leased on the first day of the tenth month of the current year, and one year's rent of $40,000 was received.   *(Continued)*

(g) Cash of $25,000 was received in the current year on the sale of gift certificates to be redeemed in merchandise in the following year.

(h) Sixty days before the end of the current fiscal year, a $150,000, 90-day, non-interest-bearing note was accepted at a discount of 12%. Proceeds in the amount of $145,500 were given to the maker of the note.

(i) Salespersons submitted orders in the current year for merchandise to be delivered in the following year. The merchandise had a cost of $30,000 and a selling price of $42,250.

Exercise 12–3

Gross profit by point of sale and installment methods.

OBJ. 2f

SPREADSHEET PROBLEM

Stratton Company makes all sales on the installment plan. Data related to merchandise sold during the current fiscal year are as follows:

Sales	$900,000
Cash received on the $900,000 of installment contracts........	325,000
Merchandise inventory, beginning of year	162,500
Merchandise inventory, end of year.................................	167,500
Purchases	635,000

Determine the amount of gross profit that would be recognized for the current fiscal year according to (a) the point of sale method and (b) the installment method.

Exercise 12–4

Determination of cost of products and services acquired.

OBJ. 2f

Properties and services acquired by an enterprise are generally recorded at cost. For each of the following, determine the cost.

(a) Equipment was purchased for $75,500 under terms of n/30, FOB shipping point. The freight charge amounted to $950, and installation costs totaled $1,500.

(b) An adjacent tract of land was acquired for $47,500 to provide additional parking for customers. The structures on the land were removed at a cost of $5,500. The salvaged material from the structures was sold for $750. The cost of grading the land was $1,750.

(c) Materials and supplies costing $4,250 were purchased for the construction of a display case. An additional $2,000 was paid to hire a carpenter to build the display case. A similar case would cost $7,500 if purchased from a manufacturer.

Exercise 12–5

Effects on financial statements of failure to accrue commission.

OBJ. 2f

Salespersons for Hall Realty receive a commission of 3% of sales, the amount due on sales of one month being paid in the middle of the following month. At the end of each of the first three years of operations, the accountant failed to record accrued sales commissions expense as follows: first year, $15,000; second year, $17,500; third year, $13,500. In each case, the commissions were paid during the first month of the succeeding year and were charged as an expense of that year. Accrued sales commissions expense was properly recorded at the end of the fourth year. (a) Determine the amount by which net income was overstated or understated for each of the four years. (b) Determine the items on the balance sheet that would have been overstated or understated at the end of each of the four years, and the amount of overstatement or understatement.

Exercise 12–6

Effect on financial statements of failure to record sales.

OBJ. 2f

Jefferson Company sells most of its products on a cash basis, but extends short-term credit to a few of its customers. Invoices for sales on account are placed in a file and are not recorded until cash is received, at which time the sale is recorded in the same manner as a cash sale. The net income reported for the first three years of operations was $89,200, $72,600, and $96,750, respectively. The total amount of the uncollected sales invoices in the file at the end of each of the three years was $9,800, $6,750, and $7,500, respectively. In each case, the entire amount was collected during the first month of the succeeding year. (a) Determine the amount by which net income was overstated or understated for each of the three years. (b) Determine the items on the balance sheet that were overstated or understated, and the amount of overstatement or understatement, as of the end of each year.

Exercise 12–7
Determination of materiality.

OBJ. 2g, i

Of the following matters, considered individually, indicate those that are material and that should be disclosed either in the financial statements or in accompanying explanatory notes.

(a) A change in estimates of the remaining usefulness of computer equipment decreased the amount of net income that would otherwise have been reported from $950,000 to $725,000.

(b) A merchandising company employs the first-in, first-out cost flow assumption and prices its inventory at the lower of cost or market.

(c) Between the end of the fiscal year and the date of publication of the annual report, a fire completely destroyed one of three principal plants. The loss was estimated at $3,000,000 and was fully covered by insurance. The net income for the fiscal year was $850,000.

(d) A change in accounting for depreciation of plant assets was adopted in the current year. The amount of net income that would otherwise have been reported decreased from $795,000 to $775,000.

(e) A company is facing litigation involving restraint of trade. Damages might amount to $5,000,000. Annual net income reported in the past few years has ranged from $12,000,000 to $15,000,000.

Exercise 12–8
Effect of different inventory cost methods on net income.

OBJ. 2g, i

The cost of merchandise inventory at the end of the first fiscal year of operations, according to three different methods, is as follows: fifo, $87,750; average, $85,000; lifo, $80,000. If the average cost method is employed, the net income reported will be $62,000. (a) What will be the amount of net income reported if the lifo method is adopted? (b) What will be the amount of net income reported if the fifo method is adopted? (c) Which of the three methods is the most conservative in terms of net income? (d) Is the particular method adopted of sufficient materiality to require disclosure in the financial statements?

Exercise 12–9
Identification of generally accepted accounting principles.

OBJ. 2

Each of the following statements represents a decision made by an accountant. State whether or not you agree with the decision. Support your answer with reference to generally accepted accounting principles that are applicable in the circumstances.

(a) In preparing the balance sheet, detailed information as to the amount due from hundreds of customers was omitted. The total amount was presented under the caption "Accounts Receivable."

(b) Used computer equipment, with an estimated useful life of 5 years and no salvage value, was purchased early in the current fiscal year for $150,000. Since the company planned to purchase new equipment, costing $250,000, to replace this equipment at the end of five years, depreciation expense of $50,000 was recorded for the current year. The depreciation expense thus provided for one fifth of the cost of the replacement.

(c) All minor expenditures for office equipment are charged to an expense account.

(d) Merchandise transferred to other parties on a consignment basis and not sold was included in merchandise inventory.

(e) Land, used as a parking lot, was purchased 10 years ago for $50,000. Since its market value is now $90,000, the land account is debited for $40,000 and a gain account is credited for a like amount. The gain is presented as an "Other income" item in the income statement.

(f) Thirty days before the end of the current year, sales catalogs were acquired for $45,000. Although the catalogs are not salable, the unused portion is included as an asset in the balance sheet at the end of the year.

(g) Merchandise inventory at the end of the current year was estimated by the general manager, who "eye-balled" the inventory on hand and then determined its cost, based on an estimate of current costs. The accountant used the general manager's estimate for recording the cost of the inventory in the accounts.

(Continued)

(h) Financial statements adjusted to eliminate the effects of inflation (using the current cost method) were presented as supplementary financial data.

(i) Net income for the current year is expected to be larger than normal. Therefore the accountant used the declining-balance method for determining depreciation for the current year to reduce the net income to a more normal amount. The accountant plans to return in future years to the use of the straight-line method that has been used in all past years for determining income.

PROBLEMS

Series A

Problem 12–1A
Installment sales.
OBJ. 2f

Menter Co. makes all sales on the installment basis and recognizes revenue at the point of sale. Condensed income statements and the amounts collected from customers for each of the first three years of operations are as follows:

	First Year	Second Year	Third Year
Sales	$402,500	$340,000	$372,000
Cost of merchandise sold	265,650	227,800	241,800
Gross profit	$136,850	$112,200	$130,200
Operating expenses	64,000	51,500	60,700
Net income	$ 72,850	$ 60,700	$ 69,500
Collected from sales of first year	$125,000	$157,500	$120,000
Collected from sales of second year		95,000	145,000
Collected from sales of third year			110,000

Instructions:

Determine the amount of net income that would have been reported in each year if the installment method of recognizing revenue had been employed, ignoring the possible effects of uncollectible accounts on the computation. Present figures in good order.

Problem 12–2A
Installment sale and repossession.
OBJ. 2f

Cone Video employs the installment method of recognizing gross profit for sales made on the installment plan. Details of a particular installment sale, amounts collected from the buyer, and the repossession of the item sold are as follows:

First year:
    Sold for $1,200 a color television set having a cost of $960; received a down payment of $200.
Second year:
    Received 12 monthly payments of $40 each.
Third year:
    The buyer defaulted on the monthly payments, the set was repossessed, and the remaining 13 installments were canceled. The set was estimated to be worth $450.

Instructions:

(1) Determine the gross profit to be recognized in the first year.
(2) Determine the gross profit to be recognized in the second year.
(3) Determine the gain or loss to be recognized from the repossession of the set. (*Suggestion:* First determine the amount of the unrecovered cost in the canceled installments. The gain or loss on repossession will then be the difference between this unrecovered cost and the value of the repossessed set.)

Problem 12–3A
Percentage-of-completion method.

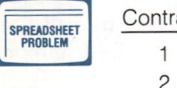

Sweeney Company began construction on three contracts during 1990. The contract prices and construction activities for 1990, 1991, and 1992 were as follows:

Contract	Contract Price	1990 Costs Incurred	1990 Percent Completed	1991 Costs Incurred	1991 Percent Completed	1992 Costs Incurred	1992 Percent Completed
1	$15,000,000	$5,575,000	40%	$4,900,000	35%	$3,400,000	25%
2	10,000,000	2,550,000	30	2,625,000	30	2,695,000	30
3	8,000,000	3,710,000	50	3,815,000	50	—	—

Instructions:

Determine the amount of revenue and the income to be recognized for each of the years, 1990, 1991, and 1992. Revenue is to be recognized by the percentage-of-completion method. Present computations in good order.

Problem 12–4A
Effect on net income from changes in three accounting principles.

OBJ. 2f

SEG Corporation was organized on January 4, 1990. During its first three years of operations, the company determined uncollectible accounts expense by the direct write-off method, the cost of the merchandise inventory at the end of the period by the first-in, first-out method, and depreciation expense by the straight-line method. The amount of net income reported and the amounts of the foregoing items for each of the three years were as follows:

	First Year	Second Year	Third Year
Net income reported.............................	$110,000	$142,000	$175,000
Uncollectible accounts expense	925	2,800	5,950
Ending merchandise inventory	72,750	82,000	112,000
Depreciation expense............................	20,000	26,800	35,000

The firm is considering the possibility of changing to the following methods in determining net income for the fourth and subsequent years: provision for doubtful accounts through the use of an allowance account, last-in, first-out inventory, and declining-balance depreciation at twice the straight-line rate. To consider the probable future effect of these changes on the determination of net income, the management requests that net income of the past three years be recomputed on the basis of the proposed methods. The uncollectible accounts expense, inventory, and depreciation expense for the past three years, computed in accordance with the proposed methods, are as follows:

	First Year	Second Year	Third Year
Uncollectible accounts expense	$ 2,625	$ 3,500	$ 5,050
Ending merchandise inventory	71,000	76,000	102,000
Depreciation expense...............................	40,000	38,840	34,100

Instructions:

Recompute the net income for each of the three years, presenting the figures in an orderly manner.

Problem 12–5A
Adjusting and correcting entries.

OBJ. 2

You are engaged to review the accounting records of Lennox Company prior to the closing of the revenue and expense accounts as of June 30, the end of the current fiscal year. The following information comes to your attention during the review:

(a) Since net income for the current year is expected to be considerably less than it was for the preceding year, depreciation on buildings has not been recorded. Buildings depreciation for the year, determined in a manner consistent with the preceding year, amounts to $40,750.

(b) Land recorded in the accounts at a cost of $100,000 was appraised at $160,000 by two expert appraisers.

(c) No interest has been accrued on a $50,000, 12%, 90-day note payable, dated May 1 of the current year.

(d) The office supplies account has a balance of $7,250. The cost of the office supplies on hand at June 30, as determined by a physical count, was $1,750.

(e) Merchandise inventory on hand at June 30 of the current year has been recorded in the accounts at cost, $197,750. Current market price of the inventory is $209,600.

(f) Accounts receivable include $12,500 owed by Baker and Wilson Inc., a bankrupt company. Lennox Company expects to receive thirty cents on each dollar owed. The allowance method of accounting for receivables is employed.

(g) The company is being sued for $5,000,000 by a customer who claims damages for personal injury allegedly caused by a defective product. Company attorneys and outside legal counsel feel extremely confident that the company will have no liability for damages resulting from this case.

(h) The company received a debit memorandum with the bank statement from First National Bank, indicating that a customer note discounted at the bank has been dishonored. The 12%, 90-day note is from Winfrey Co. and has a $50,000 face value. Lennox Company has not recorded the memorandum, which included a protest fee of $15.

Instructions:

Journalize any entries required to adjust or correct the accounts, identifying each entry by letter.

Problem 12–6A
Adjustments and corrections on work sheet; statements for sole proprietorship.

OBJ. 2

Drew Coe owns and manages The Art Mart on a full-time basis. He also maintains the accounting records. At the end of the first year of operations, he prepared the following balance sheet and income statement:

The Art Mart
Balance Sheet
December 31, 19--

Cash..	$ 7,400
Equipment...	12,600
Drew Coe..	$ 20,000

The Art Mart
Income Statement
For Year Ended December 31, 19--

Sales		$156,000
Purchases		99,500
Gross profit...		$ 56,500
Operating expenses:		
Salary expense...	$39,600	
Rent expense..	14,400	
Utilities expense	5,150	
Miscellaneous expense..	2,350	
Total operating expenses		61,500
Net loss...		$ 5,000

Because of the large net loss reported on the income statement, Coe is considering discontinuing operations. Before making a decision, he asks you to review the accounting methods employed and, if material errors are found, to prepare revised statements. The following information is obtained during the course of the review:

(a) The only transactions recorded have been those in which cash was received or disbursed.

(b) The accounts have not been closed for the year.

(c) The classification of operating expenses as "selling" and "administrative" is not considered to be sufficiently important to justify the cost of the analysis.

(d) The proprietor made no withdrawals during the year.

(e) The business was established on February 1 by an investment of $17,500 in cash by the owner. An additional investment of $7,500 was made in cash on June 1.

(f) Accounts receivable from customers at December 31 total $11,000.

(g) The merchandise inventory at December 31, as nearly as can be determined, has a cost of $23,425.

(h) Rent Expense includes an advance payment of $1,200 for the month of January in the subsequent year.

(i) Salaries owed but not paid on December 31 total $750.

(j) The equipment listed on the balance sheet at $12,600 was purchased for cash on February 2. Equipment purchased April 1 for $4,000 in cash was debited to Purchases. Equipment purchased on December 31 for $10,000, for which a 90-day, 12% note was issued, was not recorded.

(k) Uncollectible accounts are estimated at $850. The allowance method is to be used.

(l) A total of $17,500 is owed to merchandise creditors on account at December 31.

(m) Depreciation on equipment has not been recorded. The equipment is estimated to have a useful life of 10 years and no salvage value. (Use straight-line method.)

(n) Insurance premiums of $1,300 were debited to Miscellaneous Expense during the year. The unexpired portion at December 31 is $350.

(o) Supplies of $2,400 purchased during the year were debited to Purchases. An estimated $500 of supplies were on hand at December 31.

Instructions:

(1) On the basis of the financial statements presented, prepare an unadjusted trial balance, as of December 31, on an eight-column work sheet. Leave an extra line blank after "Equipment" and "Purchases."

(2) Record the adjustments and the corrections in the Adjustments columns. Complete the work sheet by extending the adjusted trial balance amounts directly to the appropriate Income Statement or Balance Sheet column.

(3) Prepare a multiple-step income statement, a statement of owner's equity, and a report form balance sheet.

Series B

Problem 12–1B
Installment sales.
OBJ. 2f

J. A. Oquendo Inc. makes all sales on the installment basis and recognizes revenue at the point of sale. Condensed income statements and the amounts collected from customers for each of the first three years of operations are as follows:

	First Year	Second Year	Third Year
Sales	$310,000	$340,000	$400,000
Cost of merchandise sold	201,500	224,400	256,000
Gross profit	$108,500	$115,600	$144,000
Operating expenses	64,000	68,500	90,500
Net income	$ 44,500	$ 47,100	$ 53,500
Collected from sales of first year	$ 85,000	$125,000	$100,000
Collected from sales of second year		110,000	161,000
Collected from sales of third year			150,000

Instructions:

Determine the amount of net income that would have been reported in each year if the installment method of recognizing revenue had been employed, ignoring the possible effects of uncollectible accounts on the computation. Present figures in good order.

Problem 12–3B
Percentage-of-completion method.
OBJ. 2f

McCarver Company began construction on three contracts during 1990. The contract prices and construction activities for each of the years 1990, 1991, and 1992 were as follows:

		1990		1991		1992	
Contract	Contract Price	Costs Incurred	Percent Completed	Costs Incurred	Percent Completed	Costs Incurred	Percent Completed
1	$6,000,000	$2,175,000	40%	$3,250,000	60%	—	—
2	8,000,000	1,200,000	20	2,750,000	40	$3,000,000	40%
3	3,500,000	455,000	15	985,000	30	1,575,000	50

Instructions:

Determine the amount of revenue and income to be recognized from the contracts for each of the years 1990, 1991, and 1992. Revenue is to be recognized by the percentage-of-completion method. Present computations in good order.

Problem 12–4B
Effect on net income from changes in three accounting principles.
OBJ. 2f

Pena Company was organized on January 3, 1989. During its first three years of operations, the company determined uncollectible accounts expense by the direct write-off method, the cost of the merchandise inventory at the end of the period by the first-in, first-out method, and depreciation expense by the straight-line method. The amounts of net income reported and the amounts of the foregoing items for each of the three years were as follows:

	First Year	Second Year	Third Year
Net income reported.................................	$47,700	$59,250	$72,500
Uncollectible accounts expense	1,150	2,350	3,750
Ending merchandise inventory	50,750	54,000	58,150
Depreciation expense...............................	19,000	19,900	20,900

The firm is considering the possibility of changing to the following methods in determining net income for the fourth and subsequent years: provision for doubtful accounts through the use of an allowance account, last-in, first-out inventory, and declining-balance depreciation at twice the straight-line rate. To consider the probable future effect of these changes on the determination of net income, the management requests that net income of the past three years be recomputed on the basis of the proposed methods. The uncollectible accounts expense, inventory, and depreciation expense for the past three years, computed in accordance with the proposed methods, are as follows:

	First Year	Second Year	Third Year
Uncollectible accounts expense	$ 2,150	$ 2,900	$ 3,500
Ending merchandise inventory	54,000	52,900	59,650
Depreciation expense...............................	38,000	32,000	27,520

Instructions:

Recompute the net income for each of the three years, presenting the figures in an orderly manner.

Problem 12–5B
Adjusting and
correcting entries.
OBJ. 2

You are engaged to review the accounting records of Elster Company prior to the closing of the revenue and expense accounts as of December 31, the end of the current fiscal year. The following information comes to your attention during the review.

(a) Accounts receivable include $12,100 owed by XL Inc., a bankrupt company. There is no prospect of collecting any of the receivable. The allowance method of accounting for receivables is employed.

(b) Land recorded in the accounts at a cost of $95,000 was appraised at $175,000 by two expert appraisers.

(c) The company is being sued for $2,500,000 by a customer who claims damages for personal injury allegedly caused by a defective product. Company attorneys and outside legal counsel retained by Elster Company feel extremely confident that the company will have no liability for damages resulting from this case.

(d) The prepaid insurance account has a balance of $9,500. At December 31, the unexpired premiums were $2,750.

(e) Since net income for the current year is expected to be considerably less than it was for the preceding year, depreciation on equipment has not been recorded. Equipment depreciation for the year, determined in a manner consistent with the preceding year, amounts to $60,500.

(f) No interest has been accrued on a $100,000, 12%, 90-day note receivable, dated December 1 of the current year.

(g) Merchandise inventory on hand at December 31 of the current year has been recorded in the accounts at cost, $301,500. Current market price of the inventory is $322,250.

Instructions:

Journalize any entries required to adjust or correct the accounts, identifying each entry by letter.

Problem 12–6B
Adjustments and
corrections on work
sheet; statements for
sole proprietorship.
OBJ. 2

Katie Molony owns and manages The Gallery on a full-time basis. She also maintains the accounting records. At the end of the first year of operations, she prepared the following balance sheet and income statement:

The Gallery
Balance Sheet
December 31, 19--

Cash..	$ 2,250
Equipment	20,000
Katie Molony	$22,250

The Gallery
Income Statement
For Year Ended December 31, 19--

Sales		$99,500
Purchases		75,000
Gross profit..		$24,500
Operating expenses:		
Salary expense......................................	$18,000	
Rent expense..	13,000	
Utilities expense	4,500	
Miscellaneous expense.............................	1,750	
Total operating expenses		37,250
Net loss...		$12,750

Because of the large net loss reported on the income statement, Molony is considering discontinuing operations. Before making a decision, she asks you to review the accounting methods employed and, if material errors are found, to prepare revised statements. The following information is discovered during the course of the review:

(a) The only transactions recorded have been those in which cash was received or disbursed.
(b) The accounts have not been closed for the year.
(c) The business was established on January 4 by an investment of $25,000 in cash by the owner. An additional investment of $10,000 was made in cash on July 20.
(d) The equipment listed on the balance sheet at $20,000 was purchased for cash on January 5. Equipment purchased July 1 for $5,000 in cash was debited to Purchases. Equipment purchased on December 31 for $6,000, for which a 60-day, 12% note was issued, was not recorded.
(e) Depreciation on equipment has not been recorded. The equipment is estimated to have a useful life of 10 years and no salvage value. (Use straight-line method.)
(f) Accounts receivable from customers at December 31 total $9,750.
(g) Uncollectible accounts are estimated at $475. The allowance method is to be used.
(h) The merchandise inventory at December 31, as nearly as can be determined, has a cost of $10,500.
(i) Insurance premiums of $750 were debited to Miscellaneous Expense during the year. The unexpired portion at December 31 is $150.
(j) Supplies of $1,000 purchased during the year were debited to Purchases. An estimated $250 of supplies were on hand at December 31.
(k) A total of $3,500 is owed to merchandise creditors on account at December 31.
(l) Rent Expense includes an advance payment of $1,000 for the month of January in the subsequent year.
(m) Salaries owed but not paid on December 31 total $350.
(n) The classification of operating expenses as "selling" and "administrative" is not considered to be sufficiently important to justify the cost of the analysis.
(o) The proprietor made no withdrawals during the year.

Instructions:

(1) On the basis of the financial statements presented, prepare an unadjusted trial balance, as of December 31, on an eight-column work sheet. Leave an extra line blank after "Equipment" and "Purchases."
(2) Record the adjustments and the corrections in the Adjustments columns. Complete the work sheet by extending the adjusted trial balance amounts directly to the appropriate Income Statement or Balance Sheet column.
(3) Prepare a multiple-step income statement, a statement of owner's equity, and a report form balance sheet.

MINI-CASE 12

R & M Parts Inc. operates twelve "cash and carry" auto parts stores in the southeast. In an effort to expand sales, the company has decided to offer two additional sales plans:

(1) credit sales to commercial enterprises, such as body and repair shops, with free twenty-four-hour delivery

(2) installment sales of major dollar items, with payments spread over 36 months.

The company president has asked you when the revenue from each of the two new plans would be recognized in the accounting records and statements.

Instructions:

(1) Indicate to the president when the revenue from each type of sale should be recorded in the accounting records.

(2) While discussing the concepts in (1), the president raised the following questions related to various accounting concepts. How would you respond to each?

(a) "Many businesses cease operating each year; so why do accountants assume a going concern concept when preparing the financial statements?"

(b) "To assume that the value of the dollar does not change and that we don't have inflation is wrong! An automatic transmission that cost $400 five years ago costs $480 today. Why wouldn't it be better to use current dollars, at least for the inventory?"

(c) "With so many different accounting methods that can be used, why can't I switch methods to improve net income this year?"

(d) "Our annual bonuses to store managers are based on store profits. It is not fair to 'anticipate no profits and provide for all losses.'"

ETHICS DISCUSSION CASE

Pacific Seaboard Inc. has negotiated the acquisition of a major trucker to supplement its shipping capabilities. The acquisition is projected to increase earnings dramatically over the next several years. Christine Oliver, controller of Pacific Seaboard Inc., is reviewing the final draft of the company's annual report, which is to be released in three days. Oliver has not informed the company's independent public accountants of the acquisition and has omitted any reference to the acquisition in the annual report. Oliver and several other top managers are planning to purchase large quantities of the acquired company's stock, prior to the public news release describing the acquisition.

Discuss whether Christine Oliver is behaving in an ethical manner.

ANSWERS TO SELF-EXAMINATION QUESTIONS

1. D In the balance sheet, the equipment should be reported at its cost less accumulated depreciation, $100,000. The effect of the declining value of the dollar on plant assets, the market value of plant assets, and the replacement cost of plant assets are not recognized in the basic historical cost statements.

2. A Under the installment basis of accounting, gross profit is realized in accordance with the amount of cash collected in each year, based on the percent of gross profit to sales. For the question, the amount of gross profit to be realized for the current year is $22,500 (answer A), determined as follows:

Percent of gross profit to sales:
$60,000 \div $200,000 = 30\%$

Gross profit realized:
$75,000 \times 30\% = $22,500$

3. A Under the percentage-of-completion method of accounting, the amount of revenue to be recognized during a period is determined on the basis of the estimated percentage of the contract that has been completed during the period. The costs incurred during the period are deducted from this revenue to yield the income from the contract. The $950,000 of income for the question is determined as follows:

Revenue to be recognized (40% × $20,000,000)	$8,000,000
Costs incurred	7,050,000
Income	$ 950,000

4. D In some situations, there are a number of accepted alternative principles that could be used. To assure a high degree of comparability of the financial statements between periods, appropriate disclosure should be made when a change is made from one accepted principle to another. A change in method of inventory pricing (answer A), a change in depreciation method for previously recorded plant assets (answer B), and a change in method of accounting for installment sales (answer C) are examples of changes in accepted alternative principles that should be appropriately disclosed.

5. D The concept of materiality (answer D) relates to the acceptance of a procedure that deviates from absolute accuracy for insignificant or immaterial items, such as reporting cents on financial statements.

Partnerships and Corporations

PART FOUR

4

CHAPTER THIRTEEN

PARTNERSHIP FORMATION, INCOME DIVISION, AND LIQUIDATION

CHAPTER OBJECTIVES

1 Identify basic characteristics of partnership organization and operation which have accounting implications.

2 Describe the advantages and disadvantages of partnerships.

3 Describe the basic accounting system for partnerships.

4 Describe and illustrate the accounting for the formation of partnerships.

5 Describe and illustrate the accounting for partnership net income and net loss.

6 Describe and illustrate the preparation of financial statements for partnerships.

7 Describe and illustrate the accounting for partnership dissolution, including admission of new partners and the withdrawal and death of partners.

8 Describe and illustrate the liquidation of partnerships.

The Uniform Partnership Act, which has been adopted by more than ninety percent of the states, defines a partnership as "an association of two or more persons to carry on as co-owners a business for profit." The partnership form of business organization is widely used for comparatively small businesses that wish to take advantage of the combined capital, managerial talent, and experience of two or more persons. In many cases, the alternative to securing the amount of investment or the various skills needed to operate a business is to adopt the corporate form of organization. The typical corporate form of organization is sometimes not permitted, however, because of restrictions in state laws. In addition, a group of physicians, attorneys, or certified public accountants who wish to band together to practice a profession often organize as a partnership. Medical and legal partnerships made up of 20 or more partners are not unusual, and the number of partners in some CPA firms exceeds 1,000.

CHARACTERISTICS OF PARTNERSHIPS

OBJECTIVE 1
Identify basic characteristics of partnership organization and operation which have accounting implications.

Partnerships have several characteristics that have accounting implications. These characteristics are described in the following paragraphs.

A partnership has a **limited life**. Dissolution of a partnership occurs whenever a partner ceases to be a member of the firm for any reason, including withdrawal, bankruptcy, incapacity, or death. Similarly, admission of a new partner dissolves the old partnership. In case of dissolution, a new partnership must be formed if the operations of the business are to be continued without interruption. This situation frequently occurs with professional partnerships. Their composition may change often as new partners are admitted and others are retired.

Most partnerships are *general partnerships,* in which the partners have **unlimited liability**. Each partner is individually liable to creditors for debts incurred by the partnership. Thus, if a partnership becomes insolvent, the partners must contribute sufficient personal assets to settle the debts of the partnership. In some states, a *limited partnership* may be formed, in which the liability of some partners may be limited to the amount of their capital investment. However, a limited partnership must have at least one general partner who has unlimited liability. In this chapter, the discussion is focused on the general partnership.

Partners have **co-ownership of partnership property**. The property invested in a partnership by a partner becomes the property of all the partners jointly. Upon dissolution of the partnership and distribution of its assets, the partners' claims against the assets are measured by the amount of the balances in their capital accounts.

Another characteristic of a partnership is **mutual agency**. This feature means that each partner is an agent of the partnership, with the authority to enter into contracts for the partnership. Thus, the acts of each partner bind the partnership and become the responsibility of all partners.

A significant right of partners is **participation in income** of the partnership. Net income and net loss are distributed among the partners according to their agreement. In the absence of any agreement, all partners share equally. If the agreement specifies profit distribution but is silent as to losses, the losses are shared in the same manner as profits.

A partnership, like a sole proprietorship, is a **nontaxable entity** and is therefore not required to pay federal income taxes. However, revenue and expense and other financial details of partnership operations must be reported annually on official Internal Revenue Service forms known as *information returns*. The individual partners must report their distributive share of partnership income on their personal tax returns.

A partnership is created by a voluntary contract containing all the elements essential to any other enforceable contract. It is not necessary that this contract be in writing, nor even that its terms be specifically expressed. However, good business practice dictates that the contract should be in writing and should clearly express the intentions of the partners. The contract, known as the **articles of partnership** or **partnership agreement**, should contain provisions regarding such matters as the amount of investment to be made, limitations on withdrawals of funds, the manner in which net income and net loss are to be divided, and the admission and withdrawal of partners.

ADVANTAGES AND DISADVANTAGES OF PARTNERSHIPS

OBJECTIVE 2
Describe the advantages and disadvantages of partnerships.

The partnership form of business organization is less widely used than are the sole proprietorship and corporate forms. For a particular business endeavor, however, the advantages of the partnership form may outweigh the disadvantages.

A partnership is relatively easy and inexpensive to organize, requiring only an agreement between two or more persons. A partnership has the advantage of being able to bring together more capital, more managerial skills, and more experience than would a sole proprietorship. Because the partnership is a nontaxable entity, the combined income taxes paid by the individual partners may be lower than the income taxes that would be paid by a corporation, which is a taxable entity.

The disadvantages of a partnership are that its life is limited, each partner has unlimited liability, and one partner can bind the partnership to contracts. Also, raising large amounts of capital is more difficult for a partnership than for a corporation.

ACCOUNTING FOR PARTNERSHIPS

OBJECTIVE 3
Describe the basic accounting system for partnerships.

Most of the day-to-day accounting for a partnership is the same as the accounting for any other form of business organization. The system described in earlier chapters may, with little change, be used by a partnership. For example, the journals described may be used without alteration. The chart of accounts, with the exception of drawing and capital accounts for each partner, does not differ from the chart of accounts of a similar business conducted by a single owner. It is in the areas of the formation, income distribution, dissolution, and liquidation of partnerships that transactions peculiar to partnerships arise. The remainder of the chapter is devoted to the accounting principles and procedures applicable to these areas.

RECORDING INVESTMENTS

OBJECTIVE 4
Describe and illustrate the accounting for the formation of partnerships.

A separate entry is made for the investment of each partner in a partnership. The various assets contributed by a partner are debited to the proper asset accounts. If liabilities are assumed by the partnership, the appropriate liability accounts are credited. The partner's capital account is credited for the net amount.

To illustrate the entry to record an initial investment, assume that Joseph A. Stevens and Earl S. Foster, who are sole owners of competing hardware stores, agree to combine their businesses in a partnership. Each is to contribute certain amounts of cash and other business assets. It is also agreed that the partnership is to assume the liabilities of the separate businesses. The entry to record the assets contributed and the liabilities transferred by Stevens is as follows:

Apr. 1	Cash	7,200	
	Accounts Receivable	16,300	
	Merchandise Inventory	28,700	
	Store Equipment	5,400	
	Office Equipment	1,500	
	Allowance for Doubtful Accounts		1,500
	Accounts Payable		2,600
	Joseph A. Stevens, Capital		55,000

A similar entry would record the assets contributed and the liabilities transferred by Foster. In each entry, the monetary amounts at which the noncash assets are stated are those agreed upon by the partners. In arriving at an appropriate amount for such assets, consideration should be given to their market values at the time the partnership is formed. The values agreed upon represent the acquisition cost to the accounting entity created by the formation of the partnership. These amounts may differ from the balances appearing in the accounts of the separate businesses before the partnership was organized. For example, the store equipment stated at $5,400 in the entry above may have had a book value of $3,500, appearing in Stevens' ledger at its original cost of $10,000 with accumulated depreciation of $6,500.

Receivables contributed to the partnership are recorded at their face amount, with a credit to a contra account if provision is to be made for possible future uncollectibility. Ordinarily, only accounts with reasonable chances of collection are transferred to the partnership. Again referring to the preceding entry, the accounts receivable on Stevens' ledger may have totaled $17,600, of which $1,300 was considered to be completely worthless. The remaining $16,300 of receivables was recorded in the partnership accounts by a debit to Accounts Receivable and by debits to the individual accounts in the subsidiary ledger. The credit of $1,500 to Allowance for Doubtful Accounts is the provision for possible future uncollectibility of the accounts receivable contributed to the partnership by Stevens.

DIVISION OF NET INCOME OR NET LOSS

OBJECTIVE 5
Describe and illustrate the accounting for partnership net income and net loss.

As in the case of a sole proprietorship, the net income of a partnership may be said to include a return for the services of the owners, for the capital invested, and for economic or pure profit. Partners are not legally employees of the partnership, nor are their capital contributions a loan. If each of two partners is to contribute equal services and amounts of capital, an equal sharing in partnership net income would be equitable. But if one partner is to contribute a larger portion of capital than the other, provision for unequal capital contributions should be given recognition in the agreement for dividing net income. Or, if the services of one partner are much more valuable to the partnership than those of the other, provision for unequal service contributions should be given recognition in their agreement.

To illustrate the division of net income and the accounting for this division, two possible agreements are to be considered. It should be noted that division of the net income or the net loss among the partners in exact accordance with their partnership agreement is of the utmost importance. If the agreement is silent on the matter, the law provides that all partners share equally, regardless of differences in amounts of capital contributed, of special skills possessed, or of time devoted to the business. The partners may, however, make any agreement they wish in regard to the division of net income and net losses.

EXECUTIVE COMPENSATION—A PARTNERSHIP VS. A CORPORATION

In a report prepared for a Congressional subcommittee, Deloitte, Haskins & Sells (a public accounting partnership) described their firm's view of partner compensation and the division of the firm's income. Excerpts from that report are as follows:

...As a general rule, compensation in major mid-sized corporations (to which we might be compared based on revenue size, number of personnel, etc.) consists of current cash, deferred payments, payments made on behalf of an individual for retirement benefits, and perquisites. In ad-

dition, options to purchase stock at potentially favorable prices may also be an attractive compensation component. Unlike a corporation, partners . . . must provide from their own earnings for their own retirement benefits, as well as paying for self-employment taxes, group insurance, and other benefit programs. As a partnership, of course, our partners . . . do not have stock options available. . . .

Each year the majority of the firm's earnings are distributed to the partners. Some small percentage is usually retained for working capital needs. No amounts are guaranteed, like a "preset" annual salary. If earnings decline, partners' . . . individual earnings also decline. Partners . . . are also required to invest capital in the firm. As such, part of their earnings represent a return on their investment. . . . With regard to their firm activities, partners have a much broader exposure to personal liability than do most corporate officers.

The factors mentioned above must be con-

sidered in making meaningful comparisons of partners' compensation with other business executives. To simply compare amounts would be misleading.

Our partnership is a private organization and many of the partners feel strongly that their compensation should not be disclosed. Nonetheless, firm management has concluded that the public may be better served if we disclose selective compensation data. We hope this disclosure demonstrates to the public that our earnings enable us to retain competent professionals, that we do not earn excessive amounts, and that we have no special agreements that would compromise our integrity or our independence.

The average earnings of all of our partners for fiscal year 1985 was approximately $143,000. As to our five most highly compensated partners, their individual earnings ranged from $385,000 to $725,000, and their average was $500,000. . . .

Source: Deloitte, Haskins & Sells, *A Report for Congress and the Public* (September, 1985).

Income Division Recognizing Services of Partners

As a means of recognizing differences in ability and in amount of time devoted to the business, articles of partnership often provide for the division of a portion of net income to the partners in the form of a salary allowance. The articles may also provide for withdrawals of cash by the partners in lieu of salary payments. A clear distinction must therefore be made between the division of net income, which is credited to the capital accounts, and payments to the partners, which are debited to the drawing accounts.

As a basis for illustration, assume that the articles of partnership of Jennifer L. Stone and Crystal R. Mills provide for monthly salary allowances of $2,500 and $2,000 respectively, with the balance of the net income to be divided equally, and that the net income for the year is $75,000. A report of the division of net income may be presented as a separate statement accompanying the balance sheet and the income statement, or it may be added at the bottom of the income statement. If the latter procedure is used, the lower part of the income statement would appear as follows:

Net income $75,000

Division of net income:	J. L. Stone	C. R. Mills	Total
Salary allowance.............................	$30,000	$24,000	$54,000
Remaining income.............................	10,500	10,500	21,000
Net income	$40,500	$34,500	$75,000

The division of net income is recorded as a closing entry, regardless of whether the partners actually withdraw the amounts of their salary allowances. The entry for the division of net income is as follows:

Dec. 31	Income Summary	75,000	
	Jennifer L. Stone, Capital......................		40,500
	Crystal R. Mills, Capital........................		34,500

If Stone and Mills had withdrawn their salary allowances monthly, the withdrawals would have accumulated as debits in the drawing accounts during the year. At the end of the year, the debit balances of $30,000 and $24,000 in their drawing accounts would be transferred to their respective capital accounts.

Income Division Recognizing Services of Partners and Investment

Partners may agree that the most equitable plan of income sharing is to allow salaries based on the services rendered and also to allow interest on the capital investments. The remainder is then shared in an arbitrary ratio. To illustrate, assume that Stone and Mills (1) are allowed monthly salaries of $2,500 and $2,000 respectively; (2) are allowed interest at 12% on capital balances at January 1 of the current fiscal year, which amounted to $80,000 and $60,000 respectively; and (3) divide the remainder of net income equally. The division of $75,000 net income for the year could then be reported on the income statement as follows:

Net income			$75,000

Division of net income:	J. L. Stone	C. R. Mills	Total
Salary allowance................................	$30,000	$24,000	$54,000
Interest allowance	9,600	7,200	16,800
Remaining income.............................	2,100	2,100	4,200
Net income	$41,700	$33,300	$75,000

On the basis of the information in the foregoing income statement, the entry to close the income summary account would be recorded as follows:

Dec. 31	Income Summary	75,000	
	Jennifer L. Stone, Capital......................		41,700
	Crystal R. Mills, Capital........................		33,300

Income Division — Allowances Exceed Net Income

In the illustrations presented thus far, the net income has exceeded the sum of the allowances for salary and interest. If the net income is less than the total of the special allowances, the "remaining balance" will be a negative figure that must be divided among the partners as though it were a net loss. The effect of this situation may be illustrated by assuming the same salary and interest allowances as in the preceding illustration, but changing the amount of net income to $50,000. The salary and interest allowances to Stone total $39,600, and the comparable figure for Mills is $31,200. The sum of these amounts, $70,800, exceeds the net income of $50,000 by $20,800. It is therefore necessary to deduct $10,400 (1/2 of $20,800) from each partner's share to arrive at the net income, as follows:

Net income $50,000

Division of net income:	J. L. Stone	C. R. Mills	Total
Salary allowance...............................	$30,000	$24,000	$54,000
Interest allowance	9,600	7,200	16,800
Total..	$39,600	$31,200	$70,800
Excess of allowances over income........	10,400	10,400	20,800
Net income	$29,200	$20,800	$50,000

In closing Income Summary at the end of the year, $29,200 would be credited to Jennifer L. Stone, Capital, and $20,800 would be credited to Crystal R. Mills, Capital.

STATEMENTS FOR PARTNERSHIPS

OBJECTIVE 6
Describe and illustrate the preparation of financial statements for partnerships.

Details of the division of net income should be disclosed in the financial statements prepared at the end of the fiscal period. This disclosure may be made by adding a section to the income statement, as illustrated in the preceding pages, or by presenting the data in a separate statement.

Details of the changes in the owner's equity of a partnership during the period should also be presented in a statement of owner's equity. The purposes of this statement and the data included in it correspond to those of the statement of owner's equity for a sole proprietorship. There are a number of variations in form. One of these variations is illustrated as follows for the Stone and Mills partnership, using assumed data and the income division shown on page 510:

Statement of Owner's Equity

Stone and Mills
Statement of Owner's Equity
For Year Ended December 31, 19--

	Jennifer L. Stone	Crystal R. Mills	Total
Capital, January 1, 19--........................	$ 80,000	$60,000	$140,000
Additional investment during the year.....		5,000	5,000
	$ 80,000	$65,000	$145,000
Net income for the year.........................	41,700	33,300	75,000
	$121,700	$98,300	$220,000
Withdrawals during the year..................	24,000	20,000	44,000
Capital, December 31, 19--....................	$ 97,700	$78,300	$176,000

PARTNERSHIP DISSOLUTION

OBJECTIVE 7
Describe and illustrate the accounting for partnership dissolution, including admission of new partners and the withdrawal and death of partners.

One of the basic characteristics of the partnership form of organization is its limited life. Any change in the personnel of the ownership results in the dissolution of the partnership. Thus, admission of a new partner dissolves the old firm. Similarly, death, bankruptcy, or withdrawal of a partner causes dissolution.

Dissolution of the partnership is not necessarily followed by the winding up of the affairs of the business. For example, a partnership composed of two partners may admit an additional partner. Or if one of three partners in a business withdraws, the remaining two partners may continue to operate the business. In all such cases, a new partnership is formed and new articles of partnership should be prepared.

Admission of a Partner

An additional person may be admitted to a partnership enterprise only with the consent of all the current partners. It does not follow, however, that a partner's interest, or part of that interest, cannot be transferred to an outside party without the consent of the remaining partners. Under common law, if a partner's interest was transferred, the partnership was automatically dissolved. Under the Uniform Partnership Act, a partner's interest *can* be transferred without the consent of the remaining partners. The person who acquires a partner's interest assumes that partner's rights to share in net income and in assets upon liquidation. The person acquiring the interest does not automatically become a partner, however, and has no voice in partnership affairs unless admitted to the firm.

An additional person may be admitted to a partnership through either of two procedures:

1. Purchase of an interest from one or more of the current partners.
2. Contribution of assets to the partnership.

When the first procedure is followed, the capital interest of the incoming partner is obtained from current partners, and *neither the total assets nor the total owner's equity of the business is affected*. When the second procedure is followed, *both the total assets and the total owner's equity of the business are increased*.

Admission by Purchase of an Interest. When an additional person is admitted to a firm by purchasing an interest from one or more of the partners, the purchase price is paid directly to the selling partners. Payment is for partnership equity owned by the partners as individuals, and hence the cash or other consideration paid is not recorded in the accounts of the partnership. The only entry needed is the transfer of the proper amounts of owner's equity from the capital accounts of the selling partners to the capital account established for the incoming partner.

As an example, assume that partners Tom Andrews and Nathan Bell have capital balances of $50,000 each. On June 1, each sells one fifth of his respective equity to Joe Canter for $10,000 in cash. The exchange of cash is not a partnership transaction and thus is not recorded by the partnership. The only entry required in the partnership accounts is as follows:

June 1	Tom Andrews, Capital	10,000	
	Nathan Bell, Capital	10,000	
	Joe Canter, Capital		20,000

The effect of the transaction on the partnership accounts is presented in the following diagram:

Partnership Accounts

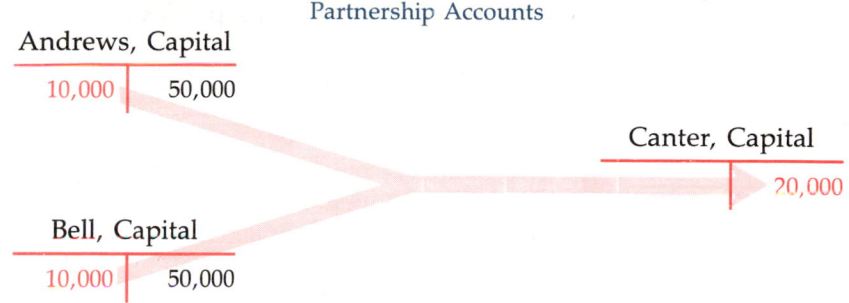

Andrews, Capital

| 10,000 | 50,000 |

Canter, Capital

| | 20,000 |

Bell, Capital

| 10,000 | 50,000 |

The foregoing entry is not affected by the amount paid by Canter for the one-fifth interest. If the firm had been earning a high rate of return on the investment and Canter had been very eager to obtain the one-fifth interest, he might have paid considerably more than $20,000. Had other circumstances prevailed, he might have acquired the one-fifth interest for considerably less than $20,000. In either event, the entry to transfer the capital interests would be as illustrated.

After the admission of Canter, the total owner's equity of the firm is $100,000, of which Canter has a one-fifth interest, or $20,000. It does not necessarily follow that he will be entitled to a similar share of the partnership net income. Division of net income or net loss will be in accordance with the new partnership agreement.

Admission by Contribution of Assets. Instead of buying an interest from the current partners, the incoming partner may contribute assets to the partnership. In this case, both the assets and the owner's equity of the firm are increased. To illustrate, assume that Donald Lewis and Gerald Morton are partners with capital accounts of $35,000 and $25,000 respectively. On June 1, Sharon Nelson invests $20,000 cash in the business, for which she is to receive an ownership equity of $20,000. The entry to record this transaction is as follows:

| June 1 | Cash.. | 20,000 | |
| | Sharon Nelson, Capital........................ | | 20,000 |

The major difference between the circumstances of the admission of Nelson and the admission of Canter in the preceding example may be observed by comparing the following diagram with the one on the preceding page:

Partnership Accounts

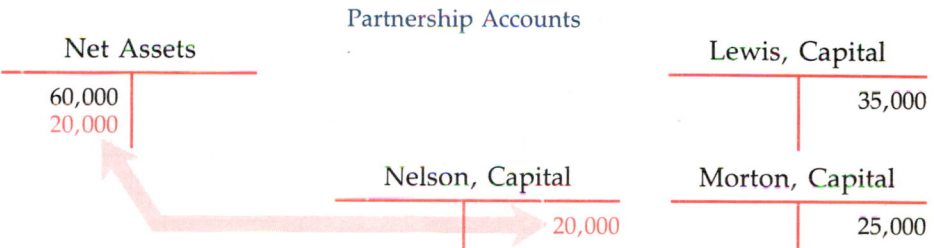

Net Assets

| 60,000 | |
| 20,000 | |

Lewis, Capital

| | 35,000 |

Nelson, Capital

| | 20,000 |

Morton, Capital

| | 25,000 |

With the admission of Nelson, the total owners' equity of the new partnership becomes $80,000, of which Nelson has a one-fourth interest, or $20,000. The extent of her participation in partnership net income will be governed by the articles of partnership.

Revaluation of Assets. If the partnership assets are not fairly stated in terms of current market value at the time a new partner is admitted, the accounts may be adjusted accordingly. The net amount of the increases and decreases in asset values are then allocated to the capital accounts of the old partners according to their income-sharing ratio. To illustrate, assume that in the preceding illustration for the Lewis and Morton partnership, the balance of the merchandise inventory account had been $14,000 and the current replacement price had been $17,000. Prior to Nelson's admission, the revaluation would be recorded as follows, assuming that Lewis and Morton share net income equally:

June 1	Merchandise Inventory	3,000	
	Donald Lewis, Capital		1,500
	Gerald Morton, Capital		1,500

If a number of assets are revalued, the adjustments may be debited or credited to a temporary account entitled Asset Revaluations. After all adjustments are made, the account is closed to the capital accounts.

It is important that the assets be stated in terms of current prices at the time of admission of a new partner. Failure to recognize current prices may result in the new partner participating in gains or losses attributable to the period prior to admission.

Goodwill. When a new partner is admitted to a partnership, goodwill attributable either to the old partnership or to the incoming partner may be recognized. Although there are various methods of estimating goodwill, such factors as the respective shares owned by the partners and the relative bargaining abilities of the partners will influence the final determination. The amount of goodwill agreed upon is recorded as an asset, with a corresponding credit to the appropriate capital accounts.

To illustrate the recognition of goodwill to the old partners, assume that on March 1 the partnership of Marsha Jenkins and Helen Kramer admits William Larson, who is to contribute cash of $15,000. After the tangible assets of the old partnership have been adjusted to current market prices, the capital balances of Jenkins and Kramer are $20,000 and $24,000 respectively. The parties agree, however, that the enterprise is worth $50,000. The excess of $50,000 over the capital balances of $44,000 ($20,000 + $24,000) indicates the existence of $6,000 of goodwill. This $6,000 should be divided between the capital accounts of the original partners according to their income-sharing agreement.

The entries to record the goodwill and the admission of the new partner, assuming that the original partners share equally in net income, are as follows:

Mar. 1	Goodwill	6,000	
	Marsha Jenkins, Capital........................		3,000
	Helen Kramer, Capital		3,000
1	Cash...	15,000	
	William Larson, Capital		15,000

If a partnership admits a new partner who is expected to improve the fortunes of the firm, the parties might agree to recognize this high earnings potential. To illustrate, assume that Sandra Ellis is to be admitted to the partnership of Cowen and Dodd for an investment of $30,000. If the parties agree to recognize $5,000 of goodwill attributable to Ellis, the entry to record her admission is as follows:

July 1	Cash...	30,000	
	Goodwill	5,000	
	Sandra Ellis, Capital............................		35,000

Withdrawal of a Partner

When a partner retires or for some other reason wishes to withdraw from the firm, one or more of the remaining partners may purchase the withdrawing partner's interest and the business may be continued without apparent interruption. In such cases, settlement for the purchase and sale is made between the partners as individuals, in a manner similar to the admission of a new partner by purchase of an interest, and thus is not recorded by the partnership. The only entry required by the partnership is a debit to the capital account of the partner withdrawing and a credit to the capital account of the partner or partners acquiring the interest.

If the settlement with the withdrawing partner is made by the partnership, the effect is to reduce the assets and the owner's equity of the firm. To determine the ownership equity of the withdrawing partner, the asset accounts should be adjusted to current market prices. The net amount of the adjustments should be divided among the capital accounts of the partners according to the income-sharing ratio. In the event that the cash or the other available assets are insufficient to make complete payment at the time of withdrawal, a liability account should be credited for the balance owed to the withdrawing partner.

Death of a Partner

The death of a partner dissolves the partnership. In the absence of any contrary agreement, the accounts should be closed as of the date of death, and the net income for the fractional part of the year should be transferred to the capital accounts. It is not unusual, however, for the partnership agreement to stipulate that the accounts remain open to the end of the fiscal year or until the affairs are wound up, if that should occur earlier. The net income of the entire period is then divided, as provided by the agreement, between the respective periods occurring before and after dissolution.

The balance in the capital account of the deceased partner is then transferred to a liability account with the deceased's estate. The surviving partner or partners may continue the business or the affairs may be wound up. If the former course is followed, the procedures for settling with the estate will conform to those outlined earlier for the withdrawal of a partner from the business.

LIQUIDATION OF PARTNERSHIPS

OBJECTIVE 8
Describe and
illustrate the
liquidation of
partnerships.

When a partnership goes out of business, it usually sells the assets, pays the creditors, and distributes the remaining cash or other assets to the partners according to their claims. The winding-up process may generally be called **liquidation**. Although liquidation refers specifically to the payment of liabilities, it is often used in a broader sense to include the entire winding-up process.

When the ordinary business activities are discontinued as the partnership goes out of business, the accounts should be adjusted and closed according to the customary procedures of the periodic summary. The only accounts remaining open then will be the various asset, contra asset, liability, and owner's equity accounts.

The sale of the assets is called **realization**. As cash is realized, it is applied first to the payment of the claims of creditors. After all liabilities have been paid, the remaining cash is distributed to the partners, based on their ownership equities as indicated by their capital accounts.

If the assets are sold piecemeal, the liquidation process may extend over a considerable period of time. This situation creates no special problem, however, if the distribution of cash to the partners is delayed until all of the assets have been sold, as assumed in the following illustrations. As a basis for the illustrations, assume that Farley, Greene, and Hall share income and losses in a ratio of 5:3:2 (5/10, 3/10, 2/10). On April 9, after discontinuing the ordinary business operations of their partnership and closing the accounts, the following summary of the general ledger is prepared:

Cash	$11,000	
Noncash Assets	64,000	
Liabilities		$ 9,000
Jean Farley, Capital		22,000
Brad Greene, Capital		22,000
Alice Hall, Capital		22,000
Total	$75,000	$75,000

Based on these facts, accounting for the liquidation of the partnership will be illustrated using three different selling prices for the noncash assets. For the sake of brevity, it will be assumed for each selling price that all noncash assets are disposed of in a single transaction, and that all liabilities are paid at one time. In addition, Noncash Assets and Liabilities will be used as account titles in place of the various asset, contra asset, and liability accounts that in actual practice would be affected by the transactions.

Gain on Realization

Between April 10 and April 30 of the current year, Farley, Greene, and Hall sell all noncash assets for $72,000, realizing a gain of $8,000 ($72,000 − $64,000). The gain is divided among the capital accounts in the income-sharing ratio of 5:3:2. The liabilities are paid, and *the remaining cash is distributed to the partners according to the balances in their capital accounts.* A statement of partnership liquidation, which summarizes the liquidation process, follows:

	Cash	+	Noncash Assets	=	Liabilities	+	Capital		
							Farley (50%)	Greene (30%)	Hall (20%)
Balances before realization..	$11,000		$64,000		$9,000		$22,000	$22,000	$22,000
Sale of noncash assets and division of gain...............	+72,000		−64,000		—		+ 4,000	+ 2,400	+ 1,600
Balances after realization....	$83,000		0		$9,000		$26,000	$24,400	$23,600
Payment of liabilities	− 9,000		—		−9,000		—	—	—
Balances after payment of liabilities........................	$74,000		0		0		$26,000	$24,400	$23,600
Distribution of cash to partners....................	−74,000		—		—		−26,000	−24,400	−23,600
Final balances..................	0		0		0		0	0	0

Farley, Greene, and Hall
Statement of Partnership Liquidation
For Period April 10–30, 19--

The entries to record the several steps in the liquidation procedure are as follows:

Sale of assets	Cash..	72,000	
	Noncash Assets..		64,000
	Loss and Gain on Realization.................................		8,000
Division of gain	Loss and Gain on Realization.....................................	8,000	
	Jean Farley, Capital..		4,000
	Brad Greene, Capital..		2,400
	Alice Hall, Capital		1,600
Payment of liabilities	Liabilities	9,000	
	Cash..		9,000
Distribution of cash to partners	Jean Farley, Capital..	26,000	
	Brad Greene, Capital..	24,400	
	Alice Hall, Capital	23,600	
	Cash..		74,000

As shown in the foregoing statement of partnership liquidation, the distribution of the cash to the partners is determined by reference to the balances of their respective capital accounts after the gain on realization has been divided among the partners. *Under no circumstances should the income-sharing ratio be used as a basis for distributing the cash.*

Loss on Realization; No Capital Deficiencies

Assume that in the foregoing example, Farley, Greene, and Hall dispose of all noncash assets for $44,000, incurring a loss of $20,000 ($64,000 − $44,000). The various steps in the liquidation of the partnership are summarized in the following statement:

Farley, Greene, and Hall
Statement of Partnership Liquidation
For Period April 10–30, 19--

	Cash	+	Noncash Assets	=	Liabilities	+	Capital Farley (50%)	+	Greene (30%)	+	Hall (20%)
Balances before realization..	$11,000		$64,000		$9,000		$22,000		$22,000		$22,000
Sale of assets and division of loss	+44,000		−64,000		—		−10,000		− 6,000		− 4,000
Balances after realization....	$55,000		0		$9,000		$12,000		$16,000		$18,000
Payment of liabilities	− 9,000		—		−9,000		—		—		—
Balances after payment of liabilities	$46,000		0		0		$12,000		$16,000		$18,000
Distribution of cash to partners.....................	−46,000		—		—		−12,000		−16,000		−18,000
Final balances..................	0		0		0		0		0		0

The entries to record the liquidation are as follows:

Sale of assets	Cash...	44,000	
	Loss and Gain on Realization.....................................	20,000	
	Noncash Assets...		64,000
Division of loss	Jean Farley, Capital...	10,000	
	Brad Greene, Capital..	6,000	
	Alice Hall, Capital	4,000	
	Loss and Gain on Realization.................................		20,000
Payment of liabilities	Liabilities...	9,000	
	Cash...		9,000
Distribution of cash to partners	Jean Farley, Capital...	12,000	
	Brad Greene, Capital..	16,000	
	Alice Hall, Capital	18,000	
	Cash...		46,000

Loss on Realization; Capital Deficiency

In the preceding illustration, the capital account of each partner was more than sufficient to absorb the appropriate share of the loss from realization. The partners shared in the distribution of cash to the extent of the remaining credit balance in their respective capital accounts. However, the share of the loss chargeable to a partner may be such that it exceeds that partner's ownership equity. The resulting debit balance in the capital account, called a **deficiency,** is a claim of the partnership against the partner. Pending collection from the deficient partner, the partnership cash will not be sufficient to pay the other partners in full. In such cases, the available cash should be distributed in such a manner that, if the claim against the deficient partner cannot be collected, each of the remaining capital balances will be sufficient to absorb the appropriate share of the deficiency.

To illustrate a situation of this type, assume that Farley, Greene, and Hall sell all of the noncash assets for $10,000, incurring a loss of $54,000 ($64,000 − $10,000). It is readily apparent that the part of the loss allocable to Farley, $27,000 (50% of $54,000), exceeds the $22,000 balance in Farley's capital account. This $5,000 deficiency of Farley's is a potential deficiency to

Greene and Hall and must be tentatively divided between them in their income-sharing ratio of 3:2 (3/5 and 2/5). The capital balances remaining represent their claims on the partnership cash. The computations may be summarized in the following manner:

	Farley (50%)	Greene (30%)	Hall (20%)	Total
			Capital	
Balances before realization.............	$ 22,000	$ 22,000	$ 22,000	$ 66,000
Division of loss on realization..........	−27,000	−16,200	−10,800	−54,000
Balances after realization................	$− 5,000	$ 5,800	$ 11,200	$ 12,000
Division of potential additional deficiency	5,000	− 3,000	− 2,000	—
Claims to partnership cash..............	0	$ 2,800	$ 9,200	$ 12,000

The various transactions that have occurred thus far in the liquidation are summarized in the following statement:

Farley, Greene, and Hall
Statement of Partnership Liquidation
For Period April 10–30, 19--

	Cash +	Noncash Assets =	Liabilities +	Farley (50%) +	Greene (30%) +	Hall (20%)
					Capital	
Balances before realization	$11,000	$64,000	$9,000	$22,000	$22,000	$22,000
Sale of assets and division of loss..	+10,000	−64,000	—	−27,000	−16,200	−10,800
Balances after realization............	$21,000	0	$9,000	$ 5,000 (Dr.)	$ 5,800	$11,200
Payment of liabilities.................	− 9,000	—	−9,000	—	—	—
Balances after payment of liabilities	$12,000	0	0	$ 5,000 (Dr.)	$ 5,800	$11,200
Distribution of cash to partners	−12,000	—	—	—	− 2,800	− 9,200
Balances	0	0	0	$ 5,000 (Dr.)	$ 3,000	$ 2,000

The entries to record the liquidation to this point are as follows:

Sale of assets	Cash..	10,000	
	Loss and Gain on Realization.....................................	54,000	
	Noncash Assets..		64,000
Division of loss	Jean Farley, Capital...	27,000	
	Brad Greene, Capital..	16,200	
	Alice Hall, Capital	10,800	
	Loss and Gain on Realization.................................		54,000
Payment of liabilities	Liabilities	9,000	
	Cash..		9,000
Distribution of cash to partners	Brad Greene, Capital...	2,800	
	Alice Hall, Capital	9,200	
	Cash..		12,000

The affairs of the partnership are not completely wound up until the claims among the partners are settled. Payments to the firm by the deficient partner are credited to that partner's capital account. Any uncollectible deficiency becomes a loss to the partnership and is written off against the capital balances of the remaining partners. Finally, the cash received from the deficient partner is distributed to the other partners according to their ownership claims.

To continue with the preceding illustration, the capital balances remaining after the $12,000 cash distribution are as follows: Farley, $5,000 debit; Greene, $3,000 credit; Hall, $2,000 credit. The various steps in the final settlement and the entries for the partnership under three different assumptions as to the final settlement are illustrated in the following paragraphs.

Assumption 1: Farley pays the entire amount of the $5,000 deficiency to the partnership (no loss).

The receipt of the $5,000 paid by Farley to the partnership and the distribution of the $5,000 to the partners are indicated in the following statement of partnership liquidation:

				Capital		
Farley, Greene, and Hall Statement of Partnership Liquidation For Period April 10–30, 19--	Cash	+ Noncash Assets	= Liabilities +	Farley (50%)	+ Greene (30%) +	Hall (20%)
Balances	0	0	0	$5,000 (Dr.)	$3,000	$2,000
Receipt of deficiency.........................	+$5,000	—	—	+5,000	—	—
Balances	$5,000	0	0	0	$3,000	$2,000
Distribution of cash to partners	−5,000	—	—	—	−3,000	−2,000
Final balances................................	0	0	0	0	0	0

The entries to record the final settlement are as follows:

Receipt of deficiency	Cash..	5,000	
	Jean Farley, Capital..		5,000
Distribution of cash to partners	Brad Greene, Capital..	3,000	
	Alice Hall, Capital	2,000	
	Cash..		5,000

After the two transactions above are completed, all of the partnership's assets will have been distributed, the liabilities paid, and the partners' capital balances reduced to zero.

Assumption 2: Farley pays $3,000 of the deficiency to the partnership, and the remainder is considered to be uncollectible ($2,000 loss).

The receipt of the $3,000 paid by Farley to the partnership, the division of the $2,000 loss, and the distribution of the $3,000 to the partners are indicated in the following statement of partnership liquidation:

	Cash +	Noncash Assets =	Liabilities +	Capital		
				Farley (50%) +	Greene (30%) +	Hall (20%)
Balances	0	0	0	$5,000 (Dr.)	$3,000	$2,000
Receipt of part of deficiency	+$3,000	—	—	+3,000	—	—
Balances	$3,000	0	0	$2,000 (Dr.)	$3,000	$2,000
Division of loss	—	—	—	+2,000	−1,200	− 800
Balances	$3,000	0	0	0	$1,800	$1,200
Distribution of cash to partners	−3,000	—	—	—	−1,800	−1,200
Final balances	0	0	0	0	0	0

(Table heading: Farley, Greene, and Hall — Statement of Partnership Liquidation — For Period April 10–30, 19--)

It should be noted that the $2,000 loss was divided between Greene and Hall in their income-sharing ratio of 3:2 (3/5 and 2/5). The entries to record the final settlement are as follows:

Receipt of part of deficiency	Cash..	3,000	
	Jean Farley, Capital..		3,000
Division of loss	Brad Greene, Capital...	1,200	
	Alice Hall, Capital	800	
	Jean Farley, Capital..		2,000
Distribution of cash to partners	Brad Greene, Capital...	1,800	
	Alice Hall, Capital	1,200	
	Cash...		3,000

After the three transactions above are completed, all of the partnership's assets will have been distributed, the liabilities paid, and the partners' capital balances reduced to zero.

Assumption 3: Farley is unable to pay any part of the $5,000 deficiency ($5,000 loss).

The division of the $5,000 loss is indicated in the following statement of partnership liquidation:

	Cash +	Noncash Assets =	Liabilities +	Capital		
				Farley (50%) +	Greene (30%) +	Hall (20%)
Balances	0	0	0	$5,000 (Dr.)	$3,000	$2,000
Division of loss	—	—	—	+5,000	−3,000	−2,000
Final balances	0	0	0	0	0	0

(Table heading: Farley, Greene, and Hall — Statement of Partnership Liquidation — For Period April 10–30, 19--)

The $5,000 loss was divided between Greene and Hall in their income-sharing ratio 3:2 (3/5 and 2/5). The following entry, which reduces the partnership account balances to zero, records this final step in the liquidation:

Division of loss

Brad Greene, Capital...	3,000	
Alice Hall, Capital	2,000	
Jean Farley, Capital...		5,000

It should be noted that the type of error most likely to occur in the liquidation of a partnership is an improper distribution of cash to the partners. Errors of this type result from confusing the distribution of cash with the division of gains and losses on realization.

Gains and losses on realization result from the disposal of assets to outsiders. *These gains and losses represent changes in partnership equity and should be divided among the capital accounts in the same manner as net income or net loss from ordinary business operations, namely, in the income-sharing ratio.* On the other hand, the distribution of cash (or other assets) to the partners is an entirely different matter and has no direct relationship to the income-sharing ratio. The distribution of assets to the partners upon liquidation is the exact reverse of the contribution of assets by the partners at the time the partnership was established. The distribution of assets to the partners is *equal to the credit balances in their respective capital accounts* after all gains and losses on realization have been divided and proper allowance has been made for any potential deficiencies.

CHAPTER REVIEW

KEY POINTS

OBJECTIVE 1

Characteristics of Partnerships

Partnership characteristics that have accounting implications are limited life, unlimited liability, co-ownership of property, mutual agency, and participation in income. In addition, a partnership is a nontaxable entity and is therefore not required to pay federal income taxes. Individual partners must report their distributive share of partnership income on their personal returns.

OBJECTIVE 2

Advantages and Disadvantages of Partnerships

The principal advantages of a partnership include the fact that it is easy and inexpensive to organize, brings together capital of one or more individuals, and is a nontaxable entity. The major disadvantages of a partnership are that its life is limited, each partner has unlimited liability, one partner can bind the partnership to contracts, and it may be difficult to raise large amounts of capital.

OBJECTIVE 3

Accounting for Partnerships

Most of the day-to-day accounting for partnerships is the same as the accounting for any other form of business organization. It is in the areas of formation, income distribution, dissolution, and liquidation of partnerships that transactions peculiar to partnerships arise.

OBJECTIVE 4   Recording Investments

To record the investment of each partner in a partnership, the various assets contributed by a partner are debited to the proper asset accounts, the liabilities assumed
are credited to the appropriate liability accounts, and the partner's capital account is
credited for the net amount. The monetary amounts at which noncash assets are
stated are those agreed upon by the partners.

OBJECTIVE 5   Division of Net Income or Net Loss

The net income of a partnership can be divided among the partners in any manner
agreed to by the partners. The net income is often divided on the basis of services
rendered by individual partners and/or on the basis of the investments of the individual partners. In the absence of any agreement, net income is divided equally
among the partners.

OBJECTIVE 6   Statements for Partnerships

Details of the division of partnership net income should be disclosed in the financial
statements prepared at the end of the fiscal period. In addition, details of changes in
the owner's equity of a partnership during the period should be presented in the
statement of owner's equity.

OBJECTIVE 7   Partnership Dissolution

Any change in the personnel of ownership results in the dissolution of the partnership. However, dissolution of the partnership is not necessarily followed by a winding up of the affairs of the business. A partnership may be dissolved by admission of
a new partner, withdrawal of a partner, or death of a partner.

OBJECTIVE 8   Liquidation of Partnerships

When a partnership goes out of business, it usually sells the noncash assets, pays the
creditors, and distributes the remaining cash or other assets to the partners according
to the balances of the partners' capital accounts. Any gain or loss on the realization
of the assets should be allocated to the partners' capital accounts in the income-
sharing ratio. The distribution of assets to the partners is equal to the credit balances
in their respective capital accounts after all gains and losses on realization have been
divided and proper allowance has been made for any potential losses.

KEY TERMS

articles of partnership 506   realization 516
liquidation 516   deficiency 518

SELF-EXAMINATION QUESTIONS

Answers at end of chapter.

1. As part of the initial investment, a partner contributes office equipment that had
    originally cost $20,000 and on which accumulated depreciation of $12,500 had
    been recorded. If the partners agree on a valuation of $9,000 for the equipment,
    what amount should be debited to the office equipment account?
    A. $7,500   C. $12,500
    B. $9,000   D. $20,000

2. X and Y agree to form a partnership. X is to contribute $50,000 in assets and to devote one-half time to the partnership. Y is to contribute $20,000 and to devote full time to the partnership. How will X and Y share in the division of net income or net loss?
   A. 5:2
   B. 1:2
   C. 1:1
   D. None of the above

3. X and Y invest $100,000 and $50,000 respectively in a partnership and agree to a division of net income that provides for an allowance of interest at 10% on original investments, salary allowances of $12,000 and $24,000 respectively, with the remainder divided equally. What would be X's share of a periodic net income of $45,000?
   A. $22,500
   B. $22,000
   C. $19,000
   D. $10,000

4. X and Y are partners who share income in the ratio of 2:1 and who have capital balances of $65,000 and $35,000 respectively. If P, with the consent of Y, acquired one half of X's interest for $40,000, for what amount would P's capital account be credited?
   A. $32,500
   B. $40,000
   C. $50,000
   D. None of the above

5. X and Y share gains and losses in the ratio of 2:1. After selling all assets for cash, dividing the losses on realization, and paying liabilities, the balances in the capital accounts were as follows: X, $10,000 Cr.; Y, $2,000 Dr. How much of the cash would be distributed to X?
   A. $2,000
   B. $8,000
   C. $10,000
   D. $12,000

ILLUSTRATIVE PROBLEM

Ryan, Shaw, and Todd, who share in income and losses in the ratio of 4:2:4, decided to discontinue business operations as of April 30 and liquidate their partnership. After the accounts were closed on April 30, the following summary of the general ledger was prepared:

Cash	$ 8,100	
Noncash Assets	70,600	
Liabilities		$27,500
Ryan, Capital		23,300
Shaw, Capital		12,100
Todd, Capital		15,800
Total	$78,700	$78,700

Between May 1 and May 18, the noncash assets were sold for $20,600, and the liabilities were paid.

Instructions:

1. Assuming that the available cash is to be distributed to the partners, prepare a statement of partnership liquidation.
2. Present entries to record (a) the sale of the assets, (b) the division of loss on the sale of the assets, (c) the payment of the liabilities, and (d) the distribution of cash to the partners.
3. Assuming that Todd pays $2,400 of the deficiency to the partnership and the remainder is considered to be uncollectible, present entries to record (a) the receipt of part of the deficiency, (b) the division of loss, and (c) the distribution of cash to the partners.

SOLUTION

(1)

Ryan, Shaw, and Todd
Statement of Partnership Liquidation
For Period May 1–18, 19--

	Cash +	Noncash Assets =	Liabilities +	Ryan (40%) +	Shaw (20%) +	Todd (40%)
					Capital	
Balances before realization	$ 8,100	$70,600	$27,500	$23,300	$12,100	$15,800
Sale of assets and division of loss.............................	+20,600	−70,600	—	−20,000	−10,000	−20,000
Balances after realization........	$28,700	0	$27,500	$ 3,300	$ 2,100	$ 4,200 (Dr.)
Payment of liabilities.............	−27,500	—	−27,500	—	—	—
Balances after payment of liabilities.........................	$ 1,200	0	0	$ 3,300	$ 2,100	$ 4,200 (Dr.)
Distribution of cash to partners	− 1,200	—	—	− 500	− 700	—
Final balances	0	0	0	$ 2,800	$ 1,400	$ 4,200 (Dr.)

(2) (a) Cash 20,600
       Loss and Gain on Realization............................ 50,000
          Noncash Assets 70,600

(b) Ryan, Capital... 20,000
     Shaw, Capital 10,000
     Todd, Capital... 20,000
        Loss and Gain on Realization........................ 50,000

(c) Liabilities 27,500
       Cash 27,500

(d) Ryan, Capital... 500
     Shaw, Capital 700
       Cash 1,200

(3) (a) Cash 2,400
       Todd, Capital... 2,400

(b) Ryan, Capital... 1,200
     Shaw, Capital 600
       Todd, Capital... 1,800

(c) Ryan, Capital... 1,600
     Shaw, Capital 800
       Cash 2,400

DISCUSSION QUESTIONS

 1. Ceal Burk and Frank Edwards joined together to form a partnership. Is it possible for them to lose a greater amount than the amount of their investment in the partnership enterprise? Explain.

2. Must a partnership (a) file a federal income tax return or (b) pay federal income taxes? Explain.

3. The partnership agreement between Barr and Chou provides for the sharing of partnership net income in the ratio of 2:1. Since the agreement is silent concerning the sharing of net losses, in what ratio will they be shared?

4. In the absence of an agreement, how will the net income be distributed between Jose Mandosa and Vincent Shore, partners in the firm of Mandosa and Shore Consultants?

5. Steven Kent, Eric Brooks, and Kurt Ross are contemplating the formation of a partnership. According to the partnership agreement, Kent is to invest $75,000 and devote one-half time, Brooks is to invest $50,000 and devote three-fourths time, and Ross is to make no investment and devote full time. Would Ross be correct in assuming that, since he is not contributing any assets to the firm, he is risking nothing? Explain.

6. What are the disadvantages of the partnership over the corporation as a form of organization for a profit-making business enterprise?

7. As a part of the initial investment, a partner contributes delivery equipment that had originally cost $35,000 and on which accumulated depreciation of $27,500 had been recorded. The partners agree on a valuation of $15,000. How should the delivery equipment be recorded in the accounts of the partnership?

8. All partners agree that $150,000 of accounts receivable invested by a partner will be collectible to the extent of 90%. How should the accounts receivable be recorded in the general ledger of the partnership?

9. Barbara Baker and Donna Carter are contemplating the formation of a partnership in which Baker is to devote full time and Carter is to devote one-half time. In the absence of any agreement, will the partners share in net income or net loss in the ratio of 2:1? Explain.

10. (a) What accounts are debited or credited to record a partner's cash withdrawal in lieu of salary? (b) At the end of the fiscal year, what accounts are debited or credited to record the division of net income among partners? (c) The articles of partnership provide for a salary allowance of $3,000 per month to partner P. If P withdrew only $2,500 per month, would this affect the division of the partnership net income?

11. How can the division of net income be disclosed in the financial statements of a partnership?

12. Elaine Gates, a partner in the firm of Edwards, Ferber, and Gates, sells her investment (capital balance of $95,000) to Martha Shook. (a) Does the withdrawal of Gates dissolve the partnership? (b) Are Edwards and Ferber required to admit Shook as a partner?

13. Explain the difference between the admission of a new partner to a partnership (a) by purchase of an interest from another partner and (b) by contribution of assets to the partnership.

14. Sue Hess and Bart Innis are partners who share in net income equally and have capital balances of $60,000 and $62,500 respectively. Hess, with the consent of Innis, sells one third of her interest to Jacob Atles. What entry is required by the partnership if the sale price is (a) $10,000? (b) $30,000?

15. Why is it important to state all partnership assets in terms of current prices at the time of the admission of a new partner?

16. When a new partner is admitted to a partnership and goodwill is attributable to the old partnership, how should the amount of the goodwill be allocated to the capital accounts of the original partners?

17. Why might a partnership attribute goodwill to a newly admitted partner?

18. (a) Differentiate between *dissolution* and *liquidation* of a partnership. (b) What does *realization* mean when used in connection with liquidation of a partnership?

19. In the liquidation process, (a) how are losses and gains on realization divided among the partners, and (b) how is cash distributed among the partners?

20. Jones and Klaus are partners, sharing gains and losses equally. At the time they decide to terminate their partnership, their capital balances are $15,000 and $30,000 respectively. After all noncash assets are sold and all liabilities are paid, there is a cash balance of $50,000. (a) What is the amount of gain or loss on realization? (b) How should the gain or loss be divided between Jones and Klaus? (c) How should the cash be divided between Jones and Klaus?

21. Lendl, Mecir, and Noah share equally in net income and net loss. After the partnership sells all the assets for cash, divides the losses on realization, and pays the liabilities, the balances in the capital accounts are as follows: Lendl, $25,000 Cr.; Mecir, $62,500 Cr.; Noah, $22,500 Dr. (a) What is the amount of cash on hand? (b) How should the cash be distributed?

22. Pate, Quinn, and Reggi are partners sharing income 3:2:1. After the firm's loss from liquidation is distributed, Pate's capital account has a debit balance of $22,500. If Pate is personally bankrupt and unable to pay any of the $22,500, how will the loss be divided between Quinn and Reggi?

Real World Focus

23. The national public accounting partnership of Deloitte, Haskins & Sells disclosed net income of $111,000,000 for the year ended June 1, 1985. The net income was attributable to 765 active partners, whose total capital as of June 1, 1985, was $116,000,000. (a) What was the average net income per active partner for the fiscal year ended June 1, 1985? (b) If the partners' total capital approximates the fair market value of the firm's net assets, what would be considered a minimum contribution for the admission of a new partner to the firm? (c) Why might the amount to be contributed by a new partner for admission to the firm exceed the amount determined in (b)?

EXERCISES

Exercise 13-1
Entry for partner's original investment.
OBJ. 4

Gayle Cowan and Kate Diaz decide to form a partnership by combining the assets of their separate businesses. Cowan contributes the following assets to the partnership: cash, $7,500; accounts receivable with a face amount of $77,500 and an allowance for doubtful accounts of $8,500; merchandise inventory with a cost of $85,000; and equipment with a cost of $125,000 and accumulated depreciation of $55,000. The partners agree that $5,000 of the accounts receivable are completely worthless and are not to be accepted by the partnership, that $8,000 is a reasonable allowance for the uncollectibility of the remaining accounts, that the merchandise inventory is to be recorded at the current market price of $81,500, and that the equipment is to be priced at $85,000. Present the partnership's entry to record Cowan's investment.

Exercise 13–2
Division of
partnership income.
OBJ. 5

Charles Berger and Mary Curren formed a partnership, investing $50,000 and $100,000 respectively. Determine their participation in the year's net income of $60,000 under each of the following assumptions: (a) no agreement concerning division of net income; (b) divided in the ratio of original capital investment; (c) interest at the rate of 12% allowed on original investments and the remainder divided in the ratio of 2:3; (d) salary allowances of $15,000 and $30,000 respectively, and the balance divided equally; (e) allowance of interest at the rate of 12% on original investments, salary allowances of $15,000 and $30,000 respectively, and the remainder divided equally.

Exercise 13–3
Division of
partnership income.
OBJ. 5

Determine the participation of Berger and Curren in the year's net income of $90,000, according to each of the five assumptions as to income division listed in Exercise 13–2.

Exercise 13–4
Division of
partnership net loss.
OBJ. 5

Allison Bunker and Martin Waldeck formed a partnership in which the partnership agreement provided for salary allowances of $25,000 and $10,000 respectively. Determine the division of $5,000 net loss for the current year.

Exercise 13–5
Partnership entries
and statement of
owner's equity.
OBJ. 6

The capital accounts of Alex Gomez and Brenda Hull have balances of $50,000 and $70,000 respectively on January 1, the beginning of the current fiscal year. On March 1, Gomez invested an additional $15,000. During the year, Gomez and Hull withdrew $36,000 and $30,000 respectively, and net income for the year was $90,000. The articles of partnership make no reference to the division of net income. (a) Present the journal entries to close (1) the income summary account and (2) the drawing accounts. (b) Prepare a statement of owner's equity for the current year.

Exercise 13–6
Admission of new
partners.
OBJ. 7

The capital accounts of Mike Cash and Ed Doerr have balances of $56,000 and $100,000 respectively. Paula Goles and Julie Howell are to be admitted to the partnership. Goles purchases one fourth of Cash's interest for $22,500 and one fifth of Doerr's interest for $30,000. Howell contributes $60,000 cash to the partnership, for which she is to receive an ownership equity of $60,000. (a) Present the entries to record the admission of (1) Goles and (2) Howell. (b) What are the capital balances of each partner after the admission of the new partners?

Exercise 13–7
Withdrawal of
partner.
OBJ. 7

Alan Wicks is to retire from the partnership of Wicks and Associates as of July 31, the end of the current fiscal year. After closing the accounts, the capital balances of the partners are as follows: Alan Wicks, $150,000; Sandra Young, $95,000; and Ralph Zimmer, $82,500. They have shared net income and net losses in the ratio of 2:1:1. The partners agreed that the merchandise inventory should be increased by $10,500, and the allowance for doubtful accounts should be increased by $2,100. Wicks agreed to accept an interest-bearing note for $100,000 in partial settlement of his ownership equity. The remainder of his claim is to be paid in cash. Young and Zimmer are to share equally in the net income or net loss of the new partnership. Present entries to record (a) the adjustment of the assets to bring them into agreement with current market prices, and (b) the withdrawal of Wicks from the partnership.

Exercise 13–8
Distribution of cash
on liquidation.
OBJ. 8

Jim Omer and Gil Arthur, with capital balances of $49,500 and $37,500 respectively, decided to liquidate their partnership. After selling the noncash assets and paying the liabilities, there is $55,000 of cash remaining. If the partners share income and losses equally, how should the cash be distributed?

Exercise 13–9
Distribution of cash
on liquidation.
OBJ. 8

Ellen Gray, Elmer Hall, and Sam Ivey arranged to import and sell orchid corsages for a university dance. They agreed to share equally the net income or net loss on the venture. Gray and Hall advanced $175 and $225 of their own respective funds to pay for advertising and other expenses. After collecting for all sales and paying creditors, they have $760 in cash. (a) How should the money be distributed? (b) Assuming that they have only $160 instead of $760, how should the money be distributed? (c) Assuming that the money was distributed as determined in (b), do any of the three have claims against another? If so, how much?

Exercise 13–10
Statement of partnership liquidation.
OBJ. 8

After closing the accounts on June 1, prior to liquidating the partnership, the capital account balances of Gertz, Hart, and Imes are $13,000, $26,000, and $31,000 respectively. Cash, noncash assets, and liabilities total $17,000, $83,000, and $30,000 respectively. Between June 1 and June 30, the noncash assets are sold for $41,000, the liabilities are paid, and the remaining cash is distributed to the partners. The partners share net income and loss in the ratio of 1:2:3. Prepare a statement of partnership liquidation for the period June 1–30.

PROBLEMS

Series A

Problem 13–1A
Entries and balance sheet for partnership.
OBJ. 4

On July 1 of the current year, Chris Victor and Dave Walls form a partnership. Victor agrees to invest $14,500 in cash and merchandise inventory valued at $45,500. Walls invests certain business assets at valuations agreed upon, transfers business liabilities, and contributes sufficient cash to bring his total capital to $40,000. Details regarding the book values of the business assets and liabilities, and the agreed valuations, follow:

	Walls' Ledger Balance	Agreed Valuation
Accounts Receivable	$23,000	$21,000
Allowance for Doubtful Accounts	550	800
Equipment	79,100	47,500
Accumulated Depreciation — Equipment	35,200	
Accounts Payable	14,500	14,500
Notes Payable	15,500	15,500

The articles of partnership include the following provisions regarding the division of net income: interest on original investments at 10%, salary allowances of $24,000 and $27,000 respectively, and the remainder equally.

Instructions:

(1) Prepare the entries to record the investments of Victor and Walls in the partnership accounts.
(2) Prepare a balance sheet as of July 1, the date of formation of the partnership.
(3) After adjustments and the closing of revenue and expense accounts at June 30, the end of the first full year of operations, the income summary account has a credit balance of $68,000, and the drawing accounts have debit balances of $24,000 (Victor) and $30,000 (Walls). Present the journal entries to close the income summary account and the drawing accounts at June 30.

Problem 13–2A
Division of partnership income.
OBJ. 5

Chin and Dyke have decided to form a partnership. They have agreed that Chin is to invest $60,000 and that Dyke is to invest $30,000. Chin is to devote one-half time to the business and Dyke is to devote full time. The following plans for the division of income are being considered:

(a) Equal division.
(b) In the ratio of original investments.
(c) In the ratio of time devoted to the business.
(d) Interest of 12% on original investments and the remainder equally.
(e) Interest of 12% on original investments, salaries of $20,000 to Chin and $30,000 to Dyke, and the remainder equally.
(f) Plan (e), except that Dyke is also to be allowed a bonus equal to 25% of the amount by which net income exceeds the salary allowances.

Instructions:

For each plan, determine the division of the net income under each of the following assumptions: (1) net income of $42,000 and (2) net income of $120,000. Present the data in tabular form, using the following columnar headings:

Plan	$42,000		$120,000	
	Chin	Dyke	Chin	Dyke

Problem 13–3A
Financial statements for partnership.
OBJ. 5, 6

The ledger of Larry Carsy and Donna Dunn, attorneys-at-law, contains the following accounts and balances after adjustments have been recorded on December 31, the end of the current fiscal year:

Cash...	$ 21,000
Accounts Receivable...	29,500
Supplies..	1,900
Land...	45,000
Building..	155,000
Accumulated Depreciation—Building.......................	77,500
Office Equipment..	40,000
Accumulated Depreciation—Office Equipment...........	22,400
Accounts Payable...	750
Salaries Payable..	1,750
Larry Carsy, Capital..	75,000
Larry Carsy, Drawing...	50,000
Donna Dunn, Capital...	55,000
Donna Dunn, Drawing..	60,000
Professional Fees...	296,750
Salary Expense..	80,500
Depreciation Expense—Building.............................	10,500
Property Tax Expense..	9,500
Heating and Lighting Expense	9,400
Supplies Expense...	5,750
Depreciation Expense—Office Equipment	5,000
Miscellaneous Expense..	6,100

An additional investment of $5,000 was made by Dunn on June 10 of the current year.

Instructions:

(1) Prepare an income statement for the current fiscal year, indicating the division of net income. The articles of partnership provide for salary allowances of $25,000 to Carsy and $35,000 to Dunn; allowances of 12% on each partner's capital balance at the beginning of the fiscal year; and equal division of the remaining net income or net loss.
(2) Prepare a statement of owner's equity for the current fiscal year.
(3) Prepare a balance sheet as of the end of the current fiscal year.

Problem 13–4A
Admission of new partner.
OBJ. 7

Don Smid and Dick Temple have operated a successful firm for many years, sharing net income and net losses equally. Judy Andrews is to be admitted to the partnership on July 1 of the current year, in accordance with the following agreement:

(a) Assets and liabilities of the old partnership are to be valued at their book values as of June 30, except for the following:
- Accounts receivable amounting to $4,250 are to be written off, and the allowance for doubtful accounts is to be increased to 5% of the remaining accounts.
- Merchandise inventory is to be valued at $61,200.
- Equipment is to be valued at $110,000.

(b) Goodwill of $30,000 is to be recognized as attributable to the firm of Smid and Temple.

(c) Andrews is to purchase $25,000 of the ownership interest of Smid for $40,000 cash and to contribute $25,000 cash to the partnership for a total ownership equity of $50,000.

(d) The income-sharing ratio of Smid, Temple, and Andrews is to be 2:1:1.

The post-closing trial balance of Smid and Temple as of June 30 is as follows:

Smid and Temple
Post-Closing Trial Balance
June 30, 19--

Cash..	12,500	
Accounts Receivable...	29,250	
Allowance for Doubtful Accounts		500
Merchandise Inventory..	59,600	
Prepaid Insurance...	1,250	
Equipment...	162,500	
Accumulated Depreciation—Equipment............................		72,500
Accounts Payable..		12,100
Notes Payable...		20,000
Don Smid, Capital...		120,000
Dick Temple, Capital		40,000
	265,100	265,100

Instructions:

(1) Present journal entries as of June 30 to record the revaluations, using a temporary account entitled Asset Revaluations. The balance in the accumulated depreciation account is to be eliminated.

(2) Present the additional entries to record the remaining transactions relating to the formation of the new partnership. Assume that all transactions occur on July 1.

(3) Present a balance sheet for the new partnership as of July 1.

Problem 13–5A
Statement of partnership liquidation.
OBJ. 8

After the accounts are closed on April 3, prior to liquidating the partnership, the capital accounts of Phil Evans, Dennis Fell, and Louis Gates are $20,000, $3,000, and $10,000 respectively. Cash and noncash assets total $2,000 and $61,000 respectively. Amounts owed to creditors total $30,000. The partners share income and losses in the ratio of 2:1:1. Between April 3 and April 25, the noncash assets are sold for $21,000, the partner with the capital deficiency pays his deficiency to the partnership, and the liabilities are paid.

Instructions:

Prepare a statement of partnership liquidation, indicating (1) the sale of assets and division of loss, (2) the receipt of the deficiency (from the appropriate partner), and (3) the payment of liabilities.

If the working papers correlating with the textbook are not used, omit Problem 13–6A.

Problem 13–6A
Partnership
liquidation.
OBJ. 8

Lori Ames, Ken Bows, and Kevin Cain decided to discontinue business operations and liquidate their partnership. A summary of the various transactions that have occurred thus far is presented in the working papers in a partial statement of liquidation.

Instructions:

(1) Assuming that the available cash is to be distributed to the partners, complete the statement of partnership liquidation through the distribution of available cash to partners.

(2) Present entries to record (a) the sale of assets, (b) the division of loss on the sale of assets, (c) the payment of liabilities, and (d) the distribution of cash to partners.

(3) Assuming that Bows pays $2,100 of his deficiency to the partnership and the remainder is considered to be uncollectible, complete the statement of partnership liquidation.

(4) Present entries to record (a) the receipt of part of the deficiency from Bows, (b) the division of loss, and (c) the distribution of cash to partners.

Problem 13–7A
Statement of
partnership
liquidation.
OBJ. 8

On July 2, the date the firm of Farr, Goss, and Hale decided to liquidate the partnership, the partners have capital balances of $30,000, $90,000, and $120,000 respectively. The cash balance is $20,000, the book values of noncash assets total $290,000, and liabilities total $70,000. The partners share income and losses in the ratio of 1:2:2.

Instructions:

Prepare a statement of partnership liquidation covering the period July 2 through July 29 for each of the following assumptions:

(1) All of the noncash assets are sold for $340,000 in cash, the creditors are paid, and the remaining cash is distributed to the partners.

(2) All of the noncash assets are sold for $190,000 in cash, the creditors are paid, and the remaining cash is distributed to the partners.

(3) All of the noncash assets are sold for $120,000 in cash, the creditors are paid, and the remaining cash is distributed to the partners. After the available cash is paid to the partners:
    (a) The partner with the debit capital balance pays the amount owed to the firm.
    (b) The additional cash is distributed.

(4) All of the noncash assets are sold for $110,000 in cash, the creditors are paid, and the remaining cash is distributed to the partners. After the available cash is paid to the partners:
    (a) The partner with the debit capital balance pays $2,000 of the deficiency to the firm.
    (b) The remaining partners absorb the remaining deficiency as a loss.
    (c) The additional cash is distributed.

Series B

Problem 13–1B
Entries and
balance sheet
for partnership.
OBJ. 4

On June 1 of the current year, Greg Alou and Ron Bowen form a partnership. Alou agrees to invest $7,500 cash and merchandise inventory valued at $62,500. Bowen invests certain business assets at valuations agreed upon, transfers business liabilities, and contributes sufficient cash to bring his total capital to $100,000. Details regarding the book values of the business assets and liabilities, and the agreed valuations, follow:

	Bowen's Ledger Balance	Agreed Valuation
Accounts Receivable...	$46,250	$45,000
Allowance for Doubtful Accounts	900	1,500
Merchandise Inventory..	22,500	18,000
Equipment	70,000⎤	52,500
Accumulated Depreciation—Equipment......................	22,200⎦	
Accounts Payable...	16,500	16,500
Notes Payable...	10,000	10,000

The articles of partnership include the following provisions regarding the division of net income: interest of 10% on original investments, salary allowances of $30,000 and $24,000 respectively, and the remainder equally.

Instructions:

(1) Prepare the entries to record the investments of Alou and Bowen in the partnership accounts.
(2) Prepare a balance sheet as of June 1, the date of formation of the partnership.
(3) After adjustments and the closing of revenue and expense accounts at May 31, the end of the first full year of operations, the income summary account has a credit balance of $75,000, and the drawing accounts have debit balances of $26,000 (Alou) and $27,500 (Bowen). Present the journal entries to close the income summary account and the drawing accounts at May 31.

Problem 13–2B
Division of partnership income.
OBJ. 5

Gwen Cole and Carol Brown have decided to form a partnership. They have agreed that Cole is to invest $40,000 and that Brown is to invest $60,000. Cole is to devote full time to the business and Brown is to devote one-half time. The following plans for the division of income are being considered:

(a) Equal division.
(b) In the ratio of original investments.
(c) In the ratio of time devoted to the business.
(d) Interest of 10% on original investments and the remainder in the ratio of 3:2.
(e) Interest of 10% on original investments, salary allowances of $40,000 to Cole and $20,000 to Brown, and the remainder equally.
(f) Plan (e), except that Cole is also to be allowed a bonus equal to 20% of the amount by which net income exceeds the salary allowances.

Instructions:

For each plan, determine the division of the net income under each of the following assumptions: (1) net income of $90,000 and (2) net income of $45,000. Present the data in tabular form, using the following columnar headings:

	$90,000		$45,000	
Plan	Cole	Brown	Cole	Brown

Problem 13–5B
Statement of partnership liquidation.
OBJ. 8

After the accounts are closed on May 5, prior to liquidating the partnership, the capital accounts of Yang Liu, Ned Mann, and Irene Nunn are $32,800, $10,800, and $16,400 respectively. Cash and noncash assets total $6,900 and $99,100 respectively. Amounts owed to creditors total $46,000. The partners share income and losses in the ratio of 2:1:1. Between May 5 and May 28, the noncash assets are sold for $33,500, the partner with the capital deficiency pays the deficiency to the partnership, and the liabilities are paid.

Instructions:

Prepare a statement of partnership liquidation indicating (1) the sale of assets and division of loss, (2) the receipt of the deficiency (from the appropriate partner), and (3) the payment of liabilities.

If the working papers correlating with the textbook are not used, omit Problem 13–6B.

Problem 13–6B
Partnership liquidation.
OBJ. 8

Lori Ames, Ken Bows, and Kevin Cain decided to discontinue business operations and liquidate their partnership. A summary of the various transactions that have occurred thus far is presented in the working papers in a partial statement of liquidation.

Instructions:

(1) Assuming that the available cash is to be distributed to the partners, complete the statement of partnership liquidation through the distribution of available cash to the partners.
(2) Present entries to record (a) the sale of assets, (b) the division of loss on the sale of assets, (c) the payment of liabilities, and (d) the distribution of cash to partners.
(3) Assuming that Bows pays $3,500 of his deficiency to the partnership and the remainder is considered to be uncollectible, complete the statement of partnership liquidation.
(4) Present entries to record (a) the receipt of part of the deficiency from Bows, (b) the division of loss, and (c) the distribution of cash to partners.

MINI-CASE 13

L & M COMPANY

Jodi Lee and Aaron Mays formed L and M Company as a partnership ten years ago by each contributing $75,000 in capital. The partnership agreement indicated the following division of net income: salary allowances of $24,000 and $36,000 to Lee and Mays respectively, and all remaining net income divided equally.

Mays recently expressed concern with the manner in which profits are being divided. Specifically, the profit-sharing agreement did not consider changes in the amounts invested by each partner as reflected in the balances of their capital accounts. Over the years, Lee has consistently withdrawn more from the partnership than Mays, with the result that the capital balances as of January 1, 1991, indicated an investment of $210,000 by Lee and $340,000 by Mays.

Lee agreed with Mays that a change in the profit-sharing agreement was warranted and accordingly proposed the following two alternatives:

Proposal I
(a) The salary allowances of Lee and Mays would be increased to $30,000 and $45,000 respectively.
(b) Interest of 10% would be allowed on the January 1 balances of the capital accounts.
(c) All remaining income would be divided equally.

Proposal II
(a) The salary allowances of Lee and Mays would not be changed.
(b) No interest would be allowed on the capital balances.
(c) Mays would be allowed a bonus of 20% of the amount by which net income exceeds salary allowances, and the remainder would be divided equally.

Mays has asked for your advice on which of the two proposals he should accept.

Instructions:

(1) For each proposal, prepare an analysis of the distribution of net income between Lee and Mays for 1991 for net income levels of $100,000, $140,000, and $200,000.
(2) Which proposal would you recommend that Mays accept?
(3) Erv Dailey has offered to purchase for $250,000 a one-third interest in the partnership capital and net income. Assuming that the net tangible assets of the partnership approximate their fair market values at January 1, 1991, how much total goodwill for the partnership is implied by Dailey's offer?

ETHICS DISCUSSION CASE	Marion Kerrey and Janson Bennett are partners in Kerrey & Bennett, CPAs. Without notifying Jason Bennett, Marion Kerrey recently signed a contract for the firm to utilize a national computerized tax preparation service. The contract, for $150,000 of use over a five-year period, provides that Kerrey & Bennett, CPAs, will have exclusive use of the service in the immediate geographic area. Discuss whether Marion Kerrey behaved in an ethical manner.

ANSWERS TO SELF-EXAMINATION QUESTIONS

1. B Noncash assets contributed to a partnership should be recorded at the amounts agreed upon by the partners. The preferable practice is to record the office equipment at $9,000 (answer B).

2. C Net income and net loss are divided among the partners in accordance with their agreement. In the absence of any agreement, all partners share equally (answer C).

3. C X's share of the $45,000 of net income is $19,000 (answer C), determined as follows:

	X	Y	Total
Interest allowance	$10,000	$ 5,000	$15,000
Salary allowance	12,000	24,000	36,000
Total	$22,000	$29,000	$51,000
Excess of allowances over income	3,000	3,000	6,000
Net income distribution	$19,000	$26,000	$45,000

4. A When an additional person is admitted to a partnership by purchasing an interest from one or more of the partners, the purchase price is paid directly to the selling partner(s). The amount of capital transferred from the capital account(s) of the selling partner(s) to the capital account of the incoming partner is the capital interest acquired from the selling partner(s). In the question, the amount is $32,500 (answer A), which is one half of X's capital balance of $65,000.

5. B Partnership cash would be equal to the net balance in the partners' capital accounts, or $8,000. This cash would be distributed in accordance with the credit balances in the partners' capital accounts, after considering the potential loss that might result from the inability to collect from a deficient partner. Therefore the $8,000 (answer B) would be distributed to X (X's $10,000 capital balance less the potential loss from Y's $2,000 deficiency).

CHAPTER FOURTEEN

CORPORATIONS: ORGANIZATION AND OPERATIONS

1 Identify basic corporation characteristics which have accounting implications.

2 Describe and illustrate the main sources of stockholders' equity.

3 Identify the common characteristics of capital stock.

4 Describe and illustrate the accounting for the issuance of capital stock.

5 Describe and illustrate the accounting for treasury stock.

6 Describe and illustrate the computation of equity per share of stock.

7 Describe and illustrate the accounting for organization costs.

In the Dartmouth College case in 1819, Chief Justice Marshall stated: "A corporation is an artificial being, invisible, intangible, and existing only in contemplation of the law." The concept underlying this definition has become the foundation for the prevailing legal doctrine that a corporation is an artificial person, created by law and having a distinct existence separate and apart from the natural persons who are responsible for its creation and operation. Almost all large business enterprises in the United States are organized as corporations.

Corporations may be classified as **nonprofit** or **profit**. Nonprofit corporations include those organized for recreational, educational, charitable, or other philanthropic purposes. For their continuation, they depend upon dues from their members or upon gifts and grants from the public at large. Other nonprofit corporations include those which render services to the public for a fee, such as cooperative-owned utility companies, but whose objective is rendering services to the public on a cost basis rather than earning a profit.[1]

Profit corporations are engaged in business activities. They depend upon profitable operations for their continued existence. Large profit corporations whose shares of stock are widely distributed and traded in a public market are often called **public corporations**. Corporations whose shares are owned by a small group are often called **nonpublic corporations**. Regardless of their nature or purpose, profit corporations are created according to state or federal statutes and are separate legal entities.

---

[1]Nonprofit organizations are discussed in more detail in Appendix F.

CHARACTERISTICS OF A CORPORATION

OBJECTIVE 1
Identify basic corporation characteristics which have accounting implications.

As a legal entity, the corporation has certain characteristics that make it different from other types of business organizations. The most important characteristics with accounting implications are described briefly in the following paragraphs.

A corporation has a **separate legal existence**. It may acquire, own, and dispose of property in its corporate name. It may also incur liabilities and enter into other types of contracts according to the provisions of its **charter** (also called **articles of incorporation**).

The ownership of a corporation, of which there may be several categories or classes, is divided into **transferable units** known as **shares of stock**. Each share of stock of a certain class has the same rights and privileges as every other share of the same class. The owners of the corporation, or **stockholders** (also called **shareholders**), may buy and sell shares without interfering with the activities of the corporation. The millions of transactions that occur daily on stock exchanges are independent transactions between buyers and sellers. Thus, in contrast to the partnership, the existence of the corporation is not affected by changes in ownership.

The stockholders of a corporation have **limited liability**. A corporation is responsible for its own acts and obligations, and therefore its creditors usually may not look beyond the assets of the corporation for satisfaction of their claims. Thus, the financial loss that a stockholder may suffer is limited to the amount invested. The phenomenal growth of the corporate form of business would not have been possible without this limited liability feature.

The stockholders, who are, in fact, the owners of the corporation, exercise control over the management of corporate affairs indirectly by electing a **board of directors**. It is the responsibility of the board of directors to meet from time to time to determine the corporate policies and to select the officers who manage the corporation. The following chart shows the **organizational structure** of a corporation:

Organizational Structure of a Corporate Enterprise

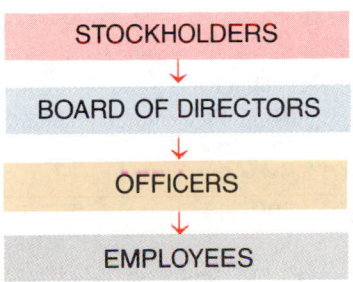

As a separate entity, a corporation is subject to **additional taxes**. It must pay a charter fee to the state at the time of its organization and annual taxes thereafter. If the corporation does business in states other than the one in which it is incorporated, it may also be required to pay annual taxes to such states. The earnings of a corporation may also be subject to a state income tax.

The earnings of a corporation are subject to the federal income tax. When the remaining earnings are distributed to stockholders as dividends, they are again taxed as income to the individuals receiving them. Under certain conditions specified in the Internal Revenue Code, a corporation with a few stockholders may elect to be treated in a manner similar to a partnership for income tax purposes. A corporation electing this optional treatment does not pay federal income taxes. Instead, its stockholders include their distributive shares of corporate income in their own taxable income, regardless of whether the income is distributed to them.

Being a creature of the state and being owned by stockholders who have limited liability, a corporation has less freedom of action than a sole proprietorship and a partnership. There may be **government regulations** in such matters as ownership of real estate, retention of earnings, and purchase of its own stock.

STOCKHOLDERS' EQUITY

OBJECTIVE 2
Describe and illustrate the main sources of stockholders' equity.

The owners' equity in a corporation is commonly called **stockholders' equity, shareholders' equity, shareholders' investment,** or **capital.** The two main sources of stockholders' equity are (1) investments contributed by the stockholders, called **paid-in capital** or **contributed capital**, and (2) net income retained in the business, called **retained earnings**. As shown in the following illustration, the stockholders' equity section of corporation balance sheets is divided into subsections based on these two sources.

Stockholders' Equity

Paid-in capital:
Common stock $330,000
Retained earnings 80,000

Total stockholders' equity $410,000

The paid-in capital contributed by the stockholders is recorded in accounts maintained for each class of stock. If there is only one class of stock, the account is entitled Common Stock or Capital Stock.

The retained earnings amount results from transferring the balance in the income summary account (the net income) to a retained earnings account at the end of a fiscal year. The dividends account, to which distributions of earnings to stockholders have been debited, is also closed to Retained Earnings. If the occurrence of net losses results in a debit balance in Retained Earnings, it is termed a **deficit**. In the stockholders' equity section of the balance sheet, a deficit is deducted from paid-in capital to determine total stockholders' equity.

There are a number of acceptable variants of the term "retained earnings," among which are *earnings retained for use in the business, earnings reinvested in the business, earnings employed in the business,* and *accumulated earnings.* For many years, the term applied to retained earnings was *earned surplus.* However, the use of this term in published financial statements has generally been discontinued. Because of its connotation as an excess, or something left over, "surplus" was sometimes erroneously interpreted by readers of financial statements to mean "cash available for dividends."

CHARACTERISTICS OF CAPITAL STOCK

OBJECTIVE 3
Identify the common characteristics of capital stock.

The general term applied to the shares of ownership of a corporation is **capital stock**. The number of shares that a corporation is *authorized* to issue is set forth in its charter. The term *issued* is applied to the shares issued to the stockholders. A corporation may, under circumstances discussed later in the chapter, reacquire some of the stock that it has issued. The stock remaining in the hands of the stockholders is then referred to as the **stock outstanding**.

The shares of capital stock are often assigned an arbitrary monetary figure, known as **par**. The par amount is printed on the **stock certificate**, which is the evidence of ownership issued to the stockholder. Stock may also be issued without par, in which case it is called **no-par** stock. Many states provide that the board of directors must assign a **stated value** to no-par stock, which makes it similar to par stock.

Because of the limited liability feature, the creditors of a corporation have no claim against the personal assets of stockholders. However, the law requires that some specific minimum contribution by the stockholders be retained by the corporation for the protection of its creditors. This amount, called **legal capital**, varies among the states but usually includes the par or stated value of the shares of capital stock issued.

Classes of Stock

The major basic rights that accompany ownership of a share of stock are (1) the right to vote in matters concerning the corporation, (2) the right to share in distributions of earnings, (3) the **preemptive right**, which is the right to maintain the same fractional interest in the corporation by purchasing a proportionate number of shares of any additional issuances of stock,[2] and (4) the right to share in assets upon liquidation.

If a corporation issues only **common stock**, each share generally has equal rights. In order to appeal to a broader investment market, a corporation may provide for one or more classes of stock with various preferential rights. The preference usually relates to the right to share in distributions of earnings. Such stock is generally called **preferred stock**.

The board of directors has the sole authority to distribute earnings to the stockholders. When such action is taken, the directors are said to *declare a dividend*. A corporation cannot guarantee that its operations will be profitable and hence it cannot guarantee dividends to its stockholders. Furthermore, the directors have wide discretionary powers in determining the extent to which earnings should be retained by the corporation to provide for expansion, to offset possible future losses, or to provide for other contingencies.

A corporation with both preferred stock and common stock may declare dividends on the common only after it meets the requirements of the stated dividend on the preferred (which may be stated in monetary terms or as a percent of par). To illustrate, assume that a corporation has 1,000 shares of $10 preferred stock (that is, the preferred has a prior claim to an annual $10 per share dividend) and 4,000 shares of common stock outstanding. Assume also that in the first three years of operations, net income was $30,000, $55,000, and $100,000 respectively. The directors authorize the retention of a portion of each year's earnings and the distribution of the remainder. Details of the dividend distribution are presented in the following tabulation:

---

[2] In recent years the stockholders of a significant number of corporations have, by formal action, given up their preemptive rights.

	First Year	Second Year	Third Year
Net income	$30,000	$55,000	$100,000
Amount retained	10,000	20,000	40,000
Amount distributed	$20,000	$35,000	$ 60,000
Preferred dividend (1,000 shares)	10,000	10,000	10,000
Common dividend (4,000 shares)	$10,000	$25,000	$ 50,000
Dividends per share:			
Preferred	$10.00	$10.00	$10.00
Common	$ 2.50	$ 6.25	$12.50

Participating and Nonparticipating Preferred Stock

In the foregoing illustration, the holders of preferred stock received an annual dividend of $10 per share, in contrast to the common stockholders, whose annual per share dividends were $2.50, $6.25, and $12.50 respectively. It is apparent from the example that holders of preferred stock have relatively greater assurance than common stockholders of receiving dividends regularly. On the other hand, holders of common stock have the possibility of receiving larger dividends than preferred stockholders. The preferred stockholders' preferential right to dividends is usually limited to a certain amount, which was assumed to be the case in the preceding example. Such stock is said to be **nonparticipating**.

Preferred stock which provides for the possibility of dividends in excess of a certain amount is said to be **participating**. Preferred shares may participate with common shares to varying degrees, and the agreement with the shareholders must be examined to determine the extent of this participation. To illustrate, assume that the contract covering the preferred stock of the corporation in the preceding illustration provides that if the total dividends to be distributed exceed the regular preferred dividend and a comparable dividend on common, the preferred shall share in the excess ratably on a share-for-share basis with the common. According to such terms, the $60,000 dividend distribution in the third year would be allocated as follows:

	Preferred Dividend	Common Dividend	Total Dividends
Regular dividend to preferred (1,000 × $10)	$10,000	—	$10,000
Comparable dividend to common (4,000 × $10)	—	$40,000	40,000
Remainder to 5,000 shares ratably ($2 per share)	2,000	8,000	10,000
Total	$12,000	$48,000	$60,000
Dividends per share	$12	$12	

Cumulative and Noncumulative Preferred Stock

As was indicated in the preceding section, most preferred stock is nonparticipating. Provision is usually made, however, to assure the continuation of the preferential dividend right if at any time the directors *pass* (do not declare) the usual dividend. The preferential dividend right is assured by providing that dividends may not be paid on the common stock if any preferred dividends have been passed (are in *arrears*). Such preferred stock is said to be **cumulative**. To illustrate, assume that a corporation has outstanding 5,000 shares of cumulative preferred 9% stock of $100 par (that is, the preferred stockholders have a prior claim to an annual 9% dividend, or $9 per share). In addition, assume that dividends have been passed for the preceding two years. In the current year, no dividend may be declared on the common stock unless the directors first declare preferred dividends of $90,000 for the past two years and $45,000 for the current year. Preferred stock not having this cumulative right is called **noncumulative**.

Other Preferential Rights

Thus far the discussion of preferential rights of preferred stock has related to dividend distributions. Preferred stock may also be given a preference in its claim to assets upon liquidation of the corporation. If the assets remaining after payment of creditors are not sufficient to return the capital contributions of both classes of stock, payment would first be made to the preferred stockholders and any balance remaining would go to the common stockholders. Another difference between preferred and common stock is that the former may have no voting rights. A corporation may also have more than one class of preferred stock, with differences as to the amount of dividends, priority of claims upon liquidation, and voting rights. In any particular case, the rights of a class of stock may be determined by reference to the charter, the stock certificate, or some other abstract of the agreement.

PREFERRED STOCK — RISKS VS. REWARDS

Preferred stocks shield shareholders somewhat from the lows of corporate fortunes. If dividend payments must be reduced, preferred stockholders receive dividends before common shareholders. However, preferred stockholders often miss out on the highs of corporate fortunes. If dividend payments are large, because most preferred stock is non-participating, preferred shareholders receive a fixed dividend and the bulk of the large dividends go to common shareholders. These "safe-but-stodgy" equities can offer dramatic profits, however, as described in the following excerpt from an article in *Business Week*:

...In times of grave financial trouble, dividends on preferreds are often suspended and placed in arrears.... If and when the company reinstates dividends, current shareholders are entitled to all the back payments, whether or not they owned stock during the arrearage period—if the preferred is cumulative....

The gains [from purchasing preferred stock with dividends in arrears] can be impressive. Bethlehem Steel announced in April that it would pay $22.5 million in arrears and resume the regular quarterly dividend on its two classes of preferred stock. Because Bethlehem had missed four payments, investors receive an extra year's worth of dividends: One class that usually pays $1.25 quarterly will return $6.25—not bad on a stock that traded in the low 30s just a few months ago.

Playing preferreds in arrears requires patience. Long Island Lighting, for instance, recently announced that it would try to resume paying dividends next year after a four-year hiatus. But the larger concern lies in the fact that you're betting on a turnaround. And all bets are off if the company goes bankrupt: You not only lose arrearages but you're also sure to see the share price plummet. On the repayment totem pole, preferreds occupy the second-lowest notch—before the common shareholders but after the creditors and bondholders....

Source: Troy Segal, "Preferred Stock: The Risky Hunt for Hidden Rewards," *Business Week* (June 13, 1988), p. 114.

ISSUING CAPITAL STOCK

OBJECTIVE 4
Describe and
illustrate the
accounting for
the issuance of
capital stock.

The entries to record investments of stockholders in a corporation are like those for investments by owners of other types of business organizations, in that cash and other assets received are debited and any liabilities assumed are credited. The credit to stockholders' equity differs, however, in that there are accounts for each class of stock. To illustrate, assume that a corporation, with an authorization of 10,000 shares of preferred stock of $100 par and 100,000 shares of common stock of $20 par, issues one half of each authorization at par for cash. The entry to record the stockholders' investment and the receipt of the cash is as follows:

Cash..	1,500,000	
Preferred Stock...		500,000
Common Stock...		1,000,000

The capital stock accounts (Preferred Stock, Common Stock) are controlling accounts. It is necessary to maintain records of each stockholder's name, address, and number of shares held in order to issue dividend checks, proxy forms, and financial reports. Individual stockholders accounts are kept in a subsidiary ledger known as the **stockholders ledger**.

Par stock is often issued by a corporation at a price other than par. When it is issued for more than par, the excess of the contract price over par is termed a **premium** on stock. When it is issued at a price that is below par, the difference is called a **discount** on stock. Thus, if stock with a par of $50 is issued at $60, the amount of the premium is $10. If the same stock is issued at $45, the amount of the discount is $5.

Theoretically, there is no reason for a newly organized corporation to issue stock at a price other than par. The par designation is merely a part of the plan of dividing owners' equity into a number of units of ownership. Hence, a group of persons investing their funds in a new corporation might all be expected to pay par for the shares. The fortunes of an enterprise do not remain the same, however, even when it is still in the process of organizing. The changing prospects for its future success may affect the price per share at which the incorporators can secure other investors.

A need for additional paid-in capital may arise long after a corporation has become established. Losses during prior fiscal periods may have depleted operating funds or the operations may have been successful enough to warrant a substantial expansion of plant and equipment. If the funds are to be obtained by the issuance of additional stock, it is apparent that the current price at which the original stock is selling in the market will affect the price that can be obtained for the new shares.

Generally speaking, the price at which stock can be sold by a corporation is influenced by (1) the financial condition, the earnings record, and the dividend record of the corporation, (2) its potential earning power, (3) the availability of money for investment purposes, and (4) general business and economic conditions and prospects.

Premium and Discount on Stock

When capital stock is issued at a premium, cash or other assets are debited for the amount received. The stock account is then credited for the par amount, and an account generally called Paid-In Capital in Excess of Par is credited for the amount of the premium.[3] For example, if Caldwell Company issues 2,000 shares of $50 par preferred stock for cash at $55, the entry to record the transaction would be as follows:

Cash...	110,000	
Preferred Stock...		100,000
Paid-In Capital in Excess of Par — Preferred Stock		10,000

The premium of $10,000 is a part of the investment of the stockholders and is therefore a part of paid-in capital. It is distinguished from the capital stock account because usually it is not a part of legal capital and in many states may be used as a basis for dividends to stockholders. However, if the premium is returned to stockholders as a dividend at a later date, it should be emphasized that the dividend is a return of paid-in capital rather than a distribution of earnings.

Most states do not permit the issuance of stock at a discount. In others, it may be done only under certain conditions. When stock is issued at less than its par, it is considered to be fully paid as between the corporation and the stockholder. In some states, however, the stockholders are contingently liable to creditors for the amount of the discount. If the corporation is liquidated and there are not enough assets to pay creditors in full, the stockholders may be assessed for an additional contribution up to the amount of the discount on their stock.

When capital stock is issued at a discount, cash or other assets are debited for the amount received, and a discount account is debited for the amount of the discount. The discount on capital stock is deducted from the par amount of capital stock in the paid-in capital subsection of stockholders' equity. Since capital stock is not often issued at a discount, transactions involving discounts are not illustrated.

Premium on Capital Stock on the Balance Sheet

The manner in which premiums on capital stock may be presented in the stockholders' equity section of the balance sheet is illustrated as follows:

Stockholders' Equity

Paid-in capital:			
Preferred 10% stock, cumulative, $50 par			
(2,000 shares authorized and issued).....	$100,000		
Excess of issue price over par	10,000	$110,000	
Common stock, $25 par (50,000 shares			
authorized, 20,000 shares issued).........	$500,000		
Excess of issue price over par	40,000	540,000	
Total paid-in capital............................		$650,000	
Retained earnings....................................		175,000	
Total stockholders' equity			$825,000

---

[3]Although the formal name of the account is Paid-In Capital in Excess of Par, the shorter term "premium" will often be used in the discussion.

The following stockholders' equity section illustrates the reporting of a deficit and some differences in terminology from that in the foregoing example:

Shareholders' Equity

Paid-in capital:		
Preferred $3 stock, cumulative, $25 par (10,000 shares authorized and issued)	$ 250,000	
Premium on preferred stock	20,000	$ 270,000
Common stock, $10 par (200,000 shares authorized, 100,000 shares issued)	$1,000,000	
Premium on common stock	100,000	1,100,000
Total paid in by stockholders		$1,370,000
Less deficit		75,000
Total shareholders' equity		$1,295,000

Issuing Stock for Assets Other Than Cash

When capital stock is issued in exchange for assets other than cash, such as land, buildings, and equipment, the assets acquired should be recorded at their fair market price or at the fair market price of the stock issued, whichever is more objectively determinable. The determination of the values to be assigned to the assets is the responsibility of the board of directors.

As a basis for illustration, assume that a corporation acquired land for which the fair market price is not determinable. In exchange, the corporation issued 10,000 shares of its $10 par common stock with a current market price of $12 per share. The transaction could be recorded as follows:

Dec. 5	Land	120,000	
	Common Stock		100,000
	Paid-In Capital in Excess of Par — Common Stock		20,000

No-Par Stock

In the early days of rapid industrial expansion and increasing use of the corporate form of business organization, it was customary to assign a par of $100 to shares of stock. It is not surprising that unsophisticated investors, mistakenly considering "par value" to be the equivalent of "value," were often induced to invest in mining and other highly speculative enterprises by the simple means of being offered $100 par stock at "bargain" prices. Another misleading practice was the use of par in assigning highly inflated values to assets acquired in exchange for stock. For example, stock with a total par of $1,000,000 might be issued in exchange for patents, mineral rights, or other properties with a conservatively estimated value of $50,000. The assets would be recorded at the full par of $1,000,000, whereas in reality the stock had been issued at a discount of $950,000. Balance sheets that were "window-dressed" in this manner were obviously deceptive.

To combat such abuses and also to eliminate the troublesome discount liability of stockholders, stock without par was conceived. The issuance of stock without par was first permitted by New York in 1912. Its use is now authorized in nearly all of the states.

Over the years, questionable practices in the issuance of securities have been virtually eliminated. Today federal and state laws and rules imposed by organized stock exchanges and governmental agencies such as the Securities and Exchange Commission combine to protect the investor from misrepresentations that were common in earlier days.

In most states, both preferred and common stock may be issued without a par designation. However, preferred stock is usually assigned a par. When no-par stock is issued, the entire proceeds may be credited to the capital stock account, even though the issuance price varies from time to time. For example, if at the time of organization a corporation issues 10,000 shares of no-par common stock at $40 a share and at a later date issues 1,000 additional shares at $36, the entries would be as follows:

Original issuance of 10,000 shares of no-par common at $40.	Cash..	400,000
	Common Stock...		400,000
Subsequent issuance of 1,000 shares of no-par common at $36.	Cash..	36,000
	Common Stock...		36,000

The laws of some states require that the entire proceeds from the issuance of no-par stock be regarded as legal capital. The preceding entries conform to this principle, which also conforms to the original concept of no-par stock. In other states, no-par stock may be assigned a stated value per share, and the excess of the proceeds over the stated value may be credited to Paid-In Capital in Excess of Stated Value. Assuming that in the previous example the stated value is $25 and the board of directors wishes to credit the common stock for stated value, the transactions would be recorded as follows. From these entries it is readily apparent that the accounting for no-par stock with a stated value may follow the same pattern as the accounting for par stock.

Original issuance of 10,000 shares of no-par common, stated value $25, at $40.	Cash..	400,000
	Common Stock...		250,000
	Paid-In Capital in Excess of Stated Value............		150,000
Subsequent issuance of 1,000 shares of no-par common, stated value $25, at $36.	Cash..	36,000
	Common Stock...		25,000
	Paid-In Capital in Excess of Stated Value............		11,000

Subscriptions and Stock Issuance

In some situations involving the initial issue of capital stock or subsequent issuances where the stockholders have waived the preemptive right, a corporation may sell its stock to an **underwriter**. The underwriter then resells the shares to investors at a price high enough to earn a profit from the sale. Under these circumstances, the corporation is relieved of the task of marketing the stock. It receives the entire amount of cash without delay and can proceed immediately with its plans for the use of the funds.

In other situations, a corporation may sell its stock directly to investors or others, such as employees, under stock purchase plans. In such cases, the buyer may enter into an agreement with the corporation to subscribe to shares at a certain price per share. The terms may provide for payment in full at some future date or for installment payments over a period of time.

When stock is subscribed for at par, the subscription price is debited to the asset account Stock Subscriptions Receivable and credited to the capital stock account Stock Subscribed. When stock is subscribed for at a price above par, the stock subscriptions receivable account is debited for the subscription price. The stock subscribed account is credited at par, and the difference between the subscription price and par is credited to Paid-In Capital in Excess of Par.

After a subscriber has completed the agreed payments, the corporation issues the stock certificate. The stock subscribed account is then debited for the total par of the shares issued, and the capital stock account is credited for the same amount.

As the basis for illustrating the entries for subscriptions and stock issuance, assume that the newly organized Ledway Corporation receives subscriptions, collects cash, and issues stock certificates according to the following transactions:

Received subscriptions to 10,000 shares of $20 par common stock from various subscribers at $21 per share, with a down payment of 40% of the subscription price.	Mar. 1	Common Stock Subscriptions Receivable.....................................	210,000	
		Common Stock Subscribed..............		200,000
		Paid-In Capital in Excess of Par—Common Stock....................		10,000
	1	Cash..	84,000	
		Common Stock Subscriptions Receivable.................................		84,000
Received 30% of subscription price from all subscribers.	May 1	Cash..	63,000	
		Common Stock Subscriptions Receivable.................................		63,000
Received final 30% of subscription price from all subscribers and issued the stock certificates.	July 1	Cash..	63,000	
		Common Stock Subscriptions Receivable.................................		63,000
	1	Common Stock Subscribed..................	200,000	
		Common Stock		200,000

A balance sheet prepared after the transactions of March 1 would list the subscriptions receivable as a current asset and the stock subscribed and the paid-in capital in excess of par as paid-in capital. While it is true that the entire amount has not been "paid in" in cash, the claim against the subscribers is an asset of equivalent value. The presentation of the items in the balance sheet of the Ledway Corporation as of March 1 is as follows:

Ledway Corporation Balance Sheet March 1, 19--			
Assets		**Stockholders' Equity**	
Current assets:		Paid-in capital:	
Cash.........................	$ 84,000	Common stock subscribed..............	$200,000
Common stock subscriptions receivable	126,000	Excess of issue price over par..................	10,000
Total assets....................	$210,000	Total stockholders' equity.	$210,000

The stock subscriptions receivable account is a controlling account. The individual accounts with each subscriber are maintained in a subsidiary ledger known as a **subscribers ledger**. It is used in much the same manner as the accounts receivable ledger.

After all the subscriptions have been collected, the common stock subscriptions receivable account will have a zero balance. The stock certificates will then be issued and the common stock subscribed account will have a zero balance. The ultimate effect of the series of transactions is a debit to Cash of $210,000, a credit to Common Stock of $200,000, and a credit to Paid-In Capital in Excess of Par of $10,000.

TREASURY STOCK

OBJECTIVE 5
Describe and illustrate the accounting for treasury stock.

Although there are some legal restrictions on the practice, a corporation may purchase shares of its own outstanding stock from stockholders. It may also accept shares of its own stock in payment of a debt owed by a stockholder, which in essence is much the same as acquisition by purchase. A corporation may buy its own stock in order to provide shares for resale to employees, to provide shares for reissuance to employees as a bonus, or to support the market price of the stock. In March, 1986, for example, General Motors announced that it would buy back as much as $1.95 billion of its common stock. General Motors officials stated that two primary uses of the treasury stock would be for incentive compensation plans and employee savings plans.

The term **treasury stock** may be applied only to the issuing corporation's stock that (1) has been issued as fully paid, (2) has later been reacquired by the corporation, and (3) has not been canceled or reissued. In the past, corporations would occasionally list treasury stock on the balance sheet as an asset. The justification for such treatment was that the stock could be reissued and was thus like an investment in the stock of another corporation. The same argument, though indefensible, might well be extended to authorized but unissued stock.

Today, it is generally agreed among accountants that treasury stock should not be reported as an asset. A corporation cannot own a part of itself. Treasury stock has no voting rights, it does not have the preemptive right to participate in additional issuances of stock, nor does it generally participate in cash dividends. When a corporation purchases its own stock, it is returning capital to the stockholders from whom the purchase was made.

There are several methods of accounting for the purchase and the resale of treasury stock. A commonly used method is the **cost basis**. When the stock is purchased by the corporation, the account Treasury Stock is debited for the price paid for it. The par and the price at which the stock was originally issued are ignored. When the stock is resold, Treasury Stock is credited at the price paid for it, and the difference between the price paid and the selling price is debited or credited to an account entitled Paid-In Capital from Sale of Treasury Stock.

As a basis for illustrating the cost method, assume that the paid-in capital of a corporation is composed of common stock issued at a premium, detailed as follows:

Common stock, $25 par (20,000 shares authorized and issued)	$500,000
Excess of issue price over par...	150,000

The assumed transactions involving treasury stock and the required entries are as follows:

Purchased 1,000 shares of treasury stock at $45. Treasury Stock...	45,000	
Cash..		45,000
Sold 200 shares of treasury stock at $60. Cash..	12,000	
Treasury Stock..		9,000
Paid-In Capital from Sale of Treasury Stock		3,000
Sold 200 shares of treasury stock at $40. Cash..	8,000	
Paid-In Capital from Sale of Treasury Stock	1,000	
Treasury Stock...		9,000

Paid-In Capital from Sale of Treasury Stock is reported in the paid-in capital section of the balance sheet. Treasury Stock is deducted from the total of the paid-in capital and retained earnings. After the foregoing transactions are completed, the stockholders' equity section of the balance sheet would appear as follows:

Stockholders' Equity

Paid-in capital:		
Common stock, $25 par		
(20,000 shares authorized and issued) ...	$500,000	
Excess of issue price over par — common		
stock	150,000	$650,000
From sale of treasury stock......................		2,000
Total paid-in capital...........................		$652,000
Retained earnings....................................		130,000
Total		$782,000
Deduct treasury stock (600 shares at cost)...		27,000
Total stockholders' equity		$755,000

The stockholders' equity section of the balance sheet indicates that 20,000 shares of stock were issued, of which 600 are held as treasury stock. The number of shares outstanding is therefore 19,400. If cash dividends are declared at this time, the declaration would apply to only 19,400 shares of stock. Similarly, 19,400 shares could be voted at a stockholders' meeting.

If sales of treasury stock result in a net decrease in paid-in capital, the decrease may be reported on the balance sheet as a reduction of paid-in capital or it may be debited to the retained earnings account.

EQUITY PER SHARE

The amount appearing on the balance sheet as total stockholders' equity can be stated in terms of the **equity per share**. Another term sometimes used in referring to the equity allocable to a single share of stock is **book value per share**. The latter term is not only less accurate but its use of "value" may also be interpreted by nonaccountants to mean "market value" or "actual worth."

When there is only one class of stock, the equity per share is determined by dividing total stockholders' equity by the number of shares outstanding. For a corporation with both preferred and common stock, it is necessary first to allocate the total equity between the two classes. In making the allocation, consideration must be given to the liquidation rights of the preferred stock, including any participating and cumulative dividend features. After the total is allocated to the two classes, the equity per share of each class may then be determined by dividing the respective amounts by the related number of shares outstanding.

To illustrate, assume that as of the end of the current fiscal year, a corporation has both preferred and common shares outstanding, that there are no preferred dividends in arrears, and that the preferred stock is entitled to receive $105 per share upon liquidation. The amounts of the stockholders' equity accounts of the corporation and the computation of the equity per share are as follows:

Stockholders' Equity

Preferred $9 stock, cumulative, $100 par (1,000 shares outstanding)...	$100,000
Excess of issue price over par—preferred stock..........................	2,000
Common stock, $10 par (50,000 shares outstanding)....................	500,000
Excess of issue price over par—common stock	50,000
Retained earnings..	253,000
Total equity	$905,000

Allocation of Total Equity to Preferred and Common Stock

Total equity	$905,000
Allocated to preferred stock:	
Liquidation price...	105,000
Allocated to common stock	$800,000

Equity Per Share

Preferred stock: $105,000 ÷ 1,000 shares = $105 per share
Common stock: $800,000 ÷ 50,000 shares = $ 16 per share

If it is assumed that the preferred stock is entitled to dividends in arrears in the event of liquidation, and that there is an arrearage of two years, the computations for the foregoing illustration would be as follows:

Allocation of Total Equity to Preferred and Common Stock

Total equity..		$905,000
Allocated to preferred stock:		
Liquidation price..	$105,000	
Dividends in arrears...	18,000	123,000
Allocated to common stock		$782,000

Equity Per Share

Preferred stock: $123,000 ÷ 1,000 shares = $123.00 per share
Common stock: $782,000 ÷ 50,000 shares = $ 15.64 per share

Equity per share, particularly of common stock, is often stated in corporation reports to stockholders and quoted in the financial press. It is one of the many factors affecting the **market price**, that is, the price at which a share is bought and sold at a particular moment. However, it should be noted that earning capacity, dividend rates, and prospects for the future usually affect the market price of listed stocks to a much greater extent than does equity per share. So-called "glamour" stocks may at times sell at more than ten times the amount of the equity per share. On the other hand, stock in corporations that have suffered severe declines in earnings or whose future prospects appear to be unfavorable may sell at prices which are much less than the equity per share.

ORGANIZATION COSTS

OBJECTIVE 7
Describe and illustrate the accounting for organization costs.

Expenditures incurred in organizing a corporation, such as legal fees, taxes and fees paid to the state, and promotional costs, are charged to an intangible asset account entitled Organization Costs. Although such costs have no realizable value upon liquidation, they are as essential as plant and equipment, for without the expenditures the corporation could not have been created. If the life of a corporation is limited to a definite period of time, the organization costs should be amortized over the period by annual charges to an expense account. However, at the time of incorporation the length of life of most corporations is indeterminate.

There are two possible extreme viewpoints on the proper accounting for organization costs and other intangibles of indeterminate life. One extreme would consider the cost of intangibles as a permanent asset until there was convincing evidence of loss in value. The other extreme would consider the cost of intangibles as an expense in the period in which the cost is incurred. The practical solution to the problem is expressed in the following quotation:

> . . . . Allocating the cost of goodwill or other intangible assets with an indeterminate life over time is necessary because the value almost inevitably becomes zero at some future date. Since the date at which the value becomes zero is indeterminate, the end of the useful life must necessarily be set arbitrarily at some point or within some range of time for accounting purposes.[4]

The Internal Revenue Code permits the amortization of organization costs equally over a period of not less than sixty months beginning with the month the corporation commences business. Since the amount of such costs is generally small in relation to total assets and the effect on net income is ordinarily not significant, amortization of organization costs over sixty months is generally accepted in accounting practice.

---

[4]*Opinions of the Accounting Principles Board*, No. 17, "Intangible Assets" (New York: American Institute of Certified Public Accountants, 1970), par. 23.

CHAPTER REVIEW

KEY POINTS

OBJECTIVE 1

Characteristics of a Corporation

The most important corporation characteristics with accounting implications are the following: separate legal existence, transferable units of stock, limited liability, and organizational structure. In addition, a corporation as a separate entity is subject to federal income taxes.

OBJECTIVE 2

Stockholders' Equity

The stockholders equity section of a corporation balance sheet is divided into two subsections: paid-in capital and retained earnings.

OBJECTIVE 3

Characteristics of Capital Stock

The stock of a corporation may be classified according to its par, right to vote, preference as to dividends, and preference as to liquidation rights. Various types of stock include par common stock, no-par common stock, participating preferred stock, nonparticipating preferred stock, cumulative preferred stock, and noncumulative preferred stock.

OBJECTIVE 4

Issuing Capital Stock

When a corporation issues stock at par, each class of stock is credited for its par amount. When a corporation issues stock at more than par, the premium is recorded by crediting Paid-In Capital in Excess of Par. Balances in the premium accounts appear with their related class of stock in the stockholders' equity section of the balance sheet.

When capital stock is issued and exchanged for assets other than cash, the assets acquired should be recorded at their fair market price or at the fair market price of the stock issued, whichever is more objectively determinable.

When no-par stock is issued, the entire proceeds may be credited to the capital stock account, even though the issue price varies from time to time. In some cases, no-par stock may be assigned a stated value per share, and the excess of the proceeds over the stated value may be credited to a separate paid-in capital account.

In some cases, investors may subscribe to shares of stock directly from a corporation. The terms of the sale usually provide for the payment in full at some future date or for installment payments over a period of time. When stock is initially subscribed, the subscription price is debited to an asset account, Stock Subscriptions Receivable, and credited to a capital stock account, Stock Subscribed. If the subscription price exceeds the par or stated value of the stock, the premium is credited to Paid-In Capital in Excess of Par. After a subscriber has completed the agreed payments, the corporation issues the stock certificate. The stock subscribed account is then debited for the total par of the shares issued, and the capital stock account is credited for the same amount.

OBJECTIVE 5

Treasury Stock

A corporation may purchase shares of its own outstanding stock from stockholders. Any treasury stock held at the end of an accounting period is deducted from the total of the paid-in capital and retained earnings of the corporation. Any difference between the price paid for and the selling price of the treasury stock is usually recorded in a paid-in capital account for treasury stock transactions.

OBJECTIVE 6

Equity per Share

The amount appearing on the balance sheet as total stockholders' equity can be stated in terms of the equity per share. For a corporation with both preferred and common stock outstanding, it is necessary to allocate the total equity between the two classes of stock. The equity allocated to each class is divided by the number of shares outstanding of the respective class to determine the equity per share.

OBJECTIVE 7

Organization Costs

Expenditures incurred in organizing a corporation are charged to an intangible asset account entitled Organization Costs. The generally accepted accounting practice is to amortize organization costs over a period of sixty months, which conforms with federal income tax regulations.

KEY TERMS

stockholders 537
stockholders' equity 538
paid-in capital 538
retained earnings 538
deficit 538
capital stock 538
stock outstanding 539
par 539
stated value 539

preemptive right 539
common stock 539
preferred stock 539
participating preferred stock 540
cumulative preferred stock 541
premium on stock 542
discount on stock 542
treasury stock 547
equity per share 549

SELF-EXAMINATION QUESTIONS

Answers at end of chapter.

1. The owners' equity in a corporation is commonly called:
   A. stockholders' equity
   B. shareholders' investment
   C. capital
   D. all of the above

2. If a corporation has outstanding 1,000 shares of $9 cumulative preferred stock of $100 par and dividends have been passed for the preceding three years, what is the amount of preferred dividends that must be declared in the current year before a dividend can be declared on common stock?
   A. $9,000
   B. $27,000
   C. $36,000
   D. None of the above

3. The stockholders' equity section of the balance sheet may include:
   A. Common Stock
   B. Common Stock Subscribed
   C. Preferred Stock
   D. all of the above

4. If a corporation reacquires its own stock, the stock is listed on the balance sheet in the:
   A. current assets section
   B. long-term liabilities section
   C. stockholders' equity section
   D. none of the above

5. A corporation's balance sheet includes 10,000 outstanding shares of $8 cumulative preferred stock of $100 par; 100,000 outstanding shares of $20 par common stock; paid-in capital in excess of par—common stock of $100,000; and retained earnings of $540,000. If preferred dividends are three years in arrears and the preferred stock is entitled to dividends in arrears plus $110 per share in the event of liquidation, what is the equity per common share?
   A. $20.00
   B. $23.00
   C. $25.40
   D. None of the above

ILLUSTRATIVE PROBLEM

The stockholders' equity and related accounts of Rockton Manufacturing Corporation as of November 1, 1990, the beginning of the fiscal year, are as follows:

Preferred Stock Subscriptions Receivable...............................	$ 120,000
Preferred 8% Stock, $50 par (100,000 shares authorized, 20,000 shares issued)...	1,000,000
Preferred Stock Subscribed (3,000 shares)	150,000
Paid-In Capital in Excess of Par—Preferred Stock.....................	80,000
Common Stock, $25 par (500,000 shares authorized, 100,000 shares issued)...	2,500,000
Paid-In Capital in Excess of Par—Common Stock.....................	600,000
Retained Earnings..	3,150,000

During the fiscal year ended October 31, 1991, Rockton Manufacturing Corporation completed the following transactions affecting stockholders' equity:

(a) Purchased 5,000 shares of treasury common for $130,000.
(b) Received balance due on preferred stock subscribed and issued the certificates.
(c) Sold 3,000 shares of treasury common for $81,000.
(d) Received subscriptions to 4,000 shares of preferred 8% stock at $51, collecting one third of the subscription price.
(e) Issued 40,000 shares of common stock at $27, receiving cash.
(f) Sold 1,000 shares of treasury common for $24,000.

Instructions:

1. Prepare the journal entries to record the transactions listed, identifying each transaction by the appropriate letter.
2. Prepare the stockholders' equity section for the October 31, 1991 balance sheet. The beginning retained earnings balance must be increased by the net income for the year, $710,000, and reduced by the dividends declared and paid, $280,000.

SOLUTION

(1)

(a) Treasury Stock	130,000	
Cash		130,000
(b) Cash	120,000	
Preferred Stock Subscriptions Receivable		120,000
Preferred Stock Subscribed	150,000	
Preferred Stock		150,000
(c) Cash	81,000	
Treasury Stock......................................		78,000
Paid-In Capital from Sale of Treasury Stock		3,000
(d) Preferred Stock Subscriptions Receivable......	204,000	
Preferred Stock Subscribed		200,000
Paid-In Capital in Excess of Par—Preferred Stock.......................		4,000
Cash	68,000	
Preferred Stock Subscriptions Receivable		68,000

(e) Cash 1,080,000
      Common Stock   1,000,000
      Paid-In Capital in Excess
        of Par—Common Stock.......................   80,000

(f) Cash 24,000
      Paid-In Capital from Sale of Treasury
        Stock...   2,000
      Treasury Stock   26,000

(2)

Stockholders' Equity

Paid-in capital:
  Preferred 8% stock, $50 par
    (100,000 shares authorized,
    23,000 shares issued) $1,150,000
  Preferred stock subscribed,
    $50 par (4,000 shares)..........   200,000
  Excess of issue price
    over par—preferred stock ...   84,000 $1,434,000

  Common stock, $25 par
    (500,000 shares authorized,
    140,000 shares issued) $3,500,000
  Excess of issue price
    over par—common stock....   680,000   4,180,000
  From sale of treasury stock   1,000
    Total paid-in capital $5,615,000
Retained earnings.....................   3,580,000
Total...................................... $9,195,000
Deduct treasury common stock
  (1,000 shares at cost)..............   26,000
Total stockholders' equity $9,169,000

DISCUSSION QUESTIONS

1. Contrast the owners' liability to creditors of (a) a partnership (partners) and (b) a corporation (stockholders).

2. Why is it said that the earnings of a corporation are subject to "double taxation"? Discuss.

3. Why are most large business enterprises organized as corporations?

4. What are the two principal sources of stockholders' equity?

5. The retained earnings account of a corporation at the beginning of the year had a credit balance of $90,000. The only other entry in the account during the year was a debit of $105,000 transferred from the income summary account at the end of the year. (a) What is the term applied to the $105,000 debit? (b) What is the balance in Retained Earnings at the end of the year? (c) What is the term applied to the balance determined in (b)?

6. The charter of a corporation provides for the issuance of a maximum of 100,000 shares of common stock. The corporation issued 80,000 shares of common stock, and two years later it reacquired 5,000 shares. After the reacquisition, what is the number of shares of stock (a) authorized, (b) issued, and (c) outstanding?

7. Of two corporations organized at approximately the same time and engaged in competing businesses, one issued $20 par common stock and the other issued $10 par common stock. Do the par designations provide any indication as to which stock is preferable as an investment? Explain.

8. What are the four basic rights that accompany ownership of a share of common stock?

9. (a) Differentiate between common stock and preferred stock. (b) Describe briefly (1) participating preferred stock and (2) cumulative preferred stock.

10. Assume that a corporation has had outstanding 100,000 shares of $2 cumulative preferred stock of $25 par and dividends were passed for the preceding three years. What amount of total dividends must be paid to the preferred stockholders before the common stockholders are entitled to any dividends in the current year?

11. If common stock of $25 par is sold for $30, what is the $5 difference between the issue price and par called?

12. What are some of the factors that influence the market price of a corporation's stock?

13. When a corporation issues stock at a premium, does the premium constitute income? Explain.

14. In which section of the corporation balance sheet would Paid-In Capital in Excess of Par — Preferred Stock appear?

15. The stockholders' equity section of a corporation balance sheet is composed of the following items:

Preferred $10 stock,		
$100 par.......................	$500,000	
Excess of issue price over		
par — preferred stock	40,000	$540,000
Common stock, $20 par......	$800,000	
Excess of issue price over		
par — common stock	70,000	870,000	$1,410,000
Retained earnings..............			330,000	$1,740,000

What is the amount of each of the following: (a) paid-in capital attributable to preferred stock, (b) paid-in capital attributable to common stock, (c) earnings retained for use in the business, and (d) total stockholders' equity?

16. Land is acquired by a corporation for 10,000 shares of its $10 par common stock, which is currently selling for $35 per share on a national stock exchange. (a) At what value should the land be recorded? (b) What accounts and amounts should be credited to record the transaction?

17. A corporation receives subscriptions to 2,500 shares of $20 par common stock from various subscribers at $24 per share, with a down payment of 25% of the subscription price. Subsequently, another payment of 25% of the subscription price was received. Assuming that financial statements are prepared at this point, determine the following account balances: (a) Subscriptions Receivable, (b) Common Stock Subscribed, (c) Paid-In Capital in Excess of Par — Common Stock, and (d) Common Stock.

18. (a) In what respect does treasury stock differ from unissued stock? (b) For what reasons might a company purchase treasury stock? (c) How should treasury stock be presented on the balance sheet?

19. A corporation reacquires 1,000 shares of its own $50 par common stock for $75,000, recording it at cost. (a) What effect does this transaction have on revenue or expense of the period? (b) What effect does it have on stockholders' equity?

20. The treasury stock in Question 19 is resold for $90,000. (a) What is the effect on the corporation's revenue of the period? (b) What is the effect on stockholders' equity?

21. A corporation that had issued 50,000 shares of $10 par common stock subsequently reacquired 5,000 shares, which it now holds as treasury stock. If the board of directors declares a cash dividend of $1 per share, what will be the total amount of the dividend?

22. At the end of the current period, a corporation has 5,000 shares of preferred stock and 50,000 shares of common stock outstanding. Assuming that there are no preferred dividends in arrears, that the preferred stock is entitled to receive $110 per share upon liquidation, and that total stockholders' equity is $2,750,000, determine the following amounts: (a) equity per share of preferred stock and (b) equity per share of common stock.

23. Common stock has a par of $20 per share, the current equity per share is $32.50, and the market price per share is $55. Suggest reasons for the comparatively high market price in relation to par and to equity per share.

24. (a) What type of expenditure is charged to the organization costs account? (b) Give examples of such expenditures. (c) In what section of the balance sheet is the balance of Organization Costs listed?

25. Identify each of the following accounts as asset, liability, stockholders' equity, revenue, or expense, and indicate the normal balance of each:
    (1) Preferred Stock
    (2) Paid-In Capital from Sale of Treasury Stock
    (3) Common Stock Subscribed
    (4) Common Stock Subscriptions Receivable
    (5) Treasury Stock
    (6) Organization Costs
    (7) Paid-In Capital in Excess of Par — Common Stock
    (8) Common Stock
    (9) Paid-In Capital in Excess of Par — Preferred Stock
    (10) Retained Earnings

Real World Focus

26. The total stockholders' equity of The Circle K Corporation was $331,021,000 as of April 30, 1988. In addition to 43,216,153 shares of common stock outstanding on April 30, 1988, The Circle K Corporation also had 475,000 shares of $8 cumulative, convertible, Series A preferred stock outstanding. The following excerpt was taken from the footnotes to The Circle K Corporation's 1988 annual report:

    In the event of liquidation, all shares related to Series A preferred stock are preferred over the common stock, and holders of Series A preferred stock will be entitled to receive, out of the assets of the Company available for distribution to shareholders, $100 per share together with an amount equal to all dividends accrued and unpaid.

    (a) If no dividends were in arrears on April 30, 1988, what was the total liquidation value of the Series A preferred stock? (b) What was the equity per share of the outstanding common stock as of April 30, 1988?

EXERCISES

Exercise 14–1
Dividends per share.
OBJ. 3

H. L. Baxter Company has stock outstanding as follows: 20,000 shares of $4 cumulative, nonparticipating preferred stock of $50 par, and 100,000 shares of $20 par common. During its first five years of operations, the following amounts were distributed as dividends: first year, none; second year, $100,000; third year, $150,000; fourth year, $200,000; fifth year, $250,000. Determine the dividends per share on each class of stock for each of the five years.

Exercise 14–2
Dividends per share.
OBJ. 3

C. C. Werner Inc. has outstanding stock composed of 1,000 shares of $9 participating preferred stock of $100 par and 10,000 shares of no-par common stock. The preferred stock is entitled to participate equally with the common, on a share-for-share basis, in any dividend distributions which exceed the regular preferred dividend and a $2 per share common dividend. The directors declare dividends of $40,000 for the current year. Determine the amount of the dividend per share on (a) the preferred stock and (b) the common stock.

Exercise 14–3
Entries for stock issuance.
OBJ. 4

On March 10, Abrams Company issued for cash 5,000 shares of no-par common stock (with a stated value of $10) at $14, and on August 7 it issued for cash 1,000 shares of $50 par preferred stock at $54. (a) Give the entries for March 10 and August 7, assuming that the common stock is to be credited with the stated value. (b) What is the total amount invested by all stockholders as of August 7?

Exercise 14–4
Stock subscriptions.
OBJ. 4

On April 1, Crystal Company received its charter authorizing 20,000 shares of $5 par common stock. On April 6, the corporation received subscriptions to 5,000 shares of stock at $20. Cash for one half of the subscription price accompanied the subscriptions. On June 5, the remaining half was received from all subscribers and the stock was issued. (a) Present entries to record the transactions of April 6. (b) Present entries to record the transactions of June 5. (c) By what amount did the corporation's stockholders' equity increase on April 1, April 6, and June 5? (d) Name two controlling accounts used in the transactions and identify the related subsidiary ledgers.

Exercise 14–5
Issuance of stock; stockholders' equity section.
OBJ. 4

IMA Company, with an authorization of 10,000 shares of preferred stock and 50,000 shares of common stock, completed several transactions involving its capital stock on February 1, the first day of operations. The trial balance at the close of the day follows:

Cash	130,000	
Common Stock Subscriptions Receivable	260,000	
Land	60,000	
Buildings	240,000	
Preferred $5 Stock, $50 par		250,000
Paid-In Capital in Excess of Par—Preferred Stock		50,000
Common Stock, $20 par		100,000
Paid-In Capital in Excess of Par—Common Stock		90,000
Common Stock Subscribed		200,000
	690,000	690,000

All shares within each class of stock were sold or subscribed at the same price, the preferred stock was issued in exchange for the land and buildings, and no cash was received on the unissued common stock subscribed. (a) Present the three compound entries to record the transactions summarized in the trial balance. (b) Prepare the stockholders' equity section of the balance sheet as of February 1.

Exercise 14–6
Treasury stock transactions.
OBJ. 5

On January 11 of the current year, Slezak Company reacquired 1,000 shares of its common stock at $30 per share. On July 2, 500 of the reacquired shares were sold at $28 per share. The remaining 500 shares were sold at $35 per share on December 19. (a) Record the transactions of January 11, July 2, and December 19. (b) What is the balance in Paid-In Capital from Sale of Treasury Stock on December 31 of the current year? (c) Where will the balance in Paid-In Capital from Sale of Treasury Stock be reported on the balance sheet?

Exercise 14–7
Equity per share.
OBJ. 6

The stockholders' equity accounts of De Vito Company at the end of the current fiscal year are as follows: Preferred $10 Stock, $100 par, $1,000,000; Common Stock, $10 par, $5,000,000; Paid-In Capital in Excess of Par — Common Stock, $200,000; Paid-In Capital in Excess of Par — Preferred Stock, $40,000; Retained Earnings, $935,000. (a) Determine the equity per share of each class of stock, assuming that the preferred stock is entitled to receive $120 upon liquidation. (b) Determine the equity per share of each class of stock, assuming that the preferred stock is to receive $120 per share plus the dividends in arrears in the event of liquidation, and that only the dividends for the current year are in arrears.

Exercise 14–8
Treasury stock and equity per share.
OBJ. 5, 6

The following items were listed in the stockholders' equity section of the balance sheet of June 30: Common stock, $25 par (20,000 shares outstanding), $500,000; Paid-in capital in excess of par — common stock, $120,000; Retained earnings, $180,000. On July 1, the corporation purchased 1,000 shares of its stock for $35,250. (a) Determine the equity per share of stock on June 30. (b) Present the entry to record the purchase of the stock on July 1. (c) Determine the equity per share on July 1.

Exercise 14–9
Equity per share; liquidation amounts.
OBJ. 6

The following items were listed in the stockholders' equity section of the balance sheet on July 31: Preferred stock, $100 par, $500,000; Common stock, $20 par, $2,000,000; Paid-in capital in excess of par — common stock, $150,000; Deficit, $250,000. On August 1, the board of directors voted to dissolve the corporation immediately. A short time later, after all noncash assets were sold and liabilities were paid, cash of $1,550,000 remained for distribution to stockholders. (a) Assuming that preferred stock is entitled to preference in liquidation of $110 per share, determine the equity per share on July 31 of (1) preferred stock and (2) common stock. (b) Determine the amount of the $1,550,000 that will be distributed for each share of (1) preferred stock and (2) common stock. (c) Explain the reason for the difference between the common stock equity per share on July 31 and the amount of the cash distribution per common share.

Exercise 14–10
Corporate organization; stockholders' equity section.
OBJ. 4, 7

Pryor Products Inc. was organized on February 17 of the current year, with an authorization of 10,000 shares of $11 noncumulative preferred stock, $100 par, and 100,000 shares of $10 par common stock.

The following selected transactions were completed during the first year of operations:

Feb. 17. Issued 25,000 shares of common stock at par for cash.
     17. Issued 750 shares of common stock to an attorney in payment of legal fees for organizing the corporation.
Mar. 4. Issued 30,000 shares of common stock in exchange for land, buildings, and equipment with fair market prices of $75,000, $205,000, and $30,000 respectively.
Aug. 15. Issued 2,000 shares of preferred stock at $106 for cash.

(a) Record the transactions. (b) Prepare the stockholders' equity section of the balance sheet as of December 31, the end of the current year. The net income for the year amounted to $64,000.

PROBLEMS

Problem 14–1A
Dividends on preferred and common stock.
OBJ. 3

The annual dividends declared by C.L. Adler Company during a six-year period are presented in the following table:

Year	Total Dividends	Preferred Dividends		Common Dividends	
		Total	Per Share	Total	Per Share
1987	$ 3,000				
1988	11,000				
1989	28,000				
1990	77,000				
1991	83,000				
1992	8,000				

During the entire period, the outstanding stock of the company was composed of 1,000 shares of cumulative, participating, $9 preferred stock, $100 par, and 10,000 shares of common stock, $50 par. The preferred stock contract provides that the preferred stock shall participate in distributions of additional dividends after allowance of a $5 dividend per share on the common stock, the additional dividends to be prorated among common and preferred shares on the basis of the total par of the stock outstanding.

Instructions:

(1) Determine the total dividends and the per share dividends declared on each class of stock for each of the six years, using the headings presented above. There were no dividends in arrears on January 1, 1987.
(2) Determine the average annual dividend per share for each class of stock for the six-year period.
(3) Assuming that the preferred stock was sold at par and common stock was sold at $62.50 at the beginning of the six-year period, determine the percentage return on initial shareholders' investment, based on the average annual dividend per share (a) for preferred stock and (b) for common stock.

Problem 14–2A

Corporate expansion; stockholders' equity section.

OBJ. 4

The following accounts and their balances appear in the ledger of A and G Inc. on June 30 of the current year:

Preferred $8 Stock, $100 par (10,000 shares authorized, 7,000 shares issued)	$ 700,000
Paid-In Capital in Excess of Par — Preferred Stock	30,000
Common Stock, $20 par (100,000 shares authorized, 75,000 shares issued)	1,500,000
Paid-In Capital in Excess of Par — Common Stock	250,000
Retained Earnings	375,000

At the annual stockholders' meeting on July 2, the board of directors presented a plan for modernizing and expanding plant operations at a cost of approximately $700,000. The plan provided (a) that the corporation borrow $250,000, (b) that 2,000 shares of the unissued preferred stock be issued through an underwriter, and (c) that a building, valued at $190,000, and the land on which it is located, valued at $50,000, be acquired in accordance with preliminary negotiations by the issuance of 10,000 shares of common stock. The plan was approved by the stockholders and accomplished by the following transactions:

July 24. Issued 10,000 shares of common stock in exchange for land and building in accordance with the plan.
30. Issued 2,000 shares of preferred stock, receiving $105 per share in cash from the underwriter.
31. Borrowed $250,000 from First National Bank, giving a 13% mortgage note.

Instructions:

Assuming for the purpose of the problem that no other transactions occurred during July:
(1) Prepare the entries to record the foregoing transactions.
(2) Prepare the stockholders' equity section of the balance sheet as of July 31.

Problem 14–3A
Stock transactions; stockholders' equity section.

OBJ. 4, 5

The following selected accounts appear in the ledger of Lowry Corporation on July 1, the beginning of the current fiscal year:

Preferred Stock Subscriptions Receivable	$ 53,500
Preferred 10% Stock, $50 par (10,000 shares authorized, 5,000 shares issued)	250,000
Preferred Stock Subscribed (4,000 shares)................................	200,000
Paid-In Capital in Excess of Par — Preferred Stock......................	35,000
Common Stock, $20 par (50,000 shares authorized, 25,000 shares issued)...	500,000
Paid-In Capital in Excess of Par — Common Stock......................	90,000
Retained Earnings..	337,000

During the year, the corporation completed a number of transactions affecting the stockholders' equity. They are summarized as follows:

(a) Purchased 1,000 shares of treasury common for $30,000.
(b) Received balance due on preferred stock subscribed and issued the certificates.
(c) Sold 500 shares of treasury common for $16,250.
(d) Issued 2,500 shares of common stock at $35, receiving cash.
(e) Received subscriptions to 1,000 shares of preferred 10% stock at $52.50, collecting 25% of the subscription price.
(f) Sold 250 shares of treasury common for $7,125.

Instructions:

(1) Prepare entries to record the transactions. Identify each entry by letter. (The use of T accounts for stockholders' equity accounts will facilitate the determination of the amounts needed in recording some of the transactions and in completing Instruction (2).)
(2) Prepare the stockholders' equity section of the balance sheet as of June 30, the end of the current fiscal year. The net income for the year was $210,000, and cash dividends declared and paid during the year were $130,000.

Problem 14–4A
Corporation organization; stockholders' equity section.

OBJ. 4, 7

Vineyards Corp. was organized by Ferber, Garr, and Hopper. The charter authorized 100,000 shares of common stock with a par of $10. The following transactions affecting stockholders' equity were completed during the first year of operations:

(a) Issued 10,000 shares of stock at par to Ferber for cash.
(b) Issued 500 shares of stock at par to Garr for promotional services rendered in connection with the organization of the corporation, and issued 7,500 shares of stock at par to Garr for cash.
(c) Purchased land and a building from Hopper. The building is encumbered by a 12%, 15-year mortgage of $100,000, and there is accrued interest of $4,000 on the mortgage note at the time of the purchase. It is agreed that the land is to be priced at $50,000 and the building at $125,000, and that Hopper's equity will be exchanged for stock at par. The corporation agreed to assume responsibility for paying the mortgage note and the accrued interest.
(d) Issued 10,000 shares of stock at $12 to various investors for cash.
(e) Purchased equipment for $75,000. The seller accepted a 6-month, 13% note for $25,000 and 5,000 shares of stock in exchange for the equipment.

Instructions:

(1) Prepare entries to record the transactions.
(2) Prepare the stockholders' equity section of the balance sheet as of the end of the first year of operations. The retained earnings balance is the net income for the year, $90,000, less dividends declared and paid during the year, $1 per share on each share of stock issued.

Problem 14–5A

Stock transactions and corrections; balance sheet.

OBJ. 4, 5, 7

Schultz Company was organized on May 1 of the current year and prepared its first financial statement, a balance sheet, the following December 31, the date that had been adopted as the end of the fiscal year. The balance sheet that was prepared by the accounting clerk is as follows:

Schultz Company
Balance Sheet
May 1 to December 31, 19--

Assets		Liabilities	
Cash......................................	$ 70,100	Accounts payable............	$ 93,000
Accounts receivable...............	190,500	Preferred stock................	200,000
Merchandise inventory............	122,500	Common stock	300,000
Prepaid insurance..................	9,100	Paid-in capital in excess	
Treasury common stock	20,000	of par — common stock..	30,000
Equipment............................	130,000		
Retained earnings (deficit)........	80,800		
Total assets	$623,000	Total liabilities...............	$623,000

You are retained by the board of directors to audit the accounts and to prepare a revised balance sheet. The relevant facts developed during the course of your engagement are:

(a) Stock authorized: 10,000 shares of $50 par, $5 preferred, and 50,000 shares of $20 par common.

(b) Stock issued: 2,000 shares of fully paid preferred at $52.50 and 15,000 shares of common at $22. The premium on preferred stock was credited to Retained Earnings.

(c) Stock subscribed but not issued: 2,000 shares of preferred at par, on which all subscribers have paid one half of the subscription price. Unpaid subscriptions are included in accounts receivable and are collectible in 60 days.

(d) The company reacquired 1,000 shares of the issued common stock at $25. The difference between par and the price paid was debited to Retained Earnings. (It is decided that the treasury stock is to be recorded at cost.)

(e) Included in merchandise inventory is $3,000 of office supplies.

(f) Land to be used as a future building site cost $30,000 and was debited to Equipment.

(g) No depreciation has been recognized. The equipment is to be depreciated for 9 months by the straight-line method, using an estimated life of 10 years.

(h) Organization costs of $6,000 were debited to Advertising Expense. (The organization costs are to be amortized over 60 months beginning with May 1 of the current year.)

(i) No dividends have been declared or paid.

(j) In balancing the common stockholders ledger with the common stock controlling account, it was discovered that the account with Janet Cline contained a posting for an issuance of 500 shares, while the copy of the stock certificate indicated that 5,000 shares had been issued. The stock certificate was found to be correct.

Instructions:

(1) Prepare journal entries where necessary to record the corrections. Corrections of net income should be recorded as adjustments to retained earnings.

(2) Prepare a six-column work sheet, with columns for (a) balances per balance sheet, (b) corrections, and (c) corrected balances. In listing the accounts, leave an extra line blank following the retained earnings account. Complete the work sheet.

(3) Prepare a corrected balance sheet in report form as of the end of the fiscal year.

Problem 14–6A
Equity per share.
OBJ. 6

Selected data from the balance sheets of six corporations, identified by letter, are as follows:

A.	Common stock, $10 par...	$ 250,000
	Paid-in capital in excess of par — common stock	50,000
	Deficit...	25,000

B.	Preferred $5 stock, $50 par..	$1,000,000
	Common stock, $20 par..	3,000,000
	Paid-in capital in excess of par — common stock	260,000
	Retained earnings...	415,000

Preferred stock has prior claim to assets on liquidation to the extent of par.

C.	Preferred $9 stock, $100 par	$1,000,000
	Paid-in capital in excess of par — preferred stock	100,000
	Common stock, no par, 25,000 shares outstanding..............	1,250,000
	Deficit...	350,000

Preferred stock has prior claim to assets on liquidation to the extent of par.

D.	Preferred 11% stock, $50 par	$1,000,000
	Paid-in capital in excess of par — preferred stock	275,000
	Common stock, $25 par...	3,000,000
	Retained earnings...	425,000

Preferred stock has prior claim to assets on liquidation to the extent of 110% of par.

E.	Preferred 9% stock, $100 par	$1,200,000
	Common stock, $50 par..	4,000,000
	Paid-in capital in excess of par — common stock	340,000
	Retained earnings...	108,000

Dividends on preferred stock are in arrears for 2 years, including the dividend passed during the current year. Preferred stock is entitled to par plus unpaid cumulative dividends upon liquidation to the extent of retained earnings.

F.	Preferred $2 stock, $25 par..	$ 500,000
	Common stock, $10 par..	2,000,000
	Deficit...	130,000

Dividends on preferred stock are in arrears for 3 years, including the dividend passed during the current year. Preferred stock is entitled to par plus unpaid cumulative dividends upon liquidation, regardless of the availability of retained earnings.

Instructions:

Determine for each corporation the equity per share of each class of stock, presenting the total shareholders' equity allocated to each class and the number of shares outstanding.

Series B

Problem 14–1B
Dividends on preferred and common stock.
OBJ. 3

The annual dividends declared by Merlin Company during a six-year period are presented in the following table:

	Total	Preferred Dividends		Common Dividends	
Year	Dividends	Total	Per Share	Total	Per Share
1987	$ 72,000				
1988	138,000				
1989	12,000				
1990	5,000				
1991	6,000				
1992	43,000				

During the entire period, the outstanding stock of the company was composed of 1,000 shares of cumulative, participating, $10 preferred stock, $100 par, and 10,000 shares of common stock, $20 par. The preferred stock contract provides that the preferred stock shall participate in distributions of additional dividends after allowance of a $5 dividend per share on the common stock, the additional dividends to be prorated among common and preferred shares on the basis of the total par of the stock outstanding.

Instructions:

(1) Determine the total dividends and the per share dividends declared on each class of stock for each of the six years, using the headings presented above. There were no dividends in arrears on January 1, 1987.
(2) Determine the average annual dividend per share for each class of stock for the six-year period.
(3) Assuming that the preferred stock was sold at par and common stock was sold at $31 at the beginning of the six-year period, determine the percentage return on initial shareholders' investment, based on the average annual dividend per share (a) for preferred stock and (b) for common stock.

Problem 14–3B

Stock transactions; stockholders' equity section.

OBJ. 4, 5

The following selected accounts appear in the ledger of Wayne Corporation on July 1, the beginning of the current fiscal year:

Preferred Stock Subscriptions Receivable	$ 63,750
Preferred $9 Stock, $100 par (20,000 shares authorized, 10,000 shares issued)	1,000,000
Preferred Stock Subscribed (2,500 shares)	250,000
Paid-In Capital in Excess of Par — Preferred Stock	45,000
Common Stock, $10 par (500,000 shares authorized, 300,000 shares issued)	3,000,000
Paid-In Capital in Excess of Par — Common Stock	600,000
Retained Earnings	975,000

During the year, the corporation completed a number of transactions affecting the stockholders' equity. They are summarized as follows:

(a) Received balance due on preferred stock subscribed and issued the certificates.
(b) Purchased 7,500 shares of treasury common for $90,000.
(c) Sold 1,500 shares of treasury common for $22,500.
(d) Received subscriptions to 2,000 shares of preferred $9 stock at $105, collecting 25% of the subscription price.
(e) Issued 50,000 shares of common stock at $15, receiving cash.
(f) Sold 1,000 shares of treasury common for $11,000.

Instructions:

(1) Prepare entries to record the transactions. Identify each entry by letter. (The use of T accounts for the stockholders' equity accounts will facilitate the determination of the amounts needed in recording some of the transactions and in completing Instruction (2).)
(2) Prepare the stockholders' equity section of the balance sheet as of June 30, the end of the current fiscal year. The net income for the year was $600,000, and cash dividends declared and paid during the year were $462,500.

Problem 14–6B

Equity per share.

OBJ. 6

Selected data from the balance sheets of six corporations, identified by letter, are as follows:

A. Common stock, no par, 100,000 shares outstanding	$ 900,000
Deficit	70,000

B. Preferred $2 stock, $25 par .... $ 500,000
    Common stock, $10 par   2,000,000
    Paid-in capital in excess of par — common stock   75,000
    Retained earnings   525,000

    Preferred stock has prior claim to assets on liquidation to the extent of par.

C. Preferred $12 stock, $100 par .... $ 750,000
    Paid-in capital in excess of par — preferred stock   40,000
    Common stock, $5 par   1,000,000
    Paid-in capital in excess of par — common stock   55,000
    Deficit   95,000

    Preferred stock has prior claim to assets on liquidation to the extent of par.

D. Preferred 10% stock, $100 par .... $ 750,000
    Paid-in capital in excess of par — preferred stock   100,000
    Common stock, $20 par   2,500,000
    Deficit   75,000

    Preferred stock has prior claim to assets on liquidation to the extent of 110% of par.

E. Preferred 11% stock, $100 par .... $ 800,000
    Common stock, $5 par   2,000,000
    Paid-in capital in excess of par — common stock   240,000
    Retained earnings   104,000

    Dividends on preferred stock are in arrears for 2 years, including the dividend passed during the current year. Preferred stock is entitled to par plus unpaid cumulative dividends upon liquidation to the extent of retained earnings.

F. Preferred $2 stock, $25 par .... $ 500,000
    Paid-in capital in excess of par — preferred stock   15,000
    Common stock, $10 par   1,500,000
    Deficit   75,000

    Dividends on preferred stock are in arrears for 3 years, including the dividend passed during the current year. Preferred stock is entitled to par plus unpaid cumulative dividends upon liquidation, regardless of the availability of retained earnings.

Instructions:

Determine for each corporation the equity per share of each class of stock, presenting the total stockholders' equity allocated to each class and the number of shares outstanding.

MINI-CASE 14

Miami Valley Cooperative Electric Corporation needs $5,000,000 to finance a major plant expansion. To raise the $5,000,000, the chairman of the board of directors suggested that the cooperative first offer common stock for sale at a price equal to the January 1, 1991 equity per share of common stock. The chairman indicated that by setting the price in this way, the value of the current common stockholders' interest in the cooperative would be preserved. Any additional funds that might be needed after this offer expired could be obtained from the issuance of preferred stock.

Since no preferred stock is authorized, the board is considering characteristics of the stock, such as the dividend rate and the cumulative and participating features. So as not to jeopardize common stockholder dividends, the board of directors tentatively approved a dividend rate of 4% for the preferred stock. The board agreed to delay any final action on other aspects of the financing plan until the legal counsel can be contacted to determine the procedures necessary to seek authorization of the preferred stock.

As of January 1, 1991, the stockholders' equity is as follows:

Paid-in capital:

Common stock, $20 par (500,000 shares authorized,
   300,000 shares issued) $6,000,000
Excess of issue price over par   450,000

Total paid-in capital $6,450,000
Retained earnings   1,650,000
Total stockholders' equity $8,100,000

Instructions:

(1) Determine the equity per share of common stock on January 1, 1991.
(2) During the board meeting, the chairman asked for your opinion of the suggestion for determining the selling price of the common stock. How would you respond?
(3) What characteristics might you suggest the board consider in designing the preferred stock? Comment on the low preferred stock dividend rate tentatively approved by the board.

ETHICS DISCUSSION CASE

Miguel Gallardo and Joseph Keker are organizing Mines Unlimited Inc. to undertake a high-risk gold mining venture in Mexico. Gallardo and Keker tentatively plan to request authorization for 100,000,000 shares of common stock to be sold to the general public. Gallardo and Keker have decided to establish a par value of $.10 per share in order to appeal to a wide variety of potential investors. Gallardo and Keker felt that investors would be more willing to invest in the company if they received a large quantity of shares for what might appear to be a "bargain" price.

Discuss whether Gallardo and Keker are behaving in an ethical manner.

ANSWERS TO SELF-EXAMINATION QUESTIONS

1. D The owners' equity in a corporation is commonly called stockholders' equity (answer A), shareholders' investment (answer B), capital (answer C), or shareholders' equity.

2. C If a corporation has cumulative preferred stock outstanding, dividends that have been passed for prior years plus the dividend for the current year must be paid before dividends may be declared on common stock. In this case, dividends of $27,000 ($9,000 × 3) have been passed for the preceding three years and the current year's dividends are $9,000, making a total of $36,000 (answer C) that must be paid to preferred stockholders before dividends can be declared on common stock.

3. D The stockholders' equity section of corporate balance sheets is divided into two principal subsections: (1) investments contributed by the stockholders and (2) net income retained in the business. Included as part of the investments by stockholders is the par of common stock (answer A); the par of stock subscribed (answer B); and the par of preferred stock (answer C).

4. C Reacquired stock, known as treasury stock, should be listed in the stockholders' equity section (answer C) of the balance sheet. The price paid for the treasury stock is deducted from the total of all of the stockholders' equity accounts.

5. B The total stockholders' equity is determined as follows:

Preferred stock	$1,000,000
Common stock	2,000,000
Excess of issue price over par—common stock	100,000
Retained earnings	540,000
Total equity	$3,640,000

The amount allocated to common stock is determined as follows:

Total equity		$3,640,000
Allocated to preferred stock:		
Liquidation price	$1,100,000	
Dividends in arrears	240,000	1,340,000
Allocated to common stock		$2,300,000

The equity per common share is determined as follows:

$$\$2,300,000 \div 100,000 \text{ shares} = \$23 \text{ per share}$$

Financial Reporting for Corporations

PART FIVE

5

CHAPTER FIFTEEN

STOCKHOLDERS' EQUITY, EARNINGS, AND DIVIDENDS

CHAPTER OBJECTIVES

1 Identify and illustrate alternative terminology used in the paid-in capital section of the balance sheet.

2 Describe and illustrate the accounting for corporate earnings and income taxes.

3 Describe and illustrate the allocation of income tax between periods.

4 Describe and illustrate the accounting for unusual items in the financial statements.

5 Describe and illustrate the computation of earnings per share.

6 Describe and illustrate the accounting for appropriations of retained earnings and the preparation of a retained earnings statement.

7 Describe and illustrate the accounting for dividends, including cash dividends, stock dividends, and liquidating dividends.

8 Describe and illustrate the accounting for stock splits.

9 Describe the accounting for dividends and stock splits for treasury stock.

As has been indicated, the stockholders' equity section of the balance sheet is divided into two major subdivisions, *paid-in capital* (or contributed capital) and *retained earnings*. Although in practice there is wide variation in the amount of detail presented and the descriptive captions used, sources of significant amounts of stockholders' equity should be properly disclosed.

The emphasis on disclosure and clarity of expression by the accounting profession has been relatively recent. In earlier days, it was not unusual to present for stockholders' equity only the amount of the par of the preferred and common stock outstanding and a balancing amount described simply as "Surplus." Readers of the balance sheet could only assume that par represented the amount paid in by stockholders and that surplus represented retained earnings. Although it was possible for a "surplus" of $1,000,000, for example, to be composed solely of retained earnings, it could represent paid-in capital from premiums on stock issued or even an excess of $1,200,000 of such premiums over an accumulated deficit of $200,000 of retained earnings.

PAID-IN CAPITAL

OBJECTIVE 1
Identify and illustrate alternative terminology used in the paid-in capital section of the balance sheet.

As illustrated in Chapter 14, the main credits to paid-in capital accounts result from the issuance of stock. If par stock is issued at a price above or below par, the difference is recorded in a separate paid-in capital account. It is also common to use two accounts in recording the issuance of no-par stock: one for the stated value and the other for the excess over stated value.

Another account for paid-in capital discussed in the preceding chapter was Paid-In Capital from Sale of Treasury Stock.

Paid-in capital may also originate from donated real estate and redemptions of a corporation's own stock. Civic organizations sometimes give land or land and buildings to a corporate enterprise as an inducement to locate in the community. In such cases, the assets are recorded in the corporate accounts at fair market value, with a credit to Donated Capital. Preferred stock contracts may give to the issuing corporation the right to redeem the stock at varying redemption prices at varying future dates. If the redemption price paid to the stockholder is greater than the original issuance price, the excess is considered to be a distribution of retained earnings. On the other hand, if the amount paid is less than the amount originally received by the corporation, the difference is a retention of capital and should be credited to Paid-In Capital from Preferred Stock Redemption or a similarly titled account.

As with other sections of the balance sheet, there are many variations in terminology and arrangement of the paid-in capital section. Some of these variations are illustrated by the following three examples. The details of each class of stock, including related stock premium or discount, are commonly listed first, followed by the other paid-in capital accounts. Instead of describing the source of each amount in excess of par or stated value, a common practice is to combine all such accounts into a single amount. It is then listed below the capital stock accounts and described as "Additional paid-in capital," "Capital in excess of par (or stated value) of shares," or by a similarly descriptive phrase.

Stockholders' Equity

Paid-in capital:			
Common stock, $20 par (50,000 shares authorized, 45,000 shares issued)	$900,000		
Excess of issue price over par	132,000	$1,032,000	
From stock redemption		60,000	
From sale of treasury stock		25,000	
Total paid-in capital			$1,117,000

Shareholders' Equity

Paid-in capital:			
Common stock, $20 par (50,000 shares authorized, 45,000 shares issued)		$ 900,000	
Premium on common stock	$132,000		
From redemption of common stock	60,000		
From transactions in own stock	25,000	217,000	
Total paid-in capital			$1,117,000

Shareholders' Investment

Contributed capital:		
Common stock, $20 par (50,000 shares authorized, 45,000 shares issued)	$ 900,000	
Additional paid-in capital	217,000	
Total contributed capital		$1,117,000

Significant changes in paid-in capital during the period should also be disclosed. The details of these changes may be presented either in a separate paid-in capital statement or in notes to other financial statements.

CORPORATE EARNINGS AND INCOME TAXES

OBJECTIVE 2
Describe and illustrate the accounting for corporate earnings and income taxes.

The determination of the net income or net loss of a corporation is comparable, in most respects, to that of other forms of business organization. Unlike sole proprietorships and partnerships, however, corporations are distinct legal entities. In general, they are subject to the federal income tax and, in many cases, to income taxes levied by states or other political subdivisions. Although the discussion that follows is limited to the income tax levied by the federal government, the basic concepts apply also to state and local income taxes.

For several years, most corporations have been required to estimate the amount of their federal income tax expense for the year and to make advance payments, usually in four installments. To illustrate, assume that a calendar-year corporation estimates its income tax expense for the year to be $84,000. The required entry for each of the four payments of $21,000 (1/4 of $84,000) would be as follows:

Income Tax..	21,000	
Cash..		21,000

At year end, the actual taxable income and the actual tax are determined. If an additional amount is owed, this liability must be recorded. Continuing with the illustration, assume that the corporation's actual tax, based on actual taxable income, is $86,000 instead of $84,000. The following entry would be required in order to include the income tax expense in the fiscal year in which the related income was earned:

Dec. 31	Income Tax	2,000	
	Income Tax Payable............................		2,000

If the amount of the advance payments exceeds the tax liability based on actual income, the amount of the overpayment would be debited to a receivable account and credited to Income Tax.

Income tax returns and related records and documents are subject to review by the taxing authority, usually for a period of three years after the return is filed. Consequently, the determination made by the taxpayer is provisional rather than final. In recognition of the possibility of an assessment for a tax deficiency, the liability for income taxes is sometimes described in the current liability section of the balance sheet as "Estimated income tax payable."

Because of its substantial size in relationship to net income, income tax is often reported on the income statement as a special deduction, as follows:

Palmer Corporation Income Statement For Year Ended December 31, 19--	
Sales	$980,000
Income before income tax.......................................	$200,000
Income tax...	82,500
Net income	$117,500

ALLOCATION OF INCOME TAX BETWEEN PERIODS

OBJECTIVE 3
Describe and illustrate the allocation of income tax between periods.

The **taxable income** of a corporation, determined according to the tax laws, is often different from the amount of income (before income tax) reported in the income statement. As a result, the amount of income tax payable based upon a corporation's income tax return may differ from the amount of income tax reported in the income statement. This difference may need to be allocated between periods, depending upon the nature of the items causing the differences.

Some items create differences between income before income tax and taxable income because the items are recognized in one period for income statement purposes and in another period for tax purposes. Such differences, called **temporary differences,** reverse or turn around in later years. Some examples of items which create temporary differences are described as follows:[1]

1. Revenues or gains that are taxable after they are reported in the income statement. Example: The point of sale method is used for reporting purposes and the installment method of determining revenue is used in determining taxable income.
2. Expenses or losses that are deducted in determining taxable income after they are reported in the income statement. Example: Product warranty expense estimated and reported in the year of the sale for reporting purposes, but is only deductible for tax purposes when paid.
3. Revenues or gains that are taxable before they are reported in the income statement. Example: Cash received in advance for magazine subscriptions is included in taxable income of the current period when received, but included in the income statement of a future period when earned.
4. Expenses or losses that are deducted in determining taxable income before they are reported in the income statement. Example: An accelerated depreciation method is used for tax purposes, and the straight-line method is used for financial reporting purposes.

Temporary differences require that the amount of the tax liability be computed at the end of each year and that the proper amount of current and postponed (deferred) liability be recognized. To illustrate the effect of temporary differences and their related effect on the amount of income tax reported in corporate financial statements, assume that a corporation that sells

---

[1]*Statement of Financial Accounting Standards No. 96,* "Accounting for Income Taxes" (Stamford: Financial Accounting Standards Board, 1987), par. 10.

its product on the installment basis recognizes the revenue at the time of sale and maintains its accounts accordingly. At the end of the first year of operations, the income before income tax according to the ledger is $300,000. Realizing the advantage of reducing current income tax, the corporation elects the installment method of determining revenue and cost of merchandise sold, which yields taxable income of only $100,000. Assuming an income tax rate of 40%, the income tax on $300,000 of income would amount to $120,000.[2] The income tax actually due for the year would only be $40,000 (40% of $100,000). The $80,000 difference between the two amounts is due to the timing difference in recognizing revenue. It represents a deferment of $80,000 of income tax to future years. As the installment accounts receivable are collected in later years, the additional $200,000 of income will be included in the taxable income, and the $80,000 deferment (40% of $200,000) will become a tax liability of those years.[3] The situation may be summarized as follows:

Income deferred to future years...	$200,000
Income tax deferred to future years (40% × $200,000).................	$ 80,000

In this example, the proof of the $80,000 deferred tax credit is shown in the following computation:

Income tax based on $300,000 reported income at 40%	$120,000
Income tax based on $100,000 taxable income at 40%	40,000
Income tax deferred to future years...	$ 80,000

The income tax to be reported on the income statement should be the total tax ($120,000 in the illustration) expected to result from the net income of the year. In this manner, the revenue reported on the income statement will be matched with the expenses (including income tax) related to that revenue, regardless of when the tax will become an actual liability to be paid. Applying the concept of the allocation of income tax between periods to the illustrative data yields the following results, stated in terms of a journal entry:

Income Tax...	120,000	
Income Tax Payable...		40,000
Deferred Income Tax Payable..............................		80,000

Continuing with the illustration, the $80,000 in Deferred Income Tax Payable will be transferred to Income Tax Payable as the remaining $200,000 of income becomes taxable in later years. If, for example, $120,000 of untaxed income of the first year of the corporation's operations becomes taxable in the second year, the effect would be as follows, stated as a journal entry:

Deferred Income Tax Payable..................................	48,000	
Income Tax Payable...		48,000

[2]For purposes of illustration, the 40% tax rate is assumed to include all federal, state, and local income taxes.

[3]If the tax rates change, companies are required to recompute their tax liabilities and to recognize the effect of the change in net income. This topic is discussed in more detail in advanced texts.

In the illustration, the amount in Deferred Income Tax Payable at the end of a year will be reported as a liability. The amount due within one year will be classified as a current liability, and the remainder will be classified as a long-term liability or reported in a Deferred Credits section following the Long-Term Liabilities section.[4]

During periods of growth, the amount of deferred income taxes for an enterprise may increase rapidly and can become a significant amount. The amounts of deferred income taxes listed as long-term liabilities on the 1988 annual reports of nine major companies were as follows:

Walgreen Co.	$119,466,000
The Pillsbury Co.	221,600,000
Circus Circus Enterprises, Inc.	39,529,000
Tandy Corporation	68,977,000
The Quaker Oats Company	250,600,000
Toys "R" Us, Inc.	53,356,000
H. J. Heinz Company	262,331,000
Super Valu Stores, Inc.	35,001,000
Delta Air Lines, Inc.	539,908,000

Differences between taxable income and income (before tax) reported on the income statement may also arise because certain revenues are exempt from tax and certain expenses are not deductible in determining taxable income.[5] For example, interest income on municipal bonds may be exempt from taxation. Such differences create no special financial reporting problems, since the amount of income tax determined in accordance with the tax laws is the amount reported on the income statement.

ARE DEFERRED TAXES REALLY A LIABILITY?

For those companies that show a significant amount of deferred taxes on their balance sheets, the question that may arise is whether such amounts are really liabilities. For example, the reporting of a liability for "deferred income taxes, $267.7 million," on an Anheuser-Busch balance sheet was discussed in *Forbes*. In this article, excerpts from which follow, it was noted that Anheuser-Busch's deferred tax liability was equal to 19% of the total liabilities and 26% of the stockholders' equity.

... Says Harvey D. Moskowitz, national director of accounting and auditing for Seidman & Seidman, "The deferred taxes on the balance sheet bear no relationship to what is actually going to be owed. So the current method of income tax accounting makes it impossible for the investor to evaluate a company's liquidity, solvency or cash flow."

Here's the explanation for this curious state of affairs: Anheuser-Busch had pretax income of $271.5 million, so, using standard corporate tax rates (less credits), it owed $99.7 million to Uncle Sam. That's what it set aside as "provision for in-

[4]In some cases, a deferred tax asset may arise for tax benefits to be received in the future. Such deferred tax assets would be reported as either a current or long-term asset, depending upon when the expected benefits are expected to be realized.

[5]Such differences, which will not reverse with the passage of time, are sometimes referred to as permanent differences.

come taxes" on its income statement. But it's not what the company actually paid. Like most businesses Anheuser keeps two sets of books, one for tax purposes, one for stock owners. It uses accelerated depreciation for taxes but straight line for reporting to investors.... So, out-of-pocket, it really had to pay only $31.9 million in taxes ... the line marked "current" on the income statement. The other $67.8 million, called "deferred," represents cash that's squirreled away in liabilities on the balance sheet, under the assumption that the company will pay those taxes eventually—when accelerated depreciation runs out, for example.

That assumption is probably wrong, though. As long as the company keeps growing—in real terms or because of inflation—it will keep adding new assets and new interest costs to replace the ones that are running out. That means those deferred taxes, instead of getting paid, will simply roll over. And over and over and over. It could almost make you dizzy.

Source: Jane Carmichael, "Rollover," *Forbes* (January 18, 1982), pp. 75, 78.

REPORTING UNUSUAL ITEMS IN THE FINANCIAL STATEMENTS

OBJECTIVE 4
Describe and illustrate the accounting for unusual items in the financial statements.

Professional accounting organizations have devoted much time to the development of guidelines for reporting unusual items in the financial statements. Generally, unusual items affect the determination of either current or prior year's net income. Accordingly, these items may be described as (1) items that affect the current year's net income and are therefore reported on the current year's income statement and (2) items that affect a prior year's net income and are therefore reported on the current year's retained earnings statement. Each of these types of unusual items are described and illustrated in the following paragraphs.

Unusual Items that Affect the Income Statement

In preparing the income statement, a company's records may show three well-defined categories of unusual items which should be presented separately from other items. These categories, which are briefly described and illustrated in the following paragraphs, are as follows:

1. The results of discontinued operations.
2. Extraordinary items of gain or loss.
3. A change from one generally accepted accounting principle to another.

Discontinued Operations. A gain or loss resulting from the disposal of a segment of a business should be identified on the income statement as a gain or loss from **discontinued operations**. The term *discontinued* refers to "the operations of a segment of a business ... that has been sold, abandoned, spun off, or otherwise disposed of or ... is the subject of a formal plan for disposal."[6] The term "segment of a business" refers to a part of an enterprise whose activities represent a major line of business, such as a division or department or a certain class of customer.[7] For example, if an enterprise owning newspapers, television stations, and radio stations were to sell its radio stations, the results of the sale would be reported as a gain or loss on discontinued operations.

[6]*Opinions of the Accounting Principles Board, No. 30*, "Reporting the Results of Operations" (New York: American Institute of Certified Public Accountants, 1973), par. 8.

[7]*Ibid.*, par. 13.

When an enterprise discontinues a segment of its operations and identifies the gain or loss therefrom, the results of "continuing operations" should also be identified in the income statement. The net income or loss from continuing operations is presented first, beginning with sales and followed by the enterprise's customary analysis of its costs and expenses. In addition to the data on discontinued operations presented in the body of the statement, such details as the identity of the segment disposed of, the disposal date, a description of the assets and liabilities involved, and the manner of disposal should be disclosed in a note to the financial statements.[8]

Extraordinary Items. Extraordinary gains and losses result from "events and transactions that are distinguished by their unusual nature *and* by the infrequency of their occurrence."[9] Such gains and losses, other than those from the disposal of a segment of a business, should be identified in the income statement as **extraordinary items**. To be so classified, an event or transaction must meet both of the following criteria:

1. Unusual nature—*the underlying event or transaction should possess a high degree of abnormality and be of a type clearly unrelated to, or only incidentally related to, the ordinary and typical activities of the entity, taking into account the environment in which the entity operates.*
2. Infrequency of occurrence—*the underlying event or transaction should be of a type that would not reasonably be expected to recur in the foreseeable future, taking into account the environment in which the entity operates.*[10]

Transactions that meet both of the criteria are uncommon. For example, the 1988 edition of *Accounting Trends & Techniques* indicated that only 127 of the 600 industrial and merchandising companies surveyed reported extraordinary items on their income statements. Usually, extraordinary items result from major casualties, such as floods, earthquakes, and other rare catastrophes not expected to recur. In addition, gains or losses that result when land or buildings are condemned for public use are considered extraordinary.

Occasionally, extraordinary events create unusual reporting in the financial statements. For example, in its 1989 income statement, Delta Air Lines reported an extraordinary gain of over $5.5 million as the result of the crash of a 727 earlier in the fiscal year. The plane that crashed was insured for $6.5 million, but its book value in Delta's accounting records was $962,000.

Gains and losses on the disposal of plant assets do not qualify as extraordinary items because (1) they are not unusual and (2) they recur from time to time in the ordinary course of business activities. Similarly, gains and losses incurred on the sale of investments are usual and recurring for most enterprises. However, if a company had owned only one investment during its entire existence, a gain or loss on its sale might qualify as an extraordinary item, provided there was no intention of acquiring other investments in the foreseeable future.

Changes in Accounting Principles. A change in accounting principle "results from adoption of a generally accepted accounting principle different from the one used previously for reporting purposes."[11] The concept of con-

---

[8]*Ibid.*, par. 18.

[9]*Ibid.*, par. 20.

[10]*Ibid.*

[11]*Opinions of the Accounting Principles Board*, No. 20, "Accounting Changes" (New York: American Institute of Certified Public Accountants, 1971), par. 7.

sistency and its relationship to changes in accounting methods were discussed in Chapter 12. A change from one generally accepted accounting principle or method to another generally accepted principle or method should be disclosed in the financial statements of the period in which the change is made. In addition to describing the nature of the change, the justification for the change should be stated and the effect of the change on net income should be disclosed.

The generally accepted procedures for disclosing the effect on net income of a change in principle are as follows: (1) report the cumulative effect of the change on net income of prior periods as a special item on the income statement and (2) report the effect of the change on net income of the current period. If the financial statements for prior periods are presented in conjunction with the current statements, the effect of the change in accounting principle should also be applied retroactively to the published statements of the prior periods and reported either on their face or in accompanying notes.

The amount of the cumulative effect on net income of prior periods should be reported in a special section of the income statement located immediately prior to the net income. If an extraordinary item or items are reported on the statement, the amount related to the change in principle should follow the extraordinary items.

The procedures should be modified for a change from the last-in, first-out assumption for inventory costing to another method or for a change in the method of accounting for long-term construction contracts. For these changes in principle, the cumulative effect on prior years' income is not reported as a special item on the income statement. Instead, the newly adopted principle should be applied retroactively to the income statements of the prior periods and the effect on income disclosed, either on the face of the statements or in accompanying notes. Financial statements of subsequent periods need not repeat the disclosures.[12]

Allocation of Income Tax to Unusual Items. The amount reported as a gain or loss from a discontinued operation, an extraordinary item, or the cumulative effect of a change in accounting principle should be net of the related income tax. The amount of income tax allocable to each of these items may be disclosed on the face of the appropriate financial statement or by an accompanying note.

Presentation of Unusual Items in the Income Statement. The manner in which gains or losses from discontinued operations, extraordinary items, and the cumulative effect of a change in accounting principle may be presented in the income statement is illustrated for Jones Corporation on page 577. Many variations in terminology and format are possible.

Unusual Items that Affect the Retained Earnings Statement

Most accountants agree that it is preferable to report all revenue and expense items occurring in the current period in the current year's income statement. Unusual or nonrecurring items, such as those described in the preceding paragraphs, are also identified and disclosed in the income statement. If nonrecurring items were "buried" in the retained earnings state-

---

[12]*Ibid.*, pars. 27 and 28.

Jones Corporation
Income Statement
For the Year Ended August 31, 19--

Net sales...	$9,600,950

Income from continuing operations before income tax.................	$1,310,000
Income tax..	620,000
Income from continuing operations...	$ 690,000
Loss on discontinued operations (Note A)..............................	100,000
Income before extraordinary item and cumulative effect of a change in accounting principle..	$ 590,000
Extraordinary item:	
Gain on condemnation of land, net of applicable income tax of $65,000	150,000
Cumulative effect on prior years of changing to a different depreciation method (Note B)...	92,000
Net income	$ 832,000

Note A. On July 1 of the current year, the entire electrical products division of the corporation was sold at a loss of $100,000, net of applicable income tax of $50,000. The net sales of the division for the current year were $2,900,000. The assets sold were composed of inventories, equipment, and plant totaling $2,100,000, and the liabilities assumed by the purchaser amounted to $600,000.

Note B. Depreciation of property, plant, and equipment has been computed by the straight-line method at all manufacturing facilities in 19--. Prior to 19--, depreciation of equipment for one of the divisions had been computed on the double-declining balance method. In 19--, the straight-line method was adopted for this division in order to achieve uniformity and to more appropriately match the remaining depreciation charges with the estimated economic utility of such assets. Pursuant to APB Opinion 20, this change in depreciation has been applied retroactively to prior years. The effect of the change was to increase income before extraordinary items for 19-- by approximately $30,000. The adjustment of $92,000 (after reduction for income tax of $88,000) to apply retroactively the new method is also included in income for 19--.

ment, they would likely be overlooked by financial statement readers. In addition, if they were included in the retained earnings statement, the total amount of the periodic net income reported over the entire life of an enterprise could not be determined from its income statements. An exception, however, is made for errors discovered in the determination of a prior period's net income.

Material errors may result from mathematical mistakes and from mistakes in the application of accounting principles or oversight or misuse of facts that existed at the time transactions were recorded. The effect of material errors that are not discovered within the same fiscal period in which they occurred should not be included in the determination of net income for the current period.[13] Corrections of this type of error, usually called **prior period adjustments**, should be reported as an adjustment of the retained earnings balance at the beginning of the period in which the correction is made.[14] Prior period adjustments would include, for example, the correction of a material error in computing depreciation expense for a prior period. In addition, a change from an unacceptable accounting principle to an acceptable accounting principle is considered to be a correction of a material error and should be treated as a prior period adjustment. An example of such a situation would be the correction resulting from changing from the cash basis to the accrual basis of accounting for a business enterprise that buys and sells merchandise.

Prior period adjustments should be distinguished from differences arising from the use of estimates. The use of estimates is inherent in the accounting process. For example, income taxes and uncollectible accounts receivable must be estimated for the timely preparation of financial statements. As a consequence, differences between the estimated and actual amounts may arise. These differences are normally minor in amount. They are not considered errors or prior period adjustments, but are included in the determination of the current period's net income.

The manner in which a prior period adjustment is presented in the retained earnings statement is illustrated as follows:

Casper Company Retained Earnings Statement For Year Ended December 31, 1990		
Retained earnings, January 1, 1990............................		$310,500
Less prior period adjustment:		
Correction of error in depreciation expense in 1989, net of applicable income tax of $13,000		29,200
Corrected retained earnings, January 1, 1990...............		$281,300
Net income for year..	$77,350	
Less dividends..	40,000	
Increase in retained earnings		37,350
Retained earnings, December 31, 1990......................		$318,650

Note that the amount reported as a prior period adjustment is reported net of the related income tax. In addition, if financial statements are presented only for the current period, the effect of the adjustment on the net income of the preceding period should also be disclosed. If financial statements for prior periods are presented, as is preferable, the statements should be adjusted and the amount of each adjustment should be disclosed.

Adjustments applicable to prior periods that meet the criteria for a prior period adjustment are rare in modern financial accounting. Annual audits by independent public accountants, combined with the internal control features of accounting systems, lessen the chances of errors justifying such treatment.

---

[13]Corrections of errors that are discovered in the same period in which they occur were discussed in Chapter 5.

[14]*Statement of Financial Accounting Standards*, No. 16, "Prior Period Adjustments" (Stamford: Financial Accounting Standards Board, 1977), par. 11.

EARNINGS PER COMMON SHARE

OBJECTIVE 5
Describe and
illustrate the
computation of
earnings per share.

The absolute amounts of net income are often useful in evaluating a company's profitability. However, these absolute amounts are difficult to use in comparing companies of different sizes. For example, a net income of $750,000 may be very satisfactory for a small computer manufacturer, but it may be very unsatisfactory for a very large computer manufacturer. Likewise, the absolute amount of net income is difficult to use in evaluating a company's profitability when the amount of stockholders' equity changes significantly. In such cases, the profitability of a company may be expressed as earnings per share. The term **earnings per share** refers to the net income per share of common stock outstanding during a given period. For public corporations, data on earnings per share of common stock must be reported on the income statement.[15] Earnings per share is often the item of greatest interest contained in corporate financial statements. These data are also often reported by the financial press and by various statistical services.

If a company has only common stock outstanding, the earnings per share of common stock is determined by dividing net income by the number of common shares outstanding. If preferred stock is outstanding, the net income must be reduced by the amount of any preferred dividend requirements before dividing by the number of common shares outstanding.

The effect of nonrecurring additions to or deductions from income of a period should be considered in computing earnings per share. Otherwise, a single per share amount based on net income would be misleading. To illustrate this point, assume that Jones Corporation, whose partial income statement for the current year was presented on page 577, reported net income of $700,000 for the preceding year, with no extraordinary or other special items. Assume also that the corporation's capital stock was composed of 200,000 common shares outstanding during the entire two-year period. If the earnings per share of $3.50 ($700,000 ÷ 200,000) for the preceding year were compared with the earnings per share of $4.16 ($832,000 ÷ 200,000) for the current year, it would appear that operations had greatly improved. However, the current year's per share amount that is comparable to $3.50 is in reality $3.45 ($690,000 ÷ 200,000), which indicates a slight downward trend in normal operations.

Data on earnings per share should be presented in conjunction with the income statement. If there are nonrecurring items on the statement, the per share amounts should be presented for (1) income from continuing operations, (2) income before extraordinary items and the cumulative effect of a change in accounting principle, (3) the cumulative effect of a change in accounting principle, and (4) net income.[16] Presentation of per share amounts is optional for the gain or loss on discontinued operations and for extraordinary items. The per share data may be shown in parentheses or added at the bottom of the statement, as in the following illustration for Jones Corporation:

[15]Nonpublic corporations are exempt from this requirement, according to *Statement of Financial Accounting Standards, No. 21*, "Suspension of the Reporting of Earnings per Share and Segment Information by Nonpublic Enterprises" (Stamford: Financial Accounting Standards Board, 1978).

[16]*Opinions of the Accounting Principles Board, No. 15*, "Earnings per Share" (New York: American Institute of Certified Public Accountants, 1969) as amended by *Opinions of the Accounting Principles Board, No. 20*, and *Opinions of the Accounting Principles Board, No. 30*.

Jones Corporation
Income Statement
For the Year Ended August 31, 19--

Income from continuing operations...	$690,000

Net income...	$832,000
Earnings per common share:	
Income from continuing operations.....................................	$3.45
Loss on discontinued operations......................................	.50
Income before extraordinary item and cumulative effect of a	
change in accounting principle.......................................	$2.95
Extraordinary item...	.75
Cumulative effect on prior years of changing to a different	
depreciation method..	.46
Net income..	$4.16

In computing the earnings per share of common stock, all factors that affect the number of common shares outstanding must be considered. If there is an issue of preferred stock or bonds (debt) with the privilege of converting to common stock, two different amounts of per share earnings should ordinarily be reported. One amount is computed without regard to the conversion privilege and is referred to as "Earnings per common share — assuming no dilution" or "Primary earnings per share." The other computation is based on the assumption that the convertible preferred stock or bonds are converted to common stock, and the amount is referred to as "Earnings per common share — assuming full dilution" or "Fully diluted earnings per share."[17]

The details of the computation of earnings per share should be disclosed in notes to the financial statements, as indicated by the following note adapted from the 1988 statements of The Pillsbury Company:

> *Net earnings per share are computed using the weighted average number of common shares, including common share equivalents of stock options, outstanding during each year. Net earnings per share assuming full dilution would be substantially the same.*

The complexities of the computation of earnings per share and other complexities of capital structure are discussed in more advanced accounting texts.

---

[17]*Opinions of the Accounting Principles Board, No. 15,* "Earnings per Share" (New York: American Institute of Certified Public Accountants, 1969) par. 16.

APPROPRIATION OF RETAINED EARNINGS

OBJECTIVE 6
Describe and illustrate the accounting for appropriations of retained earnings and the preparation of a retained earnings statement.

The amount of a corporation's retained earnings available for distribution to its shareholders may be limited by action of the board of directors. The amount restricted, which is called an **appropriation** or a **reserve**, remains a part of retained earnings and should be so classified in the financial statements. An appropriation can be effected by transferring the desired amount from Retained Earnings to a special account designating its purpose, such as Appropriation for Plant Expansion.

Appropriations may be initiated by the directors, or they may be required by law or contract. Some states require that a corporation retain earnings equal to the amount paid for treasury stock. For example, if a corporation with accumulated earnings of $200,000 purchases shares of its own issued stock for $50,000, the corporation would not be permitted to pay more than $150,000 in dividends. The restriction is equal to the $50,000 paid for the treasury stock and assures that legal capital will not be impaired by a declaration of dividends. The entry to record the appropriation would be as follows:

Apr. 24	Retained Earnings	50,000	
	Appropriation for Treasury Stock		50,000

When a part or all of an appropriation is no longer needed, the amount should be transferred back to the retained earnings account. Thus, if the corporation in the above illustration sells the treasury stock, the appropriation would be eliminated by the following entry:

Nov. 10	Appropriation for Treasury Stock	50,000	
	Retained Earnings		50,000

When a corporation borrows a large amount through the issuance of bonds (debt), the agreement may provide for restrictions on dividends until the debt is paid. The contract may stipulate that retained earnings equal to the amount borrowed be restricted during the entire period of the loan, or it may require that the restriction be built up by annual appropriations. For example, assume that a corporation borrows $700,000 on ten-year bonds. If equal annual appropriations were to be made over the life of the bonds, there would be a series of ten entries, each in the amount of $70,000, debiting Retained Earnings and crediting an appropriation account entitled Appropriation for Bonded Indebtedness. Even if the bond agreement did not require the restriction on retained earnings, the directors might decide to establish the appropriation. In that case, it would be a *discretionary* rather than a *contractual* appropriation. The entries would be the same in either case.

It must be clearly understood that the appropriation account is not directly related to any certain group of asset accounts. Its existence does not imply that there is an equivalent amount of cash or other assets set aside in a special fund. The appropriation serves the purpose of restricting dividends, but it does not assure that the cash that might otherwise be distributed as dividends will not be invested in additional inventories or other assets, or used to reduce liabilities.

Appropriations of retained earnings may be accompanied by a segregation of cash or marketable securities, in which case the appropriation is said to be **funded**. Accumulation of such funds is discussed in Chapter 16.

There are other purposes for which the directors may consider appropriations desirable. A company may earmark earnings for specific contingencies, such as inventory price declines or an adverse decision on a pending lawsuit. Some companies with properties in many locations may assume their own risk of losses from fire, windstorm, and other casualties rather than obtain protection from insurance companies. In such cases, the appropriation account would be entitled Appropriation for Self-Insurance. Such an appropriation is likely to be permanent, although its amount may vary as the total value of properties and the extent of casualty protection change. If a loss occurs, it should be debited to a special loss account rather than to the appropriation account. It is definitely a loss of the particular period and should be reported in the income statement.

The details of retained earnings may be presented in the balance sheet in the following manner. The item designated "Unappropriated" is the balance of the retained earnings account.

Retained earnings:
  Appropriated:
    For plant expansion..................................... $ 250,000
  Unappropriated...   1,800,000
    Total retained earnings................................ $2,050,000

Restrictions on retained earnings do not need to be formalized in the ledger. However, following legal requirements and contractual restrictions is necessary, and the nature and the amount of all restrictions should always be disclosed in the balance sheet. For example, the appropriations data appearing in the foregoing illustration could be presented in a note accompanying the balance sheet. Such an alternative might also be used as a means of simplifying or condensing the balance sheet, even though appropriation accounts are maintained in the ledger. The alternative balance sheet presentation, including the note, might appear as follows:

Retained earnings (see note) $2,050,000

Note: Retained earnings in the amount of $250,000 are appropriated for expansion of plant facilities; the remaining $1,800,000 is unrestricted.

When there are accounts for appropriations, it is customary to divide the retained earnings statement into two major sections: (1) appropriated and (2) unappropriated. The first section is composed of an analysis of all appropriation accounts, beginning with the opening balance, followed by the additions or the deductions during the period, and ending with the closing balance. The second section is composed of an analysis of the retained earnings account, beginning with the opening balance, followed by the period's net income, dividends, and transfers to and from the appropriation accounts, and ending with the closing balance. The final figure on the statement is the total retained earnings as of the last day of the period. This form of the statement is illustrated for Lester Corporation as follows:

Retained Earnings Statement	Lester Corporation Retained Earnings Statement For Year Ended December 31, 19--		
Appropriated:			
Appropriation for plant expansion, January 1, 19--.....		$ 180,000	
Additional appropriation (see below)		100,000	
Retained earnings appropriated, December 31, 19--..			$ 280,000
Unappropriated:			
Balance, January 1, 19--......................................	$1,414,500		
Net income for the year..	580,000	$1,994,500	
Cash dividends declared	$ 125,000		
Transfer to appropriation for plant expansion (see above)...	100,000	225,000	
Retained earnings unappropriated, December 31, 19--			1,769,500
Total retained earnings, December 31, 19--.................			$2,049,500

There are many possible variations in the form of the retained earnings statement. It may also be added to the income statement to form a combined statement of income and retained earnings, as illustrated in Chapter 5.

NATURE OF DIVIDENDS

OBJECTIVE 7
Describe and illustrate the accounting for dividends, including cash dividends, stock dividends, and liquidating dividends.

A **dividend** is a distribution by a corporation to its shareholders. On common shares, the dividend is usually stated in terms of dollars and cents rather than as a percentage of par. On preferred shares, the dividend may be stated either in monetary terms or as a percentage of par. For example, the annual dividend rate on a particular $100 par preferred stock may be stated as either $10 or 10%.

A dividend usually represents a distribution from retained earnings, and may be paid in cash, in stock of the company, or in other property. A dividend may also represent a distribution from paid-in capital. The types of dividends are discussed in the following paragraphs.

Cash Dividends

A cash distribution of earnings by a corporation to its shareholders is called a **cash dividend**. Cash dividends are the most common form of dividend. Usually there are three prerequisites to paying a cash dividend:

1. Sufficient unappropriated retained earnings
2. Sufficient cash
3. Formal action by the board of directors

A large amount of accumulated earnings does not always mean that a corporation is able to pay dividends. There must also be enough cash in excess of routine requirements. The amount of retained earnings, which represents net income retained in the business, is not directly related to cash. The cash provided by the net income may have been used to purchase assets, to reduce liabilities, or for other purposes. The directors are not required by law to declare dividends, even when both retained earnings and cash appear to be sufficient. When a dividend has been declared, however, it becomes a liability of the corporation.

Corporations with a wide distribution of stock usually try to maintain a stable dividend record. They may retain a large part of earnings in good years in order to be able to continue dividend payments in lean years. Dividends may be paid once a year or on a semiannual or quarterly basis. The tendency is to pay quarterly dividends on both common and preferred stock. In particularly good years, the directors may declare an "extra" dividend on common stock. It may be paid at one of the usual dividend dates or at some other date. The designation "extra" indicates that the board of directors does not anticipate an increase in the amount of the "regular" dividend.

Notice of a dividend declaration is usually reported in financial publications and newspapers. The notice identifies three different dates related to a declaration:

1. The date of declaration
2. The date of record
3. The date of payment

The first is the date the directors take formal action declaring the dividend, the second is the date as of which ownership of shares is to be determined, and the third is the date payment is to be made. For example, a notice read: "On June 26, the board of directors of Campbell Soup Co. declared a quarterly cash dividend of $.33 per common share to stockholders of record as of the close of business on July 8, payable on July 31."

The liability for a dividend is recorded on the declaration date, when the formal action is taken by the directors. No entry is required on the date of record, which merely fixes the date for determining the identity of the stockholders entitled to receive the dividend. The period of time between the record date and the payment date is provided to permit completion of postings to the stockholders ledger and preparation of the dividend checks. The liability of the corporation is paid by the mailing of the checks.

To illustrate the entries required in the declaration and the payment of cash dividends, assume that on December 1 the board of directors of Hiber Corporation declares the regular quarterly dividend of $2.50 on the 5,000 shares of $100 par, 10% preferred stock outstanding (total dividend of $12,500), and a quarterly dividend of 30¢ on the 100,000 shares of $10 par common stock outstanding (total dividend of $30,000). Both dividends are to stockholders of record on December 10, and checks are to be issued to stockholders on January 2. The entry to record the declaration of the dividends is as follows:

| Dec. 1 | Cash Dividends..................................... | 42,500 | |
| | Cash Dividends Payable...................... | | 42,500 |

The balance in Cash Dividends would be transferred to Retained Earnings as a part of the closing process and Cash Dividends Payable would be listed on the balance sheet as a current liability. Payment of the liability on January 2 would be recorded in the usual manner as a debit to Cash Dividends Payable and a credit to Cash for $42,500.

Dividends on cumulative preferred stock do not become a liability of the corporation until formal action is taken by the board of directors. However, dividends in arrears at a balance sheet date should be disclosed by a footnote, a parenthetical notation, or a segregation of retained earnings similar to the following:

Retained earnings:
  Required to meet dividends in arrears on
      preferred stock .... $ 50,000
  Remainder, unrestricted 116,000
     Total retained earnings..................................... $166,000

Stock Dividends

A pro rata distribution of shares of stock of a company to the stockholders, accompanied by a transfer of retained earnings to paid-in capital accounts, is called a **stock dividend**. Such distributions are usually in common stock and are issued to holders of common stock. It is possible to issue common stock to preferred stockholders or vice versa, but such stock dividends are too unusual to warrant their consideration here.

Stock dividends are quite unlike cash dividends, in that there is no distribution of cash or other corporate assets to the stockholders. They are ordinarily issued by corporations that "plow back" (retain) earnings for use in acquiring new facilities or for expanding their operations.

The effect of a stock dividend on the capital structure of the issuing corporation is to transfer accumulated earnings to paid-in capital. The statutes of most states require that an amount equivalent to the par or stated value of a stock dividend be transferred from the retained earnings account to the common stock account. Compliance with this minimum requirement is considered by accountants to be satisfactory for a nonpublic corporation, whose stockholders are presumed to have enough knowledge of the corporation's affairs to recognize the true impact of the dividend. However, many investors in the stock of public corporations are often less knowledgeable. An analysis of this latter situation, and the widely accepted viewpoint of professional accountants, has been expressed as follows:

> ...many recipients of stock dividends look upon them as distributions of corporate earnings and usually in an amount equivalent to the fair value of the additional shares received. Furthermore, it is to be presumed that such views of recipients are materially strengthened in those instances, which are by far the most numerous, where the issuances are so small in comparison with the shares previously outstanding that they do not have any apparent effect upon the share market price and, consequently, the market value of the shares previously held remains substantially unchanged. The committee therefore believes that where these circumstances exist the corporation should in the public interest account for the transaction by transferring from [retained earnings] to the category of permanent capitalization...an amount equal to the fair value of the additional shares issued. Unless this is done, the amount of earnings which the shareholder may believe to have been distributed to him will be left, except to the extent otherwise dictated by legal requirements, in [retained earnings] subject to possible further similar stock issuances or cash distributions. [18]

To illustrate the issuance of a stock dividend according to the procedure recommended above, assume the following balances in the stockholders' equity accounts of Hendrix Corporation as of December 15:

Common Stock, $20 par (2,000,000 shares issued)................. $40,000,000
Paid-In Capital in Excess of Par—Common Stock................... 9,000,000
Retained Earnings... 26,600,000

---

[18]*Accounting Research and Terminology Bulletins—Final Edition*, "No. 43, Restatement and Revision of Accounting Research Bulletins" (New York: American Institute of Certified Public Accountants, 1961), Ch. 7, Sec. B, par. 10.

On December 15, the board of directors declares a 5% stock dividend (100,000 shares, $20 par), to be issued on January 10. Assuming that the average of the high and low market prices on the declaration date is $31 a share, the entry to record the declaration would be as follows:

Dec. 15	Stock Dividends......................................	3,100,000	
	Stock Dividends Distributable...............		2,000,000
	Paid-In Capital in Excess of Par—		
	Common Stock		1,100,000

The $3,100,000 debit to Stock Dividends would be transferred to Retained Earnings as a part of the closing process. The issuance of the stock certificates would be recorded on January 10 as follows:

| Jan. 10 | Stock Dividends Distributable................... | 2,000,000 | |
| | Common Stock .... | | 2,000,000 |

The effect of the stock dividend is to transfer $3,100,000 from the retained earnings account to paid-in capital accounts and to increase by 100,000 the number of shares outstanding. There is no change in the assets, liabilities, or total stockholders' equity of the corporation. If financial statements are prepared between the date of declaration and the date of issuance, the stock dividends distributable account should be listed in the paid-in capital section of the balance sheet.

The issuance of the additional shares does not affect the total amount of a stockholder's equity and proportionate interest in the corporation. The effect of the stock dividend on the accounts of a corporation and on the equity of a stockholder owning 1,000 shares is demonstrated by the following tabulation:

The Corporation	Before Stock Dividend	After Stock Dividend
Common stock	$40,000,000	$42,000,000
Excess of issue price over par.........................	9,000,000	10,100,000
Retained earnings	26,600,000	23,500,000
Total stockholders' equity..............................	$75,600,000	$75,600,000
Number of shares outstanding..........................	2,000,000	2,100,000
Equity per share	$37.80	$36.00
A Stockholder		
Number of shares owned................................	1,000	1,050
Total equity..	$37,800	$37,800
Portion of corporation owned..........................	.05%	.05%

Liquidating Dividends

The term **liquidating dividend** is applied to a distribution to stockholders from paid-in capital. Such dividends are unusual, but in many states they may be declared from the excess of paid-in capital over par or stated value. Liquidating dividends are usually paid when a corporation permanently reduces its operations or winds up its affairs completely. Since dividends are normally paid from retained earnings, dividends that reduce paid-in capital should be identified as liquidating dividends when paid.

STOCK SPLITS

Corporations sometimes reduce the par or stated value of their common stock and issue a proportionate number of additional shares. Such a procedure is called a **stock split** or **stock split-up**. The primary purpose of a stock split is to bring about a reduction in the market price per share and thus to encourage more investors to enter the market for the company's shares. For example, when Nature's Sunshine Products Inc. declared a two-for-one stock split on November 4, 1988, the company president said: "We believe the split will place our stock price in a range attractive to both individual and institutional investors, broadening the market for the stock."

To illustrate a stock split, assume that the board of directors of Rojek Corporation, which has 10,000 shares of $100 par stock outstanding, reduces the par to $20 and increases the number of shares to 50,000. The amount of stock outstanding is $1,000,000 both before and after the stock split. Only the number of shares and the par per share are changed. Since there are no changes in the balances of any of the corporation's accounts, no entry to record the stock split is required.

Each shareholder in a corporation whose stock is split owns the same total par amount of stock before and after the stock split. For example, a Rojek Corporation stockholder who owned 100 shares of $100 par stock before the split (total par of $10,000) would own 500 shares of $20 par stock after the split (total par of $10,000).

DIVIDENDS AND STOCK SPLITS FOR TREASURY STOCK

Cash or property dividends are not paid on treasury stock. To do so would place the corporation in the position of earning income through dealing with itself. Accordingly, the total amount of a cash (or property) dividend should be based on the number of shares outstanding at the record date.

When a corporation holding treasury stock declares a stock dividend, the number of shares to be issued may be based on either (1) the number of shares outstanding or (2) the number of shares issued. In practice, the number of shares held as treasury stock represents a small percent of the number of shares issued. Also, the rate of dividend is usually small, so that the difference between the end results of both methods is usually not significant.

There is no legal, theoretical, or practical reason for excluding treasury stock when computing the number of shares to be issued in a stock split. The reduction in par or stated value would apply to all shares of the class, including the unissued, issued, and treasury shares.

CHAPTER REVIEW

KEY POINTS

Paid-In Capital

Although paid-in capital usually results from the issuance of stock, it may also originate from donated assets and redemptions of a corporation's own stock. Many variations in terminology and arrangement of the paid-in capital section of the balance sheet exist. Significant changes in paid-in capital during a period should be disclosed.

OBJECTIVE 2

Corporate Earnings and Income Taxes

Unlike sole proprietorships and partnerships, corporations are subject to federal income tax and, in many cases, to income taxes levied by states or other political subdivisions. Most corporations are required to estimate the amount of their federal income tax expense for the year and make advance payment, usually in four installments. At the end of the year, the actual taxable income and the actual tax are determined. If an additional amount is owed, a liability is recorded. If an overpayment occurs, the amount would be debited to a receivable account and credited to Income Tax.

OBJECTIVE 3

Allocation of Income Tax Between Periods

The taxable income of a corporation, determined according to the tax laws, is often different from the amount of income (before income tax) reported in the income statement. This difference may need to be allocated between periods, depending upon the nature of the items causing the difference.

Some items create differences between income before income tax and taxable income because the items are recognized in one period for income statement purposes and in another period for tax purposes. These temporary differences turn around in later years. They require special treatment in the accounts. The income tax to be reported on the income statement should be the total tax expected to result from the net income reported for that period. The amount of the income tax postponed (deferred) is accounted for in a deferred tax liability account. The deferred income tax liability is reported on the balance sheet as a current liability or a long-term liability, depending on when the items to which it relates will reverse their effects on taxable income.

OBJECTIVE 4

Reporting Unusual Items in the Financial Statements

General guidelines have been developed for reporting unusual items in the financial statements. These items may be described as (1) items that affect the current year's net income and are therefore reported on the current year's income statement and (2) items that affect a prior year's net income and are therefore reported on the current year's retained earnings statement.

A gain or loss resulting from the disposal of a segment of a business should be identified on the income statement as a gain or loss from discontinued operations. In addition, the results of continuing operations should be identified in the income statement. Details of the discontinued operations should also be disclosed in a note to the financial statements.

Extraordinary gains and losses result from events and transactions that are distinguished by their unusual nature and the infrequency of their occurrence. Such gains and losses, other than those from the disposal of a segment of a business, should be identified in the income statement as extraordinary items.

A change in accounting principle results from the adoption of a generally accepted accounting principle different from the one used previously for reporting purposes. The effect of the change in principle on net income in the current period, as well as the cumulative effect on income of prior periods, should be disclosed. Details describing the change in accounting principle are also normally disclosed in an accompanying note to the financial statements.

The amount reported as a gain or loss from discontinued operations, an extraordinary item, or the cumulative effect of a change in accounting principle should be net of the related income tax. The amount of income tax allocable to each of these items should be disclosed on the face of the income statement or by an accompanying note.

Material errors related to a prior period are termed prior period adjustments and are reported as an adjustment on the retained earnings balance at the beginning of the period in which the correction is made. Any financial statements presented for the prior period should be restated, and the current period financial statements should clearly set forth the adjustment necessary to the retained earnings account.

OBJECTIVE 5

Earnings per Common Share

Data on earnings per share of common stock are reported on the income statements of public corporations. If preferred stock is outstanding, the net income must be reduced by the amount of any preferred dividend requirements before dividing by the number of common shares outstanding. If there are nonrecurring items on the income statement, the per share amount should be presented for (1) income from continuing operations, (2) income before extraordinary items and the cumulative effect of a change in accounting principle, (3) the cumulative effect of a change in accounting principle, and (4) net income. Presentation of per share amounts is optional for a gain or loss on discontinued operations and for extraordinary items.

OBJECTIVE 6

Appropriation of Retained Earnings

The amount of a corporation's retained earnings available for distribution to its shareholders may be limited by action of the board of directors or by law or contract. The amount restricted, called an appropriation or a reserve, remains a part of retained earnings. An appropriation of retained earnings is not directly related to any certain group of assets, and its existence does not imply that there is an equivalent amount of cash or other assets set aside in a special fund. However, appropriations may be accompanied by a segregation of cash or marketable securities, in which case the appropriation is said to be funded. Appropriations of retained earnings should be clearly set forth in the retained earnings statement and should be properly identified on the face of the balance sheet or in an accompanying note.

It is customary to divide the retained earnings statement into two major sections: (1) appropriated and (2) unappropriated. Each of these sections should identify the beginning balance and any additions or deductions during the period.

OBJECTIVE 7

Nature of Dividends

A dividend is a distribution by a corporation to its shareholders. Dividends may be paid in cash, in stock of the company, or in other property. Three dates are important in the distribution of dividends. (1) The date of declaration is the date on which the directors take formal action to declare the dividend and on which the dividend is recorded in the accounting records. (2) The date of record is the date on which ownership of shares is to be determined for purposes of distribution of the dividend. (3) The date of payment is the date on which the dividend is to be distributed or paid.

Dividends on cumulative preferred stock do not become a liability of the corporation until formal action is taken by the board of directors. However, dividends in arrears at a balance sheet date should be disclosed by a footnote, a parenthetical notation, or a segregation of retained earnings.

A stock dividend is a pro rata distribution of shares of stock to stockholders. The effect of a stock dividend on the capital structure of the issuing corporation is to transfer accumulated earnings to paid-in capital. There is no change in the assets, liabilities, or total stockholders' equity of the corporation.

A dividend distribution to stockholders from paid-in capital is known as a liquidating dividend. Such dividends are usually paid when a corporation permanently reduces its operations or winds up its affairs completely. Because of the unusual nature of liquidating dividends, they should be clearly identified in the financial statements.

OBJECTIVE 8   Stock Splits

When a corporation reduces the par or stated value of its common stock and issues a proportionate number of additional shares, a stock split or stock split-up has occurred. Because only the number of shares and the par amount per share of stock is changed during a stock split, there are no changes in the balances of any corporation accounts, and no entry is required. Each shareholder owns the same total par amount of stock before and after a stock split. The primary purpose of a stock split is to reduce the market price per share and encourage more investors to enter the market for the company's shares.

OBJECTIVE 9   Dividends and Stock Splits for Treasury Stock

Cash or property dividends are not paid on treasury stock. To do so would place the corporation in a position of earning income through dealing with itself. However, when a stock dividend or a stock split occurs, treasury shares may or may not participate, depending upon action of the board of directors.

KEY TERMS

taxable income 571	funded 582
temporary differences 571	dividend 583
discontinued operations 574	cash dividend 583
extraordinary items 575	stock dividend 585
prior period adjustments 578	liquidating dividend 586
earnings per share 579	stock split 587
appropriation of retained	
earnings 581	

SELF-EXAMINATION QUESTIONS

Answers at end of chapter.

1. Paid-in capital for a corporation may originate from which of the following sources?
   A. Real estate donated to the corporation
   B. Redemption of the corporation's own stock
   C. Sale of the corporation's treasury stock
   D. All of the above

2. During its first year of operations, a corporation elected to use the straight-line method of depreciation for financial reporting purposes and the sum-of-the-years-digits method in determining taxable income. If the income tax is 40% and the amount of depreciation expense is $60,000 under the straight-line method and $100,000 under the sum-of-the-years-digits method, what is the amount of income tax deferred to future years?
   A. $16,000   C. $40,000
   B. $24,000   D. None of the above

3. A material gain resulting from the condemnation of land for public use would be reported on the income statement as:
   A. an extraordinary item   C. an item of revenue from sales
   B. an other income item   D. none of the above

4. An item treated as a prior period adjustment should be reported in the financial statements as:
    A. an extraordinary item
    B. an other expense item
    C. an adjustment of the beginning balance of retained earnings
    D. none of the above

5. An appropriation for plant expansion would be reported on the balance sheet in:

A. the plant assets section	C. the stockholders' equity section
B. the long-term liabilities section	D. none of the above

ILLUSTRATIVE PROBLEM

During its current fiscal year ended December 31, 1990, Block Inc. completed the following selected transactions:

Jan.   9. Purchased 1,500 shares of own common stock at $16, recording the stock at cost. (Prior to the purchase there were 70,000 shares of $10 par common stock outstanding.)

Mar. 16. Discovered that a receipt of $500 cash on account from I. Jonson had been posted in error to the account of I. Johnson. The transaction was recorded correctly in the journal.

May 18. Declared a semiannual dividend of $1 on the 10,000 shares of preferred stock and a 20¢ dividend on the common stock to stockholders of record on May 28, payable on June 10.

June 10. Paid the cash dividends.

Aug. 23. Sold 1,000 shares of treasury stock at $18, receiving cash.

Nov. 12. Declared semiannual dividends of $1 on the preferred stock and 20¢ on the common stock. In addition, a 5% common stock dividend was declared on the common stock outstanding, to be capitalized at the fair market value of the common stock, which is estimated at $16.

Dec.   4. Paid the cash dividends and issued the certificates for the common stock dividend.

      31. Recorded $75,000 additional federal income tax allocable to net income for the year. Of this amount, $65,600 is a current liability and $9,400 is deferred.

      31. The board of directors authorized the appropriation necessitated by the holding of treasury stock.

Instructions:

Prepare the journal entries to record the transactions for Block Inc.

SOLUTION

1990

Jan. 9	Treasury Stock..	24,000	
	Cash		24,000
Mar. 16	No entry. Error can be corrected by revising the postings in the subsidiary accounts receivable ledger.		
May 18	Cash Dividends	23,700	
	Cash Dividends Payable....................................		23,700
June 10	Cash Dividends Payable......................................	23,700	
	Cash		23,700

Aug. 23 Cash	18,000	
Treasury Stock...		16,000
Paid-In Capital from Sale of		
Treasury Stock...		2,000
Nov. 12 Cash Dividends	23,900	
Stock Dividends..	55,600	
Cash Dividends Payable.................................		23,900
Stock Dividends Distributable		34,750
Paid-In Capital in Excess of Par—Common Stock ..		20,850
Dec. 4 Cash Dividends Payable......................................	23,900	
Stock Dividends Distributable	34,750	
Cash		23,900
Common Stock..		34,750
31 Income Tax	75,000	
Income Tax Payable.......................................		65,600
Deferred Income Tax Payable............................		9,400
31 Retained Earnings..	8,000	
Appropriation for Treasury Stock		8,000

DISCUSSION QUESTIONS

1. What are the titles of the two principal subdivisions of the stockholders' equity section of a corporate balance sheet?

2. If a corporation is given land as an inducement to locate in a particular community, (a) how should the amount of the debit to the land account be determined, and (b) what is the title of the account that should be credited for the same amount?

3. A corporation has paid $200,000 of federal income tax during the year on the basis of its estimated income. What entry should be recorded as of the end of the year if it determines that (a) it owes an additional $30,000; (b) it overpaid its tax by $10,000?

4. The income before income tax reported on the income statement for the year is $750,000. Because of temporary differences between accounting and tax methods, the taxable income for the same year is $620,000. Assuming an income tax rate of 40%, determine (a) the amount of income tax to be deducted from the $750,000 on the income statement, (b) the amount of the actual income tax that should be paid for the year, and (c) the amount of the deferred income tax liability.

5. How would the amount of deferred income tax payable be reported in the balance sheet if (a) it is payable within one year, and (b) if it is payable beyond one year?

6. Indicate where the following should be reported in the financial statements, assuming that financial statements are presented only for the current year:
   (a) Loss on disposal of equipment considered to be obsolete.
   (b) Uninsured loss on building due to hurricane damage. The firm was organized in 1915, and had not previously incurred hurricane damage.

7. Classify each of the following revenue and expense items as either (a) normally recurring or (b) extraordinary. Assume that the amount of each item is material.
   (1) Interest income on notes receivable.
   (2) Loss on sale of plant assets.
   (3) Salaries of corporate officers.
   (4) Uninsured flood loss. (Flood insurance is unavailable because of periodic flooding in the area.)
   (5) Uncollectible accounts expense.
   (6) Gain on sale of land condemned for public use.

8. During the current year, twenty acres of land which cost $180,000 were condemned for construction of an interstate highway. Assuming that an award of $200,000 in cash was received and that the applicable income tax on this transaction is 25%, how would this information be presented in the income statement?

9. Indicate how prior period adjustments would be reported on the financial statements presented only for the current period.

10. A corporation reports earnings per share of $12.10 for the most recent year and $9.60 for the preceding year. The $12.10 includes $3.00 per share gain from a sale of the only investment owned since the business was organized in 1946. (a) Should the composition of the $12.10 be disclosed in the financial reports? (b) What is the earnings per share amount for the most recent year that is comparable to the $9.60 earnings per share of the preceding year? (c) On the basis of the limited information presented, would you conclude that operations had improved or declined?

11. Appropriations of retained earnings may be (a) required by law, (b) required by contract, or (c) made at the discretion of the board of directors. Give an illustration of each type of appropriation.

12. A credit balance in Retained Earnings does not represent cash. Explain.

13. The board of directors votes to appropriate $500,000 of retained earnings for bonded indebtedness. What is the effect of this action on (a) cash, (b) total retained earnings, and (c) retained earnings available for dividends?

14. What are the three prerequisites of the declaration and the payment of a cash dividend?

15. The dates in connection with the declaration of a cash dividend are September 1, October 15, and October 30. Identify each date.

16. A corporation with both cumulative preferred stock and common stock outstanding has a substantial credit balance in its retained earnings account at the beginning of the current fiscal year. Although net income for the current year is sufficient to pay the preferred dividend of $100,000 each quarter and a common dividend of $400,000 each quarter, the board of directors declares dividends only on the preferred stock. Suggest possible reasons for passing the dividends on the common stock.

17. State the effect of the following actions on a corporation's total assets, liabilities, and stockholders' equity: (a) declaration of a cash dividend; (b) payment of the cash dividend declared in (a); (c) declaration of a stock dividend; (d) issuance of stock certificates for the stock dividend declared in (c); (e) authorization and issuance of stock certificates in a stock split.

18. An owner of 500 shares of Randall Company common stock receives a stock dividend of 20 shares. (a) What is the effect of the stock dividend on the equity per share of the stock? (b) How does the total equity of 520 shares compare with the total equity of 500 shares before the stock dividend?

19. What term is used to identify a distribution to stockholders from paid-in capital?

20. A corporation with 10,000 shares of no-par common stock issued, of which 3,000 shares are held as treasury stock, declares a cash dividend of $2 a share. What is the total amount of the dividend?

21. If a corporation with 5,000 shares of common stock outstanding has a 6-for-1 stock split (5 additional shares of each share issued), what will be the number of shares outstanding after the split?

22. If the common stock in Question 21 had a market price of $150 per share before the stock split, what would be an approximate market price per share after the split?

Real World Focus

23. The annual report of Entertainment, Marketing, Incorporated disclosed the discontinuance of the company's televised home shopping operation. The estimated loss on disposal of this segment of the company is $2,567,597, net of an estimated income tax benefit of $1,641,578. Indicate how the loss from discontinued operations should be reported by Entertainment, Marketing, Incorporated on its income statement for the year ended January 31, 1988.

EXERCISES

Exercise 15–1
Income tax entries.
OBJ. 2, 3

Present entries to record the following selected transactions of Ayres Inc.:

Apr. 15. Paid the first installment of the estimated income tax for the current fiscal year ending December 31, $200,000. No entry had been made to record the liability.

June 15. Paid the second installment of $200,000.

Dec. 31. Recorded the additional income tax liability for the year just ended and the deferred income tax liability, based on the two transactions above and the following data:

Income tax rate	40%
Income before income tax	$2,100,000
Taxable income according to tax return	2,010,000
Third installment paid on September 15	200,000
Fourth installment paid on December 15	200,000

Exercise 15–2
Retained earnings statement with prior period adjustment.
OBJ. 4

Leslie Heart and Company reported the following results of transactions affecting retained earnings for the current year ended March 31, 1990:

Net income	$136,500
Dividends	30,000
Prior period adjustment for understatement of merchandise inventory on March 31, 1989, net of applicable income tax of $8,000	12,000

Assuming that the retained earnings balance reported on the retained earnings statement as of March 31, 1989, was $300,000, prepare a retained earnings statement for the year ended March 31, 1990.

Exercise 15–3
Income statement.
OBJ. 4, 5

On the basis of the following data for the current fiscal year ended April 30, prepare an income statement for Bryant Company, including an analysis of earnings per share in the form illustrated in this chapter. There were 10,000 shares of $20 par common stock outstanding throughout the year.

Administrative expenses..	$ 55,300
Cost of merchandise sold...	730,000
Cumulative effect on prior years of changing to a different depreciation method...	80,600
Gain on condemnation of land (extraordinary item).....................	70,100
Income tax applicable to change in depreciation method	24,600
Income tax applicable to gain on condemnation of land	20,100
Income tax reduction applicable to loss from discontinued operations	27,000
Income tax applicable to ordinary income...............................	110,000
Loss on discontinued operations	89,000
Sales	1,180,000
Selling expenses...	89,700

Exercise 15–4
Entries for treasury stock.
OBJ. 6

A corporation purchased for cash 3,000 shares of its own $5 par common stock at $7 a share. In the following year, it sold 1,000 of the treasury shares at $10 a share for cash. (a) Present the entries (1) to record the purchase (treasury stock is recorded at cost) and (2) to provide for the appropriation of retained earnings. (b) Present the entries (1) to record the sale of the stock and (2) to reduce the appropriation.

Exercise 15–5
Retained earnings statement.
OBJ. 6

Farmer Corporation reports the following results of transactions affecting net income and retained earnings for its first fiscal year of operations ended on December 31:

Appropriation for plant expansion	$ 40,000
Cash dividends declared	15,000
Income before income tax...	240,000
Income tax...	95,500

Prepare a retained earnings statement for the fiscal year ended December 31.

Exercise 15–6
Entries for cash dividends.
OBJ. 7

The dates in connection with a cash dividend of $18,000 on a corporation's common stock are January 12, February 2, and February 20. Present the entries required on each date.

Exercise 15–7
Stock dividends; equity per share.
OBJ. 7

The following account balances appear on the balance sheet of Kennedy Company: Common stock (10,000 shares authorized), $100 par, $500,000; Paid-in capital in excess of par — common stock, $8,000; and Retained earnings, $51,000. The board of directors declared a 4% stock dividend when the market price of the stock was $120 a share. (a) Present entries to record (1) the declaration of the dividend, capitalizing an amount equal to market value, and (2) the issuance of the stock certificates. (b) Determine the equity per share (1) before the stock dividend and (2) after the stock dividend. (c) Nancy Long owned 250 shares of the common stock before the stock dividend was declared. Determine the total equity of her holdings (1) before the stock dividend and (2) after the stock dividend.

Exercise 15–8
Stock split.
OBJ. 8

The board of directors of Pike Corporation authorized the reduction of par of its common shares from $50 to $10, increasing the number of outstanding shares to 500,000. The market price of the stock immediately before the stock split was $175 a share. (a) Determine the number of outstanding shares prior to the stock split. (b) Present the entry to record the stock split. (c) At approximately what price would a share of stock be expected to sell immediately after the stock split?

PROBLEMS

Problem 15–1A
Income tax
allocation.

OBJ. 3

Differences between the accounting methods applied to accounts and financial reports and those used in determining taxable income yielded the following amounts for the first four years of a corporation's operations:

	First Year	Second Year	Third Year	Fourth Year
Income before income tax......	$380,000	$480,000	$600,000	$570,000
Taxable income	310,000	440,000	620,000	615,500

The income tax rate for each of the four years was 40% of taxable income, and each year's taxes were promptly paid.

Instructions:

(1) Determine for each year the amounts described in the following columnar captions, presenting the information in the form indicated:

			Deferred Income Tax Payable	
Year	Income Tax Deducted on Income Statement	Income Tax Payments for the Year	Year's Addition (Deduction)	Year-End Balance

(2) Total the first three amount columns.

Problem 15–2A
Income statement.

OBJ. 4, 5

The following data were selected from the records of Leiter Inc. for the current fiscal year ended August 31, 1990:

Advertising expense..	$ 30,000
Delivery expense	11,800
Depreciation expense — office equipment	5,100
Depreciation expense — store equipment................................	13,200
Gain on condemnation of land	60,000
Income tax:	
Applicable to continuing operations	68,800
Applicable to loss from disposal of a segment of a	
business (reduction)...	6,000
Applicable to gain on condemnation of land.........................	17,000
Insurance expense..	11,000
Interest income...	16,500
Loss from disposal of a segment of the business	30,000
Merchandise inventory (September 1, 1989)............................	118,300
Merchandise inventory (August 31, 1990)...............................	126,000
Miscellaneous administrative expense	3,500
Miscellaneous selling expense	4,200
Office salaries expense..	55,200
Office supplies expense..	2,100
Purchases	722,700
Rent expense...	36,000
Sales	1,185,000
Sales commissions expense	54,800
Sales salaries expense	67,600
Store supplies expense..	3,200

Instructions:

Prepare a multiple-step income statement, concluding with a section for earnings per share in the form illustrated in this chapter. There were 100,000 shares of common stock (no preferred) outstanding throughout the year. Assume that the condemnation of land is an extraordinary item.

Problem 15–3A
Retained earnings statement.
OBJ. 6, 7

The retained earnings accounts of Palm Bay Corporation for the current fiscal year ended December 31 are as follows:

ACCOUNT APPROPRIATION FOR PLANT EXPANSION ACCOUNT NO. 3201

Date		Item	Debit	Credit	Balance Debit	Balance Credit
19--						
Jan.	1	Balance				300,000
Dec.	31	Retained earnings		65,000		365,000

ACCOUNT APPROPRIATION FOR TREASURY STOCK ACCOUNT NO. 3202

Date		Item	Debit	Credit	Balance Debit	Balance Credit
19--						
Jan.	1	Balance				500,000
Dec.	31	Retained earnings	50,000			450,000

ACCOUNT RETAINED EARNINGS ACCOUNT NO. 3301

Date		Item	Debit	Credit	Balance Debit	Balance Credit
19--						
Jan.	1	Balance				875,000
Dec.	31	Income summary		315,000		1,190,000
	31	Appropriation for plant expansion	65,000			1,125,000
	31	Appropriation for treasury stock		50,000		1,175,000
	31	Cash dividends	100,000			1,075,000
	31	Stock dividends	250,000			825,000

ACCOUNT CASH DIVIDENDS ACCOUNT NO. 3302

Date		Item	Debit	Credit	Balance Debit	Balance Credit
19--						
Apr.	12		50,000		50,000	
Oct.	17		50,000		100,000	
Dec.	31	Retained earnings		100,000	—	—

ACCOUNT STOCK DIVIDENDS ACCOUNT NO. 3303

Date		Item	Debit	Credit	Balance Debit	Balance Credit
19--						
Sept.	17		250,000		250,000	
Dec.	31	Retained earnings		250,000	—	—

Instructions:

Prepare a retained earnings statement for the fiscal year ended December 31.

Problem 15–4A
Entries for selected corporate transactions.

OBJ. 6, 7

The stockholders' equity accounts of O'Tell Enterprises Inc., with balances on January 1 of the current fiscal year, are as follows:

Common Stock, stated value $20 (100,000 shares authorized, 45,000 shares issued)	$900,000
Paid-In Capital in Excess of Stated Value	60,000
Appropriation for Plant Expansion	200,000
Appropriation for Treasury Stock	12,500
Retained Earnings	735,000
Treasury Stock (500 shares, at cost)	12,500

The following selected transactions occurred during the year:

Jan.   8. Paid cash dividends of $1 per share on the common stock. The dividend had been properly recorded when declared on December 10 of the preceding fiscal year.
Feb. 18. Sold all of the treasury stock for $14,000.
Apr. 25. Issued 5,000 shares of common stock for $150,000 cash.
May 11. Received land with an estimated fair market value of $40,000 from the Columbia City Council as a donation.
June 30. Declared a 4% stock dividend on common stock, to be capitalized at the market price of the stock, which is $30 a share.
July 31. Issued the certificates for the dividend declared on June 30.
Nov. 10. Purchased 1,000 shares of treasury stock for $32,000.
Dec. 15. Declared a $1 per share dividend on common stock.
        15. The board of directors authorized the increase of the appropriation for plant expansion by $50,000.
        20. Increased the appropriation for treasury stock to $32,000.
        31. Closed the credit balance of the income summary account, $186,000.
        31. Closed the two dividends accounts to Retained Earnings.

Instructions:

(1) Open T accounts for the stockholders' equity accounts listed and enter the balances as of January 1. Also open T accounts for the following: Paid-In Capital from Sale of Treasury Stock; Donated Capital; Stock Dividends Distributable; Stock Dividends; Cash Dividends.
(2) Prepare entries to record the transactions and post to the eleven selected accounts.
(3) Prepare the stockholders' equity section of the balance sheet as of December 31 of the current fiscal year.

Problem 15–5A
Stockholders' equity transactions and statements.

OBJ. 6, 7

The stockholders' equity section of the balance sheet of Dixon Industries as of January 1 is as follows:

Stockholders' Equity

Paid-in capital:		
Common stock, $10 par (100,000 shares authorized, 60,000 shares issued)	$600,000	
Excess of issue price over par	120,000	
Total paid-in capital		$ 720,000
Retained earnings:		
Appropriated for bonded indebtedness	$400,000	
Unappropriated	880,000	
Total retained earnings		1,280,000
Total		$2,000,000
Deduct treasury stock (5,000 shares at cost)		220,000
Total stockholders' equity		$1,780,000

The following selected transactions occurred during the fiscal year:

Mar. 15. Sold all of the treasury stock for $250,000.

Apr. 5. Issued 20,000 shares of stock in exchange for land and buildings with an estimated fair market value of $100,000 and $220,000 respectively. The property was encumbered by a mortgage of $80,000, and the company agreed to assume the responsibility for paying the mortgage note.

June 10. Declared a cash dividend of $1 per share to stockholders of record on July 10, payable on July 31.

July 31. Paid the cash dividend declared on June 10.

Sept. 12. Received additional land valued at $70,000. The land was donated for a plant site by the Fort Aikens Industrial Development Council.

Dec. 4. Issued 1,000 shares of stock to officers as a salary bonus. Market price of the stock is $13 a share. (Debit Officers Salaries Expense.)

13. Declared a 2% stock dividend on the stock outstanding to stockholders of record on December 28 to be issued on January 28. The market price of the stock is $13 a share.

31. Increased the appropriation for bonded indebtedness by $50,000.

31. Closed the income summary account. After closing all revenue and expense accounts, Income Summary has a credit balance of $315,000.

31. Closed the two dividends accounts to Retained Earnings.

Instructions:

(1) Open T accounts for the accounts appearing in the stockholders' equity section of the balance sheet and enter the balances as of January 1. Also open T accounts for the following: Paid-In Capital from Sale of Treasury Stock; Donated Capital; Cash Dividends; Stock Dividends; Stock Dividends Distributable.

(2) Prepare entries to record the transactions and post to the ten selected accounts.

(3) Prepare the stockholders' equity section of the balance sheet as of December 31, the end of the fiscal year.

(4) Prepare a retained earnings statement for the fiscal year ended December 31.

Problem 15–6A
Correcting entries and financial statements.
OBJ. 2, 4, 5, 6, 7

Oberkfell Company is in need of additional cash to expand operations. To raise the needed funds, the company is applying to Hill County Bank for a loan. For this purpose, the bank requests that the financial statements be audited. To assist the auditor, Oberkfell Company's accountant prepared the following financial statements related to the current year:

Oberkfell Company
Balance Sheet
December 31, 19--

Current assets:		
Cash..	$ 67,500	
Accounts receivable...	77,400	
Merchandise inventory..	102,900	
Supplies...	8,700	$ 256,500
Plant assets:		
Land...	$148,000	
Buildings..	390,000	
Equipment...	159,000	
Patents..	54,000	751,000
Total assets..		$1,007,500

Current liabilities:

Accounts payable	$ 55,800	
Salaries payable	4,200	$ 60,000

Deferred charges:

Accumulated depreciation — buildings	$ 87,000	
Accumulated depreciation — equipment	42,500	
Allowance for doubtful accounts	4,500	134,000

Stockholders' equity:

Common stock (50,000 shares authorized, $20 par)	$460,000	
Excess of issue price over par	54,000	
Retained earnings	198,000	
Net income	101,500	813,500
Total liabilities and stockholders' equity		$1,007,500

Oberkfell Company
Income Statement
For Year Ended December 31, 19--

Revenues:

Net sales	$867,000	
Gain on expropriation of land	50,400	
Total revenues		$917,400

Expenses:

Cost of merchandise sold	$528,600	
Salary expense	72,300	
Depreciation expense — buildings	44,300	
Loss on discontinued operations	42,600	
Utilities expense	24,900	
Insurance expense	12,500	
Depreciation expense — equipment	10,200	
Amortization expense — patents	6,000	
Uncollectible accounts expense	4,500	
Miscellaneous administrative expense	4,000	
Income tax	36,000	
Dividends expense	30,000	
Total expenses		815,900
Net income		$101,500

In the course of the audit, the auditor examined the common stock and retained earnings accounts, which appeared as follows:

ACCOUNT   COMMON STOCK ($20 Par)   ACCOUNT NO. 3200

Date		Item	Debit	Credit	Balance Debit	Balance Credit
19--						
Jan.	1	Balance — 20,000 shares				400,000
	3	Issued 1,000 shares for patents		60,000		460,000

ACCOUNT   RETAINED EARNINGS   ACCOUNT NO. 3300

Date		Item	Debit	Credit	Balance Debit	Balance Credit
19--						
Jan.	1	Balance				117,000
Mar.	1	Donation of land		60,000		177,000
	20	Error correction	9,000			168,000
Dec.	30	Appropriation for land acquisition		30,000		198,000

A closer examination of the transactions in these and other accounts revealed the following details:

(a) The patent acquired on January 3 by an issuance of 1,000 shares of common stock had a fair market value of $60,000 and an estimated useful life of 10 years.
(b) On March 1, the company received a donation of land. The land account was debited for $60,000, the fair market value of the land at that date.
(c) A computational error was made in the calculation of a prior year's dividend. The corrected amount of the dividend was paid on March 20 and debited to the retained earnings account.
(d) In anticipation of further land acquisition, the board of directors on December 30 authorized a $30,000 appropriation of retained earnings that resulted in a debit to Land and a credit to Retained Earnings.
(e) After three years of using the straight-line method of depreciation for the buildings, the company changed to the sum-of-the-years-digits method. The following entry recorded this change:

Depreciation Expense — Buildings	32,300	
Accumulated Depreciation — Buildings		32,300

(f) A $1 cash dividend declared on December 30 and payable on January 31 of the next fiscal year, was not recorded. The $30,000 of dividends expense represents the mid-year cash dividend paid on July 31 of the current year.
(g) The income tax of $36,000 is the estimated tax paid during the year. The tax based on the corrected net income was determined to be $37,300, allocated as follows:

(1) Income from continuing operations	$53,400
(2) Loss from discontinued operations	17,400
(3) Gain on expropriation of land	14,700
(4) Cumulative effect of change in depreciation method	13,400

The tax owed of $1,300 at December 31 had not been recorded.

Instructions:

(1) Prepare the necessary correcting entries for the items discovered by the independent auditor. Assume that the accounts have not been closed for the current fiscal year.
(2) Prepare a multiple-step income statement for the current fiscal year, including the appropriate earnings per share disclosure. Operating expenses need not be divided into selling and administrative expense categories.
(3) Prepare the retained earnings statement for the current fiscal year.
(4) Prepare a balance sheet as of the end of the current fiscal year.

Problem 15–7A
Entries for selected corporate transactions.
OBJ. 3, 6, 7, 8, 9

Selected transactions completed by Power Corporation during the current fiscal year are as follows:

Jan. 8. Split the common stock 4 for 1 and reduced the par from $100 to $25 per share. After the split, there were 200,000 common shares outstanding.
Feb. 1. Declared semiannual dividends of $2 on 50,000 shares of preferred stock and $1 on the 200,000 shares of $25 par common stock to stockholders of record on February 20, payable on February 27.
27. Paid the cash dividends.
Mar. 12. Purchased 25,000 shares of the corporation's own common stock at $30, recording the stock at cost.
Apr. 9. Discovered that a receipt of $4,500 cash on account from L. T. Fulton Co. had been posted in error to the account of T. Fuller Inc. The transaction was recorded correctly in the journal.

June 10. Sold 5,000 shares of treasury stock at $34, receiving cash.

July 18. Declared semiannual dividends of $2 on the preferred stock and $1 on the common stock. In addition, a 5% common stock dividend was declared on the common stock outstanding. The fair market value of the common stock, is estimated at $36.

Aug. 28. Paid the cash dividends and issued the certificates for the common stock dividend.

Oct. 15. Discovered that an invoice of $3,250 for utilities expense for the month of September was debited to Office Supplies.

Dec. 31. Recorded $168,000 additional federal income tax allocable to net income for the year. Of this amount, $92,500 is a current liability and $75,500 is deferred.

     31. The board of directors authorized the appropriation necessitated by the holding of treasury stock.

Instructions:

Record the transactions.

Series B

Problem 15–1B
Income tax allocation.
OBJ. 3

Differences between the accounting methods applied to accounts and financial reports and those used in determining taxable income yielded the following amounts for the first four years of a corporation's operations:

	First Year	Second Year	Third Year	Fourth Year
Income before income tax......	$168,500	$240,000	$360,000	$390,500
Taxable income	120,000	200,000	320,500	425,500

The income tax rate for each of the four years was 40% of taxable income, and each year's taxes were promptly paid.

Instructions:

(1) Determine for each year the amounts described in the following columnar captions, presenting the information in the form indicated:

Year	Income Tax Deducted on Income Statement	Income Tax Payments for the Year	Deferred Income Tax Payable	
			Year's Addition (Deduction)	Year-End Balance

(2) Total the first three amount columns.

Problem 15–2B
Income statement.
OBJ. 4, 5

The following data were selected from the records of Birkbeck Co. for the current fiscal year ended March 31, 1990:

Advertising expense..	$ 40,800
Delivery expense	30,600
Depreciation expense — office equipment	7,800
Depreciation expense — store equipment.................................	13,500
Gain on condemnation of land	30,000
Income tax:	
Applicable to continuing operations	70,400
Applicable to loss from disposal of a segment of a	
business (reduction)..	12,300
Applicable to gain on condemnation of land.........................	6,000

Insurance expense..	$ 13,400
Interest expense	35,000
Loss from disposal of a segment of the business	60,300
Merchandise inventory (April 1, 1989)......................................	195,000
Merchandise inventory (March 31, 1990)...................................	203,200
Miscellaneous administrative expense	6,800
Miscellaneous selling expense	12,900
Office salaries expense...	64,100
Office supplies expense...	2,500
Purchases	908,400
Rent expense..	30,000
Sales	1,500,000
Sales commissions expense	80,200
Sales salaries expense	63,700
Store supplies expense...	11,100

Instructions:

Prepare a multiple-step income statement, concluding with a section for earnings per share in the form illustrated in this chapter. There were 50,000 shares of common stock (no preferred) outstanding throughout the year. Assume that the gain on condemnation of land is an extraordinary item.

Problem 15–3B
Retained earnings statement.
OBJ. 6, 7

The retained earnings accounts of Bedrosian Corporation for the current fiscal year ended December 31 are as follows:

ACCOUNT   APPROPRIATION FOR PLANT EXPANSION   ACCOUNT NO. 3201

Date		Item	Debit	Credit	Balance Debit	Balance Credit
19--						
Jan.	1	Balance				100,000
Dec.	31	Retained earnings		75,000		175,000

ACCOUNT   APPROPRIATION FOR TREASURY STOCK   ACCOUNT NO. 3202

Date		Item	Debit	Credit	Balance Debit	Balance Credit
19--						
Jan.	1	Balance				350,000
Dec.	31	Retained earnings	80,000			270,000

ACCOUNT   RETAINED EARNINGS   ACCOUNT NO. 3301

Date		Item	Debit	Credit	Balance Debit	Balance Credit
19--						
Jan.	1	Balance				815,000
Dec.	31	Income summary		163,500		978,500
	31	Appropriation for plant expansion	75,000			903,500
	31	Appropriation for treasury stock		80,000		983,500
	31	Cash dividends	50,000			933,500
	31	Stock dividends	40,000			893,500

ACCOUNT CASH DIVIDENDS   ACCOUNT NO. 3302

Date		Item	Debit	Credit	Balance Debit	Balance Credit
19--						
Nov.	22		50,000		50,000	
Dec.	31	Retained earnings		50,000	—	—

ACCOUNT STOCK DIVIDENDS   ACCOUNT NO. 3303

Date		Item	Debit	Credit	Balance Debit	Balance Credit
19--						
Nov.	22		40,000		40,000	
Dec.	31	Retained earnings		40,000	—	—

Instructions:

Prepare a retained earnings statement for the fiscal year ended December 31.

Problem 15–4B
Entries for
selected corporate
transactions.

OBJ. 6, 7

The stockholders' equity accounts of Thurman Enterprises Inc., with balances on January 1 of the current fiscal year, are as follows:

Common Stock, stated value $100 (10,000 shares authorized, 4,000 shares issued)	$400,000
Paid-In Capital in Excess of Stated Value	150,000
Appropriation for Plant Expansion	50,000
Appropriation for Treasury Stock	25,000
Retained Earnings	372,000
Treasury Stock (200 shares, at cost)	25,000

The following selected transactions occurred during the year:

Jan. 20. Received land with an estimated fair market value of $20,000 from the city as a donation.
Feb. 1. Paid cash dividends of $5 per share on the common stock. The dividend had been properly recorded when declared on December 30 of the preceding fiscal year for $19,000.
Mar. 7. Sold all of the treasury stock for $28,000.
May 12. Issued 1,000 shares of common stock for $145,000.
July 10. Declared a 2% stock dividend on common stock, which has a market price of $150 a share.
Aug. 11. Issued the certificates for the dividend declared on July 10.
Oct. 30. Purchased 500 shares of treasury stock for $75,000.
Dec. 19. The board of directors authorized an increase of the appropriation for plant expansion by $40,000.
19. Declared a $4 per share dividend on common stock.
19. Increased the appropriation for treasury stock to $75,000.
31. Closed the credit balance of the income summary account, $108,500.
31. Closed the two dividends accounts to Retained Earnings.

Instructions:

(1) Open T accounts for the stockholders' equity accounts listed and enter the balances as of January 1. Also open T accounts for the following: Paid-in Capital from Sale of Treasury Stock; Donated Capital; Stock Dividends Distributable; Stock Dividends; Cash Dividends.
(2) Prepare entries to record the transactions and post to the eleven selected accounts.
(3) Prepare the stockholders' equity section of the balance sheet as of December 31 of the current fiscal year.

Problem 15–7B

Entries for selected corporate transactions.

OBJ. 3, 6, 7, 8, 9

Selected transactions completed by Stewart Company during the current fiscal year are as follows:

Jan. 12. Split the common stock 2 for 1 and reduced the par from $100 to $50 per share. After the split, there were 60,000 common shares outstanding.

Feb. 13. Purchased 4,000 shares of the corporation's own common stock at $55, recording the stock at cost.

Mar. 20. Discovered that a receipt of $1,500 cash on account from C. Spencer had been posted in error to the account of C. Spense. The transaction was recorded correctly in the journal.

May 9. Declared semiannual dividends of $1 on 10,000 shares of preferred stock and $2 on the common stock to stockholders of record on May 30, payable on June 22.

June 22. Paid the cash dividends.

Aug. 18. Sold 1,500 shares of treasury stock at $60, receiving cash.

Nov. 10. Declared semiannual dividends of $1 on the preferred stock and $2.20 on the common stock. In addition, a 2% common stock dividend was declared on the common stock outstanding, which had a fair market value of $62.

Dec. 30. Paid the cash dividends and issued the certificates for the common stock dividend.

30. Recorded $92,600 additional federal income tax allocable to net income for the year. Of this amount, $61,400 is a current liability and $31,200 is deferred.

30. The board of directors authorized the appropriation necessitated by the holding of treasury stock.

Instructions:

Record the transactions.

MINI-CASE 15

Kahn Co. has paid quarterly cash dividends since 1985. These dividends have steadily increased from $.10 per share to the latest dividend declaration of $1.25 per share. The board of directors would like to continue this trend and are hesitant to suspend or decrease the amount of quarterly dividends. Unfortunately, sales of Kahn Co. dropped sharply in the fourth quarter of 1990 due to worsening economic conditions and increased competition. As a result, the board is uncertain as to whether it should declare a dividend for the last quarter of 1990.

On October 1, 1990, Kahn Co. borrowed $1,000,000 from Frye National Bank to use in modernizing its retail stores and to expand its product line in reaction to its competition. The terms of the 10-year, 12% loan require Kahn Co. to

(a) Pay monthly the total interest due,

(b) Pay $100,000 of the principal each October 1, beginning in 1991,

(c) Maintain a current ratio (current assets ÷ current liabilities) of 2:1,

(d) Appropriate $1,000,000 of retained earnings until the loan is fully paid, and

(e) Maintain a minimum balance of $20,000 (called a compensating balance) in its Frye National Bank account.

On December 31, 1990, 30% of the $1,000,000 loan had been disbursed in modernization of the retail stores and in expansion of the product line, and the remainder is temporarily invested in U.S. Treasury notes. Kahn Co.'s balance sheet as of December 31, 1990, is as follows:

Kahn Co.
Balance Sheet
December 31, 1990

Assets

Current assets:			
Cash..		$ 50,000	
Marketable securities, at cost			
(market price, $706,500)....................		700,000	
Accounts receivable............................	$ 163,000		
Less allowance for			
doubtful accounts..........................	13,000	150,000	
Merchandise inventory		291,000	
Prepaid expenses		9,000	
Total current assets..........................			$1,200,000
Plant assets:			
Land..		$ 350,000	
Buildings	$1,900,000		
Less accumulated depreciation...........	430,000	1,470,000	
Equipment	$ 920,000		
Less accumulated depreciation...........	220,000	700,000	
Total plant assets..........................			2,520,000
Total assets			$3,720,000

Liabilities

Current liabilities:			
Accounts payable..............................	$ 143,600		
Notes payable			
(Frye National Bank)........................	100,000		
Salaries payable	6,400		
Total current liabilities		$ 250,000	
Long-term liabilities:			
Notes payable			
(Frye National Bank)........................		900,000	
Total liabilities.......................................			$1,150,000

Stockholders' Equity

Paid-in capital:			
Common stock, $50 par			
(50,000 shares authorized,			
20,000 shares issued).......................	$1,000,000		
Excess of issue price over par..............	80,000		
Total paid-in capital		$1,080,000	
Retained earnings:			
Appropriated for provision of			
Frye National Bank loan....................	$1,000,000		
Unappropriated..................................	490,000		
Total retained earnings......................		1,490,000	
Total stockholders' equity.........................			2,570,000
Total liabilities and			
stockholders' equity			$3,720,000

The board of directors is scheduled to meet January 8, 1991, to discuss the results of operations for 1990 and to consider the declaration of dividends for the fourth quarter of 1990. The chairman of the board has asked for your advice on the declaration of dividends.

Instructions:

(1) What factors should the board consider in deciding whether to declare a cash dividend?
(2) The board is considering the declaration of a stock dividend instead of a cash dividend. Discuss the issuance of a stock dividend from the point of view of (a) a stockholder and (b) the board of directors.

ETHICS DISCUSSION CASE	Sikes Inc. discontinued its cellular telephone operations on July 1, 1990. In preparing the income statement for the year ended December 31, 1990, Thomas Reeves, the controller, omitted the earnings per share amount for the discontinued operations. The per share loss on the discontinued operations was $1.05, while the net income per share was $4.20. Discuss whether Thomas Reeves is behaving in an ethical manner.

ANSWERS TO SELF-EXAMINATION QUESTIONS

1. **D** Paid-in capital is one of the two major subdivisions of the stockholders' equity of a corporation. It may result from many sources, including the receipt of donated real estate (answer A), the redemption of a corporation's own stock (answer B), and the sale of a corporation's treasury stock (answer C).

2. **A** The amount of income tax deferred to future years is $16,000 (answer A), determined as follows:

Depreciation expense, sum-of-the-years-digits method	$100,000
Depreciation expense, straight-line method	60,000
Excess expense in determination of taxable income	$ 40,000
Income tax rate	× 40%
Income tax deferred to future years	$ 16,000

3. **A** Events and transactions that are distinguished by their unusual nature and by the infrequency of their occurrence, such as a gain on condemnation of land for public use, are reported in the income statement as extraordinary items (answer A).

4. **C** The correction of a material error related to a prior period should be excluded from the determination of net income of the current period and reported as an adjustment of the balance of retained earnings at the beginning of the current period (answer C).

5. **C** An appropriation for plant expansion is a portion of total retained earnings and would be reported in the stockholder's equity section of the balance sheet (answer C).

CHAPTER SIXTEEN

LONG-TERM LIABILITIES AND INVESTMENTS IN BONDS

CHAPTER OBJECTIVES

1 Describe and illustrate the impact of borrowing on a long-term basis as a means of financing corporations.

2 Describe the characteristics of bonds.

3 Describe the present value concept.

4 Describe and illustrate the present value concept for bonds payable.

5 Describe and illustrate the accounting for bonds payable.

6 Describe and illustrate the use of and accounting for bond sinking funds.

7 Describe and illustrate the accounting for an appropriation for bond indebtedness.

8 Describe and illustrate the accounting for bond redemption.

9 Describe the balance sheet presentation of bonds payable.

10 Describe and illustrate the accounting for investments in bonds.

The acquisition of cash and other assets by a corporation through the issuance of its stock has been discussed in earlier chapters. Expansion of corporate enterprises through the retention of earnings, in some instances accompanied by the issuance of stock dividends, has also been explored. In addition to these two methods of obtaining relatively permanent funds, corporations may also borrow money on a long-term basis by issuing notes or **bonds**, which are a form of interest-bearing note. Long-term notes may be issued to relatively few lending agencies or to a single investor, such as an insurance company. Bonds are usually sold to underwriters (dealers and brokers in securities), who in turn sell them to investors. Although the discussion that follows will be limited to bonds, the accounting principles involved apply equally to long-term notes.

When funds are borrowed through the issuance of bonds, there is a definite commitment to pay interest and to repay the principal at a stated future date. Bondholders are creditors of the issuing corporation and their claims for interest and for repayment of principal rank ahead of the claims of stockholders.

FINANCING CORPORATIONS

OBJECTIVE 1
Describe and illustrate the impact of borrowing on a long-term basis as a means of financing corporations.

Many factors influence the incorporators or the board of directors in deciding upon the best means of obtaining funds. The subject will be limited here to a brief illustration of the effect of different financing methods on the income of a corporation and the common stockholders. To illustrate, assume that three different plans for financing a $4,000,000 corporation are under consideration by its organizers, and that in each case the securities will be issued at their par or face amount. The incorporators estimate that the enterprise will earn $800,000 annually, before deducting interest on the bonds and income tax estimated at 40% of income. The following tabulation indicates the amount of earnings that would be available to common stockholders under each of the three plans:

	Plan 1	Plan 2	Plan 3
12% bonds	—	—	$2,000,000
Preferred 9% stock, $50 par.....................	—	$2,000,000	1,000,000
Common stock, $10 par	$4,000,000	2,000,000	1,000,000
Total...	$4,000,000	$4,000,000	$4,000,000
Earnings before interest and income tax.....	$ 800,000	$ 800,000	$ 800,000
Deduct interest on bonds..........................	—	—	240,000
Income before income tax.....................	$ 800,000	$ 800,000	$ 560,000
Deduct income tax	320,000	320,000	224,000
Net income	$ 480,000	$ 480,000	$ 336,000
Dividends on preferred stock....................	—	180,000	90,000
Available for dividends on common stock ...	$ 480,000	$ 300,000	$ 246,000
Shares of common stock outstanding.........	400,000	200,000	100,000
Earnings per share on common stock........	$1.20	$1.50	$2.46

If Plan 1 is adopted and the entire financing is from the issuance of common stock, the earnings per share on the common stock would be $1.20 per share. Under Plan 2, the effect of using 9% preferred stock for half of the capitalization would result in $1.50 earnings per common share. The issuance of 12% bonds in Plan 3, with the remaining capitalization split between preferred and common stock, would yield a return of $2.46 per share on common stock.

Under the assumed conditions, Plan 3 would obviously be the most attractive for common stockholders. If the anticipated earnings should increase beyond $800,000, the spread between the earnings per share to common stockholders under Plan 1 and Plan 3 would become even greater. But if successively smaller amounts of earnings are assumed, the attractiveness of Plan 2 and Plan 3 decreases. The effect of lower earnings is illustrated by the following tabulation, in which earnings, before interest and income tax are deducted, are assumed to be $440,000 instead of $800,000:

	Plan 1	Plan 2	Plan 3
12% bonds	—	—	$2,000,000
Preferred 9% stock, $50 par.....................	—	$2,000,000	1,000,000
Common stock, $10 par	$4,000,000	2,000,000	1,000,000
Total...	$4,000,000	$4,000,000	$4,000,000
Earnings before interest and income tax.....	$ 440,000	$ 440,000	$ 440,000
Deduct interest on bonds..........................	—	—	240,000
Income before income tax.....................	$ 440,000	$ 440,000	$ 200,000
Deduct income tax	176,000	176,000	80,000
Net income	$ 264,000	$ 264,000	$ 120,000
Dividends on preferred stock....................	—	180,000	90,000
Available for dividends on common stock ...	$ 264,000	$ 84,000	$ 30,000
Shares of common stock outstanding.........	400,000	200,000	100,000
Earnings per share on common stock........	$.66	$.42	$.30

The preceding analysis focused attention on the effect of the different plans on earnings per share of common stock. There are other factors that must be considered when different methods of financing are evaluated. The issuance of bonds represents a fixed annual interest charge that, in contrast to dividends, is not subject to corporate control. Provision must also be made for the eventual repayment of the principal amount of the bonds, in contrast to the absence of any such obligation to stockholders. On the other hand, a decision to finance entirely by an issuance of common stock would require substantial investment by a single stockholder or small group of stockholders who desire to control the corporation.

HOW REFINANCING WORKS

Some of the same factors that influence a corporation's decision on financing will also be considered when a company refinances, or changes the structure of its debt and stockholders' equity. In refinancing, however, both management and the stockholders are concerned about the effect of *changes* in the debt and equity relationship. These concerns are described in the following excerpt from an article in *USA TODAY*:

When a major company like Allegis Corp. announces that it is "recapitalizing" [refinancing], many shareholders may be baffled.... Recapitalization plans aren't as complicated as they seem, however. Here are some basic questions and answers:

What is capital?

Simply put, it's a company's money. It can come from two sources: stockholders and lenders.

The stockholders' share is called equity. It represents cash the company has raised by selling stock, and profits the company has built up.

The other part of capital is money borrowed from banks or raised by selling bonds.

How companies balance equity and debt is up to them. At IBM Corp., only 11% of total capital is debt. Sears, Roebuck and Co. has 46% debt. The level of debt a company keeps depends on the risk its managers are willing to assume.

What does risk have to do with it?

It's no different for a company than for an individual. The more debt you have, the greater the risk. Reason: Any profit you earn first must go to meet interest payments. If earnings aren't sufficient to cover the interest owed, you'll have to deplete your savings—or sell something—to raise the needed cash.

What happens in a recapitalization?

A company decides to borrow heavily to raise cash for a large, one-time cash... payment to shareholders.... [In addition,]... shareholders also receive new shares to replace their old shares in the company.... [In] the process, the company generally [reduces its equity]. It's replaced with debt.

How can the company afford the debt load?

The company is forced to operate more efficiently than ever. It will have to slash expenses to keep earnings up in the face of higher interest expenses. Owens-Corning Fiberglas Corp., for example, pared its research costs significantly after its recapitalization last year....

Is there any advantage in being so heavily in debt?

Debt does have a good side. By borrowing, you gain "leverage"—the ability to control more assets by using someone else's money. That can magnify the return to shareholders, if business is good and the firm operates efficiently....

Source: Neil Budde, "How Company Recapitalization Plans Work," *USA TODAY*, (June 8, 1987).

CHARACTERISTICS OF BONDS

OBJECTIVE 2
Describe the characteristics of bonds.

When a corporation issues bonds, it executes a contract with the bondholders known as a **bond indenture** or **trust indenture**. The entire issue is divided into a number of individual bonds, which may be of varying denominations. Usually the principal of each bond, also called the **face value**, is $1,000 or a multiple thereof. The interest on bonds may be payable at annual, semiannual, or quarterly intervals. Most bonds provide for payment on a semiannual basis.

Registered bonds may be transferred from one owner to another only by endorsement on the bond certificate, and the issuing corporation must maintain a record of the name and the address of each bondholder. Interest payments are made by check to the owner of record. Title to **bearer bonds**, which are also called **coupon bonds**, is transferred merely by delivery, and the issuing corporation does not know the identity of the bondholders. Interest coupons for the entire term, in the form of checks or drafts payable to bearer, are attached to the bond certificate. At each interest date, the holder detaches the appropriate coupon and presents it to a bank for payment. Although bearer bonds were issued frequently in the past, they are rarely issued today.

When all bonds of an issue mature at the same time, they are called **term bonds**. If the maturities are spread over several dates, they are called **serial bonds**. For example, one tenth of an issue of $1,000,000, or $100,000, may mature eleven years from the issuance date, another $100,000 may mature twelve years from the issuance date, and so on until the final $100,000 matures at the end of the twentieth year.

Bonds that may be exchanged for other securities under certain conditions are called **convertible bonds**. Bonds issued by a corporation that reserves the right to redeem them before maturity are referred to as **callable bonds**.

A **secured bond** is one that gives the bondholder a claim on specific assets in case the issuing corporation fails to meet its obligations on the bonds. The properties mortgaged or pledged may be specific buildings and equipment, the entire plant, or stocks and bonds of other companies owned by the debtor corporation. Unsecured bonds issued on the basis of the general credit of the corporation are called **debenture bonds**.

PRESENT VALUE CONCEPTS

OBJECTIVE 3
Describe the present value concept.

The concept of present value plays an important role in many accounting analyses and business decisions. For example, accounting analyses based on the present value concept are useful for evaluating proposals for long-term investments in plant and equipment. Such analyses will be discussed in a later chapter. In this chapter, the concept of present value will be discussed in the context of the role that it plays in determining the selling price of bonds.

The concept of **present value** is that an amount of cash to be received at some date in the future is not the equivalent of the same amount of cash held at an earlier date. In other words, a sum of cash to be received in the future is not as valuable as the same sum on hand today, because cash on hand today can be invested to earn income. For example, $100 on hand today would be more valuable than $100 to be received a year from today. In this case, if the $100 cash on hand today can be invested to earn 10% per year, the $100 will accumulate to $110 ($100 plus $10 earnings) by one year from today. The $100 on hand today can be referred to as the present value amount that is equivalent to $110 to be received a year from today.

PRESENT VALUE CONCEPTS FOR BONDS PAYABLE

OBJECTIVE 4
Describe and illustrate the present value concept for bonds payable.

When a corporation issues bonds, it usually incurs two distinct obligations: (1) to pay the face amount of the bonds at a specified maturity date and (2) to pay periodic interest at a specified percentage of the face amount. The price that a buyer is willing to pay for these future benefits is the sum of (1) the *present value* of the face amount of the bonds at the maturity date and (2) the *present value* of the periodic interest payments.

Present Value of $1

The present value of the face amount of bonds at the maturity date is the value today of the promise to pay the face amount at some future date. To illustrate, assume that $1,000 is to be paid in one year and that the rate of earnings is 12%. The present value amount is $892.86 ($1,000 ÷ 1.12). If the $1,000 is to be paid one year later (two years in all), with the earnings compounded at the end of the first year, the present value amount would be $797.20 ($892.86 ÷ 1.12).

Instead of determining the present value of a future cash sum by a series of divisions in the manner just illustrated, it is customary to use a table of present values to find the present value of $1 for the appropriate number of periods, and to multiply that present value factor by the amount of the future cash sum. A partial table of the present value of $1 appears as follows:[1]

Present Value of $1 at Compound Interest

Periods	5%	5½%	6%	6½%	7%	10%	11%	12%	13%	14%
1	0.9524	0.9479	0.9434	0.9390	0.9346	0.9091	0.9009	0.8929	0.8850	0.8772
2	0.9070	0.8985	0.8900	0.8817	0.8734	0.8264	0.8116	0.7972	0.7831	0.7695
3	0.8638	0.8516	0.8396	0.8278	0.8163	0.7513	0.7312	0.7118	0.6931	0.6750
4	0.8227	0.8072	0.7921	0.7773	0.7629	0.6830	0.6587	0.6355	0.6133	0.5921
5	0.7835	0.7651	0.7473	0.7299	0.7130	0.6209	0.5935	0.5674	0.5428	0.5194
6	0.7462	0.7252	0.7050	0.6853	0.6663	0.5645	0.5346	0.5066	0.4803	0.4556
7	0.7107	0.6874	0.6651	0.6435	0.6228	0.5132	0.4817	0.4523	0.4251	0.3996
8	0.6768	0.6516	0.6274	0.6042	0.5820	0.4665	0.4339	0.4039	0.3762	0.3506
9	0.6446	0.6176	0.5919	0.5674	0.5439	0.4241	0.3909	0.3606	0.3329	0.3075
10	0.6139	0.5854	0.5584	0.5327	0.5083	0.3855	0.3522	0.3220	0.2946	0.2697
11	0.5847	0.5549	0.5268	0.5002	0.4751	0.3505	0.3173	0.2875	0.2607	0.2366
12	0.5568	0.5260	0.4970	0.4697	0.4440	0.3186	0.2858	0.2567	0.2307	0.2076
13	0.5303	0.4986	0.4688	0.4410	0.4150	0.2897	0.2575	0.2292	0.2042	0.1821
14	0.5051	0.4726	0.4423	0.4141	0.3878	0.2633	0.2320	0.2046	0.1807	0.1597
15	0.4810	0.4479	0.4173	0.3888	0.3624	0.2394	0.2090	0.1827	0.1599	0.1401
16	0.4581	0.4246	0.3936	0.3651	0.3387	0.2176	0.1883	0.1631	0.1415	0.1229
17	0.4363	0.4024	0.3714	0.3428	0.3166	0.1978	0.1696	0.1456	0.1252	0.1078
18	0.4155	0.3815	0.3503	0.3219	0.2959	0.1799	0.1528	0.1300	0.1108	0.0946
19	0.3957	0.3616	0.3305	0.3022	0.2765	0.1635	0.1377	0.1161	0.0981	0.0829
20	0.3769	0.3427	0.3118	0.2838	0.2584	0.1486	0.1240	0.1037	0.0868	0.0728

For the previous example, the table indicates that the present value of $1 to be received two years hence, with earnings at the rate of 12% a year, is .7972. Multiplying $1,000 by .7972 yields $797.20, which is the same amount that was determined previously by two successive divisions. In using the table, it should be noted that the "periods" column represents the number of compounding periods, while the "percentage" columns represent the compound interest rate per period. For example, 12% for two years compounded

---

[1]The tables illustrated are limited to 20 periods for a small number of interest rates, and the amounts are carried to only four decimal places. Books of tables are available with as many as 360 periods, 45 interest rates (including many fractional rates), and amounts carried to eight decimal places. More complete interest tables are provided in Appendix A.

annually, as in the preceding illustration, is 12% for two periods; 12% for two years compounded semiannually would be 6% (12% per year ÷ 2 semiannual periods) for four periods (2 years × 2 semiannual periods); and 12% for three years compounded semiannually would be 6% (12% ÷ 2) for six periods (3 years × 2 semiannual periods).

Present Value of Annuity of $1

The present value of the periodic interest payments on bonds is the value today of the promise to pay a fixed amount of interest at the end of each of a number of periods. Such a series of fixed payments at fixed intervals is called an **annuity**.

The following partial table of the present value of an annuity of $1 at compound interest indicates the value now (present value) of $1 to be received at the end of *each* period at various compound rates of interest. For example, the present value of $1,000 to be received at the end of each of the next 5 periods at 10% compound interest per period is $3,790.80 (3.7908 × $1,000).

Present Value of $1 at Compound Interest

Periods	5%	5½%	6%	6½%	7%	10%	11%	12%	13%	14%
1	0.9524	0.9479	0.9434	0.9390	0.9346	0.9091	0.9009	0.8929	0.8850	0.8772
2	1.8594	1.8463	1.8334	1.8206	1.8080	1.7355	1.7125	1.6901	1.6681	1.6467
3	2.7232	2.6979	2.6730	2.6485	2.6243	2.4869	2.4437	2.4018	2.3612	2.3216
4	3.5460	3.5052	3.4651	3.4258	3.3872	3.1699	3.1024	3.0373	2.9745	2.9137
5	4.3295	4.2703	4.2124	4.1557	4.1002	3.7908	3.6959	3.6048	3.5172	3.4331
6	5.0757	4.9955	4.9173	4.8410	4.7665	4.3553	4.2305	4.1114	3.9976	3.8887
7	5.7864	5.6830	5.5824	5.4845	5.3893	4.8684	4.7122	4.5638	4.4226	4.2883
8	6.4632	6.3346	6.2098	6.0888	5.9713	5.3349	5.1461	4.9676	4.7988	4.6389
9	7.1078	6.9522	6.8017	6.6561	6.5152	5.7590	5.5370	5.3283	5.1317	4.9464
10	7.7217	7.5376	7.3601	7.1888	7.0236	6.1446	5.8892	5.6502	5.4262	5.2161
11	8.3064	8.0925	7.8869	7.6890	7.4987	6.4951	6.2065	5.9377	5.6869	5.4527
12	8.8633	8.6185	8.3838	8.1587	7.9427	6.8137	6.4924	6.1944	5.9176	5.6603
13	9.3936	9.1171	8.8527	8.5997	8.3577	7.1034	6.7499	6.4235	6.1218	5.8424
14	9.8986	9.5896	9.2950	9.0138	8.7455	7.3667	6.9819	6.6282	6.3025	6.0021
15	10.3797	10.0376	9.7123	9.4027	9.1079	7.6061	7.1909	6.8109	6.4624	6.1422
16	10.8378	10.4622	10.1059	9.7678	9.4467	7.8237	7.3792	6.9740	6.6039	6.2651
17	11.2741	10.8646	10.4773	10.1106	9.7632	8.0216	7.5488	7.1196	6.7291	6.3729
18	11.6896	11.2461	10.8276	10.4325	10.0591	8.2014	7.7016	7.2497	6.8399	6.4674
19	12.0853	11.6077	11.1581	10.7347	10.3356	8.3649	7.8393	7.3658	6.9380	6.5504
20	12.4622	11.9504	11.4699	11.0185	10.5940	8.5136	7.9633	7.4694	7.0248	6.6231

ACCOUNTING FOR BONDS PAYABLE

OBJECTIVE 5
Describe and illustrate the accounting for bonds payable.

The interest rate specified in the bond indenture is called the **contract** or **coupon rate**, which may differ from the rate prevailing in the market at the time the bonds are issued. If the **market** or **effective rate** is higher than the contract rate, the bonds will sell at a **discount**, or less than their face amount. This discount results because buyers are unwilling to pay the face amount for bonds whose contract rate is lower than the prevailing market rate. The discount, therefore, represents the amount necessary to make up for the difference in the market and the contract interest rates. Conversely, if the market rate is lower than the contract rate, the bonds will sell at a **premium**, or more than their face amount. In this case, buyers are willing to pay more than the face amount for bonds whose contract rate is higher than the market rate.

Bonds Issued at Face Amount

To illustrate an issuance of bonds, assume that on January 1 a corporation issues for cash $100,000 of 12%, five-year bonds, with interest of $6,000 payable semiannually. The market rate of interest at the time the bonds are issued is 12%. Since the contract rate and the market rate of interest are the same, the bonds will sell at their face amount. This amount, calculated as follows, is the sum of (1) the present value of the face amount of $100,000 to be repaid in 5 years and (2) the present value of 10 semiannual interest payments of $6,000 each.[2]

Present value of face amount of $100,000 due in 5 years, at 12% compounded semiannually: $100,000 × .5584 (present value of $1 for 10 periods at 6%)	$ 55,840
Present value of 10 semiannual interest payments of $6,000, at 12% compounded semiannually: $6,000 × 7.3601 (present value of annuity of $1 for 10 periods at 6%)	44,160
Total present value of bonds	$100,000

The basic data for computing the two present values totaling $100,000 were obtained from the two present value tables presented on pages 612 and 613. The first of the two amounts, **$55,840,** is the present value of the $100,000 that is to be repaid in 5 years. The $55,840 is determined by locating the present value of $1 for 10 periods (5 years of semiannual payments) at 6% semiannually (12% annual rate) in the present value of $1 table and multiplying by $100,000. If the bond indenture provided that no interest would be paid during the entire 5-year period, the bonds would be worth only $55,840 at the time of their issuance. To express the concept of present value from a different viewpoint, if $55,840 were invested today, with interest at 12% compounded semiannually, the sum accumulated at the end of 10 semiannual periods would be $100,000.

The second of the two amounts, **$44,160,** is the present value of the series of ten $6,000 payments. The $44,160 is determined by locating the present value of an annuity of $1 for 10 periods (5 years of semiannual payments) at 6% semiannually (12% annual rate) in the present value of an annuity of $1 table and multiplying by $6,000. The present value of $44,160 can also be viewed as the amount of a current deposit earning 12% that would yield ten semiannual withdrawals of $6,000, with the original deposit being reduced to zero by the tenth withdrawal.

The entry to record the issuance of the $100,000 bonds at their face amount is as follows:

Jan. 1	Cash	100,000	
	Bonds Payable		100,000

At six-month intervals following the issuance of the 12% bonds, the interest payment of $6,000 is recorded in the usual manner by a debit to Interest Expense and a credit to Cash. At the maturity date, the payment of the principal sum of $100,000 would be recorded by a debit to Bonds Payable and a credit to Cash.

[2]Because the present value tables are rounded to four decimal places, minor rounding errors may appear in the illustrations.

Bonds Issued at a Discount

If the market rate of interest is 13% and the contract rate is 12%, the bonds will sell at a discount. The present value of the five-year, $100,000 bonds with a market rate of 13% may be calculated as follows:

Present value of $100,000 due in 5 years, at 13% compounded semiannually: $100,000 × .5327 (present value of $1 for 10 periods at 6 1/2%)..........	$53,270
Present value of 10 semiannual interest payments of $6,000 at 13% compounded semiannually: $6,000 × 7.1888 (present value of an annuity of $1 for 10 periods at 6 1/2%)...	43,133
Total present value of bonds	$96,403

The two present values that make up the total are both somewhat less than the comparable amounts in the first illustration, where the contract rate and the market rate were exactly the same. The reason for the lesser present value is that the value now of a future amount becomes less and less as the interest rate rises. In other words, the sum that would have to be invested today to equal a fixed future amount becomes less and less as the interest rate earned on the investment rises.

In the following entry to record the issuance of the 12% bonds, the bond liability is recorded at the face amount, and the discount is recorded in a separate contra account:

Jan. 1	Cash...	96,403	
	Discount on Bonds Payable	3,597	
	Bonds Payable....................................		100,000

The $3,597 discount may be viewed as the amount that is needed to compensate the investor for accepting a contract rate of interest that is below the prevailing market rate. From another view, the $3,597 represents the additional amount that must be returned by the issuer at maturity; that is, the issuer received $96,403 at the sale date but must return $100,000 at the maturity date. The $3,597 discount must therefore be amortized as additional interest expense over the five-year life of the bonds. There are two widely used methods of allocating bond discount to the various periods: (1) **straight-line** and (2) **interest**. Although the interest method is the recommended method, the straight-line method is acceptable if the results obtained by its use do not materially differ from the results that would be obtained by the use of the interest method.[3]

Amortization of Discount by the Straight-Line Method. The straight-line method is the simpler of the two methods and provides for amortization in equal periodic amounts. Application of this method to the illustration would yield amortization of 1/10 of $3,597, or $359.70, each half year. The amount of the interest expense on the bonds would remain constant for each half year at $6,000 plus $359.70, or $6,359.70. The entry to record the first interest payment and the amortization of the related amount of discount is as follows:

---

[3]*Opinions of the Accounting Principles Board, No. 21,* "Interest on Receivables and Payables" (New York: American Institute of Certified Public Accountants, 1971), par. 14.

June 30	Interest Expense	6,359.70	
	Discount on Bonds Payable		359.70
	Cash..		6,000.00

As an alternative to recording the amortization each time the interest is paid, it may be recorded only at the end of the year. When this procedure is used, each interest payment is recorded as a debit to Interest Expense and a credit to Cash. In terms of the illustration, the entry to amortize the discount at the end of the first year would be as follows:

| Dec. 31 | Interest Expense .... | 719.40 | |
| | Discount on Bonds Payable .... | | 719.40 |

The amount of the discount amortized, $719.40, is made up of the two semiannual amortization amounts of $359.70.

Amortization of Discount by the Interest Method. In contrast to the straight-line method, which provides for a constant *amount* of interest expense, the interest method provides for a constant *rate* of interest on the carrying amount (also called **book value**) of the bonds at the beginning of each period. The interest rate used in the computation is the market rate as of the date the bonds were issued, and the carrying amount of the bonds is their face amount minus the unamortized discount. The difference between the interest expense computed in this manner and the amount of the periodic interest payment is the amount of discount to be amortized for the period. Application of this method to the illustration yields the following data:

Amortization of Discount on Bonds Payable

Interest Payment	A Interest Paid (6% of Face Amount)	B Interest Expense (6½% of Bond Carrying Amount)	C Discount Amortization (B–A)	D Unamortized Discount (D–C)	E Bond Carrying Amount ($100,000–D)
				$3,597	$ 96,403
1	$6,000	$6,266(6½% of $96,403)	$266	3,331	96,669
2	6,000	6,284(6½% of $96,669)	284	3,047	96,953
3	6,000	6,302(6½% of $96,953)	302	2,745	97,255
4	6,000	6,322(6½% of $97,255)	322	2,423	97,577
5	6,000	6,343(6½% of $97,577)	343	2,080	97,920
6	6,000	6,365(6½% of $97,920)	365	1,715	98,285
7	6,000	6,389(6½% of $98,285)	389	1,326	98,674
8	6,000	6,415(6½% of $98,674)	415	911	99,089
9	6,000	6,441(6½% of $99,089)	441	470	99,530
10	6,000	6,470(6½% of $99,530)	470	—	100,000

The following important details should be observed:

1. The interest paid (column A) remains constant at 6% of $100,000, the face amount of the bonds.
2. The interest expense (column B) is computed at 6 1/2% of the bond carrying amount at the beginning of each period, yielding a gradually increasing amount.

3. The excess of the interest expense over the interest payment of $6,000 is the amount of discount to be amortized (column C).
4. The unamortized discount (column D) decreases from the initial balance, $3,597, to a zero balance at the maturity date of the bonds.
5. The carrying amount (column E) increases from $96,403, the amount received for the bonds, to $100,000 at maturity.

The entry to record the first interest payment and the amortization of the related amount of discount is as follows:

June 30	Interest Expense	6,266	
	Discount on Bonds Payable		266
	Cash...		6,000

If the amortization is recorded only at the end of the year, the amount of the discount amortized on December 31 would be $550, which is the sum of the first two semiannual amortization amounts ($266 and $284) from the preceding table.

Bonds Issued at a Premium

If the market rate of interest is 11% and the contract rate is 12%, the bonds will sell at a premium. The present value of the five-year, $100,000 bonds, with a market rate of 11%, may be calculated as follows:

Present value of $100,000 due in 5 years, at 11% compounded semi-annually: $100,000 × .5854 (present value of $1 for 10 periods at 5 1/2%)...	$ 58,540
Present value of 10 semiannual interest payments of $6,000, at 11% compounded semiannually: $6,000 × 7.5376 (present value of an annuity of $1 for 10 periods at 5 1/2%)...	45,226
Total present value of bonds	$103,766

The entry to record the issuance of the bonds is as follows:

Jan. 1	Cash..	103,766	
	Bonds Payable....................................		100,000
	Premium on Bonds Payable		3,766

Procedures for amortization of the premium and determination of the periodic interest expense are basically the same as those used for bonds issued at a discount.

Amortization of Premium by the Straight-Line Method. Application of the straight-line method to the illustration would yield amortization of 1/10 of $3,766, or $376.60, each half year. Just as bond discount can be viewed as additional interest expense, bond premium can be viewed as a reduction in the amount of interest expense. The entry to record the first interest payment and the amortization of the related amount of premium is as follows:

June 30	Interest Expense	5,623.40	
	Premium on Bonds Payable	376.60	
	Cash...		6,000.00

If the amortization of the premium is recorded only at the end of the year, each interest payment would be recorded by debiting Interest Expense and crediting Cash. The amortization of the premium at the end of the year, in the illustration, would then be recorded as follows:

Dec. 31	Premium on Bonds Payable	753.20	
	Interest Expense		753.20

The amount of the premium amortized, $753.20, is the sum of the two semiannual amounts of $376.60.

Amortization of Premium by the Interest Method. Application of the interest method of amortization yields the following data:

Amortization of Premium on Bonds Payable

Interest Payment	A Interest Paid (6% of Face Amount)	B Interest Expense (5½% of Bond Carrying Amount)	C Premium Amortization (A–B)	D Unamortized Premium (D–C)	E Bond Carrying Amount ($100,000 + D)
				$3,766	$103,766
1	$6,000	$5,707(5½% of $103,766)	$293	3,473	103,473
2	6,000	$5,691(5½% of $103,473)	309	3,164	103,164
3	6,000	$5,674(5½% of $103,164)	326	2,838	102,838
4	6,000	$5,657(5½% of $102,838)	343	2,495	102,495
5	6,000	$5,638(5½% of $102,495)	362	2,133	102,133
6	6,000	$5,618(5½% of $102,133)	382	1,751	101,751
7	6,000	$5,597(5½% of $101,751)	403	1,348	101,348
8	6,000	$5,575(5½% of $101,348)	425	923	100,923
9	6,000	$5,551(5½% of $100,923)	449	474	100,474
10	6,000	$5,526(5½% of $100,474)	474	—	100,000

The following important details should be observed:

1. The interest paid (column A) remains constant at 6% of $100,000, the face amount of the bonds.
2. The interest expense (column B) is computed at 5 1/2% of the bond carrying amount at the beginning of each period, yielding a gradually decreasing amount.
3. The excess of the periodic interest payment of $6,000 over the interest expense is the amount of premium to be amortized (column C).
4. The unamortized premium (column D) decreases from the initial balance, $3,766, to a zero balance at the maturity date of the bonds.
5. The carrying amount (column E) decreases from $103,766, the amount received for the bonds, to $100,000 at maturity.

The entry to record the first payment and the amortization of the related amount of premium is as follows:

June 30	Interest Expense	5,707	
	Premium on Bonds Payable	293	
	Cash		6,000

If the amortization is recorded only at the end of the year, the amount of the premium amortized on December 31 would be $602, which is the sum of the first two semiannual amounts ($293 and $309) from the preceding table.

Zero-Coupon Bonds

During the 1980s, some enterprises issued bonds that did not provide for periodic interest payments. In its 1987 financial statements, for example, PepsiCo Inc. reported such bonds, called **zero-coupon bonds**, with a face value of $1.1 billion and due between 1989 and 2012.

Zero-coupon bonds provide for only the payment of the face amount of the bonds at the maturity date. Because the bonds do not provide for periodic interest payments, they sell at a large discount. To illustrate, if the market rate of interest for five-year bonds which pay interest semiannually is 13%, the present value of $100,000 zero-coupon, five-year bonds may be calculated as follows:

Present value of $100,000 due in 5 years, at 13% compounded semiannually:
$100,000 × .5327 (present value of $1 for 10 periods at 6 1/2%) $53,270

The accounting for zero-coupon bonds is similar to that for interest-bearing bonds that have been sold at a discount. The entry to record the issuance of the bonds is as follows:

Cash...	53,270	
Discount on Bonds Payable.....................................	46,730	
Bonds Payable..		100,000

The discount of $46,730 is amortized as interest expense over the life of the bonds, using either the straight-line method or the interest method, as illustrated on pages 615–617.

BOND SINKING FUND

OBJECTIVE 6
Describe and illustrate the use of and accounting for bond sinking funds.

The bond indenture may provide that funds for the payment of bonds at maturity be accumulated over the life of the issue. The amounts set aside are kept separate from other assets in a special fund called a **sinking fund**. Cash deposited in the fund is usually invested in income-producing securities. The periodic deposits plus the earnings on the investments should approximately equal the face amount of the bonds at maturity. In determining the amount of these periodic deposits, the concept of future value can be used.

Future Value Concepts

Future value is the amount that will accumulate at some future date as a result of an investment or a series of investments. For example, if $1,000 is invested to earn 10% per year, the future value at the end of a year will be $1,100 ($1,000 plus $100 earnings). If the $1,100 is left to accumulate additional compounded earnings for three years, the future value at the end of the second year will be $1,210 ($1,100 plus $110 earnings), and at the end of the third year, $1,331 ($1,210 plus $121 earnings).

The future value of an investment can also be determined by using a table of future values to find the future value of $1 for the appropriate number of periods, and then multiplying the amount of the investment by this future value factor. A partial table of the future value of $1 appears as follows:

Future Value of $1 at Compound Interest

Periods	5%	5½%	6%	6½%	7%	10%	11%	12%	13%	14%
1	1.0500	1.0550	1.0600	1.0650	1.0700	1.1000	1.1100	1.1200	1.1300	1.1400
2	1.1025	1.1130	1.1236	1.1342	1.1449	1.2100	1.2321	1.2544	1.2769	1.2996
3	1.1576	1.1742	1.1910	1.2080	1.2250	1.3310	1.3676	1.4049	1.4429	1.4815
4	1.2155	1.2388	1.2625	1.2865	1.3108	1.4641	1.5181	1.5735	1.6305	1.6890
5	1.2763	1.3070	1.3382	1.3701	1.4026	1.6105	1.6851	1.7623	1.8424	1.9254
6	1.3401	1.3788	1.4185	1.4591	1.5007	1.7716	1.8704	1.9738	2.0820	2.1950
7	1.4071	1.4547	1.5036	1.5540	1.6058	1.9487	2.0762	2.2107	2.3526	2.5023
8	1.4775	1.5347	1.5939	1.6550	1.7182	2.1436	2.3045	2.4760	2.6584	2.8526
9	1.5513	1.6191	1.6895	1.7626	1.8385	2.3580	2.5580	2.7731	3.0040	3.2520
10	1.6289	1.7081	1.7909	1.8771	1.9672	2.5937	2.8394	3.1059	3.3946	3.7072
11	1.7103	1.8021	1.8983	1.9992	2.1049	2.8531	3.1518	3.4786	3.8359	4.2262
12	1.7959	1.9012	2.0122	2.1291	2.2522	3.1384	3.4985	3.8960	4.3345	4.8179
13	1.8857	2.0058	2.1329	2.2675	2.4099	3.4523	3.8833	4.3635	4.8980	5.4924
14	1.9799	2.1161	2.2609	2.4149	2.5785	3.7975	4.3104	4.8871	5.5348	6.2614
15	2.0789	2.2325	2.3966	2.5718	2.7590	4.1773	4.7846	5.4736	6.2543	7.1379
16	2.1829	2.3553	2.5404	2.7390	2.9522	4.5950	5.3109	6.1304	7.0673	8.1373
17	2.2920	2.4848	2.6928	2.9171	3.1588	5.0545	5.8951	6.8660	7.9861	9.2765
18	2.4066	2.6215	2.8543	3.1067	3.3799	5.5599	6.5436	7.6900	9.0243	10.5752
19	2.5270	2.7657	3.0256	3.3086	3.6165	6.1159	7.2633	8.6128	10.1974	12.0557
20	2.6533	2.9178	3.2071	3.5237	3.8697	6.7275	8.0623	9.6463	11.5231	13.7435

For the previous example, the table indicates that the future value of $1 three years (periods) hence, with earnings at the rate of 10% a year, is 1.331. Multiplying $1,000 by 1.331 yields $1,331, which is the same amount as determined previously.

Future value may also arise from a series of equal investments made at fixed intervals (an annuity).[4] For example, if $1,000 is invested at the end of each year to earn 10% per year compounded annually, the future value of the annuity at the end of the third year would be $3,310, determined as follows:

Year	Beginning Balance	Earnings During Year (10% × Beginning Balance)	Annual Deposit (End of Year)	Accumulation at End of Year
1	—	—	$1,000	$1,000
2	$1,000	$100	1,000	2,100
3	2,100	210	1,000	3,310

The future value of a series of investments can also be determined by using a table of future values to find the future value of an annuity of $1 for the appropriate number of periods, and then multiplying the amount of the investment by the future value factor. A partial table of the future value of an annuity of $1 appears as follows:

---

[4]As discussed in a preceding section, a series of fixed payments or investments at fixed intervals is called an annuity.

Future Value of Annuity of $1 at Compound Interest (Investments at End of Period)

Periods	5%	5½%	6%	6½%	7%	10%	11%	12%	13%	14%
1	1.0000	1.0000	1.0000	1.0000	1.0000	1.0000	1.0000	1.0000	1.0000	1.0000
2	2.0500	2.0550	2.0600	2.0650	2.0700	2.1000	2.1100	2.1200	2.1300	2.1400
3	3.1525	3.1680	3.1836	3.1992	3.2149	3.3100	3.3421	3.3744	3.4069	3.4396
4	4.3101	4.3423	4.3746	4.4072	4.4399	4.6410	4.7097	4.7793	4.8498	4.9211
5	5.5256	5.5811	5.6371	5.6936	5.7507	6.1051	6.2278	6.3529	6.4803	6.6101
6	6.8019	6.8881	6.9753	7.0637	7.1533	7.7156	7.9129	8.1152	8.3227	8.5355
7	8.1420	8.2669	8.3938	8.5229	8.6540	9.4872	9.7833	10.0890	10.4047	10.7305
8	9.5491	9.7216	9.8975	10.0769	10.2598	11.4359	11.8594	12.2997	12.7573	13.2328
9	11.0266	11.2563	11.4913	11.7319	11.9780	13.5795	14.1640	14.7757	15.4157	16.0854
10	12.5779	12.8754	13.1808	13.4944	13.8165	15.9374	16.7220	17.5487	18.4198	19.3373
11	14.2068	14.5835	14.9716	15.3716	15.7836	18.5312	19.5614	20.6546	21.8143	23.0445
12	15.9171	16.3856	16.8699	17.3707	17.8885	21.3843	22.7132	24.1331	25.6502	27.2708
13	17.7130	18.2868	18.8821	19.4998	20.1406	24.5227	26.2116	28.0291	29.9847	32.0887
14	19.5986	20.2926	21.0151	21.7673	22.5505	27.9750	30.0949	32.3926	34.8827	37.5811
15	21.5786	22.4087	23.2760	24.1822	25.1290	31.7725	34.4054	37.2797	40.4175	43.8424
16	23.6575	24.6411	25.6725	26.7540	27.8881	35.9497	39.1900	42.7533	46.6717	50.9804
17	25.8404	26.9964	28.2129	29.4930	30.8402	40.5447	44.5008	48.8837	53.7391	59.1176
18	28.1324	29.4812	30.9057	32.4104	33.9990	45.5992	50.3959	55.7497	61.7251	68.3941
19	30.5390	32.1027	33.7600	35.5167	37.3790	51.1591	56.9395	63.4397	70.7494	78.9692
20	33.0660	34.8683	36.7856	38.8253	40.9955	57.2750	64.2028	72.0524	80.9468	91.0249

For the previous example, the table indicates that the future value of an annuity of $1 three years (periods) hence, with earnings at the rate of 10% a year, is 3.310. Multiplying $1,000 by 3.310 yields $3,310, which is the same amount as determined previously.

To illustrate the concept of the future value of an annuity for the periodic deposits in a bond sinking fund, assume that a corporation issues $100,000 of 10-year bonds, dated January 1. A bond sinking fund for the payment of the bonds at maturity is established, with deposits to be made at the end of each year. If the deposits are expected to earn 14% per year, the annual deposit would be $5,171, determined as follows:

$$\text{Annual Deposit} = \frac{\text{Maturity Value of Bonds}}{\text{Future Value of Annuity of \$1 for 10 Periods at 14\%}}$$

$$\text{Annual Deposit} = \frac{\$100,000}{19.3373}$$

$$\text{Annual Deposit} = \$5,171 \text{ (rounded)}$$

Accounting for Bond Sinking Fund

When cash is transferred to the sinking fund, an account called Sinking Fund Cash is debited and Cash is credited. The purchase of investments is recorded by a debit to Sinking Fund Investments and a credit to Sinking Fund Cash. As income (interest or dividends) is received, the cash is debited to Sinking Fund Cash and Sinking Fund Income is credited.

The accounting for a bond sinking fund is illustrated by using the preceding example, in which a corporation issues $100,000 of 10-year bonds dated January 1. As indicated in the preceding section, annual deposits of $5,171, invested in securities that will yield approximately 14% per year, are sufficient to provide a fund of approximately $100,000 at the end of 10 years. A few of the typical transactions and the related entries affecting the sinking fund during the 10-year period are illustrated in the following paragraphs:

Deposit of cash in
the fund

| Sinking Fund Cash... | 5,171 | |
| Cash.. | | 5,171 |

The first deposit in the sinking fund is recorded. A similar entry would
be recorded as deposits are made at the end of each of the 9 remaining
years.

Purchase of
investments

| Sinking Fund Investments....................................... | 5,000 | |
| Sinking Fund Cash... | | 5,000 |

The purchases of securities after the first deposit was made are recorded
in a summary entry. The time of purchase and the amount invested at
any one time vary, depending upon market conditions and the unit price
of securities purchased.

Receipt of income
from investments

| Sinking Fund Cash... | 700 | |
| Sinking Fund Income.. | | 700 |

The receipt of income for the year on the securities purchased is recorded
in a summary entry. Interest and dividends are received at different
times during the year, and the amount earned per year normally increases as the fund increases.

Sale of
investments

Sinking Fund Cash...	85,100	
Sinking Fund Investments.....................................		82,480
Gain on Sale of Investments		2,620

The sale of all securities at the end of the tenth year is recorded. Investments may be sold from time to time and the proceeds reinvested. Prior
to maturity, all investments are converted into cash.

Payment of bonds

Bonds Payable..	100,000	
Cash..	1,791	
Sinking Fund Cash..		101,791

The payment of the bonds and the transfer of the remaining sinking
fund cash to the cash account is recorded. The cash available in the fund
at the end of the tenth year is assumed to be composed of the following:

Proceeds from sale of investments......................................	$ 85,100
Income earned during tenth year...	11,520
Last annual deposit	5,171
Total..	$101,791

In the illustration, the amount of the fund exceeded the amount of the liability by $1,791. This excess was transferred to the regular cash account. If the fund had been less than the amount of the liability, $99,500 for example, the regular cash account would have been drawn upon for the $500 deficiency.

Sinking fund income represents earnings of the corporation and is reported in the income statement as "Other income." The cash and the securities making up the sinking fund are classified in the balance sheet as "Investments," which usually appears immediately below the Current Assets section.

APPROPRIATION FOR BONDED INDEBTEDNESS

OBJECTIVE 7
Describe and illustrate the accounting for an appropriation for bond indebtedness.

The restriction of dividends during the life of a bond issue is another means of increasing the assurance that the obligation will be paid at maturity. Assuming that the corporation in the preceding example is required by the bond indenture to appropriate $10,000 of retained earnings each year for the 10-year life of the bonds, the following entry would be made annually:

| Dec. 31 | Retained Earnings .... | 10,000 | |
| | Appropriation for Bonded Indebtedness .. | | 10,000 |

As was indicated in Chapter 15, an appropriation has no direct relationship to a sinking fund. Each is independent of the other. When there is both a fund and an appropriation for the same purpose, the appropriation may be said to be **funded**.

BOND REDEMPTION

OBJECTIVE 8
Describe and illustrate the accounting for bond redemption.

Callable bonds are redeemable by the issuing corporation within the period of time and at the price stated in the bond indenture. Usually the call price is above the face value. If the market rate of interest declines after the issuance of the bonds, the corporation may sell new bonds at a lower interest rate and use the funds to redeem the original issue. The reduction of future interest expense is always an incentive for bond redemption. A corporation may also redeem all or a portion of its bonds before maturity by purchasing them on the open market.

When a corporation redeems bonds at a price below their carrying amount, the corporation realizes a gain. If the price is in excess of the carrying amount, a loss is incurred.[5] To illustrate redemption, assume that on June 30 a corporation has a bond issue of $100,000 outstanding, on which there is an unamortized premium of $4,000. The corporation has the option of calling the bonds for $105,000, which it exercises on this date. The entry to record the redemption is:

June 30	Bonds Payable.....................................	100,000	
	Premium on Bonds Payable	4,000	
	Loss on Redemption of Bonds.................	1,000	
	Cash...		105,000

---

[5]Gains and losses on the redemption of bonds are reported in the income statement as extraordinary items. See *Statement of Financial Accounting Standards, No. 4,* "Reporting Gains and Losses from Extinguishment of Debt" (Stamford: Financial Accounting Standards Board, 1975), par. 8.

If the bonds were not callable, the corporation might purchase a portion on the open market. Assuming that the corporation purchases one fourth ($25,000) of the bonds for $24,000 on June 30, the entry to record the redemption would be as follows:

June 30	Bonds Payable..	25,000	
	Premium on Bonds Payable	1,000	
	Cash...		24,000
	Gain on Redemption of Bonds...............		2,000

Note that only the portion of the premium relating to the bonds redeemed is written off. The excess of the carrying amount of the bonds purchased, $26,000, over the cash paid, $24,000, is recognized as a gain.

BALANCE SHEET PRESENTATION OF BONDS PAYABLE

OBJECTIVE 9
Describe the balance sheet presentation of bonds payable.

Bonds payable are usually reported on the balance sheet as long-term liabilities. If there are two or more bond issues, separate accounts should be maintained and the details of each should be reported on the balance sheet or in a supporting schedule or note. When the balance sheet date is within one year of the bond maturity date, the bonds should be transferred to the current liability classification if they are to be paid out of current assets. If they are to be paid with funds that have been set aside or if they are to be replaced with another bond issue, they should remain in the noncurrent category and their anticipated liquidation disclosed in an explanatory note.

The balance in a discount account should be reported in the balance sheet as a deduction from the related bonds payable. Conversely, the balance in a premium account should be reported as an addition to the related bonds payable. Either in the financial statements or in accompanying notes, the description of the bonds (terms, security, due date, etc.) should also include the effective interest rate and the maturities and sinking fund requirements for each of the next five years.[6]

INVESTMENTS IN BONDS

OBJECTIVE 10
Describe and illustrate the accounting for investments in bonds.

The issuance of bonds and related transactions were discussed in the preceding paragraphs from the standpoint of the issuing corporation. Whenever a corporation records a transaction between itself and the owners of its bonds, there is a reciprocal entry in the accounts of the investor.

In the following discussion, attention will be given to the principles underlying the accounting for investments in **debt securities** (bonds and notes) that are identified as long-term investments. **Long-term investments** are investments that are not intended as a ready source of cash in the normal operations of the business. These long-term investments are listed in the balance sheet under the caption "Investments," which usually follows the current assets. By contrast, temporary investments or marketable securities, which were discussed in Chapter 8, are available to meet the needs for additional cash for normal operations and are classified as current assets.

A business may make long-term investments simply because it has cash that is not needed in its normal operations. As discussed previously, cash

[6]*Statement of Financial Accounting Standards*, No. 47, "Disclosure of Long-Term Obligations" (Stamford: Financial Accounting Standards Board, 1981), par. 10.

and securities in bond sinking funds are considered long-term investments, since they are accumulated for the purpose of paying the bond liability. A corporation may also purchase bonds as a means of establishing or maintaining business relations with the issuing company.

Investments in corporate bonds may be purchased directly from the issuing corporation or from other investors. The services of a broker are usually employed in buying and selling bonds listed on the organized exchanges. The record of transactions on bond exchanges is reported daily in the financial pages of newspapers. This record usually includes data on the bond interest rate, maturity date, volume of sales, and the high, low, and closing prices for each corporation's bonds traded during the day. Prices for bonds are quoted as a percentage of the face amount. Thus, the price of a $1,000 bond quoted at 104 1/2 would be $1,045.

Accounting for Bond Investments — Purchase, Interest, and Amortization

A long-term investment in debt securities is customarily carried at cost. The cost of bonds purchased includes the amount paid to the seller plus other costs related to the purchase, such as the broker's commission. When bonds are purchased between interest dates, the buyer pays the seller the interest accrued from the last interest payment date to the date of purchase. The amount of the interest paid should be debited to Interest Income, since it is an offset against the amount that will be received at the next interest date. To illustrate, assume that a $1,000 bond is purchased at 102 plus a brokerage fee of $5.30 and accrued interest of $10.20. The transaction is recorded by the following entry. Note that the cost of the bond is recorded in a single account, i.e., the face amount of the bond and the premium paid are not recorded in separate accounts.

Apr. 2	Investment in Lewis Co. Bonds.................	1,025.30	
	Interest Income	10.20	
	Cash		1,035.50

As discussed previously, the price investors pay for bonds may be much greater or less than the face amount or the original issuance price. When bonds held as long-term investments are purchased at a price other than the face amount, the discount or premium should be amortized over the remaining life of the bonds. The amortization of discount increases the amount of the investment account and interest income. The amortization of premium decreases the amount of the investment account and interest income. The procedures for determining the amount of amortization each period correspond to those described and illustrated on pages 615 to 619.

Interest received on bond investments is recorded by a debit to Cash and a credit to Interest Income. At the end of a fiscal year, the interest accrued should be recorded by a debit to Interest Receivable and a credit to Interest Income. The adjusting entry should be reversed after the accounts are closed, so that all receipts of bond interest during the following year may be recorded without referring to the adjustment data.

As a basis for illustrating the transactions associated with long-term investments in bonds, assume that $50,000 of 8% bonds of Nowell Corporation, due in 8 3/4 years, are purchased on July 1 to yield approximately 11%. The purchase price is $41,706 plus interest of $1,000 accrued from April 1, the date of the last semiannual interest payment. Entries in the accounts of the purchaser at the time of purchase and for the remainder of the fiscal year, ending December 31, are as follows:

Payment for investment in bonds and accrued interest

July 1	Investment in Nowell Corp. Bonds............	41,706	
	Interest Income......................................	1,000	
	Cash...		42,706

Cost of $50,000 of Nowell Corp. bonds...	$41,706
Interest accrued on $50,000 at 8%, April 1–July 1 (3 months)...........	1,000
Total..	$42,706

Receipt of semi-annual interest

| Oct. 1 | Cash... | 2,000 | |
| | Interest Income................................. | | 2,000 |

Interest on $50,000 at 8%, April 1–October 1 (6 months), $2,000.

Adjusting entry

| Dec. 31 | Interest Receivable................................. | 1,000 | |
| | Interest Income................................. | | 1,000 |

Interest accrued on $50,000 at 8%, October 1–December 31 (3 months), $1,000.

Adjusting entry

| Dec. 31 | Investment in Nowell Corp. Bonds............ | 294 | |
| | Interest Income................................. | | 294 |

Discount to be amortized by interest method, July 1–December 31 (6 months):

Interest income (5 1/2% of bond carrying amount of $41,706)...	$2,294
Less interest received (4% of face amount of $50,000)................	2,000
Amount to be amortized..	$ 294

The entries in the interest income account in the above illustration may be summarized as follows:

July	1	Paid accrued interest—3 months....................................	$(1,000)
Oct.	1	Received interest payment—6 months............................	2,000
Dec. 31		Recorded accrued interest—3 months............................	1,000
	31	Recorded amortization of discount—6 months..................	294
		Interest earned—6 months...	$ 2,294

Accounting for Bond Investments—Sale

When bonds held as long-term investments are sold, the seller will receive the sales price (less commissions and other selling costs) plus the interest accrued since the last payment date. Before recording the proceeds, the seller should record the appropriate amount of the amortization of discount or premium for the current period, up to the date of sale. Then, in recording the proceeds, any gain or loss incurred on the sale can be recognized. To illustrate the recording of a sale of bonds held as a long-term investment, assume that the Nowell Corporation bonds of the preceding example are sold for $47,350 plus accrued interest on June 30, seven years after their purchase. The carrying amount of the bonds (cost plus amortized discount) as of January 1 of the year of sale is $47,080. The entries to record the amortization of discount for the current year and the sale of the bonds are as follows:

Amortization of discount for current year

| June 30 | Investment in Nowell Corp. Bonds............. | 589 | |
| | Interest Income.................................... | | 589 |

Discount to be amortized by the interest method, January 1–June 30, $589.

Receipt of interest and sale of bonds

June 30	Cash..	48,350	
	Loss on Sale of Investments.....................	319	
	Interest Income....................................		1,000
	Investment in Nowell Corp. Bonds..........		47,669

Interest accrued on $50,000 at 8%, April 1–June 30 (3 months), $1,000

Carrying amount of bonds on January 1 of current year	$47,080
Discount amortized in current year	589
Carrying amount of bonds on June 30	$47,669
Proceeds of sale...	47,350
Loss on sale	$ 319

CHAPTER REVIEW

KEY POINTS

OBJECTIVE 1

Financing Corporations

Business enterprises may raise funds for long-term financing in various ways. They may sell capital stock or issue notes or bonds, which are a form of interest-bearing note. When funds are borrowed through the issuance of bonds, there is a definite commitment to pay periodic interest and to repay the principal at a stated future date. There are many factors that must be considered when different methods of financing are evaluated. One such factor is the impact on the corporation's earnings per share of common stock.

OBJECTIVE 2

Characteristics of Bonds

When a corporation issues bonds, it executes a contract, known as a bond indenture or trust indenture, with bondholders. The principal amount of each bond is called its face value and is usually a multiple of $1,000. Different types of bonds that may be issued by a corporation include registered bonds, bearer bonds, coupon bonds, term bonds, serial bonds, convertible bonds, callable bonds, secured bonds, and debenture bonds.

OBJECTIVE 3

Present Value Concepts

The concept of present value plays an important role in many accounting analyses and business decisions. The concept of present value is that an amount of cash to be received at some date in the future is not the equivalent of the same amount of cash held at an earlier date. In other words, a sum of cash to be received in the future is not as valuable as the same sum on hand today, because cash on hand today can be invested to earn income.

OBJECTIVE 4

Present Value Concepts for Bonds Payable

When a corporation issues bonds, it incurs two distinct obligations: (1) to pay the face amount of the bonds at a specified maturity date and (2) to pay periodic interest at a specified percentage of the face amount. A price that a buyer is willing to pay for these future benefits is the sum of (1) the present value of the face amount of the bonds at the maturity date and (2) the present value of the periodic interest payments. The present value of $1 table is used to compute the present value of the face amount of the bonds at the maturity date. The present value of an annuity of $1 table is used to compute the present value of the periodic interest payments on the bonds.

OBJECTIVE 5

Accounting for Bonds Payable

The interest rate specified in the bond indenture is called the contract or coupon rate, which may differ from the rate prevailing in the market at the time the bonds are issued. If the market or effective rate is higher than the contract rate, the bonds will sell at a discount, or less than their face amount. The discount results because buyers are unwilling to pay the face amount for bonds whose contract rate is lower than the prevailing market rate. If the market rate is lower than the contract rate, the bonds will sell at a premium, or more than their face amount. In this case, buyers are willing to pay more than the face amount for bonds whose contract rate is higher than the market rate.

When bonds are issued at a discount, Discount on Bonds Payable is debited for the amount of the discount. When bonds are issued at a premium, Premium on Bonds Payable is credited for the amount of the premium. The amount of the discount or premium must be allocated to interest expense over the life of the bonds by using either the straight-line method or the interest method. The straight-line method provides for a constant amount of interest expense. The interest method provides for a constant rate of interest. A discount is amortized by crediting Discount on Bonds Payable. A premium is amortized by debiting Premium on Bonds Payable. The amortization of a discount increases interest expense, and the amortization of a premium decreases interest expense. The amortization entry may be recorded at either the date of periodic interest payments or the end of the accounting period.

OBJECTIVE 6

Bond Sinking Fund

The bond indenture may provide that funds for the payment of bonds at maturity be accumulated over the life of the issue. The amounts set aside are accounted for separately from other assets in a special fund called a sinking fund. Cash deposited in this fund is usually invested in income-producing securities. The periodic deposits plus the earnings on the investments should approximately equal the face amount of the bonds at maturity. The concept of future value may be used to determine the amount of the periodic deposits.

OBJECTIVE 7

Appropriation for Bonded Indebtedness

The bond indenture may require a board of directors to restrict dividends during the life of a bond issue through the use of an appropriation of retained earnings. This action may also be taken voluntarily. When there is both a bond sinking fund and an appropriation of retained earnings for the purpose of redeeming bonds at maturity, the appropriation is said to be funded.

OBJECTIVE 8

Bond Redemption

Callable bonds are redeemable by the issuing corporation at the price stated in the bond indenture. If the bonds are not callable, they may be purchased on the open market. When a corporation redeems bonds, any gain or loss on the redemption is recognized in the accounts.

OBJECTIVE 9

Balance Sheet Presentation of Bonds Payable

Bonds payable are usually reported on the balance sheet as long-term liabilities. When the balance sheet date is within one year of the bond maturity date, the bonds should be transferred to the current liability classification if they are to be paid out of current assets. If they are to be paid with funds that have been set aside or if they are to be replaced with another bond issue, they should remain in the noncurrent category and their anticipated liquidation disclosed in an explanatory note. The balance in a discount account should be reported in the balance sheet as a deduction from the related bonds payable, and the balance in a premium account should be reported as an addition to the related bonds payable.

OBJECTIVE 10

Investments in Bonds

A corporation may purchase bonds of another corporation as a long-term investment that is not intended as a ready source of cash in the normal operations of the business. These long-term investments are listed in the balance sheet under the caption "Investments," following the Current Assets section.

A long-term investment in debt securities is customarily carried at cost. The cost of the bonds purchased includes the amount paid to the seller plus other costs related to the purchase, such as the broker's commission. When bonds are purchased between interest dates, the buyer pays the seller the interest accrued from the last interest payment date to the date of the purchase. The amount of the interest paid should be debited to Interest Income, since it is an offset against the amount that will be received at the next interest date. When bonds held as long-term investments are purchased at a price other than the face amount, the discount or premium should be amortized over the remaining life of the bonds. The procedures for determining the amount of amortization are similar to those for bonds payable. The amortization of a discount increases the amount of the investment account and interest income. The amortization of a premium decreases the amount of the investment account and interest income.

When bonds held as long-term investments are sold, the seller will receive the sales price (less commissions and other selling costs) plus the interest accrued since the last payment date. Before recording the proceeds, the seller should record the appropriate amount of the amortization of discount or premium for the current period, up to the date of sale. Then, in recording the proceeds, any gain or loss incurred on the sale can be recognized.

KEY TERMS

bonds 608	bond premium 613
bond indenture 610	carrying amount 616
present value 611	sinking fund 619
contract rate of interest 613	future value 619
effective rate of interest 613	debt securities 624
bond discount 613	long-term investments 624

SELF-EXAMINATION QUESTIONS

Answers at end of chapter.

1. If a corporation plans to issue $1,000,000 of 12% bonds at a time when the market rate for similar bonds is 10%, the bonds can be expected to sell:
   A. at their face amount
   B. at a premium
   C. at a discount
   D. at a price below their face amount

2. If the bonds payable account has a balance of $500,000 and the discount on bonds payable account has a balance of $40,000, what is the carrying amount of the bonds?
   A. $460,000
   B. $500,000
   C. $540,000
   D. None of the above

3. The cash and the securities comprising the sinking fund established for the payment of bonds at maturity are classified on the balance sheet as:
   A. current assets
   B. investments
   C. long-term liabilities
   D. none of the above

4. If a firm purchases $100,000 of bonds of X Company at 101 plus accrued interest of $2,000 and pays broker's commissions of $50, the amount debited to Investment in X Company Bonds would be:
   A. $100,000
   B. $101,050
   C. $103,000
   D. $103,050

5. The balance in the discount on bonds payable account would usually be reported in the balance sheet in the:
   A. Current Assets section
   B. Current Liabilities section
   C. Long-Term Liabilities section
   D. none of the above

ILLUSTRATIVE PROBLEM

Dent Inc.'s fiscal year ends December 31. Selected transactions for the period 1990 through 1997 involving bonds payable issued by Dent Inc. are as follows:

1990
Nov. 30. Issued $4,000,000 of 25-year, 9% callable bonds dated November 30, 1990, for cash of $3,840,000. Interest is payable semiannually on November 30 and May 31.
Dec. 31. Recorded the adjusting entry for interest payable.
 31. Recorded amortization of $533 discount on the bonds.
 31. Closed the interest expense account.

1991
Jan. 1. Reversed the adjusting entry for interest payable.
May 31. Paid the semiannual interest on the bonds.
Nov. 30. Paid the semiannual interest on the bonds.
Dec. 31. Recorded the adjusting entry for interest payable.
 31. Recorded amortization of $6,400 discount on the bonds.
 31. Closed the interest expense account.

1997
Nov. 30. Recorded the redemption of the bonds, which were called at 102. The balance in the bond discount account is $115,200 after the payment of interest and amortization of discount have been recorded. (Record the redemption only.)

Instructions:

1. Prepare journal entries to record the preceding transactions.
2. Determine the amount of interest expense for 1990 and 1991.
3. Estimate the effective annual interest rate by dividing the interest expense for 1990 by the bond carrying amount at the time of issuance and multiplying by 12.
4. Determine the carrying amount of the bonds as of December 31, 1991.

SOLUTION

(1)

1990

Nov. 30	Cash	3,840,000	
	Discount on Bonds Payable	160,000	
	Bonds Payable		4,000,000
Dec. 31	Interest Expense	30,000	
	Interest Payable		30,000
31	Interest Expense	533	
	Discount on Bonds Payable		533
31	Income Summary	30,533	
	Interest Expense		30,533

1991

Jan. 1	Interest Payable	30,000	
	Interest Expense		30,000
May 31	Interest Expense	180,000	
	Cash		180,000
Nov. 30	Interest Expense	180,000	
	Cash		180,000
Dec. 31	Interest Expense	30,000	
	Interest Payable		30,000
31	Interest Expense	6,400	
	Discount on Bonds Payable		6,400
31	Income Summary	366,400	
	Interest Expense		366,400

1997

Nov. 30	Bonds Payable	4,000,000	
	Loss on Redemption of Bonds Payable	195,200	
	Discount on Bonds Payable		115,200
	Cash		4,080,000

(2) (a) 1990 — $30,533
     (b) 1991 — $366,400

(3) $30,533 ÷ $3,840,000 = .8% rate for one month of a year
    .8% × 12 = 9.6% annual rate

(4)
Initial carrying amount of bonds	$3,840,000
Discount amortized on December 31, 1990	533
Discount amortized on December 31, 1991	6,400
Carrying amount of bonds, December 31, 1991	$3,846,933

DISCUSSION QUESTIONS

1. When underwriters are used by the corporation issuing bonds, what function do the underwriters perform?

2. How are interest payments made to holders of (a) bearer or coupon bonds and (b) registered bonds?

3. Explain the meaning of each of the following terms as they relate to a bond issue: (a) secured, (b) convertible, (c) callable, and (d) debenture.

4. Describe the two distinct obligations incurred by a corporation when issuing bonds.

5. A corporation issues $10,000,000 of 11% coupon bonds to yield interest at the rate of 10%. (a) Was the amount of cash received from the sale of the bonds greater or less than $10,000,000? (b) Identify the following terms related to the bond issue: (1) face amount, (2) market or effective rate of interest, (3) contract or coupon rate of interest, and (4) maturity amount.

6. If bonds issued by a corporation are sold at a discount, is the market rate of interest greater or less that the coupon rate?

7. What is the present value of $1,000 due in 3 years, if the market rate of interest is 12%?

8. What is the present value of $1,000 to be received in each of the next 3 years, if the market rate of interest is 12%?

9. If the bonds payable account has a balance of $500,000 and the discount on bonds payable account has a balance of $24,500, what is the carrying amount of the bonds?

10. The following data are related to a $1,000,000, 14% bond issue for a selected semiannual interest period:

Bond carrying amount at beginning of period	$1,120,000
Interest paid at end of period...	70,000
Interest expense allocable to the period.............................	64,000

    (a) Were the bonds issued at a discount or at a premium? (b) What is the balance of the discount or premium account at the beginning of the period? (c) How much amortization of discount or premium is allocable to the period?

11. A corporation issues 12%, 10-year debenture bonds, with a face amount of $2,000,000, for 101 1/2 at the beginning of the current year. Assuming that the premium is to be amortized on a straight-line basis, what is the total amount of interest expense for the current year?

12. Indicate the title of (a) the account to be debited and (b) the account to be credited in the entry made at year end for amortization of (1) discount on bonds payable and (2) premium on bonds payable.

13. When the premium on bonds payable is amortized by the interest method, does the interest expense increase or decrease over the amortization period?

14. What is the purpose of a bond sinking fund?

15. What would be the value at the end of the second year for a $1,000 investment if the earnings rate is 12% compounded annually?

16. What would be the value at the end of the sixth year for a $5,000 investment if the earnings rate is 10% compounded annually? Use the table of the future value of $1 presented in this chapter to determine the value.

17. What would be the value at the end of the second year from a series of investments of $10,000 each to be made at the end of each of the first two years, with earnings of 12% compounded annually?

18. If Cowan Company invests $10,000 at the end of each of the next 5 years in a sinking fund, what is the value of the fund at the end of 5 years if the fund investments yield 12% per year, compounded annually? Use the table of the future value of an annuity of $1 presented in this chapter to determine the value.

19. What amount must be invested at the end of each of the next 5 years, in a sinking fund that earns 12% compounded annually, to accumulate to $10,000 at the end of the fifth year? Use the table of the future value of an annuity of $1 presented in this chapter to determine the amount.

20. If the amount accumulated in a sinking fund account exceeds the amount of liability at the redemption date, to what account is the excess transferred?

21. How are cash and securities comprising a sinking fund classified on the balance sheet?

22. Bonds Payable has a balance of $400,000 and Discount on Bonds Payable has a balance of $8,500. If the issuing corporation redeems the bonds at 98, what is the amount of gain or loss on redemption?

23. Indicate how the following accounts should be reported in the balance sheet: (a) Premium on Bonds Payable and (b) Discount on Bonds Payable.

24. Under what caption are "Long-term investments in bonds" listed on the balance sheet?

25. The quoted price of Prater Corp. bonds on June 1 is 104. On the same day the interest accrued is 5% of the face amount. (a) Does the quoted price include accrued interest? (b) If $10,000 face amount of Prater Corp. bonds is purchased on June 1 at the quoted price, what is the cost of the bonds, exclusive of commission?

26. An investor sells $50,000 of bonds of Frasier Corp. carried at $51,000 for $52,100 plus accrued interest of $500. The broker remits the balance due after deducting a commission of $250. Present the entry to record this transaction.

Real World Focus   27. Xerox Corporation 8 5/8% sinking fund debenture bonds due in 1999 were reported in *The Wall Street Journal* as selling for 92 1/4 on February 17, 1989. (a) Were the bonds selling at a premium or at a discount on February 17, 1989? (b) Was the market rate of interest for similar quality bonds higher or lower than 8 5/8% on February 17, 1989?

Real World Focus   28. A company purchased a $1,000, 20-year zero-coupon bond for $189 to yield 8.5% to maturity. How is the interest income computed? Adapted from "Technical Hotline," *Journal of Accountancy* (January 1989), p. 100.

EXERCISES

Exercise 16–1
Effect of financing on earnings per share.

OBJ. 1

Two companies are financed as follows:

	Jeter Inc.	Vessels Co.
Bonds payable, 10% (issued at face value)..........	$1,000,000	$ 500,000
Preferred 6% stock (nonparticipating).................	1,000,000	500,000
Common stock, $10 par....................................	1,000,000	2,000,000

Income tax is estimated at 40% of income. Determine for each company the earnings per share of common stock, assuming that the income before bond interest and income tax for each company is (a) $200,000, (b) $500,000, and (c) $1,000,000.

Exercise 16–2
Entries for bond issuance; amortization of discount by straight-line method.

OBJ. 5

On the first day of its fiscal year, Swindel Inc. issued $5,000,000 of 10-year, 8% bonds, interest payable semiannually, at an effective interest rate of 10%, receiving cash of $4,376,940.

(a) Present the journal entries to record the following:
  (1) Sale of the bonds.
  (2) First semiannual interest payment. (Amortization of discount is to be recorded annually.)
  (3) Second semiannual interest payment.
  (4) Amortization of discount at the end of the first year, using the straight-line method.
(b) Determine the amount of the bond interest expense for the first year.

Exercise 16–3
Amortization of discount by interest method.

OBJ. 5

Using the data presented in Exercise 16–2, compute the following:

(a) Amortization of discount at the end of the first year, using the interest method. (Round to the nearest dollar.)
(b) The amount of the bond interest expense for the first year.

Exercise 16–4
Computation of bond proceeds, entries for bond issuance, and amortization of premium by straight-line method.

OBJ. 5

On May 1, 1990, Pugh Corporation issued $1,000,000 of 10-year, 14% bonds at an effective interest rate of 13%. Interest is payable semiannually on May 1 and November 1. Present the journal entries to record the following:

(a) Sale of bonds on May 1, 1990. (Use the tables of present values appearing in the chapter to determine the bond proceeds.)
(b) First interest payment on November 1, 1990, including amortization of bond premium for 6 months, using the straight-line method. (Round to the nearest dollar.)

Exercise 16–5
Computation of bond proceeds, amortization of premium by interest method, and interest expense.

OBJ. 5

On the first day of its fiscal year, Primm Co. issued $4,000,000 of 10-year, 13% bonds at an effective interest rate of 12%, with interest payable semiannually. Compute the following, presenting figures used in your computations and rounding to the nearest dollar:

(a) The amount of cash proceeds from the sale of the bonds. (Use the tables of present values appearing in the chapter.)
(b) The amount of premium to be amortized for the first semiannual interest payment period, using the interest method.
(c) The amount of premium to be amortized for the second semiannual interest payment period, using the interest method.
(d) The amount of the bond interest expense for the first year.

Exercise 16–6
Computation of amortization of bond discount by both straight-line and interest methods.
OBJ. 5

On July 1 of the current fiscal year, Diaz Company purchased $750,000 of 10-year, 8% bonds as a long-term investment directly from the issuing company for $656,541. The effective rate of interest is 10%, and the interest is payable semiannually. Compute the amount of discount to be amortized for the first semiannual interest payment period using (a) the straight-line method and (b) the interest method.

Exercise 16–7
Determination of sinking fund deposit and entry.
OBJ. 6

C. C. Cutler Co. issued $10,000,000 of 20-year bonds on January 1 of the current year. The bond indenture requires that equal deposits be made in a bond sinking fund at the end of each of the 20 years. The fund is expected to be invested in securities that will yield 12% per year compounded annually.

(a) Determine the amount of each of the 20 deposits to be made in the bond sinking fund.
(b) Prepare the entry to record the first deposit made in the sinking fund.

Exercise 16–8
Entries for bond sinking fund and appropriation of retained earnings.
OBJ. 6, 7

Mixon Corporation issued $10,000,000 of 10-year bonds on the first day of the fiscal year. The bond indenture provides that a sinking fund be accumulated, assuming 10% interest, by 10 annual deposits of $627,455, beginning at the end of the first year.
Present the journal entries to record the following selected transactions related to the bond issue:

(a) The required amount is deposited in the sinking fund.
(b) Investments in securities from the first sinking fund deposit total $600,000.
(c) Appropriated $1,000,000 of retained earnings for bonded indebtedness.
(d) The sinking fund earned $61,500 during the year following the first deposit (summarizing entry).
(e) The bonds are paid at maturity, and excess cash of $43,800 in the fund is transferred to the cash account.
(f) Transferred the appropriation for bonded indebtedness balance of $10,000,000 back to retained earnings.

Exercise 16–9
Entries for issuance and calling of bonds.
OBJ. 5, 8

T. R. Bethel Inc. issued $10,000,000 of 20-year, 11% callable bonds on April 1, 1990, with interest payable on April 1 and October 1. The fiscal year of the company is the calendar year. Present the journal entries to record the following selected transactions:

1990
Apr. 1. Issued the bonds for cash at their face amount.
Oct. 1. Paid the interest on the bonds.
Dec. 31. Recorded accrued interest for three months.
     31. Closed the interest expense account.

1991
Jan. 1. Reversed the adjusting entry for accrued interest.
Apr. 1. Paid the interest on the bonds.

1995
Oct. 1. Called the bond issue at 101 1/2, the rate provided in the bond indenture. (Omit entry for payment of interest.)

Exercise 16–10
Entries for purchase and sale of investment in bonds.
OBJ. 10

Present journal entries to record the following selected transactions of Lauren Corporation:

(a) Purchased for cash $500,000 of Varon Co. 12% bonds at 103 plus accrued interest of $10,000.
(b) Received first semiannual interest.
(c) Amortized $750 on the bond investment at the end of the first year.
(d) Sold the bonds at 101 plus accrued interest of $5,000. The bonds were carried at $511,250 at the time of the sale.

PROBLEMS

Problem 16–1A
Effect of financing on earnings per share.
OBJ. 1

Three different plans for financing a $10,000,000 corporation are under consideration by its organizers. Under each of the following plans, the securities will be issued at their par or face amount and the income tax rate is estimated at 40% of income:

	Plan 1	Plan 2	Plan 3
14% bonds			$ 5,000,000
Preferred 8% stock, $100 par......		$ 5,000,000	2,500,000
Common stock, $25 par.............	$10,000,000	5,000,000	2,500,000
Total	$10,000,000	$10,000,000	$10,000,000

Instructions:

(1) Determine for each plan the earnings per share of common stock, assuming that the income before bond interest and income tax is $1,500,000.
(2) Determine for each plan the earnings per share of common stock, assuming that the income before bond interest and income tax is $1,100,000.
(3) What are the advantages and disadvantages of each plan?

Problem 16–2A
Entries for bonds payable transactions.
OBJ. 5

On July 1, 1990, Jones Corporation issued $10,000,000 of 10-year, 11% bonds at an effective interest rate of 10%. Interest on the bonds is payable semiannually on December 31 and June 30. The fiscal year of the company is the calendar year.

Instructions:

(1) Present the journal entry to record the amount of the cash proceeds from the sale of the bonds. Use the tables of present values appearing in this chapter to compute the cash proceeds, rounding to the nearest dollar.
(2) Present the journal entries to record the following:
   (a) The first semiannual interest payment on December 31, 1990, including the amortization of the bond premium, using the interest method.
   (b) The interest payment on June 30, 1991, including the amortization of the bond premium, using the interest method.
(3) Present the entries for Instruction (2), using the straight-line method of amortization.
(4) Determine the total interest expense for 1990 under (a) the interest method of premium amortization and (b) the straight-line method of premium amortization. (c) Will the annual interest expense using the interest method of premium amortization always be greater than the annual interest expense using the straight-line method of premium amortization?

Problem 16–3A
Entries for bond and sinking fund transactions.
OBJ. 5, 6

The following transactions relate to the issuance of $6,000,000 of 10-year, 9% bonds dated January 1, 1981, and the accumulations in a sinking fund to redeem the bonds at maturity. Interest on the bonds is payable on June 30 and December 31.

1981
Jan.   2. Sold the bond issue at 100.
June 30. Paid semiannual interest on bonds.
Dec. 31. Paid semiannual interest on bonds and deposited $435,000 in a bond sinking fund.

1982
Jan.   7. Purchased $367,500 of investments with bond sinking fund cash.
June 30. Paid semiannual interest on bonds.
Nov. 30. Received $38,725 income on investments.
Dec. 31. Paid semiannual interest on bonds.

(Assume that all intervening transactions have been properly recorded.)

1991
Jan. 2. Sold all investments in the bond sinking fund for $5,957,400. The sinking fund investments had a carrying value of $5,999,800.
     11. Paid the bonds at maturity from the sinking fund cash and the regular cash account. The cash available in the sinking fund at this date was $5,960,000.

Instructions:

Prepare journal entries to record the foregoing transactions.

Problem 16–4A
Entries for bond and sinking fund transactions, including appropriation of retained earnings.
OBJ. 5, 6, 7

During 1990 and 1991, Jordan Company completed the following transactions relating to its $30,000,000 issue of 20-year, 14% bonds dated May 1, 1990. Interest is payable on May 1 and November 1. The corporation's fiscal year is the calendar year.

1990
May 1. Sold the bond issue for $31,200,000 cash.
Nov. 1. Paid the semiannual interest on the bonds.
Dec. 31. Recorded the adjusting entry for interest payable.
     31. Recorded bond premium amortization of $40,000, which was determined by using the straight-line method.
     31. Deposited $350,000 cash in a bond sinking fund.
     31. Appropriated $1,000,000 of retained earnings for bonded indebtedness.
     31. Closed the interest expense account.

1991
Jan. 1. Reversed the adjustment for interest payable.
     15. Purchased various securities with sinking fund cash, cost $330,000.
May 1. Paid the semiannual interest on the bonds.
Nov. 1. Paid the semiannual interest on the bonds.
Dec. 18. Recorded the receipt of $22,300 of income on sinking fund securities, depositing the cash in the sinking fund.
     31. Recorded the adjusting entry for interest payable.
     31. Recorded bond premium amortization of $60,000, which was determined by using the straight-line method.
     31. Deposited $525,000 cash in the sinking fund.
     31. Appropriated $1,500,000 of retained earnings for bonded indebtedness.
     31. Closed the interest expense account.

Instructions:

(1) Prepare journal entries to record the foregoing transactions.
(2) Prepare a columnar table, using the following headings, and list the information for each of the two years.

| | | | | | Account Balances at End of Year | | |
| | Bond Interest Expense for Year | Sinking Fund Income for Year | Bonds Payable | Premium on Bonds | Sinking Fund | | Appropriation for Bonded Indebtedness |
Year					Cash	Investments	

Problem 16–5A
Entries for bonds payable transactions.
OBJ. 5, 8

The following transactions were completed by Weis Industries Inc., whose fiscal year is the calendar year:

1990
Mar. 31. Issued $5,000,000 of 10-year, 8% callable bonds dated March 31, 1990, at an effective rate of 10%, receiving cash of $4,376,940. Interest is payable semiannually on March 31 and September 30.
Sept. 30. Paid the semiannual interest on the bonds.

Dec. 31. Recorded the adjusting entry for interest payable.
   31. Recorded bond discount amortization of $28,742, which was determined by using the interest method.
   31. Closed the interest expense account.

1991
Jan. 1. Reversed the adjusting entry for interest payable.
Mar. 31. Paid the semiannual interest on the bonds.
Sept. 30. Paid the semiannual interest on the bonds.
Dec. 31. Recorded the adjusting entry for interest payable.
   31. Recorded bond discount amortization of $41,583, which was determined by using the interest method.
   31. Closed the interest expense account.

1998
Mar. 31. Recorded the redemption of the bonds, which were called at 101. The balance in the bond discount account is $177,184 after the payment of interest and amortization of discount have been recorded. (Record the redemption only.)

Instructions:

(1) Prepare journal entries to record the foregoing transactions.
(2) Indicate the amount of the interest expense in (a) 1990 and (b) 1991.
(3) Determine the effective interest rate by dividing the interest expense for 1990 by the bond carrying amount at the time of issuance and converting the result to an annual rate.
(4) Determine the carrying amount of the bonds as of December 31, 1991.

Problem 16–6A
Entries for bond investments.
OBJ. 10

The following transactions relate to certain securities acquired as a long-term investment by Gresham Company, whose fiscal year ends on December 31:

1990
Aug. 1. Purchased $300,000 of Clarke Company 10-year, 14% bonds dated June 1, 1990, directly from the issuing company for $305,900 plus accrued interest of $7,000.
Dec. 1. Received the semiannual interest on the Clarke Company bonds.
   31. Recorded the adjustment for interest receivable on the Clarke Company bonds.
   31. Recorded bond premium amortization of $250 on the Clarke Company bonds. The amortization amount was determined by using the straight-line method.

(Assume that all intervening transactions and adjustments have been properly recorded, and that the number of bonds owned has not changed from December 31, 1990, to December 31, 1995.)

1996
Jan. 1. Reversed the adjustment of December 31, 1995, for interest receivable on the Clarke Company bonds.
June 1. Received the semiannual interest on the Clarke Company bonds.
July 1. Sold one half of the Clarke Company bonds at 102 plus accrued interest. The broker deducted $700 for commission, etc., remitting the balance. Before the sale was recorded, $150 of premium on one half of the bonds was amortized, reducing the carrying amount of those bonds to $151,175.

Dec. 1. Received the semiannual interest on the Clarke Company bonds.
     31. Recorded the adjustment for interest receivable on the Clarke Company bonds.
     31. Recorded bond premium amortization of $300 on the Clarke Company bonds.

Instructions:

(1) Prepare journal entries to record the foregoing transactions.
(2) Determine the amount of interest earned on the bonds in 1990.
(3) Determine the amount of interest earned on the bonds in 1996.

Series B

Problem 16–2B
Entries for bonds payable transactions.

OBJ. 5

On July 1, 1990, Raven Corporation issued $15,000,000 of 10-year, 10% bonds at an effective interest rate of 12%. Interest on the bonds is payable semiannually on December 31 and June 30. The fiscal year of the company is the calendar year.

Instructions:

(1) Present the journal entry to record the amount of the cash proceeds from the sale of the bonds. Use the tables of present values appearing in this chapter to compute the cash proceeds, rounding to the nearest dollar.
(2) Present the journal entries to record the following selected transactions for 1990 and 1991:
   (a) The entry for the payment of interest and the amortization of the bond discount on December 31, 1990, using the interest method.
   (b) The semiannual interest payment on June 30, 1991, including the amortization of the bond discount, using the interest method.
(3) Present the entries for Instruction (2), using the straight-line method of discount amortization.
(4) What is the total interest expense for 1990 for (a) the interest method of discount amortization and (b) the straight-line method of discount amortization? (c) Will the annual interest expense using the interest method of discount amortization always be less than the annual interest expense using the straight-line method of discount amortization?

Problem 16–4B
Entries for bond and sinking fund transactions, including appropriation of retained earnings.

OBJ. 5, 6, 7

During 1990 and 1991, Bridges Company completed the following transactions relating to its $12,000,000 issue of 25-year, 10% bonds dated September 1, 1990. Interest is payable on September 1 and March 1. The corporation's fiscal year is the calendar year.

1990
Sept. 1. Sold the bond issue for $11,760,000.
Dec. 31. Recorded the adjusting entry for interest payable.
     31. Recorded bond discount amortization of $3,200, which was determined by using the straight-line method.
     31. Deposited $41,700 cash in a bond sinking fund.
     31. Appropriated $160,000 of retained earnings for bonded indebtedness.
     31. Closed the interest expense account.

1991
Jan. 1. Reversed the adjustment for interest payable.
     15. Purchased various securities with sinking fund cash, cost $40,000.
Mar. 1. Paid the semiannual interest on the bonds.
Sept. 1. Paid the semiannual interest on the bonds.

Dec. 15. Recorded the receipt of $3,120 of income on sinking fund securities, depositing the cash in the sinking fund.
    31. Recorded the adjusting entry for interest payable.
    31. Recorded bond discount amortization of $9,600, which was determined by using the straight-line method.
    31. Deposited $125,000 cash in the sinking fund.
    31. Appropriated $480,000 of retained earnings for bonded indebtedness.
    31. Closed the interest expense account.

Instructions:

(1) Prepare journal entries to record the foregoing transactions.
(2) Prepare a columnar table, using the following headings, and list the information for each of the two years.

| | | | | Account Balances at End of Year | | | |
| | Bond Interest Expense for Year | Sinking Fund Income for Year | | | Sinking Fund | | Appropriation for Bonded Indebtedness |
Year			Bonds Payable	Discount on Bonds	Cash	Investments	

Problem 16–5B
Entries for bonds payable transactions.
OBJ. 5, 8

The following transactions were completed by Skeean Co., whose fiscal year is the calendar year:

1990
Oct. 1. Issued $20,000,000 of 10-year, 14% callable bonds dated October 1, 1990, at an effective rate of 12%, receiving cash of $22,293,860. Interest is payable semiannually on October 1 and April 1.
Dec. 31. Recorded the adjusting entry for interest payable.
    31. Recorded bond premium amortization of $31,184, which was determined using the interest method.
    31. Closed the interest expense account.

1991
Jan. 1. Reversed the adjusting entry for interest payable.
Apr. 1. Paid the semiannual interest on the bonds.
Oct. 1. Paid the semiannual interest on the bonds.
Dec. 31. Recorded the adjusting entry for interest payable.
    31. Recorded bond premium amortization of $132,333, which was determined by using the interest method.
    31. Closed the interest expense account.

1996
Apr. 1. Recorded the redemption of the bonds, which were called at 106. The balance in the bond premium account is $1,360,103 after the payment of interest and amortization of premium have been recorded. (Record the redemption only.)

Instructions:

(1) Prepare journal entries to record the foregoing transactions.
(2) Indicate the amount of the interest expense in (a) 1990 and (b) 1991.
(3) Determine the effective interest rate by dividing the interest expense for 1990 by the bond carrying amount at the time of issuance and converting the result to an annual rate.
(4) Determine the carrying amount of the bonds as of December 31, 1991.

Problem 16–6B
Entries for bond investments.

OBJ. 10

The following transactions relate to certain securities acquired by Armour Company, whose fiscal year ends on December 31:

1990
Oct. 1. Purchased $500,000 of Sewell Company 20-year, 9% bonds dated August 1, 1990, directly from the issuing company for $476,200 plus $7,500 accrued interest.
Dec. 31. Recorded the adjustment for interest receivable on the Sewell Company bonds.
     31. Recorded bond discount amortization of $300 on the Sewell Company bonds. The amortization amount was determined by using the straight-line method.

(Assume that all intervening transactions and adjustments have been properly recorded, and that the number of bonds owned has not changed from December 31, 1990, to December 31, 1994.)

1995
Jan. 1. Reversed the adjustment of December 31, 1994, for interest receivable on the Sewell Company bonds.
Feb. 1. Received the semiannual interest on the Sewell Company bonds.
July 1. Sold one half of the Sewell Company bonds at 95 plus accrued interest. The broker deducted $750 for commission, etc., remitting the balance. Before the sale was recorded, $300 of discount on one half of the bonds was amortized, increasing the carrying amount of those bonds to $240,950.
Aug. 1. Received the semiannual interest on the Sewell Company bonds.
Dec. 31. Recorded the adjustment for interest receivable on the Sewell Company bonds.
     31. Recorded bond discount amortization of $600 on the Sewell Company bonds.

Instructions:

(1) Prepare journal entries to record the foregoing transactions.
(2) Determine the amount of interest earned on the bonds in 1990.
(3) Determine the amount of interest earned on the bonds in 1995.

MINI-CASE 16

BOTTLING
COMPANY

You hold a 20% common stock interest in the family-owned business, a soft drink bottling distributorship. Your father, who is the manager, has proposed an expansion of plant facilities at an expected cost of $2,000,000. Two alternative plans have been suggested as methods of financing the expansion. Each plan is briefly described as follows:
Plan 1. Issue an additional 25,000 shares of $25 par common stock at $40 per share, and $1,000,000 of 20-year, 13% bonds at face amount.
Plan 2. Issue $2,000,000 of 20-year, 13% bonds at face amount.
The balance sheet as of the end of the previous fiscal year is as follows:

CU Bottling Co.
Balance Sheet
December 31, 19--

Assets

Current assets	$ 1,800,000
Plant assets	8,700,000
Total assets	$10,500,000

Liabilities and Stockholders' Equity

Current liabilities	$ 2,700,000
Common stock, $25	1,875,000
Excess of issue price over par	225,000
Retained earnings	5,700,000
Total liabilities and stockholders' equity	$10,500,000

Net income has remained relatively constant over the past several years. The expansion program is expected to increase yearly income before bond interest and income tax from $800,000 to $1,200,000.

Your father has asked you, as the company treasurer, to prepare an analysis of each financing plan.

Instructions:

(1) Prepare a tabulation indicating the expected earnings per share on the common stock under each plan. Assume an income tax rate of 40%.
(2) List factors other than earnings per share that should be considered in evaluating the two plans.
(3) Which plan offers the greater benefit to the present stockholders? Give reasons for your opinion.

ETHICS DISCUSSION CASE

Fleming Inc. has outstanding a $25,000,000, 25-year, 12% debenture bond issue dated July 1, 1975. The bond issue is due June 30, 2000. The bond indenture requires a sinking fund which, as of February 1, 1990, has a balance of $8,000,000. Fleming Inc. is currently experiencing a shortage of funds due to a recent plant expansion. Kim Arnold, treasurer of Fleming, has suggested using the sinking fund cash to temporarily alleviate the shortage of funds. Arnold's brother-in-law, who is trustee of the sinking fund, would be willing to loan Fleming Inc. the necessary funds from the sinking fund. Discuss whether Kim Arnold is behaving in an ethical manner.

COMPREHENSIVE PROBLEM 5

Selected transactions completed by Sharp Inc. during the fiscal year ending March 31, 1990, were as follows:

(a) Issued 10,000 shares of $25 par common stock at $45, receiving cash.
(b) Received subscriptions to 5,000 shares of $100 par preferred 8% stock at $120, collecting one half of the subscription price.

(c) Collected the remaining one half of the subscriptions for the preferred stock and issued the 5,000 shares of preferred stock.

(d) Declared the first quarter dividend of $.25 per share on common stock and $2 per share on preferred stock. On the date of record, 100,000 shares of common stock were outstanding, no treasury shares were held, and 15,000 shares of preferred stock were outstanding.

(e) Paid the cash dividends.

(f) Redeemed $500,000 of 8-year, 16% bonds at 97 1/2. The balance in the bond discount account is $6,400 after the payment of interest and amortization of discount have been recorded. (Record only the redemption of the bonds payable.)

(g) Transferred $500,000 of the appropriation for bonded indebtedness back to retained earnings for the bonds redeemed in (f).

(h) Purchased 2,000 shares of treasury common stock at $40 per share.

(i) Issued $1,000,000 of 10-year, 12% bonds at an effective interest rate of 10%, with interest payable semiannually.

(j) Declared a second quarter 5% stock dividend on common stock and a $2 cash dividend per share on preferred stock. On the date of declaration, the market value of the common stock was $41 per share. On the date of record, 100,000 shares of common stock were outstanding, 2,000 shares of treasury common stock were held, and 15,000 shares of preferred stock were outstanding.

(k) Issued the stock certificates for the stock dividends declared in (j) and paid the cash dividends to the preferred stockholders.

(l) Sold, at $42 per share, 1,000 shares of treasury common stock purchased in (h).

(m) Purchased $50,000 of Wilson Inc. 10-year, 15% bonds directly from the issuing company for $48,500 plus accrued interest of $1,875.

(n) Recorded the payment of semiannual interest on the bonds issued in (i) and the amortization of the premium for six months. The amortization was determined using the interest method. (Round the amortization to the nearest dollar.)

(o) Deposited $15,000 in a bond sinking fund.

(p) Appropriated $1,000,000 of retained earnings for bonded indebtedness.

(q) Accrued interest for four months on the Wilson Inc. bonds purchased in (m). Also recorded amortization of $50.

Instructions:

(1) Record the selected transactions in general journal form.

(2) After all of the transactions for the year ended March 31, 1990 had been posted (including the transactions recorded in (1) and all adjusting entries), the following data were selected from the records of Sharp Inc.:

Income statement data:

Advertising expense	$ 90,000
Delivery expense	12,000
Depreciation expense—office equipment	12,600
Depreciation expense—store equipment	45,000
Gain on redemption of bonds	6,100
Income tax:	
Applicable to continuing operations	308,975
Applicable to loss from disposal of a	
segment of the business	21,100
Applicable to gain from redemption of bonds	1,150

(Continued)

Interest expense	68,500
Interest income	675
Loss from disposal of a segment of the business	80,500
Merchandise inventory (April 1, 1989)	380,000
Merchandise inventory (March 31, 1990)	430,000
Miscellaneous administrative expenses	1,600
Miscellaneous selling expenses	6,300
Office rent expense	25,000
Office salaries expense	85,000
Office supplies expense	5,800
Purchases	4,050,000
Sales	5,400,000
Sales commissions	125,000
Sales salaries expense	150,000
Store supplies expense	9,500

Retained earnings and balance sheet data:

Accounts payable	$ 151,000
Accounts receivable	280,500
Accumulated depreciation — office equipment	835,250
Accumulated depreciation — store equipment	2,214,750
Allowance for doubtful accounts	11,500
Bond sinking fund cash	15,000
Bonds payable, 12%, due 2001	1,000,000
Cash	120,000
Common stock, $25 par (400,000 shares authorized; 100,000 shares outstanding)	2,500,000
Deferred income tax payable (current portion, $3,200)	22,600
Dividends:	
Cash dividends for common stock	75,000
Cash dividends for preferred stock	100,000
Stock dividends for common stock	200,900
Dividends payable	25,000
Income tax payable	55,900
Interest receivable	2,500
Investment in Wilson Inc. bonds (long-term)	48,550
Marketable securities at cost, held as a short-term investment (market value, $88,300)	75,000
Merchandise inventory (March 31, 1990), at lower of cost (fifo) or market	430,000
Office equipment	2,410,100
Organization costs	60,000
Paid-in capital from sale of treasury stock	2,000
Paid-in capital in excess of par — common stock	450,000
Paid-in capital in excess of par — preferred stock	240,000
Preferred stock, $100 par (30,000 shares authorized; 15,000 shares outstanding)	1,500,000
Premium on bonds payable	120,000
Prepaid expenses	15,900
Retained earnings:	
Appropriated for bonded indebtedness (April 1, 1989)	500,000
Appropriated for bonded indebtedness (March 31, 1990)	1,000,000
Appropriated for treasury stock (April 1, 1989)	—
Appropriated for treasury stock (March 31, 1990)	40,000
Unappropriated, April 1, 1989	2,448,450
Store equipment	8,603,950
Treasury stock (1,000 shares of common stock at cost of $40 per share)	40,000

(a) Prepare a multiple-step income statement for the year ended March 31, 1990, concluding with earnings per share.
(b) Prepare a retained earnings statement for the year ended March 31, 1990.
(c) Prepare a balance sheet in report form as of March 31, 1990.

ANSWERS TO SELF-EXAMINATION QUESTIONS

1. B Since the contract rate on the bonds is higher than the prevailing market rate, a rational investor would be willing to pay more than the face amount, or a premium (answer B), for the bonds. If the contract rate and the market rate were equal, the bonds could be expected to sell at their face amount (answer A). Likewise, if the market rate is higher than the contract rate, the bonds would sell at a price below their face amount (answer D) or at a discount (answer C).

2. A The bond carrying amount, sometimes called the book value, is the face amount plus unamortized premium or less unamortized discount. For this question, the carrying amount is $500,000 less $40,000, or $460,000 (answer A).

3. B Although the sinking fund may consist of cash as well as securities, the fund is listed on the balance sheet as an investment (answer B) because it is to be used to pay the long-term liability at maturity.

4. B The amount debited to the investment account is the cost of the bonds, which includes the amount paid to the seller for the bonds (101% × $100,000) plus broker's commissions ($50), or $101,050 (answer B). The $2,000 of accrued interest that is paid to the seller should be debited to Interest Income, since it is an offset against the amount that will be received as interest at the next interest date.

5. C The balance of Discount on Bonds Payable is usually reported as a deduction from Bonds Payable in the Long-Term Liabilities section (answer C) of the balance sheet. Likewise, a balance in a premium on bonds payable account would usually be reported as an addition to Bonds Payable in the Long-Term Liabilities section of the balance sheet.

CHAPTER SEVENTEEN

INVESTMENTS IN STOCKS; CONSOLIDATED STATEMENTS; INTERNATIONAL OPERATIONS

CHAPTER OBJECTIVES

1 Describe investments in stocks.

2 Describe and illustrate the accounting for long-term investments.

3 Describe alternative methods of combining businesses.

4 Describe the accounting for parent-subsidiary affiliations.

5 Describe and illustrate the basic principles of consolidation of financial statements.

6 Illustrate a corporate balance sheet for a parent company and its subsidiaries.

7 Describe and illustrate the accounting for international operations.

In the preceding chapter, the principles of accounting for long-term investments in bonds were discussed. In this chapter, the principles of accounting for long-term investments in stocks will be presented. Accounting for the combining of operations of two corporations and the expansion of operations into international markets will also be discussed.

INVESTMENTS IN STOCKS

OBJECTIVE 1
Describe investments in stocks.

A business may make long-term investments in **equity securities** (preferred and common shares) simply because it has cash that it does not need for normal operations. A corporation may also purchase stocks as a means of establishing or maintaining business relations with the issuing company. In some cases, a corporation may acquire all or a large part of the voting stock of another corporation in order to control its activities. Similarly, a corporation may organize a new corporation for the purpose of marketing a new product or for some other business reason, receiving stock in exchange for the assets transferred to the new corporation.

Investments in stocks may be purchased directly from the issuing corporation or from other investors. Both preferred and common stocks may be *listed* on an organized stock exchange, or they may be *unlisted*, in which case they are said to be bought or sold *over the counter*. The services of a broker are usually used in buying and selling both listed and unlisted securities.

The record of transactions on the stock exchanges is reported daily by the financial press. This record usually includes, for each stock traded, the high and low price for the past year, the current annual dividend, the volume of sales for the day, and the high, low, and closing price for the day. Prices for stocks are quoted in terms of fractional dollars, with 1/8 of a dollar being the usual minimum fraction, although some low-priced stocks are sold in lower fractions of a dollar, such as 1/16 or 1/32. Thus, a price of 40 3/8 per share means $40.375; a price of 40 1/2 means $40.50.

In the following discussion, attention will be given to the principles underlying the accounting for investments in stocks that are not intended as a ready source of cash in the normal operations of the business. Such investments are identified as long-term investments and are reported in the balance sheet under the caption "Investments." The principles underlying the accounting for investments in stocks that are classified as temporary investments or marketable securities were discussed in Chapter 8.

MORE AMERICANS THAN EVER BEFORE OWN STOCK

About 47 million Americans own stock, more than ever before, but many are participants through stock mutual funds, according to a New York Stock Exchange survey.

The survey said the 47 million investors tallied as of mid-1985 were an 11 percent increase over the 42 million found in the exchange's last survey in mid-1983.

That means that one in five Americans is now a stock investor, as opposed to one of every six two years ago.

Women account for 57 percent of the new investors, the survey said; typically, she is married, employed in a technical or professional job, has an annual household income of $35,000 and a portfolio of $2,200.

Source: "More Americans Than Ever Before Own Stock," *Champaign-Urbana News Gazette,* December 5, 1985. © Associated Press.

ACCOUNTING FOR LONG-TERM INVESTMENTS IN STOCK

OBJECTIVE 2
Describe and illustrate the accounting for long-term investments.

There are two methods of accounting for long-term investments in stock: (1) the **cost method** and (2) the **equity method**. The method used depends upon whether the investor owns enough of the voting stock of the investee (company whose stock is owned by the investor) to have a significant influence over its operating and financing policies. If the investor does not have a significant influence, the cost method (with the lower of cost or market rule) must be used. If the investor can exercise a significant influence in a long-term investment situation, the equity method must be used. Evidence of such influence includes, but is not limited to, representation on the board of directors, material intercompany transactions, and interchange of managerial personnel. Guidelines to be applied in making the election are as follows:

In order to achieve a reasonable degree of uniformity in application, the Board concludes that an investment (direct or indirect) of 20% or more of the voting stock of an investee should lead to a presumption that in the absence of evidence to the contrary an investor has the ability to exercise significant influence over an investee. Conversely, an investment of less than 20% of the voting stock of an investee should lead to a presumption that an investor does not have the ability to exercise significant influence unless such ability can be demonstrated.[1]

Cost Method

The cost of stocks purchased includes not only the amount paid to the seller but also other costs related to the purchase, such as the broker's commission and postage charges for delivery. When stocks are purchased between dividend dates, there is no separate charge for the pro rata amount of

---

[1]*Opinions of the Accounting Principles Board, No. 18,* "The Equity Method of Accounting for Investments in Common Stock" (New York: American Institute of Certified Public Accountants, 1971), par. 17.

the dividend. Dividends do not accrue from day to day, since they become an obligation of the issuing corporation only when they are declared by the board of directors. The prices of stocks may be affected by the anticipated dividend as the usual declaration date approaches, but this anticipated dividend is only one of many factors that influence stock prices.

The total cost of stocks purchased should be debited to an investment account. When the cost method is used, cash dividends on capital stock held as an investment may be recorded as an increase in the appropriate income and asset accounts. To illustrate, assume that Makowski Corporation purchases 100 shares of Compton Corporation common stock at 55 plus a brokerage fee of $42. At the end of the year, Compton Corporation declares a $2 per share cash dividend. Entries in the accounts of Makowski Corporation, the investor, are as follows:

Record purchase of Compton Corp. common stock	Investment in Compton Corp. Stock 5,542	
	Cash..	5,542

Record share of cash dividends paid by Compton Corp.	Cash.. 200	
	Dividend Income..	200

In the illustration, the dividend was recorded when the cash was received. An alternative would be to record the cash dividend when it is declared by the investee corporation. If this alternative had been used, Makowski Corporation would have debited Dividends Receivable and credited Dividend Income when the dividend was declared. When the dividend was paid, Makowski Corporation would have debited Cash and credited the receivable.

A dividend in the form of additional shares of stock is usually not income, and therefore no entry is needed beyond a notation as to the additional number of shares acquired. The receipt of a stock dividend does, however, affect the carrying amount of each share of stock. Thus, if a 5-share common stock dividend is received on 100 shares of common stock with a current carrying amount of $4,200 ($42 per share), the unit carrying amount of the 105 shares becomes $40 per share ($4,200 ÷ 105).

Long-term investments in stocks of a company over which the investor does not exercise significant influence are subject to the lower of cost or market rule. In applying the rule, the carrying amount of a long-term investment in a portfolio of equity securities is the lower of the *total* cost or *total* market price of the portfolio at the date of the balance sheet. Any market value changes that are recognized are not included in net income, but are reported as a separate item in the stockholders' equity section of the balance sheet.[2] If the decline in market value below cost of an individual security as of the balance sheet date is other than temporary, the cost basis of the individual security is written down and the amount of the write-down is accounted for as a realized loss. After the write-down, the carrying amount of the individual security cannot be changed for subsequent recoveries in market value.[3]

---

[2]*Statement of Financial Accounting Standards, No. 12*, "Accounting for Certain Marketable Securities" (Stamford: Financial Accounting Standards Board, 1975), par. 11.

[3]*Ibid.*, par. 21.

Equity Method

When the equity method of accounting is used, a stock purchase is recorded at cost as under the cost method. The features that distinguish the equity method from the cost method relate to the net income and cash dividends of the investee and are summarized as follows:

1. The investor records its share of the periodic net income of the investee as an increase in the investment account and as revenue of the period. Conversely, the investor's share of the investee's periodic loss is recorded as a decrease in the investment and a loss of the period.
2. The investor records its share of cash or property dividends on the stock as a decrease in the investment account and an increase in the appropriate asset accounts.

To illustrate the foregoing, assume that as of the beginning of the fiscal years of Hally Corporation and Brock Corporation, Hally acquires 40% of the common (voting) stock of Brock for $350,000 in cash, that Brock reports net income of $105,000 for the year, and that Brock declared and paid $45,000 in cash dividends during the year. Entries in the accounts of the investor to record these transactions are as follows:

Record purchase of 40% of Brock Corp. common stock	Investment in Brock Corp. Stock........................... Cash...	350,000	350,000
Record 40% of Brock Corp. net income of $105,000	Investment in Brock Corp. Stock........................... Income of Brock Corp...........................	42,000	42,000
Record 40% of cash dividends of $45,000 paid by Brock Corp.	Cash... Investment in Brock Corp. Stock.................	18,000	18,000

The combined effect of recording 40% of Brock Corporation's income and the dividends received was to increase Cash by $18,000, Investment in Brock Corp. Stock by $24,000, and Income of Brock Corp. by $42,000.

Sale of Long-Term Investments in Stocks

When shares of stock held as a long-term investment are sold, the investment account is credited for the carrying amount of the shares sold and the cash or appropriate receivable account is debited for the proceeds (sales price less commission and other selling costs). Any difference between the proceeds and the carrying amount is recorded as a gain or loss on the sale. To illustrate, assume that an investment in Drey Corporation stock has a carrying amount of $15,700. If the proceeds from the sale of the stock are $17,500, the entry to record the transaction is as follows:

Cash	17,500	
Investment in Drey Corp. Stock		15,700
Gain on Sale of Investments		1,800

BUSINESS COMBINATIONS

OBJECTIVE 3
Describe alternative
methods of
combining
businesses.

The history of business organization in the United States has been characterized by continuous growth in the size of business entities and the combining of separate enterprises to form even larger operating units. Over the past several years, the combining of businesses has increased dramatically both in numbers and dollars. In 1987, for example, more than 3,500 combinations took place, involving the exchange of cash, debt obligations, or capital stock of approximately $170 billion.[4] These combinations were influenced by such objectives as efficiencies of large-scale production, broadening of markets and sales volume, reduction of competition, diversification of product lines, and savings in income taxes.

The combining of businesses is often announced to the public, especially if the businesses are well known. For example, the following advertisement appeared in *Barron's* (May 23, 1988) announcing the acquisition of J. P. Stevens & Co., Inc. by West Point-Pepperell, Inc.:

West Point-Pepperell, Inc.

has acquired

J. P. Stevens & Co., Inc.

We acted as financial advisor to West Point-Pepperell, Inc.
in this transaction, assisted in the negotiations and
served as Dealer Manager for the tender offer.

Merrill Lynch Capital Markets

May 7, 1988

The combining of businesses that are engaged either in similar types of activity or in totally different kinds of pursuits may be effected (1) through a joining of two or more corporations to form a single unit by merger or by consolidation or (2) through common control of two or more corporations by means of stock ownership that results in a parent-subsidiary affiliation. These methods of combining separate corporations into larger operating units are complex. Therefore, the discussion that follows is intended to be introductory, with major emphasis on the financial statements of business combinations.

---

[4] "Takeovers + Divestitures: Full Speed Ahead," Edward T. O'Toole, *Barron's*, May 23, 1988.

Mergers and Consolidations

When one corporation acquires the properties of another corporation and the latter then dissolves, the joining of the two enterprises is called a **merger**. Usually, all of the assets of the acquired company, as well as its liabilities, are taken over by the acquiring company, which continues its operations as a single unit. Payment may be in the form of cash, obligations, or capital stock of the acquiring corporation, or there may be a combination of several kinds of consideration. In any event, the consideration received by the dissolving corporation is distributed to its stockholders in final liquidation.

When two or more corporations transfer their assets and liabilities to a corporation which has been created for purposes of the takeover, the combination is called a **consolidation.** The new corporation usually issues its own securities in exchange for the properties acquired, and the original corporations are dissolved.

There are many legal, financial, managerial, and accounting problems associated with mergers and consolidations. Perhaps the most important matter is the determination of the class and amount of securities to be issued to the owners of the dissolving corporations. In resolving this problem, several factors are considered, including the relative value of the net assets contributed, the relative earning capacities, and the market price of the securities of the respective companies. Bargaining between the parties to the combination may also affect the final outcome.

Parent and Subsidiary Corporations

A common means of achieving a business combination is by one corporation owning a controlling share of the outstanding voting stock of one or more other corporations. When this method is used, none of the participants dissolves. All continue as separate legal entities. The corporation owning all or a majority of the voting stock of another corporation is known as the **parent company.** The corporation that is controlled is known as the **subsidiary company.** Two or more corporations closely related through stock ownership are sometimes called **affiliated** or **associated** companies.

The relationship of a parent and a subsidiary may be established by "purchase" or by a "pooling of interests." When a corporation acquires a controlling share of the voting common stock of another corporation in exchange for cash, other assets, issuance of notes or other debt obligations, or by a combination of these items, the transaction is treated as a purchase. It is accounted for by the **purchase method**. When this method of effecting a parent-subsidiary affiliation is used, the stockholders of the acquired company transfer their stock to the parent corporation.

Alternatively, when two corporations become affiliated by means of an exchange of voting common stock of one corporation (the parent) for substantially all (at least 90%) of the voting common stock of the other corporation (the subsidiary), the transaction is termed a pooling of interests. It is accounted for by the **pooling of interests method.** When this method of effecting a parent-subsidiary affiliation is used, the former stockholders of the subsidiary become stockholders of the parent company.

The accounting implications of the two affiliation methods are very different. The method first described is a "sale-purchase" transaction in contrast to the second method, in which there is a "joining of ownership interests" in the two companies.

The Accounting Principles Board established very strict criteria that must be met before the pooling of interests method can be used.[5] As a result, most business combinations are accounted for as a purchase. The 1988 edition of *Accounting Trends & Techniques* reported that of the applicable companies surveyed, 90% of the business combinations were accounted for by the purchase method and 10% were accounted for by the pooling of interests method.

ACCOUNTING FOR PARENT-SUBSIDIARY AFFILIATIONS

OBJECTIVE 4
Describe the accounting for parent-subsidiary affiliations.

Although the corporations that make up a parent-subsidiary affiliation may operate as a single economic unit, they continue to maintain separate accounting records and prepare their own periodic financial statements. The parent corporation uses the equity method of accounting for its investment in the stock of a subsidiary.

After the parent-subsidiary relationship has been established, the investment account of the parent is periodically increased by its share of the subsidiary's net income and decreased by its share of dividends received from the subsidiary. At the end of each fiscal year, the parent reports the investment account balance on its own balance sheet as a long-term investment, and its current share of the subsidiary's net income on its own income statement as a separate item.

In addition to the interrelationship through stock ownership, there are usually other intercorporate transactions which have an effect on the financial statements of both the parent and the subsidiary. For example, either may own bonds or other evidences of indebtedness issued by the other and either may purchase or sell goods or services to the other.

Because of the central managerial control factor and the intertwining of relationships, the results of operations and the financial position of a parent company and its subsidiaries should usually be presented as if the group were a single company with one or more branches or divisions. Such statements are likely to be more meaningful to stockholders of the parent company than separate statements for each corporation.

The financial statements resulting from the combining of parent and subsidiary statements are generally called **consolidated statements**. Specifically, such statements may be identified by the addition of "and subsidiary(ies)" to the name of the parent corporation or by modification of the title of the respective statement, as in *consolidated balance sheet* or *consolidated income statement*.[6]

BASIC PRINCIPLES OF CONSOLIDATION OF FINANCIAL STATEMENTS

OBJECTIVE 5
Describe and illustrate the basic principles of consolidation of financial statements.

When the data on the financial statements of the parent corporation and its subsidiaries are combined to form the consolidated statements, special attention should be given to the ties of relationship between the separate corporations. These ties are represented by the intercompany items appearing in their respective ledgers and statements. Examples of such intercompany items include notes receivable and notes payable, accounts receivable and accounts payable, interest receivable and interest payable, sales and pur-

---

[5]*Opinions of the Accounting Principles Board*, No. 16, "Business Combinations" (New York: American Institute of Certified Public Accountants, 1970).

[6]Examples of consolidated statements are presented in Appendix I.

chases (or cost of merchandise sold), and interest expense and interest income. The intercompany items, which are called **reciprocals**, must be eliminated from the statements that are to be consolidated. For example, a note representing a loan by a parent corporation to its subsidiary would appear as a note receivable in the parent's balance sheet and a note payable in the subsidiary's balance sheet. When the two balance sheets are combined, the note receivable and the note payable would be eliminated because the consolidated balance sheet is prepared as if the parent and subsidiary were one operating unit. After the proper eliminations are made, the remaining items on the financial statements of the subsidiary are combined with the like items on the financial statements of the parent.

The intercompany accounts of a parent and its subsidiaries may not be entirely reciprocal in amount. Differences may be caused by the manner in which the parent-subsidiary relationship was created, by the extent of the parent's ownership of the subsidiary, or by the nature of their subsequent intercompany transactions. Such factors must be considered when the financial statements of affiliated corporations are consolidated.

To direct attention to the basic concepts of consolidation, most of the data appearing in financial statements will be omitted from many of the illustrations in the following paragraphs. The term "net assets" will be used as a substitute for the specific assets and liabilities that appear in the balance sheet. Explanations will also be simplified by using the term "book equity" in referring to the monetary amount of the stockholders' equity of the subsidiary acquired by the parent. The illustrative companies will be identified as Parent and Subsidiary.

Purchase Method

When a parent-subsidiary affiliation is effected as a purchase, the parent corporation is deemed to have purchased all or a major part of the subsidiary corporation's net assets. Accordingly, the principles of accounting for a sale-purchase transaction are applied to the consolidation of the parent and the subsidiary.

Consolidated Balance Sheet at Date of Acquisition. At the date of acquisition, the assets of the subsidiary should be reported on the consolidated balance sheet at their cost to the parent, as measured by the amount of the consideration given in acquiring the stock. In the subsidiary's ledger, the reciprocal of the investment account at the date of acquisition is the composite of all of the subsidiary's stockholders' equity accounts. Any difference between the cost to the parent and the amounts reported on the subsidiary's balance sheet must be given recognition on the consolidated balance sheet.

Income from an investment in assets does not accrue to an investor until after the assets have been purchased. Therefore, subsidiary company earnings accumulated prior to the date of the parent-subsidiary purchase affiliation must be excluded from the consolidated balance sheet and the income statement. Only those earnings of the subsidiary realized subsequent to the affiliation are includable in the consolidated statements.

Wholly Owned Subsidiary Acquired at a Cost Equal to Book Equity. Assume that Parent creates Subsidiary, transferring to it $120,000 of assets and $20,000 of liabilities, and taking in exchange 10,000 shares of $10 par common stock of Subsidiary. The effect of the transaction on Parent's ledger is to replace the various assets and liabilities (net assets of $100,000) with a single account: Investment in Subsidiary, $100,000. The effect on the balance sheet of Parent, together with the balance sheet of Subsidiary prepared immediately after the transaction, is as follows:

	Assets	Stockholders' Equity
Parent:		
Investment in Subsidiary, 10,000 shares..........	$100,000	
Subsidiary:		
Net assets...	$100,000	
Common stock, 10,000 shares, $10 par		$100,000

When the balance sheets of the two corporations are consolidated, the reciprocal accounts Investment in Subsidiary and Common Stock are offset against each other, or *eliminated*. The individual assets (Cash, Equipment, etc.) and the individual liabilities (Accounts Payable, etc.) making up the $100,000 of net assets on the balance sheet of Subsidiary are then added to the corresponding items on the balance sheet of Parent. The consolidated balance sheet is completed by listing Parent's paid-in capital accounts and retained earnings.

Wholly Owned Subsidiary Acquired at a Cost Above Book Equity. Instead of creating a new subsidiary, a corporation may acquire an already established corporation by purchasing its stock. In such cases, the subsidiary stock's total cost to the parent usually differs from the book equity of such stock. To illustrate, assume that Parent acquires for $180,000 all of the outstanding stock of Subsidiary, a going concern, from Subsidiary's stockholders. Assume further that the stockholders' equity of Subsidiary is made up of common stock of $100,000 (10,000 shares, $10 par) and $50,000 of retained earnings. Parent records the investment at its cost of $180,000, regardless of the amount of the book equity of Subsidiary. It should also be noted that the $180,000 paid to Subsidiary's stockholders has no effect on the assets, liabilities, or stockholders' equity of Subsidiary. The situation immediately after the transaction may be presented as follows:

	Assets	Stockholders' Equity
Parent:		
Investment in Subsidiary, 10,000 shares..........	$180,000	
Subsidiary:		
Net assets...	$150,000	
Common stock, 10,000 shares, $10 par		$100,000
Retained earnings.......................................		50,000

It is readily apparent that the reciprocal items on the separate balance sheets differ by $30,000. If the reciprocals were eliminated, as in the preceding illustration, and were replaced solely by Subsidiary's net assets of $150,000, the consolidated balance sheet would be out of balance.

The treatment of the $30,000 difference depends upon the reason that Parent paid more than book equity for Subsidiary's stock. When the amount paid above book equity is due to an excess of fair market value over book value of Subsidiary's assets, the values of the appropriate assets should be revised upward by $30,000. For example, if land that Subsidiary had acquired several years previously at a cost of $50,000 (book value) has a current fair market value of $80,000, the book amount should be increased from $50,000 to $80,000 when the asset is reported on the consolidated balance sheet. When Parent has paid more for Subsidiary's stock because Subsidiary has prospects for high future earnings, the $30,000 should be reported on the consolidated balance sheet under a description such as "Goodwill" or "Excess of cost of business acquired over related net assets."

When the amount paid above book equity is due to both an excess of fair market value over book value of assets and high future earnings prospects, the excess of cost over book equity should be allocated accordingly.[7] To illustrate, assume that the $30,000 difference in the illustration is due to a $20,000 excess of market value over book value of Subsidiary's land and Subsidiary prospects for high future earnings. The book amount of the land, which had cost $50,000, would be increased to $70,000, and goodwill of $10,000 would be reported on the consolidated balance sheet.

Wholly Owned Subsidiary Acquired at a Cost Below Book Equity. All of the stock of a corporation may be acquired from its stockholders at a cost that is less than book equity. To illustrate, assume that the stock in Subsidiary is acquired for $130,000 and that the composition of the stockholders' equity of Subsidiary is the same as in the preceding illustration. Parent records the investment at its cost of $130,000. The situation immediately after the transaction is as follows:

	Assets	Stockholders' Equity
Parent:		
Investment in Subsidiary, 10,000 shares	$130,000	
Subsidiary:		
Net assets	$150,000	
Common stock, 10,000 shares, $10 par		$100,000
Retained earnings		50,000

Elimination of the reciprocal accounts and reporting the $150,000 of net assets of Subsidiary on the consolidated balance sheet creates an imbalance of $20,000. The possible reasons for the apparent "bargain" purchase and the treatment of the imbalance are generally the reverse of those given in explaining acquisition at a price higher than book equity. The complexities that might arise in some instances are discussed in advanced texts.

Partially Owned Subsidiary Acquired at a Cost Above or Below Book Equity. When one corporation seeks to gain control over another by purchase of its stock, it is not necessary and often not possible to acquire all of the stock. To illustrate this situation, assume that Parent acquires, at a total cost of $190,000, 80% of the stock of Subsidiary, whose book equity is composed of common stock of $100,000 (10,000 shares, $10 par) and $80,000 of retained earnings. The relevant data immediately after the acquisition of the stock are as follows:

[7] *Opinions of the Accounting Principles Board, No. 16,* "Business Combinations" (New York: American Institute of Certified Public Accountants, 1970), par. 87.

	Assets	Stockholders' Equity
Parent:		
Investment in Subsidiary, 8,000 shares	$190,000	
Subsidiary:		
Net assets	$180,000	
Common stock, 10,000 shares, $10 par...........		$100,000
Retained earnings......................................		80,000

The explanation of the $10,000 imbalance in the reciprocal items in this illustration is more complex than in the preceding illustrations. Two factors are involved: (1) the amount paid for the stock is greater than 80% of Subsidiary's book equity and (2) only 80% of Subsidiary's stock was purchased. Since Parent acquired 8,000 shares or 80% of the outstanding shares of Subsidiary, only 80% of the stockholders' equity accounts of Subsidiary can be eliminated. The remaining 20% of the stock is owned by outsiders, who are called collectively the **minority interest**. The eliminations from the partially reciprocal accounts and the amounts to be reported on the consolidated balance sheet, including the minority interest, are determined as follows:

Parent:		
Investment in Subsidiary.......................................		$190,000
Eliminate 80% of Subsidiary stock........................	$ 80,000	
Eliminate 80% of Subsidiary retained earnings	64,000	144,000
Excess of cost over book equity of		
Subsidiary interest..		$ 46,000
Subsidiary:		
Common stock	$100,000	
Eliminate 80% of Subsidiary stock........................	80,000	
Remainder...		$ 20,000
Retained earnings..	$ 80,000	
Eliminate 80% of Subsidiary retained earnings	64,000	
Remainder...		16,000
Minority interest		$ 36,000

The excess cost of $46,000 is reported on the consolidated balance sheet as goodwill or the valuation placed on other assets is increased by $46,000, according to the principles explained earlier. The minority interest of $36,000, which is the amount of Subsidiary's book equity allocable to outsiders, is reported on the consolidated balance sheet, usually preceding the stockholders' equity accounts of Parent. The 1988 edition of *Accounting Trends & Techniques* indicates that most of the companies surveyed reported minority interest in the long-term liabilities section.

Consolidated Balance Sheet Subsequent to Acquisition. Subsequent to acquisition of a subsidiary, the parent company uses the equity method to account for its investment in the subsidiary. Thus, the parent company's investment account is increased periodically for its share of the subsidiary's earnings and decreased for the related dividends received. Correspondingly, the retained earnings account of the subsidiary will be increased periodically by the amount of its net income and reduced by dividend distributions. Because of these periodic changes in the balances of the reciprocal accounts, the eliminations required in preparing a consolidated balance sheet will change each year.

To illustrate consolidation of balance sheets subsequent to acquisition, assume that Subsidiary in the preceding illustration earned net income of $50,000 and paid dividends of $20,000 during the year subsequent to Parent's acquisition of 80% of its stock. The net effect of the year's transactions on Subsidiary were as follows:

	Net Assets	Common Stock	Retained Earnings
Subsidiary:			
Date of acquisition...........................	$180,000	$100,000	$ 80,000
Add net income	50,000		50,000
Deduct dividends	(20,000)		(20,000)
Date subsequent to acquisition..........	$210,000	$100,000	$110,000

Parent's entries to record its 80% share of subsidiary's net income and dividends are as follows:

Parent entries

Investment in Subsidiary	40,000	
Income of Subsidiary..		40,000
Cash..	16,000	
Investment in Subsidiary		16,000

The net effect of the foregoing entries on Parent's investment account is to increase the balance by $24,000, as follows:

Parent:		
Investment in subsidiary, 8,000 shares:		
Date of acquisition..		$190,000
Add 80% of Subsidiary's net income....................	$40,000	
Deduct 80% of Subsidiary's dividends..................	(16,000)	24,000
One year subsequent to acquisition.....................		$214,000

Continuing the illustration, the eliminations from the partially reciprocal accounts and the amounts to be reported on the consolidated balance sheet are determined as follows:

Parent:		
Investment in Subsidiary..		$214,000
Eliminate 80% of Subsidiary stock........................	$ 80,000	
Eliminate 80% of Subsidiary retained earnings	88,000	168,000
Excess of cost over book equity of		
Subsidiary interest...		$ 46,000
Subsidiary:		
Common stock	$100,000	
Eliminate 80% of Subsidiary stock........................	80,000	
Remainder..		$ 20,000
Retained earnings	$110,000	
Eliminate 80% of Subsidiary retained earnings	88,000	
Remainder..		22,000
Minority interest		$ 42,000

A comparison of the data with the analysis as of the date of acquisition shows the following:

1. Minority interest increased $6,000 (from $36,000 to $42,000), which is equivalent to 20% of the $30,000 net increase ($50,000 of net income less $20,000 of dividends) in Subsidiary's retained earnings.
2. Excess of cost over book equity of the subsidiary interest remained unchanged at $46,000.

To avoid additional complexities, it was assumed that the $46,000 excess at the date of acquisition was not due to goodwill or to assets subject to depreciation or amortization.[8]

Work Sheet for Consolidated Balance Sheet. The preceding discussion focused on the basic concepts associated with the process of preparing consolidated balance sheets. If the consolidation process becomes quite complex or if the amount of data to be processed is substantial, all of the relevant data for the consolidated statements may be assembled on work sheets. Although a work sheet is not essential, it is used in the following illustration to show an alternate method of accumulating all relevant data for the consolidated balance sheet. Whether or not a work sheet is used, the basic concepts and the consolidated balance sheet would not be affected.

To illustrate the use of the work sheet, assume that (as was the case in the illustration in the preceding section) Parent had purchased 80% of Subsidiary stock for $190,000. Any excess of the cost of the investment over book equity is due to the excess of market value over book value of Subsidiary's land. For the year since the acquisition, Parent had debited the investment account for its share of Subsidiary earnings and had credited the investment account for its share of dividends declared by Subsidiary. Balance sheet data for Parent and Subsidiary as of December 31 of the year subsequent to acquisition appear as follows. Although these data include amounts for land, other assets, and liabilities, the net assets and stockholders' equity for Subsidiary are the same as in the preceding illustration.

	Parent	Subsidiary
Investment in Subsidiary	$214,000	
Land	100,000	$ 60,000
Other assets	400,000	200,000
	$714,000	$260,000
Liabilities	$164,000	$ 50,000
Common stock:		
Parent	300,000	
Subsidiary		100,000
Retained earnings:		
Parent	250,000	
Subsidiary		110,000
	$714,000	$260,000

---

[8]Any portion of the excess of cost over book equity assigned to goodwill must be amortized according to *Opinions of the Accounting Principles Board No. 17*, "Intangible Assets." Similarly, any excess of cost over book equity assigned to plant assets of limited life must be gradually reduced by depreciation. The application of such amortization and depreciation techniques to consolidated statements goes beyond the scope of the discussion here.

The account balances at December 31 and the eliminations from the reciprocal accounts would be entered on the work sheet and the appropriate amounts extended to the Consolidated Balance Sheet column as follows:

Parent and Subsidiary
Work Sheet for Consolidated Balance Sheet
December 31, 19--

	Parent	Subsidiary	Eliminations Debit	Eliminations Credit	Consolidated Balance Sheet	
Investment in Subsidiary...	214,000			(a) 168,000 (b) 46,000		
Land.............................	100,000	60,000	(b) 46,000		206,000	
Other Assets	400,000	200,000			600,000	
	714,000	260,000			806,000	
Liabilities	164,000	50,000			214,000	
Common Stock:						
Parent.......................	300,000				300,000	
Subsidiary..................		100,000	(a) 80,000		20,000	minority interest
Retained Earnings:						
Parent.......................	250,000				250,000	
Subsidiary..................		110,000	(a) 88,000		22,000	minority interest
	714,000	260,000	214,000	214,000	806,000	

Explanations for the entries in the Eliminations columns of the work sheet are as follows:

(a) This entry eliminates from the investment in subsidiary account the Parent's share of the Subsidiary's common stock and retained earnings. As discussed in the preceding paragraphs, the Parent's share of the Subsidiary's common stock is $80,000, and the Parent's share of the retained earnings is $88,000. After these two amounts are eliminated on the work sheet, the remaining balances in the Subsidiary's common stock and retained earnings accounts represent minority interest. The minority interests of $20,000 and $22,000 are identified in the Consolidated Balance Sheet column of the work sheet as an aid in the preparation of the consolidated balance sheet.

(b) This entry eliminates the remainder of the investment in subsidiary account and allocates the excess of cost over book equity according to the principles explained earlier. In this illustration, since the $46,000 excess of cost over book equity is due to an excess of fair value over book value of Subsidiary's land, the land account is debited for $46,000.

In the following consolidated balance sheet, the amount reported for land is $206,000 and the amount reported for minority interest is $42,000. Both of these amounts were identified on the work sheet.

Parent and Subsidiary
Consolidated Balance Sheet
December 31, 19--

Assets

Land...	$206,000
Other assets	600,000
Total assets	$806,000

Liabilities and Stockholders' Equity

Liabilities	$214,000
Minority interest in subsidiary	42,000
Common stock	300,000
Retained earnings..	250,000
Total liabilities and stockholders' equity	$806,000

It should be noted that the work sheet is only an aid for accumulating the data for the consolidated balance sheet. It is not the consolidated balance sheet. Also, if there are other intercompany items that must be eliminated from the statements that are to be consolidated, those eliminations would be entered in the Eliminations columns of the work sheet. For example, a loan by a parent to its subsidiary on a note would require an elimination of the amount of the note from both notes receivable and notes payable in the work sheet.

Pooling of Interests Method

When a parent-subsidiary affiliation is effected as a pooling of interests, the ownership of the two companies is joined together in the parent corporation. The parent deems its investment in the subsidiary to be equal to the carrying amount of the subsidiary's net assets. Any difference that may exist between such carrying amount and the fair value of the subsidiary's assets does not affect the amount recorded by the parent as the investment.

Consolidated Balance Sheet at Date of Affiliation. Since the parent's investment in the subsidiary is equal to the carrying amount of the subsidiary's net assets, no change is needed in the amounts at which the subsidiary's assets should be included in the consolidated balance sheet prepared at the date of affiliation. The subsidiary's assets are reported as they appear in the subsidiary's separate balance sheet.

The credit to the parent company's stockholders' equity accounts for the stock issued in exchange for the subsidiary company's stock corresponds to the amount debited to the investment account. In addition to the common stock account, the paid-in capital accounts may be affected, as well as the retained earnings account. According to the concept of continuity of ownership interests, subsidiary earnings accumulated prior to the affiliation should be combined with those of the parent on the consolidated balance sheet. It is as though there had been a single economic unit from the time the enterprises had begun.

To illustrate the procedure for consolidating the balance sheets of two corporations by the pooling of interests method, their respective financial positions immediately prior to the exchange of stock are assumed to be as follows:

	Assets	Stockholders' Equity
Parent:		
Net assets	$230,000	
Common stock, 4,000 shares, $25 par............		$100,000
Retained earnings......................................		130,000
Subsidiary:		
Net assets	$150,000	
Common stock, 10,000 shares, $10 par...........		$100,000
Retained earnings......................................		50,000

Since poolings must involve substantially all (90% or more) of the stock of the subsidiary, the illustration will assume an exchange of 100% of the stock. It is also assumed that the fair market value of the net assets of both companies is greater than the amounts reported above and that there appears to be an element of goodwill in both cases. Based on recent price quotations, it is agreed that for the purpose of the exchange, Parent's common stock is to be valued at $45 a share and Subsidiary's at $18 a share.[9] According to the agreement, the exchange of stock is brought about as follows:

Parent issues 4,000 shares valued at $45 per share.................... $180,000

in exchange for

Subsidiary's 10,000 shares valued at $18 per share $180,000

The excess of the $180,000 value of Parent's stock issued over the $150,000 of net assets of Subsidiary may be ignored and the investment recorded as follows:

Parent entry

Investment in Subsidiary	150,000	
Common Stock...		100,000
Retained Earnings..		50,000

After the foregoing entry has been recorded, the basic balance sheet data of the two companies are as follows:

	Assets	Stockholders' Equity
Parent:		
Investment in Subsidiary, 10,000 shares..........	$150,000	
Other net assets	230,000	
Common stock, 8,000 shares, $25 par............		$200,000
Retained earnings......................................		180,000
Subsidiary:		
Net assets	$150,000	
Common stock, 10,000 shares, $10 par...........		$100,000
Retained earnings......................................		50,000

To consolidate the balance sheets of the two companies, Parent's investment account and Subsidiary's common stock and retained earnings accounts are eliminated. The net assets of the two companies, $230,000 and

---

[9] In practice, it may be necessary to pay cash for fractional shares or for subsidiary shares held by dissenting stockholders.

$150,000, are combined without any changes in valuation, making a total of $380,000. The consolidated stockholders' equity is composed of common stock of $200,000 and retained earnings of $180,000, for a total of $380,000.

Consolidated Balance Sheet Subsequent to Affiliation. The equity method is used by the parent corporation in recording changes in its investment account subsequent to acquisition. Thus, the account is increased by the parent's share of the subsidiary's earnings and decreased by its share of dividends. Continuing the illustration of the preceding section, assume that Subsidiary's net income and dividends paid during the year subsequent to affiliation with Parent are $20,000 and $5,000 respectively. After Parent has recorded Subsidiary's net income and dividends, the Parent's investment in Subsidiary increases by $15,000, and the Subsidiary's net assets and retained earnings increase by $15,000, yielding the following account balances:

	Assets	Stockholders' Equity
Parent:		
Investment in Subsidiary, 10,000 shares..........	$165,000	
Subsidiary:		
Net assets	$165,000	
Common stock, 10,000 shares, $10 par...........		$100,000
Retained earnings		65,000

When the balance sheets of the affiliated corporations are consolidated, the reciprocal accounts are eliminated and the $165,000 of net assets of Subsidiary are combined with those of Parent.

Work Sheet for Consolidated Balance Sheet. To illustrate the use of the work sheet to assemble the relevant data for the consolidated balance sheet for an affiliation effected as a pooling of interests, assume that (as was the case in the illustration in the preceding section) Parent had exchanged 4,000 shares of its common stock for all of the 10,000 shares of Subsidiary common stock. For the year since the acquisition, Parent had debited the investment account for its share (100%) of Subsidiary earnings and had credited the investment account for its share (100%) of dividends declared by Subsidiary. Balance sheet data for Parent and Subsidiary as of December 31 of the year subsequent to acquisition appear as follows. As in the purchase illustration, amounts for land, other assets, and liabilities have been added, but the amounts for net assets and stockholders' equity for Subsidiary are the same as in the preceding illustration.

	Parent	Subsidiary
Investment in Subsidiary......................................	$165,000	
Land...	80,000	$ 40,000
Other assets	325,000	175,000
	$570,000	$215,000
Liabilities	$140,000	$ 50,000
Common stock:		
Parent..	200,000	
Subsidiary...		100,000
Retained earnings:		
Parent..	230,000	
Subsidiary...		65,000
	$570,000	$215,000

The account balances at December 31 and the eliminations from the reciprocal accounts would be entered on the work sheet and the amounts determined for the consolidated balance sheet items as follows:

Parent and Subsidiary
Work Sheet for Consolidated Balance Sheet
December 31, 19--

| | Parent | Subsidiary | Eliminations | | Consolidated Balance Sheet |
			Debit	Credit	
Investment in Subsidiary......	165,000			165,000	
Land.............................	80,000	40,000			120,000
Other Assets.....................	325,000	175,000			500,000
	570,000	215,000			620,000
Liabilities	140,000	50,000			190,000
Common Stock:					
Parent..........................	200,000				200,000
Subsidiary......................		100,000	100,000		
Retained Earnings:					
Parent..........................	230,000				230,000
Subsidiary......................		65,000	65,000		
	570,000	215,000	165,000	165,000	620,000

After 100% of Subsidiary common stock and Subsidiary retained earnings is eliminated against the Investment in Subsidiary, as indicated in the Eliminations columns of the work sheet, the amounts for the two companies are combined, without any changes in valuation, and are then reported on the consolidated balance sheet.

As previously discussed, the work sheet is only an aid for accumulating the data for the consolidated balance sheet. These data are the basis for the consolidated balance sheet, which is prepared in the normal manner.

Consolidated Income Statement and Other Statements

Consolidations of income statements and other statements of affiliated companies usually present fewer difficulties than those encountered in balance sheet consolidations. The difference is largely because of the inherent nature of the statements. The balance sheet reports cumulative effects of all transactions from the very beginning of an enterprise to a current date, whereas the income statement, the retained earnings statement, and the statement of cash flows report selected transactions only and are for a limited period of time, usually one year.

The principles used in the consolidation of the income statements of a parent and its subsidiaries are the same, regardless of whether the affiliation is deemed to be a purchase or a pooling of interests. When the income statements are consolidated, all amounts resulting from intercompany transactions, such as management fees or interest on loans charged by one affiliate to another, must be eliminated. Any intercompany profit included in inventories must also be eliminated. The remaining amounts of sales, cost of merchandise sold, operating expenses, and other revenues and expenses reported on the income statements of the affiliated corporations are then combined. The eliminations required in consolidating the retained earnings statement and other statements are based largely on data assembled in consolidating the balance sheet and income statement.

CORPORATION FINANCIAL STATEMENTS

OBJECTIVE 6
Illustrate a corporate balance sheet for a parent company and its subsidiaries.

Examples of retained earnings statements and sections of income statements affected by the corporate form of organization have been presented in preceding chapters. The consolidated balance sheet below illustrates for a corporation the balance sheet presentation of many of the items discussed in this and preceding chapters, including bond sinking funds, investments in bonds, goodwill, deferred income taxes, bonds payable and unamortized discount, minority interest in subsidiaries, and appropriation of retained earnings.

Balance Sheet of a Corporation

Escoe Corporation
Consolidated
December

Assets

Current assets:		
Cash..		$ 255,000
Marketable securities, at cost		
(market price, $160,000)...............		152,500
Accounts and notes receivable	$ 722,000	
Less allowance for		
doubtful receivables..................	37,000	685,000
Inventories, at lower of cost (first-in,		
first-out) or market......................		917,500
Prepaid expenses		70,000
Total current assets....................		$2,080,000
Investments:		
Bond sinking fund		$ 422,500
Investment in bonds of		
Dalton Company..........................		240,000
Total investments........................		662,500

	Cost	Accumulated Depreciation	Book Value	
Plant assets				
(depreciated by the straight-line method):				
Land.........................	$ 250,000	—	$ 250,000	
Buildings	920,000	$ 379,955	540,045	
Machinery and equipment.............	2,764,400	766,200	1,998,200	
Total plant assets.....	$3,934,400	$1,146,155		2,788,245

Intangible assets:		
Goodwill......................................		$ 300,000
Organization costs.........................		50,000
Total intangible assets.................		350,000
Total assets		$5,880,745

ACCOUNTING FOR INTERNATIONAL OPERATIONS

OBJECTIVE 7
Describe and
illustrate the
accounting for
international
operations.

In an effort to expand operations, many U.S. companies conduct business in foreign countries. If the operations of these multinational companies involve currencies other than the dollar, special accounting problems may arise (1) in accounting for transactions with the foreign companies and (2) in the preparation of consolidated statements for domestic and foreign companies that are affiliated. The basic principles used in such situations are presented in the following paragraphs. Details and complexities are reserved for advanced texts.

and Subsidiaries
Balance Sheet
31, 19--

Liabilities

Current liabilities:			
Accounts payable............................		$ 508,810	
Income tax payable		120,500	
Dividends payable..........................		94,000	
Accrued liabilities		81,400	
Deferred income tax payable............		10,000	
Total current liabilities			$ 814,710
Long-term liabilities:			
Debenture 8% bonds payable, due			
December 31, 19--	$1,000,000		
Less unamortized discount............	60,000	$ 940,000	
Minority interest in subsidiaries.........		115,000	
Total long-term liabilities...............			1,055,000
Deferred credits:			
Deferred income tax payable............			85,500
Total liabilities..................................			$1,955,210

Stockholders' Equity

Paid-in capital:			
Common stock, $20 par			
(250,000 shares authorized,			
100,000 shares issued)................		$2,000,000	
Excess of issue price over			
par — common stock....................		320,000	
Total paid-in capital			$2,320,000
Retained earnings:			
Appropriated:			
For bonded			
indebtedness.......	$250,000		
For plant expansion.	750,000	$1,000,000	
Unappropriated.............................		605,535	
Total retained earnings.................			1,605,535
Total stockholders' equity....................			3,925,535
Total liabilities and stockholders'			
equity..			$5,880,745

Accounting for Transactions with Foreign Companies

If transactions with foreign companies are executed in dollars, no special accounting problems arise. Such transactions would be recorded as illustrated in the text. For example, the sale of merchandise to a Japanese company that is billed in and paid in dollars would be recorded by the U.S. company in the normal manner, using dollar amounts. However, if transactions involve receivables or payables that are to be received or paid in a foreign currency, the U.S. company may incur an exchange gain or loss.

Realized Currency Exchange Gains and Losses. When a U.S. company executes a transaction with a company in a foreign country using a currency other than the dollar, one currency needs to be converted into another to settle the transaction. For example, a U.S. company purchasing merchandise from a British company that requires payment in British pounds must exchange dollars ($) for pounds (£) to settle the transaction. This exchange of one currency into another involves the use of an exchange rate. The **exchange rate** is the rate at which one unit of currency (the dollar, for example) can be converted into another currency (the British pound, for example). To continue with the illustration, if the U.S. company had purchased merchandise for £1,000 from a British company on June 1, when the exchange rate was $1.40 per British pound, $1,400 would need to be exchanged for £1,000 to make the purchase.[10] Since the U.S. company maintains its accounts in dollars, the transaction would be recorded as follows:

June 1	Purchases..	1,400	
	Cash..		1,400
	Payment of Invoice No. 1725 from W. A. Sterling Co., £1,000; exchange rate, $1.40 per British pound.		

Special accounting problems arise when the exchange rate fluctuates between the date of the original transaction (such as a purchase on account) and the settlement of that transaction in cash in the foreign currency (such as the payment of an account payable). In practice, such fluctuations are frequent. To illustrate, assume that on July 10, when the exchange rate was $.004 per yen (Y), a purchase for Y100,000 was made from a Japanese company. Since the U.S. company maintains its accounts in dollars, the entry would be recorded at $400 (Y100,000 × $.004), as follows:

July 10	Purchases..	400	
	Accounts Payable—M. Suzuki and Son ..		400
	Invoice No. 818, Y100,000, exchange rate, $.004 per yen.		

If on the date of payment, August 9, the exchange rate had increased to $.005 per yen, the Y100,000 account payable must be settled by exchanging $500 (Y100,000 × $.005) for Y100,000. In such a case, the U.S. company incurs an exchange loss of $100, because $500 was needed to settle a $400 debt (account payable). The cash payment would be recorded as follows:

---

[10]Foreign exchange rates are quoted in major financial reporting services. Because the exchange rates are quite volatile, those used in this chapter are assumed rates which do not necessarily reflect current rates.

Aug. 9	Accounts Payable — M. Suzuki and Son.....	400	
	Exchange Loss	100	
	Cash..		500
	Cash paid on Invoice No. 818, for		
	Y100,000, or $400, when exchange		
	rate was $.005 per yen.		

All transactions with foreign companies can be analyzed in the manner described above. For example, assume that on May 1, when the exchange rate was $.25 per Swiss franc (F), a sale on account for $1,000 to a Swiss company was billed in Swiss francs. The transaction would be recorded as follows:

May 1	Accounts Receivable — D. W. Robinson Co....	1,000	
	Sales..		1,000
	Invoice No. 9772, F4,000; exchange		
	rate, $.25 per Swiss franc.		

If the exchange rate had increased to $.30 per Swiss franc on May 31, the date of receipt of cash, the U.S. company would realize an exchange gain of $200. The gain was realized because the F4,000, which had a value of $1,000 on the date of sale, had increased in value to $1,200 (F4,000 × $.30) on May 31 when payment was received. The receipt of the cash would be recorded as follows:

May 31	Cash...	1,200	
	Accounts Receivable — D. W. Robinson Co.		1,000
	Exchange Gain		200
	Cash received on Invoice No. 9772, for		
	F4,000, or $1,000, when exchange rate		
	was $.30 per Swiss franc.		

Unrealized Currency Exchange Gains and Losses. In the previous illustrations, the transactions were completed by either the receipt or the payment of cash. Therefore, any exchange gain or loss was realized and, in an accounting sense, was "recognized" at the date of the cash receipt or cash payment. However, if financial statements are prepared between the date of the original transaction (sale or purchase on account, for example) and the date of the cash receipt or cash payment, and the exchange rate has changed since the original transaction, an unrealized gain or loss must be recognized in the statements. To illustrate, assume that a sale on account for $1,000 had been made to a German company on December 20, when the exchange rate was $.50 per deutsche mark (DM), and that the transaction had been recorded as follows:

Dec. 20	Accounts Receivable — T. A. Mueller Inc.....	1,000	
	Sales..		1,000
	Invoice No. 1793, DM2,000; exchange		
	rate, $.50 per deutsche mark.		

If the exchange rate had decreased to $.45 per deutsche mark on December 31, the date of the balance sheet, the $1,000 account receivable would have a value of only $900 (DM2,000 × $.45). This "unrealized" loss would be recorded as follows:

Dec. 31	Exchange Loss	100	
	Accounts Receivable—T. A. Mueller Inc..		100
	Invoice No. 1793, DM2,000 × $.05		
	decrease in exchange rate.		

Assuming that DM2,000 are received on January 19 in the following year, when the exchange rate is $.42, the additional decline in the exchange rate from $.45 to $.42 per deutsche mark must be recognized. The cash receipt would be recorded as follows:

Jan. 19	Cash	840	
	Exchange Loss ($.03 × DM2,000).............	60	
	Accounts Receivable—T. A. Mueller Inc..		900
	Cash received on Invoice No. 1793, for		
	DM2,000, or $900, when exchange rate		
	was $.42 per deutsche mark.		

If the exchange rate had increased between December 31 and January 19, an exchange gain would be recorded on January 19. For example, if the exchange rate had increased from $.45 to $.47 per deutsche mark during this period, Exchange Gain would be credited for $40 ($.02 × DM2,000).

A balance in the exchange loss account at the end of the fiscal period should be reported in the Other Expense section of the income statement. A balance in the exchange gain account should be reported in the Other Income section.

Consolidated Financial Statements with Foreign Subsidiaries

Before the financial statements of domestic and foreign companies are consolidated, the amounts shown on the statements for the foreign companies must be converted to U.S. dollars. Asset and liability amounts are normally converted to U.S. dollars by using the exchange rates as of the balance sheet date. Revenues and expenses are normally converted by using the exchange rates that were in effect when those transactions were executed. (For practical purposes, a weighted average rate for the period is generally used.) The adjustments (gains or losses) resulting from the conversion are reported as a separate item in the stockholders' equity section of the balance sheets of the foreign companies.[11]

After the foreign company statements have been converted to U.S. dollars, the financial statements of U.S. and foreign subsidiaries are consolidated in the normal manner as described previously in this chapter.

[11]*Statement of Financial Accounting Standards*, No. 52, "Foreign Currency Translation" (Stamford: Financial Accounting Standards Board, 1981).

CHAPTER REVIEW

KEY POINTS

OBJECTIVE 1

Investments in Stocks

A business may make long-term investments in equity securities (preferred and common shares) with cash that it does not need for normal operations. A corporation may also purchase stocks as a means of establishing or maintaining business relations with the issuing company. In other cases, a corporation may acquire all or a large part of the voting stock of another corporation in order to control its activities.

OBJECTIVE 2

Accounting for Long-Term Investments in Stock

There are two methods of accounting for long-term investments in stock: (1) the cost method and (2) the equity method. The method used depends upon whether the investor owns enough of the voting stock of the investee (company whose stock is owned by the investor) to have a significant influence over its operating and financing policies. If the investor does not have a significant influence, the cost method (with the lower of cost or market rule) must be used. If the investor can exercise significant influence in a long-term investment situation, the equity method must be used.

The cost of stocks purchased includes not only the amount paid to the seller but also other costs related to the purchase, such as the broker's commission and postage charges for delivery. When the cost method is used, cash dividends on capital stock held as an investment may be recorded as an increase in the appropriate income and asset accounts. Under the cost method, the lower of cost or market rule must be applied to the total cost or total market price of the stock as of the date of the balance sheet. Any market value changes that are recognized are not included in net income, but are reported as a separate item in the stockholders' equity section of the balance sheet. If the decline in market value below cost for an individual security as of the balance sheet date is other than temporary, the cost basis of the individual security is written down and the amount of the write-down is accounted for as a realized loss. After the write-down, the carrying amount of the individual security cannot be changed for subsequent recoveries in market value.

When the equity method of accounting is used, a stock purchase is recorded at cost. The investor records its share of periodic net income of the investee as an increase in the investment account and as revenue of the period. Conversely, the investor's share of the investee's periodic loss is recorded as a decrease in the investment and a loss of the period. In addition, the investor records its share of cash or property dividends on the stock as a decrease in the investment account and as an increase in the appropriate asset accounts.

When shares of stock held as a long-term investment are sold, the investment account is credited for the carrying amount of the shares sold and the cash or appropriate receivable account is debited for the proceeds (sales price less commission and other selling costs). Any difference between the proceeds and the carrying amount is recorded as a gain or loss on the sale.

OBJECTIVE 3

Business Combinations

Combinations of businesses may be effected (1) through a joining of two or more corporations to form a single unit by either merger or consolidation or (2) through common control of two or more corporations by means of stock ownership that results in a parent-subsidiary affiliation. When a corporation acquires the properties of another corporation and the latter then dissolves, the joining of the two enterprises is called a merger. When two or more corporations transfer their assets and liabilities to a corporation which has been created for purposes of the takeover, the combination is called a consolidation. When a business combination is effected by one corporation acquiring a controlling share of the outstanding voting stock of one or more other corporations, the corporation owning the majority of the voting stock is known as the parent company. The corporation that is controlled is known as the subsidiary company. When a corporation acquires a controlling share of the voting stock of another corporation in exchange for cash, other assets, issuance of notes or other debt obligations, or by a combination of these items, the transaction is accounted for by the purchase method. When two corporations are combined by exchanging the voting common stock of one corporation (the parent) for substantially all (at least 90%) of the voting common stock of the other corporation (the subsidiary), the transaction is accounted for by the pooling of interests method.

OBJECTIVE 4

Accounting for Parent-Subsidiary Affiliations

Although the corporations that make up a parent-subsidiary affiliation may operate as a single economic unit, they usually continue to maintain separate accounting records and prepare their own periodic financial statements. The parent corporation uses the equity method of accounting for its investment in the stock of the subsidiary. The financial statements resulting from combining the parent and subsidiary statements are generally called consolidated statements.

OBJECTIVE 5

Basic Principles of Consolidation of Financial Statements

When the data on the financial statements of the parent corporation and its subsidiaries are combined to form the consolidated statements, special attention should be given to the intercompany items appearing on the separate corporation financial statements. These intercompany items must be eliminated in preparing financial statements for the consolidated entity.

When a parent-subsidiary affiliation is effected as a purchase, the parent corporation is deemed to have purchased all or a major part of the subsidiary corporation's net assets. Accordingly, the assets of the subsidiary should be reported on the consolidated balance sheet at their cost to the parent. In the subsidiary's ledger, the reciprocal of the investment account at the date of acquisition is the composite of all the subsidiary's stockholders' equity accounts. In some cases, a parent corporation may pay an amount above the book equity of a subsidiary because the subsidiary has prospects for high future earnings. The amount of this excess should be identified on the consolidated balance sheet as goodwill. When a parent corporation purchases less than 100% of the subsidiary's stock, the remaining stockholders' equity is identified as minority interest. The minority interest is reported on the consolidated balance sheet, usually preceding the stockholders' equity accounts of the parent.

When a parent-subsidiary affiliation is effected as a pooling of interests, the ownership of the two companies is joined together in the parent corporation. The parent deems its investment in the subsidiary to be equal to the carrying amount of the subsidiary's net assets. Any difference that may exist between such carrying amount and the fair value of the subsidiary's assets does not affect the amount recorded by the parent as the investment. Consequently, no change is needed in the amounts at which the subsidiary's assets should be included in the consolidated balance sheet.

The principles used in the consolidation of income statements of a parent and its subsidiary are the same, regardless of whether the affiliation is deemed to be a purchase or a pooling of interests. When the income statements are consolidated, all amounts resulting from intercompany transactions, such as management fees or interest on loans charged by one affiliate to another, must be eliminated. Any intercompany profit included in inventories must also be eliminated.

OBJECTIVE 6

Corporation Financial Statements

A consolidated balance sheet of a corporation, containing many of the items discussed in this and preceding chapters, is presented on pages 664–665.

OBJECTIVE 7   Accounting for International Operations

When U.S. companies conduct business in foreign countries, special accounting problems may arise (1) in accounting for transactions with foreign companies and (2) in the preparation of consolidated statements for domestic and foreign companies that are affiliated. When a U.S. company executes a transaction with a company in a foreign country using a currency other than the dollar, an exchange rate should be used to convert one currency into another to settle the transaction. Because of this conversion process, gains and losses on foreign transactions may arise. If a foreign transaction has not been completed by the end of the year, an unrealized currency exchange gain or loss may need to be recognized, depending upon fluctuations in the exchange rates.

Before the financial statements of domestic and foreign countries are consolidated, the statements of the foreign companies must be converted to U.S. dollars. Asset and liability amounts are normally converted to U.S. dollars by using the exchange rates as of the balance sheet date. Revenues and expenses are normally converted by using the exchange rates that were in effect when those transactions were executed.

KEY TERMS

equity securities 646	subsidiary company 651
cost method 647	purchase method 651
equity method 647	pooling of interests method 651
merger 651	consolidated statements 652
consolidation 651	minority interest 656
parent company 651	exchange rate 666

SELF-EXAMINATION QUESTIONS

Answers at end of chapter.

1. Which of the following are characteristic of a parent-subsidiary relationship known as a pooling of interests?
    A. Parent acquires substantially all of the voting stock of subsidiary in exchange for cash
    B. Parent acquires substantially all of the voting stock of subsidiary in exchange for its bonds payable
    C. Parent acquires substantially all of the voting stock of subsidiary in exchange for its voting common stock
    D. All of the above

2. P Co. purchased the entire outstanding stock of S Co. for $1,000,000 in cash. If at the date of acquisition S Co.'s stockholders' equity consisted of $750,000 of common stock and $150,000 of retained earnings, what is the amount of the difference between cost and book equity of the subsidiary interest?
    A. Excess of cost over book equity of subsidiary interest, $250,000
    B. Excess of cost over book equity of subsidiary interest, $100,000
    C. Excess of book equity over cost of subsidiary interest, $250,000
    D. None of the above

3. If in Question 2 P Co. had purchased 90% of the outstanding stock of S Co. for $1,000,000, what is the amount of the difference between cost and book equity of subsidiary interest?
    A. Excess of cost over book equity of subsidiary interest, $100,000
    B. Excess of cost over book equity of subsidiary interest, $190,000
    C. Excess of cost over book equity of subsidiary interest, $250,000
    D. None of the above

4. Based on the data in Question 3, what is the amount of the minority interest at the date of acquisition?

A. $15,000   C. $100,000
B. $75,000   D. None of the above

5. On July 9, 1990, a sale on account for $10,000 to a Mexican company was billed for 25,000,000 pesos. The exchange rate was $.0004 per peso on July 9 and $.0005 per peso on August 8, 1990, when the cash was received on account. Which of the following statements identifies the exchange gain or loss for the fiscal year ended December 31, 1990?

A. Realized exchange loss, $2,500   C. Unrealized exchange loss, $2,500
B. Realized exchange gain, $2,500   D. Unrealized exchange gain, $2,500

ILLUSTRATIVE PROBLEM

All of Stereophonic Inc.'s outstanding shares of stock were acquired on October 1, 1990, by Piedmont Inc. After lengthy negotiations with Stereophonic Inc.'s major shareholder, it was agreed that (1) the current management of Stereophonic Inc. would be retained for a minimum of five years, (2) Stereophonic Inc. would be operated as an independent subsidiary, and (3) Piedmont Inc. would issue 1,200 of its own $100 par common stock in exchange for all of Stereophonic Inc.'s stock.

The balance sheets of the two corporations on September 30, 1990, were as follows:

	Piedmont Inc.	Stereophonic Inc.
Assets		
Cash..	$ 124,200	$ 18,120
Accounts receivable......................................	238,150	36,810
Inventory	405,750	61,300
Land..	120,000	50,000
Plant and equipment (net)	612,300	120,450
	$1,500,400	$286,680
Liabilities and Stockholders' Equity		
Accounts payable...	$ 136,400	$ 41,500
Common stock	900,000	120,000
Retained earnings..	464,000	125,180
	$1,500,400	$286,680

Instructions:

1. Prepare the journal entry that should be made by Piedmont Inc. to record the combination as a pooling of interests.
2. Assuming the business combination is to be recorded as a pooling of interests, prepare a consolidated balance sheet for Piedmont Inc. and Stereophonic Inc. as of October 1, 1990.
3. Assume that Piedmont Inc. paid $106,000 in cash and issued 1,500 shares of Piedmont Inc. common stock with a fair market value of $212,000 for all the common stock of Stereophonic Inc. Prepare the journal entry for Piedmont Inc. to record the combination as a purchase.
4. Assuming that the business combination is to be recorded as a purchase and that the book values of the net assets of Stereophonic Inc. are approximately equal to their fair market values, prepare a consolidated balance sheet for Piedmont Inc. and Stereophonic Inc. as of October 1, 1990.

SOLUTION

(1)

Investment in Stereophonic Inc.	245,180	
Common Stock		120,000
Retained Earnings		125,180

(2)

Piedmont Inc. and Subsidiary Stereophonic Inc.
Consolidated Balance Sheet
October 1, 1990

Assets

Current assets:		
Cash	$ 142,320	
Accounts receivable	274,960	
Inventory	467,050	
Total current assets..................................		$ 884,330
Plant assets:		
Land	$ 170,000	
Plant and equipment (net)	732,750	
Total plant assets....................................		902,750
Total assets..		$1,787,080

Liabilities

Accounts payable		$ 177,900

Stockholders' Equity

Common stock...	$1,020,000	
Retained earnings..	589,180	
Total stockholders' equity		1,609,180
Total liabilities and stockholders' equity		$1,787,080

(3)

Investment in Stereophonic Inc.	318,000	
Cash		106,000
Common Stock		150,000
Paid-In Capital in Excess of Par—Common Stock ..		62,000

(4)

Piedmont Inc. and Subsidiary Stereophonic Inc.
Consolidated Balance Sheet
October 1, 1990

Assets

Current assets:		
Cash ($124,200 + $18,120 − $106,000)	$ 36,320	
Accounts receivable	274,960	
Inventory	467,050	
Total current assets..................................		$ 778,330
Plant assets:		
Land	$ 170,000	
Plant and equipment (net)	732,750	
Total plant assets....................................		902,750
Intangible assets:		
Goodwill ($318,000 − $245,180)		72,820
Total assets..		$1,753,900

Liabilities		
Accounts payable		$ 177,900
Stockholders' Equity		
Common stock..	$1,050,000	
Excess of issue price over par—common stock.	62,000	
Retained earnings..	464,000	
Total stockholders' equity		1,576,000
Total liabilities and stockholders' equity...........		$1,753,900

DISCUSSION QUESTIONS

1. (a) What are two methods of accounting for long-term investments in stock? (b) Under what caption are long-term investments in stock reported on the balance sheet?

2. When stocks are purchased between dividend dates, does the purchaser pay the seller the dividend accrued since the last dividend payment date? Explain.

3. A stockholder owning 400 shares of Haines Co. common stock, acquired at a total cost of $11,550, receives a common stock dividend of 20 shares. What is the carrying amount per share after the stock dividend?

4. What terms are applied to the following: (a) a corporation that is controlled by another corporation through ownership of a controlling interest in its stock; (b) a corporation that owns a controlling interest in the voting stock of another corporation; (c) a group of corporations related through stock ownership?

5. What are the two methods by which the relationship of parent-subsidiary may be established?

6. P Company purchases for $12,000,000 the entire common stock of S Corporation. What type of accounts on S's balance sheet are reciprocal to the investment account on P's balance sheet?

7. Are the eliminations of the reciprocal accounts in consolidating the balance sheets of P and S in Question 6 recorded in the respective ledgers of the two companies? Explain.

8. Parks Company purchased from stockholders the entire outstanding stock of Sapp Inc. for a total of $5,150,000 in cash. At the date of acquisition, Sapp Inc. had $3,600,000 of liabilities and total stockholders' equity of $5,000,000. (a) As of the acquisition date, what was the total amount of the assets of Sapp Inc.? (b) As of the acquisition date, what was the amount of the net assets of Sapp Inc.? (c) What is the amount of difference between the investment account and the book equity of the subsidiary interest acquired by Parks Company?

9. What is the possible explanation of the difference determined in Question 8(c) and how will it affect the reporting of the difference on the consolidated balance sheet?

10. If, in Question 8, Parks Company had paid only $4,880,000 for the stock of Sapp Inc., what would the solution to part (c) have been?

11. Parent Corporation owns 85% of the outstanding common stock of Subsidiary Corporation, which has no preferred stock. (a) What is the term applied to the remaining 15% interest? (b) If the total stockholders' equity of Subsidiary Corporation is $878,000, what is the amount of Subsidiary's book equity allocable to outsiders? (c) Where is the amount determined in (b) reported on the consolidated balance sheet?

12. P Corporation owns 90% of the outstanding common stock of S Co., which has no preferred stock. Net income of S Co. was $500,000 for the year, and cash dividends declared and paid during the year amounted to $100,000. What entries should be made by P Corporation to record its share of S Co.'s (a) net income and (b) dividends? (c) What is the amount of the net increase in the equity of the minority interest?

13. (a) What purpose is served by the work sheet for a consolidated balance sheet? (b) Is the work sheet a substitute for the consolidated balance sheet?

14. At the end of the fiscal year, the amount of notes receivable and notes payable reported on the respective balance sheets of a parent and its wholly owned subsidiary are as follows:

	Parent	Subsidiary
Notes Receivable..........	$550,000	$100,000
Notes Payable..............	200,000	120,000

If $75,000 of Subsidiary's notes receivable are owed by Parent, determine the amount of notes receivable and notes payable to be reported on the consolidated balance sheet.

15. Sales and purchases of merchandise by a parent corporation and its wholly owned subsidiary during the year were as follows:

	Parent	Subsidiary
Sales	$8,250,000	$1,200,000
Purchases	4,950,000	720,000

If $110,000 of the sales of Parent were made to Subsidiary, determine the amount of sales and purchases to be reported on the consolidated income statement.

16. The relationships of parent and subsidiary were established by the following transactions. Identify each affiliation as a "purchase" or a "pooling of interests."
   (a) Company P receives 75% of the voting common stock of Company S in exchange for voting common stock of Company P.
   (b) Company P receives 90% of the voting common stock of Company S in exchange for cash.
   (c) Company P receives 100% of the voting common stock of Company S in exchange for cash and long-term bonds payable.
   (d) Company P receives 95% of the voting common stock of Company S in exchange for voting common stock of Company P.

17. Which of the following procedures for consolidating the balance sheet of a parent and wholly owned subsidiary are characteristic of acquisition of control by purchase and which are characteristic of a pooling of interests? (a) Retained earnings of subsidiary at date of acquisition are eliminated. (b) Retained earnings of subsidiary at date of acquisition are combined with retained earnings of parent. (c) Assets are not revalued. (d) Goodwill may not be recognized.

18. On March 31, Parrott Corp. issued 8,000 shares of its $100 par common stock, with a total market value of $1,000,000 to the stockholders of Shutt Inc. in exchange for all of Shutt's common stock. Parrott Corp. records its investment at $900,000. The net assets and stockholders' equities of the two companies just prior to the affiliation are summarized as follows:

	Parrott Corp.	Shutt Inc.
Net assets	$3,200,000	$900,000
Common stock	$2,000,000	$350,000
Retained earnings	1,200,000	550,000
	$3,200,000	$900,000

(a) At what amounts would the following be reported on the consolidated balance sheet as of March 31, applying the pooling of interests method: (1) Net assets, (2) Retained earnings?

(b) Assume that, instead of issuing shares of stock, Parrott Corp. had given $1,000,000 in cash and long-term notes. At what amounts would the following be reported on the consolidated balance sheet as of March 31: (1) Net assets, (2) Retained earnings?

19. Can a U.S. company incur an exchange gain or loss because of fluctuations in the exchange rate if its transactions with foreign countries, involving receivables or payables, are executed in (a) dollars, (b) the foreign currency?

20. A U.S. company purchased merchandise for 90,000 francs on account from a French company. If the exchange rate was $.18 per franc on the date of purchase and $.16 per franc on the date of payment of the account, what was the amount of exchange gain or loss realized by the U.S. company?

21. What two conditions give rise to unrealized currency exchange gains and losses from sales and purchases on account that are to be settled in the foreign currency?

Real World Focus

22. The following data were taken from the footnotes of Triton Energy Corporation's 1988 annual report:

"...At May 31, 1988...the Company owned approximately 49 1/2% of Crusader Limited, an Australian public company engaged in oil and gas exploration and production, coal mining and gas processing. The Company's investment in Crusader Limited, which is accounted for using the equity method, was $25,797,000 at May 31, 1988. ...The Company's equity in Crusader's earnings was $3,752,000 in 1988...and the Company's share of dividends declared by Crusader Limited was $327,000 in 1988..."

(a) Prepare the journal entry that Triton Energy Corporation would have made to record its interest in the earnings of Crusader Limited. (b) Prepare the journal entry that Triton Energy Corporation would have made to record its share of the dividends of Crusader Limited that were paid in cash during 1988.

EXERCISES

Exercise 17–1
Entries for invest-
ment in stock,
receipt of dividends,
and sale of shares.
OBJ. 2

On May 3, Niemyer Corporation acquired 1,000 shares of the 100,000 outstanding shares of Grace Co. common stock at 74 1/2 plus commission and postage charges of $380. On August 31, a cash dividend of $1.75 per share and a 4% stock dividend were received. On December 15, 400 shares were sold at 76 1/4 less commission and postage charges of $180. Present entries to record (a) the purchase of the stock, (b) the receipt of the dividends, and (c) the sale of the 400 shares.

Exercise 17–2
Entries using equity
method for stock
investment.
OBJ. 2

At a total cost of $1,760,000, Conn Corporation acquired 80,000 shares of Maxi-Systems Co. common stock as a long-term investment. Conn Corporation uses the equity method of accounting for this investment. Maxi-Systems Co. has 320,000 shares of common stock outstanding, including the shares acquired by Conn Corporation. Present the entries by Conn Corporation to record the following information:

(a) Maxi-Systems Co. reports net income of $500,000 for the current period.
(b) A cash dividend of $.40 per common share is paid by Maxi-Systems Co. during the current period.

Exercise 17–3
Determination and
reporting of items
related to
consolidated
statements.
OBJ. 5

On the last day of the fiscal year, Powell Inc. purchased 90% of the common stock of Singer Company for $575,000, at which time Singer Company reported the following on its balance sheet: assets, $1,000,000; liabilities, $400,000; common stock, $100 par, $100,000; retained earnings, $500,000. In negotiating the stock sale, it was determined that the book carrying amounts of Singer's recorded assets and equities approximated their current market values.

(a) Indicate for each of the following the section, the title of the item, and the amount to be reported on the consolidated balance sheet as of the date of acquisition:
(1) Difference between cost and book equity of subsidiary interest.
(2) Minority interest.
(b) During the following year, Powell Inc. realized net income of $1,250,000, exclusive of the income of the subsidiary, and Singer Company realized net income of $380,000. In preparing a consolidated income statement, indicate in what amounts the following would be reported:
(1) Minority interest's share of net income.
(2) Consolidated net income.

Exercise 17–4
Consolidated
balance sheet from
affiliation effected
as a purchase.
OBJ. 5

On December 31 of the current year, P Corporation purchased 85% of the stock of S Company. The data reported on their separate balance sheets immediately after the acquisition are as follows:

	P Corporation	S Company
Assets		
Cash...	$ 48,300	$ 32,100
Accounts receivable (net).....................................	76,200	52,500
Inventories...	211,500	93,600
Investment in S Company....................................	555,000	—
Equipment (net)...	600,000	437,300
	$1,491,000	$615,500
Liabilities and Stockholders' Equity		
Accounts payable..	$ 148,500	$ 75,500
Common stock, $100 par	1,125,000	375,000
Retained earnings..	217,500	165,000
	$1,491,000	$615,500

The fair value of S Company's assets corresponds to their book carrying amounts, except for equipment, which is valued at $480,000 for consolidation purposes. Prepare a consolidated balance sheet as of December 31, in report form, omitting captions for current assets, plant assets, etc. (A work sheet need not be used.)

Exercise 17–5
Consolidated balance sheet from affiliation effected as a pooling.
OBJ. 5

As of October 31 of the current year, Pittman Corporation exchanged 2,500 shares of its $30 par common stock for the 15,000 shares of Sisk Company $5 par common stock held by Sisk stockholders. The separate balance sheets of the two enterprises, immediately after the exchange of shares, are as follows:

	Pittman Corporation	Sisk Company
Assets		
Cash..	$ 31,500	$ 21,700
Accounts receivable (net).................................	38,150	28,000
Inventories...	106,050	45,850
Investment in Sisk Company.............................	122,500	—
Equipment (net)...	460,600	61,950
	$758,800	$157,500
Liabilities and Stockholders' Equity		
Accounts payable..	$107,800	$ 35,000
Common stock...	400,000	75,000
Retained earnings..	251,000	47,500
	$758,800	$157,500

Prepare a consolidated balance sheet as of October 31, in report form, omitting captions for current assets, plant assets, etc. (A work sheet need not be used.)

Exercise 17–6
Consolidated income statement.
OBJ. 5

For the current year ended April 30, the results of operations of Palay Corporation and its wholly owned subsidiary, Sigler Enterprises, are as follows:

	Palay Corporation		Sigler Enterprises	
Sales		$1,200,000		$500,000
Cost of merchandise sold....	$790,000		$300,000	
Selling expenses................	180,000		72,000	
Administrative expenses......	100,000		48,000	
Interest expense (income) ...	(15,000)	1,055,000	15,000	435,000
Net income		$ 145,000		$ 65,000

During the year, Palay sold merchandise to Sigler for $90,000. The merchandise was sold by Sigler to nonaffiliated companies for $120,000. Palay's interest income was realized from a long-term loan to Sigler.

(a) Prepare a consolidated income statement for the current year for Palay and its subsidiary. Use the single-step form and disregard income taxes. (A work sheet need not be used.)

(b) Assuming that none of the merchandise sold by Palay to Sigler had been sold during the year to nonaffiliated companies, and that Palay's cost of the merchandise had been $54,000, determine the amounts that would have been reported for the following items on the consolidated income statement: (1) sales, (2) cost of merchandise sold, (3) net income.

Exercise 17–7
Determination of consolidated balance sheet amounts for affiliation effected as a pooling and as a purchase.
OBJ. 5

Summarized data from the balance sheets of Peach Company and Stover Inc., as of June 30 of the current year, are as follows:

	Peach Company	Stover Inc.
Net assets	$5,000,000	$400,000
Common stock:		
25,000 shares, $50 par	1,250,000	
5,000 shares, $30 par		150,000
Retained earnings	3,750,000	250,000

(a) On July 1 of the current year, the two companies combine. Peach Company issues 3,000 shares of its $50 par common stock, valued at $450,000, to Stover's stockholders in exchange for the 5,000 shares of Stover's $30 par common stock, also valued at $450,000. Assuming that the affiliation is effected as a pooling of interests, what are the amounts that would be reported for net assets, common stock, and retained earnings as of July 1 of the current year?

(b) Assume that Peach Company had paid cash of $450,000 for all of Stover Inc.'s common stock on July 1 of the current year and that the book value of the net assets of Stover Inc. is deemed to reflect fair value. (1) What are the amounts that would be reported for net assets, common stock, and retained earnings as of July 1 of the current year, using the purchase method? (2) How much goodwill will be reported on the combined balance sheet?

Exercise 17–8
Entries for sales made in foreign currency.
OBJ. 7

Jarvis Company makes sales on account to several Israeli companies which it bills in shekels. Record the journal entries for the following selected transactions completed during the current year:

Mar. 3. Sold merchandise on account, 40,000 shekels; exchange rate, $.63 per shekel.
Apr. 8. Received cash from sale of March 3, 40,000 shekels; exchange rate, $.64 per shekel.
June 20. Sold merchandise on account, 70,000 shekels; exchange rate, $.64 per shekel.
July 31. Received cash from sale of June 20, 70,000 shekels; exchange rate, $.62 per shekel.

Exercise 17–9
Entries for purchases made in foreign currency.
OBJ. 7

Gunter Company purchases merchandise from a German company that requires payment in deutsche marks. Record the journal entries for the following selected transactions completed during the current year:

Aug. 15. Purchased merchandise on account, net 30, 10,000 deutsche marks; exchange rate, $.58 per deutsche mark.
Sept. 14. Paid invoice of August 15; exchange rate, $.59 per deutsche mark.
Nov. 13. Purchased merchandise on account, net 30, 80,000 deutsche marks; exchange rate, $.59 per deutsche mark.
Dec. 13. Paid invoice of November 13; exchange rate, $.55 per deutsche mark.

PROBLEMS

Problem 17–1A
Entries for
investments
in stock.
OBJ. 2

The following transactions relate to certain securities acquired by Norton Company, whose fiscal year ends on December 31:

1990
Jan. 7. Purchased 500 shares of the 20,000 outstanding common shares of McGinnis Corporation at 20 3/4 plus commission and other costs of $335.
Apr. 29. Received the regular cash dividend of 90¢ a share on McGinnis Corporation stock.
Oct. 30. Received the regular cash dividend of 90¢ a share plus an extra dividend of 5¢ a share on McGinnis Corporation stock.

(Assume that all intervening transactions have been recorded properly, and that the number of shares of stock owned have not changed from December 31, 1990, to December 31, 1994.)

1995
Apr. 30. Received the regular cash dividend of 90¢ a share and a 2% stock dividend on the McGinnis Corporation stock.
Aug. 10. Sold 250 shares of McGinnis Corporation stock at 31 1/2. The broker deducted commission and other costs of $75, remitting the balance.
Oct. 31. Received a cash dividend at the new rate of 95¢ a share on the McGinnis Corporation stock.

Instructions:

Record the journal entries for the foregoing transactions.

Problem 17–2A
Work sheet and
consolidated
balance sheet from
affiliation effected
as a purchase.
OBJ. 5

On May 31 of the current year, Petty Company purchased 95% of the stock of Sawyer Company. On the same date, Petty Company loaned Sawyer Company $100,000 on a 90-day note. The data reported on their separate balance sheets immediately after the acquisition and loan are as follows:

	Petty Company	Sawyer Company
Assets		
Cash	$ 90,400	$ 88,000
Accounts receivable (net)	122,400	112,000
Notes receivable	120,000	—
Inventories	286,800	156,800
Investment in Sawyer Company	862,000	—
Equipment (net)	680,000	688,000
	$2,161,600	$1,044,800
Liabilities and Stockholders' Equity		
Accounts payable	$ 336,000	$ 92,800
Notes payable	—	100,000
Common stock, $40 par	1,280,000	—
Common stock, $10 par	—	600,000
Retained earnings	545,600	252,000
	$2,161,600	$1,044,800

The fair value of Sawyer Company's assets correspond to the book carrying amounts, except for equipment, which is valued at $700,000 for consolidation purposes.

Instructions:

(1) Prepare a work sheet for a consolidated balance sheet as of May 31 of the current year.
(2) Prepare in report form a consolidated balance sheet as of May 31, omitting captions for current assets, plant assets, etc.

Problem 17–3A
Consolidated balance sheet from both pooling and purchase methods.
OBJ. 5

On July 1 of the current year, after several months of negotiations, Pear Company issued 20,000 shares of its own $10 par common stock for all of Schwab Inc.'s outstanding shares of stock. The fair market value of the Pear Company shares issued is $18.75 per share, or a total of $375,000. Schwab Inc. is to be operated as a separate subsidiary. The balance sheets of the two firms on June 30 of the current year are as follows:

	Pear Company	Schwab Inc.
Assets		
Cash..	$ 243,000	$ 28,200
Accounts receivable (net).....................................	294,000	50,300
Inventory	513,900	71,800
Land..	144,000	55,000
Plant and equipment (net)	605,100	204,700
	$1,800,000	$410,000
Liabilities and Stockholders' Equity		
Accounts payable..	$ 174,000	$ 60,000
Common stock ($10 par).....................................	1,000,000	200,000
Retained earnings...	626,000	150,000
	$1,800,000	$410,000

Instructions:

(1) (a) What entry would be made by Pear Company to record the combination as a pooling of interests? (b) Prepare a consolidated balance sheet for Pear Company and Schwab Inc. as of July 1 of the current year, assuming that the business combination has been recorded as a pooling of interests. (A work sheet is not required.)

(2) (a) Assume that Pear Company paid $75,000 in cash and issued 16,000 shares of Pear common stock with a fair market value of $300,000 for all the common stock of Schwab Inc. What entry would Pear Company make to record the combination as a purchase? (b) Prepare a consolidated balance sheet as of July 1 of the current year, assuming that the business combination has been recorded as a purchase, and that the book values of the net assets of Schwab Inc. are deemed to represent fair value. (A work sheet is not required.)

(3) Assume the same situation as in (2), except that the fair value of the land of Schwab Inc. was $70,000 for consolidation purposes. Prepare a consolidated balance sheet as of July 1 of the current year. (A work sheet is not required.)

Problem 17–4A
Eliminations for and preparation of consolidated balance sheet and income statement.
OBJ. 5

SPREADSHEET PROBLEM

On January 2 of the current year, Purdy Corporation exchanged 32,000 shares of its $12.50 par common stock for 8,000 shares (the entire issue) of Salters Company's $50 par common stock. Salters purchased from Purdy Corporation $100,000 of its $300,000 issue of bonds payable, at face amount. All of the items for "interest" appearing on the balance sheets and income statements of both corporations are related to the bonds.

During the year, Purdy Corporation sold merchandise with a cost of $240,000 to Salters Company for $320,000, all of which was sold by Salters Company before the end of the year.

Purdy Corporation has correctly recorded the income and dividends reported for the year by Salters Company. Data for the income statements for both companies for the current year are as follows:

	Purdy Corporation	Salters Company
Revenues:		
Sales	$1,920,000	$600,000
Income of subsidiary	126,000	—
Interest income	—	12,000
	$2,046,000	$612,000
Expenses:		
Cost of merchandise sold	$1,140,000	$336,000
Selling expenses	199,200	62,400
Administrative expenses	150,000	44,400
Interest expense	36,000	—
Income tax	84,000	43,200
	$1,609,200	$486,000
Net Income	$ 436,800	$126,000

Data for the balance sheets of both companies as of the end of the current year are as follows:

	Purdy Corporation	Salters Company
Assets		
Cash	$ 75,000	$ 31,000
Accounts receivable (net)	200,000	62,200
Dividends receivable	60,000	—
Interest receivable	—	3,000
Inventories	330,000	151,600
Investment in Salters Co. (8,000 shares)	800,000	—
Investment in Purdy Corp. bonds (at face amount)	—	100,000
Plant and equipment	1,380,000	682,400
Accumulated depreciation	(780,000)	(130,200)
	$2,065,000	$900,000
Liabilities and Stockholders' Equity		
Accounts payable	$ 80,300	$ 33,200
Income tax payable	34,600	6,800
Dividends payable	36,000	60,000
Interest payable	9,000	—
Bonds payable, 12% (due in 2010)	300,000	—
Common stock, $12.50 par	1,200,000	—
Common stock, $50 par	—	400,000
Excess of issue price over par—common stock	120,000	40,000
Retained earnings	285,100	360,000
	$2,065,000	$900,000

Instructions:

(1) Determine the amounts to be eliminated from the following items in preparing the consolidated balance sheet as of December 31 of the current year; (a) dividends receivable and dividends payable; (b) interest receivable and interest payable; (c) investment in Salters Co. and stockholders' equity; (d) investment in Purdy Corp. bonds and bonds payable.

(2) Prepare a detailed consolidated balance sheet as of December 31 in report form.
(3) Determine the amounts to be eliminated from the following items in preparing the consolidated income statement for the current year ended December 31: (a) sales and cost of merchandise sold; (b) interest income and interest expense; (c) income of subsidiary and net income.
(4) Prepare a single-step consolidated income statement, inserting the earnings per share in parentheses on the same line with net income.
(5) Determine the amount of the reduction in consolidated inventories, net income, and retained earnings if Salters Company's inventory had included $80,000 of the merchandise purchased from Purdy Corporation.

Problem 17–5A

Work sheet and consolidated balance sheet; year-end minority interest; increase in investment account during year.

OBJ. 5, 6

On October 31, Pruitt Company purchased 90% of the outstanding stock of Sorells Company for $975,000. Balance sheet data for the two corporations immediately after the transaction are as follows:

	Pruitt Company	Sorells Company
Assets		
Cash and marketable securities	$ 385,300	$ 53,500
Accounts receivable	554,700	138,900
Allowance for doubtful accounts	(45,200)	(18,600)
Inventories	893,600	274,700
Investment in Sorells Company	975,000	—
Land	315,000	168,750
Building and equipment	1,641,400	1,112,850
Accumulated depreciation	(522,800)	(590,100)
	$4,197,000	$1,140,000
Liabilities and Stockholders' Equity		
Accounts payable	$ 347,500	$ 126,400
Income tax payable	94,500	13,600
Bonds payable (due in 2010)	900,000	—
Common stock, $100 par	1,600,000	—
Common stock, $5 par	—	700,000
Retained earnings	1,255,000	300,000
	$4,197,000	$1,140,000

Instructions:

(1) Prepare a work sheet for a consolidated balance sheet as of the date of acquisition. The fair value of Sorells Company's assets are deemed to correspond to the book carrying amounts, except for land, which is to be increased by $31,250.
(2) Prepare in report form a detailed consolidated balance sheet as of the date of acquisition.
(3) Assuming that Sorells Company earns net income of $180,500 and pays cash dividends of $42,000 during the following fiscal year and that Pruitt Company records its share of the earnings and dividends, determine the following as of the end of the year:
   (a) The net amount added to Pruitt Company's investment account as a result of Sorells Company's earnings and dividends.
   (b) The amount of the minority interest.

Problem 17–6A
Consolidated
balance sheet from
affiliation effected
as a purchase.
OBJ. 5, 6

Several years ago, Pirkle Corporation purchased 19,000 shares of the 20,000 out-standing shares of stock of Shell Company. Since the date of acquisition, Pirkle Cor-poration has debited the investment account for its share of the subsidiary's earnings and has credited the account for its share of dividends declared. Balance sheet data for the two corporations as of December 31 of the current year are as follows:

	Pirkle Corp.	Shell Co.
Assets		
Cash	$ 69,300	$ 25,300
Notes receivable	45,000	18,000
Accounts receivable (net)	170,900	59,600
Interest receivable	3,600	800
Dividends receivable	5,700	—
Inventories	240,400	82,800
Prepaid expenses	6,200	2,000
Investment in Shell Co.	225,000	—
Land	90,000	54,000
Buildings and equipment	492,900	288,000
Accumulated depreciation	(240,000)	(115,500)
	$1,109,000	$415,000
Liabilities and Stockholders' Equity		
Notes payable	$ 54,000	$ 60,000
Accounts payable	119,400	78,600
Income tax payable	42,000	15,600
Dividends payable	18,000	6,000
Interest payable	3,100	4,800
Common stock, $50 par	720,000	—
Common stock, $10 par	—	120,000
Excess of issue price over par—common stock	—	30,000
Retained earnings	152,500	100,000
	$1,109,000	$415,000

Pirkle Corporation holds $45,000 of short-term notes of Shell Company, on which there is accrued interest of $3,600. Shell Company owes Pirkle Corporation $30,000 for a management advisory fee for the year. It has been recorded by both corporations in their respective accounts payable and accounts receivable accounts.

Instructions:

Prepare in report form a detailed consolidated balance sheet as of December 31 of the current year. (A work sheet is not required.) The excess of book equity in Shell Company over the balance of the Pirkle Corporation's investment account is attribut-able to overvaluation of Shell Company's land.

Problem 17–7A
Consolidated
balance sheet.
OBJ. 6

The following data were extracted from the records of Marin Inc. after adjustment at January 31, 1990, the end of the current fiscal year:

Accounts and notes receivable	$ 360,000
Accounts payable	250,000
Accrued liabilities	40,750
Accumulated depreciation—buildings	190,600
Accumulated depreciation—machinery and equipment	583,100
Allowance for doubtful receivables	18,500
Appropriation for bonded indebtedness	500,000
Appropriation for plant expansion	250,000
Bonds payable, 10% debenture bonds due January 31, 1998	500,000
Bond sinking fund	210,500

Buildings	$ 500,000
Cash	127,500
Common stock, $10 par, 500,000 shares authorized, 100,000 shares issued	1,000,000
Deferred income tax payable ($5,000 due within one year)	45,000
Discount on bonds payable	15,000
Dividends payable	12,500
Goodwill	400,000
Income tax payable	60,250
Inventories (lower of cost, first-in, first-out, or market)	460,750
Investment in bonds of Span Company	100,000
Land	150,000
Machinery and equipment	1,382,200
Marketable securities (at lower of cost or market; original cost, $80,000)	76,250
Minority interest in subsidiaries	57,500
Organization costs	100,000
Paid-in capital in excess of par—common stock	160,000
Prepaid expenses	20,000
Retained earnings (unappropriated)	234,000

Instructions:

Prepare a report form consolidated balance sheet for Marin Inc.

Problem 17–8A
Foreign currency transactions.

OBJ. 7

Nealy Company sells merchandise to and purchases merchandise from various Canadian and French companies. These transactions are settled in the foreign currency. The following selected transactions were completed during the current fiscal year:

Feb. 14. Sold merchandise on account to Korn Company, net 30, 400,000 francs; exchange rate, $.17 per French franc.

Mar. 16. Received cash from Korn Company; exchange rate, $.16 per French franc.

May 1. Purchased merchandise on account from Hunt Company, net 30, $12,000 Canadian; exchange rate, $.83 per Canadian dollar.

June 1. Issued check for amount owed to Hunt Company; exchange rate, $.82 per Canadian dollar.

July 31. Sold merchandise on account to Pierre Company, net 30, 150,000 francs; exchange rate, $.15 per French franc.

Aug. 30. Received cash from Pierre Company; exchange rate, $.18 per French franc.

Sept. 8. Purchased merchandise on account from Dryson Company, net 30, $30,000 Canadian; exchange rate, $.84 per Canadian dollar.

Oct. 8. Issued check for amount owed to Dryson Company; exchange rate, $.85 per Canadian dollar.

Dec. 12. Sold merchandise on account to Kammer Company, net 45, $75,000 Canadian; exchange rate, $.85 per Canadian dollar.

24. Purchased merchandise on account from Toulouise Company, net 30, 120,000 francs; exchange rate, $.18 per French franc.

31. Recorded unrealized currency exchange gain and/or loss on transactions of December 12 and 24. Exchange rates on December 31: $.87 per Canadian dollar; $.19 per French franc.

Instructions:

(1) Present entries to record the transactions and adjusting entries for the year.
(2) Present entries to record the payment of the December 24 purchase, on January 23, when the exchange rate was $.17 per French franc, and the receipt of cash from the December 12 sale, on January 26, when the exchange rate was $.88 per Canadian dollar.

Problem 17–2B
Work sheet and
consolidated
balance sheet from
affiliation effected
as a purchase.

On February 1 of the current year, Parson Company purchased 85% of the stock of Stern Company. On the same date, Parson Company loaned Stern Company $80,000 on a 120-day note. The data reported on their separate balance sheets immediately after the acquisition and loan are as follows:

	Parson Company	Stern Company
Assets		
Cash..........	$ 81,200	$ 41,200
Accounts receivable (net)...................	77,600	51,200
Notes receivable................	80,000	—
Inventories..........	263,600	83,600
Investment in Stern Company............	400,000	—
Equipment (net)........	608,000	344,000
	$1,510,400	$520,000
Liabilities and Stockholders' Equity		
Accounts payable............	$ 280,000	$ 40,000
Notes payable..........	—	80,000
Common stock, $50 par...........	800,000	—
Common stock, $10 par.........	—	320,000
Retained earnings..........	430,400	80,000
	$1,510,400	$520,000

The fair value of Stern Company's assets corresponds to the book carrying amounts, except for equipment, which is valued at $360,000 for consolidation purposes.

Instructions:

(1) Prepare a work sheet for a consolidated balance sheet as of February 1 of the current year.
(2) Prepare in report form a consolidated balance sheet as of February 1, omitting captions for current assets, plant assets, etc.

Problem 17–4B
Eliminations for
and preparation
of consolidated
balance sheet and
income statement.

On January 1 of the current year, Pulp Corporation exchanged 30,000 shares of its $10 par common stock for 15,000 shares (the entire issue) of Sego Company's $20 par common stock. Later in the year, Sego Company purchased from Pulp Corporation $50,000 of its $400,000 issue of bonds payable, at face amount. All of the items for "interest" appearing on the balance sheets and income statements of both corporations are related to the bonds.

During the year, Pulp Corporation sold merchandise with a cost of $108,000 to Sego Company for $180,000, all of which was sold by Sego Company before the end of the year.

Pulp Corporation has correctly recorded the income and dividends reported for the year by Sego Company. Data for the income statements for both companies for the current year are as follows:

	Pulp Corporation	Sego Company
Revenues:		
Sales	$1,520,000	$500,000
Income of subsidiary	111,500	—
Interest income	—	4,500
	$1,631,500	$504,500
Expenses:		
Cost of merchandise sold	$ 975,400	$252,600
Selling expenses	148,000	49,800
Administrative expenses	110,000	29,600
Interest expense	36,000	—
Income tax	104,100	61,000
	$1,373,500	$393,000
Net income	$ 258,000	$111,500

Data for the balance sheets of both companies as of the end of the current year are as follows:

	Pulp Corporation	Sego Company
Assets		
Cash	$ 70,100	$ 29,700
Accounts receivable (net)	212,400	50,100
Dividends receivable	10,000	—
Interest receivable	—	750
Inventories	405,300	159,200
Investment in Sego Co. (15,000 shares)	480,100	—
Investment in Pulp Corp. bonds (at face amount)	—	50,000
Plant and equipment	970,300	357,600
Accumulated depreciation	(184,700)	(131,850)
	$1,963,500	$515,500
Liabilities and Stockholders' Equity		
Accounts payable	$ 123,500	$ 20,900
Income tax payable	26,000	4,500
Dividends payable	18,000	10,000
Interest payable	6,000	—
Bonds payable, 9% (due in 2014)	400,000	—
Common stock, $10 par	1,000,000	—
Common stock, $20 par	—	300,000
Excess of issue price over par—common stock	120,000	40,000
Retained earnings	270,000	140,100
	$1,963,500	$515,500

Instructions:

(1) Determine the amounts to be eliminated from the following items in preparing the consolidated balance sheet as of December 31 of the current year: (a) dividends receivable and dividends payable; (b) interest receivable and interest payable; (c) investment in Sego Co. and stockholders' equity; (d) investment in Pulp Corp. bonds and bonds payable.

(2) Prepare a detailed consolidated balance sheet as of December 31 in report form.

(3) Determine the amounts to be eliminated from the following items in preparing the consolidated income statement for the current year ended December 31: (a) sales and cost of merchandise sold; (b) interest income and interest expense; (c) income of subsidiary and net income.

(Continued)

(4) Prepare a single-step consolidated income statement, inserting the earnings per share in parentheses on the same line with net income.

(5) Determine the amount of the reduction in consolidated inventories, net income, and retained earnings if Sego Company's inventory had included $40,000 of the merchandise purchased from Pulp Corporation.

Problem 17–5B
Work sheet and consolidated balance sheet; year-end minority interest; increase in investment account during year.
OBJ. 5, 6

On April 30, Price Company purchased 85% of the outstanding stock of Sales Company for $650,000. Balance sheet data for the two corporations immediately after the transaction are as follows:

	Price Company	Sales Company
Assets		
Cash and marketable securities............................	$ 173,400	$ 65,100
Accounts receivable...	240,100	118,300
Allowance for doubtful accounts...........................	(19,000)	(6,400)
Inventories..	950,000	230,800
Investment in Sales Company	650,000	—
Land..	860,000	45,000
Building and equipment.....................................	2,381,000	600,000
Accumulated depreciation..................................	(1,451,500)	(232,800)
	$3,784,000	$820,000
Liabilities and Stockholders' Equity		
Accounts payable...	$ 310,000	$108,800
Income tax payable...	83,500	11,200
Bonds payable (due in 2015)...............................	640,000	—
Common stock, $200 par	1,000,000	—
Common stock, $10 par.....................................	—	200,000
Retained earnings...	1,750,500	500,000
	$3,784,000	$820,000

Instructions:

(1) Prepare a work sheet for a consolidated balance sheet as of the date of acquisition. The fair value of Sales Company's assets are deemed to correspond to the book carrying amounts, except for land, which is to be increased by $5,000 for consolidation purposes.

(2) Prepare in report form a detailed consolidated balance sheet as of the date of acquisition.

(3) Assuming that Sales Company earns net income of $75,000 and pays cash dividends of $10,000 during the fiscal year and that Price Company records its share of the earnings and dividends, determine the following as of the end of the year:

   (a) The net amount added to Price Company's investment account as a result of Sales Company's earnings and dividends.

   (b) The amount of the minority interest.

Problem 17–8B
Foreign currency transactions.
OBJ. 7

Mills Company sells merchandise to and purchases merchandise from various Canadian and Japanese companies. These transactions are settled in the foreign currency. The following selected transactions were completed during the current fiscal year:

Jan. 8. Purchased merchandise on account from Pierce Company, net 30, $40,000 Canadian; exchange rate, $.84 per Canadian dollar.

Feb. 17. Issued check for amount owed to Pierce Company; exchange rate, $.86 per Canadian dollar.

Mar. 27. Sold merchandise on account to Nakato Company, net 30, 600,000 yen; exchange rate, $.008 per Japanese yen.

Apr. 26. Received cash from Nakato Company; exchange rate, $.009 per Japanese yen.

May   7. Purchased merchandise on account from Rutland Company, net 30, $31,000 Canadian; exchange rate, $.87 per Canadian dollar.

June 6. Issued check for amount owed to Rutland Company; exchange rate, $.86 per Canadian dollar.

Oct.   3. Sold merchandise on account to Oh Company, net 30, 1,000,000 yen; exchange rate, $.0085 per Japanese yen.

Nov.   3. Received cash from Oh Company; exchange rate, $.007 per Japanese yen.

Dec.   6. Sold merchandise on account to Claude Company, net 45, $8,000 Canadian; exchange rate, $.85 per Canadian dollar.

      20. Purchased merchandise on account from Toko Company, net 30, 3,000,000 yen; exchange rate, $.006 per Japanese yen.

      31. Recorded unrealized currency exchange gain and/or loss on transactions of December 6 and 20. Exchange rates on December 31: $.83 per Canadian dollar; $.005 per Japanese yen.

Instructions:

(1) Present the journal entries to record the transactions and adjustments for the year.
(2) Present the journal entries to record the payment of the December 20th purchase on January 19, when the exchange rate was $.0055 per Japanese yen, and the receipt of cash from the December 6th sale, on January 20, when the exchange rate was $.82 per Canadian dollar.

MINI-CASE 17

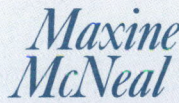
Maxine McNeal

Your grandmother recently retired, sold her home in Hartford, and moved to a retirement community in Scottsdale. With some of the proceeds from the sale of her home, she is considering investing $300,000 in the stock market.

In the process of selecting among alternative stock investments, your grandmother collected annual reports from twenty different companies. In reviewing these reports, however, she has become confused and has questions concerning several items which appear in the financial reports. She has asked for your help and has written down the following questions for you to answer:

(a) "In reviewing the annual reports, I noticed many references to 'consolidated financial statements.' What are consolidated financial statements?"

(b) "'Excess of cost of business acquired over related net assets' appears on the consolidated balance sheets in several annual reports. What does this mean? Is it an asset (it appears with other assets)?"

(c) "What is minority interest?"

(d) "A footnote to one of the consolidated statements indicated interest and the amount of a loan from one company to another had been eliminated. Is this good accounting? A loan is a loan. How can a company just eliminate a loan that hasn't been paid off?"

(e) "How can financial statements for an American company (in dollars) be combined with a British subsidiary (in pounds)?"

Instructions:

(1) Briefly respond to each of your grandmother's questions.
(2) While discussing the items in (1) with your grandmother, she asked for your advice on whether she should limit her investment to one stock. What would you advise?

ETHICS DISCUSSION CASE	Marchant Company has recently begun selling merchandise to foreign customers. Roberta Douglas, the controller, has implemented a policy that requires all foreign transactions to be executed in United States dollars. In this way, Douglas transfers to the customers all risks of foreign exchange fluctuations on sales to foreign markets. Discuss whether Roberta Douglas's policy is ethical.

ANSWERS TO SELF-EXAMINATION QUESTIONS

1. **C** When parent acquires substantially all of the voting stock of subsidiary in exchange for its voting common stock (answer C), the affiliation is termed a "pooling of interests." When parent acquires substantially all of the voting stock of subsidiary in exchange for cash (answer A), other assets, issuances of debt obligations (answer B), or a combination of the foregoing, it is termed a "purchase."

2. **B** The excess of cost over book equity of interest in S Co. is $100,000 (answer B), determined as follows:

Investment in S Co. (cost)	$1,000,000
Eliminate 100% of S Co. stock...	(750,000)
Eliminate 100% of S Co. retained earnings	(150,000)
Excess of cost over book equity of subsidiary interest..............	$ 100,000

3. **B** The excess of cost over book equity of interest in S Co. is $190,000 (answer B), determined as follows:

Investment in S Co. (cost)	$1,000,000
Eliminate 90% of S Co. stock	(675,000)
Eliminate 90% of S Co. retained earnings.............................	(135,000)
Excess of cost over book equity of subsidiary interest..............	$ 190,000

4. **D** The 10% of the stock owned by outsiders is referred to as the minority interest. It amounts to $90,000, determined as follows:

10% of common stock	$75,000
10% of retained earnings..	15,000
Total minority interest...	$90,000

5. **B** The 25,000,000 pesos ($10,000 ÷ $.0004) representing the billed price, which had a value of $10,000 on July 9, 1990, had increased in value to $12,500 (25,000,000 pesos × $.0005) on August 8, 1990, when payment was received. The gain, which was realized because the transaction was completed by the receipt of cash, was $2,500 (answer B).

CHAPTER EIGHTEEN
STATEMENT OF CASH FLOWS

The four basic financial statements are the balance sheet, the income statement, the retained earnings statement (statement of owner's equity), and the statement of cash flows. The preparation and use of the first three statements were thoroughly discussed in preceding chapters. In Chapter 1, the statement of cash flows was briefly described and illustrated for a small service enterprise. In this chapter, the nature, purpose, and preparation of the statement of cash flows are further discussed and illustrated.

NATURE OF THE STATEMENT OF CASH FLOWS

OBJECTIVE 1
Describe the nature of the statement of cash flows.

In 1987, the Financial Accounting Standards Board (FASB) issued Statement of Financial Accounting Standards No. 95, which requires the inclusion of a statement of cash flows as part of the basic set of financial statements. Such a statement is useful to managers in evaluating past and planning future investing and financing activities. It is also useful to creditors and investors in their analysis of a firm's financial condition and profitability.

The statement of cash flows replaces the statement of changes in financial position (frequently called the funds statement). The statement of changes in financial position reported a firm's significant investing and financing activities for a period. These activities were generally described in terms of the inflow or outflow of "funds," with funds defined either as "cash" or "working capital" (current assets — current liabilities). After considerable research and experimentation, the FASB decided that a statement of cash flows would better meet the objectives of financial reporting, expressed as follows:

Financial reporting should provide information to help present and potential investors and creditors and other users in assessing the amounts, timing, and uncertainty of prospective cash receipts from dividends or interest and the proceeds from the sale, redemption, or maturity of securities or loans. The prospects for those cash receipts are affected by an enterprise's ability to gen-

erate enough cash to meet its obligations when due and its other cash operating needs, to reinvest in operations, and to pay cash dividends....[1]

The **statement of cash flows** reports a firm's major sources of cash receipts and major uses of cash payments for a period.[2] Such a statement provides useful information about a firm's activities in generating cash from operations, maintaining and expanding operating capacity, meeting its financial obligations, and paying dividends. Such information, when used in conjunction with the other financial statements, assists investors, creditors, and others in assessing the entity's profitability and solvency (the ability to meet currently maturing debt). For example, the receipt of cash from issuing bonds indicates that the firm is not only committed to the payment of periodic interest expense (which affects profitability and solvency), but also to the redemption of the bonds at maturity (which affects solvency). Thus, the statement of cash flows is useful in analyzing both past and future profitability and solvency of the firm.

FOCUS ON CASH FLOW

In the past, investors have relied almost exclusively on a company's earnings information in judging the company's performance. But this information may be misleading. Therefore, as described in the following excerpt from an article in *The Wall Street Journal*, more and more investors are focusing on cash flows.

Follow the money.

That's a guiding principle for the increasing number of stock analysts and investors who study corporate cash flows. While none of them advocates using cash-flow analysis by itself, they say it can be an important tool in piercing the camouflage that sometimes makes reported earnings misleading.

As the term suggests, cash flow is basically a measure of the money flowing into—or out of—a business. If large companies were run, like lemonade stands, on a cash basis, earnings and cash flow would be identical.

Every major corporation, however, keeps its books on an accrual basis. When it builds a new plant or receives a large multiyear contract, it generally staggers the expense or income over a

period of years. That can give a truer picture of corporate profitability, but sometimes it obscures important developments.

Take a company that spent $140 million on new machinery last year. If it depreciates the equipment over a seven-year period, it will be subtracting $20 million from reported profits each year.

But if the machines will stay up-to-date and useful for 25 years, the company's reported earnings may understate its true strength....

...Sometimes the reverse is true. If a company has been neglecting capital spending, its earnings may look good. But on a cash-flow basis, it will look no better, perhaps worse, than its competitors.

Thus, focusing on cash flow makes the investor confront an important question: whether... assets being depreciated really do wear out as rapidly as they are being depreciated....

...Joseph Battipaglia, an analyst with Gruntal & Co. in New York, says that cash-flow trends gave alert investors an early warning of the auto industry's problems in the 1970's. By the end of the decade, he notes, poor earnings made those problems apparent to everyone. But by then, he says, "everyone was going through the same door at the same time."

Source: John R. Dorfman, "Stock Analysts Increase Focus on Cash Flow," *The Wall Street Journal* (February 17, 1987), Section 2, page 1.

---

[1]*Statement of Financial Accounting Concepts, No. 1*, "Objectives of Financial Reporting by Business Enterprises" (Stamford: Financial Accounting Standards Board, 1978), par. 37.

[2]Cash is the most useful concept for the statement of cash flows. However, cash in excess of immediate needs may be invested in income-producing, short-term, highly liquid investments, called cash equivalents, such as Treasury bills and money market funds. In such cases, the statement of cash flows may report changes during the period in cash and cash equivalents.

REPORTING CASH FLOWS

OBJECTIVE 2
Describe and illustrate the reporting of cash flows, including:
Cash flows from operating activities
Cash flows from investing activities
Cash flows from financing activities

The statement of cash flows classifies cash receipts and cash payments by three types of activities:

1. **Cash flows from operating activities,** which include cash transactions that enter into the determination of net income.
2. **Cash flows from investing activities,** which include receipts from the sale of investments and plant assets and other noncurrent assets; and payments for the acquisition of investments and plant assets and other noncurrent assets.
3. **Cash flows from financing activities,** which include receipts from the issuance of equity and debt securities; and payments for dividends, repurchase of equity securities, and redemption of debt securities.

By grouping cash flows by operating, investing, and financing activities, significant relationships within and among the activities can be evaluated. For example, cash receipts from borrowings can easily be related to repayments of borrowings when both are reported as financing activities. Also, the impact of each of the three activities (operating, investing, and financing) on cash flows can be evaluated. Such relationships assist investors and creditors in evaluating the effects of cash flows on profitability and solvency.

The common transactions giving rise to cash flows that would be reported in one of the three sections of the statement of cash flows are presented in the diagram below and are discussed in the following paragraphs. The focus in this chapter is on presenting the basic concept of cash flows and on providing an understanding of the preparation, interpretation, and use of the statement of cash flows.

Cash Flows

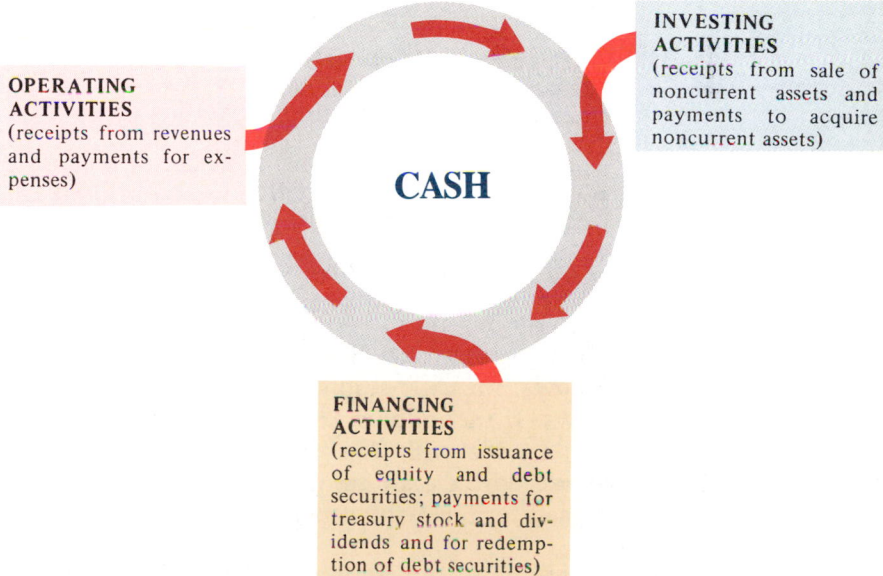

OPERATING ACTIVITIES (receipts from revenues and payments for expenses)

INVESTING ACTIVITIES (receipts from sale of noncurrent assets and payments to acquire noncurrent assets)

CASH

FINANCING ACTIVITIES (receipts from issuance of equity and debt securities; payments for treasury stock and dividends and for redemption of debt securities)

Cash Flows from Operating Activities

The most frequent and often the most important cash flows relate to the operating activities entered into for the purpose of earning net income. There are two alternatives to reporting cash flows from such operating activities in the statement of cash flows: (1) the direct method and (2) the indirect method. The **direct method** reports the major classes of operating cash receipts (cash collected from customers and cash received from interest and dividends, for example) and of operating cash payments (cash paid to suppliers for merchandise and services, to employees for wages, and to creditors for interest, for example). The difference between these operating cash receipts and cash payments would be reported as the net cash flow from operating activities. The principal advantage of the direct method is that it presents the major categories of cash receipts and cash payments. Its principal disadvantage is that the necessary data are often costly to accumulate.

When the **indirect method** is used, the effects of all deferrals of past cash receipts and payments and all accruals of expected future cash receipts and payments are removed from the net income reported on the income statement. This removal is accomplished by adjusting the amount reported as net income upward or downward to determine the net amount of cash flows from operating activities. One of the major advantages of the indirect method is that it focuses on the differences between net income and cash flows from operating activities. In addition, the data needed for the indirect method are generally more readily available and less costly to obtain than the data needed for the direct method.

Cash Flows from Investing Activities

Cash inflows from investing activities generally arise from the sale of investments, plant assets, and intangible assets. Cash outflows generally include payments to acquire investments, plant assets, and intangible assets.

In reporting cash flows from investing activities on the statement of cash flows, the cash inflows are usually reported first, followed by the cash outflows. If the inflows exceed the outflows, the net cash flow can be described as "Net cash flow provided by investing activities." If the cash outflows exceed the cash inflows, the difference can be described as "Net cash flow used for investing activities."

Cash Flows from Financing Activities

Cash inflows from financing activities include proceeds from the issuance of equity securities, such as preferred and common stocks. Cash inflows also arise from the issuance of bonds, mortgage notes payable, and notes and other long-term and short-term borrowings. Cash outflows from financing activities include the payment of cash dividends, the acquisition of treasury stock, and the repayment of amounts borrowed.

In reporting cash flows from financing activities on the statement of cash flows, the cash inflows are usually reported first, followed by the cash outflows. If the inflows exceed the outflows, the net cash flow can be described as "Net cash flow provided by financing activities." If the cash outflows exceed the cash inflows, the difference can be described as "Net cash flow used for financing activities."

Illustrations of the Statement of Cash Flows

As described in the preceding paragraphs, the statement of cash flows is divided into three sections—cash flows from operating activities, cash flows from investing activities, and cash flows from financing activities. Although different formats are possible, the cash flows from operating activities is generally presented first, followed by the cash flows from investing activities and the cash flows from financing activities. The total of the net cash flow from these activities is the net increase or decrease in cash for the period. The cash balance at the beginning of the period is added to the net increase or decrease in cash for the period to arrive at the cash balance at the end of the period.

Two illustrations of the statement of cash flows are presented below. The first illustration is the Long Taxi Corporation statement that was presented in Chapter 1 and that reports cash flows from operating activities by the direct method. The second illustration is also the Long Taxi Corporation statement, but with cash flows from operating activities reported by the indirect method. Note that regardless of which method is used, the same amount of net cash flow from operating activities is reported in the statement of cash flows.

Statement of Cash Flows— Direct Method

Long Taxi Corporation
Statement of Cash Flows
For Month Ended August 31, 1990

Cash flows from operating activities:		
Cash received from customers	$ 4,500	
Deduct cash payments for expenses and		
payments to creditors..................................	2,600	
Net cash flow from operating activities		$1,900
Cash flows from investing activities:		
Cash payments for acquisition of land................		(7,500)
Cash flows from financing activities:		
Cash received from sale of capital stock.............	$10,000	
Deduct cash payments for dividends..................	1,000	
Net cash flow from financing activities...............		9,000
Net cash flows and August 31, 1990 cash balance..		$3,400

Statement of Cash Flows— Indirect Method

Long Taxi Corporation
Statement of Cash Flows
For Month Ended August 31, 1990

Cash flows from operating activities:		
Net income, per income statement	$ 1,700	
Add increase in accounts payable	450	
	$ 2,150	
Deduct increase in supplies	250	
Net cash flow from operating activities		$1,900
Cash flows from investing activities:		
Cash payments for acquisition of land................		(7,500)
Cash flows from financing activities:		
Cash received from sale of capital stock.............	$10,000	
Deduct cash payments for dividends..................	1,000	
Net cash flow from financing activities...............		9,000
Net cash flows and August 31, 1990 cash balance..		$3,400

For small enterprises with few transactions, such as Long Taxi Corporation, the direct method of reporting cash flows from operating activities can be easily used in preparing the statement of cash flows. For large enterprises with numerous transactions, the direct method is not widely used. Therefore, the indirect method will be used in the remainder of this chapter.[3]

Noncash Investing and Financing Activities

In addition to the investing and financing activities described in the preceding sections, investing and financing may be affected by transactions that do not involve cash. If such transactions have occurred during the period, their effect, if significant, should be reported in a separate schedule to accompany the statement of cash flows. This broadened concept recognizes that some investing and financing transactions do not involve cash receipts and payments, but have a significant effect on future cash flows. For example, the issuance of common stock to retire long-term debt has no effect on cash. However, the transaction will eliminate the future cash payments to retire the bonds and future cash payments for interest. Therefore, it should be reported.

A complete discussion of the kinds of noncash transactions that usually have a significant effect on investing and financing activities is beyond the scope of discussion here. Two examples of the many possibilities are the acquisition of plant assets by the issuance of bonds or capital stock and the issuance of common stock in exchange for convertible preferred stock.

Cash Flow per Share

The term "cash flow per share" is sometimes encountered in the financial press. In many cases, the reference is to cash flows from operations per share. Such reporting of cash flow per share might mislead readers into thinking that cash flow is equivalent to or perhaps superior to earnings per share in appraising the relative success of operations. For example, users might interpret the cash flow from operations per share as being the amount available for dividends, when most of the cash generated by operations may be required for repaying loans or for reinvesting in the business. The financial statements, including the statement of cash flows, should therefore not report a cash flow per share amount.

ASSEMBLING DATA AND PREPARING THE STATEMENT OF CASH FLOWS

OBJECTIVE 3
Describe and illustrate the preparation of the statement of cash flows.

To collect the data for the statement of cash flows, all the cash receipts and disbursements for a period could be analyzed and then reported by activity (operating, investing, or financing) on the statement. However, this direct method of analyzing and reporting cash flows is expensive and time consuming. An indirect method is generally the more efficient procedure of examining the noncash balance sheet accounts and determining the type of cash flow activity that leads to changes in these accounts during the period. In performing this analysis, supplementary explanatory data can be obtained from the income statement and other records as needed. Such a procedure is not only efficient but also logical, because all transactions eventually affect

---

[3]An appendix that further discusses and illustrates the direct method of reporting cash flows from operating activities is presented at the end of this chapter.

balance sheet accounts. For example, although revenues and expenses are not shown directly on the balance sheet, the retained earnings account on the balance sheet is affected as revenues and expenses are closed at the end of a period.

Although there is no order in which the noncash balance sheet accounts must be analyzed, time can be saved and greater accuracy can be achieved by selecting the accounts in the reverse order in which they appear on the balance sheet. Therefore, the retained earnings account provides the starting point for determining the cash flows from operating activities that normally appear first on the statement of cash flows.

To illustrate this approach to assembling the data for the statement of cash flows, the comparative balance sheet on page 698 for Message Corporation for the year ended December 31, 1990, will be used. Selected ledger accounts will be presented as needed, along with supplementary data taken from the income statement.[4]

Retained Earnings

According to the comparative balance sheet for Message Corporation there was an increase of $60,500 in retained earnings during the year. The retained earnings account, as shown below, indicates the nature of the entries made during the year that resulted in this increase.

ACCOUNT RETAINED EARNINGS   ACCOUNT NO.

Date		Item	Debit	Credit	Balance Debit	Balance Credit
1990						
Jan.	1	Balance				112,000
Dec.	31	Net income		90,500		
	31	Cash dividends	30,000			172,500

The retained earnings account indicates net income of $90,500 and cash dividends declared of $30,000. The determination of the amount of cash flows from operating activities and the cash flows for the payment of dividends is discussed in the following paragraphs. It should be noted that there may be entries in the retained earnings account that do not affect cash, such as a transfer of retained earnings to paid-in capital accounts for the issuance of a stock dividend. Similarly, transfers between the retained earnings account and appropriations accounts have no effect on cash. Such transactions would not be reported on the statement of cash flows.

Cash Flows from Operating Activities. The amount of net income, $90,500, which is reported on the income statement, was determined by the accrual method of accounting. It is therefore necessary to recognize the rela-

---

[4]When the volume of data is substantial, experienced accountants may first assemble all relevant facts in working papers designed for the purpose. Specialized working papers are not essential, however. Because of their complexity, they may obscure the basic concepts of cash flow analysis for anyone who is not already familiar with the subject. For this reason, special working papers will not be used in the following discussion. Instead, the emphasis will be on the basic analyses. An appendix that discusses the use of a work sheet as an aid in assembling data for the statement of cash flows is presented at the end of this chapter.

Comparative Balance Sheet

Message Corporation
Comparative Balance Sheet
December 31, 1990 and 1989

	1990	1989	Increase Decrease*
Assets			
Cash...	$ 49,000	$ 26,000	$ 23,000
Trade receivables (net)........................	74,000	65,000	9,000
Inventories..	172,000	180,000	8,000*
Prepaid expenses	4,000	3,000	1,000
Investments (long-term)......................	—	45,000	45,000*
Land..	90,000	40,000	50,000
Building...	200,000	200,000	—
Accumulated depreciation—building......	(36,000)	(30,000)	(6,000)
Equipment	290,000	142,000	148,000
Accumulated depreciation—equipment..	(43,000)	(40,000)	(3,000)
Total assets	$800,000	$631,000	$169,000
Liabilities			
Accounts payable (merchandise creditors)...	$ 50,000	$ 32,000	$ 18,000
Income tax payable	2,500	4,000	1,500*
Dividends payable.............................	15,000	8,000	7,000
Bonds payable..................................	120,000	245,000	125,000*
Total liabilities..................................	$187,500	$289,000	$101,500*
Stockholders' Equity			
Preferred stock.................................	$150,000	—	$150,000
Excess of issue price over par— preferred stock	10,000	—	10,000
Common stock	280,000	$230,000	50,000
Retained earnings.............................	172,500	112,000	60,500
Total stockholders' equity...................	$612,500	$342,000	$270,500
Total liabilities and stockholders' equity ..	$800,000	$631,000	$169,000

tionship of the accrual method to the movement of cash. Usually, a part of some of the costs and expenses reported on the income statement, as well as a part of the revenue earned, is not accompanied by cash outflow or inflow.

There is often a period of time between the accrual of a revenue and the receipt of the related cash. Perhaps the most common example is the sale of merchandise or a service on account, for which payment is received at a later point in time. Hence, the amount reported on the income statement as revenue from sales is not likely to correspond with the amount of the related cash inflow for the same period.

Timing differences between the incurrence of an expense and the related cash outflow must also be considered in determining the amount of cash flows from operating activities. For example, the amount reported on the income statement as insurance expense is the amount of insurance premiums expired rather than the amount of premiums paid during the period. Similarly, supplies paid for in one year may be used and thus converted to an expense in a later year. Conversely, a portion of some of the expenses incurred near the end of one period, such as wages and taxes, may not require a cash outlay until the following period.

Some revenues and expenses related to noncurrent accounts do not provide or use cash. For example, depreciation expense is a proper expense for the purpose of determining net income, but it does not require an outlay of cash.

To determine the amount of cash flows from operating activities, the accrual basis net income, as reported on the income statement, must be converted to the cash basis. For purposes of illustration, the types of accounts that must be analyzed to convert net income from the accrual basis to the cash basis can be placed in two categories, described as follows:

1. Expenses affecting noncurrent accounts but not cash. For example, depreciation of plant assets and amortization of intangible assets are deducted from revenue but have no effect on cash. Similarly, the amortization of premium on bonds payable, which decreases interest expense and therefore increases operating income, does not affect cash.

2. Revenues and expenses affecting current asset and current liability accounts in amounts that differ from cash flows. For example, a sale of $10,000 on account, on which $8,000 has subsequently been collected, increases revenue by $10,000 but increases cash by only $8,000. In this case, to convert the revenue reported on the income statement ($10,000) to the cash basis, the increase in accounts receivable of $2,000 ($10,000 sale less $8,000 collection) can be deducted from the $10,000 of revenue to yield a cash flow of $8,000.

Generally accepted accounting principles require that cash flows be classified according to the nature of the underlying transaction.[5] This requirement means that cash flows from operating activities should not include transactions which are investing activities or financing activities. For example, the gain or loss from the sale of noncurrent assets would be reported as part of the total cash flows from investing activities arising from the sale of noncurrent assets. To illustrate, assume that land costing $50,000 was sold for $90,000 (a gain of $40,000). The sale should be reported in the investing activities section as "Cash receipts from the sale of land, $90,000." Since the $40,000 gain on the sale of the land is reported in the income statement, the $40,000 must be deducted from net income in converting the reported net income to cash flows from operations. Otherwise, the $40,000 gain would be reported twice on the statement of cash flows. Similarly, losses resulting from such transactions would be added to net income in determining the net cash flow from operating activities. Also, gains or losses arising from the retirement of debt would need to be deducted from or added to net income as reported on the income statement to determine the net cash flow from operating activities.

The conversion of the net income reported on the income statement to cash flows from operating activities can be summarized as follows:

---

[5]*Statement of Financial Accounting Standards, No. 95,* "Statement of Cash Flows" (Stamford: Financial Accounting Standards Board, 1987).

Net income, per income statement		$XX
Add: Depreciation of plant assets..	$XX	
Amortization of bond payable discount and intangible assets	XX	
Decreases in current assets (receivables, inventories, prepaid expenses)..	XX	
Increases in current liabilities (accounts and notes payable, accrued liabilities)	XX	
Losses on disposal of assets and retirement of debt.................	XX	XX
Deduct: Amortization of bond payable premium	$XX	
Increases in current assets (receivables, inventories, prepaid expenses)	XX	
Decreases in current liabilities (accounts and notes payable, accrued liabilities)	XX	
Gains on disposal of assets and retirement of debt.............	XX	XX
Net cash flow from operating activities		$XX

Note that two current accounts—cash and dividends payable—are not included in this conversion schedule. Cash is omitted because it is the focus of the analysis. Dividends payable is omitted because dividends are a distribution of earnings and do not affect net income. The treatment of dividends as they affect the statement of cash flows will be discussed later in the chapter. In the following paragraphs, the manner in which the net income reported by Message Corporation is converted to "Cash flows from operating activities" is discussed.

Depreciation. The comparative balance sheet for Message Corporation indicates that Accumulated Depreciation—Equipment increased by $3,000, and Accumulated Depreciation—Building increased by $6,000. Reference to these two accounts, shown as follows, indicates that depreciation for the year was $12,000 for the equipment and $6,000 for the building, or a total of $18,000.

ACCOUNT ACCUMULATED DEPRECIATION—EQUIPMENT   ACCOUNT NO.

Date		Item	Debit	Credit	Balance Debit	Balance Credit
1990						
Jan.	1	Balance				40,000
May	9	Discarded, no salvage	9,000			
Dec.	31	Depreciation for year		12,000		43,000

ACCOUNT ACCUMULATED DEPRECIATION—BUILDING   ACCOUNT NO.

Date		Item	Debit	Credit	Balance Debit	Balance Credit
1990						
Jan.	1	Balance				30,000
Dec.	31	Depreciation for year		6,000		36,000

Since the $18,000 of depreciation expense reduces net income but did not require an outlay of cash, $18,000 is added to net income in the process of determining the cash flows from operating activities, as follows:

Cash flows from operating activities:

Net income	$90,500	
Add: Depreciation...	18,000	$108,500

Current Assets and Current Liabilities. In the process of determining cash flows from operating activities, decreases in the noncash current assets and increases in the current liabilities must be added to the amount reported as net income. Conversely, increases in the noncash current assets and decreases in the current liabilities must be deducted from the amount reported as net income. The relevant current asset and current liability accounts of Message Corporation are as follows:

	December 31		Increase
Accounts	1990	1989	Decrease*
Trade receivables (net).................................	$ 74,000	$ 65,000	$ 9,000
Inventories..	172,000	180,000	8,000*
Prepaid expenses	4,000	3,000	1,000
Accounts payable			
(merchandise creditors).............................	50,000	32,000	18,000
Income tax payable	2,500	4,000	1,500*

The additions to **trade receivables** for sales on account during the year were $9,000 more than the deductions for amounts collected from customers on account. The amount reported on the income statement as sales therefore included $9,000 that did not yield cash inflow during the year. Accordingly, $9,000 must be deducted from net income.

The $8,000 decrease in **inventories** indicates that the merchandise sold exceeded the cost of the merchandise purchased by $8,000. The amount reported on the income statement as a deduction from the revenue therefore included $8,000 that did not require cash outflow during the year. Accordingly, $8,000 must be added to net income.

The outlay of cash for **prepaid expenses** exceeded by $1,000 the amount deducted as an expense during the year. Hence, $1,000 must be deducted from net income.

The effect of the increase in **accounts payable**, which is the amount owed creditors for goods and services, was to include in expired costs and expenses the sum of $18,000 for which there had been no cash outlay during the year. Income was thereby reduced by $18,000, though there was no cash outlay. Hence, $18,000 must be added to net income.

The outlay of cash for **income taxes** exceeded by $1,500 the amount of income tax deducted as an expense during the period. Accordingly, $1,500 must be deducted from net income.

The foregoing adjustments to income, including the adjustment for depreciation, may be summarized as follows:

Cash flows from operating activities:				
Net income				$ 90,500
Add: Depreciation..		$18,000		
Decrease in inventories...........................		8,000		
Increase in accounts payable...................		18,000	44,000	
				$134,500
Deduct: Increase in trade receivables		$ 9,000		
Increase in prepaid expenses...............		1,000		
Decrease in income tax payable...........		1,500	11,500	$123,000

Gain on Sale of Investments. Reference to the ledger or income statement would indicate that the sale of investments resulted in a gain of $30,000. As discussed in preceding paragraphs, to avoid the double reporting of this $30,000 in the statement of cash flows, it must be deducted from the net income reported on the income statement as follows:[6]

Cash flows from operating activities:

Net income	$90,500	
Deduct: Gain on sale of investments................................	30,000	$60,500

Reporting Cash Flows from Operating Activities. All the adjustments that are necessary to convert the net income to cash flows from operating activities for Message Corporation are presented in a format suitable for the statement of cash flows, as follows:

Cash flows from operating activities:

Net income, per income statement		$ 90,500	
Add: Depreciation...	$18,000		
Decrease in inventories...........................	8,000		
Increase in accounts payable...................	18,000	44,000	
		$134,500	
Deduct: Increase in trade receivables	$ 9,000		
Increase in prepaid expenses...............	1,000		
Decrease in income tax payable...........	1,500		
Gain on sale of investments.................	30,000	41,500	
Net cash flow from operating activities			$93,000

Cash Flows for Payment of Dividends. According to the retained earnings account of Message Corporation (page 697), cash dividends of $30,000 were declared during the year. However, according to the dividends payable account, shown as follows, dividend payments during the year totaled $23,000, revealing a timing difference between the declaration and the payment.

ACCOUNT DIVIDENDS PAYABLE   ACCOUNT NO.

Date		Item	Debit	Credit	Balance Debit	Balance Credit
1990						
Jan.	1	Balance				8,000
	10	Cash paid	8,000		—	—
June	20	Dividend declared		15,000		15,000
July	10	Cash paid	15,000		—	—
Dec.	20	Dividend declared		15,000		15,000

The $23,000 of cash dividend payments would be reported in the financing activities section and may be noted on the statement of cash flows as follows:

Cash flows from financing activities:

Cash paid for dividends...	$23,000

---

[6]The reporting of the cash flows from the sale of investments, which is an investing activity, is discussed in a later paragraph.

Common Stock

The increase of $50,000 in the common stock account, shown as follows, is the result of stock being issued in exchange for land valued at $50,000.

ACCOUNT COMMON STOCK   ACCOUNT NO.

Date		Item	Debit	Credit	Balance Debit	Balance Credit
1990 Jan.	1	Balance				230,000
Dec.	28	Issued at par in exchange for land		50,000		280,000

Although cash was not involved, the transaction represents a significant investing and financing transaction that should be reported in a separate schedule to the statement of cash flows, as discussed previously. In this schedule, the transaction may be noted as follows:

Noncash investing and financing activities:
Acquisition of land by issuance of common stock.................................... $50,000

Preferred Stock

The increase of $150,000 in the preferred stock account and the increase of $10,000 in the premium on preferred stock account, shown as follows, is the result of an issuance of preferred stock for $160,000.

ACCOUNT PREFERRED STOCK, $50 PAR   ACCOUNT NO.

Date		Item	Debit	Credit	Balance Debit	Balance Credit
1990 Nov.	1	3,000 shares issued for cash		150,000		150,000

ACCOUNT PAID-IN CAPITAL IN EXCESS OF PAR — PREFERRED STOCK   ACCOUNT NO.

Date		Item	Debit	Credit	Balance Debit	Balance Credit
1990 Nov.	1	3,000 shares issued for cash		10,000		10,000

This cash flow would be reported in the financing activities section and may be noted on the statement of cash flows as follows:

Cash flows from financing activities:
Cash received from sale of preferred stock....................................... $160,000

Bonds Payable

The next item listed on the balance sheet, bonds payable, decreased $125,000 during the year. Examination of the bonds payable account, which appears as follows, indicates that $125,000 of the bonds payable were retired by a cash payment for the face amount.

ACCOUNT   BONDS PAYABLE   ACCOUNT NO.

Date		Item	Debit	Credit	Balance Debit	Balance Credit
1990						
Jan.	1	Balance				245,000
June	30	Retired by payment of cash				
		at face amount	125,000			120,000

This cash flow would be reported in the financing activities section and may be noted as follows:

Cash flows from financing activities:
Cash paid to retire bonds payable.. **$125,000**

Equipment

The comparative balance sheet indicates that the cost of equipment increased $148,000. The following equipment account and the accumulated depreciation account reveal that the net change of $148,000 was the result of two separate transactions—the discarding of equipment that had cost $9,000 and the purchase of equipment for $157,000. The equipment discarded had been fully depreciated, as indicated by the debit of $9,000 in the accumulated depreciation account, and no salvage was realized from its disposal. Hence, the transaction had no effect on cash and is not reported on the statement of cash flows.

ACCOUNT   EQUIPMENT   ACCOUNT NO.

Date		Item	Debit	Credit	Balance Debit	Balance Credit
1990						
Jan.	1	Balance			142,000	
May	9	Discarded, no salvage		9,000		
Dec.	7	Purchased for cash	157,000		290,000	

ACCOUNT   ACCUMULATED DEPRECIATION—EQUIPMENT   ACCOUNT NO.

Date		Item	Debit	Credit	Balance Debit	Balance Credit
1990						
Jan.	1	Balance				40,000
May	9	Discarded, no salvage	9,000			
Dec.	31	Depreciation for year		12,000		43,000

The effect on cash flows from the purchase of equipment for $157,000 would be reported in the investing activities section and may be noted as follows:

Cash flows from investing activities:
Cash paid for purchase of equipment... **$157,000**

The credit in the accumulated depreciation account had the effect of reducing the book value of equipment by $12,000 but caused no change in cash. The depreciation was treated previously as an addition to net income in determining cash flows from operating activities.

Building

According to the comparative balance sheet, there was no change in the $200,000 balance in the building account between the beginning and end of the year. Reference to the ledger confirms the absence of entries in the building account during the year, and hence the account is not shown here. The credit in the related accumulated depreciation account reduced the book value of the building, but, as indicated previously, cash was not affected. The depreciation was treated previously as an addition to net income in determining cash flows from operating activities.

Land

The comparative balance sheet indicates that land increased by $50,000. The notation in the land account, which follows, indicates that the land was acquired by issuance of common stock at par.

ACCOUNT LAND   ACCOUNT NO.

Date		Item	Debit	Credit	Balance Debit	Balance Credit
1990						
Jan.	1	Balance			40,000	
Dec.	28	Acquired by issuance of common stock at par	50,000		90,000	

Although cash was not involved in this transaction, as indicated previously, the acquisition represents a significant investing and financing activity. Therefore, the transaction would be reported in a separate schedule as follows:

Noncash investing and financing activities:
Acquisition of land by issuance of common stock.................................. $50,000

Investments

The comparative balance sheet indicates that investments decreased by $45,000. The notation in the following investments account indicates that the investments were sold for $75,000 in cash.

ACCOUNT INVESTMENTS   ACCOUNT NO.

Date		Item	Debit	Credit	Balance Debit	Balance Credit
1990						
Jan.	1	Balance			45,000	
June	8	Sold for $75,000 cash		45,000	—	—

The $75,000 received from the sale of the investments must be reported as a cash flow from investing activities. Accordingly, the notation in the statement of cash flows is as follows:

Cash flows from investing activities:
Cash received from sale of investments (includes $30,000 gain reported
  in net income) $75,000

Note that the $30,000 gain on the sale is included in the net income reported on the income statement. As indicated previously, this gain was deducted from the net income in determining the cash flows from operating activities.

Preparing the Statement of Cash Flows

The statement of cash flows for Message Corporation can be prepared from the data assembled and analyzed in the preceding paragraphs. Using the indirect method of reporting cash flows from operating activities, the statement of cash flows for Message Corporation is shown below. An analysis of the statement indicates that the cash position increased by $23,000 during the year. The most significant increase in net cash flows, $93,000, was from operating activities, while the most significant use of cash, $82,000, was for investing activities.

Statement of Cash Flows

Message Corporation
Statement of Cash Flows
For Year Ended December 31, 1990

Cash flows from operating activities:			
Net income, per income statement		$ 90,500	
Add: Depreciation.............................	$ 18,000		
Decrease in inventories..............	8,000		
Increase in accounts payable	18,000	44,000	
		$134,500	
Deduct: Increase in trade receivables ...	$ 9,000		
Increase in prepaid expenses...	1,000		
Decrease in income tax payable............................	1,500		
Gain on sale of investments.....	30,000	41,500	
Net cash flow from operating activities			$93,000
Cash flows from investing activities:			
Cash received from sale of investments ..		$ 75,000	
Less: Cash paid for purchase of equipment		157,000	
Net cash flow used for investing activities..			(82,000)
Cash flows from financing activities:			
Cash received from sale of preferred stock..		$160,000	
Less: Cash paid for dividends...............	$ 23,000		
Cash paid to retire bonds payable.................................	125,000	148,000	
Net cash flow provided by financing activities..			12,000
Increase in cash			$23,000
Cash at the beginning of the year			26,000
Cash at the end of the year			$49,000

Schedule of Noncash Investing and Financing Activities	
Acquisition of land by issuance of common stock........................	$50,000

APPENDIX

THE DIRECT METHOD OF REPORTING CASH FLOWS FROM OPERATING ACTIVITIES

There are two alternative formats for reporting cash flows from operating activities on the statement of cash flows: (1) the indirect method and (2) the direct method. The amount reported as the net cash flow from operating activities will not be affected by the format used. The indirect method is more widely used in practice and was discussed and illustrated in this chapter. The basic concepts of reporting cash flows from operating activities by the direct method are briefly discussed in this appendix.

In reporting cash flows from operating activities by the direct method, the major classes of operating cash receipts (cash received from customers, for example) and operating cash payments (cash payments to suppliers for merchandise, for example) are presented on the statement of cash flows. The difference between the total cash receipts by major classes and the total cash payments by major classes is the net cash flow from operating activities.[7]

ASSEMBLING DATA FOR CASH FLOWS FROM OPERATING ACTIVITIES

To collect data for reporting cash flows from operating activities by the direct method, all of the operating cash receipts and operating cash payments for a period could be analyzed and classified for reporting on the statement of cash flows. However, this procedure would be expensive and time-consuming. A more efficient procedure is to examine the revenues and expenses reported on the income statement and to determine the cash flows related to these revenues and expenses. In performing this analysis, supplementary data can be obtained from other records as needed. To illustrate this approach to assembling data for reporting cash flows from operating activities, the following income statement for Johnson Company for the year ended December 31, 1990, will be used:

Johnson Company Income Statement For Year Ended December 31, 1990		
Sales..		$990,000
Cost of merchandise sold		580,000
Gross profit...		$410,000
Operating expenses:		
Depreciation expense	$ 38,000	
Other operating expenses.............................	256,500	
Total operating expenses.............................		294,500
Income before income tax.................................		$115,500
Income tax..		27,500
Net income		$ 88,000

---

[7]A reconciliation of net income and net cash flow from operating activities, as illustrated on page 711, should be included as a supplement to the cash flow statement when the direct method of reporting cash flows from operating activities is used.

Additional data showing the change in relevant account balances from the beginning to the end of 1990 are as follows:

Accounts	December 31 1990	December 31 1989	Increase Decrease*
Trade receivables	$ 72,500	$ 65,000	$ 7,500
Inventories..	155,000	165,000	10,000*
Prepaid expenses	6,500	5,000	1,500
Accounts payable (merchandise creditors) ...	60,000	46,000	14,000
Accrued operating expenses	13,000	8,500	4,500
Income tax payable	5,500	7,500	2,000*

The determination of the cash receipts and cash payments by major classes are discussed and illustrated in the following paragraphs.

Cash Received from Customers

The $990,000 of sales reported on the income statement for Johnson Company is determined by the accrual method. To determine the cash received from sales made to customers, the $990,000 must be converted to the cash basis. The procedure to convert the sales reported on the income statement to the cash received from customers can be summarized as follows:

Sales (reported on the income statement) ....   + decrease in trade receivables **or** − increase in trade receivables   = Cash Received from Customers

For Johnson Company, the cash received from customers is $982,500, determined as follows:

Sales..	$990,000
Less increase in trade receivables...	7,500
Cash received from customers	$982,500

The additions to **trade receivables** for sales on account during the year were $7,500 more than the deductions for amounts collected from customers on account. The amount reported on the income statement as sales therefore included $7,500 that did not yield cash inflow during the year. In other words, the increase in trade receivables of $7,500 during 1990 indicates that sales exceeded cash received from customers by $7,500. Accordingly, $7,500 must be deducted from sales to determine the cash received from customers.

The $982,500 of cash received from customers would be reported in the cash flows from operating activities section of the cash flow statement. For Johnson Company, this section is presented on page 710.

Cash Payments for Merchandise

The $580,000 of cost of merchandise sold reported on the income statement for Johnson Company is determined by the accrual method. The conversion of the cost of merchandise sold to the cash payments made during 1990 for merchandise can be summarized as follows:

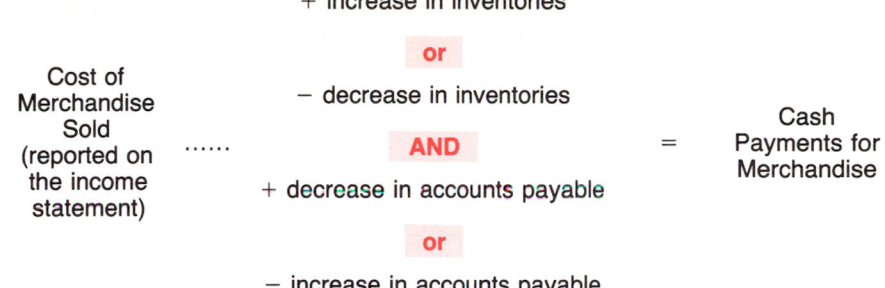

In the illustration for Johnson Company, the cash payments for merchandise is $556,000, determined as follows:

Cost of merchandise sold		$580,000
Deduct: Decrease in inventories..............................	$10,000	
Increase in accounts payable.......................	14,000	24,000
Cash payments for merchandise...............................		$556,000

The $10,000 decrease in **inventories** indicates that the merchandise sold exceeded the cost of the merchandise purchased by $10,000. The amount reported on the income statement as a deduction from sales revenue therefore included $10,000 that did not require cash outflow during the year. Accordingly, $10,000 must be deducted from cost of merchandise sold in determining the cash payments for merchandise.

The effect of the increase in **accounts payable**, which is the amount owed creditors for merchandise, was to include in merchandise purchases the sum of $14,000 for which there had been no cash outlay during the year. In other words, the increase in accounts payable indicates that cash payments for merchandise were $14,000 less than purchases made during 1990. Hence, $14,000 must be deducted from the cost of merchandise sold in determining the cash payments for merchandise.

Cash Payments for Operating Expenses

Since the $38,000 of depreciation expense reported on the income statement did not require an outlay of cash, it is not reported on the statement of cash flows. The conversion of the $256,500 reported for the other operating expenses to cash payments for operating expenses can be summarized as follows:

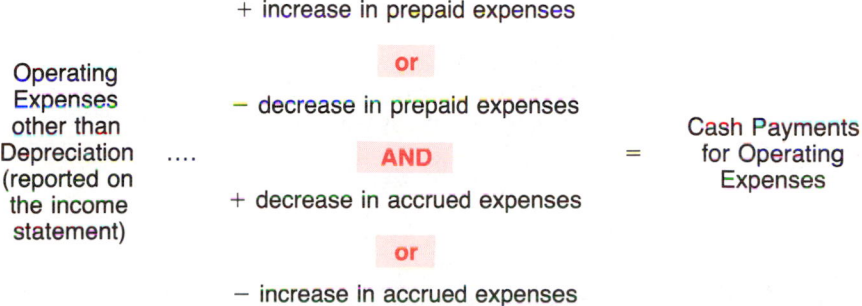

For Johnson Company, the cash payments for operating expenses is $253,500, determined as follows:

Operating expenses other than depreciation...............................	$256,500
Add increase in prepaid expenses..	1,500
	$258,000
Deduct increase in accrued operating expenses	4,500
Cash payments for operating expenses......................................	$253,500

The outlay of cash for **prepaid expenses** exceeded by $1,500 the amount deducted as an expense during the year. Hence, $1,500 must be added to the amount of operating expenses (other than depreciation) reported on the income statement in determining the cash payments for operating expenses.

The increase in **accrued operating expenses** indicates that the amount reported as an expense during the year exceeded the cash payments by $4,500. Hence, $4,500 must be deducted from the amount of operating expenses on the income statement in determining the cash payments for operating expenses.

Cash Payments for Income Taxes

The procedure to convert the amount of income tax reported on the income statement to the cash basis can be summarized as follows:

Income Tax (reported on income statement)	......	+ decrease in income tax payable **or** − increase in income tax payable	=	Cash Payments for Income Tax

For Johnson Company, the cash payments for income tax is $29,500, determined as follows:

Income tax...	$27,500
Add decrease in income tax payable	2,000
Cash payments for income tax	$29,500

The outlay of cash for **income taxes** exceeded by $2,000 the amount of income tax deducted as an expense during the period. Accordingly, $2,000 must be added to the amount of income tax reported on the income statement to determine the cash payments for income tax.

REPORTING CASH FLOWS FROM OPERATING ACTIVITIES

The main classes of operating cash receipts and operating cash payments for Johnson Company, as determined in the preceding paragraphs, may be reported in the statement of cash flows as follows:

Cash flows from operating activities:		
Cash received from customers		$982,500
Deduct: Cash payments for		
merchandise.....................	$556,000	
Cash payments for		
operating expenses............	253,500	
Cash payments for income		
tax	29,500	839,000
Net cash flow from operating activities ...		$143,500

Regardless of whether the direct method or the indirect method is used, the same amount of net cash flow from operating activities will be reported in the statement of cash flows. When the direct method is used, a reconciliation of net income and net cash flow from operating activities should be reported in a separate schedule to accompany the statement of cash flows.[8] This schedule is similar to the cash flows from operating activities section of the statement of cash flows that would be presented when the indirect method is used. For Johnson Company, such a schedule would appear as follows:

Net income, per income statement			$ 88,000
Add:	Depreciation.................................	$38,000	
	Decrease in inventories...................	10,000	
	Increase in accounts payable...........	14,000	
	Increase in accrued		
	operating expenses.....................	4,500	66,500
			$154,500
Deduct:	Increase in trade receivables	$ 7,500	
	Increase in prepaid expenses.......	1,500	
	Decrease in income tax payable...	2,000	11,000
Net cash flow from operating activities			$143,500

APPENDIX

WORK SHEET FOR STATEMENT OF CASH FLOWS

Some accountants prefer to use a work sheet to assist them in assembling data for the statement of cash flows. Although a work sheet is not essential, it is especially useful when a large number of transactions must be analyzed. Also, whether or not a work sheet is used, the concept of cash flows and the statement of cash flows are not affected.

The following sections describe and illustrate the use of the work sheet in preparing the statement of cash flows for Message Corporation, based on the data in this chapter.

WORK SHEET PROCEDURES FOR STATEMENT OF CASH FLOWS

The comparative balance sheet and additional data obtained from the accounts of Message Corporation are presented on page 712. The work sheet prepared from these data is presented on page 713. The procedures to prepare the work sheet for the statement of cash flows are outlined as follows:

1. List the titles of each balance sheet account in the Accounts column. For each account, enter the balance as of December 31, 1989, in the first column, and the balance as of December 31, 1990, in the last column. Distinguish the debit balances from the credit balances by placing the credit balances in parentheses.
2. Total the balances for both the first and last columns. The total of the debit balances should equal the total of the credit balances; thus, the totals of the first and last columns should equal zero.

---

[8]*Statement of Financial Accounting Standards, No. 95,* "Statement of Cash Flows" (Stamford: Financial Accounting Standards Board, 1987), par. 30.

3. Provide space in the bottom portion of the work sheet for later use in identifying the various cash flows from (1) operating activities, (2) investing activities, and (3) financing activities. Also, provide space at the end of the work sheet for later use in identifying items for the schedule of non-cash investing and financing activities.
4. Analyze the change during the year in each account to determine the net increase (decrease) in cash and cash flows by type of activity. Record these activities in the bottom portion of the work sheet by means of entries in the work sheet Transactions columns.
5. Complete the work sheet.

Message Corporation
Comparative Balance Sheet
December 31, 1990 and 1989

	1990	1989
Assets		
Cash	$ 49,000	$ 26,000
Trade receivables (net)	74,000	65,000
Inventories	172,000	180,000
Prepaid expenses	4,000	3,000
Investments (long-term)	—	45,000
Land	90,000	40,000
Building	200,000	200,000
Accumulated depreciation—building	(36,000)	(30,000)
Equipment	290,000	142,000
Accumulated depreciation—equipment	(43,000)	(40,000)
Total assets	$800,000	$631,000
Liabilities		
Accounts payable (merchandise creditors)	$ 50,000	$ 32,000
Income tax payable	2,500	4,000
Dividends payable	15,000	8,000
Bonds payable	120,000	245,000
Total liabilities	$187,500	$289,000
Stockholders' Equity		
Preferred stock	$150,000	—
Excess of issue price over par—preferred stock	10,000	—
Common stock	280,000	$230,000
Retained earnings	172,500	112,000
Total stockholders' equity	$612,500	$342,000
Total liabilities and stockholders' equity	$800,000	$631,000

Additional data:

(1) Net income, $90,500.
(2) Cash dividends declared, $30,000.
(3) Common stock issued at par for land, $50,000.
(4) Preferred stock issued for cash, $160,000.
(5) Bonds payable retired for cash, $125,000.
(6) Depreciation for year: equipment, $12,000; building, $6,000.
(7) Fully depreciated equipment discarded, $9,000.
(8) Equipment purchased for cash, $157,000.
(9) Book value of investments sold for $75,000 cash, $45,000.

Work Sheet for Statement of Cash Flows

Message Corporation
Work Sheet for Statement of Cash Flows
For Year Ended December 31, 1990

Accounts	Balance, Dec. 31, 1989	Transactions Debit	Transactions Credit	Balance, Dec. 31, 1990
Cash.................................	26,000	(r) 23,000		49,000
Trade Receivables....................	65,000	(q) 9,000		74,000
Inventories...........................	180,000		(p) 8,000	172,000
Prepaid Expenses....................	3,000	(o) 1,000		4,000
Investments	45,000		(n) 45,000	—
Land..................................	40,000	(m) 50,000		90,000
Building..............................	200,000			200,000
Accumulated Depreciation— Building............................	(30,000)		(l) 6,000	(36,000)
Equipment	142,000	(k) 157,000	(j) 9,000	290,000
Accumulated Depreciation— Equipment	(40,000)	(j) 9,000	(i) 12,000	(43,000)
Accounts Payable	(32,000)		(h) 18,000	(50,000)
Income Tax Payable	(4,000)	(g) 1,500		(2,500)
Dividends Payable...................	(8,000)		(f) 7,000	(15,000)
Bonds Payable	(245,000)	(e) 125,000		(120,000)
Preferred Stock......................	—		(d) 150,000	(150,000)
Paid-In Capital in Excess of Par—Preferred Stock............	—		(d) 10,000	(10,000)
Common Stock.......................	(230,000)		(c) 50,000	(280,000)
Retained Earnings...................	(112,000)	(b) 30,000	(a) 90,500	(172,500)
Totals.................................	0	405,500	405,500	0
Operating activities:				
Net Income........................		(a) 90,500		
Decrease in income tax payable...........................			(g) 1,500	
Increase in accounts payable ..		(h) 18,000		
Depreciation of equipment		(i) 12,000		
Depreciation of building..........		(l) 6,000		
Gain on sale of investments....			(n) 30,000	
Increase in prepaid expenses..			(o) 1,000	
Decrease in inventories..........		(p) 8,000		
Increase in trade receivables...			(q) 9,000	
Investing activities:				
Purchase of equipment			(k) 157,000	
Sale of investments..............		(n) 75,000		
Financing activities:				
Declaration of cash dividends..			(b) 30,000	
Issuance of preferred stock.....		(d) 160,000		
Retirement of bonds payable...			(e) 125,000	
Increase in dividends payable..		(f) 7,000		
Schedule of noncash investing and financing activities:				
Acquisition of land by issuance of common stock...............		(c) 50,000	(m) 50,000	
Net increase in cash................			(r) 23,000	
Totals.................................		426,500	426,500	

The procedures for using the work sheet are explained in detail in the following paragraphs.

Account Balances

Since cash flows can be determined by analyses of transactions affecting balance sheet accounts, the balance sheet account balances as of December 31, 1989 and 1990 are entered in the first and last columns of the work sheet. To reduce the size of the work sheet, both debit and credit balances are entered in the same column. Credit balances are identified with parentheses. The totals for both columns should equal zero, since the total of the debits in a column should equal the total of the credits in a column.

Cash Flow Activities

After the Balance columns are totaled and ruled, "Operating activities," "Investing activities," and "Financing activities" are written in the bottom portion of the work sheet. Several lines should be skipped between each category so that at a later time the various cash flows can be entered by type of activity. In addition, "Schedule of noncash investing and financing activities" is written near the bottom of the work sheet so that noncash transactions that have a significant effect on investing and financing activities can also be identified separately on the work sheet. When the work sheet is completed, the bottom portion of the work sheet will contain the data necessary to prepare the statement of cash flows.

Analysis of Accounts

As was discussed in this chapter, an efficient method of determining cash flows is to determine the type of cash flow activity that led to changes in balance sheet accounts during the period. As each noncash account is analyzed to make this determination, entries that relate specific types of cash flow activity to the noncash accounts are made in the work sheet. After all the noncash accounts have been analyzed, an entry is made to recognize the increase (decrease) in cash for the period. It should be noted that the work sheet entries are not entered into the accounts. They are, as is the entire work sheet, strictly an aid in assembling the data for later use in preparing the statement.

The sequence in which the accounts are analyzed is unimportant. However, because it is more convenient and efficient and the chance for errors is reduced, the analysis illustrated will begin with the retained earnings account and proceed upward in the listing in sequential order.

Retained Earnings. The work sheet indicates a balance of $112,000 at December 31, 1989, and $172,500 at December 31, 1990, for an increase of $60,500 in retained earnings for the year. The additional data, taken from an examination of the account, indicate that the increase was the result of two factors: (1) net income of $90,500 and (2) declaration of cash dividends of $30,000. To identify the cash flows by activity, two entries are made on the work sheet. These entries also serve to account for, or explain in terms of cash flows, the increase of $60,500.

Net Income. In closing the accounts at the end of the year, the retained earnings account was credited for $90,500, representing the net income. The $90,500 is also reported on the statement of cash flows as "cash flows from operating activities." An entry in the Transactions columns on the work sheet to debit "Operating activities—net income" and to credit retained earnings accomplishes the following: (1) the credit portion of the closing entry (to retained earnings) is accounted for and (2) the cash flow is identified in the bottom portion of the work sheet. The entry on the work sheet is as follows:

(a) Operating Activities — Net Income.............................	90,500	
Retained Earnings...		90,500

Dividends. In closing the accounts at the end of the year, the retained earnings account was debited for $30,000, representing the cash dividends declared. The $30,000 is also reported on the statement as a financing activity. An entry on the work sheet to debit retained earnings and credit "Financing activities — declaration of cash dividends" accomplishes the following: (1) the debit portion of the closing entry (to retained earnings) is accounted for and (2) the cash flow is identified in the bottom portion of the work sheet. The entry on the work sheet is as follows:

(b) Retained Earnings..	30,000	
Financing Activities — Declaration of Cash Dividends....		30,000

The cash used for the payment of dividends is also affected by a difference between the time a dividend is declared and the time it is paid. This effect is discussed later in this appendix.

Common Stock. The next item on the work sheet, common stock, increased from $230,000 to $280,000 or by $50,000 during the year. The additional data, taken from an examination of the account, indicate that the stock was exchanged for land. Although this is a noncash transaction, it should be reported in a separate schedule on the statement of cash flows. To account fully for the change of $50,000 in the common stock account and to provide the data for the separate schedule, the following entry is made on the work sheet:

(c) Schedule of Noncash Investing and Financing Activities:		
Acquisition of Land by Issuance of Common Stock	50,000	
Common Stock..		50,000

It should be noted that the effect of the exchange will also be analyzed when the land account is examined.

Preferred Stock. The work sheet indicates that the preferred stock account increased by $150,000 and the premium account increased by $10,000. The additional data indicate that these increases resulted from the sale of preferred stock for $160,000. The work sheet entry to account for these increases and to identify the cash flow is as follows:

(d) Financing Activities — Issuance of Preferred Stock.....	160,000	
Preferred Stock		150,000
Paid-In Capital in Excess of Par — Preferred Stock ..		10,000

Bonds Payable. The decrease from $245,000 to $120,000 or $125,000 in the bonds payable account resulted from the retirement of the bonds for cash. The work sheet entry to record the effect of this transaction on cash is as follows:

(e) Bonds Payable...	125,000	
Financing Activities — Retirement of Bonds Payable...		125,000

Dividends Payable. The increase in the dividends payable account from $8,000 to $15,000 during the year reveals a timing difference between the declaration and the payment of dividends. The additional data indicate that $30,000 of dividends had been declared, which was identified as a financing activity in entry (b). However, the increase in the dividends payable account of $7,000 indicates that only $23,000 ($30,000 − $7,000) of dividends were paid. The work sheet entry to adjust the dividends declared of $30,000 to reflect the dividends paid of $23,000 is as follows:

(f) Financing Activities — Declaration of Cash Dividends:
    Increase in Dividends Payable...................................... 7,000
        Dividends Payable   7,000

When the $7,000, which represents the increase in dividends payable, is deducted from the $30,000 of "Financing activities — declaration of cash dividends," $23,000 is subsequently reported on the statement as a cash flow from financing activity.

Income Tax Payable. The decrease from $4,000 to $2,500 in the income tax payable account indicates that the outlay of cash for income taxes exceeded by $1,500 the amount of income tax deducted as an expense during the period. Accordingly, $1,500 must be deducted from income to determine the amount of cash flows from operating activities. This procedure is indicated on the work sheet by the following entry:

(g) Income Tax Payable... 1,500
    Operating Activities — Net Income:
        Decrease in Income Tax Payable...............................   1,500

Accounts Payable. The accounts payable account increased by $18,000, from $32,000 to $50,000, during the year. The effect of the increase in the amount owed creditors for goods and services was to include in expired costs and expenses the sum of $18,000. Income was thereby reduced by $18,000 for which there had been no cash outlay during the year. Hence, $18,000 must be added to income to determine the amount of cash flows from operating activities. The work sheet entry is as follows:

(h) Operating Activities — Net Income:
    Increase in Accounts Payable 18,000
        Accounts Payable   18,000

Accumulated Depreciation — Equipment. The work sheet indicates that the accumulated depreciation — equipment account increased from $40,000 to $43,000 during the year. The additional data indicate that the increase resulted from (1) depreciation expense of $12,000 (credit) for the year and (2) discarding $9,000 (debit) of fully depreciated equipment. Since depreciation expense does not affect cash but does decrease the amount of net income, it should be added to net income to determine the amount of cash flows from operating activities. This effect is indicated on the work sheet by the following entry:

(i) Operating Activities — Net Income:
    Depreciation of Equipment... 12,000
        Accumulated Depreciation — Equipment...................   12,000

Since the discarding of the fully depreciated equipment did not affect cash, the following entry is made on the work sheet in order to fully account for the change of $3,000 in the accumulated depreciation—equipment account:

(j) Accumulated Depreciation—Equipment.......................... 9,000
      Equipment 9,000

It should be noted that this entry, like the transaction that was recorded in the accounts, does not affect cash. It serves only to complete the accounting for all transactions that resulted in the change in the account during the year and thus helps assure that no transactions affecting cash are overlooked in the analysis.

Equipment. The work sheet indicates that the equipment account increased from $142,000 to $290,000 or by $148,000 during the year. The additional data, determined from an examination of the ledger account, indicates that the increase resulted from (1) discarding $9,000 of fully depreciated equipment and (2) purchasing $157,000 of equipment. The discarding of the equipment was included in, or accounted for, in (j) and needs no additional attention. The use of cash to purchase equipment is recognized by the following entry on the work sheet:

(k) Equipment... 157,000
      Investing Activities—Purchase of Equipment......... 157,000

Accumulated Depreciation—Building. The work sheet indicates that the accumulated depreciation—building account increased from $30,000 to $36,000 during the year. This $6,000 increase in the accumulated depreciation—building account during the year resulted from the entry to record depreciation expense. Since depreciation expense does not affect cash but does decrease the amount of net income, it should be added to net income to determine the amount of cash flows from operating activities. This effect is accomplished by the following entry on the work sheet:

(l) Operating Activities—Net Income:
      Depreciation of Building 6,000
           Accumulated Depreciation—Building.......................... 6,000

Building. There was no change in the balance of the building account during the year, and reference to the account confirms that no entries were made in it during the year. Hence, no entry is necessary on the work sheet.

Land. As indicated in the analysis of the common stock account, the $50,000 increase in land resulted from an acquisition by issuance of common stock. To account fully for the change of $50,000 in the land account and to provide the data for the separate schedule reporting this noncash transaction, the following entry is made on the work sheet:

(m) Land.. 50,000
      Schedule of Noncash Investing and Financing
      Activities: Acquisition of Land by Issuance of
      Common Stock.. 50,000

Investments. The work sheet indicates that investments decreased from a balance of $45,000 to zero during the year. The examination of the ledger account indicates that investments were sold for $75,000. As was explained on page 702, the $30,000 gain on the sale is included in net income and must be deducted from the net income in the operating activities section. The $75,000 of cash flows from investments sold would be reported as an investing activity. To indicate this cash flow on the work sheet, the following entry is made:

(n) Investing Activities — Sale of Investments.....................	75,000	
Operating Activities — Net Income:		
Gain on Sale of Investments..................................		30,000
Investments		45,000

Prepaid Expenses. The work sheet indicates that the prepaid expenses account increased from a balance of $3,000 to $4,000 during the year. Thus, the outlay of cash for prepaid expenses exceeded by $1,000 the amount deducted as an expense during the year. Hence $1,000 must be deducted from income to determine the amount of cash flows from operating activities. The work sheet entry is as follows:

(o) Prepaid Expenses..	1,000	
Operating Activities — Net Income:		
Increase in Prepaid Expenses		1,000

Inventories. The work sheet indicates that the inventories account decreased from $180,000 to $172,000 during the year. This $8,000 decrease indicates that the merchandise sold exceeded the cost of the merchandise purchased by $8,000. The amount reported on the income statement as a deduction from the revenue therefore included $8,000 that did not require cash outflow during the year. Accordingly, $8,000 must be added to income to determine the amount of cash flows from operations. The work sheet entry is as follows:

(p) Operating Activities — Net Income:		
Decrease in Inventories...	8,000	
Inventories...		8,000

Trade Receivables (Net). The work sheet indicates that the trade receivables account increased from $65,000 to $74,000 during the year. This $9,000 increase indicates that the additions to trade receivables for sales on account during the year exceeded by $9,000 the deductions for amounts collected from customers on account. The amount reported on the income statement as sales therefore included $9,000 that did not yield cash inflow during the year. Accordingly, $9,000 must be deducted from income to determine the amount of cash flows from operating activities. The work sheet entry is as follows:

(q) Trade Receivables	9,000	
Operating Activities — Net Income:		
Increase in Trade Receivables....................................		9,000

Cash. The work sheet indicates that the cash account increased from $26,000 to $49,000 during the year. This $23,000 increase in cash is identified in the work sheet by the following entry:

(r) Cash	23,000	
Net Increase in Cash..		23,000

The credit portion of the entry is entered at the bottom of the work sheet. In preparing the statement of cash flows, the cash balance at the beginning of the year is added to this amount to determine the cash balance at the end of the year.

Completing the Work Sheet

After all the balance sheet accounts have been analyzed, all the operating, investing, and financing activities are identified in the bottom portion of the work sheet. To assure the accuracy of the work sheet entries, the debit and credit Transaction columns are totaled and compared for equality.

PREPARATION OF THE STATEMENT OF CASH FLOWS

The statement of cash flows prepared from the work sheet is identical to the statement illustrated on page 706. The data for the three sections of the statement are obtained from the bottom portion of the work sheet. Some modifications are made to the work sheet data for presentation on the statement. For example, in presenting the cash flows from operating activities, the total depreciation expense ($18,000) is reported instead of the two separate amounts ($12,000 and $6,000). In preparing the cash flows for operating activities section, the effect of depreciation is normally presented first, followed by the effects of increases and decreases in current assets and current liabilities. The effects of any gains and losses on operating activities is normally presented last. The cash paid for dividends is reported as $23,000 instead of the amount of dividends declared ($30,000) less the increase in dividends payable ($7,000). The issuance of the common stock for land ($50,000) is reported in a separate schedule.

CHAPTER REVIEW

KEY POINTS

OBJECTIVE 1

Nature of the Statement of Cash Flows

The statement of cash flows reports a firm's major sources of cash receipts and major uses of cash payments for a period. The statement of cash flows provides useful information about a firm's activities in generating cash from operations, meeting its financial obligations, paying dividends, and maintaining and expanding operating capacity. When used in conjunction with the other financial statements, the statement of cash flows is useful in analyzing both past and future profits of a firm and the ability of a firm to pay its liabilities as they become due.

OBJECTIVE 2

Types of Cash Flow Activities

The statement of cash flows classifies cash receipts and cash payments by three types of activities: cash flows from operating activities, cash flows from investing activities, and cash flows from financing activities.

Cash flows from operating activities relate to cash transactions that enter into the determination of net income. There are two alternatives to reporting cash flows from such operating activities in the statement of cash flows: (1) the direct method and

(2) the indirect method. Because of its more frequent usage, the indirect method was used in this chapter. Regardless of which method is used, the same amount of net cash flows from operating activities will be reported.

Cash inflows from investing activities generally arise from the sale of investments, plant assets, and intangible assets. Cash outflows generally include payments to acquire investments, plant assets, and intangible assets. In reporting cash flows from investing activities on the statement of cash flows, the cash inflows are usually reported first, followed by the cash outflows.

Cash inflows from financing activities include proceeds from the issuance of equity securities, such as preferred and common stock. Cash inflows also arise from the issuance of bonds, mortgage notes payable, and other long-term and short-term borrowings. Cash outflows from financing activities include the payment of cash dividends, the acquisition of treasury stock, and the repayment of amounts borrowed. In reporting cash flows from financing activities on the statement of cash flows, the cash inflows are usually reported first, followed by the cash outflows.

Investing and financing for an enterprise may be affected by transactions that do not involve cash. If such transactions have occurred during the period, their effect, if significant, should be reported in a separate schedule to accompany the statement of cash flows. This broadened concept recognizes that some investing and financing transactions do not involve cash receipts and payments, but have a significant effect on future cash flows. For example, the issuance of common stock to retire long-term debt has no effect on cash. However, the transaction will eliminate the future cash payments to retire the bonds and future cash payments for interest. Therefore, it should be reported.

OBJECTIVE 3

Assembling Data for and Preparing the Statement of Cash Flows

The common and most efficient procedure for determining the data for the statement of cash flows is to examine the noncash balance sheet accounts and determine the type of cash flow activity related to changes in these accounts.

The statement of cash flows is divided into three sections, with the cash flows from operating activities generally placed first, followed by the cash flows from investing activities and the cash flows from financing activities. A separate schedule is used to report noncash investing and financing activities.

KEY TERMS

statement of cash flows 692
cash flows from operating
    activities 693
cash flows from investing
    activities 693

cash flows from financing
    activities 693
direct method 694
indirect method 694

SELF-EXAMINATION QUESTIONS

Answers at end of chapter.

1. A full set of financial statements for a corporation would include:
   A. a balance sheet   C. a statement of cash flows
   B. an income statement   D. all of the above

2. An example of a cash flow from an operating activity is:
   A. receipt of cash from the sale of capital stock
   B. receipt of cash from the sale of bonds
   C. payment of cash for dividends
   D. none of the above

3. An example of a cash flow from an investing activity is:
   A. receipt of cash from the sale of equipment
   B. receipt of cash from the sale of capital stock
   C. payment of cash for dividends
   D. payment of cash to repurchase equity securities

4. An example of a cash flow from a financing activity is:
   A. receipt of cash from the sale of capital stock
   B. receipt of cash from the sale of bonds
   C. payment of cash for dividends
   D. all of the above

5. The net income reported on the income statement for the year was $55,000 and depreciation on plant assets for the year was $22,000. The balances of the current asset and current liability accounts at the beginning and end of the year are as follows:

	End	Beginning
Cash	$ 65,000	$ 70,000
Trade receivables	100,000	90,000
Inventories	145,000	150,000
Prepaid expenses	7,500	8,000
Accounts payable (merchandise creditors)	51,000	58,000

The total amount reported for cash flows from operating activities in the statement of cash flows would be:

A. $33,000 C. $77,000
B. $55,000 D. none of the above

ILLUSTRATIVE PROBLEM

The comparative balance sheet of Jones Inc. for December 31, 1990 and 1989, is as follows:

Assets	1990	1989
Cash	$ 65,100	$ 42,500
Trade receivables (net)	91,350	61,150
Inventories	104,500	109,500
Prepaid expenses	3,600	2,700
Land	30,000	50,000
Buildings	345,000	245,000
Accumulated depreciation—buildings	(120,600)	(110,400)
Machinery and equipment	255,000	255,000
Accumulated depreciation—machinery and equipment	(92,000)	(65,000)
Patents	35,000	40,000
	$716,950	$630,450

Liabilities and Stockholders' Equity		
Accounts payable (merchandise creditors)	$ 61,150	$ 75,000
Dividends payable	15,000	10,000
Salaries payable	6,650	7,550
Mortgage note payable, due 1995	60,000	—
Bonds payable	—	75,000
Common stock, $20 par	300,000	250,000
Excess of issue price over par—common stock	100,000	75,000
Retained earnings	174,150	137,900
	$716,950	$630,450

An examination of the income statement and the accounting records revealed the following additional information applicable to 1990:

(a) Net income, $96,250.
(b) Depreciation expense reported on the income statement: buildings, $10,200; machinery and equipment, $27,000.
(c) Land costing $20,000 was sold for $20,000.
(d) Patent amortization reported on the income statement, $5,000.
(e) A mortgage note was issued for $60,000.
(f) A building costing $100,000 was constructed.
(g) 2,500 shares of common stock were issued at 30 in exchange for the bonds payable.
(h) Cash dividends declared, $60,000.

Instructions:

Prepare a statement of cash flows.

SOLUTION

Jones Inc.
Statement of Cash Flows
For Year Ended December 31, 1990

Cash flows from operating activities:			
Net income, per income statement		$ 96,250	
Add: Depreciation..............................	$ 37,200		
Amortization of patents	5,000		
Decrease in inventories...............	5,000	47,200	
		$143,450	
Deduct: Increase in trade receivables (net)...................................	$ 30,200		
Increase in prepaid expenses ...	900		
Decrease in accounts payable...	13,850		
Decrease in salaries payable.....	900	45,850	
Net cash flow from operating activities ...			$97,600
Cash flows from investing activities:			
Cash received from sale of land		$ 20,000	
Less: Cash paid for construction of building.................................		100,000	
Net cash flow used for investing activities...			(80,000)
Cash flows from financing activities:			
Cash received from issuance of mortgage note payable		$ 60,000	
Less: Cash paid for dividends..............		55,000	
Net cash flow provided by financing activities...			5,000
Increase in cash......................................			$22,600
Cash at the beginning of the year..............			42,500
Cash at the end of the year			$65,100

Schedule of Noncash Investing and Financing Activities

Issuance of common stock to retire bonds payable.................	$75,000

DISCUSSION QUESTIONS

1. Which financial statement is most useful in evaluating past and planning future investing and financing activities?

2. What financial statement was replaced by the statement of cash flows?

3. For the statement of changes in financial position, the working capital basis was often employed. What is working capital?

4. What are the three types of activities reported on the statement of cash flows?

5. State the effect of each of the following transactions, considered individually, on cash flows (cash receipt or payment, and amount):
   (a) Sold a new issue of $300,000 of bonds at 98.
   (b) Sold equipment with a book value of $67,500 for $80,000.
   (c) Sold 1,000 shares of $100 par common stock at $120 per share.
   (d) Retired $100,000 of bonds on which there was $6,000 of unamortized bond discount for $102,000.

6. Identify each of the following as to type of cash flow activity (operating, investing, or financing):
   (a) Sale of investments
   (b) Issuance of common stock
   (c) Purchase of buildings
   (d) Net income
   (e) Issuance of bonds
   (f) Payment of cash dividends
   (g) Purchase of treasury stock
   (h) Redemption of bonds
   (i) Sale of equipment
   (j) Issuance of preferred stock
   (k) Purchase of patents

7. Name the two alternatives to reporting cash flows from operating activities in the statement of cash flows.

8. What is the principal disadvantage of the direct method of reporting cash flows from operating activities?

9. What are the major advantages of the indirect method of reporting cash flows from operating activities?

10. On the statement of cash flows, if the cash inflows from investing activities exceed the cash outflows, how is the difference described?

11. On the statement of cash flows, if the cash outflows from investing activities exceed the cash inflows, how is the difference described?

12. On the statement of cash flows, if the cash inflows from financing activities exceed the cash outflows, how is the difference described?

13. On the statement of cash flows, if the cash outflows from financing activities exceed the cash inflows, how is the difference described?

14. A corporation issued $500,000 of common stock in exchange for $500,000 of plant assets. Where would this transaction be reported on the statement of cash flows?

15. A corporation acquired as a long-term investment all of the capital stock of Jackson Inc., valued at $10,000,000, by issuance of $10,000,000 of its own common stock. Where should the transaction be reported on the statement of cash flows?

16. (a) What is the effect on cash flows of the declaration and issuance of a stock dividend?
    (b) Is the stock dividend reported on the statement of cash flows?

17. On its income statement for the current year, a company reported a net loss of $30,000 from operations. On its statement of cash flows, it reported $15,000 of cash flows from operating activities. Explain the seeming contradiction between the loss and the cash flows.

18. What is the effect on cash flows of an appropriation of retained earnings for bonded indebtedness?

19. Indicate whether each of the following would be added to or deducted from net income in determining net cash flow from operating activities:
    (a) Depreciation of plant assets
    (b) Decrease in accounts payable
    (c) Gain on retirement of long-term debt
    (d) Increase in notes payable due in 120 days
    (e) Increase in notes receivable due in 90 days
    (f) Amortization of discount on bonds payable
    (g) Increase in merchandise inventory
    (h) Decrease in accounts receivable
    (i) Loss on disposal of plant assets
    (j) Decrease in accrued salaries payable
    (k) Amortization of bonds premium
    (l) Amortization of patents
    (m) Decrease in prepaid expenses

20. A retail enterprise, employing the accrual method of accounting, owed merchandise creditors (accounts payable) $175,000 at the beginning of the year and $192,000 at the end of the year. What adjustment for the $17,000 increase must be made to net income in determining the amount of cash flows from operating activities? Explain.

21. If revenue from sales amounted to $680,000 for the year and trade receivables totaled $55,000 and $75,000 at the beginning and end of the year respectively, what was the amount of cash received from customers during the year?

22. If salaries payable was $15,000 and $22,000 at the beginning and end of the year respectively, should $7,000 be added to or deducted from income to determine the amount of cash flows from operating activities? Explain.

23. The board of directors declared cash dividends totaling $90,000 during the current year. The comparative balance sheet indicates dividends payable of $20,000 at the beginning of the year and $22,500 at the end of the year. What was the amount of cash payments to stockholders during the year?

24. A long-term investment in bonds with a cost of $115,000 was sold for $127,500 cash. (a) What was the gain or loss on the sale? (b) What was the effect of the transaction on cash flows? (c) How should the transaction be reported in the statement of cash flows?

25. A corporation issued $1,000,000 of 20-year bonds for cash at 95. How would the transaction be reported on the statement of cash flows?

26. Fully depreciated equipment costing $150,000 was discarded. What was the effect of the transaction on cash flows if (a) $6,000 cash is received, (b) there is no salvage value?

Real World Focus

27. In its 1987 financial statements, Tosco Corporation reported the issuance of common stock in payment of $7,991,000 of long-term subordinated notes payable. How would this transaction be reported on the statement of cash flows?

EXERCISES

Exercise 18–1
Cash flows from operating activities section.

OBJ. 2, 3

The net income reported on the income statement for the current year was $110,000. Depreciation recorded on equipment and a building amounted to $21,300 for the year. Balances of the current asset and current liability accounts at the beginning and end of the year are as follows:

	End of Year	Beginning of Year
Cash	$ 73,350	$ 70,500
Trade receivables (net)	105,000	96,000
Inventories	132,000	114,000
Prepaid expenses	8,300	9,200
Accounts payable (merchandise creditors)	93,000	87,300
Salaries payable	4,500	7,500

Prepare the cash flows from operating activities section of the statement of cash flows.

Exercise 18–2
Cash flows from operating activities section.

OBJ. 2, 3

The net income reported on an income statement for the current year was $73,700. Depreciation recorded on store equipment for the year amounted to $23,800. Balances of the current asset and current liability accounts at the beginning and end of the year are as follows:

	End of Year	Beginning of Year
Cash	$55,800	$50,000
Trade receivable (net)	64,400	68,000
Merchandise inventory	88,000	77,600
Prepaid expenses	6,300	6,000
Accounts payable (merchandise creditors)	55,800	58,200
Wages payable	6,000	5,000

Prepare the cash flows from operating activities section of a statement of cash flows.

Exercise 18–3
Reporting changes in equipment on statement of cash flows.

OBJ. 2, 3

An analysis of the general ledger accounts indicated that office equipment, which had cost $120,000 and on which accumulated depreciation totaled $105,000 on the date of sale, was sold for $14,000 during the year. Using this information, indicate the items to be reported on the statement of cash flows.

Exercise 18-4

Reporting changes in equipment on statement of cash flows.

OBJ. 2, 3

An analysis of the general ledger accounts indicated that delivery equipment, which had cost $56,000 and on which accumulated depreciation totaled $47,600 on the date of sale, was sold for $11,200 during the year. Using this information, indicate the items to be reported on the statement of cash flows.

Exercise 18-5

Reporting land transactions on statement of cash flows.

OBJ. 2, 3

On the basis of the details of the following plant asset account, indicate the items to be reported on the statement of cash flows.

ACCOUNT LAND   ACCOUNT NO.

Date		Item	Debit	Credit	Balance Debit	Balance Credit
19--						
Jan.	1	Balance			800,000	
Aug.	29	Purchased for cash	250,000			
Nov.	20	Sold for $80,000		50,000	1,000,000	

Exercise 18-6

Reporting stockholders' equity items on statement of cash flows.

OBJ. 2, 3

On the basis of the following stockholders' equity accounts, indicate the items, exclusive of net income, to be reported on the statement of cash flows. There were no unpaid dividends at either the beginning or end of the year.

ACCOUNT COMMON STOCK, $10 PAR   ACCOUNT NO.

Date		Item	Debit	Credit	Balance Debit	Balance Credit
19--						
Jan.	1	Balance, 65,000 shares				650,000
	20	10,000 shares issued for cash		100,000		
June	25	3,750-share stock dividend		37,500		787,500

ACCOUNT PAID-IN CAPITAL IN EXCESS OF PAR—COMMON STOCK   ACCOUNT NO.

Date		Item	Debit	Credit	Balance Debit	Balance Credit
19--						
Jan.	1	Balance				75,000
	20	10,000 shares issued for cash		20,000		
June	25	Stock dividend		7,500		102,500

ACCOUNT RETAINED EARNINGS   ACCOUNT NO.

Date		Item	Debit	Credit	Balance Debit	Balance Credit
19--						
Jan.	1	Balance				300,000
June	25	Stock dividend	45,000			
Dec.	15	Cash dividend	75,000			
	31	Net income		158,500		338,500

Exercise 18–7
Reporting land acquisition for cash and mortgage note on statement of cash flows.
OBJ. 2, 3

On the basis of the details of the following asset account, indicate the items to be reported on the statement of cash flows.

ACCOUNT LAND   ACCOUNT NO.

Date		Item	Debit	Credit	Balance Debit	Balance Credit
19--						
Jan.	1	Balance			400,000	
Mar.	2	Purchased for cash	40,000			
Oct.	29	Purchased with long-term				
		mortgage note	60,000		500,000	

Exercise 18–8
Determination of net income from net cash flow from operating activities.
OBJ. 2, 3

Brown Inc. reported a net cash flow from operating activities of $46,500 on its statement of cash flows for the year ended December 31, 1990. The following information was reported in the cash flows from operating activities section of the statement of cash flows:

Decrease in income tax payable...	$ 500
Decrease in inventories..	4,000
Depreciation	9,400
Gain on sale of investments..	15,000
Increase in accounts payable	8,800
Increase in prepaid expenses..	700
Increase in accounts receivable	4,500

Determine the net income reported by Brown Inc. for the year ended December 31, 1990.

Appendix Exercise 18–9
Cash flows from operating activities section.

The income statement of Hackett Company for the current year ended June 30 is as follows:

Sales		$1,030,000
Cost of merchandise sold.....................................		620,000
Gross profit..		$ 410,000
Operating expenses:		
Depreciation expense......................................	$ 31,500	
Other operating expenses	248,500	
Total operating expenses		280,000
Income before income tax		$ 130,000
Income tax..		40,000
Net income		$ 90,000

Changes in the balance of selected accounts from the beginning to the end of the current year are as follows:

	Increase (Decrease)
Trade receivables (net)	$(21,000)
Inventories...	11,200
Prepaid expenses..	(1,050)
Accounts payable (merchandise creditors)..................	(17,500)
Accrued operating expenses	7,000
Income tax payable..	(2,100)

Prepare the cash flows from operating activities section of the statement of cash flows, using the direct method of presentation.

**Appendix
Exercise 18–10**
Cash flows from
operating activities
section.

The income statement for Morrow Co. for the current year ended August 31 and the balances of selected accounts at the end and beginning of the year are as follows:

Sales		$200,000
Cost of merchandise sold		125,000
Gross profit		$ 75,000
Operating expenses:		
Depreciation expense	$12,500	
Other operating expenses	43,000	
Total operating expenses		55,500
Income before income tax		$ 19,500
Income tax		2,600
Net income		$ 16,900

	End of Year	Beginning of Year
Trade receivables (net)	$19,600	$17,800
Inventories	21,100	23,000
Prepaid expenses	900	600
Accounts payable (merchandise creditors)	13,500	15,000
Accrued operating expenses	1,800	1,200
Income tax payable	600	400

Prepare the cash flows from operating activities section of the statement of cash flows, using the direct method of presentation.

**Appendix
Exercise 18–11**
Cash flows from
operating activities
section.

The income statement for the current year and balances of selected accounts at the beginning and end of the current year are as follows:

Sales		$650,200
Cost of merchandise sold		382,500
Gross profit		$267,700
Operating expenses:		
Depreciation expense	$ 24,200	
Other operating expenses	160,300	
Total operating expenses		184,500
Income before income tax		$ 83,200
Income tax		17,800
Net income		$ 65,400

	End of Year	Beginning of Year
Trade receivables	$65,600	$60,000
Inventories	82,500	71,500
Prepaid expenses	5,180	5,740
Accounts payable (merchandise creditors)	57,900	54,500
Accrued operating expenses	2,810	4,690
Income tax payable	800	800

Prepare the cash flows from operating activities section of the statement of cash flows, using the direct method of presentation.

**Appendix
Exercise 18–12**
Cash flows from
operating activities
section.

The income statement for the current year and the balances of selected accounts at the beginning and end of the current year are as follows:

Sales		$1,170,000
Cost of merchandise sold		684,000
Gross profit		$ 486,000
Operating expenses:		
Depreciation expense	$ 39,150	
Other operating expenses	331,100	
Total operating expenses		370,250
Operating income		$ 115,750
Other expense:		
Interest expense		8,100
Income before income tax		$ 107,650
Income tax		27,100
Net income		$ 80,550

	End of Year	Beginning of Year
Accounts receivables (trade)	$ 72,500	$76,500
Inventories	100,000	87,300
Prepaid expenses	7,110	6,700
Accounts payable		
(merchandise creditors)	62,730	65,430
Accrued operating expenses	6,750	5,650
Interest payable	1,400	1,400
Income tax payable	2,250	3,600

Prepare the cash flows from operating activities section of the statement of cash flows, using the direct method of presentation.

PROBLEMS

Series A

Problem 18–1A
Statement of cash
flows.

OBJ. 3

The comparative balance sheet of C. W. Dodson Inc. for December 31, 1990 and 1989, is as follows:

Assets	Dec. 31, 1990	Dec. 31, 1989
Cash	$ 100,800	$ 70,700
Trade receivables (net)	123,200	112,000
Inventories	150,300	128,100
Investments	—	80,000
Land	70,000	—
Equipment	854,300	704,200
Accumulated depreciation	(208,600)	(159,600)
	$1,090,000	$935,400

Liabilities and Stockholders' Equity		
Accounts payable (merchandise creditors)	$ 74,400	$ 70,000
Accrued operating expenses	5,400	7,000
Dividends payable	21,000	14,000
Common stock, $40 par	450,000	350,000
Excess of issue price over par — common stock	23,800	16,800
Retained earnings	515,400	477,600
	$1,090,000	$935,400

The following additional information was taken from Dodson's records:

(a) The investments were sold for $85,000 cash.
(b) Equipment and land were acquired for cash.
(c) There were no disposals of equipment during the year.
(d) The common stock was issued for cash.
(e) There was a $90,300 credit to Retained Earnings for net income.
(f) There was a $52,500 debit to Retained Earnings for cash dividends declared.

Instructions:

Prepare a statement of cash flows.

Problem 18–2A
Statement of cash flows.

OBJ. 3

The comparative balance sheet of Wong Corporation at December 31, 1990 and 1989, is as follows:

Assets	Dec. 31, 1990	Dec. 31, 1989
Cash..	$ 78,900	$ 64,600
Trade receivables (net)	70,300	73,700
Merchandise inventory..	122,900	97,400
Prepaid expenses	6,660	5,860
Plant assets	472,440	425,240
Accumulated depreciation—plant assets................	(138,500)	(157,500)
	$612,700	$509,300

Liabilities and Stockholders' Equity		
Accounts payable (merchandise creditors)...............	$ 70,100	$ 53,500
Mortgage note payable..	—	60,000
Common stock, $50 par...	300,000	250,000
Excess of issue price over par—common stock	34,500	31,500
Retained earnings..	208,100	114,300
	$612,700	$509,300

Additional data obtained from the income statement and from an examination of the accounts in the ledger are as follows:

(a) Net income, $108,800.
(b) Depreciation reported on the income statement, $34,600.
(c) An addition to the building was constructed at a cost of $100,800, and fully depreciated equipment costing $53,600 was discarded, with no salvage realized.
(d) The mortgage note payable was not due until 1999, but the terms permitted earlier payment without penalty.
(e) 1,000 shares of common stock were issued at 53 for cash.
(f) Cash dividends declared and paid, $15,000.

Instructions:

Prepare a statement of cash flows.

Problem 18–3A
Statement of cash flows.
OBJ. 3

The comparative balance sheet of Monique Corporation at December 31, 1990 and 1989, is as follows:

Assets	Dec. 31, 1990	Dec. 31, 1989
Cash	$ 58,900	$ 50,800
Trade receivables (net)	90,300	74,200
Inventories	121,600	131,700
Prepaid expenses	4,400	3,100
Land	65,000	65,000
Buildings	381,500	291,500
Accumulated depreciation—buildings	(154,600)	(143,400)
Machinery and equipment	302,500	302,500
Accumulated depreciation—machinery and equipment	(101,200)	(71,500)
Patents	30,800	38,500
	$799,200	$742,400

Liabilities and Stockholders' Equity		
Accounts payable (merchandise creditors)	$ 58,000	$ 88,000
Dividends payable	9,400	8,250
Salaries payable	5,000	5,450
Mortgage note payable, due 1999	55,000	—
Bonds payable	—	110,000
Common stock, $20 par	450,000	350,000
Excess of issue price over par—common stock	80,000	70,000
Retained earnings	141,800	110,700
	$799,200	$742,400

An examination of the income statement and the accounting records revealed the following additional information applicable to 1990:

(a) Net income, $56,100.
(b) Depreciation expense reported on the income statement: buildings, $11,200; machinery and equipment, $29,700.
(c) A building was constructed for $90,000 cash.
(d) Patent amortization reported on the income statement, $7,700.
(e) A mortgage note for $55,000 was issued for cash.
(f) 5,000 shares of common stock were issued at 22 in exchange for the bonds payable.
(g) Cash dividends declared, $25,000.

Instructions:

Prepare a statement of cash flows.

Problem 18–4A
Statement of cash flows.
OBJ. 3

The comparative balance sheet of Pauley Inc. at December 31, 1990 and 1989, is as follows:

Assets	Dec. 31, 1990	Dec. 31, 1989
Cash	$ 33,700	$ 36,300
Trade receivables (net)	66,300	59,600
Inventories	131,250	115,500
Prepaid expenses	3,850	4,100
Investments	—	45,000
Land	28,500	28,500
Buildings	190,000	126,000
Accumulated depreciation—buildings	(46,200)	(41,400)
Equipment	284,000	237,300
Accumulated depreciation—equipment	(86,100)	(77,400)
	$605,300	$533,500

Liabilities and Stockholders' Equity

Accounts payable (merchandise creditors)...............	$ 38,700	$ 48,300
Income tax payable..	3,600	2,800
Bonds payable..	50,000	—
Discount on bonds payable.................................	(2,900)	—
Common stock, $20 par.......................................	315,000	300,000
Excess of issue price over par—common stock	40,200	33,000
Appropriation for plant expansion	50,000	30,000
Retained earnings..	110,700	119,400
	$605,300	$533,500

The noncurrent asset, the noncurrent liability, and the stockholders' equity accounts for 1990 are as follows:

ACCOUNT INVESTMENTS   ACCOUNT NO.

Date		Item	Debit	Credit	Balance Debit	Balance Credit
1990						
Jan.	1	Balance			45,000	
July	23	Realized $40,500 cash from sale		45,000	—	—

ACCOUNT LAND   ACCOUNT NO.

Date		Item	Debit	Credit	Balance Debit	Balance Credit
1990						
Jan.	1	Balance			28,500	

ACCOUNT BUILDINGS   ACCOUNT NO.

Date		Item	Debit	Credit	Balance Debit	Balance Credit
1990						
Jan.	1	Balance			126,000	
July	1	Acquired for cash	64,000		190,000	

ACCOUNT ACCUMULATED DEPRECIATION—BUILDINGS   ACCOUNT NO.

Date		Item	Debit	Credit	Balance Debit	Balance Credit
1990						
Jan.	1	Balance				41,400
Dec.	31	Depreciation for year		4,800		46,200

ACCOUNT EQUIPMENT   ACCOUNT NO.

Date		Item	Debit	Credit	Balance Debit	Balance Credit
1990						
Jan.	1	Balance			237,300	
Apr.	3	Discarded, no salvage		21,000		
Oct.	10	Purchased for cash	40,000			
Dec.	1	Purchased for cash	27,700		284,000	

ACCOUNT ACCUMULATED DEPRECIATION—EQUIPMENT   ACCOUNT NO.

Date		Item	Debit	Credit	Balance Debit	Balance Credit
1990						
Jan.	1	Balance				77,400
Apr.	3	Equipment discarded	21,000			
Dec.	31	Depreciation for year		29,700		86,100

ACCOUNT BONDS PAYABLE   ACCOUNT NO.

Date		Item	Debit	Credit	Balance Debit	Balance Credit
1990						
May	1	Issued 20-year bonds		50,000		50,000

ACCOUNT DISCOUNT ON BONDS PAYABLE   ACCOUNT NO.

Date		Item	Debit	Credit	Balance Debit	Balance Credit
1990						
May	1	Bonds issued	3,000		3,000	
Dec.	31	Amortization		100	2,900	

ACCOUNT COMMON STOCK, $20 PAR   ACCOUNT NO.

Date		Item	Debit	Credit	Balance Debit	Balance Credit
1990						
Jan.	1	Balance				300,000
Aug.	4	Stock dividend		15,000		315,000

ACCOUNT PAID-IN CAPITAL IN EXCESS OF PAR—COMMON STOCK ACCOUNT NO.

Date		Item	Debit	Credit	Balance Debit	Balance Credit
1990						
Jan.	1	Balance				33,000
Aug.	4	Stock dividend		7,200		40,200

ACCOUNT APPROPRIATION FOR PLANT EXPANSION   ACCOUNT NO.

Date		Item	Debit	Credit	Balance Debit	Balance Credit
1990						
Jan.	1	Balance				30,000
Dec.	31	Appropriation		20,000		50,000

ACCOUNT RETAINED EARNINGS　　　　　　　　　　　　ACCOUNT NO.

Date		Item	Debit	Credit	Balance Debit	Balance Credit
1990						
Jan.	1	Balance				119,400
Aug.	4	Stock dividend	22,200			
Dec.	31	Net income		52,400		
	31	Cash dividends	18,900			
	31	Appropriated	20,000			110,700

Instructions:

Prepare a statement of cash flows.

Problem 18–5A
Statement of cash flows.
OBJ. 3

An income statement and a comparative balance sheet for Rogers Company are as follows:

Rogers Company
Income Statement
For Current Year Ended December 31, 1990

Sales		$1,203,100
Cost of merchandise sold.......................................		772,800
Gross profit..		$ 430,300
Operating expenses (including depreciation of $39,990)		275,750
Income from operations		$ 154,550
Other income:		
Gain on sale of land..	$18,750	
Gain on sale of investments.................................	9,350	
Interest income..	2,000	30,100
		$ 184,650
Interest expense..		30,000
Income before income tax		$ 154,650
Income tax...		43,250
Net income		$ 111,400

Rogers Company
Comparative Balance Sheet
December 31, 1990 and 1989

Assets	1990	1989
Cash..	$ 49,870	$ 58,200
Trade receivables (net)	137,180	117,800
Inventories..	211,500	190,150
Prepaid expenses	5,160	6,120
Investments	34,250	93,500
Land..	87,500	75,000
Buildings..	412,500	225,000
Accumulated depreciation—buildings..................	(91,260)	(81,220)
Equipment	493,700	437,500
Accumulated depreciation—equipment...............	(179,700)	(149,750)
Total assets..	$1,160,700	$972,300

Liabilities and Stockholders' Equity		
Accounts payable (merchandise creditors)............	$ 70,340	$ 63,000
Income tax payable...	6,250	9,750
Dividends payable	15,660	12,500
Mortgage note payable....................................	175,000	—
Bonds payable...	100,000	250,000
Common stock, $50 par....................................	450,000	375,000
Excess of issue price over par—common stock	47,250	41,250
Retained earnings..	296,200	220,800
Total liabilities and stockholders' equity..............	$1,160,700	$972,300

The following additional information on cash flows during the year was obtained from an examination of the ledger:

(a) Investments (long-term) were purchased for $34,500.
(b) Investments (long-term) were sold for $103,100.
(c) Equipment was purchased for $56,200. There were no disposals.
(d) A building valued at $187,500 and land valued at $62,500 were acquired by a cash payment of $250,000.
(e) Land which cost $50,000 was sold for $68,750 cash.
(f) A mortgage note payable for $175,000 was issued for cash.
(g) Bonds payable of $150,000 were retired by the payment of their face amount.
(h) 1,500 shares of common stock were issued for cash at 54.
(i) Cash dividends of $36,000 were declared.

Instructions:

Prepare a statement of cash flows.

Problem 18–6A
Real World Focus.
OBJ. 2, 3

The current asset and current liability sections of the January 31, 1988 and 1987 balance sheets of Toys "R" Us, Inc. are as follows (dollars in thousands):

	1988	1987
Current assets:		
Cash and equivalents..	$ 45,996	$ 84,379
Receivables..	62,144	37,502
Merchandise inventories.....................................	772,833	528,939
Prepaid expenses..	5,050	3,566
Total current assets...	$886,023	$654,386
Current liabilities:		
Notes payable...	$ 17,657	—
Accounts payable...	403,105	$305,705
Accrued expenses..	167,280	118,260
Federal income taxes payable..............................	71,003	73,059
Current portion of long-term debt and other liabilities....	1,947	1,941
Total current liabilities	$660,992	$498,965

Selected data from Toys "R" Us, Inc.'s 1988 income statement (dollars in thousands) were as follows:

Net income	$203,922
Depreciation and amortization...	43,716
Deferred income taxes (expense)	13,035

Instructions:

Prepare the cash flows from operating activities section of the statement of cash flows for Toys "R" Us, Inc. for the year ended January 31, 1988.

Appendix Problem 18–7A
Statement of cash flows, applying the direct method to Problem 18–1A.

The comparative balance sheet of C. W. Dodson Inc. for December 31, 1990 and 1989, is as follows:

Assets	Dec. 31, 1990	Dec. 31, 1989
Cash	$ 100,800	$ 70,700
Trade receivables (net)	123,200	112,000
Inventories	150,300	128,100
Investments	—	80,000
Land	70,000	—
Equipment	854,300	704,200
Accumulated depreciation	(208,600)	(159,600)
	$1,090,000	$935,400

Liabilities and Stockholders' Equity		
Accounts payable (merchandise creditors)	$ 74,400	$ 70,000
Accrued operating expenses	5,400	7,000
Dividends payable	21,000	14,000
Common stock, $40 par	450,000	350,000
Excess of issue price over par—common stock	23,800	16,800
Retained earnings	515,400	477,600
	$1,090,000	$935,400

The income statement for the year ended December 31, 1990, is as follows:

Sales		$1,287,300
Cost of merchandise sold		770,000
Gross profit		$ 517,300
Operating expenses:		
Depreciation expense	$ 49,000	
Other operating expenses	364,000	
Total operating expenses		413,000
Operating income		$ 104,300
Other income:		
Gain on sale of investments		5,000
Income before income tax		$ 109,300
Income tax		19,000
Net income		$ 90,300

The following additional information was taken from C. W. Dodson's records:

(a) The investments were sold for $85,000 cash at the beginning of the year.
(b) Equipment and land were acquired for cash.
(c) There were no disposals of equipment during the year.
(d) The common stock was issued for cash.
(e) There was a $52,500 debit to Retained Earnings for cash dividends declared.

Instructions:

Prepare a statement of cash flows, using the direct method of presenting cash flows from operating activities.

Appendix
Problem 18–8A
Statement of cash flows, applying the direct method to Problem 18–1B.

The comparative balance sheet of T. E. Harber Inc. for June 30, 1990 and 1989, is as follows:

Assets	June 30, 1990	June 30, 1989
Cash..	$ 77,000	$ 59,800
Trade receivables (net)	109,800	96,000
Inventories...	127,100	108,600
Investments	—	90,000
Land...	102,000	—
Equipment...	426,000	330,000
Accumulated depreciation....................................	(178,800)	(142,800)
	$663,100	$541,600

Liabilities and Stockholders' Equity		
Accounts payable (merchandise creditors)..............	$ 68,900	$ 61,000
Accrued operating expenses	6,100	5,000
Dividends payable	14,400	12,000
Common stock, $20 par...	360,000	300,000
Excess of issue price over par—common stock	26,400	14,400
Retained earnings..	187,300	149,200
	$663,100	$541,600

The income statement for the year ended June 30, 1990, is as follows:

Sales		$1,194,000
Cost of merchandise sold...................................		708,900
Gross profit...		$ 485,100
Operating expenses:		
Depreciation expense......................................	$ 36,000	
Other operating expenses	336,000	
Total operating expenses		372,000
Operating income		$ 113,100
Other income:		
Gain on sale of investments............................		8,000
Income before income tax		$ 121,100
Income tax...		29,000
Net income		$ 92,100

The following additional information was taken from the records of T. E. Harber Inc.:

(a) Equipment and land were acquired for cash.
(b) There were no disposals of equipment during the year.
(c) The investments were sold for $98,000.
(d) The common stock was issued for cash.
(e) There was a $54,000 debit to Retained Earnings for cash dividends declared.

Instructions:

Prepare a statement of cash flows, using the direct method of presenting cash flows from operating activities.

Problem 18–1B
Statement of cash flows.
OBJ. 3

The comparative balance sheet of T. E. Harber Inc. for June 30, 1990 and 1989, is as follows:

Assets	June 30, 1990	June 30, 1989
Cash	$ 77,000	$ 59,800
Trade receivables (net)	109,800	96,000
Inventories	127,100	108,600
Investments	—	90,000
Land	102,000	—
Equipment	426,000	330,000
Accumulated depreciation	(178,800)	(142,800)
	$663,100	$541,600

Liabilities and Stockholders' Equity		
Accounts payable (merchandise creditors)	$ 68,900	$ 61,000
Accrued operating expenses	6,100	5,000
Dividends payable	14,400	12,000
Common stock, $20 par	360,000	300,000
Excess of issue price over par—common stock	26,400	14,400
Retained earnings	187,300	149,200
	$663,100	$541,600

The following additional information was taken from the records of T. E. Harber:

(a) Equipment and land were acquired for cash.
(b) There were no disposals of equipment during the year.
(c) The investments were sold for $98,000 cash.
(d) The common stock was issued for cash.
(e) There was a $92,100 credit to Retained Earnings for net income.
(f) There was a $54,000 debit to Retained Earnings for cash dividends declared.

Instructions:

Prepare a statement of cash flows.

Problem 18–2B
Statement of cash flows.
OBJ. 3

The comparative balance sheet of Lee Inc. at June 30, 1990 and 1989, is as follows:

Assets	June 30, 1990	June 30, 1989
Cash	$ 55,100	$ 74,600
Trade receivables (net)	115,300	128,300
Merchandise inventory	344,700	336,400
Prepaid expenses	5,200	3,600
Plant assets	434,000	390,800
Accumulated depreciation—plant assets	(232,300)	(266,600)
	$722,000	$667,100

Liabilities and Stockholders' Equity		
Accounts payable (merchandise creditors)	$ 72,300	$ 66,400
Mortgage note payable	—	101,300
Common stock, $30 par	300,000	270,000
Excess of issue price over par—common stock	38,800	33,800
Retained earnings	310,900	195,600
	$722,000	$667,100

Additional data obtained from the income statement and from an examination of the accounts in the ledger are as follows:

(a) Net income, $133,800.
(b) Depreciation reported on the income statement, $38,600.
(c) An addition to the building was constructed at a cost of $116,100, and fully depreciated equipment costing $72,900 was discarded, with no salvage realized.
(d) The mortgage note payable was not due until 1998, but the terms permitted earlier payment without penalty.
(e) 1,000 shares of common stock were issued at 35 for cash.
(f) Cash dividends declared and paid, $18,500.

Instructions:

Prepare a statement of cash flows.

Problem 18–3B
Statement of cash flows.

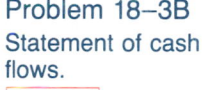

The comparative balance sheet of M. S. Terrell Corporation at December 31, 1990 and 1989, is as follows:

Assets	Dec. 31, 1990	Dec. 31, 1989
Cash	$ 67,400	$ 61,800
Trade receivables (net)	87,900	100,500
Inventories	195,100	178,600
Prepaid expenses	3,400	2,900
Land	75,000	75,000
Buildings	480,600	316,800
Accumulated depreciation—buildings	(157,500)	(144,000)
Machinery and equipment	206,300	206,300
Accumulated depreciation—machinery and equipment	(98,000)	(81,300)
Patents	35,000	37,500
	$895,200	$754,100

Liabilities and Stockholders' Equity		
Accounts payable (merchandise creditors)	$ 27,200	$ 38,900
Dividends payable	18,800	15,000
Salaries payable	7,900	14,600
Mortgage note payable, due 1995	120,000	—
Bonds payable	—	70,000
Common stock, $15 par	412,500	360,000
Excess of issue price over par—common stock	57,500	40,000
Retained earnings	251,300	215,600
	$895,200	$754,100

An examination of the income statement and the accounting records revealed the following additional information applicable to 1990:

(a) Net income, $63,200.
(b) Depreciation expense reported on the income statement: buildings, $13,500; machinery and equipment, $16,700.
(c) Patent amortization reported on the income statement, $2,500.
(d) A building was constructed for $163,800.
(e) A mortgage note for $120,000 was issued for cash.
(f) 3,500 shares of common stock were issued at 20 in exchange for the bonds payable.
(g) Cash dividends declared, $27,500.

Instructions:

Prepare a statement of cash flows.

Problem 18–4B
Statement of cash flows.

The comparative balance sheet of M. T. Wade Inc. at December 31, 1990 and 1989, is as follows:

Assets	Dec. 31, 1990	Dec. 31, 1989
Cash	$ 117,100	$ 101,400
Trade receivables (net)	168,600	150,300
Income tax refund receivable	9,000	—
Inventories	257,000	270,800
Prepaid expenses	9,300	11,100
Investments	90,000	250,000
Land	130,000	180,000
Buildings	780,000	450,000
Accumulated depreciation—buildings	(207,700)	(193,800)
Equipment	608,400	470,400
Accumulated depreciation—equipment	(218,000)	(205,700)
	$1,743,700	$1,484,500

Liabilities and Stockholders' Equity		
Accounts payable (merchandise creditors)	$ 96,000	$ 108,720
Income tax payable	—	10,880
Bonds payable	350,000	—
Discount on bonds payable	(29,000)	—
Common stock, $5 par	630,000	600,000
Excess of issue price over par—common stock	81,000	72,000
Appropriation for plant expansion	250,000	200,000
Retained earnings	365,700	492,900
	$1,743,700	$1,484,500

The noncurrent asset, the noncurrent liability, and the stockholders' equity accounts for 1990 are as follows:

ACCOUNT   INVESTMENTS   ACCOUNT NO.

Date		Item	Debit	Credit	Balance Debit	Balance Credit
1990						
Jan.	1	Balance			250,000	
Apr.	10	Realized $180,000 cash from sale		160,000	90,000	—

ACCOUNT   LAND   ACCOUNT NO.

Date		Item	Debit	Credit	Balance Debit	Balance Credit
1990						
Jan.	1	Balance			180,000	
July	8	Realized $62,500 cash from sale		50,000	130,000	

ACCOUNT   BUILDINGS   ACCOUNT NO.

Date		Item	Debit	Credit	Balance Debit	Balance Credit
1990						
Jan.	1	Balance			450,000	
June	30	Acquired for cash	330,000		780,000	

ACCOUNT ACCUMULATED DEPRECIATION — BUILDINGS   ACCOUNT NO.

Date		Item	Debit	Credit	Balance Debit	Balance Credit
1990						
Jan.	1	Balance				193,800
Dec.	31	Depreciation for year		13,900		207,700

ACCOUNT EQUIPMENT   ACCOUNT NO.

Date		Item	Debit	Credit	Balance Debit	Balance Credit
1990						
Jan.	1	Balance			470,400	
Feb.	5	Discarded, no salvage		48,000		
Aug.	8	Purchased for cash	96,000			
Sept.	30	Purchased for cash	90,000		608,400	

ACCOUNT ACCUMULATED DEPRECIATION — EQUIPMENT   ACCOUNT NO.

Date		Item	Debit	Credit	Balance Debit	Balance Credit
1990						
Jan.	1	Balance				205,700
Feb.	5	Equipment discarded	48,000			
Dec.	31	Depreciation for year		60,300		218,000

ACCOUNT BONDS PAYABLE   ACCOUNT NO.

Date		Item	Debit	Credit	Balance Debit	Balance Credit
1990						
May	1	Issued 20-year bonds		350,000		350,000

ACCOUNT DISCOUNT ON BONDS PAYABLE   ACCOUNT NO.

Date		Item	Debit	Credit	Balance Debit	Balance Credit
1990						
May	1	Bonds issued	30,000		30,000	
Dec.	31	Amortization		1,000	29,000	

ACCOUNT COMMON STOCK, $5 PAR   ACCOUNT NO.

Date		Item	Debit	Credit	Balance Debit	Balance Credit
1990						
Jan.	1	Balance				600,000
Nov.	1	Stock dividend		30,000		630,000

ACCOUNT PAID-IN CAPITAL IN EXCESS OF PAR — COMMON STOCK ACCOUNT NO.

Date		Item	Debit	Credit	Balance Debit	Balance Credit
1990						
Jan.	1	Balance				72,000
Nov.	1	Stock dividend		9,000		81,000

ACCOUNT APPROPRIATION FOR PLANT EXPANSION   ACCOUNT NO.

Date		Item	Debit	Credit	Balance Debit	Balance Credit
1990						
Jan.	1	Balance				200,000
Dec.	31	Appropriation		50,000		250,000

ACCOUNT RETAINED EARNINGS   ACCOUNT NO.

Date		Item	Debit	Credit	Balance Debit	Balance Credit
1990						
Jan.	1	Balance				492,900
Nov.	1	Stock dividend	39,000			
Dec.	31	Net loss	8,200			
	31	Cash dividends	30,000			
	31	Appropriated	50,000			365,700

Instructions:

Prepare a statement of cash flows.

MINI-CASE 18

a.j. jenkins inc.

Ann Jenkins is the president and majority shareholder of A. J. Jenkins Inc., a small retail store chain. Recently, Jenkins submitted a loan application for A. J. Jenkins Inc. to Broad State Bank. It called for a $200,000, 12%, 10-year loan to help finance the construction of a building and the purchase of store equipment costing a total of $250,000 to enable A. J. Jenkins Inc. to open a store in Cedartown. Land for this purpose was acquired last year. The bank's loan officer requested a statement of cash flows in addition to the most recent income statement, balance sheet, and retained earnings statement that Jenkins had submitted with the loan application.

As a close family friend, Jenkins asked you to prepare a statement of cash flows. From the records provided, you prepared the following statement:

A. J. Jenkins Inc.
Statement of Cash Flows
For Year Ended December 31, 19--

Cash flows from operating activities:			
Net income, per income statement		$ 45,000	
Add: Depreciation.................................	$28,600		
Decrease in trade receivables	10,800	39,400	
		$ 84,400	
Deduct: Increase in inventory	$ 9,000		
Increase in prepaid expenses.......	600		
Decrease in accounts payable......	2,400		
Gain on sale of investments.........	6,000	18,000	
Net cash flow from operating activities			$66,400
Cash flows from investing activities:			
Cash received from investments sold..........		$ 42,000	
Less: Cash paid for purchase of store equipment		35,000	
Net cash flow from investing activities.........			7,000
Cash flows from financing activities:			
Cash paid for dividends...........................		$(20,000)	
Net cash flow used for financing activities....			(20,000)
Increase in cash			$ 53,400
Cash at the beginning of the year			19,500
Cash at the end of the year			$ 72,900

Schedule of Noncash Investing and Financing Activities

Issuance of common stock at par for land.....................................	$50,000

After reviewing the statement, Jenkins telephoned you and commented, "Are you sure this statement is right?" Jenkins then raised the following questions:

(a) "How can depreciation be a cash flow?"
(b) "The issuance of common stock for the land is listed in a separate schedule. This transaction has nothing to do with cash! Shouldn't this transaction be eliminated from the statement?"
(c) "How can the gain on sale of investments be a deduction from net income in determining the cash flow from operating activities?"
(d) "Why does the bank need this statement anyway? They can compute the increase in cash from the balance sheets for the last two years."

After jotting down Jenkins' questions, you assured her that this statement was "right". However, to alleviate Jenkins' concern, you arranged a meeting for the following day.

Instructions:

(1) How would you respond to each of Jenkins' questions?
(2) Do you think that the statement of cash flows enhances the chances of A. J. Jenkins Inc. receiving the loan? Discuss.

ETHICS DISCUSSION CASE	Lee Curtis, controller of Tish Inc., has decided to add "cash flow per share" to the financial statements. He feels that such reporting, although different from past reporting, would be useful to the readers. The "cash flow per share" would be reported on the statement of cash flows. On a comparative basis with the preceding year, the "cash flow per share" figure for the current year increased by 35% (as contrasted with a slight decline in net income and earnings per share). Discuss whether Lee Curtis is behaving in an ethical manner.

ANSWERS TO SELF-EXAMINATION QUESTIONS

1. **D** A full set of financial statements for a corporation includes a balance sheet (answer A), an income statement (answer B), a statement of cash flows (answer C), and a statement of retained earnings.

2. **D** Cash flows from operating activities relate to transactions that enter into the determination of net income (answer D). Receipts of cash from the sale of capital stock (answer A) and the sale of bonds (answer B) and payments of cash for dividends (answer C) are cash flows from financing activities.

3. **A** Cash flows from investing activities include receipts from the sale of noncurrent assets, such as equipment (answer A) and payments for the acquisition of noncurrent assets. Receipts of cash from the sale of capital stock (answer B) and payments of cash for dividends (answer C) and for the repurchase of equity securities (answer D) are cash flows from financing activities.

4. **D** Cash flows from financing activities include receipts from the issuance of equity (answer A) and debt (answer B) securities and payments for dividends (answer C), repurchase of equity securities, and redemption of debt securities.

5. **D** The cash flows from operating activities section of the statement of cash flows would report net cash flow from operating activities of $65,500, determined as follows:

Net income		$55,000
Add:		
Depreciation	$22,000	
Decrease in inventories	5,000	
Decrease in prepaid expenses	500	27,500
		$82,500
Deduct:		
Increase in trade receivables	$10,000	
Decrease in accounts payable	7,000	17,000
Net cash flow from operating activities		$65,500

CHAPTER NINETEEN
FINANCIAL STATEMENT ANALYSIS AND ANNUAL REPORTS

CHAPTER OBJECTIVES

1 Describe basic financial statement analytical procedures.

2 Describe the focus of financial statement analyses.

3 Describe and illustrate the application of financial statement analysis in assessing solvency.

4 Describe and illustrate the application of financial statement analysis in assessing profitability.

5 Summarize and describe how analytical measures can be used in appraising the present performance of an enterprise and in forecasting its future.

6 Identify and illustrate the content of corporate annual reports.

The financial condition and the results of operations of business enterprises are of interest to many groups, including owners, managers, creditors, governmental agencies, employees, and prospective owners and creditors. The principal financial statements, together with supplementary statements and schedules, present much of the basic information needed to make sound economic decisions regarding business enterprises. In this chapter, the various ways in which financial statement data can be analyzed to assist in making these decisions will be discussed. In addition, annual reports that are issued by corporations and that contain the basic financial statements, a summary of activities for the past year, and an indication of plans for the future are discussed. These annual reports often contain some financial analyses as well as much of the basic information needed for additional analyses that can be used to make economic decisions regarding business enterprises.

BASIC ANALYTICAL PROCEDURES

OBJECTIVE 1
Describe basic financial statement analytical procedures.

The analytical measures obtained from financial statements are usually expressed as ratios or percentages. For example, the relationship of $150,000 to $100,000 ($150,000/$100,000 or $150,000:$100,000) may be expressed as 1.5, 1.5:1, or 150%. This ease of computation and simplicity of form for expressing financial relationships are major reasons for the widespread use of ratios and percentages in financial analysis.

Analytical procedures may be used to compare the amount of specific items on a current statement with the corresponding amounts on earlier statements. For example, in comparing cash of $150,000 on the current balance sheet with cash of $100,000 on the balance sheet of a year earlier, the current amount may be expressed as 1.5 or 150% of the earlier amount. The relationship may also be expressed in terms of change, that is, the increase of $50,000 may be stated as a 50% increase.

745

Analytical procedures are also widely used to show the relationships of individual items to each other and of individual items to totals on a single statement. To illustrate, assume that included in the total of $1,000,000 of assets on a balance sheet are cash of $50,000 and inventories of $250,000. In relative terms, the cash balance is 5% of total assets and the inventories represent 25% of total assets. Individual items in the current asset group could also be related to total current assets. Assuming that the total of current assets in the example is $500,000, cash represents 10% of the total and inventories represent 50% of the total.

Increases or decreases in items may be expressed in percentage terms only when the base figure is positive. If the base figure is zero or a negative value, the amount of change cannot be expressed as a percentage. For example, if comparative balance sheets indicate no liability for notes payable on the first, or base, date and a liability of $10,000 on the later date, the increase of $10,000 cannot be stated as a percent of zero. Similarly, if a net loss of $10,000 in a particular year is followed by a net income of $5,000 in the next year, the increase of $15,000 cannot be stated as a percent of the loss of the base year.

In the following discussion and illustrations of analytical procedures, the basic significance of the various measures will be emphasized. The measures developed are not ends in themselves; they are only guides to the evaluation of financial and operating data. Many other factors, such as trends in the industry, changes in price levels, and general economic conditions and prospects, may also need consideration in order to arrive at sound conclusions.

Horizontal Analysis

The percentage analysis of increases and decreases in corresponding items in comparative financial statements is called **horizontal analysis**. The amount of each item on the most recent statement is compared with the corresponding item on one or more earlier statements. The increase or decrease in the amount of the item is then listed, together with the percent of increase or decrease. When the comparison is made between two statements, the earlier statement is used as the base. If the analysis includes three or more statements, there are two alternatives in the selection of the base: the earliest date or period may be used as the basis for comparing all later dates or periods, or each statement may be compared with the immediately preceding statement. The two alternatives are illustrated as follows:

BASE: EARLIEST YEAR

				Increase (Decrease*)			
				1990–91		1990–92	
Item	1990	1991	1992	Amount	Percent	Amount	Percent
A	$100,000	$150,000	$200,000	$ 50,000	50%	$100,000	100%
B	100,000	200,000	150,000	100,000	100%	50,000	50%

BASE: PRECEDING YEAR

				Increase (Decrease*)			
				1990–91		1991–92	
Item	1990	1991	1992	Amount	Percent	Amount	Percent
A	$100,000	$150,000	$200,000	$ 50,000	50%	$ 50,000	33%
B	100,000	200,000	150,000	100,000	100%	50,000*	25%*

Comparison of the amounts in the last two columns of the first analysis with the amounts in the corresponding columns of the second analysis reveals the effect of the base year on the direction of change and the amount and percent of change.

A condensed comparative balance sheet for two years, with horizontal analysis, is illustrated as follows:

Comparative Balance Sheet—Horizontal Analysis

Marlea Company
Comparative Balance Sheet
December 31, 1990 and 1989

	1990	1989	Increase (Decrease*) Amount	Percent
Assets				
Current assets..................	$ 550,000	$ 533,000	$ 17,000	3.2%
Long-term investments.......	95,000	177,500	82,500*	46.5%*
Plant assets (net)..............	444,500	470,000	25,500*	5.4%*
Intangible assets...............	50,000	50,000	—	
Total assets	$1,139,500	$1,230,500	$ 91,000*	7.4%*
Liabilities				
Current liabilities	$ 210,000	$ 243,000	$ 33,000*	13.6%*
Long-term liabilities...........	100,000	200,000	100,000*	50.0%*
Total liabilities..................	$ 310,000	$ 443,000	$133,000*	30.0%*
Stockholders' Equity				
Preferred 6% stock, $100 par......................	$ 150,000	$ 150,000	—	—
Common stock, $10 par	500,000	500,000	—	—
Retained earnings.............	179,500	137,500	$ 42,000	30.5%
Total stockholders' equity....	$ 829,500	$ 787,500	$ 42,000	5.3%
Total liabilities and stockholders' equity........	$1,139,500	$1,230,500	$ 91,000*	7.4%*

The significance of the various increases and decreases in the items shown cannot be fully determined without additional information. Although total assets at the end of 1990 were $91,000 (7.4%) less than at the beginning of the year, liabilities were reduced by $133,000 (30%) and stockholders' equity increased $42,000 (5.3%). It would appear that the reduction of $100,000 in long-term liabilities was accomplished, for the most part, through the sale of long-term investments.

The foregoing balance sheet may be expanded to include the details of the various categories of assets and liabilities, or the details may be presented in separate schedules. Opinions differ as to which method presents the clearer picture. A supporting schedule with horizontal analysis is illustrated by the following comparative schedule of current assets:

Marlea Company
Comparative Schedule of Current Assets
December 31, 1990 and 1989

	1990	1989	Increase (Decrease*) Amount	Increase (Decrease*) Percent
Cash..............................	$ 90,500	$ 64,700	$25,800	39.9%
Marketable securities.........	75,000	60,000	15,000	25.0%
Accounts receivable (net) ...	115,000	120,000	5,000*	4.2%*
Inventories......................	264,000	283,000	19,000*	6.7%*
Prepaid expenses	5,500	5,300	200	3.8%
Total current assets...........	$550,000	$533,000	$17,000	3.2%

The reduction in accounts receivable may have come about through changes in credit terms or improved collection policies. Similarly, a reduction in inventories during a period of increased sales probably indicates an improvement in the management of inventories.

The changes in the current assets would appear to be favorable, particularly in view of the 24.8% increase in net sales, shown in the following comparative income statement with horizontal analysis:

Marlea Company
Comparative Income Statement
For Years Ended December 31, 1990 and 1989

	1990	1989	Increase (Decrease*) Amount	Increase (Decrease*) Percent
Sales................................	$1,530,500	$1,234,000	$296,500	24.0%
Sales returns and allowances....................	32,500	34,000	1,500*	4.4%*
Net sales.........................	$1,498,000	$1,200,000	$298,000	24.8%
Cost of goods sold	1,043,000	820,000	223,000	27.2%
Gross profit......................	$ 455,000	$ 380,000	$ 75,000	19.7%
Selling expenses...............	$ 191,000	$ 147,000	$ 44,000	29.9%
Administrative expenses.....	104,000	97,400	6,600	6.8%
Total operating expenses....	$ 295,000	$ 244,400	$ 50,600	20.7%
Operating income..............	$ 160,000	$ 135,600	$ 24,400	18.0%
Other income	8,500	11,000	2,500*	22.7%*
	$ 168,500	$ 146,600	$ 21,900	14.9%
Other expense..................	6,000	12,000	6,000*	50.0%*
Income before income tax...	$ 162,500	$ 134,600	$ 27,900	20.7%
Income tax.......................	71,500	58,100	13,400	23.1%
Net income	$ 91,000	$ 76,500	$ 14,500	19.0%

An increase in net sales, considered alone, is not necessarily favorable. The increase in Marlea Company's net sales was accompanied by a somewhat greater percentage increase in the cost of goods (merchandise) sold, which indicates a narrowing of the gross profit margin. Selling expenses increased markedly and administrative expenses increased slightly, making an overall increase in operating expenses of 20.7%, as contrasted with a 19.7% increase in gross profit.

Although the increase in operating income and in the final net income figure is favorable, it would be incorrect for management to conclude that its operations were at maximum efficiency. A study of the expenses and additional analysis and comparisons of individual expense accounts should be made.

The income statement illustrated is in condensed form. Such a condensed statement usually provides enough information for all interested groups except management. If desired, the statement may be expanded or supplemental schedules may be prepared to present details of the cost of goods sold, selling expenses, administrative expenses, other income, and other expense.

A comparative retained earnings statement with horizontal analysis is illustrated as follows:

Comparative Retained Earnings Statement — Horizontal Analysis

Marlea Company
Comparative Retained Earnings Statement
For Years Ended December 31, 1990 and 1989

	1990	1989	Increase (Decrease*) Amount	Increase (Decrease*) Percent
Retained earnings, January 1	$137,500	$100,000	$37,500	37.5%
Net income for year	91,000	76,500	14,500	19.0%
Total	$228,500	$176,500	$52,000	29.5%
Dividends:				
On preferred stock	$ 9,000	$ 9,000	—	—
On common stock	40,000	30,000	$10,000	33.3%
Total	$ 49,000	$ 39,000	$10,000	25.6%
Retained earnings, December 31	$179,500	$137,500	$42,000	30.5%

Examination of the statement reveals an increase of 30.5% in retained earnings for the year. The increase was attributable to the retention of $42,000 of the net income for the year ($91,000 net income − $49,000 dividends paid).

Vertical Analysis

Percentage analysis may also be used to show the relationship of the component parts to the total in a single statement. This type of analysis is called **vertical analysis**. As in horizontal analysis, the statements may be prepared in either detailed or condensed form. In the latter case, additional details of the changes in the various categories may be presented in supporting schedules. If such schedules are prepared, the percentage analysis may be based on either the total of the schedule or the balance sheet total. Although vertical analysis is confined within each individual statement, the significance of both the amounts and the percentages is increased by preparing comparative statements.

In vertical analysis of the balance sheet, each asset item is stated as a percent of total assets, and each liability and stockholders' equity item is stated as a percent of total liabilities and stockholders' equity. A condensed comparative balance sheet with vertical analysis is illustrated as follows:

Comparative Balance Sheet — Vertical Analysis

Marlea Company
Comparative Balance Sheet
December 31, 1990 and 1989

	1990		1989	
	Amount	Percent	Amount	Percent
Assets				
Current assets..............	$ 550,000	48.3%	$ 533,000	43.3%
Long-term investments...	95,000	8.3	177,500	14.4
Plant assets (net).........	444,500	39.0	470,000	38.2
Intangible assets...........	50,000	4.4	50,000	4.1
Total assets	$1,139,500	100.0%	$1,230,500	100.0%
Liabilities				
Current liabilities	$ 210,000	18.4%	$ 243,000	19.7%
Long-term liabilities........	100,000	8.8	200,000	16.3
Total liabilities...............	$ 310,000	27.2%	$ 443,000	36.0%
Stockholders' Equity				
Preferred 6% stock,				
$100 par...................	$ 150,000	13.2%	$ 150,000	12.2%
Common stock, $10 par..	500,000	43.9	500,000	40.6
Retained earnings.........	179,500	15.7	137,500	11.2
Total stockholders' equity	$ 829,500	72.8%	$ 787,500	64.0%
Total liabilities and				
stockholders' equity	$1,139,500	100.0%	$1,230,500	100.0%

The major relative changes in Marlea Company's assets were in the current asset and long-term investment groups. In the lower half of the balance sheet, the greatest relative change was in long-term liabilities and retained earnings. Stockholders' equity increased from 64% of total liabilities and stockholders' equity at the end of 1989 to 72.8% at the end of 1990, with a corresponding decrease in the claims of creditors.

In vertical analysis of the income statement, each item is stated as a percent of net sales. A condensed comparative income statement with vertical analysis is illustrated as follows:

Comparative Income Statement — Vertical Analysis

	Marlea Company Comparative Income Statement For Years Ended December 31, 1990 and 1989			
	1990		1989	
	Amount	Percent	Amount	Percent
Sales.........................	$1,530,500	102.2%	$1,234,000	102.8%
Sales returns and allowances...............	32,500	2.2	34,000	2.8
Net sales.....................	$1,498,000	100.0%	$1,200,000	100.0%
Cost of goods sold	1,043,000	69.6	820,000	68.3
Gross profit..................	$ 455,000	30.4%	$ 380,000	31.7%
Selling expenses...........	$ 191,000	12.8%	$ 147,000	12.3%
Administrative expenses ..	104,000	6.9	97,400	8.1
Total operating expenses .	$ 295,000	19.7%	$ 244,400	20.4%
Operating income..........	$ 160,000	10.7%	$ 135,600	11.3%
Other income	8,500	.6	11,000	.9
	$ 168,500	11.3%	$ 146,600	12.2
Other expense..............	6,000	.4	12,000	1.0
Income before income tax................	$ 162,500	10.9%	$ 134,600	11.2%
Income tax...................	71,500	4.8	58,100	4.8
Net income	$ 91,000	6.1%	$ 76,500	6.4%

Care must be used in judging the significance of differences between percentages for the two years. For example, the decline of the gross profit rate from 31.7% in 1989 to 30.4% in 1990 is only 1.3 percentage points. In terms of dollars of potential gross profit, however, it represents a decline of approximately $19,500 (1.3% × $1,498,000).

Common-Size Statements

Horizontal and vertical analyses with both dollar and percentage figures are helpful in disclosing relationships and trends in financial condition and operations of individual enterprises. Vertical analysis with both dollar and percentage figures is also useful in comparing one company with another or with industry averages. Such comparisons may be made easier by the use of **common-size statements,** in which all items are expressed only in relative terms.

Common-size statements may be prepared in order to compare percentages of a current period with past periods, to compare individual businesses, or to compare one business with industry percentages published by trade associations and financial information services. A comparative common-size income statement for two enterprises is illustrated as follows:

*Common-Size Income
Statement*

Marlea Company and Gram Corporation Condensed Common-Size Income Statement For Year Ended December 31, 1990		
	Marlea Company	Gram Corporation
Sales..	102.2%	102.3%
Sales returns and allowances..........................	2.2	2.3
Net sales..	100.0%	100.0%
Cost of goods sold	69.6	70.0
Gross profit..	30.4%	30.0%
Selling expenses......................................	12.8%	11.5%
Administrative expenses...............................	6.9	4.1
Total operating expenses..............................	19.7%	15.6%
Operating income.....................................	10.7%	14.4%
Other income	.6	.6
	11.3%	15.0%
Other expense..	.4	.5
Income before income tax.............................	10.9%	14.5%
Income tax..	4.8	5.5
Net income	6.1%	9.0%

Examination of the statement reveals that although Marlea Company has a slightly higher rate of gross profit than Gram Corporation, the advantage is more than offset by its higher percentage of both selling and administrative expenses. As a consequence, the operating income of Marlea Company is 10.7% of net sales as compared with 14.4% for Gram Corporation, an unfavorable difference of 3.7 percentage points.

Other Analytical Measures

In addition to the percentage analyses previously discussed, there are a number of other relationships that may be expressed in ratios and percentages. The items used in the measures are taken from the financial statements of the current period and hence are a further development of vertical analysis. Comparison of the items with corresponding measures of earlier periods is an extension of horizontal analysis.

FOCUS OF FINANCIAL STATEMENT ANALYSES

OBJECTIVE 2
Describe the
focus of financial
statement analyses.

Certain aspects of financial condition or of operations are of greater importance to some interested groups than to others. In general, however, all groups are interested in the ability of a business to pay its debts as they come due and to earn a reasonable amount of income. These two aspects of the status of an enterprise are called factors of **solvency** and **profitability**. An enterprise that cannot meet its obligations to its creditors on a timely basis may experience difficulty in obtaining credit, which may lead to a decline in its profitability, and it may even be forced into bankruptcy. Similarly, an enterprise whose earnings are less than those of its competitors is likely to be at a disadvantage in obtaining credit or new capital from stockholders. In addition to this interrelationship between solvency and profitability, it is important to recognize that analyses of historical data are useful in assessing the past performance of an enterprise and in forecasting its future performance. Also, the results of financial analyses may be even more useful when they are compared with those of competing enterprises and with industry averages.

The various types of financial analyses useful in evaluating the solvency and profitability of an enterprise are discussed in the following paragraphs. The examples are based on the illustrative statements presented earlier. In a few instances, data from a company's statements of the preceding year and from other sources are also used.

SOLVENCY ANALYSIS

OBJECTIVE 3
Describe and
illustrate the
application of
financial state-
ment analysis in
assessing solvency.

Solvency is the ability of a business to meet its financial obligations as they come due. Solvency analysis, therefore, focuses mainly on balance sheet relationships that indicate the ability to liquidate current and noncurrent liabilities. Major analyses used in assessing solvency include (1) current position analysis, (2) accounts receivable analysis, (3) inventory analysis, (4) the ratio of plant assets to long-term liabilities, (5) the ratio of stockholders' equity to liabilities, and (6) the number of times interest charges are earned.

Current Position Analysis

To be useful, ratios relating to a firm's solvency must show the firm's ability to liquidate its liabilities. The use of ratios showing the ability to liquidate current liabilities is called **current position analysis** and is of particular interest to short-term creditors.

Working Capital. The excess of the current assets of an enterprise over its current liabilities at a certain moment of time is called **working capital**. The amount of working capital is often used in evaluating a company's ability to meet currently maturing obligations. Although useful for making intraperiod comparisons for a company, these absolute amounts are difficult to use in comparing companies of different sizes or in comparing such amounts with industry figures. For example, working capital of $250,000 may be very adequate for a small building contractor specializing in residential construction, but it may be completely inadequate for a large building contractor specializing in industrial and commercial construction.

Current Ratio. Another means of expressing the relationship between current assets and current liabilities is through the **current ratio**, sometimes referred to as the **working capital ratio** or **bankers' ratio**. The ratio is computed by dividing the total of current assets by the total of current liabilities. The determination of working capital and the current ratio for Marlea Company is illustrated as follows:

	1990	1989
Current assets	$550,000	$533,000
Current liabilities	210,000	243,000
Working capital	$340,000	$290,000
Current ratio	2.6:1	2.2:1

The current ratio is a more dependable indication of solvency than is working capital. To illustrate, assume that as of December 31, 1990, the working capital of a competing corporation is much greater than $340,000, but its current ratio is only 1.3:1. Considering these factors alone, Marlea Company, with its current ratio of 2.6:1, is in a more favorable position to obtain short-term credit than the corporation with the greater amount of working capital.

Acid-Test Ratio. The amount of working capital and the current ratio are two solvency measures that indicate a company's ability to meet currently maturing obligations. However, these two measures do not take into account the composition of the current assets. To illustrate the significance of this additional factor, the current position data for Marlea Company and Wilson Corporation as of December 31, 1990, are as follows:

	Marlea Company	Wilson Corporation
Current assets:		
Cash..	$ 90,500	$ 45,500
Marketable securities	75,000	25,000
Accounts receivable (net)	115,000	90,000
Inventories...	264,000	380,000
Prepaid expenses	5,500	9,500
Total current assets................................	$550,000	$550,000
Current liabilities	210,000	210,000
Working capital	$340,000	$340,000
Current ratio...	2.6:1	2.6:1

Both companies have working capital of $340,000 and a current ratio of 2.6:1. But the ability of each company to meet its currently maturing debts is vastly different. Wilson Corporation has more of its current assets in inventories, which must be sold and the receivables collected before the current liabilities can be paid in full. A considerable amount of time may be required to convert these inventories into cash. Declines in market prices and a reduction in demand could also impair the ability to pay current liabilities. Conversely, Marlea Company has enough cash and current assets (marketable securities and accounts receivable) which can generally be converted to cash rather quickly to meet its current liabilities.

A ratio that measures the "instant" debt-paying ability of a company is called the **acid-test ratio** or **quick ratio**. It is the ratio of the total **quick assets**, which are the cash, the marketable securities, and the receivables, to the total current liabilities. The acid-test ratio data for Marlea Company are as follows:

	1990	1989
Quick assets:		
Cash..	$ 90,500	$ 64,700
Marketable securities	75,000	60,000
Accounts receivable (net)	115,000	120,000
Total	$280,500	$244,700
Current liabilities	$210,000	$243,000
Acid-test ratio	1.3:1	1.0:1

A thorough analysis of a firm's current position would include the determination of the amount of working capital, the current ratio, and the acid-test ratio. The current and acid-test ratios are most useful when viewed together and when compared with similar ratios for previous periods and with those of other firms in the industry.

Accounts Receivable Analysis

The size and composition of accounts receivable change continually during business operations. The amount is increased by sales on account and reduced by collections. Firms that grant long credit terms tend to have relatively greater amounts tied up in accounts receivable than those granting short credit terms. Increases or decreases in the volume of sales also affect the amount of outstanding accounts receivable.

Accounts receivable yield no revenue, hence it is desirable to keep the amount invested in them at a minimum. The cash made available by prompt collection of receivables improves solvency and may be used for purchases of merchandise in larger quantities at a lower price, for payment of dividends to stockholders, or for other purposes. Prompt collection also lessens the risk of loss from uncollectible accounts.

Accounts Receivable Turnover. The relationship between credit sales and accounts receivable may be stated as the **accounts receivable turnover**. It is computed by dividing net sales on account by the average net accounts receivable. It is preferable to base the average on monthly balances, which gives effect to seasonal changes. When such data are not available, it is necessary to use the average of the balances at the beginning and the end of the year. If there are trade notes receivable as well as accounts, the two should be combined. The accounts receivable turnover data for Marlea Company are as follows. All sales were made on account.

	1990	1989
Net sales on account	$1,498,000	$1,200,000
Accounts receivable (net):		
Beginning of year	$ 120,000	$ 140,000
End of year	115,000	120,000
Total	$ 235,000	$ 260,000
Average	$ 117,500	$ 130,000
Accounts receivable turnover	12.7	9.2

The increase in the accounts receivable turnover for 1990 indicates that there has been an acceleration in the collection of receivables, due perhaps to improvement in either the granting of credit or the collection practices used, or both.

Number of Days' Sales in Receivables. Another means of expressing the relationship between credit sales and accounts receivable is the **number of days' sales in receivables**. This measure is determined by dividing the net accounts receivable at the end of the year by the average daily sales on account (net sales on account divided by 365), illustrated as follows for Marlea Company:

	1990	1989
Accounts receivable (net), end of year	$ 115,000	$ 120,000
Net sales on account	$1,498,000	$1,200,000
Average daily sales on account	$ 4,104	$ 3,288
Number of days' sales in receivables	28.0	36.5

The number of days' sales in receivables gives a rough measure of the length of time the accounts receivable have been outstanding. A comparison of this measure with the credit terms, with figures for comparable firms in the same industry, and with figures of Marlea Company for prior years will help reveal the efficiency in collecting receivables and the trends in the management of credit.

Inventory Analysis

Although an enterprise must maintain sufficient inventory quantities to meet the demands of its operations, it is desirable to keep the amount invested in inventory to a minimum. Inventories in excess of the needs of business reduce solvency by tying up funds. Excess inventories may also cause increases in the amount of insurance, property taxes, storage, and other related expenses, further reducing funds that could be used to better advantage. There is also added risk of loss through price declines and deterioration or obsolescence of the inventory.

Inventory Turnover. The relationship between the volume of goods (merchandise) sold and inventory may be stated as the **inventory turnover**. It is computed by dividing the cost of goods sold by the average inventory. If monthly data are not available, it is necessary to use the average of the inventories at the beginning and the end of the year. The inventory turnover data for Marlea Company are as follows:

	1990	1989
Cost of goods sold	$1,043,000	$820,000
Inventories:		
Beginning of year	$ 283,000	$311,000
End of year	264,000	283,000
Total	$ 547,000	$594,000
Average	$ 273,500	$297,000
Inventory turnover	3.8	2.8

The improvement in the turnover resulted from an increase in the cost of goods sold, combined with a decrease in average inventory. The variation in types of inventories is too great to permit any broad generalizations as to what is a satisfactory turnover. For example, a firm selling food should have a much higher turnover than one selling furniture or jewelry, and the perishable foods department of a supermarket should have a higher turnover than the soaps and cleansers department. However, for each business or each department within a business, there is a reasonable turnover rate. A turnover below this rate means that the company or the department is incurring extra expenses such as those for administration and storage, is increasing its risk of loss because of obsolescence and adverse price changes, is incurring interest charges in excess of those considered necessary, and is failing to free funds for other uses.

Number of Days' Sales in Inventory. Another means of expressing the relationship between the cost of goods sold and inventory is the **number of days' sales in inventory**. This measure is determined by dividing the inventories at the end of the year by the average daily cost of goods sold (cost of goods sold divided by 365), illustrated as follows for Marlea Company:

	1990	1989
Inventories, end of year..............................	$ 264,000	$283,000
Cost of goods sold	$1,043,000	$820,000
Average daily cost of goods sold...........................	$ 2,858	$ 2,247
Number of days' sales in inventory........................	92.4	125.9

The number of days' sales in inventory gives a rough measure of the length of time it takes to acquire, sell, and then replace the average inventory. Although there was a substantial improvement in the second year, comparison of the measure with those of earlier years and of comparable firms is an essential element in judging the effectiveness of Marlea Company's inventory control.

As with many attempts to analyze financial data, it is possible to determine more than one measure to express the relationship between the cost of goods sold and inventory. Both the inventory turnover and number of days' sales in inventory are useful for evaluating the efficiency in the management of inventory. Whether both measures are used or whether one measure is preferred over the other is a matter for the individual analyst to decide.

Ratio of Plant Assets to Long-Term Liabilities

Long-term notes and bonds are often secured by mortgages on plant assets. *The **ratio of total plant assets to long-term liabilities** provides a solvency measure that shows the margin of safety of the noteholders or bondholders. It also gives an indication of the potential ability of the enterprise to borrow additional funds on a long-term basis.* The ratio of plant assets to long-term liabilities of Marlea Company is as follows:

	1990	1989
Plant assets (net).....................................	$444,500	$470,000
Long-term liabilities.................................	$100,000	$200,000
Ratio of plant assets to long-term liabilities	4.4:1	2.4:1

The marked increase in the ratio at the end of 1990 was mainly due to the liquidation of one half of Marlea Company's long-term liabilities. If the company should need to borrow additional funds on a long-term basis, it is in a stronger position to do so.

Ratio of Stockholders' Equity to Liabilities

Claims against the total assets of an enterprise are divided into two basic groups, those of the creditors and those of the owners. *The relationship between the total claims of the creditors and owners provides a solvency measure that indicates the margin of safety for the creditors and the ability of the enterprise to withstand adverse business conditions.* If the claims of the creditors are large in proportion to the equity of the stockholders, there are likely to be substantial charges for interest payments. If earnings decline to the point where the company is unable to meet its interest payments, control of the business may pass to the creditors.

The relationship between stockholder and creditor equity is shown in the vertical analysis of the balance sheet. For example, the balance sheet of Marlea Company presented on page 750 indicates that on December 31, 1990, stockholders' equity represented 72.8% and liabilities represented 27.2% of the sum of the liabilities and stockholders' equity (100.0%). Instead of expressing each item as a percent of the total, the relationship may be expressed as a ratio of one to the other, as follows:

	1990	1989
Total stockholders' equity	$829,500	$787,500
Total liabilities	$310,000	$443,000
Ratio of stockholders' equity to liabilities	2.7:1	1.8:1

The balance sheet of Marlea Company shows that the major factor affecting the change in the ratio was the $100,000 reduction in long-term liabilities during 1990. The ratio at both dates shows a large margin of safety for the creditors.

Number of Times Interest Charges Earned

Some corporations, such as public utilities, have a high ratio of debt to stockholders' equity. In analyzing such corporations, it is customary to express *the solvency measure that shows the relative risk of the debtholders in terms of the* **number of times the interest charges are earned** during the year. The higher the ratio, the greater the assurance of continued interest payments in case of decreased earnings. *The measure also provides an indication of general financial strength*, which is of concern to stockholders and employees, as well as to creditors.

In the following data, the amount available to meet interest charges is not affected by taxes on income because interest is deductible in determining taxable income.

	1990	1989
Income before income tax	$ 900,000	$ 800,000
Add interest charges	300,000	250,000
Amount available to meet interest charges	$1,200,000	$1,050,000
Number of times interest charges earned	4	4.2

Analyses like the above can be applied to dividends on preferred stock. In such cases, net income would be divided by the amount of preferred dividends to yield the number of times preferred dividends were earned. This measure gives an indication of the relative assurance of continued dividend payments to preferred stockholders.

PROFITABILITY ANALYSIS

OBJECTIVE 4
Describe and illustrate the application of financial statement analysis in assessing profitability.

Profitability is the ability of an entity to earn income. It can be assessed by computing various relevant measures, including (1) the ratio of net sales to assets, (2) the rate earned on total assets, (3) the rate earned on stockholders' equity, (4) the rate earned on common stockholders' equity, (5) earnings per share on common stock, (6) the price-earnings ratio, and (7) dividend yield.

Ratio of Net Sales to Assets

The **ratio of net sales to assets** *is a profitability measure that shows how effectively a firm utilizes its assets.* Assume that two competing enterprises have equal amounts of assets, but the amount of the sales of one is double the amount of the sales of the other. Obviously, the former is making better use of its assets. In computing the ratio, any long-term investments should be excluded from total assets because they are wholly unrelated to sales of goods or services. Assets used in determining the ratio may be the total at the end of the year, the average at the beginning and the end of the year, or the average of the monthly totals. The basic data and the ratio of net sales to assets for Marlea Company are as follows:

	1990	1989
Net sales	$1,498,000	$1,200,000
Total assets (excluding long-term investments):		
Beginning of year	$1,053,000	$1,010,000
End of year	1,044,500	1,053,000
Total	$2,097,500	$2,063,000
Average	$1,048,750	$1,031,500
Ratio of net sales to assets	1.4:1	1.2:1

The ratio improved to a minor degree in 1990, largely due to the increased sales volume. A comparison of the ratio with those of other enterprises in the same industry would be helpful in assessing Marlea Company's effectiveness in the utilization of assets.

Rate Earned on Total Assets

The **rate earned on total assets** *is a measure of the profitability of the assets, without regard to the equity of creditors and stockholders in the assets.* The rate is therefore not affected by differences in methods of financing an enterprise.

The rate earned on total assets is derived by adding interest expense to net income and dividing this sum by total assets. By adding interest expense to net income, the profitability of the assets is determined without considering the means of financing the acquisition of the assets. The rate earned by Marlea Company on total assets is determined as follows:

	1990	1989
Net income	$ 91,000	$ 76,500
Plus interest expense	6,000	12,000
Total	$ 97,000	$ 88,500
Total assets:		
Beginning of year	$1,230,500	$1,187,500
End of year	1,139,500	1,230,500
Total	$2,370,000	$2,418,000
Average	$1,185,000	$1,209,000
Rate earned on total assets	8.2%	7.3%

The rate earned on total assets of Marlea Company for 1990 indicates an improvement over that for 1989. A comparison with other companies and with industry averages would also be useful in evaluating the effectiveness of management performance.

It is sometimes preferable to determine the rate of operating income (income before nonoperating income, nonoperating expense, extraordinary items, and income tax) to total assets. If nonoperating income is not considered, the investments yielding such income should be excluded from the assets. The use of income before income tax eliminates the effect of changes in the tax structure on the rate of earnings. When considering published data on rates earned on assets, the reader should note the exact nature of the measure.

Rate Earned on Stockholders' Equity

Another relative measure of profitability is obtained by dividing net income by the total stockholders' equity. In contrast to the rate earned on total assets, **the rate earned on stockholders' equity** *emphasizes the income yield in relationship to the amount invested by the stockholders.*

The amount of the total stockholders' equity throughout the year varies for several reasons — the issuance of additional stock, the retirement of a class of stock, the payment of dividends, and the gradual accrual of net income. If monthly figures are not available, the average of the stockholders' equity at the beginning and the end of the year is used, as in the following illustration:

	1990	1989
Net income	$ 91,000	$ 76,500
Stockholders' equity:		
Beginning of year	$ 787,500	$ 750,000
End of year	829,500	787,500
Total	$1,617,000	$1,537,500
Average	$ 808,500	$ 768,750
Rate earned on stockholders' equity	11.3%	10.0%

The rate earned by a thriving enterprise on the equity of its stockholders is usually higher than the rate earned on total assets. The reason for the difference is that the amount earned on assets acquired through the use of funds provided by creditors is more than the interest charges paid to creditors. This tendency of the rate on stockholders' equity to vary disproportionately from the rate on total assets is sometimes called **leverage**. Marlea Company's rate on stockholders' equity for 1990, 11.3%, compares favorably with the rate of 8.2% earned on total assets, as reported on the preceding page. The leverage factor of 3.1% (11.3% − 8.2%) for 1990 also compares favorably with the 2.7% (10.0% − 7.3%) differential for the preceding year. These leverage factors for Marlea Company are illustrated graphically in the following chart:

Chart of Rate Earned on Stockholders' Equity and Total Assets

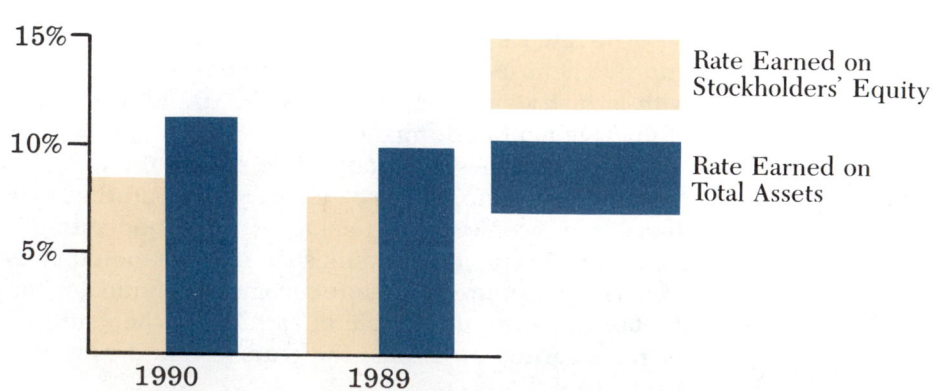

Rate Earned on Common Stockholders' Equity

When a corporation has both preferred and common stock outstanding, the holders of the common stock have the residual claim on earnings. The **rate earned on common stockholders' equity** is the net income less preferred dividend requirements for the period, stated as a percent of the average equity of the common stockholders.

Marlea Company has $150,000 of 6% nonparticipating preferred stock outstanding at both balance sheet dates, hence annual preferred dividends amount to $9,000. The common stockholders' equity is the total stockholders' equity, including retained earnings, reduced by the par of the preferred stock ($150,000). The basic data and the rate earned on common stockholders' equity are as follows:

	1990	1989
Net income	$ 91,000	$ 76,500
Preferred dividends	9,000	9,000
Remainder — identified with common stock	$ 82,000	$ 67,500
Common stockholders' equity:		
Beginning of year	$ 637,500	$ 600,000
End of year	679,500	637,500
Total	$1,317,000	$1,237,500
Average	$ 658,500	$ 618,750
Rate earned on common stockholders' equity	12.5%	10.9%

The rate earned on common stockholders' equity differs from the rates earned by Marlea Company on total assets and total stockholders' equity. This situation will occur if there are borrowed funds and also preferred stock outstanding, which rank ahead of the common shares in their claim on earnings. Thus the concept of leverage, as discussed in the preceding section, can be applied to the use of funds from the sale of preferred stock as well as from borrowing. Funds from both sources can be used in an attempt to increase the return on common stockholders' equity.

Earnings per Share on Common Stock

One of the profitability measures most commonly quoted by the financial press and included in the income statement in corporate annual reports is **earnings per share on common stock**. If a company has issued only one class of stock, the earnings per share are determined by dividing net income by the number of shares of stock outstanding. If there are both preferred and common stock outstanding, the net income must first be reduced by the amount necessary to meet the preferred dividend requirements.

Any changes in the number of shares outstanding during the year, such as would result from stock dividends or stock splits, should be disclosed in quoting earnings per share on common stock. Also, if there are any nonrecurring (extraordinary, etc.) items in the income statement, as discussed in Chapter 15, the income per share before such items should be reported along with net income per share. In addition, if there are convertible bonds or convertible preferred stock outstanding, also discussed in Chapter 15, the amount reported as net income per share should be stated without considering the conversion privilege, followed by net income per share assuming conversion had occurred.

The data on the earnings per share of common stock for Marlea Company are as follows:

	1990	1989
Net income	$91,000	$76,500
Preferred dividends	9,000	9,000
Remainder—identified with common stock	$82,000	$67,500
Shares of common stock outstanding	50,000	50,000
Earnings per share on common stock	$1.64	$1.35

Since earnings form the primary basis for dividends, earnings per share and dividends per share on common stock are commonly used by investors in weighing the merits of alternative investment opportunities. Earnings per share data can be presented in conjunction with dividends per share data to indicate the relationship between earnings and dividends and the extent to which the corporation is retaining its earnings for use in the business. The following chart shows this relationship for Marlea Company:

Chart of Earnings and Dividends per Share of Common Stock

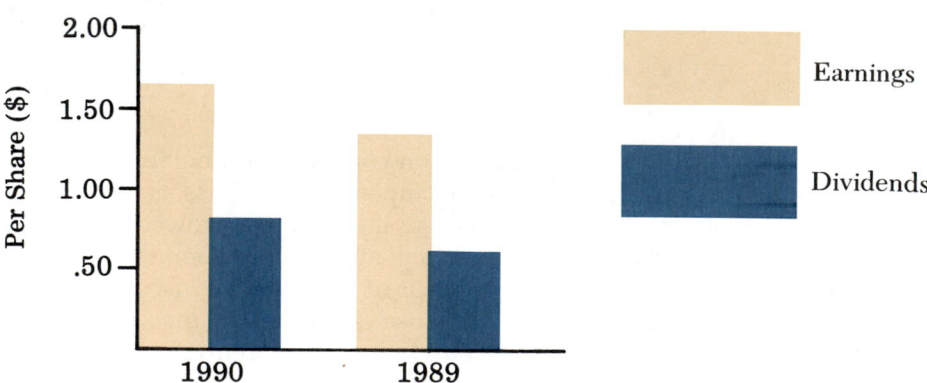

Price-Earnings Ratio

A profitability measure commonly quoted by the financial press is the **price-earnings (P/E) ratio** on common stock. *The price-earnings ratio is used as an indicator of a firm's future earnings prospects.* It is computed by dividing the market price per share of common stock at a specific date by the annual earnings per share. Assuming market prices per common share of 20 1/2 at the end of 1990 and 13 1/2 at the end of 1989, the price-earnings ratio on common stock of Marlea Company is as follows:

	1990	1989
Market price per share of common stock	$20.50	$13.50
Earnings per share on common stock	$ 1.64	$ 1.35
Price-earnings ratio on common stock	12.5	10.0

The price-earnings ratio indicates that a share of common stock of Marlea Company was selling for 12.5 and 10 times the amount of earnings per share at the end of 1990 and 1989 respectively.

Dividend Yield

The **dividend yield** on common stock is a profitability measure that shows the rate of return to common stockholders in terms of cash dividend distributions. It is of special interest to investors whose main investment objective is to receive a current return on the investment rather than an increase in the market price of the investment. The dividend yield is computed by dividing the annual dividends paid per share of common stock by the market price per share at a specific date. Assuming dividends of $.80 and $.60 per common share and market prices per common share of 20 1/2 and 13 1/2 at the end of 1990 and 1989 respectively, the dividend yield on common stock of Marlea Company is as follows:

	1990	1989
Dividends per share of common stock	$ .80	$ .60
Market price per share of common stock	$20.50	$13.50
Dividend yield on common stock	3.9%	4.4%

SUMMARY OF ANALYTICAL MEASURES

OBJECTIVE 5
Summarize and describe how analytical measures can be used in appraising the present performance of an enterprise and in forecasting its future.

The analytical measures that have been discussed and illustrated are representative of many that can be developed for a medium-size merchandising enterprise. Some of them might well be omitted in analyzing a specific firm, or additional measures could be developed. The type of business activity, the capital structure, and the size of the enterprise usually affect the measures used.

Percentage analyses, ratios, turnovers, and other measures of financial position and operating results are useful analytical devices. They are helpful in appraising the present performance of an enterprise and in forecasting its future. They are not, however, a substitute for sound judgment, nor do they provide definitive guides to action. In selecting and interpreting analytical indexes, proper consideration should be given to any conditions peculiar to the enterprise or to the industry of which the enterprise is a part. The possible influence of the general economic and business environment should also be weighed.

To determine trends, the interrelationship of the measures used in appraising a certain enterprise should be carefully studied, as should comparable indexes of earlier fiscal periods. Data from competing enterprises may also be compared in order to determine the relative efficiency of the firm being analyzed. In making such comparisons, however, it is essential to consider the potential effects of any significant differences in the accounting methods used by the enterprises.

The following presentation is a summary of the method of computation and use of the analytical measures discussed in this chapter:

	Method of Computation	Use
Solvency measures		
Working capital	Current assets − current liabilities	To indicate the ability to meet currently maturing obligations
Current ratio	Current assets / Current liabilities	

	Method of Computation	Use
Acid-test ratio	$\dfrac{\text{Quick assets}}{\text{Current liabilities}}$	**To indicate instant debt-paying ability**
Accounts receivable turnover	$\dfrac{\text{Net sales on account}}{\text{Average accounts receivable}}$	**To assess the efficiency in collecting receivables and in the management of credit**
Number of days' sales in receivables	$\dfrac{\text{Accounts receivable, end of year}}{\text{Average daily sales on account}}$	
Inventory turnover	$\dfrac{\text{Cost of goods sold}}{\text{Average inventory}}$	**To assess the efficiency in the management of inventory**
Number of days' sales in inventory	$\dfrac{\text{Inventory, end of year}}{\text{Average daily cost of goods sold}}$	
Ratio of plant assets to long-term liabilities	$\dfrac{\text{Plant assets (net)}}{\text{Long-term liabilities}}$	**To indicate the margin of safety to long-term creditors**
Ratio of stockholders' equity to liabilities	$\dfrac{\text{Total stockholders' equity}}{\text{Total liabilities}}$	**To indicate the margin of safety to creditors**
Number of times interest charges earned	$\dfrac{\text{Income before income tax + interest expense}}{\text{Interest expense}}$	**To assess the risk to debt-holders in terms of number of times interest charges were earned**

Profitability measures

Ratio of net sales to assets	$\dfrac{\text{Net sales}}{\text{Average total assets (excluding long-term investments)}}$	**To assess the effectiveness in the use of assets**
Rate earned on total assets	$\dfrac{\text{Net income + interest expense}}{\text{Average total assets}}$	**To assess the profitability of the assets**
Rate earned on stockholders' equity	$\dfrac{\text{Net income}}{\text{Average stockholders' equity}}$	**To assess the profitability of the investment by stockholders**
Rate earned on common stockholders' equity	$\dfrac{\text{Net income − preferred dividends}}{\text{Average common stockholders' equity}}$	**To assess the profitability of the investment by common stockholders**
Earnings per share on common stock	$\dfrac{\text{Net income − preferred dividends}}{\text{Shares of common stock outstanding}}$	
Dividends per share of common stock	$\dfrac{\text{Dividends}}{\text{Shares of common stock outstanding}}$	**To indicate the extent to which earnings are being distributed to common stockholders**
Price-earnings ratio	$\dfrac{\text{Market price per share of common stock}}{\text{Earnings per share on common stock}}$	**To indicate future earnings prospects, based on the relationship between market value of common stock and earnings**
Dividend yield	$\dfrac{\text{Dividends per common share}}{\text{Market price per common share}}$	**To indicate the rate of return to common stockholders in terms of dividends**

PERCEPTIONS OF FINANCIAL RATIOS

Financial statements serve as the primary financial reporting mechanism of an entity, both internally and externally. An analysis of the financial information communicated by these statements should include the computation and interpretation of financial ratios.

A survey of the views of financial executives on important issues relating to financial ratios indicated that financial ratios are an important tool in analyzing the financial results of a company and in managing a company. In addition, 93 of the 100 respondents to the survey indicated that their firms use financial ratios as part of their corporate objectives. The ratios most significant to the respondents are those that measure the ability of the firm to earn a profit.

Source: Charles H. Gibson, "How Industry Perceives Financial Ratios," *Management Accounting* (April, 1982), pp. 13–19.

Financial ratios are often more useful when they are compared with similar ratios of other companies or groups of companies. For this purpose, average ratios for many industries are compiled by various financial services and trade associations. In this process, however, it should be remembered that averages are just that—averages—and care should be taken in their use. The danger in interpreting averages was graphically illustrated by Eldon Grimm, a Wall Street analyst who said: "A statistician is an individual who has his head in the refrigerator, his feet in the oven and on the average feels comfortable."

Source: "Twenty-Five Years Ago in *Forbes*" *Forbes* (August 16, 1982), p. 107.

CORPORATE ANNUAL REPORTS

OBJECTIVE 6
Identify and illustrate the content of corporate annual reports.

Corporations ordinarily issue to their stockholders and other interested parties annual reports summarizing activities of the past year and any significant plans for the future. Although there are many differences in the form and sequence of the major sections of annual reports, one section is always devoted to the financial statements, including the accompanying notes. In addition, annual reports usually include (a) selected data referred to as financial highlights, (b) a letter from the president of the corporation, which is sometimes also signed by the chairperson of the board of directors, (c) the independent auditors' report, (d) the management report, and (e) a five- or ten-year historical summary of financial data. As a way to strengthen the relationship with stockholders, many corporations also include pictures of their products and officers or other materials. The following subsections describe the portions of annual reports commonly related to financial matters, with the exception of the principal financial statements, examples of which appear in Appendix I.

Financial Highlights

This section, sometimes called *Results in Brief*, typically summarizes the major financial results for the last year or two. It is usually presented on the first one or two pages of the annual report. Such items as sales, income before income taxes, net income, net income per common share, cash dividends, cash dividends per common share, and the amount of capital expenditures are typically presented. An example of a financial highlights section from a corporation's annual report is as follows:

FINANCIAL HIGHLIGHTS

(Dollars in thousands except per share amounts)

For the Year	Current Year	Preceding Year
Sales	$1,336,750	$ 876,400
Income before income tax	149,550	90,770
Net income	105,120	66,190
Per common share	4.03	2.62
Dividends declared on common stock	34,990	33,150
Per common share	1.48	1.40
Capital expenditures and investments	265,120	157,050
At Year-End		
Working capital	$ 415,410	$ 423,780
Total assets	1,712,170	1,457,240
Long-term debt	440,680	457,350
Stockholders' equity	840,350	692,950

There are many variations in format and content of the financial highlights section of the annual report. In addition to the selected income statement data, information about the financial position at year end, such as the amount of working capital, total assets, long-term debt, and stockholders' equity, is often provided. Other year-end data often reported are the number of common and preferred shares outstanding, number of common and preferred stockholders, and number of employees.

President's Letter

A letter by the president to the stockholders, discussing such items as reasons for an increase or decrease in net income, changes in existing plant or purchase or construction of new plants, significant new financing commitments, attention given to social responsibility issues, and future prospects, is also found in most annual reports. A condensed version of a president's letter adapted from a corporation's annual report is on page 767.

During recent years, corporate enterprises have become increasingly active in accepting environmental and other social responsibilities. In addition to the brief discussion that may be contained in the president's letter, a more detailed analysis of the company's social concerns may be included elsewhere in the annual report. Knowledgeable investors recognize that the failure of a business enterprise to meet acceptable social norms can have long-run unfavorable implications. In the near future, an important function of accounting may be to assist management in developing a statement covering the social responsibilities of corporate enterprises and what management is doing about them.

Independent Auditors' Report

Before issuing annual statements, all publicly held corporations, as well as many other corporations, engage independent public accountants, usually CPAs, to conduct an *examination* of the financial statements. Such an exami-

To the Stockholders:

FISCAL YEAR REVIEWED

The record net income in this fiscal year resulted from very strong product demand experienced for about two thirds of the fiscal year, more complete utilization of plants, and a continued improvement in sales mix. Income was strong both domestically and internationally during this period.

PLANT EXPANSION CONTINUES

Capital expenditures during the year were $14.5 million. Expansions were in progress or completed at all locations. Portions of the Company's major new expansion at one of its West Coast plants came on stream in March of this year and will provide much needed capacity in existing and new product areas. Capital expenditures will be somewhat less during next year.

ENVIRONMENTAL CONCERN

The Company recognizes its responsibility to provide a safe and healthy environment at each of its plants. The Company expects to spend approximately $1 million in the forthcoming year to help continue its position as a constructive corporate citizen.

OUTLOOK

During the past 10 years the Company's net income and sales have more than tripled. Net income increased from $3.1 million to $10.7 million, and sales from $45 million to $181 million.

The Company's employees are proud of this record and are determined to carry the momentum into the future. The current economic slowdown makes results for the new fiscal year difficult to predict. However, we are confident and enthusiastic about the Company's prospects for continued growth over the longer term.

Respectfully submitted,

Frances B. Davis

Frances B. Davis
President

March 24, 1991

nation is for the purpose of adding credibility to the statements that have been prepared by management. Upon completion of the examination, which for large corporations may engage many accountants for several weeks or longer, an **independent auditors' report** is prepared. This report accompanies the financial statements. A typical report includes three paragraphs: (1) an introductory paragraph identifying the financial statements being audited, (2) a "scope" paragraph describing the nature of the audit, and (3) an "opinion" paragraph presenting the auditor's opinion as to the fairness of the statements.[1] The wording of the following report for Winn-Dixie Stores, Inc. conforms with general usage.

---

[1]*Statements on Auditing Standards No. 58,* "Reports on Audited Financial Statements," (New York: American Institute of Certified Public Accountants, 1988), par. 8.

Independent Auditors' Report

The Shareholders and the Board of Directors
Winn-Dixie Stores, Inc.:

We have audited the accompanying consolidated balance sheets of Winn-Dixie Stores, Inc. and subsidiaries as of June 29, 1988 and June 24, 1987, and the related consolidated statements of earnings, shareholders' equity, and cash flows for each of the years in the three-year period ended June 29, 1988. These consolidated financial statements are the responsibility of the Company's management. Our responsibility is to express an opinion on these consolidated financial statements based on our audits.

We conducted our audits in accordance with generally accepted auditing standards. Those standards require that we plan and perform the audit to obtain reasonable assurance about whether the financial statements are free of material misstatement. An audit includes examining, on a test basis, evidence supporting the amounts and disclosures in the financial statements. An audit also includes assessing the accounting principles used and significant estimates made by management, as well as evaluating the overall financial statement presentation. We believe that our audits provide a reasonable basis for our opinion.

In our opinion, the consolidated financial statements referred to above present fairly, in all material respects, the financial position of Winn-Dixie Stores, Inc. and subsidiaries at June 29, 1988 and June 24, 1987, and the results of their operations and their cash flows for the years then ended in conformity with generally accepted accounting principles.

Peat Marwick Main & Co.

Certified Public Accountants

Jacksonville, Florida
August 22, 1988

In most instances, the auditors can render a report such as the one illustrated, which may be said to be "unqualified." However, it is possible that accounting methods used by a client do not conform with generally accepted accounting principles. In such cases, a "qualified" opinion must be rendered and the exception briefly described. If the effect of the departure from accepted principles is sufficiently material, an "adverse" or negative opinion must be issued and the exception described. In rare circumstances, the auditors may be unable to perform sufficient auditing procedures to enable them to reach a conclusion as to the fairness of the financial statements. In such circumstances, the auditors must issue a "disclaimer" and briefly describe the reasons for their failure to be able to reach a decision as to the fairness of the statements.

Professional accountants cannot disregard their responsibility in attesting to the fairness of financial statements without seriously jeopardizing their reputations. This responsibility is described as follows:

The report shall either contain an expression of opinion regarding the financial statements, taken as a whole, or an assertion to the effect that an opinion cannot be expressed. When an overall opinion cannot be expressed, the reasons therefor should be stated. In all cases where an auditor's name is associated with financial statements, the report should contain a clear-cut indication of the character of the auditor's examination, if any, and the degree of responsibility he is taking.[2]

Management Report

Responsibility for the accounting system and the resultant financial statements rests mainly with the principal officers of a corporation. In the **management report**, the chief financial officer or other representative of management (1) states that the financial statements are management's responsibility and that they have been prepared according to generally accepted accounting principles, (2) presents management's assessment of the company's internal accounting control system, and (3) comments on any other pertinent matters related to the accounting system, the financial statements, and the examination by the independent auditor.

Although the concept of a management report is relatively new, an increasing number of corporations are including such a report in the annual report. An example of such a report taken from the 1988 annual report for Toys "R" Us is as follows:

Management Report Section

Report of Management

Responsibility for the integrity and objectivity of the financial information presented in this Annual Report rests with Toys "R" Us management. The accompanying financial statements have been prepared from accounting records which management believes fairly and accurately reflect the operations and financial position of the Company. Management has established a system of internal controls to provide reasonable assurance that assets are maintained and accounted for in accordance with its policies and that transactions are recorded accurately on the Company's books and records.

The Company's comprehensive internal audit program provides for constant evaluation of the adequacy of and adherence to management's established policies and procedures. The Company has distributed to key employees its policies for conducting business affairs in a lawful and ethical manner.

The financial statements of the Company have been examined by Touche Ross & Co., independent certified public accountants. Their accompanying report is based on an examination conducted in accordance with generally accepted auditing standards, including a review of internal accounting controls and financial reporting matters.

Charles Lazarus
Chairman of the Board

Michael Goldstein
*Executive Vice President-
Finance and Administration*

---

[2]*Ibid.*, par. 4.

Historical Summary

This section, for which there are many variations in title, reports selected financial and operating data of past periods, usually for five or ten years. It is usually presented in close proximity to the financial statements for the current year, and the types of data reported are varied. An example of a portion of such a report is as follows:

Historical Summary Section

Five-Year Consolidated Financial and Statistical Summary for Years Ended December 31
(Dollar amounts in millions except for per share data)

For the Year	1990	1989	1986
Net sales	$1,759.7	$1,550.1	$ 997.4
Gross profit	453.5	402.8	270.8
Percent to net sales	25.8%	26.0%	27.2%
Interest expense	33.9	21.3	15.0
Income before income tax	172.7	163.4	87.5
Income tax	82.8	77.8	40.2
Net income	89.9	85.6	47.3
Percent to net sales	5.1%	5.5%	4.7%
Per common share:			
Net income	5.19	4.84	2.54
Dividends	1.80	1.65	1.40
Return on stockholders' equity	15.9%	16.4%	11.2%
Common share market price:			
High	31	41 ½	40 ⅝
Low	18	22 ⅜	22 ¼
Depreciation and amortization	43.3	41.0	23.6
Capital expenditures	98.5	72.1	55.5
At Year End			
Working capital	$ 443.9	$ 434.8	$ 254.6
Plant assets — gross	704.7	620.3	453.7
Plant assets — net	420.0	362.7	263.4
Stockholders' equity	594.3	536.9	447.6
Stockholders' equity per common share	33.07	29.69	23.02
Number of holders of common shares	39,503	39,275	43,852
Number of employees	50,225	50,134	42,826

Other Information

The preceding paragraphs described the most commonly presented sections of annual reports related to financial matters. Some annual reports may include other financial information, such as forecasts which indicate financial plans and expectations for the year ahead and supplemental data reporting the effects of price-level changes on financial statements.

CHAPTER REVIEW

KEY POINTS

OBJECTIVE 1

Basic Analytical Procedures

The analytical measures obtained from financial statements are usually expressed as ratios or percentages. The basic measures developed through the use of analytical procedures are not ends in themselves. They are only guides to the evaluation of financial and operating data. Many other factors, such as trends in the industry, changes in price levels, and general economic conditions and prospects, may also need consideration in order to arrive at sound conclusions.

The percentage analysis of increases and decreases in corresponding items in comparative financial statements is called horizontal analysis. Percentage analysis may also be used to show the relationship of the component parts to the total in a single statement. This type of analysis is called vertical analysis. Although vertical analysis is confined within each individual statement, the significance of both the amounts and the percentages is increased by preparing comparative statements. Vertical analysis with both dollar and percentage figures is also useful in comparing one company with another or with industry averages. Such comparisons may be made easier by the use of common-size statements, in which all items are expressed only in relative terms.

OBJECTIVE 2

Focus of Financial Statement Analyses

Users of financial statements are especially interested in solvency and profitability. Analyses of historical data in financial statements are useful in assessing the past performance of an enterprise and in forecasting its future performance, especially when the results of the analyses are compared with those of competing enterprises and with industry averages.

OBJECTIVE 3

Solvency Analysis

Solvency is the ability of a business to meet its financial obligations as they come due. Solvency analysis, therefore, focuses mainly on balance sheet relationships that indicate the ability to liquidate liabilities. Major analyses used in assessing solvency include (1) current position analysis, (2) accounts receivable analysis, (3) inventory analysis, (4) the ratio of plant assets to long-term liabilities, (5) the ratio of stockholders' equity to liabilities, and (6) the number of times interest charges are earned.

Current position analysis includes the assessment of working capital, the current ratio, and the acid-test ratio. Accounts receivable analysis includes the assessment of accounts receivable turnover and number of days' sales in receivables. Inventory analysis includes the assessment of inventory turnover and number of days' sales in inventory. The ratio of plant assets to long-term liabilities shows the margin of safety for the creditors. The ratio of stockholders' equity to liabilities indicates the margin of safety for the creditors and the ability of the enterprise to withstand adverse business conditions. The number of times interest charges are earned indicates the relative risk of the debtholders continuing to receive interest payments.

OBJECTIVE 4

Profitability Analysis

Profitability is the ability of an entity to earn income. It can be assessed by computing various relevant measures, including (1) the ratio of net sales to assets, (2) the rate earned on total assets, (3) the rate earned on stockholders' equity, (4) the rate earned on common stockholders' equity, (5) earnings per share on common stock, (6) the price-earnings ratio, and (7) dividend yield.

OBJECTIVE 5

Summary of Analytical Measures

The type of business activity, the capital structure, and the size of the enterprise usually affect the measures used in financial statement analysis. These analytical measures, however, are not a substitute for sound judgment, nor do they provide definitive guides to action. In selecting and interpreting analytical indexes, proper consideration should be given to any conditions peculiar to the enterprise or to the industry of which the enterprise is a part.

OBJECTIVE 6

Corporate Annual Reports

Corporations ordinarily issue to their stockholders and other interested parties annual reports summarizing activities of the past year and any significant plans for the future. These reports normally include the financial highlights section, the president's letter, the independent auditors' report, the management report, and a historical summary of operations.

KEY TERMS

horizontal analysis 746
vertical analysis 749
common-size statements 751
solvency 752
profitability 752
working capital 753
current ratio 753
acid-test ratio 754
quick assets 754
accounts receivable turnover 755
number of days' sales in
    receivables 755

inventory turnover 756
number of days' sales in
    inventory 756
rate earned on total assets 759
rate earned on stockholders'
    equity 760
leverage 760
rate earned on common stockholders'
    equity 761
earnings per share on common
    stock 761
price-earnings (P/E) ratio 762

SELF-EXAMINATION QUESTIONS

Answers at end of chapter.

1. What type of analysis is indicated by the following?

	Amount	Percent
Current assets	$100,000	20%
Plant assets	400,000	80
Total assets	$500,000	100%

    A. Vertical analysis
    B. Horizontal analysis
    C. Differential analysis
    D. None of the above

2. Which of the following measures is useful as an indication of the ability of a firm to liquidate current liabilities?
    A. Working capital
    B. Current ratio
    C. Acid-test ratio
    D. All of the above

3. The ratio determined by dividing total current assets by total current liabilities is:
    A. current ratio
    B. working capital ratio
    C. bankers' ratio
    D. all of the above

4. The ratio of the quick assets to current liabilities, which indicates the "instant" debt-paying ability of a firm, is:
    A. current ratio
    B. working capital ratio
    C. acid-test ratio
    D. none of the above

5. A measure useful in evaluating the efficiency in the management of inventories is:
    A. inventory turnover
    B. number of days' sales in inventory
    C. both A and B
    D. none of the above

ILLUSTRATIVE PROBLEM

Fleming Inc.'s comparative financial statements for the years ending December 31, 1990 and 1989, are as follows. The market price of Fleming Inc.'s common stock was $30 on December 31, 1989, and $25 on December 31, 1990.

Fleming Inc.
Comparative Income Statement
For Years Ended December 31, 1990 and 1989

	1990	1989
Sales (all on account)	$5,125,000	$3,257,600
Sales returns and allowances	125,000	57,600
Net sales	$5,000,000	$3,200,000
Cost of goods sold	3,400,000	2,080,000
Gross profit	$1,600,000	$1,120,000
Selling expenses	$ 650,000	$ 464,000
Administrative expenses	325,000	224,000
Total operating expenses	$ 975,000	$ 688,000
Operating income	$ 625,000	$ 432,000
Other income	25,000	19,200
	$ 650,000	$ 451,200
Other expense (interest)	105,000	64,000
Income before income tax	$ 545,000	$ 387,200
Income tax	300,000	176,000
Net income	$ 245,000	$ 211,200

Fleming Inc.
Comparative Retained Earnings Statement
For Years Ended December 31, 1990 and 1989

	1990	1989
Retained earnings, January 1	$ 723,000	$ 581,800
Add net income for year	245,000	211,200
Total	$ 968,000	$ 793,000
Deduct dividends:		
On preferred stock	$ 40,000	$ 40,000
On common stock	45,000	30,000
Total	$ 85,000	$ 70,000
Retained earnings, December 31	$ 883,000	$ 723,000

Fleming Inc.
Comparative Balance Sheet
December 31, 1990 and 1989

Assets	1990	1989
Current assets:		
Cash..	$ 175,000	$ 125,000
Marketable securities	150,000	50,000
Accounts receivable (net)	425,000	325,000
Inventories...	720,000	480,000
Prepaid expenses	30,000	20,000
Total current assets..	$1,500,000	$1,000,000
Long-term investments..	250,000	225,000
Plant assets	2,093,000	1,948,000
Total assets	$3,843,000	$3,173,000

Liabilities		
Current liabilities	$ 750,000	$ 650,000
Long-term liabilities:		
Mortgage note payable, 10%, due 1998	$ 410,000	—
Bonds payable, 8%, due 1999.................................	800,000	$ 800,000
Total long-term liabilities..	$1,210,000	$ 800,000
Total liabilities..	$1,960,000	$1,450,000

Stockholders' Equity		
Preferred 8% stock, $100 par.......................................	$ 500,000	$ 500,000
Common stock, $10 par	500,000	500,000
Retained earnings..	883,000	723,000
Total stockholders' equity..	$1,883,000	$1,723,000
Total liabilities and stockholders' equity	$3,843,000	$3,173,000

Instructions:

Determine the following measures for 1990:
   (1) Working capital
   (2) Current ratio
   (3) Acid-test ratio
   (4) Accounts receivable turnover
   (5) Number of days' sales in receivables
   (6) Inventory turnover
   (7) Number of days' sales in inventory
   (8) Ratio of plant assets to long-term liabilities
   (9) Ratio of stockholders' equity to liabilities
   (10) Number of times interest charges earned
   (11) Number of times preferred dividends earned
   (12) Ratio of net sales to assets
   (13) Rate earned on total assets
   (14) Rate earned on stockholders' equity
   (15) Rate earned on common stockholders' equity
   (16) Earnings per share on common stock
   (17) Price-earnings ratio
   (18) Dividend yield

SOLUTION

   (1) Working capital: $750,000
        $1,500,000 − $750,000

(2) Current ratio: 2.0:1
$1,500,000 ÷ $750,000

(3) Acid-test ratio: 1.0:1
$750,000 ÷ $750,000

(4) Accounts receivable turnover: 13.3

$$5,000,000 \div \frac{\$425,000 + \$325,000}{2}$$

(5) Number of days' sales in receivables: 31 days
$5,000,000 ÷ 365 = $13,699
$425,000 ÷ $13,699

(6) Inventory turnover: 5.7

$$3,400,000 \div \frac{\$720,000 + \$480,000}{2}$$

(7) Number of days' sales in inventory: 77.3 days
$3,400,000 ÷ 365 = $9,315
$720,000 ÷ $9,315

(8) Ratio of plant assets to long-term liabilities: 1.7:1
$2,093,000 ÷ $1,210,000

(9) Ratio of stockholders' equity to liabilities: 1.0:1
$1,883,000 ÷ $1,960,000

(10) Number of times interest charges earned: 6.2
($545,000 + $105,000) ÷ $105,000

(11) Number of times preferred dividends earned: 6.1
$245,000 ÷ $40,000

(12) Ratio of net sales to assets: 1.5:1

$$5,000,000 \div \frac{\$3,593,000 + \$2,948,000}{2}$$

(13) Rate earned on total assets: 10.0%

$$(\$245,000 + \$105,000) \div \frac{\$3,843,000 + \$3,173,000}{2}$$

(14) Rate earned on stockholders' equity: 13.6%

$$245,000 \div \frac{\$1,883,000 + \$1,723,000}{2}$$

(15) Rate earned on common stockholders' equity: 15.7%

$$(\$245,000 - \$40,000) \div \frac{\$1,383,000 + \$1,223,000}{2}$$

(16) Earnings per share on common stock: $4.10
($245,000 − $40,000) ÷ 50,000

(17) Price-earnings ratio: 6.1
$25 ÷ $4.10

(18) Dividend yield: 3.6%

$$\frac{(\$45,000 \div 50,000 \text{ shares})}{\$25}$$

DISCUSSION QUESTIONS

1. Using the following data taken from a comparative balance sheet, illustrate (a) horizontal analysis and (b) vertical analysis.

	Current Year	Preceding Year
Accounts payable	$270,000	$200,000
Total current liabilities	900,000	800,000

2. What is the advantage of using comparative statements for financial analysis rather than statements for a single date or period?

3. The current year's amount of net income (after income tax) is 15% larger than that of the preceding year. Does this indicate an improved operating performance? Discuss.

4. What are common-size financial statements?

5. In the analysis of the financial status of an enterprise, what is meant by *solvency* and *profitability*?

6. (a) Name the major ratios useful in assessing solvency and profitability.
   (b) Why is it important not to rely on only one ratio or measure in assessing the solvency or profitability of an enterprise?

7. Identify the measure of current position analysis described by each of the following: (a) the excess of the current assets over current liabilities, (b) the ratio of current assets to current liabilities, (c) the ratio of quick assets to current liabilities.

8. Selected condensed data taken from the balance sheet of North Corporation at April 30, the end of the current fiscal year, are as follows:

Cash, marketable securities, and receivables	$520,000
Other current assets	180,000
Total current assets	$700,000
Current liabilities	$400,000

At April 30, what are (a) the working capital, (b) the current ratio, and (c) the acid-test ratio?

9. For Rawlins Company, the working capital at the end of the current year is $30,000 greater than the working capital at the end of the preceding year, reported as follows:

	Current Year	Preceding Year
Current assets:		
Cash, marketable securities, and receivables...	$330,000	$240,000
Inventories	150,000	110,000
Total current assets	$480,000	$350,000
Current liabilities	300,000	200,000
Working capital	$180,000	$150,000

Has Rawlins' current position improved? Explain.

10. A company that grants terms of n/45 on all sales has an accounts receivable turnover for the year, based on monthly averages, of 5. Is this a satisfactory turnover? Discuss.

11. What does an increase in the number of days' sales in receivables ordinarily indicate about the credit and collection policy of the firm?

12. (a) Why is it advantageous to have a high inventory turnover? (b) Is it possible for the inventory turnover to be too high? Discuss. (c) Is it possible to have a high inventory turnover and a high number of days' sales in inventory? Discuss.

13. What does the following data taken from a comparative balance sheet indicate about the company's current ability to borrow additional funds on a long-term basis as compared to the preceding year?

	Current Year	Preceding Year
Plant assets (net).......................................	$2,100,000	$1,250,000
Long-term liabilities	750,000	500,000

14. What does an increase in the ratio of stockholders' equity to liabilities indicate about the margin of safety for the firm's creditors and the ability of the firm to withstand adverse business conditions?

15. In computing the ratio of net sales to assets, why are long-term investments excluded in determining the amount of the total assets?

16. In determining the number of times interest charges are earned, why are interest charges added to income before income tax?

17. In determining the rate earned on total assets, why is interest expense added to net income before dividing by total assets?

18. (a) Why is the rate earned on stockholders' equity by a thriving enterprise ordinarily higher than the rate earned on total assets?
    (b) Should the rate earned on common stockholders' equity normally be higher or lower than the rate earned on total stockholders' equity? Explain.

19. The net income (after income tax) of Smith Company was $4.20 per common share in the latest year and $8 per common share for the preceding year. At the beginning of the latest year, the number of shares outstanding was doubled by a stock split. There were no other changes in the amount of stock outstanding. What were the earnings per share in the preceding year, adjusted to place them on a comparable basis with the latest year?

20. The price-earnings ratio for the common stock of Orlando Company was 18 at December 31, the end of the current fiscal year. What does the ratio indicate about the selling price of the common stock in relation to current earnings?

21. Why would the dividend yield differ significantly from the rate earned on common stockholders' equity?

22. Favorable business conditions may bring about certain seemingly unfavorable ratios, and unfavorable business operations may result in apparently favorable ratios. For example, Arron Company increased its sales and net income substantially for the current year, yet the current ratio at the end of the year is lower than at the beginning of the year. Discuss some possible causes of the apparent weakening of the current position while sales and net income have increased substantially.

23. (a) What are the major components of an annual report? (b) Indicate the purpose of the financial highlights section and the president's letter.

24. (a) The typical independent auditors' report expressing an unqualified opinion consists of three paragraphs. What is reported in each paragraph? (b) Under what condition does an auditor give a qualified opinion?

Real World Focus

25. The rate of return on total assets based upon Fay's Drug Company, Inc.'s 1988 annual report is 7.4%. The rate of return on stockholders' equity for the same period is 10.8%. What is the explanation for the difference in the two rates?

EXERCISES

Exercise 19–1
Vertical analysis of income statement.
OBJ. 1

Revenue and expense data for W. E. Corbett Company are as follows:

	1990	1989
Sales	$1,000,000	$750,000
Cost of goods sold	600,000	420,000
Selling expenses	160,000	127,500
Administrative expenses	80,000	67,500
Income tax	50,000	30,000

(a) Prepare an income statement in comparative form, stating each item for both 1990 and 1989 as a percent of sales.
(b) Comment on the significant changes disclosed by the comparative income statement.

Exercise 19–2
Horizontal analysis of balance sheet.
OBJ. 1

Balance sheet data for Higgins Company on December 31, the end of the fiscal year, are as follows:

	1990	1989
Current assets	$436,000	$400,000
Plant assets	637,000	650,000
Intangible assets	66,500	70,000
Current liabilities	115,000	100,000
Long-term liabilities	357,200	380,000
Common stock	500,000	500,000
Retained earnings	167,300	140,000

Prepare a comparative balance sheet with horizontal analysis, indicating the increase (decrease) for 1990 when compared with 1989.

Exercise 19–3
Current position analysis.
OBJ. 3

The following data were abstracted from the balance sheet of Laskey Company:

	Current Year	Preceding Year
Cash	$202,800	$180,000
Marketable securities	112,000	80,000
Accounts and notes receivable (net)	285,200	260,000
Inventories	485,000	422,400
Prepaid expenses	15,000	17,600
Accounts and notes payable (short-term)	420,000	350,500
Accrued liabilities	80,000	49,500

(a) Determine for each year (1) the working capital, (2) the current ratio, and (3) the acid-test ratio. (Present figures used in your computations.)
(b) What conclusions can be drawn from these data as to the company's ability to meet its currently maturing debts?

Exercise 19–4
Accounts receivable analysis.
OBJ. 3

The following data are taken from the financial statements for Owen Company:

	Current Year	Preceding Year
Accounts receivable, end of year..........................	$ 496,500	$ 463,800
Monthly average accounts receivable (net)............	485,000	450,000
Net sales on account...	5,335,000	4,050,000

Terms of all sales are 1/10, n/45.

(a) Determine for each year (1) the accounts receivable turnover and (2) the number of days' sales in receivables.
(b) What conclusions can be drawn from these data concerning the composition of the accounts receivable?

Exercise 19–5
Inventory analysis.
OBJ. 3

The following data were abstracted from the income statement of Caball Corporation:

	Current Year	Preceding Year
Sales	$3,210,000	$3,120,000
Beginning inventories	490,000	418,500
Purchases	2,270,000	2,330,500
Ending inventories...	510,000	486,500

(a) Determine for each year (1) the inventory turnover and (2) the number of days' sales in inventory.
(b) What conclusions can be drawn from these data concerning the composition of the inventories?

Exercise 19–6
Six measures of solvency or profitability.
OBJ. 3, 4

SPREADSHEET PROBLEM

The following data were taken from the financial statements of Roger Clemens and Co. for the current fiscal year:

Plant assets (net)		$1,500,000
Liabilities:		
Current liabilities		$ 250,000
Mortgage note payable, 8%, issued 1985, due 1999..............		750,000
Total liabilities..		$1,000,000
Stockholders' equity:		
Preferred 5% stock, $100 par, cumulative, nonparticipating (no change during year)...		$ 300,000
Common stock, $10 par (no change during year)..................		1,200,000
Retained earnings:		
Balance, beginning of year..........	$865,000	
Net income..............................	230,000	$1,095,000
Preferred dividends....................	$ 15,000	
Common dividends	80,000	95,000
Balance, end of year		1,000,000
Total stockholders' equity		$2,500,000
Net sales..		$4,800,000
Interest expense		60,000

Assuming that long-term investments totaled $250,000 throughout the year and that total assets were $3,000,000 at the beginning of the year, determine the following, presenting figures used in your computations: (a) ratio of plant assets to long-term liabilities, (b) ratio of stockholders' equity to liabilities, (c) ratio of net sales to assets, (d) rate earned on total assets, (e) rate earned on stockholders' equity, (f) rate earned on common stockholders' equity.

Exercise 19–7
Five measures of solvency or profitability.
OBJ. 3, 4

The balance sheet for Laudner Corporation at the end of the current fiscal year indicated the following:

Bonds payable, 10% (issued in 1978, due in 1998)....................	$3,000,000
Preferred 6% stock, $100 par...	1,000,000
Common stock, $100 par	5,000,000

Income before income tax was $750,000, and income taxes were $270,000 for the current year. Cash dividends paid on common stock during the current year totaled $262,500. The common stock was selling for $105 per share at the end of the year. Determine each of the following: (a) number of times bond interest charges were earned, (b) number of times preferred dividends were earned, (c) earnings per share on common stock, (d) price-earnings ratio, and (e) dividend yield.

Exercise 19–8
Earnings per share.
OBJ. 4

The net income reported on the income statement of Martinez and Co. was $1,475,000. There were 250,000 shares of $20 par common stock and 30,000 shares of $6 cumulative preferred stock outstanding throughout the current year. The income statement included two extraordinary items: a $400,000 gain from condemnation of land and a $250,000 loss arising from flood damage, both after applicable income tax. Determine the per share figures for common stock for (a) income before extraordinary items and (b) net income.

Exercise 19–9
Real World Focus.
OBJ. 1

The following comparative income statement (in thousands of dollars) for the years ending December 31, 1988 and 1987, was adapted from the 1988 annual report of William Wrigley Jr. Company:

	1988	1987
Revenues	$901,980	$790,432
Costs and expenses:		
Cost of sales..	$392,460	$338,081
Selling, distribution, and administrative	368,266	328,737
Interest...	527	606
Total costs and expenses...	$761,253	$667,424
Earnings before income taxes	$140,727	$123,008
Income taxes	53,491	52,863
Net earnings	$ 87,236	$ 70,145

(a) Prepare a comparative income statement for 1988 and 1987 in vertical form, stating each item as a percent of revenues. (b) Based upon (a), which 1988 income statement item(s) might warrant additional investigation?

PROBLEMS

Problem 19–1A
Horizontal analysis for income statement.
OBJ. 1

For 1990, Gedman Company reported its most significant increase in net income in years. At the end of the year, Sue Gedman, the president, is presented with the following condensed comparative income statement:

Gedman Company
Comparative Income Statement
For Years Ended December 31, 1990 and 1989

	1990	1989
Sales	$741,600	$612,000
Sales returns and allowances	21,600	12,000
Net sales	$720,000	$600,000
Cost of goods sold	442,800	360,000
Gross profit	$277,200	$240,000
Selling expenses	$ 94,300	$115,000
Administrative expenses	61,000	50,000
Total operating expenses	$155,300	$165,000
Operating income	$121,900	$ 75,000
Other income	1,500	2,000
Income before income tax	$123,400	$ 77,000
Income tax	31,000	15,400
Net income	$ 92,400	$ 61,600

Instructions:

(1) Prepare a comparative income statement with horizontal analysis for the two-year period, using 1989 as the base year.
(2) To the extent the data permit, comment on the significant relationships revealed by the horizontal analysis prepared in (1).

Problem 19–2A
Vertical analysis for income statement.
OBJ. 1

For 1990, Evans Company initiated an extensive sales promotion campaign that included the expenditure of an additional $30,000 for advertising. At the end of the year, Rob Evans, the president, is presented with the following condensed comparative income statement:

Evans Company
Comparative Income Statement
For Years Ended December 31, 1990 and 1989

	1990	1989
Sales	$515,000	$354,200
Sales returns and allowances	15,000	4,200
Net sales	$500,000	$350,000
Cost of goods sold	330,000	221,900
Gross profit	$170,000	$128,100
Selling expenses	$ 93,000	$ 56,000
Administrative expenses	24,000	17,500
Total operating expenses	$117,000	$ 73,500
Operating income	$ 53,000	$ 54,600
Other income	6,000	3,500
Income before income tax	$ 59,000	$ 58,100
Income tax	11,000	10,850
Net income	$ 48,000	$ 47,250

Instructions:

(1) Prepare a comparative income statement for the two-year period, presenting an analysis of each item in relationship to net sales for each of the years.
(2) To the extent the data permit, comment on the significant relationships revealed by the vertical analysis prepared in (1).

Problem 19–3A
Common-size
income statement.
OBJ. 1

Revenue and expense data for the current calendar year for Greenwell Publishing Company and for the publishing industry are as follows. The Greenwell Publishing Company data are expressed in dollars; the publishing industry averages are expressed in percentages.

	Greenwell Publishing Company	Publishing Industry Average
Sales	$7,056,000	100.5%
Sales returns and allowances	56,000	.5%
Cost of goods sold	4,760,000	64.8%
Selling expenses	735,000	9.9%
Administrative expenses	301,000	8.9%
Other income	49,000	.6%
Other expense	91,000	1.2%
Income tax	483,000	6.8%

Instructions:

(1) Prepare a common-size income statement comparing the results of operations for Greenwell Publishing Company with the industry average.
(2) As far as the data permit, comment on significant relationships revealed by the comparisons.

Problem 19–4A
Effect of
transactions on
current position
analysis.
OBJ. 3

Data pertaining to the current position of C. Dykstra Inc. are as follows:

Cash	$ 11,600
Marketable securities	40,000
Accounts and notes receivable (net)	58,400
Inventories	101,100
Prepaid expenses	8,900
Accounts payable	43,500
Notes payable (short-term)	50,000
Accrued liabilities	6,500

Instructions:

(1) Compute (a) the working capital, (b) the current ratio, and (c) the acid-test ratio.
(2) List the following captions on a sheet of paper:

    Transaction   Working Capital   Current Ratio   Acid-Test Ratio

Compute the working capital, the current ratio, and the acid-test ratio after each of the following transactions, and record the results in the appropriate columns. Consider each transaction separately and assume that only that transaction affects the data given above.
(a) Paid accounts payable, $20,000.
(b) Sold marketable securities, $40,000.
(c) Purchased goods on account, $30,000.
(d) Paid short-term notes payable, $50,000.
(e) Declared a cash dividend, $20,000.
(f) Declared a common stock dividend on common stock, $48,500.
(g) Borrowed cash from bank on a long-term note, $100,000.
(h) Received cash on account, $15,000.
(i) Issued additional shares of stock for cash, $80,000.
(j) Paid cash for office supplies, $6,000.

Problem 19–5A

Effect of errors on current position analysis.

OBJ. 3

Prior to approving an application for a short-term loan, Toccoa National Bank required that Harvey Company provide evidence of working capital of at least $200,000, a current ratio of at least 1.8:1, and an acid-test ratio of at least 1.0:1. The chief accountant of Harvey Company compiled the following data pertaining to the current position:

Harvey Company
Schedule of Current Assets and Current Liabilities
December 31, 1990

Current assets:	
Cash..	$ 36,250
Marketable securities..	75,000
Accounts receivable..	115,250
Notes receivable...	70,000
Interest receivable..	3,500
Inventories...	192,620
Supplies...	7,380
Total current assets......................................	$500,000
Current liabilities:	
Accounts payable..	$200,000
Notes payable...	50,000
Total current liabilities..................................	$250,000

Instructions:

(1) Compute (a) the working capital, (b) the current ratio, and (c) the acid-test ratio.
(2) At the request of the bank, a firm of independent auditors was retained to examine data submitted with the loan application. This examination disclosed several errors. Prepare correcting entries for each of the following errors:
  (a) A canceled check indicates that a bill for $25,000 for repairs on factory equipment had not been recorded in the accounts.
  (b) Accounts receivable of $15,250 are uncollectible and should be immediately written off. In addition, it was estimated that of the remaining receivables, 4% would eventually become uncollectible. An allowance should be made for these future uncollectible accounts.
  (c) Six months' interest had been accrued on the $70,000, 10%, six-month note receivable dated October 1, 1990.
  (d) Supplies on hand at December 31, 1990, total $1,380.
  (e) The marketable securities portfolio includes $50,000 of Oliver Company stock that is held as a long-term investment.
  (f) The notes payable account consists of a 18%, 120-day note dated November 1, 1990. No interest had been accrued on the note.
  (g) Accrued wages as of December 31, 1990, totaled $20,000.
  (h) Rental Income had been credited upon receipt of $28,000, which was the full amount of a year's rent for warehouse space leased to F. H. Smith Inc., effective July 1, 1990.
  (i) The purchase of inventory shipped FOB shipping point on December 30, 1990, was not recorded until it was received on January 4, 1991, $22,000.
(3) Giving effect to each of the preceding errors separately and assuming that only that error affects the current position of Harvey Company, compute (a) the working capital, (b) the current ratio, and (c) the acid-test ratio. Use the following column headings for recording your answers:

| Error | Working Capital | Current Ratio | Acid-Test Ratio |

(4) Prepare a revised schedule of working capital as of December 31, 1990, and recompute the current ratio and the acid-test ratio, giving effect to the corrections of all of the preceding errors.
(5) Discuss the action you would recommend that the bank take regarding the pending loan application.

Problem 19–6A
Eighteen measures
of solvency and
profitability.

OBJ. 3, 4

The comparative financial statements of F. I. Brady Company are as follows. The market price of F. I. Brady Company's common stock was $20.30 on December 31, 1989, and $28.40 on December 31, 1990.

F. I. Brady Company
Comparative Income Statement
For Years Ended December 31, 1990 and 1989

	1990	1989
Sales (all on account)	$5,145,000	$4,120,000
Sales returns and allowances	145,000	120,000
Net sales	$5,000,000	$4,000,000
Cost of goods sold	3,000,000	2,360,000
Gross profit	$2,000,000	$1,640,000
Selling expenses	$ 450,000	$ 400,000
Administrative expenses	220,000	180,000
Total operating expenses	$ 670,000	$ 580,000
Operating income	$1,330,000	$1,060,000
Other income	30,000	40,000
	$1,360,000	$1,100,000
Other expense (interest)	260,000	200,000
Income before income tax	$1,100,000	$ 900,000
Income tax	340,000	270,000
Net income	$ 760,000	$ 630,000

F. I. Brady Company
Comparative Retained Earnings Statement
For Years Ended December 31, 1990 and 1989

	1990	1989
Retained earnings, January 1	$1,130,000	$ 750,000
Add net income for year	760,000	630,000
Total	$1,890,000	$1,380,000
Deduct dividends:		
On preferred stock	$ 50,000	$ 50,000
On common stock	240,000	200,000
Total	$ 290,000	$ 250,000
Retained earnings, December 31	$1,600,000	$1,130,000

F. I. Brady Company
Comparative Balance Sheet
December 31, 1990 and 1989

Assets	1990	1989
Current assets:		
Cash	$ 187,500	$ 287,500
Marketable securities	250,000	200,000
Accounts receivable (net)	362,500	262,500
Inventories	880,000	710,000
Prepaid expenses	80,000	115,000
Total current assets	$1,760,000	$1,575,000
Long-term investments	1,000,000	1,000,000
Plant assets	6,140,000	5,305,000
Total assets	$8,900,000	$7,880,000

Liabilities

Current liabilities..	$ 800,000	$ 750,000

Long-term liabilities:

Mortgage note payable, 12%, due 1999.............	$ 500,000	—
Bonds payable, 10%, due 1998.......................	2,000,000	$2,000,000
Total long-term liabilities..............................	$2,500,000	$2,000,000
Total liabilities...	$3,300,000	$2,750,000

Stockholders' Equity

Preferred $5 stock, $100 par...............................	$1,000,000	$1,000,000
Common stock, $15 par....................................	3,000,000	3,000,000
Retained earnings..	1,600,000	1,130,000
Total stockholders' equity	$5,600,000	$5,130,000
Total liabilities and stockholders' equity.................	$8,900,000	$7,880,000

Instructions:

Determine the following measures for 1990, presenting the figures used in your computations:
- (1) Working capital.
- (2) Current ratio.
- (3) Acid-test ratio.
- (4) Accounts receivable turnover.
- (5) Number of days' sales in receivables.
- (6) Inventory turnover.
- (7) Number of days' sales in inventory.
- (8) Ratio of plant assets to long-term liabilities.
- (9) Ratio of stockholders' equity to liabilities.
- (10) Number of times interest charges earned.
- (11) Number of times preferred dividends earned.
- (12) Ratio of net sales to assets.
- (13) Rate earned on total assets.
- (14) Rate earned on stockholders' equity.
- (15) Rate earned on common stockholders' equity.
- (16) Earnings per share on common stock.
- (17) Price-earnings ratio.
- (18) Dividend yield.

Problem 19–7A
Report on detailed financial analysis.
OBJ. 3, 4, 5

B. O'Neil is considering making a substantial investment in F. I. Brady Company. The company's comparative financial statements for 1990 and 1989 are given in Problem 19–6A. To assist in the evaluation of the company, O'Neil secured the following additional data taken from the balance sheet at December 31, 1988:

Accounts receivable (net)...	$ 250,000
Inventories..	670,000
Long-term investments..	800,000
Total assets...	6,800,000
Total stockholders' equity (preferred and common stock outstanding same as in 1989)	4,750,000

Instructions:

Prepare a report for O'Neil, based on an analysis of the financial data presented. In preparing your report, include all ratios and other data that will be useful in arriving at a decision regarding the investment.

Series B

Problem 19–2B
Vertical analysis for
income statement.

OBJ. 1

For 1990, Boggs Company initiated an extensive sales promotion campaign that included the expenditure of an additional $50,000 for advertising. At the end of the year,
Karl Boggs, the president, is presented with the following condensed comparative income statement:

Boggs Company
Comparative Income Statement
For Years Ended December 31, 1990 and 1989

	1990	1989
Sales	$947,200	$760,500
Sales returns and allowances	22,200	10,500
Net sales	$925,000	$750,000
Cost of goods sold	593,850	495,000
Gross profit	$331,150	$255,000
Selling expenses	$203,500	$135,000
Administrative expenses	27,750	42,000
Total operating expenses	$231,250	$177,000
Operating income	$ 99,900	$ 78,000
Other expense	1,850	3,000
Income before income tax	$ 98,050	$ 75,000
Income tax	24,050	18,000
Net income	$ 74,000	$ 57,000

Instructions:

(1) Prepare a comparative income statement for the two-year period, presenting an
   analysis of each item in relationship to net sales for each of the years.
(2) To the extent the data permit, comment on the significant relationships revealed by
   the vertical analysis prepared in (1).

Problem 19–4B
Effect of
transactions on
current position
analysis.

OBJ. 3

Data pertaining to the current position of Jeffries Company are as follows:

Cash	$125,500
Marketable securities	70,000
Accounts and notes receivable (net)	224,500
Inventories	348,600
Prepaid expenses	36,400
Accounts payable	196,000
Notes payable (short-term)	105,000
Accrued liabilities	49,000

Instructions:

(1) Compute (a) the working capital, (b) the current ratio, and (c) the acid-test ratio.
(2) List the following captions on a sheet of paper:

Transaction	Working Capital	Current Ratio	Acid-Test Ratio

Compute the working capital, the current ratio, and the acid-test ratio after each of
the following transactions, and record the results in the appropriate columns. Consider each transaction separately and assume that only that transaction affects the
data given above.
(a) Declared a cash dividend, $75,000.
(b) Issued additional shares of stock for cash, $245,000.   *(Continued)*

(c) Purchased goods on account, $45,000.
(d) Paid accounts payable, $30,000.
(e) Borrowed cash from bank on a long-term note, $100,000.
(f) Paid cash for office supplies, $18,000.
(g) Received cash on account, $24,800.
(h) Paid short-term notes payable, $80,000.
(i) Declared a common stock dividend on common stock, $150,000.
(j) Sold marketable securities, $70,000.

Problem 19–6B
Eighteen measures of solvency and profitability.

OBJ. 3, 4

SPREADSHEET PROBLEM

The comparative financial statements of R. J. Combs Inc. are as follows. The market price of R. J. Combs Inc.'s common stock was $54 on December 31, 1989, and $50.40 on December 31, 1990.

R. J. Combs Inc.
Comparative Income Statement
For Years Ended December 31, 1990 and 1989

	1990	1989
Sales (all on account)	$7,517,400	$6,419,200
Sales returns and allowances	37,400	19,200
Net sales	$7,480,000	$6,400,000
Cost of goods sold	4,800,000	3,840,000
Gross profit	$2,680,000	$2,560,000
Selling expenses	$1,280,000	$ 985,600
Administrative expenses	540,000	526,400
Total operating expenses	$1,820,000	$1,512,000
Operating income	$ 860,000	$1,048,000
Other income	140,000	112,000
	$1,000,000	$1,160,000
Other expense (interest)	200,000	180,000
Income before income tax	$ 800,000	$ 980,000
Income tax	320,000	400,000
Net income	$ 480,000	$ 580,000

R. J. Combs Inc.
Comparative Retained Earnings Statement
For Years Ended December 31, 1990 and 1989

	1990	1989
Retained earnings, January 1	$2,416,000	$1,936,000
Add net income for year	480,000	580,000
Total	$2,896,000	$2,516,000
Deduct dividends:		
On preferred stock	$ 30,000	$ 30,000
On common stock	50,000	70,000
Total	$ 80,000	$ 100,000
Retained earnings, December 31	$2,816,000	$2,416,000

R. J. Combs Inc.
Comparative Balance Sheet
December 31, 1990 and 1989

Assets	1990	1989
Current assets:		
Cash	$ 130,000	$ 120,000
Marketable securities	200,000	150,000
Accounts receivable (net)	440,000	400,000
Inventories	769,600	674,800
Prepaid expenses	70,400	35,200
Total current assets	$1,610,000	$1,380,000
Long-term investments	300,000	250,000
Plant assets	4,506,000	4,086,000
Total assets	$6,416,000	$5,716,000

Liabilities	1990	1989
Current liabilities	$ 700,000	$ 600,000
Long-term liabilities:		
Mortgage note payable, 10%, due 1992	$ 200,000	—
Bonds payable, 15%, due 2007	1,200,000	$1,200,000
Total long-term liabilities	$1,400,000	$1,200,000
Total liabilities	$2,100,000	$1,800,000

Stockholders' Equity	1990	1989
Preferred 6% stock, $50 par	$ 500,000	$ 500,000
Common stock, $20 par	1,000,000	1,000,000
Retained earnings	2,816,000	2,416,000
Total stockholders' equity	$4,316,000	$3,916,000
Total liabilities and stockholders' equity	$6,416,000	$5,716,000

Instructions:

Determine the following measures for 1990, presenting the figures used in your computations:
(1) Working capital.
(2) Current ratio.
(3) Acid-test ratio.
(4) Accounts receivable turnover.
(5) Number of days' sales in receivables.
(6) Inventory turnover.
(7) Number of days' sales in inventory.
(8) Ratio of plant assets to long-term liabilities.
(9) Ratio of stockholders' equity to liabilities.
(10) Number of times interest charges earned.
(11) Number of times preferred dividends earned.
(12) Ratio of net sales to assets.
(13) Rate earned on total assets.
(14) Rate earned on stockholders' equity.
(15) Rate earned on common stockholders' equity.
(16) Earnings per share on common stock.
(17) Price-earnings ratio.
(18) Dividend yield.

MINI-CASE 19

You and your sister are both presidents of companies in the same industry, RST Inc. and CDP Inc., respectively. Both companies were originally operated as a single-family business; but, shortly after your father's death in 1978, the business was divided into two companies. Your sister took over CDP Inc., located in St. Paul while you took over RST Inc., located in Des Moines.

During a recent family reunion, your sister referred to the much larger rate of return to her stockholders than was the case in your company and suggested that you consider rearranging the method of financing your corporation. The difference is highlighted by the following chart, which compares the rates earned on the stockholders' equity and the assets of the two companies:

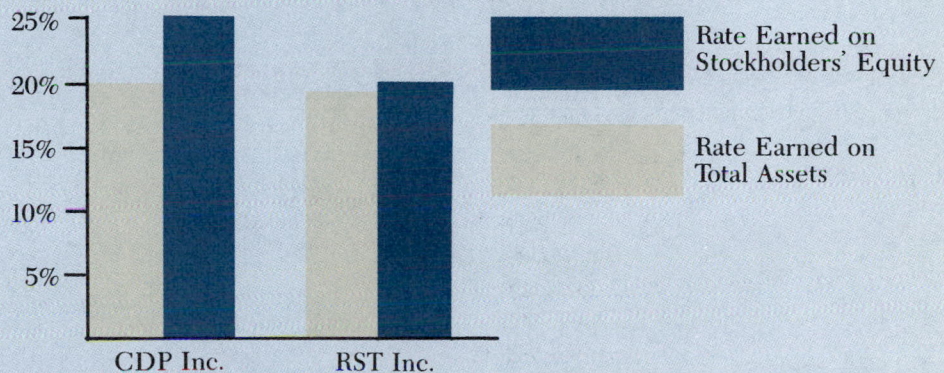

Since 1978, the growth in your sister's company has been financed largely through borrowing and yours largely through the issuance of additional common stock. Both companies have about the same volume of sales, gross profit, operating income, and total assets.

The income statements for the year ended December 31, 1990, and the balance sheets at December 31, 1990, for both companies are shown on the next page.

In addition to the 1990 financial statements, the following data were taken from the balance sheet at December 31, 1989:

	CDP Inc.	RST Inc.
Total assets	$ 960,000	$1,030,000
Total stockholders' equity....................................	500,000	900,000

Income Statements

	CDP Inc.	RST Inc.
Sales	$2,435,400	$2,343,000
Sales returns and allowances	35,400	27,000
Net sales	$2,400,000	$2,316,000
Cost of goods sold	1,470,000	1,416,000
Gross profit	$ 930,000	$ 900,000
Selling expenses	$ 400,000	$ 366,700
Administrative expenses	235,000	210,300
Total operating expenses	$ 635,000	$ 577,000
Operating income	$ 295,000	$ 323,000
Interest expense	40,000	12,000
Income before income tax	$ 255,000	$ 311,000
Income tax	100,000	124,000
Net income	$ 155,000	$ 187,000

Balance Sheets

Assets	CDP Inc.	RST Inc.
Current assets	$ 75,000	$ 78,000
Plant assets (net)	930,000	972,000
Intangible assets	15,000	30,000
Total assets	$1,020,000	$1,080,000

Liabilities		
Current liabilities	$ 30,000	$ 48,000
Long-term liabilities	400,000	100,000
Total liabilities	$ 430,000	$ 148,000

Stockholders' Equity		
Common stock ($10 par)	$ 100,000	$ 450,000
Retained earnings	490,000	482,000
Total stockholders' equity	$ 590,000	$ 932,000
Total liabilities and stockholders' equity	$1,020,000	$1,080,000

Instructions:

(1) Determine for 1990 the following ratios and other measures for both companies.
    (a) Ratio of plant assets to long-term liabilities.
    (b) Ratio of stockholders' equity to liabilities.
    (c) Ratio of net sales to assets.
    (d) Rate earned on total assets.
    (e) Rate earned on stockholders' equity.
(2) For both CDP Inc. and RST Inc., the rate earned on stockholders' equity is greater than the rate earned on total assets. Explain.
(3) Why is the rate of return on stockholders' equity for CDP Inc. approximately 25% greater than for RST Inc.?
(4) Comment on your sister's suggestion for rearranging the financing of RST Inc.

ETHICS DISCUSSION CASE	Debra Lowery, president of Logan Equipment Co., prepared a draft of the "President's Letter" to be included with Logan Equipment Co.'s 1990 annual report. The letter mentions a 15% increase in sales and a recent expansion of plant facilities, but fails to mention the net loss of $250,000 for the year.
	You have been asked to review the letter for inclusion in the annual report. How would you respond to the omission of the net loss of $250,000? Specifically, is such an action ethical?

ANSWERS TO SELF-EXAMINATION QUESTIONS

1. **A** Percentage analysis indicating the relationship of the component parts to the total in a financial statement, such as the relationship of current assets to total assets (20% to 100%) in the question, is called vertical analysis (answer A). Percentage analysis of increases and decreases in corresponding items in comparative financial statements is called horizontal analysis (answer B). An example of horizontal analysis would be the presentation of the amount of current assets in the preceding balance sheet along with the amount of current assets at the end of the current year, with the increase or decrease in current assets between the periods expressed as a percentage. Differential analysis (answer C), as discussed in Chapter 27, is the area of accounting concerned with the effect of alternative courses of action on revenue and expenses.

2. **D** Various solvency measures, categorized as current position analysis, indicate a firm's ability to meet currently maturing obligations. Each measure contributes in the analysis of a firm's current position and is most useful when viewed with other measures and when compared with similar measures for other periods and for other firms. Working capital (answer A) is the excess of current assets over current liabilities; the current ratio (answer B) is the ratio of current assets to current liabilities; and the acid-test ratio (answer C) is the ratio of the sum of cash, receivables, and marketable securities to current liabilities.

3. **D** The ratio of current assets to current liabilities is usually referred to as the current ratio (answer A) and is sometimes referred to as the working capital ratio (answer B) or bankers' ratio (answer C).

4. **C** The ratio of the sum of cash, receivables, and marketable securities (sometimes called quick assets) to current liabilities is called the acid-test ratio (answer C) or quick ratio. The current ratio (answer A) and working capital ratio (answer B) are two terms that describe the ratio of current assets to current liabilities.

5. **C** As with many attempts at analyzing financial data, it is possible to determine more than one measure that is useful for evaluating the efficiency in the management of inventories. Both the inventory turnover (answer A), which is determined by dividing the cost of goods sold by the average inventory, and the number of days' sales in inventory (answer B), which is determined by dividing the inventories at the end of the year by the average daily cost of goods sold, express the relationship between the cost of goods sold and inventory.

Managerial
Accounting
Principles
and Systems

PART SIX

6

CHAPTER TWENTY

MANAGERIAL ACCOUNTING CONCEPTS AND PRINCIPLES

CHAPTER OBJECTIVES

1   Describe managerial accounting and distinguish managerial accounting from financial accounting.

2   Describe the management process and the role of managerial accounting in this process.

3   Describe the characteristics of accounting reports prepared for use by management.

4   Describe the organization of the managerial accounting function within a business enterprise.

5   Distinguish between costs and expenses.

6   Describe and illustrate the three manufacturing costs:
    Direct materials
    Direct labor
    Factory overhead

7   Describe the common classifications of nonmanufacturing costs.

8   Distinguish between product and period costs.

9   Describe and illustrate the financial statements of a manufacturing enterprise, including the preparation of the statement of cost of goods manufactured.

10 Describe the basic cost classifications useful for planning and control:
    Variable costs and fixed costs
    Direct costs and indirect costs
    Controllable costs and noncontrollable costs
    Differential costs
    Discretionary costs
    Sunk costs
    Opportunity costs

Accounting, as described in Chapter 1, can be viewed as an information system that provides essential data about the financial activities of an entity to various users to aid them in making informed judgments and decisions. One important user of accounting information is management, who has the responsibility of directing the operations of an enterprise. The types of information needed and the use of this information by management in directing operations are the focus of most of the remainder of this text.

The preceding chapters focused on the concepts and principles of financial accounting and their application in the analysis of transactions and the preparation and interpretation of the financial statements. This chapter begins with a general description of the nature of managerial accounting and its relationship to financial accounting. The chapter then describes the management process and the role that accounting plays in this process, as well as the organization of the managerial accounting function within a business enterprise. The basic financial statements of a manufacturing enterprise are discussed, and the chapter concludes by describing and illustrating various cost concepts and principles useful in planning and controlling operations.

Most of the discussion and illustrations in the remainder of this chapter focus on manufacturing enterprises, which convert materials into finished products through the use of labor and machinery.[1] However, the concepts and principles frequently apply to service enterprises, which provide services to their customers, and to merchandising enterprises, which purchase merchandise for resale to their customers.

FINANCIAL ACCOUNTING AND MANAGERIAL ACCOUNTING

OBJECTIVE 1
Describe managerial accounting and distinguish managerial accounting from financial accounting.

Although economic information can be classified in many ways, accountants often divide accounting information into two types: financial and managerial. A brief discussion of each of these is useful in understanding the nature of the information needed by management.

Financial accounting information is presented in periodic statements that are prepared according to **generally accepted accounting principles (GAAP)**. These statements, which report the results of past financial activities, are intended primarily for the use of persons who are "outside" or external to the enterprise, such as shareholders, creditors, governmental agencies, and the general public. However, these statements are also useful to management in directing the operations of the enterprise. For example, in planning future operations, management often begins by evaluating the results of relevant past activities as reported in the basic financial statements.

Managerial accounting information includes both historical and estimated data, which management uses in conducting daily operations and in planning future operations. For example, in controlling inflows and outflows of cash, management relies upon accounting to provide information concerning the amount owed to each creditor, the amount owed by each customer, and the date each amount is due. Production managers, by comparing past performances with planned objectives, can take steps to accelerate favorable trends and reduce those trends that are unfavorable.

As indicated in the following diagram, managerial accounting overlaps financial accounting to the extent that management uses the financial statements in directing current operations and planning future operations. However, managerial accounting extends beyond financial accounting by providing additional information and reports for management's use. In providing this additional information, the accountant is *not* governed by generally accepted accounting principles. Since these data are used only by management, the accountant provides the data in the format that is most useful for management. The principle of "usefulness," then, is dominant in guiding the accountant in preparing management reports.

[1]The text focuses on the traditional managerial accounting concepts that are most useful to managers for directing the operations of a manufacturing enterprise. Recent trends in the development and use of accounting to assist management in the rapidly changing manufacturing environment are discussed in Appendix G.

*Financial and
Managerial Accounting
Functions*

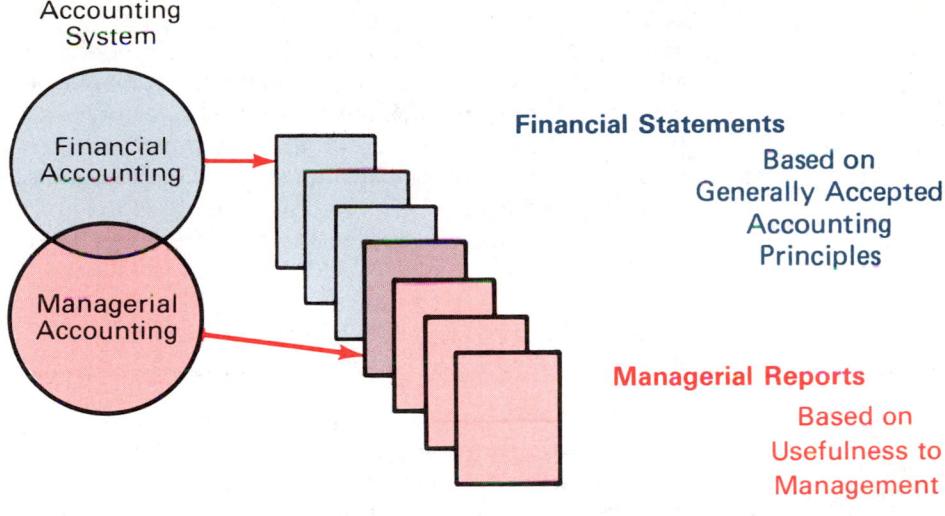

THE MANAGEMENT PROCESS

OBJECTIVE 2
Describe the
management
process and the
role of managerial
accounting in this
process.

Managerial accountants supply accounting information to assist management in the basic functions of planning and control. **Planning** is the process of setting goals for the use of an organization's resources and of developing ways to achieve these goals. Accountants provide information to enable management to plan effectively. For example, accountants provide information to assist management in setting product selling prices. In this context, projections indicating the anticipated results of alternate selling prices can be useful to management in deciding among alternatives.

Control is the process of directing operations to achieve the organization's goals and plans. For example, accounting reports comparing the actual costs with the planned costs of producing products provide management with the basis for making decisions to control costs.

A common ingredient of both planning and control is decision making, and accountants provide information useful to management in making decisions. For example, decisions need to be made in selecting from among alternate proposed plans. Decisions also need to be made to keep actual costs within the bounds of proposed costs. The relationship between managerial accounting, the management process, and decision making is shown in the following diagram:

*Managerial Accounting
and the Basic
Functions of
Management*

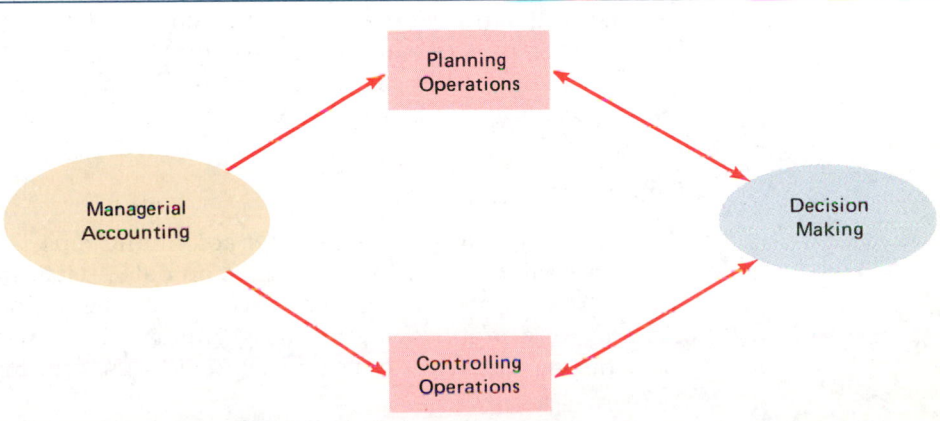

As indicated in the diagram, decisions must be made by management in planning and controlling operations. As the results of these decisions evolve and are reviewed, additional decisions may be necessary to revise plans and modify steps taken to control operations. For example, if accounting information indicates that actual performance is below planned performance, the plans may be revised or the controls modified in an attempt to improve performance. Thus, the interrelationships of the planning and control functions of management may be viewed as an endless loop, with the managerial accountant providing input for the use of management in carrying out both functions.

CHARACTERISTICS OF MANAGERIAL ACCOUNTING REPORTS

OBJECTIVE 3
Describe the characteristics of accounting reports prepared for use by management.

As indicated, accounting reports provide much of the information useful for management in planning and controlling operations. The principle of "usefulness to management" is the primary criterion for the preparation of managerial accounting reports. To be useful, these reports should possess the characteristics of (1) relevance, (2) timeliness, (3) accuracy, (4) clarity, and (5) conciseness. Each of these characteristics is described in the following paragraphs.

Relevance

Relevance means that the economic information reported must be pertinent to the specific action being considered by management. In applying this concept, the accountant must be familiar with the operations of the firm and the needs of management in order to select what is important from the masses of data that are available. Especially in this modern age of the information explosion, this selection process can be difficult. To accomplish this task, the accountant must determine the needs of management for the decision at hand, examine the available data, and select only the relevant data for reporting to management. To illustrate, assume that management is considering the replacement of fully depreciated equipment, which cost $100,000, with new equipment costing $150,000. It is the $150,000 that is relevant for an analysis of financing the replacement. The original cost, $100,000 is irrelevant.

In applying the concept of relevance, it is important to recognize that some accounting information may have little or no relevance for one use but may have a high degree of relevance for another use. For example, in the previous illustration, the $100,000 was irrelevant for purposes of evaluating the financing of the replacement equipment. For tax purposes, however, the $100,000 (and its accumulated depreciation) would be relevant for determining the amount of the gain from the sale or trade-in of the old equipment and the amount of the income tax due on any gain.

Timeliness

Timeliness refers to the need for accounting reports to contain the most up-to-date information. In many cases, outdated data can lead to unwise decisions. For example, if prior years' costs are relied upon in setting the selling price of a product, the resulting selling price may not be sufficient to cover the current year's costs and to provide a satisfactory profit.

In some cases, the timeliness concept may require the accountant to prepare reports on a prearranged schedule, such as daily, weekly, or monthly. For example, daily reports of cash receipts and disbursements assist management in effectively managing the use of cash on a day-to-day basis. On the other hand, weekly reports of the cost of products manufactured may be satisfactory to assist management in the control of costs. In other cases, reports are prepared on an irregular basis or only when needed. For example, if management is evaluating a proposed advertising promotion for the month of May, a report of current costs and other current relevant data for this specific proposal would be needed in sufficient time for management to make and implement the decision.

Accuracy

Accuracy refers to the need for the report to be correct within the constraints of the use of the report and the inherent inaccuracies in the measurement process. If the report is not accurate, management's decision may not be prudent. For example, if an inaccurate report on a customer's past payment practices is presented to management, an unwise decision in granting credit may be made.

As previously indicated, the concept of accuracy must be applied within the constraint of the use to be made of the report. In other words, there are occasions when accuracy should be sacrificed for less precise data that are more useful to management. For example, in planning production, estimates (forecasts) of future sales may be more useful than more accurate data from past sales. In addition, it should be noted that there are inherent inaccuracies in accounting data that are based on estimates and approximations. For example, in determining the unit cost of a product manufactured, an estimate of depreciation expense on factory equipment used in the manufacturing process must be made. Without this estimate, the cost of the product would be of limited usefulness in establishing the product selling price.

Clarity

Clarity refers to the need for reports to be clear and understandable in both format and content. Reports that are clear and understandable will enable management to focus on significant factors in planning and controlling operations. For example, for management's use in controlling the costs of manufacturing a product, a report that compares actual costs with expected costs and clearly indicates the differences enables management to give its attention to significant differences and to take any necessary corrective action.

Conciseness

Conciseness refers to the requirement that the report should be brief and to the point. Although the report must be complete and include all relevant information, the inclusion of unnecessary information wastes management's time and makes it more difficult for management to focus on the significant factors related to a decision. For example, reports prepared for the top level of management should usually be broad in scope and present summaries of data rather than small details.

Costs vs. Benefits of Managerial Accounting Reports

The characteristics of managerial accounting reports provide general guidelines for the preparation of reports to meet the various needs of management. In applying these guidelines, consideration must be given to the specific needs of each manager, and the reports should be tailored to meet these needs. In preparing reports, costs are incurred, and a primary consideration is that the value of the management reports must at least equal the cost of producing them. The relationship between the general guidelines and the cost-benefit consideration is illustrated as follows:

Managerial Accounting Reports

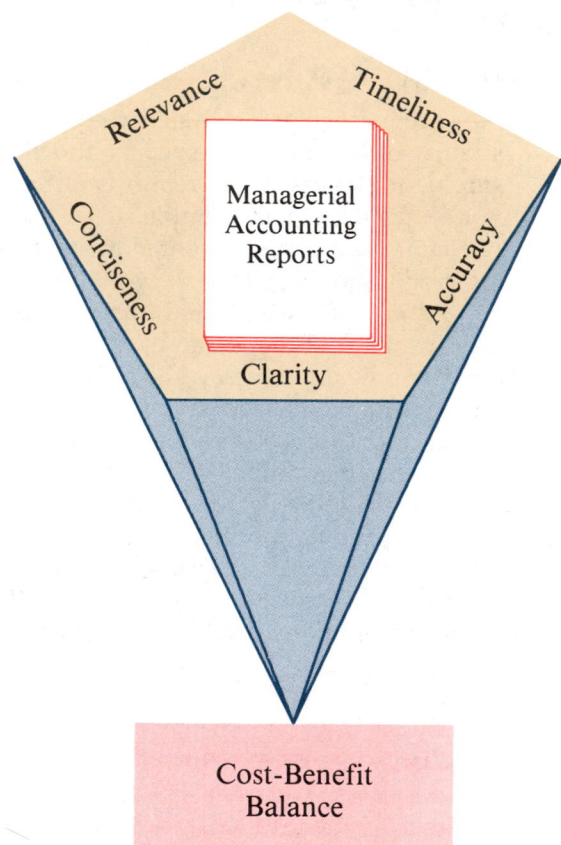

Costs and benefits must be considered, no matter how informational a report may be. A report should not be prepared if its cost exceeds the benefits derived by management.

ORGANIZATION OF THE MANAGERIAL ACCOUNTING FUNCTION

OBJECTIVE 4
Describe the organization of the managerial accounting function within a business enterprise.

Managers organize business enterprises into departments or similar units with responsibilities for specific functions or activities. This operating structure of an enterprise can be diagrammed in an **organization chart**. An organization chart for Baker Inc., a small manufacturing enterprise, is as follows:

*Organization Chart for
Baker Inc.*

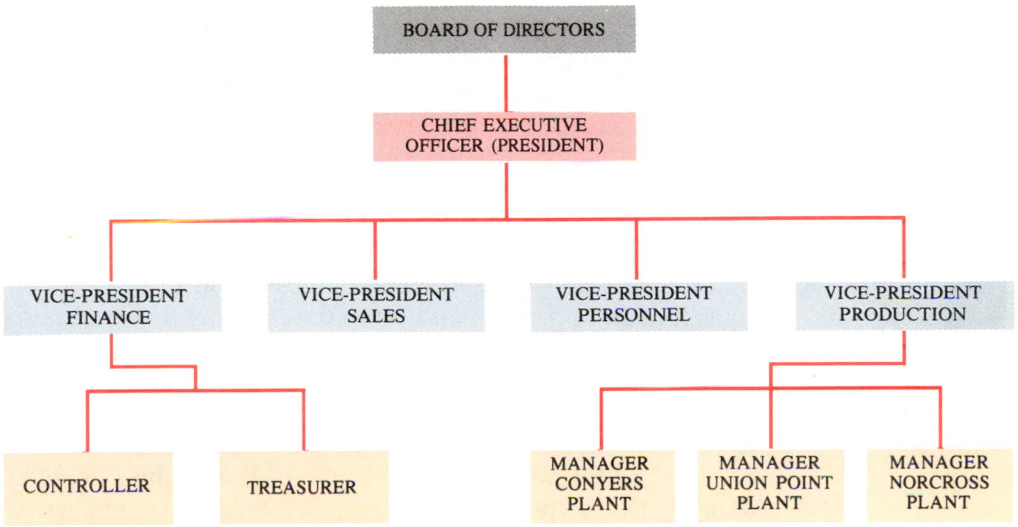

In most business organizations, the chief accountant is called the **controller**. The controller, who commonly reports to the vice-president of finance, provides advice and assistance to management but assumes no direct responsibility for the operations of the business. The controller's function might be compared to that of an airplane's navigator. The navigator, with special skills and training, assists the pilot, but the pilot is responsible for flying the airplane. Likewise, the controller, with special accounting training and skills, advises management, but management is responsible for planning and controlling operations.

The controller usually has a staff consisting of several managerial accountants. Each accountant is responsible for a specialized accounting function, such as systems and procedures, general accounting, budgets and budget analyses, special reports and analyses, and taxes. The following organization chart is typical for an accounting department that reports to the controller:

*Organization Chart—
Controller's
Department*

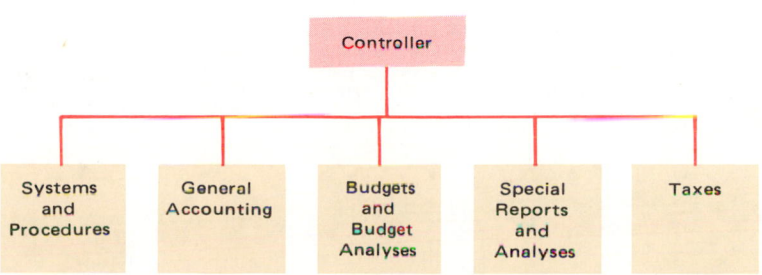

Systems and procedures is concerned with the design and implementation of procedures for the accumulation and reporting of accounting data to all interested users. In performing this function, the accountant must evaluate the usefulness of various types of data processing equipment for the firm. The systems accountant must also devise appropriate "checks and balances" to safeguard business assets and provide for an information flow that will be efficient and helpful to management.

General accounting is primarily concerned with the recording of transactions and periodic preparation of the basic financial statements. Of particular importance to this area is the gathering of data in conformity with generally accepted accounting principles for preparing the basic financial statements.

Budgets and budget analyses focuses on the plan for financial operations for future periods, and through records and summaries, focuses on the comparison of actual operations with these plans. This function provides much of the information for planning and controlling operations.

Special reports and analyses is concerned with data that will be useful to management in analyzing current problems and considering alternate courses for future operations. Much of the analysis focuses on providing data related to specific problems that confront management and identifying alternative courses of action related to proposed new projects. Often the accountants who perform this function prepare special reports according to the requirements of regulatory agencies.

Taxes encompasses the preparation of tax returns and the consideration of the tax consequences of proposed business transactions or alternate courses of action. Accountants in this area must be familiar with the tax statutes affecting their business and must also keep up-to-date on administrative regulations and court decisions on tax cases.

THE MAGIC OF 3M

3M was listed along with 61 other corporate high achievers in the best seller, *In Search of Excellence,* by Thomas J. Peters and Robert H. Waterman, Jr. In *A Passion for Excellence,* by Peters and Nancy Austin, 3M was again listed as a model for product innovation and entrepreneurship.

Some of the reasons for 3M's success, based on interviews with 3M executives, are as follows:

"Financial expertise, long recognized as one of 3M's greatest assets, is a major contributor to the corporation's success. 3M uses its financial control system to encourage rather than curtail innovation and creativity. Numbers are used to set goals and measure performance rather than to deny expenditures or punish unmet expectations."

"...we (controllers) get intimately involved with day-to-day activities...with forecasting and planning activities of business units. As an ex-

ample, in new product development we try to lay out for the managers the cost implications of bringing on a new product and what it means in relation to their total business and whether or not they can still reach their financial targets. We work with them, developing the analysis to help them prioritize what products they want to go after. . . . Our controllers view their roles as not to always challenge management, but as being a cooperative effort to develop a better business."

"3M's (division) controllers have been able to support 3M's strategic objectives while keeping management focused on operational objectives . . . we do a fair, if not a good, job of balancing strategic and operational considerations."

"Our organization is not a negatively focused accounting organization. We aren't always coming in and saying 'you can't do that.' We are supportive and positive in dealing with line management. We have tried to understand the business while doing our jobs."

"I (division controller) view the controller's function as the financial consultant . . . the person who brings to a division the financial information."

"I (vice president of finance) tell our people, 'Your job is to help the operating people achieve what they're trying to achieve. Then if you have to say no, you'll be respected for it.' The first principle is working with the operating people."

Source: Kathy Williams, "The Magic of 3M: Management Accounting Excellence," *Management Accounting* (February, 1986), pp. 20–27.

COST CONCEPTS

OBJECTIVE 5
Distinguish between costs and expenses.

As described in the preceding paragraphs, the role of managerial accounting is to provide economic information to management. This information is often related to the "costs" associated with operations. Although it can take many forms, the information provided by managerial accountants should be communicated in common cost terminology that avoids confusion and misunderstanding.[2] For example, the terms "cost" and "expense" are sometimes used interchangeably. However, the terms have different meanings.

All disbursements of cash (or the commitment to pay cash in the future) for the purpose of generating revenues are **costs**. For example, when store supplies are purchased for cash or credit (on account), the disbursement represents the cost of the supplies. In contrast, although the payment of dividends to stockholders is a disbursement, it is not a cost, since the payment of dividends does not generate revenues.

All costs initially represent assets to the enterprise. As the assets are used in generating revenues, the cost of the assets must be recognized as **expenses** in order to match revenues and expenses properly in the process of determining the net income of the period. Thus, depreciation expense is recognized as plant assets are used in generating revenues, and prepaid insurance premiums are written off as an expense over the periods benefiting from the insurance policies.

To simplify the recording process, costs that will benefit only the current period are often initially recorded as expenses rather than as assets. This procedure avoids the need to record the use of the assets as expenses, as would be the case if the costs were initially recorded as assets. For example, the payment of $1,500 for the current month's rent would be recorded by most enterprises as an expense (Rent Expense) rather than as an asset (Prepaid Rent).

[2]The terminology in this chapter is consistent with the recommendations in *Statement on Management Accounting No. 2*, "Management Accounting Terminology" (Montvale, New Jersey: National Association of Accountants, 1983).

The distinction between costs and expenses is summarized in the following diagram:

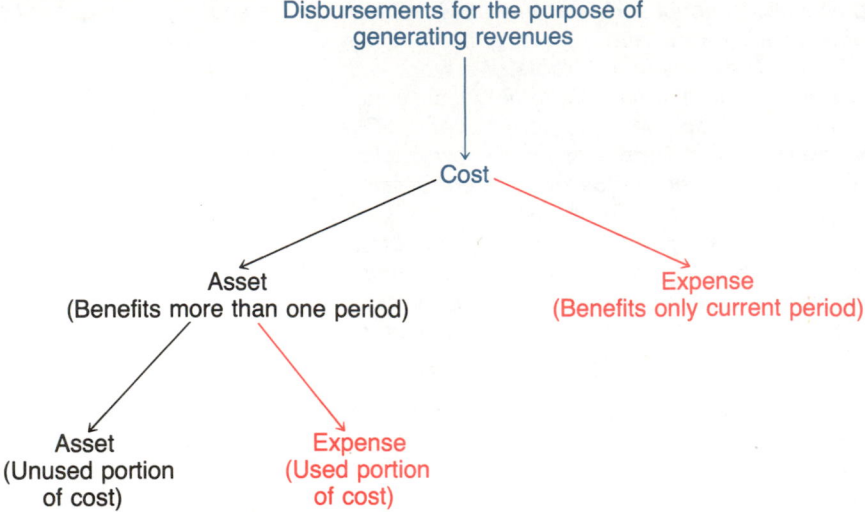

The distinction between the terms cost and expense is especially important for the preparation of financial statements for service, merchandising, and manufacturing enterprises. However, this distinction has more importance for manufacturing enterprises. Costs incurred in manufacturing products are assets, and these costs do not become expenses until the manufactured products are sold, thereby generating revenue. Likewise, products for which manufacturing has been partially or fully completed but which have not been sold should continue to be recognized as assets.

MANUFACTURING COSTS

OBJECTIVE 6
Describe and illustrate the three manufacturing costs:
Direct materials
Direct labor
Factory overhead

The cost of manufacturing a product includes not only the cost of tangible materials entering into the manufacturing process, but also the costs incurred in changing the materials into a finished product ready for sale. The cost of a manufactured product generally consists of direct materials cost, direct labor cost, and factory overhead cost.

Direct Materials Cost

The cost of materials entering directly into the manufactured product is classified as **direct materials cost,** sometimes referred to as **raw materials cost**. For example, the direct materials for Seawind Company, a manufacturer of fishing boats, would include fiberglass and paint.

As a practical matter, in order for a cost to be classified as a direct materials cost, the cost must not only be an integral part of the end product, but it must be a significant dollar portion of the total cost of the product. For Seawind Company, the costs of fiberglass and paint are a significant portion of the total cost of each boat.

Other examples of direct materials costs include the cost of paper and ink for a printer, lumber for a furniture manufacturer, silicon wafers for a producer of microcomputer chips, and steel for an automobile manufacturer. The finished product of one manufacturer may become the direct materials for another manufacturer. For example, the finished products of a lumber mill become the direct materials for a construction contractor.

Direct Labor Cost

The cost of wages paid to employees directly involved in changing direct materials into a finished product is classified as **direct labor cost**. For example, the direct labor cost of Seawind Company includes the wages of the employees who paint the boat hulls in the manufacturing process. Other examples of direct labor costs include the wages of carpenters for a construction contractor, mechanics' wages in an automotive repair shop, machine operators' wages in a tool manufacturing plant, and assemblers' wages in a microcomputer manufacturing plant.

As a practical matter, for the cost of employee wages to be classified as direct labor cost, the employee must not only be directly involved in the creation of the finished product, but the wages must be a significant portion of the total product cost. For Seawind Company, the painters' wages are a significant portion of the total cost of each boat.

Factory Overhead Cost

Costs other than direct materials cost and direct labor cost incurred in the manufacturing process are classified as **factory overhead cost**, sometimes referred to as **manufacturing overhead** or **factory burden**. For example, factory overhead cost includes the cost of heating and lighting the factory, repair and maintenance of factory equipment, and property taxes, insurance, and depreciation on factory plant and equipment. Factory overhead cost also includes materials and labor costs which do not enter directly into the finished product. For example, the cost of oil used to lubricate machinery is a materials cost which does not enter directly into finished products. Other examples of such costs include the wages of janitorial, supervisory, and quality control personnel.

As a practical matter, if the costs of direct materials or direct labor are not a significant portion of the total product cost, these costs are classified as factory overhead. In Seawind Company, for example, glue enters directly into the finished product (boats), but its cost is insignificant and it is therefore classified as factory overhead. For many industries, the increased use of automated machinery and robotics has decreased labor costs to a level where they are a small portion of total product costs. In this situation, direct labor costs of manufactured products are often included as part of factory overhead cost.

Prime Costs and Conversion Costs

As previously discussed, the total cost of a manufactured product consists of three elements: direct materials, direct labor, and factory overhead costs. These costs are often grouped in various classifications for analysis and reporting purposes. As will be illustrated in later chapters, two common classifications of manufacturing costs often reported to management for planning and decision making purposes are prime costs and conversion costs.

Prime costs are the combination of direct materials and direct labor costs. As the name implies, prime costs are generally the largest component of the total cost of a manufactured product. **Conversion costs** are the combination of direct labor and factory overhead costs. Conversion costs are the costs of converting the materials into a finished, manufactured product.

The following diagram summarizes the classification of manufacturing costs into prime costs and conversion costs:

*Prime Costs and
Conversion Costs*

PRIME COSTS

Direct Materials Cost:

(1) Enters directly into the product, and

(2) Is significant amount of total product cost.

Example: Memory chips for a microcomputer manufacturer.

Direct Labor Cost:

(1) Enters directly into manufacturing the product, and

(2) Is significant amount of total product cost.

Example: Hourly wages of assemblers of microcomputers.

CONVERSION COSTS

Factory Overhead Cost:

Is cost other than direct materials cost and direct labor cost incurred in the manufacturing of products.

Example: Depreciation on testing equipment for a microcomputer manufacturer.

NONMANUFACTURING COSTS

OBJECTIVE 7
Describe the common classifications of nonmanufacturing costs.

Nonmanufacturing costs are generally classified into two categories: selling and administrative. **Selling costs** are costs that are incurred in marketing the product and delivering the sold product to customers. Examples of selling costs include salaries of marketing personnel, advertising expenditures, sales commissions, salespersons' salaries, and depreciation on store equipment. **Administrative costs** are costs that are incurred in the administration of the business and that are not related to the manufacturing or selling functions. Examples of administrative costs include office salaries, office supplies, and depreciation on office buildings and equipment.

By classifying nonmanufacturing costs into selling and administrative, the managerial accountant enables management to establish accountability and control over the cost of two major functional activities: selling activities and administrative activities. Different levels of accountability for these activities may be shown in managerial reports. For example, selling costs may be reported by product, salespersons, departments, divisions, or geographic territories. Likewise, administrative costs may be reported by functional area, such as personnel, computer services, accounting, finance, or office support.

The accounting for nonmanufacturing costs is similar for manufacturing, merchandising, and service enterprises. Most selling and administrative costs are initially recognized as expenses because they benefit only the period in which they are incurred.

The concepts and principles discussed throughout this text for planning and controlling manufacturing costs are also applicable to selling and administrative costs. Where applicable, these concepts and principles will be illustrated for both manufacturing costs and selling and administrative costs.

PRODUCT COSTS AND PERIOD COSTS

OBJECTIVE 8
Distinguish between product and period costs.

In the preceding section, costs were classified as manufacturing or nonmanufacturing. These costs may also be classified as either product costs or period costs.

Product costs are composed of the three elements of manufacturing cost: direct materials, direct labor, and factory overhead.[3] These costs are treated as assets until the product is sold. In other words, during the period beginning when product costs are initially incurred until the products are sold, product costs are accounted for as assets and are reported as a part of inventory on the balance sheet. In this sense, product costs are sometimes referred to as **inventoriable costs**. Thus, direct materials, direct labor, and factory overhead costs incurred in one period will not appear on the income statement as expenses until the products with which they are associated are sold.

Period costs are those costs that are used up in generating revenue during the current period and that are not involved in the manufacturing process. Selling and administrative costs are period costs. They are recognized as expenses on the current period's income statement. Many period costs are time-oriented, in the sense that the costs are incurred or used as time passes.

The diagram on page 806 relates the manufacturing and nonmanufacturing cost concepts to the product cost and period cost concepts for a furniture manufacturer.

FINANCIAL STATEMENTS FOR MANUFACTURING ENTERPRISES

OBJECTIVE 9
Describe and illustrate the financial statements of a manufacturing enterprise, including the preparation of the statement of cost of goods manufactured.

The financial statements for manufacturing enterprises are more complex than those for service and merchandising enterprises. Since a manufacturing enterprise manufactures the products that it sells, the manufacturing costs described in the preceding paragraphs must be properly accounted for and reported in the financial statements. These manufacturing costs primarily affect the preparation of the balance sheet and income statement, which are described in the following paragraphs. The retained earnings and cash flow statements for the merchandising and manufacturing enterprises are similar and therefore are not discussed.

---

[3]For merchandising enterprises, product costs include the costs associated with purchasing a product in finished form and ready for sale.

*Examples of Product
Costs and Period
Costs*

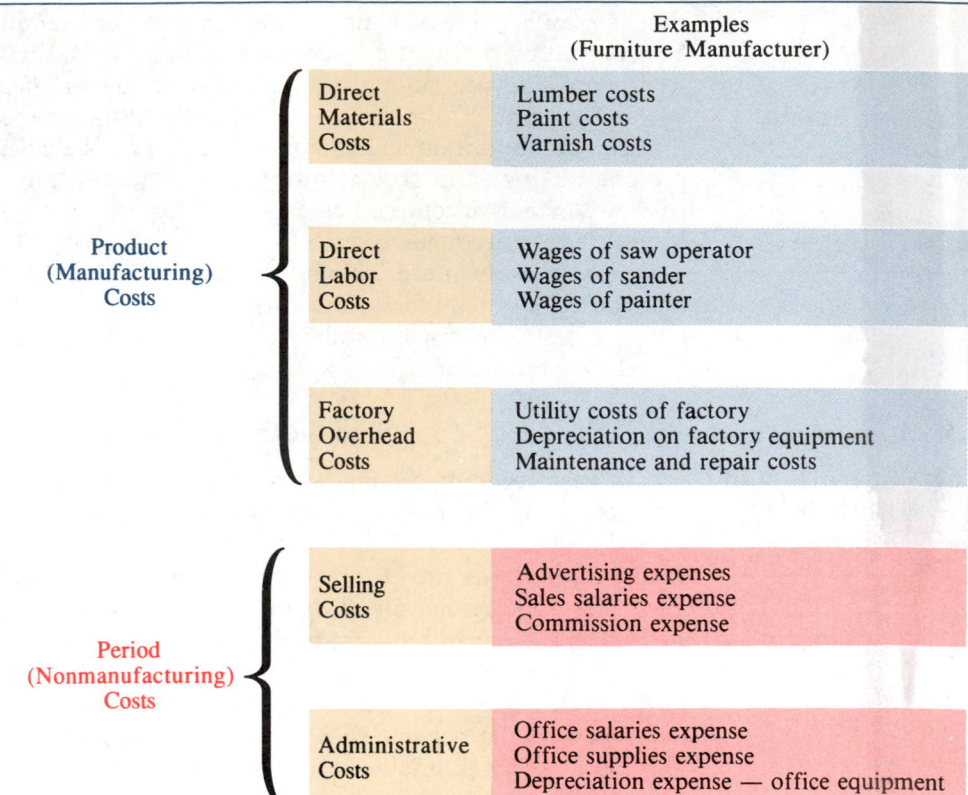

Balance Sheet for a Manufacturing Enterprise

A manufacturing enterprise reports three types of inventory on its balance sheet: direct materials inventory, work in process inventory, and finished goods inventory. The **direct materials inventory** for a manufacturing enterprise consists of the cost of the direct materials which have not yet entered into the manufacturing process.[4] The **work in process inventory** for a manufacturing enterprise consists of the direct materials costs, the direct labor costs, and the factory overhead costs which have entered into the manufacturing process, but are associated with products that have not been finished. The **finished goods inventory** of a manufacturing enterprise consists of the finished products on hand that have not been sold. For example, The Procter & Gamble Company reported the following inventories on its 1988 balance sheet:

Inventories (in millions of dollars):

Materials	$ 844
Work in process	234
Finished products	1,214

The flow of manufacturing costs into the manufacturing process and the related inventories of a manufacturing enterprise is illustrated in the following diagram:

[4]Direct materials inventory, sometimes simply called materials inventory, includes only direct materials to be used in the manufacturing process. Indirect materials are classified as factory supplies.

Flow of Manufacturing Costs to Balance Sheet

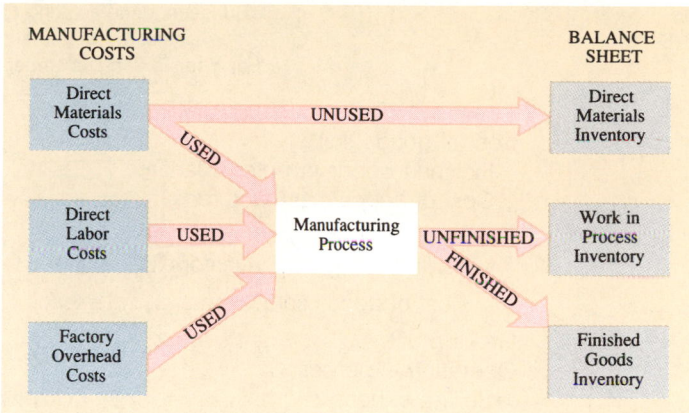

Income Statement for a Manufacturing Enterprise

The major difference in the income statements for merchandising and manufacturing enterprises is in the reporting of cost of merchandise sold for a merchandising enterprise and cost of goods sold for a manufacturing enterprise. For a merchandising enterprise, merchandise is purchased in a finished state for resale to customers. The merchandise that is sold is called the **cost of merchandise sold.**

For a manufacturing enterprise, the product to be sold is manufactured by processing direct materials, using direct labor and factory overhead. The cost of the product sold is called the **cost of goods sold.** The costs of manufacturing the product, which are comparable to the purchases reported by a merchandising enterprise, can be reported in a **statement of cost of goods manufactured.** To illustrate the difference between the income statements for a merchandising enterprise and a manufacturing enterprise, the income statements for Loose Inc., a merchandiser, and Burleson Manufacturing Company are shown below and on the following page. The Burleson Manufacturing Company income statement is supported by a statement of cost of goods manufactured.

Merchandising Enterprise — Income Statement

Loose Inc. Income Statement For the Year Ended December 31, 1990		
Sales		$1,100,000
Cost of merchandise sold:		
Merchandise inventory, Jan. 1, 1990	$ 90,000	
Purchases	900,000	
Merchandise available for sale	$990,000	
Less merchandise inventory, Dec. 31, 1990	120,000	
Cost of merchandise sold		870,000
Gross profit		$ 230,000
Operating expenses:		
Selling expenses	$ 85,000	
Administrative expenses	75,000	
Total operating expenses		160,000
Net income		$ 70,000

Manufacturing Enterprise — Income Statement

Burleson Manufacturing Company
Income Statement
For Year Ended December 31, 1990

Sales		$915,800
Cost of goods sold:		
Finished goods inventory, January 1, 1990	$ 78,500	
Cost of goods manufactured	550,875	
Cost of finished goods available for sale	$629,375	
Less finished goods inventory, December 31, 1990 ..	91,000	
Cost of goods sold		538,375
Gross profit		$377,425
Operating expenses:		
Selling expenses	$165,000	
Administrative expenses	84,425	
Total operating expenses		249,425
Net income		$128,000

Statement of Cost of Goods Manufactured

Burleson Manufacturing Company
Statement of Cost of Goods Manufactured
For Year Ended December 31, 1990

Work in process inventory, January 1, 1990			$ 55,000
Direct materials:			
Inventory, January 1, 1990	$ 62,000		
Purchases	220,800		
Cost of materials available for use	$282,800		
Less inventory, December 31, 1990	58,725		
Cost of materials placed in production		$224,075	
Direct labor		218,750	
Factory overhead:			
Indirect labor	$ 49,300		
Depreciation of factory equipment	22,300		
Heat, light, and power	21,800		
Property taxes	9,750		
Depreciation of buildings	6,000		
Insurance expense	4,750		
Factory supplies expense	2,900		
Miscellaneous factory costs	2,050		
Total factory overhead		118,850	
Total manufacturing costs			561,675
Total work in process during period			$616,675
Less work in process inventory, December 31, 1990			65,800
Cost of goods manufactured			$550,875

In Burleson's statement of cost of goods manufactured, the amount listed for the work in process inventory at the beginning of the period is composed of the estimated cost of the direct materials, the direct labor, and the factory overhead applicable to the inventory of partially processed products at the end of the preceding period. The cost of the direct materials placed in production is determined by adding the beginning inventory of direct materials and the net cost of the direct materials purchased and deducting the ending inventory. The amount of direct labor is then listed. The factory overhead costs are listed individually in the statement or in a separate schedule. The sum of the costs of direct materials placed in production, the direct labor, and the factory overhead represents the total manufacturing costs incurred during the period. Addition of this amount to the beginning inventory of work in process yields the total cost of the work that has been in process during the period. The estimated cost of the ending inventory of work in process is then deducted to yield the cost of goods manufactured.

ADDITIONAL COST CONCEPTS FOR MANAGERIAL PLANNING

OBJECTIVE 10
Describe the basic cost classifications useful for planning and control:
Variable costs and fixed costs
Direct costs and indirect costs
Controllable costs and noncontrollable costs
Differential costs
Discretionary costs
Sunk costs
Opportunity costs

The cost concepts and classifications described to this point are used primarily in the preparation of financial statements. For purposes of planning and controlling operations, managers require a variety of managerial reports in which cost data are classified in various ways. In the remainder of this chapter, the following cost concepts that are frequently reported to management for use in directing current operations and planning future operations are briefly described:

Variable costs and fixed costs	Differential costs
Direct costs and indirect costs	Discretionary costs
Controllable costs and noncontrollable costs	Sunk costs
	Opportunity costs

The use of these cost concepts by managers will be described and illustrated in more detail in later chapters.

Variable Costs and Fixed Costs

For management's use, costs are often classified by cost behavior; that is, costs are classified as to how they respond to changes in the volume of business activity. As the volume of business activity rises or falls, some costs tend to change proportionally to the rise or fall, while other costs do not change significantly as the volume of business activity changes. For directing current operations and planning future operations, a knowledge of the response pattern of costs to changing or anticipated changes in activity levels is useful.

Variable Costs. A **variable cost** varies in total dollar amount as the level of activity changes. The level of activity is normally expressed in units of production, although other activity bases may be used. Direct materials cost is a variable cost because the total direct materials cost varies directly with the number of units produced. For example, assume that Micro-Systems Inc. produces a standard microcomputer containing a 256K memory board. The cost of each memory board is a variable cost because it varies with the number of computers produced. If each memory board costs $50, the total direct materials cost of the memory boards for the production of 1,000 computers is $50,000 ($50 × 1,000); for 2,000 computers, the total cost is $100,000. Other common variable manufacturing costs include direct labor cost and factory overhead items, such as electricity, lubricants, and supplies.

The variable cost concept is also applicable to nonmanufacturing costs. For example, a 5% sales commission is a cost that varies with total sales.

Likewise, the administrative cost of billing customers is a cost that varies directly with the number of billings.

Fixed Costs. A **fixed cost** remains constant in total dollar amount as the level of activity changes. As with variable costs, the level of activity is normally expressed in units of production, although other activity bases may be used. Straight-line depreciation on manufacturing equipment is a fixed cost because the total annual depreciation does not vary with the number of units produced. For example, straight-line depreciation of $15,000 per year on Micro-Systems Inc.'s assembly and testing equipment would not vary with the number of computers produced. The total straight-line depreciation would be $15,000, regardless of whether 1,000, 2,000, or 6,000 microcomputers are produced. Other common fixed manufacturing costs include costs of renting factory equipment or buildings, property taxes on factory plant and equipment, property insurance, and salaries of factory supervisory personnel. Although these examples are factory overhead costs, some factory overhead costs, such as electricity, are variable costs.

The fixed cost concept is also applicable to nonmanufacturing costs. For example, straight-line depreciation on store equipment and a sales manager's salary do not vary with the volume of sales. Likewise, officers' salaries is a fixed cost.

Mixed Costs. Some costs have both variable and fixed characteristics. These costs are often called **mixed costs** or **semivariable** or **semifixed** costs. These mixed costs can often be separated into their variable and fixed components. For example, the rental charge for a copier might be $100 per month plus $.01 per copy. The $100 per month portion of the rental charge is a fixed cost, and the $.01 per copy portion is a variable cost.

Direct and Indirect Costs

A **direct cost** is a cost that can be traced directly to a unit within the enterprise. Costs which are not direct are said to be **indirect costs.** Critical to separating costs into direct and indirect classifications is relating costs to some unit within the enterprise. The unit may be a product line, a department, a plant, a sales territory, or some other unit.

Direct costs for a manufactured product, such as spark plugs produced by an automobile parts manufacturer, would include direct materials and direct labor because these costs can be directly traced to the spark plugs. Indirect costs for the spark plugs product line would include factory overhead costs, such as depreciation on the factory building, because these costs cannot be directly traced to the product line. For a nonmanufacturing enterprise, such as a department store, the salaries paid to the salespersons in the shoe department would be a direct cost to that department. The store's officers' salaries would be an indirect cost to the shoe department.

Controllable Costs and Noncontrollable Costs

All costs are controllable by someone within a business enterprise, but not all costs are controllable at the same level of management. For example, plant supervisors, as members of operating management, are responsible for controlling the use of direct materials in their departments. They have no control, however, over the amount of insurance coverage or premium costs related to the buildings housing their departments. For a specific level of management, **controllable costs** are costs that it controls directly, and **noncontrollable costs** are costs that another level of management controls. This distinction, as applied to specific levels of management, is useful in fixing the responsibility for the incurrence of costs and then for reporting the cost data to those responsible for cost control.

In some cases, there is a time dimension to the classification of costs as controllable or noncontrollable. Some costs cannot be controlled in the short run but can be controlled in the long run. For example, a plant manager cannot, in the short run, control the wages of factory employees who have union contracts. In the long run, however, the wages become controllable because the contracts expire and are subject to renegotiation.

Differential Costs

Differential cost, sometimes referred to as **incremental cost**, is the increase or decrease in cost that is expected from a particular course of action as compared with an alternative course of action. For example, the management of a microcomputer manufacturer must decide on whether to purchase carrying cases for the computers from an outside supplier or to produce the carrying cases. If the cost of purchasing the carrying cases is $20 per case and the cost of producing the carrying cases is $18 per case, the cost difference between the two alternatives ($2) is referred to as the differential cost. As another example, if an increase in advertising expenditures from $100,000 to $150,000 is being considered, the differential cost of the proposal would be $50,000.

Discretionary Costs

A **discretionary cost** is a cost that is not essential to short-term operations. For example, costs incurred in continuing education courses for management are classified as discretionary. Other examples of discretionary costs include advertising expenses, management consulting fees, sponsorship of employee social events (such as a company picnic), sponsorship of local athletic teams (such as a Little League team), charitable contributions to community activities, and a subsidized employee cafeteria.

Management reviews discretionary costs periodically, usually yearly, to determine whether the cost should continue to be incurred. Discretionary costs are usually the first to be reduced or eliminated during periods of worsening economic conditions, since their discontinuance does not affect short-term operations or profitability. Although discretionary costs do not have an immediate effect on short-term operations or profitability, their discontinuance can have a long-term impact on the enterprise. For example, research and development costs are often viewed as discretionary, but their discontinuance could be disastrous in the long run, especially in technologically advanced industries such as the computer industry. Likewise, the discontinuance of management continuing education could jeopardize the quality of managerial decision making in the long run.

Sunk Costs

Sunk costs are costs which have been incurred and cannot be reversed by subsequent decisions. Sunk costs are irrelevant for future decision making and are therefore excluded from managerial accounting reports prepared to assist management in making such decisions. To illustrate, assume that a major airline is currently operating a fleet of Boeing 727 passenger jets, which originally cost $300 million and on which depreciation of $250 million has been taken. In considering whether to spend $500 million to upgrade its fleet of aircraft to the newer, more fuel-efficient and technologically advanced 767 passenger jets, the original $300 million cost is irrelevant. The $300 million has been spent, and regardless of whether the original decision was wise or unwise, the $300 million expenditure cannot be reversed. For this reason, the original cost of $300 million is referred to as a sunk cost. Likewise, the $50 million book value of the 727 jets (the original cost of $300 million less accumulated depreciation of $250 million) is also irrelevant. The cost savings resulting from the use of the more fuel-efficient 767, when compared to the proposed expenditure of $500 million, are the relevant costs that would be considered by management in making the decision.

Opportunity Costs

An **opportunity cost** is the amount of income that is forgone by selecting one alternative over another. To illustrate, assume that the treasurer of Faulkner Inc. invested $100,000 in a money market account yielding 5% interest. If United States Treasury bills are currently yielding 6%, the opportunity cost of not investing in the Treasury bills is $6,000 ($100,000 × 6%). Hence, the treasurer might consider switching investments to maximize the return to Faulkner Inc. and to minimize the opportunity cost.

Opportunity cost differs fundamentally from the other classifications of costs that have been discussed previously because an opportunity cost does not represent a transaction involving a disbursement. Opportunity costs should be considered, however, in all decisions that management makes involving the commitment of resources. For example, in deciding whether to expand manufacturing capacity for the current product line, management should consider the opportunity cost of investing the resources in other product lines.

Summary of Cost Concepts

Many of the costs described in this chapter can be classified in more than one way, depending upon decision-making situations. For example, direct materials cost may be classified as a variable cost or a product cost. Each specific decision-making situation must be analyzed carefully by the managerial accountant in order to classify and report costs properly for managerial use. Such decision-making situations are discussed in the following chapters.

CHAPTER REVIEW

KEY POINTS

OBJECTIVE 1

Financial Accounting and Managerial Accounting

Financial accounting information is presented in periodic statements that are prepared according to generally accepted accounting principles. These statements are intended primarily for the use of persons who are outside or external to the enterprise. Managerial accounting information includes both historical and estimated data for management's use in conducting daily operations and in planning future operations. Since these data are used only by management, the principle of usefulness is dominant in guiding the accountant in preparing management reports.

OBJECTIVE 2

The Management Process

Managerial accountants supply accounting information to assist management in the basic functions of planning and control. A common ingredient of both planning and control is decision making, and managerial accountants provide information useful to management in making decisions.

OBJECTIVE 3

Characteristics of Managerial Accounting Reports

The principle of usefulness to management is the primary criterion for preparation of managerial accounting reports. In preparing useful managerial accounting reports, five characteristics should be considered. Relevance means that the economic information reported must be pertinent to the specific action being considered by management. Timeliness refers to the need for accounting reports to contain the most up-to-date information. Accuracy refers to the need for the report to be correct within the constraints of the use of the report and the inherent inaccuracies in the measurement process. Clarity refers to the need for the report to be clear and understandable in both format and content. Conciseness refers to the requirement that the report should be brief and to the point. A report should not be prepared if the cost of preparing it exceeds the benefits derived by management from its use.

OBJECTIVE 4

Organization of the Managerial Accounting Function

Managers organize business enterprises into departments or similar units with responsibilities for specific functions or activities. This operating structure of an enterprise can be diagrammed in an organization chart.

The chief accountant in a corporation is called the controller. The controller provides advice and assistance to management but assumes no direct responsibility for the operations of the business. The functions most commonly provided by the controller's staff include systems and procedures, general accounting, budgets and budget analyses, special reports and analyses, and taxes.

OBJECTIVE 5

Cost Concepts

All disbursements of cash (or the commitment to pay cash in the future) for the purpose of generating revenues are costs that initially represent assets to the enterprise. As the assets are used in generating revenues, the cost of the assets must be recognized as expenses in order to match revenues and expenses properly in the process of determining the net income for the period. To simplify the recording process, costs that will benefit only the current period are often initially recorded as expenses rather than as assets. This distinction between the terms cost and expense is especially important for the preparation of financial statements. This distinction has more importance for manufacturing enterprises. Costs incurred in manufacturing products are assets, and these costs do not become expenses until the manufactured products are sold.

OBJECTIVE 6

Manufacturing Costs

The cost of a manufactured product consists of direct materials cost, direct labor cost, and factory overhead cost. The cost of materials entering directly into the product is classified as direct materials cost. For a cost to be classified as a direct materials cost, the cost must not only be an integral part of the end product, but it must also be a significant dollar amount of the total cost of the product.

The cost of wages paid to employees directly involved in changing direct materials into finished products is classified as direct labor cost. For the cost of employee wages to be classified as direct labor cost, the employee must not only be directly involved in the creation of the product, but the wages must be a significant portion of the total product cost.

Costs other than direct materials cost and direct labor cost incurred in the manufacturing process are classified as factory overhead cost. If the costs of direct materials or direct labor are not a significant portion of the total product cost, these costs may be classified as factory overhead.

Two common classifications of manufacturing costs are prime costs and conversion costs. Prime costs are the combination of direct materials cost and direct labor cost. Conversion costs are the combination of direct labor cost and factory overhead cost.

OBJECTIVE 7

Nonmanufacturing Costs

Nonmanufacturing costs are generally classified into two categories: selling and administrative. These classifications enable management to establish accountability and control over the costs of each of these two major functional areas. Different levels of accountability and control may be shown in managerial reports.

OBJECTIVE 8

Product Costs and Period Costs

Product costs are composed of the three elements of manufacturing costs: direct materials, direct labor, and factory overhead. These costs are treated as assets until the product with which they are associated is sold. Product costs are sometimes referred to as inventoriable costs. Period costs are those costs that are used up in generating revenue during the current period. These costs are recognized as expenses on the current period's income statement. Many period costs are time-oriented, in the sense that the costs are incurred or used as time passes.

OBJECTIVE 9

Financial Statements for Manufacturing Enterprises

The financial statements for manufacturing enterprises are more complex than those for service and merchandising enterprises. A manufacturing enterprise reports three types of inventory on its balance sheet: direct materials, work in process, and finished goods. The direct materials inventory consists of the cost of direct materials which have not yet entered into the manufacturing process. The work in process inventory consists of direct materials costs, direct labor costs, and factory overhead costs which have entered into the manufacturing process, but are associated with products that have not been finished. The finished goods inventory consists of the finished products on hand that have not been sold.

The major difference in income statements for merchandising and manufacturing enterprises is that a merchandising enterprise reports cost of merchandise sold and a manufacturing enterprise reports cost of goods sold. For a manufacturing enterprise, the product to be sold is manufactured by processing direct materials, using direct labor and factory overhead. The cost of the product sold is called the cost of goods sold. The costs of manufacturing the product can be reported in a statement of cost of goods manufactured.

OBJECTIVE 10

Additional Cost Concepts for Managerial Planning

A variable cost varies in total dollar amount as the level of activity changes. The level of activity is normally expressed in units of production. The variable cost concept is also applicable to nonmanufacturing costs. An example of a variable cost is direct materials cost. A fixed cost remains constant in total dollar amount as the level of activity changes. The level of activity is normally expressed in units of production. The fixed cost concept is also applicable to nonmanufacturing costs. An example of a fixed cost is straight-line depreciation on factory equipment. Costs that have both variable and fixed characteristics are called mixed costs or semivariable or semifixed costs.

A direct cost is a cost that can be traced directly to a unit within the enterprise. Costs that are not direct are said to be indirect costs.

A controllable cost is one that can be controlled by a specific level of management. Over time all costs are controllable at some level of management. Therefore, when classifying a cost as controllable or noncontrollable, the time period and level of management are critical reference points.

A differential cost, sometimes referred to as an incremental cost, is the difference in cost from one course of action compared to alternative courses of action. Differential costs are an important consideration for managers in deciding among alternative courses of action.

A discretionary cost is a cost that is not essential to short-term operations. Management reviews discretionary costs periodically, usually yearly, to determine whether the costs should continue to be incurred. Although discretionary costs do not have an immediate effect on short-term operations or profitability, their discontinuance can have a long-term impact on the enterprise.

Sunk costs are costs which have been incurred and cannot be reversed by a subsequent decision. Sunk costs are irrelevant for future decision making and are therefore excluded from managerial accounting reports.

An opportunity cost is the amount of income that is forgone by selecting one alternative over another. Opportunity cost differs fundamentally from the other classifications of costs that have been discussed previously because an opportunity cost does not represent a transaction involving a disbursement. Opportunity costs should be considered in all decisions that management makes involving the commitment of resources.

Many of the costs described in this chapter can be classified in more than one way, depending upon the decision-making needs of management. Each specific decision-making situation must be analyzed carefully by the managerial accountant in order to classify and report costs properly for managerial use.

KEY TERMS

accounting 793
financial accounting 794
managerial accounting 794
planning 795
control 795
controller 799
costs 801
expenses 801
direct materials cost 802
direct labor cost 803
factory overhead cost 803
prime costs 803
conversion costs 803
product costs 805
period costs 805
direct materials inventory 806
work in process inventory 806

finished goods inventory 806
cost of merchandise sold 807
cost of goods sold 807
statement of cost of goods
    manufactured 807
variable cost 809
fixed cost 810
mixed (semivariable or semifixed)
    cost 810
direct cost 810
indirect cost 810
controllable cost 810
noncontrollable cost 810
differential cost 811
discretionary cost 811
sunk cost 811
opportunity cost 812

SELF-EXAMINATION QUESTIONS
Answers at end of chapter.

1. Which of the following is *not* a characteristic of managerial accounting reports?
    A. Timeliness   C. Conciseness
    B. Relevance   D. Cost-benefit balance

2. Which of the following expenditures would normally be recorded initially as an expense rather than as an asset?
    A. Payment of a three-year insurance premium
    B. Payment of $3,000 for the current month's rent
    C. Purchase of office equipment
    D. Purchase of direct materials to be used in manufacturing a product

3. Which of the following is not considered a cost of manufacturing a product?
    A. Direct materials cost
    B. Factory overhead cost
    C. Sales salaries
    D. Direct labor cost

4. Which of the following costs would be included as part of the factory overhead costs of a microcomputer manufacturer?
    A. The cost of memory chips
    B. Depreciation on testing equipment
    C. Wages of computer assemblers
    D. The cost of disk drives

5. Which of the following costs would normally be considered a variable cost?
    A. Direct materials cost
    B. Direct labor cost
    C. Electricity to operate factory equipment
    D. All of the above

ILLUSTRATIVE PROBLEM

The following pre-closing trial balance of Mahaney Inc. was prepared as of December 31, 1990, the end of the current fiscal year:

Cash	50,000	
Accounts Receivable	160,000	
Allowance for Doubtful Accounts		20,000
Finished Goods Inventory	180,000	
Work in Process Inventory	75,000	
Direct Materials Inventory	40,000	
Prepaid Insurance	12,000	
Factory Supplies	7,000	
Land	100,000	
Factory Buildings	400,000	
Accumulated Depreciation — Factory Buildings		220,000
Factory Equipment	250,000	
Accumulated Depreciation — Factory Equipment		125,000
Accounts Payable		30,000
Wages Payable		14,000
Income Tax Payable		10,000
Common Stock		100,000
Retained Earnings		711,000
Dividends	20,000	
Sales		1,500,000
Direct Materials Purchases	750,000	
Direct Labor	300,000	
Indirect Factory Labor	150,000	
Depreciation — Factory Equipment	25,000	
Factory Heat, Light, and Power	20,000	
Depreciation — Factory Building	20,000	
Factory Property Taxes	18,000	
Insurance Expense — Factory	12,000	
Factory Supplies Expense	6,000	
Miscellaneous Factory Costs	4,000	
Selling Expenses	60,000	
Administrative Expenses	50,000	
Income Tax	21,000	
	2,730,000	2,730,000

Inventories at December 31, 1990, were as follows:

Finished goods...	$200,000
Work in process..	70,000
Direct materials...	42,000

Instructions:

1. Prepare a statement of cost of goods manufactured.
2. Prepare an income statement.
3. Prepare a retained earnings statement.
4. Prepare a balance sheet.

SOLUTION

(1)

Mahaney Inc.
Statement of Cost of Goods Manufactured
For Year Ended December 31, 1990

Work in process inventory, January 1, 1990...			$ 75,000
Direct materials:			
Inventory, January 1, 1990..................		$ 40,000	
Purchases.......................................		750,000	
Cost of materials available for use		$790,000	
Less inventory, December 31, 1990		42,000	
Cost of materials placed in production................................		$748,000	
Direct labor...		300,000	
Factory overhead:			
Indirect labor	$150,000		
Depreciation — factory equipment	25,000		
Factory heat, light, and power...........	20,000		
Depreciation — factory buildings	20,000		
Factory property taxes......................	18,000		
Insurance expense — factory..............	12,000		
Factory supplies expense	6,000		
Miscellaneous factory costs................	4,000		
Total factory overhead...................		255,000	
Total manufacturing costs			1,303,000
Total work in process during period......			$1,378,000
Less work in process inventory December 31, 1990			70,000
Cost of goods manufactured.................			$1,308,000

(2)   Mahaney Inc.
                          Income Statement
                    For Year Ended December 31, 1990

Sales		$1,500,000
Cost of goods sold:		
Finished goods inventory, January 1, 1990	$ 180,000	
Cost of goods manufactured	1,308,000	
Cost of finished goods available for sale	$1,488,000	
Less finished goods inventory, December 31, 1990	200,000	
Cost of goods sold		1,288,000
Gross profit		$ 212,000
Operating expenses:		
Selling expenses	$ 60,000	
Administrative expenses	50,000	
Total operating expenses		110,000
Income before income tax		$ 102,000
Income tax		21,000
Net income		$ 81,000

(3)   Mahaney Inc.
                     Retained Earnings Statement
                    For Year Ended December 31, 1990

Retained earnings, January 1, 1990		$711,000
Net income for year	$81,000	
Less dividends	20,000	
Increase in retained earnings		61,000
Retained earnings, December 31, 1990		$772,000

(4)

Mahaney Inc.
Balance Sheet
December 31, 1990

Assets

Current assets:

Cash		$ 50,000	
Accounts receivable	$160,000		
Less allowance for doubtful accounts	20,000	140,000	
Inventories:			
Finished goods	$200,000		
Work in process	70,000		
Direct materials	42,000	312,000	
Prepaid insurance		12,000	
Factory supplies		7,000	
Total current assets			$521,000

Plant assets:

Land		$100,000	
Buildings	$400,000		
Less accumulated depreciation	220,000	180,000	
Factory equipment	$250,000		
Less accumulated depreciation	125,000	125,000	
Total plant assets			405,000
Total assets			$926,000

Liabilities

Current liabilities:

Accounts payable	$ 30,000	
Wages payable	14,000	
Income tax payable	10,000	
Total current liabilities		$ 54,000

Stockholders' Equity

Common stock	$100,000	
Retained earnings	772,000	
Total stockholders' equity		872,000
Total liabilities and stockholders' equity		$926,000

DISCUSSION QUESTIONS

1. In preparing reports for management's use, must the managerial accountant use generally accepted accounting principles? Discuss.

2. What is the dominant principle that guides the managerial accountant in preparing management reports?

3. Briefly describe the two basic functions of management.

4. What are the five characteristics of useful managerial accounting reports?

5. In planning production, forecasts are often used rather than data from past operations. (a) What general characteristics of managerial accounting reports support the use of forecast data? (b) What general characteristic of managerial accounting reports is sacrificed when forecasted data rather than past data are used?

6. Zarnoch Company is contemplating the expansion of its operations through the purchase of the assets of Keefe Lumber Company. Included among the assets of Keefe Lumber Company is lumber purchased for $150,000 and having a current replacement cost of $205,000. Which cost ($150,000 or $205,000) is relevant for the decision to be made by Zarnoch Company? Briefly explain the reason for your answer.

7. A bank loan officer is evaluating a request for a loan that is to be secured by a mortgage on the borrower's property. The property cost $300,000 twenty years ago and has a current market value of $450,000. Which figure, $300,000 or $450,000, is relevant for the loan officer's use in evaluating the request for the loan? Discuss.

8. What is meant by cost-benefit balance as it relates to the preparation of management reports?

9. What is the role of the controller in a business organization?

10. What term describes all disbursements of cash (or the commitment to pay cash in the future) for the purpose of generating revenues?

11. Give an example of a disbursement that is not a cost.

12. What are "expenses?"

13. What three costs make up the cost of manufacturing a product?

14. What manufacturing cost term is used to describe the cost of wages paid to employees directly involved in converting direct materials to a finished product?

15. The cost of wages paid to employees who are directly involved in converting direct materials into a finished product is not a significant portion of the total product cost. How would the wages cost normally be classified as to type of manufacturing cost?

16. Indicate whether each of the following costs of an automobile manufacturer would be classified as (a) direct materials cost, (b) direct labor cost, or (c) factory overhead cost:
    (1) tires
    (2) transmission
    (3) factory machinery lubricants
    (4) depreciation on factory machinery
    (5) wages of assembly-line worker
    (6) windshield
    (7) engine
    (8) wages of assembly-line supervisor

17. Distinguish between prime costs and conversion costs.

18. Why are nonmanufacturing costs generally classified as selling costs and administrative costs?

19. What is the difference between a product cost and a period cost?

20. Name the three inventory accounts for a manufacturing business and describe what each balance represents at the end of an accounting period.

21. What are the three categories of manufacturing costs included in the cost of finished goods and the cost of work in process?

22. What statement is used to summarize the manufacturing costs incurred during a period?

23. What are the terms used to describe (a) the merchandise sold by a merchandising enterprise and (b) the products sold by a manufacturing enterprise?

24. For a manufacturing enterprise, what is the description of the amount that is comparable to a merchandising concern's net cost of merchandise purchased?

25. "A variable cost remains constant in total dollar amount as the level of activity changes." Do you agree? Explain.

26. Classify each of the following costs as either (a) a variable cost or (b) a fixed cost:
    (1) straight-line depreciation on factory equipment
    (2) direct materials cost
    (3) $1,000 per month rent on factory building
    (4) property taxes on factory plant and equipment
    (5) electricity usage
    (6) direct labor cost
    (7) property insurance
    (8) 15% sales commission

27. For a company that produces microcomputers, would memory chips be considered a direct or an indirect cost for each microcomputer produced?

28. For a production line supervisor, would depreciation on the factory plant be considered a controllable or a noncontrollable cost?

29. In deciding between the purchase of truck A or truck B, what would be the differential cost?

30. How might the discontinuance or reduction of discretionary costs affect long-term operations? Use research and development costs as the basis for an example.

31. (a) What is meant by *sunk costs?* (b) A company is contemplating replacing an old piece of machinery which cost $620,000 and has $585,000 accumulated depreciation to date. A new machine costs $1,200,000. What is the sunk cost in this situation?

32. In considering the purchase of a new automobile, would the book value (the original cost less accumulated depreciation) of the automobile traded in be considered a sunk cost?

33. (a) What is meant by *opportunity cost?* (b) Crow Company is currently earning 9% on $100,000 invested in marketable securities. It proposes to use the $100,000 to acquire plant facilities to manufacture a new product line that is expected to add $8,000 annually to net income. What is the opportunity cost involved in the decision to manufacture the new product?

Real World Focus

34. The management of Trico Products Inc., a manufacturer of windshield wipers in Buffalo, New York, was faced with a decision on whether to locate several new plants in New York or on the Texas-Mexico border. The management decided to locate the plants on the Texas-Mexico border. Why would the employee hourly wage rate be a major differential operating cost of the two locations for purposes of this decision?

EXERCISES

Exercise 20–1
Classification as product or period costs.
OBJ. 8

For a manufacturing enterprise, classify each of the following costs as either a product (inventoriable) cost or period cost:

- (a) Sales commissions
- (b) Controller's salary
- (c) Direct materials used during production
- (d) Depreciation on factory equipment
- (e) Depreciation on office equipment
- (f) Property taxes on factory building and equipment
- (g) Advertising expenses
- (h) Factory supervisors' salaries
- (i) Repairs and maintenance costs for factory equipment
- (j) Wages of assembly workers
- (k) Oil used to lubricate factory equipment
- (l) Travel costs of salespersons
- (m) Utility costs for office building
- (n) Factory janitorial supplies
- (o) Salary of production quality control supervisor

Exercise 20–2
Statement of cost of goods manufactured.
OBJ. 9

SPREADSHEET PROBLEM

The following accounts were selected from the pre-closing trial balance of Stuart Co. at August 31, 1990, the end of the current fiscal year:

Administrative Expense	$ 65,700
Direct Labor	230,400
Direct Materials Inventory	62,000
Direct Materials Purchases	275,200
Factory Overhead	92,000
Finished Goods Inventory	91,800
Interest Expense	10,200
Sales	860,000
Selling Expense	95,000
Work in Process Inventory	67,000

Inventories at August 31 were as follows:

Finished Goods	$97,200
Work in Process	71,500
Direct Materials	64,800

Prepare a statement of cost of goods manufactured.

Exercise 20–3
Cost of goods sold.
OBJ. 9

On the basis of the data presented in Exercise 20-2, prepare the cost of goods sold section of the income statement.

Exercise 20–4
Terminology.
OBJ. 6, 8, 10

Choose (from the choices presented in parentheses) the appropriate term for completing each of the following sentences:

- (a) The wages of an assembly worker are considered an inventoriable or (fixed, product) cost.
- (b) Direct materials costs combined with direct labor costs are called (prime, conversion) costs.
- (c) Because the total wages of the assembly workers change as the level of production changes, the wages of assembly workers are considered a (fixed, variable) cost.

(d) Since the amount of overtime work by assembly workers can be determined by the production supervisor through proper scheduling, overtime pay is considered a (controllable, noncontrollable) cost for the production supervisor.

(e) Straight-line depreciation on factory equipment does not vary with changes in level of production and therefore is considered a (fixed, variable) cost.

(f) Factory overhead costs combined with direct labor costs are called (prime, conversion) costs.

(g) Sales salaries paid during the current period are shown on the income statement as an expense and are (product, period) costs.

(h) A cost that has been incurred and cannot be reversed by subsequent decisions is an example of a (fixed, sunk) cost.

(i) The (opportunity, prime) cost of not investing in U.S. Treasury securities, which are yielding 10%, is the interest forgone on the possible investment.

Exercise 20–5
Classification of costs.
OBJ. 10

The following is a list of various costs that could be incurred in producing this textbook. With respect to the manufacture and sale of this text, classify each cost as either variable or fixed, and as either indirect or direct.

(a) Paper on which the text is written
(b) Wages of vice-president of marketing
(c) Sales commissions paid to textbook representatives for each text sold
(d) Straight-line depreciation on the printing presses used to manufacture the text
(e) Electricity used to run the presses during the printing of the text
(f) Hourly wages of printing press operators during production
(g) Property taxes on the factory building and equipment
(h) Ink used to print the text
(i) Salary of staff used to develop artwork for the text
(j) Royalty paid to the authors for each text sold

Exercise 20–6
Analysis of differential costs.
OBJ. 10

Grainger Company has been purchasing carrying cases for its portable typewriters at a price of $15 per typewriter. If Grainger Company manufactures the carrying cases, the manufacturing costs are expected to be $16. (a) What is the differential cost of manufacturing the carrying cases, compared to the alternative of purchasing the cases? (b) Should Grainger Company purchase or manufacture the cases? Explain.

PROBLEMS

Series A

Problem 20–1A
Classification as product or period costs.
OBJ. 6, 7, 8

The following is a list of costs incurred by several business enterprises:

(a) Production supervisor's salary
(b) Steel for an automobile manufacturer
(c) Oil lubricants for factory plant and equipment
(d) Advertising costs
(e) Memory chips for a microcomputer manufacturer
(f) Wages of assembly worker on the production line
(g) Salary of the vice-president of marketing
(h) Wages of a machine operator on the production line
(i) Property taxes on factory building
(j) Factory operating supplies
(k) Salary of the president of the company
(l) Depreciation on factory equipment
(m) Wages of production quality control personnel
(n) Maintenance and repair costs for factory equipment

(o) Sales commissions
(p) Bonuses paid to president and other officers
(q) Health insurance premiums paid for factory workers
(r) Lumber used by furniture manufacturer
(s) Paper used by textbook publisher in printing texts
(t) Paper used by computer department in processing various managerial reports
(u) Insurance premiums paid on salespersons' automobiles
(v) Coffee for executive lounge
(w) Janitorial supplies used in cleaning the production line
(x) Protective glasses for factory machine operators
(y) Blank diskettes for the producer and distributor of microcomputer software
(z) Sales catalogs distributed free of charge to potential customers

Instructions:

Classify each of the preceding costs as product costs or period costs. For those costs classified as product costs, indicate whether the product cost is a direct materials cost, a direct labor cost, or a factory overhead cost. For those costs classified as period costs, indicate whether the period cost is a selling expense or an administrative expense. Use the following tabular headings for preparing your answer. Place an X in the appropriate column.

| | Product Cost | | | Period Cost | |
Cost	Direct Materials Cost	Direct Labor Cost	Factory Overhead Cost	Selling Expense	Administrative Expense

Problem 20–2A
Statement of cost of goods manufactured; cost of goods sold.
OBJ. 9

The following accounts related to manufacturing operations of Henry Inc. were selected from the pre-closing trial balance at June 30, 1990, the end of the current fiscal year:

Depreciation of Factory Buildings	$ 10,000
Depreciation of Factory Equipment	14,500
Direct Labor	110,000
Direct Materials Inventory	30,000
Direct Materials Purchases	145,600
Factory Supplies Expense	3,200
Finished Goods Inventory	45,000
Heat, Light, and Power	14,300
Indirect Labor	23,500
Insurance Expense	5,000
Miscellaneous Factory Costs	2,400
Property Taxes	6,100
Work in Process Inventory	28,400

Inventories at June 30 were as follows:

Finished Goods	$52,000
Work in Process	33,200
Direct Materials	32,500

Instructions:

(1) Prepare a statement of cost of goods manufactured.
(2) Prepare the cost of goods sold section of the income statement.

Problem 20–3A
Determination of missing income statement data.
OBJ. 9

Data for Gonzalez Inc. and Perrini Co., manufacturing companies, are as follows:

	Gonzalez Inc.	Perrini Co.
Work in process inventory, Jan. 1, 1990	$ 100,000	$ 80,000
Cost of direct materials placed in production	(a)	200,000
Direct labor	300,000	105,000
Total factory overhead	200,000	(f)
Total manufacturing costs	900,000	400,000
Work in process inventory, Dec. 31, 1990	(b)	(g)
Cost of goods manufactured	780,000	390,000
Finished goods inventory, Jan. 1, 1990	50,000	80,000
Finished goods inventory, Dec. 31, 1990	60,000	(h)
Cost of goods sold	(c)	370,000
Sales	1,200,000	(i)
Gross profit	(d)	380,000
Total operating expenses	140,000	(j)
Net income	(e)	180,000

Instructions:

Determine the missing items, identifying each by the letters (a) through (j).

Problem 20–4A
Financial statements for a manufacturing enterprise.
OBJ. 9

The following pre-closing trial balance of Ayers Inc. was prepared as of August 31, 1990, the end of the current fiscal year:

Cash	20,000	
Accounts Receivable	80,000	
Allowance for Doubtful Accounts		2,000
Finished Goods Inventory	85,000	
Work in Process Inventory	70,000	
Direct Materials Inventory	60,000	
Prepaid Insurance	9,000	
Factory Supplies	8,000	
Land	75,000	
Factory Buildings	300,000	
Accumulated Depreciation—Factory Buildings		150,000
Factory Equipment	450,000	
Accumulated Depreciation—Factory Equipment		210,000
Accounts Payable		60,000
Wages Payable		8,000
Income Tax Payable		5,000
Common Stock		100,000
Retained Earnings		578,000
Dividends	40,000	
Sales		800,000
Direct Materials Purchases	200,000	
Direct Labor	175,000	
Indirect Labor	50,000	
Depreciation—Factory Equipment	32,000	
Factory Heat, Light, and Power	22,000	
Factory Property Taxes	14,000	
Depreciation—Factory Buildings	18,000	
Insurance Expense—Factory	6,000	
Factory Supplies Expense	5,500	
Miscellaneous Factory Costs	3,500	
Selling Expenses	100,000	
Administrative Expenses	60,000	
Income Tax	30,000	
	1,913,000	1,913,000

Inventories at August 31, 1990 were as folllows:

Finished Goods	$90,000
Work in Process...	60,000
Direct Materials	55,000

Instructions:

(1) Prepare a statement of cost of goods manufactured.
(2) Prepare an income statement.
(3) Prepare a retained earnings statement.
(4) Prepare a balance sheet.

Problem 20–5A
Cost identification and classification.
OBJ. 10

The management of Ferguson Inc., a boat retailer and distributor, is considering expanding operations by adding a repair and maintenance department. Originally, Ferguson Inc. built its building to accommodate future expansion. For the past several years, it has rented a 2,500-foot section of the building to Ron's Motorcycle Shop for $2,000 per month. This section of the building will be converted for use by the maintenance and repair department.

New equipment costing $10,000 will be purchased. It will be depreciated using the straight-line method. Existing equipment that has no resale value or other use and has a book value of $3,000 will be converted for use by the repair and maintenance department. A supervisory mechanic will be hired for $1,500 per month, and an assistant mechanic will be hired for $6 per hour. An inventory of $20,000 of spare parts will be ordered. Ferguson Inc.'s business insurance premiums are expected to increase by $200 per month, once the repairs and maintenance department opens for business.

To obtain as much visibility as possible, a one-time special advertising promotion is planned at a cost of $2,500.

Instructions:

(1) Classify the costs of the proposed repairs and maintenance operations into the following categories:
    Variable costs
    Fixed costs
    Differential costs of expansion
    Sunk costs of expansion
(2) What is the opportunity cost for Ferguson Inc. of expanding operations?

Series B

Problem 20–1B
Classification as product or period costs.
OBJ. 6, 7, 8

The following is a list of costs incurred by several business enterprises:

(a) Disk drives for a microcomputer manufacturer
(b) Wages of a painter for an automotive repair shop
(c) Salary of the vice-president of finance
(d) Wages of a machine operator on the production line
(e) Life insurance premiums paid for company president
(f) Coal used to heat furnaces of steel manufacturer
(g) Ink used by textbook publisher in printing texts
(h) Pens, paper, and other supplies used by accounting department in preparing various managerial reports
(i) Employer's portion of factory workers' FICA taxes
(j) Electricity used to operate factory machinery
(k) Janitorial supplies used in cleaning the office building
(l) Fees paid lawn service for office grounds
(m) Wages of computer programmer for producer and distributor of microcomputer software

(n) Depreciation on copying machine used by the marketing department
(o) Production supervisor's salary
(p) Tires for an automobile manufacturer
(q) Oil lubricants for factory plant and equipment
(r) Cost of a 30-second television commercial
(s) Depreciation on robot used to assemble a product
(t) Wages of production quality control personnel
(u) Maintenance and repair costs for factory equipment
(v) Depreciation on tools used in production
(w) Bonuses paid to salespersons
(x) Insurance on factory building
(y) Salary of the secretary of the president of the company
(z) Cost of company picnic

Instructions:

Classify each of the preceding costs as product costs or period costs. For those costs classified as product costs, indicate whether the product cost is a direct materials cost, a direct labor cost, or a factory overhead cost. For those costs classified as period costs, indicate whether the period cost is a selling expense or an administrative expense. Use the following tabular headings for preparing your answer. Place an X in the appropriate column.

	Product Cost			Period Cost	
Cost	Direct Materials Cost	Direct Labor Cost	Factory Overhead Cost	Selling Expense	Administrative Expense

Problem 20–2B
Statement of cost of goods manufactured; cost of goods sold.
OBJ. 9

The following accounts related to manufacturing operations of Miles Inc. were selected from the pre-closing trial balance at March 31, 1990, the end of the current fiscal year:

Depreciation of Factory Buildings	$ 56,000
Depreciation of Factory Equipment	81,200
Direct Labor	590,000
Direct Materials Inventory	170,000
Direct Materials Purchases	800,000
Factory Supplies Expense	17,200
Finished Goods Inventory	250,000
Heat, Light, and Power	80,500
Indirect Labor	132,000
Insurance Expense	25,400
Miscellaneous Factory Costs	13,500
Property Taxes	35,000
Work in Process Inventory	160,000

Inventories at March 31 were as follows:

Finished Goods	$285,000
Work in Process	180,800
Direct Materials	200,000

Instructions:

(1) Prepare a statement of cost of goods manufactured.
(2) Prepare the cost of goods sold section of the income statement.

Problem 20–3B
Determination of missing income statement data.
OBJ. 9

Data for Bormann Inc. and Fender Co., manufacturing companies, are as follows:

	Bormann Inc.	Fender Co.
Work in process inventory, Jan. 1, 1990	$ 30,000	$ 40,000
Cost of direct materials placed in production	100,000	(f)
Direct labor	150,000	80,000
Total factory overhead	80,000	120,000
Total manufacturing costs	(a)	440,000
Work in process inventory, Dec. 31, 1990	20,000	(g)
Cost of goods manufactured	(b)	390,000
Finished goods inventory, Jan. 1, 1990	(c)	100,000
Finished goods inventory, Dec. 31, 1990	70,000	80,000
Cost of goods sold	320,000	(h)
Sales	(d)	610,000
Gross profit	280,000	(i)
Total operating expenses	150,000	(j)
Net income	(e)	80,000

Instructions:

Determine the missing items, identifying each by the letters (a) through (j).

Problem 20–4B
Financial statements for a manufacturing enterprise.
OBJ. 9

The following pre-closing trial balance of Whittier Inc. was prepared as of March 31, 1990, the end of the current fiscal year:

Cash	40,000	
Accounts Receivable	120,000	
Allowance for Doubtful Accounts		10,000
Finished Goods Inventory	170,000	
Work in Process Inventory	50,000	
Direct Materials Inventory	40,000	
Prepaid Insurance	12,000	
Factory Supplies	7,000	
Land	90,000	
Factory Buildings	350,000	
Accumulated Depreciation—Factory Buildings		220,000
Factory Equipment	175,000	
Accumulated Depreciation—Factory Equipment		80,000
Accounts Payable		45,000
Wages Payable		15,000
Income Tax Payable		10,000
Common Stock		200,000
Retained Earnings		439,000
Dividends	30,000	
Sales		1,200,000
Direct Materials Purchases	500,000	
Direct Labor	250,000	
Indirect Factory Labor	110,000	
Factory Heat, Light, and Power	18,000	
Depreciation—Factory Equipment	20,000	
Factory Property Taxes	15,000	
Depreciation—Factory Buildings	14,000	
Insurance Expense—Factory	10,000	
Factory Supplies Expense	8,000	
Miscellaneous Factory Costs	5,000	
Selling Expenses	100,000	
Administrative Expenses	60,000	
Income Tax	25,000	
	2,219,000	2,219,000

Inventories at March 31, 1990, were as follows:

Finished Goods	$160,000
Work in Process	40,000
Direct Materials	45,000

Instructions:

(1) Prepare a statement of cost of goods manufactured.
(2) Prepare an income statement.
(3) Prepare a retained earnings statement.
(4) Prepare a balance sheet.

MINI-CASE 20

Rutkosky's Pizza Inc. began operations on June 20, 1989, in the garage of Helen Rutkosky. The business specializes in fast delivery of home-made pizzas on weekends. At the request of customers, Rutkosky is considering moving to a vacant office building and devoting full time to the business. Rutkosky is currently employed at Eats' Grocery as an assistant store manager, where she makes $15,000 a year.

Rutkosky has estimated the following costs of opening the new business:

Purchase of new oven	$5,000
Purchase of additional delivery truck	$12,000
Purchase of furnishings	$8,000
Monthly rent	$1,000
Wages of employees	$5.50 per hour
Insurance	$500 per year
Local advertising	$600 per month
Additional business licenses	$300 per year

Rutkosky plans to move the existing equipment from her garage to the new business. The existing equipment has an original cost of $15,000 and accumulated depreciation of $3,000. Straight-line depreciation is used to depreciate all plant and equipment.

Instructions:

(1) Classify each of the preceeding costs of opening the new business, using the following categories:
    Variable costs
    Fixed costs
    Differential costs
    Discretionary costs
    Opportunity costs
    Sunk costs
    Note: Some costs may be classified into more than one category.
(2) Assuming that Rutkosky opens the new business, list (a) costs which are controllable on a day-to-day basis, and (b) costs which are noncontrollable on a day-to-day basis.
(3) List some direct costs and indirect costs of making pizzas.

<table>
<tr><td>ETHICS
DISCUSSION
CASE</td><td>Lyn Taos, assistant controller for Shepard Inc., is preparing a report for a proposed expansion of plant facilities at one of two possible locations—Morgan City and Pottersville. In preparing the report, Taos intentionally omitted the fact that Pottersville's property tax rates are significantly higher than Morgan City's. Taos has several relatives who own property in Pottersville. If the plant is built in Pottersville, property values should significantly increase.
Discuss whether Lyn Taos is behaving in an ethical manner.</td></tr>
</table>

ANSWERS TO SELF-EXAMINATION QUESTIONS

1. **D** Cost-benefit balance (answer D) is not a characteristic of managerial accounting reports, but is a general guideline for the preparation of managerial accounting reports. Timeliness (answer A), relevance (answer B), and conciseness (answer C) are all characteristics of useful managerial accounting reports.

2. **B** The payment of $3,000 for the current month's rent (answer B) would normally be recorded as an expense, since the disbursement benefits only the current period. Payment of a three-year insurance premium (answer A) benefits more than one period and therefore would normally be recorded initially as an asset. The purchases of office equipment (answer C) and direct materials used in manufacturing a product (answer D) would initially be recorded as assets.

3. **C** Sales salaries (answer C) is a selling expense and is not considered a cost of manufacturing a product. Direct materials cost (answer A), factory overhead cost (answer B), and direct labor cost (answer D) are costs of manufacturing a product.

4. **B** Depreciation on testing equipment (answer B) is included as part of the factory overhead costs of the microcomputer manufacturer. The cost of memory chips (answer A) and the cost of disk drives (answer D) are both considered a part of direct materials cost. The wages of microcomputer assemblers (answer C) are part of direct labor cost.

5. **D** Direct materials cost (answer A), direct labor cost (answer B), and electricity to operate factory equipment (answer C) all vary with changes in the level of activity and are therefore variable costs.

CHAPTER TWENTY-ONE

JOB ORDER COST SYSTEMS

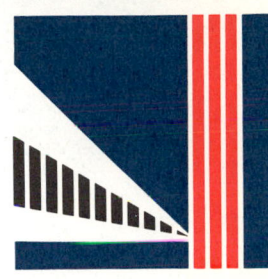

CHAPTER OBJECTIVES

1 Describe the usefulness of product costs.

2 Describe accounting systems used by manufacturing enterprises, including:
General accounting systems
Cost accounting systems

3 Describe a job order cost accounting system for a manufacturing enterprise.

4 Illustrate a job order cost accounting system for a manufacturing enterprise.

5 Describe a job order cost accounting system for a service enterprise.

A variety of cost concepts and classifications were described and illustrated in Chapter 20. For manufacturing enterprises, the importance of distinguishing between product costs and period costs was emphasized. Period costs are used up in generating revenues of the current period and are shown on the current period's income statement as expenses. Product costs are composed of the three elements of manufacturing costs: direct materials, direct labor, and factory overhead. Until the units to which they relate are sold, product costs are treated as part of inventory.

To account for product costs properly, a manufacturing enterprise must use an accounting system that will accumulate and assign all product costs to the related units of production. This chapter briefly describes the basic types of accounting systems used by manufacturing enterprises. The chapter then focuses on a discussion and illustration of one of these systems, the job order cost system. The chapter concludes with a brief description of how a job order cost accounting system can be adapted for use by service enterprises.

USEFULNESS OF PRODUCT COSTS

OBJECTIVE 1
Describe the usefulness of product costs.

In studying product costs, it is important to keep in mind that the primary function of the managerial accountant is to provide useful information to managers for planning and controlling operations. Much of this information is developed in the process of accounting for product costs.

A primary use of product costs by managers is for preparation of the financial statements of the enterprise. To present materials, work in process, and finished goods inventories properly on the balance sheet, product costs must be accounted for and assigned to the individual units in inventory. Because the cost of materials, direct labor, and factory overhead may vary throughout the period, product costs are usually assigned to inventory on the basis of an average per unit cost for the period. For example, if 1,000,000 pounds of materials were purchased throughout the period at a total cost of $2,500,000, the materials product cost per pound would be $2.50.

The product costs assigned to direct materials, work in process, and finished goods inventories are also used in the determination of net income for the period. An improper assignment of product costs to inventory would lead to a misstatement of the cost of goods sold and net income.

In addition to being used for financial statements, product costs are used by management for a variety of other purposes. For example, the per unit cost of finished goods inventory is vital information for the setting of long-term product prices. Product cost information is also necessary in deciding whether to continue making a product internally for use in further processing or to purchase the product from an outside supplier. A variety of other managerial decisions which require the use of product cost information will be illustrated throughout the remainder of this text. Without accurate product cost information, managers could not effectively or efficiently manage operations.

TYPES OF ACCOUNTING SYSTEMS

OBJECTIVE 2
Describe
accounting systems
used by
manufacturing
enterprises,
including:
General accounting
    systems.
Cost accounting
    systems.

Two basic accounting systems are commonly used by manufacturers: general accounting systems and cost accounting systems. A **general accounting system** is essentially an extension to manufacturing operations of the system for merchandising enterprises which use periodic inventory procedures. A **cost accounting system** uses perpetual inventory procedures and provides more detailed information concerning costs of production.

In the remainder of this chapter, a general accounting system is described, followed by a discussion and illustration of one of the two main types of cost accounting systems. The other main type of cost accounting system is discussed in Chapter 22.

General Accounting Systems

Although the accounting procedures for manufacturing operations are likely to be more complex than those used in merchandising operations, the complexity of such procedures varies widely. If only a single product or several similar products are manufactured, and if the manufacturing processes are neither complicated nor numerous, the accounting system may be fairly simple. In such cases, the periodic system of inventory accounting used in merchandising may be extended to the three manufacturing inventories, and the manufacturing accounts may be summarized periodically in an account entitled Manufacturing Summary. At the end of the period, the manufacturing costs are reported in the statement of cost of goods manufactured, which was described and illustrated in Chapter 20 and is reproduced at the top of page 833.

The process of adjusting the periodic inventory and other accounts of a manufacturing business is like that for a merchandising enterprise. Adjustments to the merchandise inventory account are replaced by adjusting entries for direct materials, work in process, and finished goods. The first two accounts are adjusted through Manufacturing Summary, and the third is adjusted through Income Summary.[1]

---

[1] A work sheet may be used in preparing the adjusting entries, the closing entries, and the financial statements for a manufacturing enterprise which uses periodic inventory procedures. A description and illustration of such a work sheet is presented in Appendix H.

Statement of Cost of Goods Manufactured

Burleson Manufacturing Company
Statement of Cost of Goods Manufactured
For Year Ended December 31, 1990

Work in process inventory, January 1, 1990			$ 55,000
Direct materials:			
Inventory, January 1, 1990..................	$ 62,000		
Purchases	220,800		
Cost of materials available for use.........	$282,800		
Less inventory, December 31, 1990.......	58,725		
Cost of materials placed in production		$224,075	
Direct labor		218,750	
Factory overhead:			
Indirect labor.....................................	$ 49,300		
Depreciation of factory equipment.........	22,300		
Heat, light, and power.........................	21,800		
Property taxes....................................	9,750		
Depreciation of buildings	6,000		
Insurance expense.............................	4,750		
Factory supplies expense	2,900		
Miscellaneous factory costs.................	2,050		
Total factory overhead		118,850	
Total manufacturing costs......................			561,675
Total work in process during period			$616,675
Less work in process inventory,			
December 31, 1990............................			65,800
Cost of goods manufactured			$550,875

At the end of the accounting period, the temporary accounts that appear in the statement of cost of goods manufactured are closed to Manufacturing Summary. This account's final balance, which represents the cost of goods manufactured during the period, is then closed to Income Summary. The remaining temporary accounts (sales, expenses, etc.) are then closed to Income Summary in the usual manner.

The relationship of the manufacturing summary account to the income summary account is illustrated as follows:

Cost of Goods Manufactured Closed to Income Summary

Manufacturing Summary

Dec. 31 Work in process inventory,			Dec. 31 Work in process inventory,	
Jan. 1	55,000		Dec. 31	65,800
31 Direct materials inventory,			31 Direct materials inventory,	
Jan. 1	62,000		Dec. 31	58,725
31 Direct materials purchases	220,800		31 To Income Summary	550,875
31 Direct labor	218,750			
31 Factory overhead	118,850			
	675,400			675,400

Income Summary

Dec. 31 Finished goods inventory,			Dec. 31 Finished goods inventory,	
Jan. 1	78,500		Dec. 31	91,000
31 From Manufacturing Summary	550,875			

To simplify the illustration, the individual overhead accounts are presented as a total. Note that the balance transferred from the manufacturing summary account to the income summary account, $550,875, is the same as the final figure reported on the statement of cost of goods manufactured.

Cost Accounting Systems

Through the use of perpetual inventory procedures, a cost accounting system achieves greater accuracy in the determination of product costs than is possible with a general accounting system that uses periodic inventory procedures. Cost accounting systems also permit far more effective control by supplying data on the costs incurred by each manufacturing department or process and the unit cost of manufacturing each type of product. Such systems provide not only data useful to management in minimizing costs, but also other valuable information about production methods to use and quantities to produce.

There are two main types of cost systems for manufacturing operations—job order cost and process cost. Each of the two systems is widely used, and a manufacturer may use a job order cost system for some of its products and a process cost system for others.

A **job order cost system** provides for a separate record of the cost of each particular quantity of product that passes through the factory. It is best suited to industries that manufacture goods to fill special orders from customers and to industries that produce different lines of products for stock. It is also appropriate when standard products are manufactured in batches rather than on a continuous basis. In a job order cost system, a summary such as the following would show the cost incurred in completing a job:

Job 565
1,000 Units of Product X200

Direct materials used	$2,380
Direct labor used	4,400
Factory overhead applied	3,080
Total cost	$9,860
Unit cost ($9,860 ÷ 1,000)	$ 9.86

Under a **process cost system**, the costs are accumulated for each of the departments or processes within the factory. A process system is best used by manufacturers of like units of product that are not distinguishable from each other during a continuous production process.

Perpetual Inventory Procedures

In a cost accounting system, perpetual inventory controlling accounts and subsidiary ledgers are maintained for materials, work in process, and finished goods.[2] Each of these accounts is debited for all additions and is credited for all deductions. The balance of each account thus represents the inventory on hand.

---

[2]In this chapter and in subsequent chapters, the titles of the three manufacturing inventories will be shortened to "Materials," "Work in Process," and "Finished Goods."

All expenditures incidental to manufacturing move through the work in process account, the finished goods account, and eventually into the cost of goods sold account. The flow of costs through the perpetual inventory accounts and into the cost of goods sold account is illustrated as follows:

Flow of Costs Through Perpetual Inventory Accounts

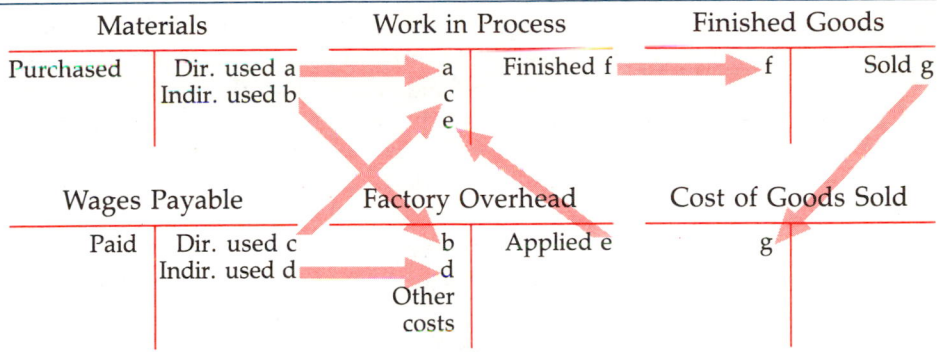

Materials and labor used in production are classified as direct and indirect. The materials and the labor used directly in the process of manufacturing are debited to Work in Process (a and c in the diagram). The materials and the labor used that do not enter directly into the finished product are debited to Factory Overhead (b and d in the diagram). Examples of indirect materials are oils and greases, abrasives and polishes, cleaning supplies, gloves, and brushes. Examples of indirect labor are salaries of supervisors, inspectors, material handlers, security guards, and janitors. The applied factory overhead cost is computed by using a predetermined factory overhead rate, as explained later in this chapter, and is debited to Work in Process (e in the diagram). The costs of the goods finished are transferred from Work in Process to Finished Goods (f in the diagram). When the goods are sold, their costs are transferred from Finished Goods to Cost of Goods Sold (g in the diagram).

The number of accounts presented in the flow chart was limited in order to simplify the illustration. In practice, manufacturing operations may require many processing departments, each requiring separate work in process and factory overhead accounts.

JOB ORDER COST SYSTEMS FOR MANUFACTURING ENTERPRISES

OBJECTIVE 3
Describe a job order cost accounting system for a manufacturing enterprise.

The basic concepts of job order cost systems are illustrated in this chapter, while process cost systems are discussed in Chapter 22. In the following paragraphs, the discussion focuses attention on the source documents that serve as the basis for the entries in the job order cost system and on the managerial uses of cost accounting in planning and controlling operations.

Materials

Procedures used in the procurement and issuance of materials differ considerably among manufacturers and even among departments of a particular manufacturer. The discussion that follows is confined to the basic principles, however, and will disregard relatively minor variations and details.

Some time in advance of the date that production of a certain commodity is to begin, the department responsible for scheduling informs the purchasing department, by means of **purchase requisitions,** of the materials that will be needed. The purchasing department then issues the necessary **purchase orders** to suppliers. After the goods have been received and inspected, the receiving department personnel prepare a **receiving report,** showing the quantity received and its condition. Quantities, unit costs, and total costs of the goods billed, as reported on the supplier's invoice are then compared with the purchase order and the receiving report to make sure that the amounts billed agree with the materials ordered and received. After such verifications, the invoice is recorded as a debit to Materials and a credit to Accounts Payable.

The account Materials in the general ledger is a controlling account. A separate account for each type of material is maintained in a subsidiary ledger called the **materials ledger**. Details as to quantity and cost of materials received are recorded in the materials ledger on the basis of the purchase invoices, or receiving reports. A typical form of materials ledger account is illustrated as follows:

Materials Ledger Account

MATERIAL NO. 23								ORDER POINT 1,000	
RECEIVED			ISSUED				BALANCE		
REC. REPORT NO.	QUAN-TITY	AMOUNT	MAT. REQ. NO.	QUAN-TITY	AMOUNT	DATE	QUAN-TITY	AMOUNT	UNIT PRICE
						JAN. 1	1,200	600.00	.50
			672	500	250.00	4	700	350.00	.50
196	3,000	1,620.00				8	700	350.00	.50
							3,000	1,620.00	.54
			704	800	404.00	18	2,900	1,566.00	.54

The accounts in the materials ledger may also be used as an aid in maintaining proper inventory quantities of stock items. Frequent comparisons of quantity balances with predetermined order points enable management to avoid costly idle time caused by lack of materials. The subsidiary ledger may also include columns for recording quantities ordered and dates of the purchase orders.

Materials are transferred from the storeroom to the factory in response to **materials requisitions,** which may be issued by the manufacturing department concerned or by a central scheduling department. Storeroom personnel record the issuances on the materials requisition by inserting the physical quantity data. Transfer of responsibility for the materials is evidenced by the signature or initials of the storeroom and factory personnel concerned. The requisition is then routed to the materials ledger clerk, who inserts unit prices and amounts. A typical materials requisition is illustrated as follows:

Materials Requisition

MATERIALS REQUISITION				
Job No. 62		Requisition No. 704		
Authorized by R. A. Sanders		Date January 18, 19--		
Description	Quantity Authorized	Quantity Issued	Unit Price	Amount
Material No. 23	800	700 100	$.50 .54	$350 54
Total issued				$404
Issued by M. K.		Received by J. B.		

The completed requisition serves as the basis for posting quantities and dollar data to the materials ledger accounts. In the illustration, the first-in, first-out costing method was used. A summary of the materials requisitions completed during the month serves as the basis for transferring the cost of the materials from the controlling account in the general ledger to the controlling accounts for work in process and factory overhead. The flow of materials into production is illustrated by the following entry:

Work in Process..	13,000	
Factory Overhead	840	
Materials		13,840

The perpetual inventory system for materials has three important advantages: (1) it provides for prompt and accurate charging of materials to jobs and factory overhead, (2) it permits the work of inventory-taking to be spread out rather than concentrated at the end of a fiscal period, and (3) it aids in the disclosure of inventory shortages or other irregularities. As physical quantities of the various materials are determined, the actual inventories are compared with the balances of the respective subsidiary ledger accounts. The causes of significant differences between the two should be determined and the responsibility for the differences assigned to specific individuals. Remedial action can then be taken.

Factory Labor

Unlike materials, factory labor is not tangible, nor is it acquired and stored in advance of its use. Hence, there is no perpetual inventory account for labor. The two main objectives in accounting for labor are (1) determination of the correct amount to be paid each employee for each payroll period and (2) appropriate allocation of labor costs to factory overhead and individual job orders.

The amount of time spent by an employee in the factory is usually recorded on **clock cards**, which are also called **in-and-out-cards**. The amount of time spent by each employee and labor cost incurred for each individual job, or for factory overhead, are recorded on **time tickets**. A typical time ticket form is illustrated as follows:

Time Ticket

Employee Name Gail Berry		No. 4521		
Employee No. 240		Date January 18, 19--		
Description of work Finishing		Job No. 62		

Time Started	Time Stopped	Hours Worked	Hourly Rate	Cost
10:00	12:00	2	$6.50	$13.00
1:00	2:00	1	6.50	6.50
Total cost				$19.50
Approved by T.D.				

The times reported on an employee's time tickets are compared with the related clock cards as an internal check on the accuracy of payroll disbursements. A summary of the time tickets at the end of each month serves as the basis for recording the direct and indirect labor costs incurred. The flow of labor costs into production is illustrated by the following entry:

Work in Process..	10,000	
Factory Overhead	2,200	
Wages Payable		12,200

Factory Overhead

Factory overhead includes all manufacturing costs except direct materials and direct labor. Examples of factory overhead costs, in addition to indirect materials and indirect labor, are depreciation, electricity, fuel, insurance, and property taxes. It is customary to have a factory overhead controlling account in the general ledger. Details of the various types of cost are accumulated in a subsidiary ledger.

Debits to Factory Overhead come from various sources. For example, the cost of indirect materials is obtained from the summary of the materials requisitions, the cost of indirect labor is obtained from the summary of the time tickets, costs of electricity and water are obtained from invoices, and the cost of depreciation and expired insurance may be recorded as adjustments at the end of the accounting period.

Although factory overhead cannot be specifically identified with particular jobs, it is as much a part of manufacturing costs as direct materials and direct labor. As the use of machines and automation has increased, factory overhead has represented an ever larger part of total costs. Many items of factory overhead cost are incurred for the entire factory and cannot be directly related to the finished product. The problem is further complicated because some items of factory overhead cost are relatively fixed in amount while others tend to vary according to changes in productivity.

To wait until the end of an accounting period to allocate factory overhead to the various jobs would be quite acceptable from the standpoint of accuracy but highly unsatisfactory in terms of timeliness. If the cost system is to be of maximum usefulness, it is imperative that cost data be available as each job is completed, even though there is a sacrifice in accuracy. It is only through timely reporting that management can make whatever adjustments seem necessary in pricing and manufacturing methods to achieve the best possible combination of revenue and cost on future jobs. Therefore, in order that job costs may be available currently, it is customary to apply factory overhead to production by using a **predetermined factory overhead rate**.

Predetermined Factory Overhead Rate. The factory overhead rate is determined by relating the estimated amount of factory overhead for the forthcoming year to some common activity base, one that will equitably apply the factory overhead costs to the goods manufactured. The common bases include direct labor costs, direct labor hours, and machine hours. For example, if it is estimated that the total factory overhead costs for the year will be $100,000 and that the total direct labor cost will be $125,000, an overhead rate of 80% ($100,000 ÷ $125,000) will be applied to the direct labor cost incurred during the year.

As factory overhead costs are incurred, they are debited to the factory overhead account. The factory overhead costs applied to production are periodically credited to the factory overhead account and debited to the work in process account. The application of factory overhead costs to production (80% of direct labor cost of $10,000) is illustrated by the following entry:

Work in Process...	8,000	
Factory Overhead		8,000

Inevitably, factory overhead costs applied and actual factory overhead costs incurred during a particular period will differ. If the amount applied exceeds the actual costs, the factory overhead account will have a credit balance and the overhead is said to be **overapplied** or **overabsorbed**. If the amount applied is less than the actual costs, the account will have a debit balance and the overhead is said to be **underapplied** or **underabsorbed**. Both cases are illustrated in the following account:

ACCOUNT FACTORY OVERHEAD   ACCOUNT NO.

Date		Item	Debit	Credit	Balance Debit	Balance Credit
May	1	Balance				200
	31	Costs incurred	8,320			
	31	Cost applied		8,000	120	

Underapplied Balance

Overapplied Balance

Disposition of Factory Overhead Balance. The balance in the factory overhead account is carried forward from month to month until the end of the year. The amount of the balance is reported on interim balance sheets as a deferred item.

The nature of the balance in the factory overhead account (underapplied or overapplied), as well as the amount, may change during the year. If there is a decided trend in either direction and the amount is substantial, the reason should be determined. If the variation is caused by alterations in manufacturing methods or by substantial changes in production goals, it may be advisable to revise the factory overhead rate. The accumulation of a large underapplied balance is more serious than a trend in the opposite direction and may indicate inefficiencies in production methods, excessive expenditures, or a combination of factors.

Despite any corrective actions that may be taken to avoid an underapplication or overapplication of factory overhead, the account will usually have a balance at the end of the fiscal year. Since the balance represents the underapplied or overapplied factory overhead applicable to the operations of the year just ended, it is not proper to report it in the year-end balance sheet as a deferred item.

There are two main alternatives for disposing of the balance of factory overhead at the end of the year: (1) by allocation of the balance among work in process, finished goods, and cost of goods sold accounts on the basis of the total amounts of applied factory overhead included in those accounts at the end of the year, or (2) by transfer of the balance to the cost of goods sold account. Theoretically, only the first alternative is sound because it represents a correction of the estimated overhead rate and brings the accounts into agreement with the costs actually incurred. On the other hand, much time and expense may be required to make the allocation and to revise the unit costs of the work in process and finished goods inventories. Furthermore, in most manufacturing enterprises, a very large part of the total manufacturing costs for the year passes through the work in process and the finished goods accounts into the cost of goods sold account before the end of the year. Therefore, unless the total amount of the underapplied or overapplied balance is great, it is satisfactory to transfer it to Cost of Goods Sold.

THE IMPLICATIONS OF AUTOMATION FOR ALLOCATING FACTORY OVERHEAD—A CASE STUDY

For some departments at Amerock Corporation, the allocation of overhead on the basis of direct labor became less accurate and less useful as manufacturing processes became more automated. The solution was to change from direct labor hours to machine hours for these departments.

Amerock Corporation, a manufacturer of cabinet and decorative hardware, found that the only disadvantages to using machine hours as a basis for allocating factory overhead were the time it would take to develop the system and the need for additional reporting by the machine operators. The potential benefits clearly outweighed any disadvantages. In the accounting area, a major advantage would be the ability to allocate overhead when one worker tended several machines. Better cost estimating would also be possible because overhead allocation would be more accurate. Forecasting and the calculation of actual costs would be easier. In the manufacturing area, machine utilization information would be more useful in understanding and controlling production and reporting.

Amerock Corporation's change in its overhead allocation basis has made it possible for accounting to capture costs accurately and for manufacturing to measure performance efficiently. The results have been so successful that Amerock plans to convert most of its departments to a machine hour basis as more of its plants become automated.

Source: Gregory Hakala, "Measuring Costs with Machine Hours," *Management Accounting* (October, 1985), pp. 57–61.

Work In Process

Costs incurred for the various jobs are debited to Work in Process. The job costs described in the preceding sections may be summarized as follows:

Direct materials, $13,000 — Work in Process debited and Materials credited; data obtained from summary of materials requisitions.

Direct labor, $10,000 — Work in Process debited and Wages Payable credited; data obtained from summary of time tickets.

Factory overhead, $8,000 — Work in Process debited and Factory Overhead credited; data obtained by applying overhead rate to direct labor cost (80% of $10,000).

The work in process account to which these costs were charged is illustrated as follows:

ACCOUNT WORK IN PROCESS   ACCOUNT NO.

Date		Item	Debit	Credit	Balance Debit	Balance Credit
May	1	Balance			3,000	
	31	Direct materials	13,000		16,000	
	31	Direct labor	10,000		26,000	
	31	Factory overhead	8,000		34,000	
	31	Jobs completed		31,920	2,080	

The work in process account is a controlling account that contains summary information only. The details concerning the costs incurred on each job order are accumulated in a subsidiary ledger known as the **cost ledger**. Each cost ledger account, called a **job cost sheet**, has spaces for recording all direct materials and direct labor chargeable to the job and for applying factory overhead at the predetermined rate. Postings to the job cost sheets are made from materials requisitions and time tickets or from summaries of these documents.

The four cost sheets in the subsidiary ledger for the work in process account illustrated are summarized as follows:

COST LEDGER

Job 71 (Summary)	
Balance............................	3,000
Direct materials..................	2,000
Direct labor	2,400
Factory overhead	1,920
	9,320

Job 73 (Summary)	
Direct materials..................	6,000
Direct labor	4,000
Factory overhead	3,200
	13,200

Job 72 (Summary)	
Direct materials..................	4,000
Direct labor	3,000
Factory overhead	2,400
	9,400

Job 74 (Summary)	
Direct materials..................	1,000
Direct labor	600
Factory overhead	480
	2,080

The relationship between the work in process controlling account on page 841 and the subsidiary cost ledger may be observed in the following tabulation:

Work in Process (Controlling)		Cost Ledger (Subsidiary)	
Beginning balance.....................	$3,000 ⟷	Beginning balance	
		Job 71...............................	$ 3,000
Direct materials........................	$13,000 ⟷	Direct materials	
		Job 71	$ 2,000
		Job 72	4,000
		Job 73	6,000
		Job 74	1,000
			$13,000
Direct labor	$10,000 ⟷	Direct labor	
		Job 71	$ 2,400
		Job 72	3,000
		Job 73	4,000
		Job 74	600
			$10,000
Factory overhead	$8,000 ⟷	Factory overhead	
		Job 71	$ 1,920
		Job 72	2,400
		Job 73	3,200
		Job 74	480
			$ 8,000
Jobs completed	$31,920 ⟷	Jobs completed	
		Job 71	$ 9,320
		Job 72	9,400
		Job 73	13,200
			$31,920
Ending balance.........................	$2,080 ⟷	Ending balance	
		Job 74	$ 2,080

The data in the cost ledger were presented in summary form for illustrative purposes. A job cost sheet for Job 72, providing for the current accumulation of cost elements entering into the job order and for a summary when the job is completed, is as follows:

Job Cost Sheet

Job No. 72						Date	May 7, 19--	
Item 5,000 Type C Containers						Date wanted	May 23, 19--	
For Stock						Date completed	May 21, 19--	

Direct Materials		Direct Labor				Summary	
Mat. Req. No.	Amount	Time Summary No.	Amount	Time Summary No.	Amount	Item	Amount
834	800.00	2202	83.60	2248	122.50	Direct	
838	1,000.00	2204	208.40	2250	187.30	materials	4,000.00
841	1,400.00	2205	167.00	2253	155.40	Direct labor	3,000.00
864	800.00	2210	229.00		3,000.00	Factory	
	4,000.00	2211	198.30			overhead	
		2213	107.20			(80% of	
		2216	110.00			direct	
		2222	277.60			labor cost)	2,400.00
		2224	217.40			Total cost	9,400.00
		2225	106.30				
		2231	153.20			No. of units	
		2234	245.20			finished	5,000
		2237	170.00			Cost per unit	1.88
		2242	261.60				

When Job 72 was completed, the direct materials costs and the direct labor costs were totaled and entered in the Summary column. Factory overhead was added at the predetermined rate of 80% of the direct labor cost, and the total cost of the job was determined. The total cost of the job, $9,400, divided by the number of units produced, 5,000, yielded a unit cost of $1.88 for the Type C Containers produced.

Upon the completion of Job 72, the job cost sheet was removed from the cost ledger and filed for future reference. At the end of the accounting period, the sum of the total costs on all cost sheets completed during the period is determined and the following entry is made:

| Finished Goods | 31,920 | |
| Work in Process | | 31,920 |

The remaining balance in the work in process account represents the total cost charged to the uncompleted job cost sheets.

Finished Goods and Cost of Goods Sold

The finished goods account is a controlling account. The related subsidiary ledger, which has an account for each kind of commodity produced, is called the **finished goods ledger** or **stock ledger**. Each account in the subsidiary finished goods ledger provides columns for recording the quantity and the cost of goods manufactured, the quantity and the cost of goods shipped, and the quantity, the total cost, and the unit cost of goods on hand. An account in the finished goods ledger is illustrated as follows:

Finished Goods Ledger Account

ITEM: TYPE C CONTAINER

	MANUFACTURED			SHIPPED			BALANCE		
JOB ORDER NO.	QUAN-TITY	AMOUNT	SHIP ORDER NO.	QUAN-TITY	AMOUNT	DATE	QUAN-TITY	AMOUNT	UNIT COST
						May 1	2,000	3,920.00	1.96
			643	2,000	3,920.00	8	—	—	—
72	5,000	9,400.00				21	5,000	9,400.00	1.88
			646	2,000	3,760.00	23	3,000	5,640.00	1.88

Just as there are various methods of costing materials entering into production, there are various methods of determining the cost of the finished goods sold. In the illustration, the first-in, first-out method is used. The quantities shipped are posted to the finished goods ledger from a copy of the shipping order or other memorandum. The finished goods ledger clerk then records on the copy of the shipping order the unit cost and the total amount of the commodity sold. A summary of the cost data on these shipping orders becomes the basis for the following entry:

Cost of Goods Sold..	30,168	
Finished Goods		30,168

If goods are returned by a buyer and are put back in stock, it is necessary to debit Finished Goods and credit Cost of Goods Sold for the cost.

Sales

For each sale of finished goods, it is necessary to maintain a record of both the cost price and the selling price of the goods sold. As previously stated, the cost data may be recorded on the shipping orders. As each sale occurs, the cost of the goods billed is recorded by debiting Cost of Goods Sold and crediting Finished Goods. The selling price of the goods sold is recorded by debiting Accounts Receivable (or Cash) and crediting Sales.

ILLUSTRATION OF JOB ORDER COST ACCOUNTING

OBJECTIVE 4
Illustrate a job order cost accounting system for a manufacturing enterprise.

To illustrate further a job order cost accounting system, assume that Amelia Co. has the following general ledger trial balance on January 1, the first day of the fiscal year.

Amelia Co. Trial Balance January 1, 19--		
Cash...	85,000	
Accounts Receivable	73,000	
Finished Goods	40,000	
Work in Process	20,000	
Materials	30,000	
Prepaid Expenses....................................	2,000	
Plant Assets..	850,000	
Accumulated Depreciation—Plant Assets................		473,000
Accounts Payable		70,000
Wages Payable...		15,000
Common Stock..		500,000
Retained Earnings....................................		42,000
	1,100,000	1,100,000

Although in practice the transactions for Amelia Co. would be recorded daily, the January transactions and adjustments are summarized as follows, along with the related journal entries:

(a) Materials purchased and prepaid expenses incurred

Materials	66,000	
Prepaid Expenses.....................................	1,000	
Accounts Payable		67,000

Summary of invoices and receiving reports:

Material A...	$29,000
Material B...	17,000
Material C...	16,000
Material D...	4,000
Total	$66,000

(b) Materials requisitioned for use

Work in Process.......................................	60,000	
Factory Overhead	3,000	
Materials		63,000

Summary of requisitions:

By Use		
Job 1001.............................	$12,000	
Job 1002.............................	26,000	
Job 1003.............................	22,000	$60,000
Factory Overhead		3,000
Total		$63,000

<u>By Types</u>

Material A............................	$27,000
Material B............................	18,000
Material C............................	15,000
Material D............................	3,000
Total..................................	$63,000

(c) Factory labor used

Work in Process..	100,000	
Factory Overhead	20,000	
Wages Payable...		120,000

Summary of time tickets:

Job 1001	$60,000	
Job 1002	30,000	
Job 1003	10,000	$100,000
Factory Overhead		20,000
Total		$120,000

(d) Other costs incurred

Factory Overhead	56,000	
Selling Expenses	25,000	
Administrative Expenses	10,000	
Accounts Payable		91,000

(e) Expiration of prepaid expenses

Factory Overhead	1,000	
Selling Expenses	100	
Administrative Expenses	100	
Prepaid Expenses		1,200

(f) Depreciation

Factory Overhead	7,000	
Selling Expenses	200	
Administrative Expenses	100	
Accumulated Depreciation—Plant Assets..............		7,300

(g) Application of factory overhead costs to jobs

Work in Process..	90,000	
Factory Overhead		90,000

The predetermined rate was 90% of direct labor cost.

Summary of factory overhead applied:

Job 1001 (90% of $60,000)...................	$54,000
Job 1002 (90% of $30,000)...................	27,000
Job 1003 (90% of $10,000)...................	9,000
Total.................................	$90,000

(h) Jobs completed

Finished Goods...................................	229,000	
Work in Process................................		229,000

Summary of completed job cost sheets:

Job 1001...	$146,000
Job 1002...	83,000
Total.................................	$229,000

(i) Sales and cost of goods sold

Accounts Receivable.............................	290,000	
Sales		290,000
Cost of Goods Sold..............................	220,000	
Finished Goods		220,000

Summary of sales invoices and shipping orders:

	Sales Price	Cost Price
Product X	$ 19,600	$ 15,000
Product Y	165,100	125,000
Product Z	105,300	80,000
Total	$290,000	$220,000

(j) Cash received

Cash...	300,000	
Accounts Receivable............................		300,000

(k) Cash disbursed

Accounts Payable................................	190,000	
Wages Payable....................................	125,000	
Cash...		315,000

The flow of costs through the manufacturing accounts, together with summary details of the subsidiary ledgers, is illustrated as follows. Entries in the accounts are identified by letters to facilitate comparisons with the foregoing summary journal entries.

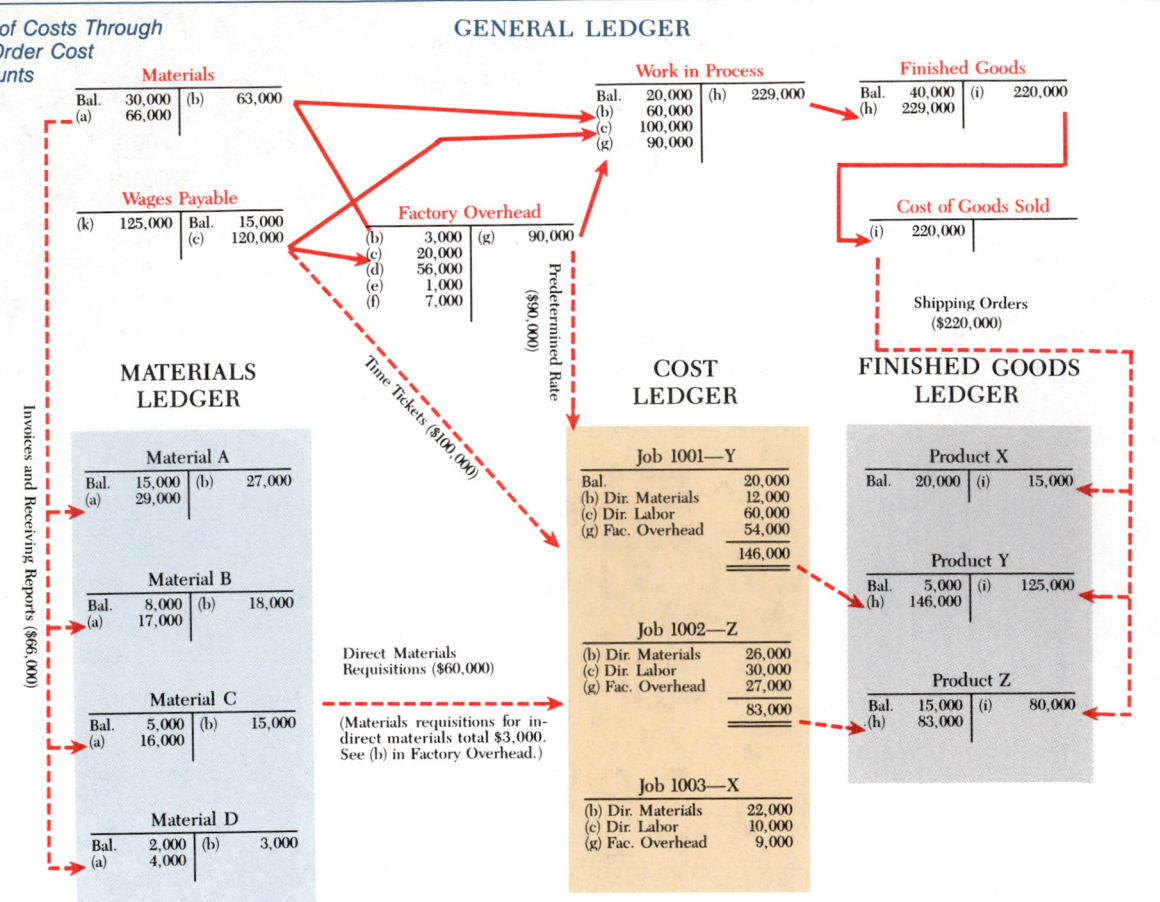

The trial balance taken from the general ledger of Amelia Co. on January 31 is as follows:

Amelia Co. Trial Balance January 31, 19--		
Cash	70,000	
Accounts Receivable	63,000	
Finished Goods	49,000	
Work in Process	41,000	
Materials	33,000	
Prepaid Expenses	1,800	
Plant Assets	850,000	
Accumulated Depreciation — Plant Assets		480,300
Accounts Payable		38,000
Wages Payable		10,000
Common Stock		500,000
Retained Earnings		42,000
Sales		290,000
Cost of Goods Sold	220,000	
Factory Overhead		3,000
Selling Expenses	25,300	
Administrative Expenses	10,200	
	1,363,300	1,363,300

The balances of the three inventory accounts—Finished Goods, Work in Process, and Materials—represent the respective ending inventories on January 31. The balances of the general ledger controlling accounts are compared with their respective subsidiary ledgers as follows:

Controlling and Subsidiary Accounts Compared

Controlling Accounts		Subsidiary Ledgers		
Account	Balance	Account		Balance
Finished Goods	$49,000 ⟷	Product X	$ 5,000	
		Product Y	26,000	
		Product Z	18,000	$49,000
Work in Process........................	$41,000 ⟷	Job 1003		$41,000
Materials	$33,000 ⟷	Material A..............	$17,000	
		Material B..............	7,000	
		Material C..............	6,000	
		Material D..............	3,000	$33,000

To simplify the Amelia Co. illustration, only one work in process account and one factory overhead account were used. Usually, a manufacturing business has several processing departments, each requiring separate work in process and factory overhead accounts. In the illustration, one predetermined rate was used in applying the factory overhead to jobs. In a factory with several processing departments, a single factory overhead rate may not provide accurate product costs and effective cost control. A single rate for the entire factory cannot take into consideration such factors as differences among departments in the nature of their operations and in amounts of factory overhead incurred. In such cases, each factory department should have a separate factory overhead rate. For example, in a factory with twenty distinct operating departments, one department might have an overhead rate of 110% of direct labor cost, another a rate of $4 per direct labor hour, and another a rate of $3.50 per machine hour.

The financial statements on the next page are based on the data for Amelia Co. It should be noted that the overapplied factory overhead on January 31 is reported on the balance sheet as a deferred item. It should also be noted that a separate statement of cost of goods manufactured, as illustrated in Chapter 20, is not shown. Under a perpetual inventory cost accounting system, the balances of the cost of goods sold, materials, work in process, and finished goods accounts are kept up to date. Hence, the finished goods ledger will indicate the costs of manufacturing the various products. Likewise, the cost ledger will indicate the costs assigned to jobs still in process. The balance of the cost of goods sold account will indicate the cost of products sold during the period. The statement of cost of goods manufactured is normally prepared only for enterprises using periodic inventory procedures under a general accounting system.

Amelia Co.
Income Statement
For Month Ended January 31, 19--

Sales		$290,000
Cost of goods sold		220,000
Gross profit		$ 70,000
Operating expenses:		
Selling expenses	$25,300	
Administrative expenses	10,200	
Total operating expenses		35,500
Income from operations		$ 34,500

Amelia Co.
Retained Earnings Statement
For Month Ended January 31, 19--

Retained earnings, January 1, 19--	$42,000
Income for the month	34,500
Retained earnings, January 31, 19--	$76,500

Amelia Co.
Balance Sheet
January 31, 19--

Assets

Current assets:			
Cash		$ 70,000	
Accounts receivable		63,000	
Inventories:			
Finished goods	$49,000		
Work in process	41,000		
Materials	33,000	123,000	
Prepaid expenses		1,800	
Total current assets			$257,800
Plant assets		$850,000	
Less accumulated depreciation		480,300	369,700
Total assets			$627,500

Liabilities

Current liabilities:			
Accounts payable	$38,000		
Wages payable	10,000		
Total current liabilities		$ 48,000	
Deferred credits:			
Factory overhead		3,000	
Total liabilities			$ 51,000

Stockholders' Equity

Common stock	$500,000	
Retained earnings	76,500	
Total stockholders' equity		576,500
Total liabilities and stockholders' equity		$627,500

JOB ORDER COST SYSTEMS FOR SERVICE ENTERPRISES

OBJECTIVE 5
Describe a job order cost accounting system for a service enterprise.

A job order cost accounting system may be useful to the management of a service enterprise in planning and controlling operations. Since the "product" of such an enterprise is service, management's focus is on direct labor and overhead costs. The cost of any materials or supplies used in rendering services for a client is usually small in amount and is normally included as part of the overhead.

The direct labor and overhead costs of rendering services to clients are accumulated in a work in process account, which is supported by a cost ledger. A job cost sheet is used to accumulate the costs for each client's job. When a job is completed and the client is billed, the costs are transferred to a cost of services account. This account is similar to the cost of merchandise sold account for a merchandising enterprise or the cost of goods sold account for a manufacturing enterprise. A finished goods account is not necessary, since the revenues associated with the services are recorded after the services have been rendered. The flow of costs through a service enterprise using a job order cost accounting system is as follows:

Flow of Costs Through a Service Enterprise

Wages Payable		Work in Process		Cost of Services
Paid XXX	Direct labor XXX	XXX	Completed jobs XXX	XXX
	Indirect labor XXX	XXX		

Supplies		Overhead	

Purchased
       XXX
	Used XXX	XXX
		XXX
			Applied
			         XXX

		Other costs XXX	

In practice, additional accounting considerations unique to service enterprises may need to be considered. For example, a service enterprise may bill clients on a weekly or monthly basis rather than waiting until a job is completed. In these situations, a portion of the costs related to each billing should be transferred from the work in process account to the cost of services account. This treatment is similar to the percentage-of-completion method used by construction contractors. A service enterprise may also have advance billings which would be accounted for as deferred revenue until the services have been completed.

CHAPTER REVIEW

KEY POINTS

OBJECTIVE 1

Usefulness of Product Costs

Product costs are useful to managers for the preparation of financial statements. Product costs are also needed by management for a wide variety of decisions, such as setting long-term product prices. Without accurate product cost information, managers could not effectively or efficiently manage operations.

OBJECTIVE 2

Types of Accounting Systems

Two basic accounting systems are commonly used by manufacturers: general accounting systems and cost accounting systems. A general accounting system uses periodic inventory procedures for materials, work in process, and finished goods inventories. For more complex manufacturing operations, a cost accounting system using perpetual inventory procedures is usually employed. A cost accounting system also uses controlling accounts and subsidiary ledgers for materials, work in process, and finished goods. The two main cost accounting systems are the job order cost and process cost systems.

OBJECTIVE 3, 4

Job Order Cost Systems for Manufacturing Enterprises

A job order cost system provides for a separate record of the cost of each particular quantity of product that passes through the factory. The details concerning the costs incurred on each job order are accumulated in a subsidiary ledger known as the cost ledger. Each cost ledger account, called a job cost sheet, has spaces for recording all direct materials and direct labor chargeable to the job and for applying factory overhead at the predetermined rate. Work in Process is the controlling account for the cost ledger. As a job is finished, it is transferred to the finished goods ledger, for which Finished Goods is the controlling account.

OBJECTIVE 5

Job Order Cost Systems for Service Enterprises

A cost accounting system may be useful to management in planning and controlling the operations of a service enterprise. The cost of any materials or supplies used in rendering services for a client is usually small in amount and is normally included as part of the overhead. The direct labor and overhead costs of rendering services are accumulated in a work in process account. When a job is completed and the client is billed, the costs are transferred to a cost of services account.

KEY TERMS

general accounting system 832
cost accounting system 832
job order cost system 834
process cost system 834
purchase requisitions 836
purchase orders 836
receiving report 836
materials ledger 836
materials requisitions 836

time tickets 838
predetermined factory
  overhead rate 839
overapplied overhead 839
underapplied overhead 839
cost ledger 841
job cost sheet 841
finished goods ledger 844

SELF-EXAMINATION QUESTIONS
Answers at end of chapter.

1. The account maintained by a manufacturing business for inventory of goods in the process of manufacture is:
   A. Finished Goods
   B. Materials
   C. Work in Process
   D. none of the above

2. For a manufacturing business, finished goods inventory includes:
   A. direct materials costs
   B. direct labor costs
   C. factory overhead costs
   D. all of the above

3. An example of a factory overhead cost is:
    A. wages of factory assembly-line workers
    B. salaries for factory plant supervisors
    C. bearings for electric motors being manufactured
    D. all of the above

4. For which of the following would the job order cost system be appropriate?
    A. Antique furniture repair shop   C. Coal manufacturer
    B. Rubber manufacturer   D. All of the above

5. If the factory overhead account has a credit balance, factory overhead is said to be:
    A. underapplied   C. underabsorbed
    B. overapplied   D. none of the above

ILLUSTRATIVE PROBLEM

Shelton Signs Inc. specializes in the production of neon signs and uses a job order cost system. The following data summarize the operations related to production for November, the first month of operations:

(a) Materials purchased on account, $21,750.
(b) Materials requisitioned and factory labor used:

	Materials	Factory Labor
Job No. 1	$2,750	$1,700
Job No. 2	3,800	2,000
Job No. 3	2,990	1,450
Job No. 4	5,950	3,800
Job No. 5	3,250	1,900
Job No. 6	900	600
For general factory use	595	500

(c) Factory overhead costs incurred on account, $4,300.
(d) Depreciation of machinery, $1,450.
(e) The factory overhead rate is 60% of direct labor cost.
(f) Jobs completed: Nos. 1, 2, 4, and 5.
(g) Jobs 1, 2, and 4 were shipped and customers were billed for $7,900, $10,500, and $18,100, respectively.

Instructions

1. Prepare entries to record the foregoing summarized operations.
2. Determine the account balances for Work in Process and Finished Goods.
3. Prepare a schedule of unfinished jobs to support the balance in the work in process account.
4. Prepare a schedule of completed jobs on hand to support the balance in the finished goods account.

SOLUTION

(1) (a) Materials	21,750	
	Accounts Payable		21,750
(b) Work in Process	31,090	
	Factory Overhead	1,095	
	Materials		20,235
	Wages Payable		11,950

(c) Factory Overhead 4,300
    Accounts Payable... 4,300

(d) Factory Overhead 1,450
    Accumulated Depreciation — Machinery 1,450

(e) Work in Process... 6,870
    Factory Overhead (60% of $11,450) 6,870

(f) Finished Goods 30,790
    Work in Process 30,790

Computation of the cost of jobs finished:

Job	Direct Materials	Direct Labor	Overhead	Total
Job No. 1................	$2,750	$1,700	$1,020	$ 5,470
Job No. 2................	3,800	2,000	1,200	7,000
Job No. 4................	5,950	3,800	2,280	12,030
Job No. 5................	3,250	1,900	1,140	6,290
				$30,790

(g) Accounts Receivable...................................... 36,500
    Sales... 36,500

Cost of Goods Sold 24,500
    Finished Goods 24,500

Computation of the cost of jobs sold:

Job No. 1................	$ 5,470
Job No. 2................	7,000
Job No. 4................	12,030
	$24,500

(2) Work in Process: $7,170 ($31,090 + $6,870 − $30,790)
    Finished Goods: $6,290 ($30,790 − $24,500)

(3)
Schedule of Unfinished Jobs

	Direct Materials	Direct Labor	Factory Overhead	Total
Job No. 3.........................	$2,990	$1,450	$870	$5,310
Job No. 6.........................	900	600	360	1,860
Balance of Work in Process, November 30				$7,170

(4)
Schedule of Completed Jobs

Job No. 5:	Direct materials	$3,250
	Direct labor...	1,900
	Factory overhead	1,140
Balance of Finished Goods, November 30..........................		$6,290

DISCUSSION QUESTIONS

1. What are two important uses of product cost information by managers?

2. What are the two basic accounting systems commonly used by manufacturers?

3. In a general accounting system, which of the following amounts is not closed to Manufacturing Summary?
   (a) Direct materials inventory as of the beginning of the year
   (b) Direct materials inventory as of the end of the year
   (c) Finished goods inventory as of the beginning of the year
   (d) Factory overhead

4. (a) Name the two principal types of cost accounting systems. (b) Which system provides for a separate record of each particular quantity of product that passes through the factory? (c) Which system accumulates the costs for each department or process within the factory?

5. Distinguish between the purchase requisition and the purchase order used in the procurement of materials.

6. Briefly discuss how the purchase order, purchase invoice, and receiving report can be used to assist in controlling cash disbursements for materials acquired.

7. What document is the source for (a) debiting the accounts in the materials ledger and (b) crediting the accounts in the materials ledger?

8. Briefly discuss how the accounts in the materials ledger can be used as an aid in maintaining appropriate inventory quantities of stock items.

9. How does use of the materials requisition help control the issuance of materials from the storeroom?

10. Discuss the major advantages of a perpetual inventory system over a periodic system for materials.

11. (a) Differentiate between the clock card and the time ticket. (b) Why should the total time reported on an employee's time tickets for a payroll period be compared with the time reported on the employee's clock cards for the same period?

12. Which of the following items are properly classified as part of factory overhead?
   (a) Factory supplies used   (d) Property taxes on factory buildings
   (b) Interest expense   (e) Sales commissions
   (c) Amortization of factory patents (f) Direct materials

13. Discuss how the predetermined factory overhead rate can be used in job order cost accounting to assist management in pricing jobs.

14. (a) How is a predetermined factory overhead rate calculated? (b) Name three common bases used in calculating the rate.

15. (a) What is (1) overapplied factory overhead and (2) underapplied factory overhead? (b) If the factory overhead account has a debit balance, was factory overhead underapplied or overapplied? (c) If the factory overhead account has a credit balance at the end of the first month of the fiscal year, where will the amount of this balance be reported on the interim balance sheet?

16. At the end of a fiscal year, there was a relatively minor balance in the factory overhead account. What is the simplest satisfactory procedure for the disposition of the balance in the account?

17. What name is given to the individual accounts in the cost ledger?

18. What document serves as the basis for posting to (a) the direct materials section of the job cost sheet, and (b) the direct labor section of the job cost sheet?

19. Describe the source of the data for debiting Work in Process for (a) direct materials, (b) direct labor, and (c) factory overhead.

20. What account is the controlling account for (a) the materials ledger, (b) the cost ledger, and (c) the finished goods ledger or stock ledger?

21. In a cost accounting system for a service enterprise, the cost of any materials or supplies used in rendering services for a client is normally debited to what account?

22. When a job is completed and the client is billed, the costs are transferred to what account in a cost accounting system for a service enterprise?

Real World Focus

23. Hewlett-Packard Company manufactures printed circuit boards in which a high volume of standardized units are fabricated, machined, assembled, and tested. Is the job order cost system appropriate in this situation?

EXERCISES

Exercise 21–1

Cost of materials issuances by fifo and lifo methods.

OBJ. 2, 3

The balance of Material F on May 1 and the receipts and issuances during May are as follows:

Balance:	May	1.............................	120 units at $12.00
Received:	May	3.............................	300 units at $12.50
		12.............................	240 units at $13.00
		29.............................	180 units at $13.80
Issued:	May	5.............................	180 units for Job 512
		19.............................	150 units for Job 528
		30.............................	200 units for Job 545

Determine the cost of each of the three issuances under a perpetual system, using (a) the first-in, first-out method and (b) the last-in, first-out method.

Exercise 21–2

Entry for issuance of materials.

OBJ. 3, 4

The issuances of materials for the current month are as follows:

Requisition No.	Material	Job. No.	Amount
711	A-06	9001	$10,280
712	I-70	9010	3,380
713	B-11	9015	7,720
714	F-12	General factory use	1,500
715	W-29	9040	8,900

Present the journal entry to record the issuances of materials.

Exercise 21–3

Entry for factory labor costs

OBJ. 3, 4

A summary of the time tickets for the current month follows:

Job. No.	Amount	Job. No.	Amount
14012	$ 3,750	14016	$ 2,400
14013	24,300	Indirect labor	3,540
14014	8,010	14017	18,750
14015	13,500	14018	10,600

Present the journal entry to record the factory labor costs.

Exercise 21–4
Factory overhead rates, entries, and account balance.
OBJ. 3, 4

Milford Company, which maintains departmental accounts for work in process and factory overhead, applies factory overhead to jobs on the basis of machine hours in Department 10 and on the basis of direct labor costs in Department 20. Estimated factory overhead costs, direct labor costs, and machine hours for April are as follows:

	Department 10	Department 20
Estimated factory overhead cost for year	$200,000	$720,000
Estimated direct labor costs for year		$600,000
Estimated machine hours for year.................	40,000	
Actual factory overhead costs for April	$ 37,150	$ 87,680
Actual direct labor costs for April.................		$ 78,500
Actual machine hours for April	7,200	

(a) Determine the factory overhead rate for Department 10. (b) Determine the factory overhead rate for Department 20. (c) Prepare the journal entries to apply factory overhead to production for April. (d) Determine the balances of the departmental factory accounts as of April 30 and indicate whether the amounts represent overapplied or underapplied factory overhead.

Exercise 21–5
Entry for jobs completed; cost of unfinished jobs.
OBJ. 3, 4

The following account appears in the ledger after only part of the postings have been completed for October:

Work in Process

Balance, October 1	51,450
Direct Materials	129,300
Direct Labor	202,500
Factory Overhead	111,000

Jobs finished during October are summarized as follows:

| Job 1903............... | $ 76,200 | Job 1930............ | $122,400 |
| Job 1908............... | 136,800 | Job 1941............ | 78,300 |

(a) Prepare the journal entry to record the jobs completed and (b) determine the cost of the unfinished jobs at October 31.

Exercise 21–6
Entries for factory costs and jobs completed.
OBJ. 3, 4

Park Enterprises Inc. began manufacturing operations on March 1. Jobs 301 and 302 were completed during the month, and all costs applicable to them were recorded on the related cost sheets. Jobs 303 and 304 are still in process at the end of the month, and all applicable costs except factory overhead have been recorded on the related cost sheets. In addition to the materials and labor charged directly to the jobs, $21,000 of indirect materials and $50,400 of indirect labor were used during the month. The cost sheets for the four jobs entering production during the month are as follows, in summary form:

Job 301		Job 302	
Direct materials	31,500	Direct materials	56,400
Direct labor........................	25,200	Direct labor......................	40,320
Factory overhead................	12,600	Factory overhead..............	20,160
Total	69,300	Total	116,880

Job 303		Job 304	
Direct materials	42,800	Direct materials	11,000
Direct labor........................	35,280	Direct labor......................	15,600
Factory overhead................		Factory overhead..............	

Prepare an entry to record each of the following operations for the month (one entry for each operation):

(a) Direct and indirect materials used.
(b) Direct and indirect labor used.
(c) Factory overhead applied (a single overhead rate is used, based on direct labor cost).
(d) Completion of Jobs 301 and 302.

Exercise 21-7
Job order cost accounting entries for service enterprise.
OBJ. 5

(a) Prepare journal entries to record the following selected transactions for September for Bateman and Sparkman, CPAs and (b) prepare a summary of jobs in work in process as of September 30.

(1) Labor incurred as reported by time reports for September:

Direct labor:
Abel Inc. (Job 1)	$ 4,000
Nobel Co. (Job 2)	2,800
Anderson Co. (Job 3)	3,500
Nash Inc. (Job 4)	12,250
Thomas Inc. (Job 5)	1,250
	$23,800
Indirect labor	6,200
Total	$30,000

(2) The following other costs were incurred on account: overhead cost, $15,000; advertising expense, $3,000; rent expense, $5,000; and office supplies expense, $1,800.
(3) Overhead is applied to individual jobs at a rate of 60% of direct labor cost.
(4) Jobs completed and billed to clients:

Client	Amount Billed
Abel Inc. (Job 1)	$ 7,000
Nobel Co. (Job 2)	5,500
Anderson Co. (Job 3)	6,000
Total billings	$18,500

PROBLEMS

Series A

Problem 21-1A
Entries and schedules for unfinished and completed jobs.
OBJ. 3, 4

Keeling Printing Company uses a job order cost system. The following data summarize the operations related to production for April, the first month of operations:

(a) Materials purchased on account, $86,130.
(b) Materials requisitioned and factory labor used:

	Materials	Factory Labor
Job 401	$17,400	$13,725
Job 402	5,100	2,940
Job 403	12,780	7,035
Job 404	6,420	2,850
Job 405	10,245	4,200
Job 406	9,270	6,915
For general factory use	1,965	4,500

(c) Factory overhead costs incurred on account, $16,950.
(d) Depreciation of machinery and equipment, $8,100.
(e) The factory overhead rate is 80% of direct labor cost.
(f) Jobs completed: 401, 402, 403, and 405.
(g) Jobs 401, 402, and 403 were shipped and customers were billed for $70,175, $17,320, and $42,405 respectively.

Instructions:

(1) Prepare entries to record the foregoing summarized operations.
(2) Open T accounts for Work in Process and Finished Goods and post the appropriate entries, using the identifying letters as dates. Insert memorandum account balances as of the end of the month.
(3) Prepare a schedule of unfinished jobs to support the balance in the work in process account.
(4) Prepare a schedule of completed jobs on hand to support the balance in the finished goods account.

If the working papers correlating with the textbook are not used, omit Problem 21–2A.

Problem 21–2A
Job order cost sheet.
OBJ. 3, 4

Douglas Furniture Company repairs, refinishes, and reupholsters furniture. A job order cost system was installed recently to facilitate (1) the determination of price quotations to prospective customers, (2) the determination of actual costs incurred on each job, and (3) cost reductions.

In response to a prospective customer's request for a price quotation on a job, the estimated cost data are inserted on an unnumbered job cost sheet. If the offer is accepted, a number is assigned to the job and the costs incurred are recorded in the usual manner on the job cost sheet. After the job is completed, reasons for the variances between the estimated and actual costs are noted on the sheet. The data are then available to management in evaluating the efficiency of operations and in preparing quotations on future jobs.

On October 7, an estimate of $342 for reupholstering a chair and couch was given to Daryl Towns. The estimate was based on the following data:

Estimated direct materials:	
9 meters at $14 per meter...	$126
Estimated direct labor:	
6 hours at $10 per hour..	60
Estimated factory overhead (70% of direct labor cost)...............	42
Total estimated costs..	$228
Markup (50% of production costs)	114
Total estimate..	$342

On October 12, the chair and couch were picked up from the residence of Daryl Towns, 1340 Bald Eagle Drive, Tucson, with a commitment to return it on October 26. The job was completed on October 20.

The related materials requisitions and time tickets are summarized as follows:

Materials Requisition No.	Description	Amount
C817	9 meters at $14	$126
C819	2 meters at $14	28

Time Ticket No.	Description	Amount
7193	5 hours at $10	$ 50
7198	2 hours at $10	20

Instructions:

(1) Complete that portion of the job order cost sheet that would be prepared when the estimate is given to the customer.
(2) Assign number 90-10-17 to the job, record the costs incurred, and complete the job order cost sheet. In commenting upon the variances between actual costs and estimated costs, assume that 2 meters of materials were spoiled, the factory overhead rate has been proved to be satisfactory, and an inexperienced employee performed the work.

Problem 21–3A
Preparation of
financial statements.
OBJ. 3, 4

The trial balance of Alpine Inc. at the beginning of the current fiscal year is as follows:

Alpine Inc.
Trial Balance
February 1, 19--

Cash..	69,520	
Accounts Receivable...............................	105,390	
Finished Goods	99,750	
Work in Process.....................................	36,540	
Materials	48,300	
Prepaid Expenses..................................	12,900	
Plant Assets..	873,600	
Accumulated Depreciation — Plant Assets......		495,780
Accounts Payable...................................		35,550
Wages Payable......................................		—
Common Stock.......................................		150,000
Retained Earnings..................................		564,670
Sales		—
Cost of Goods Sold................................	—	
Factory Overhead	—	
Selling Expenses	—	
Administrative Expenses	—	
	1,246,000	1,246,000

Transactions completed during February and adjustments required on February 28 are summarized as follows:

(a) Materials purchased on account.......................... $ 41,220
(b) Materials requisitioned for factory use:

Direct	$38,700	
Indirect	480	39,180

(c) Factory labor costs incurred:

Direct	$19,440	
Indirect	2,760	22,200

(d) Other costs and expenses incurred on account:

Factory overhead...	$10,125	
Selling expenses	9,855	
Administrative expenses	7,200	27,180

(e) Cash disbursed:

Accounts payable..	$73,800	
Wages payable	19,950	93,750

(f) Depreciation charged:

Factory equipment...	$ 6,480	
Office equipment...	540	7,020

(g) Prepaid expenses expired:
    Chargeable to factory.. $ 960
    Chargeable to selling expenses   225
    Chargeable to administrative expenses   210   1,395

(h) Applied factory overhead at a predetermined rate:
    115% of direct labor cost.

(i) Total cost of jobs completed...............................   77,400

(j) Sales, all on account:
    Selling price.. 100,800
    Cost 65,400

(k) Cash received on account................................... 102,600

Instructions:

(1) Open T accounts and record the initial balances indicated in the February 1 trial balance, identifying each as "Bal."
(2) Record the transactions directly in the accounts, using the identifying letters in place of dates.
(3) Prepare an income statement for the month ended February 28, 19--.
(4) Prepare a retained earnings statement for the month ended February 28, 19--.
(5) Prepare a balance sheet as of February 28, 19--.

Problem 21–4A
Entries, trial balance, and financial statements.
OBJ. 3, 4

The trial balance of the general ledger of Mott Corporation as of March 31, the end of the first month of the current fiscal year, is shown as follows:

Mott Corporation
Trial Balance
March 31, 19--

Cash...	82,300	
Accounts Receivable..	166,700	
Finished Goods	160,200	
Work in Process..	55,260	
Materials	66,510	
Plant Assets..	711,900	
Accumulated Depreciation—Plant Assets................		317,600
Accounts Payable...		119,700
Wages Payable...		13,500
Capital Stock..		300,000
Retained Earnings...		467,470
Sales		241,500
Cost of Goods Sold...	180,000	
Factory Overhead	1,800	
Selling and Administrative Expenses	35,100	
	1,459,770	1,459,770

As of the same date, balances in the accounts of selected subsidiary ledgers are as follows:

Finished goods ledger:
  Commodity A, 3,500 units, $63,000; Commodity B, 2,700 units, $40,500; Commodity C, 2,100 units, $56,700.
Cost ledger:
  Job 318, $55,260.
Materials ledger:
  Material X, $26,550; Material Y, $33,210; Material Z, $6,750.

The transactions completed during April are summarized as follows:

(a) Materials were purchased on account as follows:

Material X	$49,500
Material Y	34,650
Material Z	1,350

(b) Materials were requisitioned from stores as follows:

Job 318, Material X, $24,300; Material Y, $21,267	$45,567
Job 319, Material X, $12,420; Material Y, $4,986	17,406
Job 320, Material X, $19,080; Material Y, $15,177	34,257
For general factory use, Material Z	1,440

(c) Time tickets for the month were chargeable as follows:

Job 318	$17,640	Job 320	$14,760
Job 319	15,120	Indirect labor	5,400

(d) Factory payroll checks for $57,960 were issued.
(e) Various factory overhead charges of $20,150 were incurred on account.
(f) Depreciation of $8,100 on factory plant and equipment was recorded.
(g) Factory overhead was applied to jobs at 70% of direct labor cost.
(h) Jobs completed during the month were as follows: Job 318 produced 8,550 units of Commodity B; Job 320 produced 2,190 units of Commodity C.
(i) Selling and administrative expenses of $34,380 were incurred on account.
(j) Payments on account were $128,700.
(k) Total sales on account were $251,700. The goods sold were as follows (use first-in, first-out method): 1,500 units of Commodity A; 4,800 units of Commodity B; 2,400 units of Commodity C.
(l) Cash of $225,900 was received on accounts receivable.

Instructions:

(1) Open T accounts for the general ledger, the finished goods ledger, the cost ledger, and the materials ledger. Record directly in these accounts the balances as of March 31, identifying them as "Bal." Record the quantities as well as the dollar amounts in the finished goods ledger.
(2) Prepare entries to record the April transactions. After recording each transaction, post to the T accounts, using the identifying letters as dates. When posting to the finished goods ledger, record quantities as well as dollar amounts.
(3) Prepare a trial balance.
(4) Prepare schedules of the account balances in the finished goods ledger, the cost ledger, and the materials ledger.
(5) Prepare an income statement for the two months ended April 30.

Problem 21–5A
Determination of amounts missing from selected accounts in job cost system.

OBJ. 3, 4

Following are selected accounts for Bulla Products. For the purposes of this problem, some of the debits and credits have been omitted.

Accounts Receivable

Jan.	1	Balance	130,500	Jan. 31	Collections	192,800
	31	Sales	(A)			

Materials

Jan.	1	Balance	33,600	Jan. 31	Requisitions	(B)
	31	Purchases	66,400			

Work in Process

Jan.	1	Balance	38,400	Jan. 31	Goods finished	(E)
	31	Direct materials	(C)			
	31	Direct labor	77,600			
	31	Factory overhead	(D)			

Finished Goods

| Jan. | 1 | Balance | 20,700 | Jan. 31 | Cost of goods sold | (G) |
| | 31 | Goods finished | (F) | | | |

Factory Overhead

| Jan. | 1 | Balance | 400 | Jan. 31 | Applied (75% of | |
| | 1–31 | Costs incurred | 57,900 | | direct labor cost) | (H) |

Cost of Goods Sold

| Jan. | 31 | (I) | |

Sales

| | | Jan. 31 | (J) |

Selected balances at January 31:
Accounts receivable...................................... $125,000
Finished goods.. 35,200
Work in process.. 43,500
Materials 24,000

Materials requisitions for January included $2,000 of materials issued for general factory use. All sales are made on account, terms n/30.

Instructions:

(1) Determine the amounts represented by the letters (A) through (J), presenting your computations.
(2) Determine the amount of factory overhead overapplied or underapplied as of January 31.

Series B

Problem 21–1B
Entries and schedules for unfinished and completed jobs.
OBJ. 3, 4

Clardy Printing Company uses a job order cost system. The following data summarize the operations related to production for July, the first month of operations:

(a) Materials purchases on account, $275,400.
(b) Materials requisitioned and factory labor used:

	Materials	Factory Labor
Job 701	$39,600	$23,750
Job 702	25,950	17,600
Job 703	34,750	12,750
Job 704	52,375	33,450
Job 705	28,600	16,700
Job 706	17,750	7,250
For general factory use	5,750	4,400

(c) Factory overhead costs incurred on account, $49,000.
(d) Depreciation of machinery and equipment, $19,400.
(e) The factory overhead rate is 70% of direct labor cost.
(f) Jobs completed: 701, 702, 703, and 704.
(g) Jobs 701, 702, and 704 were shipped and customers were billed for $134,200, $94,100, and $182,100 respectively.

Instructions:

(1) Prepare entries to record the foregoing summarized operations.
(2) Open T accounts for Work in Process and Finished Goods and post the appropriate entries, using the identifying letters as dates. Insert memorandum account balances as of the end of the month.
(3) Prepare a schedule of unfinished jobs to support the balance in the work in process account.
(4) Prepare a schedule of completed jobs on hand to support the balance in the finished goods account.

If the working papers correlating with the textbook are not used, omit Problem 21–2B.

Problem 21–2B

Job order cost sheet.

OBJ. 3, 4

Meeks Furniture Company repairs, refinishes, and reupholsters furniture. A job order cost system was installed recently to facilitate (1) the determination of price quotations to prospective customers, (2) the determination of actual costs incurred on each job, and (3) cost reductions.

In response to a prospective customer's request for a price quotation on a job, the estimated cost data are inserted on an unnumbered job cost sheet. If the offer is accepted, a number is assigned to the job and the costs incurred are recorded in the usual manner on the job cost sheet. After the job is completed, reasons for the variances between the estimated and actual costs are noted on the sheet. The data are then available to management in evaluating the efficiency of operations and in preparing quotations on future jobs.

On August 15, an estimate of $243 for reupholstering a couch was given to Joan Holiday. The estimate was based on the following data:

Estimated direct materials:	
5 meters at $20 per meter	$100
Estimated direct labor:	
4 hours at $16 per hour..	64
Estimated factory overhead (25% of direct labor cost)...............	16
Total estimated costs...	$180
Markup (35% of production costs)	63
Total estimate...	$243

On August 16, the couch was picked up from the residence of Joan Holiday, 315 Reading Lane, Elberton, with a commitment to return it on August 30.

The job was completed on August 28. The related materials requisitions and time tickets are summarized as follows:

Materials Requisition No.	Description	Amount
2718	5 meters at $20	$100
2723	3 meters at $20	60

Time Ticket No.	Description	Amount
U8815	4 hours at $16	$ 64
U8817	2 hours at $16	32

Instructions:

(1) Complete that portion of the job order cost sheet that would be prepared when the estimate is given to the customer.
(2) Assign number U8-13 to the job, record the costs incurred, and complete the job order cost sheet. In commenting upon the variances between actual costs and estimated costs, assume that 3 meters of materials were spoiled, the factory overhead rate has been proved to be satisfactory, and an inexperienced employee performed the work.

Problem 21—4B
Entries, trial balance, and financial statements.
OBJ. 3, 4

The trial balance of the general ledger of T. Pickett Co. as of July 31, the end of the first month of the current fiscal year, is as follows:

T. Pickett
Trial Balance
July 31, 19--

Cash...	73,600	
Accounts Receivable...	148,200	
Finished Goods	150,080	
Work in Process..	49,600	
Materials	58,320	
Plant Assets...	650,000	
Accumulated Depreciation — Plant Assets................		290,000
Accounts Payable...		100,000
Wages Payable..		12,000
Capital Stock..		100,000
Retained Earnings..		556,000
Sales		250,000
Cost of Goods Sold..	145,500	
Factory Overhead	700	
Selling and Administrative Expenses	32,000	
	1,308,000	1,308,000

As of the same date, balances in the accounts of selected subsidiary ledgers are as follows:

Finished goods ledger:
   Commodity Q, 1,600 units, $32,000; Commodity R, 4,800 units, $72,000; Commodity S, 2,560 units, $46,080.
Cost ledger:
   Job 900, $49,600.
Materials ledger:
   Material G, $30,880; Material H, $25,280; Material I, $2,160.

The transactions completed during August are summarized as follows:

(a) Materials were purchased on account as follows:

Material G...	$44,000
Material H...	30,800
Material I..	1,200

(b) Materials were requisitioned from stores as follows:

Job 900, Material G, $16,832; Material H, $13,440.................	$30,272
Job 901, Material G, $21,600; Material H, $18,496.................	40,096
Job 902, Material G, $11,040; Material H, $4,904..................	15,944
For general factory use, Material I.....................................	1,280

(c) Time tickets for the month were chargeable as follows:

Job 900.....................	$15,680	Job 902....................	$13,120
Job 901.....................	13,440	Indirect labor.............	4,000

(d) Factory payroll checks for $47,500 were issued.
(e) Various factory overhead charges of $9,000 were incurred on account.
(f) Selling and administrative expenses of $30,600 were incurred on account.
(g) Payments on account were $120,000.
(h) Depreciation of $8,200 on factory plant and equipment was recorded.
(i) Factory overhead was applied to jobs at 60% of direct labor cost.
(j) Jobs completed during the month were as follows: Job 900 produced 5,120 units of Commodity Q; Job 901 produced 4,000 units of Commodity R.
(k) Total sales on account were $325,000. The goods sold were as follows (use first-in, first-out method): 3,680 units of Commodity Q; 6,000 units of Commodity R; 1,600 units of Commodity S.
(l) Cash of $200,000 was received on accounts receivable.

Instructions:

(1) Open T accounts for the general ledger, the finished goods ledger, the cost ledger, and the materials ledger. Record directly in these accounts the balances as of July 31, identifying them as "Bal." Record the quantities as well as the dollar amounts in the finished goods ledger.
(2) Prepare entries to record the August transactions. After recording each transaction, post to the T accounts, using the identifying letters as dates. When posting to the finished goods ledger, record quantities as well as dollar amounts.
(3) Prepare a trial balance.
(4) Prepare schedules of the account balances in the finished goods ledger, the cost ledger, and the materials ledger.
(5) Prepare an income statement for the two months ended August 31.

Problem 21–5B
Determination of amounts missing from selected accounts in job cost system.

OBJ. 3, 4

Following are selected accounts for Watson Products. For the purposes of this problem, some of the debits and credits have been omitted.

Accounts Receivable

Nov.	1	Balance	142,800	Nov. 30	Collections	310,000
	30	Sales	(A)			

Materials

Nov.	1	Balance	34,500	Nov. 30	Requisitions	(B)
	30	Purchases	50,700			

Work in Process

Nov.	1	Balance	63,000	Nov. 30	Goods finished	(E)
	30	Direct materials	(C)			
	30	Direct labor	67,000			
	30	Factory overhead	(D)			

Finished Goods

Nov.	1	Balance	116,700	Nov. 30	Cost of goods sold	(G)
	30	Goods finished	(F)			

Factory Overhead

Nov.	1	Balance	360	Nov. 30	Applied (40% of	
	1–30	Costs incurred	25,600		direct labor cost)	(H)

Cost of Goods Sold
Nov. 30	(I)

Sales
	Nov. 30
	(J)

Selected balances at November 30:

Accounts receivable...................................	$155,000
Finished goods..	72,000
Work in process.......................................	53,400
Materials	28,500

Materials requisitions for November included $1,200 of materials issued for general factory use. All sales are made on account, terms n/30.

Instructions:

(1) Determine the amounts represented by the letters (A) through (J), presenting your computations.
(2) Determine the amount of factory overhead overapplied or underapplied as of November 30.

MINI-CASE 21

ATKINSON INDUSTRIES

As an assistant cost accountant for Atkinson Industries, you have been assigned to review the activity base for the predetermined factory overhead rate. The president, J. C. Atkinson, has expressed concern that the over- or underapplied overhead has fluctuated excessively over the years.

An analysis of the company's operations and use of the current overhead base (direct materials usage) has narrowed the possible alternative overhead bases to direct labor cost and machine hours. For the past five years, the following data have been gathered:

	1993	1992	1991	1990	1989
Actual overhead ...	$ 672,000	$ 656,000	$ 720,000	$ 588,000	$ 564,000
Applied overhead ...	649,600	678,000	736,800	600,000	524,800
(Over) under-applied overhead.........	$ 22,400	$ (22,000)	$ (16,800)	$ (12,000)	$ 39,200
Direct labor cost	$2,680,000	$2,640,000	$2,900,000	$2,340,000	$2,240,000
Machine hours	530,400	516,000	580,800	477,600	455,200

Instructions:

(1) Calculate a predetermined factory overhead rate for each alternative base, assuming that the rates would have been determined by relating the amount of factory overhead for the past five years to the base.
(2) For each of the past five years, determine the over- or underapplied overhead, based on the two predetermined overhead rates developed in (1).
(3) Which predetermined overhead rate would you recommend? Discuss the basis for your recommendation.

ETHICS
DISCUSSION
CASE

Hillyard Manufacturing Enterprises allows employees to purchase, at cost, manufacturing materials, such as metal and lumber, for personal use. To purchase materials for personal use, an employee must complete a materials requisition form, which must then be approved by the employee's immediate supervisor. Jared Stepp, an assistant cost accountant, charges the employee an amount based upon Hillyard's net purchase cost.

Jared Stepp is in the process of replacing a deck on his home and has requisitioned lumber for personal use, which has been approved in accordance with company policy. In computing the cost of the lumber, Jared reviewed all the purchase invoices for the past year. He then used the lowest price to compute the amount due the company for the lumber.

Discuss whether Jared Stepp behaved in an ethical manner.

ANSWERS TO SELF-EXAMINATION QUESTIONS

1. C Inventory accounts are maintained by manufacturing businesses for (1) goods in the process of manufacture (Work in Process — answer C), (2) goods in the state in which they are to be sold (Finished Goods — answer A), and (3) goods in the state in which they were acquired (Materials — answer B).

2. D The finished goods inventory is composed of three categories of manufacturing costs: direct materials (answer A), direct labor (answer B), and factory overhead (answer C).

3. B Factory overhead includes all manufacturing costs, except direct materials and direct labor. Salaries of plant supervisors (answer B) is an example of a factory overhead item. Wages of factory assembly-line workers (answer A) is a direct labor item, and bearings for electric motors (answer C) are direct materials.

4. A Job order cost systems are best suited to businesses manufacturing for special orders from customers, such as would be the case for a repair shop for antique furniture (answer A). A process cost system is best suited for manufacturers of homogeneous units of product, such as rubber (answer B) and coal (answer C).

5. B If the amount of factory overhead applied during a particular period exceeds the actual overhead costs, the factory overhead account will have a credit balance and is said to be overapplied (answer B) or overabsorbed. If the amount applied is less than the actual costs, the account will have a debit balance and is said to be underapplied (answer A) or underabsorbed (answer C).

CHAPTER TWENTY-TWO
PROCESS COST SYSTEMS

CHAPTER OBJECTIVES

1 Describe and illustrate the flow of costs in a process cost accounting system.

2 Describe and illustrate the accounting for inventories of partially processed materials.

3 Describe and illustrate the preparation and use of a cost of production report.

4 Describe and illustrate the accounting for service department costs.

5 Describe and illustrate the accounting for joint products and by-products.

6 Illustrate the accounting for product costs in a process cost accounting system.

7 Describe and illustrate the use of the average cost method of inventory costing for process cost accounting systems.

In many industries, job orders as described in Chapter 21 are not suitable for scheduling production and accumulating the manufacturing costs. Companies manufacturing cement, flour, or paint, for example, do so on a continuous basis. The principal product is a homogeneous mass rather than a collection of distinct units. No useful purpose would be served by maintaining job orders for particular amounts of a product as the material passes through the several stages of production.

FLOW OF COSTS IN A PROCESS COST SYSTEM

OBJECTIVE 1
Describe and illustrate the flow of costs in a process cost accounting system.

Many of the methods, procedures, and managerial applications presented in the preceding chapter in the discussion of job order cost systems apply equally to process cost systems. For example, perpetual inventory accounts with subsidiary ledgers for materials, work in process, and finished goods are requisites of both systems. In job order cost accounting, however, the costs of direct materials, direct labor, and factory overhead are charged directly to job orders. In process cost accounting, the costs are charged to processing departments, and the cost of a finished unit is determined by dividing the total cost incurred in each process among the number of units produced. Since all goods produced in a department are identical units, it is not necessary to classify production into job orders.

In factories with departmentalized operations, costs are accumulated in factory overhead and work in process accounts maintained for each department. If there is only one processing department in a factory, the cost accounting procedures are simple. The manufacturing cost elements are charged to the single work in process account, and the unit cost of the finished product is determined by dividing the total cost by the number of units produced.

When the manufacturing procedure requires a sequence of different processes, the output of Process 1 becomes the direct materials of Process 2, the output of Process 2 becomes the direct materials of Process 3, and so on until the finished product emerges. The accumulated costs transferred from preceding departments and the costs of direct materials and direct labor incurred in each processing department are debited to the related work in process account. Each work in process account is also debited for the factory overhead applied. The costs incurred are summarized periodically, usually at the end of the month. The costs related to the output of each department during the month are then transferred to the next processing department or to Finished Goods, as the case may be. This flow of costs through a work in process account for McDermott Manufacturing Company is illustrated as follows:

Work in Process — Sanding Department

10,000 units at $9.60			To Polishing Dept., 10,000 units	160,000
from Assembly Dept.		96,000	Cost per unit:	
Direct labor	36,800		$160,000 \div 10,000 = \$16$	
Factory overhead	27,200	64,000		
		160,000		160,000

The three debits in the preceding account are normally grouped into two separate categories: (1) direct materials or partially processed materials received from another department, which in this case is composed of 10,000 units received from the Assembly Department, with a total cost of $96,000, and (2) direct labor and factory overhead applied in the Sanding Department, which in this case totaled $64,000. This second group of costs, as described in Chapter 20, is called the **conversion cost** or **processing cost**.

Again referring to the illustration, all of the 10,000 units were completely processed in the Sanding Department and were passed on to the Polishing Department. The $16 unit cost of the product transferred to the Polishing Department is made up of Assembly Department cost of $9.60 ($96,000 ÷ 10,000 units) and conversion cost of $6.40 ($64,000 ÷ 10,000 units) incurred in the Sanding Department.

A NEW WAY TO BUILD CARS

One of the major industries that uses process cost accounting is the automobile manufacturing industry. Typically, cars are built as they move along an assembly line that provides little flexibility for the installation of the many options common to today's vehicles. Therefore, automakers are turning to modern technology in modifying the traditional assembly line. For example, in two new assembly plants in Kansas City, Kansas, and Doraville, Georgia, General Motors Corporation is using hundreds of motorized, unmanned carriers to move cars through the assembly process. The effect of using these carriers, called automated guided vehicles, in the production of cars is described in the following excerpts from an article in the *New York Times*:

When Henry Ford perfected the assembly line, he was making only one type of car, the Model T, which came in just one color, black. Since then, options have proliferated and today there can be as much as a 30 percent difference in the content of a stripped-down model and one fully loaded.

Because current lines move at a constant speed, regardless of the model mix, plant managers have had to hire enough workers to build the most complex car in the assigned amount of time. This means that some people are idle when base models come down the line. And because stopping the line to fix something would idle thousands, most workers only tag an incorrectly fitting part and hope it will be repaired at the end of the line.

With the carriers, the notion of a "line" begins to fade, although the vehicles generally follow a prescribed path, receiving their instructions from wires buried in the plant floor. If a particular car has a heavy load of options, though, the vehicle may be directed to move out of the main [path] to have those parts installed, while less heavily equipped models continue along the route. G.M. engineers call this "decoupling the line." With this

flexibility, plant managers will be able to balance the work force more closely with the workload....

The carriers also fit into the modular assembly concept that G.M. officals have called one of the keys to cutting manufacturing costs in its Saturn program. Instead of installing thousands of parts, one by one, on a car, a whole module, such as an instrument panel, will be built off the line, tested and only installed if it passes the tests. Since a carrier can be programmed to stop and go as needed, it could roll to the completed instrument panels and then stop to ease the installation....

"We couldn't have done this a few years ago," said David D. Campbell, the director of operations for G.M.'s Chevrolet-Pontiac-Canada group. "We need computers that can keep track of hundreds of carriers and decide on a minute-by-minute basis what station to assign them to, based on variations in the model mix."

Source: John Holusha, "A New Way to Build Cars," *The New York Times,* March 13, 1986.

INVENTORIES OF PARTIALLY PROCESSED MATERIALS

OBJECTIVE 2
Describe and illustrate the accounting for inventories of partially processed materials.

In the preceding illustration, all materials entering a process were completely processed at the end of the accounting period. In such a case, the determination of unit costs is quite simple. The total of the costs transferred from other departments, the direct materials, the direct labor, and the factory overhead charged to a department is divided by the number of units completed and passed on to the next department or to finished goods. Often, however, some partially processed materials remain in various stages of production in a department at the end of a period. In this case, the costs in work in process must be allocated between the units that have been completed and transferred to the next process or to finished goods and those that are only partially completed and remain within the department.

Flow of Materials

To allocate direct materials and transferred costs between the output completed and transferred to the next process and inventory of goods within the department, it is necessary to determine the manner in which materials are placed in production and flow through the production processes. For some products, materials may be added to production in about the same proportion as conversion costs are incurred. In still other situations, materials may enter the process at relatively few points, which may or may not be evenly spaced throughout the process. For most manufacturing processes, however, the materials are on hand when production begins, and they move through the production processes in a first-in, first-out flow; that is, the first units entering the production process are the first to be completed. Therefore, the following discussion and illustrations will assume a normal production process, whereby all materials are placed into the process in a fifo (first-in, first-out) order. The manufacturing costs associated with such a process will also be allocated by the fifo cost method. Later in the chapter, an alternate method—the average cost method—will be discussed.

Equivalent Units of Production

To allocate processing costs between the output completed and transferred to the next process and the inventory of goods within the process, it is necessary to determine the number of *equivalent units* of production during the period. The **equivalent units of production** are the number of units that could have been manufactured from start to finish during the period. To illustrate, assume that there is no inventory of goods in process in a certain processing department at the beginning of the period, that 1,000 units of materials enter the process during the period, and that at the end of the period all of the units are 75% completed. The equivalent production in the processing department for the period would be 750 units (75% of 1,000).

Usually there is an inventory of partially processed units in the department at the beginning of a period. These units are normally completed during the period and transferred to the next department along with units started and completed in the current period. Other units started in the period are only partially processed and thus make up the ending inventory. To illustrate the computation of equivalent units under such circumstances, the following data are assumed for the Polishing Department of McDermott Manufacturing Company:

Inventory within Polishing Department on March 1 ....   600 units, 1/3 completed
Completed in Polishing Department and transferred to
    finished goods during March ....   9,800 units, completed
Inventory within Polishing Department on March 31.........   800 units, 2/5 completed

The equivalent units of production are determined as follows:

Determination of Equivalent Units of Production

To process units in inventory on March 1 (600 units × 2/3)........................   400
To process units started and completed in March (9,800 units − 600 units)...   9,200
To process units in inventory on March 31 (800 units × 2/5)   320
Equivalent units of production in March   9,920

The equivalent units of production necessary to complete the March 1 inventory is determined by multiplying the number of units, 600, by the portion that needed to be completed during March. In this example, since the 600 units were 1/3 complete on March 1, the equivalent portion that was necessary to complete production during March is 2/3. Hence, the equivalent units related to the March 1 inventory is 400 (600 units × 2/3). The units started and completed during March, 9,200, is computed by subtracting the 600 units in the March 1 inventory from the total number of units completed, 9,800. The equivalent units for the March 31 inventory is determined by multiplying the number of units, 800, by the portion that was competed during March, 2/5. The 9,920 total equivalent units of production in March represents the number of units that would have been produced if there had been no inventories within the process either at the beginning or at the end of the period.

Continuing with the illustration, the next step is to allocate the costs incurred in the Polishing Department between the units completed during March and those remaining in process at the end of the month. If all materials were introduced at the beginning of the process, the full materials cost per unit must be assigned to the uncompleted units. The conversion costs would then be allocated to the finished and the uncompleted units on the basis of equivalent units of production, as shown in the following account:

ACCOUNT WORK IN PROCESS — POLISHING DEPARTMENT   ACCOUNT NO.

Date		Item	Debit	Credit	Balance Debit	Balance Credit
Mar.	1	Bal., 600 units, 1/3 completed			10,200	
	31	Sanding Dept., 10,000 units				
		at $16	160,000		170,200	
	31	Direct labor	26,640		196,840	
	31	Factory overhead	18,000		214,840	
	31	Goods finished, 9,800 units		200,600		
	31	Bal., 800 units, 2/5 completed			14,240	

The conversion costs incurred in the Polishing Department during March total $44,640 ($26,640 + $18,000). The equivalent units of production for March, determined above, is 9,920. The conversion cost per equivalent unit is therefore $4.50 ($44,640 ÷ 9,920). Of the $214,840 debited to the Polishing Department, $200,600 was transferred to Finished Goods and $14,240 remained in the account as work in process inventory. The computation of the allocations to the finished goods and to inventory is as follows:

Allocation of Departmental Charges to Finished Goods and Inventory

Goods Finished During March

600 units: Inventory on March 1, 1/3 completed .... $ 10,200
Conversion cost in March:
  600 × 2/3, or 400 units at $4.50 1,800
Total.. $ 12,000
  (Unit cost: $12,000 ÷ 600 = $20)
9,200 units: Materials cost in March, at $16 per unit............. $147,200
Conversion cost in March:
  9,200 at $4.50 per unit............................... 41,400
Total.. 188,600
  (Unit cost: $188,600 ÷ 9,200 = $20.50)
9,800 units: Goods finished during March........................... $200,600

Polishing Department Inventory on March 31

800 units: Materials cost in March, at $16 per unit............. $ 12,800
Conversion cost in March:
  800 × 2/5, or 320 at $4.50......................... 1,440
800 units: Polishing Department inventory on March 31 ..... $ 14,240

COST OF PRODUCTION REPORT

OBJECTIVE 3
Describe and illustrate the preparation and use of a cost of production report.

A report prepared periodically for each processing department summarizes (1) the units for which the department is accountable and the disposition of these units, and (2) the costs charged to the department and the allocation of these costs. This report, termed the **cost of production report**, may be used as the source of the computation of unit production costs and the allocation of the processing costs in the general ledger to the finished and the uncompleted units. More importantly, the report is used to control costs. Each department head is held responsible for the units entering production and the costs incurred in the department. Any differences in unit product costs from one month to another are studied carefully and the causes of significant differences are determined.

The cost of production report based on the data presented in the preceding section for the Polishing Department of McDermott Manufacturing Company is shown below:

Cost of Production Report

McDermott Manufacturing Company
Cost of Production Report — Polishing Department
For the Month Ended March 31, 19--

Quantities:		
Charged to production:		
In process, March 1..		600
Received from Sanding Department		10,000
Total units to be accounted for...........................		10,600
Units accounted for:		
Transferred to finished goods		9,800
In process, March 31		800
Total units accounted for		10,600
Costs:		
Charged to production:		
In process, March 1...		$ 10,200
March costs:		
Direct materials from Sanding Department		
($16 per unit)		160,000
Conversion costs:		
Direct labor..	$ 26,640	
Factory overhead.......................................	18,000	
Total conversion costs ($4.50 per unit)...........		44,640
Total costs to be accounted for...........................		$214,840
Costs allocated as follows:		
Transferred to finished goods:		
600 units at $20...	$ 12,000	
9,200 units at $20.50	188,600	
Total cost of finished goods.............................		$200,600
In process, March 31:		
Direct materials (800 units at $16)....................	$ 12,800	
Conversion costs (800 units × 2/5 × $4.50)......	1,440	
Total cost of inventory in process, March 31.......		14,240
Total costs accounted for..................................		$214,840
Computations:		
Equivalent units of production:		
To process units in inventory on March 1:		
600 units × 2/3..		400
To process units started and completed in March:		
9,800 units − 600 units.................................		9,200
To process units in inventory on March 31:		
800 units × 2/5..		320
Equivalent units of production.......................		9,920
Unit conversion cost:		
$44,640 ÷ 9,920...		$ 4.50

SERVICE DEPARTMENTS AND PROCESS COSTS

OBJECTIVE 4
Describe and
illustrate the
accounting for
service department
costs.

In a factory with several processes, there may be one or more **service departments** that do not process the materials directly. Examples of service departments are the factory office, the power plant, and the maintenance and repair shop. These departments perform services for the benefit of other production departments. The costs that they incur, therefore, are part of the total manufacturing costs and must be charged to the processing departments.

The services performed by a service department give rise to internal transactions with the processing departments benefited. These internal transactions are recorded periodically in order to charge the factory overhead accounts of the processing departments with their share of the costs incurred by the service departments. The period usually chosen is a month, although a different period of time may be used. To illustrate, assume that the Power Department of McDermott Manufacturing Company produced 600 000 kilowatt-hours (kwh) during the month at a total cost of $30,000, or 5¢ per kilowatt-hour ($30,000 ÷ 600 000). The factory overhead accounts for the departments that used the power are accordingly charged for power at the 5¢ rate. Assuming that during the month the Assembly Department used 100 000 kwh, the Sanding Department used 300 000 kwh, and the Polishing Department used 200 000 kwh, the accounts affected by the interdepartmental transfer of cost would appear as follows:

*Service Department
Costs Charged to
Processing
Departments*

Power Department

Fuel	12,000	To Factory Overhead —	
Wages	8,500	Assembly Dept.	5,000
Depreciation	3,000	To Factory Overhead —	
Maintenance	2,500	Sanding Dept.	15,000
Insurance	2,000	To Factory Overhead —	
Taxes	1,500	Polishing Dept.	10,000
Miscellaneous	500		
	30,000		30,000

Factory Overhead — Assembly Dept.

Power	5,000

Factory Overhead — Sanding Dept.

Power	15,000

Factory Overhead — Polishing Dept.

Power	10,000

Some service departments render services to other service departments. For example, the power department may supply electric current to light the factory office and to operate data processing equipment. At the same time, the factory office provides general supervision for the power department, maintains its payroll records, buys its fuel, and so on. In such cases, the costs of the department rendering the greatest service to other service departments may be distributed first, despite the fact that it receives benefits from other service departments.

JOINT PRODUCTS AND BY-PRODUCTS

OBJECTIVE 5
Describe and illustrate the accounting for joint products and by-products.

In some manufacturing processes, more than one product is produced. In processing cattle, for example, the meat packer produces dressed beef, hides, and other products. In processing logs, the lumber mill produces several grades of lumber in addition to scraps and sawdust. When the output of a manufacturing process consists of two or more different products, the products may be joint products, or one or more of the products may be a by-product.

When two or more goods of significant value are produced from a single principal direct material, the products are termed **joint products**. Similarly, the costs incurred in the manufacture of joint products are called **joint costs**. Common examples of joint products are gasoline, naphtha, kerosene, paraffin, benzine, and other related goods, all of which come from the processing of crude oil.

If one of the products resulting from a process has little value in relation to the main product or joint products, it is known as a **by-product**. The emergence of a by-product is only incidental to the manufacture of the main product or joint products. By-products may be leftover materials, such as sawdust and scraps of wood in a lumber mill, or they may be separated from the material at the beginning of production, as in the case of cottonseed from raw cotton.

Accounting for Joint Products

In management decisions concerning the production and sale of joint products, only the relationship of the total revenue to be derived from the entire group to their total production cost is relevant. Nothing is to be gained from an allocation of joint costs to each product because one product cannot be produced without the others. A decision to produce a single joint product is in effect a decision to produce all of the joint products.

Since joint products come from the processing of a common parent material, the assignment of cost to each separate product cannot be based on actual expenditures. It is impossible to determine the amount of cost incurred in the manufacture of each separate product. However, for purposes of inventory valuation, it is necessary to allocate joint costs among the joint products.

One method of allocation commonly used is the **market (sales) value method.** Its main feature is the assignment of costs to the different products according to their relative sales values. To illustrate, assume that 10,000 units of Product X and 50,000 units of Product Y were produced at a total cost of $63,000. The sales values of the two products and the allocation of the joint costs are as follows:

Allocation of Joint Costs

Joint Costs	Joint Product	Units Produced	Sales Value per Unit	Total Sales Value
$63,000	{ X	10,000	$3.00	$30,000
	{ Y	50,000	1.20	60,000
Total sales value...				$90,000

Allocation of joint costs:

X: $\dfrac{\$30,000}{\$90,000} \times \$63,000$ $21,000

Y: $\dfrac{\$60,000}{\$90,000} \times \$63,000$ 42,000

Unit cost:
X: $21,000 ÷ 10,000 units $2.10
Y: $42,000 ÷ 50,000 units 84

Accounting for By-Products

The amount of manufacturing cost usually assigned to a by-product is the sales value of the by-product reduced by any additional costs necessary to complete and sell it. The amount of cost thus determined is removed from the proper work in process account and transferred to a finished goods inventory account. To illustrate, assume that for a certain period the costs accumulated in Department 4 total $24,400, and during the same period of time, 1,000 units of by-product B emerge from the processing in Department 4. If the estimated value of the by-product is $200, after estimated completion and selling costs have been deducted, Finished Goods—Product B would be debited for $200 and Work in Process—Department 4 would be credited for the same amount, as illustrated in the following accounts:

Work in Process—Department 4		Finished Goods—Product B	
24,400	200	200	

ILLUSTRATION OF PROCESS COST ACCOUNTING

To illustrate further the basic procedures of the process costing system, assume that Dunbar Company manufactures Product A. The manufacturing activity begins in Department 1, where all materials enter production. The materials remain in Department 1 for a relatively short time, and there is usually no inventory of work in process in that department at the end of the accounting period. From Department 1, the materials are transferred to Department 2. In Department 2, there are usually inventories at the end of the accounting period. Separate factory overhead accounts are maintained for Departments 1 and 2. Factory overhead is applied at 80% and 50% of direct labor cost for Departments 1 and 2 respectively. There are two service departments, Maintenance and Power. All inventories are costed by the first-in, first-out method.

The trial balance of the general ledger on January 1, the first day of the fiscal year, is as follows:

Dunbar Company
Trial Balance
January 1, 19--

Cash..	39,400	
Accounts Receivable..	45,000	
Finished Goods — Product A (1,000 units at $36.50)	36,500	
Work in Process — Department 2		
(800 units, 1/2 completed)	24,600	
Materials	32,000	
Prepaid Expenses...	6,150	
Plant Assets..	510,000	
Accumulated Depreciation — Plant Assets....................		295,000
Accounts Payable..		51,180
Wages Payable..		3,400
Common Stock..		250,000
Retained Earnings..		94,070
	693,650	693,650

To reduce the illustrative entries to a manageable number and to avoid repetition, the transactions and the adjustments for January are stated as summaries. In practice, the transactions would be recorded from day to day in various journals. The descriptions of the transactions, followed in each case by the entry, are as follows:

(a) Materials purchased and prepaid expenses incurred	Materials	80,500	
	Prepaid Expenses.....................................	3,300	
	Accounts Payable...............................		83,800
(b) Materials requisitioned for use	Maintenance Department	1,200	
	Power Department	6,000	
	Factory Overhead — Department 1...............	3,720	
	Factory Overhead — Department 2...............	2,700	
	Work in Process — Department 1	58,500	
	Materials		72,120
(c) Factory labor used	Maintenance Department	3,600	
	Power Department	4,500	
	Factory Overhead — Department 1...............	2,850	
	Factory Overhead — Department 2...............	2,100	
	Work in Process — Department 1	24,900	
	Work in Process — Department 2	37,800	
	Wages Payable....................................		75,750
(d) Other costs incurred	Maintenance Department	600	
	Power Department	900	
	Factory Overhead — Department 1...............	1,800	
	Factory Overhead — Department 2...............	1,200	
	Selling Expenses	15,000	
	Administrative Expenses	13,500	
	Accounts Payable...............................		33,000

(e) Expiration of prepaid expenses	Maintenance Department	300	
	Power Department	750	
	Factory Overhead — Department 1...........................	1,350	
	Factory Overhead — Department 2...........................	1,050	
	Selling Expenses	900	
	Administrative Expenses	600	
	Prepaid Expenses...		4,950

(f) Depreciation	Maintenance Department	300	
	Power Department	1,050	
	Factory Overhead — Department 1...........................	1,800	
	Factory Overhead — Department 2...........................	2,700	
	Selling Expenses	600	
	Administrative Expenses	300	
	Accumulated Depreciation — Plant Assets..............		6,750

(g) Distribution of Maintenance Department costs	Power Department	300	
	Factory Overhead — Department 1...........................	2,700	
	Factory Overhead — Department 2...........................	3,000	
	Maintenance Department		6,000

The portion of services rendered was 5%, 45%, and 50% for the Power Department, Department 1, and Department 2, respectively.

(h) Distribution of Power Department costs	Factory Overhead — Department 1...........................	5,400	
	Factory Overhead — Department 2...........................	8,100	
	Power Department		13,500

Power was provided at 5¢ per kwh for 108 000 and 162 000 kwh for Departments 1 and 2, respectively.

(i) Application of factory overhead costs to work in process	Work in Process — Department 1	19,920	
	Work in Process — Department 2	18,900	
	Factory Overhead — Department 1........................		19,920
	Factory Overhead — Department 2........................		18,900

The predetermined rates were 80% and 50% of direct labor cost for Departments 1 and 2 respectively. See transaction (c) for the monthly direct labor costs.

(j) Transfer of production costs from Department 1 to Department 2	Work in Process — Department 2.............................	103,320	
	Work in Process — Department 1		103,320

4,100 units were fully processed, and there is no work in process in Department 1 at the beginning or at the end of the month.

Total costs charged to Department 1:

Direct materials	$ 58,500
Direct labor	24,900
Factory overhead	19,920
Total costs	$103,320

Unit cost of product transferred to Department 2:

$103,320 ÷ 4,100	$ 25.20

(k) Transfer of production costs from Department 2 to Finished Goods

Finished Goods — Product A	153,840	
Work in Process — Department 2		153,840

4,000 units were completed, and the remaining 900 units were 2/3 completed at the end of the month.

Equivalent units of production:

To process units in inventory on January 1:	
800 × 1/2	400
To process units started and completed in January:	
4,000 − 800	3,200
To process units in inventory on January 31:	
900 × 2/3	600
Equivalent units of production in January	4,200

Conversion costs:

Direct labor [transaction (c)]	$ 37,800
Factory overhead [transaction (i)]	18,900
Total conversion costs	$ 56,700

Unit conversion cost:

$56,700 ÷ 4,200	$ 13.50

Allocation of costs of Department 2:

Units started in December, completed in January:		
Inventory on January 1, 800 units 1/2 completed	$24,600	
Conversion costs in January, 400 at $13.50	5,400	
Total ($30,000 ÷ 800 = $37.50 unit cost)		$ 30,000
Units started and completed in January:		
From Department 1, 3,200 units at $25.20	$80,640	
Conversion costs, 3,200 at $13.50	43,200	
Total ($123,840 ÷ 3,200 = $38.70 unit cost)		123,840
Total transferred to Product A		$153,840
Units started in January, 2/3 completed:		
From Department 1, 900 units at $25.20	$22,680	
Conversion costs, 600 at $13.50	8,100	
Total work in process — Department 2		30,780
Total costs charged to Department 2		$184,620

| *(l) Cost of goods sold* | Cost of Goods Sold... | 143,900 | |
| | Finished Goods — Product A................................ | | 143,900 |

	Product A, 3,800 units:		
	1,000 units at $36.50..		$ 36,500
	800 units at $37.50..		30,000
	2,000 units at $38.70..		77,400
	Total cost of goods sold		$143,900

| *(m) Sales* | Accounts Receivable... | 210,500 | |
| | Sales .... | | 210,500 |

| *(n) Cash received* | Cash... | 200,000 | |
| | Accounts Receivable.. | | 200,000 |

(o) Cash disbursed	Accounts Payable...	120,000	
	Wages Payable...	72,500	
	Cash...		192,500

A chart of the flow of costs from the service and processing department accounts into the finished goods account and then to the cost of goods sold account is as follows. Entries in the accounts are identified by letters to aid the comparison with the summary journal entries.

Flow of Costs Through Process Cost Accounts

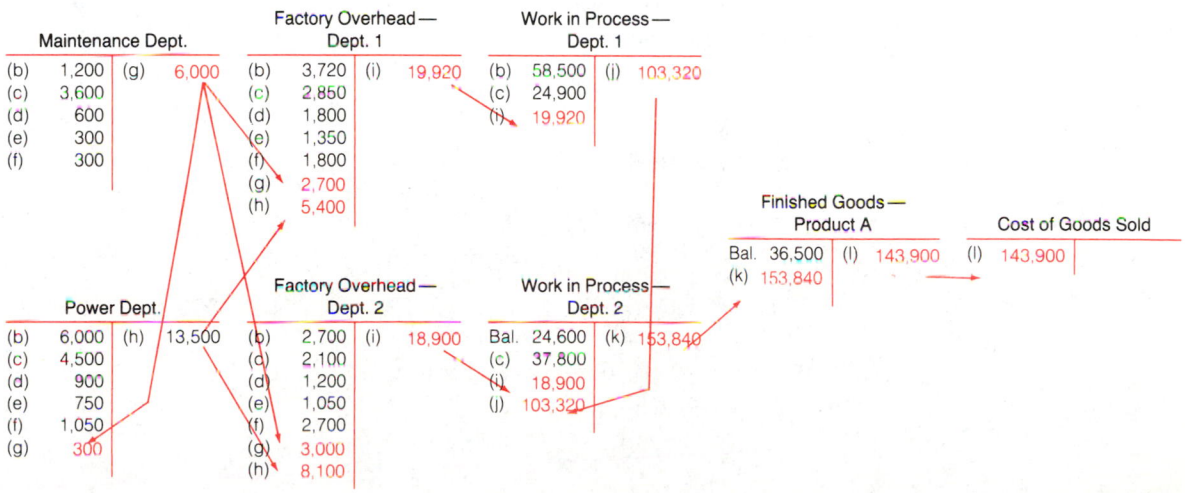

Cost of Production Reports

The cost of production reports for Departments 1 and 2 are as follows:

Dunbar Company
Cost of Production Report — Department 1
For the Month Ended January 31, 19--

Quantities:	
Units charged to production and to be accounted for	4,100
Units accounted for and transferred to Department 2	4,100
Costs:	
Costs charged to production in January:	
Direct materials...	$ 58,500
Direct labor	24,900
Factory overhead	19,920
Total costs to be accounted for..	$103,320
Total costs accounted for and transferred to Department 2	
(4,100 units × $25.20)...	$103,320

Dunbar Company
Cost of Production Report — Department 2
For the Month Ended January 31, 19--

Quantities:		
Charged to production:		
In process, January 1		800
Received from Department 1...............................		4,100
Total units to be accounted for		4,900
Units accounted for:		
Transferred to finished goods.............................		4,000
To process, January 31.......................................		900
Total units accounted for		4,900
Costs:		
Charged to production:		
In process, January 1		$ 24,600
January costs:		
Direct materials from Department 1		
($25.20 per unit)		103,320
Conversion costs:		
Direct labor	$ 37,800	
Factory overhead.......................................	18,900	
Total conversion costs ($13.50 per unit)		56,700
Total costs to be accounted for...........................		$184,620

Costs allocated as follows:
Transferred to finished goods:

800 units at $37.50...	$ 30,000	
3,200 units at $38.70....................................	123,840	
Total cost of finished goods............................		$153,840

In process, January 31:

Direct materials (900 units at $25.20)...............	$ 22,680	
Conversion costs (900 units × 2/3 × $13.50)....	8,100	
Total cost of inventory in process, January 31		30,780
Total costs accounted for.................................		$184,620

Computations:
Equivalent units of production:

To process units in inventory on January 1:	
800 units × 1/2...	400
To process units started and completed in January:	
4,000 units − 800 units..................................	3,200
To process units in inventory on January 31:	
900 units × 2/3..	600
Equivalent units of production...........................	4,200

Unit conversion cost:	
$56,700 ÷ 4,200...	$ 13.50

Financial Statements

The financial statements for process cost systems are similar to those for job order cost systems. To illustrate, the trial balance and the condensed financial statements for Dunbar Company are presented as follows. Note that the net underapplied factory overhead of $1,650 ($1,950 − $300) on January 31 is reported on the balance sheet as a deferred item.

Dunbar Company
Trial Balance
January 31, 19--

Cash..	46,900	
Accounts Receivable...	55,500	
Finished Goods — Product A (1,200 units at $38.70)	46,440	
Work in Process — Department 2		
(900 units, 2/3 completed)	30,780	
Materials	40,380	
Prepaid Expenses..	4,500	
Plant Assets...	510,000	
Accumulated Depreciation — Plant Assets.....................		301,750
Accounts Payable..		47,980
Wages Payable..		6,650
Common Stock..		250,000
Retained Earnings..		94,070
Sales		210,500
Cost of Goods Sold..	143,900	
Factory Overhead — Department 1.............................		300
Factory Overhead — Department 2.............................	1,950	
Selling Expenses	16,500	
Administrative Expenses	14,400	
	911,250	911,250

Dunbar Company
Income Statement
For Month Ended January 31, 19--

Sales		$210,500
Cost of goods sold		143,900
Gross profit		$ 66,600
Operating expenses:		
Selling expenses	$16,500	
Administrative expenses	14,400	
Total operating expenses		30,900
Income from operations		$ 35,700

Dunbar Company
Retained Earnings Statement
For Month Ended January 31, 19--

Retained earnings, January 1, 19--	$ 94,070
Income for the month	35,700
Retained earnings, January 31, 19--	$129,770

Dunbar Company
Balance Sheet
January 31, 19--

Assets

Current assets:			
Cash		$ 46,900	
Accounts receivable		55,500	
Inventories:			
Finished goods	$46,440		
Work in process	30,780		
Materials	40,380	117,600	
Prepaid expenses		4,500	
Total current assets			$224,500
Plant assets		$510,000	
Less accumulated depreciation		301,750	208,250
Deferred debits:			
Factory overhead underapplied			1,650
Total assets			$434,400

Liabilities

Current liabilities:		
Accounts payable	$ 47,980	
Wages payable	6,650	
Total liabilities		$ 54,630

Stockholders' Equity

Common stock	$250,000	
Retained earnings	129,770	
Total stockholders' equity		379,770
Total liabilities and stockholders' equity		$434,400

INVENTORY COSTING METHODS

OBJECTIVE 7
Describe and
illustrate the use of
the average cost
method of inventory
costing for process
cost accounting
systems.

In the preceding discussion and illustrations, the **first-in, first-out (fifo) cost method** was used to determine unit product costs. Another method, known as the average cost method, is sometimes used in practice. Under the **average cost method,** all costs incurred in manufacturing the goods completed during a period are averaged, and this average is used in determining the unit product cost of the goods completed during the period and the work in process at the end of the period. Although the average cost method is not as accurate and not as useful to management in controlling costs as the fifo method, it is simpler to use and is therefore encountered in practice.

First-In, First-Out (Fifo) Cost Method

In most manufacturing processes, the products flow through the processes in a first-in, first-out manner; that is, the first units entering the process are the first completed. In such processes, the work in process at the beginning of the period is completed before work is completed on additional materials entered into the process. The fifo cost method is consistent with the flow of products in such manufacturing processes and is widely used.

When the fifo cost method is used, the beginning work in process inventory costs are kept separate from the costs incurred during the current period. As a result, the fifo cost method generally provides two unit cost figures for products completed during a period: (1) units completed from the beginning work in process and (2) units started and completed during the current period. These two unit cost figures are useful to management in controlling manufacturing costs because current costs are used to determine the cost of products started and completed during the current period. Management can therefore focus on these current costs in evaluating and controlling current operations.

Using two separate costs adds some complexity to the calculation of unit costs. It also complicates the determination of product costs when the products completed by one process are used in subsequent processes. Primarily for these reasons, some enterprises prefer to use the average cost method.

Average Cost Method

The average cost method is *based on the assumption that the work in process at the beginning of the current period was started and completed during the current period.* Using this method, one unit cost figure for all products completed during the current period is determined. Although not as accurate as the fifo cost method, the average cost method avoids the problem of having two unit cost figures for products completed during a period. When the average cost method is used, it is more difficult for management to evaluate and control current operations, since past costs and current costs are averaged.

To illustrate the use of the average cost method, assume the following data for the Cutting Department of Perrin Company for July of the current year. In addition, assume that all materials used in the Cutting Department are added at the beginning of the process.

Inventory in process, July 1, 500 units:
    Materials cost, 500 units.. $24,550
    Conversion costs, 500 units, 70% completed............................ 3,600
Materials cost for July, 1,000 units.. 50,000
Conversion costs for July, 1,000 units... 9,660
Goods finished in July (includes units in process on July 1),
    1,100 units.. —
Inventory in process, July 31, 400 units, 50% completed................. —

To apply the average cost method in the determination of the unit cost for the 1,100 units finished in July and the 400 units that are 50% completed on July 31, the average materials cost and the average conversion cost are determined as follows:

Materials cost for 500 units in process at July 1............................. $24,550
Materials cost for 1,000 units for July... 50,000
    Total materials cost (1,500 units)... $74,550

    Average materials cost per unit ($74,550 ÷ 1,500)....................... $ 49.70

Conversion costs for units in process at July 1............................. $ 3,600
Conversion costs for July... 9,660
    Total conversion costs.. $13,260

Equivalent units of production:
    To process units in inventory on July 1 500
    To process units started and completed in July
        (1,100 units − 500 units)... 600
    To process units in inventory on July 31 (400 units × 50%).......... 200
        Equivalent units of production in July 1,300

    Average conversion cost per unit ($13,260 ÷ 1,300) .... $ 10.20

It should be noted that in determining the average unit materials cost, the cost of materials in work in process on July 1 (the beginning inventory) is added to the materials cost for July before dividing by the total units of materials in the cutting process during July. A similar procedure is followed for computing the average unit conversion cost. The conversion costs in work in process on July 1 (the beginning inventory) are added to the conversion costs for July before dividing by the equivalent units of production for July. As mentioned earlier, in computing these equivalent units, the units in the beginning inventory are treated as if they were all started and completed during the current period. In other words, the beginning inventory of 500 units is treated as 500 units fully completed during the current period, not 500 units 30% completed (150 units) during the current period. Alternatively, the total equivalent units, 1,300, is the total of the units completed, 1,100, and the equivalent units in the ending inventory, 200.

The average unit costs for Perrin Company are used to determine the cost of goods finished during July and the cost of the work in process on July 31 (the ending inventory) as follows:

Goods finished during July:
    1,100 units: 1,100 units at $49.70 for materials costs $54,670
               1,100 units at $10.20 for conversion costs................ 11,220
        Total (1,100 units at $59.90) $65,890

Work in process, July 31:
400 units: 400 units at $49.70 for materials costs $19,880
400 units × 50% × $10.20 for conversion costs .... <u>2,040</u>
Total .... <u>$21,920</u>

In many manufacturing processes, there is no significant difference between the unit cost figures determined under the average cost and the fifo cost methods. This similarity in unit costs is especially true where the beginning and ending work in process inventories are uniform and materials costs do not fluctuate widely from period to period. Therefore, the simplification of the calculations by using the average cost method and the lack of significant variation in unit costs under the two methods have been the principal reasons for the use of the average cost method. Computers, however, have removed much of the complexity from the calculations of unit product costs.

CHAPTER REVIEW

KEY POINTS

OBJECTIVE 1

Flow of Costs in a Process Cost System

No useful purpose would be served for companies manufacturing a homogeneous product, such as cement, flour, or paint, to maintain job orders for each particular amount of product. In these cases, a process cost system is normally utilized. In process cost accounting, costs are charged to processing departments, and the cost of the finished unit is determined by dividing the total cost incurred in each process among the number of units produced.

The accumulated costs transferred from preceding departments and the costs of direct materials and direct labor incurred in each processing department are debited to the related work in process account. Each work in process account is also debited for the factory overhead applied. The direct labor and the factory overhead applied are referred to as the conversion costs.

OBJECTIVE 2

Inventories of Partially Processed Materials

Frequently, partially processed materials remain in various stages of production in a department at the end of a period. In this case, the manufacturing costs must be allocated between the units that have been completed and those that are only partially completed and remain within the department. In allocating costs between completed products and work remaining in process, either the first-in, first-out method or the average cost method may be used. To allocate processing costs between the output completed and the inventory of goods within the department, it is necessary to determine the number of equivalent units of production during the period. The equivalent units of production are the number of units that could have been manufactured from start to finish during the period.

OBJECTIVE 3

Cost of Production Report

A report prepared periodically for each processing department summarizes (1) the units for which the department is accountable and the disposition of these units and (2) the costs charged to the department and the allocation of these costs. This report, termed the cost of production report, may be used as the source of the computation of unit production costs and the allocation of the processing costs to the finished and the uncompleted units. More importantly, the report is used to control costs.

OBJECTIVE 4

Service Departments and Process Costs

In a factory with several processes, there may be one or more service departments that do not process the materials directly. Examples include the factory office, the power plant, and the maintenance and repair shop. Periodically, the costs incurred by service departments are allocated to the factory overhead accounts of the processing departments.

OBJECTIVE 5

Joint Products and By-Products

In some manufacturing processes, more than one product is produced. When the output of a manufacturing process consists of two or more different products, the products are either joint products or by-products. When two or more goods of significant value are produced from a single principal direct material, the products are termed joint products. Similarly, the costs incurred in the manufacture of joint products are called joint costs. If one of the products resulting from a process has little value in relation to the main product or joint products, it is known as a by-product.

Since joint products come from the processing of a common parent material, the assignment of cost to each separate product cannot be based on actual expenditures. The allocation of joint costs among the joint products is usually performed using the market (sales) value method. The amount of manufacturing cost usually assigned to a by-product is the sales value of the by-product reduced by any additional costs necessary to complete and sell it.

OBJECTIVE 6

Illustration of Process Cost Accounting

In a process cost accounting system, transactions are recorded throughout the period, using perpetual inventory procedures. A cost of production report is prepared at the end of the period as support for the allocation of processing costs to work in process and finished goods.

OBJECTIVE 7

Inventory Costing Methods

The first-in, first-out (fifo) cost method of accounting for manufacturing costs is consistent with the flow of product costs through most manufacturing processes. The average cost method, although not as useful for cost control as the fifo method, is also used in practice. The simplification of the computations of unit product costs under the average cost method is the major reason for use of the method. Under the average cost method, one unit cost figure (rather than two, as under the fifo method) is computed for all products completed during a period.

KEY TERMS

conversion cost 870
equivalent units of production 872
cost of production report 873
service departments 875
joint products 876
joint costs 876

by-product 876
market (sales) value method 876
first-in, first-out (fifo) cost
    method 885
average cost method 885

SELF-EXAMINATION QUESTIONS
Answers at end of chapter.

1. For which of the following businesses would the process cost system be most appropriate?
   A. Custom furniture manufacturer
   B. Commercial building contractor
   C. Crude oil refinery
   D. None of the above

2.   The group of manufacturing costs referred to as *conversion costs* includes:
     A.   direct materials and direct labor
     B.   direct materials and factory overhead
     C.   direct labor and factory overhead
     D.   none of the above

3.   Information relating to production in Department A for May is as follows:

     May   1 Balance, 1,000 units, 3/4 completed $22,150
          31 Direct materials, 5,000 units..................................... 75,000
          31 Direct labor.. 32,500
          31 Factory overhead 16,250

     If 500 units were 1/4 completed at May 31, 5,500 units were completed during
     May, and inventories are costed by the first-in, first-out method, what was the
     number of equivalent units of production for May?
     A.   4,500   C.   5,500
     B.   4,875   D.   None of the above

4.   Based on the data presented in Question 3, what is the unit conversion cost?
     A. $10   C. $25
     B. $15   D.   None of the above

5.   If one of the products resulting from a process has little value in relation to the
     principal products, it is known as a:
     A.   joint product   C.   direct material
     B.   by-product   D.   none of the above

─────────────── ILLUSTRATIVE PROBLEM ───────────────

Tate Company manufactures Product A by a series of four processes, all materials being introduced in Department 1. From Department 1 the materials pass
through Departments 2, 3, and 4, emerging as finished Product A. All inventories
are costed by the first-in, first-out method.

The balances in the accounts Work in Process—Department 4 and Finished
Goods were as follows on May 1:

Work in Process—Department 4 (1,000 units, 1/4 completed)......... $17,800
Finished Goods (1,800 units at $23.50 a unit) 42,300

The following costs were charged to Work in Process—Department 4 during May:

Direct materials transferred from Department 3: 4,700 units at
     $16 a unit.. $75,200
Direct labor.. 25,500
Factory overhead.. 15,300

During May, 5,000 units of A were completed and 4,800 units were sold. Inventories on May 31 were as follows:

Work in Process—Department 4: 700 units, 1/2 completed
Finished Goods: 2,000 units

Instructions:

Determine the following, presenting the computations in good order:
     (a) Equivalent units of production for Department 4 during May.
     (b) Unit conversion cost for Department 4 for May.
     (c) Total and unit cost of Product A started in a prior period and finished in
         May.

                                                                    (Continued)

(d) Total and unit cost of Product A started and finished in May.
(e) Total cost of goods transferred to finished goods.
(f) Work in process inventory for Department 4, May 31.
(g) Cost of goods sold (indicate number of units and unit costs).
(h) Finished goods inventory, May 31.

SOLUTION

(a) Equivalent units of production:

To process units in inventory on May 1:	
1,000 units × 3/4	750
To process units started and completed	
in May: 5,000 units − 1,000 units	4,000
To process units in inventory on May 31:	
700 units × 1/2...	350
Equivalent units of production in May	5,100

(b) Unit conversion cost: $\dfrac{\$25,500 + \$15,300}{5,100} = \$8$

(c) Cost of Product A started in a prior period and finished in May:

1,000 units: Inventory on May 1, 1/4 completed	$ 17,800
Conversion cost in May, 750 × $8..........	6,000
Total...	$ 23,800

Unit cost: $23,800 ÷ 1,000 = $23.80

(d) Cost of Product A started and finished in May:

4,000 units: Materials from Department 3,	
4,000 × $16	$ 64,000
Conversion cost in May, 4,000 × $8	32,000
Total...	$ 96,000

Unit cost: $96,000 ÷ 4,000 = $24

(e) Total cost of goods transferred to finished goods:

Cost of Product A started in a prior period	
and finished in May (1,000 units at $23.80)	$ 23,800
Cost of Product A started and finished in May	
(4,000 units at $24)	96,000
Total	$119,800

(f) Work in process inventory, May 31:

700 units: Materials cost, 700 × $16	$ 11,200
Conversion costs in May, 350 × $8.........	2,800
Work in process inventory, May 31	$ 14,000

(g) Cost of goods sold:

1,800 units at $23.50	....	$ 42,300
1,000 units at $23.80	....	23,800
2,000 units at $24.00	....	48,000
4,800 units	....	$114,100

(h) Finished goods inventory, May 31:

2,000 units at $24	....	$ 48,000

DISCUSSION QUESTIONS

1. Which type of cost system, process or job order, would be best suited for each of the following: (a) paper manufacturer, (b) oil refinery, (c) automobile repair shop, (d) building contractor, (e) lumber mill? Give reasons for your answers.

2. Are perpetual inventory accounts for materials, work in process, and finished goods generally used for (a) job order cost systems and (b) process cost systems?

3. In job order cost accounting, the three elements of manufacturing cost are charged directly to job orders. Why is it not necessary to charge manufacturing costs in process cost accounting to job orders?

4. What two groups of manufacturing costs are referred to as conversion costs?

5. In the manufacture of 5,000 units of a product, direct materials cost incurred was $56,000, direct labor incurred was $32,000, and factory overhead applied was $11,500. (a) What is the total conversion cost? (b) What is the conversion cost per unit? (c) What is the total manufacturing cost? (d) What is the manufacturing cost per unit?

6. What is meant by the term "equivalent units"?

7. If Department F had no work in process at the beginning of the period, 16,000 units were completed during the period, and 3,000 units were 20% completed at the end of the period, what was the number of equivalent units of production for the period?

8. The following information concerns production in the Painting Department for March. All direct materials are placed in process at the beginning of production. Determine the number of units in work in process inventory at the end of the month.

WORK IN PROCESS — PAINTING DEPARTMENT

Date		Item	Debit	Credit	Balance Debit	Balance Credit
Mar.	1	Bal., 10,500 units ⅓ completed			17,500	
	31	Direct materials, 20,500 units	28,700			
	31	Direct labor	36,100			
	31	Factory overhead	9,300			
	31	Goods finished, 21,600 units		81,000		
	31	Bal., _____ units, ¼ completed			10,600	

9. For Question No. 8, determine the equivalent units of production for March, assuming that the first-in, first-out method is used to cost inventories.

10. What data are summarized in the two principal sections of the cost of production report?

11. What is the most important purpose of the cost of production report?

12. (a) How does a service department differ from a processing department? (b) Give two examples of a service department.

13. Jones Company maintains a cafeteria for its employees at a cost of $3,750 per month. On what basis would the company most likely allocate the cost of the cafeteria among the production departments?

14. Distinquish between a joint product and a by-product.

15. The Cutting Department produces two products. How should the cost be allocated (a) if the products are joint products and (b) if one of the products is a by-product?

16. In a factory with several processing departments, a separate factory overhead rate may be determined for each department. Why is a single factory overhead rate often inadequate in such circumstances?

17. What are the two common inventory costing methods used in process cost accounting?

18. What are the principal advantages of the use of the first-in, first-out method for costing inventories for process cost systems?

19. What is the principal advantage of the use of the average method for costing inventories for process cost systems?

Real World Focus

20. As production processes become more and more automated in what many see as the "age of robotics," materials may enter into and leave a production process without human intervention. For example, in the manufacture of automobiles, General Motors uses state-of-the-art paint systems, which are operated from an automated video control room. The control room supervisor monitors the preparation of the bare metal body of the automobile as it is submerged in a primer. Next, the body passes through nine pairs of robot painters teamed with other robot devices that open and close doors and paint inside surfaces. (a) In this type of production environment, would direct labor hours be an appropriate base for allocation of predetermined factory overhead? (b) Can you suggest other possible factory overhead bases?

EXERCISES

Exercise 22–1

Flowchart of accounts related to service and processing departments.

OBJ. 1

Grey Co. manufactures two products. The entire output of Department A is transferred to Department B. Part of the fully processed goods from Department B are sold as Product X and the remainder of the goods are transferred to Department C for further processing into Product Y. The service department, Factory Office, provides services for each of the processing departments.

Prepare a chart of the flow of costs from the service and processing department accounts into the finished goods accounts and then into the cost of goods sold account. The relevant accounts are as follows:

Cost of Goods Sold	Finished Goods — Product X
Factory Office	Finished Goods — Product Y
Factory Overhead — Department A	Work in Process — Department A
Factory Overhead — Department B	Work in Process — Department B
Factory Overhead — Department C	Work in Process — Department C

Exercise 22–2

Entries for flow of factory costs for process cost system.

OBJ. 1

Raser Company manufactures a single product by a continuous process, involving three production departments. The records indicate that $78,000 of direct materials were issued to and $108,000 of direct labor was incurred by Department 1 in the manufacture of the product; the factory overhead rate is 30% of direct labor cost; work in process in the department at the beginning of the period totaled $45,000; and work in process at the end of the period totaled $42,000.

Prepare entries to record (a) the flow of costs into Department 1 during the period for (1) direct materials, (2) direct labor, and (3) factory overhead; (b) the transfer of production costs to Department 2.

Exercise 22–3

Factory overhead rate, entry for application of factory overhead, and factory overhead account balance.

OBJ. 1

The chief cost accountant for G. C. Love Co. estimates total factory overhead cost for the Blending Department for the year at $18,000 and total direct labor costs at $48,000. During November, the actual direct labor cost totaled $4,000, and factory overhead cost incurred totaled $1,125. (a) What is the predetermined factory overhead rate based on direct labor cost? (b) Prepare the entry to apply factory overhead to production for November. (c) What is the November 30 balance of the account Factory Overhead — Blending Department? (d) Does the balance in (c) represent overapplied or underapplied factory overhead?

Exercise 22–4

Equivalent units of production and related costs.

OBJ. 2

The charges to Work in Process — Finishing Department for a period, together with information concerning production, are as follows. All direct materials are placed in process at the beginning of production, and the first-in, first-out method is used to cost inventories.

Work in Process — Finishing Department

2,500 units, 60% completed	94,000	To Dept. 2, 5,600 units	237,350
Direct materials, 3,100 at $26	80,600		
Direct labor	77,500		
Factory overhead	10,650		

Determine the following, presenting your computations: (a) equivalent units of production, (b) conversion cost per equivalent unit of production, (c) total and unit cost of product started in prior period and completed in the current period, and (d) total and unit cost of product started and completed in the current period.

Exercise 22–5

Cost of production report.

OBJ. 3

Prepare a cost of production report for the Assembly Department of Royal Company for June of the current fiscal year, using the following data and assuming that the first-in, first-out method is used to cost inventories:

Inventory, June 1, 8,000 units, 70% completed............................	$65,600
Materials from the Sanding Department, 20,800 units....................	87,360
Direct labor for June...	78,200
Factory overhead for June...	52,000
Goods finished during June (includes units in process, June 1) 21,300 units...	—
Inventory (June 30, 7,500 units, 80% completed).........................	—

Exercise 22–6

Entry for allocation of service department costs.

OBJ. 4

The Maintenance and Repair Department provides services to processing departments H, I, and J. During September of the current year, the total cost incurred by the Maintenance and Repair Department was $120,000. During September, it was estimated that 55% of the services were provided to Department H, 20% to Department I, and 25% to Department J.

Prepare an entry to record the allocation of the Maintenance and Repair Department cost for September to the processing departments.

Exercise 22–7

Allocation of costs for by-product and joint products.

OBJ. 5

The charges to Work in Process — Department 3, together with units of product completed during the period, are indicated in the following account:

Work in Process — Department 3

From Department 2	326,800	By-product E, 6,000 units
Direct labor	112,300	Joint product M, 12,000 units
Factory overhead	51,400	Joint product N, 20,000 units

There is no inventory of goods in process at either the beginning or the end of the period. The value of E is $1.75 a unit; M sells at $30 a unit, and N sells at $22 a unit.

Allocate the costs to the three products and determine the unit cost of each, presenting your computations.

Exercise 22–8

Unit costs of product by average cost method.

OBJ. 7

The debits to Work in Process — Melting Department for a period, together with information concerning production, are as follows:

Work in process, beginning of period:	
Materials costs, 4,500 units...	$127,100
Conversion costs, 4,500 units, 60% completed	145,160
Materials added during period, 18,200 units............................	381,380
Conversion costs during period...	580,640
Work in process, end of period, 4,000 units, 10% completed.........	—
Goods finished during period, 18,700 units	—

All direct materials are placed in process at the beginning of the process, and the average cost method is used to cost inventories. Determine the following, presenting your computations: (a) average materials cost per unit for period, (b) equivalent units of production for period, (c) average conversion cost per unit for period, (d) cost of goods finished during the period, and (e) cost of work in process at end of period.

PROBLEMS

Series A

Problem 22–1A

Work in process account data for two months and determination of difference in unit product cost between months.

OBJ. 1, 2

A process cost system is used to record the costs of manufacturing Product G, which requires a series of four processes. The inventory of Work in Process — Department 4 on April 1 and debits to the account during April were as follows:

Balance, 2,000 units, 3/4 completed....................	$18,025
From Department 3, 14,300 units	35,750
Direct labor..	94,500
Factory overhead...	10,500

During April, 2,000 units in process on April 1 were completed, and of the 14,300 units entering the department, all were completed except 3,500 units which were 1/5 completed.

Charges to Work in Process — Department 4 for May were as follows:

From Department 3, 10,500 units.......................................	$27,300
Direct labor..	95,220
Factory overhead...	10,580

During May, the units in process at the beginning of the month were completed, and of the 10,500 units entering the department, all were completed except 2,700 units, which were 1/3 completed. All inventories are costed by the first-in, first-out method.

Instructions:

(1) Set up an account for Work in Process—Department 4. Enter the balance as of April 1 and record the debits and the credits in the account for April. Present computations for the determination of (a) equivalent units of production, (b) unit conversion cost, (c) cost of goods finished, differentiating between units started in the prior period and units started and finished in April, and (d) work in process inventory.

(2) Record the transactions for May in the account. Present the computations listed in (1).

(3) Determine the difference in unit cost between the product started and completed in April and the product started and completed in May. Determine also the amount of the difference attributable collectively to operations in Departments 1 through 3 and the amount attributable to operations in Department 4.

Problem 22–2A

Equivalent units and related costs; cost of production report.

OBJ. 2, 3

Yeary Company manufactures Product P by a series of three processes, all materials being introduced in Department 1. From Department 1, the materials pass through Departments 2 and 3, emerging as finished Product P. All inventories are costed by the first-in, first-out method.

The balances in the accounts Work in Process—Department 3 and Finished Goods were as follows on October 1:

Work in Process—Department 3 (9,000 units, 1/2 completed)..	$177,300
Finished Goods (11,000 units at $25.75 a unit)....................	283,250

The following costs were charged to Work in Process—Department 3 during October:

Direct materials transferred from Department 2: 33,500 units	
at $13.80 a unit	$462,300
Direct labor..	286,130
Factory overhead...	154,070

During October, 32,500 units of P were completed and 32,900 units were sold. Inventories on October 31 were as follows:

Work in Process—Department 3: 10,000 units, 3/4 completed
Finished Goods: 10,600 units

Instructions:

(1) Determine the following, presenting computations in good order:
    (a) Equivalent units of production for Department 3 during October.
    (b) Unit conversion cost for Department 3 for October.
    (c) Total and unit cost of Product P started in a prior period and finished in October.
    (d) Total and unit cost of Product P started and finished in October.
    (e) Total cost of goods transferred to finished goods.
    (f) Work in process inventory for Department 3, October 31.
    (g) Cost of goods sold (indicate number of units and unit costs).
    (h) Finished goods inventory, October 31.

(2) Prepare a cost of production report for Department 3 for October.

Problem 22–3A
Entries for process cost system.

OBJ. 1, 2, 4, 6

Lester Company manufactures Product H. Material X is placed in process in Department 1, where it is ground and partially refined. The output of Department 1 is transferred to Department 2, where Material Y is added at the beginning of the process and the refining is completed. On April 1, Lester Company had the following inventories:

Finished Goods (6,500 units)	$136,500
Work in process — Department 1	—
Work in process — Department 2 (8,000 units, 3/4 completed)	152,400
Materials	43,700

Departmental accounts are maintained for factory overhead, and there is one service department, Factory Office. The first-in, first-out method is used to cost inventories. Manufacturing operations for April are summarized as follows:

(a) Materials purchased on account	$89,100
(b) Materials requisitioned for use:	
Material X	$67,250
Material Y	24,000
Indirect materials — Department 1	4,280
Indirect materials — Department 2	1,080
(c) Labor used:	
Direct labor — Department 1	$85,000
Direct labor — Department 2	46,500
Indirect labor — Department 1	8,400
Indirect labor — Department 2	3,800
Factory Office	2,900
(d) Depreciation charged on plant assets:	
Department 1	$37,850
Department 2	15,100
Factory Office	1,800
(e) Miscellaneous costs incurred on account:	
Department 1	$ 7,100
Department 2	2,920
Factory Office	1,200
(f) Expiration of prepaid expenses:	
Department 1	$ 2,400
Department 2	600
Factory Office	350

(g) Distribution of Factory Office costs:
    Department 1   40% of total Factory Office costs
    Department 2   60% of total Factory Office costs

(h) Application of factory overhead costs:
    Department 1   75% of direct labor cost
    Department 2   60% of direct labor cost

(i) Production costs transferred from Department 1 to Department 2:
16,000 units were fully processed, and there was no inventory of work in process in Department 1 at April 30.

(j) Production costs transferred from Department 2 to finished goods:
15,000 units, including the inventory at April 1, were fully processed. There were 9,000 units 1/3 completed at April 30.

(k) Cost of goods sold during April:
17,900 units (Use the first-in, first-out method in crediting the finished goods account.)

Instructions:

(1) Prepare entries to record the foregoing operations. Identify each entry by letter.
(2) Compute the April 30 work in process inventory for Department 2.

Problem 22–4A

Cost of production report.

OBJ. 3, 6

The data related to production during April of the current year for Department 2 of Lester Company are presented in Problem 22–3A.

Instructions:

Prepare a cost of production report for Department 2 for April.

Problem 22–5A

Entries for process cost system, including joint products.

OBJ. 4, 5, 6

A. C. Joyner Products manufactures joint products E and F. Materials are placed in production in Department 1, and after processing, are transferred to Department 2 where more materials are added. The finished products emerge from Department 2. There are two service departments: Factory Office, and Maintenance and Repair.

There were no inventories of work in process at the beginning or at the end of March. Finished goods inventories at March 1 were as follows:

Product E, 5,100 units	....	$91,800
Product F, 6,500 units	....	48,750

Transactions related to manufacturing operations for March are summarized as follows:

(a) Materials purchased on account, $256,900.

(b) Materials requisitioned for use: Department 1, $100,540 ($92,140 entered directly into the products); Department 2, $65,210 ($56,500 entered directly into the products); Maintenance and Repair, $3,680.

(c) Labor costs incurred: Department 1, $97,180 ($88,200 entered directly into the products); Department 2, $103,560 ($94,000 entered directly into the products); Factory Office, $9,380; Maintenance and Repair, $5,280.

(d) Miscellaneous costs and expenses incurred on account: Department 1, $17,000; Department 2, $16,620; Factory Office, $3,920; and Maintenance and Repair, $4,060.

(e) Depreciation charged on plant assets: Department 1, $15,320; Department 2, $14,000; Factory Office, $2,520; and Maintenance and Repair, $2,760.

(f) Expiration of various prepaid expenses: Department 1, $1,260; Department 2, $920; Factory Office, $480; and Maintenance and Repair, $340.

(g) Factory office costs allocated on the basis of hours worked: Department 1, 600 hours; Department 2, 480 hours; Maintenance and Repair, 120 hours.

(h) Maintenance and repair costs allocated on the basis of services rendered: Department 1, 70%; Department 2, 30%.

(i) Factory overhead applied to production at the predetermined rates: 80% and 65% of direct labor cost for Departments 1 and 2 respectively.

(j) Output of Department 1: 40,000 units.

(k) Output of Department 2: 20,000 units of Product E and 12,500 units of Product F. Unit selling price is $30 for Product E and $12 for Product F.

(l) Sales on account: 18,600 units of Product E at $30 and 10,700 units of Product F at $12. Credits to the finished goods accounts are to be made according to the first-in, first-out method.

Instructions:

Present entries to record the transactions, identifying each by letter. Include as an explanation for entry (k) the computations for the allocation of the production costs for Department 2 to the joint products, and as an explanation for entry (l) the number of units and the unit costs for each product sold.

Problem 22–6A

Financial statements for process cost system.

OBJ. 6

The trial balance of Raymond Inc. at March 31, the end of the first month of the current fiscal year, is as follows:

Raymond Inc.
Trial Balance
March 31, 19--

Cash..	36,300	
Marketable Securities	30,000	
Accounts Receivable...	122,500	
Allowance for Doubtful Accounts		5,000
Finished Goods — Product M	45,800	
Finished Goods — Product N...............................	77,500	
Work in Process — Department 1	9,850	
Work in Process — Department 2	16,750	
Work in Process — Department 3	14,700	
Materials	30,250	
Prepaid Insurance...	7,400	
Office Supplies...	3,570	
Land..	52,500	
Buildings..	350,000	
Accumulated Depreciation — Buildings		159,600
Machinery and Equipment....................................	171,000	
Accumulated Depreciation — Machinery and Equipment		108,300
Office Equipment	30,700	
Accumulated Depreciation — Office Equipment		12,780
Patents...	33,000	
Accounts Payable..		61,020
Wages Payable...		9,800
Income Tax Payable		3,250
Mortgage Note Payable (due 1999)........................		60,000
Common Stock ($50 par)		300,000
Retained Earnings...		279,910
Sales		380,000
Cost of Goods Sold..	251,100	
Factory Overhead — Department 1..........................	200	
Factory Overhead — Department 2..........................	180	
Factory Overhead — Department 3..........................		140
Selling Expenses	50,800	
Administrative Expenses	34,400	
Interest Expense...	6,500	
Interest Income...		200
Income Tax...	5,000	
	1,380,000	1,380,000

Instructions:

(1) Prepare an income statement.
(2) Prepare a retained earnings statement.
(3) Prepare a balance sheet.

Problem 22–7A

Unit cost of finished product by average cost method; cost of production report.

OBJ. 7

Rivero Company manufactures Product J by a series of four processes, all materials being introduced in Department 1. From Department 1, the materials pass through Departments 2, 3, and 4, emerging as finished Product J. All inventories are costed by the average cost method.

The balance in the account Work in Process — Department 4 was as follows on July 1:

Materials cost (2,000 units)...	$12,390
Conversion costs (2,000 units, 1/4 completed)	6,400

The following costs were charged to Work in Process — Department 4 during July:

Direct materials transferred from Department 3: 17,500 units
    at $6 per unit $105,000
Direct labor.. 172,800
Factory overhead... 44,800

During July, 16,500 units of Product J were completed and the work in process inventory on July 31 was 3,000 units, 1/3 completed.

Instructions:

(1) Determine the following for Department 4, presenting computations in good order:
    (a) Average materials cost per unit.
    (b) Equivalent units of production in July.
    (c) Average conversion cost per unit for July.
    (d) Cost of goods finished during July.
    (e) Cost of work in process at July 31.
(2) Prepare a cost of production report for Department 4 for July.

Series B

Problem 22–1B

Work in process account data for two months and determination of difference in unit product cost between months.

OBJ. 1, 2

A process cost system is used to record the costs of manufacturing Product Q, which requires a series of three processes. The inventory of Work in Process — Department 3 on September 1 and debits to the account during September were as follows:

Balance, 4,800 units, 1/4 completed............................... $ 21,840
From Department 2, 27,000 units..................................... 86,400
Direct labor.. 133,280
Factory overhead... 23,520

During September, 4,800 units in process on September 1 were completed, and of the 27,000 units entering the department, all were completed except 5,200 units which were 1/2 completed.

Charges to Work in Process — Department 3 for October were as follows:

From Department 2, 30,800 units..................................... $ 97,020
Direct labor.. 132,000
Factory overhead... 33,000

During October, the units in process at the beginning of the month were completed, and of the 30,800 units entering the department, all were completed except 5,100 units, which were 1/3 completed. All inventories are costed by the first-in, first-out method.

Instructions:

(1) Set up an account for Work in Process — Department 3. Enter the balance as of September 1 and record the debits and the credits in the account for September. Present computations for the determination of (a) equivalent units of production, (b) unit conversion cost, (c) cost of goods finished, differentiating between units started in the prior period and units started and finished in September, and (d) work in process inventory.
(2) Record the transactions for October in the account. Present the computations listed in (1).
(3) Determine the difference in unit cost between the product started and completed in September and the product started and completed in October. Determine also the amount of the difference attributable collectively to operations in Departments 1 and 2 and the amount attributable to operations in Department 3.

Problem 22–2B
Equivalent units and
related costs; cost of
production report.
OBJ. 2, 3

Scotch Company manufactures Product F by a series of four processes, all materials being introduced in Department 1. From Department 1, the materials pass through Departments 2, 3, and 4, emerging as finished Product F. All inventories are costed by the first-in, first-out method.

The balances in the accounts Work in Process — Department 4 and Finished Goods were as follows on May 1:

Work in Process — Department 4 (4,500 units, 2/3 completed) ...	$34,200
Finished Goods (6,200 units at $9.80 a unit).........................	60,760

The following costs were charged to Work in Process — Department 4 during May:

Direct materials transferred from Department 3: 14,000 units at $2.50 a unit...	$35,000
Direct labor...	78,000
Factory overhead...	19,500

During May, 14,500 units of F were completed and 15,600 units were sold. Inventories on May 31 were as follows:

Work in Process — Department 4: 4,000 units, 1/4 completed
Finished Goods: 5,100 units

Instructions:

(1) Determine the following, presenting computations in good order:
    (a) Equivalent units of production for Department 4 during May.
    (b) Unit conversion cost for Department 4 for May.
    (c) Total and unit cost of Product F started in a prior period and finished in May.
    (d) Total and unit cost of Product F started and finished in May.
    (e) Total cost of goods transferred to finished goods.
    (f) Work in process inventory for Department 4, May 31.
    (g) Cost of goods sold (indicate number of units and unit costs).
    (h) Finished goods inventory, May 31.
(2) Prepare a cost of production report for Department 4 for May.

Problem 22–3B
Entries for process
cost system.
OBJ. 1, 2, 4, 6

Holman Company manufactures Product T. Material A is placed in process in Department 1, where it is ground and partially refined. The output of Department 1 is transferred to Department 2, where Material B is added at the beginning of the process and the refining is completed. On November 1, Holman Company had the following inventories:

Finished Goods (8,000 units)	$72,000
Work in process — Department 1	—
Work in process — Department 2 (12,000 units, 1/3 completed).......	90,400
Materials	26,400

Departmental accounts are maintained for factory overhead, and there is one service department, Factory Office. All inventories are costed by the first-in, first-out method. Manufacturing operations for November are summarized as follows:

(a) Materials purchased on account..	$48,100
(b) Materials requisitioned for use:	
Material A..	$26,080
Material B..	21,600
Indirect materials — Department 1.....................................	1,700
Indirect materials — Department 2.....................................	1,240

(c) Labor used:

Direct labor — Department 1	$53,900
Direct labor — Department 2	38,500
Indirect labor — Department 1	4,030
Indirect labor — Department 2	1,920
Factory Office	1,830

(d) Miscellaneous costs incurred on account:

Department 1	$ 7,000
Department 2	4,100
Factory Office	2,100

(e) Expiration of prepaid expenses:

Department 1	$ 1,050
Department 2	700
Factory Office	300

(f) Depreciation charged on plant assets:

Department 1	$14,350
Department 2	12,250
Factory Office	900

(g) Distribution of Factory Office costs:

Department 1	80% of total Factory Office costs
Department 2	20% of total Factory Office costs

(h) Application of factory overhead costs:

Department 1	60% of direct labor cost
Department 2	55% of direct labor cost

(i) Production costs transferred from Department 1 to Department 2:
   21,600 units were fully processed, and there was no inventory of work in process in Department 1 at November 30.

(j) Production costs transferred from Department 2 to finished goods:
   22,140 units, including the inventory at November 1, were fully processed. 11,460 units were 1/2 completed at November 30.

(k) Cost of goods sold during November:
   25,200 units (Use the first-in, first-out method in crediting the finished goods account.)

Instructions:

(1) Prepare entries to record the foregoing operations. Identify each entry by letter.
(2) Compute the November 30 work in process inventory for Department 2.

Problem 22–4B
Cost of production report.
OBJ. 3, 6

The data related to production during November of the current year for Department 2 of Holman Company are presented in Problem 22–3B.

Instructions:

Prepare a cost of production report for Department 2 for November.

MINI-CASE 22

   H and S Inc. manufactures Product T by a series of four processes. All materials are placed in production in the Die Casting Department and, after processing, are transferred to the Tooling, Assembly, and Polishing Departments, emerging as finished Product T.

On January 1, the balance in the account Work in Process—Polishing was $213,000, determined as follows:

Direct materials: 15,000 units	$121,200
Direct labor: 15,000 units, 2/5 completed	73,440
Factory overhead: 15,000 units, 2/5 completed	18,360
Total	$213,000

The following costs were charged to Work in Process—Polishing during January:

Direct materials transferred from Assembly Dept., 145,000 units	$1,189,000
Direct labor	1,870,850
Factory overhead	330,150

During January, 144,000 units of T were completed and transferred to Finished Goods. On January 31, the inventory in the Polishing Department consisted of 16,000 units, one-fourth completed. All inventories are costed by the first-in, first-out method.

As a new cost accountant for H and S Inc., you have just received a phone call from Jill Stallings, the superintendent of the Polishing Department. She was extremely upset with the cost of production report, which she says does not balance. In addition, she commented:

"I give up! These reports are a waste of time. My department has always been the best department in the plant, so why should I bother with these reports? Just what purpose do they serve?"

The report to which Stallings referred is as follows:

H and S Inc.
Cost of Production Report—Polishing Department
For Month Ended January 31, 19--

Quantities:		
Charged to production:		
In process, January 1		6,000
Received from Assembly Department		145,000
Total units to be accounted for		151,000
Units accounted for:		
Transferred to finished goods		144,000
In process, January 31		4,000
Total units accounted for		148,000
Costs:		
Charged to production:		
In process, January 1		$ 213,000
January costs:		
Direct materials from Assembly Department ($8.20 per unit)		1,189,000
Conversion costs:		
Direct labor	$1,870,850	
Factory overhead	330,150	
Total conversion costs ($14.20 per unit)		2,201,000
Total costs to be accounted for		$3,603,000

Costs allocated as follows:
   Transferred to finished goods:
      144,000 units at $22.40 ($8.20 + $14.20)..... $3,225,600
   In process, January 31:
      Materials (4,000 units × $8.20)................... $ 32,800
      Conversion costs (4,000 units × $14.20)......   56,800
      Total cost of inventory in process...............   89,600
  Total costs accounted for............................... $3,315,200

Computations:
  Equivalent units of production:
    To process units in inventory on January 1:
      15,000 units × 2/5...................................   6,000
    To process units started and completed
      in January..   145,000
    To process units in inventory on January 31
      16,000 units × 1/4...................................   4,000
      Equivalent units of production.....................   155,000

  Unit conversion cost:
    $2,201,000 ÷ 155,000 .... $14.20

Instructions:

(1) Based upon the data for January, prepare a revised cost of production report for the Polishing Department.
(2) Assuming that all costs reported in the work in process account on January 1 were incurred in the preceding month, determine the unit direct materials cost and the unit conversion cost for December.
(3) Based on (2), determine the change in the unit direct materials cost and unit conversion cost for January as compared to December.
(4) Based on (3), what are some possible explanations for the changing unit costs?
(5) Describe how you would explain to Stallings that cost of production reports are useful.

ETHICS DISCUSSION CASE

Kathy Burchett, a cost accountant for Thacker Industries, has the responsibility of allocating service department costs. She allocates Power Department costs on a monthly basis to each of the producing departments and to the factory office. The factory office is allocated a fixed charge of $25,000 per month, and the remaining costs are allocated to the producing departments based on actual kilowatt usage. John Mercer, supervisor of the Assembly Department, recently complained to the vice-president of production that the allocations of service department costs were wrong and that the only reason the factory office was charged $25,000 was because Burchett was an employee of that department. Mercer argues that the factory office should receive at least $50,000 of the Power Department cost allocation.

Discuss the ethical issues of this case.

ANSWERS TO SELF-EXAMINATION QUESTIONS

1. **C** The process cost system is most appropriate for a business where manufacturing is conducted by continuous operations and involves a series of uniform production processes, such as the processing of crude oil (answer C). The job order cost system is most appropriate for a business where the product is made to customers' specifications, such as custom furniture manufacturing (answer A) and commercial building construction (answer B).

2. **C** The manufacturing costs that are necessary to convert direct materials into finished products are referred to as conversion costs. The conversion costs include direct labor and factory overhead (answer C).

3. **B** The number of units that could have been produced from start to finish during a period is termed equivalent units. The 4,875 equivalent units (answer B) is determined as follows:

To process units in inventory on May 1:	
1,000 units × 1/4	250
To process units started and completed	
in May: 5,500 units − 1,000 units...............................	4,500
To process units in inventory on May 31:	
500 units × 1/4	125
Equivalent units of production in May	4,875

4. **A** The conversion costs (direct labor and factory overhead) totaling $48,750 are divided by the number of equivalent units (4,875) to determine the unit conversion cost of $10 (answer A).

5. **B** The product resulting from a process that has little value in relation to the principal product or joint products is known as a by-product (answer B). When two or more commodities of significant value are produced from a single direct material, the products are termed joint products (answer A). The raw material that enters directly into the finished product is termed direct material (answer C).

Planning
and Control

PART SEVEN

7

CHAPTER TWENTY-THREE
COST BEHAVIOR CONCEPTS AND COST-VOLUME-PROFIT ANALYSIS

A variety of managerial cost terms, classifications, and concepts were introduced in Chapters 20–22. This chapter continues the discussion of cost concepts by focusing on cost behavior and its application to the relationship of costs to volume and profit.

Cost behavior refers to the manner in which a cost changes in relation to its activity base. For example, direct materials costs vary proportionately with changes in the number of units produced. If the total units produced doubles, direct materials costs will also double.

A thorough understanding of cost behavior is essential for planning and controlling operations. For example, classifying costs by their behavior as production varies allows management to establish standards for evaluating (controlling) the efficiency of current operations and for predicting (planning) the costs of future levels of operations.

Cost-volume-profit analysis is the systematic examination of the interrelationships between selling prices, volume of sales and production, costs, expenses, and profits. Management can use such information in making decisions that will improve the relationship between these variables. For example, management can use cost-volume-profit analysis to determine the effects of a change in selling prices on operations.

COST BEHAVIOR

OBJECTIVE 1
Describe and
illustrate fixed,
variable, and mixed
cost behaviors and
related concepts.

The behavior of costs can be classified in a variety of ways. The three most common cost classifications are fixed costs, variable costs, and mixed costs.[1] Each of these classifications was briefly described in Chapter 20. This chapter expands upon this discussion to include additional issues which must be considered if the managerial accountant is to classify cost behavior properly into these three types.

Fixed Costs

Fixed costs are costs that remain constant in total dollar amount as the level of activity changes. Examples of fixed manufacturing costs include straight-line depreciation on factory equipment and buildings, rent on factory plant and equipment, property insurance on factory plant and equipment, and salaries of factory supervisory personnel.

To illustrate, assume that Cottage Inc. manufactures, bottles, and distributes La Fleur Perfume at its Los Angeles plant. The production supervisor at the Los Angeles plant is Jane Sovissi, who is paid a salary of $75,000 per year. Sovissi's salary is a fixed cost that does not vary with production. Regardless of whether 50,000, 100,000, or 300,000 bottles are produced, Sovissi will still receive a salary of $75,000.

Although fixed costs remain constant in total dollar amount as the level of production changes, the fixed cost per unit changes as the level of production changes. As additional units are produced, the total fixed costs are spread over a larger number of units, and hence the fixed cost per unit decreases.

The relationship of total fixed cost and fixed cost per unit is illustrated in the following table and graphs for the $75,000 salary of Jane Sovissi:

Number of Bottles of Perfume Produced	Total Salary for Jane Sovissi	Salary per Bottle Produced
50,000 bottles	$75,000	$1.500
100,000	75,000	.750
150,000	75,000	.500
200,000	75,000	.375
250,000	75,000	.300
300,000	75,000	.350

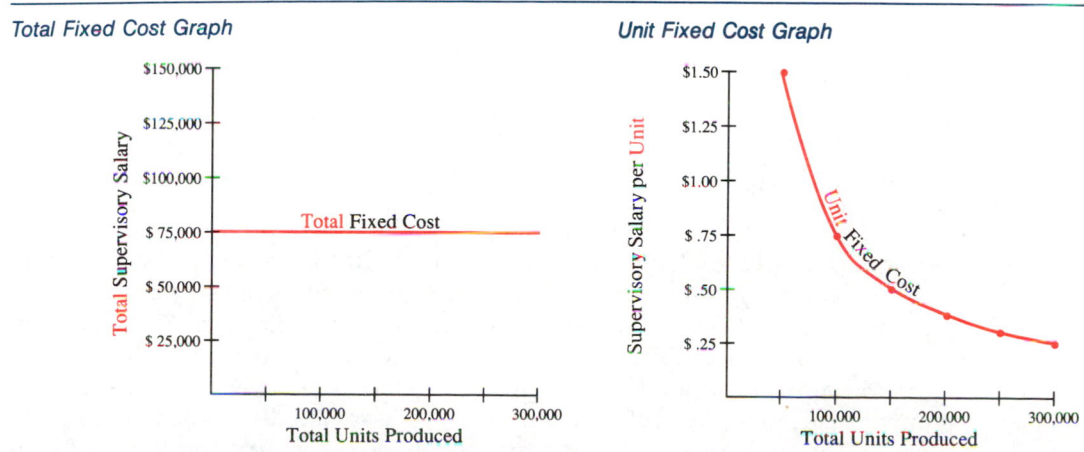

Total Fixed Cost Graph

Unit Fixed Cost Graph

[1]In this chapter, the term "costs" is often used as a convenience to represent both "costs" and "expenses."

Fixed costs are defined in terms of an **activity base,** such as bottles of perfume produced by Cottage Inc. in the preceding illustration. The appropriate activity base to be used for a cost depends on which base is most closely associated with the cost and the decision-making needs of management in using the cost in planning and controlling operations. In most situations, the activity base for fixed costs will be expressed as either units produced, units sold, or sales dollars.

In classifying costs as fixed, management focuses on a narrow range of activity within which the enterprise is planning to operate. This range of activity is referred to as the **relevant range.** For Cottage Inc., the relevant range was expressed in terms of the production of 50,000 to 300,000 bottles of perfume. Over this range of activity, the fixed costs would be $75,000. If the level of operations were to fall outside the range of 50,000 to 300,000 units, it is very likely that the fixed costs would change. To illustrate, assume that Cottage Inc. could only produce 300,000 bottles of perfume during an 8-hour shift. To produce between 300,000 and 600,000 bottles of perfume, an additional shift would be activated and another production supervisor hired at a salary of $75,000. Likewise, to produce between 600,000 and 900,000 bottles of perfume, yet another production supervisor must be hired. Graphically, the nature of the production supervisor salary costs is illustrated as follows:

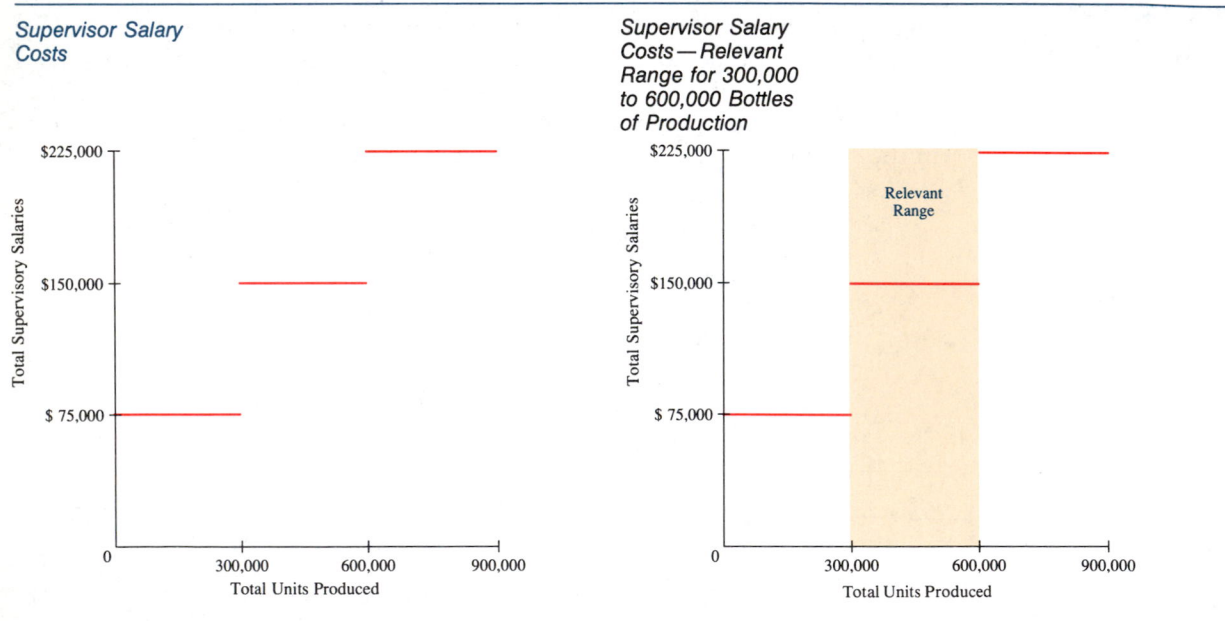

Variable Costs

Variable costs are costs that vary in total in direct proportion to changes in an activity base. As mentioned in Chapter 20, direct materials and direct labor costs are generally treated as variable costs because as production volume changes, the totals of these costs change proportionately. To illustrate, assume that Wilcox Inc. produces stereophonic sound systems under the brand name of JimBo. The parts for the stereo systems are purchased from outside suppliers for $10 per unit and are assembled in Wilcox's Augusta plant. The direct materials costs for Model JW-12 for differing levels of production are summarized in the following table:

Number of Units of Model JW-12 Produced	Direct Materials Cost per Unit	Total Direct Materials Cost
5,000 units	$10	$ 50,000
10,000 units	10	100,000
15,000 units	10	150,000
20,000 units	10	200,000
25,000 units	10	250,000
30,000 units	10	300,000

As the table illustrates, the total direct materials cost varies in direct proportion to the number of units of Model JW-12 produced. The direct materials cost for 25,000 units ($250,000) is 5 times the direct materials cost for 5,000 units ($50,000). However, the unit direct materials cost of $10 remains constant over all levels of production between 5,000 and 30,000 units. A constant per unit cost over a relevant range is a characteristic of variable costs.

The following graphs illustrate how the variable costs for direct materials for Model JW-12 behave in total and on a per unit basis as production changes:

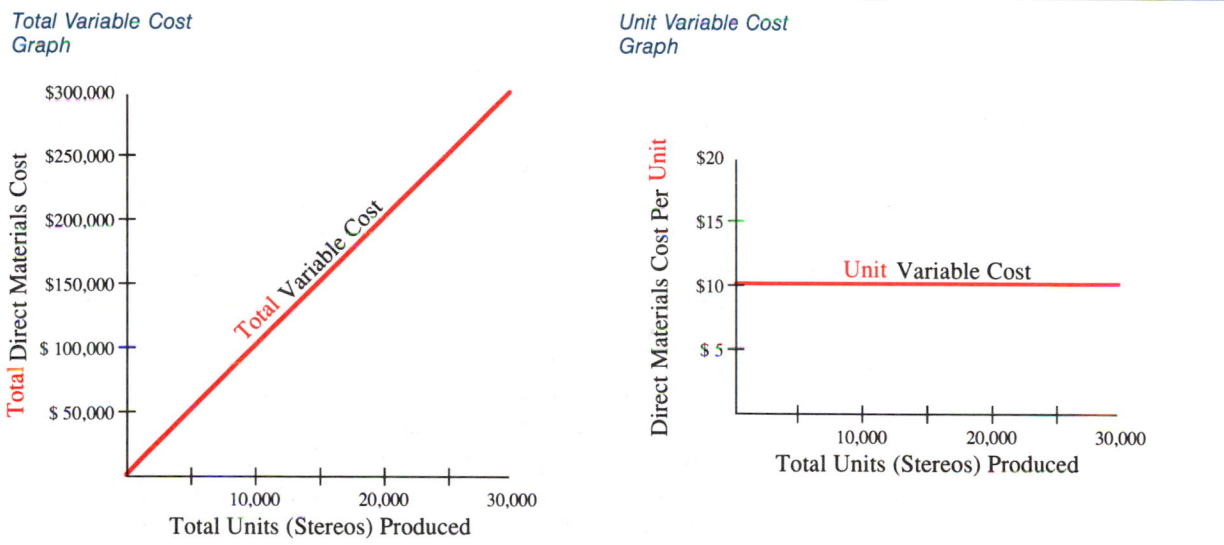

Mixed Costs

A **mixed cost** has characteristics of both a fixed and a variable cost. For example, a portion of the mixed cost may remain constant in total amount, and it will therefore be a fixed cost. Another portion of the mixed cost may change in proportion to changes in the activity base, and it will therefore be a variable cost. Mixed costs are sometimes referred to as **semivariable** or **semifixed** costs.

To illustrate, assume that Simpson Inc. manufactures sails, using rented machinery. The rental charges are $20,000 per year plus $1 for each machine hour used. If the machinery is used 20,000 hours, the total rental charge is $40,000 [$20,000 + (20,000 × $1)]. If the machinery is used 30,000 hours, the total rental charge is $50,000 [$20,000 + (30,000 × $1)], and so on. This mixed cost behavior is illustrated graphically as follows:

Mixed Costs—
$20,000 + $1 per
Hour

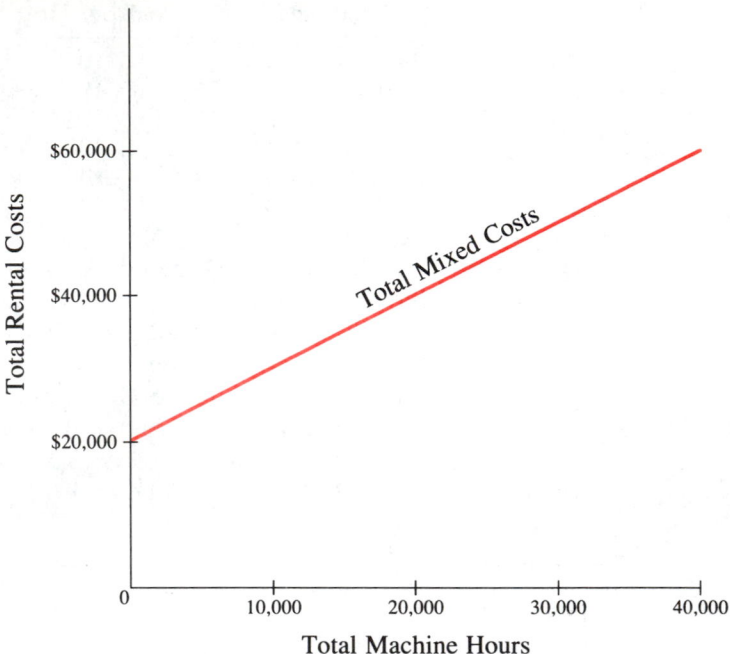

In this illustration, which is a common type of mixed cost behavior, a rental cost of $20,000 will be incurred, even if the machinery is not used at all. The $20,000 is constant over all levels of production and represents the fixed cost component of the mixed cost. The rental charge of $1 per hour, which represents the variable cost component of the mixed cost, causes the total mixed cost to increase as machine hours are used.

When mixed costs are encountered in practice, they are usually separated into their fixed and variable components for management analysis. The **high-low method** is a common cost estimation technique that can be used for this purpose.[2] The high-low method uses the highest and lowest total costs revealed by past cost patterns as the basis for estimating the variable cost per unit and the fixed cost component of a mixed cost. To illustrate, assume that the quality control department of Kason Inc. incurred the following costs during the past 5 months:

	Production	Total Cost
June	1,000 units	$45,000
July	1,500	52,500
August	2,100	61,500
September	1,800	57,000
October	750	41,250

For Kason Inc., the difference between the units produced and the difference between the total cost at the highest and lowest levels of production are as follows:

[2]Other methods of estimating costs, such as the scattergraph method and the least squares method, are discussed in cost accounting textbooks.

	Production	Total Cost
Highest level	2,100 units	$61,500
Lowest level	750	41,250
Difference	1,350 units	$20,250

Since the total fixed cost does not change with changes in volume of production, the $20,250 difference in the total cost represents the change in the total variable cost. Hence, dividing the difference in the total cost by the difference in production units provides an estimate of the variable cost per unit. For Kason Inc., the variable cost per unit is $15, as shown in the following computation:

$$\text{Variable Cost per Unit} = \frac{\text{Difference in Total Cost}}{\text{Difference in Production}}$$

$$\text{Variable Cost per Unit} = \frac{\$20,250}{1,350 \text{ units}} = \$15$$

Since the fixed cost will be the same at both the highest and the lowest levels of production, it can be estimated by subtracting the estimated total variable cost from the total cost at either the highest or the lowest levels of production, using the following total cost equation:

Total Cost = (Variable Cost per Unit × Units of Production) + Fixed Cost

Highest level:

$61,500 = ($15 × 2,100 units) + Fixed Cost
$61,500 = $31,500 + Fixed Cost
$30,000 = Fixed Cost

Lowest level:

$41,250 = ($15 × 750 units) + Fixed Cost
$41,250 = $11,250 + Fixed Cost
$30,000 = Fixed Cost

The total quality control cost for Kason Inc. can be analyzed in terms of a $30,000 fixed cost and a $15 per unit variable cost. Using these amounts in the total cost equation above, the total quality control cost at other levels of production can be estimated.

Summary of Cost Behavior Concepts

As indicated in the preceding paragraphs, costs can be classified as fixed costs, variable costs, or mixed costs. For purposes of analysis, mixed costs are generally separated into their fixed and variable cost components. The following table summarizes the cost behavior characteristics of fixed and variable costs:

	Effect of Changing Activity Level	
Cost	*Total Amount*	*Per Unit Amount*
Fixed	Remains constant regardless of activity level.	Increases and decreases inversely with activity level.
Variable	Increases and decreases proportionately with activity level.	Remains constant regardless of activity level.

COST-VOLUME-PROFIT RELATIONSHIPS

After costs have been classified into fixed and variable components, the effect on profit of these costs, along with revenues and volume, can be expressed in the form of cost-volume-profit analysis. Cost-volume-profit analysis is a commonly used tool that provides management with useful information on the relative profitability of various products, the probable effects of changes in costs and selling price, and other variables. For example, an analysis of sales and cost data can be helpful in determining the level of sales volume necessary for the business to earn a satisfactory profit, and in analyzing the effects of cost increases or decreases on the profitability of the business enterprise.

Cost-volume-profit analysis can be complex, since the relationships between costs, volume, and profits are often affected by forces that are entirely or partially beyond management's control. For example, the determination of the selling price of a product is often affected by not only the costs of production, but also by uncontrollable factors in the marketplace. On the other hand, the cost of producing the product is affected by such controllable factors as the efficiency of operations and the volume of production.

In the remainder of this chapter, cost-volume-profit analysis is applied to the calculation of the volume required to achieve the break-even point and desired profit. In addition, sales mix, the margin of safety, the contribution margin ratio, and limitations of cost-volume-profit analysis are discussed.

MATHEMATICAL APPROACH TO COST-VOLUME-PROFIT ANALYSIS

Although accountants have proposed various approaches for cost-volume-profit analysis, the mathematical aproach is one of two common approaches described and illustrated in this chapter. The mathematical approach to cost-volume-profit analysis generally uses equations (1) to indicate the revenues necessary to achieve the break-even point in operations or (2) to indicate the revenues necessary to achieve a desired or target profit. These two equations and their use by management in profit planning are described and illustrated in the paragraphs that follow.

Break-Even Point

The level of operations of an enterprise at which revenues and expired costs are exactly equal is called the **break-even point**. At this level of operations, an enterprise will neither realize an operating income nor incur an operating loss. Break-even analysis can be applied to past periods, but it is most useful when applied to future periods as a guide to business planning, particularly if either an expansion or a curtailment of operations is expected. In such cases, it is concerned with future prospects and future operations and hence relies upon estimates. The reliability of the analysis is greatly influenced by the accuracy of the estimates.

The break-even point can be computed by means of a mathematical formula which indicates the relationship between revenue, costs, and capacity. The data required are (1) total estimated fixed costs for a future period, such as a year, and (2) the total estimated variable costs for the same period, stated as a percent of net sales. To illustrate, assume that fixed costs are estimated at $90,000 and that variable costs are expected to be 60% of sales. The break-even point is $225,000 of sales, computed as follows:

Break-Even Sales (in $) = Fixed Costs (in $) + Variable Costs (as % of Break-Even Sales)

$$S = \$90,000 + 60\%S$$
$$40\%S = \$90,000$$
$$S = \$225,000$$

The validity of the preceding computation is shown in the following income statement:

Sales..		$225,000
Costs:		
Variable costs ($225,000 × 60%)..................	$135,000	
Fixed costs	90,000	225,000
Operating profit...		-0-

The break-even point can be expressed either in terms of total sales dollars, as in the preceding illustration, or in terms of units of sales. For example, in the preceding illustration, if the unit selling price is $25, the break-even point can be expressed as either $225,000 of sales or 9,000 units ($225,000 ÷ $25).

The break-even point can be affected by changes in the fixed costs, unit variable costs, and unit selling price. The effect of each of these factors on the break-even point is briefly described in the following paragraphs.

Effect of Changes in Fixed Costs. Although fixed costs do not change in total with changes in volume of activity, they may change because of other factors, such as changes in property tax rates and salary increases given to factory supervisors. Increases in fixed costs will raise the break-even point. Similarly, decreases in fixed costs will lower the break-even point.

To illustrate, assume that Bishop Co. is evaluating a proposal to budget an additional $100,000 for advertising. Fixed costs (before the additional expenditure of $100,000 is considered) are estimated at $600,000, and variable costs are estimated at 75% of sales. The break-even point (before the additional expenditure is considered) is $2,400,000, computed as follows:

Break-Even Sales (in $) = Fixed Costs (in $) + Variable Costs (as % of Break-Even Sales)

$$S = \$600,000 + 75\%S$$
$$25\%S = \$600,000$$
$$S = \$2,400,000$$

If the expenditure for advertising is increased by $100,000, the break-even point is raised to $2,800,000, computed as follows:

Break-Even Sales (in $) = Fixed Costs (in $) + Variable Costs (as % of Break-Even Sales)

$$S = \$700,000 + 75\%S$$
$$25\%S = \$700,000$$
$$S = \$2,800,000$$

The increased fixed cost of $100,000 increases the break-even point by $400,000 of sales, since 75 cents of each sales dollar must cover variable costs. Hence, $4 of additional sales are needed for each $1 increase in fixed costs if the operating profit for Bishop Co. is to remain unchanged.

Effect of Changes in Variable Costs. Although unit variable costs do not change with changes in volume of activity, they may change because of other factors, such as changes in the price of direct materials and salary increases given to factory workers providing direct labor. Increases in unit variable costs will raise the break-even point. Similarly, decreases in unit variable costs will lower the break-even point.

To illustrate, assume that Park Co. is evaluating a proposal to pay an additional 2% sales commission to its sales representatives as an incentive to increase sales. Fixed costs are estimated at $84,000, and variable costs are estimated at 58% of sales (before the additional 2% commission is considered). The break-even point (before the additional commission is considered) is $200,000, computed as follows:

Break-Even Sales (in $) = Fixed Costs (in $) + Variable Costs (as % of Break-Even Sales)
$$S = \$84,000 + 58\%S$$
$$42\%S = \$84,000$$
$$S = \$200,000$$

If the sales commission proposal is adopted, the break-even point is raised to $210,000, computed as follows:

Break-Even Sales (in $) = Fixed Costs (in $) + Variable Costs (as % of Break-Even Sales)
$$S = \$84,000 + 60\%S$$
$$40\%S = \$84,000$$
$$S = \$210,000$$

The additional 2% sales commission (a variable cost) increases the break-even point by $10,000 of sales. If the proposal is adopted, 2% less of each sales dollar is available to cover the fixed costs of $84,000.

Effect of Changing Unit Selling Price. Increases in the unit selling price will lower the break-even point, while decreases in the unit selling price will raise the break-even point. To illustrate the effect of changing the unit selling price, assume that Graham Co. is evaluating a proposal to increase the unit selling price of its product from its current price of $50 to $60 and has accumulated the following relevant data:

	Current	Proposed
Unit selling price	$50	$60
Unit variable cost	$30	$30
Variable costs (as % of break-even sales):		
$30 unit variable cost ÷ $50 unit selling price	60%	
$30 unit variable cost ÷ $60 unit selling price		50%
Total fixed costs...	$600,000	$600,000

The break-even point based on the current selling price is $1,500,000, computed as follows:

Break-Even Sales (in $) = Fixed Costs (in $) + Variable Costs (as % of Break-Even Sales)
$$S = \$600,000 + 60\%S$$
$$40\%S = \$600,000$$
$$S = \$1,500,000$$

If the selling price is increased by $10 per unit, the break-even point is decreased to $1,200,000, computed as follows:

Break-Even Sales (in $) = Fixed Costs (in $) + Variable Costs (as % of Break-Even Sales)
$$S = \$600,000 + 50\%S$$
$$50\%S = \$600,000$$
$$S = \$1,200,000$$

The increase in selling price of $10 per unit decreases the break-even point by $300,000 (from $1,500,000 to $1,200,000). In terms of units of sales, the decrease is from 30,000 units ($1,500,000 ÷ $50) to 20,000 units ($1,200,000 ÷ $60).

Desired Profit

At the break-even point, sales and costs are exactly equal. However, business enterprises do not use the break-even point as their goal for future operations. Rather, they seek to achieve the largest possible volume of sales above the break-even point. By modifying the break-even equation, the sales volume required to earn a desired amount of profit may be estimated. For this purpose, a factor for desired profit is added to the standard break-even formula. To illustrate, assume that fixed costs are estimated at $200,000, variable costs are estimated at 60% of sales, and the desired profit is $100,000. The sales volume is $750,000, computed as follows:

$$\text{Sales (in \$)} = \text{Fixed Costs (in \$)} + \text{Variable Costs (as \% of Sales)} + \text{Desired Profit}$$
$$S = \$200,000 + 60\%S + \$100,000$$
$$40\%S = \$300,000$$
$$S = \$750,000$$

The validity of the preceding computation is shown in the following income statement:

Sales..		$750,000
Costs:		
Variable costs ($750,000 × 60%)...................	$450,000	
Fixed costs	200,000	650,000
Operating profit...		$100,000

GRAPHIC APPROACH TO COST-VOLUME-PROFIT ANALYSIS

OBJECTIVE 4
Describe and illustrate the graphic approach to cost-volume-profit analysis.

Cost-volume-profit analysis can be presented graphically as well as in equation form. Many managers prefer the graphic format because the operating profit or loss for any given level of capacity can be readily determined, without the necessity of solving an equation. The following paragraphs describe two graphic approaches which managers find useful.

Cost-Volume-Profit (Break-Even) Chart

A **cost-volume-profit chart**, sometimes called a **break-even chart**, is used to assist management in understanding the relationships between costs, sales, and operating profit or loss. The cost-volume-profit chart is constructed in the following manner:

1. Percentages of capacity of the enterprise are spread along the horizontal axis and dollar amounts representing operating data are spread along the vertical axis. The outside limits of the chart represent 100% of capacity and the maximum sales potential at that level of capacity.
2. A diagonal line representing sales is drawn from the lower left corner to the upper right corner.
3. A point representing fixed costs is plotted on the vertical axis at the left, and a point representing total costs at maximum capacity is plotted at the right edge of the chart. A diagonal line representing total costs at various percentages of capacity is then drawn connecting these two points.
4. Horizontal and vertical lines are drawn at the point of intersection of the sales and cost lines, which is the break-even point, and the areas representing operating profit and operating loss are identified.

To illustrate the cost-volume-profit chart, assume that fixed costs are estimated at $90,000 and variable costs are estimated as 60% of sales. The maximum level of sales at 100% of capacity is $400,000. The following cost-volume-profit chart is based on the foregoing data:

Cost-Volume-Profit Chart

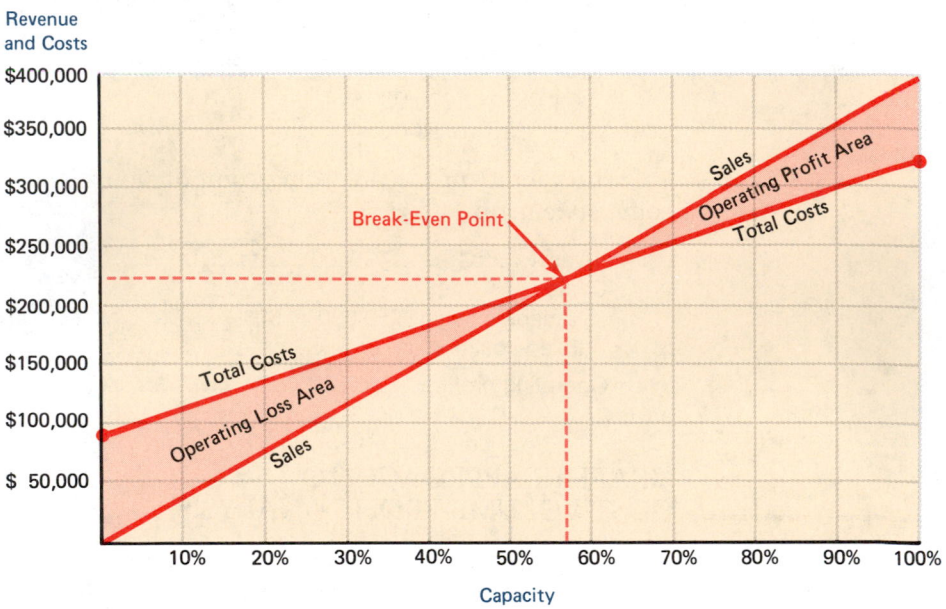

In the illustration, the total costs at maximum capacity are $330,000 (fixed costs of $90,000 plus variable costs of $240,000, which is 60% of $400,000). The dotted line drawn from the point of intersection to the vertical axis identifies the break-even sales amount of $225,000. The dotted line drawn from the point of intersection to the horizontal axis identifies the break-even point in terms of capacity of approximately 56%. Operating profits will be earned when sales levels are to the right of the break-even point (operating profit area), and operating losses will be incurred when sales levels are to the left of the break-even point (operating loss area).

Changes in the unit selling price, total fixed costs, and unit variable costs can also be analyzed using a cost-volume-profit chart. To illustrate, using the preceding example, assume that a proposal to reduce fixed costs by $42,000 is to be evaluated. In this situation, the total fixed costs would be $48,000 ($90,000 − $42,000), and the total costs at maximum capacity would amount to $288,000 ($48,000 of fixed costs plus variable costs of $240,000). The preceding cost-volume-profit chart is revised by plotting the points representing the total fixed cost and the total cost and drawing a line between the two points, indicating the proposed total cost line. The following revised chart indicates that the break-even point would decrease to $120,000 of sales (30% of capacity).

*Revised Cost-Volume-
Profit Chart*

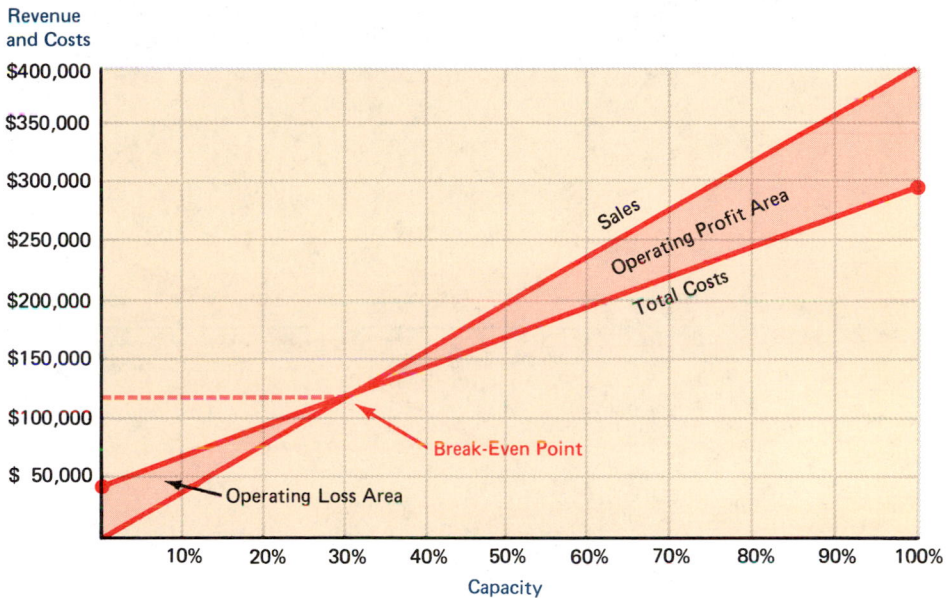

Profit-Volume Chart

Rather than focusing on sales revenues and costs, as was the case for the cost-volume-profit chart, another graphic approach to cost-volume-profit analysis, called the **profit-volume chart,** focuses on profitability. On the profit-volume chart, only the difference between total sales revenues and total costs is plotted, which enables management to determine the operating profit (or loss) for various levels of operations.

To illustrate the profit-volume chart, assume that fixed costs are estimated at $50,000, variable costs are estimated at 75% of sales, and the maximum capacity is $500,000 of sales. The maximum operating loss is equal to the fixed costs of $50,000, and the maximum operating profit at 100% of capacity is $75,000, computed as follows:

Sales..		$500,000
Costs:		
Variable costs ($500,000 × 75%)..................	$375,000	
Fixed costs...	50,000	425,000
Operating profit.......................................		$ 75,000

The following profit-volume chart is based on the foregoing data:

Profit-Volume Chart

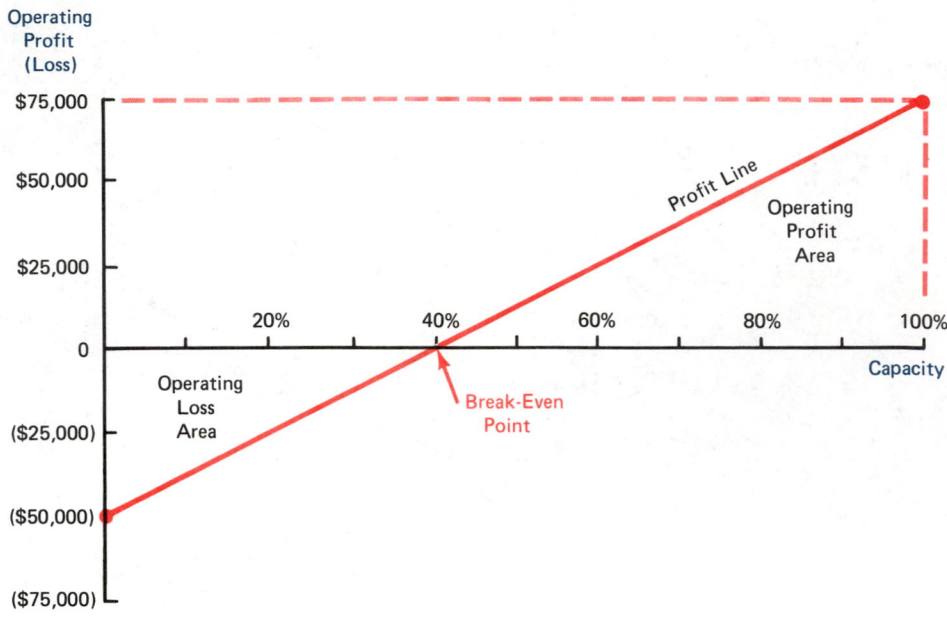

The profit-volume chart is constructed in the following manner:

1. Percentages of capacity of the enterprise are spread along the horizontal axis, and dollar amounts representing operating profits and losses are spread along the vertical axis.
2. A point representing the maximum operating loss is plotted on the vertical axis at the left. This loss is equal to the total fixed costs at 0% of capacity.
3. A point representing the maximum operating profit at 100% of capacity is plotted on the right.
4. A diagonal profit line is drawn connecting the maximum operating loss point with the maximum operating profit point.
5. The profit line intersects the horizontal axis at the break-even point expressed as a percentage of capacity, and the areas representing operating profit and operating loss are identified.

In the illustration, the break-even point is 40% of productive capacity, which can be converted to $200,000 of total sales (maximum capacity of $500,000 × 40%). Operating profit will be earned when sales levels are to the right of the break-even point (operating profit area), and operating losses will be incurred when sales levels are to the left of the break-even point (operating loss area). For example, at 60% of productive capacity, an operating profit of $25,000 will be earned, as indicated in the following profit-volume chart:

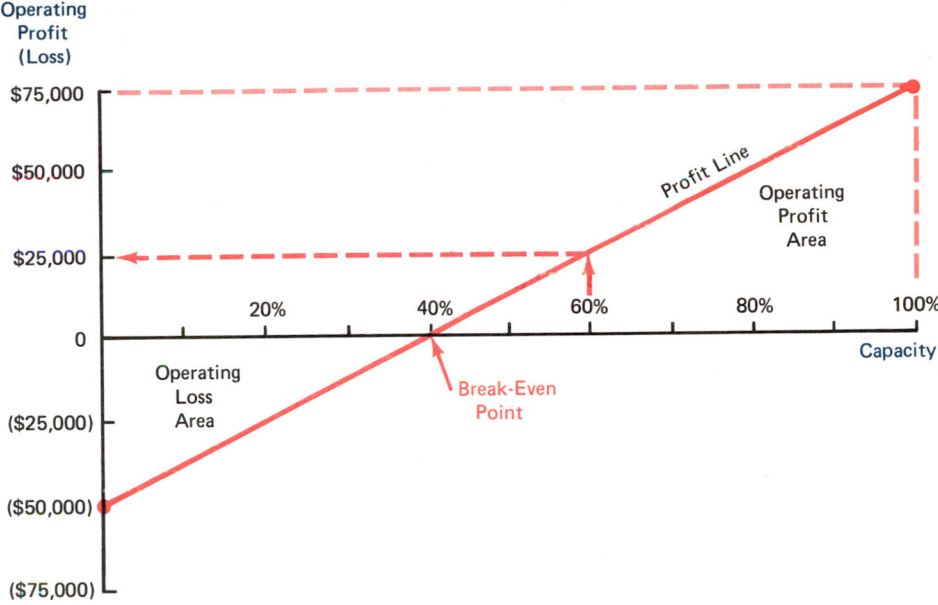

Profit-Volume Chart

The effect of changes in the unit selling price, total fixed costs, and unit variable costs on profit can be analyzed using a profit-volume chart. To illustrate, using the preceding example, assume that the effect on profit of an increase of $25,000 in fixed costs is to be evaluated. In this case, the total fixed costs would be $75,000 ($50,000 + $25,000), and the maximum operating loss at 0% of capacity would be $75,000. The maximum operating profit at 100% of capacity would be $50,000, computed as follows:

Sales..		$500,000
Costs:		
Variable costs ($500,000 × 75%)...................	$375,000	
Fixed costs..	75,000	450,000
Operating profit...		$ 50,000

A revised profit-volume chart is constructed by plotting the maximum operating loss and maximum operating profit points and drawing a line between the two points, indicating the revised profit line. The original and the revised profit-volume charts are as follows:

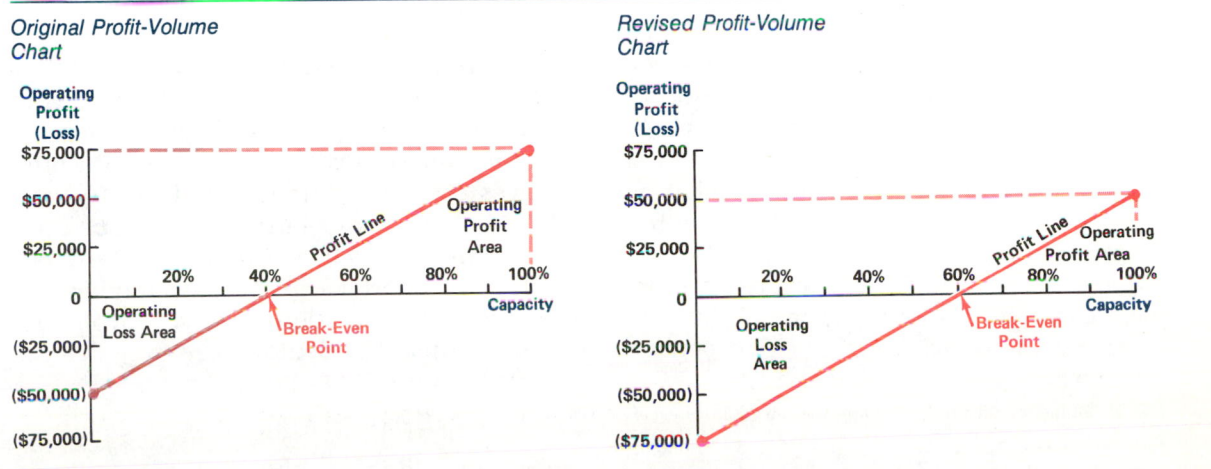

Original Profit-Volume Chart

Revised Profit-Volume Chart

The revised profit-volume chart indicates that the break-even point is 60% of capacity, which can be converted to total sales of $300,000 (maximum capacity of $500,000 × 60%). Note that the operating loss area of the chart has increased, while the operating profit area has decreased under the proposed change in fixed costs.

USE OF COMPUTERS IN COST-VOLUME-PROFIT ANALYSIS

OBJECTIVE 5
Describe the use of computers in cost-volume-profit analysis.

In the preceding paragraphs, the use of the mathematical approach to cost-volume-profit analysis and the use of the cost-volume-profit chart and the profit-volume chart for analyzing the effect of changes in selling price, costs, and volume on profits have been demonstrated. Both the mathematical and graphic approaches are becoming increasingly popular and easy to use when managers have access to a computer terminal or a microcomputer. With the wide variety of computer software that is available, managers can vary assumptions regarding selling prices, costs, and volume and can instantaneously analyze the effects of each assumption on the break-even point and profit.

BREAK-EVEN ANALYSIS—A CASE STUDY

A break-even analysis based on a multidimensional approach, rather than the traditional two-dimensional approach, was described in an article in *The Journal of Accountancy.* Such an approach is used by The Motor Convoy Inc.'s Chief Financial Officer who prepared the following break-even chart. The Motor Convoy is a Georgia-based common carrier operating primarily in the southeastern United States.

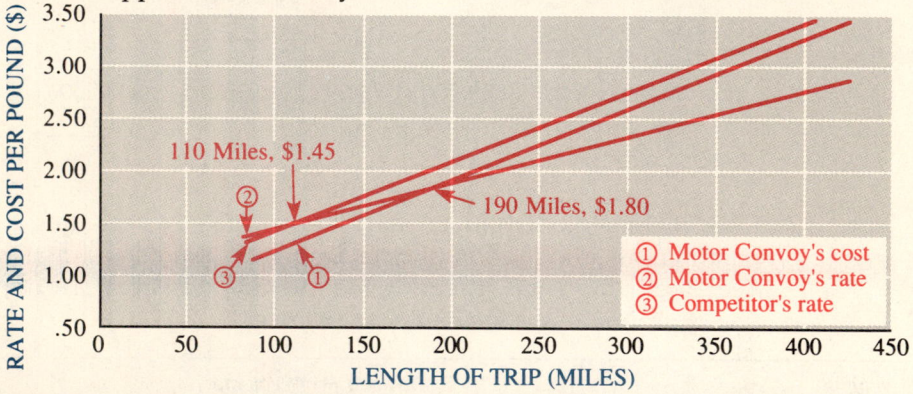

The chart illustrates a typical break-even analysis at The Motor Convoy for a normal load of 2,000 pounds over a relevant range of trips—from about 100 miles to 450 miles. The rate and cost per pound are plotted along the vertical axis, while the length of the trip (in miles) is plotted along the horizontal axis. The rate charged by The Motor Convoy's primary competitor is also graphed, so that the company can assess the effect of competition on developing its operating strategy.

In the above chart, the rate and cost curves are drawn only in the relevant range. The competitor's rate curve is parallel to The Motor Convoy's cost curve, and both rate curves cross at 110 miles. At this volume, The Motor Convoy's business should be concentrated on trips between 110 miles and 190 miles. On shorter trips, the competition is cheaper than The Motor Convoy, while on longer trips, The Motor Convoy is losing money.

Source: "Multidimensional Break-Even Analysis," *The Journal of Accountancy* (January, 1987), pp. 132–133.

SALES MIX CONSIDERATIONS

OBJECTIVE 6
Describe and illustrate the impact of sales mix considerations in cost-volume-profit analysis.

In many businesses, more than one product is sold at varying selling prices. In addition, the products often have different unit variable costs, and each product makes a different contribution to profits. Thus, the total business profit, as well as the break-even point, depends upon the proportions in which the products are sold.

Sales mix is the relative distribution of sales among the various products sold by an enterprise. For example, assume that the sales for Cascade Company during the past year, a typical year for the company, are as follows:

Product	Unit Sold	Sales Mix
A	8,000	80%
B	2,000	20
	10,000	100%

The sales mix for products A and B can be expressed as a relative percentage, as shown above, or as the ratio of 80:20. To illustrate the computation of the break-even point for Cascade Company, based on this specified sales mix, assume that fixed costs are $200,000. In addition, assume that the unit selling prices and unit variable costs for products A and B are as follows:

Product	Selling Price	Variable Cost
A	$ 90	$70
B	140	95

To compute the break-even point when several products are sold, it is useful to think of the individual products as components of one overall enterprise product. For Cascade Company, assume that this overall enterprise product is arbitrarily labeled E. The unit selling price of E can be thought of as equal to the total of the unit selling prices of the individual products A and B, each multiplied by the respective sales mix percentages. Likewise, the unit variable cost of E can be thought of as equal to the total of the unit variable costs of products A and B, multiplied by the respective sales mix percentages. The computations are as follows:

Unit selling price of E: ($90 × .8) + ($140 × .2) = $100
Unit variable cost of E: ($70 × .8) + ($95 × .2) = $75

The variable costs for enterprise product E are therefore expected to be 75% of sales ($75 ÷ $100). The break-even point can be determined in the normal manner, using the equation, as follows:

Break-Even Sales (in $) = Fixed Costs (in $) + Variable Costs (as % of Break-Even Sales)
S = $200,000 + 75%S
25%S = $200,000
S = $800,000

The break-even point of $800,000 of sales of enterprise product E is equivalent to 8,000 total sales units ($800,000 ÷ $100). Since the sales mix for products A and B is 80% and 20% respectively, the break-even quantity of A is 6,400 (8,000 × 80%) and B is 1,600 (8,000 × 20%) units.

The validity of the preceding analysis can be verified by preparing the following income statement:

Cascade Company Income Statement For Year Ended December 31, 19--			
	Product A	Product B	Total
Sales:			
6,400 units × $90	$576,000		$576,000
1,600 units × $140............................		$224,000	224,000
Total sales..	$576,000	$224,000	$800,000
Variable costs:			
6,400 units × $70	$448,000		$448,000
1,600 units × $95		$152,000	152,000
Total variable costs..........................	$448,000	$152,000	$600,000
Fixed costs			200,000
Total costs.......................................			$800,000
Operating profit................................			-0-

The effects of changes in the sales mix on the break-even point can be determined by repeating the preceding analysis, assuming a different sales mix.

SPECIAL COST-VOLUME-PROFIT RELATIONSHIPS

OBJECTIVE 7
Describe and illustrate special cost-volume-profit relationships, including the margin of safety and the contribution margin ratio.

Additional relationships can be developed from the information presented in both the mathematical and graphic approaches to cost-volume-profit analysis. Two of these relationships that are especially useful to management in decision making are discussed in the following paragraphs.

Margin of Safety

The difference between the current sales revenue and the sales at the break-even point is called the **margin of safety**. It represents the possible decrease in sales revenue that may occur before an operating loss results, and it may be stated either in terms of dollars or as a percentage of sales. For example, if the volume of sales is $250,000 and sales at the break-even point amount to $200,000, the margin of safety is $50,000 or 20%, as shown by the following computation:

$$\text{Margin of Safety} = \frac{\text{Sales} - \text{Sales at Break-Even Point}}{\text{Sales}}$$

$$\text{Margin of Safety} = \frac{\$250,000 - \$200,000}{\$250,000} = 20\%$$

The margin of safety is useful in evaluating past operations and as a guide to business planning. For example, if the margin of safety is low, management should carefully study forecasts of future sales because even a small decline in sales revenue will result in an operating loss.

Contribution Margin Ratio

Another relationship between cost, volume, and profits that is especially useful in business planning because it gives an insight into the profit potential of a firm is the **contribution margin ratio**, sometimes called the **profit-volume ratio**. This ratio indicates the percentage of each sales dollar available to cover the fixed costs and to provide operating income. For example, if the volume of sales is $250,000 and variable costs amount to $175,000, the contribution margin ratio is 30%, as shown by the following computation:

$$\text{Contribution Margin Ratio} = \frac{\text{Sales} - \text{Variable Costs}}{\text{Sales}}$$

$$\text{Contribution Margin Ratio} = \frac{\$250,000 - \$175,000}{\$250,000} = 30\%$$

The contribution margin ratio permits the quick determination of the effect on operating income of an increase or a decrease in sales volume. To illustrate, assume that the management of a firm with a contribution margin ratio of 30% is studying the effect on operating income of adding $25,000 in sales orders. Multiplying the ratio (30%) by the change in sales volume ($25,000) indicates an increase in operating income of $7,500 if the additional orders are obtained. In using the analysis in such a case, factors other than sales volume, such as the amount of fixed costs, the percentage of variable costs to sales, and the unit sales price, are assumed to remain constant. If these factors are not constant, the effect of any change must be considered in applying the analysis.

The contribution margin ratio is also useful in setting business policy. For example, if the contribution margin ratio of a firm is large and production is at a level below 100% capacity, a comparatively large increase in operating income can be expected from an increase in sales volume. On the other hand, a comparatively large decrease in operating income can be expected from a decline in sales volume. A firm in such a position might decide to devote more effort to additional sales promotion because of the large change in operating income that will result from changes in sales volume. On the other hand, a firm with a small contribution margin ratio will probably want to give more attention to reducing costs before concentrating large efforts on additional sales promotion.

LIMITATIONS OF COST-VOLUME-PROFIT ANALYSIS

OBJECTIVE 8
Describe the limitations of cost-volume-profit analysis.

The reliability of cost-volume-profit analysis depends upon the validity of several assumptions. One major assumption is that there is no change in inventory quantities during the year; that is, the quantity of units in the beginning inventory equals the quantity of units in the ending inventory. When changes in inventory quantities occur, the computations for cost-volume-profit analysis become more complex.

For cost-volume-profit analysis, a relevant range of activity is assumed, within which all costs can be classified as either fixed or variable. Within the relevant range, which is usually a range of activity within which the company is likely to operate, the unit variable costs and the total fixed costs will not change. For example, within the relevant range of activity, factory supervisory salaries are fixed. For cost-volume-profit analysis, it is assumed that a significant change in activity that would cause these salaries to change, such as adding a night shift that would double production, will not occur.

These assumptions simplify cost-volume-profit relationships, and since substantial variations in the assumptions are often uncommon in practice, cost-volume-profit analysis can be used quite effectively in decision making. Under conditions of substantial variations from the assumptions, the analysis of the cost-volume-profit relationships must be used cautiously.

CHAPTER REVIEW

KEY POINTS

OBJECTIVE 1

Cost Behavior

Cost behavior refers to the manner in which a cost changes as its activity base changes. The three most common cost classifications are fixed costs, variable costs, and mixed costs.

Fixed costs are costs that remain constant in total dollar amount as the level of activity changes. The fixed cost per unit of activity varies. As additional units are produced, the total fixed costs are spread over a larger number of units, and hence the total fixed cost per unit decreases. The appropriate activity base for a cost depends upon which base is most closely associated with the cost and the decision-making needs of management. The range of activity for which an enterprise is planning to operate is termed the enterprise's relevant range. The relevant range concept is particularly useful for analyzing cost behavior, which may change over a wide range of possible production.

Variable costs are costs that vary in total in direct proportion to changes in an activity base. Variable costs remain constant on a per unit basis with changes in the activity base.

A mixed cost has characteristics of both a fixed and a variable cost. For example, a portion of a mixed cost may remain constant in total amount, and therefore it will be a fixed cost. Another portion of a mixed cost may change in proportion to changes in the activity base, and it will therefore be a variable cost. Mixed costs are sometimes referred to as semivariable or semifixed costs. For purposes of analysis, mixed costs can generally be separated into their fixed or variable cost components.

OBJECTIVE 2

Cost-Volume-Profit Relationships

Cost-volume-profit analysis is the systematic examination of the interrelationships between selling prices, volume of sales and production, costs, expenses, and profits. It is a tool that provides management with information on the relative profitability of its various products, the probable effects of changes in selling price, and other variables.

OBJECTIVE 3

Mathematical Approach to Cost-Volume-Profit Analysis

The mathematical approach to cost-volume-profit analysis uses equations (1) to indicate the revenues necessary to achieve the break-even point in operations or (2) to indicate the revenues necessary to achieve a desired or target profit. The level of operations of an enterprise at which revenues and expired costs are exactly equal is called the break-even point. The break-even point can be determined using the following equation:

Break-Even Sales (in $) = Fixed Costs (in $) + Variable Costs (as % of Break-Even Sales)

The break-even point is raised by increases in fixed costs, increases in variable costs, or decreases in the unit selling price. The break-even point is lowered by decreases in fixed costs, decreases in variable costs, or increases in the unit selling price. By modifying the break-even equation and adding a factor for desired profit, the sales volume required to earn a desired amount of profit may be estimated.

OBJECTIVE 4

Graphic Approach to Cost-Volume-Profit Analysis

Many managers prefer to use a graphic format for cost-volume-profit analysis because the operating profit or loss for any given level of capacity can be readily determined, without the necessity of solving an equation. A cost-volume-profit chart is used to assist management in understanding the relationships between costs, sales, and operating profit or loss. Changes in the unit selling price, total fixed costs, and unit variable costs can also be analyzed using a cost-volume-profit chart. Another graphic approach to cost-volume-profit analysis, called the profit-volume chart, focuses on profitability rather than on sales revenues and costs. The effect of changes in unit selling price, total fixed costs, and unit variable costs on profit can also be analyzed using a profit-volume chart.

OBJECTIVE 5

Use of Computers in Cost-Volume-Profit Analysis

Both the mathematical and graphic approaches to cost-volume-profit analysis are becoming increasingly popular and easy to use when managers have access to a computer terminal or a microcomputer. With the wide variety of computer software that is available, managers can vary assumptions regarding selling prices, costs, and volume and can instantaneously analyze the effects of each assumption on the break-even point and profit.

OBJECTIVE 6

Sales Mix Considerations

The break-even point for an enterprise selling two or more products must be calculated on the basis of a specified sales mix. If the sales mix is assumed to be constant, the break-even point can be computed using the standard approaches.

OBJECTIVE 7

Special Cost-Volume-Profit Relationships

The difference between the current sales revenue and the sales at the break-even point is called the margin of safety. The margin of safety is useful in evaluating past operations and as a guide to business planning. Another relationship between costs, volume, and profits that is especially useful in business planning because it gives an insight into the profit potential of a firm is the contribution margin ratio. This ratio indicates the percentage of each sales dollar available to cover the fixed costs and to provide operating income. The contribution margin ratio permits the quick determination of the effect on operating income of an increase or a decrease in sales volume.

OBJECTIVE 8

Limitations of Cost-Volume-Profit Analysis

The reliability of cost-volume profit analysis depends upon the validity of several assumptions. One major assumption is that there is no change in inventory quantities during the year. Another assumption is that the analysis is conducted within a relevant range of activity within which all costs can be classified as fixed or variable. These assumptions simplify cost-volume-profit relationships, and since substantial variations in the assumptions are often uncommon in practice, cost-volume-profit analysis can be used quite effectively in decision making.

KEY TERMS

cost behavior 906
cost-volume-profit analysis 906
fixed costs 907
activity base 908
relevant range 908
variable costs 908
mixed costs 909
semivariable costs 909

high-low method 910
break-even point 912
cost-volume-profit chart 915
profit-volume chart 917
sales mix 921
margin of safety 922
contribution margin ratio 923

SELF-EXAMINATION QUESTIONS

Answers at end of chapter.

1. Which of the following statements describes variable costs?
    A. Costs that vary on a per unit basis as the activity base changes
    B. Costs that vary in total in direct proportion to changes in the activity base
    C. Costs that remain constant in total dollar amount as the level of activity changes
    D. Costs that vary on a per unit basis, but remain constant in total as the level of activity changes

2. If variable costs are 40% of sales and fixed costs are $240,000, what is the break-even point?
    A. $200,000   C. $400,000
    B. $240,000   D. None of the above

3. Based on the data presented in Question 2, how much sales would be required to realize operating profit of $30,000?
    A. $400,000   C. $600,000
    B. $450,000   D. None of the above

4. If sales were $500,000, variable costs are $200,000, and fixed costs are $240,000, what is the margin of safety?
    A. 20%   C. 60%
    B. 40%   D. None of the above

5. Based on the data presented in Question 4, what is the contribution margin ratio?
    A. 40%   C. 88%
    B. 48%   D. None of the above

ILLUSTRATIVE PROBLEM

Nissat Company expects to maintain the same inventories at the end of the year as at the beginning of the year. The estimated fixed costs for the year are $360,000 and the estimated variable costs per unit are $9. It is expected that 75,000 units will be sold at a selling price of $15 per unit. Capacity output is 80,000 units.

Instructions:

1. Determine the break-even point (a) in dollars of sales, (b) in units, and (c) in terms of capacity.
2. Construct a cost-volume-profit chart, indicating the break-even point in dollars of sales.
3. Construct a profit-volume chart, indicating the break-even point as a percentage of capacity.
4. What is the expected margin of safety?
5. What is the contribution margin ratio?

SOLUTION

(1) (a) Break-even point in dollars of sales:
$$S = \$360,000 + 60\%S$$
$$S - 60\%S = \$360,000$$
$$S = \$900,000$$

(b) Break-even point in units:
$$\$900,000 \div \$15 = 60,000 \text{ units}$$

(c) Break-even point in terms of capacity:
$$60,000 \div 80,000 = 75\%$$

(2)

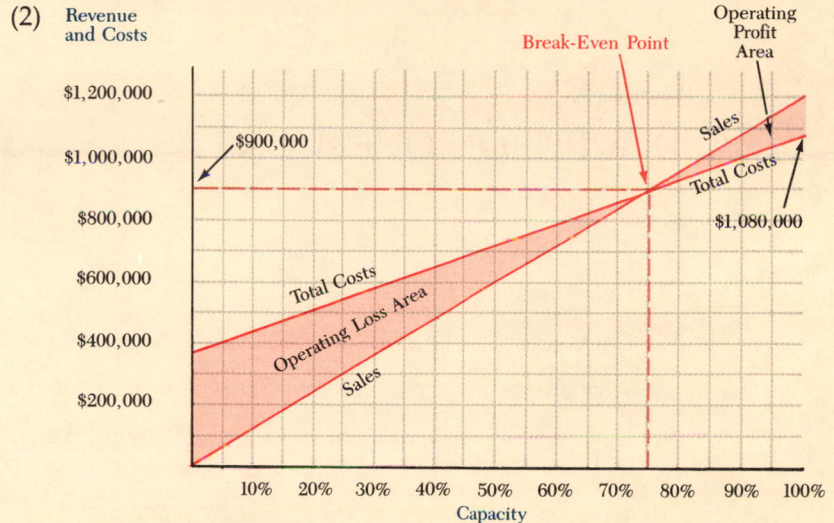

(3)

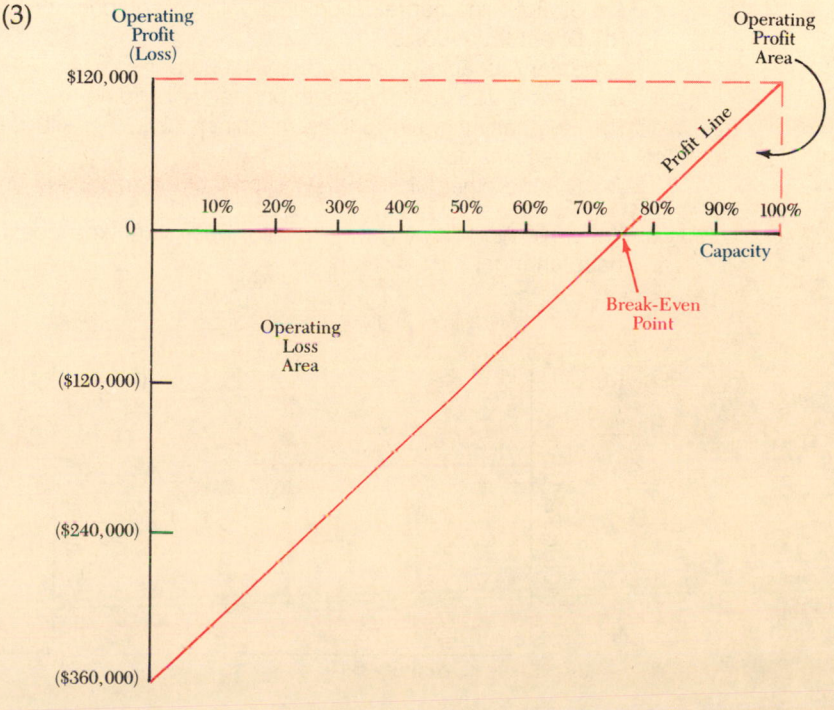

(4) Margin of safety:

Expected sales (75,000 units @ $15) $1,125,000

Break-even point 900,000

Margin of safety .... $ 225,000 or 20%

(5) Contribution margin ratio $= \dfrac{\text{Sales} - \text{Variable Costs}}{\text{Sales}}$

$$= \frac{\$1,125,000 - (75,000 \times \$9)}{\$1,125,000}$$

$$= \frac{\$450,000}{\$1,125,000}$$

$$= 40\%$$

DISCUSSION QUESTIONS

1. Define cost behavior.

2. Define cost-volume profit analysis.

3. What are the three most common classifications used for classifying cost behavior?

4. Describe the behavior of (a) total fixed costs and (b) unit fixed costs as the activity base increases.

5. Which of the following are fixed costs of production?
   (a) Property insurance premiums of $4,000 per month on plant and equipment
   (b) Straight-line depreciation on plant and equipment
   (c) Direct labor costs
   (d) Salary of factory supervisor, $40,000 per year
   (e) Rent of $25,000 per month on factory building
   (f) Electricity used in running machinery, $.02 per kilowatt-hour
   (g) Direct materials
   (h) Oil and other lubricants used on factory machinery

6. Which of the following graphs best illustrates fixed costs per unit as the activity base changes?

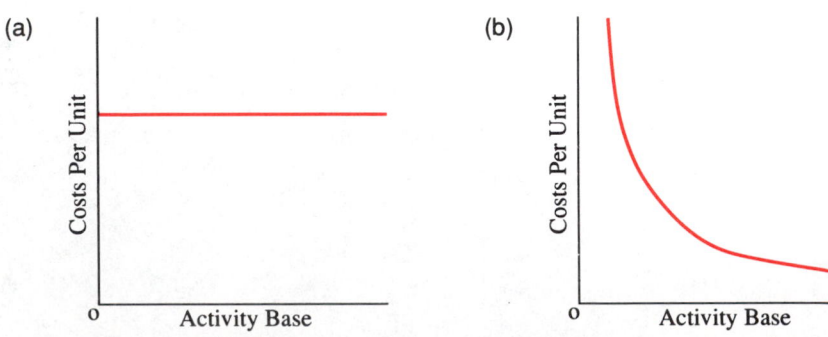

7. For Weber Tree Farm Inc., match each cost in the following table with the activity base most appropriate to it. An activity base may be used more than once.

Cost

(1) Fertilizer
(2) Dirt and packaging materials for shipping mature trees
(3) The cost of water used to water the trees
(4) Sales commissions
(5) Field managers' salaries

Activity Base

(a) Number of trees planted in the fields
(b) Number of trees shipped
(c) Number of fields
(d) Dollar amount of trees sold
(e) Dollar amount of trees planted in the fields

8. From the following list of activity bases for an automobile dealership, select the base that would be most appropriate for each of these costs: (1) preparation costs (cleaning, oil, and gasoline costs) for each car received, (2) salespersons' commission of 6% for each car sold, and (3) property taxes at the end of the year.

Activity Base

(a) Number of cars sold
(b) Number of cars received
(c) Number of cars ordered
(d) Number of cars on hand
(e) Dollar amount of cars sold
(f) Dollar amount of cars received
(g) Dollar amount of cars ordered
(h) Dollar amount of cars on hand

9. What term refers to range of activity within which the enterprise is planning to operate?

10. Describe how total variable costs and unit variable costs behave with changes in the activity base.

11. Which of the following costs would be classified as variable costs for units produced?
(a) Direct materials cost
(b) Straight-line depreciation
(c) Factory supervisor's salary
(d) Electricity costs of $.25 per kilowatt-hour
(e) Insurance premiums on factory plant and equipment of $3,000 per month
(f) Direct labor costs
(g) Oil used in operating factory machinery
(h) Janitorial supplies of $750 per month

12. Which of the following graphs illustrates how total variable costs behave with changes in total units produced?

(a)

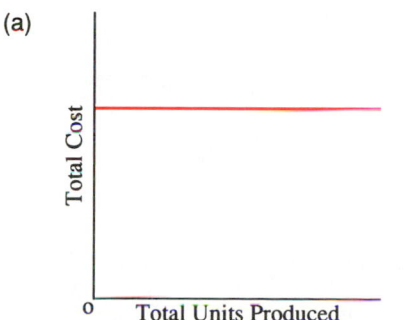

(b)

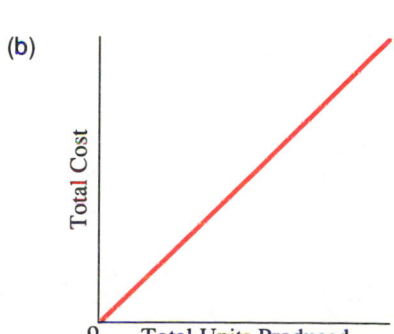

13. Which of the following graphs illustrates how unit variable costs behave with changes in total units produced?

(a)   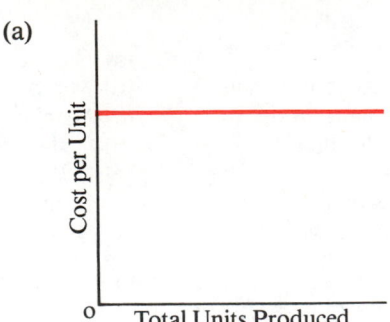   (b)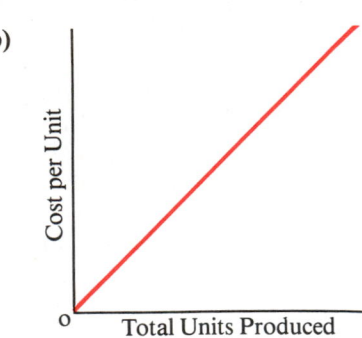

14. What type of cost has both fixed and variable cost characteristics?

15. Miller Inc. rents factory machinery for $14,000 per year and $.25 per machine hour. Which of the following graphs best illustrates the behavior of the rental costs?

(a)   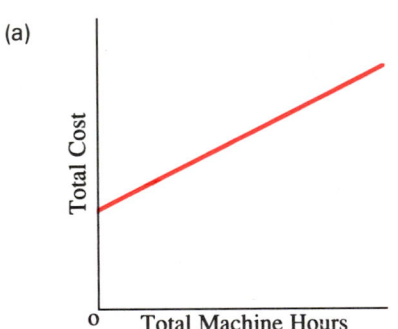   (b)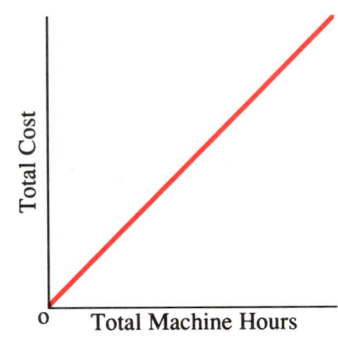

16. In applying the high-low method of estimating the fixed and variable cost components of a mixed cost, how is the variable cost component estimated?

17. In applying the high-low method of estimating the fixed and variable cost components of a mixed cost, how is the fixed cost component estimated?

18. (a) What is the break-even point? (b) What equation can be used to determine the break-even point?

19. If sales are $1,000,000, variable costs are $600,000, and fixed costs are $300,000, what is the break-even point?

20. If fixed costs are $450,000, and variable costs are 70% of sales, what is the break-even point?

21. If the unit cost of direct materials is decreased, what effect will this change have on the break-even point?

22. If the insurance rates are increased, what effect will this change in fixed costs have on the break-even point?

23. If fixed costs are $700,000 and variable costs are 80% of sales, what sales are required to realize an operating profit of $150,000?

24. What is the advantage of presenting cost-volume-profit analysis in the chart form over the equation form?

25. Name the following chart and identify the items represented by the letters *a* through *f*.

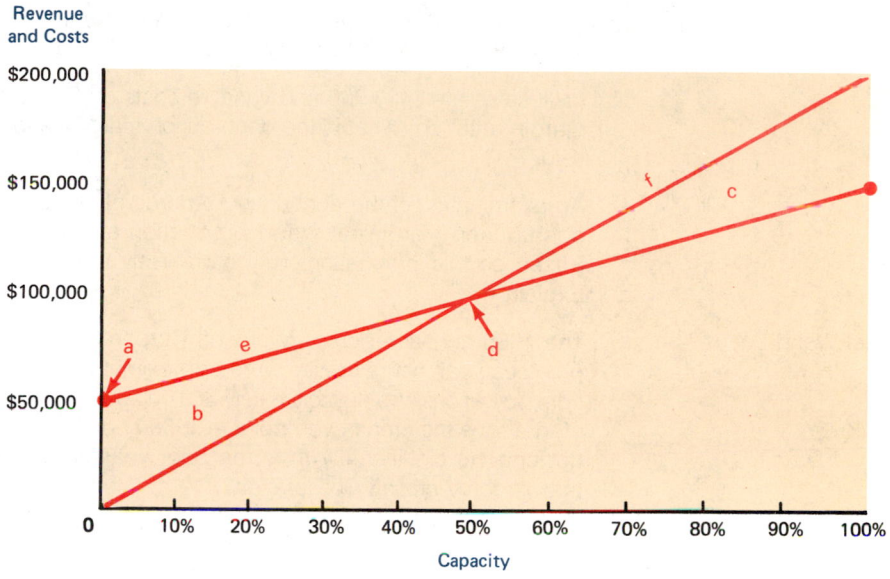

26. Name the following chart and identify the items represented by the letters *a* through *f*.

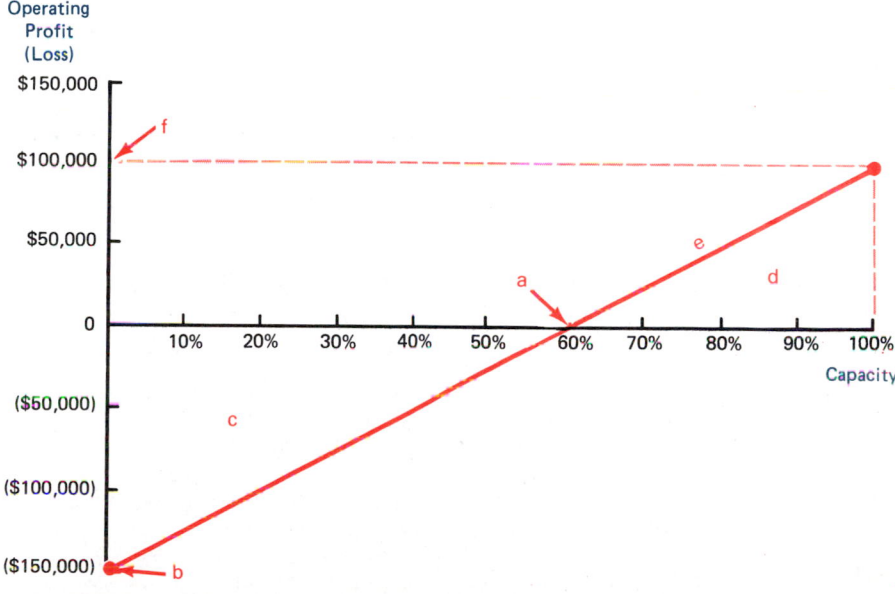

27. Both Simmons Company and Pate Company had the same sales, total costs, and operating profit for the current fiscal year, yet Simmons Company had a lower break-even point than Pate Company. Explain the reason for this difference in break-even points.

28. (a) What is meant by *sales mix*? (b) For conventional break-even analysis, is the sales mix assumed to be constant?

29. (a) What is meant by the term *margin of safety?* (b) If sales are $900,000, net income is $90,000, and sales at the break-even point are $675,000, what is the margin of safety?

30. What ratio indicates the percentage of each sales dollar that is available to cover fixed costs and provide a profit?

31. (a) If sales are $400,000 and variable costs are $272,000, what is the contribution margin ratio? (b) What is the contribution margin ratio if variable costs are 60% of sales?

32. An examination of the accounting records of Hudson Company disclosed a high contribution margin ratio and production at a level below maximum capacity. Based on this information, suggest a likely means of improving operating profit. Explain.

Real World Focus

33. The 1988 annual report of Microsoft Corporation indicates that, compared to the previous year, net revenues were approximately $240,000,000 higher and income from operations was approximately $60,000,000 higher. Microsoft Corporation operated above the break-even point in 1988 and 1987. Assuming that fixed costs did not change significantly from the prior year, what is the estimated contribution margin for Microsoft Corporation?

EXERCISES

Exercise 23–1
Classification of costs.
OBJ. 1

Following is a list of various costs incurred in producing pencils. With respect to the manufacture and sale of pencils, classify each cost as either fixed, variable, or mixed.

1. Erasers for the end of each pencil.
2. Salary of the plant superintendent.
3. Straight-line depreciation on the factory equipment.
4. Gold paint for each pencil.
5. Number 2 lead.
6. Property taxes on factory building and equipment.
7. Hourly wages of machine operators.
8. Pension cost of $.20 per employee hour on the job.
9. Lubricants used to oil machinery.
10. Rent on warehouse of $3,000 per month plus $2 per square foot of storage used.
11. Metal to hold the eraser on the end of the pencil.
12. Electricity costs of $.025 per kilowatt-hour.
13. Janitorial costs of $2,000 per month.
14. Wood costs per pencil.
15. Property insurance premiums of $1,500 per month plus $.003 for each dollar of insurance over $2,000,000.

Exercise 23–2
Identification of cost graphs.
OBJ. 1

The following cost graphs illustrate various types of cost behavior:

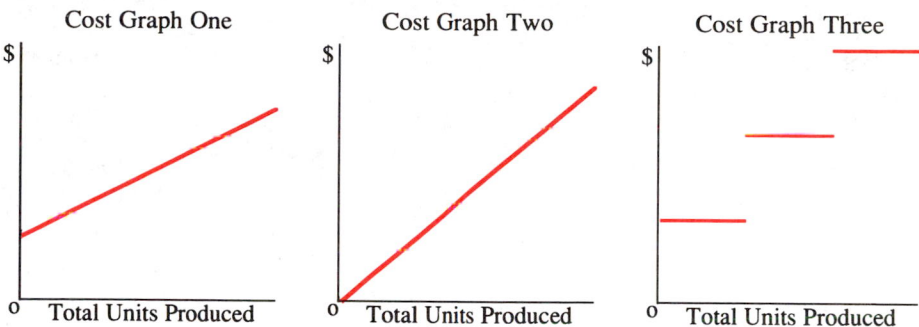

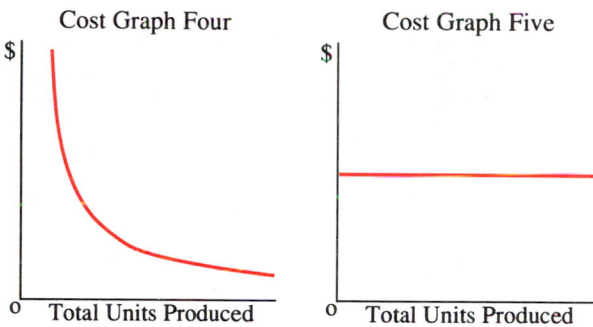

For each of the following costs, identify the cost graph that best illustrates its cost behavior as the number of units produced increases:

(a) Total direct materials cost.
(b) Per unit cost of straight-line depreciation on factory equipment.
(c) Utility costs of $2,000 per month plus $.0002 per kilowatt-hour.
(d) Salary of quality control supervisor, $2,500 per month. One quality control supervisor is needed for each 10,000 units produced.
(e) Per unit cost of direct labor.

Exercise 23–3
Relevant range and computation of fixed and variable costs.
OBJ. 1

Reynolds Inc. manufactures tool sets within a relevant range of 100,000 to 300,000 sets a year. Within this range, the following partially completed manufacturing cost schedule has been prepared:

	Tool Sets Produced		
	100,000	200,000	300,000
Total costs:			
Total variable costs	$ 700,000	(d)	(j)
Total fixed costs......................................	450,000	(e)	(k)
Total costs	$1,150,000	(f)	(l)
Cost per unit:			
Variable cost per unit..............................	(a)	(g)	(m)
Fixed cost per unit	(b)	(h)	(n)
Total cost per unit	(c)	(i)	(o)

Complete the cost schedule, identifying each cost by the appropriate letter (a) through (o).

Exercise 23–4

Analysis of a mixed cost using the high-low method of cost estimation.

OBJ. 1

McKay Company has decided to use the high-low method to estimate the fixed and variable cost components of a mixed cost. The data for the highest and lowest levels of production are as follows:

	Units Produced	Total Cost
Highest level	80,000	$370,000
Lowest level	40,000	220,000

Determine (a) the variable cost per unit and (b) the fixed cost component of the mixed cost.

Exercise 23–5

Break-even point and sales to realize operating profit.

OBJ. 3

For the current year ending March 31, Andrews Company expects fixed costs of $264,000 and variable costs equal to 67% of sales.

(a) Compute the anticipated break-even point.
(b) Compute the sales required to realize operating profit of $49,500.

Exercise 23–6

Break-even point.

OBJ. 3

SPREADSHEET PROBLEM

For the past year, Russell Company had fixed costs of $186,000 and variable costs equal to 69% of sales. All revenues and costs are expected to remain constant for the coming year, except that property taxes are expected to increase by $15,500 during the year.

(a) Compute the break-even point for the past year.
(b) Compute the anticipated break-even point for the coming year.

Exercise 23–7

Break-even point.

OBJ. 3

For the current year ending January 31, Pickett Company expects fixed costs of $140,000 and variable costs equal to 72% of sales. For the coming year, a new wage contract will increase variable costs to 75% of sales.

(a) Compute the break-even point for the current year.
(b) Compute the anticipated break-even point for the coming year, assuming that all revenues and costs are to remain constant, with the exception of the costs represented by the new wage contract.

Exercise 23–8

Break-even point.

OBJ. 3

Currently the unit selling price of a product is $24, the unit variable cost is $15, and the total fixed costs are $120,000. A proposal is being evaluated to increase the unit selling price to $25.

(a) Compute the current break-even point.
(b) Compute the anticipated break-even point, assuming that the unit selling price is increased and all costs remain constant.

Exercise 23–9

Profit-volume chart.

OBJ. 4

For the coming year, Borders Inc. anticipates fixed costs of $400,000, variable costs equal to 60% of sales, and maximum capacity of $2,000,000 of sales.

(a) What is the maximum possible operating loss?
(b) Compute the maximum possible operating profit.
(c) Construct a profit-volume chart.
(d) Estimate the break-even point as a percentage of capacity by using the profit-volume chart constructed in (c).

Exercise 23–10

Margin of safety.

OBJ. 7

(a) If Massey Company, with a break-even point at $680,000 of sales, has actual sales of $850,000, what is the margin of safety expressed (1) in dollars and (2) as a percentage of sales? (b) If the margin of safety for Rogers Company was 20%, fixed costs were $320,000, and variable costs were 75% of sales, what was the amount of actual sales?

Exercise 23–11

Contribution margin ratio.

OBJ. 7

(a) If Snowy Company budgets sales of $1,200,000, fixed costs of $100,000, and variable costs of $816,000, what is the anticipated contribution margin ratio? (b) If the contribution margin ratio for Dallas Company is 36%, sales were $950,000, and fixed costs were $185,000, what was the operating profit?

Exercise 23–12
Computation of break-even point, costs, and operating profit.

OBJ. 3, 7

For the past year, Krane Company had sales of $1,500,000, a margin of safety of 18%, and a contribution margin ratio of 36%. Compute the following:

(a) Break-even point
(b) Variable costs
(c) Fixed costs
(d) Operating profit

Exercise 23–13
Computation of break-even point, sales, and operating profit.

OBJ. 3, 7

For 1989, a company had sales of $3,000,000, fixed costs of $750,000, and a contribution margin ratio of 30%. During 1990, the variable costs were 70% of sales, the fixed costs did not change from the previous year, and the margin of safety was 20%.

(a) What was the operating profit for 1989?
(b) What was the break-even point for 1990?
(c) What was the amount of sales for 1990?
(d) What was the operating profit for 1990?

Exercise 23–14
Real World Focus.

OBJ. 3, 7

The following income statement data were taken from the 1988 financial statements of Pillsbury Company:

	(In millions)
Net sales..	$6,190.6
Costs and expenses:	
Cost of sales...	$4,322.3
Selling, general, and administrative expenses...............	1,614.5
Interest expense...	97.8
	$6,034.6
Income before income tax..	$ 156.0

Assume that the costs have been classified into the following fixed and variable components:

	Fixed	Variable
Cost of sales...	20%	80%
Selling, general, and administrative expenses............	40%	60%
Interest expense...	100%	0%

Based on the above data, determine (a) the break-even point for Pillsbury Company and (b) the margin of safety expressed in sales dollars and as a percentage of 1988 sales. Round computations to one decimal place.

PROBLEMS

Series A

Problem 23–1A
Classification of costs.

OBJ. 1

Wiley Inc. manufactures sofas for distribution to several major retail chains. The following costs are incurred in the production and sale of sofas:

(a) Fabric for sofa coverings.
(b) Springs.
(c) Hourly wages of sewing machine operators.
(d) Foam rubber for cushion fillings.
(e) Insurance premiums on property, plant, and equipment, $5,000 per year plus $.002 per insured value over $8,000,000.
(f) Straight-line depreciation on factory equipment.
(g) Wood for framing the sofas.

(h) Salary of designers.
(i) Salary of production vice-president.
(j) Rent on experimental equipment, $50 for every sofa produced.
(k) Consulting fee of $15,000 paid to efficiency specialists.
(l) Janitorial supplies, $40 for each sofa produced.
(m) Salesperson's salary, $12,000 plus 5% of the selling price of each sofa sold.
(n) Employer's FICA taxes on controller's salary of $65,000.
(o) Sewing supplies.
(p) Cartons used to ship sofas.
(q) Rental costs of warehouse, $14,000 per month.
(r) Legal fees paid to attorneys in defense of the company in a patent infringement suit, $10,000 plus $30 per hour.
(s) Property taxes on property, plant, and equipment.
(t) Electricity costs of $.00035 per kilowatt-hour.

Instructions:

Classify the preceding costs as either fixed, variable, or mixed. Use the following tabular headings and place an X in the appropriate column:

Cost	Fixed Cost	Variable Cost	Mixed Cost

Problem 23–2A
Break-even point under present and proposed conditions.
OBJ. 3

King Company operated at full capacity during 1990. Its income statement for 1990 is as follows:

Sales		$6,000,000
Cost of goods sold		3,600,000
Gross profit		$2,400,000
Operating expenses:		
Selling expenses	$1,275,000	
Administrative expenses	375,000	
Total operating expenses		1,650,000
Operating profit		$ 750,000

The division of costs between fixed and variable is as follows:

	Fixed	Variable
Cost of goods sold	30%	70%
Selling expenses	20%	80%
Administrative expenses	84%	16%

Management is considering a plant expansion program that will permit an increase of $2,000,000 in yearly sales. The expansion will increase fixed costs by $300,000, but will not affect the relationship between sales and variable costs.

Instructions:

(1) Determine for present capacity (a) the total fixed costs and (b) the total variable costs.
(2) Determine the percentage of total variable costs to sales.
(3) Compute the break-even point under present conditions.
(4) Compute the break-even point under the proposed program.
(5) Determine the amount of sales that would be necessary under the proposed program to realize the $750,000 of operating profit that was earned in 1990.
(6) Determine the maximum operating profit possible with the expanded plant.
(7) If the proposal is accepted and sales remain at the 1990 level, what will the operating profit or loss be for 1991?
(8) Based on the data given, would you recommend accepting the proposal? Explain.

Problem 23–3A
Break-even point and cost-volume-profit chart.
OBJ. 3, 4

For the coming year, Adam Company anticipates fixed costs of $75,000 and variable costs equal to 75% of sales.

Instructions:

(1) Compute the anticipated break-even point.
(2) Compute the sales required to realize an operating profit of $30,000.
(3) Construct a cost-volume-profit chart, assuming sales of $500,000 at full capacity.
(4) Determine the probable operating profit if sales total $450,000.

Problem 23–4A
Break-even point and cost-volume-profit chart.
OBJ. 3, 4

McWhorter Company operated at 80% of capacity last year, when sales totaled $800,000. Fixed costs were $240,000, and variable costs were 60% of sales. McWhorter Company is considering a proposal to spend an additional $40,000 on billboard advertising during the current year in an attempt to increase sales and utilize additional capacity.

Instructions:

(1) Construct a cost-volume-profit chart indicating the break-even point for last year.
(2) Using the cost-volume-profit chart prepared in (1), determine (a) the operating profit for last year and (b) the maximum operating profit that could have been realized during the year.
(3) Construct a cost-volume-profit chart indicating the break-even point for the current year, assuming that a noncancelable contract is signed for the additional billboard advertising. No changes are expected in unit selling price or other costs.
(4) Using the cost-volume-profit chart prepared in (3), determine (a) the operating profit if sales total $800,000 and (b) the maximum operating profit that could be realized during the year.

Problem 23–5A
Break-even point and profit-volume chart.
OBJ. 3, 4

Last year Ratcliffe Company had sales of $300,000, fixed costs of $25,000, and variable costs of $240,000. Ratcliffe Company is considering a proposal to spend $25,000 to hire a public relations firm, hoping that the company's image can be improved and sales increased. Maximum operating capacity is $500,000 of sales.

Instructions:

(1) Construct a profit-volume chart for last year.
(2) Using the profit-volume chart prepared in (1), determine for last year (a) the break-even point, (b) the operating profit, and (c) the maximum operating profit that could have been realized.
(3) Construct a profit-volume chart for the current year, assuming that the additional $25,000 expenditure is made and there is no change in unit selling price or other costs.
(4) Using the profit-volume chart prepared in (3), determine (a) the break-even point, (b) the operating profit if sales total $300,000, and (c) the maximum operating profit that could be realized.

Problem 23–6A
Sales mix and break-even point.
OBJ. 6

Data related to the expected sales of products X and Y for Crowley Company for the current year, which is typical of recent years, are as follows:

Product	Selling Price per Unit	Variable Cost per Unit	Sales Mix
X	$ 50	$30	80%
Y	125	75	20

The estimated fixed costs for the current year are $260,000.

Instructions:

(1) Determine the estimated sales revenues necessary to reach the break-even point for the current year.
(2) Based on the break-even point in (1), determine the unit sales of both X and Y for the current year.

Problem 23–7A
Break-even point
and cost-volume-
profit chart, margin
of safety, and
contribution margin
ratio.

OBJ. 3, 4, 7

MacNair Company expects to maintain the same inventories at the end of 1990 as at the beginning of the year. The total of all production costs for the year is therefore assumed to be equal to the cost of goods sold. With this in mind, the various department heads were asked to submit estimates of the costs for their departments during 1990. A summary report of these estimates is as follows:

	Estimated Fixed Cost	Estimated Variable Cost (per unit sold)
Production costs:		
Direct materials	—	$15.75
Direct labor...	—	25.50
Factory overhead.................................	$100,000	6.20
Selling expenses:		
Sales salaries and commissions	50,000	1.60
Advertising	45,200	—
Travel	31,800	—
Miscellaneous selling expense	7,000	.40
Administrative expenses:		
Office and officers' salaries...................	45,000	—
Supplies...	16,600	.25
Miscellaneous administrative expense	4,400	.30
	$300,000	$50.00

It is expected that 8,000 units will be sold at a selling price of $100 a unit. Capacity output is 15,000 units.

Instructions:

(1) Determine the break-even point (a) in dollars of sales, (b) in units, and (c) in terms of capacity.
(2) Prepare an estimated income statement for 1990.
(3) Construct a cost-volume-profit chart, indicating the break-even point in dollars of sales.
(4) What is the expected margin of safety?
(5) What is the expected contribution margin ratio?

Series B

Problem 23–1B
Classification of
costs.

OBJ. 1

Gardner Inc. manufactures blue jeans for distribution to several major retail chains. The following costs are incurred in the production and sale of blue jeans:

(a) Blue denim fabric.
(b) Insurance premiums on property, plant, and equipment, $10,000 per year plus $.003 per insured value over $5,000,000.
(c) Hourly wages of sewing machine operators.
(d) Property taxes on property, plant, and equipment.
(e) Thread.
(f) Brass buttons.
(g) Legal fees paid to attorneys in defense of the company in a patent infringement suit, $20,000 plus $50 per hour.
(h) Salary of designers.
(i) Salary of production vice-president.
(j) Rent on experimental equipment, $15,000 per year.
(k) Consulting fee of $80,000 paid to industry specialist for marketing advice.
(l) Janitorial supplies, $1,000 per month.
(m) Salesperson's salary, $12,000 plus 5% of the total sales.

(n) Electricity costs of $.00040 per kilowatt-hour.
(o) Sewing supplies.
(p) Shipping boxes used to ship orders.
(q) Rental costs of warehouse, $2,000 per month plus $.50 per square foot of storage used.
(r) Leather for patches identifying each jean style.
(s) Blue dye.
(t) Straight-line depreciation on sewing machines.

Instructions:

Classify the preceding costs as either fixed, variable, or mixed. Use the following tabular headings and place an X in the appropriate column:

Cost	Fixed Cost	Variable Cost	Mixed Cost

Problem 23–3B
Break-even point and cost-volume-profit chart.
OBJ. 3, 4

For the coming year, Melvin Company anticipates fixed costs of $280,000 and variable costs equal to 65% of sales.

Instructions:

(1) Compute the anticipated break-even point.
(2) Compute the sales required to realize an operating profit of $112,000.
(3) Construct a cost-volume-profit chart, assuming sales of $2,000,000 at full capacity.
(4) Determine the probable operating profit (loss) if sales total $700,000.

Problem 23–4B
Break-even point and cost-volume-profit chart.
OBJ. 3, 4

Purcell Company operated at 90% of capacity last year, when sales totaled $900,000. Fixed costs were $315,000, and variable costs were 55% of sales. Purcell Company is considering a proposal to spend an additional $45,000 on billboard advertising during the current year in an attempt to increase sales and utilize additional capacity.

Instructions:

(1) Construct a cost-volume-profit chart indicating the break-even point for last year.
(2) Using the cost-volume-profit chart prepared in (1), determine (a) the operating profit for last year and (b) the maximum operating profit that could have been realized during the year.
(3) Construct a cost-volume-profit chart indicating the break-even point for the current year, assuming that a noncancelable contract is signed for the additional billboard advertising. No changes are expected in unit selling price or other costs.
(4) Using the cost-volume-profit chart prepared in (3), determine (a) the operating profit if sales total $900,000 and (b) the maximum operating profit that could be realized during the year.

Problem 23–5B
Break-even point and profit-volume chart.
OBJ. 3, 4

Last year, Kaufman Company had sales of $600,000, fixed costs of $100,000, and variable costs of $450,000. Kaufman Company is considering a proposal to spend $25,000 to hire a public relations firm, hoping that the company's image can be improved and sales increased. Maximum operating capacity is $1,000,000 of sales.

Instructions:

(1) Construct a profit-volume chart for last year.
(2) Using the profit-volume chart prepared in (1), determine for last year (a) the break-even point, (b) the operating profit, and (c) the maximum operating profit that could have been realized.
(3) Construct a profit-volume chart for the current year, assuming that the additional $25,000 expenditure is made and there is no change in unit selling price or other costs.
(4) Using the profit-volume chart prepared in (3), determine (a) the break-even point, (b) the operating profit if sales total $600,000, and (c) the maximum operating profit that could be realized.

Problem 23–7B
Break-even point and cost-volume-profit chart, margin of safety, and contribution margin ratio.

OBJ. 3, 4, 7

Nexus Company expects to maintain the same inventories at the end of 1990 as at the beginning of the year. The total of all production costs for the year is therefore assumed to be equal to the cost of goods sold. With this in mind, the various department heads were asked to submit estimates of the costs for their departments during 1990. A summary report of these estimates is as follows:

	Estimated Fixed Cost	Estimated Variable Cost (per unit sold)
Production costs:		
Direct materials	—	$ 3.70
Direct labor..	—	6.50
Factory overhead.....................................	$150,000	1.20
Selling expenses:		
Sales salaries and commissions	60,000	.30
Advertising	30,000	—
Travel	14,000	—
Miscellaneous selling expense	1,700	.12
Administrative expenses:		
Office and officers' salaries....................	40,000	—
Supplies...	3,300	.16
Miscellaneous administrative expense	1,000	.02
	$300,000	$12.00

It is expected that 160,000 units will be sold at a selling price of $15 a unit. Capacity output is 200,000 units.

Instructions:

(1) Determine the break-even point (a) in dollars of sales, (b) in units, and (c) in terms of capacity.
(2) Prepare an estimated income statement for 1990.
(3) Construct a cost-volume-profit chart, indicating the break-even point in dollars of sales.
(4) What is the expected margin of safety?
(5) What is the expected contribution margin ratio?

MINI-CASE 23

Owens Company manufactures product X, which sold for $144 per unit in 1990. For the past several years, sales and operating profit have been declining. On sales of $1,008,000 in 1990, the company operated near the break-even point and used only 40% of its productive capacity. Walter Owens, your father-in-law, is considering several proposals to reverse the trend of declining sales and operating profit, and to more fully use production facilities. One proposal under consideration is to reduce the unit selling price to $120.

Your father-in-law has asked you to aid him in assessing the proposal to reduce the sales price by $24. For this purpose, he provided the following summary of the estimated fixed and variable costs for 1991, which are unchanged from 1990.

Variable costs:

Production costs	$46.50 per unit
Selling expenses	15.50 per unit
Administrative expenses	10.00 per unit

Fixed costs:

Production costs	$315,000
Selling expenses	75,000
Administrative expenses	60,000

Instructions:

(1) Determine the break-even point for 1991 in dollars, assuming (a) no change in sales price and (b) the proposed sales price.
(2) How much additional sales are necessary for Owens Company to break even in 1991 under the proposal?
(3) Determine the operating profit for 1991, assuming (a) no change in sales price and volume from 1990 and (b) the new sales price and no change in volume from 1990.
(4) Determine the maximum operating profit for 1991, assuming the proposed sales price.
(5) Briefly list factors that you would discuss with your father-in-law in evaluating the proposal.

ETHICS DISCUSSION CASE

William Keller has been controller for Yeltsin Enterprises for 18 years. Recently, Yeltsin Enterprises purchased several microcomputers to be used for analyses such as cost-volume-profit analysis. Keller does not know how to use a microcomputer, and he does not think that he should learn how to use one. He believes that he can fulfill his responsibilities as controller and adequately evaluate his staff's work on the microcomputer.

Discuss any ethical issues related to Keller's refusal to use microcomputers.

ANSWERS TO SELF-EXAMINATION QUESTIONS

1. **B** Variable costs vary in total in direct proportion to changes in the activity base (answer B). Costs that vary on a per unit basis as the activity base changes (answer A) or remain constant in total dollar amount as the level of activity changes (answer C), or both (answer D), are fixed costs.

2. **C** The break-even point of $400,000 (answer C) is that level of operations at which revenue and expired costs are exactly equal and is determined as follows:

$$\text{Break-Even Sales (in \$)} = \frac{\text{Fixed Costs (in \$)}}{+ \text{Variable Costs (as \% of Sales)}}$$

$$S = \$240,000 + 40\%S$$
$$60\%S = \$240,000$$
$$S = \$400,000$$

3. B $450,000 of sales (answer B) would be required to realize operating profit of $30,000, computed as follows:

$$\frac{\text{Sales}}{\text{(in \$)}} = \frac{\text{Fixed Costs}}{\text{(in \$)}} + \frac{\text{Variable Costs}}{\text{(as \% of Sales)}} + \frac{\text{Desired}}{\text{Profit}}$$

$$S = \$240,000 + 40\%S + \$30,000$$
$$60\%S = \$270,000$$
$$S = \$450,000$$

4. A The margin of safety of 20% (answer A) represents the possible decrease in sales revenue that may occur before an operating loss results and is determined as follows:

$$\text{Margin of Safety} = \frac{\text{Sales} - \text{Sales at Break-Even Point}}{\text{Sales}}$$

$$= \frac{\$500,000 - \$400,000}{\$500,000}$$

$$= 20\%$$

The margin of safety can also be expressed in terms of dollars and would amount to $100,000, determined as follows:

Sales	$500,000
Less sales at break-even point	400,000
Margin of safety	$100,000

5. D The contribution margin ratio indicates the percentage of each sales dollar available to cover the fixed costs and provide operating income and is determined as follows:

$$\frac{\text{Contribution Margin}}{\text{Ratio}} = \frac{\text{Sales} - \text{Variable Costs}}{\text{Sales}}$$

$$\frac{\text{Contribution Margin}}{\text{Ratio}} = \frac{\$500,000 - \$200,000}{\$500,000}$$

$$= 60\%$$

CHAPTER TWENTY-FOUR
PROFIT PLANNING FOR MANAGEMENT ANALYSIS

CHAPTER OBJECTIVES

1 Describe absorption costing and variable costing concepts.

2 Describe and illustrate the reporting of income under variable costing and absorption costing.

3 Describe and illustrate income analysis under variable costing and absorption costing.

4 Describe and illustrate management's use of variable costing and absorption costing for:

Cost control
Product pricing
Production planning
Sales analysis
Contribution margin analysis

The basic accounting systems used by manufacturers to provide accounting information useful to management in planning and controlling operations were described and illustrated in preceding chapters. In planning operations, the use of cost-volume-profit analysis, which was based on the discussion of cost behavior, was also discussed. In this chapter, two alternate concepts useful to management in planning and controlling operations— absorption costing and variable costing—are described and illustrated.

ABSORPTION COSTING AND VARIABLE COSTING

OBJECTIVE 1
Describe absorption costing and variable costing concepts.

One of the most important items affecting an enterprise's net income is the cost of goods sold. In many cases, the cost of goods sold is larger than all of the other operating expenses combined. In determining the cost of goods sold, either the absorption costing or variable costing concepts can be used.

The cost of manufactured products consists of direct materials, direct labor, and factory overhead. All such costs become a part of the finished goods inventory and remain there as an asset until the goods are sold. This conventional treatment of manufacturing costs is sometimes called **absorption costing** because all costs are "absorbed" into finished goods. Although the concept is necessary in determining historical costs and taxable income, another costing concept may be more useful to management in making decisions.

In **variable costing**, which is also termed **direct costing**, the cost of goods manufactured is composed only of variable costs—those manufacturing costs that increase or decrease as the volume of production rises or falls. These costs are the direct materials, direct labor, and only those factory overhead costs which vary with the rate of production. The remaining fac-

943

tory overhead costs, which are fixed or nonvariable items, are related to the productive capacity of the manufacturing plant and are not affected by changes in the quantity of product manufactured. Accordingly, the fixed factory overhead does not become a part of the cost of goods manufactured, but is considered an expense of the period.

The distinction between absorption costing and variable costing is illustrated in the following diagram. Note that the difference between the two costing concepts is in the treatment of the fixed manufacturing costs, which consist of the fixed factory overhead costs.

Absorption Costing Compared with Variable Costing

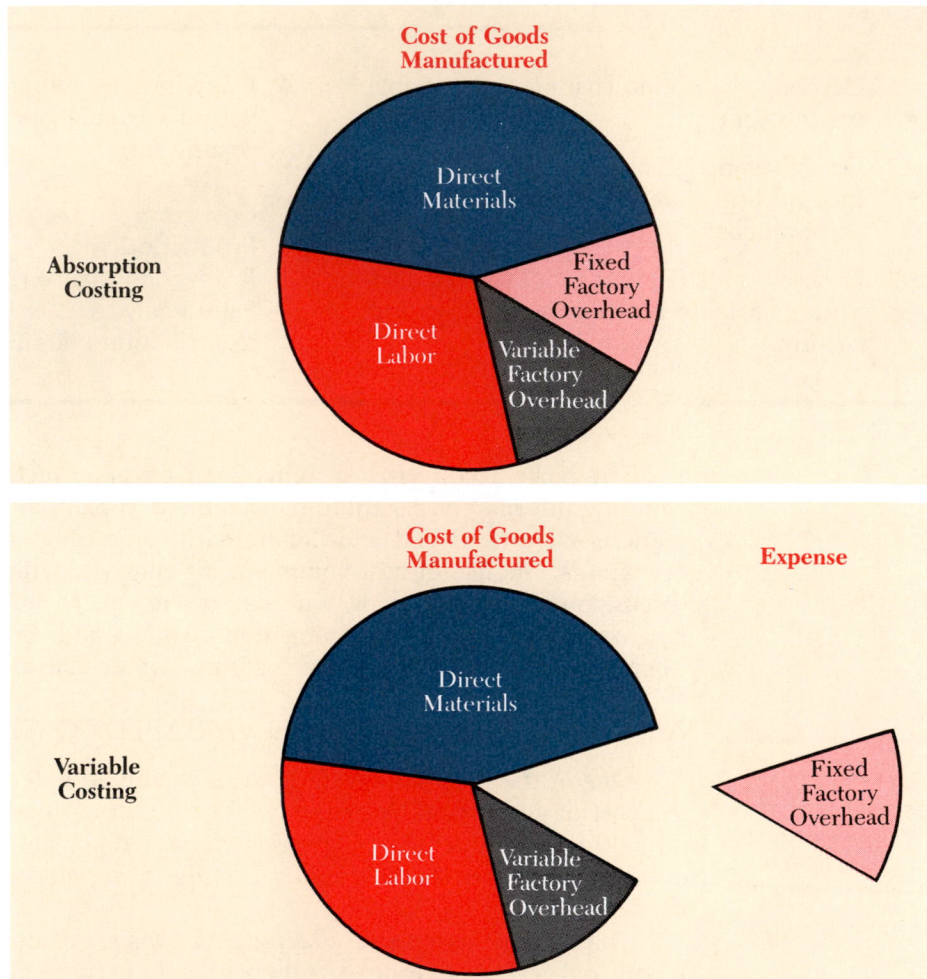

THE INCOME STATEMENT UNDER VARIABLE COSTING AND ABSORPTION COSTING

OBJECTIVE 2
Describe and illustrate the reporting of income under variable costing and absorption costing.

The arrangement of data in the variable costing income statement differs considerably from the format of the conventional absorption costing income statement. Variable costs are presented separately from fixed costs, with significant summarizing amounts inserted at intermediate points. As a basis for illustrating the differences between the two forms, assume that 15,000 units were manufactured and sold at a price of $50 and the costs were as follows:

	Total Cost	Number of Units	Unit Cost
Manufacturing costs:			
Variable...	$375,000	15,000	$25
Fixed	150,000	15,000	10
Total...	$525,000		$35
Selling and administrative expenses:			
Variable ($5 per unit sold).................	$ 75,000		
Fixed	50,000		
Total...	$125,000		

The two income statements prepared from this information are as follows. The computations in parentheses are shown as an aid to understanding.

Absorption Costing Income Statement

Absorption Costing Income Statement

Sales (15,000 × $50)..	$750,000
Cost of goods sold (15,000 × $35)...............................	525,000
Gross profit...	$225,000
Selling and administrative expenses ($75,000 + $50,000).............	125,000
Income from operations..	$100,000

Variable Costing Income Statement

Variable Costing Income Statement

Sales (15,000 × $50)		$750,000
Variable cost of goods sold (15,000 × $25)		375,000
Manufacturing margin		$375,000
Variable selling and administrative expenses...............		75,000
Contribution margin		$300,000
Fixed costs:		
Fixed manufacturing costs	$150,000	
Fixed selling and administrative expenses	50,000	200,000
Income from operations...		$100,000

The absorption costing income statement does not distinguish between variable and fixed costs. All manufacturing costs are included in the cost of goods sold. The deduction of the cost of goods sold from sales yields the intermediate amount, gross profit. Deduction of selling and administrative expenses then yields income from operations.

In contrast, the variable costing income statement includes only the variable manufacturing costs in the cost of goods sold. Deduction of the variable cost of goods sold from sales yields an intermediate amount, termed **manufacturing margin**. Deduction of the variable selling and administrative expenses yields the **contribution margin,** or **marginal income**. The fixed costs are then deducted from the contribution margin to yield income from operations.

Income Reported When Units Manufactured Equal Units Sold

In the preceding illustration, 15,000 units were manufactured and sold. Both the absorption and the variable costing income statements reported the same income from operations of $100,000. Assuming no other changes, this equality of income will always be the case when the number of units manufactured and the number of units sold are equal. Only when the number of units manufactured and the number of units sold are not equal, which creates a change in the quantity of finished goods in inventory, will the income from operations differ under the two concepts.

Income Reported When Units Manufactured Exceed Units Sold

For any period in which the number of units manufactured exceeds the number of units sold, the operating income reported under the absorption costing concept will be larger than the operating income reported under the variable costing concept. To illustrate, assume that in the preceding example only 12,000 units of the 15,000 units manufactured were sold. The two income statements that result are as follows. Computations are inserted parenthetically as an aid to understanding.

Absorption Costing Income Statement

Absorption Costing Income Statement		
Sales (12,000 × $50)...		$600,000
Cost of goods sold:		
Cost of goods manufactured (15,000 × $35)............	$525,000	
Less ending inventory (3,000 × $35)......................	105,000	
Cost of goods sold		420,000
Gross profit...		$180,000
Selling and administrative expenses		
[(12,000 × $5) + $50,000]..................................		110,000
Income from operations...		$ 70,000

Variable Costing Income Statement

Variable Costing Income Statement		
Sales (12,000 × $50)		$600,000
Variable cost of goods sold:		
Variable cost of goods manufactured		
(15,000 × $25)..	$375,000	
Less ending inventory (3,000 × $25)......................	75,000	
Variable cost of goods sold................................		300,000
Manufacturing margin		$300,000
Variable selling and administrative expenses................		60,000
Contribution margin		$240,000
Fixed costs:		
Fixed manufacturing costs	$150,000	
Fixed selling and administrative expenses	50,000	200,000
Income from operations...		$ 40,000

The $30,000 difference in the amount of income from operations ($70,000 − $40,000) is due to the different treatment of the fixed manufacturing costs. The entire amount of the $150,000 of fixed manufacturing costs is included as an expense of the period in the variable costing statement. The ending inventory in the absorption costing statement includes $30,000 (3,000 × $10) of fixed manufacturing costs. This $30,000, by being included in inventory on hand, is thus excluded from the current cost of goods sold and instead is deferred to another period.

Income Reported When Units Manufactured Are Less Than Units Sold

For any period in which the number of units manufactured is less than the number of units sold, the operating income reported under the absorption costing concept will be less than the operating income reported under the variable costing concept. To illustrate, assume that 5,000 units of inventory were on hand at the beginning of a period, 10,000 units were manufactured during the period, and 15,000 units were sold (10,000 units manufactured during the period plus the 5,000 units on hand at the beginning of the period) at $50 per unit. The manufacturing costs and selling and administrative expenses are as follows:

	Total Cost	Number of Units	Unit Cost
Beginning inventory:			
Manufacturing costs:			
Variable.....................................	$125,000	5,000	$25
Fixed	50,000	5,000	10
Total	$175,000		$35
Current period:			
Manufacturing costs:			
Variable.....................................	$250,000	10,000	$25
Fixed	150,000	10,000	15
Total	$400,000		$40
Selling and administrative expenses:			
Variable ($5 per unit sold)...............	$ 75,000		
Fixed	50,000		
Total	$125,000		

The two income statements prepared from this information are as follows. Computations are inserted parenthetically as an aid to understanding.

Absorption Costing Income Statement

Absorption Costing Income Statement

Sales (15,000 × $50)...		$750,000
Cost of goods sold:		
Beginning inventory (5,000 × $35)	$175,000	
Cost of goods manufactured (10,000 × $40)............	400,000	
Cost of goods sold		575,000
Gross profit..		$175,000
Selling and administrative expenses		
($75,000 + $50,000)		125,000
Income from operations..		$ 50,000

Variable Costing Income Statement		
Sales (15,000 × $50)		$750,000
Variable cost of goods sold:		
Beginning inventory (5,000 × $25)	$125,000	
Variable cost of goods manufactured		
(10,000 × $25)	250,000	
Variable cost of goods sold		375,000
Manufacturing margin		$375,000
Variable selling and administrative expenses		75,000
Contribution margin		$300,000
Fixed costs:		
Fixed manufacturing costs	$150,000	
Fixed selling and administrative expenses	50,000	200,000
Income from operations..		$100,000

The $50,000 difference ($100,000 − $50,000) in the amount of income from operations is attributable to the different treatment of the fixed manufacturing costs. The beginning inventory in the absorption costing income statement includes $50,000 (5,000 units × $10) of fixed manufacturing costs incurred in the preceding period. By being included in the beginning inventory, this $50,000 is included in the cost of goods sold for the current period. Under variable costing, however, this $50,000 was included as an expense in an income statement of a prior period. Therefore, none of it is included as an expense in the current period variable costing income statement.

Comparison of Income Reported Under the Two Concepts

The examples presented in the preceding sections illustrated the effects of the absorption costing and variable costing concepts on income from operations when the level of inventory changes during a period. These effects may be summarized as follows:

Units manufactured:
Equal units sold..........................	Absorption costing income equals variable costing income.
Exceed units sold.........................	Absorption costing income is greater than variable costing income.
Less than units sold......................	Absorption costing income is less than variable costing income.

INCOME ANALYSIS UNDER VARIABLE COSTING AND ABSORPTION COSTING

As was illustrated in the preceding examples, the operating income reported under the variable costing concept can differ from the operating income reported under the absorption costing concept. This difference results from changes in the quantity of the finished goods inventory, which are caused by differences in the levels of sales and production. In analyzing and evaluating operations, management should therefore be aware of the possible effects of changing inventory levels on operating income reported under the two concepts. To illustrate, assume that the following two proposed production levels are being evaluated by the management of Frand Manufacturing Company:

Proposal 1: 20,000 Units To Be Manufactured

	Total Cost	Number of Units	Unit Cost
Manufacturing costs:			
Variable..	$ 700,000	20,000	$35
Fixed	400,000	20,000	20
Total..	$1,100,000		$55
Selling and administrative expenses:			
Variable ($5 per unit sold)..................	$ 100,000		
Fixed	100,000		
Total..	$ 200,000		

Proposal 1: 20,000 Units To Be Manufactured

	Total Cost	Number of Units	Unit Cost
Manufacturing costs:			
Variable..	$ 700,000	20,000	$35
Fixed	400,000	20,000	20
Total..	$1,100,000		$55
Selling and administrative expenses:			
Variable ($5 per unit sold)..................	$ 100,000		
Fixed	100,000		
Total..	$ 200,000		

Frand Manufacturing Company has no beginning inventory and sales are estimated to be 20,000 units at $75 per unit, regardless of production levels. If the company manufactures 20,000 units, which is an amount equal to the estimated sales, income from operations under absorption costing would be $200,000. However, the reported income from operations could be increased by $80,000 by manufacturing 25,000 units and adding 5,000 units to the finished goods inventory. The absorption costing income statements illustrating this effect are as follows:

Absorption Costing Income Statements

Absorption Costing Income Statements	20,000 Units Manufactured	25,000 Units Manufactured
Sales (20,000 units × $75).........................	$1,500,000	$1,500,000
Cost of goods sold:		
Cost of goods manufactured:		
(20,000 units × $55)............................	$1,100,000	
(25,000 units × $51).............................		$1,275,000
Less ending inventory:		
(5,000 units × $51)		255,000
Cost of goods sold	$1,100,000	$1,020,000
Gross profit...	$ 400,000	$ 480,000
Selling and administrative expenses		
($100,000 + $100,000)	200,000	200,000
Income from operations.............................	$ 200,000	$ 280,000

The $80,000 increase in operating income would be caused by the allocation of the fixed manufacturing costs of $400,000 over a greater number of units of production. Specifically, an increase in production from 20,000 units to 25,000 units meant that the fixed manufacturing costs per unit decreased from $20 ($400,000 ÷ 20,000 units) to $16 ($400,000 ÷ 25,000 units). Thus, the cost of goods sold when 25,000 units are manufactured would be $4 per unit less, or $80,000 less in total (20,000 units sold times $4). Since the cost of goods sold is less, operating income is $80,000 more when 25,000 units are manufactured rather than 20,000 units.

Under the variable costing concept, income from operations would have been $200,000, regardless of the amount by which units manufactured exceeded sales, because no fixed manufacturing costs are allocated to the units manufactured. To illustrate, the following variable costing income statements are presented for Frand Manufacturing Company for the production of 20,000 units, 25,000 units, and 30,000 units. In each case, the income from operations is $200,000.

Variable Costing Income Statements

Variable Costing Income Statements			
	20,000 Units Manufactured	25,000 Units Manufactured	30,000 Units Manufactured
Sales (20,000 units × $75)....	$1,500,000	$1,500,000	$1,500,000
Variable cost of goods sold:			
Variable cost of goods manufactured:			
(20,000 units × $35).......	$ 700,000		
(25,000 units × $35).......		$ 875,000	
(30,000 units × $35).......			$1,050,000
Less ending inventory:			
(0 units × $35).............	0		
(5,000 units × $35)........		175,000	
(10,000 units × $35).......			350,000
Variable cost of goods sold..........	$ 700,000	$ 700,000	$ 700,000
Manufacturing margin	$ 800,000	$ 800,000	$ 800,000
Variable selling and administrative expenses	100,000	100,000	100,000
Contribution margin	$ 700,000	$ 700,000	$ 700,000
Fixed costs:			
Fixed manufacturing costs ..	$ 400,000	$ 400,000	$ 400,000
Fixed selling and administrative expenses ..	100,000	100,000	100,000
Total fixed costs................	$ 500,000	$ 500,000	$ 500,000
Income from operations.........	$ 200,000	$ 200,000	$ 200,000

As illustrated, if absorption costing is used, management should be careful in analyzing income from operations when large changes in inventory levels occur. Otherwise, increases or decreases in income from operations due to changes in inventory levels could be misinterpreted to be the result of operating efficiencies or inefficiencies.

BUILDING UP INVENTORY TO "HELP" EARNINGS

In conducting operations, the management of public corporations face a conflict between what is good for the business and what looks good to the public. In an effort to keep the market price of the shares of stock high, the conflict is often resolved by making decisions that look good to Wall Street. As Thomas A. Saunders III, a managing director at Morgan Stanley & Co., stated: "An enormous amount of management time in this country is devoted to managing the market price of the shares [of stock]."

In recent years, many companies have been taken private; that is, all of the shares of stock of a public corporation are acquired by a small group of investors. Frequently these companies are better managed. One reason for this better management is that the manager-owner of a private company need not worry about public perceptions of operations. The following excerpt from an article in *Business Week* illustrates one manager's reaction to a suggestion to "help" earnings by building up inventory accounted for under absorption costing.

Being private... eliminates managers' obsession with quarterly earnings and the bad habits that it creates. Shortly after he was brought in to run 12 ITT Corp. divisions that... Forstmann Little & Co. bought in 1985, CEO Richard W. Vieser was approached by a couple of the division managers who offered to "help" earnings. How? By using cash to build up inventory, they could show paper profits on increases in inventory value—just as they'd done before. Vieser laid down the law.... Don't do anything for mere appearances, especially if it wastes cash....

Source: "When Power Investors Call the Shots." *Business Week* (June 20, 1988), pp. 126–130.

MANAGEMENT'S USE OF VARIABLE COSTING AND ABSORPTION COSTING

OBJECTIVE 4
Describe and illustrate management's use of variable costing and absorption costing for:
Cost control
Product pricing
Production planning
Sales analysis
Contribution margin analysis

Both variable costing and absorption costing serve useful purposes for management. However, there are limitations to the use of both concepts in certain circumstances. Therefore, managerial accountants must carefully analyze each situation in evaluating whether variable costing reports or absorption costing reports would be more useful. In many situations, the preparation of reports under both concepts will provide useful insights. Such reports and their advantages and disadvantages are discussed in the following paragraphs.

Cost Control

As discussed in Chapter 20, all costs are controllable by someone within a business enterprise, but they are not all controllable at the same level of management. For example, plant supervisors, as members of operating management, are responsible for controlling the use of direct materials in their departments. They have no control, however, of the amount of insurance coverage or premium costs related to the buildings housing their departments. For a specific level of management, **controllable costs** are costs that it controls directly, and **noncontrollable costs** are costs that another level of management controls. This distinction, as applied to specific levels of management, is useful in fixing the responsibility for incurrence of costs and then for reporting the cost data to those responsible for cost control.

Variable manufacturing costs are controlled at the operating level because the amount of such costs varies with changes in the volume of production.

By including only variable manufacturing costs in the cost of the product, variable costing provides a product cost figure that can be controlled by operating management. The fixed factory overhead costs are ordinarily the responsibility of a higher level of management. When the fixed factory overhead costs are reported as a separate item in the variable costing income statement, they are easier to identify and control than when they are spread among units of product as they are under absorption costing.

As in the case with the fixed and variable manufacturing costs, the control of the variable and fixed operating expenses is usually the responsibility of different levels of management. Under variable costing, the variable selling and administrative expenses are reported in a separate category from the fixed selling and administrative expenses. Because they are reported in this manner, both types of operating expenses are easier to identify and control than is the case under absorption costing, where they are not reported separately.

Product Pricing

Many factors enter into the determination of the selling price of a product. The cost of making the product is clearly significant. Microeconomic theory deduces, from a set of restrictive assumptions, that income is maximized by expanding output to the volume where the revenue realized by the sale of the final unit (marginal revenue) equals the cost of that unit (marginal cost). Although the degree of exactness assumed in economic theory is rarely attainable, the concepts of marginal revenue and marginal cost are useful in setting selling prices.

In the short run, an enterprise is committed to the existing capacity of its manufacturing facilities. The pricing decision should be based upon making the best use of such capacity. The fixed costs and expenses cannot be avoided, but the variable costs and expenses can be eliminated if the company does not manufacture the product. The selling price of a product, therefore, should at least be equal to the variable costs and expenses of making and selling it. Any price above this minimum selling price contributes an amount toward covering fixed costs and expenses and providing operating income. Variable costing procedures yield data that emphasize these relationships.

In the long run, plant capacity can be increased or decreased. If an enterprise is to continue in business, the selling prices of its products must cover all costs and expenses and provide a reasonable operating income. Hence, in establishing pricing policies for the long run, information provided by absorption costing procedures is needed.

The results of a research study sponsored by the National Association of Accountants indicated that the companies studied used absorption costing in making routine pricing decisions. However, these companies regularly used variable costing as a basis for setting prices in many short-run situations.[1]

There are no simple solutions to most pricing problems. Consideration must be given to many factors of varying importance. Accounting can contribute by preparing analyses of various pricing plans for both the short run and the long run.

[1]Thomas M. Bruegelmann, Gaile A. Haessly, Michael Schiff, and Claire P. Wolfangel, *The Use of Variable Costing in Pricing Decisions*, National Association of Accountants (Montvale, New Jersey, 1986), p. vii.

VARIABLE COSTING IN PRICING DECISIONS—TWO CASE STUDIES

A firm may find it profitable to sell its existing products in new markets. For example, consumer products may be targeted for industrial usage, or the firm may decide to expand into national or international markets. Variable costing can aid management in pricing decisions related to such products, as the following case studies illustrate.

Case One

This company is a division of a Fortune 500 firm. The division identified good opportunities in Third World countries for selling its products through distributors. Since there is usually an independent agent acting as an intermediary in arranging sales between the company and the distributors in the United States, dealing with distributors eliminates the commission paid to these agents. In addition, freight costs are lower, since the distributors provide the transportation. The company passes on these cost savings and quotes prices based on variable costs rather than full costs. In this way, the company is able to meet stiff foreign competition.

Case Two

This company is engaged primarily in the manufacture and sale of wire and cable made from nonferrous metals. The company has 25 major product lines. In the initial stages of introducing a product to a new market, price is not a major factor—quality, reliability, and timeliness of delivery are far more important. Hence, in this initial introductory stage, a full cost approach is used to establish the product price. However, once a product has passed the introductory stage and has achieved a good market share, it normally runs into stiff price competition from within the market. It is at this point that variable costing enters into the pricing decision to determine the price floor. If management decides to remain in the market, a price will be set, based upon variable cost, to fight off short-run price wars from competitors.

Source: Thomas M. Bruegelmann, Gaile A. Haessly, Michael Schiff, and Claire P. Wolfangel, *The Use of Variable Costing in Pricing Decisions*, National Association of Accountants (Montvale, New Jersey, 1986), pp. 45–46.

Production Planning

Production planning also has both short-run and long-run implications. In the short run, production is limited to existing capacity, and operating decisions must be made quickly before opportunities are lost. For example, a company manufacturing products with a seasonal demand may have an opportunity to obtain an off-season order that will not interfere with its production schedule nor reduce the sales of its other products. The relevant factors for such a short-run decision are the revenues and the variable costs and expenses. If the revenues from the special order will provide a contribution margin, the order should be accepted because it will increase the company's operating income. For long-run planning, management must also consider the fixed costs and expenses.

Sales Analysis

The primary objective of the marketing and sales functions is to offer the company's products for sale at prices that will result in an adequate amount of income relative to the total assets employed. To evaluate these functions properly, management needs information concerning the profitability of various types of products and sales mixes, sales territories, and salespersons. Variable costing can make a significant contribution to management decision making in such areas:

Sales Mix Analysis. Sales mix, sometimes referred to as product mix, is generally defined as the relative distribution of sales among the various products sold. Some products are more profitable than others, and management should concentrate its sales efforts on those that will provide the maximum total operating income.

Sales mix studies are based on assumptions, such as the ability to sell one product in place of another and the ability to convert production facilities to accommodate the manufacture of one product instead of another. Proposed changes in the sales mix often affect only small segments of a company's total operations. In such cases, changes in sales mix may be possible within the limits of existing capacity, and the presentation of cost and revenue data in the variable costing form is useful in achieving the most profitable sales mix.

Two very important factors that should be determined for each product are (1) the production facilities needed for its manufacture and (2) the amount of contribution margin to be gained from its manufacture. If two or more products require equal use of limited production facilities, then management should concentrate its sales and production efforts on the product or products with the highest contribution margin per unit. The following report, which focuses on product contribution margins, is an example of the type of data needed for an evaluation of sales mix. The enterprise, which manufactures two products and is operating at full capacity, is considering whether to change the emphasis of its advertising and other promotional efforts.

Contribution Margin Statement — Unit of Product

Contribution Margin by Unit of Product
April 15, 19--

	Product A	Product B
Sales price	$6.00	$8.50
Variable cost of goods sold	3.50	5.50
Manufacturing margin	$2.50	$3.00
Variable selling and administrative expenses	1.00	1.00
Contribution margin	$1.50	$2.00

The statement indicates that Product B yields a greater amount of contribution margin per unit than Product A. Therefore, Product B provides the larger contribution to the recovery of fixed costs and expenses and realization of operating income. If the amount of production facilities used for each product is assumed to be equal, it would be desirable to increase the sales of Product B.

If two or more products require unequal use of production resources, management should concentrate its sales and production efforts on that product or products with the highest contribution margin per unit of resource. For example, assume that in the above illustration, to manufacture Product B requires twice the machine hours required for Product A. Specifically, Product B requires 2 machine hours per unit, while Product A requires only 1 machine hour per unit. Under this assumption, the contribution margin per unit of resource (machine hours) is $1.50 ($1.50 contribution margin ÷ 1 machine hour) for Product A and $1 ($2 contribution margin ÷ 2 machine hours) for Product B. Under such circumstances, a change in sales mix designed to increase sales of Product A would be desirable. To illustrate, if 2,000 additional units of Product A (requiring 2,000 machine hours) could be sold in place of 1,000 units of Product B (also requiring 2,000 machine hours), the total company contribution margin would increase by $1,000 as follows:

Additional contribution margin from sale of additional 2,000 units of Product A ($1.50 × 2,000 units)	$3,000
Less contribution margin from forgoing production and sale of 1,000 units of Product B ($2 × 1,000 units)	2,000
Increase in total contribution margin	$1,000

Sales Territory Analysis. An income statement presenting the contribution margin by sales territories is often useful to management in appraising past performance and in directing future sales efforts. The following income statement is prepared in such a format, in abbreviated form:

Contribution Margin Statement — Sales Territories

Contribution Margin Statement by Sales Territory For Month Ended July 31, 19--			
	Territory A	Territory B	Total
Sales	$315,000	$502,500	$817,500
Less variable costs	189,000	251,250	440,250
Contribution margin...........................	$126,000	$251,250	$377,250
Less fixed costs.................................			242,750
Income from operations			$134,500

In addition to the contribution margin, the **contribution margin ratio** (contribution margin divided by sales) for each territory is useful in evaluating sales territories and directing operations toward more profitable activities. For Territory A, the contribution margin ratio is 40% ($126,000 ÷ $315,000), and for Territory B the ratio is 50% ($251,250 ÷ $502,500). Consequently, more profitability could be achieved by efforts to increase the sales of Territory B relative to Territory A.

Salespersons' Analysis. A report to management for use in evaluating the sales performance of each salesperson could include total sales, gross profit, gross profit percentage, total selling expenses, and contribution to company profit. Such a report is illustrated as follows:

Salespersons' Analysis
For Six Months Ended June 30, 19--

Sales-person	Total Sales	Gross Profit	Gross Profit Percentage	Total Selling Expenses	Contribution to Company Profit
A	$300,000	$120,000	40%	$24,000	$ 96,000
B	250,000	75,000	30	22,500	52,500
C	500,000	125,000	25	35,000	90,000
D	180,000	72,000	40	18,000	54,000
E	460,000	197,800	43	27,600	170,200
F	320,000	112,000	35	22,400	89,600

The preceding report illustrates that the total sales figure is not the only consideration in evaluating a salesperson. For example, although salesperson C has the highest total sales, C's sales are not contributing as much to overall company profits as are the sales of A and E, primarily because C's sales have the lowest gross profit percentage. Of the six salespersons, E is generating the highest dollar contribution to company profit and is selling the most profitable mix of products, as measured by a gross profit percentage of 43%.

Other factors should also be considered in evaluating the performance of salespersons. For example, sales growth rates, years of experience, and actual performance compared to budgeted performance may be more important than total sales.

Contribution Margin Analysis

Another use of the contribution margin concept to assist management in planning and controlling operations focuses on differences between planned and actual contribution margins. However, mere knowledge of the differences is insufficient. Management needs information about the causes of the differences. The systematic examination of the differences between planned and actual contribution margin is termed **contribution margin analysis**.

Since contribution margin is the excess of sales over variable costs, a difference between the planned and actual contribution margin can be caused by (1) an increase or decrease in the amount of sales or (2) an increase or decrease in the amount of variable costs. An increase or decrease in either element may in turn be due to (1) an increase or decrease in the number of units sold or (2) an increase or decrease in the unit sales price or unit cost. The effect of these two factors on either sales or variable costs may be stated as follows:

1. **Quantity factor**—the effect of a difference in the number of units sold, assuming no change in unit sales price or unit cost. The quantity factor is computed as the difference between the actual quantity sold and the planned quantity sold, multiplied by the planned unit sales price or unit cost.
2. **Unit price or unit cost factor**—the effect of a difference in unit sales price or unit cost on the number of units sold. The unit price or unit cost factor is computed as the difference between the actual unit price or unit cost and the planned unit price or unit cost, multiplied by the actual quantity sold.

The following data for Noble Inc. are used as a basis for illustrating contribution margin analysis. For the sake of simplicity, a single commodity is assumed. The amount of detail entering into the analysis would be greater if several different commodities were sold, but the basic principles would not be affected.

For Year Ended December 31, 1990

	Actual	Planned	Difference (Increase or Decrease*)
Sales	$937,500	$800,000	$137,500
Less:			
Variable cost of goods sold	$425,000	$350,000	$ 75,000
Variable selling and administrative expenses	162,500	125,000	37,500
Total	$587,500	$475,000	$112,500
Contribution margin	$350,000	$325,000	$ 25,000
Number of units sold	125,000	100,000	
Per unit:			
Sales price	$7.50	$8.00	
Variable cost of goods sold	$3.40	$3.50	
Variable selling and administrative expenses	$1.30	$1.25	

The following analysis of these data shows that the favorable increase of $25,000 in the contribution margin was due in large part to an increase in the number of units sold. This increase was partially offset by a decrease in the unit sales price and an increase in the unit cost for variable selling and administrative expenses. The decrease in the unit cost for the variable cost of goods sold was an additional favorable result of 1990 operations.

Contribution Margin Analysis Report

Noble Inc.
Contribution Margin Analysis
For Year Ended December 31, 1990

Increase in amount of sales attributed to:			
Quantity factor:			
Increase in number of units sold in 1990......................................	25,000		
Planned sales price in 1990.............	× $8.00	$200,000	
Price factor:			
Decrease in unit sales price in 1990..	$.50		
Number of units sold in 1990	×125,000	62,500	
Net increase in amount of sales...........			$137,500
Increase in amount of variable cost of goods sold attributed to:			
Quantity factor:			
Increase in number of units sold in 1990......................................	25,000		
Planned unit cost in 1990	× $3.50	$ 87,500	
Unit cost factor:			
Decrease in unit cost in 1990...........	$.10		
Number of units sold in 1990	×125,000	12,500	
Net increase in amount of variable cost of goods sold			75,000
Increase in amount of variable selling and administrative expenses attributed to:			
Quantity factor:			
Increase in number of units sold in 1990......................................	25,000		
Planned unit cost in 1990	× $1.25	$ 31,250	
Unit cost factor:			
Increase in unit cost in 1990	$.05		
Number of units sold in 1990	×125,000	6,250	
Net increase in the amount of variable selling and administrative expenses..			37,500
Increase in contribution margin			$ 25,000

The data presented in the contribution margin analysis report are useful to management in evaluating past performance and in planning future operations. For example, the impact of the $.50 reduction in the unit sales price on the number of units sold and on the total sales for the year is useful information that management can use in determining whether further price reductions might be desirable. The contribution margin analysis report also highlights the impact of changes in unit variable costs and expenses. For example, the $.05 increase in the unit variable selling and administrative expenses might be a result of increased advertising expenditures. If so, the increase in the number of units sold in 1990 could be attributed to both the $.50 price reduction and the increased advertising.

CHAPTER REVIEW

KEY POINTS

OBJECTIVE 1

Absorption Costing and Variable Costing

The costs of manufacturing are direct materials, direct labor, and factory overhead. Under absorption costing, all such costs become part of the cost of goods manufactured. Under variable costing, the cost of goods manufactured is composed of only variable costs—those manufacturing costs that increase or decrease as the volume of production rises or falls. These costs are the direct materials, direct labor, and only those factory overhead costs which vary with the rate of production. The fixed factory overhead costs do not become a part of the cost of goods manufactured, but are considered an expense of the period.

OBJECTIVE 2

The Income Statement Under Variable Costing and Absorption Costing

The arrangement of data in the variable costing income statement differs considerably from the format of the conventional absorption costing income statement. The variable costing income statement includes only the variable manufacturing costs in the cost of goods sold. Deduction of the variable cost of goods sold from sales yields an intermediate amount, termed manufacturing margin. Deduction of the variable selling and administrative expenses yields the contribution margin, or marginal income. The fixed costs are then deducted from the contribution margin to yield income from operations.

A comparison of income reported under the absorption costing and variable costing concepts when the level of inventory changes during the period is summarized in the following table:

Units manufactured:
Equal units sold	Absorption costing income equals variable costing income.
Exceed units sold............	Absorption costing income is greater than variable costing income.
Less than units sold........	Absorption costing income is less than variable costing income.

OBJECTIVE 3

Income Analysis Under Variable Costing and Absorption Costing

Management should be aware of the effects of changes in inventory levels on operating income reported under variable costing and absorption costing. If absorption costing is used, increases or decreases in income from operations due to changes in inventory levels could be misinterpreted to be the result of operating efficiencies or inefficiencies.

OBJECTIVE 4

Management's Use of Variable Costing and Absorption Costing

Variable costing is especially useful at the operating level of management because the amount of variable manufacturing costs varies with changes in the volume of production and thus is controllable at this level. The fixed factory overhead costs are ordinarily controllable by a higher level of management.

In the short run, variable costing may be useful in establishing the selling price of a product. This price should be at least equal to the variable costs of making and selling the product. In the long run, however, absorption costing procedures are useful in establishing selling prices, in that all costs and a reasonable amount of operating income must be earned.

Variable costing can make a significant contribution to management decision making in analyzing and evaluating sales. Management should concentrate its sales efforts on those products that will provide the maximum total operating income. Sales mix studies emphasize the contribution margin of each product in evaluating sales territories and directing operations towards more profitable activities. In addition, a salespersons' analysis report may be useful to management in evaluating the sales performance of each salesperson. Such a report emphasizes the contribution of each salesperson to the overall company profit.

Contribution margin analysis is the systematic examination of differences between planned and actual contribution margin. Since contribution margin is the excess of sales over variable costs, a difference between the planned and actual contribution margins can be caused by (1) an increase or decrease in the amount of sales or (2) an increase or decrease in the amount of variable costs. An increase or decrease in either element may in turn be due to (1) an increase or decrease in the number of units sold or (2) an increase or decrease in the unit sales price or unit cost. The effect of these two factors on either sales or variable costs may be stated as follows:

Quantity factor—the effect of a difference in the number of units sold, assuming no change in unit sales price or unit cost. The quantity factor is computed as the difference between the actual quantity sold and the planned quantity sold, multiplied by the planned unit sales price or unit cost.

Unit price or unit cost factor—the effect of a difference in unit sales price or unit cost on the number of units sold. The unit price or unit cost factor is computed as the difference between the actual unit price or unit cost and the planned unit price or unit cost, multiplied by the actual quantity sold.

KEY TERMS

absorption costing 943
variable costing 943
manufacturing margin 945
contribution margin 945
controllable costs 951

noncontrollable costs 951
sales mix 954
contribution margin ratio 955
contribution margin analysis 956

SELF-EXAMINATION QUESTIONS

Answers at end of chapter.

1. The concept that considers the cost of products manufactured to be composed only of those manufacturing costs that vary with the rate of production is known as:
   A. absorption costing
   B. variable costing
   C. replacement cost
   D. none of the above

2. In an income statement prepared under the variable costing concept, the deduction of the variable cost of goods sold from sales yields an intermediate amount referred to as:
   A. gross profit
   B. contribution margin
   C. manufacturing margin
   D. none of the above

3.   Sales were $750,000, variable cost of goods sold was $400,000, variable selling and administrative expenses were $90,000, and fixed costs were $200,000. The contribution margin was:
     A. $60,000   C. $350,000
     B. $260,000   D.   none of the above

4.   During a year in which the number of units manufactured exceeded the number of units sold, the operating income reported under the absorption costing concept would be:
     A.   larger than the operating income reported under the variable costing concept
     B.   smaller than the operating income reported under the variable costing concept
     C.   the same as the operating income reported under the variable costing concept
     D.   none of the above

5.   If actual sales totaled $800,000 for the current year (80,000 units at $10 each) and planned sales were $765,000 (85,000 units at $9 each), the difference between actual and planned sales due to the quantity factor is:
     A.   a $50,000 increase   C.   a $45,000 decrease
     B.   a $35,000 increase   D.   none of the above

ILLUSTRATIVE PROBLEM

During the current period, McLaughlin Company sold 60,000 units of product at a selling price of $30 per unit. At the beginning of the period, there were 10,000 units in inventory and McLaughlin Company manufactured 50,000 units during the period. The manufacturing costs and selling and administrative expenses were as follows:

	Total Cost	Number of Units	Unit Cost
Beginning inventory:			
Direct materials.................................	$ 67,000	10,000	$ 6.70
Direct labor..	155,000	10,000	15.50
Variable factory overhead	18,000	10,000	1.80
Fixed factory overhead...........................	20,000	10,000	2.00
Total	$ 260,000		$26.00
Current period costs:			
Direct materials.....................................	$ 350,000	50,000	$ 7.00
Direct labor..	810,000	50,000	16.20
Variable factory overhead	90,000	50,000	1.80
Fixed factory overhead...........................	100,000	50,000	2.00
Total	$1,350,000		$27.00
Selling and administrative expenses:			
Variable..	$ 65,000		
Fixed	45,000		
Total	$ 110,000		

Instructions:

1.   Prepare an income statement based on the absorption costing concept.
2.   Prepare an income statement based on the variable costing concept.
3.   Explain the reason for the difference in the amount of operating income reported in *1* and *2*.

SOLUTION

(1) | Absorption Costing Income Statement | | |
|---|---|---|
| Sales (60,000 × $30)...................................... | | $1,800,000 |
| Cost of goods sold: | | |
| Beginning inventory (10,000 × $26).............. | $ 260,000 | |
| Cost of goods manufactured (50,000 × $27)... | 1,350,000 | |
| Cost of goods sold .... | | 1,610,000 |
| Gross profit.. | | $ 190,000 |
| Selling and administrative expenses | | |
| ($65,000 + $45,000)................................... | | 110,000 |
| Income from operations .... | | $ 80,000 |

(2) | Variable Costing Income Statement | | |
|---|---|---|
| Sales (60,000 × $30)...................................... | | $1,800,000 |
| Variable cost of goods sold: | | |
| Beginning inventory (10,000 × $24).............. | $ 240,000 | |
| Variable cost of goods manufactured | | |
| (50,000 × $25).. | 1,250,000 | |
| Variable cost of goods sold .... | | 1,490,000 |
| Manufacturing margin .... | | $ 310,000 |
| Variable selling and administrative expenses .... | | 65,000 |
| Contribution margin...................................... | | $ 245,000 |
| Fixed costs: | | |
| Fixed manufacturing costs .... | $ 100,000 | |
| Fixed selling and administrative expenses..... | 45,000 | 145,000 |
| Income from operations .... | | $ 100,000 |

(3) The difference of $20,000 ($100,000 − $80,000) in the amount of income from operations is attributable to the different treatment of the fixed manufacturing costs. The beginning inventory in the absorption costing income statement includes $20,000 (10,000 units × $2) of fixed manufacturing costs incurred in the preceding period. This $20,000 was included as an expense in a variable costing income statement of a prior period, however. Therefore, none of it is included as an expense in the current period variable costing income statement.

DISCUSSION QUESTIONS

1. What types of costs are customarily included in the cost of manufactured products under (a) the *absorption costing* concept and (b) the *variable costing* concept?

2. Which type of manufacturing cost (direct materials, direct labor, variable factory overhead, fixed factory overhead) is included in the cost of goods manufactured under the absorption costing concept but is excluded from the cost of goods manufactured under the variable costing concept?

3. At the end of the first year of operations, 1,000 units remained in the finished goods inventory. The unit manufacturing costs during the year were as follows:

Direct materials	$15.00
Direct labor...	7.50
Fixed factory overhead	3.00
Variable factory overhead...........................	1.20

What would be the cost of the finished goods inventory reported on the balance sheet under (a) the absorption costing concept and (b) the variable costing concept?

4. Which of the following costs would be included in the cost of a manufactured product according to the variable costing concept: (a) direct labor, (b) depreciation on factory building, (c) salary of factory supervisor, (d) electricity purchased to operate factory equipment, (e) property taxes on factory building, (f) rent on factory building, and (g) direct materials?

5. In the following equations, based on the variable costing income statement, identify the items designated by **X**:
   (a) Net sales $-$ **X** $=$ manufacturing margin
   (b) Manufacturing margin $-$ **X** $=$ contribution margin
   (c) Contribution margin $-$ **X** $=$ income from operations

6. In the variable costing income statement, how are the fixed manufacturing costs reported and how are the fixed selling and administrative expenses reported?

7. If the quantity of the ending inventory is larger than that of the beginning inventory, will the amount of income from operations determined by absorption costing be more than or less than the amount determined by variable costing? Explain.

8. Since all costs of operating a business are controllable, what is the significance of the term *noncontrollable cost*?

9. Discuss how financial data prepared on the basis of variable costing can assist management in the development of short-run pricing policies.

10. What term is used to refer to the relative distribution of sales among the various products manufactured?

11. A company, operating at full capacity, manufactures two products, with Product H requiring four times the production facilities as Product I. The contribution margin is $100 per unit for Product H and $30 per unit for Product I. How much would the total contribution margin be increased or decreased for the coming year if the sales of Product H could be increased by 5,000 units by changing the emphasis of promotional efforts?

12. Explain why rewarding sales personnel on the basis of total sales might not be in the best interests of an enterprise whose goal is to maximize profits.

13. Discuss the two factors affecting both sales and variable costs, to which a change in contribution margin can be attributed.

14. How is the quantity factor for an increase or decrease in the amount of sales computed in using contribution margin analysis?

15. How is the unit cost factor for an increase or decrease in the amount of variable cost of goods sold computed in using contribution margin analysis?

Real World Focus 16. Dutch Pantry Inc. operates full-service family restaurants in the eastern states. To assure consistent quality, many of the items served in the restaurants are prepared in a central food processing plant. Classify each of the following costs and expenses of the food processing plant as either variable or fixed:

(a) Garbage collection expense
(b) Salad dressing
(c) Office salaries
(d) Depreciation on equipment (straight-line method)
(e) Cooking oil
(f) Experimental costs
(g) Cleaning supplies
(h) Spices
(i) Water
(j) Property Taxes
(k) Electricity

EXERCISES

Exercise 24–1

Income statements under absorption costing and variable costing.

OBJ. 2

Northrup Company began operations on May 1 and operated at 100% of capacity during the first month. The following data summarize the results for May:

Sales (24,000 units).....................................		$900,000
Production costs (30,000 units):		
Direct materials	$225,000	
Direct labor...	270,000	
Variable factory overhead............................	75,000	
Fixed factory overhead	45,000	615,000
Selling and administrative expenses:		
Variable selling and administrative expenses ...	$206,400	
Fixed selling and administrative expenses.......	41,600	248,000

(a) Prepare an income statement in accordance with the absorption costing concept. (b) Prepare an income statement in accordance with the variable costing concept. (c) What is the reason for the difference in the amount of operating income reported in (a) and (b)?

Exercise 24–2

Cost of goods manufactured, using variable costing and absorption costing.

OBJ. 2

On August 31, the end of the first year of operations, Layton Company manufactured 50,000 units and sold 46,000 units. The following income statement was prepared, based on the variable costing concept:

Layton Company
Income Statement
For Year Ended August 31, 19--

Sales		$1,150,000
Variable cost of goods sold:		
Variable cost of goods manufactured	$750,000	
Less ending inventory.......................................	60,000	
Variable cost of goods sold		690,000
Manufacturing margin...		$ 460,000
Variable selling and administrative expenses		138,000
Contribution margin...		$ 322,000
Fixed costs:		
Fixed manufacturing costs................................	$120,000	
Fixed selling and administrative expenses............	92,000	212,000
Income from operations		$ 110,000

Determine the unit cost of goods manufactured, based on (a) the variable costing concept and (b) the absorption costing concept.

Exercise 24–3
Variable costing
income statement.
OBJ. 2

SPREADSHEET
PROBLEM

On April 30, the end of the first month of operations, Adams Company prepared the following income statement, based on the absorption costing concept:

Adams Company
Income Statement
For Month Ended April 30, 19--

Sales (9,000 units)		$720,000
Cost of goods sold:		
Cost of goods manufactured................................	$480,000	
Less ending inventory (1,000 units).......................	48,000	
Cost of goods sold..		432,000
Gross profit..		$288,000
Selling and administrative expenses..........................		140,000
Income from operations		$148,000

If the fixed manufacturing costs were $140,000 and the variable selling and administrative expenses were $108,000, prepare an income statement in accordance with the variable costing concept.

Exercise 24–4
Absorption costing
income statement.
OBJ. 2

On November 30, the end of the first month of operations, Cason Company prepared the following income statement, based on the variable costing concept:

Cason Company
Income Statement
For Month Ended November 30, 19--

Sales (15,000 units)..		$630,000
Variable cost of goods sold:		
Variable cost of goods manufactured	$450,000	
Less ending inventory (3,000 units).......................	75,000	
Variable cost of goods sold		375,000
Manufacturing margin...		$255,000
Variable selling and administrative expenses		60,000
Contribution margin..		$195,000
Fixed costs:		
Fixed manufacturing costs....................................	$ 54,000	
Fixed selling and administrative expenses..............	22,500	76,500
Income from operations		$118,500

Prepare an income statement with the absorption costing concept.

Exercise 24–5
Estimated income
statements, using
absorption and
variable costing.
OBJ. 2, 3

Prior to the first month of operations ending July 31, Godwin Company estimated the following operating results:

Sales (8,000 × $30)	$240,000
Manufacturing costs (8,000 units):	
Direct materials	48,000
Direct labor..	44,800
Variable factory overhead...	30,400
Fixed factory overhead	21,600
Fixed selling and administrative expenses.........................	11,200
Variable selling and administrative expenses	6,400

The company is evaluating a proposal to manufacture 9,000 units instead of 8,000 units.

(a) Assuming no change in sales, unit variable manufacturing costs, and fixed factory overhead and total selling and administrative expenses, prepare an estimated income statement, comparing operating results if 8,000 and 9,000 units are manufactured, in the (1) absorption costing format and (2) variable costing format. (b) What is the reason for the difference in income from operations reported for the two levels of production by the absorption costing income statement?

Exercise 24–6
Change in sales mix and contribution margin.
OBJ. 4

Van DeMark Company manufactures Products F and G and is operating at full capacity. To manufacture Product F requires three times the number of machine hours as required for Product G. Market research indicates that 6,000 additional units of Product G could be sold. The contribution margin by unit of product is as follows:

	Product F	Product G
Sales price	$200	$25
Variable cost of goods sold	120	10
Manufacturing margin	$ 80	$15
Variable selling and administrative expenses	50	6
Contribution margin	$ 30	$ 9

Prepare a tabulation indicating the increase or decrease in total contribution margin if 6,000 additional units of Product G are produced and sold.

Exercise 24–7
Contribution margin analysis — sales.
OBJ. 4

The following data for Wenstrup Inc. are available:

		For Year Ended June 30, 1990	
	Actual	Planned	Difference (Increase or Decrease*)
Sales	$544,000	$600,000	$56,000*
Less:			
Variable cost of goods sold	$289,000	$280,000	$ 9,000
Variable selling and administrative expenses	149,600	180,000	30,400*
Total	$438,600	$460,000	$21,400*
Contribution margin	$105,400	$140,000	$34,600*
Number of units sold	34,000	40,000	
Per unit:			
Sales price	$16.00	$15.00	
Variable cost of goods sold	$ 8.50	$ 7.00	
Variable selling and administrative expenses	$ 4.40	$ 4.50	

Prepare a contribution analysis of the sales quantity and price factors.

Exercise 24–8
Contribution margin analysis — variable costs.
OBJ. 4

Based upon the data in Exercise 24–7, prepare a contribution analysis of the variable costs for Wenstrup Inc. for the year ended June 30, 1990.

Exercise 24–9
Real World Focus.
OBJ. 2

The following data were adapted from the income statement of Procter & Gamble Company for the year ended June 30, 1988:

	In Millions
Net sales...	$19,336
Operating costs:	
Cost of products sold	$11,880
Marketing, administrative, and other expenses...............	5,660
Operating costs...	$17,540
Income from operations	$ 1,796

Assume that the variable amount of each category of operating costs is as follows:

Cost of products sold	$ 8,910
Marketing, administrative, and other expenses..................	4,530

Based on the above data, prepare a variable costing income statement for Proctor & Gamble Company for the year ended June 30, 1988.

PROBLEMS

Series A

Problem 24–1A
Absorption and variable costing income statements.
OBJ. 2, 3

SPREADSHEET PROBLEM

During the first month of operations ended June 30, Mattox Company manufactured 75,000 units, of which 70,000 were sold. Operating data for the month are summarized as follows:

Sales		$840,000
Manufacturing costs:		
Direct materials	$172,500	
Direct labor..	180,000	
Variable factory overhead...........................	82,500	
Fixed factory overhead	67,500	502,500
Selling and administrative expenses:		
Variable...	$224,000	
Fixed	105,000	329,000

Instructions:

(1) Prepare an income statement based on the absorption costing concept.
(2) Prepare an income statement based on the variable costing concept.
(3) Explain the reason for the difference in the amount of operating income reported in (1) and (2).

Problem 24–2A
Income statements under absorption costing and variable costing.
OBJ. 2, 3

The demand for Product M, one of numerous products manufactured by Jordan Inc., has dropped sharply because of recent competition from a similar product. The company's chemists are currently completing tests of various new formulas, and it is anticipated that the manufacture of a superior product can be started on March 1, one month hence. No changes will be needed in the present production facilities to manufacture the new product because only the mixture of the various materials will be changed.

The controller has been asked by the president of the company for advice on whether to continue production during February or to suspend the manufacture of Product M until March 1. The controller has assembled the following pertinent data:

Jordan Inc.
Estimated Income Statement—Product M
For Month Ending January 31, 19--

Sales (80,000 units).................................	$2,080,000
Cost of goods sold..................................	2,016,000
Gross profit...	$ 64,000
Selling and administrative expenses............	100,000
Loss from operations...............................	$ 36,000

The estimated production costs and selling and administrative expenses, based on a production of 80,000 units, are as follows:

Direct materials	$14.60 per unit
Direct labor...	6.75 per unit
Variable factory overhead.................................	3.10 per unit
Variable selling and administrative expenses	1.00 per unit
Fixed factory overhead	$60,000 for January
Fixed selling and administrative expenses............	20,000 for January

Sales for February are expected to drop about 40% below those of the preceding month. No significant changes are anticipated in the production costs or operating expenses. No extra costs will be incurred in discontinuing operations in the portion of the plant associated with Product M. The inventory of Product M at the beginning and end of February is expected to be inconsequential.

Instructions:

(1) Prepare an estimated income statement in absorption costing form for February for Product M, assuming that production continues during the month.
(2) Prepare an estimated income statement in variable costing form for February for Product M, assuming that production continues during the month.
(3) State the estimated operating loss arising from the activities associated with Product M for February if production is temporarily suspended.
(4) Prepare a brief statement of the advice the controller should give.

Problem 24–3A
Absorption and variable costing income statements for two months and analysis.

OBJ. 2, 3

During the first month of operations ended May 31, Addison Company manufactured 230,000 units, of which 200,000 were sold. Operating data for the month are summarized as follows:

Sales		$2,100,000
Manufacturing costs:		
Direct materials	$552,000	
Direct labor...	805,000	
Variable factory overhead.........................	253,000	
Fixed factory overhead	207,000	1,817,000
Selling and administrative expenses:		
Variable...	$120,000	
Fixed	75,000	195,000

During June, Addison Company manufactured 170,000 units and sold 200,000 units. Operating data for June are summarized as follows:

Sales		$2,100,000
Manufacturing costs:		
Direct materials	$408,000	
Direct labor...	595,000	
Variable factory overhead.........................	187,000	
Fixed factory overhead	207,000	1,397,000
Selling and administrative expenses:		
Variable...	$120,000	
Fixed	75,000	195,000

Instructions:

(1) Using the absorption costing concept, prepare income statements for (a) May and (b) June.

(2) Using the variable costing concept, prepare income statements for (a) May and (b) June.

(3) (a) Explain the reason for the differences in the amount of operating income in (1) and (2) for May.
      (b) Explain the reasons for the differences in the amount of operating income in (1) and (2) for June.

(4) Based upon your answers to (1) and (2), did Addison Company operate more profitably in May or in June? Explain.

Problem 24–4A
Salespersons' report and analysis.
OBJ. 4

Acton Company employs seven salespersons to sell and distribute its product throughout the state. Data taken from reports received from the salespersons during the current year ended June 30 are as follows:

Salesperson	Total Sales	Cost of Goods Sold	Total Selling Expenses
Barr	$540,000	$351,000	$130,500
Farmer	405,000	251,100	105,300
Griffith	340,000	207,400	71,000
Murray	360,000	226,800	84,600
Owens	225,000	135,000	46,800
Thom	290,000	171,100	67,500
York	250,000	140,000	68,400

Instructions:

(1) Prepare a report for the year, indicating total sales, gross profit, gross profit percentage, total selling expense, and contribution to company profit by salesperson.

(2) Which salesperson contributed the highest dollar amount to company profit during the year?

(3) Briefly list factors other than contribution to company profit that should be considered in evaluating the performance of salespersons.

Problem 24–5A
Variable costing income statement and effect on income of change in operations.
OBJ. 4

Fleming Company manufactures three styles of folding chairs, J, K, and L. The income statement has consistently indicated a net loss for Style K, and management is considering three proposals: (1) continue Style K, (2) discontinue Style K and reduce total output accordingly, or (3) discontinue Style K and conduct an advertising campaign to expand the sales of Style J so that the entire plant capacity can continue to be used.

If Proposal 2 is selected and Style K is discontinued and production curtailed, the annual fixed production costs and fixed operating expenses could be reduced by $45,000 and $30,000 respectively. If Proposal 3 is selected, it is anticipated that an additional annual expenditure of $60,000 for advertising Style J would yield an increase of 35% in its sales volume, and that the increased production of Style J would utilize the plant facilities released by the discontinuance of Style K.

The sales and costs have been relatively stable over the past few years, and they are expected to remain so for the foreseeable future. The income statement for the past year ended January 31 is as follows:

	Style			
	J	K	L	Total
Sales	$1,400,000	$400,000	$1,200,000	$3,000,000
Cost of goods sold:				
Variable costs...................	$ 750,000	$275,000	$ 650,000	$1,675,000
Fixed costs	250,000	85,500	210,000	545,500
Total cost of goods sold......	$1,000,000	$360,500	$ 860,000	$2,220,500
Gross profit.........................	$ 400,000	$ 39,500	$ 340,000	$ 779,500
Less operating expenses:				
Variable expenses..............	$ 130,000	$ 37,800	$ 130,000	$ 297,800
Fixed expenses	72,000	32,000	70,700	174,700
Total operating expenses	$ 202,000	$ 69,800	$ 200,700	$ 472,500
Income from operations	$ 198,000	$ (30,300)	$ 139,300	$ 307,000

Instructions:

(1) Prepare an income statement for the past year in the variable costing format. Use the following headings:

	Style		
J	K	L	Total

Data for each style should be reported through contribution margin. The fixed costs should be deducted from the total contribution margin, as reported in the "Total" column, to determine income from operations.

(2) Based on the income statement prepared in (1) and the other data presented above, determine the amount by which total annual operating income would be reduced below its present level if Proposal 2 is accepted.

(3) Prepare an income statement in the variable costing format, indicating the projected annual operating income if Proposal 3 is accepted. Use the following headings:

	Style	
J	L	Total

Data for each style should be reported through contribution margin. The fixed costs should be deducted from the total contribution margin as reported in the "Total" column. For purposes of this problem, the additional expenditure of $60,000 for advertising can be added to the fixed operating expenses.

(4) By how much would total annual income increase above its present level if Proposal 3 is accepted? Explain.

Problem 24–6A
Contribution margin analysis.
OBJ. 4

Power Inc. manufactures only one product. For the year ended December 31, 1990, the contribution margin decreased by $86,000 from the planned level of $150,000. The president of Power Inc. has expressed serious concern about the size of this decrease and has requested a follow-up report.

    The following data have been gathered from the accounting records:

		For the Year Ended December 31, 1990	
	Actual	Planned	Difference (Increase or Decrease*)
Sales	$920,000	$900,000	$ 20,000
Less:			
Variable cost of goods sold	$476,000	$450,000	$ 26,000
Variable selling and administrative			
expenses....................................	380,000	300,000	80,000
Total	$856,000	$750,000	$106,000
Contribution margin...........................	$ 64,000	$150,000	$ 86,000*
Number of units sold	80,000	75,000	
Per unit:			
Sales price	$11.50	$12.00	
Variable cost of goods sold	$ 5.95	$ 6.00	
Variable selling and administrative			
expenses....................................	$ 4.75	$ 4.00	

Instructions:

(1) Prepare a contribution margin analysis report for the year ended December 31, 1990.

(2) At a meeting of the board of directors on March 2, 1991, the president, after reviewing the contribution margin analysis report, made the following comment:

> "It looks as if the price decrease of $.50 had the effect of increasing sales. However, we lost control over the variable costs of goods sold and variable selling and administrative expenses. Let's look into these expenses and get them under control! Also, let's consider decreasing the sales price to $11 to increase sales further."

Do you agree with the president's comment? Explain.

Series B

Problem 24–1B
Absorption and variable costing income statements.
OBJ. 2, 3

During the first month of operations ended August 31, Rubin Company manufactured 320,000 units, of which 300,000 were sold. Operating data for the month are summarized as follows:

Sales		$7,500,000
Manufacturing costs:		
Direct materials	$1,600,000	
Direct labor...	2,400,000	
Variable factory overhead........................	576,000	
Fixed factory overhead	384,000	4,960,000
Selling and administrative expenses:		
Variable..	$ 720,000	
Fixed	160,000	880,000

Instructions:

(1) Prepare an income statement based on the absorption costing concept.
(2) Prepare an income statement based on the variable costing concept.
(3) Explain the reason for the difference in the amount of operating income reported in (1) and (2).

Problem 24–2B
Income statements under absorption costing and variable costing.

OBJ. 2, 3

The demand for Product K, one of numerous products manufactured by Erwin Inc., has dropped sharply because of recent competition from a similar product. The company's chemists are currently completing tests of various new formulas, and it is anticipated that the manufacture of a superior product can be started on November 1, one month hence. No changes will be needed in the present production facilities to manufacture the new product because only the mixture of the various materials will be changed.

The controller has been asked by the president of the company for advice on whether to continue production during October or to suspend the manufacture of Product K until November 1. The controller has assembled the following pertinent data:

Erwin Inc.
Estimated Income Statement — Product K
For Month Ending September 30, 19--

Sales (30,000 units)	$750,000
Cost of goods sold	690,000
Gross profit	$ 60,000
Selling and administrative expenses	92,000
Loss from operations	$ 32,000

The estimated production costs and selling and administrative expenses, based on a production of 30,000 units, are as follows:

Direct materials	$10.80 per unit
Direct labor	7.50 per unit
Variable factory overhead	2.30 per unit
Variable selling and administrative expenses	2.40 per unit
Fixed factory overhead	$72,000 for September
Fixed selling and administrative expenses	20,000 for September

Sales for October are expected to drop about 25% below those of the preceding month. No significant changes are anticipated in the production costs or operating expenses. No extra costs will be incurred in discontinuing operations in the portion of the plant associated with product K. The inventory of Product K at the beginning and end of October is expected to be inconsequential.

Instructions:

(1) Prepare an estimated income statement in absorption costing form for October for Product K, assuming that production continues during the month.
(2) Prepare an estimated income statement in variable costing form for October for Product K, assuming that production continues during the month.
(3) State the estimated operating loss arising from the activities associated with Product K for October if production is temporarily suspended.
(4) Prepare a brief statement of the advice the controller should give.

Problem 24–6B
Contribution margin analysis.

OBJ. 4

SPREADSHEET PROBLEM

Ohngren Inc. manufactures only one product. For the year ended December 31, 1990, the contribution margin decreased by $68,000 from the planned level of $180,000. The president of Ohngren Inc. has expressed serious concern about the size of this decrease and has requested a follow-up report.

The following data have been gathered from the accounting records:

| | For the Year Ended December 31, 1990 | | |
	Actual	Planned	Difference (Increase or Decrease*)
Sales	$805,000	$750,000	$ 55,000
Less:			
Variable cost of goods sold	$553,000	$480,000	$ 73,000
Variable selling and administrative expenses.................................	140,000	90,000	50,000
Total	$693,000	$570,000	$123,000
Contribution margin...........................	$112,000	$180,000	$ 68,000*
Number of units sold	700,000	600,000	
Per unit:			
Sales price	$1.15	$1.25	
Variable cost of goods sold	$ .79	$ .80	
Variable selling and administrative expenses.................................	$ .20	$ .15	

Instructions:

(1) Prepare a contribution margin analysis report for the year ended December 31, 1990.

(2) At a meeting of the board of directors on February 23, 1991, the president, after reviewing the contribution margin analysis report, made the following comment:

> "It looks as if the price decrease of $.10 had the effect of increasing sales. However, we lost control over the variable costs of goods sold and variable selling and administrative expenses. Let's look into these expenses and get them under control! Also, let's consider decreasing the sales price to $1 to increase sales further."

Do you agree with the president's comment? Explain.

MINI-CASE 24

REYNOLDS
COMPANY

Reynolds Company is a family-owned business in which you own 20% of the common stock and your brothers and sisters own the remaining shares. The employment contract of Reynolds' new president, Ellen Edward, stipulates a base salary of $75,000 per year plus 7% of income from operations in excess of $1,000,000. Reynolds uses the absorption costing method of reporting income from operations, which has averaged approximately $1,000,000 for the past several years.

Sales for 1990, Edward's first year as president of Reynolds Company, are estimated at 100,000 units at a selling price of $60 per unit. To maximize the use of Reynolds' productive capacity, Edward has decided to manufacture 150,000 units, rather than the 100,000 units of estimated sales. The beginning inventory at January 1, 1990, is insignificant in amount, and the manufacturing costs and selling and administrative expenses for the production of 100,000 and 150,000 units are as follows:

100,000 Units To Be Manufactured

	Total Cost	Number of Units	Unit Cost
Manufacturing costs:			
Variable..	$3,200,000	100,000	$32
Fixed	600,000	100,000	6
Total	$3,800,000		$38
Selling and administrative expenses:			
Variable..	$ 900,000		
Fixed	300,000		
Total	$1,200,000		

150,000 Units To Be Manufactured

	Total Cost	Number of Units	Unit Cost
Manufacturing costs:			
Variable..	$4,800,000	150,000	$32
Fixed	600,000	150,000	4
Total	$5,400,000		$36
Selling and administrative expenses:			
Variable..	$ 900,000		
Fixed	300,000		
Total	$1,200,000		

Instructions:

(1) Prepare absorption costing income statements for the year ending December 31, 1990, based upon sales of 100,000 units and the manufacture of (a) 100,000 units and (b) 150,000 units.
(2) Explain the difference in the income from operations reported in (1).
(3) Compute Edward's total salary for 1990, based on sales of 100,000 units and the manufacture of (a) 100,000 units and (b) 150,000 units.
(4) In addition to maximizing the use of Reynolds Company's productive capacity, why might Edward wish to manufacture 150,000 units rather than 100,000 units?
(5) Can you suggest an alternative way in which Edward's salary could be determined, using a base salary of $75,000 and 7% of income from operations in excess of $1,000,000, so that the salary could not be increased by simply manufacturing more units?

ETHICS DISCUSSION CASE

JoAnn Nicholas, assistant controller for Schmidt Enterprises, has been asked to prepare divisional income statements for the past 18 months. The chief executive officer intends to use the monthly statements to analyze the efficiency of each division's operations and to take corrective actions, if necessary. Nicholas did not use the variable costing format but prepared the income statements using the absorption costing format because it indicates generally more favorable operating results for the 18-month period.

Discuss whether JoAnn Nicholas is behaving in an ethical manner.

ANSWERS TO SELF-EXAMINATION QUESTIONS

1. B Under the variable costing concept (answer B), the cost of products manufactured is composed of only those manufacturing costs that increase or decrease as the volume of production rises or falls. These costs include direct materials, direct labor, and variable factory overhead. Under the absorption costing concept (answer A), all manufacturing costs become a part of the cost of the products manufactured. The absorption costing concept is required in the determination of historical cost and taxable income. The variable costing concept is often useful to management in making decisions.

2. C In the variable costing income statement, the deduction of the variable cost of goods sold from sales yields the manufacturing margin (answer C). Deduction of the variable selling and administrative expenses from manufacturing margin yields the contribution margin (answer B).

3. B The contribution margin of $260,000 (answer B) is determined by deducting all of the variable costs ($400,000 + $90,000) from sales ($750,000).

4. A In a period in which the number of units manufactured exceeds the number of units sold, the operating income reported under the absorption costing concept is larger than the operating income reported under the variable costing concept (answer A) because a portion of the fixed manufacturing costs are deferred when the absorption costing concept is used. This deferment has the effect of excluding a portion of the fixed manufacturing costs from the current cost of goods sold.

5. C A difference between planned and actual sales can be attributed to (1) a difference in the number of units sold — quantity factor and (2) a difference in the unit price — price factor. The $45,000 decrease (answer C) attributed to the quantity factor is determined as follows:

Decrease in number of units sold	5,000
Planned unit sales price	× $9
Quantity factor — decrease	$45,000

The unit price factor can be determined as follows:

Increase in unit sales price	$1
Actual number of units sold	×80,000
Price factor — increase	$80,000

The increase of $80,000 attributed to the price factor less the decrease of $45,000 attributed to the quantity factor accounts for the $35,000 increase in total sales.

CHAPTER TWENTY-FIVE

BUDGETING AND STANDARD COST SYSTEMS

CHAPTER OBJECTIVES

1 Describe the nature and objectives of budgeting.

2 Describe and illustrate the basic principles of budgeting systems.

3 Describe and illustrate the use of budget performance reports.

4 Describe and illustrate the use of flexible budgets.

5 Describe the use of computerized budgeting systems.

6 Describe the human behavioral aspects of budgeting.

7 Describe the use of standard costs in planning and controlling operations.

8 Describe and illustrate the use of variance analysis for direct materials, direct labor, and factory overhead.

9 Describe and illustrate how standards may be included in the accounts of a manufacturing enterprise.

10 Describe the importance of periodic review and revision of standards.

Effective planning and control are requisites of successful operations. Various uses of accounting data by management in performing these functions have been described and illustrated in earlier chapters. For example, the role of cost accounting in planning production and controlling costs has been discussed and illustrated. This chapter is devoted to budgeting and standard costs, two additional accounting devices that aid management in planning and controlling the operations of the business.[1]

NATURE AND OBJECTIVES OF BUDGETING

OBJECTIVE 1
Describe the nature and objectives of budgeting.

A **budget** is a formal written statement of management's plans for the future, expressed in financial terms. A budget charts the course of future action. Thus, it serves management's primary functions in the same manner that the architect's blueprints aid the builder and the navigator's flight plan aids the pilot.

A budget, like a blueprint and flight plan, should contain sound, attainable objectives. If the budget is to contain such objectives, planning must be based on careful study, investigation, and research. Management's reliance on data thus obtained lessens the role of guesswork and intuition in managing a business enterprise.

---

[1]The use of quantitative techniques to assist management in planning and controlling inventory is presented in the appendix at the end of this chapter.

In one survey, the corporate boards of directors of 600 of the 1,000 largest U.S. corporations emphasized the importance of planning to the success of a business. The results of this survey, which asked the boards to identify the most important issues facing them, are as follows:[2]

Relative Importance of Issues
Facing Boards of Directors of
Major U.S. Corporations

Issue	*Ranking as No. 1 in Importance*
Strategic planning	44%
Financial results	37
Managerial succession	17
Other	2

The essentials of budgeting are (1) the establishment of specific goals for future operations and (2) the periodic comparison of actual results with these goals. The establishment of specific goals for future operations encompasses the planning function of management. The periodic comparison of actual results with these goals encompasses the control function of management.

Although budgets are commonly associated with profit-making enterprises, they play an important role in operating most instrumentalities of government, ranging from rural school districts and small villages to gigantic agencies of the federal government. They are also an important part of the operations of churches, hospitals, and other nonprofit institutions. Individuals and family units often use budgeting techniques as an aid to careful management of resources. In this chapter, the principles of budgeting are discussed in the context of profit making enterprises.[3]

BUDGETING SYSTEMS

OBJECTIVE 2
Describe and illustrate the basic principles of budgeting systems.

The details of budgeting systems are affected by the type and degree of complexity of a particular company, the amount of its revenues, the relative importance of its various divisions, and many other factors. A budgeting system used by a large manufacturer of automobiles would obviously differ in many ways from a system designed for a small manufacturer of paper products. The differences between a system designed for factory operations of any type and a service enterprise such as an accounting firm would be even more significant.

Budgets of operating activities usually include the fiscal year of an enterprise. A year is short enough to make possible fairly dependable estimates of future operations, and yet long enough to make it possible to view the future in a reasonably broad context. However, to achieve effective control, the annual budgets must be subdivided into shorter time periods, such as quarters of the year, months, or weeks. It is also necessary to review the budgets from time to time and make any changes that become necessary as a result of unforeseen changes in general business conditions, in the particular industry, or in the individual enterprise.

---

[2]Deloitte Haskins & Sells, "Major Issues Facing Boards of Directors," *DH+S Review* (September 2, 1985), p. 6.

[3]The application of the basic budgeting principles to individuals and nonprofit organizations is presented in Appendixes D and F respectively.

A frequent variant of fiscal-year budgeting, sometimes called **continuous budgeting,** provides for maintenance of a twelve-month projection into the future. At the end of each time interval used, the twelve-month budget is revised by removing the data for the period just ended and adding the newly estimated budget data for the same period next year.

The development of budgets for the next fiscal year usually begins several months prior to the end of the current year. The responsibility for their development is ordinarily assigned to a committee made up of the budget director and such high-level executives as the controller, treasurer, production manager, and sales manager. The process is started by requesting estimates of sales, production, and other operating data from the various administrative units concerned. It is important that all levels of management and all departments participate in the preparation and submission of budget estimates. The involvement of all supervisory personnel fosters cooperation both within and among departments and also heightens awareness of each department's importance in the overall processes of the company. All levels of management are thus encouraged to set goals and to control operations in a manner that strengthens the possibilities of achieving the goals.

The process of developing budget estimates differs among enterprises. One method is to require all levels of management to start from zero and estimate sales, production, and other operating data as though operations were being started for the first time. Although this concept, called **zero-base budgeting,** has received wide attention in regard to budgeting for governmental units, it is equally useful to commercial enterprises. Another method of developing estimates is for each level of management to modify last year's budgeted amounts in light of last year's operating results and expected changes for the coming year.

The various estimates received by the budget committee are revised, reviewed, coordinated, cross-referenced, and finally put together to form the **master budget.** The estimates submitted should not be substantially revised by the committee without first giving the originators an opportunity to defend their proposals. After agreement has been reached and the master budget has been adopted by the budget committee, copies of the pertinent sections are distributed to the proper personnel in the chain of accountability. Periodic reports comparing actual results with the budget should likewise be distributed to all supervisory personnel.

As a framework for describing and illustrating budgeting, a small manufacturing enterprise will be assumed. The major parts of its master budget are as follows:

Components of Master Budget

Budgeted income statement
  Sales budget
  Cost of goods sold budget
    Production budget
    Direct materials purchases budget
    Direct labor cost budget
    Factory overhead cost budget
  Operating expenses budget

Budgeted balance sheet
  Capital expenditures budget
  Cash budget

Sales Budget

The first budget to be prepared is usually the sales budget. An estimate of the dollar volume of sales revenue serves as the foundation upon which the other budgets are based. Sales volume will have a significant effect on all of the factors entering into the determination of operating income.

The sales budget ordinarily indicates (1) the quantity of forecasted sales for each product and (2) the expected unit selling price of each product. These data are often classified by areas and/or sales representatives.

In forecasting the quantity of each product expected to be sold, the starting point is generally past sales volumes. These amounts are revised for various factors expected to affect future sales, such as a backlog of unfilled sales orders, planned advertising and promotion, expected industry and general economic conditions, productive capacity, projected pricing policy, and market research study findings. Statistical analysis can be used in this process to evaluate the effect of these factors on past sales volume. Such analysis can provide a mathematical association between past sales and the several variables expected to affect future sales.

Once the forecast of sales volume is completed, the anticipated sales revenue is then determined by multiplying the volume of forecasted sales by the expected unit sales price, as shown in the following sales budget:

Sales Budget

Product and Area	Unit Sales Volume	Unit Selling Price	Total Sales
Kennedy Company			
Sales Budget			
For Year Ending December 31, 19--			
Product X:			
Area A	208,000	$ 9.90	$2,059,200
Area B	162,000	9.90	1,603,800
Area C	158,000	9.90	1,564,200
Total	528,000		$5,227,200
Product Y:			
Area A	111,600	$16.50	$1,841,400
Area B	78,800	16.50	1,300,200
Area C	89,600	16.50	1,478,400
Total	280,000		$4,620,000
Total revenue from sales			$9,847,200

Frequent comparisons of actual sales with the budgeted volume, by product, area, and/or sales representative, will show differences between the two. Management is then able to investigate the probable cause of the significant differences and consider corrective action.

Production Budget

The number of units of each commodity expected to be manufactured to meet budgeted sales and inventory requirements is set forth in the production budget. The budgeted volume of production is based on the sum of (1) the expected sales volume and (2) the desired year-end inventory, less (3) the inventory expected to be available at the beginning of the year. A production budget is illustrated as follows:

Production Budget

Kennedy Company
Production Budget
For Year Ending December 31, 19--

	Units	
Sales	528,000	280,000
Plus desired ending inventory, December 31, 19--.....	80,000	60,000
Total	608,000	340,000
Less estimated beginning inventory, January 1, 19-- ..	88,000	48,000
Total production..	520,000	292,000

The production needs must be carefully coordinated with the sales budget to assure that production and sales are kept in balance during the period. Ideally, manufacturing operations should be maintained at capacity, and inventories should be neither excessive nor insufficient to fill sales orders.

Direct Materials Purchases Budget

The production needs shown by the production budget, combined with data on direct materials needed, provide the data for the direct materials purchases budget. The quantities of direct materials purchases necessary to meet production needs is based on the sum of (1) the materials expected to be needed to meet production requirements and (2) the desired year-end inventory, less (3) the inventory expected to be available at the beginning of the year. The quantities of direct materials required are then multiplied by the expected unit purchase price to determine the total cost of direct materials purchases.

In the following direct materials purchases budget, materials A and C are required for Product X, and materials A, B, and C are required for Product Y.

Direct Materials
Purchases Budget

Kennedy Company
Direct Materials Purchases Budget
For Year Ending December 31, 19--

	Direct Materials		
	A	B	C
Units required for production:			
Product X	390,000	—	520,000
Product Y	146,000	292,000	294,200
Plus desired ending inventory, Dec. 31, 19--......	80,000	40,000	120,000
Total	616,000	332,000	934,200
Less estimated beginning inventory, Jan. 1, 19--...	103,000	44,000	114,200
Total units to be purchased	513,000	288,000	820,000
Unit price	$ .60	$ 1.70	$ 1.00
Total direct materials purchases	$307,800	$489,600	$820,000

The timing of the direct materials purchases requires close coordination between the purchasing and production departments so that inventory levels can be maintained within reasonable limits.

Direct Labor Cost Budget

The needs indicated by the production budget provide the starting point for the preparation of the direct labor cost budget. The direct labor hours necessary to meet production needs are multiplied by the estimated hourly rate to yield the total direct labor cost. The manufacturing operations for both Products X and Y are performed in Departments 1 and 2. A direct labor cost budget is illustrated as follows:

Direct Labor Cost Budget

Kennedy Company
Direct Labor Cost Budget
For Year Ending December 31, 19--

	Department 1	Department 2
Hours required for production:		
Product X	50,000	41,600
Product Y	31,200	46,720
Total	81,200	88,320
Hourly rate	$15	$20
Total direct labor cost	$1,218,000	$1,766,400

The direct labor requirements must be carefully coordinated with available labor time to assure that sufficient labor will be available to meet production needs. Efficient manufacturing operations minimize idle time and labor shortages.

Factory Overhead Cost Budget

The factory overhead costs estimated to be necessary to meet production needs are presented in the factory overhead cost budget. For use as part of the master budget, the factory overhead cost budget usually presents the total estimated cost for each item of factory overhead. A factory overhead cost budget is illustrated as follows:

Factory Overhead Cost Budget

Kennedy Company
Factory Overhead Cost Budget
For Year Ending December 31, 19--

Indirect factory wages	$ 732,800
Supervisory salaries	360,000
Power and light	306,000
Depreciation of plant and equipment	288,000
Indirect materials	182,800
Maintenance	140,280
Insurance and property taxes	79,200
Total factory overhead cost	$2,089,080

Supplemental schedules are often prepared to present the factory overhead cost for each individual department. Such schedules enable department supervisors to direct attention to those costs for which each is solely responsible. They also aid the production manager in evaluating performance in each department.

Cost of Goods Sold Budget

The budget for the cost of goods sold is prepared by combining data on estimated inventories with the relevant estimates of quantities and costs in the budgets for (1) direct materials purchases, (2) direct labor costs, and (3) factory overhead costs. A cost of goods sold budget is illustrated as follows:

Cost of Goods Sold Budget

Kennedy Company
Cost of Goods Sold Budget
For Year Ending December 31, 19--

Finished goods inventory, January 1, 19-- ..			$1,095,600
Work in process inventory, January 1, 19-- .		$ 214,400	
Direct materials:			
Direct materials inventory, January 1, 19--	$ 250,800		
Direct materials purchases	1,617,400		
Cost of direct materials available for use ...	$1,868,200		
Less direct materials inventory, December 31, 19--	236,000		
Cost of direct materials placed in production	$1,632,200		
Direct labor	2,984,400		
Factory overhead	2,089,080		
Total manufacturing costs		6,705,680	
Total work in process during period		$6,920,080	
Less work in process inventory, December 31, 19--		220,000	
Cost of goods manufactured			6,700,080
Cost of finished goods available for sale			$7,795,680
Less finished goods inventory, December 31, 19--			1,195,000
Cost of goods sold			$6,600,680

Operating Expenses Budget

Based on past experiences, which are adjusted for future expectations, the estimated selling and administrative expenses are set forth in the operating expenses budget. For use as part of the master budget, the operating expenses budget ordinarily presents the expenses by nature or type of expenditure, such as sales salaries, rent, insurance, and advertising. An operating expenses budget is illustrated on page 983.

Detailed supplemental schedules based on departmental responsibility are often prepared for major items in the operating expenses budget. The advertising expense schedule, for example, should include such details as the advertising media to be used (newspaper, direct mail, television), quantities (column inches, number of pieces, minutes), cost per unit, frequency of use, and sectional totals. A realistic budget is prepared through careful attention to details, and effective control is achieved through assignment of responsibility to departmental supervisors.

Operating Expenses Budget

Kennedy Company
Operating Expenses Budget
For Year Ending December 31, 19--

Selling expenses:		
Sales salaries expense	$595,000	
Advertising expense	360,000	
Travel expense	115,000	
Telephone expense—selling	95,000	
Miscellaneous selling expense	25,000	
Total selling expenses		$1,190,000
Administrative expenses:		
Officers salaries expense	$360,000	
Office salaries expense	105,000	
Heating and lighting expense	75,000	
Taxes expense	60,000	
Depreciation expense—office equipment	27,000	
Telephone expense—administrative	18,000	
Insurance expense	17,500	
Office supplies expense	7,500	
Miscellaneous administrative expense	25,000	
Total administrative expenses		695,000
Total operating expenses		$1,885,000

Budgeted Income Statement

A budgeted income statement can usually be prepared from the estimated data presented in the budgets for sales, cost of goods sold, and operating expenses, with the addition of data on other income, other expense, and income tax. A budgeted income statement is illustrated as follows:

Budgeted Income Statement

Kennedy Company
Budgeted Income Statement
For Year Ending December 31, 19--

Revenue from sales		$9,847,200
Cost of goods sold		6,600,680
Gross profit		$3,246,520
Operating expenses:		
Selling expenses	$1,190,000	
Administrative expenses	695,000	
Total operating expenses		1,885,000
Income from operations		$1,361,520
Other income:		
Interest income	$ 98,000	
Other expense:		
Interest expense	90,000	8,000
Income before income tax		$1,369,520
Income tax		610,000
Net income		$ 759,520

The budgeted income statement brings together in condensed form the projection of all profit-making phases of operations and enables management to weigh the effects of the individual budgets on the profit plan for the year.

If the budgeted net income in relationship to sales or to stockholders' equity is disappointingly low, additional review of all factors involved should be undertaken in an attempt to improve the plans.

Capital Expenditures Budget

The **capital expenditures budget** summarizes future plans for acquisition of plant facilities and equipment.[4] Substantial expenditures may be needed to replace machinery and other plant assets as they wear out, become obsolete, or for other reasons fall below minimum standards of efficiency. In addition, an expansion of plant facilities may be planned to keep pace with increasing demand for a company's product or to provide for additions to the product line.

The useful life of many plant assets extends over relatively long periods of time, and the amount of the expenditures for such assets usually changes a great deal from year to year. The customary practice, therefore, is to project the plans for a number of years into the future in preparing the capital expenditures budget. A five-year capital expenditures budget is illustrated as follows:

Capital Expenditures Budget

Item	1990	1991	1992	1993	1994
Kennedy Company					
Capital Expenditures Budget					
For Five Years Ending December 31, 1994					
Machinery—					
Department 1	$400,000			$280,000	$360,000
Machinery—					
Department 2	180,000	$260,000	$560,000	200,000	
Office equipment		90,000			60,000
Total	$580,000	$350,000	$560,000	$480,000	$420,000

The various proposals recognized in the capital expenditures budget must be considered in preparing certain operating budgets. For example, the expected amount of depreciation on new equipment to be acquired in the current year must be taken into consideration when the budgets for factory overhead and operating expenses are prepared. The manner in which the proposed expenditures are to be financed will also affect the cash budget.

Cash Budget

The cash budget presents the expected inflow and outflow of cash for a day, week, month, or longer period. Receipts are classified by source and disbursements by purpose. The expected cash balance at the end of the period is then compared with the amount established as the minimum balance and the difference is the anticipated excess or deficiency for the period.

The minimum cash balance represents a safety buffer for mistakes in cash planning and for emergencies. However, the amount stated as the minimum balance need not remain fixed. It should perhaps be larger during periods of "peak" business activity than during the "slow" season. In addition, for effective cash management, much of the minimum cash balance can often be deposited in interest-bearing accounts.

---

[4]The methods of evaluating alternative capital expenditure proposals are discussed in Chapter 28.

The interrelationship of the cash budget with other budgets may be seen from the following illustration. Data from the sales budget, the various budgets for manufacturing costs and operating expenses, and the capital expenditures budget affect the cash budget. Consideration must also be given to dividend policies, plans for equity or long-term debt financing, and other projected plans that will affect cash.

Cash Budget

Kennedy Company
Cash Budget
For Three Months Ending March 31, 19--

	January	February	March
Estimated cash receipts from:			
Cash sales..........	$168,000	$185,000	$ 115,000
Collections of accounts receivable..........	699,000	712,800	572,000
Other sources (issuance of securities, interest, etc.)..........	—	—	27,000
Total cash receipts..........	$867,000	$897,800	$ 714,000
Estimated cash disbursements for:			
Manufacturing costs..........	$541,200	$557,000	$ 536,000
Operating expenses..........	150,200	151,200	140,800
Capital expenditures..........	—	144,000	80,000
Other purposes (notes, income tax, etc.)..........	47,000	20,000	160,000
Total cash disbursements..........	$738,400	$872,200	$ 916,800
Cash increase (decrease)..........	$128,600	$ 25,600	$(202,800)
Cash balance at beginning of month..........	280,000	408,600	434,200
Cash balance at end of month..........	$408,600	$434,200	$ 231,400
Minimum cash balance..........	300,000	300,000	300,000
Excess (deficiency)..........	$108,600	$134,200	$ (68,600)

In some cases, it is useful to present supplemental schedules to indicate the details of some of the amounts in the cash budget. For example, the following schedule illustrates the determination of the estimated cash receipts arising from collections of accounts receivable. For the illustration, it is assumed that the accounts receivable balance was $295,800 on January 1, and sales for each of the three months ending March 31 are $840,000, $925,000, and $575,000, respectively. Kennedy Company expects to sell 20% of its merchandise for cash. Of the sales on account, 60% are expected to be collected in the month of the sale and the remainder in the following month.

Schedule of Collections of Accounts Receivable

Kennedy Company
Schedule of Collections of Accounts Receivable
For Three Months Ending March 31, 19--

	January	February	March
January 1 balance..........	$295,800		
January sales on account (80% × $840,000):			
Collected in January (60% × $672,000)..........	403,200		
Collected in February (40% × $672,000)..........		$268,800	
February sales on account (80% × $925,000):			
Collected in February (60% × $740,000)..........		444,000	
Collected in March (40% × $740,000)..........			$296,000
March sales on account (80% × $575,000):			
Collected in March (60% × $460,000)..........			276,000
Totals..........	$699,000	$712,800	$572,000

The importance of accurate cash budgeting can scarcely be over-emphasized. An unanticipated lack of cash can result in loss of discounts, unfavorable borrowing terms on loans, and damage to the credit rating. On the other hand, an excess amount of idle cash also shows poor management. When the budget shows periods of excess cash, such funds can be used to reduce loans or purchase investments in readily marketable income-producing securities. Reference to the Kennedy Company cash budget shows excess cash during January and February and a deficiency during March.

GETTING THE MOST OUT OF YOUR CASH

Most businesses could reduce their interest expenses if they would improve their management of cash. The goal of cash management is to use the company's money to maximize earnings while paying all liabilities and maintaining adequate liquidity. Accelerating collections, delaying disbursements, and getting the needed information about the cash status are the foundation of effective cash management.

One of the most efficient cash management tools is the wire transfer, which is the safest and fastest way to move a large sum of money quickly. It is used by having your customers who monthly pay you large amounts wire the money directly to your bank.

Another efficient cash management tool is the lockbox, which is a system that has your customers mail their remittance checks directly to a post office box in the name of your company. You authorize your bank to collect the customers' payments, and each item is deposited directly to the bank, according to your instructions. A lockbox greatly accelerates the transformation of your receivables into cash, and it eliminates delays from mail and processing.

If your company is borrowing from a bank and not using its cash as effectively as it can, your company is losing interest every day. If the money is not needed on a day-by-day basis, you should invest the excess money in overnight, one- or two-week or 30-day instruments. If you are required to keep a compensating balance, monitor the account so that you do not keep more than the required amount.

Every morning, through phone calls or through a third party, you can receive information on your previous night's bank balances, credits, and disbursements in order to determine what you have available for investments that day. You can arrange for your bank to transfer the money out of your account and into investments every day.

Source: Allen E. Fishman, "Getting the Most Out of Your Cash," *St. Louis Post-Dispatch* (May 5, 1986), p. 14A.

Budgeted Balance Sheet

The budgeted balance sheet presents estimated details of the financial condition at the end of a budget period, assuming that all budgeted operating and financing plans are fulfilled. It need not differ in form and arrangement from a balance sheet based on actual data in the accounts and hence is not illustrated. If the budgeted balance sheet shows weaknesses in financial position, such as an abnormally large amount of current liabilities in relation to current assets, or excessive long-term debt in relation to stockholders' equity, the relevant factors should be given further study so that corrective action may be taken.

BUDGET PERFORMANCE REPORTS

A **budget performance report** comparing actual results with the budgeted figures should be prepared periodically for each budget. This "feedback" enables management to determine the cause of significant differences and to seek means of preventing their recurrence. If corrective action cannot be taken because of changed conditions that have occurred since the budget was prepared, future budget figures should be revised accordingly.

A budget performance report for Kennedy Company is illustrated as follows:

Budget Performance Report

Kennedy Company Budget Performance Report—Factory Overhead Cost, Department 1 For Month Ended June 30, 19--	Budget	Actual	Over	Under
Indirect factory wages	$30,200	$30,400	$200	
Supervisory salaries	15,000	15,000		
Power and light	12,800	12,750		$ 50
Depreciation of plant and equipment	12,000	12,000		
Indirect materials	7,600	8,250	650	
Maintenance	5,800	5,700		100
Insurance and property taxes	3,300	3,300		
	$86,700	$87,400	$850	$150

The amounts reported in the "Budget" column were obtained from supplemental schedules accompanying the master budget. The amounts in the "Actual" column are the costs actually incurred. The last two columns show the amounts by which actual costs exceeded or were below budgeted figures. As shown in the illustration, there were differences between the actual and budgeted amounts for some of the items of overhead cost. The cause of the significant difference in indirect materials cost should be investigated, and an attempt to find means of corrective action should be made. For example, if the difference in indirect materials cost were found to be caused by a marketwide increase in the price of materials used, a corrective action may not be possible. On the other hand, if the difference resulted from the inefficient use of materials in the production process, it may be possible to eliminate the inefficiency and effect a savings in future indirect materials costs.

FLEXIBLE BUDGETS

In the discussion of budget systems, it has been assumed that the amount of sales and the level of manufacturing activity achieved during a period approximated the goals established in the budgets. When substantial changes in expectations occur during a budget period, the budgets should be revised to give effect to such changes. Otherwise, they will be of questionable value as incentives and instruments for controlling costs and expenses.

The effect of changes in volume of activity can be "built in" to the budget system by what are termed **flexible budgets**. Particularly useful in estimating and controlling factory overhead costs and operating expenses, a flexible budget is in reality a series of budgets for varying rates of activity. To illustrate, assume that because of extreme variations in demand and other uncontrollable factors, the output of a particular manufacturing enterprise fluctuates widely from month to month. In such circumstances, the total factory overhead costs incurred during periods of high activity are certain to be greater than during periods of low activity. It is equally certain, however, that fluctuations in total factory overhead costs will not be exactly proportionate to the volume of production. For example, if $100,000 of factory overhead costs are usually incurred during a month in which production totals 10,000 units, the factory overhead for a month in which only 5,000 units are produced would unquestionably be more than $50,000.

Although there are many approaches to the preparation of a flexible budget, the first step is to identify the fixed and variable components of the various factory overhead and operating expenses being budgeted. The costs and expenses can then be presented in variable and fixed categories. For example, in the following flexible budget for factory overhead cost for one department and one product, "electric power" is broken down into its fixed and variable cost components for three different levels of production. The fixed portion is $10,000 for all levels of production. The variable portion is $30,000 for 10,000 units of product, $27,000 ($30,000 × 9,000/10,000) for 9,000 units of product, and $24,000 ($30,000 × 8,000/10,000) for 8,000 units of product.

Flexible Budget for Factory Overhead Cost

Colter Manufacturing Company Monthly Factory Overhead Cost Budget			
Units of product...	8,000	9,000	10,000
Variable cost:			
Indirect factory wages	$ 32,000	$ 36,000	$ 40,000
Electric power	24,000	27,000	30,000
Indirect materials	12,000	13,500	15,000
Total variable cost..................................	$ 68,000	$ 76,500	$ 85,000
Fixed cost:			
Supervisory salaries	$ 40,000	$ 40,000	$ 40,000
Depreciation of plant and equipment.............	25,000	25,000	25,000
Property taxes...	15,000	15,000	15,000
Insurance	12,000	12,000	12,000
Electric power	10,000	10,000	10,000
Total fixed cost......................................	$102,000	$102,000	$102,000
Total factory overhead cost............................	$170,000	$178,500	$187,000

In practice, the number of production levels and the interval between levels in a flexible budget will vary with the range of production volume. For example, instead of budgeting for 8,000, 9,000, and 10,000 units of product, it might be necessary to provide for levels, at intervals of 500, from 6,000 to 12,000 units. Alternative bases, such as machine hours or direct labor hours, may also be used in measuring the volume of activity.

In preparing budget performance reports, the actual results would be compared with the flexible budget figures for the level of operations achieved. For example, if Colter Manufacturing Company manufactured 10,000 units during a month, the budget figures reported in the budget performance report would be those appearing in the "10,000 units" column of Colter's flexible budget.

COMPUTERIZED BUDGETING SYSTEMS

OBJECTIVE 5
Describe the use of computerized budgeting systems.

Many firms use computers in the budgeting process. Computers can not only speed up the budgeting process, but they can also reduce the cost of budget preparation when large quantities of data need to be processed. Computers are especially useful in preparing flexible budgets and in continuous budgeting. Budget performance reports can also be prepared on a timely basis by the use of the computer.

By using the computerized simulation models, which are mathematical statements of the relationships among various operating activities, management can determine the impact of various operating alternatives on the master budget. For example, if management wishes to evaluate the impact of a proposed change in direct labor wage rates, the computer can quickly provide a revised master budget that reflects the new rates. If management wishes to evaluate a proposal to add a new product line, the computer can quickly update current budgeted data and indicate the effect of the proposal on the master budget.

BUDGETING AND HUMAN BEHAVIOR

OBJECTIVE 6
Describe the human behavioral aspects of budgeting.

In the budgeting process, overall goals of the business as well as specific goals for individual units within the business are established. Significant human behavior problems can develop if managers view these goals as unrealistic or unachievable. In such a case, managers may become discouraged as well as uncommitted to the achievement of the goals. As a result, the budget becomes less effective as a tool for planning and controlling operations. On the other hand, goals set within a range that managers consider attainable are likely to inspire managers to achieve the goals. Therefore, it is important that all levels of management be involved in establishing the goals which they will be expected to achieve. In such an environment, the budget is a planning tool that will favorably affect human behavior and increase the possibility of achieving the goals.

Human behavior problems can also arise when the budgeted and actual results are compared in budget performance reports. These problems can be minimized if budgets are revised when substantial changes in expectations occur during a budget period. Otherwise, the budgets will be of questionable value as incentives and instruments for controlling costs and expenses.

STANDARD COSTS

OBJECTIVE 7
Describe the use of standard costs in planning and controlling operations.

The determination of the unit cost of products manufactured is basic to cost accounting. The process cost and job order cost systems discussed in the preceding chapters were designed to determine *actual* or *historical* unit costs. The aim of both systems is to provide management with timely data on actual manufacturing costs and to aid in cost control and profit maximization.

The use of budgetary control procedures is often extended to the point of unit cost projections for each commodity produced. Cost systems using detailed estimates of each element of manufacturing cost entering into the finished product are sometimes called **standard cost systems**. Such systems enable management to determine how much a product should cost (standard), how much it does cost (actual), and the causes of any difference (variance) between the two. **Standard costs** thus serve as a measuring device for determination of efficiency. If the standard cost of a product is $5 per unit and its current actual cost is $5.50 per unit, the factors responsible for the excess cost can be determined and remedial measures taken. Thus, supervisors have a device for controlling the costs for which they are responsible, and employees become more cost conscious.

Standard costs may be used in either the process type of production or the job order type of production. For more effective control, standard costs should be used for each department or cost center in the factory. It is possible, however, to use standard costs in some departments and actual costs in others.

A wide variety of management skills are needed in setting standards, and the joint effort of accounting, engineering, personnel administration, and other managerial areas is also needed. Time and motion studies of each operation are made, and the work force is trained to use the most efficient methods. Direct materials and productive equipment are subjected to detailed study and tests in an effort to achieve maximum productivity for a given level of costs.

VARIANCES FROM STANDARDS

OBJECTIVE 8
Describe and illustrate the use of variance analysis for direct materials, direct labor, and factory overhead.

One of the primary purposes of a standard cost system is to facilitate control over costs by comparing actual costs with standard costs. Control is achieved by the action of management in investigating significant deviations of performance from standards and taking corrective action. Differences between the standard costs of a department or product and the actual costs incurred are termed **variances**. If the actual cost incurred is less than the standard cost, the variance is favorable. If the actual cost exceeds the standard cost, the variance is unfavorable. When actual costs are compared with standard costs, only the "exceptions" or variances are reported to the person responsible for cost control. This reporting by the "principle of exceptions" enables the one responsible for cost control to concentrate on the cause and correction of the variances.

When manufacturing operations are automated, standard cost data can be integrated with the computer that directs operations. Variances can then be detected and reported automatically by the computer system, and adjustments can be made to operations in progress.

The total variance for a certain period is usually made up of several variances, some of which may be favorable and some unfavorable. There may be variances from standards in direct materials costs, in direct labor costs, and in factory overhead costs. Illustrations and analyses of these variances for Mayer Company, a manufacturing enterprise, are presented in the following paragraphs. For illustrative purposes, it is assumed that only one type of direct material is used, that there is a single processing department, and that Product X is the only commodity manufactured by the enterprise. The standard costs for direct materials, direct labor, and factory overhead for a unit of Product X are as follows:

Direct materials:	
2 pounds at $1 per pound.............................	$ 2.00
Direct labor:	
.4 hour at $16 per hour	6.40
Factory overhead:	
.4 hour at $8.40 per hour..............................	3.36
Total per unit..	$11.76

Direct Materials Cost Variance

Two major factors enter into the determination of standards for direct materials cost: (1) the quantity (usage) standard and (2) the price standard. If the actual quantity of direct materials used in producing a commodity differs from the standard quantity, there is a **quantity variance**. If the actual unit price of the materials differs from the standard price, there is a **price variance**. To illustrate, assume that the standard direct materials cost of producing 10,000 units of Product X and the direct materials cost actually incurred during June were as follows:

Actual:	20,600 pounds at $1.04....................	$21,424
Standard:	20,000 pounds at $1.00...................	20,000

The unfavorable variance of $1,424 resulted in part from an excess usage of 600 pounds of direct materials and in part from an excess cost of $.04 per pound. The analysis of the direct materials cost variance is as follows:

Direct Materials Cost Variance

Quantity variance:

Actual quantity....................	20,600 pounds	
Standard quantity...............	20,000 pounds	
Variance—unfavorable	600 pounds × standard price, $1........	$ 600

Price variance:

Actual price.......................	$1.04 per pound	
Standard price...................	1.00 per pound	
Variance—unfavorable	$ .04 per pound × actual quantity, 20,600.	824
Total direct materials cost variance—unfavorable...................................		$1,424

Direct Materials Quantity Variance. The direct materials quantity variance is the difference between the actual quantity used and the standard quantity, multiplied by the standard price per unit. If the standard quantity exceeds the actual quantity used, the variance is favorable. If the actual quantity of materials used exceeds the standard quantity, the variance is unfavorable, as shown for Mayer Company in the following illustration:

Direct Materials Quantity Variance

$$\text{Direct Materials Quantity Variance} = \frac{\text{Actual Quantity Used} -}{\text{Standard Quantity}} \times \frac{\text{Standard Price}}{\text{per Unit}}$$

Quantity variance = (20,600 pounds − 20,000 pounds) × $1.00 per pound
Quantity variance = 600 pounds × $1.00 per pound
Quantity variance = $600 unfavorable

Direct Materials Price Variance. The direct materials price variance is the difference between the actual price per unit and the standard price per unit, multiplied by the actual quantity used. If the standard price per unit exceeds the actual price per unit, the variance is favorable. If the actual price per unit exceeds the standard price per unit, the variance is unfavorable, as shown for Mayer Company in the following illustration:

Direct Materials Price Variance

$$\text{Direct Materials Price Variance} = \frac{\text{Actual Price Per Unit} -}{\text{Standard Price}} \times \frac{\text{Actual Quantity}}{\text{Used}}$$

Price variance = ($1.04 per pound − $1.00 per pound) × 20,600 pounds
Price variance = $.04 per pound × 20,600 pounds
Price variance = $824 unfavorable

Reporting Direct Materials Cost Variance. The physical quantity and the dollar amount of the quantity variance should be reported to the factory superintendent and other personnel responsible for production. If excessive amounts of direct materials were used because of the malfunction of equipment or some other failure within the production department, those responsible should correct the situation. However, an unfavorable direct materials quantity variance is not necessarily the result of inefficiency within the production department. If the excess usage of 600 pounds of materials in the example above had been caused by inferior materials, the purchasing department should be held responsible.

The unit price and the total amount of the materials price variance should be reported to the purchasing department, which may or may not be able to control this variance. If materials of the same quality could have been purchased from another supplier at the standard price, the variance was controllable. On the other hand, if the variance resulted from a marketwide price increase, the variance was not subject to control.

Direct Labor Cost Variance

As in the case of direct materials, two major factors enter into the determination of standards for direct labor cost: (1) the time (usage or efficiency) standard and (2) the rate (price or wage) standard. If the actual direct labor hours spent producing a product differ from the standard hours, there is a **time variance**. If the wage rate paid differs from the standard rate, there is a **rate variance**. The standard cost and the actual cost of direct labor in the production of 10,000 units of Product X during June are assumed to be as follows:

Actual:	3,950 hours at $16.40......................	$64,780
Standard:	4,000 hours at $16.00.....................	64,000

The unfavorable direct labor variance of $780 is made up of a favorable time variance and an unfavorable rate variance, determined as follows:

Direct Labor Cost Variance

Time variance:		
Actual time........................	3,950 hours	
Standard time....................	4,000 hours	
Variance—favorable........	−50 hours × standard rate, $16............	$ 800
Rate variance:		
Actual rate........................	$16.40 per hour	
Standard rate	16.00 per hour	
Variance—unfavorable	$ .40 per hour × actual time, 3,950 hours	1,580
Total direct labor cost variance—unfavorable..		$ 780

Direct Labor Time Variance. The direct labor time variance is the difference between the actual hours worked and the standard hours, multiplied by the standard rate per hour. If the actual hours worked exceed the standard hours, the variance is unfavorable. If the actual hours worked are less than the standard hours, the variance is favorable, as shown for Mayer Company in the following illustration:

Direct Labor Time Variance

| Direct Labor Time Variance | = | Actual Hours Worked − Standard Hours | × | Standard Rate per Hour |

Time variance = (3,950 hours − 4,000 hours) × $16 per hour
Time variance = −50 hours   × $16 per hour
Time variance = $800 favorable

In the illustration, when the standard hours (4,000) are subtracted from the actual hours worked (3,950), the difference is "−50 hours." The minus sign indicates that the variance of 50 hours, or $800 (50 hours × $16), is favorable.

Direct Labor Rate Variance. The direct labor rate variance is the difference between the actual rate per hour and the standard rate per hour, multiplied by the actual hours worked. If the standard rate per hour exceeds the actual rate per hour, the variance is favorable. If the actual rate per hour exceeds the standard rate per hour, the variance is unfavorable, as shown for Mayer Company in the following illustration:

Direct Labor Rate Variance

| Direct Labor Rate Variance | = | Actual Rate per Hour − Standard Rate | × | Actual Hours Worked |

Rate variance = ($16.40 per hour − $16.00 per hour) × 3,950 hours
Rate variance = $.40 per hour   × 3,950 hours
Rate variance = $1,580 unfavorable

Reporting Direct Labor Cost Variance. The control of direct labor cost is often in the hands of production supervisors. To aid them, periodic reports analyzing the cause of any direct labor variance may be prepared. A comparison of standard direct labor hours and actual direct labor hours will provide the basis for an investigation into the efficiency of direct labor (time variance). A comparison of the rates paid for direct labor with the standard rates highlights the efficiency of the supervisors or the personnel department in scheduling and selecting the proper level of direct labor for production (rate variance).

Factory Overhead Cost Variance

Some of the difficulties encountered in allocating factory overhead costs among products manufactured have been considered in Chapter 21. These difficulties stem from the great variety of costs that are included in factory overhead and their nature as indirect costs. For the same reasons, the procedures used in determining standards and variances for factory overhead cost are more complex than those used for direct materials cost and direct labor cost.

A flexible budget is used to establish the standard factory overhead rate and to aid in determining subsequent variations from standard. The standard rate is determined by dividing the standard factory overhead costs by the standard amount of productive activity, generally expressed in direct labor hours, direct labor cost, or machine hours. A flexible budget showing the standard factory overhead rate for a month is as follows:

*Factory Overhead
Cost Budget Indicating
Standard Factory
Overhead Rate*

Mayer Company Factory Overhead Cost Budget For Month Ending June 30, 19--				
Percent of productive capacity..............	80%	90%	100%	110%
Direct labor hours	4,000	4,500	5,000	5,500
Budgeted factory overhead:				
Variable cost:				
Indirect factory wages	$12,800	$14,400	$16,000	$17,600
Power and light	5,600	6,300	7,000	7,700
Indirect materials	3,200	3,600	4,000	4,400
Maintenance	2,400	2,700	3,000	3,300
Total variable cost.....................	$24,000	$27,000	$30,000	$33,000
Fixed cost:				
Supervisory salaries	$ 5,500	$ 5,500	$ 5,500	$ 5,500
Depreciation of plant and equipment..	4,500	4,500	4,500	4,500
Insurance and property taxes..........	2,000	2,000	2,000	2,000
Total fixed cost.........................	$12,000	$12,000	$12,000	$12,000
Total factory overhead cost...............	$36,000	$39,000	$42,000	$45,000
Factory overhead rate per direct labor hour ($42,000 ÷ 5,000).....			$8.40	

The standard factory overhead cost rate is determined on the basis of the projected factory overhead costs at 100% of productive capacity, where this level of capacity represents the general expectation of business activity under normal operating conditions. In the illustration, the standard factory overhead rate is $8.40 per direct labor hour. This rate can be subdivided into $6 per hour for variable factory overhead ($30,000 ÷ 5,000 hours) and $2.40 per hour for fixed factory overhead ($12,000 ÷ 5,000 hours).

Variances from standard for factory overhead cost result (1) from operating at a level above or below 100% of capacity and (2) from incurring a total amount of factory overhead cost greater or less than the amount budgeted for the level of operations achieved. The first factor results in the **volume variance,** which is a measure of the penalty of operating at less than 100% of productive capacity or the benefit from operating at a level above 100% of productive capacity. The second factor results in the **controllable variance**, which is the difference between the actual amount of factory overhead incurred and the amount of factory overhead budgeted for the level of production achieved during the period. To illustrate, assume that the actual cost and standard cost of factory overhead for Mayer Company's production of 10,000 units of Product X during June were as follows:

Actual:	Variable factory overhead	$24,600	
	Fixed factory overhead.........................	12,000	$36,600
Standard: 4,000 hours at $8.40............................			33,600

The unfavorable factory overhead cost variance of $3,000 is made up of a volume variance and a controllable variance, determined as follows:

Factory Overhead Cost Variance

Volume variance:		
Productive capacity of 100%	5,000	hours
Standard for amount produced	4,000	hours
Productive capacity not used	1,000	hours
Standard fixed factory overhead cost rate	×$2.40	
Variance — unfavorable		$2,400
Controllable variance:		
Actual factory overhead cost incurred $36,600		
Budgeted factory overhead for standard product produced. 36,000		
Variance — unfavorable		600
Total factory overhead cost variance — unfavorable		$3,000

Factory Overhead Volume Variance. The factory overhead volume variance is the difference between the productive capacity at 100% and the standard productive capacity, multiplied by the standard fixed factory overhead rate. If the standard capacity for the amount produced exceeds the productive capacity at 100%, the variance is favorable. If the productive capacity at 100% exceeds the standard capacity for the amount produced, the variance is unfavorable, as shown for Mayer Company in the following illustration:

Factory Overhead Volume Variance

$$\frac{\text{Factory Overhead}}{\text{Volume Variance}} = \frac{\text{Productive Capacity at 100\%} -}{\text{Standard Capacity for Amount Produced}} \times \frac{\text{Standard Fixed Factory}}{\text{Overhead Rate}}$$

Volume variance = (5,000 hours − 4,000 hours)   × $2.40 per hour
Volume variance = 1,000 hours   × $2.40 per hour
Volume variance = $2,400 unfavorable

In the illustration, the unfavorable volume variance of $2,400 can be viewed as the cost of the available but unused productive capacity (1,000 hours). It should also be noted that the variable portion of the factory overhead cost rate was ignored in determining the volume variance. Variable factory overhead costs vary with the level of production. Thus, a curtailment of production should be accompanied by a comparable reduction of such costs. On the other hand, fixed factory overhead costs are not affected by changes in the volume of production. The fixed factory overhead costs represent the costs of providing the capacity for production, and the volume variance measures the amount of the fixed factory overhead cost due to the variance between capacity used and 100% of capacity.

The idle time that resulted in a volume variance may be due to such factors as failure to maintain an even flow of work, machine breakdowns or repairs causing work stoppages, and failure to obtain enough sales orders to keep the factory operating at full capacity. Management should determine the causes of the idle time and should take corrective action. A volume variance caused by failure of supervisors to maintain an even flow of work, for example, can be remedied. Volume variances caused by lack of sales orders may be corrected through increased advertising or other sales effort, or it may be advisable to develop other means of using the excess plant capacity.

Factory Overhead Controllable Variance. The factory overhead controllable variance is the difference between the actual factory overhead and the budgeted factory overhead for the standard amount produced. If the budgeted factory overhead for the standard amount produced exceeds the actual factory overhead, the variance is favorable. If the actual factory overhead exceeds the budgeted factory overhead for the standard amount produced, the variance is unfavorable. For Mayer Company, the standard direct labor hours for the amount produced during June was 4,000 (80% of productive capacity). Therefore, the factory overhead budgeted at this level of production, according to the budget on page 994, was $36,000. When this budgeted factory overhead is compared with the actual factory overhead, as shown in the following illustration for Mayer Company, an unfavorable variance results.

Factory Overhead Controllable Variance

| Factory Overhead Controllable Variance | = | Actual Factory Overhead | − | Budgeted Factory Overhead for Standard Amount Produced |

Controllable variance = $36,600
Controllable variance = $600 unfavorable

The amount and the direction of the controllable variance show the degree of efficiency in keeping the factory overhead costs within the limits established by the budget. Most of the controllable variance is related to the cost of the variable factory overhead items because generally there is little or no variation in the costs incurred for the fixed factory overhead items. Therefore, responsibility for the control of this variance generally rests with department supervisors.

Reporting Factory Overhead Cost Variance. The best means of presenting standard factory overhead cost variance data is through a factory overhead cost variance report. Such a report, illustrated as follows, can present both the controllable variance and the volume variance in a format that pinpoints the causes of the variances and aids in placing the responsibility for control.

Factory Overhead Cost Variance Report

Mayer Company
Factory Overhead Cost Variance Report
For Month Ended June 30, 19--

| | | | Productive capacity for the month | 5,000 hours |
Actual production for the month.. 4,000 hours

	Budget	Actual	Variances Favorable	Variances Unfavorable
Variable cost:				
Indirect factory wages	$12,800	$13,020		$ 220
Power and light	5,600	5,550	$50	
Indirect materials	3,200	3,630		430
Maintenance	2,400	2,400		
Total variable cost.................	$24,000	$24,600		
Fixed cost:				
Supervisory salaries	$ 5,500	$ 5,500		
Depreciation of plant and				
equipment	4,500	4,500		
Insurance and property taxes.....	2,000	2,000		
Total fixed cost.....................	$12,000	$12,000		
Total factory overhead cost...........	$36,000	$36,600		
Total controllable variances...			$50	$ 650
Net controllable variance — unfavorable...				$ 600
Volume variance — unfavorable:				
Idle hours at the standard rate for fixed factory overhead —				
1,000 × $2.40				2,400
Total factory overhead cost variance — unfavorable				$3,000

The variance in many of the individual cost items in factory overhead can be subdivided into quantity and price variances, as were the variances in direct materials and direct labor. For example, the indirect factory wages variance may include both time and rate variances, and the indirect materials variance may be made up of both a quantity variance and a price variance.

The foregoing brief introduction to analysis of factory overhead cost variance suggests the many difficulties that may be encountered in actual practice. The rapid increase of automation in factory operations has been accompanied by increased attention to factory overhead costs. The use of predetermined standards and the analysis of variances from such standards provides management with the best possible means of establishing responsibility and controlling factory overhead costs.

STANDARDS IN THE ACCOUNTS

OBJECTIVE 9
Describe and illustrate how standards may be included in the accounts of a manufacturing enterprise.

Although standard costs can be used solely as a statistical device apart from the ledger, it is generally considered preferable to include them in the accounts. One approach, when this plan is used, is to debit the work in process account for the actual cost of direct materials, direct labor, and factory overhead entering into production. The same account is credited for the standard cost of the product completed and transferred to the finished goods account. The balance remaining in the work in process account is then made up of the ending inventory of work in process and the variances of actual cost from standard cost. In the following illustrative accounts, there is assumed to be no ending inventory of work in process. The balance in the account is the sum of the variances (unfavorable) between standard and actual costs.

Standard Costs in Accounts

ACCOUNT   WORK IN PROCESS   ACCOUNT NO.

Date		Item	Debit	Credit	Balance Debit	Balance Credit
June	30	Direct materials (actual)	21,424		21,424	
	30	Direct labor (actual)	64,780		86,204	
	30	Factory overhead (actual)	36,600		122,804	
	30	Units finished (standard)		117,600		
	30	Balance (variances)			5,204	

ACCOUNT   FINISHED GOODS   ACCOUNT NO.

Date		Item	Debit	Credit	Balance Debit	Balance Credit
June	1	Inventory (standard)			88,200	
	30	Units finished (standard)	117,600		205,800	
	30	Units sold (standard)		111,720	94,080	

Variances from standard costs are usually not reported to stockholders and others outside of management. However, it is customary to disclose the variances on income statements prepared for management. An interim monthly income statement prepared for Mayer Company's internal use is illustrated as follows:

Variances from Standards In Income Statement

Mayer Company Income Statement For Month Ended June 30, 19--			
Sales...			$190,000
Cost of goods sold—at standard.........			111,720
Gross profit—at standard...................			$ 78,280
	Favorable	Unfavorable	
Less variances from standard cost:			
Direct materials quantity..................		$ 600	
Direct materials price......................		824	
Direct labor time	$800		
Direct labor rate.............................		1,580	
Factory overhead volume		2,400	
Factory overhead controllable...........		600	5,204
Gross profit....................................			$ 73,076
Operating expenses:			
Selling expenses............................		$22,500	
Administrative expenses..................		19,225	41,725
Income before income tax..................			$ 31,351

At the end of the fiscal year, the variances from standard are usually transferred to the cost of goods sold account. However, if the variances are significant or if many of the products manufactured are still on hand, the variances should be allocated to the work in process, finished goods, and cost of goods sold accounts. The result of such an allocation is to convert these account balances from standard cost to actual cost.

REVISION OF STANDARDS

OBJECTIVE 10
Describe the importance of periodic review and revision of standards.

Standard costs should be continuously reviewed, and when they no longer represent the conditions that were present when the standards were set, they should be changed. Standards should not be revised merely because they differ from actual costs, but because they no longer reflect the conditions that they were intended to measure. For example, the direct labor cost standard would not be revised simply because workers were unable to meet properly determined standards. On the other hand, standards should be revised when prices, product designs, labor rates, manufacturing methods, or other circumstances change to such an extent that the current standards no longer represent a useful measure of performance.

APPENDIX

QUANTITATIVE TECHNIQUES FOR INVENTORY CONTROL

The chapters of this textbook have discussed many ways in which accounting data can be used by management in planning and controlling business operations. These analyses have usually involved a limited number of objectives and variables. This appendix focuses on the use of quantitative techniques that rely on more sophisticated mathematical relationships and statistical methods. Such techniques enable management to consider a larger number of objectives and variables in planning and controlling operations.

The discussions and illustrations in this appendix relate to the use of quantitative techniques in controlling inventory. These techniques often lead to a clarification of management decision alternatives and their expected effects on the business enterprise. For example, the most economical plan for purchasing materials for a single plant may be easily determined, based on the lowest overall cost per unit of materials. However, the most economical plan for purchasing materials for several plants may not be easily determined, because transportation costs to the various plant locations may be different, and the amount of purchases from any one supplier may be limited. In this latter case, a quantitative technique known as linear programming may be useful in determining the most economical plan for purchasing materials.

The primary disadvantages of quantitative techniques are their complexity and their reliance on mathematical relationships and statistical methods which may be understood by only the most highly trained experts. When computers are used, however, it is less important to understand these complexities, so that quantitative techniques can be used by all levels of management.

For a business enterprise that needs large quantities of inventory to meet sales orders or production requirements, inventory is one of its most important assets. The lack of sufficient inventory can result in lost sales, idle production facilities, production bottlenecks, and additional purchasing costs due to placing special orders or rush orders. On the other hand, excess inventory can result in large storage costs and large spoilage losses, which reduce the profitability of the enterprise. Thus, it is important for a business enterprise to know the ideal quantity to be purchased in a single order and the minimum and maximum quantities to be on hand at any time. Such factors as economies of large-scale buying, storage costs, work interruption due to shortages, and seasonal and cyclical changes in production schedules need to be considered. Three quantitative techniques that are especially useful in inventory control are (1) the economic order quantity formula, (2) the inventory order point formula, and (3) linear programming.

ECONOMIC ORDER QUANTITY

The optimum quantity of inventory to be ordered at one time is termed the **economic order quantity (EOQ)**. Important factors to be considered in determining the optimum quantity are the costs involved in processing an order for the materials and the costs involved in storing the materials.

The annual cost of processing orders for a specified material (cost of placing orders, verifying invoices, processing payments, etc.) increases as the number of orders placed increases. On the other hand, the annual cost of storing the materials (taxes, insurance, occupancy of storage space, etc.) decreases as the number of orders placed increases. The economic order quantity is therefore that quantity that will minimize the combined annual costs of ordering and storing materials.

The combined annual cost incurred in ordering and storing materials can be computed under various assumptions as to the number of orders to be placed during a year. To illustrate, assume the following data for an inventoriable material which is used at the same rate during the year:

Units required during the year	1,200
Ordering cost, per order placed	$10.00
Annual storage cost, per unit................	$.60

If a single order were placed for the entire year's needs, the cost of ordering the 1,200 units would be $10. The average number of units held in inventory during the year would therefore be 600 (1,200 units ÷ 2) and would result in an annual storage cost of $360 (600 units × $.60). The combined order and storage costs for placing only one order during the year would thus be $370 ($10 + $360). If, instead of a single order, two orders were placed during the year, the order cost would be $20 (2 × $10), 600 units would need to be purchased on each order, the average inventory would be 300 units, and the annual storage cost would be $180 (300 units × $.60). Accordingly, the combined order and storage costs for placing two orders during the year would be $200 ($20 + $180). Successive computations will disclose the EOQ when the combined cost reaches its lowest point and starts upward. The following table shows an optimum of 200 units of materials per order, with 6 orders per year, at a combined cost of $120:

Tabulation of Economic Order Quantity

Number of Orders	Number of Units per Order	Average Units in Inventory	Order Cost	Storage Cost	Combined Cost
				Order and Storage Costs	
1	1,200	600	$10	$360	$370
2	600	300	20	180	200
3	400	200	30	120	150
4	300	150	40	90	130
5	240	120	50	72	122
6	200	100	60	60	120
7	171	86	70	52	122

The economic order quantity may also be determined by a formula based on differential calculus. The formula and its application to the illustration is as follows:

Economic Order Quantity Formula

$$EOQ = \sqrt{\frac{2 \times \text{Annual Units Required} \times \text{Cost per Order Placed}}{\text{Annual Storage Cost per Unit}}}$$

$$EOQ = \sqrt{\frac{2 \times 1,200 \times \$10}{\$.60}}$$

$$EOQ = \sqrt{40,000}$$

$$EOQ = 200 \text{ units}$$

INVENTORY ORDER POINT

The **inventory order point,** usually expressed in units, is the level to which inventory is allowed to fall before an order for additional inventory is placed. The inventory order point depends on the (1) daily usage of inventory that is expected to be consumed in production or sold, (2) number of production days that it takes to receive an order for inventory, termed the **lead time,** and (3) **safety stock,** which is the amount of inventory that is available for use when unforeseen circumstances arise, such as delays in receiving ordered inventory as a result of a national truckers' strike. Once the order point is reached, the most economical quantity should be ordered.

The inventory order point is computed by using the following formula:

Inventory Order Point = (Daily Usage × Days of Lead Time) + Safety Stock

To illustrate, assume that Beacon Company, a printing company, estimates daily usage of 3,000 pounds of paper and a lead time of 30 days to receive an order of paper. Beacon Company desires a safety stock of 10,000 pounds. The inventory order point for the paper is 100,000 pounds, computed as follows:

Inventory Order Point = (Daily Usage × Lead Time) + Safety Stock
Inventory Order Point = (3,000 lbs. × 30 days) + 10,000 lbs.
Inventory Order Point = 90,000 lbs + 10,000 lbs.
Inventory Order Point = 100,000 lbs.

In this illustration, a safety stock of 10,000 pounds of paper was assumed. This level of safety stock should be established by management after considering many factors, such as the uncertainty in the estimates of daily inventory usage and lead time. If management were 100% certain that estimates of the daily usage and lead time were correct, no safety stock would be required. As the uncertainty in these estimates increases, the amount of safety stock normally increases. In addition, the level of safety stock carried by an enterprise will also depend on the costs of carrying inventory and the costs of being out of inventory when materials are needed for production or sales. If the costs of carrying inventory are low and the costs of being out of inventory are high, then relatively large amounts of safety stock would normally be carried by a business enterprise.

Quantitative techniques using statistics and probability theory may be useful to managers in establishing order point and safety stock levels. Such techniques are described in advanced texts.

LINEAR PROGRAMMING FOR INVENTORY CONTROL

Linear programming is a quantitative method that can provide data for solving a variety of business problems in which management's objective is to minimize costs or maximize profits, subject to several limiting factors. Although a thorough discussion of linear programming is appropriate for more advanced courses, the following simplified illustration demonstrates the way in which linear programming can be applied to determine the most economical purchasing plan. In this situation, management's objective is to minimize the total cost of purchasing materials for several branch locations, subject to the availability of materials from suppliers.

Assume that a manufacturing company purchases Part P for use at both its West Branch and East Branch. Part P is available in limited quantities from two suppliers. The total unit cost price varies considerably for parts acquired from the two suppliers mainly because of differences in transportation charges. The relevant data for the decision regarding the most economical purchase arrangement are summarized in the following diagram:

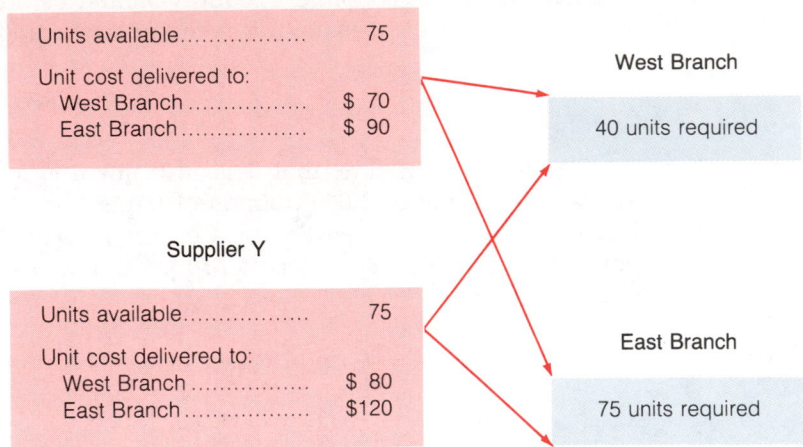

Supplier X

Units available	75
Unit cost delivered to:	
West Branch	$ 70
East Branch	$ 90

West Branch

40 units required

Supplier Y

Units available	75
Unit cost delivered to:	
West Branch	$ 80
East Branch	$120

East Branch

75 units required

It might appear that the most economical course of action would be to purchase (1) the 40 units required by West Branch from Supplier X at $70 a unit, (2) 35 units for East Branch from Supplier X at $90 a unit, and (3) the remaining 40 units required by East Branch from Supplier Y at $120 a unit. If this course of action were followed, the total cost of the parts needed by the two branches would amount to $10,750, as indicated by the following computation:

	Cost of Purchases		
	By West Branch	By East Branch	Total
From Supplier X:			
40 units at $70	$2,800		$ 2,800
35 units at $90		$3,150	3,150
From Supplier Y:			
40 units at $120		4,800	4,800
Total	$2,800	$7,950	$10,750

Although many different purchasing programs are possible, the most economical course of action would be to purchase (1) the 75 units required by East Branch from Supplier X at $90 a unit and (2) the 40 units required by West Branch from Supplier Y at $80 a unit. If this plan were used, no units would be purchased at the lowest available unit cost, and the total cost of the parts would be $9,950, calculated as follows:

	Cost of Purchases		
	By West Branch	By East Branch	Total
From Supplier X:			
75 units at $90		$6,750	$6,750
From Supplier Y:			
40 units at $80	$3,200		3,200
Total	$3,200	$6,750	$9,950

Linear programming can be applied to this situation by using a mathematical equation approach. This approach, called the **simplex method,** uses algebraic equations and is often used more practically with a computer. The simplex method is described in advanced texts.

CHAPTER REVIEW

KEY POINTS

OBJECTIVE 1

Nature and Objectives of Budgeting

The essentials of budgeting are (1) the establishment of specific goals for future operations and (2) the periodic comparison of actual results with these goals. The establishment of specific goals for future operations encompasses the planning function of management. The periodic comparison of actual results with these goals encompasses the control function of management.

OBJECTIVE 2

Budgeting Systems

Although budgets may be prepared for quarters of the year, months, or weeks, budgets of operating activities usually include the fiscal year of an enterprise. A variant of fiscal-year budgeting, continuous budgeting, provides for maintenance of a twelve-month projection into the future.

All levels of management should be encouraged to participate in the budgeting process. Usually a budget committee has final responsibility for preparation of the master budget.

The sales budget is usually the first component of the master budget that is prepared. The production budget sets forth the number of units of each commodity expected to be manufactured to meet budgeted sales and inventory requirements. The direct materials purchases budget is based on the needs shown by the production budget. The production budget also serves as a starting point for the preparation of the direct labor cost budget and factory overhead cost budget. The cost of goods sold budget is prepared by combining data on estimated inventories with the relevant estimates of quantities and costs in the budgets for (1) direct materials purchases, (2) direct labor costs, and (3) factory overhead costs. After the operating expenses budget is prepared, the budgeted income statement can be prepared.

The capital expenditures budget summarizes future plans for the acquisition of plant facilities and equipment, while the cash budget represents the expected inflow and outflow of cash for a day, week, month, or a longer period. The budgeted balance sheet presents estimated details of financial condition at the end of a budget period, assuming that all the budgeted operating and financing plans are fulfilled.

OBJECTIVE 3

Budget Performance Reports

A budget performance report provides feedback to management by reporting actual results compared with budgeted figures. Significant differences can then be investigated and corrective action taken.

OBJECTIVE 4

Flexible Budgets

Through the use of flexible budgets, the effect of changes in volume of activity can be built into the budgetary system. The preparation of flexible budgets requires the separation of costs and expenses into fixed and variable components. The use of flexible budgets facilitates the preparation of budget performance reports based on the actual level of operations achieved.

OBJECTIVE 5

Computerized Budgeting Systems

Computers can be useful in speeding up the budgetary process and in preparing timely budget performance reports. In addition, through the use of simulation models, management can determine the impact of operating alternatives on the various budgets.

OBJECTIVE 6

Budgeting and Human Behavior

Significant human behavior problems can develop if managers view a budget as unrealistic or unachievable. Human behavior problems can also arise when budgeted and actual results are compared. These problems can be minimized if managers are involved in establishing budgets initially and budgets are revised for changes and expectations that occur during a budget period.

OBJECTIVE 7

Standard Costs

Standard cost systems use detailed estimates of each element of manufacturing cost to measure efficiency. The establishment of standards requires a joint effort by management, accounting, engineering, personnel, administration, and other managerial areas.

OBJECTIVE 8

Variances from Standards

One of the primary purposes of a standard cost system is to facilitate control over costs by comparing actual costs with standard costs and thus determining variances. The two major variances for direct materials cost are the (1) direct materials quantity variance and (2) direct materials price variance. The two major variances for direct labor costs are the (1) direct labor time variance and (2) direct labor rate variance. The two major variances for factory overhead costs are the (1) factory overhead volume variance and (2) factory overhead controllable variance.

OBJECTIVE 9

Standards in the Accounts

It is generally preferable to include standards in the accounts. One approach is to debit the work in process account for the actual costs of direct materials, direct labor, and factory overhead entering into production. The same account is then credited for the standard costs of the product completed and transferred to the finished goods account. Thus, the variances of actual costs from standard costs are isolated along with the ending inventory in the work in process account. At the end of the fiscal year, the variances are usually transferred to the cost of goods sold account.

OBJECTIVE 10   Revision of Standards

Established standards should be continually reviewed. If the standards no longer represent present conditions, they should be revised.

KEY TERMS

budget 976
continuous budgeting 978
zero-base budgeting 978
master budget 978
capital expenditures budget 984
budget performance report 987
flexible budgets 987
standard costs 989
variances 990

direct materials quantity
   variance 991
direct materials price variance 991
direct labor time variance 992
direct labor rate variance 993
factory overhead volume
   variance 995
factory overhead controllable
   variance 995

SELF-EXAMINATION QUESTIONS

Answers at end of chapter.

1. The budget that summarizes future plans for acquisition of plant facilities and equipment is the:
    A. cash budget
    B. sales budget
    C. capital exenditures budget
    D. none of the above

2. The system that "builds in" the effect of fluctuations in volume of activity into the various budgets is termed:
    A. budget performance reporting
    B. continuous budgeting
    C. flexible budgeting
    D. none of the above

3. The actual and standard direct labor costs for producing a specified quantity of product are as follows:

    Actual: 990 hours at $10.90....................... $10,791
    Standard: 1,000 hours at $11.00....................... 11,000

    The direct labor cost time variance is:
    A. $99 favorable
    B. $99 unfavorable
    C. $110 favorable
    D. $110 unfavorable

4. The actual and standard factory overhead costs for producing a specified quantity of product are as follows:

Actual:	Variable factory overhead	$72,500	
	Fixed factory overhead	40,000	$112,500
Standard: 19,000 hours at $6			
	($4 variable and $2 fixed).............		114,000

If 1,000 hours of productive capacity were unused, the factory overhead volume variance would be:

A. $1,500 favorable   C. $4,000 unfavorable
B. $2,000 unfavorable   D. none of the above

5. Based on the data in Question 4, the factory overhead controllable variance would be:

A. $3,500 favorable   C. $1,500 favorable
B. $3,500 unfavorable   D. none of the above

ILLUSTRATIVE PROBLEM

Partin Company prepared the following factory overhead cost budget for the Finishing Department for June of the current year:

Partin Company
Factory Overhead Cost Budget—Finishing Department
For Month Ending June 30, 19--

Machine hours:		
Normal productive capacity		10,000
Hours budgeted		9,000
Variable cost:		
Indirect factory wages	$9,450	
Indirect materials	6,750	
Power and light	5,400	
Total variable cost		$21,600
Fixed cost:		
Supervisory salaries	$8,000	
Indirect factory wages	3,300	
Depreciation of plant and equipment	3,100	
Insurance	1,500	
Power and light	1,200	
Property taxes	900	
Total fixed cost		18,000
Total factory overhead cost		$39,600

Instructions:

1. Prepare a flexible budget for the month of July, indicating capacities of 8,000, 9,000, 10,000 and 11,000 machine hours and the determination of a standard factory overhead rate per machine hour.
2. Prepare a standard factory overhead cost variance report for July. The Finishing Department was operated for 8,000 machine hours and the following factory overhead costs were incurred:

Indirect factory wages	$11,500
Supervisory salaries	8,000
Power and light	6,350
Indirect materials	6,050
Depreciation of plant and equipment	3,100
Insurance	1,500
Property taxes	900
Total factory overhead costs incurred	$37,400

SOLUTION

(1)   Partin Company
        Factory Overhead Cost Budget—Finishing Department
                    For Month Ending July 31, 19--

Percent of normal productive capacity	80%	90%	100%	110%
Machine hours	8,000	9,000	10,000	11,000
Budgeted factory overhead:				
Variable cost:				
Indirect factory wages	$ 8,400	$ 9,450	$10,500	$11,550
Indirect materials	6,000	6,750	7,500	8,250
Power and light	4,800	5,400	6,000	6,600
Total variable cost	$19,200	$21,600	$24,000	$26,400
Fixed cost:				
Supervisory salaries	$ 8,000	$ 8,000	$ 8,000	$ 8,000
Indirect factory wages	3,300	3,300	3,300	3,300
Depreciation of plant and equipment	3,100	3,100	3,100	3,100
Insurance	1,500	1,500	1,500	1,500
Power and light	1,200	1,200	1,200	1,200
Property taxes	900	900	900	900
Total fixed cost	$18,000	$18,000	$18,000	$18,000
Total factory overhead cost	$37,200	$39,600	$42,000	$44,400

Factory overhead rate per machine hour
    ($42,000 ÷ 10,000 hours) $4.20

(2)   Partin Company
     Factory Overhead Cost Variance Report—Finishing Department
                    For Month Ended July 31, 19--

Normal productive capacity for the month......................... 10,000 hours
Actual production for the month................................... 8,000 hours

			Variances	
	Budget	Actual	Favorable	Unfavorable
Variable cost:				
Indirect factory wages	$ 8,400	$ 8,200	$200	
Indirect materials	6,000	6,050		$ 50
Power and light	4,800	5,150		350
Total variable cost	$19,200	$19,400		
Fixed cost:				
Supervisory salaries	$ 8,000	$ 8,000		
Indirect factory wages	3,300	3,300		
Depreciation of plant and equipment	3,100	3,100		
Insurance	1,500	1,500		
Power and light	1,200	1,200		
Property taxes	900	900		
Total fixed cost	$18,000	$18,000		
Total factory overhead cost..	$37,200	$37,400		
Total controllable variances			$200	$ 400

Net controllable variance — unfavorable .... $ 200
Volume variance — unfavorable:
  Idle hours at standard rate for fixed factory overhead —
    2,000 × $1.80   3,600
Total factory overhead cost variance — unfavorable $3,800

DISCUSSION QUESTIONS

1. What is a budget?

2. (a) Name the two basic functions of management in which accounting is involved.
   (b) How does a budget aid management in the discharge of these basic functions?

3. What is meant by *continuous budgeting*?

4. Why should all levels of management and all departments participate in the preparation and submission of budget estimates?

5. Which budgetary concept requires all levels of management to start from zero and estimate sales, production, and other operating data as though the operations were being initiated for the first time?

6. Why should the production requirements as set forth in the production budget be carefully coordinated with the sales budget?

7. Why should the timing of direct materials purchases be closely coordinated with the production budget?

8. Merriam Inc., which estimates that 130,000 units will be sold during the current year, desires an ending inventory of 15,000 units. If 12,500 units are in the beginning inventory, what is the estimated production for the current year?

9. What are the three budgets from which data on relevant estimates of quantities and costs are combined with data on estimated inventories in preparing the budget for the cost of goods sold?

10. What is a capital expenditures budget?

11. (a) Discuss the purpose of the cash budget. (b) If the cash for the first quarter of the fiscal year indicates excess cash at the end of each of the first two months, how might the excess cash be used.

12. What is a budget performance report?

13. What is a flexible budget?

14. Owens Corporation uses flexible budgets. For each of the following variable operating expenses, indicate whether there has been a saving or an excess of expenses, assuming that actual sales were $800,000.

Expense Item	Actual Amount	Budget Allowance Based on Sales
Factory supplies expense............	$ 8,250	1%
Uncollectible accounts expense ...	21,750	3%

15. How can computerized budgeting systems aid firms in the budgeting process?

16. Briefly discuss the type of human behavior problem that might arise if goals used in developing budgets are unrealistic or unachievable.

17. What are the basic objectives in the use of standard costs?

18. As the term is used in reference to standard costs, what is a *variance*?

19. What is meant by reporting by the "principle of exceptions" as the term is used in reference to cost control?

20. (a) What are the two variances between the actual cost and the standard cost for direct materials? (b) Discuss some possible causes of these variances.

21. (a) What are the two variances between the actual cost and the standard cost for direct labor? (b) Who generally has control over the direct labor cost?

22. (a) Describe the two variances between the actual costs and the standards costs for factory overhead. (b) What is a factory overhead cost variance report?

23. If standards are recorded in the accounts and Work in Process is debited for the actual manufacturing costs and credited for the standard cost of products produced, what does the balance in Work in Process represent?

24. Are variances from standard costs usually reported in financial statements issued to stockholders and others outside the firm?

25. Assuming that the variances from standards are not significant at the end of the period, to what account are they transferred?

Real World Focus 26. During the ten-year period, 1978–1987, the ratio of cost of sales to net sales for PepsiCo Inc. decreased from 48.4% to 38.8%. During this same period, the net sales of PepsiCo increased by almost 400%. As sales increase, why would management normally expect the ratio of cost of sales to net sales to decrease?

EXERCISES

Exercise 25–1
Sales and
production budgets.
OBJ. 2

Coker Company manufactures two models of humidifiers, H10 and H20. Based on the following production and sales data for April of the current year, prepare (a) a sales budget and (b) a production budget.

	H10	H20
Estimated inventory (units), April 1	54,700	13,100
Desired inventory (units), April 30	65,000	10,000
Expected sales volume (units):		
Northern Region	100,000	50,000
Southern Region	80,000	20,000
Unit sales price	$8.50	$11.40

Exercise 25–2
Professional fees budget.
OBJ. 2

Mitchell and Momper, CPAs, offer three types of services to clients: auditing, tax, and computer installation. Based upon past experience and projected growth, the following billable hours have been estimated for the year ending December 31, 1990:

	Billable Hours
Audit Department:	
Staff..	18,000
Partners	6,000
Tax Department:	
Staff..	15,000
Partners	3,000
Computer Installation:	
Staff..	12,000
Partners	2,000

The average billing rate for staff is $40 per hour, and the average billing rate for partners is $80 per hour.

Prepare a professional fees budget for Mitchell and Momper, CPAs, for the year ending December 31, 1990, using the following columnar headings and showing the estimated professional fees by type of service rendered:

Billable Hours	Hourly Rate	Total Revenue

Exercise 25–3
Direct labor cost budget.
OBJ. 2

Based upon the data in Exercise 25–2 and assuming that the average compensation per hour for staff and partners is $25 and $50 respectively, prepare a direct labor cost budget for Mitchell and Momper, CPAs, for the year ending December 31, 1990. Use the following columnar headings:

Billable Hours Required	
Staff	Partners

Exercise 25–4
Schedule of cash collections of accounts receivable.
OBJ. 2

McNeely Company was organized on September 1 of the current year. Projected sales for each of the first three months of operations are as follows:

September............................	$240,000
October...............................	300,000
November............................	420,000

The company expects to sell 20% of its merchandise for cash. Of sales on account, 70% are expected to be collected in the month of the sale, 25% in the month following the sale, and the remainder in the following month. Prepare a schedule indicating cash collections of accounts receivable for September, October, and November.

Exercise 25–5
Schedule of cash disbursements.
OBJ. 2

Sussex Company was organized on March 31 of the current year. Projected operating expenses for each of the first three months of operations are as follows:

April	$156,800
May.....................................	195,200
June....................................	217,600

Depreciation, insurance, and property taxes represent $28,800 of the estimated monthly operating expenses. Insurance was paid on March 31, and property taxes will be paid in November. Three fourths of the remainder of the operating expenses are expected to be paid in the month in which they are incurred, with the balance to be paid in the following month. Prepare a schedule indicating cash disbursements for operating expenses for April, May, and June.

Exercise 25–6
Flexible budget for operating expenses.
OBJ. 4

Wang Company uses flexible budgets that are based on the following data:

Sales commissions.....................................	4% of sales
Advertising expense...................................	$20,000 for $400,000 of sales
	$30,000 for $500,000 of sales
	$40,000 for $600,000 of sales
Miscellaneous selling expense	$3,000 plus 3/4% of sales
Office salaries expense..............................	$35,000
Office supplies expense.............................	3% of sales
Miscellaneous administrative expense	$600 plus 1/2% of sales

Prepare a flexible operating expenses budget for July of the current year for sales volumes of $400,000, $500,000, and $600,000.

Exercise 25–7
Budget performance report.
OBJ. 3

The operating expenses incurred during July of the current year by Wang Company were as follows:

Sales commissions..	$21,250
Advertising expense......................................	29,100
Miscellaneous selling expense	7,000
Office salaries expense.................................	35,000
Office supplies expense................................	15,300
Miscellaneous administrative expense	3,000

Assuming that the total sales for July were $500,000, prepare a budget performance report for operating expenses on the basis of the data presented above and in Exercise 25–6.

Exercise 25–8
Direct materials variances.
OBJ. 8

The following data related to the direct materials cost for the production of 50,000 units of product:

Actual:	87,500 pounds at $3.40................	$297,500
Standard:	90,000 pounds at $3.20................	288,000

Determine the quantity variance, price variance, and total direct materials cost variance.

Exercise 25–9
Standard direct materials cost per unit from variance data.
OBJ. 8

The following data relating to direct materials cost for August of the current year are taken from the records of Hammar Company:

Quantity of direct materials used	17,760 pounds
Unit cost of direct materials	$3.50 per pound
Units of finished product manufactured...........................	15,000 units
Standard direct materials per unit of finished product.........	1.2 pounds
Direct materials quantity variance — favorable..................	$720
Direct materials price variance — unfavorable	$8,880

Determine the standard direct materials cost per unit of finished product, assuming that there was no inventory of work in process at either the beginning or the end of the month. Present your computations.

Exercise 25–10
Direct labor variances.
OBJ. 8

The following data relate to direct labor cost for the production of 25,000 units of product:

Actual:	61,200 hours at $13.25................	$810,900
Standard:	60,000 hours at $13.50	810,000

Determine the time variance, rate variance, and total direct labor cost variance.

Exercise 25–11
Factory overhead cost variances.
OBJ. 8

The following data relate to factory overhead cost for the production of 75,000 units of product:

Actual: Variable factory overhead............. $127,500
            Fixed factory overhead   98,000
Standard: 30,000 hours at $7......................   210,000

If productive capacity of 100% was 35,000 hours and the factory overhead costs budgeted at the level of 30,000 standards hours was $224,000, determine the volume variance, controllable variance, and total factory overhead cost variance. The fixed factory overhead rate was $2.80 per hour.

Exercise 25–12
Income statement indicating standard cost variances.
OBJ. 9

The following data were taken from the records of Comer Company for January of the current year:

Administrative expenses...	$ 62,500
Cost of goods sold (at standard)	975,000
Direct materials quantity variance — favorable...................	6,400
Direct materials price variance — favorable......................	3,300
Direct labor time variance — unfavorable..........................	8,175
Direct labor rate variance — unfavorable	2,250
Factory overhead volume variance — unfavorable..............	25,000
Factory overhead controllable variance — favorable	4,000
Sales	1,250,000
Selling expenses...	105,000

Prepare an income statement for presentation to management.

Appendix Exercise 25–13
Economic order quantity.

Assuming that Product T is used at the same rate throughout the year, 8,100 units are required during the year, the cost per order placed is $3, and the storage cost per unit is $1.50, what is the economic order quantity for Product T? Use the formula on page 1000.

Appendix Exercise 25–14
Inventory order point.

Assuming that Smith Co. estimates daily usage of 3,000 pounds of Material F, the lead time to receive an order of Material F is 15 days, and a safety stock of 12,000 pounds is desired, what is the inventory order point?

Appendix Exercise 25–15
Economic order quantity and inventory order point.

McKean Company estimates that 2,040 units of Material H will be required during the coming year. The materials will be used at the rate of 20 units per day throughout the 272-day period of budgeted production for the year. Past experience indicates that the annual storage cost is $.30 per unit, the cost to place an order is $34, the lead time to receive an order is 15 days, and the desired amount of safety stock is 700 units. Determine (a) the economic order quantity, (b) the inventory order point, and (c) the number of units to be purchased when the inventory order point is reached.

PROBLEMS

Series A

Problem 25–1A
Sales, production, direct materials, and direct labor budgets.
OBJ. 2

The budget director of DeBow Company requests estimates of sales, production, and other operating data from the various administrative units every month. Selected information concerning sales and production for April of the current year are summarized as follows:

(a) Estimated sales for April by sales territory:
  Northeast:
    Product E: 12,000 units at $50 per unit
    Product F: 10,000 units at $70 per unit
  Southeast:
    Product E: 9,000 units at $50 per unit
    Product F: 13,500 units at $70 per unit
  Southwest:
    Product E: 19,000 units at $50 per unit
    Product F: 21,500 units at $70 per unit

(b) Estimated inventories at April 1:
  Direct materials:
    Material P: 8,500 lbs.   Material R: 7,000 lbs.
    Material Q: 18,000 lbs.   Material S: 6,500 lbs.
  Finished products:
    Product E: 7,500 units   Product F: 8,000 units

(c) Desired inventories at April 30:
  Direct materials:
    Material P: 9,000 lbs.   Material R: 8,000 lbs.
    Material Q: 16,500 lbs.   Material S: 6,000 lbs.
  Finished Products:
    Product E: 9,100 units   Product F: 10,500 units

(d) Direct materials used in production:
  In manufacture of Product E:
    Material P: 2.4 lbs. per unit of product
    Material Q: 1.2 lbs. per unit of product
    Material R: .9 lbs. per unit of product
  In manufacture of Product F:
    Material Q: 1.8 lbs. per unit of product
    Material R: 1.0 lbs. per unit of product
    Material S: 1.3 lbs. per unit of product

(e) Anticipated purchase price for direct materials:
    Material P: $1.50 per lb.   Material R: $5.00 per lb.
    Material Q: $ .75 per lb.   Material S: $2.60 per lb.

(f) Direct labor requirements:
  Product E:
    Department 20: 2.0 hours at $12 per hour
    Department 30:   .5 hours at $10 per hour
  Product F:
    Department 10: 1.8 hours at $16 per hour
    Department 20: 1.2 hours at $12 per hour

Instructions:

(1) Prepare a sales budget for April.
(2) Prepare a production budget for April.
(3) Prepare a direct materials purchases budget for April.
(4) Prepare a direct labor cost budget for April.

Problem 25–2A
Budgeted income
statement and
supporting budgets.

OBJ. 2

The budget director of Gear Inc., with the assistance of the controller, treasurer, production manager, and sales manager, has gathered the following data for use in developing the budgeted income statement for May:

(a) Estimated sales for May:
    Product H: 40,000 units at $75 per unit
    Product I: 60,000 units at $60 per unit

(b) Estimated inventories at May 1:

Direct materials:
- Material A: 8,500 lbs.
- Material B: 11,200 lbs.
- Material C: 10,000 lbs.

Finished products:
- Product H: 5,000 units at $50 per unit
- Product I: 7,500 units at $36 per unit

(c) Desired inventories at May 31:

Direct materials:
- Material A: 10,000 lbs.
- Material B: 12,000 lbs.
- Material C: 8,000 lbs.

Finished products:
- Product H: 4,500 units at $50 per unit
- Product I: 8,000 units at $36 per unit

(d) Direct materials used in production:

In manufacture of Product H:
- Material A: .8 lbs. per unit of product
- Material B: 1.2 lbs. per unit of product

In manufacture of Product I:
- Material B: 1.4 lbs. per unit of product
- Material C: 2.0 lbs. per unit of product

(e) Anticipated cost of purchases and beginning and ending inventory of direct materials:
- Material A: $15.50 per lb.
- Material B: 2.00 per lb.
- Material C: 7.20 per lb.

(f) Direct labor requirements:

Product H:
- Department 100: 1.5 hours at $18 per hour
- Department 200: .6 hours at $10 per hour

Product I:
- Department 200: .8 hours at $10 per hour
- Department 300: .2 hours at $9 per hour

(g) Estimated factory overhead costs for May:

Indirect factory wages	$225,000
Depreciation of plant and equipment	110,000
Supervisory salaries	50,000
Power and light	36,000
Indirect materials	32,000
Maintenance	15,000
Insurance and property taxes	7,000

(h) Estimated operating expenses for May:

Sales salaries expense	$381,000
Officers salaries expense	270,000
Advertising expense	250,000
Office salaries expense	125,000
Depreciation expense—office equipment	80,000
Telephone expense—selling	37,200
Telephone expense—administrative	21,400
Travel expense—selling	13,250
Travel expense—administrative	7,750
Office supplies expense	3,350
Miscellaneous selling expense	8,000
Miscellaneous administrative expense	6,000

(i) Estimated other income and expense for May:

Interest income.. $200,000
Interest expense...   150,000

(j) Estimated tax rate: 40%.

Instructions:

(1) Prepare a sales budget for May.
(2) Prepare a production budget for May.
(3) Prepare a direct materials purchases budget for May.
(4) Prepare a direct labor cost budget for May.
(5) Prepare a factory overhead cost budget for May.
(6) Prepare a cost of goods sold budget for May. Work in process at the beginning of May is estimated to be $80,000, and work in process at the end of May is estimated to be $65,000.
(7) Prepare an operating expenses budget for May. Classify the expenses as either selling or administrative expenses.
(8) Prepare a budgeted income statement for May.

Problem 25–3A

Cash budget.

OBJ. 2

SPREADSHEET PROBLEM

The treasurer of Brady Company instructs you to prepare a monthly cash budget for the next three months. You are presented with the following budget information:

	May	June	July
Sales	$120,000	$180,000	$200,000
Manufacturing costs	70,000	110,000	125,000
Operating expenses	20,000	27,000	30,000
Capital expenditures.....................	—	18,000	—

The company expects to sell about 25% of its merchandise for cash. Of sales on account, 60% are expected to be collected in full in the month following the sale and the remainder the following month. Depreciation, insurance, and property taxes represent $10,000 of the estimated monthly manufacturing costs and $4,000 of the probable monthly operating expenses. Insurance and property taxes are paid in February and October respectively. Of the remainder of the manufacturing costs and operating expenses, 60% are expected to be paid in the month in which they are incurred and the balance in the following month.

Current assets as of May 1 are composed of cash of $15,000, marketable securities of $25,000, and accounts receivable of $90,000 ($60,000 from April sales and $30,000 from March sales). Current liabilities as of May 1 are composed of a $20,000, 9%, 120-day note payable due June 10, $38,000 of accounts payable incurred in April for manufacturing costs, and accrued liabilities of $6,000 incurred in April for operating expenses.

It is expected that $5,000 in dividends will be received in May. An estimated income tax payment of $3,500 will be made in June. Brady Company's regular quarterly dividend of $1,000 is expected to be declared in June and paid in July. Management desires to maintain a minimum cash balance of $20,000.

Instructions:

(1) Prepare a monthly cash budget for May, June, and July.
(2) On the basis of the cash budget prepared in (1), what recommendation should be made to the treasurer?

Problem 25–4A
Budgeted income statement and balance sheet.

OBJ. 2

As a preliminary to requesting budget estimates of sales, costs, and expenses for the fiscal year beginning January 1, 1990, the following tentative trial balance as of December 31 of the preceding year is prepared by the accounting department of Crymes Company:

Cash	41,000	
Accounts Receivable	54,000	
Finished Goods	90,000	
Work in Process	47,200	
Materials	31,300	
Prepaid Expenses	6,100	
Plant and Equipment	480,400	
Accumulated Depreciation — Plant and Equipment		192,000
Accounts Payable		60,000
Notes Payable		40,000
Common Stock, $20 par		100,000
Retained Earnings		358,000
	750,000	750,000

Factory output and sales for 1990 are expected to total 50,000 units of product, which are to be sold at $24 per unit. The quantities and costs of the inventories (lifo method) at December 31, 1990, are expected to remain unchanged from the balances at the beginning of the year.

Budget estimates of manufacturing costs and operating expenses for the year are summarized as follows:

	Estimated Costs and Expenses	
	Fixed (Total for Year)	Variable (Per Unit Sold)
Cost of goods manufactured and sold:		
Direct materials	—	$7.10
Direct labor	—	3.90
Factory overhead:		
Depreciation of plant and equipment	$15,000	—
Other factory overhead	10,000	1.75
Selling expenses:		
Sales salaries and commissions	25,000	.80
Advertising	20,000	—
Miscellaneous selling expense	2,000	.18
Administrative expenses:		
Office and officers salaries	30,000	.20
Supplies	1,000	.05
Miscellaneous administrative expense	500	.02

Balances of accounts receivable, prepaid expenses, and accounts payable at the end of the year are expected to differ from the beginning balances by only inconsequential amounts.

For purposes of this problem, assume that federal income tax of $160,000 on 1990 taxable income will be paid during 1990. Regular quarterly cash dividends of $.15 a share are expected to be declared and paid in March, June, September, and December. It is anticipated that plant and equipment will be purchased for $250,000 cash in November.

Instructions:

(1) Prepare a budgeted income statement for 1990.
(2) Prepare a budgeted balance sheet as of December 31, 1990.

Problem 25–5A

Flexible factory overhead cost budget and variance report.

OBJ. 4, 8

Webster Inc. prepared the following factory overhead cost budget for the Polishing Department for July of the current year:

Webster Inc.
Factory Overhead Cost Budget — Polishing Department
For Month Ending July 31, 19--

Machine hours:		
Productive capacity of 100%....................................		10,000
Hours budgeted		11,500
Variable cost:		
Indirect factory wages	$7,475	
Indirect materials	3,680	
Power and light	2,875	
Total variable cost...		$14,030
Fixed cost:		
Supervisory salaries	$5,500	
Indirect factory wages	3,100	
Depreciation of plant and equipment.........................	2,090	
Insurance	1,260	
Power and light	1,120	
Property taxes...	730	
Total fixed cost..		13,800
Total factory overhead cost...		$27,830

During July, the Polishing Department was operated for 11,500 machine hours, and the following factory overhead costs were incurred:

Indirect factory wages	$10,700
Supervisory salaries	5,500
Power and light	4,100
Indirect materials	3,500
Depreciation of plant and equipment...................................	2,090
Insurance	1,260
Property taxes..	730
Total factory overhead cost incurred	$27,880

Instructions:

(1) Prepare a flexible budget for July, indicating capacities of 7,000, 8,500, 10,000, and 11,500 hours and the determination of a standard factory overhead rate per machine hour.

(2) Prepare a standard factory overhead cost variance report for July.

Problem 25–6A

Direct materials, direct labor, and factory overhead cost variance analysis.

OBJ. 8

Standard costs and actual costs for direct materials, direct labor, and factory overhead incurred for the manufacture of 8,000 units of product were as follows:

	Standard Costs	Actual Costs
Direct materials	14,400 pounds at $7.50	14,600 pounds at $7.95
Direct labor......................	5,600 hours at $15	5,250 hours at $15.80
Factory overhead..............	Rates per machine hour, based on 100% of capacity of 20,000 machine hours:	
	Variable cost, $3.70	$60,100 variable cost
	Fixed cost, $2.50	$50,000 fixed cost

Two machine hours are required per unit.

Instructions:

Determine (a) the quantity variance, price variance, and total direct materials cost variance; (b) the time variance, rate variance, and total direct labor cost variance; and (c) the volume variance, controllable variance, and total factory overhead cost variance.

Problem 25–7A
Entries and standard cost variance analysis.

OBJ. 9

Alexander Inc. maintains perpetual inventory accounts for materials, work in process, and finished goods and uses a standard cost system based on the following data:

	Standard Cost per Unit
Direct materials: 5 kilograms at $1.80 per kg	$ 9
Direct labor: 3/4 hour at $20 per hour	15
Factory overhead: $8.00 per direct labor hour..............	6
Total	$30

There was no inventory of work in process at the beginning or end of November, the first month of the current fiscal year. The transactions relating to production completed during November are summarized as follows:

(a) Materials purchased on account, $130,700.
(b) Direct materials used, $108,240. This represented 61 500 kilograms at $1.76 per kilogram.
(c) Direct labor paid, $182,310. This represented 8,850 hours at $20.60 per hour. There were no accruals at either the beginning or the end of the period.
(d) Factory overhead incurred during the month was composed of depreciation on plant and equipment, $24,500; indirect labor, $18,500; insurance, $12,000; and miscellaneous factory costs, $9,500. The indirect labor and miscellaneous factory costs were paid during the period, and the insurance represents an expiration of prepaid insurance. Of the total factory overhead of $64,500, fixed costs amounted to $30,000, and variable costs were $34,500.
(e) Goods finished during the period, 12,000 units.

Instructions:

(1) Prepare entries to record the transactions, assuming that the work in process account is debited for actual production costs and credited with standard costs for goods finished.
(2) Prepare a T account for Work in Process and post to the account, using the identifying letters as dates.
(3) Prepare schedules of variances for direct materials cost, direct labor cost, and factory overhead cost. Productive capacity for the plant is 10,000 direct labor hours.
(4) Total the amount of the standard cost variances and compare this total with the balance of the work in process account.

Appendix
Problem 25–8A
Economic order quantity and inventory order point.

Daniel Company has recently decided to implement a policy designed to control inventory better. Based on past experience, the following data have been gathered for materials, which are used at a uniform rate throughout the year:

Units required during the year...	2,160
Units of safety stock	240
Days of scheduled production..	270
Days of lead time to receive an order	20
Ordering cost, per order placed	$27
Annual storage cost, per unit	$.40

Instructions:

(1) Complete the following table for "number of orders" of 1 through 6.

Number of Orders	Number of Units per Order	Average Units in Inventory	Order and Storage Costs		
			Order Cost	Storage Cost	Combined Cost
1	2,160	1,080	$27.00	$432.00	$459.00

(2) Determine the economic order quantity, based on the table completed in (1).
(3) Determine the economic order quantity, using the formula on page 1000.
(4) Determine the inventory order point.

Appendix Problem 25–9A
Economic order quantity under present and proposed conditions.

Based on the data presented in Appendix Problem 25–8A, assume that Daniel Company is considering the purchase of new automated storage equipment to facilitate access to materials and to increase storage capacity. In addition, the manager of the purchasing department has requested authorization to purchase five microcomputers to expedite the processing of purchase orders.

Instructions:

(1) Assuming that the new storage equipment will increase the storage cost from $.40 to $1.60 per unit, determine the economic order quantity for Daniel Company, using the formula on page 1000.
(2) Assuming that the new storage equipment is not purchased and the acquisition of the microcomputer equipment will decrease the cost per order placed from $27.00 to $12.00, determine the economic order quantity, using the formula on page 1000.
(3) Assuming that both the new storage equipment and the microcomputer equipment are purchased, determine the economic order quantity, using the formula on page 1000. As indicated in (1) and (2), the purchase of the storage equipment is expected to increase the storage cost per unit from $.40 to $1.60, and the microcomputer equipment is expected to decrease the cost per order placed from $27.00 to $12.00.
(4) Based on the answers to Appendix Problem 25–8A and (1), (2), and (3) above, what generalizations can be made concerning how changes in the cost per order placed and the storage cost per unit affect the economic order quantity?

Series B

Problem 25–1B
Sales, production, direct materials, and direct labor budgets.
OBJ. 2

The budget director of Kotch Company requests estimates of sales, production, and other operating data from the various administrative units every month. Selected information concerning sales and production for May of the current year are summarized as follows:

(a) Estimated sales for May by sales territory:
   Northeast:
      Product E: 5,000 units at $120 per unit
      Product F: 40,000 units at $ 40 per unit
   Southeast:
      Product E: 6,000 units at $120 per unit
      Product F: 36,000 units at $ 40 per unit
   Southwest:
      Product E: 3,000 units at $120 per unit
      Product F: 50,000 units at $ 40 per unit

(b) Estimated inventories at May 1:
  Direct materials:
    Material W: 18,200 lbs.   Material Y: 7,700 lbs.
    Material X: 4,600 lbs.   Material Z: 13,250 lbs.
  Finished products:
    Product E: 2,000 units   Product F: 11,000 units

(c) Desired inventories at May 31:
  Direct materials:
    Material W: 20,000 lbs.   Material Y: 8,000 lbs.
    Material X: 5,000 lbs.   Material Z: 14,000 lbs.
  Finished products:
    Product E: 1,500 units   Product F: 12,000 units

(d) Direct materials used in production:
  In manufacture of Product E:
    Material X: 3.6 lbs. per unit of product
    Material Y: 1.4 lbs. per unit of product
    Material Z: .5 lbs. per unit of product
  In manufacture of Product F:
    Material W: 1.6 lbs. per unit of product
    Material Y: .4 lbs. per unit of product
    Material Z: 1.0 lb. per unit of product

(e) Anticipated purchase price for direct materials:
    Material W: $10.00 per lb.   Material Y: $2.50 per lb.
    Material X: $ .30 per lb.   Material Z: $ .80 per lb.

(f) Direct labor requirements:
  Product E:
    Department 20: 3.2 hours at $15 per hour
    Department 30: .4 hours at $12 per hour
  Product F:
    Department 10: .2 hours at $9 per hour
    Department 20: .1 hours at $15 per hour

Instructions:

(1) Prepare a sales budget for May.
(2) Prepare a production budget for May.
(3) Prepare a direct materials purchases budget for May.
(4) Prepare a direct labor cost budget for May.

Problem 25–2B
Budgeted income statement and supporting budgets.
OBJ. 2

The budget director of Gonzales Inc., with the assistance of the controller, treasurer, production manager, and sales manager, has gathered the following data for use in developing the budgeted income statement for June:

(a) Estimated sales for June:
    Product G: 100,000 units at $50 per unit
    Product H: 20,000 units at $15 per unit

(b) Estimated inventories at June 1:
  Direct materials: Finished products:
    Material A: 15,800 lbs.   Product G: 9,000 units at $34 per unit
    Material B: 9,500 lbs.   Product H: 3,000 units at $11 per unit

(c) Desired inventories at June 30:

Direct materials: Finished products:
   Material A: 18,000 lbs.   Product G: 11,000 units at $34 per unit
   Material B: 9,000 lbs.   Product H: 1,500 units at $11 per unit

(d) Direct materials used in production:

In manufacture of Product G:
   Material A: 1.5 lbs. per unit of product
   Material B: .7 lbs. per unit of product
In manufacture of Product H:
   Material B: .8 lbs. per unit of product

(e) Anticipated cost of purchases and beginning and ending inventory of direct materials:

   Material A: $7 per lb.
   Material B: $4 per lb.

(f) Direct labor requirements:

Product G:
   Department 100: 1.2 hours at $12 per hour
   Department 200:   .1 hours at $8 per hour
Product H:
   Department 200:   .2 hours at $8 per hour
   Department 300:   .5 hours at $9 per hour

(g) Estimated factory overhead costs for June:

Indirect factory wages	$150,000
Depreciation of plant and equipment	110,000
Supervisory salaries	90,000
Power and light	80,000
Indirect materials	40,000
Maintenance	25,000
Insurance and property taxes	15,000

(h) Estimated operating expenses for June:

Sales salaries expense	$230,000
Officers salaries expense	150,000
Advertising expense	110,000
Office salaries expense	70,000
Depreciation expense — office equipment	42,000
Telephone expense — selling	24,000
Telephone expense — administrative	10,000
Travel expense — selling	7,500
Travel expense — administrative	6,500
Office supplies expense	3,000
Miscellaneous selling expense	2,000
Miscellaneous administrative expense	1,000

(i) Estimated other income and expense for June:

Interest income	$100,000
Interest expense	90,000

(j) Estimated tax rate: 40%.

Instructions:

(1) Prepare a sales budget for June.
(2) Prepare a production budget for June.
(3) Prepare a direct materials purchases budget for June.
(4) Prepare a direct labor cost budget for June.
(5) Prepare a factory overhead cost budget for June.
(6) Prepare a cost of goods sold budget for June. Work in process at the beginning of June is estimated to be $28,500, and work in process at the end of June is estimated to be $29,000.
(7) Prepare an operating expenses budget for June. Classify the expenses as either selling or administrative expenses.
(8) Prepare a budgeted income statement for June.

Problem 25–3B
Cash budget.
OBJ. 2

The treasurer of Grayson Company instructs you to prepare a monthly cash budget for the next three months. You are presented with the following budget information:

	July	August	September
Sales	$300,000	$250,000	$400,000
Manufacturing costs	200,000	130,000	250,000
Operating expenses	40,000	25,000	60,000
Capital expenditures	—	240,000	—

The company expects to sell about 20% of its merchandise for cash. Of sales on account, 75% are expected to be collected in full in the month following the sale and the remainder the following month. Depreciation, insurance, and property taxes represent $25,000 of the estimated monthly manufacturing costs and $4,000 of the probable monthly operating expenses. Insurance and property taxes are paid in December. Of the remainder of the manufacturing costs and operating expenses, 60% are expected to be paid in the month in which they are incurred and the balance in the following month.

Current assets as of July 1 are composed of cash of $35,100, marketable securities of $20,000 and accounts receivable of $282,000 ($210,000 from June sales and $72,000 from May sales). Current liabilities as of July 1 are composed of a $70,000, 15%, 180-day note payable due September 15, $42,000 of accounts payable incurred in June for manufacturing costs, and accrued liabilities of $10,300 incurred in June for operating expenses.

It is expected that $5,000 in dividends will be received in August. An estimated income tax payment of $8,000 will be made in September. Grayson Company's regular semiannual dividend of $10,000 is expected to be declared in August and paid in September. Management desires to maintain a minimum cash balance of $30,000.

Instructions:

(1) Prepare a monthly cash budget for July, August, and September.
(2) On the basis of the cash budget prepared in (1), what recommendation should be made to the treasurer?

Problem 25–5B
Flexible factory overhead cost budget and variance report.
OBJ. 4, 8

Zuber Company prepared the following factory overhead cost budget for the Painting Department for March of the current year:

Zuber Company
Factory Overhead Cost Budget—Painting Department
For Month Ending March 31, 19--

Machine hours:		
Productive capacity of 100%.................................		70,000
Hours budgeted		56,000
Variable cost:		
Indirect factory wages	$84,000	
Indirect materials	33,600	
Power and light	16,800	
Total variable cost...		$134,400
Fixed cost:		
Supervisory salaries	$63,000	
Indirect factory wages	43,400	
Depreciation of plant and equipment......................	26,250	
Insurance	21,700	
Power and light	14,350	
Property taxes...	13,300	
Total fixed cost..		182,000
Total factory overhead cost......................................		$316,400

During March, the Painting Department was operated for 56,000 machine hours, and the following factory overhead costs were incurred:

Indirect factory wages	$133,000
Supervisory salaries	63,000
Indirect materials	32,900
Power and light	32,000
Depreciation of plant and equipment...............................	26,250
Insurance	21,700
Property taxes...	13,300
Total factory overhead cost incurred	$322,150

Instructions:

(1) Prepare a flexible budget for March, indicating capacities of 49,000, 56,000, 63,000, and 70,000 hours and the determination of a standard factory overhead rate per machine hour.
(2) Prepare a standard factory overhead cost variance report for March.

Problem 25–6B
Direct materials, direct labor, and factory overhead cost variance analysis.
OBJ. 8

Standard costs and actual costs for direct materials, direct labor, and factory overhead incurred for the manufacture of 12,000 units of product were as follows:

	Standard Costs	Actual Costs
Direct materials	9,000 pounds at $23	9,250 pounds at $22.20
Direct labor......................	3,000 hours at $18	2,800 hours at $18.50
Factory overhead..............	Rates per machine hour, based on 100% of capacity of 50,000 machine hours:	
	Variable cost, $2.60	$130,000 variable cost
	Fixed cost, $1.80	$90,000 fixed cost

Four machine hours are required per unit.

Instructions:

Determine (a) the quantity variance, price variance, and total direct materials cost variance; (b) the time variance, rate variance, and total direct labor cost variance; and (c) the volume variance, controllable variance, and total factory overhead cost variance.

Problem 25–7B
Entries and standard cost variance analysis.

OBJ. 9

Johns Inc. maintains perpetual inventory accounts for materials, work in process, and finished goods and uses a standard cost system based on the following data:

	Standard Cost per Unit
Direct materials: 6 kilograms at $2.80 per kg	$16.80
Direct labor: 1 hour at $18 per hour	18.00
Factory overhead: $3.10 per machine hour..................	6.20
Total	$41.00

Each unit of product uses a standard of 2 machine hours. There was no inventory of work in process at the beginning or end of March, the first month of the current fiscal year. The transactions relating to production completed during March are summarized as follows:

(a) Materials purchased on account, $98,300.
(b) Direct materials used, $93,000. The amount represented 31 000 kilograms at $3.00 per kilogram.
(c) Direct labor paid, $88,690. This amount represented 4,900 hours at $18.10 per hour. There were no accruals at either the beginning or the end of the period.
(d) Factory overhead incurred during the month was composed of depreciation on plant and equipment, $14,300; indirect labor, $12,700; insurance, $4,960; and miscellaneous factory costs, $2,940. The indirect labor and miscellaneous factory costs were paid during the period, and the insurance represents an expiration of prepaid insurance. Of the total factory overhead of $34,900, fixed costs amounted to $18,000, and variable costs were $16,900.
(e) Goods finished during the period, 5,000 units.

Instructions:

(1) Prepare entries to record the transactions, assuming that the work in process account is debited for actual production costs and credited with standard costs for goods finished.
(2) Prepare a T account for Work in Process and post to the account, using the identifying letters as dates.
(3) Prepare schedules of variances for direct materials cost, direct labor cost, and factory overhead cost. Productive capacity for the plant is 15,000 machine hours.
(4) Total the amount of the standard cost variances and compare this total with the balance of the work in process account.

MINI-CASE 25

BARNES MANUFACTURING COMPANY

Your father is president and chief operating officer of Barnes Manufacturing Company and has hired you as a summer intern to assist the controller. The controller has asked you to visit with the production supervisor of the Polishing Department and evaluate the supervisor's concern with the budgeting process. After this evaluation, you are to meet with the controller to discuss suggestions for improving the budgeting process.

This morning, you met with the supervisor, who expressed dissatisfaction with the budgets and budget performance reports prepared for the factory overhead costs for the Polishing Department. Specifically, March's budget performance report was mentioned as an example. The supervisor indicated that this report is not useful in evaluating the efficiency of the department, because most of the overages for the individual factory overhead items are not caused by inefficiencies, but by variations in the volume of activity between actual and budget. Although you were not provided with a copy of the budget for March, the supervisor indicated that it is standard practice for the plant manager to prepare a budget based on the production of 10,000 units. Actual production varies widely, however, with approximately 12,000 to 15,000 units being produced each month for the past several months. You are provided with the following budget performance report for March of the current year, when actual production was 15,000 units. All of the overages relate to variable costs, and the other costs are fixed.

Barnes Manufacturing Company
Budget Performance Report—Factory Overhead Cost, Polishing Department
For Month Ended March 31, 19--

	Budget	Actual	Over	Under
Indirect factory wages....................	$28,000	$ 41,700	$13,700	
Electric power..............................	17,800	27,000	9,200	
Supervisory salaries	16,000	16,000		
Depreciation of plant assets...........	12,000	12,000		
Indirect materials..........................	8,200	12,400	4,200	
Insurance and property taxes	4,000	4,000		
	$86,000	$113,100	$27,100	$0

In your discussion, you learned that the department supervisor has little faith in the budgeting process. The supervisor views the budgets as worthless and the budget performance reports as a waste of time, because they require an explanation of the budget overages, which, for the most part, are not departmentally controlled.

Instructions:

Prepare a list of suggestions for improving the budgeting process. Include any reports that you might find useful when you meet with the controller to discuss your suggestions.

ETHICS DISCUSSION CASE	Jan Himmel, a cost accounting clerk for Icahn Inc., has been assigned the task of preparing the first draft of the cost of goods sold and related budgets for the manufacturing operations. Himmel has received budget estimates for the forthcoming year from the various production supervisors. Because she thinks that the production supervisors probably over-estimated their costs in order to have some cushion for possible production problems, she decided to cut all the supervisors' estimates by 15%.
	Discuss whether Jan Himmel behaved in an ethical manner by cutting all the budget estimates by 15%.

ANSWERS TO SELF-EXAMINATION QUESTIONS

1. **C** The capital expenditures budget (answer C) summarizes the plans for the acquisition of plant facilities and equipment for a number of years into the future. The cash budget (answer A) presents the expected inflow and outflow of cash for a budget period, and the sales budget (answer B) presents the expected sales for the budget period.

2. **C** Flexible budgeting (answer C) provides a series of budgets for varying rates of activity and thereby builds into the budgeting system the effect of fluctuations in volume of activity. Budget performance reporting (answer A) is a system of reports that compares actual results with budgeted figures. Continuous budgeting (answer B) is a variant of fiscal-year budgeting that provides for continuous twelve-month projections into the future. This twelve-month projection is achieved and maintained by periodically deleting from the current budget the data for the elapsed period and adding newly estimated budget data for the same period next year.

3. **C** The favorable direct labor cost time variance of $110 (answer C) is determined as follows:

Actual time	990 hours
Standard time...	1,000 hours
Time variance — favorable	−10 hours
10 hours × $11 standard	$110

4. **B** The unfavorable factory overhead volume variance of $2,000 (answer B) is determined as follows:

Productive capacity not used.............................	1,000 hours
Standard fixed factory overhead cost rate.............	×$2
Factory overhead volume variance — unfavorable...	$2,000

5. **A** The favorable factory overhead controllable variance of $3,500 (answer A) is determined as follows:

Actual factory overhead cost incurred	$112,500
Budgeted factory overhead for standard product produced [(19,000 hours at $4 variable) + (20,000 hours at $2 fixed)]...................................	116,000
Factory overhead controllable variance — favorable	$ −3,500

CHAPTER TWENTY-SIX
RESPONSIBILITY ACCOUNTING

CHAPTER OBJECTIVES

1 Describe the nature of centralized and decentralized operations.

2 Describe the three types of decentralized operations.

3 Describe and illustrate responsibility accounting for cost centers.

4 Describe and illustrate responsibility accounting for profit centers.

5 Describe and illustrate responsibility accounting for investment centers.

In a small business, virtually all plans and decisions can be made by one individual. As a business grows or its operations become more diverse, it becomes difficult, if not impossible, for one individual to perform these functions. For example, the responsibility for planning and controlling operations is clear in a one-person real estate agency. If the agency expands by opening an office in a distant city, some of the authority and responsibility for planning and decision making in a given area of operations might be delegated to others. In other words, if centralized operations become unwieldy as a business grows, the need to delegate responsibility for portions of operations arises. This separation of a business into more manageable units is termed **decentralization**. In a decentralized business, an important function of the managerial accountant is to assist individual managers in evaluating and controlling their areas of responsibility.

A term frequently applied to the process of measuring and reporting operating data by areas of responsibility is **responsibility accounting**. Some of the concepts useful in responsibility accounting were presented in preceding chapters. For example, in discussing budgetary control of operations, the use of the master budget, budgets for various departments, and budget performance reports in controlling operations by areas of responsibility were discussed. In this chapter, the concept of responsibility accounting as it relates to three types of decentralized operations is described and illustrated.

CENTRALIZED AND DECENTRALIZED OPERATIONS

OBJECTIVE 1
Describe the nature of centralized and decentralized operations.

A completely centralized business organization is one in which all major planning and operating decisions are made by the top echelon of management. For example, a one-person, owner-manager-operated business is centralized because all plans and decisions are made by one person. In a small owner-manager-operated business, centralization may be desirable, since the

1027

owner-manager's close supervision ensures that the business will be operated in conformity with the manager's wishes and desires.

In a decentralized business organization, responsibility for planning and controlling operations is delegated among managers. These managers have the authority to make decisions without first seeking the approval of higher management. The level of decentralization varies significantly, and there is no one best level of decentralization for all businesses. In some companies, for example, plant managers have authority over all plant operations, including plant asset acquisitions and retirements. In other companies, a plant manager may only have authority for scheduling production and for controlling the costs of direct materials, direct labor, and factory overhead. The proper level of decentralization for a company depends on the advantages and disadvantages of decentralization as they apply to a company's specific, unique circumstances.

Advantages of Decentralization

As a business grows, it becomes more difficult for top management to maintain close daily contact with all operations. Hence, a top management that delegates authority in such circumstances has a better chance of sound decisions being made, and the managers closest to the operations may anticipate and react to operating information more quickly. In addition, as a company diversifies into a wide range of products and services, it becomes more difficult for top management to maintain operating expertise in all product lines and services. In such cases, decentralization allows managers to concentrate on acquiring expertise in their areas of responsibility. For example, in a company that maintains diversified operations in oil refining, banking, and the manufacture of office equipment, individual managers could become "expert" in the area of their responsibility.

The delegation of responsibility for day-to-day operations from top management to middle management frees top management to concentrate more on strategic planning. **Strategic planning** is the process of establishing long-term goals for an enterprise and developing plans to achieve these goals. For example, a goal to expand an enterprise's product line into new markets and to plan to finance this expansion through the issuance of long-term debt rather than additional common stock are examples of strategic planning decisions. As the business environment becomes more complex and as companies grow, strategic planning assumes an increasingly important role in the long-run success of a company.

Decentralized decision making provides excellent training for managers, which may be a factor in enabling a company to retain quality managers. Since the art of management can best be acquired through experience, the delegation of responsibility enables managers to acquire and develop managerial expertise early in their careers. Also, the operating personnel may be more creative in suggesting operating improvements, since personnel in a decentralized company tend to identify closely with the operations for which they are responsible.

The delegation of responsibility also serves as a positive reinforcement for managers, in that they may view such delegation as an indication of top management's confidence in their abilities. Thus, manager morale tends to increase because managers feel that they have more control over factors affecting their careers and their performance evaluation.

Disadvantages of Decentralization

The primary disadvantage of decentralized operations is that decisions made by one manager may affect other managers in such a way that the profitability of the entire company may suffer. For example, two managers competing in a common product market may engage in price cutting to win customers. As a result, the overall company profits may be less than the profits that could have been if the price cutting had not occurred.

Other potential disadvantages of decentralized operations may be the duplication of various assets and costs in the operating division. For example, each manager of a product line might have a separate sales force and administrative office staff, but centralization of these personnel could save money. Likewise, the costs of gathering and processing operating information in a decentralized operation might be greater than if such information were gathered and processed centrally.

THINKING SMALL

One company that experienced positive results from decentralizing was NCR (formerly National Cash Register Co.), a Dayton-based multinational electronics and computer manufacturing corporation. In 1979, NCR was a troubled company. Management began to examine NCR's problems and to reevaluate the company's structure, which appeared to be inhibiting NCR's ability to innovate and adapt. Additional background and the results of NCR's changes were reported in *Inc.*, as follows:

As part of this reevaluation process, NCR commissioned the McKinsey & Co. consulting group to study the attributes of a number of highly successful companies. The researchers looked at such corporations as Sperry, IBM, and Hewlett-Packard, to determine what they had done that might be applied to NCR.

*Using this study as background, NCR developed a plan for restructuring itself. Analyzing the path of a product from idea to implementation, it discovered some obvious impediments. The de-*velopment, production, and marketing of a new product involved three separate divisions. This cumbersome system created opportunities for false starts and misinterpreting . . . the market. . . . It took a long time to get a product through this entire process, and sometimes products got lost in translation. . . .

So NCR proceeded to break up its product-management organization and move the parts to units that would develop, manufacture, and market products. In consulting jargon, this is called shifting from a "functional" to a "divisional" organization, and it has been done many times before in other industries. . . .

These changes transformed NCR Corp. from a highly centralized operation into a series of stand-alone [or decentralized] units. Today there is no requirement that one unit buy components from another NCR unit if it can find better or cheaper products outside the company. Moreover, based upon the nature of their products, the different divisions make their own decisions about how they want to structure themselves with regard to such activities as marketing.

Source: Eugene Linden, "Let a Thousand Flowers Bloom," *Inc.* (April, 1984), pp. 64–76.

TYPES OF DECENTRALIZED OPERATIONS

OBJECTIVE 2
Describe the three types of decentralized operations.

Decentralized operations can be classified by the scope of responsibility assigned and the decision-making authority given to individual managers. The three common types of decentralized operations are referred to as cost centers, profit centers, and investment centers. Each of these types of decentralized operations is briefly described in the following paragraphs. Responsibility accounting for each type is then discussed and illustrated in the remainder of this chapter.

Cost Centers

In a **cost center**, the department or division manager has responsibility for the control of costs incurred and the authority to make decisions that affect these costs. For example, the marketing manager has responsibility for the costs of the Marketing Department, and the supervisor of the Power Department has responsibility for the costs incurred in providing power. The department manager does not make decisions concerning sales of the cost center's output, nor does the department manager have control over the plant assets available to the cost center.

Cost centers are the most widely used type of decentralization, because the organization and operation of most businesses allow for an easy identification of areas where managers can be assigned responsibility for and authority over costs. Cost centers may vary in size from a small department with a few employees to an entire manufacturing plant. In addition, cost centers may exist within other cost centers. For example, a manager of a manufacturing plant organized as a cost center may treat individual departments within the plant as separate cost centers, with the department managers reporting directly to the plant manager.

Profit Centers

In a **profit center**, the manager has the responsibility and the authority to make decisions that affect both costs and revenues (and thus profits) for the department or division. For example, a retail department store might decentralize its operations by product line. The manager of each product line would have responsibility for the cost of merchandise and decisions regarding revenues, such as the determination of sales prices. The manager of a profit center does not make decisions concerning the plant assets available to the center. For example, the manager of the Sporting Goods Department does not make the decision to expand the available floor space for that department.

Profit centers are widely used in businesses in which individual departments or divisions sell products or services to those outside the company. A partial organization chart for a department store decentralized by retail departments as profit centers is as follows:

Partial Organization Chart for Department Store with Profit Centers

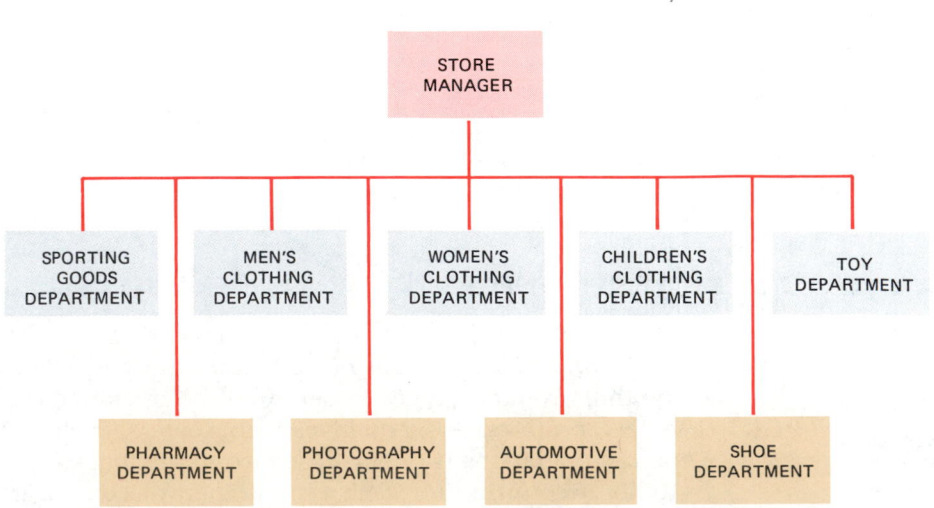

Occasionally, profit centers are established when the center's product or service is consumed entirely within the company. For example, a Repairs and Maintenance Department of a manufacturing plant could be treated as a profit center if its manager were allowed to bill other departments, such as the various production departments, for services rendered. Likewise, the Data Processing Department of a company might bill each of the company's administrative and operating units for computing services.

In a sense, a profit center may be viewed as a business within a business. While the primary concern of a cost center manager is the control of costs, the profit center is concerned with both revenues and costs.

Profit centers are often viewed as an excellent training assignment for new managers. For example, Lester B. Korn, Chairman and Chief Executive Officer of Korn/Ferry International, recently offered the following strategy for young executives en route to top management positions:

> *Get Profit-Center Responsibility — Obtain a position where you can prove yourself as both a specialist with particular expertise and a generalist who can exercise leadership, authority, and inspire enthusiasm among colleagues and subordinates.*

Investment Centers

In an **investment center**, the manager has the responsibility and the authority to make decisions that affect not only costs and revenues, but also the plant assets available to the center. For example, a plant manager sets selling prices of products and establishes controls over costs. In addition, the plant manager could, within general constraints established by top management, expand production facilities through equipment acquisitions and retirements.

The manager of an investment center has more authority and responsibility than the manager of either a cost center or a profit center. The manager of an investment center occupies a position similar to that of a chief operating officer or president of a separate company. As such, an investment center manager is evaluated in much the same way as a manager of a separate company is evaluated.

Investment centers are widely used in highly diversified companies. A partial organizational chart for a diversified company with divisions organized as investment centers is as follows:

Partial Organization Chart for Diversified Company with Investment Centers

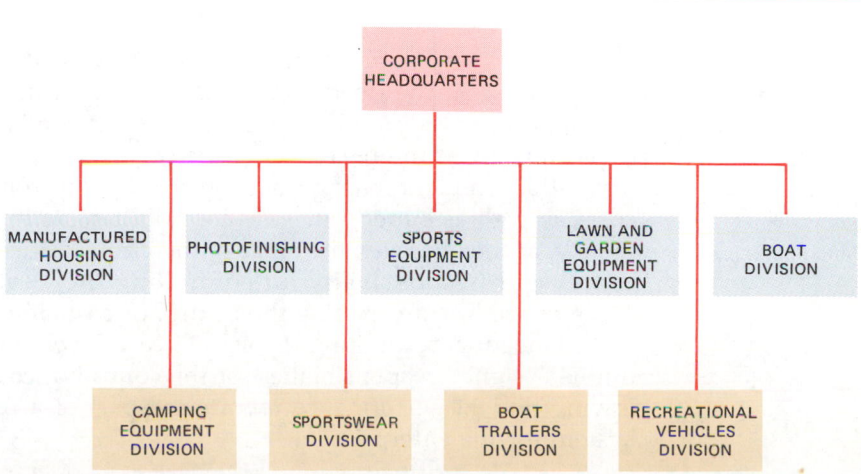

RESPONSIBILITY ACCOUNTING FOR COST CENTERS

OBJECTIVE 3
Describe and
illustrate
responsibility
accounting for cost
centers.

Since managers of cost centers have responsibility for and authority to make decisions regarding costs, responsibility accounting for cost centers focuses on costs. The primary accounting tools appropriate for controlling and reporting costs are budgets and standard costs. Since budgets and standard costs were described and illustrated in Chapter 25, they will not be discussed in detail in this chapter. Instead, responsibility accounting for a cost center which uses budgeting to assist in the control of costs will be illustrated. The basic concepts of responsibility accounting, as illustrated, are equally applicable to cost centers that use standard cost systems to aid in cost control.

For purposes of illustration, assume that the responsibility for the manufacturing operations of an enterprise is as represented in the following organization chart:

*Organization Chart
Depicting
Management
Responsibility for
Production*

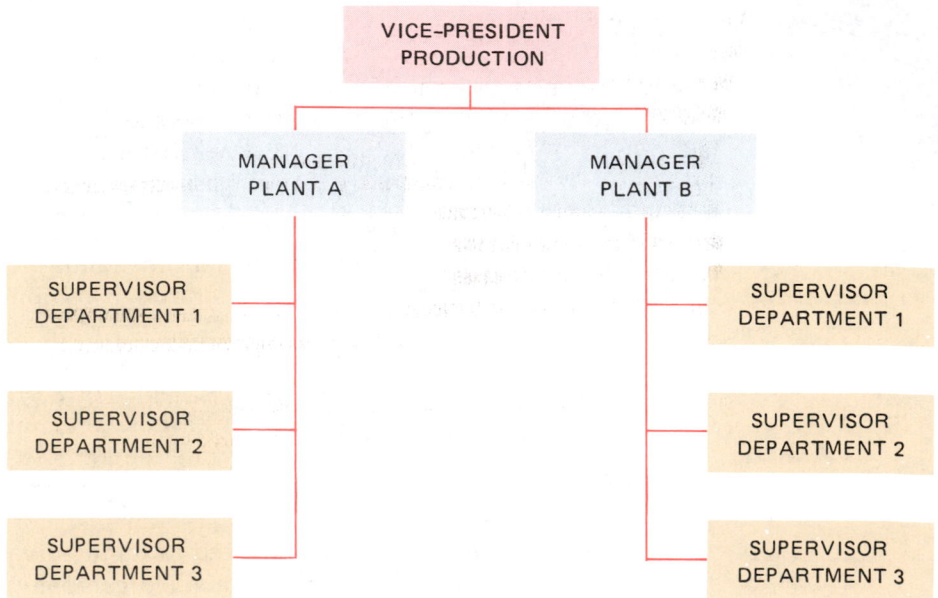

Within the organizational structure illustrated, there are three levels of cost centers. At the operating level, each department is a cost center, with the department supervisors responsible for controlling costs within their departments. At the next level of the organization, each plant is a cost center, with each plant manager responsible for controlling plant administrative costs as well as supervising the control of costs in the plant departments. Finally, at the top level, the office of the vice-president of production is a cost center with responsibility for controlling the administrative costs of the office as well as supervising the control of costs in each plant.

Managerial accounting reports aid each level of management in carrying out its assigned responsibilities for the control of costs. To illustrate, the following budget performance reports are part of a responsibility accounting system for the enterprise:

Responsibility
Accounting
Reports

Budget Performance Report—
Vice-President, Operations
For Month Ended October 31, 19--.

	Budget	Actual	Over	Under
Administration................	$ 19,500	$ 19,700	$ 200	
Plant A........................	467,475	470,330	2,855	
Plant B........................	395,225	394,300		$925
	$882,200	$884,330	$3,055	$925

Budget Performance Report—Manager, Plant A
For Month Ended October 31, 19--

	Budget	Actual	Over	Under
Administration................	$ 17,500	$ 17,350		$150
Department 1	109,725	111,280	$1,555	
Department 2	190,500	192,600	2,100	
Department 3	149,750	149,100		650
	$467,475	$470,330	$3,655	$800

Budget Performance Report—
Supervisor, Department 1-Plant A
For Month Ended October 31, 19--

	Budget	Actual	Over	Under
Factory wages................	$ 58,100	$ 58,000		$100
Materials	32,500	34,225	$1,725	
Supervisory salaries	6,400	6,400		
Power and light..............	5,750	5,690		60
Depreciation of plant and equipment............	4,000	4,000		
Maintenance	2,000	1,990		10
Insurance and property taxes	975	975		
	$109,725	$111,280	$1,725	$170

The amount of detail presented in the budget performance report depends upon the level of management to which the report is directed. The reports prepared for the department supervisors present details of the budgeted and actual manufacturing costs for their departments. Each supervisor can then concentrate on the individual items that resulted in significant variations. In the illustration, the budget performance report for Department 1-Plant A indicates a significant variation between the budgeted and actual amounts for materials. It is clear that supplemental reports providing detailed data on the causes of the variation would aid the supervisor in taking corrective action. One such report, a scrap report, is illustrated as follows. This report indicates the cause of a significant part of the variation.

Scrap Report

Materials Scrap Report—Department 1-Plant A
For Month Ended October 31, 19--

Material No.	Units Spoiled	Unit Cost	Dollar Loss	Remarks
A392	50	$3.10	$ 155.00	Machine malfunction
C417	76	.80	60.80	Inexperienced employee
G118	5	1.10	5.50	
J510	120	8.25	990.00	Substandard materials
K277	2	1.50	3.00	
P719	7	2.10	14.70	
V112	22	4.25	93.50	Machine malfunction
			$1,322.50	

The scrap report is one example of the type of supplemental report that can be provided to department supervisors. Other examples would include reports on factory wages and the cost of idle time.

The budget performance reports for the plant managers contain summarized data on the budgeted and actual costs for the departments under their jurisdiction. These reports enable them to identify the department supervisors responsible for significant variances. The report for the vice-president in charge of operations summarizes the data by plant. The persons responsible for plant operations can thus be held accountable for significant variations from predetermined objectives.

RESPONSIBILITY ACCOUNTING FOR PROFIT CENTERS

OBJECTIVE 4
Describe and illustrate responsibility accounting for profit centers.

Since managers of profit centers have responsibility for and authority to make decisions regarding expenses and revenues, responsibility accounting reports for profit centers are normally in the form of income statements. These income statements for individual profit centers report expenses and revenues by departments through either gross profit or operating income. Alternatively, profit center income statements may include a breakdown of revenues and expenses by responsibility for their incurrence, and may identify contributions made by each department to overall company profit.

Since profit centers are widely used by merchandising enterprises, such as department stores, a merchandising enterprise is used as the basis for the following discussion and illustration of responsibility accounting for profit centers. Although the degree to which profit centers are used by a merchandising enterprise varies, profit centers are typically established for each major retail department. The enterprise in the illustrations, Harris Company, has established Departments A and B as profit centers.

Gross Profit by Departments

To compute gross profit by departments, it is necessary to determine by departments each element entering into gross profit. An income statement showing gross profit by departments for Harris Company appears on pages 1036 and 1037. For illustrative purposes, the operating expenses are shown in condensed form. Usually they would be listed in detail.

For a merchandising enterprise, the gross profit is one of the most significant figures in the income statement. Since the sales and the cost of goods sold are both controlled by departmental management, the reporting of gross profit by departments is useful in cost analysis and control. In addition, such reports aid management in directing its efforts toward obtaining a mix of sales that will maximize profits. For example, after studying the reports, management may decide to change sales or purchases policies to achieve a higher gross profit for each department. Caution must be exercised in the use of such reports to insure that proposed changes affecting gross profit do not have an adverse effect on net income. A change that increases gross profit could result in an even greater increase in operating expenses and thereby decrease net income.

Operating Income by Departments

Departmental reporting may be extended to operating income. In such cases, each department must be assigned not only the related revenues and the cost of goods sold (as in the preceding illustration), but also that part of operating expenses incurred for its benefit. Some of these expenses may be easily identified with the department benefited. For example, if each salesperson is restricted to a certain sales department, the sales salaries may be assigned to the proper departmental salary accounts each time the payroll is prepared. On the other hand, the salaries of company officers, executives, and office personnel are not identifiable with specific sales departments and must therefore be allocated if an equitable and reasonable basis for allocation exists.

When operating expenses are allocated, they should be apportioned to the respective departments as nearly as possible in accordance with the cost of services rendered to them. Determining the amount of an expense chargeable to each department is not always a simple matter. In the first place, it requires the exercise of judgment; and accountants of equal ability may well differ in their opinions as to the proper basis for the apportionment of operating expenses. Second, the cost of collecting data for use in making an apportionment must be kept within reasonable bounds. Consequently, information that is readily available and is substantially reliable may be used instead of more accurate information that would be more costly to collect.

To illustrate the apportionment of operating expenses, assume that Harris Company extends its departmental reporting through income from operations. The company's operating expenses for the year and the methods used in apportioning them are presented in the paragraphs that follow.

Sales Salaries Expense is apportioned to the two departments according to the distributions shown in the payroll records. Of the $84,900 total in the account, $54,000 is chargeable to Department A and $30,900 is chargeable to Department B.

Advertising Expense, covering billboard advertising and newspaper advertising, is apportioned according to the amount of advertising incurred for each department. The billboard advertising totaling $5,000 emphasizes the name and the location of the company. This expense is allocated on the basis of gross sales, the assumption being that this basis represents a fair allocation of billboard advertising to each department. Analysis of the newspaper space costing $14,000 indicates that 65% of the space was devoted to Department A and 35% to Department B. The computations of the apportionment of the total advertising expense are as follows:

	Total	Department A	Department B
Sales—dollars	$900,000	$630,000	$270,000
Sales—percent	100%	70%	30%
Billboard advertising ..	$ 5,000	$ 3,500	$1,500
Newspaper space— percent...................	100%	65%	35%
Newspaper advertising	14,000	9,100	4,900
Advertising expense	$19,000	$12,600	$6,400

Income Statement Departmentalized through Gross Profit

Harris
Income
For Year Ended

		Department A	
Revenue from sales:			
Sales...	....	$630,000	....
Less sales returns and allowances..........	....	15,300	....
Net sales...	....	....	$614,700
Cost of goods sold:			
Inventories, January 1, 19--.....................	....	$ 80,150	....
Purchases	$334,550	....	....
Less purchases discounts......................	6,200	328,350	....
Goods available for sale...........................	....	$408,500	....
Less inventories, December 31, 19--........	....	85,150	....
Cost of goods sold	....	....	323,350
Gross profit...	....	....	$291,350
Operating expenses:			
Selling expenses...................................	....	....	....
Administrative expenses.........................	....	....	....
Total operating expenses....................	....	....	....
Income from operations........................	....	....	....
Other expense:			
Interest expense	....	....	....
Income before income tax.......................	....	....	....
Income tax..	....	....	....
Net income	....	....	....

Depreciation Expense—Store Equipment is apportioned according to the average cost of the equipment in each of the two departments. The computations for the apportionment of the depreciation expense are as follows:

	Total	Department A	Department B
Cost of store equipment:			
January 1	$28,300	$16,400	$11,900
December 31	31,700	19,600	12,100
Total	$60,000	$36,000	$24,000
Average	$30,000	$18,000	$12,000
Percent	100%	60%	40%
Depreciation expense	$ 4,400	$ 2,640	$ 1,760

Officers' Salaries Expense and **Office Salaries Expense** are apportioned on the basis of the relative amount of time devoted to each department by the officers and by the office personnel. Obviously, this can be only an approximation. The number of sales transactions may have some bearing on the matter, as may billing and collection procedures and other factors such as promotional campaigns that might vary from period to period. Of the total

Company
Statement
December 31, 19--

Department B				Total	
....	$270,000	....	....	$900,000	....
....	7,100	....	....	22,400	....
....	....	$262,900	....	....	$877,600
....	$ 61,750	....	....	$141,900	....
$200,350	....	....	$534,900	....	....
2,400	197,950	....	8,600	526,300	....
....	$259,700	....	....	$668,200	....
....	78,950	....	....	164,100	....
....	....	180,750	....	....	504,100
....	....	$ 82,150	....	....	$373,500
....	....	....	....	$113,000	....
....	....	....	....	110,200	....
....	....	....	....	....	223,200
....	....	....	....	....	$150,300
....	....	....	....	....	2,500
....	....	....	....	....	$147,800
....	....	....	....	....	64,444
....	....	....	....	....	$ 83,356

officers' salaries of $52,000 and office salaries of $17,600, it is estimated that 60%, or $31,200 and $10,560 respectively, is chargeable to Department A and that 40%, or $20,800 and $7,040 respectively, is chargeable to Department B.

Rent Expense and **Heating and Lighting Expense** are usually apportioned on the basis of floor space devoted to each department. In apportioning rent expense for a multistory building, differences in the value of the various floors and locations may be taken into account. For example, the space near the main entrance of a department store is more valuable than the same amount of floor space located far from the elevator on the sixth floor. For Harris Company, rent expense is apportioned on the basis of floor space used because there is no significant difference in the value of the floor areas used by each department. In allocating heating and lighting expense, it is assumed that the number of lights, their wattage, and the extent of use are uniform throughout the sales departments. If there are major variations and the total lighting expense is material, further analysis and separate apportionment may be advisable. The rent expense and the heating and lighting expense are apportioned as follows:

	Total	Department A	Department B
Floor space, square feet.........	160,000	104,000	56,000
Percent	100%	65%	35%
Rent expense........................	$15,400	$10,010	$5,390
Heating and lighting expense ..	$ 5,100	$ 3,315	$1,785

Property Tax Expense and **Insurance Expense** are related primarily to the cost of the inventories and the store equipment. Although the cost of these assets may differ from their assessed value for tax purposes and their value for insurance purposes, the cost is most readily available and is considered to be satisfactory as a basis for apportioning these expenses. The computations of the apportionment of the personal property tax expense and the insurance expense are as follows:

	Total	Department A	Department B
Inventories:			
January 1	$141,900	$ 80,150	$ 61,750
December 31	164,100	85,150	78,950
Total............................	$306,000	$165,300	$140,700
Average	$153,000	$ 82,650	$ 70,350
Average cost of store equipment (computed previously).......	30,000	18,000	12,000
Total	$183,000	$100,650	$ 82,350
Percent	100%	55%	45%
Property tax expense...........	$ 6,800	$ 3,740	$ 3,060
Insurance expense	$ 3,900	$ 2,145	$ 1,755

Uncollectible Accounts Expense, Miscellaneous Selling Expense, and **Miscellaneous Administrative Expense** are apportioned on the basis of gross sales. Although the uncollectible accounts expense may be apportioned on the basis of an analysis of accounts receivable written off, it is assumed that the expense is closely related to gross sales. The miscellaneous selling and administrative expenses are apportioned on the basis of gross sales, which are assumed to be a reasonable measure of the benefit to each department. The computation of the apportionment is as follows:

	Total	Department A	Department B
Sales	$900,000	$630,000	$270,000
Percent	100%	70%	30%
Uncollectible accounts expense	$ 4,600	$ 3,220	$ 1,380
Miscellaneous selling expense	$ 4,700	$ 3,290	$ 1,410
Miscellaneous administrative expense	$ 4,800	$ 3,360	$ 1,440

An income statement presenting income from operations by departments for Harris Company appears on pages 1040 and 1041. The amounts for sales and the cost of goods sold are presented in condensed form. Details could be reported, if desired, in the manner illustrated on pages 1036 and 1037.

Departmental Margin

In a research study, 85% of the companies surveyed indicated that they allocate some operating expenses to profit centers (departments), as discussed in the preceding section.[1] Caution should be used, however, in relying on income statements departmentalized through income from operations, since the use of arbitrary bases in allocating operating expenses is likely to yield incorrect amounts of departmental operating income. In addition, the reporting of operating income by departments may be misleading, since the departments are not independent operating units. The departments are segments of a business enterprise, and no single department of a business can earn an income independently. For these reasons, income statements of segmented businesses may follow a somewhat different format than the one illustrated on pages 1040 and 1041. The alternative format emphasizes the contribution of each department to overall company net income and to covering the overall operating expenses incurred on behalf of the business. Income statements prepared in this alternative format are said to follow the **departmental margin** approach to responsibility accounting.

Prior to the preparation of an income statement in the departmental margin format, it is necessary to differentiate between operating expenses that are direct and those that are indirect. As discussed in Chapter 20, these two categories may be described in general terms as follows:

---

[1]James M. Fremgen and Shu S. Liao, *The Allocation of Corporate Indirect Costs* (New York: National Association of Accountants, 1981), pp. 33–34.

1. **Direct expense** — Operating expenses directly traceable to or incurred for the sole benefit of a specific department and usually subject to the control of the department manager.
2. **Indirect expense** — Operating expenses incurred for the entire enterprise as a unit and hence not subject to the control of individual department managers.

The details of departmental sales and the cost of goods sold are presented on the income statement in the usual manner. The direct expenses of each department are then deducted from the related departmental gross profit, yielding balances which are identified as the departmental margin. The remaining expenses, including the indirect operating expenses, are not departmentalized. They are reported separately below the total departmental margin.

An income statement in the departmental margin format for Harris Company is presented on page 1042. The basic revenue, cost, and expense

Income Statement Departmentalized through Income from Operations

Harris
Income
For Year Ended

			Department A
Net sales	....	....	$614,700
Cost of goods sold	....	....	323,350
Gross profit	....	....	$291,350
Operating expenses:			
Selling expenses:			
Sales salaries expense	$ 54,000	....	....
Advertising expense	12,600	....	....
Depreciation expense — store equipment	2,640	....	....
Miscellaneous selling expense	3,290	....	....
Total selling expenses	....	$ 72,530	....
Administrative expenses:			
Officers' salaries expense	$ 31,200	....	....
Office salaries expense	10,560	....	....
Rent expense	10,010	....	....
Property tax expense	3,740	....	....
Heating and lighting expense	3,315	....	....
Uncollectible accounts expense	3,220	....	....
Insurance expense	2,145	....	....
Miscellaneous administrative expense	3,360	....	....
Total administrative expenses	....	67,550	....
Total operating expenses	....	....	140,080
Income (loss) from operations	....	....	$151,270
Other expense:			
Interest expense	....	....	....
Income before income tax	....	....	....
Income tax	....	....	....
Net income	....	....	....

data for the period are identical with those reported in the earlier illustration. The expenses identified as "direct" are sales salaries, property tax, uncollectible accounts, insurance, depreciation, and the newspaper advertising portion of advertising. The billboard portion of advertising, which is for the benefit of the business as a whole, as well as officers' and office salaries, and the remaining operating expenses, are identified as "indirect." Although a $970 net loss from operations is reported for Department B below, a departmental margin of $38,395 is reported for the same department on the statement on page 1042.

With departmental margin income statements, the manager of each department can be held responsible for operating expenses traceable to the department. A reduction in the direct expenses of a department will have a favorable effect on that department's contribution to the net income of the enterprise.

Company
Statement
December 31, 19--

Department B			Total		
....	....	$262,900	....	....	$877,600
....	....	180,750	....	....	504,100
....	....	$ 82,150	....	....	$373,500
$ 30,900	....	....	$ 84,900	....	....
6,400	....	....	19,000	....	....
1,760	....	....	4,400	....	....
1,410	....	....	4,700	....	....
....	$ 40,470	....	....	$113,000	....
$ 20,800	....	....	$ 52,000	....	....
7,040	....	....	17,600	....	....
5,390	....	....	15,400	....	....
3,060	....	....	6,800	....	....
1,785	....	....	5,100	....	....
1,380	....	....	4,600	....	....
1,755	....	....	3,900	....	....
1,440	....	....	4,800	....	....
....	42,650	....	....	110,200	....
....	....	83,120	....	....	223,200
....	....	$ (970)	....	....	$150,300
....	....	....	....	....	2,500
....	....	....	....	....	$147,800
....	....	....	....	....	64,444
....	....	....	....	....	$ 83,356

The departmental margin income statement may also be useful to management in making plans for future operations. For example, this type of analysis can be used when the discontinuance of a certain operation or department is being considered. If a specific department yields a departmental margin, it generally should be retained, even though the allocation of the indirect operating expenses would result in a net loss for that department. This observation is based upon the assumption that the department in question represents a relatively small segment of the enterprise. Its termination, therefore, would not cause any significant reduction in the amount of indirect expenses.

Income Statement Departmentalized through Departmental Margin

Harris Company
Income Statement
For Year Ended December 31, 19--

	Department A		Department B		Total	
Net sales.............................	....	$614,700	....	$262,900	....	$877,600
Cost of goods sold	....	323,350	....	180,750	....	504,100
Gross profit.............................	....	$291,350	....	$ 82,150	....	$373,500
Direct departmental expenses:						
Sales salaries expense	$54,000	....	$30,900	....	$84,900	....
Advertising expense	9,100	....	4,900	....	14,000	....
Property tax expense............	3,740	....	3,060	....	6,800	....
Uncollectible accounts expense	3,220	....	1,380	....	4,600	....
Depreciation expense—store equipment........................	2,640	....	1,760	....	4,400	....
Insurance expense	2,145	....	1,755	....	3,900	....
Total direct departmental expenses......................	....	74,845	....	43,755	....	118,600
Departmental margin	....	$216,505	....	$ 38,395	....	$254,900
Indirect expenses:						
Officers' salaries expense......	....	....	....	....	$52,000	....
Office salaries expense	....	....	....	....	17,600	....
Rent expense......................	....	....	....	....	15,400	....
Heating and lighting expense .	....	....	....	....	5,100	....
Advertising expense	....	....	....	....	5,000	....
Miscellaneous selling expense	....	....	....	....	4,700	....
Miscellaneous administrative expense	....	....	....	....	4,800	....
Total indirect expenses	....	....	....	....	....	104,600
Income from operations............	....	....	....	....	....	$150,300
Other expense:						
Interest expense	....	....	....	....	....	2,500
Income before income tax.........	....	....	....	....	....	$147,800
Income tax.............................	....	....	....	....	....	64,444
Net income	....	....	....	....	....	$ 83,356

RESPONSIBILITY ACCOUNTING FOR INVESTMENT CENTERS

OBJECTIVE 5
Describe and illustrate responsibility accounting for investment centers.

Since investment center managers have responsibility for revenues and expenses, operating income is an essential part of investment center reporting. In addition, because the investment center manager also has responsibility for the assets invested in the center, two additional measures of performance are often used. These additional measures are the rate of return on investment and residual income. In practice, most companies use some combination of all these measures. In the following paragraphs, each measure of investment center performance is described and illustrated for Waller Company, a diversified company with three operating divisions, A, B, and C.

Operating Income

Because investment centers are evaluated as if they were separate companies, traditional financial statements are normally prepared for each center. For purposes of assessing profitability, operating income is the focal point of analysis. Since the determination of operating income for decentralized operations was described and illustrated in the preceding paragraphs, only condensed divisional income statements will be used for illustrative purposes. The condensed divisional income statements for Waller Company are as follows:

Waller Company Divisional Income Statements For Year Ended December 31, 19--			
	Division A	Division B	Division C
Sales	$560,000	$672,000	$750,000
Cost of goods sold	336,000	470,400	562,500
Gross profit	$224,000	$201,600	$187,500
Operating expenses	154,000	117,600	112,500
Operating income	$ 70,000	$ 84,000	$ 75,000

Based on the amount of divisional operating income, Division B is the most profitable of Waller Company's divisions, with income from operations of $84,000. Divisions A and C are less profitable, with Division C reporting $5,000 more operating income than Division A.

Although operating income is a useful measure of investment center profitability, it does not reflect the amount of investment in assets committed to each center. For example, if the amount of assets invested in Division B is twice that of the other divisions, then Division B is the least profitable of the divisions in terms of the rate of return on investment. Since investment center managers also control the amount of assets invested in their centers, they should be held accountable for the use of invested assets.

Rate of Return on Investment

One of the most widely used measures of divisional performance for investment centers is the **rate of return on investment (ROI)**, or **rate of return on assets**. This rate is computed as follows:

$$\text{Rate of Return on Investment (ROI)} = \frac{\text{Operating Income}}{\text{Invested Assets}}$$

The rate of return on investment is useful because the three factors subject to control by divisional managers (revenues, expenses, and invested assets) are considered in its computation. By measuring profitability relative to the amount of assets invested in each division, the rate of return on investment can be used to compare divisions. The higher the rate of return on investment, the more effectively the division is utilizing its assets in generating income. To illustrate, the rate of return on investment for each division of Waller Company, based on the book value of invested assets, is as follows:

	Operating Income	Invested Assets	Rate of Return on Investment
Division A..................	$70,000	$350,000	20%
Division B..................	84,000	700,000	12
Division C..................	75,000	500,000	15

Although Division B generated the largest operating income, its rate of return on investment (12%) is the lowest. Hence, relative to the assets invested, Division B is the least profitable division. In comparison, the rates of return on investment of Divisions A and C are 20% and 15% respectively. These differences in the rates of return on investment may be analyzed by restating the expression for the rate of return on investment in expanded form, as follows:

$$\text{Rate of Return on Investment (ROI)} = \frac{\text{Operating Income}}{\text{Sales}} \times \frac{\text{Sales}}{\text{Invested Assets}}$$

In the expanded form, the rate of return on investment is the product of two factors: (1) the ratio of operating income to sales, often termed the **profit margin**, and (2) the ratio of sales to invested assets, often termed the **investment turnover**. As shown in the following computation, the use of this expanded expression yields the same rate of return for Division A, 20%, as the previous expression for the rate of return on investment:

$$\text{Rate of Return on Investment (ROI)} = \frac{\text{Operating Income}}{\text{Sales}} \times \frac{\text{Sales}}{\text{Invested Assets}}$$

$$\text{ROI} = \frac{\$70,000}{\$560,000} \times \frac{\$560,000}{\$350,000}$$

$$\text{ROI} = 12.5\% \times 1.6$$

$$\text{ROI} = 20\%$$

The expanded expression for the rate of return on investment is useful in management's evaluation and control of decentralized operations because the profit margin and the investment turnover focus on the underlying operating relationships of each division. The profit margin component focuses on profitability by indicating the rate of profit earned on each sales dollar. When efforts are aimed at increasing a division's profit margin by changing the division's sales mix, for example, the division's rate of return on investment may increase.

The investment turnover component focuses on efficiency in the use of assets and indicates the rate at which sales are being generated for each dollar of invested assets. The more sales per dollar invested, the greater the efficiency in the use of the assets. When efforts are aimed at increasing a division's investment turnover through special sales promotions, for example, the division's rate of return on investment may increase.

The rate of return on investment, using the expanded expression for each division of Waller Company, is summarized as follows:

	Rate of Return on Investment (ROI) =	Profit Margin	× Investment Turnover

	ROI	$= \dfrac{\text{Operating Income}}{\text{Sales}} \times$	$\dfrac{\text{Sales}}{\text{Invested Assets}}$
Division A:	ROI	$= \dfrac{\$70,000}{\$560,000} \times$	$\dfrac{\$560,000}{\$350,000}$
	ROI	= 12.5% ×	1.6
	ROI	= 20%	
Division B:	ROI	$= \dfrac{\$84,000}{\$672,000} \times$	$\dfrac{\$672,000}{\$700,000}$
	ROI	= 12.5% ×	.96
	ROI	= 12%	
Division C:	ROI	$= \dfrac{\$75,000}{\$750,000} \times$	$\dfrac{\$750,000}{\$500,000}$
	ROI	= 10% ×	1.5
	ROI	= 15%	

Although Divisions A and B have the same profit margins, Division A's investment turnover is larger than that of Division B (1.6 to .96). Thus, by more efficiently utilizing its invested assets, Division A's rate of return on investment is higher than Division B's. Division C's profit margin of 10% and investment turnover of 1.5 are lower than the corresponding factors for Division A. The product of these factors results in a return on investment of 15% for Division C, as compared to 20% for Division A.

To determine possible ways of increasing the rate of return on investment, the profit margin and investment turnover for a division should be analyzed. For example, if Division A is in a highly competitive industry where the profit margin cannot be easily increased, the division manager should concentrate on increasing the investment turnover. To illustrate, assume that sales of Division A could be increased by $56,000 through changes in advertising expenditures. The cost of goods sold is expected to be 60% of sales, and operating expenses will increase to $169,400. If the advertising changes are undertaken, Division A's operating income would increase from $70,000 to $77,000, as shown in the following condensed income statement:

Sales ($560,000 + $56,000)	$616,000
Cost of goods sold ($616,000 × 60%)	369,600
Gross profit...	$246,400
Operating expenses.....................................	169,400
Operating income...	$ 77,000

The rate of return on investment for Division A, using the expanded expression, is recomputed as follows:

$$\text{Rate of Return on Investment (ROI)} = \frac{\text{Operating Income}}{\text{Sales}} \times \frac{\text{Sales}}{\text{Invested Assets}}$$

$$\text{ROI} = \frac{\$77,000}{\$616,000} \times \frac{\$616,000}{\$350,000}$$

$$\text{ROI} = 12.5\% \times 1.76$$

$$\text{ROI} = 22\%$$

Although Division A's profit margin remains the same (12.5%), the division's investment turnover has increased from 1.6 to 1.76, an increase of 10% (.16 ÷ 1.6). The 10% increase in investment turnover has the effect of also increasing the rate of return on investment by 10% (from 20% to 22%).

The major advantage of the use of the rate of return on investment instead of operating income as a divisional performance measure is that the amount of divisional investment is directly considered. Thus, divisional performances can be compared, even though the sizes of the divisions may vary significantly.

In addition to its use as a performance measure, the rate of return on investment can assist management in other ways. For example, in considering a decision to expand the operations of Waller Company, management should consider giving priority to Division A because it earns the highest rate of return on investment. If the current rates of return on investment can be maintained in the future, an investment in Division A will return 20 cents (20%) on each dollar invested, while investments in Divisions B and C will return only 12 cents and 15 cents respectively.

A major disadvantage of the rate of return on investment as a performance measure is that it may lead divisional managers to reject new investment proposals, even though the rate of return on these investments exceeds the minimum considered acceptable by the company. For example, a division might have an overall rate of return on investment of 25%, and the company might have an overall rate of return on investment of 15%. If the division accepts a new investment that would earn a 20% rate of return on investment, the overall rate of return for the division would decrease, but the overall rate of return for the company as a whole would increase. Thus, the division manager might reject the proposal, even though its acceptance would be in the best interests of the company.

Residual Income

In the previous illustration for Waller Company, two measures of evaluating divisional performance were discussed and illustrated. The advantages and disadvantages of both measures were also discussed. An additional measure, residual income, is useful in overcoming some of the disadvantages associated with the operating income and rate of return on investment measures.

Residual income is the excess of divisional operating income over a minimum amount of desired operating income. The minimum amount of desired divisional operating income is set by top management by establishing a minimum rate of return for the invested assets and then multiplying this rate by the amount of divisional assets. To illustrate, assume that the top management of Waller Company has established 10% as the minimum rate of return on divisional assets. The residual incomes for Divisions A, B, and C are computed as follows:

Residual Income by Division	Division A	Division B	Division C
Divisional operating income...................	$70,000	$84,000	$75,000
Minimum amount of divisional operating income:			
$350,000 × 10%...........................	35,000		
$700,000 × 10%...........................		70,000	
$500,000 × 10%...........................			50,000
Residual income	$35,000	$14,000	$25,000

The major advantage of residual income as a performance measure is that it gives consideration not only to a minimum rate of return on investment, but also to the total magnitude of the operating income earned by each division. For example, Division A has more residual income than the other divisions of Waller Company, even though it has the least operating income. Also, Division C earns $11,000 more residual income than Division B, even though Division B generates more operating income than Division C. The reason for this difference is that Division B has $200,000 more assets than Division C. Hence, Division B's operating income is reduced by $20,000 ($200,000 × 10%) more than Division C's operating income in determining residual income.

CHAPTER REVIEW

KEY POINTS

OBJECTIVE 1

Centralized and Decentralized Operations

Responsibility accounting is the process of measuring and reporting operating data to management by areas of responsibility. In a centralized business organization, all major planning and operating decisions are made by the top echelon of management. In a decentralized business organization, the responsibility for planning and controlling operations is delegated among managers who have authority to make decisions without first seeking the approval of higher management. In a decentralized organization, an important function of the managerial accountant is to assist managers in the process of measuring and reporting data by their areas of responsibility.

OBJECTIVE 2

Types of Decentralized Operations

Decentralized operations can be classified by the scope of the responsibility assigned and the decision-making authority given to individual managers. In a cost center, the manager has the responsibility for the control of costs incurred and the authority to make decisions that affect those costs. In a profit center, the manager has the responsibility and the authority to make decisions that affect both costs and revenue (and thus profits) for the department or division. In an investment center, the manager has the responsibility and the authority to make decisions that affect not only costs and revenues, but also the plant assets available to the center.

OBJECTIVE 3

Responsibility Accounting for Cost Centers

Since managers of cost centers have responsibility for and authority to make decisions regarding costs, responsibility accounting for cost centers focuses on costs. The primary accounting tools for planning and controlling costs for a cost center are budgets and standard costs.

OBJECTIVE 4   Responsibility Accounting for Profit Centers

Since managers of profit centers have responsibility for and authority to make decisions regarding expenses and revenues, responsibility accounting reports for profit centers are normally in the form of income statements. One such statement determines gross profit by departments. Departmental reporting may be extended to operating income, in which case the operating expenses incurred by the company must be allocated to the departments. These expenses are usually allocated on the basis of the departmental benefit received from the expenditure. Some accountants, who consider the allocation of operating expenses to be arbitrary, advocate the preparation of departmental income statements based upon departmental margin. Departmental margin is determined by deducting the direct expenses of each department from departmental gross profit. The remaining expenses are not allocated to a department, but are reported in the income statement separately below the total departmental margin.

OBJECTIVE 5   Responsibility Accounting for Investment Centers

Because investment centers are evaluated as if they were separate companies, traditional financial statements which report operating income are normally prepared for each center. A measure of performance for investment centers is the rate of return on investment. The rate of return on investment is computed by dividing operating income by invested assets. In addition, the rate of return on investment may be considered as the product of two factors: (1) the profit margin and (2) the investment turnover. An additional measure of investment center performance, residual income, is the excess of divisional operating income over a minimum amount of desired operating income.

KEY TERMS

decentralization 1027
responsibility accounting 1027
strategic planning 1028
cost center 1030
profit center 1030
investment center 1031
departmental margin 1039

direct expense 1040
indirect expense 1040
rate of return on investment
  (ROI) 1043
profit margin 1044
investment turnover 1044
residual income 1046

SELF-EXAMINATION QUESTIONS

Answers at end of chapter.

1. When the manager has the responsibility for and authority to make decisions that affect costs and revenues, but no responsibility for or authority over assets invested in the department, the department is referred to as:
   A. a cost center
   B. a profit center
   C. an investment center
   D. none of the above

2. Which of the following would be the most appropriate basis for allocating rent expense for use in arriving at operating income by departments?
   A. Departmental sales
   B. Physical space occupied
   C. Cost of inventory
   D. Time devoted to departments

3. The term used to describe the excess of departmental gross profit over direct departmental expenses is:
   A. income from operations
   B. net income
   C. departmental margin
   D. none of the above

4. Division A of Kern Co. has sales of $350,000, cost of goods sold of $200,000, operating expenses of $30,000, and invested assets of $600,000. What is the rate of return on investment for Division A?

   A. 20%
   B. 25%
   C. 40%
   D. None of the above

5. Division L of Liddy Co. has a rate of return on investment of 24% and an investment turnover of 1.6. What is the profit margin?

   A. 6%
   B. 15%
   C. 24%
   D. None of the above

ILLUSTRATIVE PROBLEM

Perry Home Appliances operates two sales departments—Department F for freezers and refrigerators and Department R for ranges and ovens. The following trial balance was prepared as of April 30, the end of the current fiscal year, after all adjustments, including those for inventories, were recorded and posted.

Perry Home Appliances
Trial Balance
April 30, 19--

Cash	72,650	
Accounts Receivable	97,450	
Inventories—Department F	17,600	
Inventories—Department R	41,200	
Prepaid Insurance	4,400	
Store Supplies	625	
Store Equipment	45,000	
Accumulated Depreciation—Store Equipment		25,800
Accounts Payable		34,300
Income Tax Payable		6,400
Common Stock		100,000
Retained Earnings		80,375
Cash Dividends	25,000	
Income Summary	53,200	58,800
Sales—Department F		350,000
Sales—Department R		650,000
Sales Returns and Allowances—Department F	6,400	
Sales Returns and Allowances—Department R	10,200	
Purchases—Department F	280,600	
Purchases—Department R	532,000	
Sales Salaries	43,400	
Advertising Expense	10,800	
Depreciation Expense—Store Equipment	8,800	
Store Supplies Expense	1,250	
Miscellaneous Selling Expense	800	
Office Salaries	10,000	
Rent Expense	9,800	
Heating and Lighting Expense	4,000	
Property Tax Expense	3,000	
Insurance Expense	1,800	
Uncollectible Accounts Expense	1,100	
Miscellaneous Administrative Expense	900	
Interest Income		1,000
Income Tax	24,700	
	1,306,675	1,306,675

Inventories at the beginning of the year were as follows: Department F, $17,200; Department R, $36,000.

The bases to be used in apportioning expenses, together with other essential information, are as follows:

Sales salaries — payroll records: Department F, $17,300; Department R, $26,100.
Advertising expense — usage: Department F, $4,000; Department R, $6,800.
Depreciation expense — average cost of equipment. Equipment balances at beginning of year: Department F, $17,000; Department R, $26,000. Equipment balances at end of year: Department F, $18,200; Department R, $26,800.

SOLUTION

PERRY HOME
Income
For Year Ended

	Department F		
Revenue from sales:			
Sales	....	$350,000	....
Less sales returns and allowances..	....	6,400	....
Net sales....................................	....	....	$343,600
Cost of goods sold:			
Inventories, May 1, 19--	....	$ 17,200	....
Purchases	....	280,600	....
Goods available for sale	....	$297,800	....
Less inventories, April 30, 19--....	....	17,600	....
Cost of goods sold	....	....	280,200
Gross profit.................................	....	....	$ 63,400
Operating expenses:			
Selling expenses:			
Sales salaries	$17,300	....	....
Advertising expense	4,000	....	....
Depreciation expense—			
store equipment..................	3,520	....	....
Store supplies expense............	550	....	....
Miscellaneous selling expense ..	280	....	....
Total selling expenses	....	$ 25,650	....
Administrative expenses:			
Office salaries.........................	$ 3,000	....	....
Rent expense.........................	2,940	....	....
Heating and lighting expense...	1,200	....	....
Property tax expense	1,050	....	....
Insurance expense...................	630	....	....
Uncollectible accounts expense .	385	....	....
Miscellaneous administrative			
expense	315	....	....
Total administrative expenses .	....	9,520	....
Total operating expenses	....	....	35,170
Income from operations	....	....	$ 28,230
Other income:			
Interest income...........................	....	....	....
Income before income tax..............	....	....	....
Income tax	....	....	....
Net income	....	....	....

Store supplies expense — requisitions: Department F, $550; Department R, $700.

Office salaries — Department F, 30%; Department R, 70%.

Rent expense and heating and lighting expense — floor space: Department F, 1,200 sq. ft.; Department R, 2,800 sq. ft.

Property tax expense and insurance expense — average cost of equipment plus average cost of inventories.

Uncollectible accounts expense, miscellaneous selling expense, and miscellaneous administrative expense — volume of gross sales.

Instructions:

Prepare an income statement departmentalized through income from operations.

APPLIANCES
Statement
April 30, 19--

Department R			Total		
....	$650,000	....	....	$1,000,000	....
....	10,200	....	....	16,600	....
....	....	$639,800	....	....	$983,400
....	$ 36,000	....	....	$ 53,200	....
....	532,000	....	....	812,600	....
....	$568,000	....	....	$ 865,800	....
....	41,200	....	....	58,800	....
....	....	526,800	....	....	807,000
....	....	$113,000	....	....	$176,400
$26,100	....	....	$43,400	....	....
6,800	....	....	10,800	....	....
5,280	....	....	8,800	....	....
700	....	....	1,250	....	....
520	....	....	800	....	....
....	$ 39,400	....	....	$ 65,050	....
$ 7,000	....	....	$10,000	....	....
6,860	....	....	9,800	....	....
2,800	....	....	4,000	....	....
1,950	....	....	3,000	....	....
1,170	....	....	1,800	....	....
715	....	....	1,100	....	....
585	....	....	900	....	....
....	21,080	....	....	30,600	....
....	....	60,480	....	....	95,650
....	....	$ 52,520	....	....	$ 80,750
....	....	....	....	....	1,000
....	....	....	....	....	$ 81,750
....	....	....	....	....	24,700
....	....	....	....	....	$ 57,050

DISCUSSION QUESTIONS

1. What is responsibility accounting?

2. What is a decentralized business organization?

3. Name three common types of responsibility centers for decentralized operations.

4. Differentiate between a cost center and a profit center.

5. Differentiate between a profit center and an investment center.

6. In what major respect would budget performance reports prepared for the use of plant managers of a manufacturing enterprise with cost centers differ from those prepared for the use of the various department supervisors who report to the plant managers?

7. The newly appointed manager of the Clothing Department in a department store is studying the income statements presenting gross profit by departments in an attempt to adjust operations to achieve the highest possible gross profit for the department. (a) Suggest ways in which an income statement departmentalized through gross profit can be used in achieving this goal. (b) Suggest reasons why caution must be exercised in using such statements.

8. Describe the underlying principle of apportionment of operating expenses to departments for income statements departmentalized through income from operations.

9. For each of the following types of expenses, select the allocation basis listed that is most appropriate for use in arriving at operating income by departments:

   Expense:
   (a) Advertising expense
   (b) Rent expense
   (c) Property tax expense
   (d) Sales salaries

   Basis of allocation:
   (1) Cost of inventory and equipment
   (2) Departmental sales
   (3) Time devoted to departments
   (4) Physical space occupied

10. Describe an appropriate basis for apportioning Officers' Salaries Expense among departments for purposes of the income statement departmentalized through income from operations.

11. Differentiate between a direct and an indirect operating expense.

12. Indicate whether each of the following operating expenses incurred by an individual department within a merchandising enterprise is a direct or an indirect expense:
    (a) Depreciation of store equipment
    (b) General manager's salary
    (c) Heating and lighting expense
    (d) Insurance expense on building
    (e) Sales commissions
    (f) Uncollectible accounts expense

13. What term is applied to the dollar amount representing the excess of departmental gross profit over direct departmental expenses?

14. Recent income statements departmentalized through income from operations report operating losses for Department E, a relatively minor segment of the business. Management studies indicate that discontinuance of Department E would not affect sales of other departments or the volume of indirect expenses. Under what circumstances would the discontinuance of Department E result in a decrease of net income of the enterprise?

15. Name three performance measures useful in evaluating investment centers.

16. What is the major shortcoming of using operating income as a performance measure for investment centers?

17. Why should the factors under the control of the investment center manager (revenues, expenses, and invested assets) be considered in the computation of the rate of return on investment?

18. Wenstrup Co. has $500,000 invested in Division Q, which earned $90,000 of operating income. What is the rate of return on investment for Division Q?

19. If Wenstrup Co. in Question 18 had sales of $1,500,000, what is (a) the profit margin and (b) the investment turnover for Division Q?

20. What are two ways of expressing the rate of return on investment?

21. In evaluating investment centers, what does multiplying the profit margin by the investment turnover equal?

22. In a decentralized company in which the divisions are organized as investment centers, how could a division be considered the least profitable, even though it earned the largest amount of operating income?

23. Which component of the rate of return on investment (profit margin factor or investment turnover factor) focuses on efficiency in the use of assets and indicates the rate at which sales are generated for each dollar of invested assets?

24. Division D of Shaut Co. has a rate of return on investment of 10%. (a) If Division D increases its investment turnover by 40%, what would be the new rate of return on investment? (b) If Division D also increases its profit margin from 6% to 9%, what would be the new rate of return on investment?

25. How does the use of the rate of return on investment facilitate comparability of divisions of decentralized companies?

26. The rates of return on investment for Sauter Co.'s three divisions, A, B, and C, are 25%, 20%, and 17%, respectively. In expanding operations, which of Sauter Co.'s divisions should be given priority? Explain.

27. What term is used to describe the excess of divisional operating income over a minimum amount of desired operating income?

28. Division L of Jaffe Co. reported operating income of $350,000, based on invested assets of $1,600,000. If the minimum rate of return on divisional investments is 20%, what is the residual income for Division L?

Real World Focus 29. Tandy Corporation's annual report for the year ended June 30, 1988 reports a profit margin of 7.0% and an investment turnover rate of 1.76. (a) What was the rate of return on investment for the year ended June 30, 1988? (b) If the investment turnover rate does not change for the year ended June 30, 1989, what must the profit margin be to earn a rate of return on investment of 15%? (Round to the nearest tenth of one percent.)

EXERCISES

Exercise 26–1
Budget performance report.
OBJ. 3

The budget for Department R of Elgin Plant for the current month ended June 30 is as follows:

Factory wages..	$250,000
Materials	220,000
Power and light	75,000
Supervisory salaries	55,000
Depreciation of plant and equipment.............	30,000
Maintenance	27,500
Insurance and property taxes......................	17,500

During June, the costs incurred in Department R of Elgin Plant were as follows: factory wages, $261,300; materials, $219,100; power and light, $75,100; supervisory salaries, $55,000; depreciation of plant and equipment, $30,000; maintenance, $27,650; insurance and property taxes, $17,500. (a) Prepare a budget performance report for the supervisor of Department R, Elgin Plant, for the month of June. (b) For what significant variations in costs might the supervisor be expected to request supplemental reports?

Exercise 26–2
Apportionment of rent expense to departments.
OBJ. 4

Aldrich Company occupies a two-story building. The departments and the floor space occupied by each department are as follows:

Receiving and Storage.................basement		2,100 sq. ft.
Department A.............................basement		3,900
Department B.............................first floor..................		12,000
Department C.............................first floor..................		8,000
Department D.............................second floor............		3,500
Department E.............................second floor............		4,200
Department F.............................second floor............		6,300

The building is leased at an annual rental of $160,000, allocated to the floors as follows: basement, 15%; first floor, 50%; second floor, 35%. Determine the amount of rent to be apportioned to each department.

Exercise 26–3
Apportionment of depreciation and property tax expense to departments.
OBJ. 4

In income statements prepared for Wong Company, depreciation expense on equipment is apportioned on the basis of the average cost of the equipment, and property tax expense is apportioned on the basis of the combined total of the average cost of the equipment and the average cost of the inventories. Depreciation expense on equipment amounted to $300,000, and property tax expense amounted to $45,000 for the year. Determine the apportionment of the depreciation expense and the property tax expense, based on the following data:

	Average Cost	
Departments	Equipment	Inventories
Service:		
S1......................	$ 420,000	
S2......................	280,000	
Sales:		
R10......................	840,000	$ 70,000
R11......................	560,000	140,000
R12......................	700,000	490,000
Total	$2,800,000	$700,000

Exercise 26–4
Departmental
income statement.
OBJ. 4

SPREADSHEET
PROBLEM

The following data were summarized from the accounting records for Ricks Company for the current year ended August 31:

Cost of goods sold:

Department P..	$250,200
Department Q	355,500

Direct expenses:

Department P..	132,000
Department Q	178,800

Income tax...	54,000
Indirect expenses	115,500
Interest income...	24,000

Net sales:

Department P..	492,600
Department Q	699,400

Prepare an income statement departmentalized through departmental margin.

Exercise 26–5
Determination of
missing items on
income statements.
OBJ. 5

One item is omitted from each of the following condensed divisional income statements of Dominion Company:

	Division J	Division K	Division L
Sales	$500,000	$750,000	$ (e)
Cost of goods sold.........................	310,000	(c)	440,000
Gross profit..................................	$ (a)	$350,000	$360,000
Operating expenses	120,000	(d)	250,000
Operating income	$ (b)	$140,000	$ (f)

(a) Determine the amount of the missing items, identifying them by letter. (b) Based on operating income, which division is the most profitable?

Exercise 26–6
Rate of return on
investment.
OBJ. 5

The operating income and the amount of invested assets in each division of Karsten Company are as follows:

	Operating Income	Invested Assets
Division H............	$151,200	$ 840,000
Division I	180,000	1,200,000
Division J.............	107,800	490,000

(a) Compute the rate of return on investment for each division. (b) Which division is the most profitable per dollar invested?

Exercise 26–7
Residual income.
OBJ. 5

Based on the data in Exercise 26–6, assume that management has established a minimum rate of return for invested assets of 12%. (a) Determine the residual income for each division. (b) Based on residual income, which of the divisions is the most profitable?

Exercise 26–8
Determination of
missing items for
computations of rate
of return on
investment.
OBJ. 5

One item is omitted from each of the following computations of the rate of return on investment:

Rate of Return on Investment	=	Profit Margin	×	Investment Turnover
18%		15%		(a)
(b)		18%		1.5
20%		(c)		2.5
17%		10%		(d)
(e)		25%		.6

Determine the missing items, identifying each by the appropriate letter.

Exercise 26–9
Profit margin,
investment turnover,
and rate of return on
investment.
OBJ. 5

The condensed income statement for Division G of Dunlop Company is as follows:

Sales	$1,500,000
Cost of goods sold...................................	900,000
Gross profit...	$ 600,000
Operating expenses	330,000
Operating income	$ 270,000

The manager of Division G is considering ways to increase the rate of return on investment. (a) Using the expanded expression, determine the profit margin, investment turnover, and rate of return on investment of Division G, assuming that $1,250,000 of assets have been invested in Division G. (b) If expenses could be reduced by $30,000 without decreasing sales, what would be the impact on the profit margin, investment turnover, and rate of return on investment for Division G?

Exercise 26–10
Determination of
missing items for
computations of rate
of return on
investment and
residual income.
OBJ. 5

One or more items is missing from the following tabulation of rate of return on investment and residual income:

Invested Assets	Operating Income	Rate of Return on Investment	Minimum Rate of Return	Minimum Amount of Operating Income	Residual Income
$ 900,000	$153,000	(a)	15%	(b)	(c)
$ 500,000	(d)	18%	(e)	$55,000	$35,000
$1,200,000	(f)	(g)	(h)	$96,000	$60,000
$ 750,000	$120,000	(i)	9%	(j)	(k)

Determine the missing items, identifying each item by the appropriate letter.

PROBLEMS

Series A

If the working papers correlating with the textbook are not used, omit Problem 26–1A.

Problem 26–1A
Budget performance
reports.
OBJ. 3

The organization chart for the manufacturing operations of Hawkins Inc. is presented in the working papers, along with the completed budget performance reports for the Foundry and Plating Departments of Plant 3. Partially completed budget performance reports prepared for the Finishing Department of Plant 3 and the vice-president in charge of operations are also presented.

Instructions:

(1) Complete the budget performance report for the supervisor of the Finishing Department of Plant 3.
(2) Prepare a budget performance report for the use of the manager of Plant 3, detailing the relevant data from the three departments in the plant. Assume that the budgeted and actual administration expenses for the plant were $11,300 and $11,875, respectively.
(3) Complete the budget performance report for the vice-president in charge of operations.

Problem 26–2A
Departmental
income statement
through income from
operations.
OBJ. 4

Goldblum Appliances operates two sales departments—Department H for small appliances, such as radios and televisions, and Department I for large appliances, such as refrigerators and washing machines. The following trial balance was prepared as of March 31, the end of the current fiscal year, after all adjustments, including those for inventories, were recorded and posted.

Cash...	39,260	
Accounts Receivable....................................	90,100	
Inventories—Department H...........................	18,200	
Inventories—Department I............................	64,300	
Prepaid Insurance.......................................	2,040	
Store Supplies..	2,000	
Store Equipment...	85,000	
Accumulated Depreciation—Store Equipment..		19,100
Accounts Payable..		15,900
Income Tax Payable.....................................		11,300
Common Stock..		100,000
Retained Earnings.......................................		21,200
Cash Dividends..	5,200	
Income Summary...	97,500	82,500
Sales—Department H		420,000
Sales—Department I.....................................		780,000
Sales Returns and Allowances—Department H...	3,800	
Sales Returns and Allowances—Department I..	6,200	
Purchases—Department H	252,000	
Purchases—Department I.............................	507,000	
Sales Salaries Expense................................	50,800	
Advertising Expense....................................	18,000	
Depreciation Expense—Store Equipment	9,500	
Store Supplies Expense	2,400	
Miscellaneous Selling Expense.......................	2,800	
Office Salaries Expense	50,000	
Rent Expense..	18,000	
Heating and Lighting Expense	15,000	
Property Tax Expense...................................	6,000	
Insurance Expense.......................................	3,000	
Uncollectible Accounts Expense.....................	2,400	
Miscellaneous Administrative Expense.............	2,200	
Interest Expense..	5,000	
Income Tax...	92,300	
	1,450,000	1,450,000

Inventories at the beginning of the year were as follows: Department H, $23,400; Department I, $74,100.

The bases to be used in apportioning expenses, together with other essential information, are as follows:

Sales salaries expense—payroll records: Department H, $17,700; Department I, $33,100.

Advertising expense—usage: Department H, $6,300; Department I, $11,700.

Depreciation expense—average cost of equipment. Equipment balances at beginning of year: Department H, $30,000; Department I, $45,000. Equipment balances at end of year: Department H, $37,200; Department I, $47,800.

Store supplies expense—requisitions: Department H, $870; Department I, $1,530.

Office salaries expense—Department H, 45%; Department I, 55%.

Rent expense and heating and lighting expense—floor space: Department H, 11,100 sq. ft.; Department I, 18,900 sq. ft.

Property tax expense and insurance expense—average cost of equipment plus average cost of inventories.

Uncollectible accounts expense, miscellaneous selling expense, and miscellaneous administrative expense—volume of gross sales.

Instructions:

Prepare an income statement departmentalized through income from operations.

Problem 26–3A
Departmental income statement through departmental margin.
OBJ. 4

Moffett Corporation consists of two departments, S and T. The bases to be used in apportioning expenses between the two departments, together with other essential data, are as follows:

Sales salaries and commissions expense—basic salary plus 6% of sales. Basic salaries for Department S, $80,000; Department T, $36,000.

Advertising expense for brochures—usage within each department advertising specific products: Department S, $13,000; Department T, $8,000.

Depreciation expense—average cost of store equipment: Department S, $122,500; Department T, $52,500.

Insurance expense—average cost of store equipment plus average cost of inventories. Average cost of inventories was $42,500 for Department S and $82,500 for Department T.

Uncollectible accounts expense—.3% of sales. Departmental managers are responsible for the granting of credit on the sales made by their respective departments.

The following data are obtained from the ledger on October 31, the end of the current fiscal year:

Sales—Department S		1,250,000
Sales—Department T		450,000
Cost of Goods Sold—Department S	750,000	
Cost of Goods Sold—Department T	300,000	
Sales Salaries and Commissions Expense	218,000	
Advertising Expense	21,000	
Depreciation Expense—Store Equipment	18,000	
Miscellaneous Selling Expense	4,000	
Administrative Salaries Expense	60,000	
Rent Expense	35,000	
Utilities Expense	11,250	
Insurance Expense	10,000	
Uncollectible Accounts Expense	5,100	
Miscellaneous Administrative Expense	1,500	
Interest Income		15,000
Income Tax	110,700	

Instructions:

(1) Prepare an income statement departmentalized through departmental margin.
(2) Determine the rate of gross profit for each department.
(3) Determine the rate of departmental margin to sales for each department.

Problem 26–4A
Divisional income statements and rate of return on investment analysis.
OBJ. 5

SPREADSHEET PROBLEM

Lambert Company is a diversified company with three operating divisions organized as investment centers. Condensed data taken from the records of the three divisions for the year ended March 31 are as follows:

	Division P	Division Q	Division R
Sales	$1,050,000	$2,250,000	$1,800,000
Cost of goods sold	630,000	1,800,000	1,350,000
Operating expenses	336,000	247,500	261,000
Invested assets	750,000	1,500,000	1,125,000

The management of Lambert Company is evaluating each division as a basis for planning a future expansion of operations.

Instructions:

(1) Prepare condensed divisional income statements for Divisions P, Q, and R.
(2) Using the expanded expression, compute the profit margin, investment turnover, and rate of return on investment for each division.
(3) If available funds permit the expansion of operations of only one division, which of the divisions would you recommend for expansion, based on (1) and (2)?

Problem 26–5A
Effect of proposals on divisional performance.
OBJ. 5

A condensed income statement for Division J of Siegel Company for the year ended January 31 is as follows:

Sales	$3,200,000
Cost of goods sold.................................	2,000,000
Gross profit..	$1,200,000
Operating expenses................................	880,000
Operating income	$ 320,000

The president of Siegel Company is concerned with Division J's rate of return on invested assets of $2,000,000, and has indicated that the division's rate of return on investment must be increased to at least 18% by the end of the next year if operations are to continue. The division manager is considering the following three proposals:

Proposal 1: Transfer equipment with a book value of $400,000 to other divisions at no gain or loss and lease similar equipment. The annual lease payments would exceed the amount of depreciation expense on the old equipment by $48,000. This increase in expense would be included as part of the cost of goods sold. Sales would remain unchanged.

Proposal 2: Reduce invested assets by discontinuing a product line. This action would eliminate sales of $1,325,000, cost of goods sold of $1,060,000, and operating expenses of $207,500. Assets of $500,000 would be transferred to other divisions at no gain or loss.

Proposal 3: Purchase new and more efficient machinery and thereby reduce the cost of goods sold by $153,600. Sales would remain unchanged, and the old machinery, which has no remaining book value, would be scrapped at no gain or loss. The new machinery would increase invested assets by $560,000 for the year.

Instructions:

(1) Using the expanded expression, determine the profit margin, investment turnover, and rate of return on investment for Division J for the past year.
(2) Prepare condensed estimated income statements for Division J for each proposal.
(3) Using the expanded expression, determine the profit margin, investment turnover, and rate of return on investment for Division J under each proposal.
(4) Which of the three proposals would meet the required 18% rate of return on investment?
(5) If Division J were in an industry where the profit margin could not be increased, how much would the investment turnover have to increase to meet the president's required 18% rate of return on investment?

Problem 26–6A
Determination of missing items from computations.
OBJ. 5

Data for Divisions R, S, T, U, and V of Van Spyk Company are as follows:

	Sales	Operating Income	Invested Assets	Rate of Return on Investment	Profit Margin	Investment Turnover
Division R	$ 660,000	$ 99,000	$ 550,000	(a)	(b)	(c)
Division S	$1,120,000	(d)	$ 800,000	21%	(e)	(f)
Division T	(g)	$180,000	(h)	(i)	12%	1.25
Division U	$1,210,000	(j)	(k)	22%	20%	(l)
Division V	(m)	$300,000	$1,200,000	(n)	(o)	2.5

Instructions:

(1) Determine the missing items, identifying each by letters (a) through (o).
(2) Determine the residual income for each division, assuming that the minimum rate of return established by management is 15%.
(3) Which division is the most profitable?

Problem 26–7A
Divisional performance analysis and evaluation.

OBJ. 5

SPREADSHEET PROBLEM

The vice-president of operations of Argo Company is evaluating the performance of two divisions organized as investment centers. Division B has the highest rate of return on investment, but generates the smallest amount of operating income. Division C generates the largest operating income, but has the lowest rate of return on investment. Invested assets and condensed income statement data for the past year for each division are as follows:

	Division B	Division C
Sales	$2,160,000	$3,000,000
Cost of goods sold	1,620,000	1,875,000
Operating expenses	172,800	735,000
Invested assets	1,800,000	2,000,000

Instructions:

(1) Prepare condensed divisional income statements for each division for the year ended January 31.
(2) Using the expanded expression, determine the profit margin, investment turnover, and rate of return on investment for each division.
(3) If management desires a minimum rate of return of 15%, determine the residual income for each division.
(4) Discuss the evaluation of Divisions B and C, using the performance measures determined in (1), (2), and (3).

Problem 26–8A
Divisional performance analysis and evaluation.

OBJ. 5

The vice-president of operations of Bristol Inc. recently resigned, and the president is considering which one of two division managers to promote to the vacated position. Both division managers have been with the company approximately ten years. Operating data for each division for the past three years are as follows:

	1990	1989	1988
Division P:			
Sales	$ 2,500,000	$ 1,800,000	$ 950,000
Cost of goods sold	1,500,000	1,000,000	570,000
Gross profit	$ 1,000,000	$ 800,000	$ 380,000
Operating expenses	750,000	638,000	304,000
Operating income	$ 250,000	$ 162,000	$ 76,000
Invested assets	$ 1,000,000	$ 900,000	$ 500,000
Total industry sales	$12,500,000	$12,000,000	$9,500,000
Division Q:			
Sales	$ 2,100,000	$ 2,000,000	$1,575,000
Cost of goods sold	1,500,000	1,400,000	1,100,000
Gross profit	$ 600,000	$ 600,000	$ 475,000
Operating expenses	432,000	430,000	317,500
Operating income	$ 168,000	$ 170,000	$ 157,500
Invested assets	$ 1,200,000	$ 1,000,000	$ 750,000
Total industry sales	$14,000,000	$10,000,000	$6,300,000

Instructions:

(1) For each division for each of the three years, use the expanded expression to determine the profit margin, investment turnover, and rate of return on investment.
(2) Assuming that 12% has been established as a minimum rate of return, determine the residual income for each division for each of the three years.
(3) Determine each division's market share (division sales divided by total industry sales) for each of the three years.
(4) Based on (1), (2), and (3), which division manager would you recommend for promotion to vice-president of operations?
(5) What other factors should be considered in the promotion decision?

Problem 26–9A
Real World Focus.
OBJ. 5

The following data (in millions) for the three primary product groups of Procter & Gamble Company were taken from Procter & Gamble's 1988 financial statements:

	Net Sales	Operating Earnings	Invested Assets
Laundry and Cleaning	$6,668	$699	$2,852
Personal Care	8,676	888	7,114
Food and Beverage..............	2,963	32	1,721

Instructions:

(1) For each of the three product groups, use the expanded expression to determine the profit margin, investment turnover, and rate of return on investment. Round the profit margin and rate of return on investment to one decimal place. Round the investment turnover to two decimal places and determine the rate of return on investment by multiplying the profit margin by the investment turnover.
(2) Rank the product groups from the highest to the lowest in terms of rate of return on investment.

Series B

If the working papers correlating with the textbook are not used, omit Problem 26–1B.

Problem 26–1B
Budget performance reports.
OBJ. 3

The organization chart for the manufacturing operations of Hawkins Inc. is presented in the working papers, along with the completed budget performance reports for the Foundry and Plating Departments of Plant 3. Partially completed budget performance reports prepared for the Finishing Department of Plant 3 and the vice-president in charge of operations are also presented.

Instructions:

(1) Complete the budget performance report for the supervisor of the Finishing Department of Plant 3.
(2) Prepare a budget performance report for the use of the manager of Plant 3, detailing the relevant data from the three departments in the plant. Assume that the budgeted and actual administration expenses for the plant were $14,500 and $13,800, respectively.
(3) Complete the budget performance report for the vice-president in charge of operations.

Problem 26–2B
Departmental income statement through income from operations.
OBJ. 4

Smolinski Co. operates two sales departments—Department K for sporting goods and Department W for camping equipment. The following trial balance was prepared as of April 30, the end of the current fiscal year, after all adjustments, including those for inventories, were recorded and posted:

Cash	29,600	
Accounts Receivable	64,200	
Inventories — Department K	36,400	
Inventories — Department W	20,600	
Prepaid Insurance	2,250	
Store Supplies	2,150	
Store Equipment	128,400	
Accumulated Depreciation — Store Equipment		33,300
Accounts Payable		25,900
Income Tax Payable		6,550
Common Stock		100,000
Retained Earnings		77,250
Cash Dividends	10,000	
Income Summary	62,000	57,000
Sales — Department K		450,000
Sales — Department W		150,000
Sales Returns and Allowances — Department K	4,000	
Sales Returns and Allowances — Department W	2,200	
Purchases — Department K	200,000	
Purchases — Department W	108,000	
Sales Salaries Expense	80,000	
Advertising Expense	16,500	
Depreciation Expense — Store Equipment	10,000	
Store Supplies Expense	5,400	
Miscellaneous Selling Expense	4,100	
Office Salaries Expense	45,000	
Rent Expense	15,000	
Heating and Lighting Expense	9,000	
Property Tax Expense	4,800	
Insurance Expense	4,200	
Uncollectible Accounts Expense	3,400	
Miscellaneous Administrative Expense	1,600	
Interest Expense	5,000	
Income Tax	26,200	
	900,000	900,000

Inventories at the beginning of the year were as follows: Department K, $41,400; Department W, $17,600.

The bases to be used in apportioning expenses, together with other essential information, are as follows:

Sales salaries expense — payroll records: Department K, $50,000; Department W, $30,000.

Advertising expense — usage: Department K, $10,800; Department W, $5,700.

Depreciation expense — average cost of equipment. Balances of equipment at beginning of year: Department K, $71,600; Department W, $40,000. Balances at end of year: Department K, $82,000; Department W, $46,400.

Store supplies expense — requisitions: Department K, $3,600; Department W, $1,800.

Office salaries expense — Department K, 70%; Department W, 30%.

Rent expense and heating and lighting expense — floor space: Department K, 17,400 sq. ft.; Department W, 12,600 sq. ft.

Property tax expense and insurance expense — average cost of equipment plus average cost of inventories.

Uncollectible accounts expense, miscellaneous selling expense, and miscellaneous administrative expense — volume of gross sales.

Instructions:

Prepare an income statement departmentalized through income from operations.

Problem 26–4B
Divisional income
statements and rate
of return on
investment analysis.

OBJ. 5

Colton Company is a diversified company with three operating divisions organized as investment centers. Condensed data taken from the records of the three divisions for the year ended July 31 are as follows:

	Division X	Division Y	Division Z
Sales	$1,250,000	$750,000	$2,250,000
Cost of goods sold...................	800,000	550,000	1,575,000
Operating expenses.................	300,000	80,000	405,000
Invested assets	1,000,000	600,000	1,500,000

The management of Colton Company is evaluating each division as a basis for planning a future expansion of operations.

Instructions:

(1) Prepare condensed divisional income statements for Divisions X, Y, and Z.
(2) Using the expanded expression, compute the profit margin, investment turnover, and rate of return on investment for each division.
(3) If available funds permit the expansion of operations of only one division, which of the divisions would you recommend for expansion, based on (1) and (2)?

Problem 26–6B
Determination of
missing items from
computations.

OBJ. 5

Data for Divisions G, H, I, J, and K of Beacon Company are as follows:

	Sales	Operating Income	Invested Assets	Rate of Return on Investment	Profit Margin	Investment Turnover
Division G	$ 800,000	$128,000	$640,000	(a)	(b)	(c)
Division H	(d)	(e)	$750,000	14%	(f)	1.75
Division I	$1,800,000	(g)	(h)	(i)	12%	1.50
Division J	$ 650,000	(j)	(k)	(l)	10%	1.3
Division K	(m)	$120,000	(n)	25%	12.5%	(o)

Instructions:

(1) Determine the missing items, identifying each by letters (a) through (o).
(2) Determine the residual income for each division, assuming that the minimum rate of return established by management is 12%.
(3) Which division is the most profitable?

Problem 26–7B
Divisional
performance
analysis and
evaluation.

OBJ. 5

The vice-president of operations of DeRoma Company is evaluating the performance of two divisions organized as investment centers. Division W generates the largest amount of operating income, but has the lowest rate of return on investment. Division S has the highest rate of return on investment, but generates the smallest operating income. Invested assets and condensed income statement data for the past year for each division are as follows:

	Division S	Division W
Sales	$18,750,000	$16,000,000
Cost of goods sold............	14,000,000	12,000,000
Operating expenses..........	3,250,000	2,480,000
Invested assets	7,500,000	8,000,000

Instructions:

(1) Prepare condensed divisional income statements for each division for the year ended August 31.
(2) Using the expanded expression, determine the profit margin, investment turnover, and rate of return on investment for each division.   *(Continued)*

(3) If management desires a minimum rate of return of 16%, determine the residual income for each division.

(4) Discuss the evaluation of Divisions S and W, using the performance measures determined in (1), (2), and (3).

MINI-CASE 26

Your father is the president of Newman Company, a privately held, diversified company with five separate divisions organized as investment centers. A condensed income statement for the Carpet Division for the past year is as follows:

Newman Company—Carpet Division
Income Statement
For Year Ended December 31, 19--

Sales	$12,000,000
Cost of goods sold	7,800,000
Gross profit	$ 4,200,000
Operating expenses	2,520,000
Operating income	$ 1,680,000

The manager of the Carpet Division was recently presented with the opportunity to add an additional product line, which would require invested assets of $2,000,000. A projected income statement for the new product line is as follows:

New Product Line
Projected Income Statement
For Year Ended December 31, 19--

Sales	$ 2,500,000
Cost of goods sold	1,500,000
Gross profit	$ 1,000,000
Operating expenses	680,000
Operating income	$ 320,000

The Carpet Division currently has $8,000,000 in invested assets, and Newman Company's overall rate of return on investment, including all divisions, is 12%. Each division manager is evaluated on the basis of divisional rate of return on investment, and a bonus equal to $5,000 for each percentage point by which the division's rate of return on investment exceeds the company average is awarded each year.

Your father is concerned that the manager of the Carpet Division rejected the addition of the new product line, when all estimates indicated that the product line would be profitable and would increase overall company income. You have been asked to analyze the possible reasons why the Carpet Division manager rejected the new product line.

Instructions:

(1) Determine the rate of return on investment for the Carpet Division for the past year.
(2) Determine the Carpet Division manager's bonus for the past year.
(3) Determine the estimated rate of return on investment for the new product line.
(4) Why might the manager of the Carpet Division decide to reject the new product line?

(Continued)

> **(5)** Can you suggest an alternative performance measure for motivating division managers to accept new investment opportunities that would increase the overall company income and rate of return on investment?

ETHICS DISCUSSION CASE	Vernon Baxter, the assistant controller for Loucks Enterprises, prepares responsibility accounting reports for the various divisions of the company. On December 20th, a case of wine with a card wishing "Merry Christmas" from John Potts, manager of the beverage division, was delivered to Baxter's home. Baxter accepted the wine and sent a note of thanks to Potts.

Discuss whether Baxter behaved in an ethical manner.

ANSWERS TO SELF-EXAMINATION QUESTIONS

1. **B** The manager of a profit center (answer B) has responsibility for and authority over costs and revenues. If the manager has responsibility and authority for only costs, the department is referred to as a cost center (answer A). If the responsibility and authority extend to the investment in assets as well as costs and revenues, it is referred to as an investment center (answer C).

2. **B** Operating expenses should be apportioned to the various departments as nearly as possible in accordance with the cost of services rendered to them. For rent expense, generally the most appropriate basis is the floor space devoted to each department (answer B).

3. **C** When the departmental margin approach to income reporting is employed, the direct departmental expenses for each department are deducted from the gross profit for each department to yield departmental margin for each department (answer C). The indirect expenses are deducted from the total departmental margin to yield income from operations (answer A). The final total income is identified as net income (answer B).

4. **A** The rate of return on investment for Division A is 20% (answer A), computed as follows:

$$\text{Rate of Return on Investment (ROI)} = \frac{\text{Operating Income}}{\text{Invested Assets}}$$

$$\text{ROI} = \frac{\$350,000 - \$200,000 - \$30,000}{\$600,000}$$

$$\text{ROI} = \frac{\$120,000}{\$600,000}$$

$$\text{ROI} = 20\%$$

5. **B** The profit margin for Division L of Liddy Co. is 15% (answer B), computed as follows:

$$\text{Rate of Return on Investment (ROI)} = \text{Profit Margin} \times \text{Investment Turnover}$$

$$24\% = \text{Profit Margin} \times 1.6$$

$$15\% = \text{Profit Margin}$$

Decision Making

PART EIGHT

8

CHAPTER TWENTY-SEVEN
DIFFERENTIAL ANALYSIS AND PRODUCT PRICING

CHAPTER OBJECTIVES

1 Describe and illustrate differential analysis for decisions involving:
   Leasing or selling
   Discontinuing an unprofitable segment
   Making or buying
   Replacing equipment
   Processing or selling
   Accepting business at a special price.

2 Describe and illustrate the setting of normal product prices, using the total cost, product cost, and variable cost concepts.

3 Describe the economic theory of product pricing.

A primary objective of accounting is to provide management with analyses that will be useful in solving current problems and in planning for the future. The types of analyses depend on the nature of the decisions to be made. In this chapter, differential analysis—which provides management with data on the differences between total revenues and total costs associated with alternative courses of action—is discussed and illustrated. The relationship of economic theory to product pricing is also briefly discussed. The chapter concludes with a discussion and illustration of practical approaches used by managers in setting normal product prices.

DIFFERENTIAL ANALYSIS

OBJECTIVE 1
Describe and illustrate differential analysis for decisions involving:
Leasing or selling
Discontinuing an unprofitable segment
Making or buying
Replacing equipment
Processing or selling
Accepting business at a special price.

Planning for future operations is chiefly decision making. For some decisions, revenue and cost information drawn from the general ledger and other basic accounting records is very useful. For example, historical cost data in the absorption costing format are helpful in planning production for the long run. Historical cost data in the variable costing format are useful in planning production for the short run. However, the revenue and cost data needed to evaluate courses of future operations or to choose among competing alternatives are often not available in the basic accounting records.

The relevant revenue and cost data in the analysis of future possibilities are the differences between the alternatives under consideration. The amounts of such differences are called **differentials** and the area of accounting concerned with the effect of alternative courses of action on revenues and costs is called **differential analysis**.

Differential revenue is the amount of increase or decrease in revenue expected from a particular course of action as compared with an alternative. To illustrate, assume that certain equipment is being used to manufacture a product that provides revenue of $150,000. If the equipment could be used to make another product that would provide revenue of $175,000, the differential revenue from the alternative would be $25,000.

Differential cost is the amount of increase or decrease in cost that is expected from a particular course of action as compared with an alternative. For example, if an increase in advertising expenditures from $100,000 to $150,000 is being considered, the differential cost of the action would be $50,000.

The main advantage of differential analysis is its selection of relevant revenues and costs related to alternative courses of action. Differential analysis reports emphasize the significant factors bearing on the decision, help to clarify the issues, and save the time of the reader.

Differential analysis can aid management in making decisions on a variety of alternatives, including (1) whether equipment should be leased or sold, (2) whether to discontinue an unprofitable segment, (3) whether to manufacture or purchase a needed part, (4) whether to replace usable plant assets, (5) whether to process further or sell an intermediate product, and (6) whether to accept additional business at a special price. The following discussion relates to the use of differential analysis in analyzing these alternatives.

Lease or Sell

Management often has a choice between leasing or selling a piece of equipment that is no longer needed in the business. In deciding which option is best, management can use differential analysis. To illustrate, assume that Company A is considering the disposal of equipment that originally cost $200,000 and has been depreciated a total of $120,000 to date. Company A can sell the equipment through a broker for $100,000 less a 6% commission. Alternatively, Company B has tentatively offered to lease the equipment for a number of years for a total of $160,000, after which it would have no residual value. During the period of the lease, Company A would incur repair, insurance, and property tax expenses estimated at $35,000. Company A's analysis of whether to lease or sell the equipment is as follows:

Differential Analysis Report—Lease or Sell

Proposal To Lease or Sell Equipment
June 22, 19--

Differential revenue from alternatives:		
Revenue from lease..	$160,000	
Revenue from sale	100,000	
Differential revenue from lease		$60,000
Differential cost of alternatives:		
Repair, insurance, and property tax expenses	$ 35,000	
Commission expense on sale.................................	6,000	
Differential cost of lease......................................		29,000
Net advantage of lease alternative............................		$31,000

It should be noted that it was not necessary to consider the $80,000 book value ($200,000 − $120,000) of the equipment. The $80,000 is a **sunk cost**; that is, it is a cost that will not be affected by later decisions. In the illustration, the expenditure to acquire the equipment had already been made, and the choice is now between leasing or selling the equipment. The relevant factors to be considered are the differential revenues and differential costs associated with the lease or sell decision. The undepreciated cost of the equipment is irrelevant. The validity of the foregoing report can be shown by the following conventional analysis:

Lease alternative:			
Revenue from lease		$160,000	
Depreciation expense	$80,000		
Repair, insurance, and property tax expenses ..	35,000	115,000	
Net gain			$45,000
Sell alternative:			
Sales price..		$100,000	
Book value of equipment.............................	$80,000		
Commission expense...................................	6,000	86,000	
Net gain			14,000
Net advantage of lease alternative			$31,000

The alternatives presented in the illustration were relatively uncomplicated. Regardless of the number and complexity of the additional factors that may be involved, the approach to differential analysis remains basically the same. Two factors that often need to be considered are (1) the differential revenue from investing the funds generated by the alternatives and (2) the income tax differential. In the example, there would undoubtedly be a differential advantage to the immediate investment of the $94,000 net proceeds ($100,000 − $6,000) from the sale over the investment of the net proceeds from the lease arrangement, which would become available over a period of years. The income tax differential would be that related to the differences in timing of the income from the alternatives and the differences in the amount of investment income.

Discontinuance of an Unprofitable Segment

When a department, branch, territory, or other segment of an enterprise has been operating at a loss, management should consider eliminating the unprofitable segment. It might be natural to assume (sometimes mistakenly) that the total operating income of the enterprise would be increased if the operating loss could be eliminated. Discontinuance of the unprofitable segment will usually eliminate all of the related variable costs. However, if the segment represents a relatively small part of the enterprise, the fixed costs (depreciation, insurance, property taxes, etc.) will not be reduced by its discontinuance. It is entirely possible in this situation for the total operating income of a company to be reduced rather than increased by eliminating an unprofitable segment. As a basis for illustrating this type of situation, the following income statement is presented for the year just ended, which was a normal year. For purposes of the illustration, it is assumed that discontinuance of Product A, on which losses are incurred annually, will have no effect on total fixed costs.

	Condensed Income Statement For Year Ended August 31, 19--			
	Product			
	A	B	C	Total
Sales	$100,000	$400,000	$500,000	$1,000,000
Cost of goods sold:				
Variable costs	$ 60,000	$200,000	$220,000	$ 480,000
Fixed costs	20,000	80,000	120,000	220,000
Total cost of goods sold	$ 80,000	$280,000	$340,000	$ 700,000
Gross profit	$ 20,000	$120,000	$160,000	$ 300,000
Operating expenses:				
Variable expenses	$ 25,000	$ 60,000	$ 95,000	$ 180,000
Fixed expenses	6,000	20,000	25,000	51,000
Total operating expenses	$ 31,000	$ 80,000	$120,000	$ 231,000
Income (loss) from operations	$ (11,000)	$ 40,000	$ 40,000	$ 69,000

Data on the estimated differential revenue and differential cost related to discontinuing Product A, on which an operating loss of $11,000 was incurred during the past year, may be assembled in a report such as the following. This report emphasizes the significant factors bearing on the decision.

Differential Analysis Report— Discontinuance of Unprofitable Segment

Proposal To Discontinue Product A September 29, 19--		
Differential revenue from annual sales of product:		
Revenue from sales		$100,000
Differential cost of annual sales of product:		
Variable cost of goods sold	$60,000	
Variable operating expenses	25,000	85,000
Annual differential income from sales of Product A		$ 15,000

Instead of an increase in annual operating income to $80,000 (Product B, $40,000; Product C, $40,000) that might seem to be indicated by the income statement, the discontinuance of product A would reduce operating income to an estimated $54,000 ($69,000 − $15,000). The validity of this conclusion can be shown by the following conventional analysis:

Proposal To Discontinue Product A September 29, 19--				
	Current Operations			Discontinuance of Product A
	Product A	Products B and C	Total	
Sales	$100,000	$900,000	$1,000,000	$900,000
Cost of goods sold:				
Variable costs.................	$ 60,000	$420,000	$ 480,000	$420,000
Fixed costs	20,000	200,000	220,000	220,000
Total cost of goods sold .	$ 80,000	$620,000	$ 700,000	$640,000
Gross profit.......................	$ 20,000	$280,000	$ 300,000	$260,000
Operating expenses:				
Variable expenses...........	$ 25,000	$155,000	$ 180,000	$155,000
Fixed expenses	6,000	45,000	51,000	51,000
Total operating expenses	$ 31,000	$200,000	$ 231,000	$206,000
Income (loss) from operations	$ (11,000)	$ 80,000	$ 69,000	$ 54,000

For purposes of the illustration, it was assumed that the discontinuance of Product A would not cause any significant reduction in the volume of fixed costs. If plant capacity made available by discontinuance of a losing operation can be used in some other manner or if plant capacity can be reduced, with a resulting reduction in fixed costs, additional analysis would be needed.

In decisions involving the elimination of an unprofitable segment, management must also consider such other factors as its effect on employees and customers. If a segment of the business is discontinued, some employees may have to be laid off and others may have to be relocated and retrained. Also important is the possible decline in sales of the more profitable products to customers who were attracted to the firm by the discontinued product.

Make or Buy

The assembly of many parts is often a substantial element in manufacturing operations. Many of the large factory complexes of automobile manufacturers are specifically called assembly plants. Some of the parts of the finished automobile, such as the motor, are produced by the automobile manufacturer, while other parts, such as tires, are often purchased from other manufacturers. Even in manufacturing the motors, such items as spark plugs and nuts and bolts may be acquired from suppliers in their finished state. When parts or components are purchased, management has usually evaluated the question of "make or buy" and has concluded that a savings in cost results from buying the part rather than manufacturing it. However, "make or buy" options are likely to arise anew when a manufacturer has excess productive capacity in the form of unused equipment, space, and labor.

As a basis for illustrating such alternatives, assume that a manufacturer has been purchasing a component, Part X, for $5 a unit. The factory is currently operating at 80% of capacity, and no significant increase in production is anticipated in the near future. The cost of manufacturing Part X, determined by absorption costing methods, is estimated at $1 for direct materials, $2 for direct labor, and $3 for factory overhead (at the predetermined rate of 150% of direct labor cost), or a total of $6. The decision based on a simple comparison of a "make" price of $6 with a "buy" price of $5 is obvious. However, to the extent that unused capacity could be used in manufacturing the part, there would be no increase in the total amount of fixed factory overhead costs. Hence, only the variable factory overhead costs need to be considered. Variable factory overhead costs such as power and maintenance are determined to amount to aproximately 65% of the direct labor cost of $2, or $1.30. The cost factors to be considered are summarized in the following report:

<table>
<tr><td>*Differential Analysis
Report — Make or Buy*</td><td></td></tr>
</table>

Proposal To Manufacture Part X
February 15, 19--

Purchase price of part..		$5.00
Differential cost to manufacture part:		
Direct materials	$1.00	
Direct labor..	2.00	
Variable factory overhead...	1.30	4.30
Cost reduction from manufacturing Part X		$ .70

Other possible effects of a change in policy should also be considered, such as the possibility that a future increase in volume of production would require the use of the currently idle capacity of 20%. The possible effect of the alternatives on employees and on future business relations with the supplier of the part, who may be providing other essential components, are additional factors that might need study.

Equipment Replacement

The usefulness of plant assets may be impaired long before they are considered to be "worn out." Equipment may no longer be ideally adequate for the purpose for which it is used, but on the other hand it may not have reached the point of complete inadequacy. Similarly, the point in time when equipment becomes obsolete may be difficult to determine. Decisions to replace usable plant assets should be based on studies of relevant costs rather than on whims or subjective opinions. The costs to be considered are the alternative future costs of retention as opposed to replacement. The book values of the plant assets being replaced are sunk costs and are irrelevant.

To illustrate some of the factors involved in replacement decisions, assume that an enterprise is considering the disposal of several identical machines having a total book value of $100,000 and an estimated remaining life of five years. The old machines can be sold for $25,000. They can be replaced by a single high-speed machine at a cost of $250,000, with an estimated useful life of five years and no residual value. Analysis of the specifications of the new machine and of accompanying changes in manufacturing methods indicate an estimated annual reduction in variable manufacturing costs from $225,000 to $150,000. No other changes in the manufacturing costs or the operating expenses are expected. The basic data to be considered are summarized in the following report:

Differential Analysis
Report—Equipment
Replacement

Proposal To Replace Equipment November 28, 19--		
Annual variable costs—present equipment...............	$225,000	
Annual variable costs—new equipment...................	150,000	
Annual differential decrease in cost.........................	$ 75,000	
Number of years applicable...................................	× 5	
Total differential decrease in cost	$375,000	
Proceeds from sale of present equipment.................	25,000	$400,000
Cost of new equipment..		250,000
Net differential decrease in cost, 5-year total		$150,000
Annual net differential decrease in cost—new equipment.		$ 30,000

Complicating features could be added to the foregoing illustration, such as a disparity between the remaining useful life of the old equipment and the estimated life of the new equipment, or possible improvement in the product due to the new machine, with a resulting increase in selling price or volume of sales. Another factor that should be considered is the importance of alternative uses for the cash outlay needed to obtain the new equipment. The amount of income that would result from the best available alternative to the proposed use of cash or its equivalent is sometimes called **opportunity cost**. If, for example, it is assumed that the cash outlay of $250,000 for the new equipment, less the $25,000 proceeds from the sale of the present equipment, could be used to yield a 10% return, the opportunity cost of the proposal would amount to 10% of $225,000, or $22,500.

The term "opportunity cost" introduces a new concept of "cost." In reality, it is not a cost in any usual sense of the word. Instead, it represents the forgoing of possible income associated with a lost opportunity. Although opportunity cost computations do not appear as a part of historical accounting data, they are unquestionably useful in analyses involving choices between alternative courses of action.

Process or Sell

When a product is manufactured, it progresses through various stages of production. Often a product can be sold at an intermediate stage of production, or it can be processed further and then sold. In deciding whether to sell a product at an intermediate stage or to process it further, the differential revenues that would be provided and the differential costs that would be incurred from further processing must be considered. Since the costs of producing the intermediate product do not change, regardless of whether the intermediate product is sold or processed further, these costs are not differential costs and are not considered.

To illustrate, assume that an enterprise produces Product Y in batches of 4,000 gallons by processing standard quantities of 4,000 gallons of direct materials, which cost $1.20 per gallon. Product Y can be sold without further processing for $2 per gallon. It is possible for the enterprise to process Product Y further to yield Product Z, which can be sold for $5 per gallon. Product Z will require additional processing costs of $5,760 per batch, and 20% of the gallons of Product Y will evaporate during production. The differential revenues and costs to be considered in deciding whether to process Product Y to produce Product Z are summarized in the following report:

Proposal To Process Product Y Further October 1, 19--		
Differential revenue from further processing per batch:		
Revenue from sale of Product Z [(4,000 gallons − 800 gallons evaporation) × $5]	$16,000	
Revenue from sale of Product Y (4,000 gallons × $2)	8,000	
Differential revenue		$8,000
Differential cost per batch:		
Additional cost of producing Product Z		5,760
Net advantage of further processing Product Y per batch..		$2,240

The net advantage of further processing Product Y into Product Z is $2,240 per batch. Note that the initial cost of producing the intermediate Product Y, $4,800 (4,000 gallons × $1.20), is not considered in deciding whether to process Product Y further. This initial cost will be incurred regardless of whether Product Z is produced.

Acceptance of Business at a Special Price

In determining whether to accept additional business at a special price, management must consider the differential revenue that would be provided and the differential cost that would be incurred. If the company is operating at full capacity, the additional production will increase both fixed and variable production costs. But if the normal production of the company is below full capacity, additional business may be undertaken without increasing fixed production costs. In the latter case, the variable costs will be the differential cost of the additional production. Variable costs are the only costs to be considered in making a decision to accept or reject the order. If the operating expenses are likely to increase, these differentials must also be considered.

To illustrate, assume that the usual monthly production of an enterprise is 10,000 units of a certain commodity. At this level of operation, which is well below capacity, the manufacturing cost is $20 per unit, composed of variable costs of $12.50 and fixed costs of $7.50. The normal selling price of the product in the domestic market is $30. The manufacturer receives an offer from an exporter for 5,000 units of the product at $18 each. Production can be spread over a three-month period without interfering with normal production or incurring overtime costs. Pricing policies in the domestic market will not be affected. Comparison of a sales price of $18 with the present unit cost of $20 would indicate that this offer should be rejected. However, if attention is limited to the differential cost, which in this case is composed of the variable costs, the conclusion is quite different. The essentials of the analysis are presented in the following brief report:

Proposal To Sell to Exporter March 10, 19--	
Differential revenue from acceptance of offer:	
Revenue from sale of 5,000 additional units at $18	$90,000
Differential cost of acceptance of offer:	
Variable costs of 5,000 additional units at $12.50	62,500
Gain from acceptance of offer	$27,500

Proposals to sell an increased output in the domestic market at a reduction from the normal price may require additional considerations of a difficult nature. It would clearly be unwise to increase sales volume in one territory by means of a price reduction if sales volume would thereby be jeopardized in other areas. Manufacturers must also exercise care to avoid violations of the Robinson-Patman Act, which prohibits price discrimination within the United States unless the difference in price can be justified by a difference in the cost of serving different customers.

SETTING NORMAL PRODUCT PRICES

OBJECTIVE 2
Describe and illustrate the setting of normal product prices, using the total cost, product cost, and variable cost concepts.

Differential analysis, as illustrated, is useful to management in setting product selling prices for special short-run decisions, such as whether to accept business at a price lower than the normal price. In such situations, the short-run price is set high enough to cover all variable costs plus provide an excess to cover some of the fixed costs and perhaps provide for profit. Such a pricing plan will improve profits in the short run. In the long run, however, the normal selling price must be set high enough to cover all costs and expenses (both fixed and variable) and provide a reasonable amount for profit. Otherwise, the long-run survival of the firm may be jeopardized.

The normal selling price can be viewed as the target selling price which must be achieved in the long run, but which may be deviated from in the short run because of such factors as competition and general market conditions. A practical approach to setting the normal price is the cost-plus approach. Using this approach, managers determine product prices by adding to a "cost" amount a plus, called a **markup,** so that all costs plus a profit are covered in the price.

Three cost concepts commonly used in applying the cost-plus approach are (1) total cost, (2) product cost, and (3) variable cost. Each of these cost concepts is described and illustrated in the following paragraphs.

Total Cost Concept

Using the **total cost concept** of determining the product price, all costs of manufacturing a product plus the selling and general expenses are included in the cost amount to which the markup is added. Since all costs and expenses are included in the cost amount, the dollar amount of the markup equals the desired profit.

The first step in applying the total cost concept is to determine the total cost of manufacturing the product. Under the absorption costing system of accounting for manufacturing operations, the costs of direct materials, direct labor, and factory overhead should be available from the accounting records. The next step is to add the estimated selling and administrative expenses to the total cost of manufacturing the product. The cost amount per unit is then computed by dividing the total costs by the total units expected to be produced and sold.

After the cost amount per unit has been determined, the dollar amount of the markup is determined. For this purpose, the markup is expressed as a percentage of cost. This percentage is then multiplied by the cost amount per unit. The dollar amount of the markup is then added to the cost amount per unit to arrive at the selling price.

The markup percentage for the total cost concept is determined by applying the following formula:

$$\text{Markup Percentage} = \frac{\text{Desired Profit}}{\text{Total Costs}}$$

The numerator of the markup percentage formula includes only the desired profit, since all costs and expenses will be covered by the cost amount to which the markup will be added. The denominator of the formula includes the total costs, which are covered by the cost amount.

To illustrate the use of the total cost concept, assume that the costs for Product R of Pellit Co. are as follows:

Variable costs:	
Direct materials	$ 3.00 per unit
Direct labor..	10.00
Factory overhead...............................	1.50
Selling and administrative expenses.......	1.50
Total	$16.00 per unit
Fixed costs:	
Factory overhead...............................	$50,000
Selling and administrative expenses.......	20,000

Pellit Co. desires a profit equal to a 20% rate of return on assets, $800,000 of assets are devoted to producing Product R, and 100,000 units are expected to be produced and sold. The cost amount for Product R is $1,670,000, or $16.70 per unit, computed as follows:

Variable costs ($16.00 × 100,000 units)............................		$1,600,000
Fixed costs:		
Factory overhead...	$50,000	
Selling and administrative expenses.............................	20,000	70,000
Total costs...		$1,670,000
Cost amount per unit ($1,670,000 ÷ 100,000 units)		$16.70

The desired profit is $160,000 (20% × $800,000), and the markup percentage for Product R is 9.6%, computed as follows:

$$\text{Markup Percentage} = \frac{\text{Desired Profit}}{\text{Total Costs}}$$

$$\text{Markup Percentage} = \frac{\$160,000}{\$1,670,000}$$

$$\text{Markup Percentage} = 9.6\%$$

Based on the cost amount per unit and the markup percentage for Product R, Pellit Co. would price Product R at $18.30 per unit, as shown in the following computation:

Cost amount per unit..............	$16.70
Markup ($16.70 × 9.6%).........	1.60
Selling price...........................	$18.30

The ability of the selling price of $18.30 to generate the desired profit of $160,000 is shown in the following condensed income statement for Pellit Co.:

Pellit Co. Income Statement For Year Ended December 31, 19--		
Sales (100,000 units × $18.30)		$1,830,000
Expenses:		
Variable (100,000 units × $16.00)....................	$1,600,000	
Fixed ($50,000 + $20,000)	70,000	1,670,000
Income from operations..................................		$ 160,000

The total cost concept of applying the cost-plus approach to product pricing is sometimes used by contractors who sell products to government agencies. In many cases, government contractors are required by law to be reimbursed for their products on a total-cost-plus-profit basis.

Product Cost Concept

Using the **product cost concept** of determining the product price, only the costs of manufacturing the product, termed the product cost, are included in the cost amount to which the markup is added. Selling expenses, administrative expenses, and profit are covered in the markup. The markup percentage is determined by applying the following formula:

$$\text{Markup Percentage} = \frac{\text{Desired Profit} + \text{Total Selling and Administrative Expenses}}{\text{Total Manufacturing Costs}}$$

The numerator of the markup percentage formula includes the desired profit plus the total selling and administrative expenses. Selling and administrative expenses must be covered by the markup, since they are not covered by the cost amount to which the markup will be added. The denominator of the formula includes the costs of direct materials, direct labor, and factory overhead, which are covered by the cost amount.

To illustrate the use of the product cost concept, assume the same data that were used in the preceding illustration. The cost amount for Pellit Co.'s Product R is $1,500,000, or $15 per unit, computed as follows:

Direct materials ($3 × 100,000 units)		$ 300,000
Direct labor ($10 × 100,000 units)................................		1,000,000
Factory overhead:		
Variable ($1.50 × 100,000 units)................................	$150,000	
Fixed	50,000	200,000
Total manufacturing costs..		$1,500,000
Cost amount per unit ($1,500,000 ÷ 100,000 units)		$15

The desired profit is $160,000 (20% × $800,000), and the total selling and administrative expenses are $170,000 [(100,000 units × $1.50 per unit) + $20,000]. The markup percentage for Product R is 22%, computed as follows:

$$\text{Markup Percentage} = \frac{\text{Desired Profit} + \text{Total Selling and Administrative Expenses}}{\text{Total Manufacturing Costs}}$$

$$\text{Markup Percentage} = \frac{\$160,000 + \$170,000}{\$1,500,000}$$

$$\text{Markup Percentage} = \frac{\$330,000}{\$1,500,000}$$

Markup Percentage = 22%

Based on the cost amount per unit and the markup percentage for Product R, Pellit Co. would price Product R at $18.30 per unit, as shown in the following computation:

Cost amount per unit...............................	$15.00
Markup ($15 × 22%)...............................	3.30
Selling price...	$18.30

Variable Cost Concept

Using the **variable cost concept** of determining the product price, only variable costs are included in the cost amount to which the markup is added. All variable manufacturing costs, as well as variable selling and administrative expenses, are included in the cost amount. Fixed manufacturing costs, fixed selling and administrative expenses, and profit are covered in the markup.

The markup percentage for the variable cost concept is determined by applying the following formula:

$$\text{Markup Percentage} = \frac{\text{Desired Profit} + \text{Total Fixed Costs}}{\text{Total Variable Costs}}$$

The numerator of the markup percentage formula includes the desired profit plus the total fixed manufacturing costs and the total fixed selling and administrative expenses. Fixed manufacturing costs and fixed selling and administrative expenses must be covered by the markup, since they are not covered by the cost amount to which the markup will be added. The denominator of the formula includes the total variable costs, which are covered by the cost amount.

To illustrate the use of the variable cost concept, assume the same data that were used in the two preceding illustrations. The cost amount for Product R is $1,600,000, or $16.00 per unit, computed as follows:

Variable costs:	
Direct materials ($3 × 100,000 units)	$ 300,000
Direct labor ($10 × 100,000 units)..............................	1,000,000
Factory overhead ($1.50 × 100,000 units)....................	150,000
Selling and administrative expenses	
($1.50 × 100,000 units)	150,000
Total variable costs	$1,600,000
Cost amount per unit ($1,600,000 ÷ 100,000 units)	$16.00

The desired profit is $160,000 (20% × $800,000), the total fixed manufacturing costs are $50,000, and the total fixed selling and administrative expenses are $20,000. The markup percentage for Product R is 14.4%, computed as follows:

$$\text{Markup Percentage} = \frac{\text{Desired Profit + Total Fixed Costs}}{\text{Total Variable Costs}}$$

$$\text{Markup Percentage} = \frac{\$160,000 + \$50,000 + \$20,000}{\$1,600,000}$$

$$\text{Markup Percentage} = \frac{\$230,000}{\$1,600,000}$$

Markup Percentage = 14.4%

Based on the cost amount per unit and the markup percentage for Product R, Pellit Co. would price Product R at $18.30 per unit, as shown in the following computation:

Cost amount per unit..	$16.00
Markup ($16.00 × 14.4%)	2.30
Selling price...	$18.30

The variable cost concept emphasizes the distinction between variable and fixed costs in product pricing. This distinction is similar to the distinction between absorption and variable costing described in Chapter 24.

Choosing a Cost-Plus Approach Cost Concept

The three cost concepts commonly used in applying the cost-plus approach to product pricing are summarized as follows:

Cost Concept	Covered in Cost Amount	Covered in Markup
Total cost	Total costs	Desired profit
Product cost	Total manufacturing costs	Desired profit + Total selling and administrative expenses
Variable cost	Total variable costs	Desired profit + Total fixed costs

As demonstrated in the Pellit Co. illustration, all three cost concepts will yield the same selling price ($18.30) when the concepts are properly applied. Which of the three cost concepts should be used by management depends on such factors as the cost of gathering the data and the decision needs of management. For example, the data for the product cost concept can be easily gathered by a company using an absorption cost accounting system.

To reduce the costs of gathering data, standard costs rather than actual costs may be used with any of the three cost concepts. However, caution should be exercised by management when using standard costs in applying the cost-plus approach. The standards should be based on normal (attainable) operating levels and not theoretical (ideal) levels of performance. In product pricing, the use of standards based on ideal or maximum capacity operating levels might lead to the establishment of product prices which are too low, since the costs of such factors as normal spoilage or normal periods of idle time would not be covered in the price. As a result, the desired profit would be reduced by these costs.

ECONOMIC THEORY OF PRODUCT PRICING

In addition to costs, as discussed in the preceding paragraphs, other factors may influence the pricing decision. In considering these factors, which include the general economic conditions of the marketplace, a knowledge of the economic theory underlying product pricing is useful to the managerial accountant. Although the study of **price theory** is generally considered a separate discipline in the area of microeconomics, the following paragraphs present an overview of the economic concepts for explaining pricing behavior.

Maximization of Profits

In microeconomic theory, management's primary objective is assumed to be the maximization of profits. Profits will be maximized at the point at which the difference between total revenues and total costs is the greatest amount. Consequently, microeconomic theory focuses on the behavior of total revenues as price and sales volume vary and the behavior of total costs as production varies.

Revenues

Generally, it is not possible to sell an unlimited number of units of product at the same price. At some point, price reductions will be necessary in order to sell more units. Total revenue may increase as the price is reduced, but there comes a point when further price decreases will reduce total revenue. To illustrate, the following revenue schedule shows the effect on revenue when each $1 reduction in the unit selling price increases the number of units sold:

Revenue Schedule

Price	Units Sold	Total Revenue	Marginal Revenue
$11	1	$11	$11
10	2	20	9
9	3	27	7
8	4	32	5
7	5	35	3
6	6	36	1
5	7	35	−1

In the revenue schedule illustrated, a price reduction from $11 to $10 increases total revenue by $9 (from $11 to $20). This increase (or decrease) in total revenue realized from the sale of an additional unit of product is called the **marginal revenue**. With each successive price reduction from $11 to $6, the total revenue increase is less. Finally, a price reduction from $6 to $5 decreases total revenue by $1.

Costs

As production and sales increase, the total cost increases. The amount by which total cost increases, however, varies as more and more production and sales are squeezed from limited facilities. Economists assume that as the total number of units produced and sold increases from a relatively low level, the total cost increases but in decreasing amounts. This assumption is based on efficiencies created by **economies of scale.** Economies of scale generally imply that, for a given amount of facilities, it is more efficient to produce and sell large quantities than small quantities. At some point, however, the total cost will begin to increase by increasing amounts because of inefficiencies created by such factors as employees getting in each other's way and machine breakdowns caused by heavy use. The increase in total cost from producing and selling an additional unit of product is known as **marginal cost.** To illustrate, the following cost schedule shows the effect on cost when one additional unit is produced and sold:

Cost Schedule

Units Produced and Sold	Total Cost	Marginal Cost
1	$ 9	$9
2	17	8
3	24	7
4	30	6
5	37	7
6	45	8
7	54	9

In the cost schedule, the cost of producing 1 unit is $9, and for each additional unit the total cost per unit increases by $8, $7, $6, $7, $8, and $9 respectively. The marginal cost of producing and selling the second unit is $8, which is the difference between the total cost of producing and selling 2 units ($17) and the total cost of 1 unit ($9). As production and sales increase from 1 unit to 4 units, the marginal cost decreases from $9 to $6. After the production and sale of 4 units, however, the marginal cost increases from $6 for the fourth unit to $9 for producing and selling the seventh unit.

Product Price Determination

A price-cost combination that maximizes the total profit of an enterprise will occur when marginal revenues and marginal costs are equal. In the illustration, the marginal revenue equals the marginal cost for 3 units of sales and production, as shown in the following table:

Price	Units Produced and Sold	Total Revenue	Marginal Revenue	Total Cost	Marginal Cost
$11	1	$11	$11	$ 9	$9
10	2	20	9	17	8
9	3	27	7	24	7
8	4	32	5	30	6
7	5	35	3	37	7
6	6	36	1	45	8
5	7	35	−1	54	9

For the third unit of sales and production, marginal revenue and marginal cost equal $7. To sell 3 units, the revenue schedule on page 1080 indicates that the price should be set at $9 per unit, which will provide total revenue of $27. The cost schedule on page 1081 indicates that the total cost of the 3 units will be $24. Thus, profit will be $3, as follows:

Total revenue (3 units × $9).............	$27
Total cost (from cost schedule).........	24
Profit...	$ 3

The more theoretical economic approach is not often used for product pricing because the data required by this approach are often unavailable. For example, it is difficult to predict the amount that customers will purchase over a range of prices without actually offering the product for sale at those prices. Therefore, since total cost data can be estimated reliably from accounting records, the cost-plus aproach to product pricing is frequently used.

THE ART OF PRICING AIR FARES

One industry in which pricing plays a very significant role is the airline industry. Fare wars and constantly changing fares are commonplace among the major airlines. The fine tuning involved in pricing fares is described in the following excerpt from an article in *The Wall Street Journal:*

The latest round of fare wares... has put a spotlight on how carriers use state-of-the-art computer software, complex forecasting techniques and a little intuition to [determine] how many seats at what prices they will offer on any given flight....

Too many wrong projections can lead to huge losses of revenue, or even worse. The inability of People Express to manage its inventory of seats properly, for example, was one of the major causes of its demise.

"It's a sophisticated guessing game," said [the] vice president of pricing and product planning at American Airlines.... "You don't want to sell a seat to a guy for $69 when he's willing to pay $400."

With the industry now adopting very low discount but nonrefundable fares, the complex task of managing seat inventory may become easier because airlines will be better able to predict how many people will show up for a flight.

Some airlines have already seen a drop in their no-shows, which means they can overbook less and spare more customers from being bumped.

The nonrefundable fares could also enable carriers to sell more discount seats weeks before a flight, rather than putting them on sale at the last minute in an effort to fill up the plane.

American's [pricing] operation illustrates just how complicated the process can be. At the airline's corporate headquarters [in Dallas], 90 yield managers are linked by terminals to five International Business Machines mainframe computers in Tulsa, Okla. The managers monitor and adjust the fare mixes on 1,600 daily flights as well as 528,000 future flights involving nearly 50 million passengers. Their work is hectic: A fare's average life span is two weeks, and industrywide about 200,000 fares change daily.

American and the other airlines base their forecasts largely on historical profiles of each flight. Business travelers, for example, book heavily on many Friday afternoon flights, but often not until the day of departure. The airlines reserve blocks of seats for those frequent fliers. Few, if any, discounts are made available....

For the bargain hunter, finding a discount will increasingly depend on the season, day and time of travel, destination and length of stay....

The following table indicates the difference between the number of seats sold at each fare for a Wednesday and Friday flight of American Airlines:

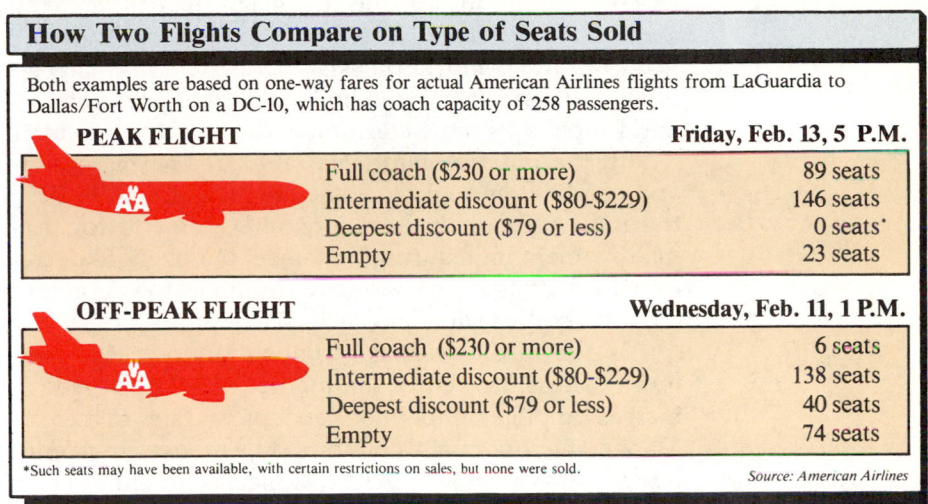

How Two Flights Compare on Type of Seats Sold

Both examples are based on one-way fares for actual American Airlines flights from LaGuardia to Dallas/Fort Worth on a DC-10, which has coach capacity of 258 passengers.

PEAK FLIGHT   **Friday, Feb. 13, 5 P.M.**

Full coach ($230 or more)	89 seats
Intermediate discount ($80-$229)	146 seats
Deepest discount ($79 or less)	0 seats*
Empty	23 seats

OFF-PEAK FLIGHT   **Wednesday, Feb. 11, 1 P.M.**

Full coach ($230 or more)	6 seats
Intermediate discount ($80-$229)	138 seats
Deepest discount ($79 or less)	40 seats
Empty	74 seats

*Such seats may have been available, with certain restrictions on sales, but none were sold.

Source: American Airlines

Pricing Strategies

Within the constraints of market conditions, managers must decide upon a pricing strategy for a company's various products. The pricing strategy chosen for a product depends upon the factors previously discussed. In addition, the stage in the product's life cycle at which the product is offered for sale has an important effect. The **product life cycle** concept is based on the idea that a product normally passes through various stages from the time that it is introduced until the time that it disappears from the market.

The normal life cycle for a product is divided into five stages: the introductory stage, the rapid growth stage, the turbulent stage, the maturity stage, and the terminating stage. Graphically, the relationship of these stages to total dollar sales during a product's life cycle can be illustrated as follows:

Product Life Cycle

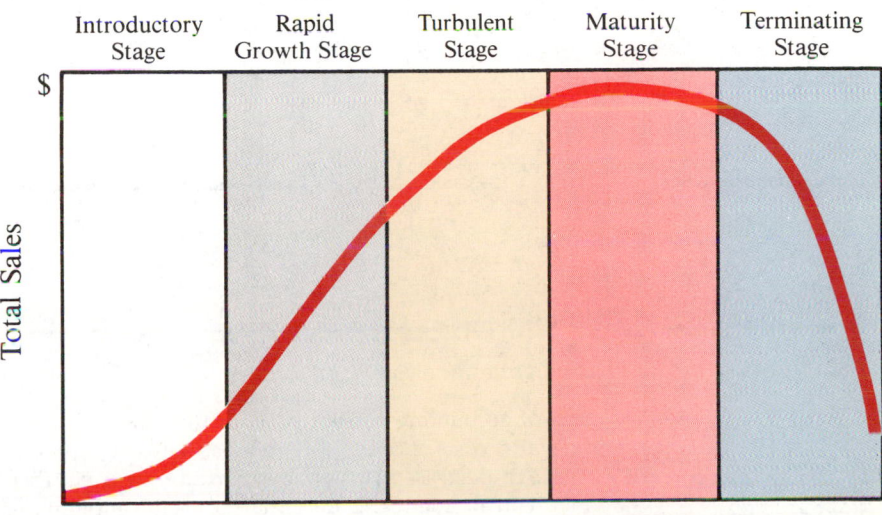

In the introductory stage, the product is new to the market and no direct competition exists. During this stage, management normally spends large amounts on promotional activities in order to develop a market for the product. Since no competition exists, prices are normally set to provide coverage of all costs and to provide high profit margins. Total sales begin low and expand rapidly as more consumers discover the product.

In the rapid growth stage, the product has caught on with consumers and competitors begin to enter the market. Total sales expand rapidly, since the industry cannot meet consumer demand for the product. Prices normally remain high during this stage, but begin to decrease as competition increases. Management normally continues to set prices high enough to cover all costs and provide for a reasonable profit.

In the turbulent stage, competition increases dramatically as more and more competitors enter the market. Although sales continue to be strong, increasing price competition causes total sales to increase at a decreasing rate. Management normally continues to set prices high enough to cover all costs, but profit margins are reduced to meet competition. For short periods of time, management may offer the product for sale at special prices that cover only variable costs. During this stage, one or two companies may achieve dominant positions in the market as less efficient competitors are driven out of the market.

In the maturity stage, competition stabilizes and few, if any, new competitors enter the market. Management normally sets prices at a relatively low level to cover all costs and to allow for a low profit margin. The consumer demand for the product levels off and may decline. Total sales reach a maximum and begin to decline.

In the terminating stage, the strategy of management is to reduce the chance of any losses and to get as much profit out of the remaining product demand as possible. Near the end of this stage, prices are often set to cover only product variable costs in order to reduce the chance that the company will be left with excess inventories after consumer demand has disappeared.

One example of the product life cycle concept is the market for the IBM personal computer during the early and mid-1980's. During this period, the price of a standard IBM personal computer decreased from approximately $3,500 in 1980, when it was first introduced, to less than $1,000 in 1990. IBM attempted to prolong the computer's relatively brief life cycle by introducing new enhancements, such as hard disk drives, additional memory, and color monitors.

CHAPTER REVIEW

KEY POINTS

OBJECTIVE 1   Differential Analysis

The area of accounting concerned with the effect of alternative courses of action on revenues and costs is called differential analysis. Differential revenue is the amount of increase or decrease in revenue expected from a particular course of action as compared with an alternative. Differential cost is the amount of increase or decrease in cost that is expected from a particular course of action as compared with an alternative.

Differential analysis can aid management in making decisions on a variety of alternatives, including (1) whether equipment should be leased or sold, (2) whether to discontinue an unprofitable segment, (3) whether to manufacture or purchase a needed part, (4) whether to replace plant assets, (5) whether to process further or sell an intermediate product, and (6) whether to accept additional business at a special price.

OBJECTIVE 2

Setting Normal Product Prices

The normal selling price can be viewed as the target selling price, which must be achieved in the long run but may be deviated from in the short run because of such factors as competition and general market conditions. A practical approach to setting the normal price is the cost-plus approach. Using this approach, managers determine product prices by adding to a "cost" amount a markup, so that all costs plus a profit are covered in the price.

The three cost concepts commonly used in applying the cost-plus approach to product pricing are summarized as follows:

Cost Concept	Covered in Cost Amount	Covered in Markup
Total cost	Total costs	Desired profit
Product cost	Total manufacturing costs	Desired profit + Total selling and administrative expenses
Variable cost	Total variable costs	Desired profit + Total fixed costs

The markup percentage for each cost concept is determined by dividing the amount covered in the markup by the amount covered in the cost.

OBJECTIVE 3

Economic Theory of Product Pricing

The theory underlying product pricing is a separate economic discipline known as price theory. In this theory, management's primary objective is assumed to be the maximization of profits. The increase (decrease) in total revenue realized from the sale of an additional unit of product is called marginal revenue. The increase in total cost from producing and selling an additional unit of product is called marginal cost. The point where marginal revenue and marginal cost are equal is the level of sales and production at which profits are maximized.

The stage in its life cycle at which a product is offered for sale has an important effect on management's choice of a pricing strategy. During the introductory stage, product prices are set to cover all costs and to provide for high profit margins. During the rapid growth stage, product prices remain high, but begin to decrease as new competitors enter the market. During the turbulent stage, profit margins are reduced as prices fall and special prices covering only variable costs may be established for short periods. During the maturity stage, prices remain at low levels as total sales reach a maximum and begin to fall. During the terminating stage, prices may be lowered to cover only variable costs in order to reduce losses and excess inventories.

KEY TERMS

differential analysis 1067
differential revenue 1068
differential cost 1068
sunk cost 1069
opportunity cost 1073
markup 1075
total cost concept 1075

product cost concept 1077
variable cost concept 1078
price theory 1080
marginal revenue 1080
economies of scale 1081
marginal cost 1081
product life cycle 1083

SELF-EXAMINATION QUESTIONS

Answers at end of chapter.

1. The amount of increase or decrease in cost that is expected from a particular course of action as compared with an alternative is referred to as:
    A. differential cost
    B. replacement cost
    C. sunk cost
    D. none of the above

2. Victor Company is considering the disposal of equipment that was originally purchased for $200,000 and has accumulated depreciation to date of $150,000. The same equipment would cost $310,000 to replace. What is the sunk cost?
    A. $50,000
    B. $150,000
    C. $200,000
    D. None of the above

3. The amount of income that would result from the best available alternative to a proposed use of cash or its equivalent is referred to as:
    A. actual cost
    B. historical cost
    C. opportunity cost
    D. none of the above

4. For which cost concept used in applying the cost-plus approach to product pricing are fixed manufacturing costs, fixed selling and administrative expenses, and desired profit allowed for in the determination of markup?
    A. Total cost
    B. Product cost
    C. Variable cost
    D. None of the above

5. According to microeconomic theory, profits of a business enterprise will be maximized at the point where:
    A. marginal revenue equals marginal cost
    B. the change in total revenue is greater than the change in total cost
    C. the change in total cost is greater than the change in total revenue
    D. none of the above

ILLUSTRATIVE PROBLEM

Berry Company recently began production of a new product, M, which required the investment of $2,000,000 in assets. The costs of producing and selling 100,000 units of Product M are estimated as follows:

Variable costs:	
Direct materials	$ 2.40 per unit
Direct labor..	6.50
Factory overhead..	.90
Selling and administrative expenses	.20
Total..	$10.00 per unit

Fixed costs:	
Factory overhead..	$ 60,000
Selling and administrative expenses	140,000

Berry Company is currently considering the establishment of a selling price for Product M. The president of Berry Company has decided to use the cost-plus approach to product pricing and has indicated that Product M must earn an 18% rate of return on invested assets.

Instructions:

1. Determine the amount of desired profit from the production and sale of Product M.
2. Assuming that the total cost concept is used, determine (a) the cost amount per unit, (b) the markup percentage, and (c) the selling price of Product M.

(Continued)

3. Assuming that the product cost concept is used, determine (a) the cost amount per unit, (b) the markup percentage, and (c) the selling price of Product M.
4. Assuming that the variable cost concept is used, determine (a) the cost amount per unit, (b) the markup percentage, and (c) the selling price of Product M.
5. Assume that for the current year, the selling price of Product M was $15.60 per unit. To date, 80,000 units have been produced and sold and analysis of the domestic market indicates that 15,000 additional units are expected to be sold during the remainder of the year. Recently, Berry Company received an offer from Wong Inc. for 4,000 units of Product M at $11.50 each. Wong Inc. will market the units in Korea under its own brand name and no additional selling and administrative expenses associated with the sale will be incurred by Berry Company. The additional business is not expected to affect the domestic sales of Product M and the additional units could be produced during the current year, using existing capacity. (a) Prepare a differential analysis report of the proposed sale to Wong Inc. (b) Based upon the differential analysis report in (a), should the proposal be accepted?

SOLUTION

(1) $360,000 ($2,000,000 × 18%)

(2) (a) Total costs:

Variable ($10 × 100,000 units)	$1,000,000
Fixed ($60,000 + $140,000)	200,000
Total	$1,200,000

Cost amount per unit: $1,200,000 ÷ 100,000 units = $12

(b) $$\text{Markup Percentage} = \frac{\text{Desired Profit}}{\text{Total Costs}}$$

$$\text{Markup Percentage} = \frac{\$360,000}{\$1,200,000}$$

Markup Percentage = 30%

(c)

Cost amount per unit	$12.00
Markup ($12 × 30%)	3.60
Selling price	$15.60

(3) (a) Total manufacturing costs:

Variable ($9.80 × 100,000 units)	$ 980,000
Fixed factory overhead	60,000
Total	$1,040,000

Cost amount per unit: $1,040,000 ÷ 100,000 units = $10.40

(b) Markup Percentage = $\dfrac{\text{Desired Profit} + \begin{array}{c}\text{Total Selling and}\\\text{Administrative Expenses}\end{array}}{\text{Total Manufacturing Costs}}$

Markup Percentage = $\dfrac{\$360{,}000 + \$140{,}000 + (\$.20 \times 100{,}000 \text{ units})}{\$1{,}040{,}000}$

Markup Percentage = $\dfrac{\$360{,}000 + \$140{,}000 + \$20{,}000}{\$1{,}040{,}000}$

Markup Percentage = $\dfrac{\$520{,}000}{\$1{,}040{,}000}$

Markup Percentage = 50%

(c) Cost amount per unit $10.40
    Markup ($10.40 × 50%) 5.20
    Selling price $15.60

(4) (a) Variable cost amount per unit: $10
     Total variable costs: $10 × 100,000 units = $1,000,000

(b) Markup Percentage = $\dfrac{\text{Desired Profit} + \text{Total Fixed Costs}}{\text{Total Variable Costs}}$

Markup Percentage = $\dfrac{\$360{,}000 + \$60{,}000 + \$140{,}000}{\$1{,}000{,}000}$

Markup Percentage = $\dfrac{\$560{,}000}{\$1{,}000{,}000}$

Markup Percentage = 56%

(c) Cost amount per unit $10.00
    Markup ($10 × 56%) 5.60
    Selling price $15.60

(5) (a)

Proposal To Sell to Wong Inc.

Differential revenue from acceptance of offer:	
Revenue from sale of 4,000 additional units at $11.50	$46,000
Differential cost of acceptance of offer:	
Variable costs of 4,000 additional units at $9.80	39,200
Gain from acceptance of offer	$ 6,800

(b) The proposal should be accepted.

DISCUSSION QUESTIONS

1. What term is applied to the type of analysis that emphasizes the difference between the revenues and costs for proposed alternative courses of action?

2. Explain the meaning of (a) *differential revenue* and (b) *differential cost*.

3. Edmunds Lumber Company incurs a cost of $90 per thousand board feet in processing a certain "rough-cut" lumber, which it sells for $130 per thousand board feet. An alternative is to produce a "finished-cut" at a total processing cost of $115 per thousand board feet, which can be sold for $180 per thousand board feet. What is the amount of (a) the differential revenue and (b) the differential cost associated with the alternative?

4. (a) What is meant by *sunk costs*? (b) A company is contemplating replacing an old piece of machinery which cost $450,000 and has $420,000 accumulated depreciation to date. A new machine costs $750,000. What is the sunk cost in this situation?

5. The condensed income statement for Hass Company for the current year is as follows:

| | Product | | | |
	R	S	T	Total
Sales	$300,000	$120,000	$450,000	$870,000
Less variable costs	160,000	90,000	270,000	520,000
Contribution margin	$140,000	$ 30,000	$180,000	$350,000
Less fixed costs	90,000	75,000	110,000	275,000
Income (loss) from operations	$ 50,000	$(45,000)	$ 70,000	$ 75,000

Management decided to discontinue the manufacture and sale of Product S. Assuming that the discontinuance will have no effect on the total fixed costs or on the sales of Products R and T, has management made the correct decision? Explain.

6. (a) What is meant by *opportunity cost*? (b) Jablow Company is currently earning 12% on $300,000 invested in marketable securities. It proposes to use the $300,000 to acquire plant facilities to manufacture a new product that is expected to add $60,000 annually to net income. What is the opportunity cost involved in the decision to manufacture the new product?

7. In the long run, the normal selling price must be set high enough to cover what factors?

8. What are three cost concepts commonly used in applying the cost-plus approach to product pricing?

9. In using the product cost concept of applying the cost-plus approach to product pricing, what factors are included in the markup?

10. The variable cost concept used in applying the cost-plus approach to product pricing includes what costs in the cost amount to which the markup is added?

11. In determining the markup percentage for the variable cost concept of applying the cost-plus approach, what is included in the denominator?

12. Why might the use of ideal standards in applying the cost-plus approach to product pricing lead to setting product prices which are too low?

13. Although the cost-plus approach to product pricing may be used by management as a general guideline, what are some examples of other factors that managers should also consider in setting product prices?

14. In microeconomic theory, what is assumed to be management's primary objective for a business enterprise?

15. As the terms are used in microeconomic theory, what is meant by (a) marginal revenue and (b) marginal cost?

16. If the total revenue for selling 5 units of Product Q is $50 and the total revenue for selling 6 units is $54, what is the marginal revenue associated with selling the sixth unit?

17. What does the concept of economies of scale generally imply?

18. For a given amount of facilities, why will the total costs begin to increase by increasing amounts at some point?

19. According to microeconomic theory, at what point is profit maximized?

20. Why is the more theoretical economic approach to product pricing not used as often as the cost-plus approach?

21. For the following graph of total sales for a product, identify each stage of the product's life cycle.

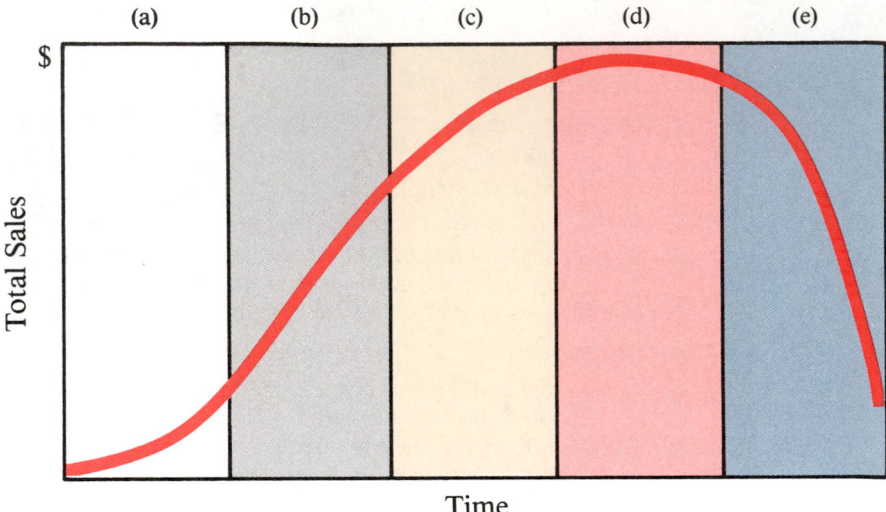

Real World Focus

22. In the personal computer hardware market, at what stage in the product life cycle is the 5 1/4-inch disk drive and at what stage is the 3 1/2-inch drive?

Real World Focus

23. In July, 1986, *The Wall Street Journal* reported that the brakes that General Motors produces at its Delco Moraine division for its automobile assembly plants cost up to 15% more to make than they would cost to buy from an outside supplier. The same article reported that Ford Motor Co. and Chrysler Corp. buy almost all their brakes from outside suppliers as far away as Brazil, and these companies save money in the process. The decision of General Motors to produce its brakes internally is an example of what type of decision illustrated in this chapter?

EXERCISES

Exercise 27–1
Lease or sell decision.
OBJ. 1

Hayes Corporation is considering selling excess machinery with a book value of $150,000 (original cost of $325,000 less accumulated depreciation of $175,000) for $90,000 less a 10% brokerage commission. Alternatively the machinery can be leased for a total of $115,000 for five years, after which it will have no estimated residual value. During the period of the lease, the costs of repairs, insurance, and property tax expenses expected to be incurred by Hayes Corporation are estimated at $20,000. (a) Prepare a differential analysis report, dated January 4 of the current year, for the lease or sell decision. (b) On the basis of the data presented, would it be advisable to lease or sell the machinery? Explain.

Exercise 27–2

Differential analysis report for discontinuance of product.

OBJ. 1

A condensed income statement by product line for Alvarez Co. indicated the following for Product K for the past year:

Sales	$300,000
Cost of goods sold	175,000
Gross profit	$125,000
Operating expenses	150,000
Loss from operations	$ (25,000)

It is estimated that 24% of the cost of goods sold represents fixed factory overhead costs and that 20% of operating expenses is fixed. Since Product K is only one of many products, the fixed costs will not be materially affected if the product is discontinued. (a) Prepare a differential analysis report, dated January 7 of the current year, for the proposed discontinuance of Product K. (b) Should Product K be retained? Explain.

Exercise 27–3

Make or buy decision.

OBJ. 1

LeTrec Company has been purchasing carrying cases for its portable typewriters at a delivered cost of $15 per unit. The company, which is currently operating below full capacity, charges factory overhead to production at the rate of 35% of direct materials cost. The direct materials and direct labor costs per unit to produce comparable carrying cases are expected to be $8 and $5 respectively. If LeTrec Company manufactures the carrying cases, fixed factory overhead costs will not increase and variable factory overhead costs associated with the cases are expected to be 5% of direct materials costs. (a) Prepare a differential analysis report, dated February 3 of the current year, for the make or buy decision. (b) On the basis of the data presented, would it be advisable to make or to continue buying the carrying cases? Explain.

Exercise 27–4

Differential analysis report for machine replacement.

OBJ. 1

SPREADSHEET PROBLEM

Mortner Company produces a commodity by applying a machine and direct labor to the direct materials. The original cost of the machine is $320,000, the accumulated depreciation is $200,000, its remaining useful life is 8 years, and its salvage value is negligible. On November 4, a proposal was made to replace the present manufacturing procedure with a fully automatic machine that will cost $650,000. The automatic machine has an estimated useful life of 8 years and no significant salvage value. For use in evaluating the proposal, the accountant accumulated the following annual data on present and proposed operations:

	Present Operations	Proposed Operations
Sales	$1,300,000	$1,300,000
Direct materials	550,000	550,000
Direct labor	250,000	—
Power and maintenance	40,000	100,000
Taxes, insurance, etc.	18,500	25,000
Selling and administrative expenses	110,000	110,000

(a) Prepare a differential analysis report for the proposal to replace the machine. Include in the analysis both the net differential decrease in costs anticipated over the 8 years and the net annual differential decrease in costs anticipated. (b) Based only on the data presented, should the proposal be accepted? (c) What are some of the other factors that should be considered before a final decision is made?

Exercise 27–5

Decision on acceptance of additional business.

OBJ. 1

OH Company has a plant capacity of 100,000 units, and current production is 75,000 units. Monthly fixed costs are $250,000, and variable costs are $18.50 per unit. The present selling price is $24 per unit. On October 11, the company received an offer from JMC Company for 15,000 units of the product at $20 each. The JMC Company will market the units in a foreign country under its own brand name. The additional business is not expected to affect the regular selling price or quantity of sales of OH Company. (a) Prepare a differential analysis report for the proposed sale to JMC Company. (b) Briefly explain the reason why the acceptance of this additional business will increase operating income. (c) What is the minimum price per unit that would produce a contribution margin?

Exercise 27–6
Use of absorption costing or variable costing in bidding on contract.
OBJ. 1

Sinclair Company expects to operate at 85% of productive capacity during September. The total manufacturing costs for September for the production of 17,000 grinders are budgeted as follows:

Direct materials	$110,500
Direct labor	34,000
Variable factory overhead	25,500
Fixed factory overhead	40,000
Total manufacturing costs	$210,000

The company has an opportunity to submit a bid for 2,500 grinders to be delivered by September 30 to a government agency. If the contract is obtained, it is anticipated that the additional activity will not interfere with normal production during September or increase the selling or administrative expenses. (a) What is the unit cost below which Sinclair Company should not go in bidding on the government contract? (b) Is a unit cost figure based on absorption costing or one based on variable costing more useful in arriving at a bid on this contract? Explain.

Exercise 27–7
Total cost concept of product pricing.
OBJ. 2

Hargrave Company uses the total cost concept of applying the cost-plus approach to product pricing. The costs of producing and selling 10,000 units of Product M are as follows:

Variable costs:	
Direct materials	$ 5.60 per unit
Direct labor	2.80
Factory overhead	.60
Selling and administrative expenses	1.50
Total	$10.50 per unit

Fixed costs:	
Factory overhead	$30,000
Selling and administrative expenses	15,000

Hargrave Company desires a profit equal to an 18% rate of return on invested assets of $100,000. (a) Determine the amount of desired profit from the production and sale of Product M. (b) Determine the total costs and the cost amount per unit for the production and sale of 10,000 units of Product M. (c) Determine the markup percentage for Product M. (d) Determine the selling price of Product M.

Exercise 27–8
Product cost concept of product pricing.
OBJ. 2

Based on the data presented in Exercise 27–7, assume that Hargrave Company uses the product cost concept of applying the cost-plus approach to product pricing. (a) Determine the total manufacturing costs and the cost amount per unit for the production and sale of 10,000 units of Product M. (b) Determine the markup percentage for Product M. (c) Determine the selling price of Product M.

Exercise 27–9
Variable cost concept of product pricing.
OBJ. 2

Based on the data presented in Exercise 27–7, assume that Hargrave Company uses the variable cost concept of applying the cost-plus approach to product pricing. (a) Determine the cost amount per unit for the production and sale of 10,000 units of Product M. (b) Determine the markup percentage for Product M. (c) Determine the selling price of Product M.

Exercise 27–10
Economic concept of pricing.
OBJ. 3

For the following revenue schedule and cost schedule for Product E, (a) determine the level of sales and production at which marginal cost is equal to marginal revenue, (b) determine the unit sales price at the level of sales determined in (a), and (c) determine the maximum profit for Product E at the level of sales determined in (a).

Revenue Schedule

Price	Units Sold	Total Revenue	Marginal Revenue
$10	1	$10	$10
9	2	18	8
8	3	24	6
7	4	28	4
6	5	30	2
5	6	30	0
4	7	28	−2

Cost Schedule

Units Produced and Sold	Total Cost	Marginal Cost
1	$ 7	$7
2	13	6
3	18	5
4	22	4
5	25	3
6	29	4
7	34	5

PROBLEMS

Series A

Problem 27–1A
Differential analysis report involving opportunity costs.
OBJ. 1

SPREADSHEET PROBLEM

On January 2, Kurowski Company is considering leasing a building and purchasing the necessary equipment to operate a public warehouse. The project would be financed by selling $400,000 of 9% U.S. Treasury bonds that mature in 15 years. The bonds were purchased at face value and are currently selling at face value. The following data have been assembled:

Cost of equipment...	$400,000
Life of equipment...	15 years
Estimated residual value of equipment...	$ 80,000
Yearly costs to operate the warehouse, in addition to depreciation of equipment	$ 28,000
Yearly expected revenues—first 9 years	$120,000
Yearly expected revenues—next 6 years...	$ 80,000

Instructions:

(1) Prepare a differential analysis report presenting the differential revenue and the differential cost associated with the proposed operation of the warehouse for the 15 years as compared with present conditions.
(2) Based on the results disclosed by the differential analysis, should the proposal be accepted?
(3) If the proposal is accepted, what is the total estimated income from operation of the warehouse for the 15 years?

Problem 27–2A
Differential analysis report for machine replacement proposal.
OBJ. 1

Pally Company is considering the replacement of a machine that has been used in its factory for five years. Relevant data associated with the operations of the old machine and the new machine, neither of which has any estimated residual value, are as follows:

Old Machine

Cost of machine, 15-year life	$ 870,000
Annual depreciation	58,000
Annual manufacturing costs, exclusive of depreciation	320,000
Related annual operating expenses	150,000
Associated annual revenue	2,100,000
Current estimated selling price	500,000

New Machine

Cost of machine, 10-year life	$1,250,000
Annual depreciation	125,000
Estimated annual manufacturing costs, exclusive of depreciation	200,000

Annual operating expenses and revenue are not expected to be affected by purchase of the new machine.

Instructions:

(1) Prepare a differential analysis report as of May 18 of the current year, comparing operations utilizing the new machine with operations using the present equipment. The analysis should indicate the total net differential decrease or increase in costs that would result over the 10-year period if the new machine is acquired.
(2) List other factors that should be considered before a final decision is reached.

Problem 27–3A
Differential analysis report for sales promotion proposal.
OBJ. 1

Vaughn Company is planning a one-month campaign for November to promote sales of one of its two products. A total of $50,000 has been budgeted for advertising, contests, redeemable coupons, and other promotional activities. The following data have been assembled for their possible usefulness in deciding which of the products to select for the campaign:

	Product F	Product Q
Unit selling price	$40	$120
Unit production costs:		
Direct materials	$17	$50
Direct labor	8	32
Variable factory overhead	3	7
Fixed factory overhead	2	2
Total unit production costs	$30	$ 91
Unit variable operating expenses	5	5
Unit fixed operating expenses	1	4
Total unit costs	$36	$100
Operating income per unit	$ 4	$ 20

No increase in facilities would be necessary to produce and sell the increased output. It is anticipated that 20,000 additional units of Product F or 5,000 additional units of Product Q could be sold without changing the unit selling price of either product.

Instructions:

(1) Prepare a differential analysis report as of October 7 of the current year, presenting the additional revenue and additional costs anticipated from the promotion of Product F and Product Q.
(2) The sales manager had tentatively decided to promote Product Q, estimating that operating income would be increased by $50,000 ($20 operating income per unit for 5,000 units, less promotion expenses of $50,000). It was also believed that the selection of Product F would increase operating income by only $30,000 ($4 operating income per unit for 20,000 units, less promotion expenses of $50,000). State briefly your reasons for supporting or opposing the tentative decision.

Problem 27–4A
Differential analysis report for further processing.
OBJ. 1

The management of Avanti Company is considering whether to process further Product S into Product W. Product W can be sold for $150 per pound, and Product S can be sold without further processing for $80 per pound. Product S is produced in batches of 375 pounds by processing 500 pounds of raw material, which costs $30 per pound. Product W will require additional processing costs of $12.00 per pound of Product S, and 1.5 pounds of Product S will produce 1 pound of Product W.

Instructions:

(1) Prepare a differential analysis report as of August 15, presenting the differential revenue and differential cost per batch associated with the further processing of Product S to produce Product W.
(2) Briefly report your recommendations.

Problem 27–5A
Differential analysis report for further processing.
OBJ. 1

Eldridge Refining Inc. refines Product M in batches of 50,000 gallons, which it sells for $5 per gallon. The associated unit costs are currently as follows:

Direct materials	$2.40
Direct labor	1.20
Variable factory overhead	.30
Fixed factory overhead	.15
Sales commissions	.25
Fixed selling and administrative expenses	.08

The company is presently considering a proposal to put Product M through several additional processes to yield Products M and R. Although the company had determined such further processing to be unwise, new processing methods have now been developed. Existing facilities can be used for the additional processing, but since the factory is operating at full 8-hour-day capacity, the processing would have to be performed at night. Additional costs of processing would be $10,000 per batch, and there would be an evaporation loss of 20%, with 45% of the processed material evolving as Product M and 35% as Product R. The selling price of Product R is $9 per gallon. Sales commissions are a uniform percentage based on the sales price.

Instructions:

(1) Prepare a differential analysis report as of December 16, presenting the differential revenue and the differential cost per batch associated with the processing to produce Products M and R, compared with processing to produce Product M only.
(2) Briefly report your recommendations.

Problem 27–6A
Product pricing using the cost-plus approach concepts; differential analysis report for acceptance of additional business.
OBJ. 1, 2

Wilson Company recently began production of a new product, J, which required the investment of $500,000 in assets. The costs of producing and selling 50,000 units of Product J are estimated as follows:

Variable costs per unit:	
Direct materials	$ 6.20
Direct labor	7.40
Factory overhead	1.40
Selling and administrative expenses	1.00
Total	$16.00
Fixed costs:	
Factory overhead	$150,000
Selling and administrative expenses	50,000

Wilson Company is currently considering the establishment of a selling price for Product J. The president of Wilson Company has decided to use the cost-plus approach to product pricing and has indicated that Product J must earn a 16% rate of return on invested assets.

Instructions:

(1) Determine the amount of desired profit from the production and sale of Product J.
(2) Assuming that the total cost concept is used, determine (a) the cost amount per unit, (b) the markup percentage, and (c) the selling price of Product J.
(3) Assuming that the product cost concept is used, determine (a) the cost amount per unit, (b) the markup percentage, and (c) the selling price of Product J.
(4) Assuming that the variable cost concept is used, determine (a) the cost amount per unit, (b) the markup percentage, and (c) the selling price of Product J.
(5) Comment on any additional considerations that could influence the establishment of the selling price for Product J.
(6) Assume that as of September 1, 40,000 units of Product J have been produced and sold during the current year. Analysis of the domestic market indicates that 6,500 additional units are expected to be sold during the remainder of the year at the normal product price determined under the total cost concept. On September 2, Wilson Company received an offer from Yu Inc. for 3,000 units of Product J at $15.80 each. Yu Inc. will market the units in Japan under its own brand name and no additional selling and administrative expenses associated with the sale will be incurred by Wilson Company. The additional business is not expected to affect the domestic sales of Product J and the additional units could be produced using existing capacity. (a) Prepare a differential analysis report of the proposed sale to Yu Inc. (b) Based upon the differential analysis report in (a), should the proposal be accepted?

Series B

Problem 27–1B
Differential analysis report involving opportunity costs.

OBJ. 1

On February 1, Runge Company is considering leasing a building and purchasing the necessary equipment to operate a public warehouse. The project would be financed by selling $500,000 of 8% U.S. Treasury bonds that mature in 10 years. The bonds were purchased at face value and are currently selling at face value. The following data have been assembled:

Cost of equipment..	$500,000
Life of equipment...	10 years
Estimated residual value of equipment..	$ 50,000
Yearly costs to operate the warehouse, in addition to depreciation of equipment...	$ 30,000
Yearly expected revenues—first 6 years	$120,000
Yearly expected revenues—next 4 years...	$ 90,000

Instructions:

(1) Prepare a differential analysis report presenting the differential revenue and the differential cost associated with the proposed operation of the warehouse for the 10 years as compared with present conditions.
(2) Based on the results disclosed by the differential analysis, should the proposal be accepted?
(3) If the proposal is accepted, what is the total estimated income from operation of the warehouse for the 10 years?

Problem 27–2B
Differential analysis report for machine replacement proposal.

OBJ. 1

Jost Company is considering the replacement of a machine that has been used in its factory for four years. Relevant data associated with the operations of the old machine and the new machine, neither of which has any residual value, are as follows:

Old Machine

Cost of machine, 12-year life..	$ 600,000
Annual depreciation	50,000
Annual manufacturing costs, exclusive of depreciation.......................	480,000
Related annual operating expenses	220,000
Associated annual revenue...	1,200,000
Current estimated selling price..	360,000

New Machine

Cost of machine, 8-year life	$1,500,000
Annual depreciation	187,500
Estimated annual manufacturing costs, exclusive of depreciation.........	275,000

Annual operating expenses and revenue are not expected to be affected by purchase of the new machine.

Instructions:

(1) Prepare a differential analysis report as of July 20 of the current year, comparing operations utilizing the new machine with operations using the present equipment. The analysis should indicate the total net differential decrease or increase in costs that would result over the 8-year period if the new machine is acquired.
(2) List other factors that should be considered before a final decision is reached.

Problem 27–6B
Product pricing using the cost-plus approach concepts; differential analysis report for acceptance of additional business.

OBJ. 1, 2

Alman Company recently began production of a new product, W, which required the investment of $800,000 in assets. The costs of producing and selling 25,000 units of Product W are estimated as follows:

Variable costs per unit:	
Direct materials	$ 6.00
Direct labor..	2.75
Factory overhead..	1.25
Selling and administrative expenses............................	2.00
Total	$12.00

Fixed costs:	
Factory overhead...	$70,000
Selling and administrative expenses.............................	30,000

Alman Company is currently considering the establishment of a selling price for Product W. The president of Alman Company has decided to use the cost-plus approach to product pricing and has indicated that Product W must earn a 10% rate of return on invested assets.

Instructions:

(1) Determine the amount of desired profit from the production and sale of Product W.
(2) Assuming that the total cost concept is used, determine (a) the cost amount per unit, (b) the markup percentage, and (c) the selling price of Product W.
(3) Assuming that the product cost concept is used, determine (a) the cost amount per unit, (b) the markup percentage, and (c) the selling price of Product W. Round to the nearest cent.
(4) Assuming that the variable cost concept is used, determine (a) the cost amount per unit, (b) the markup percentage, and (c) the selling price of Product W.
(5) Comment on any additional considerations that could influence the establishment of the selling price for Product W. *(Continued)*

(6) Assume that as of June 1, 22,000 units of Product W have been produced and sold during the current fiscal year. Analysis of the domestic market indicates that 1,500 additional units of Product W are expected to be sold during the remainder of the fiscal year ending June 30, at the normal product price determined under the total cost concept. On June 1, Alman Company received an offer from Sanchez Inc. for 1,000 units of Product W at $9.50 each. Sanchez Inc. will market the units in Mexico under its own brand name and no additional selling and administrative expenses associated with the sale will be incurred by Alman Company. The additional business is not expected to affect the domestic sales of Product W and the additional units could be produced using existing capacity. (a) Prepare a differential analysis report of the proposed sale to Sanchez Inc. (b) Based upon the differential analysis report in (a), should the proposal be accepted?

MINI-CASE 27

SCHOOLCRAFT MOTORS

Your father operates a family-owned automotive dealership. Recently, the city government has requested bids on the purchase of 10 sedans for use by the city police department. Although the city prefers to purchase from local dealerships, state law requires the acceptance of the lowest bid. The past several contracts for automotive purchases have been granted to dealerships from surrounding communities.

The following data were taken from the dealership records for the normal sale of the automobile for which current bids have been requested:

Retail list price of sedan...	$13,600
Costs allocated to normal sale:	
Dealer cost from manufacturer..	10,800
Fixed overhead...	500
Shipping charges from manufacturer................................	420
Preparation charges	100
Sales commission based on selling price..........................	6%

Your father has asked you to help him in arriving at a "winning" bid price for this contract. In the past, your father has always bid $300 above the total cost (including fixed overhead). No sales commissions will be paid if the bid is accepted, and your father has indicated that the bid price must contribute at least $300 per car to the profits of the dealership.

Instructions:

(1) Do you think that your father has used good bidding procedures for prior contracts? Explain.
(2) What should be the bid price, based upon your father's profit objectives?
(3) Explain why the bid price determined in (2) would not be an acceptable price for normal customers.

ETHICS DISCUSSION CASE	Sarah Gingell is a cost accountant for Norboru Enterprises. Ed Yu, vice-president of marketing, has asked Sarah to meet with representatives of Norboru's major competitor to discuss product cost data. Yu indicates that the sharing of this data will enable Norboru to determine a fair and equitable price for its products.
	Would it be ethical for Gingell to attend the meeting and share the relevant cost data?

ANSWERS TO SELF-EXAMINATION QUESTIONS

1. **A** Differential cost (answer A) is the amount of increase or decrease in cost that is expected from a particular course of action compared with an alternative. Replacement cost (answer B) is the cost of replacing an asset at current market prices, and sunk cost (answer C) is a past cost that will not be affected by subsequent decisions.

2. **A** A sunk cost is not affected by later decisions. For Victor Company, the sunk cost is the $50,000 (answer A) book value of the equipment, which is equal to the original cost of $200,000 (answer C) less the accumulated depreciation of $150,000 (answer B).

3. **C** The amount of income that could have been earned from the best available alternative to a proposed use of cash is called opportunity cost (answer C). Actual cost (answer A) or historical cost (answer B) is the cash or equivalent outlay for goods or services actually acquired.

4. **C** Under the variable cost concept of product pricing (answer C), fixed manufacturing costs, fixed administrative and selling expenses, and desired profit are allowed for in the determination of the markup. Only desired profit is allowed for in the markup under the total cost concept (answer A). Under the product cost concept (answer B), total selling and administrative expenses and desired profit are allowed for in the determination of markup.

5. **A** Microeconomic theory indicates that profits of a business enterprise will be maximized at the point where marginal revenue equals marginal cost (answer A). At lower levels of production and sales, the change in total revenue is greater than the change in total cost (answer B); hence, more profit can be achieved by manufacturing and selling more units. At higher levels of production and sales, the change in total cost is greater than the change in total revenue (answer C); hence, less profit will be achieved by manufacturing and selling more units.

CHAPTER TWENTY-EIGHT
CAPITAL INVESTMENT ANALYSIS

CHAPTER OBJECTIVES

1 Describe the nature and importance of capital investment analysis.

2 Describe and illustrate the following methods of evaluating capital investment proposals:
Average rate of return
Cash payback
Discounted cash flow
Discounted internal rate of return.

3 Describe factors that complicate capital investment analysis.

4 Describe and illustrate the capital rationing process.

5 Describe the basic concepts for planning and controlling capital investment expenditures.

With the accelerated growth of American industry, increasing attention has been given to long-term investment decisions involving property, plant, and equipment. The process by which management plans, evaluates, and controls such investments is called **capital investment analysis**, or **capital budgeting**. This chapter describes analyses useful for making capital investment decisions, which may involve thousands, millions, or even billions of dollars. The similarities and differences between the most commonly used methods of evaluating capital investment proposals, as well as the uses of each method, are emphasized. Finally, considerations complicating capital investment analyses, the process of allocating available investment funds among competing proposals (capital rationing), and planning and controlling capital expenditures are briefly discussed.

NATURE OF CAPITAL INVESTMENT ANALYSIS

OBJECTIVE 1
Describe the nature and importance of capital investment analysis.

Capital investment expenditures normally involve a long-term commitment of funds and thus affect operations for many years. These expenditures must earn a reasonable rate of return so that the enterprise can meet its obligations to creditors and provide dividends to stockholders. Because capital investment decisions are some of the most important decisions that management makes, the systems and procedures for evaluating, planning, and controlling capital investments must be carefully developed and implemented.

A capital investment program should include a plan for encouraging employees at all levels of an enterprise to submit proposals for capital investments. The plan should provide for communicating to the employees the long-range goals of the enterprise so that useful proposals are submitted. In addition, the plan may provide for rewarding employees whose proposals are implemented. All reasonable proposals should be given serious consideration and the effects of the economic implications expected from these proposals should be identified.

METHODS OF EVALUATING CAPITAL INVESTMENT PROPOSALS

The methods of evaluating capital investment proposals can be grouped into two general categories that can be referred to as (1) methods that ignore present value and (2) present value methods. The characteristic that distinguishes one category from the other is the way in which the concept of the time value of money is treated. Both the time value of money and the concept of present value are discussed in more detail later in this chapter. Because cash on hand can be invested to earn more cash while cash to be received in the future cannot, money has a time value. However, the methods that ignore present value do not give consideration to the fact that cash on hand is more valuable than cash to be received in the future. The two methods in this category are (1) the average rate of return method and (2) the cash payback method.

By converting dollars to be received in the future into current dollars, using the concept of present value, the present value methods take into consideration the fact that money has a time value. The two common present value methods used in evaluating capital investment proposals are (1) the discounted cash flow method and (2) the discounted internal rate of return method.

Often management will use some combination of the four methods in evaluating the various economic aspects of capital investment proposals. Each of the methods has both advantages and limitations. In addition, some of the computations can become rather complex. By use of the computer, however, the calculations can be performed easily and quickly. More importantly, the computer can be used in developing models that indicate the effect of changes in key factors on the results of capital investment proposals.

Methods That Ignore Present Value

The average rate of return and the cash payback methods of evaluating capital investment proposals are simple to use and are especially useful in screening proposals. Management often establishes a minimum standard, and proposals not meeting this minimum standard are dropped from further consideration. When several alternative proposals meet the minimum standard, management will often rank the proposals from the most desirable to the least desirable.

The methods that ignore present value are also useful in evaluating capital investment proposals that have relatively short useful lives. In such situations, the timing of the cash flows is less important and management generally focuses its attention on the amount of income to be earned from the investment and the total net cash flows to be received from the investment.

Average Rate of Return Method. The expected **average rate of return,** sometimes referred to as the **accounting rate of return,** is a measure of the expected profitability of an investment in plant assets. The amount of income expected to be earned from the investment is stated as an annual average over the number of years the asset is to be used. The amount of the investment may be considered to be the original cost of the plant asset, or recognition may be given to the effect of depreciation on the amount of the investment. According to the latter view, the investment gradually declines from the original cost to the estimated residual value at the end of its useful life. If straight-line depreciation and no residual value are assumed, the average investment would be equal to one half of the original expenditure.[1]

To illustrate, assume that management is considering the purchase of a certain machine at a cost of $500,000. The machine is expected to have a useful life of 4 years, with no residual value, and its use during the 4 years is expected to yield total income of $200,000. The estimated average annual income is therefore $50,000 ($200,000 ÷ 4), and the average investment is $250,000 [($500,000 + $0 residual value) ÷ 2]. Accordingly, the expected average rate of return on the average investment is 20%, computed as follows:

$$\text{Average Rate of Return} = \frac{\text{Estimated Average Annual Income}}{\text{Average Investment}}$$

$$\text{Average Rate of Return} = \frac{\$200,000 \div 4}{(\$500,000 + \$0) \div 2}$$

$$\text{Average Rate of Return} = 20\%$$

The expected average rate of return of 20% should be compared with the rate established by management as the minimum reward for the risks involved in the investment. The attractiveness of the proposed purchase of additional equipment is indicated by the difference between the expected rate and the minimum desired rate.

When several alternative capital investment proposals are being considered, the proposals can be ranked by their average rates of return. The higher the average rate of return, the more desirable the proposal. For example, assume that management is considering the following alternative capital investment proposals and has computed the indicated average rates of return:

	Proposal A	Proposal B
Estimated average annual income	$ 30,000	$ 36,000
Average investment	$120,000	$180,000
Average rate of return:		
$30,000 ÷ $120,000	25%	
$36;000 ÷ $180,000		20%

If only the average rate of return is considered, Proposal A, based on its average rate of return of 25%, would be preferred over Proposal B.

---

[1]The average investment is the midpoint of the depreciable portion of the cost of the asset. Since a plant asset is never depreciated below its residual value, this midpoint is determined by adding the original cost of the asset to the estimated residual value and dividing by 2.

The primary advantages of the average rate of return method are its ease of computation and the fact that it emphasizes the amount of income earned over the entire life of the proposal. Its main disadvantages are its lack of consideration of the expected cash flows from the proposal and the timing of these cash flows. These cash flows are important because cash coming from an investment can be reinvested in other income-producing activities. Therefore, the more funds and the sooner the funds become available, the more income that can be generated from their reinvestment.

Cash Payback Method. The expected period of time that will pass between the date of a capital investment and the complete recovery in cash (or equivalent) of the amount invested is called the **cash payback period**. To simplify the analysis, the revenues and the out-of-pocket operating expenses expected to be associated with the operation of the plant assets are assumed to be entirely in the form of cash. The excess of the cash flowing in from revenue over the cash flowing out for expenses is termed **net cash flow**. The time required for the net cash flow to equal the initial outlay for the plant asset is the payback period.

For purposes of illustration, assume that the proposed investment in a plant asset with an 8-year life is $200,000 and that the annual net cash flow is expected to be $40,000. The estimated cash payback period for the investment is 5 years, computed as follows:

$$\frac{\$200,000}{\$40,000} = 5 \text{ year cash payback period}$$

In the preceding illustration, the annual net cash flows were equal ($40,000 per year). If these annual net cash flows are not equal, the cash payback period is determined by summing the annual net cash flows until the cumulative sum equals the amount of the proposed investment. To illustrate, assume that for a proposed investment of $400,000, the annual net cash flows and cumulative net cash flows over the proposal's 6-year life are as follows:

Year	Net Cash Flow	Cumulative Net Cash Flow
1	$ 60,000	$ 60,000
2	80,000	140,000
3	105,000	245,000
4	155,000	400,000
5	140,000	540,000
6	90,000	630,000

The cumulative net cash flow at the end of the fourth year equals the amount of the investment, $400,000. Therefore, the payback period is 4 years.

The cash payback method is widely used in evaluating proposals for expansion and for investment in new projects. A relatively short payback period is desirable, because the sooner the cash is recovered the sooner it becomes available for reinvestment in other projects. In addition, there is likely to be less possibility of loss from changes in economic conditions, obsolescence, and other unavoidable risks when the commitment is short-term. The cash payback concept is also of interest to bankers and other creditors who may be dependent upon net cash flow for the repayment of claims associated with the initial capital investment. The sooner the cash is recovered, the sooner the debt or other liabilities can be paid. Thus, the cash payback method would be especially useful to managers whose primary concern is liquidity.

One of the primary disadvantages of the cash payback method as a basis for decisions is its failure to take into consideration the expected profitability of a proposal. A project with a very short payback period, coupled with relatively poor profitability, would be less desirable than one with a longer payback period but with satisfactory profitability. Another disadvantage of the cash payback method is that the cash flows occurring after the payback period are ignored. A 5-year project with a 3-year payback period and two additional years of substantial cash flows is more desirable than a 5-year project with a 3-year payback period that has lower cash flows in the last two years.

Present Value Methods

An investment in plant and equipment may be viewed as the acquisition of a series of future net cash flows composed of two elements: (1) the recovery of the initial investment and (2) income. The period of time over which these net cash flows will be received may be an important factor in determining the value of an investment.

The concept of the time value of money is that any specified amount of cash to be received at some date in the future is not the equivalent of the same amount of cash held at an earlier date. A sum of cash to be received in the future is not as valuable as the same sum on hand today, because cash on hand today can be invested to earn income. For example, $10,000 on hand today would be more valuable than $10,000 to be received a year from today. In other words, if cash can be invested to earn 10% per year, the $10,000 on hand today will accumulate to $11,000 ($10,000 plus $1,000 earnings) by one year from today. The $10,000 on hand today can be referred to as the **present value** amount that is equivalent to $11,000 to be received a year from today.

Discounted Cash Flow Method. The **discounted cash flow method,** sometimes referred to as the **net present value method,** uses present value concepts to compute the present value of the cash flows expected from a proposal. To illustrate, if the rate of earnings is 12% and the cash to be received in one year is $1,000, the present value amount is $892.86 ($1,000 ÷ 1.12). If the cash is to be received one year later (two years in all), with the earnings compounded at the end of the first year, the present value amount would be $797.20 ($892.86 ÷ 1.12).

Instead of determining the present value of future cash flows by a series of divisions in the manner just illustrated, it is customary to find the present value of $1 from a table of present values and to multiply it by the amount of the future cash flow. Reference to the following partial table indicates that the present value of $1 to be received two years hence, with earnings at the rate of 12% a year, is .797. Multiplication of .797 by $1,000 yields $797, which is the same amount that was determined in the preceding paragraph by two successive divisions. The small difference is due to rounding the present value factors in the table to three decimal places.[2]

---

[2]More complete tables of both present values and future values are in Appendix A.

Present Value of $1 at
Compound Interest

Year	6%	10%	12%	15%	20%
1	.943	.909	.893	.870	.833
2	.890	.826	.797	.756	.694
3	.840	.751	.712	.658	.579
4	.792	.683	.636	.572	.482
5	.747	.621	.567	.497	.402
6	.705	.564	.507	.432	.335
7	.665	.513	.452	.376	.279
8	.627	.467	.404	.327	.233
9	.592	.424	.361	.284	.194
10	.558	.386	.322	.247	.162

The particular rate of return selected in discounted cash flow analysis is affected by the nature of the business enterprise and its relative profitability, the purpose of the capital investment, the cost of securing funds for the investment, the minimum desired rate of return, and other related factors. If the present value of the net cash flow expected from a proposed investment, at the selected rate, equals or exceeds the amount of the investment, the proposal is desirable. For purposes of illustration, assume a proposal for the acquisition of $200,000 of equipment with an expected useful life of 5 years and a minimum desired rate of return of 10%. The anticipated net cash flow for each of the 5 years and the analysis of the proposal are as follows. The calculation shows that the proposal is expected to recover the investment and provide more than the minimum rate of return.

Discounted Cash Flow
Analysis

Year	Present Value of $1 at 10%	Net Cash Flow	Present Value of Net Cash Flow
1	.909	$ 70,000	$ 63,630
2	.826	60,000	49,560
3	.751	50,000	37,550
4	.683	40,000	27,320
5	.621	40,000	24,840
Total		$260,000	$202,900

Amount to be invested 200,000

Excess of present value over amount to be invested ..... $ 2,900

When several alternative investment proposals of the same amount are being considered, the one with the largest excess of present value over the amount to be invested is the most desirable. If the alternative proposals involve different amounts of investment, it is useful to prepare a relative ranking of the proposals by using a **present value index**. The present value index for the previous illustration is computed by dividing the total present value of the net cash flow by the amount to be invested, as follows:

$$\text{Present Value Index} = \frac{\text{Total Present Value of Net Cash Flow}}{\text{Amount To Be Invested}}$$

$$\text{Present Value Index} = \frac{\$202,900}{\$200,000}$$

$$\text{Present Value Index} = 1.01$$

To illustrate the ranking of the proposals by use of the present value index, assume that the total present values of the net cash flow and the amounts to be invested for three alternative proposals are as follows:

	Proposal A	Proposal B	Proposal C
Total present value of net cash flow......	$107,000	$86,400	$93,600
Amount to be invested........................	100,000	80,000	90,000
Excess of present value over amount to be invested..................................	$ 7,000	$ 6,400	$ 3,600

The present value index for each proposal is as follows:

	Present Value Index
Proposal A..............................	1.07 ($107,000 ÷ $100,000)
Proposal B..............................	1.08 ($ 86,400 ÷ $ 80,000)
Proposal C..............................	1.04 ($ 93,600 ÷ $ 90,000)

The present value indexes indicate that although Proposal A has the largest excess of present value over the amount to be invested, it is not as attractive as Proposal B in terms of the amount of present value per dollar invested. It should be noted, however, that Proposal B requires an investment of only $80,000, while Proposal A requires an investment of $100,000. The possible use of the $20,000 if B is selected should be considered before a final decision is made.

The primary advantage of the discounted cash flow method is that it gives consideration to the time value of money. A disadvantage of the method is that the computations are more complex than those for the methods that ignore present value. In addition, this method assumes that the cash received from the proposal during its useful life will be reinvested at the rate of return used to compute the present value of the proposal. Because of changing economic conditions, this assumption may not always be reasonable.

Discounted Internal Rate of Return Method. The **discounted internal rate of return method,** sometimes called the **internal rate of return** or **time-adjusted rate of return method**, uses present value concepts to compute the rate of return from the net cash flows expected from capital investment proposals. Thus, it is similar to the discounted cash flow method in that it focuses on the present value of the net cash flows. However, the discounted internal rate of return method starts with the net cash flows and, in a sense, works backwards to determine the discounted rate of return expected from the proposal. The discounted cash flow method requires management to specify a minimum rate of return, which is then used to determine the excess (deficiency) of the present value of the net cash flow over the investment.

To illustrate the use of the discounted internal rate of return method, assume that management is evaluating a proposal to acquire equipment costing $33,530, which is expected to provide annual net cash flows of $10,000 per year for 5 years. If a rate of return of 12% is assumed, the present value of the net cash flows can be computed using the present value of $1 table on page 1105, as follows:

Year	Present Value of $1 at 12%	Net Cash Flow	Present Value of Net Cash Flow
1	.893	$10,000	$ 8,930
2	.797	10,000	7,970
3	.712	10,000	7,120
4	.636	10,000	6,360
5	.567	10,000	5,670
Total.............................		$50,000	$36,050

Since the present value of the net cash flow based on a 12% rate of return, $36,050, is greater than the $33,530 to be invested, 12% is obviously not the discounted internal rate of return. The following analysis indicates that 15% is the rate of return that equates the $33,530 cost of the investment with the present value of the net cash flows:

Year	Present Value of $1 at 15%	Net Cash Flow	Present Value of Net Cash Flow
1	.870	$10,000	$ 8,700
2	.756	10,000	7,560
3	.658	10,000	6,580
4	.572	10,000	5,720
5	.497	10,000	4,970
Total.............................		$50,000	$33,530

In the illustration, the discounted internal rate of return was determined by trial and error. A rate of 12% was assumed before the discounted internal rate of return of 15% was identified. Such procedures are tedious and time consuming. When equal annual net cash flows are expected from a proposal, as in the illustration, the computations can be simplified by using a table of the present value of an annuity.[3]

A series of equal cash flows at fixed intervals is termed an **annuity**. The **present value of an annuity** is the sum of the present values of each cash flow. From another point of view, the present value of an annuity is the amount of cash that would be needed today to yield a series of equal cash flows at fixed intervals in the future. For example, reference to the following table of the present value of an annuity of $1 shows that the present value of cash flows at the end of each of five years, with a discounted internal rate of return of 15% per year, is 3.353. Multiplication of $10,000 by 3.353 yields the same amount ($33,530) that was determined in the preceding illustration by five successive multiplications.

---

[3]In the illustration, equal annual net cash flows are assumed, so that attention can be focused on the basic concepts. If the annual net cash flows are not equal, the procedures are more complex, but the basic concepts are not affected. In such cases, computers can be used to perform the computations.

*Present Value of an
Annuity of $1 at
Compound Interest*

Year	6%	10%	12%	15%	20%
1	.943	.909	.893	.870	.833
2	1.833	1.736	1.690	1.626	1.528
3	2.673	2.487	2.402	2.283	2.106
4	3.465	3.170	3.037	2.855	2.589
5	4.212	3.791	3.605	3.353	2.991
6	4.917	4.355	4.111	3.785	3.326
7	5.582	4.868	4.564	4.160	3.605
8	6.210	5.335	4.968	4.487	3.837
9	6.802	5.759	5.328	4.772	4.031
10	7.360	6.145	5.650	5.019	4.192

The procedures for using the present value of an annuity of $1 table to determine the discounted internal rate of return are as follows:

1. A present value factor for an annuity of $1 is determined by dividing the amount to be invested by the annual net cash flow, as expressed in the following formula:

$$\text{Present Value Factor for an Annuity of \$1} = \frac{\text{Amount To Be Invested}}{\text{Annual Net Cash Flow}}$$

2. The present value factor determined in (1) is located in the present value of an annuity of $1 table by first locating the number of years of expected useful life of the investment in the Year column and then proceeding horizontally across the table until the present value factor determined in (1) is found.
3. The discounted internal rate of return is then identified by the heading of the column in which the present value factor in (2) is located.

To illustrate the use of the present value of an annuity of $1 table, assume that management is considering a proposal to acquire equipment costing $97,360, which is expected to provide equal annual net cash flows of $20,000 for 7 years. The present value factor for an annuity of $1 is 4.868, computed as follows:

$$\text{Present Value Factor for an Annuity of \$1} = \frac{\text{Amount To Be Invested}}{\text{Annual Net Cash Flow}}$$

$$\text{Present Value Factor for an Annuity of \$1} = \frac{\$97,360}{\$20,000}$$

$$\text{Present Value Factor for an Annuity of \$1} = 4.868$$

For a period of 7 years, the following table for the present value of an annuity of $1 indicates that the factor 4.868 is associated with a percentage of 10%. Thus, 10% is the discounted internal rate of return for this proposal.

	Year	6%	10%	12%
Present Value of an Annuity of $1 at Compound Interest	1	9.43	.909	.893
	2	1.833	1.736	1.690
	3	2.673	2.487	2.402
	4	3.465	3.170	3.037
	5	4.212	3.791	3.605
	6	4.917	4.355	4.111
	7	5.582	4.868	4.564
	8	6.210	5.335	4.968
	9	6.802	5.759	5.328
	10	7.360	6.145	5.650

If the minimum acceptable rate of return for similar proposals is 10% or less, then the proposed equipment acquisition should be considered desirable. When several proposals are under consideration, management often ranks the proposals by their discounted internal rates of return, and the proposal with the highest rate is considered the most attractive.

The primary advantage of the discounted internal rate of return method is that the present values of the net cash flows over the entire useful life of the proposal are considered. An additional advantage of the method is that by determining a rate of return for each proposal, all proposals are automatically placed on a common basis for comparison, without the need to compute a present value index as was the case for the discounted cash flow method. The primary disadvantage of the discounted internal rate of return method is that the computations are somewhat more complex than for some of the other methods. In addition, like the discounted cash flow method, this method assumes that the cash received from a proposal during its useful life will be reinvested at the discounted internal rate of return. Because of changing economic conditions, this assumption may not always be reasonable.

THE DISCOUNTED INTERNAL RATE OF RETURN METHOD— AN APPLICATION USING THE MICROCOMPUTER

The complexity of using the present value methods of evaluating capital investment proposals can be significantly reduced by using a microcomputer. The following computer program, which was written in the BASIC programming language, computes the discounted internal rate of return for an investment proposal with a series of equal net cash flows:

```
10   INPUT "periods";N: INPUT "investment";I: INPUT "annual net cash flow";C
20   INPUT "guess";G
30   X=(X+G)/100+1:S=I
40   FOR J=1 TO N:S=S+C/X^J:NEXT:X=(X-1)*100
50   IF ABS(Y-X)<=.001 THEN END
60   LPRINT X:Y=X:RESTORE:IF S>0 THEN 30
70   X=X-G:G=G/3:GOTO 30
```

To run this program, the user must have access to the BASIC programming system. The manual accompanying this system will describe the procedures for calling up the system and entering, saving, loading, and running a program. In using the above program, the program steps must be keyboarded exactly as shown. When the program is run, the user will be required to input (1) the number of periods for which the proposed capital investment will yield annual cash inflows, (2) the cost of the investment expressed as a negative initial cash flow, (3) the annual net cash flows, and (4) an initial guess as to the approximate discounted internal rate of return. The initial guess does not necessarily have to be close to the true value, since the computer will estimate the true value regardless of the accuracy of the initial guess. The initial guess only adds efficiency to the estimation process. An example of the use of this computer program for the illustration presented on pages 1108–1109 is as follows:

```
periods? 7
investment? -97360
annual net cash flow? 20000
guess? 15
 15
 4.999995
 9.999991
 14.99999
 11.66666
 10.55554
 10.18517
 10.06172
 10.02057
 10.00685
 10.00227
 10.00456
 10.00303
```

The program will stop computing the estimated discounted internal rate of return when successive estimates are reasonably close to one another and additional precision is not warranted. In the above example, the approximate discounted internal rate of return is 10%. Note that the difference between the above estimate and the illustration in the text is due to rounding within the computer program.

Note: This program was written for the BASIC programming language using the IBM personal computer.

FACTORS THAT COMPLICATE
CAPITAL INVESTMENT ANALYSIS

OBJECTIVE 3
Describe factors that complicate capital investment analysis.

In the preceding paragraphs, the basic concepts for four widely used methods of evaluating capital investment proposals were discussed. In practice, additional factors may have an impact on the outcome of a capital investment decision. Some of the most important of these factors, which are described in the following paragraphs, are the federal income tax, unequal lives of alternative proposals, the leasing alternative, uncertainty, and changes in price levels.

Income Tax

In many cases, the impact of the federal income tax on capital investment decisions can be very significant. One provision of the Internal Revenue Code (IRC) which should be considered in capital investment analysis is depreciation.

For determining depreciation for federal income tax purposes, useful lives that are much shorter than the actual useful lives can often be used. Also, depreciation can be calculated by methods that approximate the 200 percent declining-balance method. Thus, depreciation for tax purposes often exceeds the depreciation for financial statement purposes in the early years of an asset's use. The tax reduction in these early years is offset by higher taxes as the annual cost recovery allowance decreases, so that accelerated depreciation does not effect a long-run saving in taxes.

Unequal Proposal Lives

In the preceding sections, the discussion of the methods of analyzing capital investment proposals was based on the assumption that alternative proposals had the same useful lives. In practice, however, alternative proposals may have unequal lives. In such cases, the proposals must be made comparable. One widely used method is to adjust the lives of projects with the longest lives to a time period that is equal to the life of the project with the shortest life. In this manner, the useful lives of all proposals are made equal. To illustrate, assume that the discounted cash flow method is being used to compare the following two proposals, each of which has an initial investment of $100,000:

Net Cash Flows

Year	Proposal X	Proposal Y
1	$30,000	$30,000
2	30,000	30,000
3	25,000	30,000
4	20,000	30,000
5	15,000	30,000
6	15,000	—
7	10,000	—
8	10,000	—

If the desired rate of return is 10%, the proposals have an excess of present value over the amount to be invested, as follows:

Proposal X

Year	Present Value of $1 at 10%	Net Cash Flow	Present Value of Net Cash Flow
1	.909	$ 30,000	$ 27,270
2	.826	30,000	24,780
3	.751	25,000	18,775
4	.683	20,000	13,660
5	.621	15,000	9,315
6	.564	15,000	8,460
7	.513	10,000	5,130
8	.467	10,000	4,670
Total..		$155,000	$112,060
Amount to be invested			100,000
Excess of present value over amount to be invested			$ 12,060

Proposal Y

Year	Present Value of $1 at 10%	Net Cash Flow	Present Value of Net Cash Flow
1	.909	$ 30,000	$ 27,270
2	.826	30,000	24,780
3	.751	30,000	22,530
4	.683	30,000	20,490
5	.621	30,000	18,630
Total...		$150,000	$113,700
Amount to be invested			100,000
Excess of present value over amount to be invested			$ 13,700

The two proposals cannot be compared by focusing on the amount of the excess of the present value over the amount to be invested, because Proposal Y has a life of 5 years while Proposal X has a life of 8 years. Proposal X can be adjusted to a 5-year life by assuming that it is to be terminated at the end of 5 years and the asset sold. This assumption requires that the residual value of Proposal X be estimated at the end of 5 years and that this value be considered a cash flow at that date. Both proposals will then cover 5 years, and the results of the discounted cash flow analysis can be used to compare the relative attractiveness of the two proposals. For example, assume that Proposal X has an estimated residual value at the end of year 5 of $40,000. For Proposal X, the excess of the present value over the amount to be invested is $18,640 for a 5-year life, as follows:

Proposal X

Year	Present Value of $1 at 10%	Net Cash Flow	Present Value of Net Cash Flow
1	.909	$ 30,000	$ 27,270
2	.826	30,000	24,780
3	.751	25,000	18,775
4	.683	20,000	13,660
5	.621	15,000	9,315
5 (Residual value)	.621	40,000	24,840
Total...		$160,000	$118,640
Amount to be invested			100,000
Excess of present value over amount to be invested			$ 18,640

Since the present value over the amount be be invested for Proposal X exceeds that for Proposal Y by $4,940 ($18,640 − $13,700), Proposal X may be viewed as the more attractive of the two proposals.

Lease Versus Capital Investment

Leasing of plant assets has become common in many industries in recent years. Leasing allows an enterprise to acquire the use of plant assets without the necessity of using large amounts of cash to purchase them. In addition, if management believes that a plant asset has a high degree of risk of becoming obsolete before the end of its useful life, then leasing rather than purchasing the asset may be more attractive. By leasing the asset, management reduces the risk of suffering a loss due to obsolescence. Finally, the Internal Revenue Code provisions which allow the lessor (the owner of the asset) to pass tax deductions on to the lessee (the party leasing the asset) have increased the popularity of leasing in recent years. For example, a company that leases for its use a $200,000 plant asset with a life of 8 years for $50,000 per year is permitted to deduct the annual lease payments of $50,000.

In many cases, before a final decision is made, management should consider the possibility of leasing assets instead of purchasing them. Ordinarily, leasing assets is more costly than purchasing because the lessor must include in the rental price not only the costs associated with owning the assets but also a profit. Nevertheless, using the methods of evaluating capital investment proposals, management should consider whether or not the profitability and cash flows from the lease alternative with its risks compares favorably to the profitability and cash flows from the purchase alternative with its risks.

Uncertainty

All capital investment analyses rely on factors that are uncertain; that is, the accuracy of the estimates involved, including estimates of expected revenues, expenses, and cash flows, are uncertain. Although the estimates are subject to varying degrees of risk or uncertainty, the long-term nature of capital investments suggests that many of the estimates are likely to involve considerable uncertainty. Errors in one or more of the estimates could lead to unwise decisions.

Changes in Price Levels

The past three decades, which have been characterized by increasing price levels, are described as periods of **inflation**. In recent years, the rates of inflation have fluctuated widely, making the estimation of future revenues, expenses, and cash flows more difficult. Therefore, management should consider the expected future price levels and their likely effect on the estimates used in capital investment analyses. Fluctuations in the price levels assumed could significantly affect the analyses.

CAPITAL RATIONING

OBJECTIVE 4
Describe and illustrate the capital rationing process.

Capital rationing refers to the process by which management allocates available investment funds among competing capital investment proposals. Generally, management will use various combinations of the evaluation methods described in this chapter in developing an effective approach to capital rationing.

In capital rationing, an initial screening of alternative proposals is usually performed by establishing minimum standards for the cash payback and the average rate of return methods. The proposals that survive this initial screening are subjected to the more rigorous discounted cash flow and discounted internal rate of return methods of analysis. The proposals that survive this final screening are evaluated in terms of nonfinancial factors, such as employee morale. For example, the acquisition of new, more efficient equipment which eliminates several jobs could lower employee morale to a level that could decrease overall plant productivity.

The final step in the capital rationing process is a ranking of the proposals and a comparison of proposals with the funds available to determine which proposals will be funded. The unfunded proposals are reconsidered if funds subsequently become available. The following flowchart portrays the capital rationing decision process:

Capital Rationing Decision Process

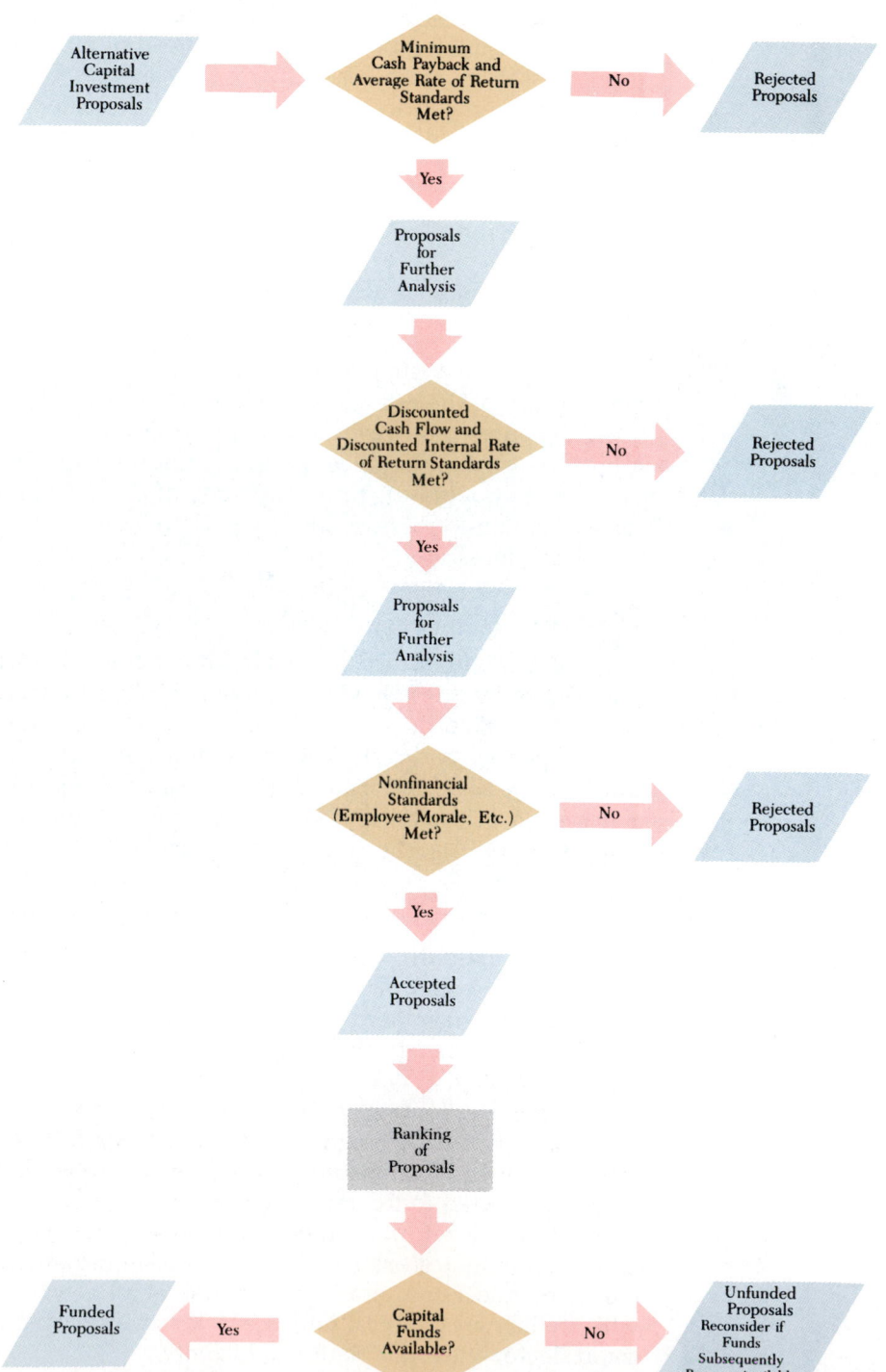

PLANNING AND CONTROLLING CAPITAL INVESTMENT EXPENDITURES

OBJECTIVE 5
Describe the basic concepts for planning and controlling capital investment expenditures.

Proposals that are funded in the capital rationing process should be included in the budget to facilitate the planning of operations and the financing of capital expenditures. A capital expenditures budget, which is integrated with the master budget as discussed in Chapter 25, summarizes acquisition decisions for a period typically ranging from one to five years. The following capital expenditures budget was prepared for Hovey Company:

Capital Expenditures Budget

Hovey Company
Capital Expenditures Budget
For Five Years Ending December 31, 1995

Item	1991	1992	1993	1994	1995
Machinery — Department A..	$240,000	—	—	$168,000	$216,000
Machinery — Department B..	108,000	$156,000	$336,000	120,000	—
Delivery equipment	—	54,000	—	—	36,000
Total	$348,000	$210,000	$336,000	$288,000	$252,000

The capital expenditures budget does not authorize the acquisition of plant assets. Rather, it serves as a planning device to determine the effects of the capital expenditures on operations after management has evaluated the alternative proposals, using the methods described in this chapter. Final authority for capital expenditures must come from the proper level of management. In some corporations, large capital expenditures must be approved by the board of directors.

Once the capital expenditures have been approved, control must be established over the costs of acquiring the assets, including the costs of installation and testing before the assets are placed in service. Throughout this period of acquiring the assets and readying them for use, actual costs should be compared to planned (budgeted) costs. Timely reports should be prepared, so that management can take corrective actions as quickly as possible and thereby minimize cost overruns and operating delays.

After the assets have been placed in service, attention should be focused on comparisons of actual operating expenses with budgeted operating expenses. Such comparisons provide opportunities for management to follow up on successful expenditures or to terminate or otherwise attempt to salvage failing expenditures.

CHAPTER REVIEW

KEY POINTS

OBJECTIVE 1

Nature of Capital Investment Analysis

The process by which management plans, evaluates, and controls investments involving property, plant, and equipment is called capital investment analysis. A capital investment program should include a plan for encouraging employees at all levels of an enterprise to submit proposals for capital investments. All reasonable proposals should be given serious consideration, and the effects of the economic implications expected from these proposals should be identified.

Methods of Evaluating Capital Investment Proposals

The methods of evaluating capital investment proposals can be grouped into two general categories: (1) methods that ignore present value and (2) present value methods. The methods that ignore present value include (1) the average rate of return method and (2) the cash payback method. Methods that use present values in evaluating capital investment proposals are (1) the discounted cash flow method and (2) the discounted internal rate of return method.

The expected average rate of return is a measure of the expected profitability of an investment in plant assets. When several alternative capital investment proposals are being considered, the proposals can be ranked by their average rates of return. The higher the average rate of return, the more desirable the proposal. The primary advantage of the average rate of return method is its simplicity, and its primary disadvantage is its lack of consideration of expected cash flows from a proposal and the timing of those cash flows.

The cash payback method measures the cash payback period, which is the expected period of time that will pass between the date of a capital investment and the complete recovery in cash (or equivalent) of the amount invested. The cash payback method is especially useful to managers whose primary concern is liquidity. The primary disadvantage of the cash payback method is its failure to take into consideration the expected profitability of a proposal. Another disadvantage of the cash payback method is that the cash flows occurring after the payback period are ignored.

The discounted cash flow method uses present value concepts to compute the present value of the cash flows expected from a proposal. When several alternative investment proposals of the same amount are being considered, the one with the largest excess of present value over the amount to be invested is the most desirable. If the alternative proposals involve different amounts of investment, it is useful to prepare a ranking of the proposals by using a present value index. The primary advantage of the discounted cash flow method is that it gives consideration to the time value of money. A disadvantage of the method is that the computations are more complex than those for the methods that ignore present value. In addition, it assumes that the cash received from the proposal during its useful life will be reinvested at the rate of return used to compute the present value of the proposal.

The discounted internal rate of return method uses present value concepts to compute the rate of return from the net cash flows expected from capital investment proposals. When several proposals are under consideration, management often ranks proposals by their discounted internal rates of return, and the proposal with the highest rate is considered the most attractive. The primary advantage of the discounted internal rate of return method is that the present values of the net cash flows over the entire useful life of the proposal are considered. The primary disadvantage of the discounted internal rate of return method is that the computations are somewhat more complex than for some of the other methods. In addition, like the discounted cash flow method, this method assumes that the cash received from a proposal during its useful life will be reinvested at the discounted internal rate of return.

Factors that Complicate Capital Investment Analysis

Factors that may complicate capital investment analysis include the impact of the federal income tax, unequal lives of alternative proposals, the leasing alternative, uncertainty, and changes in price levels.

Capital Rationing

Capital rationing refers to the process by which management allocates available investment funds among competing capital investment proposals. In capital rationing, an initial screening of alternative proposals is usually performed by establishing minimum standards for the cash payback and the average rate of return methods.

The final step in the capital rationing process is a ranking of the proposals and a comparison of proposals with the funds available to determine which proposals will be funded.

OBJECTIVE 5   Planning and Controlling Capital Investment Expenditures

Proposals that are funded in the capital rationing process should be included in the master budget. Throughout the period of acquiring plant assets and readying them for use, actual costs should be compared to planned costs, and timely reports should be prepared so that management can minimize cost overruns and operating delays.

KEY TERMS

capital investment analysis 1100
average rate of return 1102
cash payback period 1103
present value 1104
discounted cash flow method 1104
present value index 1105

discounted internal rate of return
    method 1106
annuity 1107
present value of an annuity 1107
inflation 1113
capital rationing 1113

SELF-EXAMINATION QUESTIONS
Answers at end of chapter.

1. Methods of evaluating capital investment proposals that ignore present value include:
   A. average rate of return
   B. cash payback
   C. both A and B
   D. neither A nor B

2. Management is considering a $100,000 investment in a project with a 5-year life and no residual value. If the total income from the project is expected to be $60,000 and recognition is given to the effect of straight-line depreciation on the investment, the average rate of return is:
   A. 12%
   B. 24%
   C. 60%
   D. none of the above

3. As used in the analysis of proposed capital investments, the expected period of time that will elapse between the date of a capital investment and the complete recovery of the amount of cash invested is called:
   A. the average rate of return period
   B. the cash payback period
   C. the discounted cash flow period
   D. none of the above

4. Which method of analyzing capital investment proposals determines the total present value of the cash flows expected from the investment and compares this value with the amount to be invested?
   A. Average rate of return
   B. Cash payback
   C. Discounted cash flow
   D. Discounted internal rate of return

5. The process by which management allocates available investment funds among competing capital investment proposals is referred to as:
   A. capital rationing
   B. capital expenditure budgeting
   C. leasing
   D. none of the above

ILLUSTRATIVE PROBLEM

The capital investment committee of Bormann Company is currently considering two projects. The estimated operating income and net cash flows expected from each project are as follows:

	Project A		Project B	
Year	Operating Income	Net Cash Flow	Operating Income	Net Cash Flow
1	$ 9,000	$19,000	$ 5,000	$15,000
2	7,000	17,000	6,000	16,000
3	6,000	16,000	8,000	18,000
4	5,000	15,000	7,000	17,000
5	3,000	13,000	4,000	14,000
	$30,000	$80,000	$30,000	$80,000

Each project requires an investment of $50,000. Straight-line depreciation will be used, and no residual value is expected. The committee has selected a rate of 15% for purposes of the discounted cash flow analysis.

Instructions:

1. Compute the following:
   a. The average rate of return for each project, giving effect to depreciation on the investment.
   b. The excess or deficiency of present value over the amount to be invested, as determined by the discounted cash flow method for each project. Use the present value of $1 table appearing in this chapter.
2. Prepare a brief report for the capital investment committee, advising it on the relative merits of the two projects.

SOLUTION

(1) (a) Average annual rate of return for both projects:

$$\frac{\$30,000 \div 5}{(\$50,000 + \$0) \div 2} = 24\%$$

(b) Discounted cash flow analysis:

Year	Present Value of $1 at 15%	Net Cash Flow Project A	Net Cash Flow Project B	Present Value of Net Cash Flow Project A	Present Value of Net Cash Flow Project B
1	.870	$19,000	$15,000	$16,530	$13,050
2	.756	17,000	16,000	12,852	12,096
3	.658	16,000	18,000	10,528	11,844
4	.572	15,000	17,000	8,580	9,724
5	.497	13,000	14,000	6,461	6,958
Total		$80,000	$80,000	$54,951	$53,672
Amount to be invested..........................				50,000	50,000
Excess of present value over amount to be invested...........................				$ 4,951	$ 3,672

(2) (a) Both projects offer the same average annual rate of return.
   (b) Although both projects exceed the selected rate established for discounted cash flows, Project A offers a larger excess of present value over the amount to be invested. Thus, if only one of the two projects can be accepted, Project A would be the more attractive.

DISCUSSION QUESTIONS

1. Which two methods of capital investment analysis ignore present value?

2. Which two methods of capital investment analysis can be described as present value methods?

3. What is the "time value of money" concept?

4. (a) How is the average rate of return computed for capital investment analysis, assuming that consideration is given to the effect of straight-line depreciation on the amount of the investment? (b) If the amount of a 10-year investment is $900,000, the straight-line method of depreciation is used, there is no residual value, and the total income expected from the investment is $810,000, what is the average rate of return?

5. What are the principal objections to the use of the average rate of return method in evaluating capital investment proposals?

6. (a) As used in analyses of proposed capital investments, what is the cash pay-back period? (b) Discuss the principal limitations of the cash payback method for evaluating capital investment proposals.

7. What is the present value of $8,625 to be received one year from today, assuming an earnings rate of 15%.

8. Which method of evaluating capital investment proposals reduces their expected future net cash flows to present values and compares the total present values to the amount of the investment?

9. A discounted cash flow analysis used to evaluate a proposed equipment acquisition indicated a $12,600 excess of present value over the amount to be invested. What is the meaning of the $12,600 as it relates to the desirability of the proposal?

10. How is the present value index for a proposal determined?

11. What are the major disadvantages of the use of the discounted cash flow method of analyzing capital investment proposals?

12. What is an annuity?

13. What are the major disadvantages of the use of the discounted internal rate of return method of analyzing capital investment proposals?

14. What provision of the Internal Revenue Code is especially important for consideration in analyzing capital investment proposals?

15. What method can be used to place two capital investment proposals with unequal useful lives on a comparable basis?

16. What are the major advantages of leasing a plant asset rather than purchasing it?

17. What is capital rationing?

18. Which budget summarizes the acquisition decisions for a period?

Real World Focus

19. Boston Metal Products, a small manufacturer in Medford, Mass., was considering the purchase of a robot. The company controller was asked to calculate whether the $200,000 investment made financial sense. Using traditional accounting techniques, the controller concluded that the investment did not meet the financial criteria that had been established. However, the company went ahead and made the investment. What qualitative considerations could Boston Metal Products have used to justify the capital investment in a robot?

EXERCISES

Exercise 28–1
Average rate of return.
OBJ. 2

The following data are accumulated by Sumner Company in evaluating two competing capital investment proposals:

	Proposal C	Proposal L
Amount of investment	$500,000	$860,000
Useful life	7 years	10 years
Estimated residual value	–0–	–0–
Estimated total income	$332,500	$731,000

Determine the expected average rate of return for each proposal, giving effect to straight-line depreciation on each investment.

Exercise 28–2
Cash payback period.
OBJ. 2

Noakes Company is evaluating two capital investment proposals, each requiring an investment of $320,000 and each with a 9-year life and expected total net cash flows of $720,000. Proposal 1 is expected to provide equal annual net cash flows of $80,000, and Proposal 2 is expected to have the following unequal annual net cash flows:

Year 1	$145,000
Year 2	90,000
Year 3	85,000
Year 4	85,000
Year 5	75,000
Year 6	70,000
Year 7	60,000
Year 8	55,000
Year 9	55,000

Determine the cash payback period for both proposals.

Exercise 28–3
Discounted cash flow method.
OBJ. 2

The following data are accumulated by Gresham Company in evaluating the purchase of $240,000 of equipment having a 4-year useful life:

	Net Income	Net Cash Flow
Year 1	$40,000	$100,000
Year 2	20,000	80,000
Year 3	6,000	66,000
Year 4	4,000	64,000

(a) Assuming that the desired rate of return is 10%, determine the excess (deficiency) of present value over the amount to be invested for the proposal. Use the table of the present value of $1 appearing in this chapter. (b) Would management be likely to look with favor on the proposal? Explain.

Exercise 28–4
Present value index.
OBJ. 2

Tasker Company has computed the excess of present value over the amount to be invested for capital expenditure proposals H and J, using the discounted cash flow method. Relevant data related to the computation are as follows:

	Proposal H	Proposal J
Total present value of net cash flow	$189,000	$296,800
Amount to be invested..	175,000	280,000
Excess of present value over amount to be invested........	$ 14,000	$ 16,800

Determine the present value index for each proposal.

Exercise 28–5
Average rate of return, cash payback period, discounted cash flow method.
OBJ. 2

Freer Company is considering the acquisition of machinery at a cost of $750,000. The machinery has an estimated life of 5 years and no residual value. It is expected to provide yearly income of $37,500 and yearly net cash flows of $187,500. The company's minimum desired rate of return for discounted cash flow analysis is 6%. Compute the following:

(a) The average rate of return, giving effect to straight-line depreciation on the investment.
(b) The cash payback period.
(c) The excess (deficiency) of present value over the amount to be invested, as determined by the discounted cash flow method. Use the table of the present value of $1 appearing in this chapter.

Exercise 28–6
Discounted internal rate of return method.
OBJ. 2

The discounted internal rate of return method is used by Kang Company in analyzing a capital expenditure proposal that involves an investment of $288,400 and annual net cash flows of $80,000 for each of the 7 years of useful life. (a) Determine a "present value factor for an annuity of $1" which can be used in determining the discounted internal rate of return. (b) Using the factor determined in (a) and the present value of an annuity of $1 table appearing in this chapter, determine the discounted internal rate of return for the proposal.

Exercise 28–7
Discounted cash flow method and discounted internal rate of return method.
OBJ. 2

Mulvey Inc. is evaluating a proposed expenditure of $158,500 on a 4-year project whose estimated net cash flows are $50,000 for each of the four years.
(a) Compute the excess (deficiency) of present value over the amount to be invested, using the discounted cash flow method and an assumed rate of return of 12%.
(b) Based on the analysis prepared in (a), is the rate of return (1) more than 12%, (2) 12%, or (3) less than 12%? Explain. (c) Determine the discounted internal rate of return by computing a "present value factor for an annuity of $1" and using the table of the present value of an annuity of $1 presented in the text.

PROBLEMS

Series A

Problem 28–1A
Average rate of return method, discounted cash flow method, and analysis.
OBJ. 2

The capital investment budget committee is considering two projects. The estimated operating income and net cash flows from each project are shown as follows:

	Project S		Project W	
Year	Operating Income	Net Cash Flow	Operating Income	Net Cash Flow
1	$ 50,000	$130,000	$ 40,000	$120,000
2	45,000	125,000	40,000	120,000
3	35,000	115,000	35,000	115,000
4	25,000	105,000	35,000	115,000
5	25,000	105,000	30,000	110,000
Total	$180,000	$580,000	$180,000	$580,000

Each project requires an investment of $400,000. Straight-line depreciation will be used, and no residual value is expected. The committee has selected a rate of 10% for purposes of the discounted cash flow analysis.

Instructions:

(1) Compute the following:
    (a) The average rate of return for each project, giving effect to depreciation on the investment.
    (b) The excess (deficiency) of present value over the amount to be invested, as determined by the discounted cash flow method for each project. Use the present value of $1 table appearing in this chapter.
(2) Prepare a brief report for the capital investment committee, advising it on the relative merits of the two projects.

Problem 28–2A
Cash payback period, discounted cash flow method, and analysis.
OBJ. 2

Hemrick Company is considering two projects. The estimated net cash flows from each project are as follows:

Year	Project M	Project N
1	$150,000	$125,000
2	100,000	125,000
3	40,000	70,000
4	40,000	15,000
5	20,000	15,000
Total	$350,000	$350,000

Each project requires an investment of $250,000, with no residual value expected. A rate of 10% has been selected for the discounted cash flow analysis.

Instructions:

(1) Compute the following for each project:
    (a) Cash payback period.
    (b) The excess (deficiency) of present value over the amount to be invested, as determined by the discounted cash flow method. Use the present value of $1 table appearing in this chapter.
(2) Prepare a brief report advising management on the relative merits of each of the two projects.

Problem 28–3A
Discounted cash flow method, present value index, and analysis.
OBJ. 2

Joiner Company wishes to evaluate three capital investment projects by using the discounted cash flow method. Relevant data related to the projects are summarized as follows:

	Project J	Project K	Project L
Amount to be invested.....................	$500,000	$400,000	$200,000
Annual net cash flows:			
Year 1..	320,000	250,000	100,000
Year 2..	220,000	200,000	80,000
Year 3..	100,000	70,000	40,000

Instructions:

(1) Assuming that the desired rate of return is 10%, prepare a discounted cash flow analysis for each project. Use the present value of $1 table appearing in this chapter.
(2) Determine a present value index for each project.
(3) Which project offers the largest amount of present value per dollar of investment? Explain.

Problem 28–4A
Discounted cash
flow method,
discounted internal
rate of return
method, and
analysis.

Management is considering two capital investment projects. The estimated net cash flows from each project are as follows:

Year	Project D	Project E
1	$180,000	$50,000
2	180,000	50,000
3	180,000	50,000
4	180,000	50,000

Project D requires an investment of $513,900, while Project E requires an investment of $129,450.

Instructions:

(1) Compute the following for each project:
  (a) The excess (deficiency) of present value over the amount to be invested, as determined by the discounted cash flow method. Use a rate of 12% and the present value of $1 table appearing in this chapter.
  (b) A present value index.
(2) Determine the discounted internal rate of return for each project by (a) computing a "present value factor for an annuity of $1" and (b) using the present value of an annuity of $1 table appearing in this chapter.
(3) What advantage does the discounted internal rate of return method have over the discounted cash flow method in comparing projects?

Problem 28–5A
Evaluation of
alternative capital
investment
decisions.

The investment committee of Beaver Company is evaluating two projects. The projects have different useful lives, but each requires an investment of $160,000. The estimated net cash flows from each project are as follows:

	Net Cash Flows	
Year	Project A	Project B
1	$45,000	$60,000
2	45,000	60,000
3	45,000	60,000
4	45,000	60,000
5	45,000	
6	45,000	

The committee has selected a rate of 15% for purposes of discounted cash flow analysis. It also estimates that the residual value at the end of each project's useful life is $0, but at the end of the fourth year, Project A's residual value would be $90,000.

Instructions:

(1) For each project, compute the excess (deficiency) of present value over the amount to be invested, as determined by the discounted cash flow method. Use the present value of $1 table appearing in this chapter. (Ignore the unequal lives of the projects.)
(2) For each project, compute the excess (deficiency) of present value over the amount to be invested, as determined by the discounted cash flow method, assuming that Project A is adjusted to a four-year life for purposes of analysis. Use the present value of $1 table appearing in this chapter.
(3) In reporting to the investment committee, what advice would you give on the relative merits of the two projects?

Problem 28–6A
Capital rationing
decision involving
six proposals.

Shaut Inc. is considering the allocation of a limited amount of capital investment funds among six proposals. The amount of proposed investment, estimated operating income, and net cash flow for each proposal are as follows:

Proposal A:	Investment	Year	Operating Income	Net Cash Flow
	$100,000	1	$20,000	$40,000
		2	10,000	30,000
		3	10,000	30,000
		4	5,000	25,000
		5	5,000	25,000

Proposal B:	Investment	Year	Operating Income	Net Cash Flow
	$500,000	1	$40,000	$140,000
		2	25,000	125,000
		3	20,000	120,000
		4	15,000	115,000
		5	12,500	112,500

Proposal C:	Investment	Year	Operating Income	Net Cash Flow
	$200,000	1	$50,000	$90,000
		2	20,000	60,000
		3	10,000	50,000
		4	5,000	45,000
		5	5,000	45,000

Proposal D:	Investment	Year	Operating Income	Net Cash Flow
	$75,000	1	$3,750	$18,750
		2	3,750	18,750
		3	3,750	18,750
		4	3,750	18,750
		5	3,750	18,750

Proposal E:	Investment	Year	Operating Income	Net Cash Flow
	$50,000	1	$20,000	$30,000
		2	10,000	20,000
		3	4,000	14,000
		4	2,500	12,500
		5	1,000	11,000

Proposal F:	Investment	Year	Operating Income	Net Cash Flow
	$300,000	1	$12,000	$72,000
		2	12,000	72,000
		3	12,000	72,000
		4	12,000	72,000
		5	12,000	72,000

Shaut Inc.'s capital rationing policy requires a minimum cash payback period of 4 years for projects of $100,000 and over, and a minimum cash payback period of 3 years for projects under $100,000. In addition, a minimum average rate of return of 10% is required on all projects. If the preceding minimum standards are met, the discounted cash flow method and present value indexes are used to rank the remaining proposals.

Instructions:

(1) Compute the cash payback period for each of the six proposals.

(2) Giving effect to straight-line depreciation on the investments and assuming no estimated residual value, compute the average rate of return for each of the six proposals.
(3) Using the following format, summarize the results of your computations in (1) and (2). Indicate which proposals should be accepted for further analysis and which should be rejected by placing a check mark in the appropriate column at the right.

Proposal	Cash Payback Period	Average Rate of Return	Accept for Further Analysis	Reject
A				
B				
C				
D				
E				
F				

(4) For the proposals accepted for further analysis in (3), compute the excess (deficiency) of present value over the amount to be invested, as determined by the discounted cash flow method. Use a rate of 10% and the present value of $1 table appearing in this chapter.
(5) Compute the present value index for each of the proposals in (4).
(6) Rank the proposals from most attractive to least attractive, based on the present values of net cash flows computed in (4).
(7) Rank the proposals from most attractive to least attractive, based on the present value indexes computed in (5).
(8) Based upon the analyses, comment on the relative attractiveness of the proposals ranked in (6) and (7).

Series B

Problem 28–1B
Average rate of return method, discounted cash flow method, and analysis.

OBJ. 2

The capital investments budget committee is considering two projects. The estimated operating income and net cash flows from each project are shown as follows:

	Project F		Project K	
Year	Operating Income	Net Cash Flow	Operating Income	Net Cash Flow
1	$ 75,000	$195,000	$ 80,000	$200,000
2	70,000	190,000	60,000	180,000
3	60,000	180,000	60,000	180,000
4	40,000	160,000	60,000	180,000
5	40,000	160,000	25,000	145,000
Total	$285,000	$885,000	$285,000	$885,000

Each project requires an investment of $600,000. Straight-line depreciation will be used, and no residual value is expected. The committee has selected a rate of 15% for purposes of the discounted cash flow analysis.

Instructions:

(1) Compute the following:
  (a) The average rate of return for each project, giving effect to depreciation on the investment.
  (b) The excess (deficiency) of present value over the amount to be invested, as determined by the discounted cash flow method for each project. Use the present value of $1 table appearing in this chapter.
(2) Prepare a brief report for the capital investment committee, advising it on the relative merits of the two projects.

Problem 28–2B

Cash payback period, discounted cash flow method, and analysis.

OBJ. 2

Woburn Company is considering two projects. The estimated net cash flows from each project are as follows:

Year	Project G	Project R
1	$200,000	$190,000
2	175,000	185,000
3	50,000	90,000
4	50,000	30,000
5	50,000	30,000
Total	$525,000	$525,000

Each project requires an investment of $375,000, with no residual value expected. A rate of 15% has been selected for the discounted cash flow analysis.

Instructions:

(1) Compute the following for each project:
    (a) Cash payback period.
    (b) The excess (deficiency) of present value over the amount to be invested, as determined by the discounted cash flow method. Use the present value of $1 table appearing in this chapter.
(2) Prepare a brief report advising management on the relative merits of each of the two projects.

Problem 28–3B

Discounted cash flow method, present value index, and analysis.

OBJ. 2

Zarzeski Company wishes to evaluate three capital investment proposals by using the discounted cash flow method. Relevant data related to the proposals are summarized as follows:

	Proposal T	Proposal U	Proposal V
Amount to be invested.............	$750,000	$600,000	$800,000
Annual net cash flows:			
Year 1................................	400,000	350,000	475,000
Year 2................................	380,000	320,000	340,000
Year 3................................	100,000	110,000	220,000

Instructions:

(1) Assuming that the desired rate of return is 12%, prepare a discounted cash flow analysis for each proposal. Use the present value of $1 table appearing in this chapter.
(2) Determine a present value index for each proposal.
(3) Which proposal offers the largest amount of present value per dollar of investment? Explain.

Problem 28–4B

Discounted cash flow method, discounted internal rate of return method, and analysis.

OBJ. 2

Management is considering two capital investment proposals. The estimated net cash flows from each proposal are as follows:

Year	Proposal I	Proposal J
1	$40,000	$120,000
2	40,000	120,000
3	40,000	120,000
4	40,000	120,000

Proposal I requires an investment of $121,480, while Proposal J requires an investment of $380,400.

Instructions:

(1) Compute the following for each proposal:
    (a) The excess (deficiency) of present value over the amount to be invested, as determined by the discounted cash flow method. Use a rate of 6% and the present value of $1 table appearing in this chapter.
    (b) A present value index.
(2) Determine the discounted internal rate of return for each project by (a) computing a "present value factor for an annuity of $1" and (b) using the present value of an annuity of $1 table appearing in this chapter.
(3) What advantage does the discounted internal rate of return method have over the discounted cash flow method in comparing projects?

MINI-CASE 28

PLUNKETT INDUSTRIES INC.

Your father is considering an investment of $500,000 in either Project B or Project F. In discussing the two projects with an advisor, it was decided that, for the risk involved, a return of 10% on the cash investment would be required. For this purpose, your father estimated the following economic factors for the projects:

	Project B	Project F
Useful life	4 years	4 years
Residual value	–0–	–0–
Net income:		
Year 1	$ 85,000	$ 30,000
2	55,000	30,000
3	25,000	70,000
4	15,000	60,000
Net cash flows:		
Year 1	$210,000	$155,000
2	180,000	155,000
3	150,000	195,000
4	140,000	185,000

Although the average rate of return exceeded 10% on both projects, your father has tentatively decided to invest in Project F because the rate was higher for Project F. Although he doesn't fully understand the importance of cash flow, he has heard others talk about its importance in evaluating investments. In this respect, he noted that the total net cash flow from Project F is $690,000, which exceeds that of Project B by $10,000.

Instructions:

(1) Determine the average rate of return for both projects.
(2) How would you explain the importance of net cash flows in the analysis of investment projects? Include a specific example to demonstrate the importance of net cash flows and their timing to these two projects.

ETHICS DISCUSSION CASE	Richard Kasner, the controller of Mandelstam Inc., has recently prepared Mandelstam's federal income tax return for the preceding year. In determining depreciation for federal income tax purposes, Kasner used shorter useful lives for several assets than the estimated useful lives used in preparing the company's income statement. In addition, Kasner deducted as expenses several expenditures which were related to depreciable assets acquired during the year. Kasner believes it is highly unlikely that the company's tax return will be audited by the Internal Revenue Service. Discuss whether Kasner behaved in an ethical manner.

ANSWERS TO SELF-EXAMINATION QUESTIONS

1. **C** Methods of evaluating capital investment proposals that ignore the time value of money are categorized as methods that ignore present value. This category includes the average rate of return method (answer A) and the cash payback method (answer B).

2. **B** The average rate of return is 24% (answer B), determined by dividing the expected average annual earnings by the average investment, as follows:

$$\frac{\$60,000 \div 5}{(\$100,000 + \$0) \div 2} = 24\%$$

3. **B** Of the three methods of analyzing proposals for capital investments, the cash payback method (answer B) refers to the expected period of time required to recover the amount of cash to be invested. The average rate of return method (answer A) is a measure of the anticipated profitability of a proposal. The discounted cash flow method (answer C) reduces the expected future net cash flows originating from a proposal to their present values.

4. **C** The discounted cash flow method (answer C) uses the concept of present value to determine the total present value of the cash flows expected from a proposal and compares this value with the amount to be invested. The average rate of return method (answer A) and the cash payback method (answer B) ignore present value. The discounted internal rate of return method (answer D) uses the present value concept to determine the discounted internal rate of return expected from the proposal.

5. **A** Capital rationing (answer A) is the process by which management allocates available investment funds among competing capital investment proposals. Capital expenditure budgeting (answer B) is the process of summarizing the decisions that have been made for the acquisition of plant assets and preparing a capital expenditures budget to reflect these decisions. Leasing (answer C) is an alternative that management should consider before making a final decision on the acquisition of assets.

APPENDIX A

INTEREST TABLES

The following present value and future value tables contain factors carried to six decimal places for interest rates of 5% to 14% for 50 periods.

Present Value of 1 at Compound Interest Due in n Periods: $p_{\overline{n}|i} = \dfrac{1}{(1+i)^n}$

n	5%	5.5%	6%	6.5%	7%	8%	9%	10%	11%	12%	13%	14%
1	0.952381	0.94787	0.943396	0.93897	0.934580	0.925926	0.917431	0.909091	0.90090	0.892857	0.88496	0.87719
2	0.907029	0.89845	0.889996	0.88166	0.873439	0.857339	0.841680	0.826446	0.81162	0.797194	0.78315	0.76947
3	0.863838	0.85161	0.839619	0.82785	0.816298	0.793832	0.772183	0.751315	0.73119	0.711780	0.69305	0.67497
4	0.822702	0.80722	0.792094	0.77732	0.762895	0.735030	0.708425	0.683013	0.65873	0.635518	0.61332	0.59208
5	0.783526	0.76513	0.747258	0.72988	0.712986	0.680583	0.649931	0.620921	0.59345	0.567427	0.54276	0.51937
6	0.746215	0.72525	0.704961	0.68533	0.666342	0.630170	0.596267	0.564474	0.53464	0.506631	0.48032	0.45559
7	0.710681	0.68744	0.665057	0.64351	0.622750	0.583490	0.547034	0.513158	0.48166	0.452349	0.42506	0.39964
8	0.676839	0.65160	0.627412	0.60423	0.582009	0.540269	0.501866	0.466507	0.43393	0.403883	0.37616	0.35056
9	0.644609	0.61763	0.591898	0.56735	0.543934	0.500249	0.460428	0.424098	0.39092	0.360610	0.33288	0.30751
10	0.613913	0.58543	0.558395	0.53273	0.508349	0.463193	0.422411	0.385543	0.35218	0.321973	0.29459	0.26974
11	0.584679	0.55491	0.526788	0.50021	0.475093	0.428883	0.387533	0.350494	0.31728	0.287476	0.26070	0.23662
12	0.556837	0.52598	0.496969	0.46968	0.444012	0.397114	0.355535	0.318631	0.28584	0.256675	0.23071	0.20756
13	0.530321	0.49856	0.468839	0.44102	0.414964	0.367698	0.326179	0.289664	0.25751	0.229174	0.20416	0.18207
14	0.505068	0.47257	0.442301	0.41410	0.387817	0.340461	0.299246	0.263331	0.23199	0.204620	0.18068	0.15971
15	0.481017	0.44793	0.417265	0.38883	0.362446	0.315242	0.274538	0.239392	0.20900	0.182696	0.15989	0.14010
16	0.458112	0.42458	0.393646	0.36510	0.338735	0.291890	0.251870	0.217629	0.18829	0.163122	0.14150	0.12289
17	0.436297	0.40245	0.371364	0.34281	0.316574	0.270269	0.231073	0.197845	0.16963	0.145644	0.12522	0.10780
18	0.415521	0.38147	0.350344	0.32189	0.295864	0.250249	0.211994	0.179859	0.15282	0.130040	0.11081	0.09456
19	0.395734	0.36158	0.330513	0.30224	0.276508	0.231712	0.194490	0.163508	0.13768	0.116107	0.09806	0.08295
20	0.376889	0.34273	0.311805	0.28380	0.258419	0.214548	0.178431	0.148644	0.12403	0.103667	0.08678	0.07276
21	0.358942	0.32486	0.294155	0.26648	0.241513	0.198656	0.163698	0.135131	0.11174	0.092560	0.07680	0.06383
22	0.341850	0.30793	0.277505	0.25021	0.225713	0.183941	0.150182	0.122846	0.10067	0.082643	0.06796	0.05599
23	0.325571	0.29187	0.261797	0.23494	0.210947	0.170315	0.137781	0.111678	0.09069	0.073788	0.06014	0.04911
24	0.310068	0.27666	0.246979	0.22060	0.197147	0.157699	0.126405	0.101526	0.08170	0.065882	0.05323	0.04308
25	0.295303	0.26223	0.232999	0.20714	0.184249	0.146018	0.115968	0.092296	0.07361	0.058823	0.04710	0.03779
26	0.281241	0.24856	0.219810	0.19450	0.172195	0.135202	0.106393	0.083905	0.06631	0.052521	0.04168	0.03315
27	0.267848	0.23560	0.207368	0.18263	0.160930	0.125187	0.097608	0.076278	0.05974	0.046894	0.03689	0.02908
28	0.255094	0.22332	0.195630	0.17148	0.150402	0.115914	0.089548	0.069343	0.05382	0.041869	0.03264	0.02551
29	0.242946	0.21168	0.184557	0.16101	0.140563	0.107328	0.082155	0.063009	0.04849	0.037383	0.02889	0.02237
30	0.231377	0.20064	0.174110	0.15119	0.131367	0.099377	0.075371	0.057309	0.04368	0.033378	0.02557	0.01963
31	0.220359	0.19018	0.164255	0.14196	0.122773	0.092016	0.069148	0.052099	0.03935	0.029802	0.02262	0.01722
32	0.209866	0.18027	0.154957	0.13329	0.114741	0.085200	0.063438	0.047362	0.03545	0.026609	0.02002	0.01510
33	0.199873	0.17087	0.146186	0.12516	0.107235	0.078889	0.058200	0.043057	0.03194	0.023758	0.01772	0.01325
34	0.190355	0.16196	0.137912	0.11752	0.100219	0.073045	0.053395	0.039143	0.02878	0.021212	0.01568	0.01162
35	0.181290	0.15352	0.130105	0.11035	0.093663	0.067635	0.048986	0.035584	0.02592	0.018940	0.01388	0.01019
40	0.142046	0.11746	0.097222	0.08054	0.066780	0.046031	0.031838	0.022095	0.01538	0.010747	0.00753	0.00529
45	0.111297	0.08988	0.072650	0.05879	0.047613	0.031328	0.020692	0.013719	0.00913	0.006098	0.00409	0.00275
50	0.087204	0.06877	0.054288	0.04291	0.033948	0.021321	0.013449	0.008519	0.00542	0.003460	0.00222	0.00143

Present Value of Ordinary Annuity of 1 per Period: $P_{\overline{n}|i} = \dfrac{1 - \dfrac{1}{(1+i)^n}}{i}$

n	5%	5.5%	6%	6.5%	7%	8%	9%	10%	11%	12%	13%	14%
1	0.952381	0.94787	0.943396	0.93897	0.934579	0.925926	0.917431	0.909091	0.90090	0.892857	0.88496	0.87719
2	1.859410	1.84632	1.833393	1.82063	1.808018	1.783265	1.759111	1.735537	1.71252	1.690051	1.66810	1.64666
3	2.723248	2.69793	2.673012	2.64848	2.624316	2.577097	2.531295	2.486852	2.44371	2.401831	2.36115	2.32163
4	3.545951	3.50515	3.465106	3.42580	3.38721	3.312127	3.239720	3.169865	3.10245	3.037349	2.97447	2.91371
5	4.329477	4.27028	4.212364	4.15568	4.100197	3.992710	3.889651	3.790787	3.69590	3.604776	3.51723	3.43308
6	5.075692	4.99553	4.917324	4.84101	4.766540	4.622880	4.485919	4.355261	4.23054	4.111407	3.99755	3.88867
7	5.786373	5.68297	5.582381	5.48452	5.389289	5.206370	5.032953	4.868419	4.71220	4.563757	4.42261	4.28830
8	6.463213	6.33457	6.209794	6.08875	5.971299	5.746639	5.534819	5.334926	5.14612	4.967640	4.79677	4.63886
9	7.107822	6.95220	6.801692	6.65610	6.515232	6.246888	5.995247	5.759024	5.53705	5.328250	5.13166	4.94637
10	7.721735	7.53763	7.360087	7.18883	7.023582	6.710081	6.417658	6.144567	5.88923	5.650223	5.42624	5.21612
11	8.306414	8.09254	7.886875	7.68904	7.498674	7.138964	6.805191	6.495061	6.20652	5.937699	5.68694	5.45273
12	8.863252	8.61852	8.383844	8.15873	7.942686	7.536078	7.160725	6.813692	6.49236	6.194374	5.91765	5.66029
13	9.393573	9.11708	8.852683	8.59974	8.357651	7.903776	7.486904	7.103356	6.74987	6.423548	6.12181	5.84236
14	9.898641	9.58965	9.294984	9.01384	8.745468	8.224237	7.786150	7.366687	6.96187	6.628168	6.30249	6.00207
15	10.379658	10.03758	9.712249	9.40267	9.107914	8.559479	8.060688	7.606080	7.19087	6.810864	6.46238	6.14217
16	10.837770	10.46216	10.105895	9.76776	9.446649	8.851369	8.312558	7.823709	7.37916	6.973986	6.60388	6.26506
17	11.274066	10.86461	10.477260	10.11058	9.763223	9.121638	8.543631	8.021553	7.54879	7.119630	6.72909	6.37286
18	11.689587	11.24607	10.827603	10.43247	10.059087	9.371887	8.755625	8.201412	7.70162	7.249670	6.83991	6.46742
19	12.085321	11.60765	11.158116	10.73471	10.335595	9.603599	8.950115	8.364920	7.83929	7.365777	6.93797	6.55037
20	12.462210	11.95038	11.469921	11.01851	10.594014	9.818147	9.128546	8.513564	7.96333	7.469444	7.02475	6.62313
21	12.821153	12.27524	11.764077	11.28498	10.835527	10.016803	9.292244	8.648694	8.07507	7.562003	7.10155	6.68696
22	13.163003	12.58317	12.041582	11.53520	11.061241	10.200744	9.442425	8.771540	8.17574	7.644646	7.16951	6.74294
23	13.488574	12.87504	12.303379	11.77014	11.272187	10.371059	9.580207	8.883218	8.26643	7.718434	7.22966	6.79206
24	13.798642	13.15170	12.550358	11.99074	11.469334	10.528758	9.706612	8.984744	8.34814	7.784316	7.28288	6.83514
25	14.093945	13.41393	12.783356	12.19788	11.653583	10.674776	9.822580	9.077040	8.42174	7.843139	7.32998	6.87293
26	14.375185	13.66250	13.003166	12.39237	11.825779	10.809978	9.928972	9.160945	8.48806	7.895660	7.37167	6.90608
27	14.643034	13.89810	13.210534	12.57500	11.986709	10.935165	10.026580	9.237223	8.54780	7.942554	7.40856	6.93515
28	14.898127	14.12142	13.406164	12.74648	12.137111	11.051078	10.116128	9.306567	8.60162	7.984423	7.44120	6.96066
29	15.141074	14.33310	13.590721	12.90749	12.277674	11.158406	10.198283	9.369606	8.65011	8.021806	7.47009	6.98304
30	15.372451	14.53375	13.764831	13.05868	12.409041	11.257783	10.273654	9.426914	8.69379	8.055184	7.49565	7.00266
31	15.592811	14.72393	13.929086	13.20063	12.531814	11.349799	10.342802	9.479013	8.73315	8.084986	7.51828	7.01988
32	15.802677	14.90420	14.084043	13.33393	12.646555	11.434999	10.406240	9.526376	8.76860	8.111594	7.53830	7.03498
33	16.002549	15.07507	14.230230	13.45909	12.753790	11.513888	10.464441	9.569432	8.80054	8.135352	7.55602	7.04823
34	16.192904	15.23703	14.368141	13.57661	12.854009	11.586934	10.517835	9.608575	8.82932	8.156564	7.57170	7.05985
35	16.374194	15.39055	14.498246	13.68696	12.947672	11.654568	10.566821	9.644159	8.85524	8.175504	7.58557	7.07005
40	17.159086	16.04612	15.046297	14.14553	13.331709	11.924613	10.757360	9.779051	8.95105	8.243777	7.63438	7.10504
45	17.774070	16.54773	15.455832	14.48023	13.605522	12.108402	10.881197	9.862808	9.00791	8.282516	7.66086	7.12322
50	18.255925	16.93152	15.761861	14.72452	13.800746	12.233485	10.961683	9.914814	9.04165	8.304498	7.67524	7.13266

Future Amount of 1 at Compound Interest Due in n Periods: $a_{\overline{n}|i} = (1 + i)^n$

n	5%	5.5%	6%	6.5%	7%	8%	9%	10%	11%	12%	13%	14%
1	1.050000	1.05500	1.060000	1.06500	1.070000	1.080000	1.090000	1.100000	1.11000	1.120000	1.13000	1.14000
2	1.102500	1.11303	1.123600	1.13423	1.144900	1.166400	1.188100	1.210000	1.23210	1.254400	1.27690	1.29960
3	1.157625	1.17424	1.191016	1.20795	1.225043	1.259712	1.295029	1.331000	1.36763	1.404928	1.44290	1.48154
4	1.215506	1.23882	1.262477	1.28647	1.310796	1.360489	1.411582	1.464100	1.51807	1.573519	1.63047	1.68896
5	1.276282	1.30696	1.338226	1.37009	1.402552	1.469328	1.538624	1.610510	1.68506	1.762342	1.84244	1.92541
6	1.340096	1.37884	1.418519	1.45914	1.500730	1.586874	1.677100	1.771561	1.87041	1.973823	2.08195	2.19497
7	1.407100	1.45468	1.503630	1.55399	1.605781	1.713824	1.828039	1.948717	2.07616	2.210681	2.35261	2.50227
8	1.477455	1.53469	1.593848	1.65500	1.718186	1.850930	1.992563	2.143589	2.30454	2.475963	2.65844	2.85259
9	1.551328	1.61909	1.689479	1.76257	1.838459	1.999005	2.171893	2.357948	2.55804	2.773079	3.00404	3.25195
10	1.628895	1.70814	1.790848	1.87714	1.967151	2.158925	2.367364	2.593742	2.83942	3.105848	3.39457	3.70722
11	1.710339	1.80209	1.898299	1.99915	2.104852	2.331639	2.580426	2.853117	3.15176	3.478550	3.83586	4.22623
12	1.795856	1.90121	2.012196	2.12910	2.252192	2.518170	2.812665	3.138428	3.49845	3.895976	4.33452	4.81790
13	1.885649	2.00577	2.132928	2.26749	2.409845	2.719624	3.065805	3.452271	3.88328	4.363493	4.89801	5.49241
14	1.979932	2.11609	2.260904	2.41487	2.578534	2.937194	3.341727	3.797498	4.31044	4.887112	5.53475	6.26135
15	2.078928	2.23248	2.396558	2.57184	2.759032	3.172169	3.642482	4.177248	4.78459	5.473566	6.25427	7.13794
16	2.182875	2.35526	2.540352	2.73901	2.952164	3.425943	3.970306	4.594973	5.31089	6.130394	7.06733	8.13725
17	2.292018	2.48480	2.692773	2.91705	3.158815	3.700018	4.327633	5.054470	5.89509	6.866041	7.98608	9.27646
18	2.406619	2.62147	2.854339	3.10665	3.379932	3.996019	4.717120	5.559917	6.54355	7.689966	9.02427	10.57517
19	2.526950	2.76565	3.025600	3.30859	3.616528	4.315701	5.141661	6.115909	7.26334	8.612762	10.19742	12.05569
20	2.653298	2.91776	3.207135	3.52365	3.869684	4.660957	5.604411	6.727500	8.06231	9.646293	11.52309	13.74349
21	2.785963	3.07823	3.399564	3.75268	4.140562	5.033834	6.108808	7.400250	8.94917	10.803848	13.02109	15.66758
22	2.925261	3.24754	3.603537	3.99661	4.430402	5.436540	6.658600	8.140275	9.93357	12.100310	14.71383	17.86104
23	3.071524	3.42615	3.819750	4.25639	4.740530	5.871464	7.257874	8.954302	11.02627	13.552347	16.62663	20.36158
24	3.225100	3.61459	4.048935	4.53305	5.072367	6.341181	7.911083	9.849733	12.23916	15.178629	18.78809	23.21221
25	3.386355	3.81339	4.291871	4.82770	5.427433	6.848475	8.623081	10.834706	13.58546	17.000064	21.23054	26.46192
26	3.555673	4.02313	4.549383	5.14150	5.807353	7.396353	9.399158	11.918177	15.07986	19.040072	23.99051	30.16658
27	3.733456	4.24440	4.822346	5.47570	6.213868	7.988061	10.245082	13.109994	16.73865	21.324881	27.10928	34.38991
28	3.920129	4.47784	5.111687	5.83162	6.648838	8.627106	11.167140	14.420994	18.57990	23.883866	30.63349	39.20449
29	4.116136	4.72412	5.418388	6.21067	7.114257	9.317275	12.172182	15.863093	20.62369	26.749930	34.61584	44.69312
30	4.321942	4.98395	5.743491	6.61437	7.612255	10.062657	13.267678	17.449402	22.89230	29.959922	39.11590	50.95016
31	4.538039	5.25807	6.088101	7.04430	8.145113	10.867669	14.461770	19.194342	25.41045	33.555113	44.20096	58.08318
32	4.764941	5.54726	6.453387	7.50218	8.715271	11.737083	15.763329	21.113777	28.20560	37.581726	49.94709	66.21483
33	5.003189	5.85236	6.840590	7.98982	9.325340	12.676050	17.182028	23.225154	31.30821	42.091533	56.44021	75.48490
34	5.253348	6.17424	7.251025	8.50916	9.978114	13.690134	18.728411	25.547670	34.75212	47.142517	63.77744	86.05279
35	5.516015	6.51383	7.686087	9.06225	10.676581	14.785344	20.413968	28.102437	38.57485	52.799620	72.06851	98.10018
40	7.039989	8.51331	10.285718	12.41607	14.974458	21.724521	31.409420	45.259256	65.00087	93.050970	132.78155	188.88351
45	8.985008	11.12655	13.764611	17.01110	21.002452	31.920449	48.327286	72.890484	109.53024	163.987604	244.64140	363.67907
50	11.467400	14.54196	18.420154	23.30668	29.457025	46.901613	74.357520	117.390853	184.56483	289.002190	450.73593	700.23299

Future Amount of Ordinary Annuity of 1 per Period: $A_{\overline{n}|i} = \dfrac{(1+i)^n - 1}{i}$

n	5%	5.5%	6%	6.5%	7%	8%	9%	10%	11%	12%	13%	14%
1	1.000000	1.00000	1.000000	1.00000	1.000000	1.000000	1.000000	1.000000	1.00000	1.000000	1.00000	1.00000
2	2.050000	2.05500	2.060000	2.06500	2.070000	2.080000	2.090000	2.100000	2.11000	2.120000	2.13000	2.14000
3	3.152500	3.16802	3.183600	3.19922	3.214900	3.246400	3.278100	3.310000	3.34210	3.374400	3.40690	3.43960
4	4.310125	4.34227	4.374616	4.40717	4.439943	4.506112	4.573129	4.641000	4.70973	4.779328	4.84980	4.92114
5	5.525631	5.58109	5.637093	5.69364	5.750740	5.866601	5.984711	6.105100	6.22780	6.352847	6.48027	6.61010
6	6.801913	6.88805	6.975319	7.06373	7.153291	7.335929	7.523335	7.715610	7.91286	8.115189	8.32271	8.53552
7	8.142008	8.26686	8.393838	8.52287	8.654021	8.922803	9.200435	9.487171	9.78327	10.089012	10.40466	10.73049
8	9.549109	9.72157	9.897468	10.07686	10.259803	10.636628	11.028474	11.435888	11.85943	12.299693	12.75726	13.23276
9	11.026564	11.25626	11.491316	11.73185	11.977989	12.487558	13.021036	13.579477	14.16397	14.775656	15.41571	16.08535
10	12.577893	12.87535	13.180795	13.49442	13.816448	14.486562	15.192930	15.937425	16.72201	17.548735	18.41975	19.33730
11	14.206787	14.58350	14.971643	15.37156	15.783599	16.645487	17.560293	18.531167	19.56143	20.654583	21.81432	23.04452
12	15.917127	16.38559	16.869941	17.37071	17.888451	18.977126	20.140720	21.384284	22.71319	24.133133	25.65018	27.27075
13	17.712983	18.28680	18.882138	19.49981	20.140643	21.495297	22.953385	24.522712	26.21164	28.029109	29.98470	32.08865
14	19.598632	20.29257	21.015066	21.76730	22.550488	24.214920	26.019189	27.974983	30.09492	32.392602	34.88271	37.58107
15	21.578564	22.40866	23.275970	24.18217	25.129022	27.152114	29.360916	31.772482	34.40536	37.279715	40.41746	43.84241
16	23.657492	24.64114	25.672528	26.75401	27.888054	30.324283	33.003399	35.949730	39.18995	42.753280	46.67173	50.98035
17	25.840366	26.99640	28.212880	29.49302	30.840217	33.750226	36.973705	40.544703	44.50084	48.883674	53.73906	59.11760
18	28.132385	29.48120	30.905653	32.41007	33.999033	37.450244	41.301338	45.599173	50.39594	55.749715	61.72514	68.39407
19	30.539004	32.10267	33.759992	35.51672	37.378965	41.446263	46.018458	51.159090	56.93949	63.439681	70.74941	78.96923
20	33.065954	34.86832	36.785591	38.82531	40.995492	45.761964	51.160120	57.274999	64.20283	72.052442	80.94683	91.02493
21	35.719252	37.78608	39.992727	42.34895	44.865177	50.422921	56.764530	64.002499	72.26514	81.698736	92.46992	104.76842
22	38.505214	40.86431	43.392290	46.10164	49.005739	55.456755	62.873338	71.402749	81.21431	92.502584	105.49101	120.43600
23	41.430475	44.11185	46.995828	50.09824	53.436141	60.893296	69.531939	79.543024	91.14788	104.602894	120.20484	138.29704
24	44.501999	47.53800	50.815577	54.35463	58.176671	66.764759	76.789813	88.497327	102.17415	118.155241	136.83147	158.65862
25	47.727099	51.15250	54.864512	58.88768	63.249038	73.105940	84.700896	98.347059	114.41331	133.333870	155.61956	181.87083
26	51.113454	54.96598	59.156383	63.71538	68.676470	79.954415	93.323977	109.181765	127.99877	150.333934	176.85010	208.33274
27	54.669126	58.98911	63.705766	68.85688	74.483823	87.350768	102.723135	121.099942	143.07864	169.374007	200.84061	238.49933
28	58.402583	63.23351	68.528112	74.33257	80.697691	95.338830	112.968217	134.209936	159.81729	190.698887	227.94989	272.88923
29	62.322712	67.71135	73.629798	80.16419	87.346529	103.965936	124.135356	148.630930	178.39719	214.582754	258.58338	312.09373
30	66.438848	72.43548	79.058186	86.37486	94.460786	113.283211	136.307539	164.494023	199.02088	241.332684	293.19922	356.78685
31	70.760790	77.41943	84.801677	92.98923	102.073041	123.345868	149.575217	181.943425	221.91317	271.292606	332.31511	407.73701
32	75.298829	82.67750	90.889778	100.03353	110.218154	134.213537	164.036987	201.137767	247.32362	304.847719	376.51608	465.82019
33	80.063771	88.22476	97.343165	107.53571	118.933425	145.950620	179.800315	222.251544	275.52922	342.429446	426.46317	532.03501
34	85.066959	94.07712	104.183755	115.52553	128.258765	158.626670	196.982344	245.476699	306.83744	384.520979	482.90338	607.51991
35	90.320307	100.25136	111.434780	124.03469	138.236878	172.316804	215.710755	271.024368	341.58955	431.663496	546.68082	693.57270
40	120.799774	136.60561	154.761966	175.63192	199.635112	259.056519	337.882445	442.592556	581.82607	767.091420	1013.70424	1342.02510
45	159.700156	184.11917	212.743514	246.32459	285.749311	386.505617	525.858734	718.904837	986.63856	1358.230032	1874.16463	2590.56480
50	209.347996	246.21748	290.335905	343.17967	406.528929	573.770156	815.083556	1163.908529	1668.77115	2400.018249	3459.50712	4994.52135

CODES OF PROFESSIONAL ETHICS
FOR ACCOUNTANTS

In recent years, governments, businesses, and the public have given increased attention to ethical conduct. They have insisted upon a level of human behavior that goes beyond that required by laws and regulations. Thus many businesses, as well as professional groups (such as accountants) and governmental organizations, have established standards of ethical conduct. This text emphasizes the ethical conduct of accountants, who serve various business interests as well as the public.

This appendix sets forth the standards of professional conduct expected of accountants in public accounting and private accounting. For accountants employed in public accounting, the American Institute of Certified Public Accountants' *Code of Professional Conduct* is presented.[1] For accountants employed in private accounting, the National Association of Accountants' *Standards of Ethical Conduct for Management Accountants* is presented as a guide to professional conduct.[2]

Supplementing the codes of professional ethics are ethics discussion cases that appear at the end of each chapter. These cases represent "real world" examples of ethical issues facing accountants. It should be noted that codes of professional ethics are general guides to good behavior and their application to specific situations often requires the exercise of professional judgment. In some cases, the line between right and wrong may be quite fine, and reasonable people may disagree. In addition, business is dynamic and everchanging, and what society considers to be acceptable behavior changes from time to time.

---

[1]*Code of Professional Conduct* (New York: American Institute of Certified Public Accountants, 1988), pp. 3–8.
[2]*Statements on Management Accounting*, No. 1C, "Standards of Ethical Conduct for Management Accountants" (New York: National Association of Accountants, 1983), pp. 1–2.

Code of Professional Conduct
as adopted January 12, 1988

Composition, Applicability, and Compliance

The Code of Professional Conduct of the American Institute of Certified Public Accountants consists of two sections—(1) the Principles and (2) the Rules. The Principles provide the framework for the Rules, which govern the performance of professional services by members. The Council of the American Institute of Certified Public Accountants is authorized to designate bodies to promulgate technical standards under the Rules, and the bylaws require adherence to those Rules and standards.

The Code of Professional Conduct was adopted by the membership to provide guidance and rules to all members—those in public practice, in industry, in government, and in education—in the performance of their professional responsibilities.

Compliance with the Code of Professional Conduct, as with all standards in an open society, depends primarily on members' understanding and voluntary actions, secondarily on reinforcement by peers and public opinion, and ultimately on disciplinary proceedings, when necessary, against members who fail to comply with the Rules.

Section I—Principles

Preamble

Membership in the American Institute of Certified Public Accountants is voluntary. By accepting membership, a certified public accountant assumes an obligation of self-discipline above and beyond the requirements of laws and regulations.

These Principles of the Code of Professional Conduct of the American Institute of Certified Public Accountants express the profession's recognition of its responsibilities to the public, to clients, and to colleagues. They guide members in the performance of their professional responsibilities and express the basic tenets of ethical and professional conduct. The Principles call for an unswerving commitment to honorable behavior, even at the sacrifice of personal advantage.

Article I

Responsibilities

In carrying out their responsibilities as professionals, members should exercise sensitive professional and moral judgments in all their activities.

As professionals, certified public accountants perform an essential role in society. Consistent with that role, members of the American Institute of Certified Public Accountants have responsibilities to all those who use their professional services. Members also have a continuing responsibility to cooperate with each other to improve the art of account-ing, maintain the public's confidence, and carry out the profession's special responsibilities for self-governance. The collective efforts of all members are required to maintain and enhance the traditions of the profession.

Article II

The Public Interest

Members should accept the obligation to act in a way that will serve the public interest, honor the public trust, and demonstrate commit-ment to professionalism.

A distinguishing mark of a profession is acceptance of its responsibility to the public. The accounting profession's public consists of clients, credit grantors, governments, employers, investors, the business and financial community, and others who rely on the objectivity and integrity of certified public accountants to maintain the orderly functioning of commerce. This reliance imposes a public interest responsibility on certified public accountants. The public interest is defined as the col-lective well-being of the community of people and institutions the pro-fession serves.

In discharging their professional responsibilities, members may en-counter conflicting pressures from among each of those groups. In resolving those conflicts, members should act with integrity, guided by the precept that when members fulfill their responsibility to the public, clients' and employers' interests are best served.

Those who rely on certified public accountants expect them to dis-charge their responsibilities with integrity, objectivity, due professional care, and a genuine interest in serving the public. They are expected to provide quality services, enter into fee arrangements, and offer a range of services—all in a manner that demonstrates a level of profes-sionalism consistent with these Principles of the Code of Professional Conduct.

All who accept membership in the American Institute of Certified Public Accountants commit themselves to honor the public trust. In return for the faith that the public reposes in them, members should seek continually to demonstrate their dedication to professional excel-lence.

Article III

Integrity

To maintain and broaden public confidence, members should per-form all professional responsibilities with the highest sense of integrity.

Integrity is an element of character fundamental to professional recog-nition. It is the quality from which the public trust derives and the benchmark against which a member must ultimately test all decisions.

Integrity requires a member to be, among other things, honest and candid within the constraints of client confidentiality. Service and the public trust should not be subordinated to personal gain and advantage. Integrity can accommodate the inadvertent error and the honest difference of opinion; it cannot accommodate deceit or subordination of principle.

Integrity is measured in terms of what is right and just. In the absence of specific rules, standards, or guidance, or in the face of conflicting opinions, a member should test decisions and deeds by asking: "Am I doing what a person of integrity would do? Have I retained my integrity?" Integrity requires a member to observe both the form and the spirit of technical and ethical standards; circumvention of those standards constitutes subordination of judgment.

Integrity also requires a member to observe the principles of objectivity and independence and of due care.

Article IV

Objectivity and Independence

A member should maintain objectivity and be free of conflicts of interest in discharging professional responsibilities. A member in public practice should be independent in fact and appearance when providing auditing and other attestation services.

Objectivity is a state of mind, a quality that lends value to a member's services. It is a distinguishing feature of the profession. The principle of objectivity imposes the obligation to be impartial, intellectually honest, and free of conflicts of interest. Independence precludes relationships that may appear to impair a member's objectivity in rendering attestation services.

Members often serve multiple interests in many different capacities and must demonstrate their objectivity in varying circumstances. Members in public practice render attest, tax, and management advisory services. Other members prepare financial statements in the employment of others, perform internal auditing services, and serve in financial and management capacities in industry, education, and government. They also educate and train those who aspire to admission into the profession. Regardless of service or capacity, members should protect the integrity of their work, maintain objectivity, and avoid any subordination of their judgment.

For a member in public practice, the maintenance of objectivity and independence requires a continuing assessment of client relationships and public responsibility. Such a member who provides auditing and other attestation services should be independent in fact and appearance. In providing all other services, a member should maintain objectivity and avoid conflicts of interest.

Although members not in public practice cannot maintain the appearance of independence, they nevertheless have the responsibility to maintain objectivity in rendering professional services. Members employed by others to prepare financial statements or to perform auditing, tax, or consulting services are charged with the same responsibility for objectivity as members in public practice and must be scrupulous in their application of generally accepted accounting principles and candid in all their dealings with members in public practice.

Article V

Due Care

A member should observe the profession's technical and ethical standards, strive continually to improve competence and the quality of services, and discharge professional responsibility to the best of the member's ability.

The quest for excellence is the essence of due care. Due care requires a member to discharge professional responsibilities with competence and diligence. It imposes the obligation to perform professional services to the best of a member's ability with concern for the best interest of those for whom the services are performed and consistent with the profession's responsibility to the public.

Competence is derived from a synthesis of education and experience. It begins with a mastery of the common body of knowledge required for designation as a certified public accountant. The maintenance of competence requires a commitment to learning and professional improvement that must continue throughout a member's professional life. It is a member's individual responsibility. In all engagements and in all responsibilities, each member should undertake to achieve a level of competence that will assure that the quality of the member's services meets the high level of professionalism required by these Principles.

Competence represents the attainment and maintenance of a level of understanding and knowledge that enables a member to render services with facility and acumen. It also establishes the limitations of a member's capabilities by dictating that consultation or referral may be required when a professional engagement exceeds the personal competence of a member or a member's firm. Each member is responsible for assessing his or her own competence—of evaluating whether education, experience, and judgment are adequate for the responsibility to be assumed.

Members should be diligent in discharging responsibilities to clients, employers, and the public. Diligence imposes the responsibility to render services promptly and carefully, to be thorough, and to observe applicable technical and ethical standards.

Due care requires a member to plan and supervise adequately any professional activity for which he or she is responsible.

Article VI

Scope and Nature of Services

A member in public practice should observe the Principles of the Code of Professional Conduct in determining the scope and nature of services to be provided.

The public interest aspect of certified public accountants' services requires that such services be consistent with acceptable professional behavior for certified public accountants. Integrity requires that service and the public trust not be subordinated to personal gain and advantage. Objectivity and independence require that members be free from conflicts of interest in discharging professional responsibilities. Due care requires that services be provided with competence and diligence.

Each of these Principles should be considered by members in determining whether or not to provide specific services in individual circumstances. In some instances, they may represent an overall constraint on the nonaudit services that might be offered to a specific client. No hard-and-fast rules can be developed to help members reach these judgments, but they must be satisfied that they are meeting the spirit of the Principles in this regard.

In order to accomplish this, members should

- Practice in firms that have in place internal quality-control procedures to ensure that services are competently delivered and adequately supervised.

- Determine, in their individual judgments, whether the scope and nature of other services provided to an audit client would create a conflict of interest in the performance of the audit function for that client.

- Assess, in their individual judgments, whether an activity is consistent with their role as professionals (for example, Is such activity a reasonable extension or variation of existing services offered by the member or others in the profession?).

Standards of Ethical Conduct for Management Accountants

Management accountants have an obligation to the organizations they serve, their profession, the public, and themselves to maintain the highest standards of ethical conduct. In recognition of this obligation, the National Association of Accountants has promulgated the following standards of ethical conduct for management accountants. Adherence to these standards is integral to achieving the *Objectives of Management Accounting.*[1] Management accountants shall not commit acts contrary to these standards nor shall they condone the commission of such acts by others within their organizations.

Competence

Management accountants have a responsibility to:

- Maintain an appropriate level of professional competence by ongoing development of their knowledge and skills.

- Perform their professional duties in accordance with relevant laws, regulations, and technical standards.

- Prepare complete and clear reports and recommendations after appropriate analyses of relevant and reliable information.

---

[1] National Association of Accountants, *Statements on Management Accounting: Objectives of Management Accounting*, Statement No. 1B, New York, N.Y., June 17, 1982.

Confidentiality

Management accountants have a responsibility to:

- Refrain from disclosing confidential information acquired in the course of their work except when authorized, unless legally obligated to do so.
- Inform subordinates as appropriate regarding the confidentiality of information acquired in the course of their work and monitor their activities to assure the maintenance of that confidentiality.
- Refrain from using or appearing to use confidential information acquired in the course of their work for unethical or illegal advantage either personally or through third parties.

Integrity

Management accountants have a responsibility to:

- Avoid actual or apparent conflicts of interest and advise all appropriate parties of any potential conflict.
- Refrain from engaging in any activity that would prejudice their ability to carry out their duties ethically.
- Refuse any gift, favor, or hospitality that would influence or would appear to influence their actions.
- Refrain from either actively or passively subverting the attainment of the organization's legitimate and ethical objectives.
- Recognize and communicate professional limitations or other constraints that would preclude responsible judgment or successful performance of an activity.
- Communicate unfavorable as well as favorable information and professional judgments or opinions.
- Refrain from engaging in or supporting any activity that would discredit the profession.

Objectivity

Management accountants have a responsibility to:

- Communicate information fairly and objectively.
- Disclose fully all relevant information that could reasonably be expected to influence an intended user's understanding of the reports, comments, and recommendations presented. ☐

ALTERNATIVE METHOD OF RECORDING
MERCHANDISE INVENTORIES

The recording of adjusting entries for merchandise inventory at the end of the accounting period is described and illustrated in Chapter 4. The alternative method presented in this appendix classifies the entries for the beginning and the ending merchandise inventories as *closing* entries instead of *adjusting* entries. The difference in viewpoint has a minor effect on the work sheet, the sequence of entries in the journal, and the income summary account. It does not alter the financial statements in any way.

WORK SHEET

The merchandise inventory at the beginning of the period is to be reported on the income statement as a part of the cost of merchandise sold. On the work sheet, merchandise inventory at the beginning of the period is therefore extended from the Trial Balance Debit column to the Adjusted Trial Balance Debit column and the Income Statement Debit column.

The merchandise inventory at the end of the period is to be reported on the balance sheet as an asset and on the income statement as a deduction from the cost of merchandise available for sale. The ending merchandise inventory is therefore entered on the work sheet as a debit in the Balance Sheet Debit column and as a credit in the Income Statement Credit column. Both the debit and the credit amounts are placed on the same line as that used for the beginning merchandise inventory.

All adjustments are recorded in the Adjustments columns of the work sheet in the same manner as was illustrated on pages 156 and 157, except that by this method no entries are required in the Adjustments columns for merchandise inventory. The balances are then extended to the Income Statement and Balance Sheet columns, and the work sheet is completed. A work sheet employing this alternative procedure is illustrated on page C-2. Note that the Income Statement and Balance Sheet columns, including column totals and the amount of net income, are the same as those on the work sheet on pages 156 and 157.

ADJUSTING ENTRIES

The adjusting entries made from the alternative work sheet are illustrated on page C-3. They are exactly the same as those illustrated on page 186, except for the exclusion of adjustments for inventory.

Work Sheet

Cox Co.
Work Sheet
For Year Ended December 31, 1990

Account Title	Trial Balance Debit	Trial Balance Credit	Adjustments Debit	Adjustments Credit	Adjusted Trial Balance Debit	Adjusted Trial Balance Credit	Income Statement Debit	Income Statement Credit	Balance Sheet Debit	Balance Sheet Credit
Cash	62,950				62,950				62,950	
Notes Receivable	40,000				40,000				40,000	
Accounts Receivable	60,880				60,880				60,880	
Interest Receivable			(a) 200		200				200	
Merchandise Inventory	59,700				59,700		59,700	62,150	62,150	
Office Supplies	1,090			(b) 610	480				480	
Prepaid Insurance	4,560			(c) 1,910	2,650				2,650	
Store Equipment	27,100				27,100				27,100	
Accumulated Depreciation—Store Equipment		2,600		(d) 3,100		5,700				5,700
Office Equipment	15,570				15,570				15,570	
Accumulated Depreciation—Office Equipment		2,230		(e) 2,490		4,720				4,720
Accounts Payable		22,420				22,420				22,420
Salaries Payable				(f) 1,140		1,140				1,140
Unearned Rent		2,400	(g) 600			1,800				1,800
Note Payable (final payment, 1994)		25,000				25,000				25,000
Capital Stock		100,000				100,000				100,000
Retained Earnings		53,800				53,800				53,800
Dividends	18,000				18,000				18,000	
Sales		720,185				720,185		720,185		
Sales Returns and Allowances	6,140				6,140		6,140			
Sales Discounts	5,790				5,790		5,790			
Purchases	521,980				521,980		521,980			
Purchases Returns and Allowances		9,100				9,100		9,100		
Purchases Discounts		2,525				2,525		2,525		
Transportation In	17,400				17,400		17,400			
Sales Salaries Expense	59,250		(f) 780		60,030		60,030			
Advertising Expense	10,860				10,860		10,860			
Depreciation Expense—Store Equipment			(d) 3,100		3,100		3,100			
Miscellaneous Selling Expense	630				630		630			
Office Salaries Expense	20,660		(f) 360		21,020		21,020			
Rent Expense	8,100				8,100		8,100			
Depreciation Expense—Office Equipment			(e) 2,490		2,490		2,490			
Insurance Expense			(c) 1,910		1,910		1,910			
Office Supplies Expense			(b) 610		610		610			
Miscellaneous Administrative Expense	760				760		760			
Interest Income				(a) 200		600		600		
Rent Income		3,600		(g) 600		3,800		3,800		
Interest Expense	2,440				2,440		2,440			
	943,860	943,860	10,050	10,050	950,790	950,790	722,960	798,360	289,980	214,580
Net Income							75,400			75,400
							798,360	798,360	289,980	289,980

Adjusting Entries

	DATE		DESCRIPTION	POST. REF.	DEBIT	CREDIT	
1			Adjusting Entries				1
2	1990 Dec.	31	Interest Receivable	114	2 0 0 00		2
3			Interest Income	811		2 0 0 00	3
4							4
5		31	Office Supplies Expense	717	6 1 0 00		5
6			Office Supplies	116		6 1 0 00	6
7							7
8		31	Insurance Expense	716	1 9 1 0 00		8
9			Prepaid Insurance	117		1 9 1 0 00	9
10							10
11		31	Depreciation Expense — Store Equip.	613	3 1 0 0 00		11
12			Accumulated Depr. — Store Equip.	122		3 1 0 0 00	12
13							13
14		31	Depreciation Expense — Office Equip.	715	2 4 9 0 00		14
15			Accumulated Depr. — Office Equip.	124		2 4 9 0 00	15
16							16
17		31	Sales Salaries Expense	611	7 8 0 00		17
18			Office Salaries Expense	711	3 6 0 00		18
19			Salaries Payable	213		1 1 4 0 00	19
20							20
21		31	Unearned Rent	214	6 0 0 00		21
22			Rent Income	812		6 0 0 00	22

JOURNAL   PAGE 28

CLOSING ENTRIES

All accounts with balances in the Income Statement Credit column of the work sheet are closed in one compound journal entry by debiting each account and crediting Income Summary. All accounts with balances in the Income Statement Debit column are closed in one entry by debiting Income Summary and crediting each account. The income summary and the dividends accounts are then closed to the retained earnings account. All of the closing entries for the alternative procedure are as follows:

Closing Entries

JOURNAL   PAGE 29

	DATE		DESCRIPTION	POST. REF.	DEBIT	CREDIT	
1			Closing Entries				1
2	1990 Dec.	31	Merchandise Inventory	114	62 1 5 0 00		2
3			Sales	411	720 1 8 5 00		3
4			Purchases Returns and Allowances	512	9 1 0 0 00		4
5			Purchases Discounts	518	2 5 2 5 00		5
6			Interest Income	811	3 8 0 0 00		6
7			Rent Income	812	6 0 0 00		7
8			Income Summary	313		798 3 6 0 00	8

Closing Entries Continued

	Date	Account	Post. Ref.	Debit	Credit	
9						9
10	31	Income Summary	313	722 9 6 0 00		10
11		Merchandise Inventory	114		59 7 0 0 00	11
12		Sales Returns and Allowances	412		6 1 4 0 00	12
13		Sales Discounts	413		5 7 9 0 00	13
14		Purchases	511		521 9 8 0 00	14
15		Transportation In	514		17 4 0 0 00	15
16		Sales Salaries Expense	611		60 0 3 0 00	16
17		Advertising Expense	612		10 8 6 0 00	17
18		Depreciation Exp. — Store Equip.	613		3 1 0 0 00	18
19		Miscellaneous Selling Expense	619		6 3 0 00	19
20		Office Salaries Expense	711		21 0 2 0 00	20
21		Rent Expense	712		8 1 0 0 00	21
22		Depreciation Exp. — Office Equip.	715		2 4 9 0 00	22
23		Insurance Expense	716		1 9 1 0 00	23
24		Office Supplies Expense	717		6 1 0 00	24
25		Miscellaneous Administrative				25
26		Expense	719		7 6 0 00	26
27		Interest Expense	911		2 4 4 0 00	27
28						28
29	31	Income Summary	313	75 4 0 0 00		29
30		Retained Earnings	311		75 4 0 0 00	30
31						31
32	31	Retained Earnings	311	18 0 0 0 00		32
33		Dividends	312		18 0 0 0 00	33

The income summary account, as it will appear after the closing entries have been posted, is as follows:

Income Summary Account

ACCOUNT **Income Summary**   ACCOUNT NO. **313**

Date	Item	Post. Ref.	Debit	Credit	Balance Debit	Balance Credit
1990 Dec. 31	Revenue, etc.	29		798 3 6 0 00		798 3 6 0 00
31	Expenses, etc.	29	722 9 6 0 00			75 4 0 0 00
31	Net Income	29	75 4 0 0 00			

APPENDIX D

ACCOUNTING FOR INDIVIDUALS

The focus of the discussion and illustrations in the text is the business enterprise organized to make a profit. The concepts and principles applicable to accounting for individuals is the focus of this appendix.

ACCOUNTING SYSTEMS FOR INDIVIDUALS

The term **individuals**, as used in the appendix title, may refer to a person or to a family unit, such as a husband, wife, and children. Accounting systems for these individuals differ widely. Some individuals may use a system based on the accrual method and double-entry accounting, with a complete set of journals, ledgers, and reports. Such an elaborate system is needed by individuals who have complex reporting obligations and many financial transactions of large amounts. For other individuals, a rather simple system based on the cash method is sufficient. The basics of such a system are described briefly in the sections that follow.

Budgets for Individuals

The use of budgets by an individual or a family unit is an important part of successful financial planning. A budget provides a systematic and orderly method of managing money. It enables individuals to spend their money wisely and to live within their income. The cash basis is ordinarily used in preparing budgets for individuals because most of their transactions are cash transactions evidenced by bank deposits and checks. In addition, the cash basis is required for an individual's reports to state taxing authorities and to the Internal Revenue Service for income taxes and FICA taxes.

The first step in preparing a budget is to determine as accurately as possible the cash income expected during a certain period of time, ordinarily a calendar year. Money to be received from salary or wages (net take-home pay), interest on bonds or savings accounts, dividends on shares of stock, and any other cash income should be included in the estimate. The second step is to develop a realistic plan for allocating the estimated income among the various goods and services most wanted by the individual or family and to provide for savings. There is no magic formula for determining the amount to be saved or the allocation of expenditures among various "essentials" and "luxuries." Much depends on such factors as the size of the family unit, its needs, tastes, wants, and the priorities assigned to each.

The process of estimating income and expenditures is often complicated by the fact that not all income is received on a regularly recurring basis and not all expenditures are incurred on a regularly recurring basis. Some income may be received on a weekly, biweekly, monthly, quarterly, or semiannual basis. For example, if salary is received biweekly, twenty-six amounts are used in determining the yearly amount. On the other hand, dividends on shares of stock are ordinarily received quarterly and four amounts would be used in estimating the yearly amount. Heating and lighting expenses ordinarily vary as the seasons change, thus requiring the consideration of twelve different monthly estimates to determine the yearly amount.

After the estimate of total income and expenditures for the year has been completed, the next step is to divide total income and each category of expenditure by 12, which provides the data for the monthly budget. Such a budget for a family composed of a husband, a wife, and two children is illustrated as follows:

Monthly Budget

Susan and Henry Rice
Monthly Budget

Income..	$3,900
Allocations for expenditures:	
Housing and house operation	$1,350
Food and sundries..	1,120
Transportation	400
Clothing	260
Medical care...	180
Recreation and education..	160
Contributions and gifts...	140
Savings..	140
Miscellaneous	150
Total allocations for expenditures..	$3,900

Basic to the budgeting process is the requirement that the budget balance, that is, that the allocations among planned expenditures and savings do not exceed cash income. The need to maintain a balanced budget requires that priorities on spending be established if the individual or family unit is to be able to do those things that give it the most satisfaction. Thus, if the preliminary budget shows an excess of cash outflow over cash income, as is often the case, consideration should be given to possibilities of increasing earnings, reducing expenditures, omitting savings, borrowing money, or drawing upon accumulated savings from earlier periods. If the reverse situation occurs, the excess cash income may be added to savings or used to reduce outstanding liabilities.

Budget Performance Record for Individuals

An essential part of budgeting is the necessity of keeping a record of actual expenditures and making frequent comparisons with budgeted amounts. This record, termed the **budget performance record**, is then used to help control expenditures and to help the individuals to live within their budget.

The budget performance record is a multicolumn form that shows (1) the monthly budget allocations for each category of expenditures, (2) the actual individual expenditures made during the month and the end-of-month total of each category, and (3) the amount by which each total is over or under the budgeted amounts. Budget performance records for January, the first month of the budget period, and for a portion of February are illustrated as follows. The budget allocations are based on the budget appearing above.

Susan and Henry Rice
Budget Performance Record—January, 19--

	Housing & house operation	Food & sundries	Transportation	Clothing	Medical care	Recreation & education	Contributions & gifts	Savings	Miscellaneous
January allocation...........	1,350	1,120	400	260	180	160	140	140	150
January payments:									
January 1.....................						36			16
2.....................		114	136						14
4.....................					24				
5.....................		82							
7.....................		50							22
8.....................	30		16		20	24			
9.....................	166	160		130					
10....................	110						100		
12....................		94							10
14....................		64				18			
15....................	62	76	14						
17....................		70							30
19....................		90	49			10			
21....................						22			36
23....................	60	74	15	42					
26....................	150								
27....................		104					60		
29....................		72	12						
30....................	970				70			140	
31....................		116	102	36		48			16
Total.....................	1,548	1,166	344	208	114	158	160	140	144
Over* or under budget, February 1..................	198*	46*	56	52	66	2	20*	—	6

Susan and Henry Rice
Budget Performance Record—February, 19--

	Housing & house operation	Food & sundries	Transportation	Clothing	Medical care	Recreation & education	Contributions & gifts	Savings	Miscellaneous
Over* or under budget, February 1..................	198*	46*	56	52	66	2	20*	—	6
February allocation..........	1,350	1,120	400	260	180	160	140	140	150
Total budget, February.....	1,152	1,074	456	312	246	162	120	140	156
February payments:									
February 1.....................		30				34			
2.....................			14	36					32
3.....................		38							16
5.....................		62							
7.....................	28						20		
8.....................		50	18			48			
9.....................	82				10				14
10....................		82		80					10

The January payments were recorded during the month and totaled at the end of the month for each category. These totals were then subtracted from the budget allocations to determine the over or under budget amounts as of February 1. For example, the allocation for housing and house operation for January was $1,350, and the total payments made during January amounted to $1,548. The payments exceeded the budgeted amount by $198. An investigation determined that this budget variance was the result of seasonal fluctuations in expenditures, namely, higher than average expenditures necessary for heat and light during the month and payment of a semiannual premium on property insurance. The over budget amount of $198, therefore, was carried forward to the budget performance record for February.

The actual expenditures will often vary from the monthly allocations, and the causes of the "over budget" amounts should be carefully examined. If they are fairly small in amount and are the result of seasonal fluctuations in expenditures, as in the illustration, the balances should be carried forward to the next month and no revisions of the monthly budget are necessary. On the other hand, if the balances are significant and cannot be attributed to seasonal fluctuations, the monthly budget for the succeeding months should be revised accordingly. For example, a large expenditure for medical care that had not been anticipated may require a revision of the budgeted allocations for expenditures and savings for the next several months.

Records for Individuals

In addition to the budget performance record described in the preceding section, the record keeping system ordinarily consists of (1) a checkbook, (2) a file for bills and statements of account representing unpaid liabilities, (3) a file for documents supporting cash payments, and (4) a property inventory record.

As cash is received, it is deposited in the checking account and the amount is recorded in the checkbook, either on a "stub" or "check register" provided by the bank for the purpose of keeping a record of deposits, checks, and cash balance. As each check is written, the amount of the disbursement and its purpose should be entered on the stub or check register and the remaining balance recorded. The disbursement should be entered in the budget performance record. The checkbook "cash balance" should be reconciled with the monthly bank statement as described in Chapter 7.

Individuals, like business enterprises, often need to make small expenditures. Payment by check in such cases would result in delay, annoyance, and excessive writing of checks. Instead, a check for a moderate sum can be "cashed" and the money used for small disbursements in a manner similar to a business enterprise's use of a petty cash fund. A pocket note pad may be carried for purposes of recording such expenditures. As a check is written to replenish the "pocket" cash, the memoranda recorded in the note pad may be summarized for recording on the stub or check register and in the budget performance record.

A simple but effective method of handling unpaid liabilities is to maintain a file box or folder in which bills and statements of account are placed. When the liabilities are paid, the documents are marked with the number of the check written to make the payment and are filed in a paid file. This file should be retained as long as is legally required for such purposes as verification of income tax deductions claimed, or as long as it may be needed for informational purposes.

The property inventory record contains detailed information, including description and cost data, about valuable pieces of property, such as personal residence (including improvements), investments, jewelry, silverware, and china. Such a record is especially useful for insurance purposes and for establishing gain or loss on sale of property.

FINANCIAL STATEMENTS FOR INDIVIDUALS

Financial statements are often prepared for an individual or for related individuals, such as a husband and wife as a family unit. Such statements may be used in arranging a loan of a large amount, as an aid in planning for retirement, for estate and income tax planning, or for disclosure by public officials or candidates for public office.

Financial statements for individuals should be prepared according to generally accepted accounting principles for personal financial statements.[1] These principles primarily focus on an individual's assets and liabilities, which are reported at estimated current values rather than historical costs.

Statement of Financial Condition

The main financial statement for individuals is the **statement of financial condition,** sometimes called the statement of assets and liabilities. This statement, illustrated below and on pages D-6 and D-7 presents the (1) estimated current values of assets, (2) estimated current amounts of liabilities, (3) estimated income tax on unrealized appreciation of assets, and (4) estimated net worth.

The assets and liabilities are reported on the accrual basis. Current and noncurrent classifications are not used, because working capital is generally not relevant to users of personal financial statements. The notes accompanying the statement describe the methods used in determining the current values and other relevant details.

Bruce A. and Jennifer S. McCord
Statement of Financial Condition
December 31, 19--

Assets

Cash (Note 2)...	$ 18,250
Marketable securities (Note 3)	115,600
Cash value of life insurance ($300,000 face value)....................	36,500
Investment in real estate (Note 4)	130,000
Equity interest in McCord and Associates (Note 5)	183,000
Automobiles	17,000
Residence, pledged against mortgage (Note 4)........................	225,000
Household furnishings..	28,500
Jewelry and paintings (Note 4)	50,000
Vested interest in AB Corp. pension trust	49,700
Total assets	$853,550

---

[1]*Statement of Position, No. 82-1,* "Accounting and Financial Reporting for Personal Financial Statements" (New York: American Institute of Certified Public Accountants, 1982).

Liabilities

Accounts payable and accrued liabilities...................................	$ 7,700
Income tax payable	8,775
Note payable, 12%, due May 31, 19--....................................	40,000
Mortgage note payable, 11%, final payment due July 1, 19-- (Note 6)..	148,500
Total liabilities..	$204,975
Estimated income tax on unrealized appreciation of assets (Note 7)....	28,000
Net worth...	620,575
Total liabilities, estimated income tax on unrealized appreciation of assets, and net worth..	$853,550

Note 1—Current values and amounts

The accompanying statement of financial condition includes the assets and liabilities of Bruce A. and Jennifer S. McCord. Assets are stated at their estimated current values and liabilities at their estimated current amounts.

Note 2—Cash

The cash amount of $18,250 includes $17,500 deposited in money market accounts. These accounts allow unrestricted withdrawal without penalty.

Note 3—Marketable securities

Marketable securities consist of the following (estimated current value is the quoted market price on December 31, 19--, less estimated broker commissions):

	Shares or Face Amount	Current Value
Stocks:		
American Manufacturing......................................	500	$ 48,700
Jackson Tool Company.......................................	200	9,800
Pontiac Power Company	100	5,500
United Products Inc.	50	20,900
Bonds:		
Pontiac Power Company, 10⅛%, due 20--..............	$10,000	10,300
U.S. Government, 9½%, due 19--	20,000	20,400
Total...		$115,600

Note 4—Investment in real estate and residence and personal effects

The estimated market price of investment in real estate and residence, jewelry, and paintings is based on independent appraisals made by Hunt and Associates.

Note 5–Equity interest in McCord and Associates

The estimated market price of the equity interest of Bruce A. McCord in McCord and Associates partnership is based on an offer made on October 10, 19-- to purchase the net assets of the partnership. The offer was rejected.

Note 6–Mortgage note payable

The terms of the mortgage note provide for monthly payments of $1,460, which include the interest accrued on the loan.

Note 7–Estimated income tax on unrealized appreciation of assets

Estimated income taxes have been provided on the unrealized appreciation of the estimated current values of assets over their tax bases as if the estimated current values of the assets had been realized on the statement date, using applicable tax laws and regulations. This estimate will probably differ from the amounts of income taxes that eventually might be paid because of possible changes in the current values of the assets and in the tax laws which might be in effect at the time of disposal of the assets.

Assets. Assets, such as real estate and securities, are reported in the order of liquidity at their estimated current values. The current values of most assets other than listed securities may be estimated by examining recent transactions involving similar assets or by using appraisals by independent experts in particular fields, such as art or jewelry. Any estimated costs of disposal of an asset, such as commissions, are deducted in arriving at estimated current values.

Investments. The estimated current values of corporate securities, real estate, interests in sole proprietorships or partnerships, and life insurance must be determined as accurately as possible. Quoted market prices of marketable securities are usually available in the financial press. The estimated current market value of real estate can be obtained from a competent real estate appraiser. Data on recent sales of similar real estate may also be available. An offer to purchase the net assets of a sole proprietorship or other business unit or an estimate of liquidation values may be used as the estimated market price of such investments. Life insurance is reported at its cash surrender value, which is obtainable from the policy contract or from the insurer, less the amount of any loans against it. The face amount of life insurance should also be disclosed.

Residences and Personal Effects. Ordinarily, a residence and household furnishings, automobiles, objects of art, and jewelry are reported in the statement of financial condition if their value is material in relation to total assets. The estimated current values of especially significant assets may be determined by independent appraisers or estimated on the basis of advertised prices of similar items.

Future Interests. Individuals may have future interests in pensions, profit-sharing plans, trusts, or similar future rights. If the individual has a definite (rather than contingent) legal right to future benefits, such a right is said to be "vested" in the individual. The present value of such interests should be reported on the statement.

Liabilities. Commitments to pay future sums that are fixed in amount are listed on the statement of financial condition at their present values in the order of dates of maturity. Examples of such commitments include fixed amounts of alimony and charitable pledges. Commitments that depend upon a future contingency or the rendering of services by others should be disclosed in a note.

Estimated Income Tax on Unrealized Appreciation of Assets. An estimate of the income tax that could be owed if the assets were sold at their current values should be reported as a separate item below the total liabilities. This provision is necessary because the current values of the assets cannot be realized without the incurrence of a tax liability.

Net Worth. The equity of the individual(s) is called **net worth**. At the financial statement date, net worth can be determined as the difference between (1) the total assets and (2) the total of the liabilities plus the estimated income tax on the unrealized appreciation of the assets. On the statement of financial condition, net worth is reported below the estimated income tax on unrealized appreciation of assets.

Other Financial Statements for Individuals

For most uses, a single statement of financial condition is sufficient. In some situations, comparative statements for at least two years may be useful. When comparative statements are presented, an additional statement is often included. This statement, referred to as the statement of changes in net worth, presents the major sources of increases and decreases in net worth.

Although personal financial statements are presented on the basis of estimated current values, users may sometimes request certain historical cost data. Such data may be included as supplementary information in the statements.

DISCUSSION QUESTIONS

1. How does the use of budgets assist an individual or family unit in financial planning?

2. If the preliminary monthly budget for an individual indicates an excess of cash outflow over cash income, what courses of action might the individual consider to achieve a balanced budget?

3. What name is given to the record that indicates the relationship between actual expenditures made by an individual and the allocations for expenditures provided in the budget?

4. In addition to a budget performance record, what four other records are ordinarily included in an individual's record keeping system?

5. In what respects does the statement of financial condition prepared for individuals differ from the conventional balance sheet prepared for commercial enterprises?

6. In what order are (a) assets and (b) liabilities listed in the statement of financial condition?

7. Why should the statement of financial condition include an amount for estimated income tax on unrealized appreciation of assets?

8. In the statement of financial condition, what caption is used to identify the equity of an individual?

EXERCISES

Exercise D–1
Statement of financial condition.

Linda and Van Johnson applied to the Concord National Bank for a loan. The bank requested a statement of financial condition. Summary financial data accumulated as of February 1 are as follows:

(a) Present value of accounts payable and accrued liabilities, $14,250.
(b) Automobiles: cost, $30,800; estimated market price, $17,500.
(c) Cash, including money market funds, $20,200.
(d) Cash value of $250,000 face value life insurance policy, $37,500.
(e) Household furnishings: cost, $102,200; estimated market price, $78,000.
(f) Marketable securities: cost, $230,000; estimated current value, $310,000.
(g) Present value of 10% mortgage note payable, final payment due June 1, 19--, $134,100.
(h) Residence (pledged against mortgage note): cost, $150,000; estimated market price, $250,000.

Prepare a statement of financial condition (exclusive of notes to the statement) as of February 1. Assume that the estimated income tax on unrealized appreciation of assets is $24,000.

Exercise D–2
Statement of financial condition.

Ann Goss is a partner in the firm of Goss and Associates, and Tom Goss owns and manages The Loft. They applied to First City Bank for a loan to be used to build an apartment complex. The bank requested a statement of financial condition, and they assembled the following data for this purpose at April 30:

(a) Cash in bank, savings, and money market accounts, $23,500. (Unrestricted withdrawals are allowed without penalty.)
(b) Marketable securities (current value is quoted market price on April 30, 19--, less estimated broker commissions):

	Cost	Current Value
Stocks:		
ICM Industries, 500 shares	$12,500	$15,500
Thompson Manufacturing Inc., 200 shares	7,100	6,050
Choice Food Stores Inc., 300 shares	18,000	23,700
Bonds:		
U.S. Treasury, 8%, $50,000 face amount, due 19--	46,300	48,100
Carson Motors Inc., 10%, $20,000 face amount, due 20--	20,000	22,600

(c) Ann Goss's equity interest in Goss and Associates: cost, $75,000; estimated market, $140,000. Tom Goss's equity interest in The Loft: cost, $60,000; estimated market, $95,000. Estimated market prices were determined by an independent appraisal made by Fender Realty.
(d) Cash value of $500,000 face value life insurance policy, $92,000.

(e) Residence: cost, $175,000; estimated market, $300,000. The estimated market price was determined by an independent appraisal made by Reynolds and Associates. The residence is pledged against a 9% mortgage note payable, final installment due July 1, 19--. The present value of the monthly mortgage payments of $1,250, including interest, is $97,600.

(f) Household furnishings: cost, $81,000; estimated market, $50,000.

(g) Automobiles: cost, $32,600; estimated market, $16,000.

(h) Jewelry and paintings: cost, $40,000; estimated market, $60,000. The estimated market price was determined by an independent appraisal made by Reynolds and Associates.

(i) Present value of vested interest in Vance Inc. Pension Trust, $17,500.

(j) Present value of accounts payable and accrued liabilities, $9,500.

(k) Income tax payable, $7,500.

(l) Present value of 12% note payable, due March 1, 19--, $24,000.

(m) Estimated income tax on unrealized appreciation of salable assets, $42,600.

Prepare a statement of financial condition as of April 30 of the current year. Notes to the statement should be presented as appropriate.

Exercise D–3
Budget performance record for individual.

Pam Conrad maintains a budget performance record. The over-under budget amounts as of September 1 and the monthly allocations for expenditures as indicated by the monthly budget are as follows:

	Over*-Under Budget	Allocations
Housing and house operation	$50*	$2,000
Food and sundries	50	480
Transportation	30*	200
Clothing	40*	100
Medical care	30	100
Recreation and education	10	95
Contributions and gifts	20*	60
Savings	—	200
Miscellaneous	10*	50

The expenditures for September are summarized as follows:

Sept. 2. Food and sundries, $40.
    5. Medical care, $45; miscellaneous, $15.
    6. Food and sundries, $82; recreation and education, $40.
    7. Transportation, $40; miscellaneous, $6.
   10. Food and sundries, $58; clothing, $60.
   12. Housing and house operation, $900; food and sundries, $74; transportation, $35.
   14. Transportation, $18; recreation and education, $25.
   16. Housing and house operation, $220; food and sundries, $110; miscellaneous, $5.
   18. Food and sundries, $30; transportation, $40.
   19. Clothing, $30; miscellaneous, $12.
   22. Housing and house operation, $150; recreation and education, $40.
   23. Food and sundries, $43; transportation, $10; contributions, $50.
   25. Transportation, $25; clothing, $20.
   27. Housing and house operation, $300; food and sundries, $27.
   28. Food and sundries, $40; medical care, $45; miscellaneous, $10.
   30. Housing and house operation, $750; transportation, $30; savings, $200.

Prepare a budget performance record for September.

APPENDIX E

INCOME TAXES

The federal government and more than three fourths of the states levy an income tax. In addition, some of the states permit municipalities or other political subdivisions to levy income taxes. In operating a business or determining one's personal income tax, it is only good management to plan to keep these taxes to a minimum. This idea was expressed by Judge Learned Hand in *Newman* [35 AFTR 857], as follows:

> *Over and over again courts have said that there is nothing sinister in so arranging one's affairs as to keep taxes as low as possible. Everybody does so, rich or poor; and all do right, for nobody owes any public duty to pay more than the law demands; taxes are enforced exactions, not voluntary contributions. To demand more in the name of morals is mere cant.*

An understanding of any but the simplest aspects of income taxes is almost impossible without some knowledge of accounting concepts. Conversely, an understanding of the basic concepts of income taxes enable an individual or business to minimize taxes. In many cases, this understanding of the basic concepts leads one to seek the advice and assistance of professional accountants who specialize in determining the tax or developing plans to minimize the tax.

The explanations and illustrations of the federal system presented in this appendix are illustrative of the nature of income taxes. They are brief and relatively free of the many complexities encountered in actual practice. In addition, it should be noted that the federal tax laws are often changed, and that major tax bills have been enacted on the average of every 18 months since the original tax law was passed in 1913. The tax law upon which this discussion is based is the Tax Reform Act of 1986 (as amended by the Revenue Act of 1987 and the Technical and Miscellaneous Revenue Act of 1988). The current tax law and the current tax rates should be examined before tax-related decisions are made.

FEDERAL INCOME TAX SYSTEM

The present system of federal income tax began with the Revenue Act of 1913, which was enacted soon after the ratification of the Sixteenth Amendment to the Constitution. All current income tax statutes, as well as other federal tax laws, are now codified in the Internal Revenue Code (IRC).

The Treasury Department is charged with responsibility in federal tax matters. The division of the Department concerned specifically with enforcement and collection of the income tax is the Internal Revenue Service (IRS), headed by the Commissioner of Internal Revenue. Interpretations of the law and directives formulated according to express provisions of the IRC are issued in various forms. The most important and comprehensive are the "Regulations," which extend to more than two thousand pages.

The data required for the determination of income tax liability are supplied by the taxpayer on official forms and supporting schedules that are referred to collectively as a tax return. Failure to receive the forms from the

IRS or failure to maintain adequate records does not relieve taxpayers of their legal obligations to file annual tax returns. Willful failure to comply with the income tax laws may result in the imposition of severe civil and criminal penalties.

Taxpayers alleged by the IRS to be deficient in reporting or paying their tax may, if they disagree with the determination, present their case in informal conferences at district and regional levels. Unresolved disputes may be taken to the federal courts for settlement. The taxpayer may seek relief in the Tax Court or may pay the disputed amount and sue to recover it.

The income tax is not imposed upon business units as such, but upon taxable entities. The principal taxable entities are individuals, corporations, estates, and trusts. Business enterprises organized as sole proprietorships are not taxable entities. The revenues and expenses of such business enterprises are reported in the individual tax returns of the owners. Partnerships are not taxable entities but are required to report on an informational return the details of their revenues, expenses, and allocations to partners. The partners then report on their individual tax returns the amount of net income and other special items allocated to them on the partnership return.

Corporations engaged in business for profit are generally treated as distinct taxable entities. However, it is possible for two or more corporations with common ownership to join in filing a consolidated return. Subchapter S of the IRC also permits a nonpublic corporation that conforms to specified requirements to elect to be treated in a manner similar to a partnership. The effect of the election is to tax the shareholders on their distributive shares of the net income instead of taxing the corporation.

ACCOUNTING METHODS

Although neither the IRC nor the Regulations provide uniform systems of accounting for use by all taxpayers, detailed procedures are prescribed in certain cases. In addition, the IRS has the authority to prescribe accounting methods where those used by a taxpayer fail to yield a fair determination of taxable income. In general, taxpayers have the option of using either the cash basis or the accrual basis.

Cash Basis

Because of its greater simplicity, the cash basis of determining taxable income is usually used by individuals whose sources of income are limited to salary, dividends, and interest. Professional and other service enterprises (e.g., physicians, attorneys, insurance agencies) also ordinarily use the cash basis in determining taxable income. One of the advantages is that the fees charged to clients or customers are not considered to be earned until payment is received. Similarly, it is not necessary to accrue expenses incurred but not paid within the tax year. It is not permissible, however, to treat the entire cost of long-lived assets as an expense of the period in which the cash payment is made.[1] Deductions for depreciation on equipment and buildings used for business purposes may be claimed in the same manner as under the accrual basis, regardless of when payment is made.

---

[1]The current tax law allows small businesses to write off as an expense as much as $10,000 of annual equipment purchases.

Recognition of revenue according to the cash basis is not always contingent upon the actual receipt of cash. In some cases, revenue is said to be constructively received at the time it becomes available to the taxpayer, regardless of when it is actually converted to cash. For example, a check for services rendered which is received before the end of a taxable year is income of that year, even though the check is not deposited or cashed until the following year. Other examples of constructive receipt are bond interest coupons due within the taxable year and interest credited to a savings account as of the last day of the taxable year.

Accrual Basis

For businesses in which production or trading in merchandise is an important factor, purchases and sales must be accounted for on the accrual basis. Thus, revenues from sales must be reported in the year in which the goods are sold, regardless of when the cash is received. Similarly, the cost of goods purchased must be reported in the year in which the liabilities are incurred, regardless of when payment is made. The usual adjustments must also be made for the beginning and ending inventories in order to determine the cost of goods sold and the gross profit. However, manufacturing and merchandising enterprises are not required to extend the accrual basis to all phases of their operations. A mixture of the cash and accrual methods of accounting is permissible, if it yields reasonable results and is used consistently from year to year.

INCOME TAX ON INDIVIDUALS

Methods of accounting in general, as well as many of the regulations affecting the determination of net business or professional income, are not affected by the legal nature or the organizational structure of the taxpayer. On the other hand, the tax base and the tax rate structure for individuals differ markedly from those which apply to corporations.

The individual's tax base, upon which the amount of income tax is determined, is called taxable income. Taxable income is gross income less certain deductions as specified by the IRC. It is determined as follows:

Determination of Taxable Income for Individuals

GROSS INCOME
minus
DEDUCTIONS FROM GROSS INCOME
equals
ADJUSTED GROSS INCOME
minus
ITEMIZED DEDUCTIONS AND EXEMPTIONS
equals
TAXABLE INCOME

The basic concepts underlying the determination of taxable income are discussed in the paragraphs that follow.

Gross Income

Items of gross income subject to tax are sometimes called taxable gross income. Some of the taxable and nontaxable items of gross income of individuals are as follows:

TAXABLE ITEMS	NONTAXABLE ITEMS
Wages and other remuneration from employer.	All or portions of federal old-age pension benefits, depending on amounts of other income.
Tips and gratuities for services rendered.	Value of property received as a gift.
Cash dividends.	Value of property received by bequest, devise, or inheritance.
Rents and royalties.	
Income from a business or profession.	Life insurance proceeds received because of death of insured.
Gains from the sale of real estate, securities, and other property.	Interest on most obligations of a state or political subdivision.
Distributive share of partnership income.	Scholarships for tuition and fees.
Income from an estate or trust.	Compensation for injuries or for damages related to personal or family rights.
Prizes won in contests.	Worker's compensation insurance for sickness or injury.
Gambling winnings.	
Jury fees.	
Gains from illegal transactions.	
Unemployment compensation.	

Deductions from Gross Income

Business expenses and other expenses related to earning revenue are deductible in full or in part from gross income to yield adjusted gross income. For example, ordinary and necessary expenses incurred in the operations of a sole proprietorship are deductible from gross income. Also, expenses that are directly connected with earning rent or royalty income are allowable as deductions from gross income.

A self-employed individual may establish a qualified retirement fund (called a Keogh plan) and deduct the annual contribution from gross income in determining adjusted gross income. Also, certain employees may deduct contributions to plans provided by employers (called 401K plans), and low- and middle-income workers can deduct contributions to individual retirement accounts (called IRAs). The IRC and related regulations state many limitations on the amount of such deductions from gross income.

Adjusted Gross Income

The expenses described in the preceding section are deducted from an amount of related gross income. The resulting figure is the adjusted gross income. The amount of adjusted gross income is used in determining the amount of some of the deductions described in the following section. For example, the medical deduction is limited to the portion of total medical expenses which exceed 7 1/2% of adjusted gross income.

Itemized Deductions, the Standard Deduction, and Exemptions

After the amount of adjusted gross income of an individual is determined, two categories of deductions are subtracted to yield taxable income: (1) itemized deductions or the standard deductions and (2) exemptions. These two deductions from adjusted gross income are described in the following paragraphs.

Itemized Deductions. Certain specified expenditures and losses may be *itemized* and deducted from adjusted gross income. The deductions that are generally available to individuals who itemize deductions are described in the paragraphs that follow.

Charitable Contributions. Contributions made by an individual to domestic organizations created exclusively for religious, charitable, scientific, literary, or educational purposes, or for the prevention of cruelty to children or animals are deductible, provided the organization is nonprofit and does not devote a substantial part of its activities to influencing legislation. Contributions to domestic governmental units and to organizations of war veterans are also deductible.

The limitation on the amount of qualified contributions that may be deducted ranges from 20% of adjusted gross income for contributions to private foundations to 50% of adjusted gross income for contributions to public charities, with 50% being the overall maximum. There are other intermediate limitations related to contributions of various types of property other than cash.

Interest Expense. Interest expense on indebtedness for the taxpayer's principal and second residences is deductible, subject to certain limitations. Interest expense on indebtedness used for investment purposes is fully deductible up to an amount equal to investment income.

Taxes. Most of the taxes levied by the federal government are *not* deductible from adjusted gross income. Some of the taxes of a nonbusiness or personal nature levied by states or their political subdivisions are deductible from adjusted gross income. The common deductible state and local taxes are real estate, personal property, and income taxes.

Medical Expenses. Amounts paid for prescription drugs and insulin and other medical expenses are generally deductible to the extent that they exceed 7 1/2% of adjusted gross income. Other medical expenses deductible in total or in part include medical care insurance, doctors' fees, hospital expenses, etc.

Standard Deduction. As an alternative to itemizing deductions, the taxpayer may take a standard deduction. The amount of the deduction depends upon whether the taxpayer is filing as a single taxpayer, as a head of household, or with a spouse (joint return). In 1989, for example, the standard deduction for a single taxpayer is $3,000. The deduction is adjusted annually for inflation.

Exemptions. In general, each taxpayer is entitled to a personal exemption.[2] An additional exemption is allowed for each dependent. The amount of the personal exemption is $2,000 in 1989 and is adjusted annually for inflation.

Taxable Income and Determination of Income Tax

After the taxable income is determined, the taxpayer uses various tax rate schedules to determine the amount of the income tax. For example, the individual tax rates for a single taxpayer are as follows for 1989:

Taxable Income	Tax Rate[3]
$0– $17,850	15%
Over $17,850	28%

To illustrate the use of the tax rate schedules, assume that a single taxpayer has taxable income of $27,850. The tax is determined as follows:

---

[2]For certain high-income taxpayers, a surtax is added to offset the benefits of the personal exemption.
[3]For certain high-income taxpayers, a surtax is added to offset the benefit of the initial 15% tax rate.

Individual Tax Rates — Single Taxpayer		
Tax on	$17,850 at 15%	$2,678 (rounded)
Tax on	10,000 at 28%	2,800
Total on	$27,850	$5,478

Credits Against the Tax

After the amount of the income tax has been determined, the tax may be reduced on a dollar-for-dollar basis by the amount of various credits. These credits are therefore quite different from deductions and exemptions, which are reductions of the income subject to tax. The most common credits are described in the paragraphs that follow.

Credit for the Elderly. Some elderly taxpayers receive nontaxable retirement income, while others receive taxable retirement income. The credit for the elderly is an attempt to overcome this perceived inequity. The formula for determining the credit is complex and the IRC should be consulted for the details.

Child and Disabled Dependent Care Expenses Credit. Taxpayers who maintain a household are allowed a tax credit for expenses, including household expenses, involved in the care of a dependent child under age 13 or a physically or mentally incapacitated dependent or spouse, provided the expenses were incurred to enable the taxpayer to be gainfully employed. The amount of the credit is on a sliding scale, depending on the amount of adjusted gross income and the number of dependents.

Earned Income Credit. This credit against the tax is available to low-income workers who maintain a household for at least one of their dependent children and who have earned income (wages and self-employment income). Unlike the other credits, which cannot exceed the amount of the tax before applying the credit, if the earned income credit reduces the tax liability below zero, the negative amount is paid to the taxpayer. For example, if a worker's tax liability before applying the credit is $150 and the earned income credit is $375, the taxpayer will receive a direct payment of $225. Direct payments of tax revenues to individuals who have no liability for federal income tax is a concept with significant socioeconomic implications. The concept is often called a "negative income tax."

Filing Returns; Payment of Tax

The income tax withheld from an employee's earnings by an employer represents current payments on account. An individual whose income is not subject to withholding, or only partially so, or an individual whose income is fairly large must estimate the income tax in advance. The estimated tax for the year, after deducting the estimated amount to be withheld and any credit for overpayment from prior years, must be paid currently, usually in quarterly installments.

Annual income tax returns must be filed at the appropriate Internal Revenue Service office within 3 1/2 months following the end of the taxpayer's taxable year. Any balance owed must accompany the return. If there has been an overpayment of the tax liability, the taxpayer may request that the overpayment be refunded or credited against the estimated tax for the following year.

INCOME TAX ON CORPORATIONS

The taxable income of a corporation is determined, in general, by deducting its ordinary business expenses from the total amount of its includable gross income. The corporate tax rates, in general, are as follows for 1989:

Corporate Income Tax Rates

Taxable Income	Tax Rate[4]
$0–$50,000	15%
$50,001–$75,000	25%
Over $75,000	34%

TAX PLANNING TO MINIMIZE INCOME TAXES

There are various legal means of minimizing or reducing federal income taxes, some of which are of broader applicability than others. Much depends upon the volume and the sources of a taxpayer's gross income, the nature of the expenses and other deductions, and the accounting methods used. Examples of means to minimize income taxes are presented in the following paragraphs.

Alternative Accounting Principles

There are many cases in which an enterprise may choose from among two or more optional accounting principles in determining the amount of its taxable income. The particular principle chosen may have an effect on the amount of income tax, not only in the year in which the choice is made but also in later years. To illustrate, the tax law generally permits an enterprise to choose its method of determining the cost of inventory. Two widely used methods are fifo (first-in, first-out) and lifo (last-in, first-out). The more traditional method is fifo, while the more widely used method is lifo. The method chosen may have a significant effect on income and the tax on income in periods of changing price levels.

Under fifo, the first goods purchased during a year are assumed to be the first goods sold. During a period of rising prices, the first goods purchased are the least costly. If the least costly goods are sold, they are charged against revenue, and the most costly goods are included in inventory. Under lifo, however, the last goods purchased during a year are assumed to be the first goods sold. During a period of rising prices, the last goods purchased are the most costly. If the most costly goods are sold, they are charged against revenue, and the least costly goods are included in inventory. Thus, in periods of rising prices, lifo results in higher cost of goods sold, lower income, and lower taxes than fifo. During periods of declining prices, lifo results in lower cost of goods sold, higher income, and higher taxes than fifo.

In times of inflation, which has been the long-term trend in the United States since World War II, the use of lifo not only results in a lower annual income tax, but it also permits the taxpayer to retain more funds, by lowering tax payments, to replace goods sold with higher-priced goods. Clearly, this advantage is one of the most important reasons for lifo's popularity.

[4]The benefits of the initial 15% and 25% tax rates are phased out for companies whose income exceeds $100,000. For those companies, a 5% tax on income over $100,000 would be added until the tax is equal to a flat rate of 34%.

Use of Corporate Debt

If a corporation is in need of relatively permanent funds, it generally considers borrowing money on a long-term basis or issuing stock. Since interest on debt is a deductible expense in determining taxable income and dividends paid on stock are not, this impact on income tax is one of the important factors to consider in evaluating the two methods of financing. To illustrate, assume that a corporation which expects a tax rate of 34% is considering issuing (1) $1,000,000 of 10% bonds or (2) $1,000,000 of 10% cumulative preferred stock. If the bonds are issued, the deduction of the yearly $100,000 of interest in determining taxable income results in an annual net borrowing cost of $66,000 ($100,000 less tax savings of 34% of $100,000). If the preferred stock is issued, the dividends are not deductible in determining taxable income and the net annual outlay for this method of financing is $100,000. Thus, issuing bonds instead of preferred stock reduced the annual financing expenditures by $34,000 ($100,000 − $66,000).

Nontaxable Investment Income

Interest on bonds issued by a state or political subdivision is exempt from the federal income tax. To illustrate, the following table compares the income after tax on a $100,000 investment in a 10% industrial bond and a $100,000 investment in an 8% municipal bond for a corporation with a tax rate of 34%.

	Taxable 10% Industrial Bond	Nontaxable 8% Municipal Bond
Income...	$10,000	$8,000
Tax (34% of $10,000)	3,400	—
Income after tax............................	$ 6,600	$8,000

Although the interest rate on the municipal bond (8%) is less than the rate on the industrial bond (10%), the aftertax income is larger from the investment in the municipal bond.

GENERAL IMPACT OF INCOME TAXES

The foregoing description of the federal income tax system and discussion of tax minimization demonstrates the importance of income taxes to individuals and to business enterprises. Many accountants, in both private and public practice, devote their entire attention to tax planning for their employers or their clients. The statutes and the administrative regulations, which are often changed, must be studied continuously by anyone who engages in this phase of accounting.

DISCUSSION QUESTIONS

1. (a) Does the failure to receive the tax forms from the IRS qualify as a legitimate means of tax avoidance? (b) Does the failure to maintain adequate records qualify as a legitimate means of tax avoidance?

2. (a) What are the principal taxable entities subject to the federal income tax? (b) How is the income of a sole proprietorship taxed?

3. Describe briefly the system employed in subjecting the income of partnerships to the federal income tax.

4. The adjusted gross income of a sole proprietorship for the year was $75,000, of which the owner withdrew $48,000. What amount of income from the business enterprise must be reported on the owner's income tax return?

5. Do corporations electing partnership treatment (Subchapter S) pay federal income tax? Discuss.

6. Which of the two methods of accounting, cash or accrual, is more commonly used by individual taxpayers?

7. Describe constructive receipt of gross income as it applies to (a) a salary check received from an employer, (b) interest credited to a savings account, and (c) bond interest coupons.

8. Arrange the following items in their proper sequence for the determination of taxable income of an individual.
(a) Adjusted gross income
(b) Taxable income
(c) Itemized deductions and exemptions
(d) Gross income
(e) Expenses related to business or specified revenue

9. Which inventory method (lifo or fifo) would result in the lower income tax during a period of rising prices? Explain.

EXERCISES

Exercise E–1
Determination of income using cash method and accrual method.

Janet Long, MD, opened her office after graduation from medical school in early January of the current year. On December 30, the accounting records indicated the following for the current year to date:

	Total	Cash Received	Cash Paid
Fees earned..	$113,000	$95,000	—
Lease of office and equipment....................	30,000	—	$27,500
Medical assistant salary...........................	24,000	—	22,000
Medical supplies, utilities, etc....................	9,500	—	8,700

(a) Determine the amount of net income Long would report from her practice for the current year under the (a) cash method and (b) accrual method.
(b) List the advantages of using the cash method rather than the accrual method in accounting for Long's practice.
(c) What is the principal advantage of using the accrual method rather than the cash method in accounting for Long's practice?

Exercise E-2
Determination of income tax for sole proprietor.

Don McFarlane opened a business which he operated as a sole proprietorship in early January of the current year. On December 31, the accounting records indicated the following for the current year:

Administrative expenses.	$ 17,100
Cost of merchandise sold.	172,500
Sales	255,250
Selling expenses.	31,600
Withdrawals by owner.	24,000

Determine the amount of taxable income from the business that McFarlane should include on his tax return for the current year.

Exercise E-3
Determination of corporation income tax.

During the current year, three corporations realized the following taxable income:

Corporation X.	$90,000
Corporation Y.	10,000
Corporation Z.	60,000

Using the tax rates indicated in the chapter, determine the amount of income tax owed by each corporation.

Exercise E-4
Effects of using fifo and lifo for inventory costing.

A-1 Limousine Sales sold 30 limousines for $25,000 each during the first year of operations. Data related to purchases during the year are as follows:

	Quantity	Unit Cost
January 5	5	$20,000
March 15.	7	20,500
June 30.	9	20,750
September 3.	10	20,800
November 10	5	20,900

Sales of limousines are the company's only source of income, and operating expenses for the current year are $52,500.

(a) Determine the net income for the current year, using the fifo (first-in, first-out) inventory method.
(b) Determine the net income for the current year, using the lifo (last-in, first-out) inventory method.
(c) Which method of inventory costing, fifo or lifo, would you recommend for tax purposes? Discuss.

Exercise E-5
Effects of corporation income tax on two financing plans.

The board of directors of Wayne Inc. is planning an expansion of plant facilities expected to cost $2,500,000. The board is undecided about the method of financing this expansion and is considering two plans:

Plan 1. Issue 25,000 shares of $100, 9% cumulative preferred stock at par.
Plan 2. Issue $2,500,000 of 20-year, 11% bonds at face amount.

The condensed balance sheet of the corporation at the end of the most recent fiscal year is as follows:

Wayne Inc.
Balance Sheet
December 31, 19--

Assets		Liabilities and Stockholders' Equity	
Current assets.................	$1,400,000	Current liabilities..............	$1,140,000
Plant assets	4,600,000	Common stock, $25 par....	2,500,000
		Paid-in capital in excess	
		of par.........................	1,000,000
		Retained earnings............	1,360,000
		Total liabilities and stock-	
Total assets	$6,000,000	holders' equity..............	$6,000,000

Net income has remained relatively constant over the past several years. As a result of the expansion program, yearly income after tax but before bond interest and related income tax is expected to increase to $475,000.

(a) Prepare a tabulation indicating the net annual outlay (dividends and interest after tax) for financing under each plan. (Use the 34% income tax rate indicated in the chapter.)

(b) List factors other than the net cost of financing that the board should consider in evaluating the two plans.

ACCOUNTING FOR NONPROFIT ORGANIZATIONS

Entities engaged in business transactions may be classified as profit-making or nonprofit. Profit-making organizations respond to a demand for a product or a service with the expectation of earning net income. The accounting concepts and procedures applicable to such organizations are discussed in the text. Although many of these concepts and procedures apply to nonprofit organizations, there are also differences, which are described and illustrated in this appendix.

CHARACTERISTICS OF NONPROFIT ORGANIZATIONS

Nonprofit, or **not-for-profit**, entities are usually organized as informal associations or as corporations in accordance with applicable laws and regulations. Such organizations may be classified as either (1) governmental units or (2) charitable, religious, or philanthropic units (hereafter referred to simply as "charitable"). The first category includes the federal government and state, county, and city governments. The second category includes churches, hospitals, private schools and universities, medical research facilities, and many other types of organizations that are financed wholly or in part by donations.

The distinguishing characteristics of nonprofit organizations are as follows: (1) there is neither a conscious profit motive nor an expectation of earning net income, (2) no part of any excess of revenues over expenditures is distributed to those who contributed support through taxes or voluntary donations, and (3) any excess of revenues over expenditures that results from operations in the short run is ordinarily used in later years to further the purposes of the organization.

Nonprofit organizations provide goods or services that fulfill a social need, often for those who do not have the purchasing power to acquire these goods or services for themselves. Some nonprofit organizations, such as a government-owned electric utility or a public transportation company, are created to provide services to the citizens of the area for a fee that is close to the cost of providing the service. After the initial investment, they tend to be self-sustaining; that is, the revenues earned support their operations. Because the activities of such organizations are financed mainly by charges to the customers using the services, the accounting concepts and procedures used are those appropriate to a commercial enterprise. Most nonprofit organizations, however, are established to provide a service to society without levying against the user a direct charge equal to the full cost of the service. The concepts and procedures applicable to nonprofit organizations of the latter type are discussed in this appendix. The explanations and illustrations presented are necessarily brief and relatively free of the complexities encountered in actual practice.

ACCOUNTING FOR NONPROFIT ORGANIZATIONS

With the increase in the sense of social responsibility in society has come a corresponding increase in the number of nonprofit organizations and in the volume of their activities. Approximately one third of the volume of business in the United States is conducted by governmental units and charitable organizations. As such organizations play an increasingly significant role, accounting for these organizations is receiving more and more attention. For example, the Governmental Accounting Standards Board (GASB), similar to the Financial Accounting Standards Board (FASB), was established in 1984. This body is responsible for establishing accounting standards for state and local governmental units,[1] and it has issued *Concepts Statement No. 1,* "Objectives of Financial Reporting," which provides a framework for developing such standards. To the extent that nonprofit organizations issue general-purpose external financial statements, the pronouncements of the Financial Accounting Standards Board may apply.[2] Accounting issues for nonprofit organizations have also been addressed by the American Institute of Certified Public Accountants and other professional accounting groups.

The accounting systems for all nonprofit organizations must provide financial data to internal management for use in planning and controlling operations and to external parties, such as taxpayers and donors, for use in determining the effectiveness of operations. The basic double-entry system, an effective system of internal control, and the periodic determination of and reporting of financial position and results of operations are essential for nonprofit organizations. In addition, accounting systems for nonprofit organizations should include mechanisms (1) to ensure that management observes the restrictions imposed upon it by law, charter, by-laws, etc., and (2) to provide for reports to taxpayers and donors that such restrictions have been respected. For these reasons, a nonprofit organization often applies the concept of "fund accounting" in conjunction with a budget and appropriations technique to account for the assets received by the organization and to ensure that expenditures are made only for authorized purposes.

Fund Accounting

In this book, the term "fund" has been used with a variety of meanings. Fund has been used to denote segregations of cash for a special purpose, for example, in "petty cash fund," or to designate the amount of cash and marketable securities segregated in a "sinking fund" to pay long-term obligations at maturity.

In accounting for nonprofit organizations, **fund** is defined as an accounting entity with accounts maintained for recording assets, liabilities, **fund equity** (the excess of assets over liabilities), revenues, and expenditures for a particular purpose according to specified restrictions or limitations. The following description of fund accounting appeared in an annual report for the District of Columbia:

---

[1] *Statement No. 1,* "Authoritative Status of NCGA Pronouncements and AICPA Industry Audit Guide" (Stamford: Governmental Accounting Standards Board, 1984).
[2] For example, Statement of Financial Accounting Standards, No. 93, "Recognition of Depreciation by Not-for-Profit Organizations" (Stamford: Financial Accounting Standards Board, 1987), requires charitable organizations to recognize depreciation on long-lived tangible assets in general-purpose external financial statements.

The accounts of the District are organized in funds and account groups, each of which is considered a separate accounting entity. The accompanying financial statements include all funds and account groups of the District.

The operations of each fund are accounted for with a separate set of self-balancing accounts that comprise its assets, liabilities, fund equity, revenues, and expenditures.... Government resources are allocated to and accounted for in individual funds based upon the purposes for which they are to be spent.

Funds may be established by law, provisions of a charter, administrative action, or by a special contribution to a charitable organization. Most nonprofit organizations maintain a General Fund in which to record transactions related to day-to-day operations. For example, cities usually maintain a "General Fund" for recording transactions related to many community services, such as fire and police protection, street lighting and repairs, and maintenance of water and sewer mains. Cities may maintain additional funds for special tax assessments, bond redemption, and for other specified purposes. It is possible to have transactions between funds, as when one fund borrows money from another fund, in which case the transaction is recorded in the accounts of both funds.

Both public and private universities usually maintain a number of separate funds in addition to a General Fund. For example, there may be a number of scholarship funds, named for alumni or other donors, with many restrictions concerning the recipients, such as high scholastic attainment, residence in a specified area, and enrollment in a particular course of study.

Charitable organizations often have a number of funds, sometimes called "endowment funds," from which only the income may be spent. The amounts contributed to such funds are often invested in various income-yielding bonds and stocks. For fund balances of modest amount, however, it is not feasible to identify each bond or share with a particular fund. In such situations, the investments are commingled, each fund having a claim on the investment pool equal to its fund balance. The income is periodically divided among the various participating funds in proportion to the respective fund balances at the beginning of the period. The same technique is used by governmental units, such as state universities, for the temporary investment of large amounts of cash that would otherwise yield no income.

Estimated Revenues and Appropriations. Budgeting is an important part of an accounting system for nonprofit organizations. The budget is prepared by management and subsequently reviewed, revised, and approved by the governing body (council, directors, trustees, etc.) of the organization. The official budget sets the specific goals for the fiscal period and, through appropriations, designates the manner in which the revenues of each fund are to be used to accomplish these goals. The estimated revenues may be viewed as potential assets and the **appropriations** as potential liabilities.

Many governmental units apply the concept of **zero-base budgeting** in developing budget estimates. This concept requires all levels of management to start from zero and estimate revenues and appropriations as if there had been no previous activities in their unit.

After the budget for the General Fund has been approved by the governing body, the estimated revenues and appropriations are recorded in controlling accounts. Any difference between the estimated revenues and appropriations is recorded in the fund equity account, Fund Balance. The amount in the fund balance account represents unrestricted, spendable resources of the General Fund. An example of such an entry is as follows:

Estimated Revenues...	1,900,000	
Appropriations..		1,850,000
Fund Balance..		50,000

The effect of the recording of the budgeted amounts in the General Fund accounts is presented in the following diagram:

GENERAL FUND ACCOUNTS

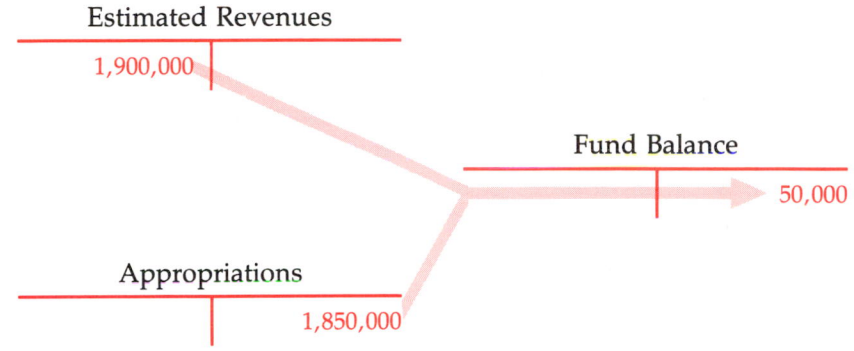

When the budget shows an excess of estimated revenues over appropriations, as in the preceding illustration, Fund Balance is credited. If the budget had shown an excess of appropriations over estimated revenues, the excess would be debited to Fund Balance. The subsidiary ledgers for Estimated Revenues and Appropriations contain accounts for the various sources of expected revenue (property taxes, sales taxes, etc.) and the various purposes of appropriations (general government, street and roads, libraries, etc.). By recording this budgetary information in the accounts, periodic reports comparing actual amounts with budgeted amounts can be prepared readily.

Revenues. The realization of revenues requires an entry debiting accounts for the assets acquired and crediting the revenues account. For example, a portion of the estimated revenues from property taxes, sales taxes, etc., may be realized in the form of cash during the first month of the fiscal year. To summarize these receipts, an entry would be made as follows:

Cash..	152,500	
Revenues		152,500

Revenues is a controlling account. In practice, it is customary to use a single subsidiary ledger, called the **revenue ledger**, for both Estimated Revenues and Revenues. Each subsidiary account is used for recording the estimated revenues and the actual revenues. The relationship between the general ledger accounts and the subsidiary revenue ledger is illustrated in the following diagram:

GENERAL LEDGER ACCOUNTS

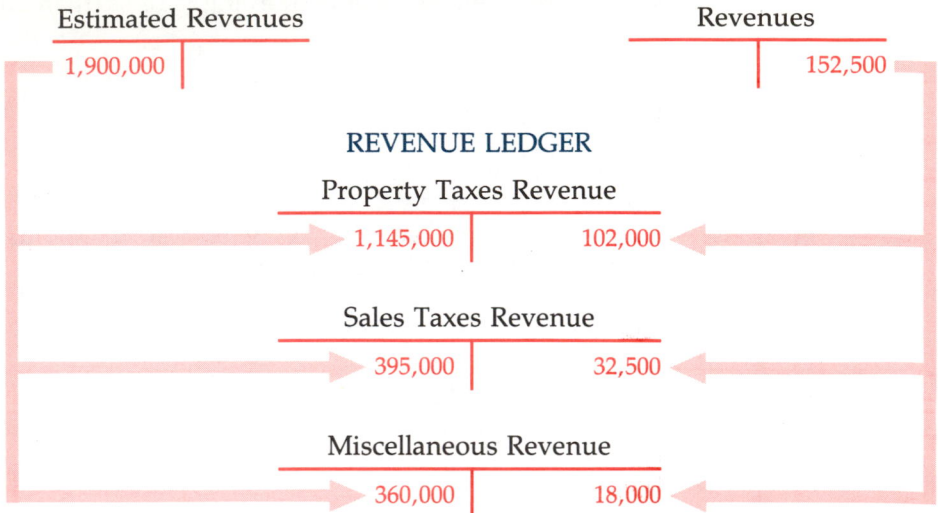

At any point in time, the difference between the two general ledger controlling accounts, Estimated Revenues and Revenues, would be equal to the sum of the balances of the accounts in the subsidiary revenue ledger. A debit balance in a subsidiary ledger account indicates the amount of the excess of estimated revenues over actual revenues. If actual revenues exceed the amount estimated, the account balance would be a credit.

Expenditures. As regularly recurring expenditures, such as payrolls, are incurred, the account Expenditures is debited and the appropriate liability accounts or cash are credited. For example, the entry for the biweekly payroll would be as follows:

Expenditures..	31,200	
Wages Payable		31,200

Encumbrances. There is usually a lapse of time between the placing of an order and delivery of the goods or services ordered. When contracts such as those for road or building construction are executed, the time lag may extend over relatively long periods. All legally binding commitments to pay money eventually become expenditures. These commitments, called **encumbrances**, should be recorded in the accounts when a contract is entered into in order to ensure that expenditures do not exceed amounts appropriated. The means of preventing overexpenditures is illustrated by the following entry:

Encumbrances	10,000	
Fund Balance Reserved for Encumbrances		10,000

When orders are filled or contracts completed for amounts encumbered, the entry that recorded the encumbrance is reversed and the expenditure is recorded, as illustrated by the following entries:

Fund Balance Reserved for Encumbrances................	10,000	
Encumbrances..		10,000
Expenditures...	10,000	
Accounts Payable...		10,000

The effect of these two entries is to (1) cancel the original entry in which the encumbrance was recorded and (2) record the expenditure and the related liability.

When encumbrances are recorded, the sum of the balances of the accounts Encumbrances and Expenditures can be viewed as offsets to the account Appropriations. The difference obtained by subtracting the balances of Encumbrances and Expenditures from the amount of Appropriations is the amount of commitments that can still be made. For example, if appropriations of $1,850,000 were approved when the budget was adopted and $1,500,000 and $240,000 have been recorded in Expenditures and Encumbrances, respectively, only $110,000 is available for commitment during the remainder of the fiscal year.

Expenditure Ledger. Appropriations, Encumbrances, and Expenditures are controlling accounts. In practice, it is customary to use a single subsidiary ledger, called the **expenditure ledger**, in which each account indicates appropriations, encumbrances, and expenditures.

When a budget is approved, appropriations are recorded in the proper accounts in the expenditure ledger to indicate the unencumbered or uncommitted balance. As order commitments are made, the amounts of the encumbrances are recorded in the proper expenditure ledger account (by a debit) and the unencumbered balance is adjusted accordingly. When orders are filled, the expenditure and the credit to encumbrances are recorded in the proper columns. At any point in time, the accounts in the expenditure ledger indicate the balance of the encumbrances outstanding and the unencumbered balance.

In the following illustration of an account in the expenditure ledger, the budget appropriation for police department supplies is $250,000 as of July 1. On July 5, a purchase order that encumbered $10,000 was recorded and the encumbrances balance of $10,000 and the unencumbered balance of $240,000 were recorded. When the invoice of $10,000 was received on July 17, the encumbrances balance was reduced to zero and the $10,000 expenditure was recorded.

ACCOUNT   POLICE DEPARTMENT—SUPPLIES   ACCOUNT NO. 200-21

Date		Item	Encumbrances			Expenditures		Unencumbered
			Debit	Credit	Balance	Item	Total	Balance
July	1	Budget appropriation						250,000
	5	Purchase order	10,000		10,000			240,000
	17	Invoice		10,000	—	10,000	10,000	240,000
	30	Purchase order	7,500		7,500			232,500

Long-Lived Assets. When long-lived assets are purchased, they are usually recorded as debits to the account Expenditures in the same manner as supplies and other ordinary expenses. A separate record, called the General

Fixed Assets Account Group, can be maintained for the purpose of assigning responsibility for the custody and use of the individual assets.

The practice of recording the purchase of long-lived assets as an expenditure and the related failure to record depreciation expense has been debated for many years. Most governmental units do not differentiate between long-lived assets and ordinary recurring expenses. This practice is supported by the fact that the acquisition of plant assets is often authorized by a special appropriation, perhaps financed by a bond issue for a local government unit.[3]

Periodic Reporting

A nonprofit organization should prepare interim statements comparing actual revenues and expenditures with the related budgeted amounts. Variations between the two should be investigated immediately to determine their cause and to consider possible corrective actions.

At the end of the fiscal year, closing entries are recorded and the operating data are summarized and reported. The entry to close the revenues and estimated revenues accounts is illustrated as follows:

Revenues	1,920,000	
Estimated Revenues		1,900,000
Fund Balance		20,000

In the illustration, actual revenues exceeded the amount estimated. If the actual revenues had been less than the amount estimated, the fund equity account, Fund Balance, would have been decreased by a debit. The effect of this entry is to adjust Fund Balance to the actual amount of the revenues for the period.

The entry to close the appropriations and expenditures accounts is illustrated as follows:

Appropriations	1,850,000	
Expenditures		1,825,000
Fund Balance		25,000

In the illustration, appropriations exceeded the actual expenditures. If the appropriations had been less than the actual expenditures, Fund Balance would have been decreased by a debit. The effect of this entry is to adjust Fund Balance to the actual amount of the expenditures for the period.

The entry to close the encumbrances account, which represents the commitments outstanding at the end of the year, is illustrated as follows:

Fund Balance	20,000	
Encumbrances		20,000

Inevitably, some orders placed during the year will remain unfilled at the end of the year. To indicate the commitment to pay for these orders, Fund Balance Reserved for Encumbrances is not closed and is included in

---

[3]Most charitable organizations are required to recognize depreciation for general-purpose external financial statements (Statement of Financial Accounting Standards, No. 93). In such cases, the recording and reporting of depreciation follows the concepts for profit-making enterprises.

the fund equity section of the year-end balance sheet. When the orders are filled in the next year, Fund Balance Reserved for Encumbrances will be debited and Accounts Payable credited.

Financial Statements

Financial statements for each fund and combined financial statements for all funds should be prepared periodically. The principal financial statements prepared at the end of each fiscal year are (1) a balance sheet, which is similar to a commercial enterprise balance sheet, and (2) a statement of revenues, expenditures, and changes in fund balance. The objective of the **statement of revenues, expenditures, and changes in fund balance** is to provide users with information on a nonprofit entity's operating performance for a period. The nature of this statement emphasizes the absence of the profit motive and the importance of controlling expenditures within the revenue limits imposed by law or the dictate of donors. The first part of the statement presents a comparison of the budgeted and actual revenues and expenditures, but not a net income amount. The second part, which is similar to the retained earnings statement for a commercial enterprise, presents the effects of operations and encumbrances on the unreserved fund balance. Both the balance sheet and the statement of revenues, expenditures, and changes in fund balance are illustrated in the following section.

The financial statements for the funds should also be accompanied by adequate disclosures, including a summary of significant accounting policies. Two excerpts from the summary of significant accounting policies section of the District of Columbia's annual report are as follows:

Encumbrances

Encumbrances are commitments to acquire goods and services. The recording of purchase orders and contracts in order to reserve that portion of the applicable appropriation is employed as an extension of allocation in the General Fund.

Fixed Assets

Costs to acquire fixed assets used in governmental funds are charged as current expenditures in the General Fund.

ILLUSTRATION OF NONPROFIT ACCOUNTING

To illustrate further the concepts and procedures that have been described, assume that the trial balance of the General Fund of the City of Lewiston, as of July 1, 1990, the beginning of the fiscal year, is as follows:

City of Lewiston — General Fund
Trial Balance
July 1, 1990

Cash	242,500	
Savings Accounts	250,000	
Property Taxes Receivable	185,000	
Investment in U.S. Treasury Notes	350,000	
Accounts Payable		162,600
Wages Payable		30,000
Fund Balance		834,900
	1,027,500	1,027,500

The transactions completed during the year for the General Fund are summarized and recorded as follows, in general journal form. In practice, the transactions would be recorded from day to day in various journals.

(a) Estimated revenues and appropriations	Estimated Revenues... Appropriations.. Fund Balance...	9,100,000	9,070,000 30,000
(b) Revenues from property tax levy	Property Taxes Receivable .... Revenues	6,500,000	6,500,000
(c) Collection of property taxes and other taxes on a cash basis	Cash.. Property Taxes Receivable .... Revenues	9,105,000	6,470,000 2,635,000
(d) Expenditures for payrolls	Expenditures... Wages Payable	3,280,000	3,280,000
(e) Expenditures encumbered	Encumbrances .... Fund Balance Reserved for Encumbrances	5,800,000	5,800,000
(f) Liquidation of encumbrances and receipt of invoices	Fund Balance Reserved for Encumbrances .... Encumbrances .... Expenditures... Accounts Payable	5,785,000 5,785,000	5,785,000 5,785,000
(g) Cash disbursed	Accounts Payable .... Wages Payable .... Cash..	5,800,000 3,270,000	9,070,000
(h) Revenues and estimated revenues accounts closed	Revenues .... Estimated Revenues.................................... Fund Balance...	9,135,000	9,100,000 35,000
(i) Appropriations and expenditures accounts closed	Appropriations... Expenditures... Fund Balance...	9,070,000	9,065,000 5,000
(j) Encumbrances account closed	Fund Balance.. Encumbrances	15,000	15,000

After the foregoing entries have been posted, the general ledger accounts and the trial balance for the General Fund appear as follows. Entries in the accounts are identified by letters to facilitate comparison with the preceding summary journal entries.

Cash

Balance	242,500	(g)	9,070,000
(c)	9,105,000	Balance	277,500
	9,347,500		9,347,500
Balance	277,500		

Savings Accounts

Balance	250,000

Property Taxes Receivable

Balance	185,000	(c)	6,470,000
(b)	6,500,000	Balance	215,000
	6,685,000		6,685,000
Balance	215,000		

Investment in U.S. Treasury Notes

Balance	350,000

Accounts Payable

(g)	5,800,000	Balance	162,600
Balance	147,600	(f)	5,785,000
	5,947,600		5,947,600
		Balance	147,600

Wages Payable

(g)	3,270,000	Balance	30,000
Balance	40,000	(d)	3,280,000
	3,310,000		3,310,000
		Balance	40,000

Fund Balance Reserved for Encumbrances

(f)	5,785,000	(e)	5,800,000
Balance	15,000		
	5,800,000		5,800,000
		Balance	15,000

Fund Balance

(j)	15,000	Balance	834,900
Balance	889,900	(a)	30,000
		(h)	35,000
		(i)	5,000
	904,900		904,900
		Balance	889,900

Estimated Revenues

(a)	9,100,000	(h)	9,100,000

Revenues

(h)	9,135,000	(b)	6,500,000
		(c)	2,635,000
	9,135,000		9,135,000

Appropriations

(i)	9,070,000	(a)	9,070,000

Expenditures

(d)	3,280,000	(i)	9,065,000
(f)	5,785,000		
	9,065,000		9,065,000

Encumbrances

(e)	5,800,000	(f)	5,785,000
		(j)	15,000
	5,800,000		5,800,000

City of Lewiston—General Fund
Trial Balance
June 30, 1991

Cash..	277,500	
Savings Accounts	250,000	
Property Taxes Receivable	215,000	
Investment in U.S. Treasury Notes.........................	350,000	
Accounts Payable..		147,600
Wages Payable		40,000
Fund Balance Reserved for Encumbrances..............		15,000
Fund Balance...		889,900
	1,092,500	1,092,500

The balance sheet for the City of Lewiston General Fund, as of June 30, 1991, is as follows. On the balance sheet, the fund balance reserved for encumbrances is reported as a separate item in the fund equity section. The balance of the account Fund Balance, $889,900, is described as "Unreserved fund balance." As mentioned previously, this amount represents the unrestricted, spendable resources of the General Fund.

Balance Sheet

City of Lewiston—General Fund
Balance Sheet
June 30, 1991

Assets

Cash...		$ 277,500
Savings accounts[4]...		250,000
Property taxes receivable		215,000
Investment in U.S. Treasury notes.....................		350,000
Total assets		$1,092,500

Liabilities

Accounts payable...	$147,600	
Wages payable...	40,000	
Total liabilities...		$ 187,600

Fund Equity

Fund balance reserved for encumbrances	$ 15,000	
Unreserved fund balance....................................	889,900	
Total fund equity		904,900
Total liabilities and fund equity............................		$1,092,500

Although there are many variations in form, the statement of revenues, expenditures, and changes in fund balance reports the following:

1. Differences (in terms of over or under budget) between budgeted revenues and actual revenues.
2. Differences (in terms of over or under budget) between budgeted expenditures and actual expenditures.

---

[4]*Statement No. 3,* "Deposits with Financial Institutions, Investments (including Repurchase Agreements), and Reverse Repurchase Agreements" (Stamford: Governmental Accounting Standards Board, 1986), requires specific disclosures about deposits with financial institutions. A discussion of these disclosures is beyond the scope of this appendix.

3. The excess or deficiency of revenues (both actual and budgeted) over expenditures.
4. The fund balance at the beginning of the year and the amount of the encumbrances closed to fund balance at the end of the year.
5. The fund balance at the end of the year.

The statement of revenues, expenditures, and changes in fund balance for the City of Lewiston General Fund is as follows:

Statement of Revenues, Expenditures, and Changes in Fund Balance

City of Lewiston — General Fund
Statement of Revenues, Expenditures, and Changes in Fund Balance
For Year Ended June 30, 1991

	Budget	Actual	Over	Under
Revenues:				
General property taxes	$6,480,000	$6,500,000	$20,000	
Sales taxes	1,835,500	1,850,500	15,000	
Motor vehicle licenses	312,250	310,250		$ 2,000
Municipal court fines	257,000	255,750		1,250
Interest	35,000	35,000		
Building permits	27,100	27,500	400	
Miscellaneous	153,150	156,000	2,850	
Total revenues	$9,100,000	$9,135,000	$38,250	$ 3,250
Expenditures:				
General government	$2,450,000	$2,465,250	$15,250	
Police department— personnel services	1,250,000	1,256,000	6,000	
Police department—supplies	299,000	290,500		$ 8,500
Police department—equipment	190,000	182,750		7,250
Police department— other charges	30,000	27,500		2,500
Fire department— personnel services	1,035,000	1,039,000	4,000	
Fire department—supplies	320,600	315,600		5,000
Fire department—equipment	200,500	197,750		2,750
Fire department— other charges	16,400	18,200	1,800	
Streets and roads	1,530,000	1,521,850		8,150
Sanitation	741,000	739,500		1,500
Public welfare	630,000	632,600	2,600	
Libraries	377,500	378,500	1,000	
Total expenditures	$9,070,000	$9,065,000	$30,650	$35,650
Excess of revenues over expenditures	$ 30,000	$ 70,000		
Fund balance, July 1, 1990		834,900		
		$ 904,900		
Less encumbrances		15,000		
Fund balance, June 30, 1991		$ 889,900		

The data for the preparation of the preceding statement would be provided by the various subsidiary ledgers for the City of Lewiston General Fund. These ledgers were not presented in order to simplify the illustration.

DISCUSSION QUESTIONS

1. What entity is responsible for establishing accounting standards for state and local governmental units?

2. What characteristics distinguish commercial enterprises from nonprofit organizations?

3. As the term is used in reference to accounting for nonprofit organizations, what is meant by "fund accounting"?

4. What concept requires all levels of management of a governmental unit to start from zero and estimate revenues and appropriations as if there had been no previous activities in their unit?

5. In recording estimated revenues and appropriations as expressed in the budget, would Fund Balance be debited or credited if appropriations exceed estimated revenues?

6. If an account in the revenue ledger indicated that estimated revenues exceeded revenues, will the account have a debit balance or a credit balance?

7. What is the purpose of recording encumbrances in the accounts?

8. If the appropriations, expenditures, and encumbrances accounts have balances of $875,000, $750,000, and $50,000, respectively, what amount is available for commitments during the remainder of the fiscal year?

9. In the subsidiary expenditure ledger, the libraries account shows an unencumbered balance. Does this balance indicate that appropriations for the year exceed the sum of encumbrances outstanding and expenditures incurred to date?

10. What account in the "general fund" of a governmental organization is debited for purchases of long-lived assets?

11. When the closing entry for the appropriations and expenditures accounts is prepared, in what account is the difference between the balances in the two accounts recorded?

12. If, in the closing process, the appropriations are $2,800,000 and the expenditures are $2,760,000, will the fund balance account be debited or credited?

13. At the end of the fiscal year, to what account is the balance in Encumbrances closed?

14. In which financial statements will the year-end balance of the following accounts appear: (a) Expenditures and (b) Fund Balance Reserved for Encumbrances?

15. What are the two principal financial statements for nonprofit organizations?

16. Describe the two parts of the statement of revenues, expenditures, and changes in fund balance.

EXERCISES

Exercise F–1

Entries from budget for nonprofit enterprise.

The budget approved for the fiscal year by the city council of Buckley for the General Fund indicated appropriations of $1,525,000 and estimated revenues of $1,540,000. Present the entry to record the financial data indicated by the budget.

Exercise F–2

Entries from budget and for revenues and expenditures.

Present entries to record the following selected data related to the General Fund of Villa Grove:

(a) The budget indicated appropriations of $3,350,000 and estimated revenues of $3,400,000.
(b) Cash received from revenues, $490,000.
(c) Cash paid for regularly recurring expenditures, $275,000.

Exercise F–3

Entries for placement of orders and their receipt for nonprofit enterprise.

An order was placed by a nonprofit organization for $9,250 of supplies. Subsequently, $8,750 of the supplies were received and $500 were back ordered. Present entries to record (a) the placement of the order and (b) the receipt of the supplies and the invoice of $8,750, terms n/eom.

Exercise F–4

Closing entries for nonprofit enterprise.

Selected account balances from the General Fund ledger of McNair Park District at the end of the current fiscal year are as follows:

Appropriations..	$670,000
Encumbrances	30,000
Estimated Revenues..................................	690,000
Expenditures...	632,000
Fund Balance..	65,750
Fund Balance Reserved for Encumbrances....	30,000
Revenues	698,500

Prepare the appropriate closing entries.

Exercise F–5

Balance sheet for General Fund of governmental organization.

Selected account balances from the ledger of the Paxton Forest Preserve District—General Fund are as follows:

Accounts Payable	$ 11,800
Cash in Bank	14,750
Fund Balance...	168,450
Marketable Securities	150,000
Petty Cash...	500
Fund Balance Reserved for Encumbrances....	10,000
Savings Accounts	25,000

Prepare a balance sheet as of July 31.

Exercise F–6

Statement of revenues, expenditures, and changes in fund balance.

Data from two subsidiary ledgers of Village of Savoy—General Fund, at August 31, 1991, are as follows:

Revenue Ledger		
	Debits	Credits
Property taxes.............................	100,000	102,100
Sales taxes	350,000	334,800
Other...	10,000	12,200

Expenditure Ledger

	Expenditures	Budget Appropriations
Administration	38,750	40,000
Fire............................	75,300	75,000
Library	15,800	13,200
Police	235,900	240,000
Streets and roads	55,600	50,000
Other	27,400	30,000

The beginning balance of the fund balance account as of September 1, 1990, was $187,500. Assuming that the encumbrances account has a balance of $5,000 on August 31, 1991, prepare a statement of revenues, expenditures, and changes in fund balance for the year ended August 31, 1991.

Exercise F–7
Computation of unreserved fund balance.

Selected account balances before closing on June 30, the end of the current fiscal year for Rankin — General Fund, are as follows. The fund balance account had a balance of $371,400 on July 1, 1990, the beginning of the current year.

Appropriations...	$2,333,000
Encumbrances	10,000
Estimated Revenues................................	2,370,000
Expenditures..	2,298,000
Revenues	2,310,000

Compute the balance of the fund balance account as of June 30, 1991, the end of the current fiscal year.

MAJOR TRENDS IN MANUFACTURING

During the 1970s and throughout the 1980s, the competitive advantage in the manufacture and production of goods shifted from the United States to foreign producers. In 1970, the United States exported $42.5 billion of merchandise and imported $39.9 billion, for a net surplus of exports over imports of $2.6 billion. In 1985, the United States exported $214.4 billion of merchandise and imported $338.9 billion, for a net trade deficit (i.e., imports exceeded exports) of $124.5 billion.[1] This shift in exports and imports has been blamed on such factors as the high cost of American labor, trade barriers to foreign markets, unfavorable exchange rates, and the poor quality of American goods.

In response to competitive world markets, many manufacturers have been forced to adopt new manufacturing techniques and processes. In turn, the managerial accounting methods which provide the basic information that management uses in planning and controlling operations have changed. Many of these changes are briefly described in this appendix.

The major trends in manufacturing in the United States in recent years can be grouped into five general categories: (1) just-in-time manufacturing systems, (2) automation, (3) product quality, (4) inventory control, and (5) information technology. In the following paragraphs, each of these trends is briefly described, and its implications for managerial accounting are discussed.

JUST-IN-TIME MANUFACTURING SYSTEMS

Recently, manufacturers have begun to reorganize the traditional production line to achieve greater efficiency and to improve quality. One such system that has received much attention by industry is the **just-in-time manufacturing system**, sometimes referred to as the **flexible flow manufacturing system**.

In a traditional production process, a product moves through the process according to functional flows along a continuous production line. That is, the product moves from process to process as each function or step is completed. Each worker is assigned a specific job, which is performed repeatedly as unfinished products are received from the preceding department. In such a process, a product is often said to be "pushed through" production, since each manufacturing department "pushes" the unfinished product to the next stage (department) of manufacturing. For example, a furniture manufacturer might use seven production departments to perform the operating functions necessary to manufacture furniture, as shown in the following diagram.

[1]Council of Economic Advisers, *Economic Report of the President* (United States Printing Office: Washington, D.C., 1987), p. 358.

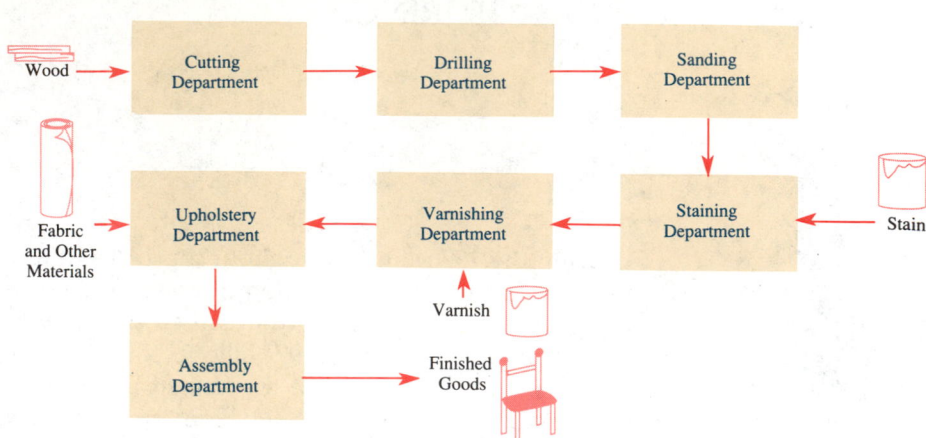

For the furniture maker in the illustration, manufacturing would begin in the Cutting Department, where the wood would be cut to design specifications. Next, the Drilling Department would perform the drilling function, after which the Sanding Department would sand the wood, the Staining Department would stain the furniture, and the Varnishing Department would apply varnish and other protective coatings. Then, the Upholstery Department would add fabric and other materials. Finally, the Assembly Department would assemble the furniture to complete the manufacturing process.

In the traditional production process, production supervisors attempt to enter enough materials into the manufacturing process to keep all the manufacturing departments operating. Some departments, however, may process materials more rapidly than others. In addition, if one department stops production because of machine breakdowns, for example, the preceding departments usually continue production in order to avoid idle time. This unevenness may result in a build-up of work in process between departments. Furthermore, if bottlenecks occur, the entire production line stops because the unfinished product is not passed on to the successive departments.

In a just-in-time manufacturing system, a primary emphasis is on the reduction of work in process inventories. Large amounts of work in process represent a large dollar investment in inventory that is not earning a return to the enterprise. Ideally, no work in process would exist among departments, but each department's processing finishes "just in time" for the next department's processing to begin. In a just-in-time system, the product is often said to be "pulled through" production, since a department finishing its processing "pulls" (demands) more materials from the preceding department.

One way in which just-in-time manufacturing systems attempt to reduce work in process is by combining processing functions into **work centers**. The seven departments illustrated above for the furniture manufacturer might be reorganized into three work centers, for example. As shown in the following diagram, Work Center One would perform the cutting, drilling, and sanding functions; Work Center Two would perform the staining and varnishing functions; and Work Center Three would perform the upholstery and assembly functions.

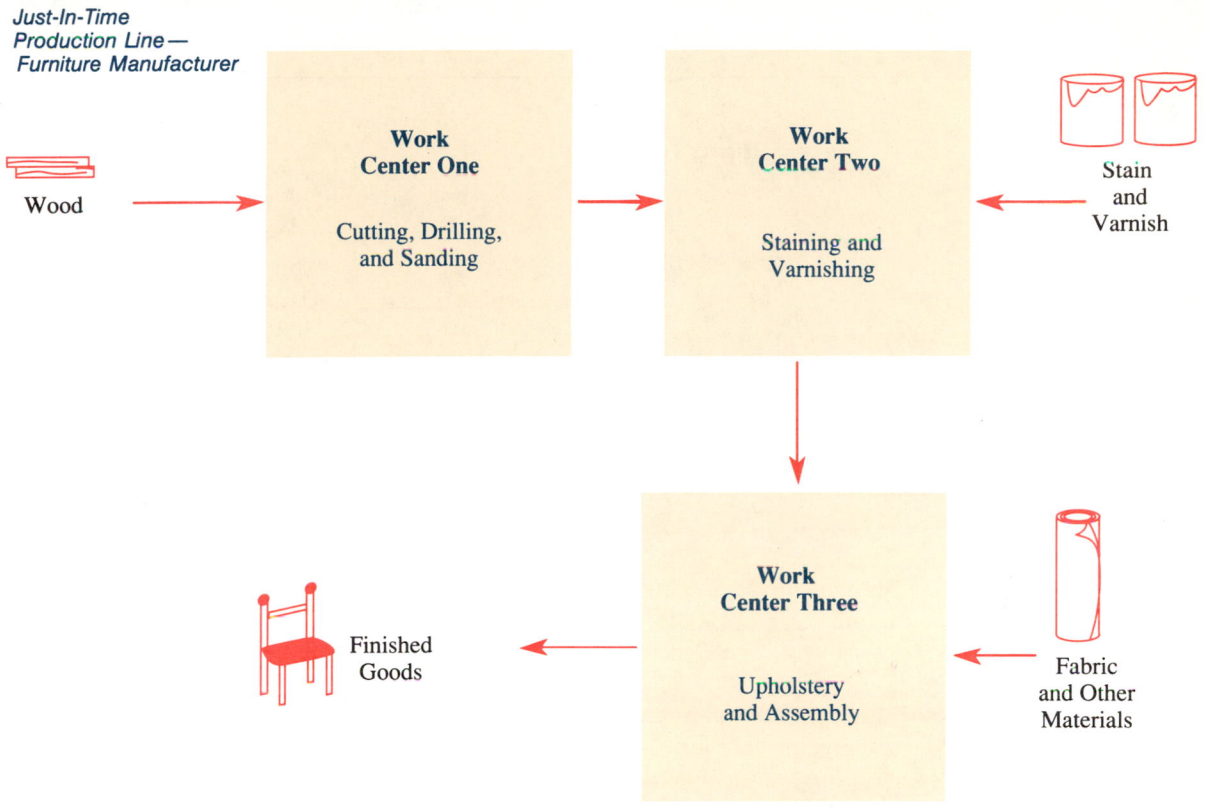

Just-In-Time Production Line — Furniture Manufacturer

In the traditional production line, as described previously, a worker typically performs only one function on a continuous basis. However, in a work center in which several manufacturing functions take place, the workers are often cross-trained to perform more than one function. Research has indicated that workers who perform several manufacturing functions identify better with the end product. This identification creates pride in the products and improves quality and productivity.

The just-in-time reorganization of the manufacturing departments may also result in a reorganization of activities involving services to these departments. Specifically, the service activities may be assigned to individual work centers, rather than to the traditional centralized service departments. For example, each work center may be assigned the responsibility for the repair and maintenance of its machinery and equipment. The acceptance of this responsibility creates an environment in which workers gain a better understanding of the production process and machinery limitations. In turn, workers tend to take better care of the machinery, which decreases repairs and maintenance costs, reduces machine downtime, and improves product quality.

Another trend in just-in-time manufacturing systems is the splitting or "decoupling" of the traditional production process into one or more mini-production lines. For example, the mini-production lines of General Motors were described on pages 870–871. Each mini-production line operates as if it were independent of the other production lines. Thus, the continuous nature of the traditional production line is eliminated, and there is less emphasis on pushing materials into production to keep all departments operating. Examples of a traditional production line and a decoupled, just-in-time manufacturing system are shown in the following diagrams.

Traditional Production System—Continuous Production Line

Just-In-Time Manufacturing System—Decoupled Production Line

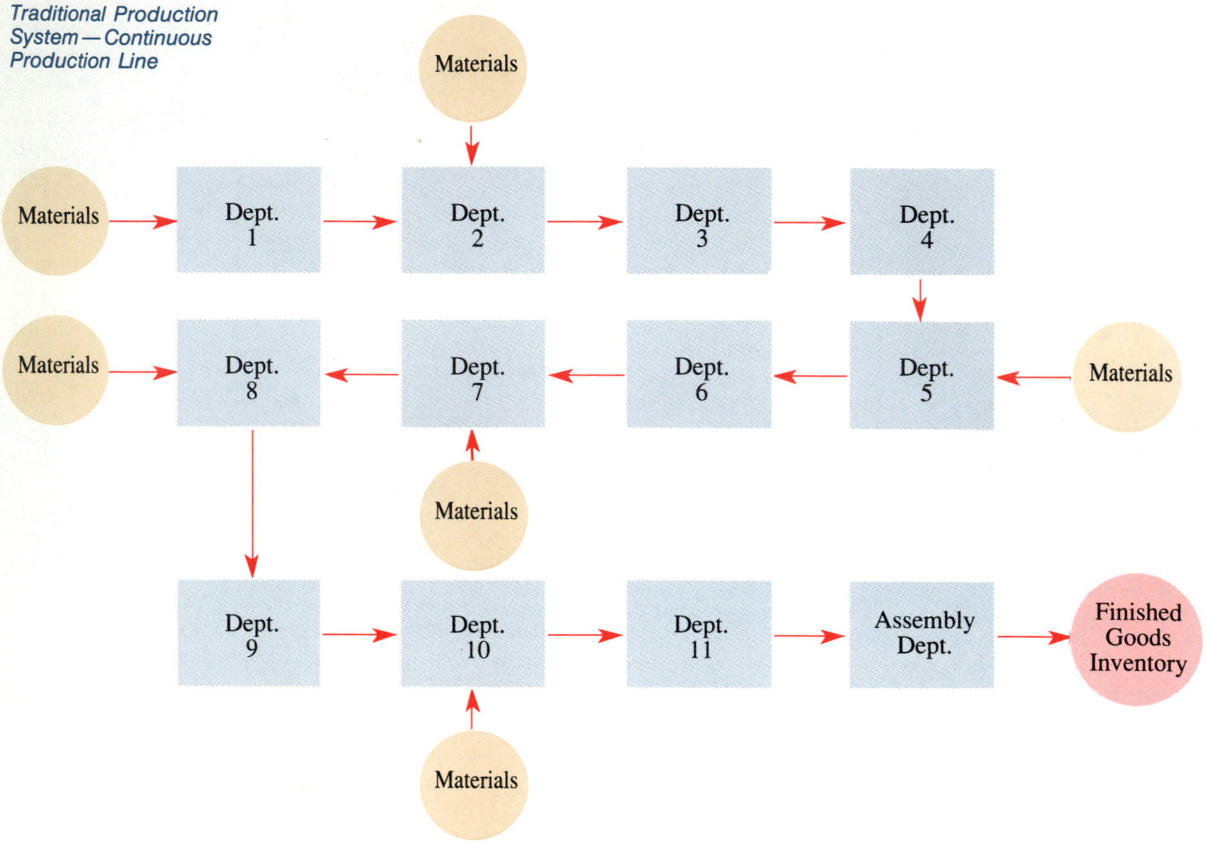

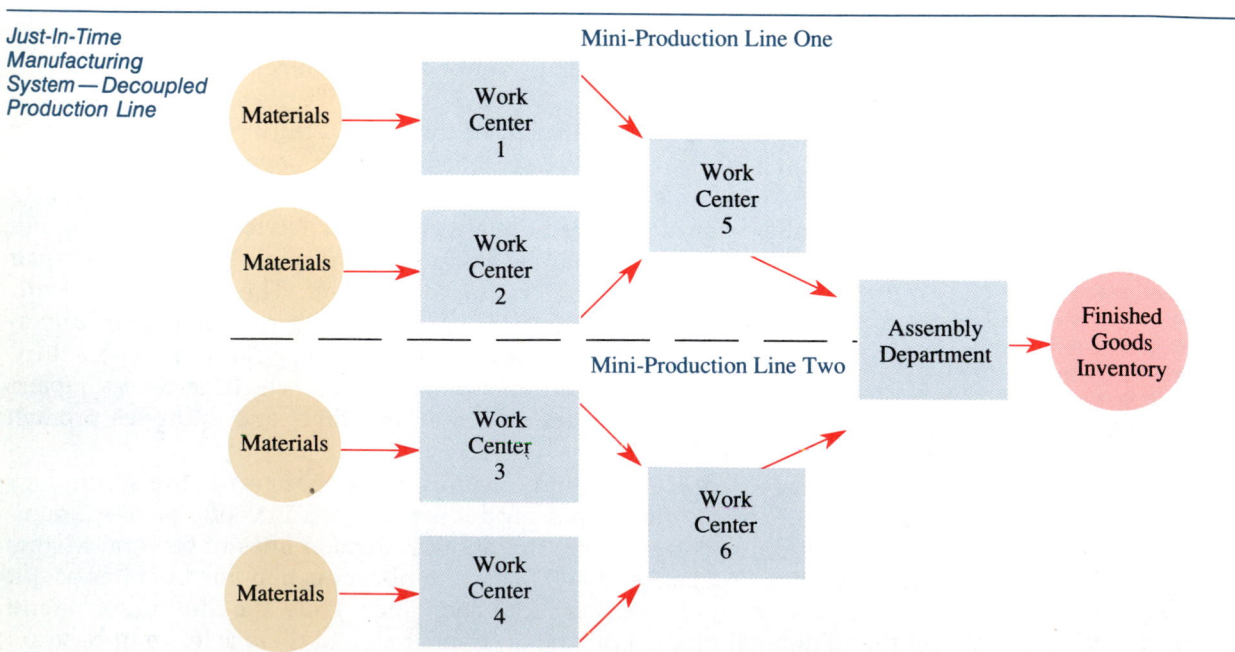

In a just-in-time manufacturing system, handling costs are reduced because the product is not moved as frequently as in a traditional production line. The mini-production line is often set up so that the product is on a movable carrier that is centrally located in the work center. When the workers in each work center have completed their activities with the product, the entire carrier is then moved to the next work center.

Mini-production lines also provide additional flexibility in the manufacturing process. Since each line is viewed as separate from the other lines, a line having a slow period might contract for special jobs outside the company.

The important implications of just-in-time manufacturing systems for managerial accountants are in the areas of cost allocation, cost accumulation, and cost control. When service functions, such as repairs and maintenance, are assigned to individual work centers, the costs of the services are accumulated in each work center, rather than allocated from a service department. As a result, the direct costs for each work center are determined more easily and are more accurate. In turn, cost control by work center and by mini-production line are facilitated.

The reduction of the amount of work in process inventory may make it unnecessary to account for work in process as a separate inventory item. Costs are accumulated in each work center as they enter the manufacturing process, and at the end of the period, these costs are transferred directly to finished goods inventory and to cost of goods sold, without flowing through the work in process account. Any work in process at the end of the period could be reported with the materials as "Materials and In Process Inventory."

AUTOMATION

One of the more visible trends in manufacturing is the increased use of automated machinery to perform routine, repetitive tasks with minimum human involvement in the manufacturing process. Automated machinery can take many forms, including computer-aided machinery and robots.

The use of automated machinery in the manufacturing process is often justified on the basis of labor and material savings. Other factors, however, such as improved quality control and reduced product development time, are often benefits of the use of automated machinery. For example, with the use of robotics, changes in products can be easily introduced into the manufacturing process by reprogramming robots. This ability to add or modify products quickly allows a company to react to changing market preferences and conditions.

The use of automated machinery increases overhead costs through increases in depreciation, maintenance, repairs, property taxes, and insurance. Automation also reduces the amount of direct labor required in the manufacturing process. Twenty-five years ago, for example, direct labor costs frequently accounted for 40% of production costs. With the use of automated machinery, direct labor costs may now represent no more than 5% of production costs. In such an environment, direct labor costs may be charged to overhead rather than accounted for as a separate product cost.[2] As a result, overhead as a percentage of product costs increases.

When a manufacturing process is automated, there is likely to be a greater emphasis on the control of overhead costs through analysis of cost trends. Activity measures may be developed to aid managers in determining

[2]Ford S. Worthy, "Accounting Bores You? Wake Up," *Fortune* (October 12, 1987), p. 44.

the nature of overhead costs for control and allocation purposes. These activity measures, known as **cost drivers,** may include the number of orders received and processed for Receiving Department costs; the number of pounds, gallons, or liters shipped for Shipping Department costs; the number of repairs for Maintenance Department costs; and the number of engineering orders completed for Engineering Department costs. These cost drivers rather than traditional allocation bases, such as direct labor hours, direct labor costs, or units produced, would be used for allocating overhead costs to products.

An example of the results of a cost analysis brought about by automation was a company that found that 23% of its products accounted for 85% of its total sales and all of its profits. The remaining 77% of its products lost money. The cost analysis revealed that the direct-labor-based overhead allocation system was shifting costs from low-volume, special-order products to more profitable high-volume products. The allocation system was thereby disguising the true profitability of the products. The company immediately analyzed its product line and discontinued those products that were losing money.[3]

PRODUCT QUALITY

During the 1950s and 1960s, price was a primary vehicle for competition among manufacturers. During that period, for example, Japanese products were primarily known for their low prices. During the last decade, however, some foreign competitors, such as Japan, have implemented new manufacturing techniques and stringent quality control standards and have supplied world markets with higher quality products at lower prices than those of U.S. manufacturers. As a result, many U.S. manufacturers have been forced to move toward superior product quality as a major manufacturing goal in order to compete effectively.

To improve product quality, U.S. manufacturers have begun to use a Japanese method of organizing workers into **quality circles,** sometimes referred to as **quality control teams**. A quality circle is a group of employees who meet periodically to identify and discuss problems and, when appropriate, to implement solutions to those problems. The use of such quality circles generates greater worker interest and commitment to the manufacturing process and to product quality. The team concept also generates a greater number of suggestions for improving manufacturing processes and cutting costs.

Quality control may be enhanced through the automation of manufacturing processes that allow robots or computer-controlled machinery to monitor the manufacturing process directly. When a weakness or defect in the manufactured product is detected, production is stopped and corrective action is taken.

Managerial accountants aid managers in their efforts to control product quality by analyzing defects and defective rates and by providing timely information on customer complaints, service calls, and warranty expenses. The monitoring of scrap provides managers with information on the quality of materials received from suppliers. In a quality control environment, less emphasis is placed on the price of materials and more emphasis is placed on how the quality of the materials affects the final product.

[3]H. Thomas Johnson and Robert S. Kaplan, *Relevance Lost,* Harvard Business School Press (Boston: 1987).

The managerial accountant also aids managers in the control of the quality of production by preparing and interpreting quality control charts. **Quality control charts,** which may be developed by using statistical methods, show desired operating conditions and limits within which production may vary. Production observations outside these limits require investigation and possible corrective action.

INVENTORY CONTROL

Inventory control has been a major concern for managers for many years. Two modern techniques of inventory control—materials requirements planning and just-in-time inventory systems—are briefly described in the following paragraphs.

Materials Requirements Planning

Materials requirements planning (MRP), also known as **materials resource planning**, is a system developed in the 1970s. An MRP system uses computers to project materials requirements by developing purchasing schedules and manufacturing schedules based on projected demand. Included in the materials projections are allowances for such factors as machine breakdowns, which cause shortages or delays in processing materials. An MRP system is also reviewed and updated for such factors as changes in the product and in customer demand for the product.

The major disadvantages of MRP are that the models used to project materials requirements are often complex, require lengthy periods to develop, and must be used with computers. Therefore, an MRP system is costly. Although these disadvantages are significant, it has been estimated that between 2,000 and 5,000 companies in the United States are using an MRP system.[4] Most of these companies have annual sales exceeding $20 million. Black & Decker, for example, with sales of over $1 billion and nearly 20,000 products, has had remarkable success in using MRP.[5]

In the development of materials requirements planning systems, managerial accountants provide the product cost information necessary for the development of the computer models that are used to minimize materials and inventory costs. For example, the purchase cost of each item of material going into the final product must be estimated, along with handling and storage costs. Managerial accountants must also notify managers of any significant changes in costs, so that the system can be updated.[6]

Just-In-Time Inventory Systems

Just-in-time inventory systems were initially developed by the Japanese, who refer to such systems as **Kanban systems**. The goal of just-in-time inventory systems is to reduce inventories to the lowest possible point. The optimum of just-in-time systems would be to acquire just enough materials to keep the production line moving on a continuous basis. No inventory would ever exist, and no interruptions in the production process would occur because of inventory shortages. The impact of a just-in-time inventory

---

[4]Sumer C. Aggarwal, "MRP, JIT, OPT, FMS?" *Harvard Business Review* (September-October, 1985), p. 8.
[5]*Ibid.,* p. 9.
[6]Billy B. Bowers, "Product Costing in the MRP Environment," *Management Accounting* (December, 1982), pp. 24–27.

system on the profitability of an enterprise can be significant. For example, General Motors has used a just-in-time inventory approach since 1980 and has reduced its annual inventory-related costs from $8 billion to $2 billion.[7]

The implementation of a just-in-time inventory system usually requires major changes in an enterprise's purchasing system. These changes generally involve agreements with suppliers that will assure the receipt of high quality materials and a timely (just-in-time) delivery of the materials. Manufacturers may require suppliers to locate warehouses near production facilities in order to expedite delivery of materials. In some cases, a manufacturer's computer system is connected directly to a supplier's system, so that purchases may be made electronically when production reaches predetermined levels.

Just-in-time inventory systems are normally implemented with just-in-time manufacturing systems. In these cases, the managerial accountant provides input into the selection of suppliers and the design of innovative purchasing systems. Since materials may be shipped directly from suppliers to mini-production lines, where they will immediately enter production, methods are needed to assure the enterprise that proper quantities of materials have been received. Rather than delaying production by counting materials at the point of receipt, emphasis is likely to be placed on an analysis of the output of the manufacturing process and a reconciliation of the output quantities with the invoices received from the suppliers.

With just-in-time inventory and manufacturing systems emphasis is placed on the timely delivery of materials. Long-term supplier-manufacturer relationships are negotiated with an emphasis on the timely delivery of quality materials rather than the lowest possible price. As inventories are reduced, relevant product costs become more significant for managerial decision making in such areas as product pricing, cost control, and discontinuance of unprofitable products. The emphasis also changes in performance evaluations, where more nonfinancial measures are used, such as the time to produce a product from start to finish, or **throughput time**, the quantity of scrap generated, and numbers of service calls.

INFORMATION TECHNOLOGY

The use of advanced computer information technology in the manufacturing process allows managers to maintain real-time contact with the manufacturing process. With this information, managers can monitor and control operations on a minute-by-minute basis. This continuous monitoring of inputs and outputs of the manufacturing process increases production efficiency and product quality. For example, production supervisors can monitor the amount of scrap that is being generated at each stage of production and can take any corrective action that might be necessary on a timely basis. In contrast, in a traditional manufacturing system, managers often receive weekly or monthly scrap reports.

A primary concern of managerial accountants is providing managers with accurate and timely information on which to base decisions. Managerial accountants may need to become directly involved in the development and implementation of the advanced computer systems that are integrated with the manufacturing process. The challenge to managerial accountants is

[7]David Whiteside and Jules Arbose, "Unsnarling Industrial Production: Why Top Management Is Starting to Care?" *International Management* (March, 1984), p. 20.

to develop innovative methods for providing information, so that managers are not overwhelmed by the amount of data, but are able to identify the essential information for decision-making purposes.

DESIGNING THE FACTORY FLOOR

Computer simulations can be used to design manufacturing operations to maximize efficiency and productivity. The following excerpts were taken from an article in *Business Week* that described how these simulations are used.

You pass by the factory manager's office, and what do you see? He and his top engineers are huddled around a computer screen where cute little symbols are threading their way through mazes. Are these well-paid professionals playing video games on company time?

Look again: The screen display is a recreation of the factory floor, replete with machine tools, robots, flexible manufacturing cells, and materials-handling vehicles. The goal of this game is to exploit those resources in the most efficient way and turn out the highest-quality, lowest-cost product. Welcome to the era of manufacturing simulation.

While the exercise may have make-believe overtones, the payoff can be real. That's what the engineers at Northern Research & Engineering Corp., a consulting subsidiary of Ingersoll-Rand Co., learned when they designed a complicated line for making ball bearings. They figured they would need 77 machine tools performing 16 different processes. But when they fed the information into a computer and simulated the line in operation, they quickly realized the plan could be improved. They were able to [save] $750,000 for their client, Torrington Co. With computer simulation, says Northern Research senior engineer James M. Hanson, savings of several million dollars are "not unusual...."

Source: William G. Wild, Jr. and Otis Port, "This Video 'Game' Is Saving Manufacturers Millions," *Business Week* (August 17, 1987), pp. 82 and 84.

DISCUSSION QUESTIONS

1. How has the United States economy responded in recent years to competitive pressures from world-wide producers of goods?

2. What term is sometimes used to refer to just-in-time manufacturing systems?

3. Describe the differences in worker assignments for a traditional production line and a just-in-time manufacturing system.

4. What term is used to describe the combined processing functions in a just-in-time manufacturing system?

5. In a just-in-time manufacturing system, what is the primary advantage of assigning repair and maintenance responsibilities directly to individual work centers?

6. For managerial accountants, what are two implications of just-in-time manufacturing systems?

7. What is a primary characteristic of automated machinery?

8. What term is used to refer to an activity measure used to allocate overhead costs for cost control and allocation purposes?

9. In allocating overhead costs for an engineering department to individual production departments, what would be a good cost driver?

10. During the 1950s and 1960s, what was the primary vehicle for competition among manufacturers?

11. What are some of the benefits of using quality circles to improve product quality?

12. The managerial accountant can aid managers in controlling the quality of production through the preparation and interpretation of what type of chart?

13. What term is given to inventory systems that use computers to project materials requirements and then develop purchase schedules and manufacturing schedules?

14. What is the ultimate goal of just-in-time inventory systems?

15. Why does the implementation of a just-in-time inventory system usually require major changes in an enterprise's purchasing system?

16. How can a managerial accountant aid in the implementation of a just-in-time inventory system?

17. What are some nonfinancial indicators of product quality?

18. What is a primary managerial accounting concern with respect to advanced computer information technology?

Real World Focus

19. The bar codes designed to speed groceries through checkout lanes are now being applied to manufacturing assembly lines. For example, North American automobile makers now require the use of bar codes by virtually all their suppliers. Why would manufacturers insist on the use of bar codes by their suppliers?

MANUFACTURING WORK SHEET

Many accountants use a work sheet to assist them in the preparation of financial statements. The use of a work sheet for a merchandising enterprise was illustrated in Chapter 4. In a like manner, a work sheet may be used for a manufacturing enterprise. Such a work sheet was not illustrated in Chapter 21, so that the discussion could focus on the basic concepts applicable to accounting for manufacturing operations.

The following sections describe and illustrate the use of a work sheet for manufacturing operations. The illustration is based on the presentation of a general accounting system, which is described on pages 832–834.

WORK SHEET PROCEDURES

The work sheet used in preparing financial statements for a merchandising business is expanded for manufacturing enterprises using periodic inventory procedures by adding a pair of columns for the statement of cost of goods manufactured, as shown on page H–2. All items that enter into the determination of the cost of goods manufactured are extended to these two columns. After all these data have been extended, the two cost of goods manufactured columns should be totaled and the difference determined. This difference, which is labeled "Cost of Goods Manufactured" in the account title column, is transferred to the income statement columns by entries in the statement of cost of goods manufactured credit column and the income statement debit column. The remainder of the work sheet is completed in the same manner as is followed for a merchandising business.

To illustrate the use of a work sheet for a manufacturing enterprise, data are taken from the accounts and records of Burleson Manufacturing Company, which uses periodic inventory procedures. The unadjusted trial balance at the end of 1990 is reported in the first two columns of the work sheet presented on page H–2. The data needed for year-end adjustments on December 31, 1990, are summarized as follows:

Inventories on December 31, 1990:	
Finished goods	$91,000
Work in process	65,800
Direct materials	58,725
Factory supplies	1,800
Depreciation for the year:	
Factory buildings	6,000
Factory equipment	22,300
Accruals on December 31, 1990:	
Wages and salaries:	
Direct labor	4,500
Indirect labor	950

Adjusting Entries

The adjusting entries are recorded on the work sheet in the usual manner illustrated in the merchandising enterprise chapters, except for inventories of work in process and direct materials. Each of the adjusting entries pertaining to the inventories of finished goods, work in process, and direct materials is briefly described in the following paragraphs.

Burleson Manufacturing Company
Work Sheet
For Year Ended December 31, 1990

ACCOUNT TITLE	TRIAL BALANCE DEBIT	TRIAL BALANCE CREDIT	ADJUSTMENTS DEBIT	ADJUSTMENTS CREDIT	STATEMENT OF COST OF GOODS MANUFACTURED DEBIT	STATEMENT OF COST OF GOODS MANUFACTURED CREDIT	INCOME STATEMENT DEBIT	INCOME STATEMENT CREDIT	BALANCE SHEET DEBIT	BALANCE SHEET CREDIT
Cash	18,200								18,200	
Accounts Receivable	66,100								66,100	
Allowance for Doubtful Accounts		1,500								1,500
Finished Goods	78,500		(b) 91,000	(a) 78,500					91,000	
Work in Process	55,000		(d) 65,800	(c) 55,000					65,800	
Direct Materials	62,000		(f) 58,725	(e) 62,000					58,725	
Factory Supplies	4,700			(g) 2,900					1,800	
Prepaid Insurance	1,250								1,250	
Land	50,000								50,000	
Factory Buildings	240,000								240,000	
Accumulated Depreciation — Factory Buildings		30,000		(h) 6,000						36,000
Factory Equipment	446,000								446,000	
Accumulated Depreciation — Factory Equipment		111,500		(i) 22,300						133,800
Accounts Payable		45,600								45,600
Wages and Salaries Payable				(j) 5,450						5,450
Income Tax Payable		13,200								13,200
Common Stock ($10 par)		200,000								200,000
Retained Earnings		537,325								537,325
Dividends	40,000								40,000	
Income Summary			(a) 78,500	(b) 91,000			78,500	91,000		
Manufacturing Summary			(c) 55,000; (e) 62,000	(d) 65,800; (f) 58,725	55,000; 62,000	65,800; 58,725				
Sales		915,800						915,800		
Direct Materials Purchases	220,800				220,800					
Direct Labor	214,250		(j) 4,500		218,750					
Indirect Factory Labor	48,350		(j) 950		49,300					
Depreciation — Factory Equipment			(i) 22,300		22,300					
Factory Heat, Light, and Power	21,800				21,800					
Factory Property Taxes	9,750				9,750					
Depreciation — Factory Buildings			(h) 6,000		6,000					
Insurance Expense — Factory	4,750				4,750					
Factory Supplies Expense			(g) 2,900		2,900					
Miscellaneous Factory Expense	2,050				2,050					
Selling Expenses	130,500						130,500			
Administrative Expenses	88,700						88,700			
Income Tax	52,225						52,225			
	1,854,925	1,854,925	447,675	447,675	675,400	124,525	550,875		900,800	1,078,875	972,875
Cost of Goods Manufactured					675,400	550,875	550,875			
						675,400	900,800	1,006,800	1,078,875	972,875
Net Income							106,000			106,000
							1,006,800	1,006,800	1,078,875	1,078,875

The finished goods inventory account is adjusted through the income summary account in the same manner as the merchandise inventory of a merchandising enterprise. The beginning finished goods inventory is transferred to the income summary account by crediting Finished Goods and debiting Income Summary for $78,500 (entry (a) on the work sheet). The ending finished goods inventory is recorded by debiting Finished Goods and crediting Income Summary for $91,000 (entry (b) on the work sheet).

As explained in Chapter 21, the work in process inventory account is adjusted through Manufacturing Summary. The inventory of work in process at the beginning of the period is transferred to the manufacturing summary account by crediting Work in Process and by debiting Manufacturing Summary for $55,000 (entry (c) on the work sheet). The ending work in process inventory is recorded by debiting Work in Process and by crediting Manufacturing Summary for $65,800 (entry (d) on the work sheet).

Like the work in process inventory, the direct materials inventory at the beginning of the fiscal period is transferred to the manufacturing summary account by crediting Direct Materials and by debiting Manufacturing Summary for $62,000 (entry (e) on the work sheet). The direct materials inventory at the end of the period is recorded by debiting Direct Materials and crediting Manufacturing Summary for $58,725 (entry (f) on the work sheet).

Completing the Work Sheet

After all the adjustments have been entered on the work sheet, each account balance, as adjusted, is then extended to the appropriate column. In this illustration, the adjusted trial balance columns which appear in the work sheets illustrated in Chapters 3, 4, and 5 have been eliminated. Experienced accountants often omit these columns in order to save time in preparing the work sheet. Under this approach, the adjusted account balances are entered directly into the proper financial statement columns. The temporary accounts that appear in the statement of cost of goods manufactured are extended to the statement of cost of goods manufactured columns. The other accounts are extended to the income statement and balance sheet columns in the usual manner. Note that the beginning and ending inventory amounts appearing opposite Income Summary and Manufacturing Summary in the adjustments column are extended individually rather than as the net figure, since both amounts will be used in preparing the statements.

After all of the amounts have been extended to the appropriate columns, the work sheet is completed in the following manner:

1. The statement of cost of goods manufactured columns are totaled. In the illustration, the total of the Dr. column is $675,400 and the total of the Cr. column is $124,525.
2. The amount of the difference between the two statement of cost of goods manufactured columns is determined and entered in the statement of cost of goods manufactured Cr. column and the income statement Dr. column. This amount ($550,875 in the illustration) is the cost of goods manufactured for the period.
3. The totals of the columns are entered. The statement of cost of goods manufactured columns should now be in balance.
4. The amount of net income is determined and is recorded in the income statement Dr. column and in the balance sheet Cr. column.
5. The totals of the last four columns, which should now be in balance, are entered.

Financial Statements

The completed work sheet provides the information necessary for preparing the financial statements. For Burleson Manufacturing Company, the income statement, statement of cost of goods manufactured, retained earnings statement, and balance sheet are shown below and on page H-5.

Income Statement

Burleson Manufacturing Company
Income Statement
For Year Ended December 31, 1990

Sales		$915,800
Cost of goods sold:		
Finished goods inventory, January 1, 1990	$ 78,500	
Cost of goods manufactured	550,875	
Cost of finished goods available for sale	$629,375	
Less finished goods inventory, December 31, 1990	91,000	
Cost of goods sold		538,375
Gross profit		$377,425
Operating expenses:		
Selling expenses	$130,500	
Administrative expenses	88,700	
Total operating expenses		219,200
Income before income tax		$158,225
Income tax		52,225
Net income (per share, $5.30)		$106,000

Statement of Cost of Goods Manufactured

Burleson Manufacturing Company
Statement of Cost of Goods Manufactured
For Year Ended December 31, 1990

Work in process inventory, January 1, 1990			$ 55,000
Direct materials:			
Inventory, January 1, 1990		$ 62,000	
Purchases		220,800	
Cost of materials available for use		$282,800	
Less inventory, December 31, 1990		58,725	
Cost of materials placed in production		$224,075	
Direct labor		218,750	
Factory overhead:			
Indirect labor	$49,300		
Depreciation of factory equipment	22,300		
Heat, light, and power	21,800		
Property taxes	9,750		
Depreciation on buildings	6,000		
Insurance expired	4,750		
Factory supplies used	2,900		
Miscellaneous factory costs	2,050		
Total factory overhead		118,850	
Total manufacturing costs			561,675
Total work in process during period			$616,675
Less work in process inventory, December 31, 1990			65,800
Cost of goods manufactured			$550,875

Retained Earnings
Statement

Burleson Manufacturing Company
Retained Earnings Statement
For Year Ended December 31, 1990

Retained earnings, January 1, 1990		$537,325
Net income for year...	$106,000	
Less dividends..	40,000	
Increase in retained earnings		66,000
Retained earnings, December 31, 1990.....................		$603,325

Balance Sheet

Burleson Manufacturing Company
Balance Sheet
December 31, 1990

Assets

Current assets:			
Cash...		$ 18,200	
Accounts receivable............................	$ 66,100		
Less allowance for doubtful accounts..	1,500	64,600	
Inventories:			
Finished goods	$ 91,000		
Work in process.............................	65,800		
Direct materials..............................	58,725	215,525	
Factory supplies.................................		1,800	
Prepaid insurance		1,250	
Total current assets			$301,375
Plant assets:			
Land...		$ 50,000	
Buildings	$240,000		
Less accumulated depreciation..........	36,000	204,000	
Factory equipment..............................	$446,000		
Less accumulated depreciation..........	133,800	312,200	
Total plant assets............................			566,200
Total assets			$867,575

Liabilities

Current liabilities:		
Accounts payable..............................	$ 45,600	
Wages and salaries payable	5,450	
Income tax payable	13,200	
Total current liabilities		$ 64,250

Stockholders' Equity

Common stock, $10 par	$200,000	
Retained earnings................................	603,325	
Total stockholders' equity.......................		803,325
Total liabilities and stockholders' equity		$867,575

ADJUSTING ENTRIES

    At the end of the accounting period, the adjusting entries appearing in the work sheet are recorded in the journal and posted to the ledger, bringing the ledger into agreement with the data reported in the financial statements. The adjusting entries for Burleson Manufacturing Company are as follows:

Adjusting Entries

(a)	Income Summary	78,500	
	Finished Goods		78,500
(b)	Finished Goods	91,000	
	Income Summary		91,000
(c)	Manufacturing Summary	55,000	
	Work in Process		55,000
(d)	Work in Process	65,800	
	Manufacturing Summary		65,800
(e)	Manufacturing Summary	62,000	
	Direct Materials		62,000
(f)	Direct Materials	58,725	
	Manufacturing Summary		58,725
(g)	Factory Supplies Expense	2,900	
	Factory Supplies		2,900
(h)	Depreciation — Factory Buildings	6,000	
	Accumulated Depreciation — Factory Buildings.		6,000
(i)	Depreciation — Factory Equipment	22,300	
	Accumulated Depreciation — Factory Equipment		22,300
(j)	Direct Labor	4,500	
	Indirect Factory Labor	950	
	Wages and Salaries Payable		5,450

CLOSING ENTRIES

The closing entries are recorded in the journal immediately following the adjusting entries, as follows:

Closing Entries

Manufacturing Summary	558,400	
Direct Materials Purchases		220,800
Direct Labor		218,750
Indirect Factory Labor		49,300
Depreciation — Factory Equipment		22,300
Factory Heat, Light, and Power		21,800
Factory Property Taxes		9,750
Depreciation — Factory Buildings		6,000
Insurance Expense — Factory		4,750
Factory Supplies Expense		2,900
Miscellaneous Factory Expense		2,050
Sales	915,800	
Income Summary		915,800

Income Summary	822,300	
Selling Expenses		130,500
Administrative Expenses		88,700
Income Tax		52,225
Manufacturing Summary		550,875
Income Summary	106,000	
Retained Earnings		106,000
Retained Earnings	40,000	
Dividends		40,000

The manufacturing accounts are closed to Manufacturing Summary. The revenue account, Sales, is closed to Income Summary. The expense accounts, including the balance in Manufacturing Summary ($550,875, which represents the cost of goods manufactured), are also closed to Income Summary. The final steps in the closing process are to close the balances in Income Summary (representing the net income) and Dividends to Retained Earnings.

PROBLEMS

Problem H–1
Manufacturing work sheet and financial statements.

The accounts in the ledger of Rex Manufacturing Inc., with unadjusted balances on December 31, the end of the current year, are as follows:

Cash	25,600
Accounts Receivable	47,450
Allowance for Doubtful Accounts	220
Finished Goods	61,500
Work in Process	28,750
Direct Materials	40,200
Prepaid Expenses (Controlling)	8,000
Land	67,450
Factory Buildings	360,000
Accumulated Depreciation — Factory Buildings	90,000
Factory Equipment	275,000
Accumulated Depreciation — Factory Equipment	112,350
Office Equipment	30,000
Accumulated Depreciation — Office Equipment	10,000
Accounts Payable	52,320
Income Tax Payable	—
Wages Payable	—
Common Stock ($10 par)	500,000
Retained Earnings	74,160
Dividends	20,000
Income Summary	—
Manufacturing Summary	—
Sales	710,300
Direct Materials Purchases	212,000
Direct Labor	81,730
Factory Overhead (Controlling)	154,170
Selling Expenses (Controlling)	72,000
Administrative Expenses (Controlling)	48,000
Interest Income	5,000
Income Tax	22,500

The data needed for the year-end adjustments on December 31 are as follows:

Inventories on December 31:		
Finished goods..	$58,000	
Work in process...	29,100	
Direct materials	43,580	$130,680
Income tax owed at December 31		7,500
Doubtful accounts at December 31 from analysis of		
accounts receivable		1,150
Prepaid insurance expired during year:		
Factory overhead..	$ 3,500	
Administrative expenses......................................	700	4,200
Accrued wages at December 31:		
Direct labor...	$ 1,800	
Indirect labor..	900	2,700
Depreciation expense for year:		
Factory building...	$ 8,000	
Factory equipment	16,700	
Office equipment	2,600	27,300

Instructions:

(1) Prepare a manufacturing work sheet. (Leave one extra line after Manufacturing Summary and two extra lines after Factory Overhead and Administrative Expenses for use in recording the adjusting entries.)
(2) Prepare a statement of cost of goods manufactured.
(3) Prepare an income statement.
(4) Prepare a retained earnings statement.
(5) Prepare a balance sheet.

Problem H–2
Manufacturing financial statements.

The chief accountant for Abbey Co. prepared the manufacturing work sheet shown on page H-9 for the current year.

Instructions:

(1) Prepare a statement of cost of goods manufactured.
(2) Prepare an income statement.
(3) Prepare a retained earnings statement.
(4) Prepare a balance sheet.

Problem H–3
Adjusting and closing entries.

The work sheet for Abbey Co. for the current year is presented on page H–9.

Instructions:

(1) Prepare the journal entries to adjust the accounts at the end of the year.
(2) Prepare the journal entries to close the appropriate accounts at the end of the year.

Abbey Co.
Work Sheet
For Year Ended May 31, 19--

ACCOUNT TITLE	TRIAL BALANCE DEBIT	TRIAL BALANCE CREDIT	ADJUSTMENTS DEBIT	ADJUSTMENTS CREDIT	STATEMENT OF COST OF GOODS MANUFACTURED DEBIT	STATEMENT OF COST OF GOODS MANUFACTURED CREDIT	INCOME STATEMENT DEBIT	INCOME STATEMENT CREDIT	BALANCE SHEET DEBIT	BALANCE SHEET CREDIT
Cash	20,450								20,450	
Accounts Receivable	75,500								75,500	
Allowance for Doubtful Accounts		1,800								1,800
Finished Goods	92,000		(b) 94,500	(a) 92,000					94,500	
Work in Process	70,000		(d) 67,000	(c) 70,000					67,000	
Direct Materials	61,200		(f) 59,700	(e) 61,200					59,700	
Prepaid Insurance	8,700			(g) 5,900					2,800	
Factory Supplies	7,900			(h) 5,250					2,650	
Land	75,000								75,000	
Factory Buildings	335,000								335,000	
Accumulated Depreciation—Factory Buildings		170,000		(i) 16,000						186,000
Factory Equipment	450,000								450,000	
Accumulated Depreciation—Factory Equipment		211,500		(j) 22,300						233,800
Accounts Payable		55,900								55,900
Wages Payable				(k) 4,550						4,550
Income Tax Payable		8,200								8,200
Common Stock ($10 par)		221,000								221,000
Retained Earnings		431,100								431,100
Dividends	15,000								15,000	
Income Summary			(a) 92,000	(b) 94,500			92,000	94,500		
Manufacturing Summary			(c) 70,000 (e) 61,200	(d) 67,000 (f) 59,700	70,000 61,200	67,000 59,700				
Sales		785,500						785,500		
Direct Materials Purchases	184,800				184,800					
Direct Labor	160,000		(k) 3,800		163,800					
Indirect Factory Labor	82,500		(k) 750		83,250					
Depreciation—Factory Equipment			(j) 22,300		22,300					
Factory Heat, Light, and Power	31,800				31,800					
Factory Property Taxes	12,750				12,750					
Depreciation—Factory Buildings			(i) 16,000		16,000					
Insurance Expense—Factory			(g) 5,900		5,900					
Factory Supplies Expense			(h) 5,250		5,250					
Miscellaneous Factory Expense	3,400				3,400					
Selling Expenses	100,500						100,500			
Administrative Expenses	78,500						78,500			
Income Tax	20,000						20,000			
	1,885,000	1,885,000	498,400	498,400	660,450	126,700				
Cost of Goods Manufactured						533,750	533,750			
					660,450	660,450	824,750	880,000	1,197,600	1,142,350
Net Income							55,250			55,250
							880,000	880,000	1,197,600	1,197,600

Problem H–4
Statement of
cost of goods
manufactured;
adjusting entries and
closing entries.

The following accounts related to manufacturing operations were selected from the pre-closing trial balance of Presley Co. at March 31, the end of the current fiscal year:

Depreciation of Factory Buildings	$ 30,000
Depreciation of Factory Equipment	115,700
Direct Labor	320,150
Direct Materials Inventory	55,000
Direct Materials Purchases	410,800
Factory Supplies Expense	12,300
Finished Goods Inventory	115,000
Heat, Light, and Power Expense	33,900
Indirect Labor	61,400
Insurance Expense	18,000
Miscellaneous Factory Costs	7,600
Property Taxes Expense	25,000
Work in Process Inventory	72,900

Inventories at March 31 were as follows:

Finished Goods	$127,200
Work in Process	81,100
Direct Materials	62,750

Instructions:

(1) Prepare a statement of cost of goods manufactured.
(2) Prepare journal entries to adjust the work in process and direct materials inventories.
(3) Prepare journal entries to close the appropriate accounts to Manufacturing Summary.
(4) Prepare the journal entry to close Manufacturing Summary.

SPECIMEN FINANCIAL STATEMENTS

This appendix contains selected statements and notes for real companies.

Pages I-6 through I-16 contain the complete financial statements for Minnesota Mining and Manufacturing Company.

Consolidated Statements of Income

Tandy Corporation and Subsidiaries

In thousands, except per share amounts.
Restated for consolidation of credit and insurance subsidiaries.

	1988 Dollars	% of Revenues
Net sales and operating revenues	$3,793,767	100.0%
Cost of products sold	1,870,429	49.3
Gross profit	1,923,338	50.7
Expenses:		
Selling, general and administrative	1,341,090	35.3
Depreciation and amortization	68,156	1.8
Interest expense, net of interest income and interest allocated to operations spun off	(588)	—
	1,408,658	37.1
Income before income taxes and equity in operations spun off	514,680	13.6
Provision for income taxes	198,326	5.3
Net income	$ 316,354	8.3%
Net income per average common share	$3.54	
Average common shares outstanding	89,466	

Consolidated Balance Sheets

Coca-Cola Enterprises Inc.

(In thousands except share data)	**December 30, 1988**	January 1, 1988

Assets

Current

Cash and cash equivalents, at cost (approximates market)	$ **162**	$ 11,297
Trade accounts receivable, less allowances of $8,766 in 1988 and $6,140 in 1987	**293,890**	262,508
Inventories	**124,852**	117,724
Prepaid expenses and other assets	**69,558**	60,462
Total Current Assets	**488,462**	451,991
Investments and Other Long-Term Assets	**65,674**	68,949

Property, Plant and Equipment

Land	**135,293**	124,831
Buildings and improvements	**436,322**	365,607
Machinery and equipment	**1,124,981**	943,917
Containers	**41,374**	63,044
	1,737,970	1,497,399
Less allowances for depreciation	**558,233**	459,265
	1,179,737	1,038,134
Goodwill and Other Intangible Assets	**2,935,334**	2,690,950
	$4,669,207	$4,250,024

	December 30, 1988	January 1, 1988

Liabilities and Shareholders' Equity

Current

Accounts payable and accrued expenses	$ 399,777	$ 376,448
Accounts payable to The Coca-Cola Company	1,849	31,475
Current maturities of long-term debt	148,495	66,091
Total Current Liabilities	550,121	474,014
Long-Term Debt	2,062,022	2,091,089
Deferred Income Taxes	221,543	152,992
Other Long-Term Obligations	27,144	5,782

Shareholders' Equity

Preferred stock, $1 par value		
Authorized – 100,000,000 shares;		
Issued and outstanding – 2,500 shares,		
at aggregate liquidation preference	250,000	–
Common stock, $1 par value		
Authorized – 500,000,000 shares;		
Issued – 140,260,000 shares	140,260	140,260
Paid-in capital	1,260,814	1,264,965
Reinvested earnings	264,394	127,513
Common stock in treasury, at cost		
(7,378,835 shares at December 30, 1988		
and 471,800 shares at January 1, 1988)	(107,091)	(6,591)
	1,808,377	1,526,147
	$4,669,207	$4,250,024

Statements of Consolidated Cash Flows

(In thousands)			Fiscal Year Ended
	January 31 1988	February 1 1987	February 2 1986
CASH FLOWS FROM OPERATING ACTIVITIES			
Net income	$203,922	$152,217	$119,774
Adjustments to reconcile net income to net cash provided by operating activities:			
Depreciation and amortization	43,716	33,288	26,074
Deferred taxes	13,035	14,184	9,669
Change in operating assets and liabilities:			
Accounts and other receivables	(24,642)	(11,531)	(2,564)
Merchandise inventories	(243,894)	(115,446)	(15,580)
Prepaid expenses	(1,484)	(320)	(1,215)
Accounts payable, accrued expenses and taxes	144,364	102,382	(153)
Total adjustments	(68,905)	22,557	16,231
Net cash provided by operating activities	135,017	174,774	136,005
CASH FLOWS FROM INVESTING ACTIVITIES			
Capital expenditures-net	(314,827)	(259,388)	(221,794)
Other net	13,792	10,952	11,053
Net cash used in investing activities	(301,035)	(248,436)	(210,741)
CASH FLOWS FROM FINANCING ACTIVITIES			
Short-term borrowings-net	17,663	(1,136)	(19,118)
Long-term borrowings	96,611	—	2,493
Long-term debt repayments	(1,860)	(2,027)	(3,819)
Exercise of stock options	15,221	25,033	16,072
Net cash provided by financing activities	127,635	21,870	(4,372)
CASH AND SHORT-TERM INVESTMENTS			
Decrease during year	(38,383)	(51,792)	(79,108)
Beginning of year	84,379	136,171	215,279
End of year	$ 45,996	$ 84,379	$136,171

SUPPLEMENTAL DISCLOSURES OF CASH FLOW INFORMATION

The Company considers all highly liquid investments purchased as part of its daily cash management activities to be short-term investments.

During the years ended January 31, 1988, February 1, 1987 and February 2, 1986, the Company made income tax payments of $119,722,000, $79,934,000 and $70,205,000 and interest payments (net of amounts capitalized) of $9,610,000, $8,044,000 and $6,857,000 respectively.

Consolidated Balance Sheet
Chrysler Corporation and Consolidated Subsidiaries

Assets

	December 31	
	1988	**1987**
	(In millions of dollars)	
Cash and cash equivalents	$ 1,643.8	$ 1,702.1
Marketable securities	1,612.2	878.5
Finance and accounts receivables (Note 2)	27,689.0	24,426.1
Inventories (Note 3)	2,971.4	2,552.1
Property and equipment (Note 4)	6,687.1	6,306.5
Special tools	2,465.2	2,462.8
Intangible assets (Note 5)	2,687.8	2,296.0
Other assets (Note 6)	2,810.3	2,134.6
Total Assets	$ 48,566.8	$ 42,758.7

Liabilities and Shareholders' Equity

	1988	1987
Liabilities:		
Short-term debt (Note 7)	$ 10,511.2	$ 8,978.4
Accounts payable and accrued liabilities (Note 8)	9,139.1	7,996.2
Long-term debt (Note 9)	16,635.6	15,494.6
Other liabilities	2,463.9	1,810.6
Deferred income taxes (Note 10)	1,934.7	1,676.0
Commitments and contingent liabilities (Note 11)	—	—
Minority interest in consolidated subsidiary (Note 13)	300.0	300.0
Shareholders' Equity (Note 14): *(Shares in millions)*		
Preferred stock — $1 per share par value; authorized 20.0 shares; $2.375 cumulative convertible preferred stock issued: 1988 — 0.3 shares; 1987 — 0.3 shares	0.3	0.3
Common stock — $1 per share par value; authorized 500.0 shares; issued: 1988 — 244.6 shares; 1987 — 244.7 shares	244.6	244.7
Additional paid-in capital	2,376.3	2,374.3
Retained earnings	5,357.6	4,581.3
Treasury stock — common stock; at cost: 1988 — 11.5 shares; 1987 — 23.4 shares	(396.5)	(697.7)
Total Shareholders' Equity	7,582.3	6,502.9
Total Liabilities and Shareholders' Equity	$ 48,566.8	$ 42,758.7

Statement of Income

Minnesota Mining and Manufacturing Company and Consolidated Subsidiaries for the Years Ended December 31, 1988, 1987 and 1986

(Amounts in millions, except per share data)	1988	1987	1986
Net Sales	**$10,581**	$9,429	$8,602
Operating Expenses			
Cost of goods sold	**6,105**	5,513	5,074
Selling, general and administrative expenses	**2,593**	2,338	2,118
Total	**8,698**	7,851	7,192
Operating Income	**1,883**	1,578	1,410
Other Income and Expense			
Interest expense	**95**	95	106
Investment and other income-net	**(94)**	(82)	(44)
Total		13	62
Income Before Income Taxes	**1,882**	1,565	1,348
Provision for Income Taxes	**728**	647	569
Net Income	**$ 1,154**	$ 918	$ 779
Average Number of Shares Outstanding	**226.9**	228.6	229.3
Earnings Per Share	**$ 5.09**	$ 4.02	$ 3.40

Balance Sheet

Minnesota Mining
and Manufacturing
Company and
Consolidated
Subsidiaries as of
December 31, 1988
and 1987

(Dollars in millions)	1988	1987
ASSETS		
Current Assets		
Cash and cash equivalents	$ 522	$ 432
Other securities	375	274
Accounts receivable – net	1,727	1,615
Inventories	1,831	1,770
Other current assets	286	252
Total current assets	4,741	4,343
Investments	720	586
Property, Plant and Equipment – net	3,073	2,932
Other Assets	388	365
Total	$8,922	$8,226

	1988	1987
LIABILITIES AND STOCKHOLDERS' EQUITY		
Current Liabilities		
Accounts payable	$ 572	$ 586
Payrolls	295	284
Income taxes	299	277
Short-term debt	347	264
Other current liabilities	858	693
Total current liabilities	2,371	2,104
Deferred Income Taxes	264	312
Other Liabilities	367	315
Long-Term Debt	406	435
Stockholders' Equity – net	5,514	5,060
Shares outstanding – 1988: 224,332,865; 1987: 227,492,769		
Total	$8,922	$8,226

Statement of Cash Flows

Minnesota Mining and Manufacturing Company and Consolidated Subsidiaries for the Years Ended December 31, 1988, 1987 and 1986

(Dollars in millions)	1988	1987	1986
Cash Flows from Operating Activities:			
Net income	$1,154	$ 918	$ 779
Adjustments to reconcile net income to net cash provided by operating activities:			
Depreciation	632	564	507
Amortization	43	45	41
Deferred income taxes	(52)	(96)	13
Accounts receivable	(190)	(124)	(54)
Inventories	(113)	(50)	20
Accounts payable and other liabilities	291	279	203
Other	(109)	(155)	61
Net cash provided by operating activities	1,656	1,381	1,570
Cash Flows from Investing Activities:			
Acquisition of businesses and investments	(160)	(154)	(175)
Dividends received and other proceeds	39	52	47
Capital expenditures	(841)	(722)	(704)
Disposals of property, plant and equipment	58	82	112
Net cash used in investing activities	(904)	(742)	(720)
Cash Flows from Financing Activities:			
Net change in short-term debt	98	(57)	(152)
Repayments of long-term debt	(65)	(113)	(33)
Proceeds from long-term debt	34	13	124
Purchases of treasury stock	(344)	(215)	(199)
Issuances of common stock	96	112	129
Payments of dividends	(481)	(425)	(412)
Other	(51)	–	(100)
Net cash used in financing activities	(713)	(685)	(643)
Effect of exchange rate changes on cash	51	77	53
Net increase in cash and cash equivalents	90	31	260
Cash and cash equivalents at beginning of year	432	401	141
Cash and cash equivalents at end of year	$ 522	$ 432	$ 401

Notes to Financial Statements

Accounting Policies

Consolidation: All significant subsidiaries are consolidated. Subsidiaries outside the United States are consolidated on the basis of their fiscal years ended October 31. Unconsolidated subsidiaries and affiliates are included on the equity basis.

During 1988, the company adopted Statement of Financial Accounting Standards (SFAS) No. 94, "Consolidation of All Majority-Owned Subsidiaries." Financial statements for prior years have been restated to reflect the consolidation of Eastern Heights State Bank. This adoption did not have a significant impact on those statements.

In the first quarter of 1989, 3M will consolidate its Japanese joint-venture company, Sumitomo 3M Ltd. The results of Sumitomo 3M's operations have been accounted for on the equity basis. This consolidation will not change 3M's reported net income and will have no material impact on the Balance Sheet. Resulting increases in 3M's net sales are estimated to be less than 10 percent. With the consolidation in 1989, the results of prior years will be restated.

Cash and Cash Equivalents: Cash and cash equivalents consist of cash, bank deposits and temporary cash investments with a maturity of three months or less when purchased.

Other Securities: Other securities consist of marketable securities stated at cost which approximates market.

Inventories: Inventories are stated at lower of cost or market, with cost generally determined on a first-in, first-out basis.

Other Assets: Other assets include goodwill, patents, other intangibles and other noncurrent assets. Goodwill is generally amortized on a straight-line basis over 10 years. Other items are amortized on a straight-line basis over their estimated economic lives.

Deferred Income Taxes: Deferred income taxes arise from items recorded in different periods for tax and financial reporting purposes. These items consist primarily of currently nondeductible expenses net of depreciation differences.

The company expects to adopt SFAS No. 96, "Accounting for Income Taxes," in the first quarter of 1990. The adoption is not expected to have a significant impact on net income.

Depreciation: Depreciation of property, plant and equipment is generally computed on a straight-line basis over the estimated useful lives of these assets.

Research and Development: Research and development costs were $689 million in 1988, $624 million in 1987 and $564 million in 1986.

Foreign Currency Translation: Financial information relating to subsidiaries outside the United States is reported under SFAS No. 52, "Foreign Currency Translation." Local currencies are generally considered the functional currencies outside the United States, except in countries with highly inflationary economies.

Statement of Cash Flows: The company adopted SFAS No. 95, "Statement of Cash Flows," in its 1988 financial statements. Prior years' Statements of Changes in Financial Position have been restated to reflect this adoption.

Income Taxes

Income Before Income Taxes
(Millions)

	U.S.	Foreign	Total
1988	**$1,101**	**$781**	**$1,882**
1987	$ 909	$656	$1,565
1986	$ 838	$510	$1,348

Provision for Income Taxes
(Millions)

1988	Current	Deferred	Total
Federal	$ 395	$(41)	$ 354
State	69	(4)	65
Foreign	312	(3)	309
Total	$ 776	$(48)	$ 728
1987			
Federal	$ 395	$(63)	$ 332
State	59	(4)	55
Foreign	267	(7)	260
Total	$ 721	$(74)	$ 647
1986			
Federal	$ 303	$ 6	$ 309
State	47	1	48
Foreign	197	15	212
Total	$ 547	$ 22	$ 569

Income tax payments included in the Statement of Cash Flows were $754 million in 1988, $699 million in 1987 and $462 million in 1986.

A reconciliation of the statutory U.S. income tax rate to the worldwide consolidated effective tax rate appears below. At December 31, 1988, there were approximately $1.915 billion of reinvested earnings of subsidiaries outside the United States that are considered to be permanently invested. No provision has been made for taxes that might be payable upon their remittance.

	1988	1987	1986
Statutory U.S. tax rate	**34.0%**	40.0%	46.0%
State income taxes	**2.3**	2.1	1.9
All other—net	**2.4**	(.8)	(5.7)
Effective worldwide tax rate	**38.7%**	41.3%	42.2%

Balance Sheet Information

(Millions)	1988	1987
Accounts receivable		
Accounts receivable	$1,827	$1,709
Less allowances	100	94
Accounts receivable – net	$1,727	$1,615
Inventories		
Finished goods	$ 939	$ 878
Work in process	491	511
Raw materials and supplies	401	381
Total inventories	$1,831	$1,770
Investments		
Equity in unconsolidated subsidiaries and affiliates	$ 448	$ 375
Other investments – at cost	272	211
Total investments	$ 720	$ 586
Property, plant and equipment – at cost		
Land	$ 99	$ 99
Buildings and leasehold improvements	1,480	1,305
Machinery and equipment	4,932	4,475
Construction in progress	154	243
	$6,665	$6,122
Less accumulated depreciation	3,592	3,190
Property, plant and equipment – net	$3,073	$2,932
Short-term debt		
Commercial paper	$ 259	$ 151
Long-term debt – current portion	16	19
Other borrowings	72	94
Total short-term debt	$ 347	$ 264
Long-term debt		
Sinking fund debentures, 8.85%, due 1990-2005	$ 126	$ 132
Notes, 9.75%, due 1990	97	97
Notes, 5.75%, due 1991	100	100
Other borrowings, due 1990-2025	83	106
Total long-term debt	$ 406	$ 435

Maturities of long-term debt through 1993 are shown below:

(Millions) 1989	1990	1991	1992	1993
$ 16	$ 114	$ 122	$ 16	$ 11

In 1986, the company borrowed 18 billion yen ($100 million), due 1991, at 5.75 percent and entered into an agreement to convert the yen principal and interest obligations on this debt into U.S. dollars and the fixed interest rate into a variable interest rate below commercial paper rates. This resulted in a net interest cost of approximately 7.2 percent in 1988, 6.4 percent in 1987 and 5.9 percent in 1986.

During 1985, the company issued $100 million of 9.75 percent dual currency notes, due 1990, with interest payable in U.S. dollars and the principal repayable in pound sterling. The company has entered into a forward exchange contract to provide protection against changes in currency exchange rates at maturity of this obligation, resulting in an annual net interest cost of 9.5 percent.

Sinking fund deposits are required for the 8.85 percent debentures. The deposits must be adequate to redeem at least $6 million of principal, with an option to redeem up to an additional $6 million of principal, annually. During 1988, the company reacquired debentures totaling $6.3 million to satisfy the sinking fund deposit requirements through 1989.

Interest payments, net of amounts capitalized, included in the Statement of Cash Flows were $72 million in 1988, $87 million in 1987 and $97 million in 1986.

Performance by Business Sectors

Financial information relating to the company's business sectors for 1988, 1987 and 1986 appears below. Additional information on these sectors appears in the Review of Operations beginning on page 14.

3M is an integrated enterprise characterized by substantial intersector cooperation, cost allocations and inventory transfers. Therefore, management does not represent that these sectors, if operated independently, could earn the operating income shown.

(Millions)		Industrial and Electronic	Information and Imaging Technologies	Life Sciences	Commercial and Consumer	Eliminations and Other	Total Company
Net Sales	1988	$3,825	$2,978	$2,285	$1,483	$ 10	$10,581
	1987	3,448	2,648	2,001	1,327	5	9,429
	1986	3,055	2,680	1,667	1,199	1	8,602
Operating Income	1988	767	312	510	367	(73)	1,883
	1987	699	192	444	320	(77)	1,578
	1986	611	185	381	275	(42)	1,410
Identifiable Assets as of December 31*	1988	2,469	2,001	1,514	856	146	6,986
	1987	2,280	2,059	1,323	810	169	6,641
	1986	2,102	2,008	1,061	759	134	6,064
Depreciation	1988	216	230	99	70	17	632
	1987	186	218	83	63	14	564
	1986	160	211	65	58	13	507
Capital Expenditures	1988	307	227	186	88	33	841
	1987	258	216	157	88	3	722
	1986	242	228	104	110	20	704

*Excludes certain corporate assets, primarily cash and cash equivalents, other securities, certain other current assets, and investments.

In accordance with company policy, operating expenses incurred at the corporate level totaling $88 million in 1988, $89 million in 1987 and $75 million in 1986 have been allocated to business sectors in determining operating income.

Performance by Geographic Areas

Discussions of operating performance by geographic area in the Review of Operations and Financial Review are based on data used by management. These data include export sales and certain income and expense items in the geographic area where the sale is made. The table below presents information on 3M's operations by geographic area for the years ended December 31, 1988, 1987 and 1986, and is based on accounting standards that require the previously mentioned items to be reported in the geographic area where they originate.

(Millions)		United States	Europe	Other Areas	Eliminations	Total Company
Net Sales to Customers, Including Export	1988	$6,351	$2,911	$1,319		$10,581
	1987	5,813	2,489	1,127		9,429
	1986	5,383	2,227	992		8,602
Transfers Between Geographic Areas	1988	669	141	66	$(876)	—
	1987	533	114	52	(699)	—
	1986	481	86	34	(601)	—
Operating Income	1988	1,133	477	273		1,883
	1987	929	405	244		1,578
	1986	897	322	191		1,410
Identifiable Assets*	1988	4,667	1,923	746	(350)	6,986
	1987	4,452	1,835	624	(270)	6,641
	1986	4,167	1,530	568	(201)	6,064

*Excludes certain corporate assets, primarily cash and cash equivalents, other securities, certain other current assets, and investments.

Net assets of subsidiaries outside the United States totaled $1.963 billion at year-end 1988, $1.734 billion in 1987 and $1.449 billion in 1986.

Retirement Plans

3M has various company-sponsored retirement plans covering substantially all U.S. employees and many employees outside the United States. Pension benefits are principally based on an employee's years of service and compensation near retirement. The charge to income relating to these plans was $60 million in 1988, $41 million in 1987 and $8 million in 1986.

U.S. Plan: The company's funding policy is to deposit with an independent trustee amounts at least equal to those required by federal law and regulations. A trust fund is maintained to provide pension benefits to plan participants and their beneficiaries. Plan assets consist primarily of equity-oriented securities with the balance in fixed income and real estate investments.

Assumptions used to calculate costs and actuarial present values include an 8.5 percent expected long-term rate of return on plan assets; a graduated long-term rate of compensation increases approximating 6 percent; settlement rates of 9.25 percent in 1988 and 1987, and 9.0 percent in 1986; and projections for inflation, retirement ages and other factors.

Non-U.S. Plans: In 1987, the company adopted SFAS No. 87 for certain of its pension plans outside the United States. The company will adopt SFAS No. 87 for the remainder of its non-U.S. plans in 1989. For these plans, at the date of the latest actuarial valuations, total pension fund assets exceeded the present value of vested benefits.

The assumptions used to calculate costs and actuarial present values for these plans reflect the economic environments within the various countries involved. Assumptions include expected long-term rates of return on plan assets ranging from 5.3 percent to 10.0 percent; graduated long-term rates of compensation increases ranging from 4.5 percent to 9.0 percent; settlement rates ranging from 4.5 percent to 9.25 percent; and projections for inflation, retirement ages and other factors.

At year-end, the funded status of plans that have adopted SFAS No. 87 was as follows:

(Millions)	U.S. Plan		Non-U.S. Plans	
	1988	1987	**1988**	1987
Actuarial present value of:				
Vested benefit obligation	**$1,162**	$1,013	**$318**	$281
Nonvested benefit obligation	**363**	315	**28**	26
Accumulated benefit obligation	**$1,525**	$1,328	**$346**	$307
Projected benefit obligation	**$1,753**	$1,555	**$499**	$415
Plan assets at fair value	**2,173**	2,035	**476**	425
Plan assets in excess of (less than) the projected benefit obligation	**$ 420**	$ 480	**$(23)**	$ 10
Unrecognized net transition asset	**(410)**	(447)	**(35)**	(36)
Other adjustments and unrecognized items	**59**	29	**56**	17
Prepaid (accrued) pension expense recognized in the Balance Sheet	**$ 69**	$ 62	**$ (2)**	$ (9)

Net pension cost for plans that have adopted SFAS No. 87 was as follows:

(Millions)	U.S. Plan			Non-U.S. Plans	
	1988	1987	1986	**1988**	1987
Service cost (employee benefits earned during the year)	**$ 54**	$ 53	$ 42	**$ 29**	$ 23
Interest cost on projected benefit obligation	**147**	131	119	**31**	26
Return on assets – actual	**(217)**	(120)	(312)	**(45)**	(21)
Net amortization and deferral	**16**	(52)	130	**7**	(11)
Net pension expense (income)	**$ —**	$ 12	$ (21)	**$ 22**	$ 17

Other Postretirement Benefits

The company provides health care and life insurance benefits for substantially all of its U.S. employees who reach retirement age while employed by the company. The estimated cost of these benefits is actuarially determined and accrued over the employees' service periods as a level percentage of compensation for employees expected to qualify for benefits. An 8.5 percent investment rate of return is used in the calculation; other assumptions relate to inflation in medical costs and assumptions similar to those used in the determination of pension expense.

Amounts charged against income were $15 million in 1988 and $14 million in each of the two prior years. 3M's funding policy is to deposit with an independent trustee amounts deductible for federal income tax purposes. Employees outside the United States are covered principally by government-sponsored plans, and the cost of company-provided plans is not material.

Stock Option Plans

Participants in the General Employees' Stock Purchase Plan are granted options at 85 percent of market value at the date of grant. Management stock options are granted at 100 percent of market value. A summary of significant option information follows.

General Employees' Stock Purchase Plan: At December 31, 1988, there were 14,187 participants in the 1987 and 1982 plans, with about 56,500 employees eligible to participate. Options must be exercised within 27 months from date of grant.

	Shares	Price Range
Under Option–		
January 1, 1988	174,551	$35.73 - $69.92
Granted	898,844	48.51 - 55.95
Exercised	(871,027)	35.73 - 65.88
Cancelled	(33,486)	35.73 - 69.92
Under Option–		
December 31, 1988	168,882	46.38 - 69.92
Shares available for grant–		
December 31, 1988	3,788,413	

Management Stock Ownership Program: At December 31, 1988, there were 4,253 participants in the 1987 plan and 3,686 in the 1982 and 1978 plans. A total of 353 individuals participated in all plans. All outstanding options expire between May 1989 and May 1998.

	Shares			
	1987 Plan	1982 Plan	1978 Plan	Price Range
Under Option–				
January 1, 1988	1,812,600	3,399,606	462,492	$25.50 - $63.70
Granted	1,836,900	—	—	$58.90
Exercised	(4,200)	(366,817)	(274,501)	25.50 - 63.70
Retired or Forfeited	(19,600)	(5,412)	(13,344)	25.50 - 63.70
Under Option–				
December 31, 1988	3,625,700	3,027,377	174,647	26.91 - 63.70
Options Exercisable–				
December 31, 1988	1,831,400	3,027,377	174,647	26.91 - 63.70
Shares available for grant–				
December 31, 1988	1,868,300			

In addition to shares in the above plans, 34,983 shares are under option in two subsidiary plans.

Stockholders' Equity

Common stock, without par value, of 500,000,000 shares is authorized, with 236,008,264 shares issued in 1988, 1987 and 1986.

Treasury stock of 11,675,399 shares at December 31, 1988, 8,515,495 shares in 1987 and 7,475,502 shares in 1986 is reported at cost.

Preferred stock of 10,000,000 shares, without par value, is authorized but unissued.

(Dollars in millions)	Common Stock	Reinvested Earnings	Cumulative Translation	Treasury Stock	Total
Balance, December 31, 1985	$296	$4,389	$(412)	$(265)	$4,008
Net income		779			779
Dividends paid ($1.80 per share)		(412)			(412)
Reacquired stock (3,783,386 shares)				(199)	(199)
Issuances pursuant to stock option and benefit plans (3,160,708 shares)		(22)		151	129
Acquisition of businesses in exchange for stock (10,866 shares)		—		—	—
Translation adjustments			158		158
Balance, December 31, 1986	$296	$4,734	$(254)	$(313)	$4,463
Net income		918			918
Dividends paid ($1.86 per share)		(425)			(425)
Reacquired stock (3,336,411 shares)				(215)	(215)
Issuances pursuant to stock option and benefit plans (2,286,643 shares)		(32)		144	112
Acquisition of businesses in exchange for stock (9,775 shares)		—		1	1
Translation adjustments			206		206
Balance, December 31, 1987	$296	$5,195	$ (48)	$(383)	$5,060
Net income		1,154			1,154
Dividends paid ($2.12 per share)		(481)			(481)
Reacquired stock (5,659,369 shares)				(344)	(344)
Issuances pursuant to stock option and benefit plans (1,910,377 shares)		(26)		122	96
Acquisition of businesses in exchange for stock (589,088 shares)		(1)		37	36
Translation adjustments			(7)		(7)
Balance, December 31, 1988	$296	$5,841	$ (55)	$(568)	$5,514

Litigation and Claims

Various legal actions, governmental proceedings and other claims are pending against the company and certain of its subsidiaries. In some cases, these actions seek damages as well as other relief which, if granted, would require sizable expenditures.

Although the total amount of liability at December 31, 1988, with respect to such matters cannot be ascertained, it is the opinion of counsel for the company that any resulting liability will not materially affect the financial statements of the company.

Quarterly Data (Unaudited)

(Dollars in millions, except per share data)	1988	1987	1986
Net Sales			
First	$ 2,602	$2,207	$2,069
Second	2,711	2,381	2,185
Third	2,689	2,466	2,236
Fourth	2,579	2,375	2,112
Year	$10,581	$9,429	$8,602

	1988	1987	1986
Cost of Goods Sold			
First	$ 1,506	$1,285	$1,231
Second	1,557	1,374	1,282
Third	1,552	1,425	1,301
Fourth	1,490	1,429	1,260
Year	$ 6,105	$5,513	$5,074

	1988	1987	1986
Net Income			
First	$ 277	$ 213	$ 181
Second	309	240	198
Third	296	249	215
Fourth	272	216	185
Year	$ 1,154	$ 918	$ 779

	1988	1987	1986
Earnings Per Share			
First	$ 1.22	$ .93	$ .79
Second	1.36	1.05	.86
Third	1.30	1.09	.94
Fourth	1.21	.95	.81
Year	$ 5.09	$ 4.02	$ 3.40

Management's Report

Management is responsible for the integrity and objectivity of the data included in this report. The financial statements have been prepared in accordance with generally accepted accounting principles. Where necessary, they reflect estimates based on management judgment.

Established accounting procedures and related systems of internal control provide reasonable assurance that assets are safeguarded, that the books and records properly reflect all transactions, and that policies and procedures are implemented by qualified personnel. Internal auditors continually review the accounting and control systems.

The Audit Committee, composed of four members of the Board of Directors who are not employees of the company, meets regularly with representatives of management, the independent certified public accountants and the company's internal auditors to monitor the functioning of the accounting and control systems and to review the results of the auditing activities. The Audit Committee recommends independent accountants for appointment by the Board, subject to stockholder ratification. The independent accountants and the internal auditors have full and free access to the Audit Committee.

The independent accountants conduct an objective, independent audit of the financial statements. Their report appears at right.

R. W. Roberts

Roger W. Roberts
Senior Vice President, Finance

Report of Independent Certified Public Accountants

To the Stockholders of Minnesota Mining and Manufacturing Company:

We have audited the balance sheets of Minnesota Mining and Manufacturing Company and consolidated subsidiaries as of December 31, 1988 and 1987, and the related statements of income and cash flows for each of the three years in the period ended December 31, 1988. These financial statements are the responsibility of the company's management. Our responsibility is to express an opinion on these financial statements based on our audits.

We conducted our audits in accordance with generally accepted auditing standards. Those standards require that we plan and perform the audit to obtain reasonable assurance about whether the financial statements are free of material misstatement. An audit includes examining, on a test basis, evidence supporting the amounts and disclosures in the financial statements. An audit also includes assessing the accounting principles used and significant estimates made by management, as well as evaluating the overall financial statement presentation. We believe that our audits provide a reasonable basis for our opinion.

In our opinion, the financial statements referred to above (pages 32, 34, 36 and 38 to 44) present fairly, in all material respects, the financial position of Minnesota Mining and Manufacturing Company and consolidated subsidiaries as of December 31, 1988 and 1987, and the results of their operations and their cash flows for each of the three years in the period ended December 31, 1988, in conformity with generally accepted accounting principles.

Coopers & Lybrand

St. Paul, Minnesota
February 6, 1989

GLOSSARY

A

Absorption costing. The concept that considers the cost of manufactured products to be composed of direct materials, direct labor, and factory overhead. (943)

Accelerated depreciation method. A depreciation method that provides for a high depreciation charge in the first year of use of an asset and gradually declining periodic charges thereafter. (392)

Account. The form used to record additions and deductions for each individual asset, liability, owner's equity, revenue, and expense. (48)

Account form of balance sheet. A balance sheet with assets on the left-hand side and liabilities and owner's equity on the right-hand side. (24, 185)

Accounting. The process of identifying, measuring, and communicating economic information to permit informed judgments and decisions by users of the information. (7, 793)

Accounting cycle. The sequence of principle accounting procedures employed to process transactions during a fiscal period. (118)

Accounting equation. The expression of the relationship between assets, liabilities, and owner's equity; most commonly stated as Assets = Liabilities + Owner's Equity. (17)

Accounting system. The system that provides the information for use in conducting the affairs of the business and reporting to owners, creditors, and other interested parties. (224)

Account payable. A liability created by a purchase made on credit. (18, 49)

Account receivable. A claim against a customer for sales made on credit. (19, 49)

Accounts payable ledger. The subsidiary ledger containing the individual accounts with suppliers (creditors). (230)

Accounts receivable ledger. The subsidiary ledger containing the individual accounts with customers (debtors). (230)

Accounts receivable turnover. The relationship between credit sales and accounts receivable, computed by dividing net sales on account by the average net accounts receivable. (755)

Accrual. An expense or a revenue that gradually increases with the passage of time. (151)

Accrual basis. Revenues are recognized in the period earned and expenses are recognized in the period incurred in the process of generating revenues. (94)

Accrued asset (accrued revenue) or accrued liability (accrued expense). An asset (revenue) or a liability (expense) that gradually increases with the passage of time and that is recorded at the end of the accounting period by an adjusting entry. (99)

Accumulated depreciation account. The contra asset account used to accumulate the depreciation recognized to date on plant assets. (98, 153, 154)

Acid-test ratio. The ratio of the sum of cash, receivables, and marketable securities to current liabilities. (754)

Activity base. The base which is most closely associated with a cost and the decision-making needs of management in using the cost in planning and controlling operations. (908)

Adequate disclosure. The concept that financial statements and their accompanying footnotes should contain all of the pertinent data believed essential to the reader's understanding of an enterprise's financial status. (478)

Adjusting entry. An entry required at the end of an accounting period to record an internal transaction and to bring the ledger up to date. (95)

Administrative expense. An expense incurred in the administration or general operations of the business. (180)

Aging the receivables. The process of analyzing the accounts receivable and classifying them according to various age groupings, with the due date being the base point for determining age. (328)

Allowance method. The method of accounting for uncollectible receivables, by which advance provision for the uncollectibles is made. (325)

American Institute of Certified Public Accountants (AICPA). The national professional organization of CPAs. (469)

Amortization. The periodic expense attributed to the decline in usefulness of an intangible asset or the allocation of bond premium or discount over the life of a bond issue. (405, 615)

Annuity. A series of equal cash flows at fixed intervals. (1107)

Appropriation of retained earnings. The amount of a corporation's retained earnings that has been restricted and therefore is not available for distribution to shareholders as dividends. (581)

Articles of partnership. The formal written contract creating a partnership. (506)

Asset. Property owned by a business enterprise. (16)

Average cost method. The method of inventory costing that is based on the assumption that costs should be charged against revenue in accordance with the weighted average unit costs of the commodities sold. (357, 885)

Average rate of return. A method of evaluating capital investment proposals that focuses on the expected profitability of the investment. (1102)

─────────────── **B**

Balance of an account. The amount of difference between the debits and the credits that have been entered into an account. (52)

Balance sheet. A financial statement listing the assets, liabilities, and owner's equity of a business entity as of a specific date. (22)

Bank reconciliation. The method of analysis that details the items that are responsible for the difference between the cash balance reported in the bank statement and the balance of the cash account in the ledger. (283)

Betterments. Expenditures that increase operating efficiency or capacity for the remaining useful life of a plant asset. (399)

Bond. A form of interest-bearing note employed by corporations to borrow on a long-term basis. (608)

Bond indenture. The contract between a corporation issuing bonds and the bondholders. (610)

Boot. The balance owed the supplier when an old asset is traded for a new asset. (402)

Break-even point. The level of operations of an enterprise at which revenues and expired costs are equal. (912)

Budget. A formal written statement of management's plans for the future, expressed in financial terms. (976)

Budget performance report. A report comparing actual results with budget figures. (987)

Business entity concept. The concept that assumes that accounting applies to individual economic units and that each unit is separate and distinct from the persons who supply its assets. (15, 470)

Business transaction. The occurrence of an event or of a condition that must be recorded in the accounting records. (16)

By-product. A product resulting from a manufacturing process and having little value in relation to the principal product or joint products. (876)

─────────────── **C**

Capital. The rights (equity) of the owners in a business enterprise. (50)

Capital expenditure. A cost that adds to the utility of an asset for more than one accounting period. (398)

Capital expenditures budget. The budget summarizing future plans for acquisition of plant facilities and equipment. (984)

Capital investment analysis. The process by which management plans, evaluates, and controls long-term capital investments involving property, plant, and equipment. (1100)

Capital lease. A lease which includes one or more of four provisions that result in treating the leased asset as a purchased asset in the accounts. (404)

Capital rationing. The process by which management allocates available investment funds among competing capital investment proposals. (1113)

Capital stock. Shares of ownership of a corporation. (50, 538)

Carrying amount. The amount at which a temporary or a long-term investment or a long-term liability is reported on the balance sheet; also called basis or book value. (331, 616)

Cash. Any medium of exchange that a bank will accept at face value. (49)

Cash basis. Revenue is recognized in the period cash is received, and expenses are recognized in the period cash is paid. (94)

Cash discount. The deduction allowable if an invoice is paid by a specified date. (139)

Cash dividend. A cash distribution of earnings by a corporation to its shareholders. (583)

Cash flows from financing activities. The section of the statement of cash flows in which is reported the transactions involving cash receipts from the issuance of equity and debt securities; and cash payments for dividends, repurchase of equity securities, and redemption of debt securities. (693)

Cash flows from investing activities. The section of the statement of cash flows in which is reported the activities involving cash receipts from the sale of investments, plant assets, and other noncurrent assets; and cash payments for the acquisition of investments, plant assets, and other noncurrent assets. (693)

Cash flows from operating activities. The section of the statement of cash flows in which is reported the cash transactions that entered into the determination of net income. (693)

Cash payback period. The expected period of time that will elapse between the date of a capital expenditure and the complete recovery in cash (or equivalent) of the amount invested. (1103)

Cash payments journal. The journal in which all cash payments are recorded. (236)

Cash receipts journal. The journal in which all cash receipts are recorded. (241)

Certified Public Accountant (CPA). An accountant who meets state licensing requirements for engaging in the practice of public accounting as a CPA. (11)

Chart of accounts. A listing of all the accounts used by a business enterprise. (51)

Check register. A modified form of the cash payments journal used to record all transactions paid by check. (290)

Closing entry. An entry necessary to eliminate the balance of a temporary account in preparation for the following accounting period. (111)

Codes of professional conduct. Standards of conduct established by professional organizations of CPAs to guide CPAs in the conduct of their practices. (11)

Common-size statement. A financial statement in which all items are expressed only in relative terms. (751)

Common stock. The basic ownership class of corporate capital stock. (539)

Completed-contract method. The method that recognizes revenue from long-term construction contracts when the project is completed. (476)

Composite-rate depreciation method. A method of depreciation based on the use of a single rate that applies to entire groups of assets. (397)

Conservatism. The concept that dictates that in selecting among alternatives, the method or procedure that yields the lesser amount of net income or asset value should be selected. (485)

Consistency. The concept that assumes that the same generally accepted accounting principles have been applied in the preparation of successive financial statements. (483)

Consolidated statement. A financial statement resulting from combining parent and subsidiary company statements. (652)

Consolidation. The creation of a new corporation by the transfer of assets and liabilities from two or more existing corporations. (651)

Constant dollar. Historical costs that have been converted into dollars of constant value through the use of a price-level index. (473)

Contingent liability. A potential obligation that will materialize only if certain events occur in the future. (323)

Continuous budgeting. A method of budgeting that provides for maintenance of a twelve-month projection into the future. (978)

Contra account. An account that is offset against another account. (98)

Contract rate of interest. The interest rate specified on a bond. (613)

Contribution margin. Sales less variable cost of goods sold and variable selling and administrative expenses. (945)

Contribution margin analysis. The systematic examination of the differences between planned and actual contribution margin. (956)

Contribution margin ratio. The percentage of each sales dollar that is available to cover the fixed expenses and provide an operating income. (923, 955)

Control. The process of directing operations to achieve the organization's goals and plans. (795)

Controllable cost. For a specific level of management, a cost that can be directly controlled. (810, 951)

Controller. The chief managerial accountant of an organization. (799)

Controlling account. The account in the general ledger that summarizes the balances of a subsidiary ledger. (230)

Conversion costs. The combination of direct labor and factory overhead costs. (803, 870)

Corporation. A separate legal entity that is organized in accordance with state or federal statutes and in which ownership is divided into shares of stock. (15)

Cost accounting system. An accounting system which uses the perpetual system of inventory accounting for the three manufacturing inventories: direct materials, work in process, and finished goods. (832)

Cost behavior. The manner in which a cost changes in relation to its activity base. (906)

Cost center. A decentralized unit in which the department or division manager has responsibility for control of costs incurred and the authority to make decisions that affect these costs. (1030)

Cost ledger. A subsidiary ledger employed in a job order cost system and which contains an account for each job order. (841)

Cost method. A method of accounting for an investment in stock, by which the investor recognizes as income its share of cash dividends of the investee. (647)

Cost of goods sold. The cost of the manufactured product sold. (807)

Cost of merchandise sold. The cost of the merchandise purchased by a merchandise enterprise and sold. (179, 807)

Cost of production report. A report prepared periodically by a processing department, summarizing (1) the units for which the department is accountable and the disposition of these units and (2) the costs charged to the department and the allocation of these costs. (873)

Cost principle. The principle that assumes that the monetary record for properties and services purchased by a business should be maintained in terms of cost. (15)

Costs. The disbursement of cash (or the commitment to pay cash in the future) for the purpose of generating revenues. (801)

Cost-volume-profit analysis. The systematic examination of the interrelationships between selling prices, volume of sales and production, costs, expenses, and profits. (906)

Cost-volume-profit chart. A chart used to assist management in understanding the relationships between costs, expenses, sales, and operating profit or loss. (915)

Credit. (1) The right side of an account; (2) the amount entered on the right side of an account; (3) to enter an amount on the right side of an account. (52)

Credit memorandum. The form issued by a seller to inform a debtor that a credit has been posted to the debtor's account receivable. (141)

Cumulative preferred stock. Preferred stock that is entitled to current and past dividends before dividends may be paid on common stock. (541)

Current asset. Cash or another asset that may reasonably be expected to be realized in cash or sold or consumed, usually within a year or less, through the normal operations of a business. (49)

Current cost. The amount of cash that would have to be paid currently to acquire assets of the same age and in the same condition as existing assets. (473)

Current liability. A liability that will be due within a short time (usually one year or less) and that is to be paid out of current assets. (49)

Current ratio. The ratio of current assets to current liabilities. (753)

D

Debit. (1) The left side of an account; (2) the amount entered on the left side of an account; (3) to enter an amount on the left side of an account. (52)

Debit memorandum. The form issued by a buyer to inform a creditor that a debit has been posted to the creditor's account payable. (141)

Debt security. A bond or a note payable. (624)

Decentralization. The separation of a business into more manageable units. (1027)

Declining-balance depreciation method. A method of depreciation that provides declining periodic depreciation charges to expense over the estimated life of an asset. (391)

Deferral. A postponement of the recognition of an expense already paid or a revenue already received. (151)

Deficiency. The debit balance in the owner's equity account of a sole proprietor or a partner. (518)

Deficit. A debit balance in the retained earnings account. (538)

Departmental margin. Departmental gross profit less direct departmental expenses. (1039)

Depletion. The cost of metal ores and other minerals removed from the earth. (404)

Depreciation. The decrease in usefulness of all plant assets except land. (97, 388)

Differential analysis. The area of accounting concerned with the effect of alternative courses of action on revenues and costs. (1067)

Differential cost. The amount of increase or decrease in cost that is expected from a particular course of action compared with an alternative. (811, 1068)

Differential revenue. The amount of increase or decrease in revenue expected from a particular course of action as compared with an alternative. (1068)

Direct cost. A cost that can be traced directly to a unit within an enterprise or organization. (810)

Direct expense. An expense directly traceable to or incurred for the sole benefit of a specific department and ordinarily subject to the control of the department manager. (1040)

Direct labor cost. Wages of factory workers who convert materials into a finished product. (803)

Direct labor rate variance. The cost associated with the difference between the standard rate and the actual rate paid for direct labor used in producing a commodity. (992)

Direct labor time variance. The cost associated with the difference between the standard hours and actual hours of direct labor spent producing a commodity. (992)

Direct materials cost. The cost of materials that enter directly into the finished product. (802)

Direct materials inventory. The cost of direct materials which have not yet entered into the manufacturing process. (806)

Direct materials price variance. The cost associated with the difference between the standard price and the actual price of direct materials used in producing a commodity. (991)

Direct materials quantity variance. The cost associated with the difference between the standard quantity and the actual quantity of direct materials used in producing a commodity. (991)

Direct method. A method of reporting the cash flows from operating activities as the difference between the operating cash receipts and the operating cash payments. (694)

Direct write-off method. A method of accounting for uncollectible receivables, whereby an expense is recognized only when specific accounts are judged to be uncollectible. (325)

Discontinued operations. The operations of a business segment that have been disposed of. (574)

Discount. (1) The interest deducted from the maturity value of a note; (2) excess of par value of stock over its sales price; (3) excess of the face amount of bonds over their issue price. (322, 445, 542, 613)

Discounted cash flow method. A method of analysis of proposed capital investments that focuses on the present value of the cash flows expected from the investment. (1104)

Discounted internal rate of return method. A method of analysis of proposed capital investments that focuses on using present value concepts to compute the rate of return from the net cash flows expected from the investment. (1106)

Discount rate. The rate used in computing the interest to be deducted from the maturity value of a note. (445)

Discretionary cost. A cost that is not essential to short-term operations. (811)

Dishonored note receivable. A note which the maker fails to pay on the due date. (324)

Dividend. A distribution of earnings of a corporation to its owners (stockholders). (26, 50, 583)

Double-entry accounting. A system for recording transactions based on recording increases and decreases in accounts so that debits always equal credits. (54)

Drawings. The amount of withdrawals made by a sole proprietor or partner. (50)

E

Earnings per share (EPS) on common stock. The profitability ratio of net income available to common shareholders to the number of common shares outstanding. (599, 761)

Economies of scale. An economic concept that recognizes that over a wide range of production, costs vary in differing proportions to changes in an activity base. When production facilities are limited, costs tend to increase but at a decreasing rate as production increases from a relatively low level. (1081)

Effective rate of interest. The market rate of interest at the time bonds are issued. (613)

Electronic funds transfer (EFT). A payment system that uses computerized electronic impulses rather than paper (money, checks, etc.) to effect a cash transaction. (294)

Employee's earnings record. A detailed record of each employee's earnings. (437)

Equity. The right or claim to the properties of a business enterprise. (17)

Equity method. A method of accounting for investments in common stock, by which the investment account is adjusted for the investor's share of periodic net income and property dividends of the investee. (647)

Equity per share. The ratio of stockholders' equity to the related number of shares of stock outstanding. (549)

Equity security. Preferred or common stock. (646)

Equivalent units of production. The number of units that could have been manufactured from start to finish during a period. (872)

Exchange rate. The rate at which one unit of currency can be converted into another currency. (666)

Expense. The amount of assets consumed or services used in the process of earning revenue. (19, 50, 801)

Extraordinary item. An event or transaction that is unusual and infrequent. (575)

Extraordinary repairs. Expenditures that increase the useful life of an asset beyond the original estimate. (399)

F

Factory overhead cost. All of the costs of operating the factory except for direct materials and direct labor. (803)

Factory overhead controllable variance. The difference between the actual amount of factory overhead cost incurred and the amount of factory overhead budgeted for the level of operations achieved. (994)

Factory overhead volume variance. The cost or benefit associated with operating at a level above or below 100% of productive capacity. (994)

FICA tax. Federal Insurance Contributions Act tax used to finance federal programs for old-age and disability benefits and health insurance for the aged. (430)

Financial accounting. The branch of accounting that is concerned with the recording of transactions using generally accepted accounting principles (GAAP) for a business enterprise or other economic unit and with a periodic preparation of various statements from such records. (794)

Financial Accounting Standards Board (FASB). The current authoritative body for the development of accounting principles for all entities except state and municipal governments. (15, 467)

Finished goods inventory. The cost of finished products on hand that have not been sold. (806)

Finished goods ledger. The subsidiary ledger that contains the individual accounts for each kind of commodity produced. (844)

First-in, first-out (fifo) method. A method of inventory costing based on the assumption that the costs of merchandise sold should be charged against revenue in the order in which the costs were incurred. (356, 885)

Fiscal year. The annual accounting period adopted by an enterprise. (117)

Fixed expense (cost). An expense (cost) that tends to remain constant in amount regardless of variations in volume of activity. (810, 907)

Flexible budget. A series of budgets for varying rates of activity. (987)

FOB destination. Terms of agreement between buyer and seller, whereby ownership passes when merchandise is received by the buyer, and the seller absorbs the transportation costs. (145)

FOB shipping point. Terms of agreement between buyer and seller, whereby ownership passes when merchandise is delivered to the shipper, and the buyer absorbs the transportation costs. (145)

Funded. An appropriation of retained earnings accompanied by a segregation of cash or marketable securities. (582)

Future value. The amount that will accumulate at some future date as a result of an investment or a series of investments. (619)

G–H

General accounting system. An accounting system which extends the periodic system of inventory accounting used by merchandising enterprises to the three manufacturing inventories: direct materials, work in process, and finished goods. (832)

General journal. The two-column form used to record journal entries that do not "fit" in any special journals. (231)

General ledger. The principal ledger, when used in conjunction with subsidiary ledgers, that contains all of the balance sheet and income statement accounts. (230)

Generally accepted accounting principles (GAAP). Generally accepted guidelines for the preparation of financial statements. (13)

Going concern concept. The concept that assumes that a business entity has a reasonable expectation of continuing in business at a profit for an indefinite period of time. (470)

Goodwill. An intangible asset that attaches to a business as a result of such favorable factors as location, product superiority, reputation, and managerial skill. (406)

Government Accounting Standards Board (GASB). The current authoritative body for the development of accounting principles for state and municipal governments. (468)

Gross pay. The total earnings of an employee for a payroll period. (429)

Gross profit. The excess of net revenue from sales over the cost of merchandise sold. (179)

Gross profit method. A means of estimating inventory on hand without the need for a physical count. (369)

High-low method. A technique that uses the highest and lowest total costs as a basis for estimating the variable cost per unit and fixed cost component of a mixed cost. (910)

Horizontal analysis. The percentage of increases and decreases in corresponding items in comparative financial statements. (746)

------ I

Income from operations. The excess of gross profit over total operating expenses. (181)

Income statement. A summary of the revenues and expenses of a business entity for a specific period of time. (22)

Income summary account. The account used in the closing process for summarizing the revenue and expense accounts. (111)

Indirect cost. A cost that for a specific unit within an enterprise or organization cannot be traced directly to that unit. (810)

Indirect expense. An expense that is incurred for an entire business enterprise as a unit and that is not subject to the control of individual department managers. (1040)

Indirect method. A method of reporting the cash flows from operating activities as the net income from operations adjusted for all deferrals of past cash receipts and payments and all accruals of expected future cash receipts and payments. (694)

Inflation. A period when prices in general are rising and the purchasing power of money is declining. (1113)

Installment method. The method of recognizing revenue, whereby each receipt of cash from installment sales is considered to be composed of partial pay-

ment of cost of merchandise sold and gross profit. (476)

Intangible asset. A long-lived asset that is useful in the operations of an enterprise, is not held for sale, and is without physical qualities. (386)

Interim statement. A financial statement issued for a period covering less than a fiscal year. (192)

Internal controls. The detailed procedures adopted by an enterprise to control its operations. (225)

Internal Revenue Service (IRS). The branch of the U.S. Treasury Department concerned with enforcement and collection of the income tax. (469)

Inventory turnover. The relationship between the volume of goods sold and inventory, computed by dividing the cost of goods sold by the average inventory. (756)

Investment center. A decentralized unit in which the manager has the responsibility and authority to make decisions that affect not only costs and revenues, but also the plant assets available to the center. (1031)

Investment turnover. A component of the rate of return on investment, computed as the ratio of sales to invested assets. (1044)

Invoice. The bill provided by the seller (who refers to it as a sales invoice) to a buyer (who refers to it as a purchase invoice) for items purchased. (139)

------ J

Job cost sheet. An account in the cost ledger in which the costs charged to a particular job order are recorded. (841)

Job order cost system. A type of cost system that provides for a separate record of the cost of each particular quantity of product that passes through the factory. (834)

Joint cost. The cost common to the manufacture of two or more products (joint products). (876)

Joint products. Two or more commodities of significant value produced from a single principal direct material. (876)

Journal. The initial record in which the effects of a transaction on accounts are recorded. (53)

Journalizing. The process of recording a transaction in a journal. (53)

------ L

Last-in, first-out (lifo) method. A method of inventory costing based on the assumption that the most recent merchandise costs incurred should be charged against revenue. (357)

Ledger. The group of accounts used by an enterprise. (48)

Leverage. The tendency of the rate earned on stockholders' equity to vary from the rate earned on total assets because the amount earned on assets acquired through the use of funds provided by creditors varies from the interest paid to these creditors. (760)

Liability. A debt of a business enterprise. (17)

Liquidating dividend. A distribution out of paid-in capital when a corporation permanently reduces its operations or winds up its affairs completely. (586)

Liquidation. The winding-up process when a partnership goes out of business. (516)

Long-term investment. An investment that is not intended to be a ready source of cash in the normal operations of a business and that is listed in the "investments" section of the balance sheet. (624)

Long-term liability. A liability that is not due for a comparatively long time (usually more than one year). (49)

Lower of cost or market. A method of costing inventory or valuing temporary investments that carries those assets at the lower of their cost or current market prices. (366)

M

Managerial accounting. The branch of accounting that uses both historical and estimated data in providing information which management· uses in conducting daily operations and in planning future operations. (794)

Manufacturing margin. Sales less variable cost of goods sold. (945)

Marginal cost. The increase in total cost of producing and selling an additional unit of product. (1081)

Marginal revenue. The increase in total revenue realized from the sale of an additional unit of product. (1080)

Margin of safety. The difference between current sales revenue and the sales at the break-even point. (922)

Marketable security. An investment in a security that can be readily sold when cash is needed. (331)

Market (sales) value method. A method of allocating joint costs among products according to their relative sales values. (876)

Markup. An amount which is added to a "cost" amount to determine product price. (1075)

Master budget. The comprehensive budget plan encompassing all the individual budgets related to sales, cost of goods sold, operating expenses, capital expenditures, and cash. (978)

Matching. The principle of accounting that all revenues should be matched with the expenses incurred in earning those revenues during a period of time. (22, 94, 475)

Materiality. The concept that recognizes the practicality of ignoring small or insignificant deviations from generally accepted accounting principles. (483)

Materials ledger. The subsidiary ledger containing the individual accounts for each type of material. (836)

Materials requisition. The form used by the appropriate manufacturing department to authorize the issuance of materials from the storeroom. (836)

Maturity value. The amount due at the maturity or due date of a note. (320)

Merchandise inventory. Merchandise on hand and available for sale. (349)

Merger. The fusion of two corporations by the acquisition of the properties of one corporation by another, with the dissolution of one of the corporations. (651)

Minority interest. The portion of a subsidiary corporation's capital stock that is not owned by the parent corporation. (656)

Mixed cost. A cost with both variable and fixed characteristics, sometimes referred to as semivariable or semifixed cost. (810, 909)

Multiple-step income statement. An income statement with numerous sections and subsections with several intermediate balances before net income. (179)

N

Natural business year. A year that ends when a business's activities have reached the lowest point in its annual operating cycle. (117)

Net income. The final figure in the income statement when revenues exceed expenses. (22, 183)

Net loss. The final figure in the income statement when expenses exceed revenues. (22, 183)

Net pay. Gross pay less payroll deductions; the amount the employer is obligated to pay the employee. (429)

Net realizable value. The amount at which merchandise that can be sold only at prices below cost should be valued, determined as the estimated selling price less any direct cost of disposition. (367)

Net worth. The owner's equity in a business. (50)

Nominal account. A revenue or expense account periodically closed to the income summary account; a temporary owner's equity account. (56)

Noncontrollable cost. For a specific level of management, a cost that cannot be directly controlled. (810, 951)

Note payable. A written promise to pay, representing an amount owed by a business. (49)

Note receivable. A written promise to pay, representing an amount to be received by a business. (49, 317)

Number of days' sales in inventory. The relationship between the volume of sales and inventory, computed by dividing the inventory at the end of the year by the average daily cost of goods sold. (756)

Number of days' sales in receivables. The relationship between credit sales and accounts receivable, computed by dividing the net accounts receivable at the end of the year by the average daily sales on account. (755)

O

Operating lease. A lease which does not meet the criteria for a capital lease, and thus which is accounted for as an operating expense, so that neither future lease obligations nor future rights to use the leased asset are recognized in the accounts. (404)

Opportunity cost. The amount of income that would result from the best available alternative to a proposed use of cash or its equivalent. (812, 1073)

Other expense. An expense that cannot be associated definitely with operations. (183)

Other income. Revenue from sources other than the principal activity of a business. (183)

Overapplied factory overhead. The amount of factory overhead applied in excess of the actual factory overhead costs incurred for production during a period. (839)

Owner's equity. The rights of the owners in a business enterprise. (17, 50)

P–Q

Paid-in capital. The capital acquired from stockholders. (538)

Par. The arbitrary monetary figure printed on a stock certificate. (539)

Parent company. The company owning all or a majority of the voting stock of another corporation. (651)

Participating preferred stock. Preferred stock that could receive dividends in excess of the specified amount granted by its preferential rights. (540)

Partnership. An unincorporated business owned by two or more individuals. (15)

Payroll. The total amount paid to employees for a certain period. (426)

Payroll register. A multi-column form used to assemble and summarize payroll data at the end of each payroll period. (433)

Percentage-of-completion method. The method of recognizing revenue from long-term contracts over the entire life of the contract. (477)

Period costs. Those costs that are used up in generating revenue during the current period and that are not involved in the manufacturing process. These costs are recognized as expenses on the current period's income statement. (805)

Periodic inventory system. A system of inventory accounting in which only the revenue from sales is recorded each time a sale is made; the cost of merchandise on hand at the end of a period is determined by a detailed listing (physical inventory) of the merchandise on hand. (148, 352)

Perpetual inventory system. A system of inventory accounting that employs records that continually disclose the amount of the inventory on hand. (148, 352)

Petty cash fund. A special cash fund used to pay relatively small amounts. (293)

Physical inventory. The detailed listing of merchandise on hand. (148, 352)

Planning. The process of setting goals for the use of an organization's resources and developing ways to achieve these goals. (795)

Plant asset. A tangible asset of a relatively fixed or permanent nature owned by a business enterprise. (49, 386)

Point of sale method. The method of recognizing revenue, whereby the revenue is determined to be realized at the time that title passes to the buyer. (475)

Pooling of interests method. A method of accounting for an affiliation of two corporations resulting from an exchange of voting stock of one corporation for substantially all of the voting stock of the other corporation. (651)

Post-closing trial balance. A trial balance prepared after all ot the temporary accounts have been closed. (116)

Posting. The process of transferring debits and credits from a journal to the accounts. (53)

Predetermined factory overhead rate. The rate used to apply factory overhead costs to the goods manufactured. (839)

Preemptive right. The right of each shareholder to maintain the same fractional interest in the corporation by purchasing a proportionate number of shares of any additional issuances of stock. (539)

Preferred stock. A class of stock with preferential rights over common stock. (539)

Premium. (1) The excess of the sales price of stock over its par amount; (2) excess of the issue price of bonds over the face amount. (542, 613)

Prepaid expense. A purchased commodity or service that has not been consumed at the end of an accounting period. (18, 49, 151)

Present value. The estimated present worth of an amount of cash to be received (or paid) in the future. (611, 1104)

Present value index. An index computed by dividing the total present value of the net cash flow to be received from a proposed capital investment by the amount to be invested. (1105)

Present value of an annuity. The sum of the present values of a series of equal cash flows to be received at fixed intervals. (1107)

Price-earnings (P/E) ratio. The ratio of the market price per share of common stock, at a specific date, to the annual earnings per share. (762)

Price-level index. The ratio of the total cost of a group of commodities prevailing at a particular time to the total cost of the same group of commodities at an earlier base time. (473)

Price theory. A separate discipline in the area of microeconomics which studies the setting of product prices. (1080)

Prime costs. The combination of direct materials and direct labor costs. (803)

Prior period adjustment. Correction of a material error related to a prior period or periods, excluded from the determination of net income. (578)

Private accounting. The profession whose members are accountants employed by a business firm or nonprofit organization. (10)

Proceeds. The net amount available from discounting a note. (322, 445)

Process cost system. A type of cost system that accumulates costs for each of the various departments or processes within a factory. (834)

Product cost concept. A concept used in applying the cost-plus approach to product pricing in which only the costs of manufacturing the product, termed the product cost, are included in the cost amount to which the markup is added. (1077)

Product costs. The three components of manufacturing cost: direct materials, direct labor, and factory overhead costs. (805)

Product life cycle. A concept that assumes that a product passes through various stages from the time that it is introduced until the time it disappears from the market. (1083)

Profitability. The ability of a firm to earn income. (752)

Profit center. A decentralized unit in which the manager has the responsibility and the authority to make decisions that affect both costs and revenues (and thus profits). (1030)

Profit margin. A component of the rate of return on investment, computed as the ratio of operating income to sales. (1044)

Profit-volume chart. A chart used to assist management in understanding the relationship between profit and volume. (917)

Promissory note. A written promise to pay a sum in money on demand or at a definite time. (316)

Public accounting. The profession whose members render accounting services on a fee basis. (10)

Purchase method. The accounting method employed when a parent company acquires a controlling share of the voting stock of a subsidiary other than by the exchange of voting common stock. (651)

Purchase order. The form issued by the purchasing department to suppliers, requesting the delivery of materials. (836)

Purchase requisition. The form used to inform the purchasing department that items are needed by a business. (836)

Purchases discounts. An available discount taken by the purchaser for early payment of an invoice; a contra account to Purchases. (140)

Purchases journal. The journal in which all items purchased on account are recorded. (232)

Purchases returns and allowances. Reduction in purchases, resulting from merchandise returned to the vendor or from the vendor's reduction in the original purchase price; a contra account to Purchases. (141)

Quick assets. The sum of cash, receivables, and marketable securities. (754)

R

Rate earned on common stockholders' equity. A measure of profitability computed by dividing net income, reduced by preferred dividend requirements, by common stockholders' equity. (761)

Rate earned on stockholders' equity. A measure of profitability computed by dividing net income by total stockholders' equity. (760)

Rate earned on total assets. A measure of the profitability of assets, without regard to the equity of creditors and stockholders in the assets. (759)

Rate of return on investment (ROI). A measure of managerial efficiency in the use of investments in assets. (1043)

Real account. A balance sheet account. (56)

Realization. The sale of assets when a partnership is being liquidated. (516)

Receiving report. The form used by the receiving department to indicate that materials have been received and inspected. (836)

Relevant range. The range of activity within which the enterprise is planning to operate. (908)

Report form of balance sheet. The form of balance sheet with the liability and owner's equity sections presented below the asset section. (24, 185)

Residual income. The excess of divisional operating income over a "minimum" amount of desired operating income. (1046)

Residual value. The estimated recoverable cost of a depreciable asset as of the time of its removal from service. (388)

Responsibility accounting. The process of measuring and reporting operating data by areas of responsibility. (1027)

Retail inventory method. A method of inventory costing based on the relationship of the cost and retail price of merchandise. (368)

Retained earnings. Net income retained in a corporation. (26, 50, 538)

Retained earnings statement. A statement for a corporate enterprise, summarizing the changes in retained earnings during a specific period of time. (26, 184)

Revenue expenditure. An expenditure that benefits only the current period. (398)

Revenues. The gross increases in owner's equity as a result of business and professional activities entered into for the purpose of earning income. (19, 50)

Reversing entry. An entry that reverses a specific adjusting entry to facilitate the recording of routine transactions in the subsequent period. (188)

S

Sales discounts. An available discount granted by the seller for early payment of an invoice; a contra account to Sales. (144)

Sales journal. The journal in which all sales of merchandise on account are recorded. (239)

Sales mix. The relative distribution of sales among the various products available for sale. (921, 954)

Sales returns and allowances. Reductions in sales, resulting from merchandise returned by customers or from the seller's reduction in the original sales price; a contra account to Sales. (144)

Securities and Exchange Commission (SEC). The federal agency that exercises a dominant influence over the development of accounting principles for most companies whose securities are traded in interstate commerce. (469)

Selling expense. An expense incurred directly and entirely in connection with the sale of merchandise. (180)

Semivariable cost. A cost with both variable and fixed characteristics, sometimes referred to as a mixed or semifixed cost. (810, 909)

Service department. A factory department that does not process materials directly but renders services for the benefit of production departments. (875)

Single-step income statement. An income statement with the total of all expenses deducted from the total of all revenues. (179)

Sinking fund. Assets set aside in a special fund to be used for a specific purpose. (619)

Slide. The erroneous movement of all digits in a number, one or more spaces to the right or the left, such as writing $542 as $5,420. (67)

Sole proprietorship. A business owned by one individual. (15)

Solvency. The ability of a firm to pay its debts as they come due. (752)

Special journal. A journal designed to record a single type of transaction. (231)

Standard costs. Detailed estimates of what a product should cost. (989)

Stated value. An amount assigned by the board of directors to each share of no-par stock. (539)

Statement of cash flows. A summary of the major cash receipts and cash payments for a period. (22, 692)

Statement of cost of goods manufactured. A separate statement for a manufacturer that reports the cost of goods manufactured during a period. (807)

Statement of owner's equity. A summary of the changes in the owner's equity of a business entity that have occurred during a specific period of time. (22)

Stock dividend. Distribution of a company's own stock to its shareholders. (585)

Stockholders. The owners of a corporation. (537)

Stockholders' equity. The equity of the shareholders in a corporation. (26, 50, 538)

Stock outstanding. The stock that has been issued to stockholders. (539)

Stock split. A reduction in the par or stated value of a share of common stock and the issuance of a proportionate number of additional shares. (587)

Straight-line depreciation method. A method of depreciation that provides for equal periodic charges to expense over the estimated life of an asset. (390)

Strategic planning. The development of a long-range course of action to achieve enterprise goals. (1028)

Subsidiary company. The corporation that is controlled by a parent company. (651)

Subsidiary ledger. A ledger containing individual accounts with a common characteristic. (230)

Sum-of-the-years-digits depreciation method. A method of depreciation that provides for declining periodic depreciation charges to expense over the estimated life of an asset. (392)

Sunk cost. A cost that is not affected by subsequent decisions. (811, 1069)

T

T account. A form of account resembling the letter T. (51)

Taxable income. The base on which the amount of income tax is determined. (571)

Temporary account. A revenue or expense account periodically closed to the income summary account; a nominal account. (56)

Temporary differences. Differences between income before income tax and taxable income created by items that are recognized in one period for income statement purposes and in another period for tax purposes. Such differences reverse or turn around in later years. (571)

Temporary investment. An investment in securities that can be readily sold when cash is needed. (331)

Time tickets. The form on which the amount of time spent by each employee and the labor cost incurred for each individual job, or for factory overhead, are recorded. (838)

Total cost concept. A concept used in applying the cost-plus approach to product pricing in which all costs of manufacturing a product plus the selling and administrative expenses are included in the cost amount to which the markup is added. (1075)

Transposition. The erroneous arrangement of digits in a number, such as writing $542 as $524. (67)

Treasury stock. A corporation's own outstanding stock that has been reacquired. (547)

Trial balance. A summary listing of the balances and the titles of the accounts. (66)

U

Underapplied factory overhead. The amount of actual factory overhead in excess of the factory overhead applied to production during a period. (839)

Unearned revenue. Revenue received in advance of its being earned. (152)

Units-of-production depreciation method. A method of depreciation that provides for depreciation expense based on the expected productive capacity of an asset. (390)

V

Variable cost. A cost that varies in total dollar amount as the level of activity changes. (809, 908)

Variable cost concept. A concept used in applying the cost-plus approach to product pricing in which only variable costs and expenses are included in the cost amount to which the markup is added. (1078)

Variable costing. The concept that considers the cost of products manufactured to be composed only of those manufacturing costs that increase or decrease as the volume of production rises or falls (direct materials, direct labor, and variable factory overhead). (943)

Variances from standard. Difference between standard cost and actual cost. (990)

Vertical analysis. The percentage analysis of component parts in relation to the total of the parts in a single financial statement. (749)

Voucher. A document that serves as evidence of authority to pay cash. (288)

Voucher register. The journal in which all vouchers are recorded. (289)

Voucher system. Records, methods, and procedures employed in verifying and recording liabilities and paying and recording cash payments. (288)

W–Z

Working capital. The excess of total current assets over total current liabilities at some point in time. (753)

Work in process inventory. The direct materials costs, the direct labor costs, and the factory overhead costs which have entered into the manufacturing process, but are associated with products that have not been finished. (806)

Work sheet. A working paper used to assist in the preparation of financial statements. (100)

Zero-base budgeting. A concept of budgeting that requires all levels of management to start from zero and estimate budget data as if there had been no previous activities in their unit. (978)

INDEX

A

Absorption costing, 943
  and variable costing, 943
  compared with variable
    costing, *illus.*, 944
  income statement, *illus.*, 945,
    946, 947
  income statements, *illus.*, 949
Absorption costing and variable
    costing, 943
  income analysis under, 948
  income statement under, 944
  management's use of, 951
Accelerated methods of
    depreciation, 392
Acceptance of business at a
    special price, 1074,
  illus., 1074
Account,
  balance of, 52
  controlling, 230
  def., 48
  in office equipment ledger,
    illus., 396
  nature of, 51
  with corrected posting, *illus.*,
    194
Accounting, profession of, 10
Account balances,
  on work sheet for statement of
    cash flows, 714
Account form of balance sheet, 185
Accounting, 793
  allowance method for
    uncollectibles, 325
  budgetary, 14
  cost, 13
  def., 7
  development of concepts and
    principles, 466
  direct charge-off method for
    uncollectibles, 325
  direct write-off method for
    uncollectibles, 325, 330
  double entry, 54
  financial, 13, 794
  financial and managerial
    functions, *illus.*, 795
  for bonds payable, 613
  for deferrals, 243
  for international operations,
    665
  for long-term investments in
    stocks, 647
  for notes receivable, 320
  for parent-subsidiary
    affiliations, 652
  for purchases, 138
  for sales, 142
  for transactions with foreign
    companies, 666
  future of, 5
  instruction, 14
  international, 5, 14
  managerial, 13, 794
  not-for-profit, 14
  principles and practices, 14
  private, 10
  provider of information to
    users, *illus.*, 8
  public, 3, 10, 11
  relationship to other
    disciplines, 9
  responsibility, 1027
  social, 14
  socioeconomic, 5
  specialist fields, 12
  tax, 13
Accounting cycle,
  def., 118
  illus., 119
Accounting equation, 17
Accounting for by-products, 877
Accounting for joint products, 876
  market (sales) value method,
    876
Accounting for long-term
    investments in stock,
  cost method, 647
  equity method, 647
Accounting for transactions with
    foreign companies, 666
Accounting information system, 7
Accounting information, users of, 8
Accounting methods employed,
    478
Accounting organizations, 469
  American Accounting
    Association (AAA), 469
  American Institute of Certified
    Public Accountants
    (AICPA), 469
Accounting period, 474
Accounting Principles Board (APB),
    467
Accounting principles, generally
    accepted, 13
Accounting rate of return, 1102
Accounting systems, 13
  computerized, 5, 246
  cost accounting, 832
  def., 224
  for payroll and payroll taxes,
    433
  general, 832
  installation and revision, 225
  other modifications, 243
  principles of, 224
  types of, 832
Account payable, 18
Account receivable, 19
Accounts,
  balance sheet, 52
  chart of, 50
  classification of, 49
  controlling and subsidiary
    compared, *illus.*, 849
  doubtful, 324
  four-column, 58
    illus., 59
  income statement, 55
  nominal, 56
  normal balances, *illus.*, 56
  process cost, flow of costs
    through, *illus.*, 881
  real, 56
  temporary, 56
  two-column, 58,
    illus., 59
  uncollectible, 324
Accounts payable, 49, 701, 709
  account, in general ledger at
    end of month, *illus.*,
    237–239
  control and subsidiary ledger,
    237
  schedule, *illus.*, 239
Accounts payable ledger, 230
Accounts receivable,
  account, in general ledger at
    end of month, *illus.*, 243
  analysis of, *illus.*, 329
  def., 49
  on the balance sheet, *illus.*,
    327
  schedule of collections of,
    illus., 985
  turnover, 755
Accounts receivable analysis, 755
Accounts receivable ledger, 230
  account in, *illus.*, 240
Accounts receivable turnover, 755
Accrual,
  adjusting entries for, 153
  def., 151
  on financial statements, 151
Accrual basis of accounting, 94
Accrued assets, 151
  adjusting entries for, 154
  reversing entries for, 190
Accrued expenses, 99
  adjusting entries for, 153
  adjustment for, *illus.*, 99
  def., 99
Accrued liabilities, 99, 151
  adjusting entries for, 153
  reversing entries for, 188
Accrued operating expenses, 710
Accrued revenues,
  adjusting entries for, 154
Accrued salaries,
  adjustment and reversal, *illus.*,
    190
Accumulated depreciation, 98
  as a contra asset account, 98
Accuracy, 797
Acid-test ratio, 754
Activity base, 908
Adaptation to organizational
    structure, 225
Adequate disclosure, 478
  accounting methods employed,
    478
  changes in accounting
    estimates, 479
  contingent liabilities, 479
  events subsequent to date of
    statement, 481
  segment of a business, 481
Adequate internal controls, 225
Adjusted trial balance, on work
    sheet, 104
Adjusting entries,
  accrued assets, 154
  accrued expenses, 153
  accrued liabilities, 153
  accrued revenues, 154
  def., 95
  for prepaid expenses, 151
  for unearned revenues, 152
  illus., 111, 186
  journalizing and posting, 110
  prepaid expenses, 151
  unearned revenues, 152
Adjusting process, nature of, 95
Adjustments,
  for deferrals and accruals, 151
  on work sheet, 154
  prior period, 578
Administrative costs, 804
Administrative expenses, 180
Admission of a partner, 512
Affiliated companies, 651
Aging the receivables, 328
Allocation of costs, 477
Allocation of departmental charges
    to finished goods and
    inventory, *illus.*, 873
Allocation of income tax between
    periods, 571
Allowance account,
  write-offs to, 327
Allowance method of accounting
    for uncollectibles, 325
American Accounting Association
    (AAA), 469
American Institute of Certified
    Public Accountants
    (AICPA), 11, 469
Amortization, 405
  of discount on bonds payable,
    illus., 616
  of premium on bonds payable,
    illus., 618
Analysis of accounts,
  on work sheet for statement of
    cash flows, 714
Analysis of accounts receivable,
    illus., 329
Annuity,
  def., 613, 1107
  future value of, $1 at
    compound interest, *illus.*,
    621
  present value of, 1107
  present value of, $1, 613
  present value of, $1 at
    compound interest, *illus.*,
    613
Appropriation, 581
  for bonded indebtedness, 623
Appropriation of retained earnings,
    581
Articles of incorporation, 537
Articles of partnership, 506
Assets, 49
  accrued, 151
  current, 49
  def., 17
  fixed, 49, 386
  intangible, 386, 405
  plant, 49, 386,
    acquisition of, 387
  quick, 754
  rate earned on, 759
  ratio of net sales to, 758
Associated companies, 651
Auditing, 13
Automated perpetual inventory
    systems, 365
Average cost method, 885
Average inventory costing method,
    355, 357
Average rate of return, 1102

B

Bad debts, 324
Balance,
  compensating, *def.*, 280
  of the account, 52
Balance sheet, 185
  account form, 24, 185
  budgeted, 986
  columns of work sheet, 105
  comparative, *illus.*, 698

comparative, horizontal analysis, *illus.,* 747
comparative vertical analysis, *illus.,* 750
corporation, *illus.,* 27
def., 22
flow of manufacturing costs to, *illus.,* 807
illus., 109
manufacturing enterprise, 806
merchandise inventory, *illus.,* 367
of a corporation, *illus.,* 664–665
plant assets and intangible assets, *illus.,* 407
presentation of bonds payable, 624
report form, 24, *illus.,* 185
sole proprietorship, *illus.,* 23
Balance sheet accounts, 52
Bank account, as a tool for controlling cash, 280
Bankers' ratio, 753
Bank reconciliation, 283
format for, *illus.,* 284
Bank statement, 282
illus., 283
Basic analytical procedures, financial statements, 745
summary of, 763
Basic principles of consolidation of financial statements, 652
Basis, 331
Bearer bonds, 611
Betterments, 399
Bill, 139
Board of directors, 537
Bond discount,
amortization by interest method, 616
amortization by straight-line method, 615
Bonded indebtedness, appropriation for, 623
Bond indenture, 610
Bond investments,
accounting for purchase, interest, and amortization, 625
accounting for sale, 626
Bond premium, 613
Bond redemption, 623
Bonds, 331, 608
bearer, 611
callable, 611
characteristics of, 610
convertible, 611
coupon, 611
debenture, 611
discount, 613
indenture, 610
investments in, 624
issued at a discount, 615
issued at a premium, 617
issued at face amount, 614
premium, 613
redemption, 623
registered, 611
secured, 611
serial, 611
sinking fund, 619
term, 611
zero-coupon, 619
Bond sinking fund, 619
accounting for, 621
Bonds payable,
accounting for, 613
amortization of discount, *illus.,* 616
amortization of premium on, *illus.,* 618
balance sheet presentation, 624
determining cash flows, 703
present value concepts for, 612

Book inventories, 352
Book value, 616
of asset, 98
Book value per share, 549
Boot, 402
Break-even chart, 915
Break-even point, 912
def., 912
desired profit, 915
Budget,
capital expenditures, 984, *illus.,* 984, 1115
cash, 984, *illus.,* 985
cost of goods sold, 982, *illus.,* 982
direct labor cost, 981, *illus.,* 981
direct materials purchases, 980, *illus.,* 980
factory overhead cost, 981, *illus.,* 981
flexible, 987, *illus.,* 988
master, 978
operating expenses, 982, *illus.,* 983
performance reports, 987, *illus.,* 987
production, 979, *illus.,* 980
sales, 979, *illus.,* 979
Budgeted balance sheet, 986
Budgeted income statement, 983, *illus.,* 983
Budgeting,
and human behavior, 989
continuous, 978
nature and objectives of, 976
systems, 977
zero-base, 978
Budgeting and human behavior, 989
Budgeting systems, 977
computerized, 989
Budget performance report, 987 *illus.,* 987
Budgets and budget analyses, 800
Building,
determining cash flows, 705
Business combinations, 650
mergers and consolidations, 651
parent and subsidiary corporations, 651
Business entity concept, 15, 470
By-products, 876
accounting for, 877
and joint products, 876

_____ C

Callable bonds, 611
Capital, 538
contributed, 538
def., 50
paid-in, 538, 568
Capital and revenue expenditures, 398
illus., 400
summary of, 399
Capital budgeting, 1100
Capital expenditures, 398, 984
def., 398
illus., 984
summary of, 399
Capital investment analysis, 1100
factors that complicate, 1110
nature of, 1100
Capital investment expenditures, budget, *illus.,* 1115
planning and controlling, 1115
Capital leases, 404
Capital rationing, 1113
decision process, *illus.,* 1114
Capital stock, 538
characteristics of, 538
def., 50
issuing, 542

Carrying amount, 331, 616
Cash, 280
bank account as a tool for controlling, 280
change funds, 287
control over, 280
other funds, 294
petty, 293
short and over, 287
Cash basis of accounting, 94
Cash budget, 984
illus., 985
Cash change funds, 287
Cash discount, 139
Cash dividend, 583
Cash flow activities,
on work sheet for statement of cash flows, 714
Cash flow per share, 696
Cash flows,
from financing activities, 694, *def.,* 693
from investing activities, 694, *def.,* 693
from operating activities, *def.,* 693, *illus.,* 693
reporting, 693, 710
Cash flows from financing activities, 694, *def.,* 693
Cash flows from investing activities, 694, *def.,* 693
Cash flows from operating activities, 693,
assembling data for, 707
cash payments for income taxes, 710
cash payments for merchandise, 708
cash payments for operating expenses, 709
cash received from customers, 708
def., 693
direct method of reporting, 694, 707, *illus.,* 695
indirect method of reporting, 694, *illus.,* 695
reporting, 710
Cash payback period, 1103
Cash payments, internal control of, 287
Cash payments journal,
after posting, *illus.,* 236
Cash receipts,
internal control of, 286
Cash receipts journal, 241
after posting, *illus.,* 241
flow of data from, to ledgers, *illus.,* 242
Cash short and over, 287
Cash transactions and electronic funds transfer, 294
Centralized and decentralized operations, 1027
Certified public accountants, (CPAs), 11
professional conduct or ethics, codes of, 11
qualifications of, 11
Changes in accounting estimates, 479
Changes in price levels, 472, 1113
Characteristics of a corporation, 537
additional taxes, 537
articles of incorporation, 537
board of directors, 537
charter, 537
government regulations, 538
limited liability, 537
organizational structure, 537, *illus.,* 537
separate legal existence, 537
shareholders, 537

shares of stock, 537
stockholders, 537
transferable units, 537
Characteristics of managerial accounting reports, 796
accuracy, 797
clarity, 797
conciseness, 797
relevance, 796
timeliness, 796
Characteristics of notes receivable, 318
Charge, 52
Charter, 537
Chart of accounts, 50
def., 51
illus., 1
Check,
and remittance advice, *illus.,* 282
def., 281
register, 290
Check register, 290
illus., 290
Clarity, 797
Classes of stock, 539
Classification of receivables, 316
Clock cards, 837
Closing entries, 186
def., 111
illus., 113, 187
journalizing and posting, 111
Closing process,
flowchart of, *illus.,* 112
nature of, 111
Combined income and retained earnings statement, 184
Common-size statements, 751
income statement, *illus.,* 752
Common stock, 539
chart of earnings and dividends per share, *illus.,* 762
determining cash flows, 703
earnings per share, 761
Comparative balance sheet,
horizontal analysis, *illus.,* 747
illus., 698
vertical analysis, *illus.,* 750
Comparative income statement,
horizontal analysis, *illus.,* 748
vertical analysis, *illus.,* 751
Compensating balance, *def.,* 280
Completed-contract method, 476
Composite-rate depreciation method, 397
illus., 397
Compound journal entry, 53
Computerized budgeting systems, 989
Concepts and principles,
accounting period concept, 474
adequate disclosure concept, 478
business entity concept, 470
conservatism, 485
consistency, 482, 483
development of, 466
going concern concept, 470
matching revenue and expired costs principle, 474
materiality, 483
objective evidence concept, 471
unit of measurement concept, 472
Conciseness, 797
Conservatism, 485
Consistency, 482, 483
Consolidated income statement, and other statements, 663
Consolidated statements, 652
basic principles of, 652
income statement, 663
with foreign subsidiaries, 668
Consolidations, 651
Constant dollar, 473

Constant dollar equivalent, 473
Contingent liabilities, 323, 479
Continuous budgeting, 978
Contra account, 98
Contract rate of interest, 613
Contributed capital, 538
Contribution margin, 945
    analysis, 956
    analysis report, *illus.*, 958
    ratio, 955
Contribution margin analysis, 956
    report, *illus.*, 958
Contribution/margin analysis report, *illus.*, 958
Contribution margin ratio, 923, 955
Contribution margin statement,
    sales territories, *illus.*, 955
    unit of product, *illus.*, 954
Contributory plan, 442
Control,
    def., 795
    environment, 227
    over receivables, 317
    procedures, 228
Control environment, 227
Controllable costs, 810, 951
Controllable variance, 994
Controller, 799
Controlling account, 230
Controlling and subsidiary accounts
    compared, *illus.*, 849
Control procedures, 228
Conversion costs, 803, 870
    and prime costs, *illus.*, 804
Convertible bonds, 611
Co-ownership of partnership
    property, 506
Copyright, 406
Corporate annual reports, 765
    financial highlights, 765,
        illus.,766
    historical summary, 770, *illus.*,
        770
    independent auditors' report,
        766, 767, *illus.*, 768
    management report, 769, *illus.*,
        769
    other information, 770
    president's letter, 766, *illus.*,
        767
Corporate earnings and income
    taxes, 570
Corporate organization, 3
Corporation financial statements,
    664
    balance sheet, *illus.*, 664–665
Corporations, 15
    characteristics of, 537
    financing, 608
    nonprofit, 536
    nonpublic, 536
    profit, 536
    public, 536
Correcting entry, *illus.*, 194
Correction of errors, 193
    procedures for, *illus.*, 195
Cost accounting system, 832, 834
    job order, 834
    process cost, 834
Cost basis, 547
Cost behavior, 907
    def., 906
    summary of concepts, 911
Cost center, 1030
Cost concepts,
    additional, for managerial
        planning, 809
    choosing a cost-plus approach,
        1079
    product, 1077
    summary, 812
    total, 1075
    variable, 1078
Cost control, 951
    controllable costs, 951
    noncontrollable costs, 951
Cost-effectiveness balance, 224
Cost ledger, 841

Cost method,
    of accounting for long-term
        investments in stocks, 647
Cost of goods manufactured closed
        to income summary, *illus.*,
        833
Cost of goods sold, 179, 807
Cost of goods sold budget, 982,
    illus.,, 982
Cost of merchandise purchased,
    149
Cost of merchandise sold, 149,
    179, 807
    beginning and ending
        inventory, *illus.*, 149
Cost of merchandise sold,
    ending inventory but no
        beginning inventory, *illus.*,
        149
Cost of production report, 873, 882
    illus., 874, 882
Cost of sales, 179
Cost principle, 15
Costs, 1080
    administrative, 804
    controllable, 810, 951
    conversion, 803, 870
    current, 473
    def., 801
    differential, 811, 1068
    direct, 810
    direct labor, 803
    direct materials, 802
    discretionary, 811
    expired, 805
    factory overhead, 803
    fixed, 809, 810, 907
    incremental, 811
    indirect, 810
    inventoriable, 805
    joint, 876
    manufacturing, 802
    marginal, 1081
    mixed, 810, 909
    noncontrollable, 810, 951
    nonmanufacturing, 804
    opportunity, 812, 1073
    organization, 550
    period, 805
    prime, 803
    processing, 870
    product, 805
    raw materials, 802
    selling, 804
    semifixed, 810, 909
    semivariable, 810, 909
    standard, 989
    sunk, 811, 1069
    total fixed, *illus.*, 907
    total variable, *illus.*, 909
    transportation, 145
    unit fixed, *illus.*, 907
    unit variable, *illus.*, 909
    variable, 809, 908
Costs and expenses distinguished,
    illus.,, 802
Cost-volume-profit analysis, 906
    break-even point, 912
    cost-volume-profit chart, *illus.*,
        916
    def., 906
    desired profit, 915
    graphic approach, 915
    limitations of, 923
    mathematical approach to, 912
    relationships, 912
    revised cost-volume-profit
        chart, *illus.*, 917
    use of computers, 920
Cost-volume-profit chart, 915
    illus., 916
    revised, *illus.*, 917
Cost-volume-profit relationships,
    912
    special, 922
Coupon bonds, 611
Coupon rate, 613
Credit, *def.*, 52

Credit memorandum, 141, 144,
    illus., 145
Creditors ledger, 230
Credit period, 139
Credit terms,
    def., 139
    illus., 139
Cumulative preferred stock, 540,
    541
Current cost, 473
Current liabilities, 49
Current position analysis, 753
Current ratio, 753
Customers ledger, 230

——— D

Data base, *def.*, 229
Data processing methods, 229
Death of a partner, 515
Debenture bonds, 611
Debit,
    def., 52
    posting of, *illus.*, 60
Debit and credit,
    expanded rules, balance sheet
        accounts, *illus.*, 55
    expanded rules, income
        statement accounts, *illus.*,
        56
    general rules, *illus.*, 54
Debit balance, 52
Debit memorandum, 141
    illus., 141
Debt securities, 624
Decentralization, 1027
    advantages of, 1028
    disadvantages of, 1029
Decentralized operations,
    cost centers, 1030
    investment centers, 1031
    profit centers, 1030
    types of, 1029
Declining-balance method of
        depreciation, 391
    comparison with straight-line
        and sum-of-the-years-digits
        methods, *illus.*, 393
Deductions, 429
Deductions from employee
        earnings, 429
Deferrals,
    accounting for, 243
    adjusting entries for, 151, 152
    alternative methods of
        recording, 246
    def., 151
    on financial statements, 151
Deferred charges, 151
Deferred credits, 151
Deficiency, 518
Departmental margin, 1039
Depletion, 404
Deposit tickets, 281
Depreciation,
    accounting for, 388
    adjustment for, *illus.*, 98
    def., 97, 388
    for federal income tax, 393
    low unit cost plant assets, 397
    MACRS rate schedule, *illus.*,
        394
    nature of, 388
    periodic revision, 394
    recording, 395
Depreciation expense,
    factors that determine, *illus.*,
        389
    reporting in financial
        statements, 407
Depreciation methods,
    accelerated, 392
    comparison of, 392, *illus.*, 393
    composite-rate, 397, *illus.*, 397
    declining balance, 391

    straight-line, 390
    sum-of-the-years-digits, 392
    units-of-production, 390
    use of, *illus.*, 390
Development of concepts and
        principles, 466
Differential analysis,
    acceptance of business at a
        special price, 1074, *illus.*,
        1074
    discontinuance of an
        unprofitable segment,
        1069, *illus.*, 1070
    equipment replacement, 1072,
        illus., 1073
    lease or sell, 1068, *illus.*, 1068
    make or buy, 1071, *illus.*, 1072
    process or sell, 1073, *illus.*,
        1074
Differential analysis report,
    discontinuance of an
        unprofitable segment,
        illus., 1070
    equipment replacement, *illus.*,
        1073
    lease or sell, *illus.*, 1068
    make or buy, *illus.*, 1072
    process or sell, *illus.*, 1074
    sale at special price, *illus.*,
        1074
Differential cost, 811, 1068
Differential revenue, 1068
Differentials, 1067
Direct change-off method,
    accounting for
        uncollectibles, 325
Direct cost, 810
Direct costing, 943
Direct expense, 1040
Direct labor cost, 803
Direct labor cost budget, 981, *illus.*,
    981
Direct labor cost variance, 992,
    illus., 992
Direct labor rate variance, 993,
    illus., 993
Direct labor time variance, 992,
    illus., 993
Direct materials cost, 802
Direct materials cost variance, 991,
    illus., 991
Direct materials inventory, 806
Direct materials price variance,
    991, *illus.*, 991
Direct materials purchases budget,
    980, *illus.*, 980
Direct materials quantity variance,
    991, *illus.*, 991
Direct method of reporting cash
        flows from operating
        activities, 694, 707, *illus.*,
        695
Direct write-off method,
    accounting for uncollectibles,
        325, 330
Discontinuance of an unprofitable
        segment, 1069
    differential analysis report,
        illus., 1070
Discontinued operations, 574
Discount, 322, 445, 542
    cash, 139
    on stock, 542
    purchases, 139, 292, *def.*, 140
    sales, 144
Discounted cash flow analysis,
    illus., 1105
Discounted cash flow method, 1104
Discounted internal rate of return
        method, 1106
Discounting, 445
    notes receivable, 322, *illus.*,
        323
Discounting notes receivable, 322
    diagram of, *illus.*, 323
Discount on stock, 542
Discount rate, 445
Discretionary cost, 811

Dishonored notes receivable, 324
Dividends, 26, 50
    and stock splits for treasury
        stock, 587
    cash, 583
    chart, with earnings per share
        of common stock, *illus.*,
        762
    def., 583
    liquidating, 586
    nature of, 583
    stock, 585
Dividend yield, 763
Double-entry accounting, 54
Double-entry system, 1
Doubtful accounts, 324
Drawee, *def.*, 281
Drawer, *def.*, 281
Drawings, *def.*, 50
Due date, 318
    determination of, *illus.*, 318

——— E ———

Earnings,
    corporate, 570
    per common share, 579
Earnings per common share, 579
Earnings per share, 579
Earnings per share on common
        stock, 761
    chart, with dividends per
        share, *illus.*, 762
Economic order quantity (EOQ),
        999
    formula, *illus.*, 1000
    tabulation of, *illus.*, 1000
Economic order quantity formula,
        illus., 1000
Economic theory of product pricing,
        1080
Economies of scale, 1081
Effective rate of interest, 613
Effective reporting, 225
Electronic funds transfer (EFT),
        294
Employee earnings,
    deductions from, 429
    liability for, 426
Employee's earnings record, 436,
        437, *illus.*, 438–439
Employees' fringe benefits, 441
    liability for, 441
    pensions, liability for, 442
    vacation pay, liability for, 441
Employer's payroll taxes, liability
        for, 432
Entries,
    adjusting, 95, *illus.*, 186
    closing, 111, 186, *illus.*, 187
    correcting, *illus.*, 194
    reversing, 188
    use of reversing, 251
Equipment,
    determining cash flows, 704
Equipment replacement, 1072
    differential analysis report,
        illus., 1073
Equities, 17
    def., 17
Equity method, 647
    of accounting for long-term
        investments in stock, 649
Equity per share, 549
Equity securities, 646
Equivalent units of production, 872
    determination of, *illus.*, 872
Errors,
    correction of, 193
    discovery of, 67
    procedures for correcting,
        illus., 195
Estimating inventory cost, 368
    gross profit method, 369; *illus.*,
        369
    retail method, 368, *illus.*, 368

Estimating uncollectibles, 328
Events subsequent to date of
        statements, 481
Exchange rate, 666
Expected realizable value, 326
Expenditures,
    capital, 398
    revenue, 398, 399
    summary of capital and
        revenue, 399
Expenses, 19
    accrued, 99
    administrative, 180
    def., 50, 801
    direct, 1040
    general, 180
    indirect, 1040
    nonoperating, 183
    other, 183
    prepaid, 246
    selling, 180
Extraordinary items, 575
Extraordinary repairs, 399

——— F ———

Face value, 611
Factors that complicate capital
        investment analysis, 1110
    changes in price levels, 1113
    income tax, 1110
    lease versus capital
        investment, 1112
    uncertainty, 1113
    unequal proposal lives, 1111
Factory labor, in job order cost
        system, 837
Factory overhead,
    controllable variance, 995,
        illus., 996
    cost budget indicating standard
        factory overhead rate,
        illus., 994
    cost variance, 993, *illus.*, 995
    cost variance report, *illus.*, 996
    in a job order cost system, 838
    overapplied, 839
    predetermined rate, 839
    underapplied, 839
    volume variance, 994, *illus.*,
        995
Factory overhead controllable
        variance, 995, *illus.*, 996
Factory overhead cost, 803
    flexible budget for, *illus.*, 988
Factory overhead cost budget, 981,
        illus., 981
Factory overhead cost variance,
        993
    illus., 995
    report, *illus.*, 996
Factory overhead cost variance
        report, *illus.*, 996
Factory overhead volume variance,
        994, *illus.*, 995
Federal income tax,
    depreciation, 393
FICA tax, 430
Financial accounting, 794
    and managerial, functions,
        illus., 795
Financial Accounting Standards
        Board (FASB), 15, 467
Financial Analysts Federation, 469
Financial Executives Institute (FEI),
        469
Financial highlights, 765, *illus.*, 766
Financial statement analysis, 745
    basic analytical procedures, 745
    common-size statements, 751
    focus of, 752
    horizontal analysis, 746
    other analytical measures, 752
    summary of analytical
        measures, 763
    vertical analysis, 749

Financial statements,
    analysis of, basic analytical
        procedures, 745
    basic principles of
        consolidation of, 652
    consolidated statements, 652
    consolidated, with foreign
        subsidiaries, 668
    corporation, 26, 664
    for partnerships, 511
    for sole proprietorships, 22
    manufacturing enterprises, 805
    merchandising enterprises, 179
    process cost systems, 883
    unusual items reported in, 574
    work sheet for, 100
Financial statements for
        manufacturing enterprises,
        805
    balance sheet, 806
Financing corporations, 608
Finished goods and cost of goods
        sold, in a job order cost
        system, 844
Finished goods inventory, 806
Finished goods ledger, 844
First-in, first-out (fifo) cost method,
        885
First-in, first-out (fifo) method of
        costing inventory, 355,
        356
Fiscal year,
    illus., 117
Fixed assets, 386, *def.*, 49
Fixed costs, 809, 810, 907
    total fixed, *illus.*, 907
    unit fixed, *illus.*, 907
Fixed liabilities, 49
Flexibility to meet future needs,
        224
Flexible budgets, 987
    for factory overhead cost,
        illus., 988
Flow diagram of a payroll system,
        illus., 440
Flow of costs through a service
        enterprise, *illus.*, 851
Flow of costs through job order
        cost accounts, *illus.*, 848
Flow of costs through perpetual
        inventory accounts, *illus.*,
        835
Flow of costs through process cost
        accounts, *illus.*, 881
Flow of manufacturing costs to
        balance sheet, *illus.*, 807
Flow of materials, 871
FOB destination, 145, 353
FOB shipping point, 145, 353
Foreign companies,
    accounting for transactions
        with, 666
Foreign subsidiaries,
    consolidated statements with,
        668
Fringe benefits, 441
Full disclosure, 478
Funded, 582, 623
Funded plan, 442
Future value, 619
    concepts, 619
    of an annuity of $1 at
        compound interest, *illus.*,
        621
    of $1 at compound interest,
        illus., 620

——— G ———

Gain on realization, 516
General accounting, 800
General accounting system, 832
General expenses, 180
General journal, 231
    entry for returns and
        allowances, *illus.*, 235

entry, sales returns and
        allowances, *illus.*, 240
General ledger, 230
    accounts payable, at end of
        month, *illus.*, 237–239
    accounts receivable, at end of
        month, *illus.*, 243
General ledger accounts, after
        posting from purchases
        journal, *illus.*, 234
Generally accepted accounting
        principles (GAAP), 13,
        794
Going concern, 388
Going concern concept, 470
Goodwill, 406
Governmental Accounting
        Standards Board (GASB),
        468
Government influence, 4
Government organizations, 469
    Internal Revenue Service,
        (IRS), 469
    Securities and Exchange
        Commission (SEC), 469
Graphic approach to
        cost-volume-profit
        analysis, 915
Gross margin, 179
Gross pay, 429
Gross profit, 179
    by department, 1035
    on sales, 179
Gross profit by department, 1035
Gross profit method, 369
    estimate of inventory, *illus.*,
        369

——— H ———

High-low method, 910
Historical summary, 770, *illus.*, 770
Horizontal analysis, 746
    comparative balance sheet,
        illus., 747
    comparative income statement,
        illus., 748
    comparative retained earnings
        statement, 749
    comparative schedule of
        current assets, *illus.*, 748

——— I ———

In-and-out-cards, 837
Income,
    from operations, 181
    net, 183
    nonoperating, 183
    operating, 180
    other, 183
    taxable, 571
Income analysis under variable
        costing and absorption
        costing, 948
Income division,
    allowances exceed net
        income, 510
    partnership, 508
    recognizing services of
        partners, 509
    recognizing services of
        partners and investment,
        510
Income reported when units
        manufactured are less
        than units sold, 947
    absorption costing income
        statement, *illus.*, 947
    variable costing income
        statement, *illus.*, 948
Income reported when units
        manufactured equal units
        sold, 946

Income reported when units manufactured exceed units sold, 946
  absorption costing income statement, *illus.,* 946
  variable costing income statement, *illus.,* 946
Income statement,
  absorption costing, *illus.,* 945, 946, 947, 949
  budgeted, 983, *illus.,* 983
  columns of work sheet, 105
  combined with retained earnings statement, *illus.,* 184
  common-size, *illus.,* 752
  comparative, horizontal analysis, *illus.,* 748
  comparative, vertical analysis, *illus.,* 751
  consolidated, 663
  def., 22
  departmentalized through departmental margin, *illus.,* 1042
  departmentalized through gross profit, *illus.,* 1036–1037
  departmentalized through income from operations, *illus.,* 1040–1041
  illus., 23, 109
  manufacturing enterprise, 807, *illus.,* 808
  merchandising enterprise, *illus.,* 807
  multiple-step, 179, *illus.,* 182
  single-step, 179, *illus.,* 183
  under variable costing and absorption costing, 944
  unusual items that affect it, 574
  variable costing, *illus.,* 945, 946, 948, 950
Income statement accounts, 55
Income summary, account, 111, *illus.,* 188
Income taxes, 4, 701, 710, 1110
  allocation between periods, 571
  cash payments for, 710
  corporate earnings and, 570
Incremental cost, 811
Independent auditors' report, 766, 767, *illus.,* 768
Indirect costs, 810
Indirect expense, 1040
Indirect method of reporting cash flows from operating activities, 694, *illus.,* 695
Industrial revolution, 2
Inflation, 1113
Influential organizations, other, 469
  Financial Analysts Federation, 469
  Financial Executives Institute (FEI), 469
  National Association of Accountants (NAA), 469
  Securities Industry Associates, 470
Installment method, 476, *illus.,* 476
Intangible assets, 386, 405
  copyrights, 406
  goodwill, 406
  in balance sheet, *illus.,* 407
  patents, 405
Interest, 319
Interest-bearing notes, 319
Interest-bearing notes receivable, 321
Interim statements, *def.,* 192
Internal controls,
  adequate, 225
  of cash payments, 287
  of cash receipts, 286
  payroll systems, 441
  perpetual inventory system and, 364
Internal control structure, 227

Internal rate of return method, 1106
Internal Revenue Service (IRS), 469
International operations, accounting for, 665
Inventoriable costs, 805
Inventories, 701, 709
  book, 352
  def., 349
  importance of, 349
  of partially processed materials, 871
Inventories of partially processed materials, 871
Inventory,
  accounting for and reporting under perpetual system, 361
  analysis, 756
  determining actual quantities in, 353
  determining cost of, 354
  direct materials, 806
  effect on current period's statements, 350
  effect on following period's statements, 351
  finished goods, 806
  ledger, 362
  merchandise, 349
  number of days' sales in, 756
  periodic system, 148
  perpetual system, 148
  physical, 148, 352
  systems, 352
  turnover, 756
  valuation at lower of cost or market, 366, *illus.,* 367
  valuation at net realizable value, 367
  work in process, 806
Inventory analysis, 756
Inventory control,
  linear programming for, 1001
  quantitative techniques, 998
Inventory costing methods, 885
  average, 355, 357
  average cost method, 885
  comparison of, 358
  first-in, first-out (fifo), 355, 357, 885
  illus., 355
  last-in, first-out (lifo), 355, 357
  periodic system, 354
  perpetual system, 362
  retail, 368, *illus.,* 368
  weighted average, 357
Inventory ledger, 362
Inventory order point, 1000
Inventory systems, 352
  comparison of periodic and perpetual, *illus.,* 361–362
  merchandise, 148
  periodic, 352
  perpetual, 352
Inventory turnover, 756
Investment center, 1031
  partial organization chart for diversified company, *illus.,* 1031
Investments,
  determining cash flows, 705
  in bonds, 624
  in stocks, 646
  long-term, 624
  recording, for partnership, 507
  shareholders', 538
  temporary, 331
Investment turnover, 1044
Invoice, 139
  illus., 140
Issuing stock for assets other than cash, 544

J

Job cost sheet, 841, *illus.,* 843
Job order cost accounting,

flow of costs through, *illus.,* 848
  illustration of, 845
Job order cost system, 834
  cost of goods sold, 844
  factory labor, 837
  factory overhead, 838
  finished goods, 844
  for manufacturing enterprises, 835
  for service enterprises, 851
  materials, 835
  sales, 844
  work in process, 841
Joint costs, 876
  allocation of, *illus.,* 876
Joint products, 876
  accounting for, 876
  and by-products, 876
Journal, 57, 231
  cash payments, 236
  cash receipts, 241
  def., 53
  general, 231
  multi-column, 230
  purchases, 232, *illus.,* 232–233
  sales, 239, *illus.,* 240
  special, 230, 231
  two-column, 57, *illus.,* 58
  with corrected entry, *illus.,* 193
Journal entry, 53
  compound, 53
Journalizing, 53
Journalizing and posting, 60
  adjusting entries, 110
  closing entries, 111
  illustration of process, 60

L

Land,
  determining cash flows, 705
Last-in, first-out (lifo) inventory costing method, 355, 357
Lead time, 1000
Lease or sell, 1068
  differential analysis report, *illus.,* 1068
Leases, 404
  capital, 404
  operating, 404
Lease versus capital investment, 1112
Leasing,
  plant assets, 404
Ledgers,
  accounts payable, 230
  accounts receivable, 230, *illus.,* 240
  after accounts have been adjusted and closed, *illus.,* 113–116
  after posting, *illus.,* 64–66
  creditors, 230
  customers, 230
  def., 48
  flow of credits to, from purchases journal, *illus.,* 234
  flow of data to, from cash receipts journal, *illus.,* 241
  flow of data to, from purchases journal, *illus.,* 235
  general, 230
  inventory, 362
  stockholders, 542
  subscribers, 547
  subsidiary, 230
Legal capital, 539
Lessee, 404
Lessor, 404
Leverage, 760
Liabilities, 49
  accrued, 99, 151
  contingent, 323, 479
  current, 49
  def., 17, 49

  limited, 537
  long-term, 49
  ratio of stockholders' equity to, 757
  unlimited, 506
Liability for employee's earnings, 426
Limited liability, 537
Limited life, 505
Linear programming, 1001
  for inventory control, 1001
Liquidating dividends, 586
Liquidation, 516
Liquidation of partnerships, 516
  gain on realization, 516
  loss on realization; capital deficiency, 518
  loss on realization; no capital deficiencies, 517
Long-term investments, 624
Long-term investments in stock, accounting for, 647
  sale of, 649
Long-term liabilities, 49
  ratio of plant assets to, 757
Loss,
  from operations, 183
  net, 183
Loss on realization; capital deficiency, 518
Loss on realization; no capital deficiencies, 517

M

MACRS depreciation rate schedule, *illus.,* 394
Make or buy, 1071
  differential analysis report, *illus.,* 1072
Maker, 318
Management process, 795
Management report, 769, *illus.,* 769
Managerial accounting, 794
  and financial, functions, *illus.,* 795
  and the basic functions of management, *illus.,* 795
  characteristics of reports, 796
  organization of the function, 798
Managerial accounting functions, 798
  budgets and budget analyses, 800
  general accounting, 800
  special reports and analyses, 800
  systems and procedures, 800
  taxes, 800
Managerial accounting reports, characteristics, 796
  costs vs. benefits, 798
  illus., 798
Manufacturing burden, 803
Manufacturing costs, 802
  flow to balance sheet, *illus.,* 807
Manufacturing enterprises, financial statements, 805
  income statement, 807, *illus.,* 808
  job order cost system, 835
Manufacturing margin, 945
Manufacturing overhead, 803
Marginal cost, 1081
Marginal income, 945
Marginal revenue, 1080
Margin of safety, 922
Marketable securities, 331
Market price, 550
Market rate, 613
Market (sales) value method, 876
  of allocating joint costs, 876
Markup, 1075
Master budget, 978
  components of, *illus.,* 978
Matching, 22, 475

Matching principle, 94
Matching revenue and expired costs, 474
 allocation of costs, 477
 recognition of revenue, 475
Materiality, 483
Materials,
 in job order cost system, 835
Materials ledger, 836
Materials ledger account, *illus.*, 836
Materials requisition, 836
 illus., 837
Mathematical approach to cost-volume-profit analysis, 912
Maturity value, 320
Maximization of profits, 1080
Merchandise available for sale, 149
Merchandise, cash payments for, 708
Merchandise inventory, 349
 adjustments, 150
 on balance sheet, *illus.*, 367
 systems, 148
Merchandising enterprise,
 financial statements, 179
 income statement, *illus.*, 807
 periodic reporting, 148
 reversing entries for, 191, *illus.*, 192
Merger, 651
Mergers and consolidations, 651
Methods of evaluating capital investment proposals, 1101
 average rate of return, 1102
 cash payback period, 1103
 discounted cash flow, 1104, *illus.*, 1105
 discounted internal rate of return, 1106
 internal rate of return, 1106
 methods that ignore present value, 1101
 net present value, 1104
 present value methods, 1104
 time-adjusted rate of return, 1106
Methods that ignore present value, 1101
 average rate of return, 1102
 cash payback period, 1103
Minority interest, 656
Mixed costs, 810, 909, *illus.*, 910
Moving average, 364
Multi-column journal, 230
Multiple-step income statement, 179, *illus.*, 182
Mutual agency, 506

——— N

National Association of Accountants (NAA), 469
Natural business year, 117
Nature and objectives of budgeting, 976
Net cash flow, 1103
Net income,
 def., 22, 183
 division in partnership, 508
Net loss,
 def., 22, 183
 division in partnership, 508
Net pay, 429, 430
 computation of, 430
Net periodic pension cost, 442
Net present value method, 1104
Net profit, *def.*, 22
Net purchases, 149
Net realizable value, 326, 367
Net sales,
 ratio to assets, 758
Net worth, 50
Nominal accounts, 56
Noncash financing activities, 696
Noncash investing and financing activities, 696

Noncontributory plan, 442
Noncontrollable costs, 810, 951
Noncumulative preferred stock, 540, 541
Non-interest-bearing notes, 319
Nonmanufacturing costs, 804
Nonoperating expense, 183
Nonoperating income, 183
Nonparticipating preferred stock, 540
Nonprofit, 536
Nonpublic corporations, 536
Nontaxable entity, 506
No-par stock, 539, 544
Notes, 316
 interest-bearing, 319
 non-interest-bearing, 319
 promissory, 316, *illus.*, 316
 receivable, 317
Notes payable, 49
 short-term, 443
Notes receivable, 317
 accounting for, 320
 characteristics of, 318
 def., 49
 discounting, 322
 dishonored, 324
 interest-bearing, 321
Number of days' sales in inventory, 756
Number of days' sales in receivables, 755
Number of times interest charges earned, 758

——— O

Objective evidence concept, 471
Office equipment ledger, account in, *illus.*, 396
Operating expenses, cash payments for, 709
Operating expenses budget, 982, *illus.*, 983
Operating income, 180, 1043
Operating income by department, 1035
Operating leases, 404
Operations,
 centralized and decentralized, 1027
 discontinued, 574
 loss from, 183
Opportunity cost, 812, 1073
Organizational structure,
 adaptation to, 225
 of a corporate enterprise, *illus.*, 537
Organization chart, 798
 controller's department, *illus.*, 799
 depicting management responsibility for production, *illus.*, 1032
 for Baker Inc., *illus.*, 799
 for department store with profit centers, *illus.*, 1030
 for diversified company with investment centers, *illus.*, 1031
Organization costs, 550
Other income, 183
Overapplied factory overhead, 839
Owner's equity, 50
 def., 17, 50
 statement of, 22, 24, *illus.*, 23, 109, 511

——— P

Paid-in capital, 538, 568
Par, 539
Parent and subsidiary corporations, 651
 pooling of interests method, 651, 660
 purchase method, 651, 653

Parent company, 651
Parent-subsidiary affiliations,
 accounting for, 652
 consolidated statements, 652
Partial organization chart for department store with profit centers, *illus.*, 1030
Partial organization chart for diversified company with investment centers, *illus.*, 1031
Participating preferred stock, 540
Participation in income, 506
Partnership agreement, 506
Partnership dissolution, 511
 admission of a partner, 512
 death of a partner, 515
 withdrawal of a partner, 515
Partnerships, 15
 accounting for, 507
 advantages and disadvantages, 506
 characteristics of, 505
 dissolution, 511
 division of net income or net loss, 508
 liquidation, 516
 recording investments, 507
 statements, 511
Patents, 405
Payee, 318, *def.*, 281
Payroll, 426
 accounting systems for, 433
 and payroll taxes, 426
 checks, 437
 distribution, 434
 register, 433, *illus.*, 434–435
Payroll checks, 437
Payroll distribution, 434
Payroll register, 433, *illus.*, 434–435
Payroll system,
 diagram, 439
 flow of, *illus.*, 440
 internal controls, 441
Payroll taxes, 426
 accounting systems for, 433
 and payroll, 426
Pencil footing, 52
Pensions,
 contributory plan, 442
 funded plan, 442
 liability for, 442
 noncontributory plan, 442
 qualified plan, 442
 unfunded plan, 442
Percentage-of-completion method, 477
Period costs, 805
 examples of, *illus.*, 806
Periodic inventory system, 148, 352
 comparison to perpetual, *illus.*, 361–362
 inventory costing methods under, 354
Periodic reporting,
 merchandising enterprises, 148
Periodic revision,
 of depreciation, 394
Perpetual inventory account, (FIFO), *illus.*, 363
 (LIFO), *illus.*, 364
Perpetual inventory accounts, flow of costs, *illus.*, 835
Perpetual inventory procedures, 834
Perpetual inventory system, 148, 352
 accounting and reporting under, 361
 automated, 365
 comparison to periodic, *illus.*, 361–362
 internal control and, 364
 inventory costing methods under, 362
Petty cash, 293
Petty cash receipt, *illus.*, 293
Physical inventory, 148, 352

Planning, *def.*, 795
Plant assets, 97, 386
 acquisition of, 387
 acquisition through leasing, 404
 def., 49
 depreciation when low unit cost, 397
 discarding, 400
 disposal of, 400
 exchange, 402
 in balance sheet, *illus.*, 407
 ratio to long-term liabilities, 757
 reporting in financial statements, 407
 sale, 401
Point of sale method, 475, *illus.*, 476
Pooling of interests method, 651, 660
Post-closing trial balance, 116, *illus.*, 116
Posting, 53, 60
 of debit, *illus.*, 60
Predetermined factory overhead rate, 839
Preemptive right, 539
Preferential rights, preferred stock, 541
Preferred stock, 539
 cumulative, 540, 541
 determining cash flows, 703
 noncumulative, 540, 541
 nonparticipating, 540
 participating, 540
 preferential rights, 541
Premium, 542
 on capital stock on the balance sheet, 543
 on stock, 542
Premium on stock, 542
Prepaid expenses, 18, 49, 151, 246, 701, 710
 adjusting entries for, 151
 adjustment of, *illus.*, 96, 97
Prepaid expenses,
 recorded as asset, *illus.*, 247–248
 recorded as expense, *illus.*, 248
Present value, 611, 1104
 concepts, 611
 concepts for bonds payable, 612
 index, 1105
 of an annuity, 1107
 of an annuity of $1, 613
 of an annuity of $1 at compound interest, *illus.*, 613, 1108, 1109
 of $1, 612
 of $1 at compound interest, *illus.*, 612, 1105
Present value index, 1105
Present value methods, 1104
 discounted cash flow, 1104, *illus.*, 1105
 discounted internal rate of return, 1106
 internal rate of return, 1106
 net present value, 1104
 time-adjusted rate of return, 1106
Present value of an annuity, 1107
 of $1 at compound interest, *illus.*, 1108, 1109
Present value of $1 at compound interest, *illus.*, 1105
President's letter, 766, *illus.*, 767
Price-earnings (P/E) ratio, 762
Price-level index, 473
Price theory, 1080
Price variance, 991
 direct materials, 991, *illus.*, 991
Pricing strategies, 1083
Prime costs, 803
 and conversion costs, *illus.*, 804
Primitive accounting, 1

Prior period adjustments, 578
Proceeds, 322, 445
Process cost accounting,
    illustration of, 877
Process costs,
    and service departments, 875
Process cost system, 834
    financial statements, 883
    flow of costs in, 869
Processing cost, 870
Process or sell, 1073
    differential analysis report,
        illus., 1074
Product cost concept, 1077
Product costs, 805
    examples of, *illus.*, 806
    usefulness of, 831
Production budget, 979
    illus., 980
Production planning, 953
Product life cycle, 1083, *illus.*, 1083
Product price determination, 1081
Product pricing, 952
Product warranty liability, 445
Profit, 536
Profitability, 752
    analysis, 758
    def., 758
Profitability analysis, 758
Profit center, 1030
    partial organization chart for
        department store, *illus.*,
        1030
Profit-making businesses, *illus.*, 16
Profit margin, 1044
Profit-volume chart, 917
    illus., 918, 919
    original, *illus.*, 919
    revised, *illus.*, 919
Profit-volume ratio, 923
Promissory note, 316
    illus., 318
Property, plant, and equipment,
    386
Public corporations, 536
Purchase method, 651, 653
Purchase orders, 836
Purchase requisitions, 836
Purchases, accounting for, 138
Purchases discounts, 139, 292,
    def., 140
Purchases journal, 232
    flow of credits from, to ledgers,
        illus., 233
    flow of data from, to ledgers,
        illus., 235
    illus., 232–233
Purchases returns and allowances,
    141

——— Q

Qualified plan, 442
Quantitative techniques for
    inventory control, 998
    economic order quantity
        (EOQ), 999
    inventory order point, 1000
    linear programming, 1001
Quantity variance, 991
    direct materials, 991, *illus.*, 991
Quick assets, 754
Quick ratio, 754

——— R

Rate,
    contract, 613
    coupon, 613
        effective, 613
        exchange, 666
        market, 613
Rate earned on common
    stockholders' equity, 761

Rate earned on stockholders'
    equity, 760, *illus.*, 760
Rate earned on stockholders'
    equity and total assets,
    illus., 760
Rate earned on total assets, 759,
    illus., 760
Rate of return on assets, 1043
Rate of return on investment (ROI),
    1043
Rate variance, 992
    direct labor, 993, *illus.*, 993
Ratio,
    acid-test, 754
    bankers', 753
    contribution margin, 923
    current, 753
    net sales to assets, 758
    price earnings (P/E)
    profit-volume, 923
    quick, 754
    stockholders' equity to
        liabilities, 757
    total plant assets to long-term
        liabilities, 757
    working capital, 753
Ratio of net sales to assets, 758
Ratio of stockholders' equity to
    liabilities, 757
Ratio of total plant assets to
    long-term liabilities, 757
Raw materials costs, 802
Real accounts, 56
Realizable value,
    expected, 326
    net, 326
Realization, 516
Receivables,
    aging, 328
    and temporary investments in
        the balance sheet, 332,
        illus., 332
    classification of, 316
    control over, 317
    def., 316
    trade, 317
    uncollectible, 324
Receiving report, 836
Reciprocals, 653
Recognition of revenue, 475
    completed-contract method,
        476
    installment method, 475, *illus.*,
        476
    percentage-of-completion
        method, 477
    point of sale method, 475,
        illus., 476
    receipt of payment, 475
Recording investments,
    partnership, 507
Registered bonds, 611
Relevance, 796
Relevant range, 908
    supervisor salary costs, for
        300,000 to 600,000 bottles
        of production,
        illus., 908
Remittance advice, 281
    and check, *illus.*, 282
Report form of balance sheet, *illus.*,
    185
Reporting cash flows, 693
    direct method, 694, *illus.*, 695
    from operating activities, 710
    indirect method, 694, *illus.*,
        695
Reporting unusual items in financial
    statements, 574
Research and development costs,
    406
Reserve, 581
Reserve method, accounting for
    uncollectibles, 325
Residual income, 1046
    by division, *illus.*, 1047
Residual value, 388
Responsibility accounting, 1027

for cost centers, 1032
    for investment centers, 1043
    for profit centers, 1034
    illus., 1033
Responsibility accounting for cost
    centers, 1032, *illus.*, 1033
Responsibility accounting for
    investment centers, 1043
    operating income, 1043
    rate of return on investment
        (ROI), 1043
    residual income, 1046, *illus.*,
        1047
Responsibility accounting for profit
    centers,
    departmental margin, 1039
    gross profit by department,
        1035
    income statement
        departmentalized through
        departmental margin,
        illus., 1042
    income statement
        departmentalized through
        gross profit, *illus.*,
        1036–1037
    income statement
        departmentalized through
        income from operations,
        illus., 1040–1041
    operating income by
        departments, 1035
Retail inventory method, 368
    determination of inventory,
        illus., 368
Retail method of inventory costing,
    368, *illus.*, 368
Retained earnings, 26, 538
    appropriation of, 581
    def., 50
    determining cash flows, 697
Retained earnings statement, 26,
    110, 184
    combined with income
        statement, *illus.*, 184
    corporation, *illus.*, 27
    illus., 184, 583
    unusual items that affect it,
        576
Returns and allowances,
    general journal entry for, *illus.*,
        235
Returns and allowances,
    purchases, 141
Returns and allowances, sales, 144
Revenue expenditures, 399
    def., 398
    summary of, 399
Revenues, 19, 1080
    def., 50
    differential, 1068
    marginal, 1080
    unearned, 151, 152, 249
Revenues received in advance, 151
Reversing entries, 188
    for accrued assets, 190
    for accrued liabilities, 188
    for a merchandising enterprise,
        191, *illus.*, 192
    use of, 251
Revision of standards, 998

——— S

Safety stock, 1000
Salary, 426
Sales,
    accounting for, 142
    in a job order cost system, 844
Sales analysis, 954
Sales budget, 979, *illus.*, 979
Sales discounts, *def.*, 144
Sales journal, 239
    after posting, *illus.*, 240
Sales mix, 921, 954
Sales mix considerations, 921

Salespersons' analysis, *illus.*, 956
Sales returns and allowances, 144
    general journal entry, *illus.*,
        240
Sales tax,
    for buyer, 147
    for seller, 147
Salvage value, 388
Schedule of collection of accounts
    receivable, *illus.*, 985
Scope of accounting reports, 472
Scrap report, *illus.*, 1034
Scrap value, 388
Secured bonds, 611
Securities,
    marketable, 331
Securities and Exchange
    Commission (SEC), 469
Securities Industry Associates, 470
Segment of a business, 481
Selling costs, 804
Selling expenses, 180
Semifixed costs, 810, 909
Semivariable costs, 810, 909
Separate legal existence, 537
Serial bonds, 611
Service departments, 875
    and process costs, 875
    costs charged to processing
        departments, *illus.*, 875
Service enterprises,
    flow of costs through, *illus.*,
        851
    job order cost systems for, 851
Setting normal product prices, 1075
    choosing a cost-plus approach,
        1079
    product cost concept, 1077
    total cost concept, 1075
    variable cost concept, 1078
Shareholders, 537
Shareholders' equity, 538
Shareholders' investment, 538
Shares of stock, 537
Shipping terms, *illus.*, 146
Short-term notes payable, 443
Signature card, 281
Single-step income statement, 183,
    illus., 183
Sinking fund, 619
Slides, *def.*, 67
Sole proprietorship, 15
Solvency, 752
    def., 753
    analysis, 753
Solvency analysis, 753
Special journals, 230, 231
    and subsidiary ledgers, 230
Special reports and analyses, 800
Standard costs, 989
    in the accounts, 997, *illus.*, 997
    systems, 989
Standard costs in accounts, *illus.*,
    997
Standard cost systems, 989
Standards, 989
    in the accounts, 997
    revision of, 998
    variances from, in income
        statement, *illus.*, 998
Standards in the accounts, 997
Stated value, 539
Statement of cash flows, 25, 691
    assembling data and
        preparing, 696, 706
    bonds payable, 703
    building, 705
    common stock, 703
    corporation, *illus.*, 28
    def., 22, 692
    direct method, *illus.*, 695
    equipment, 704
    illus., 706
    illustrations of, 694
    indirect method, *illus.*, 695
    investments, 705
    land, 705
    nature of, 691

preferred stock, 703
preparing, 706, 719
retained earnings, 697
sole proprietorship, *illus.,* 23
work sheet for, 711, *illus.,* 713
Statement of cost of goods
manufactured, 807,
illus., 808, 833
Statement of owner's equity, 24,
def., 22
illus., 109, 511
sole proprietorship, *illus.,* 23
Stock,
accounting for long-term
investments in, 647
classes of, 539
common, 539
cumulative, 540, 541
investment in, 646
issuing for assets other than
cash, 544
noncumulative, 540, 541
nonparticipating, 540
no-par, 544
participating, 540
preferred, 539
treasury, 547
Stock certificate, 539
Stock dividend, 585
Stockholders, 537
Stockholders' equity, 50, 538
changes in, 26
common, rate earned on, 761
rate earned on, 760
ratio to liabilities, 757
Stockholders' ledger, 542
Stock ledger, 844
Stock outstanding, 539
Stock splits, 587
and dividends, for treasury
stock, 587
Stock split-up, 587
Straight-line method of
depreciation, 390
comparison with
declining-balance and
sum-of-the-years-digits
methods, *illus.,* 393
illus., 390
Strategic planning, 1028
Subscribers ledger, 547
Subscriptions and stock issuance,
545
Subsidiary company, 651
Subsidiary corporations, 651
Subsidiary ledgers, 230
and special journals, 230
plant assets, 396
Sum-of-the-years-digits method of
depreciation, 392
comparison with straight-line
and declining-balance
methods, *illus.,* 393
illus., 392
Sunk costs, 811, 1069
Supervisor salary costs,
illus., 908
relevant range for 300,000 to
600,000 bottles of
production, *illus.,* 908
Systems,
analysis, 226
design, 226
implementation, 226
Systems and procedures, 800

T

T account, 51
illus., 51
Take-home pay, 430
Taxable income, 571
Taxes, 800
income, 570
sales, 147

Temporary accounts, 56
Temporary differences, 571
Temporary investments, 331
and receivables in balance
sheet, 332, *illus.,* 332
Term bonds, 611
Time-adjusted rate of return
method, 1106
Timeliness, 796
Time tickets, 838, *illus.,* 838
Time variance, 992
direct labor, 992, *illus.,* 993
Total cost concept, 1075
Total fixed cost graph, *illus.,* 907
Total variable cost, *illus.,* 909
Trade-in value, 388
Trade receivables, 317, 701, 708
Transactions,
and the accounting equation,
17
business, 16
effect on owner's equity, *illus.,*
21
internal, 17
Transferable units, 537
Transportation costs, 145
Transpositions, *def.,* 67
Treasury stock, 547
Trial balance,
def., 66
post-closing, *illus.,* 116
proof provided by, 66
Trust indenture, 610
Turnover,
accounts receivable, 755
inventory, 756
investment, 1044

U

Uncertainty, 1113
Uncollectible accounts, 324
estimate of, *illus.,* 329
Uncollectible receivables, 324
allowance method of
accounting for, 325
estimating, 328
Underapplied factory overhead,
839
Underwriter, 545
Unearned revenues, 151, 152, 249
adjusting entries for, 152
adjustment and reversal for,
recorded as revenue,
illus., 250–251
adjustment for, recorded as
liability, *illus.,* 249
adjustment for, recorded as
revenue, *illus.,* 250
comparison of systems of
recording, 251
recorded initially as liabilities,
249
recorded initially as revenues,
249
systems of recording, *illus.,*
251
Unequal proposal lives, 1111
Unfunded plan, 442
Unit fixed cost graph, *illus.,* 907
Unit of measurement, 472
changes in price levels, 472
scope of accounting reports,
472
Units-of-production method of
depreciation, 390, *illus.,*
391
Unit variable cost, *illus.,* 909
Unlimited liability, 506
Unusual items,
reporting in financial
statements, 574
that affect the income
statement, 574
that affect the retained
earnings statement, 576

V

Vacation pay, liability for, 441
Valuation of inventory,
other than cost, 366
lower of cost or market, 366,
illus., 367
net realizable value, 367
Value,
residual, 388
salvage, 388
scrap, 388
trade-in, 388
Variable cost concept, 1078
Variable costing, 943
compared with absorption
costing, *illus.,* 944
income statement, *illus.,* 945,
946, 948
income statements, *illus.,,* 950
Variable costing and absorption
costing,
income analysis under, 948
income statement under, 944
management's use of, 951
Variable costs, 809, 908
total variable, *illus.,* 909
unit variable, *illus.,* 909
Variances, 990
controllable, 995, *illus.,* 996
direct labor cost, 992, *illus.,*
992
direct labor rate, 993, *illus.,*
993
direct labor time, 992, *illus.,*
993
direct materials cost, 991,
illus., 991
direct materials price, 991,
illus., 991
direct materials quantity, 991,
illus., 991
factory overhead controllable,
995, *illus.,* 996
factory overhead cost, 993,
illus., 995
factory overhead volume, 994,
illus., 995
from standards, 990
from standards in income
statement, *illus.,* 998
price, 991
quantity, 991
rate, 992
time, 992
volume, 994, *illus.,* 995
Variances from standards, 990
Vertical analysis, 749
comparative balance sheet,
illus., 750
comparative income statement,
illus., 751
Volume variance, 994
Voucher,
def., 288
illus., 288
register, 289
system, 288
Voucher register, 288
illus., 290–291
Voucher system, 288
basic features, 288

W

Wage and tax statement, *illus.,* 437
Wages, 427
Weighted average inventory costing
method, 357
Withdrawal of a partner, 515
Working capital ratio, 753
Working papers, 100
Work in process, in a job order cost
system, 841
Work in process inventory, 806

Work sheet,
adjusted trial balance columns,
104
adjustments, 154
adjustments columns, 102
balance sheet columns, 105
completing, 155
completing for statement of
cash flows, 719
def., 100
for financial statements, 100
for merchandising enterprises,
154, *illus.,* 156–157
for statement of cash flows,
711, *illus.,* 713
illus., 180–181
income statement columns,
105
procedures for statement of
cash flows, 711
ten-column, *illus.,* 100–101
trial balance columns, 101
Work sheet procedures for
statement of cash flows,
711,
account balances, 714
cash flow activities, 714
analysis of accounts, 714
Write-offs to allowance account,
327

Y

Year-end procedures, completion,
156

Z

Zero-base budgeting, 978
Zero-coupon bonds, 619

INDEX OF REAL COMPANIES

Allegis Corp., 610
American Airlines, 1082–1083
Amerock Corporation, 840–841
Amoco, 143
Anheuser-Busch, 573–574
Apple Computer Inc., 480
Bethlehem Steel Corporation, 480,
542
Black & Decker, G-7
Boston Metal Products, 1120
Campbell Soup Co., 584
Chrysler Corp., 359, 368, 479,
1090
Circus Circus Enterprises, Inc., 573
Coca-Cola Enterprises Inc., 35
Colt Industries Inc., 429
Crazy Eddie Inc., 352
Crusader Limited, 676
Deloitte, Haskins & Sells, 508–509,
527, 768, 977
Delta Air Lines, Inc., 573
Digital Equipment Corporation, 479
Dutch Pantry Inc., 963
Entertainment Marketing,
Incorporated, 594
Equity Funding Corporation of
America, 258
Exxon, 143
Fay's Drug Company, Inc., 492,
778
Federated Department Stores, 127
Ford Motor Co., 1090
Forstmann Little & Co., 951
General Electric Co., 295
General Motors Corporation, 548,
870–871, 892, 1090
Gruntal & Co., 692

Gulf, 165
Hewlett-Packard Company, 856, 1029
H. J. Heinz Company, 573
Humana Corp., 429
Hilton Hotels Corporation, 338
IBM Corp., 610, 1029
Ingersoll-Rand Co., G-9
ITT Corp., 951
J. C. Penney, 127
J. P. Stevens & Co., Inc., 650
K mart Corporation, 127, 204, 281
Korn/Ferry International, 1031
La-Z-Boy Chair Company, 414
Long Island Lighting, 542
Martin Marietta Corporation, 477
McKinsey & Co., 1029
Merck & Co., Inc., 360
Merrill Lynch Capital Markets, 650

Microsoft Corporation, 932
Mobil, 143, 165
Morgan Stanley & Co., 951
NCR Corp., 1029
Northern Research & Engineering Corp., G-9
Owens-Corning Fiberglas Corp., 610
Peat Marwick Main & Co., 768
People Express, 1082
PepsiCo, Inc., 1009
Perini Corporation, 301
Procter & Gamble Company, 806, 966–967, 1061
Reebok International Ltd., 429
Rose's Stores Inc., 229
Sears, Roebuck and Co., 610
Seidman & Seidman, 573–574
Sohio, 143

Sperry Corp., 1029
Super Valu Stores, Inc., 573
Tandy Corporation, 165, 573, 725, 1053
Texaco, 165
The Circle K Corporation, 557
The Limited, Inc., 127
The Motor Convoy Inc., 920
The Pillsbury Co., 78, 474, 573, 580, 935
The Price Club, 204
The Quaker Oats Company, 573
The Walgreen Co., 359, 375–376, 573
The Walt Disney Company, 481–482
The Washington Post Company, 481
The Wurlitzer Company, 471,

480–481
3M, 800–801
Time Incorporated, 479
Torrington Co., G-9
Touche Ross & Co., 12, 769
Toys "R" Us, 127, 573, 735–736, 769
Tribune Company, 483
Trico Products Inc., 821
Triton Energy Corporation, 676
West Point-Pepperell, Inc., 650
Whirlpool Corporation, 450
William Wrigley Jr. Company, 780
Winn-Dixie Stores, Inc., 767–768
Woodside Design Associates, Inc., 480
Wyatt Co., 429
Xerox Corporation, 633
Zayre Corp., 127

CHECK FIGURES FOR SELECTED PROBLEMS

Problem	Check Figure
1–1A	John Allen, Capital, $3,920 at end of the month
1–2A	Net income, $1,970
1–3A	Net income, $2,475
1–4A	Net income, $2,105
1–5A	Net income, $14,300
1–6A	Net income, $33,450
1–7A	Net income, $9,800
1–1B	John Herr, Capital, $1,770 at end of the month
1–2B	Net income, $1,550
1–4B	Net income, $1,930
1–5B	Net income, $31,450
1–6B	Net income, $93,375
2–1A	Trial balance totals, $19,150
2–2A	Trial balance totals, $22,265
2–3A	Trial balance totals, $103,015
2–4A	Trial balance totals, $177,325
2–5A	Trial balance totals, $311,450
2–6A	Trial balance totals, $33,138.10
2–7A	Trial balance totals, $122,380
2–1B	Trial balance totals, $23,210
2–2B	Trial balance totals, $29,100
2–4B	Trial balance totals, $293,670
2–6B	Trial balance totals, $33,138.10
2–7B	Trial balance totals, $109,940
3–1A	Net income, $16,435
3–2A	Capital, Dec. 31, $115,020
3–3A	Net income, $1,775.34
3–4A	Net income, $22,590
3–5A	Net income, $42,130
3–1B	Net income, $23,850
3–2B	Capital, June 30, $51,335
3–3B	Net income, $2,870.24
Comprehensive Problem 1	Net income, $3,200
4–3A	Trial balance totals, $219,590
4–6A	Cost of merchandise sold, $489,700
4–7A	Net income, $32,590
4–6B	Cost of merchandise sold, $479,500
4–7B	Net income, $53,350
5–1A	Net income, $52,490
5–2A	Retained earnings, Dec. 31, $167,700
5–3A	Retained earnings, Dec. 31, $192,600
5–4A	Total assets, $455,800
5–5A	Capital, Mar. 31, $180,810
5–7A	Net income, $139,805
5–8A	Net income, $139,805
5–9A	Net income for Sept., $5,067
5–1B	Net income, $80,000
5–2B	Retained earnings, Mar. 31, $187,250
5–3B	Retained earnings, Apr. 30, $323,760
5–5B	Retained earnings, June 30, $174,520
Comprehensive Problem 2	Total assets, May 31, $236,720
6–1A	Accounts payable, May 31, $51,681.35
6–2A	Accounts payable, Mar. 31, $12,727
6–3A	Accounts receivable, May 31, $14,570
6–4A	Accounts receivable, July 31, $10,860
6–5A	Accounts receivable, June 30, $19,950
6–6A	Trial balance totals, $171,760
6–2B	Accounts payable, June 30, $9,725
6–4B	Accounts receivable, July 31, $10,860
6–5B	Accounts receivable, June 30, $11,550
6–6B	Trial balance totals, $176,738

Problem	Check Figure
Comprehensive Problem 3	Trial balance totals, $153,162
7–1A	Adjusted balance, $16,341
7–2A	Adjusted balance, $12,986.09
7–3A	Accounts payable, May 31, $25,950
7–5A	Accounts payable, June 30, $14,550
7–6A	Accounts payable, June 30, $7,800
7–1B	Adjusted balance, $22,627.55
7–2B	Adjusted balance, $9,398.02
7–3B	Accounts payable, May 31, $21,700
7–5B	Accounts payable, June 30, $24,550
7–6B	Accounts payable, June 30, $5,700
8–3A	Interest income, Mar. 16, $873
8–4A	Allowance for doubtful accounts, Dec. 31, $12,500
8–5A	Allowance for doubtful accounts, end of 4th year, $12,800
8–6A	Total assets, $521,300
8–3B	Interest income, Mar. 11, $1,260
8–4B	Allowance for doubtful accounts, Dec. 31, $31,250
9–1A	Net income, $85,000
9–2A	Inventory (2), $12,767
9–3A	Inventory (4), $2,900
9–4A	Total inventory, lower of C or M, $49,710
9–5A	Net income, $77,000
9–6A	Inventory (1), $299,520; (2), $422,750
9–2B	Inventory (2), $7,870
9–3B	Inventory (4), $150,250
9–4B	Total inventory, lower of C or M, $49,855
9–6B	Inventory (1), $213,500; (2), $627,500
10–5A	Accum. deprec., June 30, 1993, $2,250
10–6A	Accum. deprec., Sept. 30, 1991, $266,250
10–7A	Net income, $186,806
10–5B	Accum. deprec., Dec. 31, 1992, $1,525
10–6B	Accum. deprec., Mar. 31, 1991, $269,700
11–4A	FICA tax payable, Dec. 28, $6,622
11–5A	Total payroll taxes expense, $19,415.10
11–5B	Total payroll taxes expense, $19,352.50
Comprehensive Problem 4	Total assets, $997,390
12–1A	Income from operations, 3rd year, $66,450
12–2A	Gain on repossession, $34
12–3A	Income from contracts, 1992, $655,000
12–4A	Net income as recomputed, 3rd year, $172,800
12–6A	Income from operations, $14,920
12–1B	Income from operations, 3rd year, $53,240
12–3B	Income from contracts, 1992, $375,000
12–4B	Net income as recomputed, 3rd year, $68,730
12–6B	Income from operations, $7,325
13–1A	Total assets, $130,000
13–3A	Total owner's equity, $190,000
13–4A	Total owner's equity, $231,600
13–1B	Total assets, $196,500
14–1A	Total common dividends per share, $15
14–2A	Total stockholders' equity, $3,305,000
14–3A	Total stockholders' equity, $1,625,375
14–4A	Total stockholders' equity, $470,900
14–5A	Total stockholders' equity, $426,900
14–1B	Total common dividends per share, $18.60
14–3B	Total stockholders' equity, $6,911,000

Check Figures-2

Problem	Check Figure
15–1A	Deferred income tax payable, end of 4th year, $17,800
15–2A	Net income, $139,000
15–3A	Total retained earnings, $1,640,000
15–4A	Total stockholders' equity, $2,202,000
15–5A	Total stockholders' equity, $2,588,000
15–6A	Net income, $130,200
15–1B	Deferred income tax payable, end of 4th year, $37,200
15–2B	Net income, $93,000
15–3B	Total retained earnings, $1,338,500
15–4B	Total stockholders' equity, $1,180,100
16–1A	Earnings per share on common stock, Plan 3 (2), .40
16–4A	Premium on bonds, end of 1991, $1,100,000
16–5A	Carrying amount of bonds, Dec. 31, 1991, $4,447,265
16–4B	Discount on bonds, end of 1991, $227,200
16–5B	Carrying amount of bonds, Dec. 31, 1991, $22,130,343
Comprehensive Problem 5	Net Income, $400,950
17–2A	Total assets, $2,297,000
17–3A	Total assets: (1), $2,210,000; (2), $2,160,000; (3), $2,160,000
17–4A	Total assets, $2,002,000; net income, $436,800
17–5A	Total assets, $4,437,000
17–6A	Total assets, $1,202,200
17–7A	Total assets, $3,095,000
17–2B	Total assets, $1,610,400
17–4B	Total assets, $1,938,150; net income, $258,000
17–5B	Total assets, $4,009,000
18–1A	Net cash flow from operating activities, $103,700
18–2A	Net cash flow from operating activities, $137,100
18–3A	Net cash flow from operating activities, $66,950
18–4A	Net cash flow from operating activities, $60,500
18–5A	Net cash flow from operating activities, $87,360
18–6A	Net cash flow from operating activities, $135,017
18–1B	Net cash flow from operating activities, $96,800
18–2B	Net cash flow from operating activities, $181,400
18–3B	Net cash flow from operating activities, $73,100
18–4B	Net cash flow from operating activities, −$800
19–5A	Working capital, Dec. 31, 1990, $112,500
20–2A	Cost of goods manufactured, $327,300
20–4A	Cost of goods manufactured, $541,000
20–2B	Cost of goods manufactured, $1,780,000
20–4B	Cost of goods manufactured, $955,000
21–1A	Finished goods, $17,805
21–3A	Total assets, $765,991
21–4A	Trial balance totals, $1,725,860
21–1B	Finished goods, $56,425
21–4B	Trial balance totals, $1,637,704
22–1A	Work in process, May 31, $15,300
22–2A	Equivalent units of production, 35,500
22–4A	Equivalent units of production, 12,000
22–6A	Total assets, $746,380
22–7A	Equivalent units of production, 17,500
22–1B	Work in process, October 31, $25,415
22–2B	Equivalent units of production, 12,500
22–4B	Equivalent units of production, 23,870

Problem	Check Figure
23–2A	Present break-even point, $4,125,000
23–3A	Anticipated break-even point, $300,000
23–4A	Maximum operating profit: (2), $160,000; (4), $120,000
23–5A	Maximum operating profit: (2), $75,000; (4), $50,000
23–7A	Break-even point, $600,000
23–3B	Anticipated break-even point, $800,000
23–4B	Maximum operating profit: (2), $135,000; (4), $90,000
23–5B	Maximum operating profit: (2), $150,000; (4), $125,000
23–7B	Break-even point, $1,500,000
24–1A	Income from operations (2), $37,500
24–2A	Operating loss, $53,600
24–3A	Income from operations for June (2b), $298,000
24–4A	Contribution to company profit, Thom, $51,400
24–5A	Total contribution margin (1), $1,027,200; (3), $1,122,000
24–6A	Decrease in contribution margin, $86,000
24–1B	Income from operations (2), $1,946,000
24–2B	Operating loss, $47,000
24–6B	Decrease in contribution margin, $68,000
25–1A	Total production, Product E, 41,600 units
25–2A	Net income, $857,070
25–3A	Deficiency, June, $16,900
25–4A	Net income, $236,500; cash, $39,500
25–6A	Total factory overhead cost variance — unfavorable, $10,900
25–7A	Work in process, $4,950 CR.
25–1B	Total production, Product E, 13,500 units
25–2B	Net income, $670,170
25–3B	Excess, August, $3,200
25–6B	Total factory overhead cost variance — unfavorable, $8,800
25–7B	Work in process, $11,590
26–2A	Net income, $138,600
26–3A	Total departmental margin, $377,900
26–4A	ROI, Division R, 16.8%
26–5A	ROI, Proposal 3, 18.5%
26–6A	Division V is most profitable
26–7A	ROI, Division C, 19.5%
26–2B	Net income, $53,600
26–4B	ROI, Division Z, 18%
26–7B	ROI, Division W, 19%
27–1A	Gain from operating warehouse, $280,000
27–2A	Net cost reduction, $450,000
27–3A	Gain from promotion campaign, Product F, $90,000
27–4A	Net advantage, $3,000
27–5A	Net advantage, $9,000
27–6A	Selling price, $21.60
27–1B	Loss from operating warehouse, $70,000
27–2B	Net cost reduction, $500,000
27–6B	Selling price, $19.20
28–1A	Excess of present value over amount to be invested, Project W, $41,420
28–2A	Excess of present value over amount to be invested, Project N, $39,005
28–3A	Present value index, Proposal L, .94
28–4A	Discounted internal rate of return, Proposal E, 20%
28–5A	Excess of present value over amount to be invested, B (2), $11,360
28–6A	Excess of present value over amount to be invested, Proposal E, $19,673
28–1B	Excess of present value over amount to be invested, Project K, $3,545
28–2B	Excess of present value over amount to be invested, Project R, $21,450
28–3B	Present value index, Proposal V, 1.06
28–4B	Discounted internal rate of return, Proposal J, 10%